Imperial War Museum Film Catalogue
Volume 1
The First World War Archive

Imperial War Museum Film Catalogue
VOLUME 1
The First World War Archive

Edited by Roger Smither

KEEPER, DEPARTMENT OF FILM

Introduction by Stephen Badsey

ROYAL MILITARY ACADEMY, SANDHURST

Catalogue entries compiled by
Stephen Badsey
with Neil Pilfold, John Kerr,
Kay Gladstone and Roger Smither

Bibliographies and Indexes in Military Studies, Number 7

GREENWOOD PRESS
WESTPORT, CONNECTICUT

Published in the United States and Canada by
Greenwood Press, 88 Post Road West, Westport, CT 06881
an imprint of Greenwood Publishing Group, Inc.

English language edition, except the United States and Canada,
published by Flicks Books, England.

First published 1994

Library of Congress Cataloging-in-Publication Data

Imperial War Museum film catalogue I / edited by Roger Smither.
      p.   cm. -- (Bibliographies and indexes in military studies,
  ISSN 1040-7995; no. 7)
   Includes bibliographical references.
   ISBN 0-313-29379-1 (alk. paper)
   1. World War, 1914-1918--Sources--Film catalogs. 2. World War,
1914-1918--Film catalogs. 3. Imperial War Museum (Great Britain)--
Film catalogs. 4. World War, 1914-1918--Great Britain--Film
catalogs. I. Smither, Roger B. N. II. Imperial War Museum (Great
Britain) III. Series.
D522.22.I46   1994
016.9403--dc20   94-4046
                                          CIP

Library of Congress Catalog Card Number: 94-4046

ISBN: 0-313-29379-1

Printed and bound in Great Britain by Bookcraft (Bath) Ltd.

Contents

Foreword   vi
Introduction   vii
Bibliography   xxi
How to Use the Catalogue   xxiii
Abbreviations   xxvi

The Catalogue

IWM Series   1
Topical Budget Newsreel   454

Indexes

How to Use the Indexes   522
Title Index   523
Personality Index   548
Place Index   562
Unit and Organisation Index   573

Foreword

Dr Alan Borg CBE FSA
Director General of the Imperial War Museum

The First World War film collection in the Imperial War Museum constitutes one of the first film archives in the world. The Museum was founded in 1917 to record a war that was perceived as different in many ways from its predecessors and which, it was vainly imagined, was the war to end all wars. Vast collections were assembled, from aircraft and artillery to documents and works of art. The importance of the film record had been realised immediately, so it was natural that the new Museum should take on the task of preserving and conserving the archive. Today, of course, the unique importance of this record is even more widely recognised and it is constantly used by scholars, researchers and educational programme makers.

It is therefore very appropriate that this first full published catalogue should coincide both with the 75th anniversary of the establishment of the archive itself and with the 100th anniversary of the birth of cinema. It is our intention to continue to publish catalogues of all our collections, so that more and more people can easily discover the wealth of historical material we hold. Film catalogues are especially important in this regard, providing the first essential point of entry to the archive.

I should like to take this opportunity of thanking all those who have been involved in this enterprise, especially the Keeper of Film, Roger Smither, and his staff. The service which a Museum offers to its public is directly proportional to the efforts of the staff. In these terms, the Department of Film enjoys a very high reputation, for which this catalogue provides further support.

Introduction

Stephen Badsey

Perhaps the most surprising fact about the Imperial War Museum's First World War film archive, commonly known as the IWM Series, is that it has survived when so many other films from the silent era have vanished. Consisting chiefly of contemporary silent actuality film taken by British and Dominion cameramen during the First World War (1914-18), and lodged at the Department of Film of the Imperial War Museum in London, it is both a unique primary source for contemporary British film propaganda of the First World War, and also the world's first official national film archive, being preserved from an era in which the entire culture of film production was based on rapid commercial exploitation. It is hoped that this new catalogue will introduce even more researchers to the IWM Series. The collection is open to the public by appointment, although a charge is made for those viewing a large amount of material or working on behalf of commercial productions.

Historical research undertaken since 1980 has considerably improved understanding of British propaganda in the First World War, including the official propaganda films and the organisations which produced them. The belief, found or implied in earlier writings, in a well prepared and elaborate British Government propaganda organisation deliberately manipulating home public opinion from the very start of the war has now been largely discredited. Instead, British propaganda organisations have been shown as evolving throughout the war in response to the increasing demands on British society and its institutions of the country's first experience of total war. This was particularly true of institutions dealing with film, the great popular mass medium of the era.

It is a constant source of disappointment to researchers that there is little or no extant film of British armed forces during the first eighteen months of the First World War. In 1914 there was no official British organisation to oversee documentary or newsreel film production, and the IWM Series itself holds only a few short pieces from newsreels or private sources which can be convincingly dated before the middle of 1915. Compilation films of the war made from official sources towards its end, or in its immediate aftermath, often made use of post-1915 film to cover this awkward gap. It is indicative of the British official attitude to film in the early stages of the war, which was a mixture of indifference and concern about security, that the only film of the Gallipoli campaign of 1915-16 was shot by Ellis Ashmead Bartlett, a still photographer for the Newspaper Proprietors Association who also possessed a cine camera, with help from the Royal Navy still photographer Ernest Brooks, and that the only surviving original copy of this was obtained by the Australian War Memorial in 1919. A copy of this film, edited and with intertitles by the Australians, is now held in the IWM Series as film IWM 1058.

The first major achievement of British film propaganda was the full-length documentary *Britain Prepared* (IWM 580) in December 1915, showing the work of the Royal Navy, the British munitions and shipbuilding industry, and the Army in training. This was the product of the Foreign Office propaganda organisation based at Wellington House, formed just after the start of the war under Charles Masterman, the Chancellor of the Duchy of Lancaster. In August 1915 the Wellington House Cinema Committee was formed by Masterman. Chaired by J Brooke Wilkinson, Secretary of the British Board of Film Censors, it consisted of three owners of prominent British film companies, including William F Jury, head of Jury's Imperial Pictures, who became the leading figure in British wartime official film production. Access to the Western Front was denied to all cameramen by the British Army until July 1915, when Hilton deWitt Girdwood, a Canadian sponsored by the India Office, was allowed to film with Indian troops in France for two months. Girdwood's motives were entirely commercial, and arguments with the War Office over copyright and faked scenes delayed the release of his film *With the Empire's Fighters* until September 1916, by which time it had been overtaken by events. No copy of Girdwood's film exists in the IWM Series and, like a number of other British semi-official propaganda films of the 1914-15 period, it appears not to have survived at all.

Meanwhile, in parallel and in competition with the Wellington House Cinema Committee, a second organisation was created in October 1915 in association with the War Office. This was the British Topical Committee for War Films, comprising the seven most prominent British newsreel or documentary film companies (including Jury's once more), with Brooke Wilkinson as its secretary. This committee was granted official status to film the Western Front by Reginald Brade, Permanent Secretary at the War Office, in return for a share of its profits to be given to War Office charities. Its first two official cameramen, Geoffrey Malins and E G Tong, left for the front in November 1915 to film six series of *Official Pictures of the British Army in France*, short films of various aspects of Army activity, at the rate of one series a month. All of these short films, which concentrated principally on satisfying public curiosity about the novelties of war on the Western Front, are still preserved in the IWM Series, although some are not in their original versions. In June Tong fell ill and was replaced by J B McDowell of the British & Colonial Kinematograph Company, who served on for another two years to become the doyen of British official cameramen on the Western Front, winning the Military Cross for bravery in 1918. The Royal Navy's first official cameraman was F W Engholm, appointed by the Chief Censor, Rear-Admiral Sir Douglas Brownrigg, in 1915.

In July 1916 the Canadian War Records Office under W Maxwell Aitken (created Lord Beaverbrook in January 1917), a Canadian-born British MP who was heavily involved in British War Office propaganda, sent out Oscar Bovill as the first Canadian official cameraman on the Western Front. The British official cameramen also filmed Australian forces on the Western Front after April 1916. The first Australian still photographer on the Western Front, H Baldwin, was appointed in November 1916 and his role extended to cine cameraman in April 1917. The first New Zealand official still photographer and cameraman, Henry A Sanders, was recruited from Pathé Frères in March 1917 and served with the New Zealand Division until replaced by Charles D Barton in December 1918. During the same period Thomas F Scales filmed New Zealand training depots and activities in Great Britain.

In June 1916 British propaganda film underwent a major development when the rough film shot by Malins and McDowell at the start of the Somme offensive was turned into the full-length documentary *The Battle of the Somme* (IWM 191) rather than short films. The unprecedented popular and commercial success of this film established a pattern of major documentaries, with *The King Visits His Armies In The Great Advance* (IWM 192) being released in October. It also led to a streamlining of the War Office official film organisation. In December 1916 the agreement between the War Office and the British Topical Committee for War Films, which had proved unsatisfactory for both sides, was dissolved. In its place the War Office Cinema Committee was established, consisting of Beaverbrook, Brade and Jury, who took over the production of official film through his own company. The War Office Cinema Committee continued the big battle documentary style with *The Battle of the Ancre and the Advance of the Tanks* (IWM 116), released in January 1917; the series *Sons of Our Empire* (IWM 130), released in five weekly parts in April; and *The German Retreat and the Battle of Arras* (IWM 113) in June.

In February 1917 the Foreign Office expanded the Wellington House organisation into the Department of Information under the novelist John Buchan, and this became the main controller of British overseas propaganda. The Wellington House Cinema Committee was dissolved, and the Department of Information Cinema Section became dependent for documentary film of the fighting fronts on the War Office Cinema Committee, which remained the dominant organisation in the production of British official film for the remainder of the war. In April 1917 the War Office Cinema Committee established a monopoly over official filming on all fronts, with Sir Graham Greene, the Permanent Secretary at the Admiralty, becoming its nominal fourth member. This monopoly included films of the Dominion forces (although pressure for a seat on the committee from the head of the Australian War Records Section, Dr C E W Bean, was firmly resisted) and the Home Front, of which several films were made by commercial film companies for the War Office Cinema Committee or by service film units in Britain (such as those belonging to the Air Ministry) towards the end of the war.

As the heralded British offensives of 1916 and 1917 failed to produce any decisive result, public interest in the big battle picture faded, and British official propaganda film policy changed once again. In May 1917 the War Office Cinema Committee entered into an agreement with William Jeapes, owner of the Topical Film Company, for control of its newsreel the *Topical Budget,* and finally bought the company outright for the duration of the war in September. The short items of the *War Office Official Topical Budget* newsreel became the main outlet for British and Empire official actuality film for the remainder of the war. In May a reciprocal agreement was made with the French Government for an exchange of the *War Office Official Topical Budget* with its French equivalent, the *Annales de la Guerre* newsreel.

By September 1917 Beaverbrook and the War Office Cinema Committee had obtained the acceptance of a permanent, if very small organisation for controlling all British and Dominion cameramen and still photographers under Major Andrew Holt as part of the Press Section at General Headquarters in France. Thereafter two or three British official cameramen normally served on the Western Front at any one time, together with a single cameraman each for the Canadians, Australians and New Zealanders. Editing and production took place in Britain through the Topical Film Company, with censorship and general policy being decided by the War Office. Malins was replaced in March 1917 as an official cameraman by H C Raymond (who filmed on the Western and Italian Fronts for the remainder of the war), and himself replaced Bovill as Canadian official cameraman in June. A third British cameraman, Bertram Brooks-Carrington, served briefly with McDowell in France from April to June 1917. Other British official cameramen who served on the Western Front include Frank Bassill from November 1917, and Walter Buckstone from May 1918, joined by Frederick Wilson shortly before the end of the war. Hubert Wilkins and Frank Hurley replaced Baldwin as the Australian official cameramen in summer 1917, working as both still photographers and cine cameramen. By this time the acceptance of cameramen by military authorities was much greater than at the war's start, and they would sometimes take the initiative in securing the services of a cameraman to film a particular event.

With Beaverbrook as both head of the Canadian War Records Section and a member of the War Office Cinema Committee, there was considerable overlap between British and Canadian official film arrangements, and agreements were also reached with the Australian and New Zealand Governments for a mutual exchange of films by November 1917. Harold Jeapes (the brother of William Jeapes) was appointed as the British official cameraman in Egypt and Palestine in April 1917 and continued there until the end of the war. In December 1917 he was joined by Frank Hurley, transferred from the Western Front as the Australian official cameraman and photographer. Under the agreement between the Australian War Records Section and the War Office Cinema Committee, Australian film was sent directly to London and incorporated into British productions, but not into the *War Office Official Topical Budget*. This arrangement continued until June 1918 when Hurley filmed and edited an entirely Australian production, *With the Australian Forces In Palestine* (IWM 28), being replaced as Australian official cameraman in Palestine by J R Campbell, who served until the end of the war. The quality of the work done by these men in Palestine and Egypt suffered greatly from the effects of the desert heat on film stock and the primitive developing facilities available in Cairo. From July 1918 the undeveloped film was sent directly to London for processing.

In addition to its official cameramen, the War Office concluded a reciprocal filming agreement with the American newsman Lowell Thomas, who together with his cameraman Harry Chase also covered the Palestine region, in particular the activities of T E Lawrence ('of Arabia'). Another American citizen, Ariel Varges of the International Film Service, was contracted by the War Office on the Salonika Front in late March or early April 1917 as both a still photographer and cameraman, and transferred to the Mesopotamian Front shortly afterwards. Varges continued to film British and Indian troops in Mesopotamia from May 1917 until the end of the war.

In theory the organisation of still photographers, both on the Western Front and elsewhere, came under the Department of Information and was entirely separate from that of the cameramen. In practice a considerable overlap of functions between the two was both necessary and desirable. It was the normal working arrangement for the Australian and New Zealand cameramen, and for most British cameramen outside the Western Front, to duplicate both functions in one man. The still photographers and cine cameramen often went on assignment together, and their work is often complementary.

Other than the *War Office Official Topical Budget*, the major British official film production for autumn 1917 onwards was the *British Regiments* series, each episode of which looked at the life of one battalion of a regiment serving on the Western Front. These films were released in pairs of films in three series, in December 1917, January 1918 and February 1918. Films of major battles were rare, and on a much smaller scale than the earlier big documentaries, and the whole style of official actuality film production had become generally more intimate by the end of 1918. Lack of supporting documentation makes it uncertain how many films in the IWM Series that are obviously of official origin and date from 1917-18 were ever released to the public in Britain or overseas. In addition, the Topical Film Company continued to function in its pre-war role as a newsreel production studio, providing cameramen to film events on the Home Front as required. Dramatised or other non-actuality propaganda films, including cartoons, were either produced for the War Office Cinema Committee by the Topical Film Company or contracted out to other British film studios.

The final stage in the evolution of British propaganda organisation came in February 1918 with the creation of the Ministry of Information under Beaverbrook, which amalgamated most of the existing propaganda departments, leaving only the Directorate of Enemy Propaganda at Crewe House under Lord Northcliffe outside Beaverbrook's control. The final organisation for filming and photographing the Western Front was established at General Headquarters in France in April 1918, when the cameramen (who had worn military uniform from the start) were given honorary commissions as lieutenants or second-lieutenants. Beaverbrook appointed Jury as head of the Ministry of Information Cinematograph Section, and the War Office Cinema Committee continued only in nominal existence for administrative and legal reasons before being wound up in 1919.

Several of the films made by the Ministry of Information in 1918 and preserved in the IWM Series give a clear indication of the direction in which British film propaganda was heading when the war ended. The short item and the *War Office Official Topical Budget* newsreel, renamed the *Pictorial News (Official)* in February 1918, remained the preferred format for actuality film. But there was also a new emphasis on short fictional dramas and cartoons, all on the theme of the need for a greater civilian war effort. The Ministry also produced its 'Film Tags', very short pieces to be shown during intervals in a normal commercial film show offering tips on rationing, encouragement to buy War Bonds, and so on. The tone of these films was increasingly anti-German, and outright hate propaganda, although very rare, was just starting to appear at the war's end.

Coverage by the British official cameramen of the final victories of 1918, on the Western Front and elsewhere, appears disappointing until one takes into account how few they were and the technological limitations of the cameras that they were using. They were better equipped to film victory parades than battles. Compilation films such as *The Great British Offensive* (IWM 322) and *How The British Army Broke The Famous Hindenburg Line* (IWM 332), made from material shot in August and September 1918, provided a valuable record but lacked the scale and inspiration of *The Battle of the Somme*.

In October 1918 Beaverbrook resigned as Minister of Information due to ill health, and in December the Ministry closed down, leaving only a rump organisation which became part of the Foreign Office. Since 1917, the Ministry had worked in close collaboration with the Imperial (originally National) War Museum, which was established in that year. Some of the Ministry's collections, such as photographs and pictorial art, were transferred directly to the Museum together with their associated departments. This did not happen to the official film collection for two reasons: the Museum did not have anywhere to store or show the films; and part of Jury's agreement with the War Office Cinema Committee was that his firm would enjoy three years' exclusive commercial exploitation of the films in Britain after the war. The first reels of the film collection, held in War Office storage vaults at Aldershot, came under Museum control in 1919 virtually as an unknown quantity with very little documentation, and extra material arrived from Jury's and other newsreel firms over the next few years. Post-war compilations now in the IWM Series, such as *The World's Greatest Story* (IWM 420) and *Our Empire's Fight for Freedom* (IWM 440), about which little is known, fall into this category. Other films, such as *The Advance Through Nazareth and Damascus* (IWM 37), which has very detailed intertitles, may represent Jury's reworking of the original official films.

In 1920 a viewing room and storage vaults were made available to the Museum at the War Office and a small permanent staff employed under E Foxen Cooper, the Government's 'Cinematography Adviser', who acted as part-time custodian of the collection. The Museum's terms of reference were to preserve the achievements of Britain and its Empire during the war. It concluded reciprocal arrangements with Canada, Australia and New Zealand for exchange of film, but declined to enter into similar agreements with the United States or Germany, on the grounds that neither was part of the British Empire. Nevertheless, the IWM Series does include both American and German official films of the war, possibly acquired by the Topical Film Company before the collection was handed over to the Museum.

From late 1921 until early 1923, as detailed memories of the war faded, the Museum made its first serious attempt to evaluate the official film collection as history. Under Foxen Cooper's direction, viewing sessions were arranged at the War Office and Admiralty for officers who would identify fakes and pass judgement on the films. As part of this process, efforts were made to question the official cameramen on the locations and dates of their original material for the big battle pictures, although after four years their replies were not necessarily accurate. But however well intentioned, these viewing sessions appear to have been conducted in a very unsystematic manner, and to have yielded few useful results. To judge from their written notes, the Royal Navy and Army officers (including, on one occasion, the famous Colonel J F C Fuller of the Tank Corps) treated the sessions as little more than a pleasant afternoon's recreation, and – like a surprising number of battlefield veterans – they failed to distinguish accurately between genuine actuality film and reconstruction. The broad conclusion was that the films were of little or no military or historical value, and that apart from a few extracts they should be destroyed.

To its credit, the Imperial War Museum refused to take this advice, although it had no way of presenting its films to the public, and they were of no obvious commercial value. Despite repeated requests and some complaints, the Museum also refused to allow the use of its material in commercial feature films. It collected or accepted very few films in the inter-war period, and did so with reluctance. However, until the foundation in 1935 of the National Film Library (later the National Film Archive, and now the National Film and Television Archive) the Museum was the only British national repository for official films of a historic nature. Foxen Cooper suggested on several occasions that systematic filming of important events for the official record should be continued or resumed after the war, but with little success. Two events – the signing of the Locarno Pact in 1925, and a visit to England by the King of Afghanistan in 1928 – were filmed, the latter certainly under Foxen Cooper's supervision, but these two items (held in the collection as IWM 811 and IWM 809 respectively) apparently represent his only successes in this field. At least one film, on the funeral of Marshal Foch of France (IWM 509), was deposited with the Museum at the request of the Prince of Wales (later Edward VIII) in 1930. The IWM Series includes other films of non-military subjects from this period, including the 1924 Olympic Games, and it is at least a plausible hypothesis that these were also royal gifts.

The Museum's main policy towards film in this period was simply to preserve the collection entrusted to it, starting in 1921 by making archive master prints. In the late 1920s a second investigation was made into the state of the films, leading to the assignment of new can numbers for the collection. According to lists still extant, this made the following subdivisions to the series:

IWM 1 – 60	Palestine (including Egypt)
IWM 61 – 94	Mesopotamia
IWM 95 – 100	Salonika
IWM 101 – 500	Western Front (including Italy and Britain)
IWM 501 – 549	Miscellaneous subjects (including presentation films)
IWM 550 – 600	Admiralty
IWM 601 – 650	Air Force (Air Ministry Films)
IWM 651 – 700	Topical Films
IWM 701 – 725	War Office
IWM 726 – 750*	Board of Trade
IWM 751 – 800*	Board of Agriculture
IWM 801 – 850*	Various (Industrial Films etc)

A very few films on these lists have not survived to the present day. Also now largely missing are the government or industrial films (marked *) from after the First World War, which came only indirectly within the Museum's terms of reference. These were either given up to other institutions or possibly left unpreserved in the 1930s. The numbering sequence was also deliberately left with some blank numbers into which additional films were slotted as appropriate after their acquisition at a later date.

After further investigations, the Museum began a major film preservation programme between 1930 and 1933, which was resumed and completed in 1938. As part of this process, in 1934 W J G Maloney, who had originally joined Foxen Cooper's staff in 1920 as a messenger, was given the task of viewing the collection, and assembling a card index and shotsheets (detailed lists of the contents of the film on a scene-by-scene basis) for each film. Taking about four years to complete, Maloney's work represented the first catalogue of the series. He was designated Film Librarian in 1937. Foxen Cooper died in 1934 and was succeeded as the Government's Cinematography Adviser by J G Hughes-Roberts. Like Foxen Cooper before him, Hughes-Roberts was actually employed by His Majesty's Stationery Office (HMSO), the agency responsible for government publications and Crown copyright. In 1939 it was reported that HMSO was responsible for some 2 million feet of film, ninety percent of which was the Museum's collection.

The Second World War vastly increased the Museum's film holdings, and what previously had been simply its film collection became known as the IWM Series, a term used specifically for films taken and acquired before 1939. The film collection was transferred to the direct control of the Museum in 1953, with Maloney joining the Museum staff and remaining Film Librarian until his retirement in 1962. Understanding of the collection depended very heavily on his personal knowledge, and that of his successor John Sutters, who died in 1971. A year before this, the Museum created a Department of Film under Clive Coultass, who was succeeded by Anne Fleming in 1983.

In 1958, under the terms of the Public Records Act, the Museum became the recognised repository for official films of conflicts involving British or Commonwealth forces since 1914. A virtually simultaneous extension of the Museum's terms of reference empowered it to acquire films of the First World War other than those official films in the original IWM Series. The series has never been closed or completed, although its growth is now measured in terms of a handful of films each decade. In the same year, the film collection was moved to new vaults with greatly improved preservation facilities at the Public Record Office site at Hayes in Middlesex. By the end of the 1960s a major preservation programme to generate new acetate safety masters from the nitrate originals of the IWM Series was nearing completion at Hayes. Viewing facilities using Steenbeck editing tables were established in the Department of Film at the Museum's main building in London, and a public cinema was opened there to show films from the collection.

These changes meant that the Museum was unusually well placed for the next major development in the history of the IWM Series – its exploitation by television. In 1964 the BBC first screened its television series *The Great War*, which drew heavily on the IWM Series as a primary source. Indeed, some accounts give the highly misleading impression that television researchers discovered a hitherto unknown collection at the Museum. The full historical significance of *The Great War* in British cultural understanding of the First World War has yet to be properly assessed, although there is evidence that it has been considerable. For the IWM Series as a historical record this television exposure was a mixed blessing. It introduced the film images of the First World War once more to a mass audience, and provided the Museum with an important source of revenue for film preservation. But, whereas since the 1920s the War Office and Museum staff, with inadequate resources, had made efforts to evaluate the films in context and to identify fakes, *The Great War* set the documentary television convention of using images from authentic archive and old feature film indiscriminately, purely for dramatic visual effect. Although there have been honourable exceptions, most notably the 1973 Thames Television series *The World At War*, the demand for 'good shots' rather than historical accuracy has remained dominant. In this respect, television programme makers have followed the same imperatives as the original editors and exploiters of the compilation official films under Beaverbrook.

Partly in response to the increasing importance of television exploitation of its film archive following *The Great War*, the Museum established a Department of Information Retrieval, the main duty of which became the researching and cataloguing of the film collection on a systematic basis. The cataloguers were generally recruited for an interest in military history rather than formal training in librarianship or knowledge of film theory. In 1990 the Keeper of Information Retrieval, Roger Smither, succeeded Anne Fleming as Keeper of the Department of Film.

In 1980 I was myself recruited into Information Retrieval principally to research and recatalogue the IWM Series. This was the first comprehensive attempt to catalogue the series since Maloney's in 1934, adding to work in the late 1970s on cataloguing its naval material by Neil Pilfold, also of Information Retrieval. The new catalogue took from October 1980 to December 1983 to complete, being based on the systematic viewing (using a Steenbeck film table) and research of every film in the collection. Daily responsibility for the actual handling of each film as it arrived lay with the cutting room staff of the Department of Film under Alice 'Queenie' Turner as Film Librarian. Queenie, who retired in 1984 after 50 years working with film, had begun her career in a newsreel firm employing Frank Bassill, the former Western Front official cameraman.

The principal research aid in cataloguing the film was the Museum's own excellent military library held by the Department of Printed Books (together with the specialist knowledge of many of the Museum staff). In addition, because of the close partnership between still photographers and cine cameramen, the collection held by the Department of Photographs frequently deals with the same subjects as the films, often with more detailed captions than the intertitles of the films. The shotsheets produced by Maloney sometimes provide information which has otherwise since been lost, and further information comes from the original Topical Film Company store ledgers, recording the commercial details of each film. The Department of Film also holds 'dope sheets' for a few of the major IWM Series films. Strictly, a dope sheet is a detailed written record made by the cameraman at the time of what he has filmed. These sheets, however, are believed to have been compiled by Foxen Cooper and his staff in discussions with the cameramen in the early 1920s as part of the first viewing and assessment process, and should be treated with caution.

In addition to the IWM Series films themselves, the Department of Film also holds at least part of the working papers of the Topical Film Company for the period that it was owned by the War Office Cinema Committee, together with the early papers of the Imperial War Museum dealing with its film collection up to about 1930. Although these papers are available to researchers they remain working papers of the Department of Film rather than a historical source, and there is no generally accepted reference system for them. I have referred to them in this catalogue and elsewhere as the MoI(Film) and IWM(Film) Papers. In 1983 the Australian War Memorial kindly supplied the Department of Film with copies of Australian War Records Section papers relating to film, referred to as AWRS(Film) Papers.

While I was cataloguing the IWM Series I was fortunate that other researchers were busy uncovering the story of the War Office Cinema Committee and the various ancestors of the Ministry of Information. In particular, Dr Nicholas Hiley was then working on his own doctoral thesis on British propaganda 1914-16, and has spent many years since in search of details on the official photographers and cameramen. In 1993 he provided the introduction to a facsimile reprint of Geoffrey Malins's memoirs *How I Filmed the War*, published by the Museum. Dr Nicholas Reeves of Thames Valley University published his own detailed account, *Official British Propaganda During the First World War*, in association with the Museum in 1986.

As this introduction has already made clear, the newsreel *Topical Budget* became the vehicle for much British film activity during the war. Luke McKernan, a cataloguer at the National Film and Television Archive, has worked extensively in recent years on the newsreel, as the surviving issues from the non-War Office period, together with the company's records, are now in the Archive's collections. Both his book *Topical Budget: the Great British News Film,* published by the British Film Institute in 1992, and his other work – including the presently unpublished *Catalogue of the Topical Budget Newsreel* (1911-31) – have been invaluable to the Museum in the preparation of this publication.

Christopher Pugsley, a military historian currently working on a research project at the New Zealand Film Archive, has been most helpful in correcting the Museum's identification and attribution of New Zealand official film. His detailed comments, which are incorporated into the entries and notes for New Zealand films in the catalogue that follows, will be expanded upon in his forthcoming book, *The Camera in the Crowd.*

For the three years that I worked on the IWM Series, and for a decade afterwards, Roger Smither has provided unfailing support, some sharp insights, and the most gentle of correctives.

The cataloguing process used to recatalogue the IWM Series was based on an off-line system producing computer-generated microfiche. At the time the Department of Film was changing over from APPARAT, a computer system designed specifically for the Museum, to the Museum Documentation Association system GOS which was used to produce the final microfiche catalogue. This catalogue, which is available to be consulted by researchers in the Department of Film, includes comprehensive index listings for the contents of the IWM Series films which could not be included in this printed catalogue. Since 1983 further work has been done on the IWM Series notably, by Neil Pilfold, who has catalogued most of the additional *Topical Budget* newsreels included in this catalogue as the NTB Series. The individual cataloguers for each film are identified by their initials as follows:

SDB	Stephen Badsey
KGTG	Kay Gladstone
JCK	John Kerr
NAP	Neil Pilfold
RBNS	Roger Smither
DW	David Walsh

The final version of this published catalogue was completed by Roger Smither and John Kerr in 1992-93. The catalogue has been derived from the Museum Documentation Association MODES system and further processed using Microsoft Word. The cataloguing conventions used are those established in the Museum for its own use. Some of these may require explanation – see the section *How to Use the Catalogue* following this introduction.

The recataloguing process uncovered both errors and discrepancies in the original IWM Series catalogue. In particular, a single film number was found on occasions to cover more than one film, either in several reels or on the same reel. It was neither practical nor necessary to embark for a second time on large scale renumbering of the collection, which would have involved at least three copies (the fine grain master, the negative and the viewing print) for each film, and would have produced considerable disruption. Instead, individual films were identified as sub-items of a specific number. The extreme examples of this phenomenon are the *Annales de la Guerre* newsreel, held under a single number as IWM 508 reels 10 to 92, and the single reel IWM 700, which contains news stories from five different issues of the *War Office Official Topical Budget* with intertitles in Spanish, catalogued as films IWM 700a-e. There are more than enough instances of such multiple entries to compensate for the intentional or accidental gaps in the numbering sequence. As a result, although that sequence now runs from IWM 1 to IWM 1218 (with more films being added all the time) the actual number of individual films held in the collection is rather greater.

Following the recataloguing of the 1980s, the IWM Series is at present divided as follows:

IWM 1 – 58	Palestine, including Egypt
IWM 59 – 100	Mesopotamia and Salonika
IWM 101 – 200	Western Front (including Italy and Britain)
IWM 201 – 419	Western Front continued (including early material)
IWM 420 – 507	Western Front continued (including compilations)
IWM 508	The *Annales de la Guerre* newsreel
IWM 509 – 549	Ministry of Information
IWM 550 – 603	Admiralty
IWM 604 – 650	Air Force (Air Ministry Films)
IWM 651 – 700	The *War Office Official Topical Budget* newsreel
IWM 706 – 859	Films of an official or semi-official nature acquired in the 1920s
IWM 860 – 989	RAF instructional or newsreel films of 1917-36
IWM 990 – 1060	Films mainly of the First World War acquired 1951-70
IWM 1061	The Foulkes collection
IWM 1062 – 1142	Films mainly of the First World War acquired since 1970
IWM 1143 – 1166	Admiralty
IWM 1167 – 1218	Films mainly of the First World War acquired or renumbered since 1970

The core of the IWM Series remains the uncut footage shot by the British and Dominion official cameramen on the Western, Italian, Salonika, Palestine and Mesopotamian Fronts from late 1915 to 1918. The typical film of the collection is silent actuality material of the First World War, either unedited or with the contemporary editing left intact, sometimes with intertitles, but often without them.

While the catalogue itself forms the most complete guide to the IWM Series, the following overview, in which a few of the more notable films have been indicated, will give an idea of its scope and may be helpful to browsers.

IWM 1-58. This section consists largely of the films shot by British and Australian official cameramen in Egypt and Palestine between about April 1917 and the end of the war, including the famous *General Allenby's Entry into Jerusalem* (IWM 13). The film taken by Lowell Thomas and his cameraman Harry Chase of T E Lawrence is also in the collection, at least after a fashion. What Thomas provided as his part of the bargain with the British Government was 90 minutes of off-cuts and short sections which may represent a complete set of his original rushes, but were in no logical sequence. Reconstruction work by the Museum staff in the 1980s has joined matching sequences together and generally made the film (IWM 41) more accessible. A later Museum acquisition dating from 1927, the two short films *With Lawrence in Arabia* and *With Allenby in Palestine*, both on the same reel (IWM 1131), show the use which Lowell Thomas made of his material and that of the official cameramen.

IWM 59-100. This section consists largely of the film shot by Ariel Varges in Salonika and Mesopotamia. There is inevitably some overlap between the Palestine and Mesopotamia material, which was treated in Britain as being from the same exotic part of the world. One remarkable inclusion is the uncut film taken by Varges of the 'Dunsterforce' expedition under Brigadier-General Lionel Dunsterville to Baku in Azerbaijan in August 1918 at the height of the Russian Civil War (IWM 73). Two unofficial films from 1916 have also became part of the collection, probably in the initial transfer from Jury's Imperial Pictures. These are Gaumont's *With the Kut Relief Force in Mesopotamia* (IWM 83), which includes a number of suspect scenes, and Cherry Kearton's *Operations of the British Expeditionary Forces in East Africa* (IWM 84). A mixture of British and French official films of the Salonika Front occupies the end of the sequence.

IWM 101-200. This section consists largely of film by British and Dominion official cameramen on the Western Front from late 1915 to the end of the war. These films are frequently uncut rushes missing their intertitles, and poorly supported by documentation. Generally they provide considerable problems for the viewer. They are in no particular logical or sequence, and include occasional films from the Home Front and the Italian Front. The three main British official production films of the war, *The Battle of the Somme* (IWM 191), *The Battle of the Ancre and the Advance of the Tanks* (IWM 116) and *The German Retreat and the Battle of Arras* (IWM 113), are in this sequence, together with the early 1917 series *Sons of Our Empire* (IWM 130) and the less well recognised industrial classic, *Woolwich Arsenal and Its Workers* (IWM 161). An unusual inclusion is the visit of D W Griffith to the Western Front (IWM 122) as part of the filming of his own feature film *Hearts of the World*. This film was partly reconstructed in 1981 with the inclusion of some previously missing sections. Another unexpected inclusion is a film taken of the immediate aftermath of the Dublin Easter Rising of 1916 (IWM 194).

IWM 201-419. This section is a continuation of the official First World War material, with a rather higher proportion of completed films. It includes many of the short films made by the British Topical Committee For War Films before *The Battle of the Somme*, which are otherwise generally scattered throughout the collection. The most notable items are one of the few existing films of Lord Kitchener, who died in June 1916 (IWM 213), and several reels of rushes dealing with American troops on the Western Front, some of them clearly by American cameramen. This part of the collection also includes the uncut British rushes from the German offensive of March 1918, and the British offensive of August and September 1918, which make an interesting comparison with the earlier battle films. It ends with most of the *British Regiments* series, largely in sequence.

IWM 420-507. As well as Western Front material and more of the *British Regiments* series this part of the collection has several large compilation films of the First World War. Among these are *The World's Greatest Story* (IWM 420) which includes the intervention in Russia in 1918-19, and *Our Empire's Fight For Freedom* (IWM 440), together with *America's Answer to the Hun* (IWM 458) and *Pictorial History of the World War* (IWM 501) from the United States. The compilation film *Five Years Ago* (IWM 442), made in 1923, is the first example of the Museum attempting to exploit its own collection. Two rare soundtrack films in this part of the collection are *The First World War* (IWM 484), made by Truman Talley and Laurence Stallings for the Fox Film Corporation in 1934, and *The Soul of a Nation* (IWM 485) made by J B Williams for Associated British Film Distributors on behalf of the Conservative Party in 1933, both gifts to the Museum for the use of some of its material. Generally, this part of the collection marks an area of distinct but uneven transition from official British and Dominion films taken during the war to films acquired by the Museum in the war's immediate aftermath.

IWM 508-10–508-92. This is an almost complete run of the French official newsreel of the war, *Annales de la Guerre* from Issue 10 in May 1917 to the final Issue 92 in December 1918, in exchange for the *War Office Official Topical Budget*. Intertitles are usually in French, and it is possible to compare French and British treatments of the same events, and even the same film, by comparison with the *War Office Official Topical Budget*.

IWM 509-549. Almost all of the films in this sequence are British official dramatised or cartoon propaganda films of 1918, including the Ministry of Information 'Film Tags'. The British official view of role of women in the later part of the war is well covered in the IWM Series in general, and *Mrs John Bull Prepared* (IWM 521) and *The Woman's Portion* (IWM 522) are of particular interest. The level of sophistication reached by the propagandists in 1918 is well illustrated by *The Adventures of Dick Dolan* (IWM 537), a fictional romance made to encourage the purchase of War Bonds.

IWM 551-603. This section consists almost entirely of British official Admiralty film shot during the war from 1916 onwards, mainly in British home waters, in a mixture of rushes and completed films. One interesting inclusion (IWM 560) is a British adaptation of the German film of submarine U.35 operating in the Mediterranean in 1917. It is significant that *Britain Prepared* (IWM 580) was included among this naval material, reflecting its concentration on the Royal Navy. Although distinctly out of place in the series, the films on the 1924 Olympic Games all come under the same number (IWM 594) as part of this sequence.

IWM 604-650. This section consists largely of films made by the Royal Flying Corps and Royal Air Force during and just after the First World War, including trial flights of airships and aircraft filmed by the Air Ministry. Among the most impressive of these films is *HMS Argus Alighting Trials* (IWM 627), showing experiments in autumn 1918 in landing aircraft on an aircraft carrier. Also included in this section are *Surrender of the German High Seas Fleet* (IWM 637), and *The Arrival of the German Submarines Off Harwich* (IWM 646). The section ends with a Pathé film, *War In the Air* (IWM 650), showing a seaplane of the Russian Imperial Navy on the Black Sea during the war.

IWM 651-700. The section contains much of the *War Office Official Topical Budget* newsreel held in the IWM Series, although other examples will be found elsewhere. Languages for the intertitles in the *Topical Budgets* in the IWM Series, where they appear, vary between English, French and Spanish. Comparison with contents lists for the English language versions shown in Britain suggests that several of the reels in French or Spanish contain stories from more than one issue. (Another possibility is that they are complete issues prepared for overseas release, with a different running order from the domestic version.) Some of the material in these newsreels is clearly identifiable from the earlier rushes in the collection, but several sequences, in particular of the Home Front, do not appear elsewhere. It is a reflection of the manner in which the IWM Series was passed to the Museum that other films unrelated to the *War Office Official Topical Budget* have found their way into the collection from Jury's or the Topical studios in the same cans. Since 1984 more complete examples of *War Office Official Topical Budget* newsreels have been placed in their own series, the NTB Series.

IWM 706-859. This section includes most of the films acquired by the Museum in the 1920s, including the notable *Modern Warfare in China 1924-1925* (IWM 712), a film produced in the Soviet Union with intertitles in English, Russian and Chinese, showing the army of a Soviet-backed Chinese warlord, and *Kaiser Wilhelm Visits Turkey* (IWM 772), a copy of a German film made in 1917. As the area of the collection originally intended for Board of Trade and Ministry of Agriculture films, this sequence still includes such unwarlike items as *The Harvest of the Sugar Maple Tree* (IWM 812) and *50,000 Miles With The Prince of Wales* (IWM 843), made in 1920.

IWM 860-989. This is the first section to go beyond the numbering of the 1920s, and consists largely of RAF films from 1917 through to 1936. Some of these are instructional or training films, others are extracts from newsreels or completed films of general interest. The section includes several films of rare or unusual interwar aircraft.

IWM 990-1060. This section marks the known start of the collection following the Second World War with the *Sapper Reunion Film* (IWM 990), a compilation which can be firmly dated to 1951. It also shows the change in acquisition policy, with a widening of the collection including a reel of Second Boer War material (IWM 1025) and *Heroes of Gallipoli* (IWM 1058), the Australian edited version of the Ashmead Bartlett film. The collection also contains several reels of European archive film connected with *The Great War* series.

IWM 1061-01–1061-09o. This section consists of a bequest to the Museum by a Welsh private collector, Mr E G Foulkes, in the 1970s, and contains a number of fragments from the *War Office Official Topical Budget* and other newsreels, particularly the *Gaumont Graphic* of the First World War.

IWM 1062-IWM 1142. This section consists of the continuing acquisitions for the IWM Series within the last two decades, and for self-evident reasons it follows no common theme or logical progression. The collection held as IWM 1062-01 to IWM 1062-22 was donated to the Museum in the 1970s by Mrs Bing Maddicks. Material dealing with other nations than Britain, or with events before 1916, is more likely to be found in this part of the collection than among the earlier official material. One film of particular interest is the *Landung auf Osel 1917* (IWM 1124), a German film of their successful amphibious landings in the Baltic in 1917.

IWM 1143-1166. This section consists of additional British official naval material of the First World War, transferred to the Museum in the 1970s. Some of the material, described in documentation as being of the Battle of Jutland, appears to be of that era, but no film was taken of the battle itself.

IWM 1167-1218. This section, which ends the IWM Series to date, shows the same random pattern of recent acquisitions to the collection. It also includes a few films from earlier in the collection which were renumbered for various reasons during the cataloguing of the 1980s, in particular some material of tests of prototype First World War tanks. Also notable is one of the few genuinely virulent anti-German propaganda films produced by the Ministry of Information at the end of the war, *The Leopard's Spots* (IWM 1209).

NTB Series. As has already been noted, a number of more complete English-language examples of *War Office Official Topical Budget* newsreels acquired since 1984 have been placed in their own series, the NTB Series.

It is hoped that the new catalogue has produced a general improvement in knowledge of the IWM Series, and made the series more accessible to researchers. At the very least, it has improved the quality (and sometimes the accuracy) of the stockshots of the First World War offered on British television, starting to reverse the process begun by *The Great War*. It also uncovered some small historical nuggets. For the military historian, an anonymous column of troops in *Britain Prepared* was unexpectedly identified as the 36th Ulster Division (recruited from the original Ulster Volunteer Force which in 1914 had been prepared to fight the British Army to prevent Irish independence) loyally marching past King George V in 1915. For the film historian, a most unexpected inclusion among the *War Office Official Topical Budget* cans was *The Police Dog* (IWM 670c), a cartoon on the adventures of 'Pinkerton Pup' produced by J R Bray for Pathé in the United States in 1916, which may be the only surviving print of this previously lost film. For the historian of film propaganda, a can of apparently unrelated and meaningless segments (IWM 383) turned out to be the censored sections from two of the early 1916 British official films, showing censorship policy in action. A film originally catalogued as "Martyred Belgium" (IWM 714) was recognised following publication in 1985 of an article by Nicholas Hiley as an incomplete copy of the 'lost' propaganda film *For the Empire*.

One additional spin-off from work on the IWM Series has been continuing detailed research into the film *The Battle of the Somme* in particular. Released on video with viewing notes by the Museum in 1987, this film is now achieving its proper place at the centre of any discussion of British perspectives on the First World War, both at the time and in the modern television era. A further video released by the Museum in the course of 1991 was entitled *War Women of Britain* and features eight short films and 'Film Tags' dealing with the Home Front, 1917-18. A new video edition of *The Battle of the Somme*, packaged with its sequel *The Battle of the Ancre and the Advance of the Tanks* with a specially recorded piano accompaniment, was released through a commercial distributor, DD Video, in November 1993.

Viewed as a film historical record, the main value of the IWM Series films is the wealth of social history that they contain, most of it revealed unintentionally by the camera. Although several of the films are valuable to military specialists researching the First World War, they are much less spectacular than feature film representations of war, something which again often disappoints researchers. But in addition to its value as a social record, it is hoped that the film collection represented by this catalogue, placed together in context with other work done on British propaganda in the First World War, will also continue to contribute to the major changes in our understanding of Britain during the war that are at present taking place within British historical study.

Cataloguing the unedited silent film with little supporting documentation which is typical of the IWM Series may best be compared to the work of an archaeologist translating the corrupt text of an inscription in a dead language carved on the wall of some decaying monument. It is remarkable how much was forgotten and has had to be rediscovered since 1918. But it is also, I am sure, remarkable how much has still been missed. It is a feature of the IWM Series films that something new can be found at every viewing, depending on the interests and expertise brought by the viewer. No one who has worked on this catalogue would pretend that it is definitive, and I earnestly recommend that researchers should treat it only as the starting place for their own investigations. Comments, corrections and suggestions should be communicated to the Department of Film in writing, and are more than welcome.

The last word should be left to the review of *The Battle of the Somme* which appeared in *The Times* on its first release in August 1916, and has become something of a slogan for all those connected with the IWM Series:

> In years to come, when historians want to know the conditions under which the great offensive was launched, they will only have to send for these films and a complete idea of the situation will be revealed before their eyes – for we take it as a matter of course that a number of copies of them will be carefully preserved in the national archives.

■ **Dr Stephen Badsey** is currently a Senior Lecturer in the Department of War Studies at the Royal Military Academy, Sandhurst. He was formerly with the Department of Information Retrieval at the Imperial War Museum and has worked as a film researcher and consultant for the BBC. He has written extensively on military-media matters and modern warfare. His recent books include *The Gulf War Assessed*, with John Pimlott (London: Arms and Armour Press, 1992).

Bibliography

S D Badsey, 'Battle of the Somme: British War Propaganda' in *Historical Journal of Film, Radio and Television* 3: 2 (1983).

Kevin Brownlow, *The War, The West and the Wilderness*, Secker and Warburg (London, 1979).

Jane Carmichael, *First World War Photographers*, Routledge (London, 1989).

[E Foxen Cooper], 'Historical Film Records: The Life of the Nation: A Heritage for Posterity' (article by "A Correspondent" from *The Times* of 19 March 1929), reprinted in *Researcher's Guide to British Newsreels Vol III*, editor James Ballantyne, British Universities Film and Video Council (London, 1993).

Kay Gladstone, 'Film as Allied assistance: Captain Bromhead's mission to Russia, 1916-1917' in *Imperial War Museum Review* 9 (1994).

Cate Haste, *Keep The Home Fires Burning*, Allen Lane (London, 1977).

Nicholas Hiley, '*The British Army Film, You!* and *For the Empire*: reconstructed propaganda films' in *Historical Journal of Film, Radio and Television* 5: 2 (1985).

Nicholas Hiley, *Making War: The British News Media and Government Control 1914-1916* (Open University, unpublished PhD thesis, 1985).

Rachael Low, *The History of the British Film 1914-1918*, Allen and Unwin (1950; subsequent edition 1973).

Luke McKernan, *Topical Budget: The Great British News Film*, British Film Institute (London, 1992).

Luke McKernan, *Catalogue of the Topical Budget newsreel (1911-1931)* (National Film and Television Archive, London, unpublished work in progress).

Geoffrey H Malins, *How I Filmed the War*, Herbert Jenkins (London, 1920; reprinted with an introduction by Nicholas Hiley by the Imperial War Museum, London, 1993).

Gary S Messinger, *British Propaganda and the State in the First World War*, Manchester University Press (Manchester, 1992).

Christopher Pugsley, *The Camera in the Crowd* (New Zealand Film Archive, Wellington, unpublished work in progress).

Nicholas Reeves, *Official British Film Propaganda During the First World War*, Croom Helm (London, 1986).

M L Sanders, 'British Film Propaganda in Russia 1916-1918' in *Historical Journal of Film, Radio and Television* 3: 2 (1983).

M L Sanders and Philip M Taylor, *British Propaganda During the First World War*, Macmillan (London 1982).

Roger Smither (ed), *The Battles of the Somme and Ancre*, DD Video (London, 1993).

Roger Smither and David Walsh, 'Unknown Pioneer: Edward Foxen Cooper and the Imperial War Museum Film Archive, 1919-1934' in *Imperial War Museum Review* 9 (1994).

David Walsh, 'The Imperial War Museum Film Archive' in *Image Technology* 75: 3 (1993).

A slightly different version of this introduction appeared as an article in the *Historical Journal of Film, Radio and Television* 13: 2 (1993). This was a special issue on Britain and the cinema in the First World War, and also included the following articles:

Gary S Messinger, 'An Inheritance Worth Remembering: The British Approach to Official Propaganda during the First World War'.

Nicholas Hiley, 'Hilton DeWitt Girdwood and the origins of British official filming'.

Roger Smither, '"A Wonderful Idea of the Fighting": the question of fakes in *The Battle of the Somme*'.

Luke McKernan, '"The Supreme Moment of the War": *General Allenby's Entry into Jerusalem*'.

Nicholas Reeves, 'The Power of Film Propaganda – Myth or Reality?'

Andrew Kelly, 'The Brutality of Military Incompetence: *Paths of Glory* (1957)'.

How to Use the Catalogue

A typical entry has the following appearance:

IWM 163 · GB, (prod) 1918
a BOMB PROOF LODGING

b/w · 1 reel · 66' (1 min) · silent
intertitles: none

sp War Office Cinema Committee *pr* Topical Film Company *cam* Bassill, F A

■ Gunners of 51st (Highland) Division enter by ladder a temporary shelter they
have constructed in a large overturned water tower at Riencourt near Bapaume,
Western Front, 5 January 1918.

[shotsheet available]
catalogued SDB: 6/1982

It is hoped that such entries are reasonably self-explanatory. However, the following
notes describe the entry, area by area.

(1) Reference number
IWM 163 · GB, (prod) 1918

The first item of information is the reference number by which the film is identified in
Museum records. This catalogue is arranged in numerical order, and all the indexes
refer to the reference number. Note that, for reasons explained in the *Introduction*,
"reference numbers" are sometimes quite complex codes. Because of the catalogue's
numerical arrangement, notes are included to explain gaps in the sequence.

The remainder of the line gives the country of origin of the film and the date of
release if known. If a release date is not known, a date of production (prod) is supplied.
Dates are given as precisely as possible: in many cases, however, only a general estimate
is possible. Estimated dates may be qualified by a question mark (indicating a probable
date), by the abbreviation ca. (for circa), or by the terms "before" or "after" (more
precise than ca., in that a definite cut-off point can be determined). Occasionally, no
more accurate estimate than a span of years can be given.

(2) Title
a BOMB PROOF LODGING

Information is next given on the title(s) by which the film is identified: that given in bold
type is considered the main title. When known, this is the title used for the film on its
original release. An allocated title, which is always clearly identified as such, is one
invented by the cataloguer to describe the film when no title exists, or the existing title is
misleading.

Other titles, which appear in ordinary type on subsequent lines, usually with an explanatory note, may include a series title, an alternative title, a translation for a title in a foreign language, or a related title. A related title indicates, for example, that one film contains or consists of rough material for another.

(3) Technical description
b/w · 1 reel · 66' (1 min) · silent
intertitles: none

Technical information is provided on the colour, length (in number of reels, and as a total length measured in feet), running time and sound of the film: terms used are explained in *Abbreviations*, and as follows:

tinted   this entry indicates that the original nitrate material held by the Museum is or was wholly or partly tinted – *ie* colour was added to the film stock to create or enhance a particular mood. Note that such tinting is not commonly reproduced in acetate viewing prints made from the same material.

           lengths are expressed in the 'Imperial' unit of measurement, feet, to the nearest foot. Metric equivalents may be calculated using the formulae 1 foot = 0.3048 metres; 1 metre = 3.2809 feet.

mins   running times are expressed to the nearest minute; for silent film, running times are calculated at the notional running speed of 16 frames per second.

silent   film without sound, with full frame pictures extending the complete width of the film between the sprocket holes.

comopt   (*ie* combined optical): optical soundtrack printed onto a picture-carrying film.

mute   film without sound, printed with reduced frame size leaving space for an optical soundtrack.

(4) Credits
sp War Office Cinema Committee *pr* Topical Film Company *cam* Bassill, F A

Production credits are given to the best of the Museum's current knowledge. Credits rarely appear on screen and have been researched as far as possible in sources considered authoritative. Such documentation is itself often incomplete and the information given is, therefore, often a statement of probability (indicated by a question mark) or a statement that one of two cameramen would have been responsible, etc. Terms used are explained in *Abbreviations*.

(5) Summary
■ Gunners of 51st (Highland) Division enter by ladder a temporary shelter they have constructed in a large overturned water tower at Riencourt near Bapaume, Western Front, 5 January 1918.

A descriptive summary of the film is provided. When a film is of more than one reel, the summary will usually indicate the location of reel changes, but does not otherwise indicate the location of any given shot in the film. Given the subject matter of the collection, there is much military terminology in these entries: no attempt has been made to supply a comprehensive dictionary of such terms. In some entries, however, abbreviations are used to describe the camera angles etc. Such terms are explained in *Abbreviations*.

(6) Notes
[shotsheet available]
catalogued SDB: 6/1982

The final area of information will include some or all of the following:

Notes, including the following:
- notes on aspects of the catalogue entry, such as the sources for data, particularly titles, not apparent from the film itself;
- notes on the events portrayed;
- cross-references to other films;
- the Museum's cataloguing rules allow (perhaps unusually) the cataloguer's own personal views on a film, entered as specifically identified "remarks". Note: these "remarks" have been retained in the published catalogue but do not reflect or constitute an official Museum evaluation of the film.

References to books, journal articles, newspapers or unpublished sources relevant to or used in compiling the catalogue entry.

Indications of other documentation (most frequently a shotsheet) which is not published but is available in the Museum's Department of Film.

The identity of the cataloguer and the date the entry was completed.

CURRENCY

Several of the films contain references to prices given in the currency system used in Britain before decimalisation in 1971. One pound (£) was divided into twenty shillings (s), each of which contained twelve pence (d). A price could be written as £2 10s 6d or as £2/10/6; 15s 6d or 15/6. By convention, prices were often described in terms of smaller units – "forty shillings" meaning two pounds, or "three ha'pence" meaning 1½d.

Coins in circulation had the following values:
¼d; ½d; 1d; 3d; 6d; 1s; 2s; 2s6d; 10s; £1 (a sovereign).

Abbreviations

The following abbreviations have been used in the catalogue:

AA	anti-aircraft	cal	calibre
AAC	Australian Air Corps	*cam*	cameraman
ADC	aide de camp	CB	(1) Companion of the Bath*
ADM	the 'Admiralty' series of films in the Imperial War Museum film archive		(2) model designation of British C-type airship
ADS	Advanced Dressing Station	CCS	Casualty Clearing Station
adv	adviser	CE1	model designation of a flying boat produced by the Royal
AEF	American Expeditionary Force		Aircraft Factory; "CE" stood
AEG	Allgemeine Elektrizitäts Gesellschaft		for "Coastal Experiment".
ALH	Australian Light Horse	CIGS	Chief of the Imperial General Staff
ANZAC	Australian and New Zealand Army Corps	C-in-C	Commander-in-Chief
APTC	Army Physical Training Corps	CIV	City Imperial Volunteers
ARS	appareil respiratoire spécial (French gas mask)	CMB	Coastal Motor Boat
		CMG	Companion of the Order of St Michael and St George*
AS	anti-submarine	COI	the 'Central Office of
ASC	Army Service Corps		Information' series of films in
ASW	anti-submarine warfare		the Imperial War Museum film
AUX MT	Auxiliary Motor Transport		archive
AWRS	Australian War Records Section	*comm*	commentary
Bde	Brigade	*comm sp*	commentary spoken
BE2, BE2C		comopt	combined optical (optical
	model designation of a fighter aircraft produced by the Royal Aircraft Factory; "BE" stood for "Blériot Experimental".		soundtrack printed onto a picture-carrying film)
		comp	compiler
		CoS	Chief of Staff
BEF	British Expeditionary Force	Coy	Company
BFI	British Film Institute	Cpt	Captain
Bn	Battalion	CSM	Company Sergeant-Major
BSA	Birmingham Small Arms Company	CSMI	Company Sergeant-Major Instructor
BSMAF	British Sportsmen's Motor Ambulance Fund	CU	close up
		cwt	hundredweight (unit of 'Imperial' measurement, equivalent to 50.8 kg)
BTCFWF	British Topical Committee for War Films		
Bty	Battery	DC3	model designation of a transport aircraft produced by the Douglas Company, also known as the Dakota or C-47.
BUNAV	Bureau of Navigation		
C	type designation of British airship; "C" stood for "Coastal".		
		DCL	Doctor of Civil Law

DCM   Distinguished Conduct Medal**

DFW   Deutsche Flugzeug Werke

DH4, DH6, DH9
    model designations of aircraft produced by De Havilland factories

dir   director

dist   distributor

DoI   Department of Information

DrI   model designation of a fighter aircraft produced by Fokker; "Dr" stood for "Dreidecker" *ie* Triplane.

DSC   Distinguished Service Cross**

DSO   Distinguished Service Order**

ed   (film) editor

EEF   Egyptian Expeditionary Force

FANY   First Aid Nursing Yeomanry

FBA   Franco-British Aviation (aircraft manufacturer)

FDCO   Flight Deck Control Officer

FE2b, FE2d
    model designation of a fighter aircraft produced by the Royal Aircraft Factory; "FE" stood for "Farman Experimental".

FLAK/flak
    Fliegerabwehrkanone: German equivalent of "anti-aircraft".

FO   Foreign Office

FOO   forward observation officer

ft   feet

GB   Great Britain

GBE   Knight Grand Cross of the Order of the British Empire*

GCB   Knight Grand Cross of the Order of the Bath*

GCMG   Knight Grand Cross of the Order of St Michael and St George*

GHQ   General Headquarters

GII, GIII, GIV, GV
    model designation of bomber aircraft produced by AEG and Gotha; "G" stood for "Grossflugzeug". "G" designations were also used by the French manufacturer Caudron.

GOC   General Officer Commanding

GOC-in-C
    General Officer Commanding-in-Chief

GRV   Georgius Rex V

GS   general service

HA   high angle – *ie* with the camera looking down on its subject

HAC   Honourable Artillery Company

HA.MS   high angle medium shot

HIJMS   His Imperial Japanese Majesty's Ship

HM   His Majesty

HMAS   His Majesty's Australian Ship

HMG   His Majesty's Gun (a nickname, not an official designation)

H/MGC   Heavy Section (or Heavy Branch), Machine Gun Corps – forerunner to the Royal Tank Corps

HMLS   His Majesty's Land Ship

HMS   His Majesty's Ship

HMSO   His (or Her) Majesty's Stationery Office

HM.TMS   His Majesty's Trawler Mine-Sweeper

hp   horsepower

HP   Handley-Page (British aircraft manufacturer)

HQ   Headquarters

HRH   His Royal Highness

ICC   Imperial Camel Corps

I(Lt)Bn   Number 1 (Light) Battalion

IRB   Irish Republican Brotherhood

IWT   Inland Water Transport

KBE   Knight Commander of the Order of the British Empire*

KC   King's Counsel

KCMG   Knight Commander of the Order of St Michael and St George*

KOSB   King's Own Scottish Borderers (Regiment)

KOYLI   King's Own Yorkshire Light Infantry (Regiment)

LA   low angle – *ie* with the camera looking up to its subject

LA.MS   low angle medium shot

LCC   London County Council

LF   London Fire [Brigade]

LOOB   Left Out of Battle

LS   long shot

LVG   Luft-Verkehrs Gesellschaft

M	Monsieur	*prod*	producer
MAS	Motor Anti-Submarine [boat]	PT	physical training
MC	Military Cross**	Pte.	Private
MCU	medium close-up	PV5	model designation of a sea plane
MDS	Main Dressing Station		produced by Port Victoria
MEF	Mesopotamian Expeditionary	QMAAC	Queen Mary's Auxiliary Army
	Force		Corps
MG	machine gun	R	type designation of British
MGC	Machine Gun Corps		airship; "R" stood for "Rigid".
MGH	the 'Modern General History'	R and R	rest and recreation
	series of films in the Imperial	RA	Royal Artillery
	War Museum film archive	RAMC	Royal Army Medical Corps
Mgr	Monsignor	RAP	Regimental Aid Post
mins	minutes	RCAF	Royal Canadian Air Force
Mk	mark (as in production model –	RE	Royal Engineers
	eg Tank Mk V)	RE8	model designation of a fighter
ML	Motor Launch		aircraft produced by the Royal
Mlle	Mademoiselle		Aircraft Factory; "RE" stood
MLS	medium long shot		for "Reconnaissance
Mme	Madame		Experimental".
MO	Medical Officer	*rec*	(sound) recordist
MP	Member of Parliament	Regt	Regiment
M/S	mine-sweeper	RFA	Royal Field Artillery
MS	(1) medium shot (2) manuscript	RFC	Royal Flying Corps
MT	Motor Transport	RGA	Royal Garrison Artillery
MTV	Motor Transport Volunteers	RHA	Royal Horse Artillery
NAAFI	Navy, Army and Air Force	RM	Royal Marines
	Institute	RMA	(1) Royal Military Academy
NACB	National Army Canteen Board		(2) Royal Marine Artillery
NCO	non-commissioned officer	RMLI	Royal Marine Light Infantry
n.d.	not dated	RMO	Regimental Medical Officer
NFTVA	National Film and Television	RMS	Royal Mail (steam)ship
	Archive	RN	Royal Navy
NS	type designation of British	RNAS	Royal Naval Air Service
	airship; "NS" stood for "North	RNR	Royal Naval Reserve
	Sea".	RNVR	Royal Naval Volunteer Reserve
NZ	New Zealand	RS	'Royal Sovereign' class of
NZEF	New Zealand Expeditionary		battleships (RN)
	Force	RSM	Regimental Sergeant-Major
NZMC	New Zealand Medical Corps	RSPCA	Royal Society for the Prevention
OBE	Officer of the Order of the		of Cruelty to Animals
	British Empire*	SC	Special Constable
OC	Officer Commanding	SCAF	Section Cinématographique de
OP	observation post		l'Armée Française
OTC	Officers' Training Corps	*scr*	script
PC	coastal escort or patrol craft	SE5a	model designation of a fighter
PG	prisonnier de guerre		aircraft produced by the Royal
PH	type of gas mask		Aircraft Factory; "SE" stood
PMA	"print/mute/acetate" – technical		for "Scout Experimental".
	description of a copy of a film	Sgr	Signor
POW	prisoner of war		
pr	production company or unit		

SIA	model designation of aircraft produced by the Società Italiana Aeroplani
SL	searchlight
SL11	model designation of a German airship; "SL" stood for "Schütte-Lanz".
SMLE	short magazine Lee-Enfield (rifle)
SMS	Seiner Majestät Schiff
SOS	internationally recognised distress signal – conventionally "Save Our Souls"
sp	sponsor (*ie* the agency responsible for initiating the making of the film)
Sqdn	Squadron
SS	(1) steamship (2) type designation of British airship, of which SSZ was a sub-type; "SS" stood for "Sea Scout".
TA	Territorial Army
TBD	model designation of the Douglas torpedo-bomber (TB) aircraft also known as the Devastator
TDS	Torpedo Dropping School
TGWU	Transport and General Workers' Union
TMB	Trench Mortar Battery
TNT	trinitrotoluene
TUC	Trades Union Congress
UB, UC, UE	classes of German U-boat
UKY	the 'United Kingdom' series of films in the Imperial War Museum film archive
US	United States (of America)
USA	United States of America
USAAC	United States Army Air Corps
USN	United States Navy
USS	United States Ship
USSR	Union of Soviet Socialist Republics
VAD	Voluntary Aid Detachment
VC	Victoria Cross**
VIP	Very Important Person
VTC	Volunteer Training Corps
WAAC	Women's Army Auxiliary Corps (British)
WAC	Women's Army Corps (US)
WOCC	War Office Cinema Committee
WRAF	Women's Royal Air Force

WRNS	Women's Royal Naval Service
XLS	extreme long shot
YMCA	Young Men's Christian Association

*	a rank in one of the various Orders of Chivalry within the British system of honours
**	a decoration or gallantry award conferred on personnel serving in British or Commonwealth forces

IWM Series

IWM 1 · GB, (prod) 8/1917
PRESENTATION OF FRENCH DECORATIONS TO BRITISH TROOPS IN EGYPT BY GENERAL BAILLOUD

b/w · 1 reel · 205' (4 mins) · silent
intertitles: none

sp War Office Cinema Committee *pr* Topical Film Company (?) *cam* Jeapes, Harold (?)

- General Bailloud decorates three soldiers of British 7th Mounted Brigade at Ismailia, Egypt, 1 August 1917.

A street scene, civilians, mainly dressed in white, walk along the pavement. A car bearing General Bailloud and General Sir Edmund Allenby arrives, they mount horses and leave with an escort. At Ismailia General Bailloud inspects the 7th Mounted Brigade, Desert Mounted Corps with Allenby watching. Bailloud presents the Knight's Cross, Légion d'honneur, to Captain R C Layton and the Médaille Militaire to Sergeant-Major J East and to Corporal R Thornton, all of the 1/1st Sherwood Rangers. The officer helping is probably Lieutenant-Colonel H Thorpe, in command of the regiment. (Note that 7th Mounted Brigade, as Corps reserve troops, recently returned from Salonika, did not carry swords.)

Notes
Title: this is taken from the shotsheet.
[shotsheet available]
catalogued SDB: 10/1980

IWM 2 · GB, (?) 1917
the 44TH REMOUNT SQUADRON ON THE EGYPTIAN COAST

b/w · 1 reel · 1189' (20 mins) · silent
intertitles: English

sp War Office Cinema Committee (?)
pr Topical Film Company (?) *prod* Jury, William F (?) *cam* Jeapes, Harold (?)

- Training and loading methods of a British Army remount squadron in Egypt, probably 1917.

The squadron exists to train fresh horses and mules for British Army war service. The horses are taught to keep at a steady walk in formation when other horses are galloping past at an angle. Various manœuvres of a squadron in column of troops (according to the 1912 Cavalry Training Manual). Horses and large mules being taught to get up and down a steep embankment with a rider, and horses being exercised in the shallows of the sea. There is a brief shot of horses drinking from a trough, then a sequence of a large herd of mules "being taught to play follow the leader" at a gallop behind a single horseman. There follows "breaking obstinate animals" in a manège, both to the saddle and to pull a wagon, teaching mules to jump low walls and fences while being ridden, a general inspection, and the squadron loading horses onto a transport train, ending with a message held up to the camera on a board, "44th Remount Squadron, loading 100 horses, time 2 minutes 32 seconds".

Notes
Summary: nothing can be discovered about this film, and it is possibly not British official film at all. See **IWM 634** for a different use of the same scenes.
Remarks: the film is poorly edited in parts but the sequence showing the squadron drilling is both interesting and impressive.
[shotsheet available]
catalogued SDB: 10/1980

IWM 3 · GB, 12/1917
an EGYPTIAN LABOUR CONTINGENT

b/w · 1 reel · 920' (16 mins) · silent
intertitles: English

sp War Office Cinema Committee *pr* Topical Film Company (?) *cam* Jeapes, Harold; and/or Hurley, Frank (?)

- A contingent of the Egyptian Labour Corps from recruitment in Egypt to arrival and work in France, 1917.

A pan of the assembly camp in Egypt, tented and open, where the "recruits of all provinces dressed in various types of garb" arrive and are given Egyptian Labour Corps uniform, "the men are delighted with its quality". A squad of Egyptian Labour Corps police drilling. A company of volunteers, in uniform with blanket rolls, marches to the quayside to board the SS *Minnetonka* at Alexandria. The ship leaves the harbour. The final scene shows members of the Egyptian Labour Corps in France at a harbour, unloading hay from nets. They watch a single-stick bout followed by a "native dance".

Notes
Summary: the shotsheet gives the ship as
SS *Minnetonka* and the information that she
was sunk on the journey. The *Minnetonka*
was in fact sunk on 31 January 1918, but
was not carrying troops at the time. The
scenes in France were probably not shot by
Jeapes, nor connected with those shot in
Egypt.
[shotsheet available]
catalogued SDB: 10/1980

IWM 4 · GB, (?) 1917
a TURKISH PRISONER OF WAR CAMP

b/w · 1 reel · 894' (15 mins) · silent
intertitles: English

sp War Office Cinema Committee (?)
pr Topical Film Company (?) *cam* Jeapes,
Harold and/or Hurley, Frank (?)

■ Prisoner of war camp at El Maadi (or
Heliopolis ?) in Egypt for Turkish other
ranks prisoners, 1917 (?).

Views of the camp, showing that "prisoners
have ample room for exercise". The
prisoners' band of mandolins, violins and
drums plays to an audience of prisoners in
the open. Prisoners help to unload a ration
wagon. Prisoners march "to their dinners"
across the compound. The "shower baths
and washing places". A wrestling bout
staged for entertainment between two of the
prisoners, while others watch. Half-way
through, this is speeded up (for comic
effect ?) by undercranking the camera. The
same audience watches two prisoners
dancing. The film ends with two prisoners
kicking a football about.

Notes
Summary: the appearance of the camp is
consistent with descriptions of both El
Maadi and Heliopolis, but closer to the first.
Remarks: fairly mild propaganda, consistent
with the British approach of 'the
propaganda of facts' in handling prisoner of
war subjects which can be seen in **IWM
436** and **IWM 441**.
[*Report on British Prisoner of War Camps in
Egypt*, International Red Cross, 1/1917]
[shotsheet available]
catalogued SDB: 10/1980

IWM 5 · GB, (prod) 1917
SIWA EXPEDITION
the NEW CRUSADERS (rough material)

b/w · 1 reel · 658' (11 mins) · silent
intertitles: English

sp War Office Cinema Committee (?)
pr Topical Film Company (?) *cam* Jeapes,
Harold (?)

■ Rough material of the Siwa Expedition of
February and events in Gaza and El Arish
of March and April, Egypt and Palestine
Front, 1917.

A British column of Rolls-Royce armoured
cars and Ford Model T light cars prepares
for the expedition. This is followed by their
arrival in El Arish with "notables" assembling
before the governor. In the desert the motor
column signals with semaphore to part of a
flanking column. The film then jumps back
to a bedouin encampment outside El Arish.
Inside El Arish the Sinai Police prepare to
set out on patrol. Doctors work in a
dressing station. In the desert there are a
mounted patrol, a laden camel train, and
more scenes of the motor column. Finally, a
large number of prisoners, some in Turkish
uniform, being gathered inside an open
square at El Arish.

Notes
Title: this is taken from the shotsheet.
Summary: The British official cameraman
did not arrive in Egypt until April 1917, and
it seems unlikely that these scenes are
actually of the expedition in February. See
also **IWM 17**, **IWM 58** and **IWM 60**.
[shotsheet available]
catalogued SDB: 10/1980

IWM 6 · GB, (?) 1918
**INSPECTION OF THE IMPERIAL CAMEL
CORPS**
ON THE PALESTINE FRONT (series)

b/w · 1 reel · 1094' (18 mins) · silent
intertitles: English

sp War Office Cinema Committee (?)
pr Topical Film Company *cam* Jeapes,
Harold

■ Probably 3rd or 4th Battalion, Imperial
Camel Corps, with its camel battery, the
Hong Kong-Singapore Mountain Battery,
training on the Palestine Front, early
1917.

The display begins with a parade and
march past, followed by men of the ICC
setting out for a patrol in the desert and
drawing river water for their camels. This is

broken by sequences of horse and mule riders in the desert, and a demonstration of assembling its guns by the Hong Kong-Singapore Mountain Battery of the Indian Army, attached to the Imperial Camel Corps (this was the only camel-mounted battery equipped with 10-pounder breechloading mountain guns on active service).

Notes
Intertitles: these are flashframes.
Summary: see also **IWM 58** and **IWM 60**.
Technical: most of the film appears as slightly out-of-focus.
[shotsheet available]
catalogued SDB: 10/1980

IWM 7 · GB, (prod) 1917
AUSTRALIANS, ITALIANS, AND FRENCH COLONIAL TROOPS IN PALESTINE

b/w · 1 reel · 503' (9 mins) · silent
intertitles: none

sp War Office Cinema Committee (?)
pr Topical Film Company *cam* Jeapes, Harold

▪ Jumbled, unedited film of the training and camp life of the French Contingent of the Egyptian Expeditionary Force, Palestine Front, 1917.

The film opens with an unrelated scene of Australian troops exploding a shell or mine in a training exercise. 1st Spahi Cavalry Regiment 'charges' the camera. One of the men demonstrates steadiness by standing on his saddle. More French Cavalry in tropical kit. General scenes in the Spahi encampment. French colonial troops, probably Algerian, being instructed in the use of the Mitrailleuse Saint Etienne machinegun (?). A race in full pack between French colonial troops and Italian Bersaglieri. The film ends with portrait shots of General Bailloud, commanding the French Contingent, and of Lieutenant-General Sir Philip Chetwode, commanding the Desert Column.

Notes
Title: this is taken from the shotsheet.
Date: Chetwode's presence suggests that the film was taken before July 1917, when the French and Italian Contingents were still part of the Desert Column, prior to their transfer to Bulfin's XXI Corps.
[shotsheet available]
catalogued SDB: 10/1980

IWM 8 · GB, (?) 1917
WITH THE ITALIAN FORCES IN PALESTINE

b/w · 1 reel · 754' (13 mins) · silent
intertitles: none

sp War Office Cinema Committee (?)
pr Topical Film Company (?) *cam* Jeapes, Harold

▪ Training and camp life of the Italian Contingent of the Egyptian Expeditionary Force, Palestine Front, 1917 (?).

The film opens with the Italians practising grenade throwing. Next are scenes of the contingent's field kitchens. The hospital tent, with wounded arriving for treatment. Bersaglieri marching at the double. Some Carabinieri mounting guard on the camp. A camel train arrives with supplies. Bersaglieri practise musketry from a shallow trench, finishing with a bayonet charge. There are general scenes of life in the camp, soldiers washing, a barber, and troops practising physical training.

Notes
Title: this is taken from the shotsheet.
[shotsheet available]
catalogued SDB: 10/1980

IWM 9 · GB/USA (?), (prod) 1917
[NORTON'S COLUMN IN MESOPOTAMIA]
(allocated)

b/w · 1 reel · 624' (11 mins) · silent
intertitles: English

sp War Office Cinema Committee (?)
pr International Film Service (?)
cam Varges, Ariel L (?)

▪ Jumbled film apparently of the raid into Kurdistan by Norton's Column of the Mesopotamian Expeditionary Force, September 1917.

A limbered 13-pounder battery followed by a vehicle column. Soldiers standing beside one of the cars in the column hold up a written notice for the camera "Norton's Column". This is probably the column commanded by Brigadier-General C E G Norton, consisting mainly of the 7th Indian Cavalry Brigade, 14th Light Armoured Motor Battery and 'S' Battery Royal Horse Artillery, conducting operations towards Mandali in September 1917. The film continues with Indian drivers loading wagons, a column of horsemen (7th Indian Cavalry Brigade ?) moving along a desert road, and Indian troops with wagons and pack mules. An 18-pounder battery crosses a small river by a bridge of boats. A "Turkish spy" (from the flashframe but apparently wearing British uniform) is brought blindfold into the camp. A column of soldiers moves off into the distance. A final scene of troops resting in a shallow scrape trench beside a Rolls-Royce armoured car.

Notes
Title: the film was originally listed on the store ledger as *Palestine* and in the shotsheet as *With the Forces in Palestine*, which is a series title. It also opens with an MS flashframe "Palestine". Despite this, and given that, according to the store ledger, Varges was the cameraman, it is most probably Norton's Column in Mesopotamia. [shotsheet available]
catalogued SDB: 10/1980

IWM 10 · GB, (?) 1918
DEIR EL BELAH

b/w · 1 reel · 990' (17 mins) · silent
intertitles: English

sp Ministry of Information (?) *pr* Topical Film Company *cam* Jeapes, Harold

- Gurkha and British troops during the Third Battle of Gaza, Palestine Front, November 1917.

Gurkhas in a trench prepare for the assault and attack. They are probably 3/3rd Battalion, the Gurkha Rifles, 75th Division, before the fall of Gaza on 18 November 1917. This is followed by a sequence of 8-inch howitzers being taken over a bridge at Belah, unlimbered, and fired. A sequence giving the view through a telescope shows a heliograph and mounted sentries on the move. The inside of the pumping station at Shellal. A press for printing British Army maps of the Palestine Front. Some West Indians, part of 1st Battalion, British West Indies Regiment (?), loaned to XXI Corps on 75th Division Front, marching down a road. There are brief views of officers on a hill surveying with binoculars and signalling, an outside view of the pumping station, and a final view of British troops in dug-outs on a hillside, possibly 1/5th Battalion, the Devonshire Regiment, 75th Division but possibly men of 60th (London) Division instead. Finally, stores being landed from a ship using surf boats, perhaps at Gaza.

Notes
Title: this is taken from the shotsheet.
Intertitles: these are MS flashframes.
Shotsheet: this and the subtitles bear little relation to each other. The troops described as Devonshires by the shotsheet are given by the flashframe as "lads from the streets of London", *ie* 60th (London) Division. *Remarks:* the Gurkha sequence is quite good, the film is otherwise a mess. [shotsheet available]
catalogued SDB: 10/1980

IWM 11 · GB, (?) 1918
GAZA

b/w · 2 reels · 1353' (22 mins) · silent
intertitles: English

sp War Office Cinema Committee (?) *pr* Topical Film Company *cam* Jeapes, Harold

- Scenes of Gaza and its surroundings shortly after its capture by British forces, Palestine Front, November 1917.

(Reel 1) A panorama of Gaza under British occupation. (The two ships described as shallow draft monitors which bombarded Gaza are HMS *Moth* and HMS *Caddis Fly* (?) serving in Mesopotamia.) The ruins of the Great Mosque: "information was received that the Turks were using the Great Mosque as an ammunition dump" and so "the Turks paid the penalty for their sacrilegious trickery, our guns fired five rounds at the Mosque, with disastrous results". British and Indian troops with Turkish Army prisoners. A final portrait shot of General Sir Edmund Allenby, commanding the Egyptian Expeditionary Force. *(Reel 2)* A series of stockshots. A camel train carrying water, another camel train encamped. 60-pounder guns of 75th Division (?) in action. Limbered 18-pounders entering Gaza. The old trenches around Gaza shown by night and day. British soldiers in part of the ruins of Gaza. Two German prisoners taken along with the Turks. Australian Light Horse, probably in a training exercise, making a dismounted charge in the sand dunes. British Lewis machinegunners training.

Notes
Title: this is taken from the store ledger.
Intertitles: these are all flashframes.
Date: the shotsheet refers to Allenby as "Lord Allenby", a title he did not receive until after the war.

Summary: see also **IWM 6**, **IWM 58**, **IWM 60**, **IWM 71** and **IWM 79**.
[shotsheet available]
catalogued SDB: 10/1980

IWM 12 · GB, (prod) 1917
EL MEJDEL, JAFFA AND WEST COUNTRY TROOPS

b/w · 1 reel · 952' (16 mins) · silent
intertitles: none

sp War Office Cinema Committee *pr* Topical Film Company *cam* Jeapes, Harold

■ Jumbled material of the British capture of Jaffa, Palestine Front, November 1917.

I. Troops and transport camels of 52nd (Lowland) Division in the streets of El Mejdel (captured 9 November), including the well inside a mosque. Part of a squadron of 1st Hyderabad Lancers riding through the streets of Jaffa (the shotsheet gives this as Jericho), followed by troops of 75th Division. A shot of "Jaffa town hall and clock tower within half an hour of its capture". (Jaffa was captured by the Wellington Mounted Rifle Regiment, New Zealand Mounted Rifle Brigade, ANZAC Mounted Division, at 10am on 16 November.) A view of the ANZAC Mounted Division bivouacs, and a panorama of Jaffa filmed from the sea.
II. From here the film breaks up into brief scenes of the pontoon bridge at El Ghoranyeh, some British troops (60th Division ?) on the march, the ANZAC Mounted Division leading its horses, and Turkish prisoners being put on trains at the railway station at Jerusalem by troops of 52nd Division.

Notes
Title: this is taken from the shotsheet.
Date: the store ledger gives this film as arriving in Great Britain in December 1917. Since Jericho was not captured until February 1918 it seems unlikely that the reference to it in the shotsheet is correct.
[shotsheet available]
catalogued SDB: 10/1980

IWM 13 · GB, 21/2/1918
GENERAL ALLENBY'S ENTRY INTO JERUSALEM
WAR OFFICE OFFICIAL TOPICAL BUDGET 339-2 (alternative)

b/w · 1 reel · 826' (14 mins) · silent
intertitles: English

sp War Office Cinema Committee *pr* Topical Film Company *cam* Jeapes, Harold

I. The entry of General Allenby into Jerusalem and the reading of his proclamation, Palestine, 11 December 1917. Views of the honour guard at the Jaffa Gate, composed of English, Welsh, Scottish, Indian, Australian and New Zealand troops, with twenty soldiers each from Italy and France continuing the line inside the gate. Allenby meets the military governor of Jerusalem, Brigadier-General W M Borton, at the gate and walks in procession through the streets. The group is headed by two ADCs, Captain W L Naper and Lieutenant R H Andrew, then General Allenby flanked by the heads of the French and Italian Contingents, Lieutenant-Colonel P de Piepape and Lieutenant-Colonel F D'Agostio, each with one staff officer. Then come Lieutenant-Colonel Lord Dalmeny and Lieutenant-Colonel A P Wavell (the future Field Marshal Lord Wavell). The remaining group includes the French High Commissioner, M Picot, Major T E Lawrence ('Lawrence of Arabia'), Major-General L J Bols, Lieutenant-General Sir Philip Chetwode and Brigadier-General G P Dawnay, Allenby's Chief of Staff. After the group has conversed amongst itself and Allenby has greeted civil dignitaries, his proclamation is read out with Allenby himself, de Piepape and d'Agostio on the platform. Allenby and his staff, who made a point of walking into the city, then leave on horseback via the Jaffa Gate. Allenby had been less than fifteen minutes in the city.
II. The Duke of Connaught decorates Allenby and some of his officers at the Turkish barracks at Mount Zion, Palestine, 20 March 1918. Allenby receives the GCMG from Connaught, Major-General L J Bols receives the KCMG and Lieutenant-General Bulfin the KCMG also. A final portrait shot of Allenby closes the film.

Notes
Date: the release date is for the original British release, the second item was presumably added later.
Shotsheet: this bears only passing relation to the film.
Production: it is apparent that more than one cameraman was responsible for the Allenby material, but the identity of the second cameraman is not known. For a full account, see the article by Luke McKernan cited below.
Technical: the P 1 16mm version of this film

has the same scenes in a slightly different order.

[Luke McKernan, "'The Supreme Moment of the War': General Allenby's Entry into Jerusalem", *Historical Journal of Film, Radio and Television* 13: 2 (1993): 169-180]
[shotsheet available]
catalogued SDB: 10/1980

IWM 14 · GB, 1917
ALLENBY IN CAIRO (1917)

b/w · 1 reel · 246' (5 mins) · silent
intertitles: none

sp War Office Cinema Committee *pr* Topical Film Company *cam* Jeapes, Harold

- Arrival of General Sir Edmund Allenby, the new commander of the Egyptian Expeditionary Force, in Cairo, 27 June 1917.

Allenby's train pulls into the station and he gets down to meet with some civilian dignitaries. He inspects an honour guard of Infantry and a boy scout troop. Allenby drives away from the station in company with two other cars. (Note the civilian press photographers at work.) The rest of the parade, including the Infantry and boy scouts, then leaves.

Notes
Title: this is taken from the shotsheet.
Summary: see also **IWM 40**.
[shotsheet available]
catalogued SDB: 10/1980

IWM 15 · GB, (prod) 1917
BETHLEHEM, SOLOMON'S POOL AND JERUSALEM

b/w · 1 reel · 630' (11 mins) · silent
intertitles: English

sp War Office Cinema Committee *pr* Topical Film Company *cam* Jeapes, Harold (and Hurley, Frank ?)

- Scenes of Bethlehem, Solomon's Pool and Jerusalem, including General Allenby's visit to Bethlehem on Christmas Day, Palestine Front, 1917.

I. A long sequence of 2/4th Battalion, the Dorset Regiment, with its band leading, marching into Bethlehem (poor quality film).
II. Allenby's visit to Bethlehem, 25

December 1917. He can be seen among a large crowd, getting into his car and leaving. (Note the official still photographer, Sergeant Westmoreland, at work.)
III. The 'Solomon's Pool' reservoir. A flashframe reads "the reservoirs built by Solomon 3,000 years ago were cleaned and the waters sent into Jerusalem by the aqueduct built by Herod and Pontius Pilate".
IV. Turkish prisoners on the march guarded by Indian lancers.
V. Interior shots of the Church of the First Prison of Christ at Jerusalem.

Notes
Title: this is taken from the shotsheet.
Intertitles: these are all flashframes.
Summary: Allenby attempted to make his visit to Bethlehem secret, and the cameramen did not arrive until just as he was due to leave.
[shotsheet available]
catalogued SDB: 10/1980

IWM 16 · GB, (prod) 1917
CROSSING OF THE AUJA, MULEBBIS, GUNS NEAR JERUSALEM

b/w · 1 reel · 624' (11 mins) · silent
intertitles: none

sp War Office Cinema Committee *pr* Topical Film Company *cam* Jeapes, Harold and Hurley, Frank

I. The bridging of the Auja River north of Jaffa by 52nd (Lowland) Division, Palestine Front, 20 December 1917. The film follows the construction of the bridge by the divisional sappers from first start in the early morning mists to completion and the first ammunition mules making the crossing.
II. The Jewish settlement at Mulebbis on the day after it was first occupied by British troops, Palestine Front, 23 December 1917.
III. British positions north-east of Jerusalem, Palestine Front, 24 December 1917. A captured German 77mm field gun is used to shell Turkish positions north of Jerusalem. Further towards Jericho 'A' and 'B' Batteries of CCLXVII Brigade Royal Field Artillery, part of 53rd (Welsh) Division, are shelling the Turkish positions.

Notes
Title: this is taken from the shotsheet.
[shotsheet available]
catalogued SDB: 10/1980

IWM 17 · GB, 4/1918
the NEW CRUSADERS : with the British forces on the Palestine Front

b/w · 3 reels · 2394' (40 mins) · silent
intertitles: English

sp Ministry of Information *pr* Topical Film Company *prod* Jury, William F *cam* Jeapes, Harold and Hurley, Frank (?)

- British campaign on the Palestine Front, February to November 1917.

(Reel 1) The raid against the stronghold of Sayad Ahmed of the Sennusi tribesmen at Siwa, made in February 1917 by a force of three light armoured batteries and three light car patrols under Brigadier-General H W Hodgson. The force, consisting of Rolls-Royce armoured cars, Ford Model T light cars, Napier light cars and Vauxhall D staff cars, leaves the assembly area and crosses the Shegga pass on 2 February. A field wireless is set up. Hodgson, in Siwa on 3 February, addresses the local leaders. This is followed by scenes prior to First Battle of Gaza. A pan of El Arish with soldiers of 52nd (Lowland) Division in the foreground, street scenes of El Arish, and British Yeomanry (with New Zealand Mounted Rifles ?) patrols on the road from Magdhaba to El Arish. Royal Engineers laying a telegraph wire from a limber across the desert. RAMC men dressing wounds. *(Reel 2)* A Yeomanry bivouac at El Arish, surf boats landing supplies on the beaches, and an RE officer directing the building of a railway by members of the Egyptian Labour Corps. Men of 1/8th Battalion, the Hampshire Regiment, 54th (East Anglia) Division eating. Three Mk I tanks, two Males (including HMLS 'Otazel') and one Female (HMLS 'Nutty') in a trench crossing trial near the Suez Canal in July 1917, filmed from inside the trench as they cross. A 13-pounder Mk III anti-aircraft gun on a motor lorry mounting in action. Also 8-inch and 6-inch howitzers and 60-pounder guns in action, during the Battle of Gaza. Men of 1/4th Battalion, the Norfolk Regiment, in the front trenches preparing for the Second Battle of Gaza on 19 April 1917, followed by a panorama of Gaza. *(Reel 3)* British troops building a railway. Troops of the Imperial Camel Corps entering Beersheba in November 1917. General Sir Edmund Allenby, Lieutenant-General Sir Philip Chetwode, and Lieutenant-General Sir Harry Chauvel (commanding the Desert Mounted Corps) leaving their headquarters at Beersheba, ending with a portrait shot of Chauvel.

Notes
Summary: the 5 February 1917 entry in the War Diary in the Public Record Office (PRO 95/4438) says "cinema operator much evidence", but does not give a name (information from David List). No official cameraman has been identified as being in the country at that date. See also **IWM 5**, **IWM 58** and **IWM 60**. An incomplete copy of a version of this film with French subtitles is held as **IWM 658a**.
Remarks: disjointed to the point of incoherence, the film depends chiefly on the novelty value of desert scenes rather than any message or narrative of events for its impact.
[shotsheet available]
catalogued SDB: 10/1980

IWM 18 · GB, (prod) 1917
JEWISH COLONIES IN PALESTINE : Rishon Le Zion

b/w · 1 reel · 136' (3 mins) · silent
intertitles: English

sp War Office Cinema Committee *pr* Topical Film Company *cam* Jeapes, Harold (and Hurley, Frank ?)

- Brief film of the Jewish settlement at Rishon le Zion, Palestine Front, autumn 1917.

Saturday afternoon in the settlement, the name of which means 'Zion's First'. People wander about and a brass band of the Australian Light Horse plays on a bandstand. A general panorama of Rishon le Zion filmed from "the top of the refrigerator building where the famous wines are kept".

Notes
Title: this is taken from the shotsheet.
Intertitles: there is a single flashframe, quoted in the summary.
Remarks: extremely interesting as a historical record, but poor quality film.
[shotsheet available]
catalogued SDB: 10/1980

IWM 19 · GB, (prod) 1917
JERUSALEM

b/w · 1 reel · 194' (4 mins) · silent
intertitles: English

sp War Office Cinema Committee *pr* Topical

Film Company *cam* Jeapes, Harold (and Hurley, Frank ?)

- Views of the Mosque of Omar in Jerusalem guarded by Indian troops, Palestine Front, 1917.

A pan over the Mosque of Omar taken from the front of the Mosque of El Aska, followed by a view of the courtyard of the Mosque of Omar. Two Indian Infantry regiments, one of them probably 58th (Vaughan's) Rifles, are seen changing guard at the Mosque. According to the caption, "the Mosque is guarded by British Indian troops all of whom are Mohammedans".

Notes
Title: this is taken from the shotsheet.
Intertitles: these are all flashframes.
Summary: see also **IWM 45.**
[shotsheet available]
catalogued SDB: 10/1980

IWM 20 · GB, (prod) 1917
CAMELS AND JAFFA

b/w · 1 reel · 246' (4 mins) · silent
intertitles: none

sp War Office Cinema Committee (?)
pr Topical Film Company (?) *cam* Jeapes, Harold and/or Hurley, Frank (?)

- Scenes in Jaffa under British occupation, Palestine Front, probably late 1917.

A camel train approaches and enters the city. A panorama of the city taken from the sea. Tiffin (compressed camel or horse fodder) being unloaded from ships lying out to sea by surf boats. The men working to unload the tiffin onto the beach appear to be Egyptian Labour Corps under British direction.

Notes
Title: this is taken from the shotsheet.
[shotsheet available]
catalogued SDB: 10/1980

IWM 21 · GB, (after) 4/1918
HIS ROYAL HIGHNESS THE DUKE OF CONNAUGHT INSPECTS CADETS AT THE IMPERIAL SCHOOL OF INSTRUCTION, ZEITOUN

b/w · 1 reel · 580' (10 mins) · silent
intertitles: none

sp Ministry of Information *pr* Topical Film Company *prod* Jury, William F *cam* Jeapes, Harold and/or Hurley, Frank (?)

- Visit of the Duke of Connaught to the Imperial School of Instruction at Zeitoun to review the cadets, part of his tour of Egypt and the Palestine Front between January and March 1918.

The camp prepares with the cadets drawn up on parade. The Duke's car arrives and he gets out. He and his staff watch demonstrations of heliograph and semaphore signalling, and the firing of Hotchkiss automatic rifles, Lewis machineguns and Vickers machineguns. The march past at the end includes a band and an Indian Army contingent.

Notes
Summary: see also **IWM 60.**
Remarks: a very pleasant, well filmed piece, worlds away from war photography, and a good illustration of the quality the cameramen could provide if not working under the constraints of active service filming.
[shotsheet available]
catalogued SDB: 10/1980

IWM 22 · GB, (prod) 1917
JERICHO

b/w · 1 reel · 862' (15 mins) · silent
intertitles: English

sp War Office Cinema Committee *pr* Topical Film Company *cam* Jeapes, Harold

- Mixed film of 60th Division at Jerusalem and the ANZAC Mounted Division at Jericho, Palestine Front, late 1917.

A portrait shot of an unidentified junior officer of the Australian Light Horse. Next is an inspection of 60th (London) Division by its commander, Major-General Sir John Shea, outside Jerusalem. Civilian labourers are shown "voluntarily assisting to repair" the Jerusalem-Jericho Road (according to the shotsheet), with men of 60th Division repairing a bridge on the road and Major-General Shea's car driving past up an incline. A panorama of Jericho followed by "natives returning from the funeral of an Arab who was killed by the Turks for refusing to hand over his money", one of them carrying a spade. Men of the Australian Light Horse (or New Zealand Mounted Rifles ?) are seen mounting first guard over their headquarters at Jericho and saluting as a senior officer, possibly Major-General E C W Chaytor, leaves the building. The Auckland Regiment of the New Zealand Mounted Brigade, ANZAC Mounted Division, is seen galloping through the town. (Identification uncertain, the same scene is shown shortly afterwards as "Australian troops".) There are staged scenes of Australians in the Jericho market place, a brief scene of a Red Cross hospital, a panorama of Jericho, an Australian Light Horse patrol coming into Jericho and a final scene of civilians repairing roads in the area.

Notes
Title: this is taken from the shotsheet.
[shotsheet available]
catalogued SDB: 10/1980

IWM 23 · GB, 1917
the SULTAN OF EGYPT'S FUNERAL

b/w · 1 reel · 382' (6 mins) · silent
intertitles: none

sp War Office Cinema Committee *pr* Topical Film Company *cam* Jeapes, Harold

■ Funeral of Hussein Kemal, first Sultan of Egypt, in Cairo, 10 October 1917.

The chief mourner is the Sultan's brother and successor, Ahmed Fuad I. The road to the palace has many spectators, and British soldiers lining the route as an honour guard. Lancers of the Sultan's bodyguard lead the parade, followed by Sultan Fuad in a landau, the Lancers of the Guard, and other carriages. The next scene is the funeral procession on foot to the Rifai Mosque, with many Egyptian mourners in black, the coffin being carried by Egyptian Marines, and British naval and military representatives (including one Australian officer) as official mourners. The coffin comes to the front of the mosque and is taken up the steps and inside. Finally, the new Sultan leaves the mosque, enters a car and drives away.

Notes
Title: this is taken from the shotsheet.
[shotsheet available]
catalogued SDB: 10/1980

IWM 24 · GB, (prod) 1918
HEBRON

b/w · 1 reel · 104' (2 mins) · silent
intertitles: none

sp Ministry of Information (?) *pr* Topical Film Company *cam* Jeapes, Harold

■ An RAMC doctor, probably Major Paterson, who was a doctor in Hebron for 31 years before the war, talking to a group of Arabs; followed by a slow panorama of Hebron, ending at the mosque. Palestine Front, 1918.

Notes
Title: this is taken from the shotsheet.
Shotsheet: this bears little relation to the film, which is probably incomplete. One of the scenes on the shotsheet, the Tomb of Abraham and Solomon's Pool, marked "not to be exhibited", is now **IWM 72**.
[shotsheet available]
catalogued SDB: 10/1980

IWM 25 · GB, (prod) 1918
[the DUKE OF CONNAUGHT AND ALLENBY INSPECTING TROOPS ON THE PALESTINE FRONT, MARCH 1918]
(allocated)

b/w · 2 reels · 1505' (25 mins) · silent
intertitles: English

sp Ministry of Information *pr* Topical Film Company *cam* Jeapes, Harold (and Hurley, Frank ?)

■ Duke of Connaught, on a tour of Egypt and the Palestine Front, inspects units of the Egyptian Expeditionary Force with General Allenby, March 1918.

I. The film opens with an attached scene of mule transport and horses of 5th Cavalry Division being watered.
II. *(Reel 1)* The Duke and Allenby ride to a saluting base to inspect the 7th (Meerut) Division, commanded by Major-General V B Fane, at Ismailia. This includes a march past by 2nd Battalion, the Black Watch, and a guard of honour of 2nd Battalion, the Leicestershire Regiment, which is inspected by the Duke. Major-General V B Fane escorts the Duke to the landing stage and he leaves by launch across Lake Timsah. Allenby and the Duke arrive by another launch at Kantara, for their inspection of 24th Stationary Hospital, meeting the officer commanding, Lieutenant-Colonel Powell RAMC, and the matron, Miss Stewart. The reel ends with a trooptrain arriving at Kantara, carrying uninjured Australian Light

Horse who detrain and carry away their equipment on foot. *(Reel 2)* Connaught at Belah on 14 March, reviewing a march past of 4th Cavalry Division (?) and the ANZAC Mounted Division (?). This is followed by the Duke's inspection of 157th Brigade, 52nd (Lowland) Division on 18 March. Finally, the Duke presents awards to a number of officers and soldiers at an old Turkish camp at Mount Zion on 20 March. Allenby receives the GCMG, Major-General L J Bols receives the KCMG, and a number of other officers the CMG. Awards are also given to several other soldiers, including some Indian soldiers.

Notes
Summary: see also **IWM 13**.
[shotsheet available]
catalogued SDB: 10/1980

IWM 26 · GB, 1918
the OCCUPATION OF ES SALT

b/w · 1 reel · 1042' (18 mins) · silent
intertitles: English

sp Ministry of Information *pr* Topical Film Company *cam* Jeapes, Harold (and Hurley, Frank ?)

■ Occupation of Es Salt by 60th (London) Division, Palestine Front, March or April 1918.

British troops of 60th Division occupied Es Salt twice, between 26 and 28 March, and between 30 April and 3 May. This film may show either or both occasions together with some stock material. It opens with camels carrying supplies over the pontoon bridge at El Ghoranyeh, followed by troops of 179th Brigade and 181st Brigade, 60th Division, on the march. A brief view of "the world famous Imperial Camel Corps" (in fact showing an Arab camel train), followed by British soldiers on the march in hill country halting to shoot at a Turkish aeroplane (not in shot). Camels bearing stretchers, known as 'cacolets', on the march. A panorama of Es Salt with 2/14th Battalion, the London Regiment, better known as 2nd London Scottish, of 179th Brigade, marching through its streets "headed by their famous band of pipers" (not in shot). One company commander tells his men to march to attention as they pass the camera. There are brief shots of a captured German 77mm field gun, a Ford Model T car "arrived from GHQ", and an ASC soldier showing a copy of the *Daily Mirror* newspaper to a group of

Arabs. Continuing with a camel train at El Ghoranyeh bridge, a Rolls-Royce armoured car advancing against shellfire, and more troops of 60th Division marching up the road to Es Salt. It ends with two mule carts and Indian soldiers transporting stores.

Notes
Remarks: a valuable piece of historical evidence for the Palestine campaign. But this film contains too many obvious stock, staged and faked items to make its remaining material entirely credible.
[shotsheet available]
catalogued SDB: 10/1980

IWM 27 · GB, (prod) 1918
1ST BATTALION EGYPTIAN ARMY VISITS THE MOSQUE OF OMAR (sic)
the NEBI-NUSA FESTIVALS (rough material)

b/w · 1 reel · 1364' (23 mins) · silent
intertitles: none

sp Ministry of Information *pr* Topical Film Company *cam* Jeapes, Harold (and Hurley, Frank ?)

■ Unedited film of the Nebi-Nusa festivals, the arrival of the International Zionist Commission, and the visit of Egyptian 1st Infantry Regiment to the Mosque of Omar, Jerusalem, April 1918.

This is the unedited material used in **IWM 45** *The Nebi-Nusa Festivals*, taken by the British official cameraman. Apart from this material, the film also contains portrait shots of the military governor of Jerusalem, Lieutenant-Colonel Ronald Storrs, and of Major-General L J Bols.

Notes
Title: this is taken from the shotsheet.
Summary: just after the Wailing Wall sequence in this film appears an MS flashframe "Lowell Thomas to join here". This suggests that some of the film in the finished version may be by Lowell Thomas. See **IWM 41** and **IWM 45**.
[shotsheet available]
catalogued SDB: 10/1980

IWM 28 · Australia, 6/1918
WITH THE AUSTRALIAN FORCES IN PALESTINE

b/w · 5 reels · 3290' (56 mins) · silent
intertitles: English

sp Australian War Records Section
ed Hurley, Frank *cam* Hurley, Frank

- Australian airmen, horsemen and members of the Imperial Camel Corps on the Palestine Front, 1918.

I. The first part shows 1 Squadron Australian Flying Corps in Palestine. *(Reel 1)* The squadron prepares for a patrol in its Martinsyde Elephants, Bristol F2B Fighters, RE8s and BE2s. The camera is in the rear gunner's position of a Bristol Fighter to film the take-off from the airfield and the flight from Jaffa to the River Jordan. *(Reel 2)* The flight continues over the Judean hills to the vicinity of Jerusalem. The plane passes a Martinsyde Elephant and a BE2 in flight, and a tethered observation balloon of Number 49 Balloon Section (?). The flight continues over the Dead Sea and up the Jordan valley to Jericho (where a stockshot of the streets is included). The plane returns to its airfield and makes a spin dive down to land. Finally, the planes are all wheeled to their hangars.
II. The next three reels show Australian Light Horse (more likely the Australian Mounted Division than the ANZAC Mounted Division) and the Australian Contingents of the Imperial Camel Corps. *(Reel 3)* Australian troopers looking at the view of Jerusalem from the Mount of Olives; continuing with other troopers returning from Bethlehem to their camp near Jerusalem and watering their horses, riding down the Jerusalem road to the Jaffa Gate, walking dismounted down the Via Dolorosa, and camped among the Judaean hills. A Vickers machinegun team fires behind earth cover. ALH on the march. "The descent into the Jordan valley" of an ALH brigade marching along with Red Cross wagons in column. Flooding that has washed away a railway in the valley. *(Reel 4)* ICC unloading stores from camels. Surf boats unloading stores and fodder at Gaza (?). An Arab camel train and men unloading more stores at Jaffa (?). Men and camels of the ICC on the march in column. The Red Cross facilities of the ICC. (An extra shot of the British 60th (London) Division on the march.) Some combat training of the Hong Kong-Singapore Mountain Battery, attached to the ICC. *(Reel 5)* An ICC bivouac. Men of the ALH moving through the ruins of Gaza. The film ends with a long sequence of a brigade of ALH on the march.

Notes
Summary: the film shows evidence of interpolation. The scene of the surf boats appears in **IWM 20** and that of 60th Division

in **IWM 26**. Both may have been filmed by the British official cameraman Harold Jeapes and have had no place in the original version of this film. See **IWM 634** for a different use of the first two reels. [AWRS(Film) Papers, File 4375/60/3] [shotsheet available]
catalogued SDB: 10/1980

IWM 29 · NO FILM

IWM 30 · GB, (prod) 1918
[ALLENBY MEETS WEIZMANN : Tel-el-Jelil, and Arsulf] (allocated)

b/w · 4 reels · 3976' (67 mins) · silent
intertitles: English

sp Ministry of Information *pr* Topical Film Company *cam* Jeapes, Harold and Hurley, Frank

- Mixed film of British, Indian and Jewish forces, including the meeting of General Allenby with Chaim Weizmann in Jerusalem, Palestine Front, May 1918.

(Reel 1) An auction of British Army horses to civilians. A trooptrain arrives in Lod, British soldiers climb out, form up and march away, 5 May. An Indian battalion on the march through the hills. More British troops marching away from Lod railway. A fire in an officer's quarters at a tented camp. British troops resting in a dry wadi. Indians clearing undergrowth from a small river, described as Wadi Auja (compare with the same scene in **IWM 80**, captioned as "a tributary of the Tigris"). *(Reel 2)* Jewish recruits for 40th (Jewish) Battalion, Royal Fusiliers, leaving their settlements and being taken by train through the Judean hills to Jerusalem station, where they are greeted by Jewish officials and sent out to train with a British escort. General Sir Edmund Allenby arrives in Jerusalem to share the platform at a Jewish meeting with Chaim Weizmann and the Chief Rabbi of Jerusalem. After the speeches Weizmann accompanies Allenby to his car. A portrait shot of the Japanese military attaché to the Egyptian Expeditionary Force. An observation kite balloon at Tel-el-Jelil being inflated on 21 June, near 7th (Meerut) Division camp. The balloon is lowered to change the observer and moved by its winch cable to a different site. 60-pounder guns, possibly under control from the balloon, fire under scrim netting. *(Reel 3)*

British troops and Egyptian labourers build a light railway through to Beersheba. Indian troops dig ditches by the side. More Indian troops on the march through the desert. Back to the kite balloon at Tel-el-Jelil, showing the view from the observer's basket as the balloon ascends and descends again. A portrait shot of Major-General V B Fane commanding 7th (Meerut) Division. A pay parade for men of 7th (Meerut) Division. Men of 121st Pioneer Regiment on the march. A horse race for men of the division on 22 June. Arsulf, captured by the British on 8 June, showing Turkish prisoners being escorted to the rear. Indian wounded are placed on narrow gauge trucks and taken to a dressing station by men of 128th, 129th and 130th Field Ambulances, then back to the base hospital at Ramleh. *(Reel 4)* 21st Brigade advanced headquarters is positioned covering a stretch of beach between the cliff-face and the sea; men of 2nd Battalion, the Black Watch, man a sandbag breastwork while the transport mules wait. A training exercise with Lewis machineguns for 2nd Battalion, Leicestershire Regiment. Indian soldiers, followed by their camel transport, near Jericho. Transport horses at Elijah's Well, Jerusalem. A fast-travelling car throws up dust in the desert as a type of screen. British troops practise a mock attack and bayonet fighting. Transport horses being groomed. Indian troops practise throwing Mills bombs. British troops practise with the 3-inch trench mortar.

Notes
Intertitles: only the third and fourth reels have titles.
Remarks: the meeting of Allenby and Weizmann and the forming of the Jewish Battalion are of great historical importance.
[shotsheet available]
catalogued SDB: 12/1980

IWM 31 · GB, (?) 1918
INLAND WATER TRANSPORT, EGYPT

b/w · 1 reel · 389' (7 mins) · silent
intertitles: none

sp Ministry of Information (?) *pr* Topical Film Company (?) *cam* Jeapes, Harold and/or Hurley, Frank (?)

■ Unedited film of boats on the River Nile carrying compressed horse fodder ('tiffin'), Egypt, 1918 (?).

The first boat, a steamer, tows two barges, followed by a Victoria Shipping Line steamer 'pushing' its barges. A small steamer, marked as S35, and two melon boats pass through a swing-bridge. Two converted passenger steamers, SS *Fostat* and SS *Serapis*, carry sacks on deck. Finally, some boats being towed by a small steamer.

Notes
Title: this is taken from the shotsheet.
Summary: see also **IWM 31** sections and **IWM 634**.
[shotsheet available]
catalogued SDB: 11/1980

IWM 32 · GB, (?) 1918
47TH STATIONARY HOSPITAL, GAZA, AND TROOPS IN PALESTINE

b/w · 1 reel · 857' (15 mins) · silent
intertitles: none

sp Ministry of Information (?) *pr* Topical Film Company *cam* Jeapes, Harold (and Hurley, Frank and/or Campbell, J R ?)

I. The British Army 47th Stationary Hospital, showing the ward tents, the patients' dining tents, the nurses' dining tent and the local Arab helpers. Gaza, Palestine Front, 1918 (?).
II. Arab soldiers and an officer wearing British-style uniforms with burnouses, as new recruits to the King of Hejaz's Army, Palestine Front, 1918.
III. Almond picking in the Jewish settlement at Rishon le Zion, Palestine Front, probably 1918. A study of the inhabitants as they pick almonds, including a lady "of low caste" (according to the shotsheet), a girl and a veiled lady of high caste. It is not clear whether these are Jewish or Moslem women.
IV. German prisoners being escorted through Jerusalem by Australian and Indian horsemen, Palestine Front, 1918. Some of the prisoners are taken away in lorries from the Turkish barracks at Mount Zion, escorted by Australian Light Horse. Other German prisoners are led through the streets of Jerusalem by an escort of Hyderabad Lancers and Australian Light Horse. (According to the shotsheet, the prisoners were "hooted by the Jews".)

Notes
Title: this is taken from the shotsheet.
Summary: see also **IWM 18** and **IWM 33**.
[shotsheet available]
catalogued SDB: 11/1980

IWM 33 · GB, (prod) 1918
HORSE SHOW AND SPORTS

b/w · 1 reel · 613' (11 mins) · silent
intertitles: none

sp Ministry of Information *pr* Topical Film
Company *cam* Jeapes, Harold (and Hurley,
Frank and/or Campbell, J R ?)

I. An out-of-focus sequence of General Sir
Edmund Allenby (?) reviewing a march past
by British or Indian Cavalry of the Desert
Mounted Corps, Palestine Front, 1918.
II. Arab workers filling bottles and operating
machinery in the British National Army
Canteen Board mineral water factory,
Palestine Front, 1918.
III. Locals gathering grapes at the Jewish
settlement of Rishon le Zion, Palestine
Front, 1918.
IV. The sports and horse show of 7th
(Meerut) Division, including gun limbers,
mule teams and horses jumping, Palestine
Front, 1918.

Notes
Title: this is taken from the shotsheet.
Summary: see also **IWM 18** and **IWM 32**.
[shotsheet available]
catalogued SDB: 11/1980

IWM 34 · GB, (prod) 1918
BOMBING SCHOOL AND SPORTS

b/w · 1 reel · 550' (9 mins) · silent
intertitles: none

sp Ministry of Information *pr* Topical Film
Company *cam* Jeapes, Harold (and
Campbell, J R ?)

■ Unedited film of British, Indian and
Australian forces, mainly playing various
sports, Palestine Front, July 1918.

Australian troops practising bomb (hand-
grenade) throwing from slit trenches. The
explosions are filmed at various angles and
distances. The 'cup final' of 7th (Meerut)
Division football championships, in which
(according to the shotsheet) the Royal
Engineers team defeats the team from 1st
Battalion, Seaforth Highlanders. Tel-el-Jelil,
13 July 1918. More sports at Bereit Salaam
for GHQ, including a pillow fight over water,
a test of lance skill on a wheelbarrow,
bareback wrestling on horses, and running.
Finally, a British sentry silhouetted against a
rising moon.

Notes
Title: this is taken from the shotsheet.
Remarks: the final shot of the sentry,
although a cliché, is nevertheless a very
attractive one.
[shotsheet available]
catalogued SDB: 11/1980

IWM 35 · GB, (prod) 1918
**WINE INDUSTRY AND LAYING OF THE
FOUNDATION STONE OF THE JEWISH
UNIVERSITY**

b/w · 1 reel · 287' (5 mins) · silent
intertitles: none

sp Ministry of Information (?) *pr* Topical Film
Company *cam* Jeapes, Harold

■ Wine production at the Jewish settlement
of Rishon le Zion, followed by the arrival
of dignitaries for the ceremonial laying of
the foundation stone of the Jewish
University, both Palestine, summer 1918.

A group of about eight men and women
picking grapes in a vineyard – the
atmosphere is relaxed and cheerful, with
only an overseer figure taking the task
completely seriously; a close-up of a girl
with a basket balanced on her head.
Outside the wine press building, full baskets
are unloaded from a cart; inside
(underexposed scenes) baskets are
emptied into the press, a meeting takes
place, and there is some sort of inspection
by a visiting party, some wearing topees. At
a ceremonial gathering, civilian dignitaries
(some in topees) and military officers arrive
between lines of members of the Maccabi
Athletic Association, some of whom hold
banners with Hebrew text. The shotsheet
describes the event as in the title, though
there is no film of any actual stone-laying,
and identifies "General Allenby and staff"
arriving.

Notes
Title: this is taken from the shotsheet.
Summary: the shotsheet is the source for
Rishon le Zion as the specific location of
the vineyard and wine press scenes.
[shotsheet available]
catalogued RBNS: 11/1986

IWM 36 · GB, (prod) 8/1918
**ANNUAL PROCESSION OF THE
MANUNAL (HOLY CARPET) FROM THE
CITADEL OF CAIRO TO MECCA**

b/w · 1 reel · 474' (8 mins) · silent
intertitles: none

sp Ministry of Information pr Topical Film
Company cam Jeapes, Harold (and
Campbell, J R ?)

- Procession of the Manunal leaving Cairo,
August 1918.

The Manunal was a covering mat or carpet
for the Kaa'ba outside the Great Mosque at
Mecca. Very highly decorated, a new one
was made in Cairo each year and
transported in ceremonial procession to
Port Said, by ship to Jidda, and on to
Mecca. This film shows the start of the
journey, with Egyptian troops and police
lining the streets of Cairo through which the
procession, led by a military band, passes.
The procession pauses before a mosque to
receive a blessing. The carpet itself, which
must not be seen or touched, is enclosed in
a large ornate box.

Notes
Title: this is taken from the shotsheet.
Summary: further information on the
Manunal was provided by the Islamic
Cultural Centre, London.
[shotsheet available]
catalogued SDB: 12/1980

IWM 37 · GB, (?) 2/1919
**the ADVANCE THROUGH NAZARETH
AND DAMASCUS, SEPTEMBER 20TH-
OCTOBER 1ST 1918**

b/w · 3 reels · 1125' (19 mins) · silent
intertitles: English

pr Jury's Imperial Pictures (?) prod Jury,
William F cam Jeapes, Harold and
Campbell, J R

- Compilation film of the final British victory
over the Turks and the visit of the
Maharajah of Patiala to his own regiment,
Palestine Front, September and October
1918.

I. (Reel 1) A panorama of Nazareth. Men of
4th Regiment, Australian Light Horse,
entering Tiberias on 25 September. The
bridge at Jisr Benat Yakub (which means
'the bridge of the daughters of Jacob'). A
Vickers machinegun of the ALH 4th
Machine Gun Squadron being sighted into
position. The Essex Battery, Royal Horse
Artillery of 5th Cavalry Division crossing the
Jordan River below Jisr Benat Yakub. The

mayor of El Kuneitra surrendering the town
to 5th Regiment, Australian Light Horse, on
28 September. The arrival in Kuneitra of
Major-General H W Hodgson (no good
view) commanding the Australian Mounted
Division. Men of 5th ALH and some Indian
lancers enter the town. Part of the
Australian Mounted Division continues the
advance over the open plains. A crowd
outside the Serail (the Sultan's Palace) in
Damascus on 1 October. Arab horsemen of
Prince Faisal's forces chase out looters.
(Reel 2) The bulk of Prince Faisal's force
arrives in Damascus on 1 October, English-
language newspapers are distributed
through the city, and troops of the
Australian Mounted Division and 5th Cavalry
Division also arrive. Faisal and General
Allenby (just glimpsed) arrive for their
meeting at the Victoria Hotel, and are later
seen leaving the building.
II. (Reel 3) The Maharajah of Patiala,
wearing British uniform and a turban,
inspects the Patiala Infantry Regiment, part
of 20th Brigade in Chaytor's Force of the
Egyptian Expeditionary Force. He is shown
a Lewis machinegun section and a
demonstration of rapid rifle shooting by a
senior NCO of the regiment.

Notes
Production: this may just be one of the last
of the Ministry of Information films, but the
captions are too detailed for British wartime
censor's regulations, there does not appear
to be a record of its release during the war,
and the Australian War Records Section did
not see a copy until February 1919. It is
probable that it was one of the post-war
compilations made by Jury from official
material as part of his reward for controlling
wartime film production. The War Office
Cinema Committee, which remained in
paper existence after the end of the war,
appears to have been connected with the
making of the film.
[shotsheet available]
catalogued SDB: 11/1980

IWM 38 · GB, (?) 2/1919
the ADVANCE IN PALESTINE

b/w · 6 reels · 4785' (80 mins) · silent
intertitles: English

pr Jury's Imperial Pictures (?) prod Jury,
William F cam Jeapes, Harold; and
Campbell, J R

I. The advance of the Desert Mounted
Corps from Nablus to Haifa following the

Battle of Megiddo, Palestine Front, 21-27 September 1918. *(Reel 1)* Most of the scenes are of Indian troops of 15th Cavalry Brigade, 5th Cavalry Division. Also shown in the advance are the Nottinghamshire Battery, Royal Horse Artillery and 'A' Battery of the Honourable Artillery Company; part of 5th Mounted Brigade, Australian Mounted Division; and 1st Spahi Cavalry Regiment of the French Contingent. *(Reel 2)* There is a brief scene of Lieutenant-General Sir Philip Chetwode arriving at the Jewish settlement of Zimmaria. The advance continues along the Sea of Galilee, Lake Tiberias, and to Haifa. Indian Cavalry bring in German and Turkish prisoners.
II. Recruit training by the Royal Air Force at the Senior Officers' School at Heliopolis and the Imperial School of Instruction at Zeitoun, Egypt, late 1918. *(Reel 3)* Recruits are given a medical examination, then instruction as pilots and training with the Lewis machinegun as air-gunners. *(Reel 4)* A training flight by a DH6 bomber and a demonstration of the assembly of an Airco DH9 by Royal Air Force and Women's Royal Air Force personnel, aided by Arab workers. The aircraft is assembled from parts sent out from Britain. *(Reel 5)* More scenes of the work done by the Zeitoun and Heliopolis training schools in instructing RAF personnel. *(Reel 6)* An Avro 504A aircraft takes off and demonstrates stunt flying. Part of the sequence is filmed from an aircraft in flight. The film ends with a montage of aircraft in flight, in no particular order, including a Martinsyde Elephant and a Farman Shorthorn, probably all stockshots.

Notes
Title: it seems likely that the title of the film originally referred only to the first two reels, and the remainder has become attached to these.
Intertitles: the first two reels are unusually well subtitled, the third and fourth reels have flashframes and the final reels have no titles at all.
Production: the subtitles on the first two reels seem to be too detailed for British wartime censor's regulations, suggesting another of the post-war compilations made by Jury from official material as part of his reward for controlling wartime film production (*cf.* **IWM 37** *the Advance through Nazareth and Damascus, September 20th-October 1st 1918*). The War Office Cinema Committee, which remained in paper existence after the end of the war, appears to have been connected with the making of the film.
[shotsheet available]

catalogued SDB: 11/1980

IWM 39 · GB, (prod) 1918
[BAALBEC AND BEIRUT/TRIPOLI MATERIAL] (allocated)

b/w · 1 reel · 927' (16 mins) · silent
intertitles: none

sp Ministry of Information (?) *pr* Topical Film Company

- Somewhat muddled footage principally showing the ruins at Baalbec, and the arrival of British troops in a Middle-Eastern town, presumably also in the same area, 1918.

Views of the ruins of Baalbec, with occasional glimpses of a visiting British officer and enthusiastic local guides who make great efforts to excite his (and the camera's) interest in a lion's head carving. A panorama of a valley, showing some terrace farming and groves of trees, then another panorama from a mountain over the lowlands to the seashore. A British officer and two (Indian ?) troops pose by a coastal defence gun; watched by some local children, they traverse and elevate the barrel. A military column led by a mounted officer moves through a small town street watched by a crowd of onlookers, many in fezzes; this is followed by several more units in an informal parade with fewer onlookers past a mounted officer. The troops include both Indian troops and Highlanders, the latter led by pipers. Views of a city square, then more shots of the ruins, and more of the march past. Panning view over a city waterfront with some sunken ships. High angle shot of activity around a bandstand in a wooded park, panning right to street with tramlines. A final return to the city square.

Notes
Summary: in the absence of any clues (even from the shotsheet) the interpretation of this film remains very conjectural. Assuming the material does belong all together – not necessarily a safe assumption in this part of the collection – the undoubted identification of Baalbec suggests a location in what is now Lebanon, and thus a date at the end of the Palestine campaign. This in turn suggests that the coastal scenes could be in or around Beirut, and the parade of troops in Beirut or Tripoli. The composition of the parade does not conflict with such a theory

– the only Highlanders in the EEF were the Black Watch and Seaforth Battalions in 7th (Meerut) Division, which did finish the campaign in this area.
[shotsheet available]
catalogued RBNS: 11/1986

IWM 40 · GB, (?) 1918
ALLENBY IN CAIRO (1918)

b/w · 1 reel · 780' (13 mins) · silent
intertitles: none

sp Ministry of Information (?) *pr* Topical Film Company (?) *cam* Jeapes, Harold and/or Campbell, J R (?)

■ Unedited film of General Sir Edmund Allenby's arrival in Cairo following the Armistice with Turkey, November 1918.

The film may be out of time-sequence. It shows General Allenby talking to senior officers (none identifiable) in Cairo. This is followed by a procession of cars through the streets of the city. Allenby's train arrives at Cairo station. He gets out and inspects an honour guard of Egyptian soldiers. The procession of cars arrives at Lunar Park. The film ends with a still shot of a model, composed of a wreath of the flags of all the Allies behind a cannon, and a Union Jack being hoisted, twice, to the top of a flagpole.

Notes
Summary: see also **IWM 14**.
[shotsheet available]
catalogued SDB: 11/1980

IWM 41 · USA, (prod) 1917
[LOWELL THOMAS'S FILM OF LAWRENCE OF ARABIA (rough material)]
(allocated)

b/w · 7 reels · 5412' (90 mins) · silent
intertitles: none

cam Thomas, Lowell; and Chase, H A

■ Extremely jumbled and mixed rough material – now also held in more coherent form as **IWM 42** – of the visit of Lowell Thomas to the deserts of the Middle East, autumn 1917.

The film runs in segments of varying length, with sequences often breaking, to continue later in the reel or another reel. It shows the voyage of Lowell Thomas out from Salonika to Cairo, where Sultan Hussein Kemal conducts the 'ceremony of the drums', granting a new set of parade drums to an Infantry regiment. While in Egypt Thomas also takes an aeroplane flight to get aerial views of the River Nile and the Pyramids, and watches a divisional horse show and sports, possibly 7th (Meerut) Division. He and his companions take a ship from Port Said to Jidda, and are greeted on arrival by Faisal's Arab horsemen. A variety of location shots of the desert, including rock caves and the ruined city of Petra. Thomas meets with Prince Faisal and with Major Lawrence, and films both them and their men on the march and in acted combat. Thomas returns via Jerusalem, where he films the arrival of General Sir Edmund Allenby for his ceremonial entry into the city, 11 December 1917, and his decoration with the GCB by the Duke of Connaught. The film also includes various shots of British, Australian and Arab troops, and local scenes.

Notes
Production: Lowell Thomas used his film for a series of lectures, 1918-19. William F Jury arranged for the British Government to receive copies of this film in exchange for British official material of Palestine.
Summary: the film as it now stands clearly represents material held in the most convenient form for re-editing, in short segments. It is unlikely that a definitive version of the complete film ever existed, and, if so, it is now lost, although copies of two short "Lowell Thomas Adventure Films", *With Lawrence in Arabia* and *With Allenby in Palestine* (which are held as **IWM 1131a** and **1131b** respectively), may give some idea of the uses to which the film was put post-war. It is also not clear how much of the existing scenes of Allenby and the British forces in Palestine were filmed by Lowell Thomas himself, rather than British and Australian official cameramen.
Shotsheet: in its present form this film is extremely difficult to interpret and virtually impossible to catalogue fully. See the detailed shotsheet for a scene-by-scene description.
[Lowell Thomas, *With Lawrence In Arabia*, Century (1924)]
[Kevin Brownlow, *The War, the West and the Wilderness*, Secker and Warburg (1979): 441-451]
[shotsheet available]
catalogued SDB: 4/1982

IWM 42 · USA, (prod) 1917
**[LOWELL THOMAS'S FILM OF
LAWRENCE OF ARABIA (reassembled by
Imperial War Museum)]** (allocated)

b/w · 5 reels · 5471' (90 mins) · silent
intertitles: none

cam Thomas, Lowell; and Chase, H A

- Alternative version of the film held as
  IWM 41, assembled by IWM staff to
  restore some approximate coherence to
  the material.

The assembly groups the films into
episodes as follows: *(Reel 1)* Salonika, the
voyage to Egypt, the ceremony of the
drums, the aeroplane flight. *(Reel 2)* the
horse show, scenes at a 'cactus patch'
location, a transport ship carrying Egyptian
Labour Corps from Port Said to Jidda,
scenes at a beach location. *(Reel 3)* the
main Lawrence material, with material on
Arab cavalry and camels, and armoured
cars, on a community living in rock caves,
and on Faisal and Lawrence (and Thomas),
ending with various parade scenes. *(Reel 4)*
Jerusalem, camel train scenes, and lengthy
coverage of British soldiers enjoying the
discovery of a spilt wine keg on a road.
(Reel 5) the Imperial Camel Corps, and an
assembly of shots describable as local
colour and general background.

Notes
Production: see **IWM 41** for production
details and additional references.
Summary: this assembly places together
film of compatible subjects or of the same
location in a loose approximation to
chronological order, with the intention of
providing researchers with something easier
to view than **IWM 41**. It does not aspire to
re-create or restore Lowell Thomas's original
film as to either chronology or narrative
continuity, as no records of such an original
or definitive form have been found.
[shotsheet available]
catalogued RBNS: 11/1986

IWM 43 · GB/USA, (prod) 1918
**[BRITISH GENERALS IN MESOPOTAMIA
AND PALESTINE 1918]** (allocated)

b/w · 1 reel · 212' (4 mins) · silent
intertitles: none

sp Ministry of Information *pr* International
Film Service *cam* Varges, Ariel L

- Portrait shots of British generals of the
  Mesopotamian Expeditionary Force and
  of General Sir Edmund Allenby, 1918.

I. Lieutenant-General Sir William R Marshall,
C-in-C of the MEF, filmed wearing a cap,
then a sun helmet.
II. Major-General W Gillman, chief of staff of
the MEF.
III. Major-General H T Brooking,
commanding 15th Indian Division, MEF.
IV. Major-General the Honourable R Stuart
Wortley, the Deputy Quartermaster-General
of the MEF.
V. Major-General F F Ready, the Deputy
Adjutant-General of the MEF.
VI. General Sir Edmund Allenby, C-in-C of
the Egyptian Expeditionary Force.

Notes
Summary: the scene of Allenby appears
also in **IWM 13**, and was probably not
taken by Varges, but attached to this film at
a later date.
[shotsheet available]
catalogued SDB: 11/1980

IWM 44 · GB, (prod) 1918
ARMAGEDDON

b/w · 1 reel · 606' (11 mins) · silent
intertitles: none

sp Ministry of Information *pr* Topical Film
Company *cam* Jeapes, Harold (and Hurley,
Frank and/or Campbell, J R ?)

- Jumbled material of the British forces on
  the Palestine Front, 1918 (?).

All very dark, poor quality film. It includes
scenes of Gurkhas in trenches, 60-pounder
guns firing, British soldiers walking through
a lemon grove and other British soldiers
resting. This is followed by two soldiers
using a field telephone, some pack camels,
a French mounted formation on the march,
a panorama of a city with a castle (probably
Aleppo), ruins in the desert, and a trench
scene, finishing with a scene of Arab
women carrying water jars on their heads
down a road.

Notes
Title: this is taken from the shotsheet.
Summary: see also **IWM 10** and **IWM 45**.
[shotsheet available]
catalogued SDB: 11/1980

IWM 45 · GB, (?) 1919
the NEBI-NUSA FESTIVALS : scenes and incidents en route

b/w · 1 reel · 1122' (20 mins) · silent
intertitles: English

pr Jury's Imperial Pictures (?) *prod* Jury, William F *cam* Jeapes, Harold (and Thomas, Lowell and/or Chase, H A and/or Hurley, Frank ?)

■ Scenes of the Nebi-Nusa festivals, the arrival of the Zionist Commission, and the Grand Mosque of Omar, all in Jerusalem, April 1918.

I. The Nebi-Nusa festivals of 26 April. Lieutenant-Colonel Ronald Storrs, the military governor of Jerusalem, helps assemble the sacred banners, and they are taken in a procession, which includes some Arab soldiers, to the Mount of Olives with much dancing and singing.
II. The arrival of the Zionist Commission, headed by Dr Chaim Weizmann, in Jerusalem on 3 April. The commission includes Major E A de Rothschild. On 11 April they go in procession to the Mount of Olives to deliver speeches, accompanied by members of the Maccabi Athletic Association and the banners of various Jewish workers' associations. The West Wall (or Wailing Wall) of the Temple of Solomon is also shown.
III. The Great Mosque of Omar, guarded by 58th (Vaughan's) Rifles. Soldiers of Egyptian 1st Infantry Regiment, headed by a band, including bagpipers, march to the mosque. The Egyptians remove their boots before entering the mosque. Lieutenant-Colonel Storrs converses with the officers of the battalion while they wait.

Notes
Production: this appears to be one of the post-war compilations made by Jury from official material as part of his reward for controlling wartime film production. It may, however, be an official film sponsored by the MoI before the end of 1918.
Summary: see also **IWM 19** and **IWM 27**, which contain most of the rough material for this film.
Remarks: A good example of the difference that editing can make to sometimes indifferent material. Also of considerable historical value.
[shotsheet available]
catalogued SDB: 11/1980

IWM 46-57 · NO FILM

IWM 58 · GB, (prod) 1917
[PALESTINE (rough material)] (allocated)
the NEW CRUSADERS (rough material)

b/w · 2 reels · 1757' (30 mins) · silent
intertitles: English

sp War Office Cinema Committee *pr* Topical Film Company *cam* Jeapes, Harold (and Hurley, Frank ?)

■ Rough material of British forces on the Palestine Front, 1917.

Most of the film is identical, including the captions, to **IWM 17** *The New Crusaders*. Additional scenes are of rifles firing from concealed loopholes, General Sir Edmund Allenby greeting dignitaries on his entry into Jerusalem (from **IWM 13** *General Allenby's Entry into Jerusalem*), a panorama of Alexandria (?), soldiers of the French Contingent of the Egyptian Expeditionary Force disembarking from a train, General Bailloud, their commander, leaving his headquarters, and the Hong Kong-Singapore Mountain Battery in training (from **IWM 6** *Inspection of the Imperial Camel Corps*) and using their 10-pounder mountain guns in an anti-aircraft role.

[shotsheet available]
catalogued SDB: 11/1980

IWM 59 · GB/USA, (prod) 1917
[MESOPOTAMIA (rough material)] (allocated)
WITH THE FORCES IN MESOPOTAMIA (offcuts)

b/w · 2 reels · 1193' (20 mins) · silent
intertitles: English

sp War Office Cinema Committee
pr International Film Service *cam* Varges, Ariel L

■ Very jumbled film of British forces in the Battle of Ramadi, Mesopotamian Front, 28-29 September 1917.

Probably offcuts from **IWM 61** *With the Forces in Mesopotamia. (Reel 1)* Camouflaged 60-pounder guns firing dug in. A gunner observing from a perch, possibly close to Ramadi. Indian troops unload sacks from a train. A prone Lewis machinegunner firing. British soldiers filling water buckets. A close-up of the feed action on a Vickers machinegun as it fires from a trench. An 18-pounder battery firing in the desert. Turkish 1-pounder pom-pom guns and machineguns captured at Ramadi and put on display. Shells bursting in the desert filmed from a trench. A walled city by the River Tigris with a railway station, probably Samarra. Indian troops fire through loopholes in a heavily sand-bagged trench. An observation tower made from sandbags. A 6-inch 30cwt howitzer being loaded and fired. Highlanders, probably 2nd Battalion, Black Watch of 7th (Meerut) Division, march through the streets of Samarra with Lieutenant-General Sir William Marshall (?) accompanying them. A Holt tractor hauls a 60-pounder through the desert. *(Reel 2)* Turkish prisoners captured during the Battle of Ramadi are marched by 1/5th Battalion, the Queen's Own (Royal West Kent Regiment) through the desert, over a bridge of boats across the River Tigris at Baghdad, through 'Piccadilly Circus' and 'New Street', Baghdad and on to a prisoner of war camp.

Notes
Remarks: some imaginative camerawork, even if this example is confused. Varges seems, generally, to be a better cameraman than Jeapes or Hurley in Palestine.
[shotsheet available]
catalogued SDB: 12/1980

IWM 60 · GB/USA, (prod) 1917
[PALESTINE SECTIONS]
the NEW CRUSADERS (rough material)

b/w · 4 reels · 2924' (50 mins) · silent
intertitles: English

sp War Office Cinema Committee
cam Jeapes, Harold and Varges, Ariel L
(and Hurley, Frank ?)

■ Very jumbled film of British forces, mainly on the Palestine Front, otherwise Mesopotamian or Salonika Fronts, 1917-18.

Some of the film comes directly, including the captions, from **IWM 17** *The New Crusaders*. Most of the segments are of only a few seconds' duration. Most of the film is of ancient ruins such as Babylon and Baalbec. Unique material includes: *(Reel 1)* A party of Highland soldiers dancing a fling, a bullock-drawn sledge threshing corn, and a Stokes trench mortar being fired from a trench – probably at a training school in

Mesopotamia. *(Reel 2)* Further scenes of 4.5-inch howitzers of the Indian Army in Mesopotamia (?) and a long sequence of Turkish prisoners of war and refugees from the desert. The Australian Light Horse, or possibly the single British Cavalry regiment in Mesopotamia, 7th Hussars, appear in several scenes. *(Reel 3)* A further panorama of the city of Baghdad, salt pans and fish drying on racks, and another panorama of a shell-damaged town. Also included is a long sequence of a town on fire, possibly the great fire at Salonika on 18 August 1917. Arab camels are inspected by a British vet. Further scenes of Turkish prisoners. *(Reel 4)* This reel begins with a panorama of El Arish, and a sequence of a Highland battalion led by a pipe band, "the Palestine highlands is now occupied by Scottish Highlanders" (one of the few captions in the film). It also includes part of the Siwa expedition from **IWM 17** *The New Crusaders*, a 6-inch howitzer being fired at the Battle of Ramadi, 8-inch howitzers being transported and unloaded from railway flatcars in Mesopotamia, and a 1-pounder Vickers Mk III anti-aircraft gun being fired from a railway flatcar not far from Baghdad.

Notes
Title: this is taken from the shotsheet.
Summary: see also **IWM 5**, **IWM 6**, **IWM 11**, **IWM 17**, **IWM 21**, **IWM 39**, **IWM 65**, **IWM 80**, **IWM 81** and **IWM 131**.
Remarks: this film is a typical example of the very confused material obtained as a result of the wartime habit of keeping stockshots and short segments together in one can, and of regarding Palestine and Mesopotamia as interchangeable locations.
[shotsheet available]
catalogued SDB: 12/1980

IWM 61 · GB/USA, (?) 1917
WITH THE FORCES IN MESOPOTAMIA – SERIES 1 (?)

b/w · 2 reels · 1834' (31 mins) · silent
intertitles: English

sp War Office Cinema Committee
pr International Film Service *prod* Jury, William F *cam* Varges, Ariel L

■ British forces on the Mesopotamian Front during and after the Battle of Ramadi, 28-29 September 1917.

(Reel 1) An Indian Infantry battalion (probably from 7th (Meerut) Division, as are all identifiable troops) marching down 'New

Street' in Baghdad. This is followed by the bridge of boats built by the Royal Engineers over the River Tigris at Baghdad to replace that destroyed by the Turks. "A motley crowd" in the bazaar, followed by refugees from the countryside boarding a steamer in Baghdad to take them to Basra. A further Indian battalion, possibly 20th Punjab Infantry, followed by 2nd Battalion, the Black Watch, led by its pipers. A regimental soda water making machine in operation. The Guides Infantry Regiment, crossing a pontoon bridge over the River Tigris not far from Ramadi. Gunfire from 60-pounders and a 6-inch 26cwt (?) howitzer. *(Reel 2)* A scene (acted) of Indian troops moving into a sand-bagged trench system, cleaning their rifles, one man in a sniper's position with a fixed rifle, and a Lewis machinegunner firing from a dugout. An 18-pounder position in the desert, not far from Samarra, with a mobile observation post and two guns. A captured Turkish shell-dump near Ramadi. A 60-pounder being pulled by a Holt tractor. An advanced position workshop shrinking a heated iron tyre onto a light spoked wheel. 60-pounders and 18-pounders firing with the shell-bursts seen in the distance. A 2-inch 'plum pudding' mortar being fired by British soldiers from a trench. A Lewis machinegun team firing from their trench, with the sergeant acting as a spotter. Indian troops crossing a pontoon bridge at Ramadi. Three wagons full of Indian troops being pulled along a light railway by a mule team, and the troops disembarking. Turkish prisoners being led through 'Piccadilly Circus', and 'New Street', Baghdad. The film ends with the partially destroyed railway station at Samarra, with its rolling stock.

Notes
Title: only the series title appears on the film. The episode number has been added from the shotsheet.
Summary: see also **IWM 59, IWM 63, IWM 68, IWM 79, IWM 80** and **IWM 82**.
[shotsheet available]
catalogued SDB: 12/1980

IWM 62 · NO FILM

IWM 63 · GB/USA, (prod) 1917
[MESOPOTAMIA – CTESIPHON AND SAMARRA] (allocated)

b/w · 2 reels · 1557' (26 mins) · silent
intertitles: none

sp War Office Cinema Committee
pr International Film Service *cam* Varges, Ariel L

■ Unedited film of British forces on the Mesopotamian Front, and of the Arch of Chosroess at Ctesiphon, 1917.

I. *(Reel 1)* Mainly unrelated scenes. A British 6-inch 26cwt (?) howitzer. Turkish prisoners being searched by British troops. A dressing station with Indian orderlies, a motor ambulance and a doctor performing first aid. Observers on the ground signalling to an aeroplane by laying out large strips of cloth in the shape of letters.
II. The main subject of the film is the architecture. Firstly, the Al Malwaiyah tower, 9th century, part of the Great Mosque of Samarra, contrasted with a British observation post built of sandbags. There is another unrelated scene of Rolls-Royce armoured cars recovering a damaged Martinsyde G 100 Elephant bomber of 72 Squadron RFC from the desert. A water supply column filling its trucks from the River Tigris by means of hand pumps and hoses. Then more architecture: detailed views of the Arch of Chosroess, built by Seleucus Nicator on the right bank of the River Tigris, 280 feet high, 300 feet in length, and 78 feet in breadth, it probably functioned as the royal presence chamber.
III. *(Reel 2)* The remaining film shows scenes of the area: observers in a captured Turkish post, Indian and British troops – together with the crew of a Rolls-Royce armoured car – inspecting and burying dead soldiers, collecting those still alive in stretchers, and a chaplain in vestments conducting a burial service outside a field dressing station. Indian troops on the march in the desert, Turkish prisoners of war, scenes in Baghdad and Samarra of pottery making, knife grinding, cotton separating and other crafts.

Notes
Title: the title as it appeared on the shotsheet was simply *Mesopotamia*, which has been altered. The title in the store ledger is *Tikrit and Deur Operations*, which does not match the film.
Summary: see also **IWM 59, IWM 60, IWM 61, IWM 64, IWM 77, IWM 78** and **IWM 80**.
[shotsheet available]
catalogued SDB: 12/1980

IWM 64 · GB/USA, (prod) 1918
WITH THE FORCES IN MESOPOTAMIA – SERIES 4

WITH THE FORCES IN MESOPOTAMIA
(rough material)

b/w · 1 reel · 528' (9 mins) · silent
intertitles: none

sp Ministry of Information *pr* International
Film Service *cam* Varges, Ariel L

■ Jumbled material of British troops on the
Mesopotamian Front, 1917-18.

The material was mainly used in the *With
the Forces in Mesopotamia* series. It opens
with two Holt tractors of 13th Indian Division
hauling a 6-inch 30cwt (?) howitzer across
the Narim River at Narim Kopris, beside the
bridge destroyed by the Turks. A British
cyclist unit on the move in the desert. Pack
mules led by British and Indian soldiers. 1st
Battalion, Connaught Rangers on the march
through the desert in the winter of 1917
(note the considerable variety of dress).
Indian stretcher-bearers carry wounded
across the Diyala River. A pontoon bridge
across the Tigris with British troops and a
cart crossing. Indian soldiers of 31st
Brigade wade through the Khasradala ford
at Aq Su on 29 April 1918. Indian troops in
a water-carrying column filling their trucks
from a river by hoses and hand pumps. A
Holt tractor being put through trials while
towing a 6-inch 26cwt (?) howitzer.

Notes
Summary: see the remainder of the *With the
Forces in Mesopotamia* series, and also
IWM 63, IWM 68 and **IWM 78**.
[shotsheet available]
catalogued SDB: 12/1980

IWM 65 · GB/USA, (?) 1918
**WITH THE FORCES IN MESOPOTAMIA –
SERIES 6**

b/w · 2 reels · 1579' (27 mins) · silent
intertitles: none

sp Ministry of Information (?) *pr* International
Film Service *cam* Varges, Ariel L

■ British film of the inhabitants of the River
Tigris shoreline from Basra to Kut al
Amara, mostly filmed from a moving
boat, 1918 (?).

I. *(Reel 1)* The opening is filmed from the
river. Firstly, Ezra's Tomb, a landmark at
Qurna, about 200km down river from Kut,
followed by Qurna itself. The boat continues
downstream, passing several smaller craft,

known as 'ballams', *Hospital Paddle
Steamer 5*, a high-sterned yawl or 'mahaila',
and finally passes into the port of Basra. At
the Inland Water Transport yard a small
ship rests on a slipway, ballams move in
Khandar creek (?), a helmeted diver is at
work, so is a dredger, and an Insect Class
gunboat is on patrol.
II. *(Reel 2)* The remaining scenes are mainly
on land. British Military Police control a
pontoon footbridge, probably over the Tigris
at Basra. Marsh Arabs follow the boat as it
moves, trying to sell eggs and fowl. In the
market place at Baghdad, Zahroam of
Amara, the silversmith known to the troops
as 'the silver identity-disk man', works with
his tiny furnace. At the Base Ordnance
Depot in the city refugee women work,
sewing.
III. The film ends with scenes of Kut al
Amara after its capture by the British,
showing the remains of the liquorice
factory, Indian labourers leaving work, and
two Turkish memorials to their dead.

Notes
Summary: see also the remainder of the
With the Forces in Mesopotamia series, and
also **IWM 60, IWM 61, IWM 71, IWM 75**
and **IWM 81**.
[shotsheet available]
catalogued SDB: 12/1980

IWM 66 · GB/USA, (?) 1918
**[MESOPOTAMIA – BABYLON AND
BAGHDAD]** (allocated)

b/w · 1 reel · 613' (11 mins) · silent
intertitles: none

sp Ministry of Information (?) *pr* International
Film Service *cam* Varges, Ariel L

■ Ruins of Babylon and the town of
Baghdad under British occupation, 1918
(?).

The ruins of Babylon, concentrating on the
Temple of E'Sagilo and the basalt lion
statue, including some close-up views of
relief carvings and mouldings. This is
followed by a panorama of Baghdad, from
the River Tigris inland, taken from a high
point, probably the Tower of Seria. Local
inhabitants load mules with grain and lead
them out of the city. The film ends with
British gunners repairing a captured Turkish
gun, probably an anti-aircraft gun of an
obsolete design.

Notes
Title: the title as originally given on the shotsheet for this film was, as with several similar films, simply *Mesopotamia*.
Summary: see also **IWM 60**, **IWM 75** and **IWM 81**.
Remarks: of considerable historical interest.
[shotsheet available]
catalogued SDB: 12/1980

IWM 67 · NO FILM

IWM 68 · GB/USA, (?) 1918
MESOPOTAMIA – DIYALA RIVER, KIFRIE ROAD, TUZ KERMATLI (sic)

b/w · 2 reels · 1447' (25 mins) · silent
intertitles: none

sp Ministry of Information (?) *pr* International Film Service (?) *cam* Varges, Ariel L

- British and Indian troops on the Mesopotamian Front, April 1918.

(Reel 1) A poor quality scene showing a company of Burma Sappers building a trestle bridge over the River Diyala on 16 April. Punjabis (of 14th Indian Division ?) making chapattis, also on 16 April. An Indian Lewis machinegunner using his gun in an anti-aircraft role from a trench, a second using a fixed anti-aircraft mount and a third firing out over no man's land. (The shotsheet describes the machinegunners as Sikhs of Patalia, Ferozopore and Ludiana, and Jats of the Hissar and Bikanir districts.) Punjabi soldiers from Hazara in a trench using rifle grenades. Two 18-pounder field guns with an observation post in the desert. A kite balloon of 23rd Kite Balloon Company, guarded by a 13-pounder Mk IV anti-aircraft gun, about to ascend. Indian batteries of 4.5-inch howitzers and a 6-inch howitzer. Soldiers of the Gurkha Rifles moving past an RFA park. A temporary ferry platform transporting a limber and some mules across the River Diyala on 22 April. 2nd Battalion, the Norfolk Regiment, of 14th Division, crossing the river at Masina on the same day. A 60-pounder being hauled across at the same place on 26 April. *(Reel 2)* Soldiers, perhaps of 13th Division, bathing by the Narim Kopris bridge. A convoy of Ford light cars along a desert road. Prisoners taken in the action at Tuz Khurmatli on 28 April, one being attended to by a doctor. British soldiers, apparently under fire, salvaging the engine from a crashed RE8 reconnaissance aircraft, and burning the airframe. Turkish prisoners of war in camp, and crossing a stream. A Rolls-Royce armoured car being pulled through a river. 6th Battalion, the East Lancashire Regiment, and 6th Battalion, the King's Own (Royal Lancaster Regiment) of 13th Division crossing the River Diyala with Turkish prisoners, some on camels. Troopers of the Indian Cavalry Division entering Tuz. A staged sequence of Turkish troops surrendering. Lewis machinegunners in action with a Rolls-Royce armoured car. The final scene is of British troops in camp giving three cheers to the camera.

Notes
Title: this is taken from the shotsheet.
Production: the film has very detailed captions, and is possibly one of the post-war compilations made by Jury from official material as part of his reward for controlling wartime film production.
Summary: see also **IWM 61**, **IWM 64**, **IWM 79** and **IWM 80**.
[shotsheet available]
catalogued SDB: 12/1980

IWM 69 · GB/USA, (?) 1918
KURKUCH

b/w · 1 reel · 287' (5 mins) · silent
intertitles: none

sp Ministry of Information *pr* International Film Service *cam* Varges, Ariel L

- Award of decorations to British and Indian soldiers in Kurkuch, Mesopotamian Front, 7-11 May 1918.

The British held Kurkuch only for a few days in 1918. This film shows British soldiers of 38th Brigade entering the town, followed by a number of soldiers being decorated by the commander of III Corps, Lieutenant-General Sir E G Egerton, in the square at Kurkuch, focussing on an Indian Cavalry officer at the end of the line. The film ends with more British troops marching into Kurkuch, and with a panorama of the town and the interior of the bazaar.

Notes
Title: this is taken from the shotsheet.
Remarks: if identification of the location is correct, this is a most remarkable and valuable film, although entirely for the rarity value of its location, not for its content.
[shotsheet available]
catalogued SDB: 12/1980

IWM 70 · GB/USA, (prod) 1918
[MESOPOTAMIA – INDIAN TROOPS BUILD A RAILWAY] (allocated)

b/w · 1 reel · 308' (5 mins) · silent
intertitles: none

sp Ministry of Information *pr* International Film Service *cam* Varges, Ariel L

- Short film of Indian sappers laying a railway line, Mesopotamian Front, 1918.

Flatcars carry the rails, sleepers and the troops themselves forward, as they build the line across the desert. The sappers wave and applaud for the camera. For the final shot the camera is mounted on the leading flatcar as it moves forward.

[shotsheet available]
catalogued SDB: 12/1980

IWM 71 · GB/USA, (prod) 1918
[HMS MOTH AND HMS CADDIS FLY (?)] (allocated)

b/w · 1 reel · 544' (10 mins) · silent
intertitles: none

sp Ministry of Information *pr* International Film Service *cam* Varges, Ariel L

- Gunboats HMS *Moth* and HMS *Caddis Fly* (?) on the River Tigris and the River Euphrates, Mesopotamian Front, 1918.

The film starts with a slow pan of a Fly Class river gunboat, probably HMS *Caddis Fly*. An Insect Class gunboat, HMS *Moth*, which is larger, is moored by the river bank, and bombards the area with its 6-inch and 12-pounder guns. HMS *Caddis Fly* is shown on patrol, and making smoke while at anchor. The river shown may be the Tigris, or the Euphrates, or both.

Notes
Title: the shotsheet gives the title *HMS Moth and Vardis*. The store ledger, which is of an earlier date, gives it as just KARDIS. Neither name fits the Fly Class river gunboat shown. HMS *Caddis Fly*, which served in the area, seems the most likely candidate.
Summary: see also **IWM 5**, **IWM 6**, **IWM 11** and **IWM 82**.
Remarks: the light and shade contrast between the sunlight, the water and the ships themselves is very beautiful.
[shotsheet available]
catalogued SDB: 12/1980

IWM 72 · GB, (?) 1918
SCENES ON THE EUPHRATES – MESOPOTAMIA
ADVANCE OF THE CRUSADERS INTO MESOPOTAMIA (further episode)

b/w · 1 reel · 616' (11 mins) · silent
intertitles: English

pr Jury's Imperial Pictures (?) *prod* Jury, William F (?) *cam* Varges, Ariel L (and Hurley, Frank and/or Jeapes, Harold ?)

- Everyday life in the Euphrates valley, at the Jewish settlement of Rishon le Zion, and at Hebron and Abraham's Tomb on the Palestine Front, 1917-18.

I. The film opens with the Hindiya barrage dam across the Euphrates. The local population fish from small circular coracles, called 'sufas', while others carry pots and loads of fish, and wash the fish roes using a sieve. Others hang up the fish to dry on racks. Near Babylon, grain harvesting is taking place, with the grain being threshed and the chaff winnowed by hand. Pottery is made on a handwheel.
II. This is followed by a street scene at the Jewish settlement of Rishon le Zion shortly after its capture by the British in September 1917. It is a Saturday afternoon, a brass band from the Australian Light Horse arrives and begins to play from the bandstand.
III. A final scene shows the streets of Hebron, followed by a view of the entrance to the mosque of the Tombs of Abraham, Isaac and Jacob.

Notes
Production: the format of this film closely resembles that of **IWM 78**, **IWM 79** and **IWM 80**, which comprise the series *Advance of the Crusaders into Mesopotamia*. It is possible that this is the first episode of the series.
Summary: see also **IWM 18**, **IWM 61**, **IWM 81** and **IWM 82**.
[shotsheet available]
catalogued SDB: 12/1980

IWM 73 · GB, (prod) 1918
[BAKU – THE OCCUPATION BY 'DUNSTERFORCE' 17TH AUGUST TO 14TH SEPTEMBER 1918] (allocated)

b/w · 2 reels · 1345' (23 mins) · silent
intertitles: none

sp Ministry of Information *pr* International Film Service *cam* Varges, Ariel L

- Occupation by the British 'Dunsterforce' expedition of Baku in southern Russia, August-September 1918.

(Reel 1) Russian, or possibly Armenian, soldiers assisted by British troops to fire a 76.2mm Russian field gun. A wounded soldier on a stretcher is loaded into a lorry. A group of Armenian soldiers, one of whom is very young, grouped with a British soldier around a 4-inch Russian howitzer. British troops marching through Baku, possibly 7th Battalion, the North Staffordshire Regiment, on 17 August. A Russian light gun being fired from a railway flatcar. A panorama of the town, with a British soldier semaphoring and men in Russian Army uniform at rest. A British camp, showing Armenians firing Russian 152mm howitzers under instruction. A British doctor gives local recruits a medical inspection. Local women collect new clothing. A column of civilian refugees, many mounted on asses, moving through the mountains. The exterior of the mosque at Baku, and the light gun firing from the railway flatcar, interspersed with more of the refugee column. Recruits at Baku being taught drill interspersed with views of the mosque. (Note that some of the 'British' drill instructors may be Australians.) Refugees board a ship at the quayside. Its name, written in Cyrillic characters, is given as SAGA on the bow, with HAMED-AGA written across below the bridge. The oil wells at Binagadi near Baku. More of the refugees, possibly Armenians who had fled across the Assadabad Pass to Baku. (Reel 2) Russian troops, in uniform, drilling and posing in the main square at Baku. More scenes of the 152mm howitzers firing. A squad of local recruits being inspected by the British and taught how to march in step by an Australian officer. The refugee train still moving through the mountains. At a military camp a British soldier bangs an alarm and the Armenian troops come rushing out and form up. Horses are lifted on board one of the ships using a sling. Irregular troops gather around their leader.

Notes
Summary: 'Dunsterforce' was assembled from volunteer specialists in the forces of the British Empire to train and organise a local defence force at Baku against possible German or Bolshevik Russian attack on the oilfields nearby. Dunsterville's own account does not mention a cameraman. The Australian War Records Section Papers confirm that Varges took the film, but photograph Q 24909 shows Dunsterville himself holding a still camera and it is possible that other still photographs were

taken by officers of the expedition, rather than by Varges.
Remarks: this film has every appearance of being genuine, and as such is absolutely priceless as a historical record of a very little-known event. It is noteworthy that, in contrast to the attitudes of 1914, although this was a highly secret mission, a film camera and still cameras were taken along deliberately to record it for posterity.
[L C Dunsterville, The Adventures of Dunsterforce, Edward Arnold (1920)]
[AWRS(Film) Papers, File 4375/60/27]
[shotsheet available]
catalogued SDB: 1/1983

IWM 74 · NO FILM

IWM 75 · GB/USA, (prod) 1918
MESOPOTAMIA – EXAMPLES OF ANCIENT ARCHITECTURE

b/w · 1 reel · 433' (8 mins) · silent
intertitles: English

sp Ministry of Information pr International Film Service cam Varges, Ariel L

- Ancient ruins, including Babylon and Ctesiphon, in Mesopotamia, 1918.

The film opens with views of two sets of ruins, one with children playing. This is followed by close-ups, probably in both Babylon and Ctesiphon, of "carvings, depicting biblical incidents, hewn out of the solid rock by ancient workmen with their primitive implements, more than a thousand years ago". In fact this shows some fairly sophisticated Assyrian relief carvings made in about 750 BC. These show, among other items, a sun-symbol (with spread wings), and men hunting boar from the backs of elephants. Some British soldiers are in shot for part of the film.

Notes
Title: this is taken from the shotsheet.
Summary: see also **IWM 60**, **IWM 65** and **IWM 81**.
[shotsheet available]
catalogued SDB: 12/1980

IWM 76 · NO FILM

IWM 77 · GB/USA, (?) 1918
MESOPOTAMIA – BAGHDAD AND RIVER SCENES

b/w · 3 reels · 3010' (51 mins) · silent
intertitles: English

sp Ministry of Information (?) *pr* International Film Service (?) *cam* Varges, Ariel L

- Everyday life in Mesopotamia under the British occupation, 1918.

(Reel 1) The film's only caption, "Indian troops marching through Baghdad". They are wearing winter clothing. A British horse-drawn fire-engine leaves for a (staged ?) emergency. On the river there are light canoes, known as 'ballams', and larger craft. In the streets can be seen mule transport. Lieutenant-General Sir W R Marshall, the commander of the Mesopotamian Expeditionary Force, rides through the city with his aides. Captured Turks are brought in on a river transport craft. Other craft on the river, between scenes of the streets, include a Fly Class gunboat. Marsh-dwellers sell eggs to a passing river-boat. *(Reel 2)* Further up the river is a village and a pontoon bridge. More street scenes are shown. The cameraman's car stuck in the mud on the road outside the city. The Turkish memorials to their dead at Kut al Amara, and the remains of the liquorice factory. *(Reel 3)* The River Tigris at Qurna, taken from a boat which moves downstream, past a pontoon bridge, and past a swing-bridge, 'the MacMunn bridge'. Indian troops, members of the Egyptian Labour Corps and local workers help unload stores from a ship and are given gifts from British officers at the Baghdad Depot of the Women's Branch, Bombay Presidency War and Relief Fund. A British soldier trims the beard of a grizzled Arab with clippers. The outside of the Baghdad Station Library, part of the War Gifts Depot.

Notes
Title: this is taken from the shotsheet.
Production: although bearing no definite signs either way, it is possible that this film is not a wartime official production, but one of the post-war compilations made by Jury from official material as part of his reward for controlling wartime film production.
Summary: see also **IWM 78**.
[shotsheet available]
catalogued SDB: 12/1980

IWM 78 · GB, (?) 1919
ADVANCE OF THE CRUSADERS INTO MESOPOTAMIA – 2

b/w · 1 reel · 852' (15 mins) · silent
intertitles: English

pr Jury's Imperial Pictures (?) *prod* Jury, William F *cam* Varges, Ariel L and Jeapes, Harold (and Thomas, Lowell and/or Chase, H A and/or Hurley, Frank ?)

I. British and Indian forces, and the Arch of Chosroess, Mesopotamian Front, 1918. Indian soldiers resting after a march. An Indian water-truck column refilling their trucks from a river using hose-pipes and pumps. The construction of a sandbag observation tower, and British troops observing the fire of a 6-inch howitzer from the tower, near Ramadi. British Army ground observers signal to aircraft, using strips of cloth laid out as letters on the ground. A 6-inch howitzer and an 18-pounder firing from behind scrim netting. The Al Malwaiyah tower, part of the Great Mosque at Samarra (described in the film as "a Turkish spiral observation tower"). British soldiers checking the belongings of Turkish prisoners. A long sequence showing the Arch of Chosroess at Ctesiphon.
II. The Jewish settlement at Mulebbis under British control, Palestine Front, December 1917.
The British captured the settlement on 22 December. The people return to the settlement with their possessions, "restoring their goods and shackles (sic) to their homes". British soldiers buy oranges from a street stall.

Notes
Title: only the series title appears on the film. The episode number has been taken from the shotsheet.
Production: this appears to be one of the post-war compilations made by Jury from official material as part of his reward for controlling wartime film production.
Summary: It is unclear whether otherwise unidentified material is official film or not. See also **IWM 72**, **IWM 79** and **IWM 80**.
Remarks: Jury has some odd ideas as to where Mesopotamia is, and a cavalier disregard for consistency in describing his films' locations and events. If wartime captioning was as inaccurate as this, the implications for wartime film identification are grim indeed.
[shotsheet available]
catalogued SDB: 12/1980

IWM 79 · GB, (?) 1920
ADVANCE OF THE CRUSADERS INTO MESOPOTAMIA – 3

b/w · 1 reel · 881' (15 mins) · silent
intertitles: English

pr Jury's Imperial Pictures (?) *prod* Jury, William F *cam* Varges, Ariel L

- British forces on the Mesopotamian Front, September 1917.

A balloon of 23rd Kite Balloon Company defended by a 13-pounder anti-aircraft gun on a lorry mount. A crashed RE8 reconnaissance aircraft (compare with the same scene in **IWM 68** *Mesopotamia – Diyala River, Kifrie Road, Tuz Kermatli*). A Holt tractor hauling a 60-pounder through the desert near Ramadi. A 60-pounder firing in the desert. Turkish soldiers surrendering to a British 18-pounder battery. More 60-pounders, described as "naval guns". A British battalion resting in camp. British soldiers swimming in the River Narim close to the damaged bridge at Narim Kopris. Women refugees in Baghdad sewing clothing and sorting munitions under the direction of ASC personnel. Ezra's Tomb at Qurna, described as "a Turkish Mosque". Marsh Arabs trying to sell eggs to passing boats. A panorama of Baghdad. A dredger on the River Tigris. A diver "repairing boats captured from the Turks". (Compare with the same scene in **IWM 65** *With the Forces in Mesopotamia – Series 6*.) Local boats, 'ballams', in Khora creek. A street in Baghdad, including the silversmith Zahroam of Amara. The monuments erected by the Turks at Kut to their war dead.

Notes
Title: only the series title appears on the film. The episode number has been taken from the shotsheet.
Production: this film appears to be one of the post-war compilations made by Jury from official material as part of his reward for controlling wartime film production.
Summary: see also **IWM 59, IWM 61, IWM 64, IWM 68, IWM 72, IWM 80, IWM 81** and **IWM 82**. The "naval guns" 60-pounder scene appears as a stockshot in **IWM 116**.
[shotsheet available]
catalogued SDB: 12/1980

IWM 80 · GB, (?) 1920
ADVANCE OF THE CRUSADERS INTO MESOPOTAMIA – 4

b/w · 1 reel · 1470' (26 mins) · silent
intertitles: English

pr Jury's Imperial Pictures (?) *prod* Jury, William F *cam* Varges, Ariel L

- Indian and some British forces on the Mesopotamian Front, 1917-18.

British "Territorials" in winter clothes march along a road in Mesopotamia, followed by a unit of cyclists. Indian soldiers marching. A 1-pounder Vickers anti-aircraft gun on a rail flatcar at Kahm Baghdadie in action. An 18-pounder in action in the desert near Ramadi. Two British observation posts, one of sandbags, the other improvised by tilting a field gun's limber. The "famous Bengal Lancers escorting prisoners" (poor film quality, no prisoners visible with the horsemen). Turkish prisoners on the march, escorted by British and Indian troops. Turkish soldiers surrendering to a Rolls-Royce armoured car. More Turkish prisoners drinking from a river and being shown by British officers how to cook chapattis for themselves. A series of shots edited together to produce a long column of Turkish prisoners. Indian Red Cross orderlies helping wounded Turks. Indian soldiers shown "clearing one of the tributaries of the Tigris of overgrown bushes and weeds". (Compare with **IWM 30** in which the same scene is described as Wadi Auja in Palestine.) Horsemen, probably men of 7th (Queen's Own) Hussars, watering their horses. Turkish prisoners being escorted through 'Exchange Square' in Baghdad, together with a captured battery of German 77mm field guns. A pay parade for an Indian battalion. Indian troops unloading stores from a light railway wagon which is drawn by mules. Turkish prisoners being led over a pontoon bridge into Baghdad, ending at a prisoner of war camp.

Notes
Title: only the series title appears on the film. The episode number has been taken from the shotsheet.
Production: this film appears to be one of the post-war compilations made by Jury from official material as part of his reward for controlling wartime film production.
Summary: see also **IWM 30, IWM 59, IWM 60, IWM 61, IWM 63, IWM 68, IWM 72, IWM 78, IWM 79, IWM 81** and **IWM 82**.
Remarks: entertaining, after a fashion, but with no plot or message. Simply one scene after another, with little regard even for accurate description of what is being shown.
[shotsheet available]
catalogued SDB: 12/1980

IWM 81 · GB, (?) 1920
BAGHDAD, BABYLON AND BAALBEC
ADVANCE OF THE CRUSADERS INTO
MESOPOTAMIA (further episode)

b/w · 1 reel · 841' (15 mins) · silent
intertitles: English

pr Jury's Imperial Pictures (?) prod Jury,
William F cam Varges, Ariel L; and Jeapes,
Harold

■ Views of Baghdad and Babylon in
Mesopotamia and of Baalbec on the
Palestine Front, 1918.

I. A panorama of Baghdad from the Tigris
inland, filmed from the Tower of Seria.
Indian soldiers (described as British
territorial troops) wander about. The bazaar
is shown.
II. Babylon, showing the palace of
Nebuchadnezzar II and a basalt statue of a
lion. "Our British Tommies were always
interested in anything that had a Biblical
connection."
III. A car in the desert throwing up dust as
"an improvised smoke screen" and a scene
of a ziggurat. Views of Birs Nimrud, known
as the Tower of Babel, showing the
decorated inner walls.
IV. Ancient ruins of Baalbec, given as "built
nearly nine thousand years ago, when King
Solomon ruled over Israel". (Solomon
reigned in the early 10th century BC.)

Notes
Title: the shotsheet describes this film,
loaned by Jury, as being part of the series
With the Forces in Mesopotamia, which may
be an error for Advance of the Crusaders
into Mesopotamia. It is certainly post-1918.
The main title is taken from the shotsheet.
Summary: see also **IWM 72**, **IWM 78**, **IWM
79**, **IWM 80** and **IWM 82**.
Remarks: probably the best of the films
which show the ancient architecture of
Mesopotamia and Palestine.
[shotsheet available]
catalogued SDB: 12/1980

IWM 82 · GB, (?) 1920
**BRITISH ADVANCE ON THE EUPHRATES
UNDER THE COMMAND OF MAJOR-
GENERAL BROOKING**
ADVANCE OF THE CRUSADERS INTO
MESOPOTAMIA – 9 (?) (alternative)

b/w · 1 reel · 860' (15 mins) · silent
intertitles: English

pr Jury's Imperial Pictures (?) prod Jury,
William F cam Varges, Ariel L

■ Advance of 15th Indian Division up the
Euphrates valley, Mesopotamian Front,
1918.

A column of Ford light trucks carrying
"supplies". (Compare with the same scene
in **IWM 68**.) Men of the Gurkha Rifles
moving through an RFA park. Soldiers of
2nd Battalion, the Norfolk Regiment, wading
across the River Diyala at Masina on 22
April. Armoured cars being towed across
the river. Turkish prisoners on camels
crossing the river. One 60-pounder being
pulled across the river by British troops,
another being transported by a tow ferry.
Burmese sappers building a trestle bridge
over the river on 16 April. Indian and British
soldiers starting to dig a trench system.
Indian machinegunners practising with the
Lewis machinegun. A 6-inch howitzer being
fired. A view of the river gunboat HMS
Caddis Fly (?). Shell fire on the Turkish
positions, followed by a staged Turkish
surrender and the prisoners being escorted
through the desert. A small British soda-
water machine, to produce drinks "for the
wounded". (Compare with the same scene
in **IWM 61**.) An ass-drawn scoop and water-
channel drawing water from the River
Diyala.

Notes
Title: the shotsheet describes this as
'Mesopotamia Reel 9', loaned by Jury. It is
possibly part of the series Advance of the
Crusaders into Mesopotamia.
Summary: see also **IWM 61**, **IWM 68** (which
duplicates most of the material in this film),
IWM 71, **IWM 72** and **IWM 77-81**.
[shotsheet available]
catalogued SDB: 12/1980

IWM 83 · GB, 14/8/1916
**WITH THE KUT RELIEF FORCE IN
MESOPOTAMIA**

b/w · 1 reel · 1003' (17 mins) · silent
intertitles: English

pr Gaumont

■ Advance of the Kut Relief Force from
Basra upriver until the fall of Kut al
Amara, 5 December 1915 to 29 April
1916.

Basra, showing 'The Strand', followed by
people in the bazaar and by light canoes,

'ballams', on the river (both scenes probably acted). Genuine film of troops in barges being towed upriver by paddle steamers, passing Ezra's Tomb, half-way between Basra and Kut. Marsh Arabs follow the boat. A bows-on shot of a British river gunboat, probably Insect Class. Troops on a paddle steamer with improvised mosquito nets. An acted scene of a soldier eating while surrounded by flies. Genuine scene of Arab 'mahaila' sailboats. Indian soldiers on board a paddle steamer. The British advanced position at Fallahiya on or about 5 April, showing a Napier light lorry and an Indian converted 1915 Fiat armoured car being unloaded from a ship, together with an 18-pounder being manhandled into position. Mule wagons with Indian drivers moving up. British troops in the trenches at Abu Rumman, captured on 5 April. A hospital ship docking at Fallahiya, and some of the 1136 sick and wounded evacuated from Kut after the surrender disembarking and being taken to a field hospital. (Note the packing case in the field hospital scene, marked "OC Flying Column Oran". This might be Ora, near Fallahiya, but there is no record of a field hospital there.)

Notes
Remarks: an extremely interesting illustration of the limitations of 'war films' in the First World War, using a mixture of behind-the-lines material, fakes and acted scenes, prior to the establishing of an official organisation for obtaining front line material. It is difficult to estimate just how much of this film is genuine, but probably not very much.
[*The Bioscope*, 26 July 1916: 200]
[shotsheet available]
catalogued SDB: 12/1980

IWM 84 · GB, (?) 1916
OPERATIONS OF THE BRITISH EXPEDITIONARY FORCES IN EAST AFRICA
OUR GRIP ON THE HUNS : Cherry Kearton War Series (series)

b/w · 1 reel · 580' (10 mins) · silent
intertitles: English

pr Academy Moving Picture Bureau

■ British campaign in German East Africa, 1916 (?).

Soldiers of the King's African Rifles patrolling into the bush, supplied by light canoes bringing equipment up to the frontier outposts. The 25th Battalion, the Royal Fusiliers, better known as 'The Frontiersmen' or 'Driscoll's Scouts', moving up country and encamping. Wheeled mortars being cast and scratch-built from molten metal, and later test-fired. A horse being camouflaged using potassium permanganate to darken its coat. An aeroplane (described as belonging to the RFC) apparently a Caudron GIII with French markings, taking off, in flight and landing. African scouts stalking on patrol. The Frontiersmen acting out the drill for a night alarm. A 4.7-inch coastal defence gun mounted on a field carriage being fired.

Notes
Production: probably a private purchase by the IWM. Cherry Kearton was a noted wildlife film-maker who had filmed Theodore Roosevelt's pre-war African safari, etc. According to *Who's Who in Filmland* (1931), "In 1916 [CK] went out as an officer with the Twenty-Fifth Royal Fusiliers to German East Africa, and served to the end of the war." He evidently took a camera with him.
Remarks: a well made film of considerable interest.
[shotsheet available]
catalogued SDB: 12/1980

IWM 85-94 · NO FILM

IWM 95 · GB/USA (?), (?) 1917
[BRITISH TROOPS IN SALONIKA – 1]
(allocated)

b/w · 1 reel · 558' (10 mins) · silent
intertitles: none

sp War Office Cinema Committee (?)
pr International Film Service (?)
cam Varges, Ariel L (?)

■ British guns and forces on the Salonika Front, probably early 1917.

An Indian mountain battery with 10-pounder mountain guns. A British 2.75-inch mountain gun (?) dug in on a hillside under scrim netting. Another 2.75-inch on a raised platform. A 13-pounder anti-aircraft gun. Gunners fusing shells. A 60-pounder being fired under scrim. A group of officers of various Allied nationalities watching a British march past.

Notes
Production: although possibly a private

acquisition, this is most likely one of the films taken by Varges for the British Government in spring 1917 before his transfer to the Mesopotamian Front.
[shotsheet available]
catalogued SDB: 12/1980

IWM 96 · GB/USA (?), (?) 1917
[BRITISH TROOPS IN SALONIKA – 2]
(allocated)

b/w · 1 reel · 1185' (20 mins) · silent
intertitles: none

sp War Office Cinema Committee (?)
pr International Film Service (?)
cam Varges, Ariel L (?)

- British troops in action on the Salonika Front, probably early 1917.

Two 13-pounder anti-aircraft guns firing on raised platforms. An 18-pounder field gun behind scrim netting firing. A senior officer (possibly Major-General C J Briggs) decorating British soldiers. An open-air church parade. A Vickers machinegun on an improvised anti-aircraft mount. British troops march past the brigadier-general. A 6-inch howitzer firing. A Yeomanry dismounted outpost (a 'cossack post'). British soldiers on the march and waiting in trenches, including a scene of an officer firing a Very pistol from the mouth of a dug-out. British horsemen on the march. Serbian (?) troops on the march. British transport wagons crossing a ford. British ASC troops loading supplies onto a pack mule. A canteen being filled from a pump. A wounded soldier being carried on a stretcher. A horse being helped to its feet by British soldiers. Wagon limbers being manhandled down a slope.

Notes
Production: this may be a private purchase by the IWM, but is more likely to have been filmed by Varges for the British Government in spring 1917.
[shotsheet available]
catalogued SDB: 12/1980

IWM 97 · France, (?) 1917
SUR LA STRUMA AVEC L'ARMEE GRECQUE

b/w · 3 reels · 1925' (33 mins) · silent
intertitles: French

- French film of Greek forces on the Salonika Front, 1916-17.

(Reel 1) General Paraskevopoulos directs his country's forces in the River Struma valley, which includes the Rupel Pass, supported by fire from British 6-inch howitzers and French 155mm howitzers. The French General Nider surveying the area. King Alexander of Greece visiting the front with General Gérome. *(Reel 2)* Premier Venizelos at the 1st Division headquarters in Athens, presenting new colours to the Greek 34th Infantry Regiment. Colonel Tsolacopolos receives the colours for his regiment. Among the gathering are an Orthodox priest and General Bordeaux, the head of the French mission. *(Reel 3)* General Zymbrakakis directs operations in the Skra valley (showing his own troops, fire support from French 155mm howitzers, and Bulgarian prisoners of war). King Alexander inspecting Greek soldiers. The King in Athens with the Duke of Connaught, visiting as Britain's representative, inspecting a parade, meeting with Venizelos and taking the salute. Finally, a group of refugees arriving at a temporary camp and repairing or building their houses there.

Notes
Technical: a few sections from **IWM 98** have become attached to the end of reel 3. *Remarks:* a very revealing demonstration of the superiority of the French approach to the techniques of wartime propaganda in films over that of the British at around the same date.
[shotsheet available]
catalogued SDB: 12/1980

IWM 98 · GB, (?) 1917
[BRITISH TROOPS IN SALONIKA – 3]
(allocated)

b/w · 3 reels · 2119' (35 mins) · silent
intertitles: English

sp War Office Cinema Committee
cam LaVoy, Merl (?)

- British troops, mainly 22nd Division, on the Salonika Front, 1917-18 (?).

(Reel 1) Wounded soldiers with mule transport, snow-covered mountains filmed from an aircraft (Mount Olympus ?). A 13-pounder anti-aircraft gun showing the rangefinder in use. A British Army camp, with a bakery and soldiers washing and eating. Three soldiers in a trench fusing

Mills grenades. A Royal Engineers wagon laying a line. A view from the rear gunner's position of a two-seater aircraft taking off, flying over Salonika harbour, the nearby mountains, and a military camp. *(Reel 2)* Brigadier-General F S Montague-Bates (66th Brigade, 22nd Division) in a posed position. A return shot of the three soldiers fusing Mills grenades. They change to fitting magazines on Lewis machineguns and using a trench periscope. General Guillaumat inspects a British battalion. General scenes of the British Army camp. A Red Cross wagon on the move. A heavily camouflaged gun (possibly a 60-pounder) and a 6-inch howitzer. More soldiers in trenches. Major-General J Duncan, commanding 22nd Division, and Lieutenant-General H F M Wilson posed together. British soldiers at bayonet practice. *(Reel 3)* A Highland battalion, probably Black Watch, with its pipe band, and a single piper playing. A French general decorates British troops, who march past.

Notes
Cameraman: the shotsheet, mis-numbered as **IWM 135**, identifies the cameraman as Merl LaVoy. He was a US freelance cameraman who visited the Salonika Front in early 1917. There is some evidence that he was briefly employed on a semi-official basis by the British Government but he could not have filmed all this material (see last Note).
Intertitles: the film has only one title, before the mule scene.
Summary: the scene of mules transporting wounded appears also in **IWM 96**.
Remarks: quite interesting material, but almost impossible to put in a precise context of date or location. If correct, the identification of LaVoy as the cameraman suggests a date of early 1917 (see earlier Note), but Guillaumat's presence means a date between 10/12/1917 and 9/6/1918.
[shotsheet available]
catalogued SDB: 1/1981

IWM 99 · GB/USA, (?) 1916
READY FOR THE ENEMY

b/w · 1 reel · 415' (7 mins) · silent
intertitles: English

sp War Office (?) *pr* International Film Service for Topical Film Company
cam Varges, Ariel L (?)

■ British and French troops on the Salonika Front, probably 1916.

A British column of mules and wagons moves down a hill road. British soldiers and Greek civilians unloading and stacking stores. French 105mm howitzers, limbered up, moving along a dirt road. British soldiers hauling an 18-pounder field gun into position. A French shell-dump with 75mm shells being fused on a special machine. A British soldier throwing Mills grenades from a trench. A Vickers machinegun team in action (note the machinegunner 'tapping' the gun handles to spread the cone of fire). A heavily camouflaged "huge gun", possibly a British 6-inch Mk VII field gun, shown from front and rear.

Notes
Production: probably made by the Topical Film Company before it was taken over by the British Government as a production company, and the establishing of an official cameraman on the Salonika Front. The identification of Varges as the cameraman is tentative, based on work by Nicholas Hiley. It appears that Varges was in 1916 already employed by the British on a semi-official basis in Salonika.
[shotsheet available]
catalogued SDB: 1/1981

IWM 100 · GB, (?) 1916
WITH THE ALLIED TROOPS IN SALONIKA

b/w · 1 reel · 442' (8 mins) · silent
intertitles: English

pr Pathé

■ British and French troops on the Salonika Front soon after the Allied landing in October 1915.

French Chasseurs Alpins dismantling a mountain gun. French Infantry, probably from 156th Division, resting (they appear to be wearing dark blue tunics and red trousers rather than horizon blue). Greek civilians passing a dump of 75mm shells, "no shortage of shells here". The British Army camp. Greek civilians building wooden huts. A British fatigue party of about forty men pulling a wagon through their camp. British ASC troops checking the harness of their wagons before moving off. A British battalion marching in column. A meal from British field kitchens. British troops resting, possibly 10th (Irish) Division (note the high proportion of marksman's badges worn). A semaphore flag "signalling the arrival of troops in the Bay". A view of the French Army camp.

Notes
Production: probably made in late 1915 or early 1916 before the appointment of an official cameraman to the Salonika Front.
[shotsheet available]
catalogued SDB: 1/1981

IWM 101 · GB, (?) 1917
INLAND WATER TRANSPORT

b/w · 1 reel · 220' (4 mins) · silent
intertitles: none

sp War Office Cinema Committee (?)
pr Topical Film Company

- Barges and construction work of the Inland Water Transport on the La Bassée Canal, Western Front, probably 1917.

A pile-driver on the canal bank builds a landing stage. A road swing-bridge across the canal on the section between Béthune and Givenchy opens to let IWT barge AS 174 pass through. Two mobile cranes, one marked IWT 32, unload roadfill material from the barge, with soldiers assisting.

Notes
Title: this is taken from the shotsheet.
Date: although very difficult to date, this is more probably 1917 than earlier or later.
Summary: compare with **IWM 31** *Inland Water Transport, Egypt.*
[shotsheet available]
catalogued SDB: 1/1981

IWM 102 · GB, (after) 7/1917
SCENES ON THE YSER CANAL

b/w · 1 reel · 361' (6 mins) · silent
intertitles: English

sp War Office Cinema Committee *pr* Topical Film Company *cam* McDowell, J B or Raymond, H C (?)

- Royal Engineers field companies and men of the Guards Division crossing the Yser Canal, Western Front, 31 July 1917.

Parties of the Irish Guards with Royal Engineers of either 55th Company or 76th Company RE carry coils of wire past defences and over the Yser Canal by a small footbridge. They are followed by Grenadier Guards and by men of the RAMC returning with wounded. On another part of the canal, possibly Bois de Crapouillots, a main road bridge is under construction. There is general wreckage, including a lorry (possibly of 36th Division, note the unit sign) and an RFA limber with all the horses dead, and a digging party clearing up.

Notes
Cameraman: the cameraman was either McDowell or Raymond.
Summary: see also **IWM 103** *The Advance on St Julien.* Following the policy change in spring 1917, the British abandoned their previously successful 'big battle' film format in favour of a more intimate approach, culminating in the major project for autumn 1917, the *British Regiments* series. As a result of this, there is very little coverage of the Third Battle of Ypres, and this item represents one of the few films of an event in the battle.
[shotsheet available]
catalogued SDB: 1/1981

IWM 103 · GB, (after) 7/1917
the ADVANCE ON ST JULIEN

b/w · 1 reel · 215' (4 mins) · silent
intertitles: none

sp War Office Cinema Committee *pr* Topical Film Company *cam* McDowell, J B or Raymond, H C (?)

- Attack on St-Julien by 39th Division, Western Front, 31 July 1917.

A very broken film. A gunner with two horses out of control plunges past startled soldiers in a trench. Explosions in the distance. A view of no man's land. 18-pounder field guns are brought up past a trench and wounded on stretchers come back the other way. Behind the lines, German prisoners are used as stretcher-bearers. Horses carrying 18-pounder shells in panniers move up.

Notes
Cameraman: the cameraman was either McDowell or Raymond.
Summary: see also **IWM 102** *Scenes on the Yser Canal.* Following a policy change in spring 1917, the British abandoned their previously successful 'big battle' film format in favour of a more intimate approach, culminating in the major project for autumn 1917, the *British Regiments* series. As a result there is very little coverage of the

Third Battle of Ypres, and this item represents one of the very few films of an event in the battle.
Remarks: confused, very vague, possibly faked film, with very poor quality camerawork. Were it not for the rarity value of its subject, it would be worthless.
[shotsheet available]
catalogued SDB: 1/1981

IWM 104 · GB, (?) 1917
THIRD ARMY INFANTRY TRAINING SCHOOL

b/w · 1 reel · 1104' (19 mins) · silent
intertitles: English

sp War Office Cinema Committee (?) *pr* Topical Film Company

■ Demonstrations of mounted and dismounted drill at Third Army Infantry Training School, probably 1917.

I. An officer shows the correct methods of mounting a horse, sitting at attention and at ease, trotting, the extended trot, leading off alternate legs, and a dressage test. Following this, other riders jump.
II. A party of six drill sergeants shows the correct and incorrect postures for attention, stand at ease, marching in file and halting, marking time, dressing, and saluting, all without weapons. Carrying rifles, they demonstrate the attention and at ease positions, fixing bayonets, bayonet guards and practise with "the blob", and against straw dummies. This ends with a demonstration of rushing a dummy trench system.

Notes
Title: this is taken from the shotsheet.
Intertitles: some of these are slightly out of sequence.
Remarks: a noteworthy, and in some ways frightening, demonstration of the extent to which the British Army of the period sought to ritualise the most trivial action, completely unconscious of the absurdity of its appearance.
[shotsheet available]
catalogued SDB: 1/1981

IWM 105 · GB, (?) 1916
SCENES OF THE WESTERN FRONT

b/w · 1 reel · 548' (10 mins) · silent
intertitles: English

sp War Office Cinema Committee *pr* Topical Film Company *cam* McDowell, J B

■ British forces and German prisoners on the Western Front, 1916 (?).

A narrow gauge railway carries 9.2-inch shells and troops forward. A poor middle-distance view of a tank flying a flag moving up with supporting troops on foot. Soldiers moving into a devastated wood supported by smoke (?) bomb explosions. German prisoners help to load equipment onto British lorries. British RFA limbers take captured German guns down a road, mainly 77mm field guns. French 75mm field guns firing. German prisoners shown for the camera, together with captured light guns, mortars and Maxim machineguns. German prisoners repair a road as an 18-pounder battery moves through. The prisoners rest and eat by the roadside.

Notes
Summary: this film appears to be a mixture from several sources, rather than film taken deliberately in one location at one time.
[shotsheet available]
catalogued SDB: 1/1981

IWM 106 · GB, (?) 1916
[WESTERN FRONT CHRISTMAS – 1915 (?)] (allocated)

b/w · 1 reel · 356' (6 mins) · silent
intertitles: English

sp War Office (?) *pr* British Topical Committee for War Films (?) *cam* Malins, Geoffrey H (?)

■ Christmas scenes on the Western Front, probably 1915.

The Prince of Wales leaves a house to enter a car. A steam pump in operation by a canal lock, probably the Yser Canal. Troops, possibly new arrivals, entering billets. A field kitchen. Soldiers digging. A "Christmas ride to Berlin" (flashframe) showing British soldiers riding horses while wearing gas masks. A horse obstacle-race. A "ride of the Amazons" (flashframe) of soldiers wearing skirts riding through shallow water. A ship coming into harbour. An RHA troop waiting to move off. British soldiers using a hand pump to clear a waterlogged trench.

Notes
Date: that of Christmas 1915 is uncertain,

but the format is that of early British official film, and Christmas 1916 seems too late. Furthermore, there is the Prince of Wales, recorded by Malins as filmed at Christmas 1915.
Intertitles: these are all flashframes.
[Geoffrey H Malins, *How I Filmed the War*, Herbert Jenkins (1920)]
[shotsheet available]
catalogued SDB: 1/1981

IWM 107 · GB, (?) 1916
GENERAL DE LISLE PRESENTING MEDALS TO OFFICERS AND MEN

b/w · 1 reel · 398' (7 mins) · silent
intertitles: none

sp War Office Cinema Committee (?)
pr Topical Film Company *cam* Malins, Geoffrey H (?)

■ Major-General de Lisle presenting medals, probably Western Front, 1916 (?).

An officer, possibly Major-General H B de Lisle, presenting medals to a kilted battalion, who then march past. A pan over a group from the battalion sitting and smoking. They are possibly the Canadian 16th Battalion (Canadian Scottish).

Notes
Title: this is taken from the shotsheet.
Cameraman: Malins is given as the cameraman in the store ledger. If this is correct the film was taken either before February 1917, when he retired as a British official cameraman, or after December 1917, when he returned to the Western Front as a Canadian official cameraman.
Summary: all information has been taken from the shotsheet. Nothing further can be discovered about the film, and it is a mystery why de Lisle should present decorations to Canadians.
[shotsheet available]
catalogued SDB: 1/1981

IWM 108 · GB, (prod) 1916
CHAPPERTON DOWN ARTILLERY SCHOOL

b/w · 1 reel · 686' (11 mins) · silent
intertitles: English

sp War Office (?)

■ Demonstration firings of 6-inch, 8-inch and 9.2-inch howitzers with the new Type 106 fuse at Chapperton Down near Aldershot, spring 1916.

Taken at the school on 9 March 1916, this film shows in detail the firing procedures for the 6-inch 26cwt howitzer, the 8-inch Mk VI howitzer and the 9.2-inch Mk I howitzer with the new Type 106 graze fuse (not shown). It shows the effects of the fall of shot, giving the distance and line of camera to the point of impact with the direction of wind for each firing. In each case the result is a surface burst.

Notes
Production: probably an internal Army training film made for the War Office rather than any part of the official propaganda film programme.
Remarks: concerned with ballistics rather than tactics. The new graze fuse removed the need for extremely complex calculations in setting bombardments to cut enemy wire, and led to greatly improved results, but did not arrive on the Western Front in significant numbers until nearly a year after this film was made.
[shotsheet available]
catalogued SDB: 1/1981

IWM 109 · GB, 1917
the KING HOLDS AN INVESTITURE IN HYDE PARK, LONDON

b/w · 1 reel · 829' (14 mins) · silent
intertitles: none

sp Department of Information

■ Royal Investiture for Imperial Military and Naval Forces, Hyde Park, London, 2 June 1917.

The film opens with the front row of officers awaiting the investiture, sitting on wooden chairs in the park. They are, from right to left: Major Henry Murray of the Australian forces, Lieutenant-Colonel James Forbes-Robertson of the Border Regiment, Captain Ambrose Peck of the destroyer HMS *Swift*, Captain Edward Evans of the destroyer HMS *Broke*, Lieutenant-Colonel Agar Adamson of the Canadian forces, and Lieutenant-Colonel Albert Fewtrell of the Australian forces. In the investiture 351 awards were given, including 11 Victoria Crosses, 4 of them posthumous. 313 servicemen received their awards personally, 26 were received by relatives.

There were 12 awards of the Royal Red Cross to nurses. The film shows the King arriving and taking the salute. On the platform with him is the Queen. The Duke of Connaught, Viscount French and Sir William Robertson inspect with him the guard of the Scots Guards. Back on the platform he presents the awards with the Queen seated beside him. Finally, all those decorated give three cheers for the King.

Notes
Title: this is taken from the shotsheet.
[Programme of Investiture, 2/6/1917, held by Department of Film]
[shotsheet available]
catalogued SDB: 1/1981

IWM 110 · GB, (prod) 1917
SPORTS OF THE 7TH BLACK WATCH

b/w · 1 reel · 330' (6 mins) · silent
intertitles: none

sp War Office Cinema Committee *pr* Topical Film Company *cam* Raymond, H C

- 7th Battalion, the Black Watch, sports at Bailleul, Western Front, 10 May 1917.

The sports are watched by the Divisional GOC, Major-General Harper of 51st (Highland) Division, and by Field Marshal Haig. The pipe band marches past the watching troops. Haig, after looking around, leaves on horseback. The finish of the mile race is watched by the senior officers, including Harper. There is also a wheelbarrow race, a race in gas masks, a pillow fight on a greasy pole, a race for local children, a race for bandsmen in full kit, and a tug of war. The prizes are given to the children by officers of the regiment, and to the men by Major-General Harper.

Notes
Title: this is taken from the shotsheet.
[shotsheet available]
catalogued SDB: 1/1981

IWM 111 · GB, 1917
CARDINAL BOURNE VISITS THE IRISH TROOPS IN FRANCE

b/w · 1 reel · 326' (6 mins) · silent
intertitles: English

sp War Office Cinema Committee *pr* Topical Film Company *prod* Jury, William F

cam McDowell, J B or Raymond, H C (?)

- Cardinal Bourne's visit to 16th (Irish) Division at Ervillers, Western Front, on 27 October 1917.

The Cardinal meets regimental chaplains outside a barn marked as a Catholic church. (Note the official photographer, J Warwick Brooke, at work.) The Cardinal walks towards the camera for a posed shot. Together with Brigadier-General Ramsey of 48th Dublin Fusiliers Brigade, he inspects the men and gives them an address standing in a wagon, finishing with a benediction. The Cardinal talks to one of the soldiers. The film ends with the brigade marching past.

Notes
Remarks: a surprisingly interesting film.
[shotsheet available]
catalogued SDB: 1/1981

IWM 112 · GB, 1917
RIBEMONT GAS SCHOOL

b/w · 2 reels · 1872' (32 mins) · silent
intertitles: English

sp War Office *cam* McDowell, J B

- Training film, using Australian troops, on the use of the small box respirator, Western Front, November 1916.

I. *(Reel 1)* The opening shows a demonstration by a group of soldiers of the correct methods of carrying, wearing, cleaning and removing the gas mask, including running at the double while wearing it. They test the fit of their gas masks by entering a room full of tear gas. One soldier in close-up then repeats the full drill. A similar drill is shown for the horse respirator. This is followed by an acted scene in the school's training trenches showing precautions to be taken if the wind is dangerous for a gas attack. In the trench an officer inspects the gas masks and an NCO tests the Strombos warning horn, the Vermorel sprayer to lay the gas, the Ayrton fans to clear the gas out of dug-outs and the bottom of trenches, and the blanket 'door' of a gas-proof dugout.
II. *(Reel 2)* The remainder of the film is an acted gas attack in the training trenches, with smoke substituting for gas. The sentry gives the gas alert, soldiers come to the fire-step in their gas masks, but there is one casualty from a badly-fitting mask. A fatigue

party responds to the gas alert. After the attack the gas is cleared using Ayrton fans, and rifles are cleaned. At the film's end there are two further demonstrations as troops enter a gas-filled chamber, firstly with full head cover and then without respirators, to demonstrate the temporary effects of tear gas.

Notes

Production: according to the AWRS(Film) Papers, this film was made by British cameramen and at the request of the British War Office, but filmed at the Australian 5th Division Gas School, since no British gas training unit was able, or prepared, to make the same facilities available to the cameramen. The dopesheet, prepared in 1922 after conversations with McDowell, contradicts the Australian version by saying that the dates of filming were 2-11 February 1917.
Summary: the use of any type of gas would have corroded the cameras, and it is most probable that some type of smoke was used.
Remarks: given that, for technical reasons, film of a genuine gas attack could not be obtained, the demonstration in this film is an excellent substitute, and surprisingly realistic by the standards of the time.
[AWRS(Film) Papers, File 4375/60/14]
[dopesheet available]
[shotsheet available]
catalogued SDB: 1/1981

IWM 113 · GB, 6/6/1917
the GERMAN RETREAT AND THE BATTLE OF ARRAS
the BATTLE OF ARRAS (alternative)
the BATTLE OF THE SCARPE (alternative)

b/w · 4 reels · 4129' (68 mins) · silent
intertitles: English

sp War Office Cinema Committee *pr* Topical Film Company *prod* Jury, William F
cam Malins, Geoffrey H; McDowell, J B; and Raymond, H C

■ Aftermath of the German retreat to the Hindenburg Line, and the Battle of Arras, Western Front, March-April 1917.

(Reel 1) The opening shows the destruction near Bapaume and Péronne caused by the German retreat. Buildings have been blown up, and trees cut down. A British cyclist patrol is greeted by the population of a newly liberated village. French soldiers in another liberated village, probably Roye. A

British 6-inch howitzer battery near Henin is shown, together with its 21 year old commander (possibly Major A Gordon of 11th Siege Battery RGA). Batteries of 18-pounders and 9.2-inch howitzers are also in action in the Henin area. *(Reel 2)* South African 1st Regiment during a trench raid (their leader, Captain Rolf, was awarded the MC), taking three prisoners. Another trench raid, possibly by 9th Battalion, the Cameronians. Behind the lines near Arras 19th Hussars wait. *(Reel 3)* Soldiers of 10th (London Stock Exchange) Battalion, Royal Fusiliers and Royal West Kents march up to the battlefield for the attack. German prisoners and wounded come back, but no fighting is shown. Men of the King's Liverpool Regiment and King's Own Shropshire Light Infantry move up. *(Reel 4)* In the aftermath, captured German gun positions are shown together with British howitzers moving to Monchy-le-Preux. The first train arrives at Arras station, played in by the pipe band of a battalion of Gordon Highlanders. Australians and men of 29th Division rest after the attack. On 13 April men of 29th Division are taken to rest by buses.

Notes

Dopesheet: a dopesheet for this film exists in the Department of Film, but is suspect in many respects.
Remarks: the last, and least successful, of the three 'big battle' pictures made between summer 1916 and spring 1917 by British official cameramen. Compare with **IWM 116** *The Battle of the Ancre and the Advance of the Tanks* and **IWM 191** *The Battle of the Somme.* The film is patchy, without drama and lacks scenes of actual combat. It was a recognition of these limitations which led to the shift away from the 'big battle' format.
[A J Peacock, "Evidence In Camera", *Stand To!*, 3 (winter 1981)]
[W Alex Frame, "Unknown Raiders", *Stand To!*, 4 (spring 1982)]
[dopesheet available]
[shotsheet available]
catalogued SDB: 10/1980

IWM 114 · GB, 12/6/1916
the WORK OF THE ARMY VETERINARY CORPS : and how it is helped by the RSPCA
OFFICIAL PICTURES OF THE BRITISH ARMY IN FRANCE – FIFTH SERIES (series)

b/w · 1 reel · 590' (9 mins) · silent
intertitles: English

sp War Office *pr* British Topical Committee for War Films *cam* Malins, Geoffrey H or Tong, Edward G (?)

- British Army Veterinary Hospital at Neufchâtel, near Dieppe, spring 1916.

An unfinished stable at the hospital, "will you help the RSPCA to complete it ?". A group of three horses. A wounded horse being attended to at a mobile veterinary section near the front. Wounded horses are entrained, then detrained at the hospital and loaded into a horsebox. The hospital itself includes an operating theatre, with horses being operated on, treatment for shrapnel wounds, and a horse-dip. The horses are then fed and exercised. A remount officer inspects the cured horses and they are led out of the stables.

Notes
Cameraman: the cameraman was either Malins or Tong.
[shotsheet available]
catalogued SDB: 1/1981

IWM 115 · GB, 10/1917
VISIT OF SPANISH GENERALS TO THE WESTERN FRONT

b/w · 1 reel · 775' (13 mins) · silent intertitles: none

sp War Office Cinema Committee *pr* Topical Film Company

- Spanish generals being shown over the British sector of the Western Front, March-April 1917.

At Fourth Army headquarters, Querrieu Château, on 15 April 1917 General Henry Rawlinson shows the visiting generals some captured German trench mortars and a new Mk I Female tank. Leading the Spanish party are General Primo de Rivera, General Aranaz and also Brigadier-General Martinez Anido. After this comes the visit of the generals to the old Somme battlefield in March, escorted by Colonel Hulton Wilson. They drive up the Albert-Bapaume road, getting out at La Boisselle to tour the battlefield. The film jumps twice, to the debris of Le Sars and to the party standing on the Butte de Warlencourt. The generals go on to inspect the veterinary hospital at Abbeville, watch British and Indian Cavalry (either 4th or 5th Cavalry Division) practising close-order charges on the training ground at Rouen, and pose beside

the canteen at No 6 Veterinary Hospital in Rouen.

Notes
Title: this is taken from the shotsheet.
Summary: the General Primo de Rivera mentioned is the future Spanish dictator.
[shotsheet available]
catalogued SDB: 1/1981

IWM 116 · GB, 1/1917
the BATTLE OF THE ANCRE AND THE ADVANCE OF THE TANKS
BATTLE OF THE ANCRE (alternative)

b/w · 5 reels · 4472' (76 mins) · silent intertitles: English

sp War Office *pr* British Topical Committee for War Films *prod* Jury, William F
cam Malins, Geoffrey H; and McDowell, J B

- British operations in the Somme offensive between the Battle of Flers-Courcelette and the Battle of the Ancre, Western Front, September-November 1916.

(Reel 1) Material from various phases of the Somme offensive without regard for logical or chronological continuity. The film opens with the unloading of supply trains, and soldiers on the march to the battlefield, horses being used to carry 18-pounder shells to the guns in saddle-panniers as the mud is impassable for wheeled transport, and the first appearance of the tanks. *(Reel 2)* 18-pounder guns, 6-inch and 8-inch howitzers fire under the control of battery officers and forward observation officers. A sequence of "Irish troops" attacking Martinpuich is shown (fake ?). *(Reel 3)* The tanks and Highlanders take Martinpuich on 15 September. *(Reel 4)* Scenes of ruins and a field dressing station after the battle. A German colonel captured with his staff on 13 November. Men of 63rd (Royal Naval) Division rest after capturing Beaumont Hamel. *(Reel 5)* General views of the Ancre battlefield and troops cleaning up and resting in the aftermath. The final sequence is of silhouetted supply columns moving on up the road. Among the various units in the film, those which are identified are three tanks, HMLS 'Oh I Say !', HMLS 'Daphne' and HMLS 'Dodo', the Australian 1st and 2nd Divisions, Howe and Hawke Battalions from 63rd (Royal Naval) Division, 29th Division, and several Infantry regiments. These include 4th Battalion, the Worcestershire Regiment, 2nd Battalion, the Northamptonshire Regiment, 2nd Battalion,

the West Yorkshire Regiment, 7th and 8th Battalions, the King's Own Scottish Borderers, 13th Battalion, the Royal Scots, 11th Battalion, the Argyll and Sutherland Highlanders, 6th and 10th Battalions, the Cameron Highlanders, 8th and 9th Battalions, the Durham Light Infantry, the Essex Regiment and the Royal Welch Fusiliers.

Notes
Shotsheet: a detailed shotsheet and analysis of this film has been published to accompany video distribution of this film (1993).
Remarks: the second of the three 'big battle' films made between summer 1916 and spring 1917 by British official organisations, and that which conforms most closely to the 'big battle' format. Compare with **IWM 113** *The German Retreat and the Battle of Arras* and **IWM 191** *The Battle of the Somme.* Extremely patchy, it shows evidence of the use of fakes, particularly in the 'Irish' attack, while some close-ups of tanks are clearly filmed in a training ground. Nevertheless it has some good moments, such as the long ride to take shells to the guns in reel 1 and the attack of the Highlanders in reel 3. The novelty value of the tanks is heavily played upon.
[Geoffrey H Malins, *How I Filmed the War*, Herbert Jenkins (1920)]
[dopesheet available]
[shotsheet available]
catalogued SDB: 10/1980

IWM 117 · GB, (?) 1917
the DUKE OF CONNAUGHT REVIEWS THE GUARDS

b/w · 1 reel · 513' (9 mins) · silent
intertitles: English

sp War Office Cinema Committee *pr* Topical Film Company *prod* Jury, William F *cam* McDowell, J B (?)

■ Duke of Connaught reviews men of the Guards Division at Lumbres, near Wizernes, Western Front, 1 November 1916.

All three Guards brigades were at the inspection. The film opens with the men, including the massed bands of the division, assembling in position. Connaught arrives on horseback with an escort of Indian lancers and is greeted by the divisional commander, Major-General G P T Fielding, himself riding a white horse. They inspect the division, Connaught addresses the men,

and the bands lead a march past (one officer's horse shies at the camera). Connaught takes the salute and leads three cheers for the King. An extract from **IWM 119** *The Duke of Connaught's Visit to the Armies* has become attached to the end of the film.

Notes
Summary: see also **IWM 119**.
[shotsheet available]
catalogued SDB: 1/1981

IWM 118 · GB, 17/4/1916
the EYES OF THE ARMY : with the RFC at the front
OFFICIAL PICTURES OF THE BRITISH ARMY IN FRANCE – THIRD SERIES (series)

b/w · 1 reel · 420' (8 mins) · silent
intertitles: English

sp War Office *pr* British Topical Committee for War Films *cam* Malins, Geoffrey H or Tong, Edward G (?)

■ Royal Flying Corps workshops and aeroplanes, Western Front, spring 1916.

An RFC mobile repair shop. A wrecked BE2 has its wings removed by mechanics and is taken to the repair sheds where its fabric is stripped off. A French officer, being escorted round the shop, passes the fuselage of a Bristol Scout C type. The mechanics march off to eat. RFC personnel inspect the wreckage of a crashed "Albatros" (?). A rotary engine is fitted to a BE2 (?). An RE7 reconnaissance aircraft goes out on a flight, sending signals to two wireless operators on the ground, and comes back to land.

Notes
Cameraman: this was either Malins or Tong.
Summary: only a few of the type of RE7 shown, with the Beardmore engine, ever flew, and it is an extremely rare aircraft. This one belonged either to 21 Squadron or 12 Squadron RFC.
Remarks: a finely executed piece, with the accident of recording a rare aircraft making it doubly valuable.
[shotsheet available]
catalogued SDB: 1/1981

IWM 119 · GB, (after) 9/1917
the DUKE OF CONNAUGHT'S VISIT TO THE ARMIES

b/w · 1 reel · 287' (5 mins) · silent
intertitles: English

sp War Office Cinema Committee pr Topical
Film Company cam McDowell, J B or
Raymond, H C (?)

- Duke of Connaught's visit to the Trench
  School of Instruction at Helfaut and to 1st
  Battalion, the Grenadier Guards, Western
  Front, November 1917.

I. The Duke of Connaught, together with his
son Prince Arthur of Connaught, on 20
November, coming out of Tramecourt
Château and posing on the steps.
II. Following this is the arrival of Connaught
(without the Prince) at the Trench School of
Instruction, Helfaut, also on 20 November.
He watches a demonstration of the 3-inch
mortar by British troops with American
officers under training.
III. The Duke, also in November, arrives at
Zudroye to inspect 1st Battalion, the
Grenadier Guards. He is accompanied by
its commanding officer, Lieutenant-Colonel
Maitland-Makgill-Crichton. Connaught leads
the battalion in three cheers for the King.
IV. The film ends with a scene (also in **IWM
117** The Duke of Connaught Reviews the
Guards) of the Duke, apparently at Helfaut,
inspecting a type of shell or mine with a
group of officers, one of whom is American.

Notes
Title: this is taken from the shotsheet.
Intertitles: there is only one title, a
flashframe.
Cameraman: the cameraman was either
McDowell or Raymond.
[shotsheet available]
catalogued SDB: 1/1981

IWM 120 · GB, 1917
the GRAVE OF MAJOR W REDMOND

b/w · 1 reel · 275' (5 mins) · silent
intertitles: English

sp War Office Cinema Committee pr Topical
Film Company prod Jury, William F
cam McDowell, J B or Raymond, H C (?)

- Visit of an Irish delegation to the grave of
  Major William Redmond at Locre,
  Belgium, 21 September 1917.

Redmond died of wounds on 7 June 1917
and was buried in Locre cemetery. The film
shows the deputation from Ireland visiting
his grave which is tended by nuns and has

been extremely highly decorated for the
ceremony. The members of the deputation
are Dr James Ashe, Mayor Nicholas Byrne
of Wexford and High Sheriff Myles Keogh of
Dublin. Also present are officers of 36th
(Ulster) Division, 16th (Irish) Division, and
French, Belgian and American
representatives. Dr Ashe places a piece of
Irish soil on the grave and gives a speech
(there is no indication of the words). The
delegates shake hands with the foreign
representatives as they leave.

Notes
Cameraman: the cameraman was either
McDowell or Raymond.
Summary: see also **IWM 212**.
Remarks: British official film tended to avoid
the problem of Ireland, and this is a good
example. The film itself is a simple record
and almost any attitude or conclusion can
be read into it, according to existing
conviction.
[shotsheet available]
catalogued SDB: 1/1981

IWM 121 · GB, (before) 12/1917
the GERMAN RETREAT TO ST QUENTIN

b/w · 3 reels · 2703' (46 mins) · silent
intertitles: English

sp War Office Cinema Committee pr Topical
Film Company prod Jury, William F

- British pursuit of the German retreat to
  the Hindenburg Line, Western Front,
  March 1917.

I. (Reel 1) Craters left by the Germans in
order to hinder pursuit and the flooding
from the Omignon River at Caulaincourt.
The wrecked sugar factory at Jeancourt. A
battalion of the Leicestershire Regiment
resting. A mounted patrol coming to a
village, possibly 1/1st Surrey Yeomanry at
Vermand. Officers inspect the wreckage of
an Albatros DIII. Scenes of wreckage and
German prisoners being gathered. (Reel 2)
A cyclist and mounted patrol at Roisel. A
detachment of pontoon wagons moves out
of Etreillers.
II. The film is broken here by events on 15
May. King Albert of Belgium and Prince
Alexander of Teck visit Fourth Army
headquarters at Villers-Carbonnel. A day
later, with Generals Sir Henry Rawlinson
and Sir Hubert Gough, they visit Pozières
and Mouquet Farm, and inspect an
Australian guard of honour led by
Lieutenant-General Sir William Birdwood.

On 15 May the King and the Prince inspect 2nd Guards Brigade at Curlu, and are met by its corps commander, Lieutenant-General the Earl of Cavan.
III. The film continues again with patrols of British and Indian Cavalry of 4th Cavalry Division entering another village, possibly Vraignes. The Cavalry patrols bring in German prisoners. *(Reel 3)* More soldiers, including a Highland Light Infantry battalion, are ordered forward. Men of the Leicestershire Regiment hold a trench. A comic acted sequence of British soldiers holding a position wearing gas masks. The men play cards, and two officers discover that they cannot smoke in the masks. British and French soldiers rest in the fortified quarry at Le Verguier. A battalion of the Royal Warwickshire Regiment holds a trench near St-Quentin. The film ends with troops in silhouette marching along a road near Arras.

Notes
Date: the release date given is for the appearance of the film overseas. It would have appeared in Britain before this.
Remarks: the captions are violent in tone compared to the usual British practice. However, this is a well-made, well-captioned, extremely interesting and imaginative propaganda film. It is marred by the scenes of King Albert, obviously added as a makeweight. Unfortunately, from comparison with the photographs taken, most of the scenes were probably filmed about a month after the German retreat and do not depict the actual British pursuit.
[shotsheet available]
catalogued SDB: 1/1981

IWM 122 · GB, (prod) 1917
GRIFFITH AT THE FRONT
HEARTS OF THE WORLD (production scenes)

b/w · 1 reel · 685' (11 mins) · silent
intertitles: none

prod Griffith, D W

■ Visit of D W Griffith to the Western Front while filming *Hearts of the World*, October-November 1917.

The film starts with Griffith talking to the abbot and another monk outside the Cistercian abbey at Mont des Cats, used as a casualty clearing station. Griffith is then shown with two British officers entering and leaving a Red Cross station on Kemmel

Ridge. The main part of the film shows Griffith's tour over the Ypres ridges. This begins in a trench with British soldiers "sixty yards from the Germans, four miles from Ypres", probably on Wytschaete Ridge south of Hill 60. Griffith goes to the top of the observation post and comes down to set up his camera. There is a test scene of two British soldiers rushing down the trench and slamming a barbed wire screen behind them. Griffith is taken by an escort through Polygon Wood. He watches 6-inch Mk VII guns firing in the Elverdinghe area. With his production crew he surveys the ruins of Ypres Cloth Hall. He talks to Belgian soldiers in a reserve trench in Houthulst Wood. Finally, he inspects a German pillbox, probably at Shrewsbury Forest. He and his escorts try on their gas masks for the camera. The last scene is of Griffith meeting with British official war correspondents in Cassel, Porte de Bergue area. One of these may be Philip Gibbs.

Notes
Title: this is taken from the shotsheet.
Summary: see also Department of Film correspondence files for 1973, correspondence between A Fleming and J Deslaudes, 26 February 1973 et seq., concerning the authenticity of some of these sections. They are now regarded as authentic.
[Kevin Brownlow, *The War, the West and the Wilderness*, Secker and Warburg (1979)]
[Beaverbrook Papers, Series E, in House of Lords Record Office]
[shotsheet available]
catalogued SDB: 9/1981

IWM 123 · GB, (prod) 1918
[WESTERN FRONT (rough material)]
(allocated)
SONS OF OUR EMPIRE (offcuts)
the WORLD'S GREATEST STORY (offcuts)

b/w · 2 reels · 1232' (20 mins) · silent
intertitles: English

■ Rough material, mainly of the Western Front, 1916-18.

This 2-reel film consists largely of duplicates from the series **IWM 130** *Sons of Our Empire* and **IWM 420** *The World's Greatest Story*, including the remains of the missing original first episode of **IWM 130**, and of stockshots of unidentified British marching columns on the Western Front. In the second reel one possibly unique scene shows three British soldiers clowning for the camera, pushing and driving a car without an engine through the cleared square of a town which is otherwise mostly rubble.

Notes
Shotsheet: this film has no shotsheet. Many of its scenes are of a few seconds' duration.
catalogued SDB: 7/1982

IWM 124 · GB, 1917
MAJOR HRH PRINCE ARTHUR OF CONNAUGHT PRESENTS BRITISH DECORATIONS TO FRENCH OFFICERS AND OTHER RANKS

b/w · 1 reel · 130' (3 mins) · silent
intertitles: none

sp War Office Cinema Committee *pr* Topical Film Company *cam* McDowell, J B (?)

■ Prince Arthur decorating French soldiers at Méricourt, Western Front, on 12 November 1916.

Prince Arthur decorates the French soldiers in an open square, following which the decorated men pose as a group. The Prince, declining to enter his car, walks off.

[shotsheet available]
catalogued SDB: 1/1981

IWM 125 · GB, (ca) 1917
BUILDING A NISSEN HUT

b/w · 1 reel · 344' (6 mins) · silent
intertitles: English

sp War Office Cinema Committee (?)

■ Film on the assembly of a Nissen hut, probably 1917.

Men of the Royal Engineers, watched by three officers (one of them a colonel with a staff armband) assemble a Nissen hut, which is described as being "cool in summer and warm in winter" and as housing 24 men.

Notes
Remarks: an inadequate film, which fails to explain the precise method of construction of a Nissen hut, the principles on which it is designed, and the uses to which it can be put.
[shotsheet available]
catalogued SDB: 1/1981

IWM 126 · GB, (?) 1917
OFF TO ENGLAND

b/w · 1 reel · 283' (5 mins) · silent
intertitles: none

sp War Office Cinema Committee (?)
pr Topical Film Company

■ Departure of a British leave boat from a French port, probably 1917.

British soldiers of various regiments and branches, all wearing life-jackets, embark on leave boats. One group is on board a small side-wheeler CD-8, and others on a larger vessel E0826. The larger ship moves out of harbour with ladies on the quayside waving as it clears the harbour mouth.

Notes
Remarks: the final shot is a cliché, but an attractive one.
[shotsheet available]
catalogued SDB: 1/1981

IWM 127 · GB, (?) 1917
SCENES ON THE MENIN ROAD

b/w · 1 reel · 665' (12 mins) · silent
intertitles: English

sp War Office Cinema Committee (?)
pr Topical Film Company

■ General views of the area around Ypres, Western Front, probably 1917.

I. German prisoners escorted by Yeomanry over an iron bridge. A metre-gauge railway train holding a platoon of the Queen's Regiment. A repair workshop for guns and howitzers. A group of soldiers shaving in a field of horses. Royal Engineers in combat gear coming up a trench. Soldiers clearing mud from a narrow gauge railway track. Guns, hidden by scrim netting, firing, followed by mules being led past them. A poor quality shot of a 6-inch howitzer (?). A party of Durham Light Infantry falling in by a roadside. Men of the King's Royal Rifle Corps and Royal Engineers digging a trench. Soldiers eating in the open. A chaplain assisting in the treatment of a man with a wounded arm. German prisoners sitting with British stretcher-bearers. II. The film ends with a poor quality scene of German prisoners carrying Australians on stretchers to the rear, from **IWM 158** *Fighting in Flanders*.

Notes
Summary: see also **IWM 158**.
[shotsheet available]
catalogued SDB: 1/1981

IWM 128 · GB, 1918
WITH THE SOUTH AFRICAN FORCES

b/w · 4 reels · 3513' (60 mins) · silent
intertitles: English

sp Ministry of Information pr Topical Film
Company prod Jury, William F cam
McDowell, J B; Raymond, H C; and
Buckstone, Walter A and/or Brooks-
Carrington, Bertram (?)

■ South African Brigade and South African
Native Labour Contingent in Britain and
on the Western Front, 1916-18.

(Reel 1) Replacements, probably in Britain
October-December 1917, drill and train. The
brigade itself in France, probably early
March 1918, resting, marching, eating and
swimming. The brigade horse-show,
probably near Ostreville in March 1917,
including Brigadier-General F S Dawson.
(Reel 2) Logging in France by the South
African Native Labour Contingent. One
black sergeant, singled out, is probably
Muti, son of Ntshingwayo of Zululand. (Reel
3) The officers and NCOs of the contingent
presented to George V and Queen Mary at
Abbeville, 10 July 1917. The South African
Military Hospital in Richmond Park, London.
(Reel 4) At the hospital the amputees and
injured men of the South African Brigade
recover from their wounds and are retrained
in civilian skills. The South African Native
Labour Contingent under Captain Gilfillan
give a demonstration of Zulu dance on the
beach at Dannes on 24 June 1917. The end
of the film breaks up into a series of
unrelated scenes of soldiers marching past
a windmill and of the King's visit to the
South African Native Labour Contingent.

Notes
Title: this is taken from the shotsheet.
Cameraman: the shotsheet describes the
cameraman as Buckstone, who did not
reach the Western Front until May 1918. He
may have filmed the scenes in Britain. This
is one of the few films which, from the
approximate shooting dates, may have
been worked on by Bertram Brooks-
Carrington.
Summary: see also **IWM 217** and **IWM 413**.
[shotsheet available]
catalogued SDB: 1/1981

IWM 129 · GB, 1917
the PRESIDENT OF PORTUGAL IN FRANCE

b/w · 1 reel · 315' (6 mins) · silent
intertitles: none

sp War Office Cinema Committee pr Topical
Film Company prod Jury, William F
cam McDowell, J B or Raymond, H C (?)

■ Visit of President Bernardino Machado of
Portugal to the British and Portuguese
forces on the Western Front, October
1917.

The film starts with the President leaving his
guest château at Montreuil to the salute of
the British escort, tipping his hat to the
camera and driving off. At 4pm on 11
October he and Field Marshal Haig inspect
the guard of honour of the Queen's (Royal
West Surrey Regiment) at Lillers station.
With Haig are Brigadier-General John
Charteris and Brigadier-General John
'Tavish' Davidson (?), his heads of
Intelligence and Operations respectively.
Again Machado acknowledges the camera,
leaving by car. Two days later the President
arrives at Roquetoire to decorate four
Portuguese officers, the first to be awarded
the Croix de guerre. Portuguese troops
march past. The President leaves by car
(notice the official photographer, J Warwick
Brooke, in the crowd).

Notes
Title: this is taken from the shotsheet.
Cameraman: this was either McDowell or
Raymond.
Summary: Haig did not like Machado's
behaviour towards the camera: he wrote in
his diary that "the whole performance was
like a comedy".
[Robert Blake, The Private Papers of
Douglas Haig 1914-1919, Eyre and
Spottiswoode (1952)]
[shotsheet available]
catalogued SDB: 1/1981

IWM 130-01+2 · GB, 1917
**SONS OF OUR EMPIRE EPISODE 1 :
Winter on the Western Front**
WINTER ON THE WESTERN FRONT
(alternative)

b/w · 2 reels · 2002' (34 mins) · silent
intertitles: English

sp War Office Cinema Committee pr Topical
Film Company prod Jury, William F

cam McDowell, J B; and Raymond, H C

- Winter training for British troops, and Bapaume after its capture, Western Front, early 1917

I. *(Reel 1)* Winter training for British troops. Infantry guns and Highlanders move in columns along the roads up to the snow-covered trenches. Hot soup is brought to troops in the trenches. A dawn 'stand to'. Rifle grenades and a 3-inch Stokes mortar are test-fired. A bombardment in snow by various British guns: 6-inch howitzers, 9.2-inch howitzers, 18-pounders and 60-pounders, directed by air observation. A major daylight trench raid through the snow, covered by smoke grenades. The raid is in four waves, including wiring parties. Meanwhile other trenches are repaired and 6-inch howitzers continue the harassing fire.

II. *(Reel 2)* Damage to Bapaume shown after its capture. Highland Light Infantry (?) repair the Bapaume Road. A panorama of the town starting with the railway station. Views from rue de Casernes and rue de Bapaume. Some buildings are still smouldering and parties of British troops who walk by warm themselves by the fires. A detailed scene of the railway station. A German observation post on top of the sugar factory. More damage, including the town hall, and a Vickers machinegun emplacement on rue de Péronne. British troops, including lorry-mounted 13-pounder anti-aircraft guns, move through the town. Australians, probably of Australian 5th Division, enter the town.

Notes
Date: the original version of Episode 1 of *Sons of Our Empire*, which was devoted entirely to winter training, was first shown at the Scala Theatre, London, on 21 March 1917. Shortly afterwards the Germans abandoned Bapaume in their retreat to the Siegfried Stellung (or Hindenburg Line) and film of the captured town was included in the version of the episode released to the public on 9 April 1917. Some fragments of the original version of Episode 1 can be found in **IWM 123**.
Summary: by extensive use of stock footage, this episode and the remander of the series seek to give the impression that Bapaume fell as the direct consequence of a major British offensive, which it did not. In effect, the series portrays a non-existent battle. Furthermore, the decision to include the material of Bapaume as soon as it was received has meant that the series shows this material, of April 1917, considerably

before the episode on the capture of Courcelette in November 1916.
Remarks: generally, the series is an improvement on both **IWM 116** *The Battle of the Ancre and the Advance of the Tanks* and **IWM 113** *The German Retreat and the Battle of Arras* in representing warfare between late 1916 and early 1917. In this episode, the trench raid sequence, in starkly contrasting black and white against a snow setting, is very lovely and quite 'surreal' in appearance. The film of Bapaume should have been used to better effect rather than being fitted into a completed series in this manner.
[shotsheet available]
catalogued SDB: 6/1982

IWM 130-03+4 · GB, 1917
SONS OF OUR EMPIRE EPISODE 2 :
Glimpses of the British Navy in war time
GLIMPSES OF THE BRITISH NAVY IN WAR TIME (alternative)

b/w · 2 reels · 2473' (42 mins) · silent
intertitles: English

sp War Office Cinema Committee *pr* Topical Film Company *prod* Jury, William F
cam Engholm, F W

- British battle-cruiser squadron base at Rosyth, July-August 1916.

I. *(Reel 1)* The Royal Naval Air Service at Rosyth. Firstly, their marching band. Then aircrew running a Felixstowe F2A flying boat out of its hangar for launch, followed by a Short 184 seaplane. These and other seaplanes in the air, including a Sopwith Baby. The Felixstowe practises bomb runs against a partly sunken wreck. The Short and the Felixstowe are brought in by tugs. Commodore Caley and Flight-Commander Porte pose in a group with Commander Lynes. The seaplane carrier HMS *Engadine* launches a Sopwith Baby, which flies on patrol and returns to the ship. Some of the seaplanes stunt flying.
II. The submarine service. E.23 is loaded with torpedoes, and moves off surfaced, submerges, surfaces and fires her 12-pounder, before returning to the base and being dry docked.
III. *(Reel 2)* The battle-cruiser force, starting with a view of HMS *Lion*. Admiral Beatty's dog. Filming from a small boat in the harbour, the camera shows HMS *Tiger*, HMS *Chester*, with the 5.5-inch gun beside which Jack Cornwell died, and some of his shipmates, HMS *Birmingham* with a

destroyer escort passing under a bridge, the hospital ship HMS *Garth Castle* collecting wounded from a drifter, and unloading others onto the shore. The wounded are taken by train to a convalescent home. HMS *Princess Royal* at medium distance in sunlight on a dappled sea, and at anchor. HMS *Yarmouth* (? possibly HMS *Phaeton*) at anchor. Torpedoes being loaded and fired from the destroyer HMS *Firedrake*, in rough weather at "15 knots an hour" (sic). Members of the crew display the ensign and a lifebelt captured from the submarine UC.5. A King Edward VII Class battleship fires a broadside.

Notes
Intertitles: it is unthinkable that a Royal Navy censoring bureau could make the mistake of "15 knots an hour", and this points strongly to censoring by MI7 at the War Office.
Summary: for this episode see the naval material in **IWM 577**, **IWM 580** and **IWM 595**. Note that despite the claims of this episode, although submarine E23 did torpedo SMS *Westfalen* on 19 August 1916, the ship did not sink.
[shotsheet available]
catalogued SDB & NAP: 6/1982

IWM 130-05+6 · GB, 1917
SONS OF OUR EMPIRE EPISODE 3 : the King's message to his troops
the KING'S MESSAGE TO HIS TROOPS (alternative)

b/w · 2 reels · 2172' (35 mins) · silent
intertitles: English

sp War Office Cinema Committee *pr* Topical Film Company *prod* Jury, William F
cam Raymond, H C and McDowell, J B

■ British preparations during the later Somme offensive, Western Front, autumn 1916.

I. *(Reel 5)* Impressionistic to the point of incoherence. Starting with troops disembarking at a harbour. Marching columns, some of them identified: the Devonshire Regiment, some Scots, the Bedfordshire Regiment, the Black Watch (?), joined by 18-pounders and a Mk I Female tank of 'A' Company H/MGC. British Cavalry move up along a road. A Mk I Female tank, identified by the caption as HMLS 'Créme [sic] de Menthe' of 'C' Company H/MGC. West Africans of the Labour Corps unload shells at a dump.

Other shells, from 15-inch to 18-pounder, are distributed. Another tank, a Mk I Male, identified by the caption as HMLS 'Devil's Own' (by implication, of 'D' Company H/MGC) but apparently marked with an 'A'. A 60-pounder stuck in mud. Canadian 15th Battalion (Royal Highlanders of Canada) (?) and 17th Battalion, Royal Scots Fusiliers of 35th (Bantam) Division (?) on the march. An observation kite balloon is raised. Two 6-inch guns fire. Pioneers of the Royal Sussex Regiment, Durham Light Infantry and "Northants" (? possibly Loyal North Lancashire Regiment) march along. Australians (?) on the march. A Mk I Female tank moving up.
II. *(Reel 6)* Indians of 4th or 5th Cavalry Division relax at their camp. "New Zealanders" (? possibly Australian 2nd Division) entraining. 6-inch howitzers being pulled forwards by their teams. An 18-pounder shell-dump. FE2b and FE2d bombers, probably 20 Squadron RFC, take off on patrol. Men of the Guards Division march to their positions. A 12-inch railway gun, probably 'HMG Boche Buster', fires. More men of the Guards Division. 9.2-inch howitzers of 55th Royal Australian Siege Artillery (?) fire. The bombardment includes also 60-pounders, 6-inch Mk VII guns, 18-pounders and 8-inch howitzers. The Cavalry wait to move up. An RE7 observation plane takes off, showing the view down onto the waiting battlefield.

Notes
Title: the title sequence is missing from all copies of this episode, as is the end sequence.
Summary: this episode and the two following form a highly impressionistic account of the later stages of the Somme offensive. No attempt has been made to preserve chronological or geographical integrity, and all the unit identifications given in these episodes must be partly suspect.
Remarks: dreadful – some occasionally interesting material of horsemen or guns relieves the tedium of endless stockshots.
[shotsheet available]
catalogued SDB: 6/1982

IWM 130-07+8 · GB, 1917
SONS OF OUR EMPIRE EPISODE 4 : Preparations for the Great Offensive
PREPARATIONS FOR THE GREAT OFFENSIVE (alternative)

b/w · 2 reels · 1764' (21 mins) · silent
intertitles: English

sp War Office Cinema Committee pr Topical Film Company prod Jury, William F cam Raymond, H C; and McDowell, J B

- Preparations in the Somme offensive leading to the Canadian capture of Courcelette, Western Front, autumn 1916.

I. (Reel 7) Preparations for the battle. 8-inch and 6-inch howitzers fire a bombardment. Mk I tanks, Males and Females, move forwards. 13-pounder anti-aircraft guns provide air defence. A motor machinegun section moves in its cycle combinations out of camp. British Cavalry trot forwards. Men of the Leicestershire Regiment and Northumberland Fusiliers move through the rear of the battle zone. The bombardment by 8-inch howitzers and 18-pounders continues. Mules bring water to the gun positions. Men of the Norfolk Regiment at rest. Indian lancers of 4th or 5th Cavalry Division also resting. 13-pounders RHA trotting along a road. A Mk I Male tank on the move. 1/14th Battalion, the London Regiment (London Scottish), 56th Division, on the march. Grenades are handed out in the front trenches. Men of the Guards Division attend an open-air church parade. "Who dies if England lives ? Who lives if England dies ?"
II. (Reel 8) The moment of the attack. The heavy bombardment by various guns and howitzers continues. A Mk I Male tank in position. "The day...the hour...three minutes more then...the minute, and for God, King and Empire the Canadians swept forward." The Canadian troops go over the top. Vickers machineguns give covering fire. Distant views across no man's land, including a German surrender. A Mk I Male tank damaged, with part of its steering wheels missing. 56th Division rear areas, with wiring parties going forward. An officer controlling an 18-pounder battery's fire with a megaphone. More views of no man's land. A heliograph team signals to the guns. The 18-pounders continue to fire and ammunition is brought up to them.

Notes
Remarks: a good illustration of the technical problems of filming across no man's land which led to the virtual abandonment of any attempt to portray major battles other than in very personal terms. A promising opening leads to an exciting attack sequence, and then the film falls apart in incoherence.
[shotsheet available]
catalogued SDB: 6/1982

IWM 130-09+10 · GB, 1917
SONS OF OUR EMPIRE EPISODE 5 :
Attacking hard
ATTACKING HARD (alternative)

b/w · 2 reels · 1741' (32 mins) · silent
intertitles: English

sp War Office Cinema Committee pr Topical Film Company prod Jury, William F cam Raymond, H C; and McDowell, J B

- Wounded, prisoners and captured ground from the British Somme offensive, Western Front, autumn 1916.

(Reel 9) A bombardment in progress. Mk I tanks move up. Fatigue parties (described as "doctors") move forwards. Prisoners are brought in and the captured area mopped up. The German Crown Prince's HQ at Péronne shows shell damage. A Guards Division dressing station. The formal search of prisoners by Australians, "the Intelligence officer returns an Iron Cross to a prisoner". The troops return to their rest camps. A chaplain takes a message from a wounded man on a stretcher. Tanks and soldiers return. (Reel 10) The remains of Trones Wood and the unidentifiable rubble of villages. German dead in their trenches. A ditched Mk I tank. "Australians," "London Irish" and "Civil Service Rifles" (of 56th Division) return. An open-air funeral service, "the inevitable price of victory". Mk I tanks of 'D' Company H/MGC being serviced and maintained. Aircraft return from their observation flights. An observation kite balloon lands. Men of 35th (Bantam) Division and the New Zealand Division rest. A final shot of Prime Minister Lloyd George on a balcony with H Samuel Homer Stacy, with a policy speech: "our sword was not lightly drawn, and will never be sheathed until our terms – Restitution, Reparation and Guarantees – are fully assured".

Notes
Summary: note that a version of reel 10 with German subtitles is held as **IWM 670a**.
Remarks: a better and more coherent end than the series perhaps deserved. A non-contemporary or non-British observer would be puzzled as to precisely which battle he was watching.
[shotsheet available]
catalogued SDB: 6/1982

IWM 131 · GB, 1917
the GREAT GERMAN RETREAT
the CAPTURE OF PERONNE (alternative)

b/w · 2 reels · 1027' (17 mins) · silent
intertitles: English

sp War Office Cinema Committee *pr* Topical
Film Company *prod* Jury, William F
cam McDowell, J B or Raymond, H C (?)

■ Péronne shortly after its capture by the
British, Western Front, 17 March 1917.

I. *(Reel 1)* The Lincolnshire Regiment clear
a road lined with damaged trees. Nine men
of the Royal Munster Fusiliers cross a
damaged bridge over the Somme. A
column of the Loyal North Lancashire
Regiment marches down a dirt road over
the old battlefield. (No battalions of any of
these regiments were involved in the
capture of Péronne.)
II. "Burning houses in Péronne" with British
soldiers passing by in twos and threes. The
damaged cathedral. On a monument in the
main square have been chalked the names
of formations passing through the town.
(1/8th Battalion, the Royal Warwickshire
Regiment, of 48th Division, was the first to
enter Péronne on 17 March. This is shortly
after.) A battalion of Sherwood Foresters
(59th Division ?) in marching column. A
motor machinegun company in its motor-
cycle combinations. A French village where
British officers self-consciously fraternise
with local women and children. *(Reel 2)*
Barbed wire defences at "Buiches" (Biaches
?). A damaged bridge over the Somme. A
Yeomanry detachment crosses a wooden
bridge at Péronne, followed by a Vauxhall
staff car, "the first motor car to cross the
Somme". A cyclist patrol moves forward. A
group of officers fraternises with French
peasants. More scenes of Péronne,
including the famous sign placed by the
Germans on the town hall in the main
square, "Nicht Ärgern, Nur Wundern" (don't
be angry, just wonder).

Notes
Cameraman: the cameraman was either
McDowell or Raymond.
[shotsheet available]
catalogued SDB: 6/1982

IWM 132 · GB, 1918
**[HAIG AND HIS ARMY COMMANDERS
ON 11TH NOVEMBER 1918]** (allocated)

b/w · 1 reel · 309' (5 mins) · silent
intertitles: none

sp Ministry of Information *pr* Topical Film
Company

■ Events in Field Marshal Haig's day, 11
November 1918.

I. The film opens with a very brief portrait
shot of Haig, taken by a French official
cameraman in August 1917.
II. The Army Commanders arrive by car at
Haig's temporary headquarters at Cambrai
for their final conference, shortly before
11am. General Birdwood (Fifth Army)
arrives first, then Byng (Third Army), Plumer
(Second Army) then Byng with Horne (First
Army), Rawlinson (Fourth Army) and Haig.
At 11am General Plumer is pictured in
close-up, left profile, with General Byng next
to him, trying to make him laugh. A posed
group on a flight of steps: Plumer, Haig and
Rawlinson in front, Byng, Birdwood and
Horne behind, with staff officers to the rear,
including Lieutenant-Generals Sir John
'Tavish' Davidson, Montgomery, and Sir
Louis Vaughan. The next scene shows Haig
back at his command train near Iwuy at
12.50pm, greeting Prince Fushimi of Japan,
Prince Arthur of Connaught, and Count
Inouye. The Prince of Wales arrives at
2.15pm and Haig also greets him. Finally,
Haig's departure from Cambrai at about
11.30am following his Army Commanders'
conference. The Army Commanders, except
Plumer, are visible saying goodbye, and the
troops cheer him. The other generals leave.

Notes
Summary: a very precious historical record,
well complemented by Haig's diary and the
official photographs. For the first scene see
IWM 508-24 *Annales de la Guerre* material.
According to Haig's diary, he told his
generals at 11am to "go off and be
cinemaed", and Byng was trying hard to
make Plumer laugh.
[Robert Blake, *The Private Papers of
Douglas Haig 1914-1919*, Eyre and
Spottiswoode (1952)]
[shotsheet available]
catalogued SDB: 6/1982

IWM 133 · GB, 15/5/1916
**the WONDERFUL ORGANISATION OF
THE RAMC**
OFFICIAL PICTURES OF THE BRITISH
ARMY IN FRANCE – FOURTH SERIES
(series)

b/w · 1 reel · 630' (11 mins) · silent
intertitles: English

sp War Office *pr* British Topical Committee
for War Films *cam* Malins, Geoffrey H or
Tong, Edward G (?)

■ RAMC system for dealing with casualties, France, April 1916.

The casualties occur in a forward trench in 51st (Highland) Division sector between Roclincourt and Neuville-St-Vaast. An RAMC captain bandages the head of one man who, with other walking wounded and two stretcher cases, is taken to the Regimental Aid Post. From this, coming out of the trench system, the wounded are placed on a 60cm railway trolley and pushed to the Advanced Dressing Station. Here they pass through the Patients' Entrance, and after preliminary treatment are loaded onto an ambulance. This takes them to 18th Casualty Clearing Station on the outskirts of Arras (belonging to 18th Division, recently relieved by the Highland Division). The ambulances are from 8th Motor Ambulance Convoy, attached to the Highland Division. RAMC men unload the stretchers, "each man's equipment is labelled and carefully kept". Four doctors and a nurse conduct an operation in the tented operating theatre. After preliminary treatment the wounded, including the stretcher cases, are when sufficiently recovered taken to board a train at Arras which takes them to Dieppe station (the film starts to break up here). More severe cases are taken by Red Cross barges down the canals. At Dieppe the men are loaded onto a hospital ship which steams out of harbour "off to England".

Notes
Cameraman: the cameraman was either Malins or Tong.
Remarks: although tending to break up into misplaced scenes and pull-backs as it ends, this is a well made film.
[shotsheet available]
catalogued SDB: 6/1982

IWM 134 · GB, 1916
the RESULT OF CINEMA DAY, NOVEMBER 9TH 1915

b/w · 1 reel · 622' (11 mins) · silent
intertitles: English

sp Wellington House (?) *cam* Woods-Taylor, G (?)

■ Manufacture of ambulances bought through the donation by British cinemas of a day's takings on 9 November 1915, and their presentation to King George V, 22 March 1916.

I. The film opens disjointedly, showing a poster appealing for funds for the Red Cross and St John Ambulance Brigade for Cinema Day. The fifty ambulances built were sent to Mesopotamia, and Lord Montagu of Beaulieu, Chief Inspector of Mechanical Transport for India, Persia and Mesopotamia, visits the Star Engineering Company at Wolverhampton where they are being constructed. The workers leave the factory gates at "dinnertime".
II. Twenty of the fifty ambulances donated form a procession in the Mall at 10am on 22 March 1916 and move off at 11.15am for a drive past King George V, Queen Mary and Lord Montagu in front of Buckingham Palace, and down the Mall escorted by a troop of Royal Horse Guards. Each ambulance is marked "British Red Cross Society" and "St John Ambulance Ass.".
III. There is an additional scene at the end of the film of "Second Field Ambulance, Leicesters" Red Cross men on foot marching down a tree-lined road with horse-drawn Red Cross wagons behind them (a 'field ambulance' was a military unit, not a vehicle).

[*The Bioscope*, 4 November 1915: 496c]
[*The Bioscope*, 11 November 1915: 629]
[*The Bioscope*, 23 March 1916: 1261, 1359]
[*The Bioscope*, 30 March 1916: 1443]
[shotsheet available]
catalogued SDB: 6/1982

IWM 135 · NO FILM

IWM 136 · GB, 1917
DUTCH GENERALS VIEWING THE BATTLEFIELD

b/w · 1 reel · 471' (8 mins) · silent
intertitles: English

sp War Office Cinema Committee *pr* Topical Film Company

■ Visit of Dutch generals to the old British Somme battlefield, Western Front, 1917 (?).

I. A group of four Dutch generals with two British escorts walking over the battlefield. The soil is very chalky and the battlefield is heavily cratered but old enough to have telephone wires erected over it. The visitors investigate a captured German dug-out.
II. An honour guard of British Cavalry with lances, very smartly dressed but off parade, walking their horses along a road, then

moving off mounted, then stationary mounted with their horses browsing off roadside bushes.
III. A final scene of the Dutch generals standing in the rain watching British 8-inch howitzers fire from across a road.

Notes
Title: this is taken from the shotsheet.
Summary: nothing can be discovered about the Dutch generals, the date of their visit, or its relationship to the horsemen, who are themselves unidentified.
[shotsheet available]
catalogued SDB: 6/1982

IWM 137 · GB, 1917
[GENERAL PERSHING'S ARRIVAL IN FRANCE] (allocated)

b/w · 1 reel · 196' (4 mins) · silent
intertitles: none

sp War Office Cinema Committee *pr* Topical Film Company

■ Arrival of General John J Pershing at Boulogne, France, 13 June 1917.

The film is presented, uncut, in reverse order of events. It begins with Pershing saying goodbye to the British Adjutant-General, Sir G H Fowke, and the French General Peltier, prior to entering his car and leaving the harbour-side where his ship has docked. This is followed by Pershing meeting Fowke on board ship. Pershing inspecting the honour guard of French sailors as he leaves the ship. A final scene, chronologically the first, of Pershing meeting with Peltier on board ship.

[shotsheet available]
catalogued SDB: 6/1982

IWM 138 · Australia, 1/1918
WITH THE AUSTRALIAN FORCES IN FRANCE

b/w · 2 reels · 2373' (40 mins) · silent
intertitles: English

sp Australian War Records Section
prod Jury, William F (?) *ed* Bean, C E W (?)

■ I ANZAC Corps before and during the First Battle of the Somme, Western Front, May-October 1916.

(Reel 1) Men of Australian 1st Division marching to Pozières, 16 July, followed by a cyclist patrol and a motorised machinegun battery. Men of the New Zealand Division resting briefly in a village square, with an impromptu triple-jump contest. 12-inch shells are assembled at a dump and 18-pounder shells loaded into limbers. Australian troops load and shovel roadfill from a barge onto wheelbarrows. A 12-inch Mk I railway howitzer fires in a gun-pit. Men of Australian 1st Division arrive at their billet, a farm near Fleurbaix, May 1916, and settle in. The training trenches at Fleurbaix, where troops of the division practise the charge through a smokescreen. A tree-felling contest in the woods near Conty in August between Australians, Canadians, and the victorious New Zealanders. General William Birdwood, commanding I ANZAC Corps, is present. West Australians, probably of 3rd Brigade, Australian 1st Division, watch the Somme offensive from behind a parapet. Other members of the division rest on the way to Pozières. A chaplain conducts an open-air service. An 18-pounder battery moves up at a canter. Men of 1st and 2nd Divisions (11th, 20th and 18th Battalions ?) resting. A 9.2-inch howitzer fires, followed by an 18-pounder marked "Wandering Willie". More troops of 1st Division (9th Battalion ?) resting. German prisoners, probably of XIX Saxon Corps, are helped into lorries by men of 2nd Division. *(Reel 2)* Shells bursting in front of Pozières. A New South Wales battalion (19th Battalion of 2nd Division?) in a wooded area. Wounded of both divisions are treated at Bécourt dressing station. An improvised burial service at the roadside, "all honour to the glorious dead". Two wrecked German 155mm howitzers. Australians inspecting German trenches after capture. Views of Pozières chalk pit and Mouquet farm. Men of 2nd Division pose for the camera wearing German helmets and other trophies. Men of 1st Division resting. The visit of the Australian Prime Minister, William Hughes, to Birdwood's headquarters at Fleurbaix in June. A panorama of the battlefield. Men of 1st Division resting.

Notes
Production: according to Dr Bean's account in the AWRS(Film) Papers, he was able, in January 1918, to convince Lord Beaverbrook as head of the War Office Cinema Committee and William Jury as its technical expert to use the existing Australian film record to make a major film. Bean 'composed' this film entirely on paper, working from shotsheets, and left the rest to

Jury. When Bean first saw the film after a year he complained that Jury had disregarded his instructions and produced instead "a most miserable hotch potch". Although the identification is not positive, this film appears to be the one referred to by the file.
Remarks: despite Bean's complaints, the film is quite good by the standards of the time. His disappointment perhaps reflects his own lack of experience in thinking that he could compose a film with no direct involvement in the editing process.
[AWRS(Film) Papers, File 4375/60/36]
[shotsheet available]
catalogued SDB: 6/1982

IWM 139 · Australia, 1918
the AUSTRALIAN PREMIER ACCOMPANIED BY THE MINISTER FOR THE NAVY PAYS A VISIT TO THE TROOPS IN FRANCE

b/w · 1 reel · 286' (5 mins) · silent
intertitles: English

sp Australian War Records Section
cam Wilkins, G H (?)

■ Premier William Hughes and Sir Joseph Cook visit Australian headquarters, and General Monash replaces Birdwood, Western Front, 1918.

I. The visit of Premier William Hughes and Minister of the Navy Sir Joseph Cook to Australian Corps headquarters at Allonville on 2 July 1918. They arrive by car and are greeted by Lieutenant-General Sir John Monash. Hughes poses with Monash and his staff on the steps of the building before driving off to visit the troops. Cook is shown addressing one of the three bands of 200 selected soldiers (from 4th, 6th or 11th Brigade, all of which were visited) with Hughes and Monash looking on.
II. Portrait shots of General Sir William Birdwood and his Chief of Staff, Lieutenant-General Sir C B Brudenell White, in front left profile. Both Birdwood and Brudenell White shake hands with their staff in front of headquarters before driving off to take command of Fifth Army, 11am 31 May 1918. A portrait shot of General Monash, who replaced Birdwood.
III. An unattached sequence of Australian troops collecting fresh vegetables, transporting them by punt and loading them onto lorries.

Notes
Production: probably Australian official film.
[shotsheet available]
catalogued SDB: 6/1982

IWM 140 · GB, (?) 1918
HM THE KING ON THE CLYDE

b/w · 2 reels · 1609' (27 mins) · silent
intertitles: English

sp Department of Information (?)

■ King George V's visit to Clydeside, 17-20 September 1917.

(Reel 1) Starting with the King, in Field Marshal's uniform, decorating soldiers in Ibrox Park, Glasgow, on 18 September, assisted by Lieutenant-General Sir J S Ewart, commanding Central Scottish Command. Among those receiving decorations are Private George McIntosh of the Gordon Highlanders and Sergeant Sam Frickleton of the New Zealand Rifle Brigade, both VCs. The next scene is the King in Admiral's uniform on 17 September greeting a group of workers, possibly at J G Kincaid & Co of Greenock. Next is the King in Field Marshal's uniform on 18 September leaving Kirklees station with his staff, and again at Ibrox Park. Lord Strathclyde is awarded a GBE, and Sir John S Samuel a KBE. Private Harry Christian, Royal Lancashire Fusiliers, carried on a litter, is given a Victoria Cross.
(Reel 2) The King in Field Marshal's uniform on 18 September at the Greenock & Grangemouth Dockyard (?), talking to a riveter of Messrs Boys, Gilson Ltd. The King in Field Marshal's uniform at the Clydeside Steel Works on 19 September. In Admiral's uniform again on 18 September the King drives past a cheering crowd and meets with Royal Navy officers at Central Station, Glasgow. A final return to Ibrox Park where the King inspects the guard of honour from "the Highland Regiment" (Highland Light Infantry ?). In Field Marshal's uniform on 19 September the King visits the Lanarkshire Steel Company smelting works and other factories in Motherwell, Mossend and Cathcart, including the laying of the foundation stone at the new Beardmore & Co works, assisted by Sir William Beardmore. The King in Admiral's uniform on 20 September visits the Dunsmuir & Jackson works. The film ends with the Royal Standard flying.

Notes
Title: this is taken from the shotsheet.
Production: since the Department of Information was at this date employing cameramen on a temporary basis, it is not possible to determine whether this is official or private newsreel film.
[*The Times*, 17 September 1917: 6A]
[*The Times*, 18 September 1917: 7D, 9B]
[*The Times*, 19 September 1917: 7C, 9B]
[*The Times*, 20 September 1917: 7C, 9B]
[*The Times*, 21 September 1917: 6D, 9B]
[shotsheet available]
catalogued SDB: 6/1982

Notes
Cameraman: the cameraman was either McDowell or Raymond.
Summary: the damaged Nieuport is B1629, for which Lieutenant W Jenkins was the usual pilot. This aircraft was credited with the shooting-down of an Albatros on 15 July 1917. Jenkins was himself killed on 17 November 1917. See also **IWM 118**.
[William Bishop, *The Courage of the Early Morning*, David McKay (1966)]
[*The Times*, 6 September 1917]
[shotsheet available]
catalogued SDB: 6/1982

IWM 141 · GB, 12/1917
WITH THE ROYAL FLYING CORPS (SOMEWHERE IN FRANCE)

b/w · 1 reel · 911' (16 mins) · silent
intertitles: English

sp War Office Cinema Committee *pr* Topical Film Company *prod* Jury, William F
cam McDowell, J B or Raymond, H C (?)

■ RFC base at Ste-Marie-Cappel, Western Front, late August 1917.

A Nieuport 17 of 'B' Flight, 60 Fighter Squadron, badly damaged outside a hangar; mechanics removing a damaged wing. Three men working in a mobile repair shop (see the same scene in **IWM 118** *The Eyes of the Army*). A new wing is fitted to a FE2d of 20 Night Bomber Squadron outside a hangar. A posed group of members of 60 Squadron, left to right: Frank 'Mongoose' Soden (with dog), Captain William A 'Billy' Bishop VC DSO MC, Keith 'Grid' Caldwell, E W 'Moley' Molesworth, Spencer 'Nigger' Horn. Pan over a larger group of the squadron's pilots. (Bishop left the squadron at the end of August, when it was moved from Filescamp Farm to Ste-Marie-Cappel, and this may still be Filescamp.) An FE2d of 20 Squadron (indistinctly marked "Presented by the Sultan of Mysore" ?) is wheeled out of its hangar. Other FE2ds of the squadron are armed, bombed up with 20-pounder and 112-pounder bombs; the pilot and gunner board one plane and the flight of five takes off. A Sopwith 1½ Strutter of 45 Fighter Squadron is prepared for flight and the squadron takes off. One 1½ Strutter is shown stunt flying. Two FE2ds come in to land at Ste-Marie-Cappel past a line of 1½ Strutters. (This scene dates the film, as by 1 September 45 Squadron had been completely re-equipped with Sopwith Camels.)

IWM 142 · GB, (?) 1918
AMERICAN CONGRESSMEN VISIT FRANCE

b/w · 1 reel · 398' (7 mins) · silent
intertitles: none

sp War Office Cinema Committee *pr* Topical Film Company

■ Visit of some American congressmen to Vimy Ridge and the Somme battlefield, Western Front, 9-10 November 1917.

Seven congressmen with a British officer escort walk through an ordnance workshop with a light railway terminal, past 6-inch howitzers (presumably being repaired). They go on to tour Vimy Ridge on foot, wearing shrapnel helmets, walking up the ridge to see the view from the top described by their escort. The group visits the inside of the damaged Arras Cathedral and Albert Cathedral (showing the Leaning Virgin very clearly). In civilian clothes they tour the Somme battlefield close to Fricourt Farm, including a visit to Péronne. The film ends with a shot of the US flag flying in the wind.

Notes
Title: this is taken from the shotsheet.
Summary: none of the congressmen can be identified. They may be part of Colonel House's mission to Europe, but the main body of this mission did not leave London for Paris until 23 November.
[*The Times*, 24 November 1917]
[shotsheet available]
catalogued SDB: 6/1982

IWM 143 · GB (?), (prod) 1917
WITH A CANADIAN BRIGADE AT YPRES

b/w · 1 reel · 126' (2 mins) · silent
intertitles: none

I. Canadian rear areas during the Third Battle of Ypres, Western Front, late 1917. Isolated Canadian soldiers walking over very muddy ground at Ypres between water-filled craters. The cameraman's comments are on the shotsheet: "Took a few pieces of wounded and prisoners coming back over bad ground. I do not think the film will be very good. Conditions were all against any good results. Could get no help – runners being killed or wounded almost every time they went out. I was at advanced Brigade GHQ".
II. The visit of Cardinal Bourne to an Australian unit on the Western Front, late 1917. The Cardinal arrives by car and walks past a military unit to a hut marked "Catholic Club – open to all", followed by the soldiers.

Notes
Title: this is taken from the shotsheet.
Production: most probably British official film, but may have been taken by cameramen from the Dominions.
[shotsheet available]
catalogued SDB: 7/1982

IWM 144 · GB, (?) 1918
CAMBRAI OFFENSIVE

b/w · 2 reels · 1403' (24 mins) · silent
intertitles: none

sp War Office Cinema Committee *pr* Topical Film Company *prod* Jury, William F
cam McDowell, J B; and Raymond, H C

- Events in 6th and 15th Division rear areas between the British offensive and the German counteroffensive at Cambrai, Western Front, November 1917.

A German 150mm gun is towed into a wood east of Ribécourt on the Marcoing Road by a Mk IV Female tank HMLS 'Intimidate' (of 'I' Company, Tank Corps ?) and met by men of the Royal Artillery and (probably) 6th Division on 29 November. (Note the tankmen still wear H/MGC shoulder titles.) A donkey-cart arrives marked "captured by 16th TMB", 16th Trench Mortar Battery, 6th Division. Royal Engineers clear obstructions on the waterless Canal du Nord near Mœuvres on 28 November. 8th (Pioneer) Battalion, the Royal Scots, of 51st (Highland) Division cuts a road through the canal's banks. An iron bridge over the canal at Mœuvres has been blown by the Germans. Wagon traffic crosses over the dry canal bed. A group of British soldiers repairs an old trench. Mechanical and hand pumps fill a water trough for horses near Mœuvres. Royal Field Artillery limbers canter along a road. Another view of the bridge at Mœuvres. Horse and mechanical transport moves British soldiers along a road. German prisoners (including a group of gunner officers wearing the new regulation tunic). Two Mk IV tanks, apparently unarmed supply tanks, in a rear area with British Infantry. A knocked out Mk IV Female being used as an observation post at Ribécourt on 23 November. Horses of CCXXXV Brigade RFA, 47th Division, watering at a pool in the middle of Flesquières (see **IWM 146** *Scenes in Captured Villages on the Cambrai Front*). Soldiers gathered around a small well. *(Reel 2)* British wounded, probably of the Highland Division, walk through Flesquières. 18-pounders are moved up by limbers. A Cavalry regiment, perhaps 8th Hussars of 5th Cavalry Division, held up by guns crossing its front. More German prisoners are brought in. A large mine crater left by the Germans. A French liaison officer talks to evacuated civilians. British soldiers advance through a captured village. An observation post looking out towards no man's land. Two 18-pounders firing. British Cavalry pass German prisoners on the road. A crashed German Albatros CIII is inspected by the British. More British soldiers, some lay a water-pipe. The structure in ferroconcrete for an incomplete German bunker at Flesquières on 23 November.

Notes
Title: this is taken from the shotsheet.
Cameraman: unusually for so late in the war, two cameramen appear to have been assigned to different divisions, 6th and 51st Divisions respectively, in different corps.
Intertitles: there are some manuscript flashframes on the film.
Summary: see also **IWM 146**.
[B H Liddell Hart, *The Tanks – the History of the Royal Tank Regiment ...*, Vol I, Cassell (1959)]
[John Ewing, *The Royal Scots 1914-1919*, 2 vols, Oliver and Boyd (1925)]
[Bryan Cooper, *The Ironclads at Cambrai*, Souvenir Press (1967)]
[shotsheet available]
catalogued SDB: 6/1982

IWM 145 · NO FILM

IWM 146 · GB, (?) 1918
**SCENES IN CAPTURED VILLAGES ON
THE CAMBRAI FRONT**

b/w · 1 reel · 344' (6 mins) · silent
intertitles: none

sp War Office Cinema Committee pr Topical
Film Company prod Jury, William F
cam Raymond, H C

▪ Villages of Marcoing, Flesquières and
  Havrincourt, Cambrai area, Western
  Front, 20-24 November 1917.

Ambulances in the main square at Marcoing
shortly after its capture, 20 November.
There is no great damage to the square
apart from broken windows, a hall with the
sign "Justice de Paix" over it and a badly
damaged church. Unsaddled horses of
CCXXXV Brigade RFA drinking from a pool
in the centre of Flesquières. Soldiers of 51st
(Highland) Division, probably Gordon
Highlanders, with a captured German
210mm mortar. Royal Artillery draught
horses, paddocked by a damaged building
in Havrincourt, being fed. A possibly
unrelated scene ends the film: a pioneer
battalion gathers up picks, shovels and
rifles before marching off in loose order,
and a Royal Horse Artillery troop poses
limbered up for the camera.

Notes
Title: this is taken from the shotsheet.
Summary: see also **IWM 144** Cambrai
Offensive.
[shotsheet available]
catalogued SDB: 6/1982

IWM 147 · GB, (?) 1917
NEWFOUNDLAND TROOPS

b/w · 1 reel · 338' (7 mins) · silent
intertitles: English

sp War Office Cinema Committee (?)
pr Topical Film Company

▪ Royal Newfoundland Regiment in billets
  at Berneville, Western Front, 9 May 1917.

A posed group of the regiment's officers, six
lying down, at least eleven standing up.
These include the commanding officer,
Lieutenant-Colonel A L Hadow, and the
second in command, Lieutenant-Colonel J
Forbes-Robertson, who was in command
on 14 April 1917 during the counter-attack
at Monchy in the Battle of Arras. Also

present is Lieutenant K J Keegan,
decorated for bravery during the Monchy
counter-attack. Rations are served out to
the regiment in its rest billets. A posed
group of men decorated as a result of
Monchy (ranks given as for April 1917,
some had been promoted by May), left to
right, lying down: Private F Curran, Corporal
J H Hillier, Private J Hounsell. Standing, left
to right: Corporal A S Rose, Sergeant W
Pitcher, Lieutenant-Colonel J Forbes-
Robertson, Lieutenant K J Keegan,
Sergeant C Parsons, Sergeant J R
Waterfield. There is a posed group of all the
officers and men of the regiment who
fought at Monchy and were still serving in
May 1917. The regimental bootmaker at
work. The regiment on the march with full
kit, pack mules, wagons and mounted
officers, through the streets of Berneville (?).

Notes
Remarks: almost a forerunner of the British
Regiments series which began shooting in
autumn 1917.
[G W L Nicholson, The Fighting
Newfoundlander, Government of
Newfoundland (1964)]
[shotsheet available]
catalogued SDB: 6/1982

IWM 148 · GB, (?) 1918
**REFUGEES FROM VILLAGES ON THE
CAMBRAI FRONT**

b/w · 1 reel · 115' (2 mins) · silent
intertitles: none

sp War Office Cinema Committee pr Topical
Film Company cam McDowell, J B

▪ The family of Jules Copin, and a baby
  born after evacuation from the Cambrai
  area, Western Front, November 1917.

A nursing home behind the lines with Jules
Copin, his wife and child, and two blind
aunts, led by two nurses. Copin was a
French soldier captured by the Germans in
September 1914 who escaped and was
hidden by his wife in his own home at
Masnières near Cambrai until the village
was captured by the British in November
1917. Also shown is a baby born one day
after its mother was evacuated by the
British from a captured village, posed with
its mother, three other children, and two
nurses at the home.

Notes
Title: the title and some of the details of the

film have been taken from the shotsheet. *Remarks:* a useful example of the basic British principle of 'the propaganda of facts' when dealing with the enemy. catalogued SDB: 6/1982

IWM 149 · NO FILM

IWM 150 · GB, (?) 1918
SOLDIERS VOTING AND AMERICAN HEROES AT CAMBRAI

b/w · 1 reel · 384' (17 mins) · silent intertitles: none

sp War Office Cinema Committee (?) *pr* Topical Film Company *cam* Bassill, F A

■ Men of Canadian 3rd Division voting in the Canadian General Election, and American Railway Engineers, Western Front, December 1917.

A poster lists the various "Electoral Districts in Canada". Polling took place between 1 and 17 December. Men of 7th Brigade, Canadian 3rd Division read the poster. The brigade is 49th (Edmonton) Battalion, 42nd (5th Royal Highlanders of Canada) Battalion, the Royal Canadian Regiment, and the Princess Patricia's Canadian Light Infantry. Outside, a line of men of the brigade wait to vote. At 3rd Division Salvage Company at Norrent-Fontes, a hut has a sign painted over it, "Bring your salvage to this dump and vote for the Government !!! Both will help win the war". Underneath this is a sign reading "a vote against the Government means you are here for life; a vote for the Government means another man is coming to take your place". Next to this is a sign advertising Canadian War Bonds. A soldier of 42nd Battalion reads the notice on voting.
II. American Railway Engineers of 'F' Company, 11th Engineers, who took part in the defence against the German counterattack at Cambrai in November 1917, now at work repairing a track. The men pose for the camera in a group. A portrait shot of Sergeant McDonald and Private McDonald, who were captured and escaped after killing their guards. Posed group of the officers, led by Captain C Raymond Hulsart. The company on the march in full kit.

Notes
Title: this is taken from the shotsheet.

[shotsheet available] catalogued SDB: 6/1982

IWM 151 · Australia, (?) 1917
GENERAL BIRDWOOD PRESENTING MEDALS TO THIRD AUSTRALIAN DIVISION

b/w · 1 reel · 219' (4 mins) · silent intertitles: none

sp Australian War Records Section *cam* Wilkins, G H

■ Australians of 3rd Division being decorated by General Sir William Birdwood, Lumbres training area, Western Front, August 1917.

Australians parade in the open air in front of Birdwood, who stands with his staff at a table covered by a Union Flag. The soldiers approach and receive decorations. Other Australian troops at rest (possibly an unrelated scene). The men of the division, led by their band, march past Birdwood.

Notes
Title: this is taken from the shotsheet.
Production: apparently Australian official film.
[shotsheet available] catalogued SDB: 6/1982

IWM 152 · NO FILM

IWM 153 · GB, 1917
[SAINT OMER, SPANISH VISITORS AND CHRISTMAS SCENES, 1917] (allocated)

b/w · 1 reel · 725' (12 mins) · silent intertitles: none

sp War Office Cinema Committee *pr* Topical Film Company *cam* McDowell, J B

I. Recreational clubs for British soldiers in the town of St-Omer, Western Front, late 1917. A wooden house, the "Church Army Club and Military Church", with British and American troops wandering in front of it. Two permanent buildings, the Roberts Club (named after Field Marshal Lord Roberts) and the Monro Club (named after General Sir Charles Monro), both for servicemen. All the buildings are in St-Omer.
II. Spanish civilians being escorted over the

old Vimy Ridge battlefield, Western Front, late 1917. A British officer escorts the party, whose names (from the shotsheet) are José Clare, Luis Clare, André Triand, Manuel Azaña and Pierre Ynglanda, over the deserted remains of the battlefield. III. British soldiers behind the lines on the Western Front celebrating Christmas, 1917. British soldiers at Christmas buying turkeys and ducks from a French farm. One, with a sprig of mistletoe, kisses a French girl at the farm. Other British soldiers with an American (?) liaison officer march through the snow, and others rest in a snow-covered field. Scottish troops led by their pipe band march through the snow. British soldiers cut mistletoe down from a tree.

Notes

Summary: it is presumed that the Spaniard identified by the shotsheet as Manuel Azena (sic) is in fact Manuel Azaña, the future President of the Spanish Republic.
[shotsheet available]
catalogued SDB: 6/1982

IWM 154 · GB, 1918
BRITISH TROOPS IN ITALY

b/w · 1 reel · 1341' (23 mins) · silent
intertitles: English

sp War Office Cinema Committee *pr* Topical Film Company *cam* Raymond, H C

■ British troops in the Piave River area of the Italian Front, December 1917.

2nd Battalion, King's Own Scottish Borderers of 5th Division, including four bagpipers, detraining and resting at Legnano, 20 December 1917. 1st Battalion, the Bedfordshire Regiment (?) of 5th Division marching through Legnano in column of fours. Men of 11th Battalion, West Yorkshire Regiment, 23rd Division, taking an outdoor wash in wooded country behind the River Piave. Men of 41st Division (?) in a village behind the River Piave buying trinkets from outdoor stalls and helping the local women draw water from a large domed well in the street. A line-laying wagon of the Royal Engineers moves along a street with Italian Carabinieri watching. A group of soldiers from the Machine Gun Corps and RAMC pluck geese for Christmas, with an Italian girl, wearing an RAMC cap, helping. A British 18-pounder battery passes one way along a tree-lined road and Italian troops bring a bullock cart of fodder the other way. Brigadier-General

Peppino Garibaldi addresses British troops. Six French, British and Italian company officers talk together in a square "within a mile of the enemy". British and French troops move along shallow trenches (probably training). The wreckage of three aeroplanes guarded by British and Italian troops after they were shot down in an air raid, probably all Albatros CIII with Austrian markings. The wreckage of two cottages after another Albatros had crashed on top of them. The aerodrome of 45 Fighter Squadron RFC, probably at Padova or San Pelagio. The pilots pose beside their Sopwith Camels, after which two of the Camels take off. British soldiers wearing their shrapnel helmets and gas mask satchels dig reserve trenches in a wooded area behind the Piave.

Notes

Date: Raymond was in Italy from 11 December 1917 to January 1918, and again in June 1918, but was only able to film for about two weeks on the first occasion.
[MoI(Photo) Papers, file on Ernest Brooks]
[shotsheet available]
catalogued SDB: 6/1982

IWM 155 · GB, (prod) 1917
TOMMY SECURES SUITABLE FARE FOR THIS SEASON

b/w · 1 reel · 36' (1 min) · silent
intertitles: none

sp War Office Cinema Committee *pr* Topical Film Company *cam* McDowell, J B (?)

■ Very brief scene of a British soldier walking towards the camera carrying two live turkeys, Western Front, December 1917.

Notes

Title: this is taken from the shotsheet.
Summary: probably originally part of **IWM 153.**
Technical: although clearly a single scene from a larger film, this is now held in a separate can by itself.
[shotsheet available]
catalogued SDB: 6/1982

IWM 156 · New Zealand, 1917
INSPECTION OF NEW ZEALAND TROOPS BY FIELD MARSHAL SIR DOUGLAS HAIG

b/w · 1 reel · 402' (7 mins) · silent
intertitles: none

cam Sanders, Henry A

■ Field Marshal Haig's inspection of the
New Zealand Division near Fromental in
the Lumbres training area in France, 14
September 1917.

Haig, on horseback, with staff and lancer
escort, accompanied by Major-General Sir
Andrew Russell, the New Zealand divisional
commander, inspects the division and takes
the salute during the march past. Also
present is Winston Churchill, the Minister of
Munitions, in tweeds.

Notes
Production: New Zealand official film.
Summary: Haig wrote in his diary (14
September 1917) "At 10.00am I inspected
the New Zealand Division on the training
ground E of Halettes (N of the Boulogne–St-
Omer Road) .... The 1st, 2nd and 4th
Brigades were on parade. The men were
well turned out and handled their arms
smartly. They are a sturdy, thick set type of
man. After my inspection, the troops
marched past by platoons. A very fine show
in fine style. Mr Winston Churchill
accompanied me and seemed much
impressed."
Authority: additional detail from Christopher
Pugsley, 12/1993.
Remarks: Sanders reported problems with
his camera, but this is a poorly filmed,
blurred, uninteresting and dull piece of
work. Sanders may have been told to keep
back from the official party – certainly the
camera was held too far from the action
and angled badly throughout. The effect is
like looking over someone's shoulder from
the back of a densely packed crowd.
[shotsheet available]
catalogued SDB: 6/1982

IWM 157 · New Zealand, 1917
**VISIT OF SIR THOMAS MACKENZIE
KCMG HIGH COMMISSIONER FOR NEW
ZEALAND TO THE NEW ZEALAND
DIVISION, SEPTEMBER 9TH AND 10TH
1917**

b/w · 1 reel · 567' (10 mins) · silent
intertitles: English

cam Sanders, Henry A

■ Sir Thomas MacKenzie's visit to the New
Zealand Division in its training area near

Lumbres west of St-Omer, France,
September 1917.

2nd Battalion Otago Regiment, led by its
band, marching easy along a road with high
wooded banks. There is an open-air church
parade for the battalion, attended by
MacKenzie, Lieutenant-General Sir
Alexander Godley, Commander II ANZAC
Corps, Major-General Sir Andrew Russell
and Captain Malcolm Ross the official NZEF
Press Correspondent. The service is led by
a chaplain in khaki and vestments, whose
makeshift altar is covered with a Union
Jack. MacKenzie talks to Otago soldiers
after the parade. Visiting the 2nd NZ Field
Ambulance, he talks, with his back to the
camera, to a line of slightly wounded New
Zealanders sitting on a bench, one with a
head bandage. He inspects 3rd Battalion
Auckland Regiment accompanied by the
divisional commander, Major-General Sir
Andrew Russell and Brigadier-General H
Hart, commanding 4 NZ Infantry Brigade.
Russell, on horseback, addresses 3rd
Battalion Otago Regiment, followed by a
further address by MacKenzie, on foot,
while Ross takes notes. MacKenzie departs
by car – the last vehicle to leave is the
official photographer's van with the
divisional sign, a silver fern, below the side
window.

Notes
Title: this is taken from the shotsheet.
Production: New Zealand official film,
released in New Zealand (censor date) 15
April 1918. The New Zealand Government
first appointed an official photographer-
cinematographer in 1907, and had
commissioned official films of important
events since 1901. In the First World War,
the NZ public expected to see their soldiers
on film. In 1916 the authorities negotiated
for the British official cameramen to film
New Zealand military activities. Although
initially agreed to (see **IWM 196**), this
proved too difficult and New Zealand then
made its own arrangements. Sir Thomas
MacKenzie was the patron of government
film-making in New Zealand before 1914,
when he was Minister of Tourist and Health
Resorts. As High Commissioner, he
negotiated an agreement with Pathé Frères
in 1912 to use New Zealand official film in
the *Pathé Gazette*. It was this connection
that led to the appointment of Henry A
Sanders (the original *Pathé Gazette*
cameraman in Great Britain) as the NZEF
official photographer on the Western Front
from April 1917 until early 1919, and of
Thomas A Scales as "cinema expert" in the
United Kingdom from April 1917 until late

1918. Both were recommended by Pathé Frères to act as official New Zealand cameramen, and both returned to work for Pathé after the war. Sanders was appointed as an honorary lieutenant and promoted to captain in October 1917; Scales was made a sergeant, and paid an additional £5 per week out of regimental funds to make up the difference between his NZEF pay and allowances and the income he had previously enjoyed with Pathé. Pathé Frères retained the negatives and world distribution rights except for New Zealand: three copies of each film were provided to the NZ Government for screening in New Zealand. Films taken by Scales in the UK were widely shown in New Zealand, and individual films and extracts from them were included in the Pathé Gazette; however, WOCC regulations resulted in many of Sanders's films not being shown in New Zealand until after the Armistice of 1918.
Summary: Russell noted in his diary "The whole visit has been successful, fine weather – just enough speechifying but not too much".
Authority: additional detail from Christopher Pugsley, 12/1993.
[shotsheet available]
catalogued SDB: 7/1982

IWM 158 · Australia, 1917
FIGHTING IN FLANDERS : with the Australian Imperial Forces on the Western Front

b/w · 2 reels · 1502' (26 mins) · silent
intertitles: English

sp Australian War Records Section
cam Hurley, J F

- Australian troops preparing for and in action during the Third Battle of Ypres (Passchendaele), Western Front, 1917.

(Reel 1) Australian 2nd Division at outdoor physical training and Swedish drill, followed by bayonet training and Lewis machinegun practice, probably in 'W' training area, Bouvelinghem, August 1917. 18-pounder field guns of 2nd Division (?) come into a park. Field Marshal Haig (on horseback) reviews 5th Division in 'W' area on 29 August. Men of 2nd Division, in slouch hats, march down a road towards the front. (They are probably 28th Battalion.) An extended sequence of a 6-inch howitzer being fired. (Reel 2) More of 2nd Division marching to the front. Australians in battle equipment move through the ruins of trenches carrying

supplies close to the front at Ypres. A Mk IV Male tank, HMLS 'Amethyst' of 'A' Company, H/MGC, moves up. Supporting troops of 2nd Division (?) consolidate their position, digging supports and having a brief meal. Stretcher-bearers helped by a chaplain bandage wounded of 1st and 2nd Divisions, who are taken to a dressing station. The German prisoners are marched to the rear, fed, and talk with their guards. (Some of these scenes may be of the Messines area rather than the Ypres salient.)

Notes
Production: Australian official film.
Summary: see also **IWM 127**. According to Captain Gill, his battalion was filmed by Hurley on 8 September as being the best battalion in the division.
[Papers of Captain R H Gill – letter to his parents, 8 September 1917, in IWM Department of Documents]
[shotsheet available]
catalogued SDB: 6/1982

IWM 159 · GB, 1918
MR BEN TILLET MP VISITS BRITISH SOLDIERS IN YPRES (sic)

b/w · 1 reel · 264' (5 mins) · silent
intertitles: none

sp War Office Cinema Committee pr Topical Film Company cam McDowell, J B

- Ben Tillett meets British troops at Hellfire Corner in Ypres, Western Front, at noon on 9 January 1918.

Tillett, in raincoat, helmet and gas mask satchel, talks to gunners transporting stores in horse-drawn wagons at Hellfire Corner, on the Menin Road out of Ypres. He goes on to talk to other soldiers, probably all VI Corps ASC, and inspects the ruins of Ypres Cloth Hall. Finally, he is seen shaking hands with drivers and passengers in VI Corps ASC lorries (note the bulldog formation sign) and with French soldiers.

Notes
Title: this is taken from the shotsheet.
Remarks: everything is rather posed and camera-conscious. The film is mainly noteworthy in that from associated documents it is possible to identify each event to the minute.
[Mol(Photo) Papers, File on David McClellan, memorandum 8 January 1918]
[shotsheet available]
catalogued SDB: 6/1982

IWM 160 · New Zealand, 1918
**NEW ZEALAND FIELD ARTILLERY IN
ACTION, NEW YEAR'S DAY 1918**
VISIT TO THE NEW ZEALAND INFANTRY
BASE DEPOT AT ETAPLES (extracts)

b/w · 1 reel · 459' (8 mins) · silent
intertitles: none

cam Sanders, Henry A

■ Jumble of shots from two separate films
showing scenes of the New Zealand
Infantry and General Training Base Depot
at Etaples in France and a New Zealand
howitzer battery in the Ypres salient
during the winter of 1917/18.

The first scene is double-exposed and
shows cookhouse fatigues and a squad of
soldiers marching at the New Zealand
Depot at Etaples. A 4.5-inch howitzer of a
forward New Zealand battery on the Menin
Road near Westhoek in the Ypres Salient is
shown to cease firing, and then the gun
crew covers it with white camouflage
tarpaulin and a scrim net. The gunners
open tinned Christmas cakes and
puddings, and pass around cigarettes. The
scene shifts back to Etaples and the New
Zealand Commandant, Lieutenant-Colonel
G 'Hoppy' Mitchell, inspecting a
reinforcement draft in full kit. The men
shoulder arms and march off to entrain for
the front. A bugler sounds a bugle call with
the NZ Depot accommodation tents and
cookhouse as background, and a flag is
raised, the film cutting half-way through the
ceremony. A reinforcement parade at the
Depot and soldiers practising Swedish drill.

Notes
Title: this is taken from the shotsheet.
Intertitles: scratched on negative.
Production: this film is actually a jumble of
scenes from two films, *New Zealand Field
Artillery in Action, New Year's Day 1918* and
*Visit to the New Zealand Infantry Base Depot
at Etaples,* both filmed by the NZ official
cinematographer Captain Henry A Sanders
in late 1917 and early 1918. Similar
Christmas shots filmed at the same time
were used in *The New Zealand Field Artillery
in France* (held as **IWM 166**). The lack of
intertitling and the mis-editing of this and
other New Zealand films suggests that the
NZ film in the IWM archive has survived
from negatives deposited with the WOCC,
rather than from the collection of edited and
titled films sent to the IWM from New
Zealand in the post-war film exchange. This
may also explain why none of Scales's film
of the New Zealanders in the United

Kingdom (see **Notes** to **IWM 157**) forms
part of the IWM collection.
Authority: additional detail from Christopher
Pugsley, 12/1993.
Remarks: the 'Christmas' scene is a superior
example of the genre.
[shotsheet available]
catalogued SDB: 6/1982

IWM 161 · GB, 3/1918
**WOOLWICH ARSENAL AND ITS
WORKERS**

b/w & (partly) tinted · 5 reels · 4053' (68
mins) · silent
intertitles: English

sp Ministry of Information *pr* Topical Film
Company

■ Munitions manufacture at Woolwich
Arsenal West, London, early 1918.

(Reel 1) The arsenal entrance in Beresford
Square, with the internal train taking the
workers to various departments. Women
and boys in the Tailors' Shop make gloves,
felt "buttons" for 15-inch shells, and
cartridge bags of various sizes. Other
women make and assemble time fuses and
impact fuses for the various types of shell.
(Reel 2) The workers (who, except in the
heavy jobs, are women with men as
supervisors) making small arms cartridges,
showing in detail the process involved in
making an 18-pounder shell-case from first
casting. *(Reel 3)* Men in the Leather Shop
making leather, canvas and cork items,
including saddlery and cartridge carrying
cases. Logs are brought to the sawmill
where they are cut into sheets, then to the
Carpenters' Shop where they are cut into
planks and into the basic shapes for wheels
and barrels. *(Reel 4)* On to the Coopers'
Shop where wheels and barrels are
repaired. Old, very young and disabled men
are seen at work. Inside the Iron Foundry a
Bessemer Converter is at work, and steel is
shaped using drop hammers and giant
shears. *(Reel 5)* Casting in the Brass
Foundry, with guns' ends shaped and
bored by an automatic rifling tool,
mountings being tested in the Fitters' Shop
and finished shells and guns being taken
out of the factory by train and barge. The
film ends with workers leaving the factory at
the end of the day.

Notes
Colour: reel 1 is tinted purple and red; the
remaining reels are untinted.

Summary: compare with **IWM 460** *The Other Italian Army*, the equivalent film from the Italians, which is technically much more accomplished but also more flamboyant. See also **IWM 499**, consisting of duplicate material and out-takes, some of which show that the mechanical processes were not always as smooth as the finished film suggests.
Technical: received by the IWM in 1921 as a Spanish export version, *Uno de los Arsenales Britanicos, Woolwich y sus Trabajadores*, with subtitles that were a direct translation from the English. In 1982 the film was restored to its original English-language version, new subtitles being made from the original records.
Remarks: a very interesting film. The complexity of shell and gun manufacture is well brought out. The tinting on the first reel is beautiful.
[shotsheet available]
catalogued SDB: 6/1982

IWM 162 · GB, (?) 1918
the CARE OF OUR WOUNDED

b/w · 2 reels · 1853' (32 mins) · silent
intertitles: English

sp Ministry of Information (?) *pr* Topical Film Company

■ British medical services on the Western Front, 1916-18.

(Reel 1) "Stretcher bearers" (most probably a wiring party) crossing no man's land. An RAMC doctor in a shell-hole attends to two heavily bandaged patients. Wounded, some walking and some on stretchers, are brought into the trenches. One blinded soldier is helped across the battlefield by a chaplain. Wounded, including some Germans, pass through trenches. Walking wounded of the Australian 2nd Division. RAMC men try to manœuvre a stretcher across a wide dug-out while a soldier in the foreground tries to sleep. A stretcher party crosses a narrow canal by footbridge. Wounded troops at a forward dressing station. Wounded being transported by wheeled stretchers. A medical corpsman joking with a wounded German prisoner. Walking wounded at a dressing station are attended to by a doctor. A man on a stretcher dictates a letter to a chaplain. Men of the Australian 1st and 2nd Divisions on stretchers being loaded into an ambulance. Ambulances driving to a Casualty Clearing Station. A doctor at work in the CCS. The patients are labelled and taken out to a hospital ship. *(Reel 2)* Other patients are loaded into a Red Cross train, some of them walking, others on stretchers. Scenes of the Princess Louise Convalescent Home for Nurses in France with its matron, Lady Gifford. A VAD ambulance convoy at work at Etaples in June 1917. "The two women of Pervyse", Baroness T'Serclaes (previously Mrs Elsie Knocker) and Marie Chisholm, at work with Belgian troops. A hospital train being unloaded and wounded being taken on board a hospital ship (number E 8106) by members of the RAMC and FANY. The ship then leaves harbour.

Notes
Date: this film was released not later than September 1918.
Summary: a compilation from earlier material. Scenes used in this film can be found in **IWM 102**, **IWM 113**, **IWM 116**, **IWM 130**, **IWM 158** and **IWM 191**.
Remarks: a good example of the manner in which, even before the war's end, compilation films used material from the period 1916-18 indiscriminately and without regard for chronological or geographical consistency, producing an 'endless war' effect.
[shotsheet available]
catalogued SDB: 6/1982

IWM 163 · GB, (prod) 1918
a BOMB PROOF LODGING

b/w · 1 reel · 66' (1 min) · silent
intertitles: none

sp War Office Cinema Committee *pr* Topical Film Company *cam* Bassill, F A

■ Gunners of 51st (Highland) Division enter by ladder a temporary shelter they have constructed in a large overturned water tower at Riencourt near Bapaume, Western Front, 5 January 1918.

[shotsheet available]
catalogued SDB: 6/1982

IWM 164 · GB, (ca) 1918
[a KITE BALLOON AND THE BELLE OF ARQUES] (allocated)

b/w · 1 reel · 581' (10 mins) · silent
intertitles: none

sp War Office Cinema Committee (?)

pr Topical Film Company

I. A British observation kite balloon on the Western Front in the second half of the First World War. An RFC kite balloon in the air. It appears to be attacked by an aeroplane, and the balloon's observer parachutes to earth while the balloon itself bursts into flames and collapses. Further scenes of the balloon being inflated by a gas generator, rising and descending safely, the observer getting out and the balloon being secured. The headphone cable link between the observer and the ground is tested before the balloon is raised. The item ends with further scenes of the aeroplane attack on the balloon and the balloon in the air.
II. The "Belle of Arques", a young lady operating a swing-bridge at Arques, Western Front, 1916-18. The young lady, a refugee from Arras, operates by hand a swing-bridge across a canal in the centre of Arques. A British Red Cross barge A 108 passes under the bridge when it is raised and British lorries drive over it when it is lowered.

Notes
Summary: see also **IWM 217** *Observing for our Heavy Guns.*
[shotsheet available]
catalogued SDB: 6/1982

IWM 165 · Australia, (?) 1918
AUSTRALIAN CORPS TRAINING SCHOOL

b/w · 1 reel · 311' (6 mins) · silent
intertitles: none

sp Australian War Records Section

- Demonstration by Australian Infantry of tactics used in trench fighting on the Western Front, early 1918 (?).

Opening with a pan over a group of Australian soldiers of various divisions wearing their bush hats and watching the exercise. This is followed by the exercise itself. Australian troops in full battle equipment run past a cloud of earth thrown up by an explosion. Some go over a bayonet assault course wearing their gas masks. Two, with bush hats, fire rifle grenades from a kneeling position. The final scene is platoon training. In a very realistic exercise the platoon, led by its officer, practises bombing up the traverses in a training trench, a grenade being thrown and the men dashing forward to arrive just after

the explosion. Finally, a 3-inch mortar is fired from a trench.

Notes
Title: this is taken from the shotsheet.
Production: Australian official film.
Remarks: an extremely valuable demonstration of the tactics in use by the British and Imperial forces during the final stages of trench warfare.
[shotsheet available]
catalogued SDB: 6/1982

IWM 166 · New Zealand, 1917
the NEW ZEALAND FIELD ARTILLERY IN FRANCE
NEW ZEALAND RIFLE BRIGADE ON THE MARCH (extracts)

b/w · 1 reel · 670' (12 mins) · silent
intertitles: none

cam Sanders, Henry A

- Jumble of scenes from two films showing the New Zealand Field Artillery and the new Zealand Rifle Brigade on the Western Front in 1917 and early 1918.

The opening scenes show New Zealand Field Artillery horses being watered at a river and fed at horse lines. This is followed by a scene of a gunner officer emerging from a sand-bagged command post and directing fire using a megaphone. An 18-pounder fires (viewed from the rear with a detailed close-up of the aiming and firing mechanism). A Forward Observation Officer directs fire through his signaller using a field telephone. A soldier emerges from his dug-out and fires a rifle grenade (the recoil knocks his shrapnel helmet off). This is followed by two long sequences of two different battalions marching. One wearing shrapnel helmets marches through a village. The second is the New Zealand Rifle Brigade marching along a country road. A brief scene of gunners riding their horses bareback. The route march continues. A scene of gunners being issued Christmas parcels by the Battery Quartermaster Sergeant. The film ends with an extended sequence of two 18-pounders in the snow firing at the intense rate.

Notes
Title: this is taken from the shotsheet.
Intertitles: scratched on negative.
Production: this film is actually a jumble of scenes from two films, *The New Zealand Field Artillery in France* and *New Zealand*

Rifle Brigade on the March, both filmed by the NZ official cinematographer Captain Henry A Sanders (*cf.* **IWM 160**).
Remarks: the 18-pounder firing sequence is particularly fine, but the starring role is given to the horses (watch for the bugler being nudged by his horse). New Zealand sent 10 117 horses overseas during the war, 2655 for the New Zealand Field Artillery. Because of quarantine regulations, only three horses are known to have returned.
Authority: additional detail from Christopher Pugsley, 12/1993.
[shotsheet available]
catalogued SDB: 6/1982

IWM 167 · GB, 1918
HUNTINGDON WORKSHOP

b/w · 1 reel · 240' (5 mins) · silent
intertitles: none

sp War Office Cinema Committee

- Aircraft manufacture in Britain, 1918.

Workers in a Huntingdon aircraft factory in February 1918, mainly women, use a former and pegs to construct the basic wooden frame for the rear fuselage of a Sopwith Camel. Men replace the fabric on the wings of another Camel. A third Camel has its basic fuselage doped and painted. The film then returns to another basic body being assembled.

Notes
Summary: see also **IWM 200** *Aero Engines*.
[shotsheet available]
catalogued SDB: 6/1982

IWM 168 · GB, 1918
CHINESE NEW YEAR CELEBRATIONS IN FRANCE

b/w · 1 reel · 197' (4 mins) · silent
intertitles: none

sp War Office Cinema Committee *pr* Topical Film Company *cam* Bassill, F A

- Chinese Labour Corps celebrate New Year in Noyelles, Western Front, 11 February 1918.

The townspeople and some British officers and NCOs watch as the members of the Corps celebrate the Chinese New Year with a procession, including two 'Junks' carried by one man each, a tug of war, a group of four stilt walkers and an improvised percussion band.

[shotsheet available]
catalogued SDB: 6/1982

IWM 169 · GB, 1917
SOUTH AFRICANS HOLD A MEMORIAL SERVICE IN DELVILLE WOOD

b/w · 1 reel · 321' (6 mins) · silent
intertitles: none

sp War Office Cinema Committee *pr* Topical Film Company

- Memorial service held by the South African Brigade for its members killed in taking Delville Wood during the First Battle of the Somme, Western Front, the service taking place in early 1917.

The brigade is drawn up in hollow square around the wooden memorial in Delville Wood. The three chaplains – Anglican, Dutch Reform and Presbyterian – conduct the service. The divisional commander, Major-General H T Lukin (9th Division) and Brigadier-General F S Dawson commanding the brigade are both present. The buglers blow the last post. Lukin presents medals won in the taking of Delville Wood while another officer reads the citations (one officer appears to be crying). Members of VAD place wreaths at the foot of the memorial. One of them, shown in close-up, is the High Commissioner's daughter, Miss Schreiner. The brigade then marches past its divisional and brigade commanders, along a corduroy road. The 4th (South African Scottish) Regiment, which is also shown at rest at the end of the film, is prominent with its kilts and springbok mascot.

Notes
Title: the title and some of the details of the film come from the shotsheet.
[shotsheet available]
catalogued SDB: 7/1982

IWM 170 · GB, 1918
VISIT OF HRH THE PRINCE OF WALES TO EBBW VALE, FEBRUARY 21ST 1918

b/w · 1 reel · 314' (6 mins) · silent
intertitles: English

- Prince of Wales's visit to Ebbw Vale, 21 February 1918.

The Prince's car arrives at Ebbw Vale. He wears Army uniform and is accompanied by the Honourable Sir Sidney Greville and Lord Treowan. He greets the assembled dignitaries and inspects a guard of honour from the local Cadet Corps and the Monmouthshire volunteers. Wearing collier's overalls and cap, and carrying a safety lamp, he emerges from a visit to the underground coalface at Victoria Colliery. He inspects Lord Treowan's nearby steelworks and meets a group of VAD nurses at the local hospital. At Cardiff docks he is shown various light naval weapons, including a mine projector (?). He leaves to the cheers of the people. In the last scene he greets one of the workers of Guest, Keene and Nettlefold Ltd.

Notes
Production: possibly a private newsreel film rather than official material.
Intertitles: some of these are obviously missing.
[*The Times,* 21 February 1918: 9B]
[*The Times,* 22 February 1918: 3B]
[*Daily Mirror,* 22 February 1918]
[*Daily Mirror,* 23 February 1918]
[shotsheet available]
catalogued SDB: 6/1982

IWM 171 · GB, (?) 1918
SOUTH AFRICAN ARTILLERY IN ACTION

b/w · 1 reel · 254' (5 mins) · silent
intertitles: none

sp Ministry of Information (?) *pr* Topical Film Company *cam* Bassill, F A

- 6-inch 26cwt howitzer of the South African Brigade in action, Western Front, probably 1918.

In detail, the howitzer is loaded and fired, probably in the Péronne area. The gun crew uncovers the camouflage sheet from the howitzer. Then a posed group of the gunners, showing their cap badges clearly. Finally, the gun is fired, cleaned out, reloaded and fired again six times.

Notes
Title: this is taken from the shotsheet.
[shotsheet available]
catalogued SDB: 6/1982

IWM 172 · New Zealand, 1918
NEW ZEALAND DIVISIONAL RUGBY TEAM

b/w · 1 reel · 608' (11 mins) · silent
intertitles: none

cam Sanders, Henry A

- Rugby match between the New Zealand Division 'All Blacks' and a French Army selection, played in Paris on Sunday 17 February 1918, the New Zealanders winning 5 points to 3.

The film covers three of the six days the New Zealand team spent in Paris. The first scenes show their tour of the city by horse-drawn charabanc on 16 February, visiting the Bois de Boulogne and Les Invalides. A visit to Versailles, which actually took place on 18 February, is seen next. The match takes place at the Parc des Princes stadium, the spectators being mainly soldiers. The New Zealand team comes out first and performs a 'haka' dance, after which the French team comes out. The kick-off is made by Miss Violet Russell, daughter of the New Zealand divisional commander. The match itself is shown in detail. The New Zealand team is then seen in its charabanc turning past the Arc de Triomphe and into the Champs Elysées (possibly more of the 16 February city tour). II. To the end of the film is attached a brief, unrelated scene of a British Cavalry patrol on the Western Front.

Notes
Title: this is taken from the shotsheet.
Intertitles: sequence of scenes scratched on negative.
Production: New Zealand official film.
Summary: A contemporary match report (see reference) names the French try scorer as Shohl, with New Zealand's try scored by Carnegie and converted by Capper. The result is described as "a lucky New Zealand win".
Remarks: this is one of several films of the NZEF 'All Blacks' taken in France during the First World War by the NZEF official cinematographer. Similar films were taken of the NZEF (UK) team by Scales (see **IWM 157**). This particular film clearly demonstrates the difficulties of filming a rugby match from the sideline, but Sanders's filming of the two teams taking the field captures the spirit of the two nationalities – the dour, workaday look of the New Zealanders, and the almost embarrassed way they perform the haka, compared to their opponents' Gallic

insouciance, conscious of rank and superiority, coats draped over shoulders, all marvellously French.
Authority: additional detail from Christopher Pugsley, 12/1993.
[*Chronicles of the NZEF*, 4: 39 (13 March 1918): 56]
[shotsheet available]
catalogued SDB: 7/1982

IWM 173 · Australia, 1918
AUSTRALIAN ENGINEERS PREPARE A DEFENSIVE SYSTEM

b/w · 1 reel · 362' (6 mins) · silent
intertitles: English

cam Wilkins, G H (?)

■ Construction of a trench system and pillbox by Australian Engineers, Western Front, early 1918.

Australian sappers wearing shrapnel helmets dig a trench system traced out with a line, shoring up the completed trenches with corrugated iron and A-frames, and fitting duckboards. An Australian digging party works beside a light railway system. An armoured engine arrives and collects them. (Note the canvas screens on the ridgeline protecting them from observation.) At a supply dump sacks are unloaded from a light railway onto a light tramway, a 'Decanville' cart, and pulled forward to the beginning of the trench system. More men build a reinforced dug-out and pillbox from corrugated iron sheeting and concrete.

Notes
Production: Australian official film.
[shotsheet available]
catalogued SDB: 6/1982

IWM 174 · GB, 1918
INSPECTION OF VOLUNTEER REGIMENTS AT BEDFORD, MARCH 1918, BY FIELD MARSHAL VISCOUNT FRENCH

b/w · 1 reel · 513' (9 mins) · silent
intertitles: English

sp Ministry of Information *cam* Raymond, H C (?)

■ Field Marshal Viscount French's inspection of the Volunteer Training Corps battalions of Number Nine District, Eastern Command, March 1918.

French as GOC Home Forces with the VTC battalions commanded by Brigadier-General W G Carter. French is on foot with his staff. Firstly, he inspects a battalion of the Bedfordshire Regiment drawn up on parade, addresses the officers and presents an award to a private. Then he and his staff wait on a suburban road as the four battalions of the district, from the Bedfordshire, Northamptonshire, Herefordshire and Huntingdonshire regiments, march past. Several men wear civilian clothes or New Army navy blue greatcoats instead of khaki. The film ends with a Union Flag fluttering in the breeze.

Notes
Cameraman: the store ledger identifies Raymond as the cameraman. If this is correct he must have been on leave in England and called in for this particular assignment.
[shotsheet available]
catalogued SDB: 6/1982

IWM 175 · GB, (?) 1918
PREPARING A BOMBING RAID

b/w · 1 reel · 501' (9 mins) · silent
intertitles: none

sp Ministry of Information (?) *pr* Topical Film Company *cam* Bassill, F A (?)

I. Preparations for a bombing raid by an RFC Squadron, Western Front, early 1918. Probably 27 Night Bomber Squadron RFC at Serny in early 1918. An Airco DH4 is brought out of its hangar and fitted with 20-pound bombs. The pilot and gunner board the plane. A light tramway is used for the bomb trolleys bringing 112-pound bombs across the airfield, and one of these is fitted to another DH4. The propeller of the original aircraft is turned over and the chocks removed (out of sequence). The gunner is handed two aerial cameras. The aircraft takes off.
II. British Army steam tractors ploughing a field on the Western Front, early 1918. Two British steam tractors ploughing a field, very close to a barbed wire entanglement. One tractor becomes ditched and the other is used to pull it out of the mud. Rakes or harrows drawn by horses are at work on the same land.

Notes
Title: this is taken from the shotsheet.
[shotsheet available]
catalogued SDB: 6/1982

IWM 176 · GB, 1918
RAILWAYMEN IN FRANCE

b/w · 1 reel · 531' (10 mins) · silent
intertitles: English

sp Ministry of Information *pr* Topical Film
Company

I. The BEF locomotive shop at St-Etienne-
du-Rouvray, France, March 1918. The
soldiers employed at the shop form into
their squads prior to leaving work. Views
inside and outside the workshops of the
various engines, one "an American giant"
being repaired, maintained and run.
II. Canadian Engineers and men of the
Chinese Labour Corps use horse-drawn
scoops to excavate a cutting, Western
Front, 1918.

Notes
Title: this is taken from the shotsheet.
[shotsheet available]
catalogued SDB: 6/1982

IWM 177 · GB, (?) 1918
**[CANADIAN CORPS HQ AND SCENES
NEAR BAPAUME, MARCH 1918]**
(allocated)

b/w · 1 reel · 472' (8 mins) · silent
intertitles: none

sp Ministry of Information *pr* Topical Film
Company *cam* Bassill, F A (?)

I. US delegates visit Canadian Corps
headquarters, Western Front, March 1918.
A visit by six American delegates of the
Loyal Order of the Moose, one of them in
uniform, to the headquarters of the
Canadian Corps on 17 March 1918. They
are met by (possibly) Prince Arthur of
Connaught and watch a close order drill
demonstration on a football pitch.
II. British troops in the rear areas near
Bapaume during the Kaiserschlacht
Offensive, Western Front, 22 and 23 March
1918. Between Péronne and Bapaume, Holt
tractors pull a battery of 6-inch 26cwt
howitzers down the road, followed by
supply lorries. Horses of the RFA and two
battalions of Infantry also come down the
road. There is much dust. A group of
soldiers rest on board a lorry. One sleeps
on the trail of a 18-pounder field gun. A
battery, probably of 6-inch howitzers, waits
in column, and the opportunity is taken to
issue hay to the horses.

Notes
Remarks: the second subject gives a very
good visual impression of rear areas during
a Western Front battle.
[shotsheet available]
catalogued SDB: 7/1982

IWM 178 · GB, (prod) 1918
GERMAN OFFENSIVE 1

b/w · 1 reel · 499' (9 mins) · silent
intertitles: none

sp Ministry of Information *pr* Topical Film
Company *cam* Bassill, F A (?)

■ British Mk IV Female tank and a 6-inch
  howitzer battery, probably Amiens area,
  Western Front, late March 1918.

One continuous shot, without a cut, of a Mk
IV Female tank, number 2558, moving away
across a narrow gauge railway line, up a
grassy incline and into the distance across
a flat grassy plain. It is accompanied by a
handful of soldiers who lift a wire for the
tank to pass underneath without cutting it.
Two men sit on the tank and an officer rides
beside it on a white horse. Probably
considerably behind the lines.
II. 6-inch 26cwt howitzers firing in the yard
of a farmhouse, while in the vehicle park
their gunners fuse the shells and Royal
Engineer wagons gallop forward past the
battery. With each firing the vibration
shakes slates from the farmhouse roof. An
18-pounder battery is brought forward past
the scene.

Notes
Title: this is taken from the shotsheet.
[shotsheet available]
catalogued SDB: 7/1982

IWM 179 · GB, (prod) 1918
GERMAN OFFENSIVE 2

b/w · 1 reel · 379' (7 mins) · silent
intertitles: none

sp Ministry of Information *pr* Topical Film
Company *cam* Bassill, F A (?)

■ British Whippet tanks and some Infantry
  moving towards the battlefield, probably
  the Bray-Serre Road, Western Front, 26
  March 1918.

Three Medium A Whippet tanks of 3rd

Battalion, Tank Corps (numbers A262, A277 and A212), moving across an open field, probably not far from the road between Bray and Serre. A second scene shows the tanks moving on the road itself, being passed by an Army car and passing a light cart. The Whippets have difficulty turning off the road down a slight bank between quite widely-spaced trees, having to back and turn to get through the gap. The three continue quite rapidly over open country. On the same road a company of Highland troops, possibly Argyll and Sutherland Highlanders, resting by the roadside, eating bread and jam. There are several 'old soldier' types among them. A final scene shows British soldiers escorting German prisoners, some with bicycles, down the same road.

Notes
Title: this is taken from the shotsheet.
[shotsheet available]
catalogued SDB: 7/1982

IWM 180 · GB, (prod) 1918
GERMAN OFFENSIVE 3

b/w · 1 reel · 556' (10 mins) · silent
intertitles: none

sp Ministry of Information *pr* Topical Film Company *cam* McDowell, J B (?)

■ British troops, predominantly Cavalry, Amiens area, Western Front, late March or early April 1918.

Royal Engineers start to dig a trench in open country. Men of the Machine Gun Corps (?) rest by the roadside. More soldiers dig trenches in the open. A column of horsemen, possibly 1st Cavalry Division, on patrol quite close to the front, pass others waiting dismounted in a leafless wood. A soldier asleep in a foxhole while others nearby rest and eat (they have mud covers on their rifles – probably a safe area). Infantry lining a scrape trench are approached by a group of prisoners (?) while in the background horsemen gallop past. Soldiers holding a more substantial trench. A group of Cavalry officers holds an open-air briefing while German prisoners rest nearby. A Cavalryman escorts three prisoners who are on foot. More Cavalry trot along a road. At a dressing station some wounded, including two French soldiers, are given tea (?). A smashed 18-pounder with its limber overturned on the roadside and the dead bodies of its horses and crew

beside it. In a railway siding two French and one British soldier inspect a burnt-out ammunition train hit by a German bomb. Refugees from Amiens, some quite smartly dressed, wheeling handcarts and loading furniture onto a lorry.

Notes
Title: this is taken from the shotsheet.
[shotsheet available]
catalogued SDB: 7/1982

IWM 181 · GB, (prod) 1918
GERMAN OFFENSIVE 4

b/w · 1 reel · 322' (5 mins) · silent
intertitles: none

sp Ministry of Information *pr* Topical Film Company *cam* McDowell, J B (?)

■ British and French forces on the Amiens Front behind Villers-Bretonneux, Western Front, probably 1-3 April 1918.

Filmed on 3 April, the remaining evidence of the famous charge of Lord Strathcona's Horse of the Canadian Cavalry Brigade, 3rd Cavalry Division, at Moreuil Ridge on 30 March. The dismounted survivors of the regiment (?) come out of line in marching column, wearing greatcoats, caps and helmets (one wears a balmoral). Their horses are led to safety by the 'number 3s' of each group. The dead horses left behind in the charge are still in position. A mixed battalion, possibly pioneers, a day or so earlier, gets up from resting by a tree line and walks uphill into a leafless wood. A few soldiers dig a trench-line in open country. The pioneers emerge from the trees into open country again (possibly near Corbie). Staged meeting between French, probably 29th Division, and British, probably 18th Division, beside their gun limbers. A street damaged by shell fire, with a dead horse and wrecked cart in it and a British cyclist moving past, possibly Villers-Bretonneux.

Notes
Title: this is taken from the shotsheet.
[J E B Seely, *Adventure*, Heinemann (1920)]
[John Toland, *No Man's Land: the Story of 1918*, Eyre Methuen (1980)]
[shotsheet available]
catalogued SDB: 7/1982

IWM 182 · GB, (prod) 1918
GERMAN OFFENSIVE 5

b/w · 1 reel · 253' (5 mins) · silent
intertitles: none

sp Ministry of Information pr Topical Film
Company cam Bassill, F A

- British troops in the Arras area, behind
  the lines, Western Front, 30 March 1918.

A very brief scene of British soldiers and
French civilians walking along a street,
possibly Arras. A Mk IV Female tank, with
two soldiers riding on it, moving away
across a field. A Highland battalion,
probably 1/14th (London Scottish) Battalion,
the London Regiment, digging a reserve
trench in an open field. Two 13-pounder
anti-aircraft guns on rail mountings firing. A
marching column in shrapnel helmets and
battle order, probably 56th (1st London)
Division retiring out of the line at Durham
Camp, Mont-St-Eloi, with a transport column
of lorries passing the other way. A rear view
of a 6-inch Mk VII howitzer being fired
under scrim netting. A column of lorries and
two buses carrying troops down a road.

Notes
Title: this is taken from the shotsheet.
[shotsheet available]
catalogued SDB: 7/1982

IWM 183 · GB, (prod) 1918
GERMAN OFFENSIVE 6

b/w · 1 reel · 621' (10 mins) · silent
intertitles: none

sp Ministry of Information pr Topical Film
Company cam McDowell, J B

- British and French troops in and around
  Amiens, Western Front, ca. 5-7 April
  1918.

British and French troops camped in
woods, with one man being shaved,
probably close to Boves. French soldiers
drive two abandoned cows in past British
18-pounders. A French armoured car of II
Cavalry Corps, (?) a special model based
on the White chassis, halted while two
British soldiers talk to the occupants.
German shells bursting over open country
with a wood in the background, near
Moreuil. A mule cart on the road with all the
mules dead. A panorama of Amiens taken
from the north-east across the river,
showing the cathedral. A close-up pan, top
to bottom, of the cathedral itself. British and
French soldiers camped in woodland with a

cow and a few horses, the men sleeping or
resting, probably 2/10th Battalion, the
London Regiment, of 58th Division with
soldiers of the French 29th Division (?). A
camouflaged 6-inch howitzer battery firing
from a tree line out across a plain. A French
75mm battery firing in the open, showing
the firing mechanism of one gun, probably
near Domart. A French naval gun (?) on a
railway carriage mount firing, near Boves.

Notes
Title: this is taken from the shotsheet.
Intertitles: the film has some manuscript
flashframes.
[shotsheet available]
catalogued SDB: 7/1982

IWM 184 · GB, (prod) 1918
GERMAN OFFENSIVE 7

b/w · 1 reel · 522' (9 mins) · silent
intertitles: none

sp Ministry of Information pr Topical Film
Company cam Bassill, F A

- British forces in the Béthune area,
  including gas casualties, Western Front,
  9-10 April 1918.

A head-on shot of a Mk IV Female tank 146
HMLS 'Inviolate' of 9th Battalion, Tank
Corps, equipped with unditching
equipment, crossing over a bank, followed
by three other Mk IV tanks, all being driven
with doors and hatches open. Men of the
Chinese Labour Corps at a railway goods
siding unload stores from goods wagons
onto flatcars of a light railway. British troops
help them unload 9.2-inch shells. A light US
Baldwin 4-60 PT locomotive passes pulling
truckloads of troops. A long column of
German prisoners marches down a road
with a British escort. Refugees pulling carts
(without horses) followed by other refugees
going up one side of a street, probably
Béthune, while a British marching column,
including a limbered 60-pounder battery
and some wagons goes in the other
direction. Some refugees ride in army
wagons, others push carts or lead donkeys.
A posed shot of a German prisoner,
standing with a blanket over his shoulders
between a soldier of the Portuguese 2nd
Division and one of 51st (Highland)
Division. A line of walking wounded of 51st
and 55th Divisions, mostly temporarily
blinded by gas, others with flesh wounds,
smiling at the camera. The gassed men
move off in the classic posture of the blind,

each with his hand on the shoulder of the man in front.

Notes
Title: this is taken from the shotsheet.
[shotsheet available]
catalogued SDB: 7/1982

IWM 185 · GB, (prod) 1918
GERMAN OFFENSIVE 8

b/w · 1 reel · 553' (9 mins) · silent
intertitles: none

sp Ministry of Information *pr* Topical Film Company *cam* McDowell, J B

■ British forces in the Villers-Bretonneux and Béthune areas, Western Front, about 8-10 April 1918.

I. Open country, very flat with a few low woods and shells on the horizon moving closer. In the foreground a Red Cross ambulance moves down a road – probably Villers-Bretonneux. Small parties of British troops move into the village itself, which has suffered some shell damage. They examine a child's stuffed toy. Two soldiers build a roadblock of wood and wire cheveux-de-frise. Other soldiers of 58th (2/1st London) Division rest by the side of a road, then move forward to enter a dug-out in a railway embankment – probably close to Amiens.
II. Refugees at Béthune being shepherded by British troops across the La Bassée Canal bridge. A column of men from 4th or 5th Battalion, the Kings Own Royal Lancasters, of 55th Division, march across the bridge in full kit, move in single file down the road and into the beginnings of a trench system. Four soldiers, one of them Scottish, watch while a limbered-up 18-pounder battery moves down the road. A small group of refugees with prams and handcarts comes into the village, and a boy asks directions of a British corporal. An 18-pounder battery moves along parallel to the canal so that its reflection shows in the water, and finally crosses over the bridge.

Notes
Title: this is taken from the shotsheet.
Summary: shot on about 8-10 April, this film shows McDowell's move from Third to First Army front as the offensive spreads northward.
Remarks: the two scenes of the 18-pounder batteries in Béthune are extremely good and attractive examples of their type. The

shells 'walking' towards the camera are also most impressive, if rather too far away to be frightening.
[shotsheet available]
catalogued SDB: 7/1982

IWM 186 · GB, (prod) 1918
GERMAN OFFENSIVE 9

b/w · 1 reel · 771' (12 mins) · silent
intertitles: none

sp Ministry of Information *pr* Topical Film Company *cam* Bassill, F A

■ British 51st and 55th Divisions in the Béthune area, Western Front, about 10-14 April 1918.

I. Soldiers haul a ditched Thornycroft lorry out into the roadside by using sheerlegs. They are passed by refugees in carts and on foot as they work. Soldiers resting and eating in an open field. Two exhausted soldiers resting with a dog. Two more soldiers posed with a fox terrier on a lead, and one of them posed again holding the terrier while eating. Gunners build up a small dump of 18-pounder shells by the roadside, limbers draw up and they refill them. Refugees, filmed through the open doors of railway goods wagons, clamber inside. Some British soldiers carry a few of the refugees, old ladies unable to walk, in their chairs to the train, which then leaves. A lancer regiment, probably of 1st Cavalry Division, rides down a tree-lined road.
II. Two soldiers of 51st (Highland) Division escort a colleague with a thigh wound across the La Bassée Canal bridge. A sergeant inspects the leg of the wounded soldier who is wearing a kilt. Two officers of 55th Division pose with a baby goat. A battery of French armoured cars (the White chassis type) are parked on a verge to allow British troops to move past. A column of French lancers, probably from II Cavalry Corps, on the road.
III. A squadron of DH4 light bombers lined up at their aerodrome, with 112-pound bombs being fitted under the wings of some and 16-pound bombs under the wings of others. Possibly they are 27 Squadron RFC in early 1918.

Notes
Title: this is taken from the shotsheet.
[shotsheet available]
catalogued SDB: 7/1982

IWM 187 · GB, (prod) 1918
GERMAN OFFENSIVE 10

b/w · 1 reel · 676' (11 mins) · silent
intertitles: none

sp Ministry of Information *pr* Topical Film
Company *cam* McDowell, J B

- British troops on the La Bassée Canal
  and the Mont des Cats area, and the
  Funeral of Manfred von Richthofen ('the
  Red Baron') at Bertangles, all Western
  Front, mid-April 1918.

I. The La Bassée Canal sector. British
troops commencing barbed wire defences
in open country on 17 April. On the same
day troops in Béthune (?) dig a trench-line,
with shells bursting over the houses. Two
stretcher-bearers carry a wounded man out
of the garden of a house and put him in an
ambulance (they are probably 51st
Division). Soldiers of the Portuguese 2nd
Division wheel their bicycles through
Béthune on 20 April while men of 51st
Division line the route.
II. Two small groups of British soldiers rest
in foxholes in the Mont des Cats area,
perhaps 2nd Battalion, Argyll and
Sutherland Highlanders of 33rd Division.
Shells fall on Mont des Cats (?) filmed out-
of-focus from the far side of barbed wire
entanglements on 22 April.
III. The funeral of Baron Manfred von
Richthofen at Bertangles on 22 April. Two
ground crew of the RAF display the
wreckage of his Fokker triplane and its two
Spandau machineguns. Members of six
RAF squadrons carry wreaths along the
road to the cemetery. The burial party
consists of men of 3 Squadron, Australian
Flying Corps. The party takes the coffin and
places it covered with flowers on a lorry.
The cortège moves off at a slow march. At
the burial place itself a chaplain in
vestments conducts the service while the
burial party stands with reversed arms. The
party then fires three volleys over the grave.

Notes
Title: this is taken from the shotsheet.
[John Toland, *No Man's Land: the Story of
1918*, Eyre Methuen (1980)]
[P J Carisella and James W Ryan, *Who
Killed the Red Baron?*, Fawcett (1969)]
[shotsheet available]
catalogued SDB: 7/1982

IWM 188 · GB, (prod) 1918
GERMAN OFFENSIVE 11

b/w · 1 reel · 639' (11 mins) · silent
intertitles: none

sp Ministry of Information *pr* Topical Film
Company *cam* Bassill, F A

- British and French forces in the Mont des
  Cats-Cassel area, Second Army sector,
  Western Front, about 21 April 1918.

Soldiers, possibly 16th Battalion, King's
Royal Rifle Corps, 33rd Division, in the later
stages of digging a trench. Some of the
men use long poles to fix barbed wire
entanglements across a small stream. Three
light railway trains carrying soldiers on
flatcars pass along an embankment. A
company of troops, possibly Royal Irish
Rifles, march in column through a damaged
village. A damaged farm building marked
"Cinema Nightly", used as a behind-the-lines
cinema for troops until the German
offensive. Prime Minister Clemenceau says
farewell to the officers of the British 33rd
Division and its commander Major-General
Pinney at Cassel on 21 April, gets into his
car and drives off. Two battalions of the
same division, possibly 1st Battalion, the
Middlesex Regiment 2nd Battalion, the
Argyll and Sutherland Highlanders, march
past Clemenceau's car. Nearer to Mont des
Cats, British troops rest at the roadside by a
village while French military wagons pass.
British soldiers marching parallel to a light
railway track. French lancers trotting along
a road. Other lancers leading their horses
(note that in the French Army one mounted
horsesoldier remains out of every three
men). French Cavalry, possibly 2nd Light
Cavalry Division, in marching column along
a road.

Notes
Title: this is taken from the shotsheet.
[shotsheet available]
catalogued SDB: 7/1982

IWM 189 · GB, (prod) 1918
GERMAN OFFENSIVE 12

b/w · 1 reel · 434' (7 mins) · silent
intertitles: none

sp Ministry of Information *pr* Topical Film
Company *cam* Bassill, F A

- British forces in the Amiens area, and
  possibly further north, Western Front, in
  the last week of April 1918.

A Scottish cyclist battalion on a wooded

road. A French 75mm field gun limbered up but stuck in a ditch, with French and British troops trying to free it, probably Arras area. A battalion on the march down a road – possibly not British. Shell damage to a street being inspected by British and French troops, probably Amiens. The shell damage to Amiens Cathedral, both inside and outside. A battalion of the Suffolk Regiment resting in a square in the city. A French Infantry band carrying their instruments on the march.

Notes
Title: this is taken from the shotsheet.
Remarks: compared to the remainder of the series, this is an uninteresting film.
[shotsheet available]
catalogued SDB: 7/1982

IWM 190 · GB, (prod) 1918
GERMAN OFFENSIVE 13

b/w · 1 reel · 919' (16 mins) · silent
intertitles: none

sp Ministry of Information *pr* Topical Film Company *cam* McDowell, J B

I. British troops in and near Amiens in the Somme area, Western Front, in the first days of May 1918. The village of Ebblinghem under German shell fire, the shells 'walking' towards the target over open fields. French soldiers marching through a crossroads on the outskirts of Amiens watched by idle British troops. They are followed by a British battalion also on the march. Damage to the law courts at Béthune and the St-Roche station at Amiens. A cage of live canaries is taken from the wreckage of a building by British soldiers. Amiens town hall in use as a temporary British headquarters. The interior of Amiens Cathedral with the sun shining through a hole in the roof. A pan over the town, including the cathedral.
II. A British monthly Army Commanders' Conference, possibly at Amiens, Western Front, June 1918. The assembled Army Commanders leave the Town Commandant's headquarters and pose for the camera. They are, left to right: General Sir Henry Rawlinson (Fourth Army), General Sir Julian Byng (Third Army), Field Marshal Sir Douglas Haig (GOC-in-C), General Sir Henry Horne (First Army), Major-General Sir Herbert Lawrence (Chief-of-Staff), General Sir William Birdwood (Fifth Army). (General Sir Herbert Plumer of Second Army is not in sight.)

Notes
Title: this is taken from the shotsheet.
Date: the presence of Birdwood means that the Army Commanders' Conference cannot be earlier than June 1918. The absence of Plumer, whose Army was heavily engaged in that month, makes it the most likely date.
[shotsheet available]
catalogued SDB: 7/1982

IWM 191 · GB, 11/8/1916
the BATTLE OF THE SOMME

b/w · 5 reels · 4694' (79 mins) · silent
intertitles: English

sp War Office *pr* British Topical Committee for War Films *prod* Jury, William F *ed* Urban, C A and Malins, Geoffrey H *cam* Malins, Geoffrey H; and McDowell, J B

■ British forces, chiefly 7th and 29th Divisions, on the first day of the Somme offensive, Western Front, 1 July 1916.

The 'big battle' structure of the film opens with the preparatory bombardment for the days before the attack, the Infantry marching to their final positions, the attack itself, the casualties, prisoners and consolidation of the next few days as the attacking troops are withdrawn for rest. The bombardment, shown in the opening reels, is by a variety of guns from a giant 15-inch howitzer to trench mortars. The attack by 29th Division at Beaumont Hamel is shown, including the explosion of a mine under Hawthorn Redoubt. The remainder of the film shows the British and German wounded being treated at the Minden Post dressing station in 7th Division sector and the consolidation of captured German positions at Fricourt and Mametz. The British soldiers come out of the line to rest, and they and their German prisoners retire to the rear.

Notes
Shotsheet: a detailed shotsheet and analysis of the film has been published to accompany video distribution of this film (1993).
Remarks: the classic First World War film in every sense, widely used for stockshots even today. It established the basic structure of the 'big battle' film, which was to continue for a further two productions until the spring of 1917. The only British official film to have a major impact on the perception of the war, both at the time and in historical terms. Also the only official film

of the war with a claim to be regarded as great art in its own right. The unprecedented and unexpected public success of this film established cinema as a major factor in British propaganda for the remainder of the war.

[Geoffrey H Malins, *How I Filmed the War*, Herbert Jenkins (1920)]
[Martin Middlebrook, *The First Day on the Somme*, Allen Lane (1971)]
[Rachael Low, *The History of the British Film 1914-1918*, Allen and Unwin (1950)]
[Kevin Brownlow, *The War, the West and the Wilderness*, Secker and Warburg (1979)]
[S D Badsey, "Battle of the Somme: British War Propaganda", *Historical Journal of Film, Radio and Television* 3: 2 (1983): 109-115]
[Roger Smither, "'A Wonderful Idea of the Fighting': the question of fakes in *The Battle of the Somme*", *Historical Journal of Film, Radio and Television* 13: 2 (1993): 149-168]
[dopesheet available]
[shotsheet available]
catalogued SDB: 7/1982

IWM 192 · GB, 10/1916
the KING VISITS HIS ARMIES IN THE GREAT ADVANCE

b/w · 2 reels · 2497' (40 mins) · silent
intertitles: English

sp War Office *pr* British Topical Committee for War Films *prod* Jury, William F *cam* Malins, Geoffrey H; (and McDowell, J B ?)

■ King George V's visit to the British forces on the Western Front, 8-15 August 1916.

The King arrives at Calais and meets various military and civilian dignitaries. He is taken to General Haig's château at Beauquesne where, with Haig and the Prince of Wales, he meets President Poincaré and Generals Joffre and Foch (Lloyd George is seen arriving also – see **Notes** below). The King visits troops of II ANZAC Corps, a Casualty Clearing Station in Second Army area, a church at Cassel and the Canadian Corps area. At La Panne he meets with the Prince of Wales and the Belgian royal family to present decorations to Belgian soldiers. He tours parts of Second Army area and the Somme battlefield, escorted by General Sir Henry Rawlinson, while the battle is in progress. The King then returns to Calais and crosses the English Channel in safety.

Notes
Summary: see also **IWM 198** and **IWM 192**

sections. Although Lloyd George is shown on the film arriving with the others, he did not in fact attend the meeting and was not in France at the time.
Shotsheet: a detailed shotsheet and analysis of the film has been prepared and is held on file in the Department of Film.
[Geoffrey H Malins, *How I Filmed the War*, Herbert Jenkins (1920)]
[Robert Blake, *The Private Papers of Douglas Haig 1914-1919*, Eyre and Spottiswoode (1952)]
[shotsheet available]
catalogued SDB: 7/1982

IWM 193a · GB, 26/12/1917
WAR OFFICE OFFICIAL TOPICAL BUDGET 331-1 (Spanish version)

b/w · 1 reel · 88' (2 mins) · silent
intertitles: Spanish

sp War Office Cinema Committee *pr* Topical Film Company

■ Four members of a Chinese military mission to British GHQ are shown how to use their gas masks before setting off on a tour of the Western Front, November 1917.

[shotsheet available]
catalogued SDB: 6/1983

IWM 193b · GB, 29/12/1917
WAR OFFICE OFFICIAL TOPICAL BUDGET 331-2 (Spanish version)

b/w · 1 reel · 118' (2 mins) · silent
intertitles: Spanish

sp War Office Cinema Committee *pr* Topical Film Company

I. The Lord Mayor of London holding a Christmas raffle for children at Harrods store, London, December 1917.
II. A volunteer battalion of the Bedfordshire Regiment marching past, probably at Bedford, December 1917.

Notes
Summary: compare with **IWM 174** *Inspection of Volunteer Regiments at Bedford, March 1918, by Field Marshal Viscount French* for the Bedford item.
[shotsheet available]
catalogued SDB: 6/1983

IWM 193c · GB, 2/1/1918
**WAR OFFICE OFFICIAL TOPICAL
BUDGET 332-1 (Spanish version)**

b/w · 1 reel · 189' (3 mins) · silent
intertitles: Spanish

sp War Office Cinema Committee *pr* Topical
Film Company

I. A French soldier silhouetted against the
sunset with palm trees, and a French
battalion marching into the outskirts of
Jerusalem, Palestine, December 1917.
II. Fund raising for War Bonds, Trafalgar
Square, London, November and December
1917.
Cardinal Bernard Vaughan is first shown on
4 December, then Sir Arthur Yapp on 29
November, speaking from the top of the
'tank bank' in Trafalgar Square, exhorting
people to buy War Bonds.

Notes
Summary: see also **IWM 508-39** for the
French item.
[shotsheet available]
catalogued SDB: 6/1983

IWM 193d · GB, 5/1/1918
**WAR OFFICE OFFICIAL TOPICAL
BUDGET 332-2 (Spanish version)**

b/w · 1 reel · 291' (5 mins) · silent
intertitles: Spanish

sp War Office Cinema Committee *pr* Topical
Film Company

I. Mrs C S Peel, Director of the Women's
Section of the Ministry of Food, seen
walking down a staircase into the Ministry
gardens with two assistants, London, 1918.
II. The Lord Mayor of London entertains
convalescent soldiers at the Guildhall,
London, January 1918. The soldiers enter
the Guildhall, followed by the Lord Mayor,
who leaves his coach. Some of the soldiers
improvise a Highland fling for the camera.
III. British soldiers of 41st Division (?) help
Italian women draw water from a well, in a
village near the Piave River, Italy, early
1918.

Notes
Summary: see also **IWM 154** *British Troops
in Italy* for the Italian item.
[shotsheet available]
catalogued SDB: 6/1983

IWM 194 · GB, (prod) 1916
EASTER RISING, DUBLIN 1916

b/w · 1 reel · 848' (14 mins) · silent
intertitles: none

■ Aftermath of the Dublin Easter Rising,
Ireland, 1916.

O'Connell Street before the rising (black
segments block out part of the film).
Members of the Irish Volunteers in civilian
clothes with webbing pouches and rifles
drill and march past in the open. More of
the Irish Volunteers in their paramilitary
uniform (introduced in August 1914)
marching off in a parade. Two columns of
Irish Volunteers, filmed from a high window,
marching through a crowded Dublin square
in civilian clothes. The damage done to
Liberty Hall, the head office of the Irish
TGWU and headquarters of the rising.
O'Connell Bridge in the aftermath, with
damage to a number of buildings. British
soldiers halt outside the Customs House.
Other soldiers unload an ammunition
wagon outside Liberty Hall. The interior of a
hospital, probably Dublin Castle, showing
three wounded men in beds – all British
soldiers (?). Men of the Australian Division
(?) march through the crowded streets.
Three British soldiers set up a Vickers
machinegun by a sand-bagged barricade.
Another barricade made of overturned cars.
A pan out from the O'Connell monument to
show the damage done to the Post Office.
An improvised armoured car made from
railway boilers bolted onto a Guinness lorry.
A further pan over Liberty Hall and other
buildings in Liffey Street – masonry is pulled
away from burnt-out buildings for safety.
The film ends with a posed shot of Thomas
Clark with Miss O'Donovan Rossa.

Notes
Summary: see also the videotapes of the
relevant episode of the television series *The
Troubles*, held by the Department of Film,
and the accompanying book.
[shotsheet available]
catalogued SDB: 7/1982

IWM 195 · GB, (ca) 1917
**[SOUTH AFRICAN LABOUR
CONTINGENT AT SIDING] (allocated)**

b/w · 1 reel · 25' (1 min) · silent
intertitles: none

sp War Office Cinema Committee (?) *pr*
Topical Film Company

- Men of the South African Labour Contingent carrying boxes, some marked with the Red Cross, from a stationary goods train in a siding. They are overseen by a black sergeant and white officers. Probably Western Front 1916-18.

Notes
Summary: nothing can be discovered about this very short film, which is clearly only a fragment of a larger sequence.
[shotsheet available]
catalogued SDB: 7/1982

IWM 196 · GB, (prod) 1917
REVIEW OF NEW ZEALAND TROOPS BY SIR WALTER LONG

b/w · 1 reel · 963' (16 mins) · silent
intertitles: none

- New Zealand Division on the Western Front, March 1917.

This is the first film devoted to the New Zealand Division. It was taken on 8-15 March 1917. It opens with Major-General Sir Andrew Russell, the divisional commander, with Sir Walter Long, Secretary of State for the Colonies, reviewing the division on 9 March on the Armentières–Bailleul Road. They are accompanied by Lieutenant-General Sir Alexander Godley, GOC II ANZAC Corps. Units of 2 NZ Infantry Brigade march past led by their band. This is followed by an inspection of the NZ Pioneer Battalion, where Long is escorted by the second in command and senior Maori officer in this unit, Major Peter Buck. After this the film becomes increasingly difficult to interpret (see **Notes**). Trench scenes show a single soldier firing a Lewis machinegun over a parapet, and the firing of rifle grenades. A view of no man's land. A group of unarmed soldiers walk through a deep muddy pool in a shell crater. A party of soldiers coming out of the line is shown walking down a duckboard footpath in single file with snow on the ground. 15th Battery NZ Field Artillery of 18-pounder field guns shown firing from concealed positions in a village, matched with bursting shells throwing up mud in no man's land. The film ends with scenes from a rugby match between the NZ Divisional 'All Blacks' and 38th (Welsh) Division, with a crowd, including several officers watching. The match was played on 15 March 1917, the New Zealanders winning 10-3.

Notes
Title: this is taken from the negative.
Intertitles: scratched on negative.
Production: in 1916 the NZ authorities negotiated for British official cameramen to film New Zealand military activities. This arrangement proved unsatisfactory and New Zealand subsequently made its own arrangements – see **IWM 157**. This is the one film specifically taken by a British official cameraman of the New Zealand Division.
Summary: Russell was conscious that this was the first film the New Zealand public would see of their division in France, and his staff detailed a comprehensive programme for the cameraman showing all aspects of trench life. Much of this programme is included in the resulting film – hence the scenes of mud etc.
Authority: additional detail from Christopher Pugsley, 12/1993.
[shotsheet available]
catalogued SDB: 7/1982

IWM 197 · GB, 7/1917
the CAPTURE OF MESSINES

b/w · 2 reels · 1766' (29 mins) · silent
intertitles: English

sp War Office Cinema Committee *pr* Topical Film Company *prod* Jury, William F
cam Raymond, H C

I. Sports and horse-show of 15th (Scottish) Division, which took no part in the Battle of Messines, at Liencourt, Western Front, 13 May 1917.
II. British preparations and conduct of the Battle of Messines, Western Front, 5-12 June 1917. Men of Australian 3rd Division, probably 4th Brigade, 13th (New South Wales) Battalion, inspecting from an observation tower the scale model of the battlefield laid out near Scherpenberg, about the size of a croquet lawn. The preliminary bombardment for the battle on 5 June filmed from the Australian positions across the Douve River valley. A gunner FOO on the edge of Ploegsteert Wood using a field telephone. The dirt road from Ploegsteert to Messines on 11 June, with shells bursting on the ridge in the distance. A few walking wounded, stretcher-bearers and a water cart come up the track away from the battle and ammunition mules are led towards it. A few men of 25th Division (?) rest in the rear areas in mud-holes. The crater left by one of the nineteen large mines blown in the attack, filmed from

above and the bottom of the crater on 11 June. The ruins of Messines itself, taken by the New Zealand Division, with trenches still being consolidated. The ruins of Wytschaete village, with the wood on its left, probably filmed on 8 June. A battalion of 16th (Irish) Division marches back to its rest area at Locre where it is greeted by its Left Out of Battle (LOOB) contingent. Some of the men wash in a nearby duck pond. Two more marching columns led by their bands return to their rest areas, probably 7th or 8th Battalion, Royal Inniskilling Fusiliers, and 6th Royal Irish Rifles. A posed shot of Major-General O S W Nugent with his staff of 36th (Ulster) Division, followed by posed groups of officers and men of the division. A group of soldiers from 8th or 9th Battalion, Royal Dublin Fusiliers clowning for the camera with captured trophies in a rest area near Dranoutre. Men of 7th Battalion, the Royal Irish Rifles who served with Major William Redmond MP in their rest area. Redmond's grave at the hospice in Locre tended by two nuns.

Notes
Remarks: the only attempt by the WOCC to return to the 'big battle' format of films, on a far smaller scale than before, after dropping it in spring 1917. In its way this is an attractive and intelligent film, although it does not in itself provide a very clear idea of the course of the battle.
[Lyn MacDonald, *They Called It Passchendaele*, Michael Joseph (1978)]
[shotsheet available]
catalogued SDB: 7/1982

IWM 198 · GB, 3/9/1917
the ROYAL VISIT TO THE BATTLEFIELDS OF FRANCE, JULY 1917

b/w · 4 reels · 3689' (62 mins) · silent
intertitles: English

sp War Office Cinema Committee *pr* Topical Film Company *prod* Jury, William F
cam McDowell, J B; and Raymond, H C

■ Visit of King George V and Queen Mary to France 3-14 July 1917.

The King and Queen arrive in Calais to start the visit. The King inspects war trophies at Bailleul with General Sir Herbert Plumer, then goes on to watch a tank demonstration and talk with a group of French officers. The Queen watches a flame-thrower demonstration at Helfaut. The King and Prince of Wales meet the King of

Belgium at La Panne then go on to inspect aircraft at Bray Dunes with General Sir Henry Rawlinson. The Queen inspects aircraft with Brigadier-General Sir Hugh Trenchard, commander of the RFC, and goes on to meet briefly with Sir Douglas Haig, and later to visit an American hospital. The King visits an RNAS base. The Queen visits a Casualty Clearing Station and the Tank Corps central stores and tank park. The King and Prince arrive at Tramecourt Château and are joined by the Queen, together with the King and Queen of Belgium. On the following day they go their various ways, the King to St-Sixte Monastery (used as a CCS) and on to an aerodrome and the Gas School at Helfaut. Haig meets with the King, the Queen, and President and Madame Poincaré at Abbeville. The Queen and Prince visit the Asiatic Petrol Company factories near Rouen. The King tours Vimy Ridge and the Somme battlefield. At Albert the King knights two Corps commanders, General Currie of the Canadian Corps and General Fanshawe, and decorates a number of French officers. The King goes on to visit Australian 5th Division headquarters. The Queen visits the South African hospital at Abbeville. The King continues his tour of Vimy Ridge and the Somme area. Finally, the King, Queen and Prince call in at the Duchess of Sutherland's hospital prior to leaving for Britain from Calais.

Notes
Shotsheet: a detailed shotsheet and analysis of the film has been prepared and is held on file in the Department of Film.
Remarks: the film is less tedious than the simple list of Royal visits might suggest, and contains a few good and interesting moments, but these only serve to highlight a vast bulk of routine.
[*The Times*, 16 July 1917: 7A, 7B]
[B H Liddell Hart, *The Tanks – the History of the Royal Tank Regiment ...*, Vol I, Cassell (1959): 108-109]
[shotsheet available]
catalogued SDB: 7/1982

IWM 199 · GB, (?) 1917
SECOND ARMY BOMBING SCHOOL

b/w · 1 reel · 512' (9 mins) · silent
intertitles: none

sp War Office Cinema Committee (?)
pr Topical Film Company (?)

■ Training in minor tactics, 2nd Army
  Bombing School, Western Front,
  probably early 1917.

A series of explosions in an open field (no
indication of scale). British gunners loading
and firing a 9.45-inch 'flying pig' mortar,
repeated several times and filmed from
various angles and distances to show the
variations in explosions. Helmeted British
(or Australian ?) soldiers coming over the
top from a training trench moving in single
file. Others, some in slouch hats, stay in the
trenches. Several more stock explosions
providing a barrage. The advancing troops
arrive at the ground, cratered from the
barrage, and start to dig in and wire the
position.

Notes
Title: this is taken from the shotsheet.
Production: this is almost certainly British
but may be Australian official film.
[shotsheet available]
catalogued SDB: 7/1982

IWM 200 · GB, (?) 1918
AERO ENGINES

b/w · 1 reel · 1275' (21 mins) · silent
intertitles: English

sp Ministry of Information (?) *pr* Topical Film
Company

■ Four subjects: all on production of
  aircraft or aero engines, principally by
  women workers on the British Home
  Front, 1918.

I. "Aero Engines" – women assembly
workers operating various kinds of precision
lathes and equipment in the manufacture of
engines, ending with men testing a rotary
engine, possibly a Le Rhône made under
licence, on a test bed.
II. "Aeroplanes – Flying Scouts" – women
making the basic frame fuselage for
Sopwith Camels at a Huntingdon workshop
in early 1918, using large frame formers,
then covering the frames with fabric, doping
and painting.
III. "Engines" – a badly undercranked film of
women performing precision work on
specialist machines, including the use of
high-quality optical equipment, and "lady
draughtsmen" under training. IV "Bombing
Planes" – filmed at the Handley Page works
in Cricklewood, this shows women workers
assembling the parts and fabric for a
Handley Page 0/400 long range bomber,

ending with a stockshot of the finished
aircraft outside a hangar.

Notes
Summary: see also **IWM 167** *Huntingdon
Workshop* and notes on the shotsheet to
this film.
[shotsheet available]
catalogued SDB: 7/1982

IWM 201 · GB, (?) 1917
ROYAL VISIT TO DEAL

b/w · 1 reel · 368' (6 mins) · silent
intertitles: English

sp Department of Information (?)

■ King George V inspects Royal Marine
  cadets and officers of the Dover Patrol at
  Deal, 1917 (?).

I. The King, in Field Marshal's uniform, with
a number of Royal Marine officers also in
khaki, inspects the cadets. Older cadets are
drawn up on parade in blues for a drill
demonstration. Another group does
physical training. Young cadets march past
the King and establishment staff at a table
covered with Union Flags (one upside
down). A posed group of the King with the
staff. Cadets in blues on an assault training
course.
II. The King presents medals to three
officers of the Dover Patrol (not identified).

Notes
Summary: very little can be discovered out
about this film. It is probably British official
material taken by a private company. The
visit does not appear in any Court circular
for the war years and may have been
unofficial.
[shotsheet available]
catalogued SDB: 11/1982

IWM 202-01 · GB, 17/1/1916
**WITH THE INDIAN TROOPS AT THE
FRONT PART I**
OFFICIAL PICTURES OF THE BRITISH
ARMY IN FRANCE – FIRST SERIES (series)

b/w · 1 reel · 522' (9 mins) · silent
intertitles: English

sp War Office *pr* British Topical Committee
for War Films *cam* Malins, Geoffrey H or
Tong, Edward G (?)

- Units of the former Indian Corps, just
  after its disbandment, in rear areas
  before their departure from France,
  November and December 1915.

The officers' mess, a building away from the
battle zone, of 58th (Vaughan's) Rifles, with
officers entering and leaving. Pan over a
group of soldiers from 57th (Wilde's) Rifles.
An outdoor "durbar" (orderly room) for 47th
Sikhs – some officers sit while three new
soldiers are paraded before them and
perform the ritual of offering the blades of
their bayonets for each officer in turn to
touch as a symbol of loyalty. An open-air
workshop for the Sappers and Miners at
which they shape wood, making wooden
trench periscopes. Gurkhas sharpen their
kukris on a grindstone. A demonstration of
a "Khattak" or ritual sword dance. Sikhs in
formal wrestling bouts which others watch.
34th Sikh Pioneers dig shallow trenches
from start to completion with a sandbag
parapet and coiled wire in front. 57th
(Wilde's) Rifles machinegun section
demonstrates setting up its two Maxims in a
wood and then retiring with them. At a
"refilling point" on a muddy road British and
Indian soldiers collect food and fodder for
their horses. 4th Cavalry entrains its horses
and waits for the order to load its men.

Notes
Date: this film was the very first of the
Official Pictures of the British Army in France
and so represents the first British official film
record of any of the war zones released for
public viewing.
Cameraman: this was either Malins or Tong.
Summary: this film was subject to
censorship at GHQ France. The resulting
censored sections are now in **IWM 383**.
[shotsheet available]
catalogued SDB: 11/1982

IWM 202-02 · GB, 24/1/1916
**WITH THE INDIAN TROOPS AT THE
FRONT PART II**
OFFICIAL PICTURES OF THE BRITISH
ARMY IN FRANCE – FIRST SERIES (series)

b/w · 1 reel · 407' (7 mins) · silent
intertitles: English

sp War Office *pr* British Topical Committee
for War Films *cam* Malins, Geoffrey H or
Tong, Edward G (?)

- Units of the former Indian Corps, mainly
  7th (Meerut) Division, just after the
  Corps's disbandment, in rear areas

before their departure from France,
November and December 1915.

Lieutenant-Colonel G H Bell, with his
adjutant Lieutenant Gray, taking the salute
at the side of the road as his battalion, 69th
Punjab Infantry, marches past, 14
November. 58th (Vaughan's) Rifles
marching in column across a field. 1st
Battalion, Seaforth Highlanders with its
transport marching through a village in wet
weather. An Indian battalion of 7th Division
on the march in road column in wet
weather, followed by one of the division's
Gurkha battalions. 93rd Burma Infantry
resting by the roadside in the rain and wet.
Nearby, 1st Seaforths also relax, and three
bagpipers give an improvised performance,
at which one or two of the men begin
dancing. Also nearby, another of the
division's Indian battalions rests by a
stream.

Notes
Cameraman: this was either Malins or Tong.
Summary: this film was subject to
censorship at GHQ France. The resulting
censored sections are now in **IWM 383**.
[shotsheet available]
catalogued SDB: 11/1982

IWM 203 · GB, 31/1/1916
**the MAKING OF AN OFFICER : with the
Artists Rifles at the Front**
OFFICIAL PICTURES OF THE BRITISH
ARMY IN FRANCE – FIRST SERIES (series)

b/w · 1 reel · 543' (10 mins) · silent
intertitles: English

sp War Office *pr* British Topical Committee
for War Films *cam* Tong, E G

- British basic officer training in the Artists
  Rifles, St-Omer, Western Front,
  December 1915.

Drill and musketry instruction. On sentry
training British and French sentries together
stop a staff car to check the occupants. Out
in the country, the trainees cut brushwood
for hurdles. They learn how to make
bridges from tree trunks and rafts from gas
capes filled with straw. They repair trench
systems, and construct wire entanglements.
An officer teaches them the elements of
map reading. After a final address by the
commanding officer they leave the training
battalion in a bus of 16th AUX MT
Company. On arrival at an officer cadet
school they are instructed in using and

stripping the Vickers machinegun and throwing hand-grenades.

Notes
Production: the BTCFWF symbol appears on this film as a single negative flashframe. *Summary:* by this date the Artists Rifles, or 1/28th (County of London) Battalion of the London Regiment, enjoyed a unique status not as a fighting unit but as a holding battalion entirely for men undergoing officer training in France. This film was subject to censorship at GHQ France. The resulting censored sections are now in **IWM 383**. See also **IWM 414**.
[shotsheet available]
catalogued SDB: 11/1982

IWM 204 · GB, 7/2/1916
a MACHINE GUN SCHOOL AT THE FRONT
OFFICIAL PICTURES OF THE BRITISH ARMY IN FRANCE – FIRST SERIES (series)

b/w · 1 reel · 399' (8 mins) · silent
intertitles: English

sp War Office *pr* British Topical Committee for War Films *cam* Malins, Geoffrey H or Tong, Edward G (?)

■ British Army Machine Gun School in France, December 1915.

A posed group of the school staff. A training exercise: the men run forward to set up their Vickers machineguns under cover or in a prone position. One of the groups of trainees sets out with their machineguns over their shoulders. At the range, they go through weapons practice with the Lewis, Maxim and Vickers machineguns, including both firing and tabletop instruction. A line of Vickers machineguns fires at a range, with an instructor giving a demonstration (showing the target he is aiming at). The group returns from the ranges carrying the machineguns.

Notes
Cameraman: this was either Malins or Tong.
[shotsheet available]
catalogued SDB: 11/1982

IWM 205 · GB, 14/2/1916
WITH OUR TERRITORIALS AT THE FRONT
OFFICIAL PICTURES OF THE BRITISH ARMY IN FRANCE – FIRST SERIES (series)

b/w · 1 reel · 495' (9 mins) · silent
intertitles: English

sp War Office *pr* British Topical Committee for War Films *cam* Malins, Geoffrey H or Tong, Edward G (?)

■ Civil Service Rifles and Post Office Rifles of 47th (London) Division coming out of the line at Loos, and Number 1 Motor Ambulance Convoy concert party, Western Front, January 1916.

I. The two battalions, otherwise respectively 15th and 8th Battalions, the London Regiment, march in very muddy greatcoats and caps through a rear area village, followed by their Red Cross contingent. They are being relieved by "Welsh Territorials", probably 4th Battalion, Royal Welch Fusiliers, who march in the opposite direction along the road. The Loos Crassier (?) can be seen on the horizon. The two London Regiment battalions continue on their march and board a trooptrain (carriages rather than trucks) back to their billets. Arriving there, they relax and start to scrape the mud off their equipment. They play improvised football among themselves, with a few French soldiers joining in.
II. A small concert party of Number 1 Motor Ambulance Convoy entertains the rest of the convoy. It begins with an introduction by an officer leading into a joke conductor for the band and a comedy sketch involving a cowboy. In the middle of this a despatch rider on a motor-cycle arrives with an urgent message, the men rush to their ambulances and drive off (acted).

Notes
Cameraman: this was either Malins or Tong.
[shotsheet available]
catalogued SDB: 11/1982

IWM 206 · GB, 3/1916
YPRES – THE SHELL SHATTERED CITY OF FLANDERS [1916]
OFFICIAL PICTURES OF THE BRITISH ARMY IN FRANCE – SECOND SERIES (series)

b/w · 1 reel · 299' (5 mins) · silent
intertitles: English

sp War Office *pr* British Topical Committee for War Films *cam* Malins, Geoffrey H or Tong, Edward G (?)

■ Damage to the town of Ypres, Western Front, February 1916.

A panorama of the city. Views of the main square taken from the area of Hellfire Corner. The Cloth Hall, most of it still intact. Exterior and interior scenes of the cathedral, showing the west door and the fact that the organ has been destroyed. British soldiers pet two black and white puppies abandoned in the ruins.

Notes
Title: a longer version with the same title, now held as **IWM 344**, was released in 1918, showing scenes up to the end of the war.
Cameraman: this was either Malins or Tong.
[shotsheet available]
catalogued SDB: 11/1982

IWM 207 · GB, 13/3/1916
HRH THE PRINCE OF WALES WITH THE GUARDS IN THE FRONT LINE
OFFICIAL PICTURES OF THE BRITISH ARMY IN FRANCE – SECOND SERIES (series)

b/w · 1 reel · 594' (10 mins) · silent
intertitles: English

sp War Office *pr* British Topical Committee for War Films *cam* Malins, Geoffrey H or Tong, Edward G (?)

- Front line trenches of the Guards Division in front of Aubers Ridge, and the Prince of Wales with the Earl of Cavan, December 1915.

1st or 4th Battalion, Grenadier Guards, with 1st Battalion, Welsh Guards, in a street, probably Richebourg-St-Vaast, about to be led off by a pipe and drum band for a Christmas service, 25 December 1915. They enter the temporary church at La Gorge (?). After the service a number of officers emerge, including the divisional commander, Major-General the Earl of Cavan, and the Prince of Wales, who served on the divisional staff. About two days later, a party led by Cavan and the Prince visits a concealed battery headquarters (no sign of guns) in a leafless wood. Men of the Scots Guards grease their feet as a protection against trench foot and put on waders before going into the line. A battalion of Irish Guards gets up and pulls on its packs after resting by the roadside. Coldstream Guards in the second line work in the rain with shovels to clear a swamped "trench road". The second line trenches are all flooded to between knee and waist depth. An Irish Guards chaplain

makes his rounds. In a forward trench one of the Irish Guards uses a sniperscope to fire at the enemy. Another sniper with a head wound is taken away on a stretcher. A rear view of a Vickers machinegun team firing, then removing the gun. A platoon of 1st Battalion, the Welsh Guards, is checked by its officer for trench foot after coming out of the line.

Notes
Cameraman: this was either Malins or Tong.
[Geoffrey H Malins, *How I Filmed the War*, Herbert Jenkins (1920)]
[C Headlam, *The Guards Division in the Great War: 1915-1918*, Vol I, John Murray (1924)]
[*The Bioscope*, 17 February 1916: 674]
[shotsheet available]
catalogued SDB: 11/1982

IWM 208 · GB, 27/3/1916
LIVELINESS ON THE BRITISH FRONT
OFFICIAL PICTURES OF THE BRITISH ARMY IN FRANCE – THIRD SERIES (series)

b/w · 1 reel · 471' (8 mins) · silent
intertitles: English

sp War Office *pr* British Topical Committee for War Films *cam* Malins, Geoffrey H or Tong, Edward G (?)

- Guards Division in the line in front of Aubers Ridge, Western Front, early 1916.

A New Army battalion of Royal Welch Fusiliers, 38th (Welsh) Division (attached to the Guards Division for training) arrives by bus and gets out in the Guards area. Grenadier Guards in the rubble of Epinette Château filling sandbags and clearing debris. A wooden tramway on the La Bassée Road is used to move corrugated iron for strong points. At Rouge Croix crossroads, about two miles from the front, soldiers race across to avoid German shells. A first aid post in the front lines with canvas screens and a water pump. 2nd Battalion, Irish Guards, at "Southerland Avenue" (sic) trench with the flag they carried in the Battle of Loos. Men of the battalion work on the drainage system in the trenches: showing interest in the camera is Captain the Honourable H R L Alexander (the future Field Marshal Earl Alexander). Wooden crosses mark graves just by the second line trenches. A Grenadier sniper in a front line trench. Men of a tunnelling company enter and leave a trench minehead.

II. A final sequence, almost certainly a training exercise, of New Army troops throwing smoke grenades forward from their trenches and then rushing forward into the smoke (note the caps rather than helmets and lack of equipment).

Notes
Cameraman: this was either Malins or Tong.
Remarks: generally valuable, like all the early film of the war. The training exercise 'attack' at the end is quite attractive.
[shotsheet available]
catalogued SDB: 11/1982

IWM 209 · GB, 3/4/1916
VILLAGES IN FLANDERS, THE SCENES OF HARD FIGHTING, NOW HELD BY THE BRITISH
OFFICIAL PICTURES OF THE BRITISH ARMY IN FRANCE – THIRD SERIES (series)

b/w · 1 reel · 585' (10 mins) · silent
intertitles: English

sp War Office *pr* British Topical Committee for War Films *cam* Malins, Geoffrey H or Tong, Edward G (?)

■ Damage done to the villages and churches in the Ypres area, Western Front, by March 1916.

Scenes of damaged houses and churches, with British troops clearing away the rubble. The first church is late perpendicular with its roof missing, possibly Neuve Eglise. The second church, neo-Norman, has, in December 1915, its tower blown off and graveyard damaged. It is filmed again three months later "showing how completely it has been destroyed by German guns". A British soldier attends to a "blind" (unexploded) shell in a graveyard, possibly Voormezele. A 19th century Gothic church, showing both interior and exterior with roof missing, possibly Mont St-Eloi. More general damage to one village, including a destroyed brewery. A damaged railway station, possibly at Mont Kemmel. A church interior, possibly also Kemmel, showing damage to the Stations of the Cross. Finally, the grave of Captain F O Grenfell, 9th Lancers, who won one of the first Victoria Crosses of the war and was killed doing trench duty in May 1915.

Notes
Cameraman: this was either Malins or Tong.
Summary: most of the village identifications are very uncertain. As the film makes clear,

the appearance of a building could change completely in a few months' fighting.
[shotsheet available]
catalogued SDB: 11/1982

IWM 210 · GB, 10/4/1916
WITH THE ROYAL FIELD ARTILLERY IN ACTION
OFFICIAL PICTURES OF THE BRITISH ARMY IN FRANCE – THIRD SERIES (series)

b/w · 1 reel · 546' (9 mins) · silent
intertitles: English

sp War Office *pr* British Topical Committee for War Films *cam* Malins, Geoffrey H or Tong, Edward G (?)

■ Royal Field Artillery in action in Flanders, early 1916.

An 18-pounder field gun battery emerges head-on out of a farm courtyard onto a very wet and muddy road. RFA gunners pack 18-pounder shells into wooden boxes for transportation. A 4.5-inch field howitzer fires from brushwood cover. At an observation post a Forward Observation Officer (FOO) with his team, one with a trench periscope, relays firing orders with a notepad and field telephone. Men of an 18-pounder battery run to enter a gun-pit entirely concealed in reeds. The battery fires, shown visible from the rear but almost completely hidden from the front. View from a front trench of shells bursting over the German lines 200 yards away – the ground is flat and without cover. The FOO relays fresh orders to the battery which continues its shoot. Another view of the 4.5-inch howitzer firing.

Notes
Cameraman: this was either Malins or Tong.
Remarks: the opening shot of the battery emerging from the farm is a very attractive one.
[shotsheet available]
catalogued SDB: 11/1982

IWM 211 · GB, 24/4/1916
the BATTLEFIELD OF NEUVE CHAPELLE
OFFICIAL PICTURES OF THE BRITISH ARMY IN FRANCE – THIRD SERIES (series)

b/w · 1 reel · 432' (8 mins) · silent
intertitles: English

sp War Office *pr* British Topical Committee for War Films *cam* Malins, Geoffrey H

■ Battlefield of Neuve Chapelle, Western Front, filmed by the British a year after the battle, which began on 10 March 1915.

The battlefield forms part of the British reserve line, and is still under intermittent German shell fire. The British assembly trenches, one with a very clean white cross "To An Unknown British Hero" (probably not genuine). The captured German trenches are substantially deeper and better revetted. The village itself is mostly rubble though the Calvary outside it is still intact.

[Geoffrey H Malins, *How I Filmed the War*, Herbert Jenkins (1920)]
[shotsheet available]
catalogued SDB: 11/1982

IWM 212 · GB, (?) 1918
WITH THE NORTH AND SOUTH IRISH AT THE FRONT
OFFICIAL PICTURES OF THE BRITISH ARMY IN FRANCE – FOURTH SERIES (series)

b/w · 2 reels · 1767' (29 mins) · silent
intertitles: English

sp Ministry of Information *pr* British Topical Committee for War Films

■ Compilation showing Irish Guards, 16th (Irish) Division and 36th (Ulster) Division on the Western Front between late 1915 and the middle of 1917, and a Canadian battalion touring Ireland, 1917.

(Reel 1) Connaught Rangers eating in billets near Hulluch, March 1916. Royal Inniskilling Fusiliers near Messines, June 1917. Royal Munster Fusiliers march to Mass near Hulluch, March 1916. 2nd Battalion, the Irish Guards, near Aubers Ridge, December 1915. Troops of 16th Division at Messines. A march past of 7th Battalion, Royal Irish Rifles in early 1915 showing Major William Redmond leading his company. More of the Irish Guards clearing water from their trenches near Aubers Ridge. *(Reel 2)* Connaught Rangers (?) probably in a training area, throwing smoke grenades and charging forward. Damage done to a "well constructed German dugout". A British 60-pounder battery being shelled. German soldiers helping to carry trophies and wounded of 16th Division, Somme area, late 1916. 36th (Ulster) Division staff, including Major-General Nugent, and some of its troops.

Graves just behind the Irish Guards line. A church parade in memory of the dead. Major Redmond's grave in the Hospice at Locre. Irish and Australian walking wounded, posed for the camera, just arrived at Dover (?).
II. A tour round Ireland in June 1917 of Canadian 55th Battalion, (Duchess of Connaught's Own Irish Canadian Rangers), under Colonel O'Donoughie. They go through Cork, Belfast, Blarney Castle and Limerick, ending with a sermon preached for them by Cardinal Logue in Armagh Cathedral where the battalion colours were laid up for the war's duration.

Notes
Production: in its original form this was a 1-reel film *With the Irish at the Front*, released on 1 May 1916 by the War Office as part of its fourth series of official films, and dealing only with 16th Division. This version has been re-edited to include material of 36th Division and events of 1917.
Summary: see also **IWM 116** *The Battle of the Ancre and the Advance of the Tanks*, **IWM 197** *The Capture of Messines* and **IWM 208** *Liveliness on the British Front*.
Remarks: British propaganda towards Ireland during the war was understated and covert, at least in films. This episode makes no effort to enlist sympathy for the British cause or the Irish soldiers. It merely provides evidence for the fact that the British Army on the Western Front contained a number of organised formations made up exclusively of Irishmen.
[shotsheet available]
catalogued SDB: 11/1982

IWM 213 · GB, 8/5/1916
WITH LORD KITCHENER IN FRANCE
OFFICIAL PICTURES OF THE BRITISH ARMY IN FRANCE – FOURTH SERIES (series)

b/w · 1 reel · 544' (10 mins) · silent
intertitles: English

sp War Office *pr* British Topical Committee for War Films *cam* Malins, Geoffrey H or Tong, Edward G (?)

■ Field Marshal Lord Kitchener, Secretary of State for War, on a visit to France inspecting troops, and in England, February 1916 and possibly earlier in the First World War.

I. Kitchener visits France between 9 and 12 February. He leaves a "headquarters" (possibly of a division) by car. He inspects a brigade of New Army Infantry which cheers him as he leaves. He watches wounded on stretchers being taken on board ship at Calais, and watches the ship leave harbour.

II. In Britain, King George V, Kitchener and General Sir William Robertson, the new Chief of Imperial General Staff, in full dress uniform wait on a saluting base next to a railway carriage.

III. Kitchener on board a ship (no clear shot but probably a destroyer) leaving Dover for Calais. He walks on deck.

IV. Kitchener in Britain inspecting a New Army battalion, probably of Argyll and Sutherland Highlanders, volunteer motorcar drivers, and VAD ambulance drivers – this may by as early as 1914.

Notes
Cameraman: this was either Malins or Tong.
Summary: see also the P 2 version which has an additional scene of Kitchener and Robertson passing on the gangplank of a ship. The existing version of this film is probably not the original release version.
[P Magus, *Kitchener – Portrait of an Imperialist*, John Murray (1958): 371]
[Robert Blake, *The Private Papers of Douglas Haig 1914-1919*, Eyre and Spottiswoode (1952): 128]
[shotsheet available]
catalogued SDB: 11/1982

IWM 214 · GB, 22/5/1916
LETTERS FROM HOME : the work of the Postal Department at the Front
OFFICIAL PICTURES OF THE BRITISH ARMY IN FRANCE – FOURTH SERIES (series)

b/w · 1 reel · 537' (9 mins) · silent
intertitles: English

sp War Office *pr* British Topical Committee for War Films *cam* Malins, Geoffrey H or Tong, Edward G (?)

■ Partially dramatised account of a letter being sent from a mother in Britain to her son serving in a trench on the Western Front, early 1916.

The young 'mother', at a table, begins her letter, "dear son" (acted). British troops unload sacks of mail for France at one of the Channel ports. The mail is taken across the Channel by ship and unloaded at a French port. A special "express" lorry is loaded with mail for headquarters, while

British troops and French officials load other mail into goods trains. The express lorry arrives at GHQ Army Post Office at St-Omer where the mail is unloaded and sorted. At the railhead the sacks of letters for the troops are unloaded from the train onto lorries. At a "refilling point" soldiers crowd round the lorry, the sacks are distributed and battalion orderlies sort the mail. At a field post office, a brick building beyond German shell range, soldiers queue to collect mail from pigeon-holes. In a final scene (acted) letters are distributed to Highland troops in a front line trench while under shell fire.

Notes
Production: in this film the BTCFWF symbol appears only as a single flashframe.
Cameraman: this was either Malins or Tong.
Remarks: the British made an important point, for morale reasons among the troops, of having postal deliveries even in the very front lines. However, most of this film, particularly the last scene, has either been staged or acted in training camps.
[shotsheet available]
catalogued SDB: 11/1982

IWM 215 · GB, 5/6/1916
the FIGHT AT ST ELOI
OFFICIAL PICTURES OF THE BRITISH ARMY IN FRANCE – FIFTH SERIES (series)

b/w · 1 reel · 605' (10 mins) · silent
intertitles: English

sp War Office *pr* British Topical Committee for War Films *cam* Malins, Geoffrey H

■ Attack by 1st Battalion, Northumberland Fusiliers, at St-Eloi, Western Front, 27 March 1916.

A major commanding one of the supporting batteries receives orders to fire from a field telephone. 18-pounder field guns, completely hidden by brushwood, open fire. The view from the front line trench about an hour after the British dawn attack showing the newly-formed mine craters. A column of German prisoners, mostly 18th Jaeger Battalion, being marched to the rear by escorts of 1st Battalion, Northumberland Fusiliers. Men of the Northumberland Fusiliers posed two days after the attack, back in their rest area, displaying their trophies which include Jaeger dress helmets. The official photographer, Second-Lieutenant Ernest Brooks, walks among the men with his camera, posing them for the picture, and then moves out of shot. (No members of the other battalion in the attack, 4th Royal Fusiliers, are clearly identified in the film.)

[Geoffrey H Malins, *How I Filmed the War*, Herbert Jenkins (1920)]
[H R Sandilands, *The Fifth in the Great War*, G W Grigg and Sons (1938): 139-142]
[shotsheet available]
catalogued SDB: 11/1982

IWM 216 · GB, 26/6/1916
SCENES IN AND AROUND BRITISH HEADQUARTERS
OFFICIAL PICTURES OF THE BRITISH ARMY IN FRANCE – FIFTH SERIES (series)

b/w · 1 reel · 318' (6 mins) · silent
intertitles: English

sp War Office *pr* British Topical Committee for War Films *cam* Malins, Geoffrey H or Tong, Edward G (?)

■ Arrival of General Cadorna, the Italian C-in-C, on the British zone of the Western Front for the Allied Commanders' Conference of 12 March 1916.

Cadorna arrives at Calais on board a British destroyer, met by British, French and Italian liaison officers. He leaves for British headquarters at St-Omer. In the main square of the town Cadorna (described as "the French commander") presents medals to men of the Canadian Corps. A march past follows and the decorated men are chaired across the square by their fellows. On leaving, Cadorna walks with Field Marshal Haig past a guard of honour of the Artists Rifles into the railway station, where the two men shake hands in farewell. (Note in the scene of Cadorna's arrival at Calais the British official photographer, Ernest Brooks, at work.)

Notes
Title: BTCFWF publicity for this film adds a subtitle "The Spirit which animates the Allies is one of complete and cordial co-operation". *Cameraman:* this was either Malins or Tong.
[shotsheet available]
catalogued SDB: 11/1982

IWM 217 · GB, 3/7/1916
OBSERVING FOR OUR HEAVY GUNS
OFFICIAL PICTURES OF THE BRITISH ARMY IN FRANCE – FIFTH SERIES (series)

b/w · 1 reel · 469' (8 mins) · silent
intertitles: English

sp War Office *pr* British Topical Committee for War Films *cam* Malins, Geoffrey H or Tong, Edward G (?)

■ Semi-dramatised account of British aerial spotting techniques for guns on the Western Front, early 1916.

A kite balloon is positioned by RFC ground staff and ascends over a small village. The view down from the basket and a (faked) close-up of the observer and signaller spotting from the basket. A 60-pounder battery receives the signal and the observer directs its fire. The gun fires several times, and a 6-inch Mk VII gun joins in, "note its tremendous recoil". The balloon is lowered and the basket touches ground bumpily.

Notes
Cameraman: this was either Malins or Tong.
Summary: see also **IWM 128** *With the South African Forces*, **IWM 130** *Sons of Our Empire* and **IWM 164** *Kite Balloon and the Belle of Arques*.
[shotsheet available]
catalogued SDB: 11/1982

IWM 218 · GB, (?) 1918
WITH BRITAIN'S MONSTER GUNS IN ACTION
OFFICIAL PICTURES OF THE BRITISH ARMY IN FRANCE – SIXTH SERIES (series)

b/w · 1 reel · 877' (15 mins) · silent
intertitles: English

sp Ministry of Information (?) *pr* British Topical Committee for War Films (?)

■ Compilation film of heavy British guns on the Western Front, 1916-18.

Two aircrew with their backs to the camera walk towards their BE2 aircraft before an artillery spotting mission – jump cut to the plane flying. A 12-inch Mk I railway howitzer of 89th Siege Battery RGA (?) at Dickebusch in June 1916 being elevated and loaded. In the aircraft's cockpit "8,000 feet up" (fake) the observer sends Morse messages to a receiver on the ground, relayed by field telephone to the gun, which opens fire (possibly a blank – the wadding can be seen leaving the barrel). The whole sequence is repeated correcting for range, including a view down from the observer's position showing trench-lines, and repeated again. A second battery, of 12-inch Mk II siege howitzers, also fires, is loaded and fired again, and some maintenance work is carried out on one gun. The BE2 returns home (the aircraft actually shown landing is an RE7 with a Beardmore engine). A line of shells is loaded into another 12-inch railway gun under a camouflage awning.

II. King George V's visit to the 14-inch railway gun 'HMG Boche Buster' of 471st Siege Battery RGA at Brayon on 8 August 1918. With him is the GOC First Army, General Horne. The hawk-nosed man behind George V is the battery commander, Major S Montague Cleve.

Notes
Production: a film with this title was released on 17 July 1916 as part of the sixth War Office series of *Official Films*. This version has the appearance of being a re-edited re-release, including material up to the end of the war. The additional material is probably marked by the various changes in caption style throughout the film.
Title: the BTCFWF publicity for this film adds the subtitle "Their fire is directed by wireless from aeroplanes".
[Montague Cleve file in IWM Department of Film]
[shotsheet available]
catalogued SDB: 11/1982

IWM 219 · GB, 24/7/1916
MINING ACTIVITY ON THE BRITISH FRONT
OFFICIAL PICTURES OF THE BRITISH ARMY IN FRANCE – SIXTH SERIES (series)

b/w · 1 reel · 764' (13 mins) · silent
intertitles: English

sp War Office *pr* British Topical Committee for War Films *cam* Malins, Geoffrey H or Tong, Edward G (?)

■ Largely dramatised account of a tunnelling company of Royal Engineers planting and exploding a mine under a German position on the Western Front, early 1916.

I. The tunnelling company loads itself and its equipment into lorries, unloads at the end of the journey, and enters the trench system. At the minehead shaft one man wearing breathing apparatus checks for gas. The men dig at the tunnel face until the captain in charge hears, through a tube, German countermining going on. Explosive charges are brought down the shaft, set in

position, the men retire to the surface and a young second-lieutenant checks the electric firing circuit. Highlanders close by take cover in the crater of "the Hohenzollern redoubt" (?). The mine is exploded, followed by two more scenes of mine or shell explosions. The Highlanders run forward to take the crater. Other British troops run forward through a trench system and a machinegun opens fire. Two more mines explode by a tree line.

II. At this point the film breaks up into random scenes. A party of British soldiers walks down a shallow trench as if on patrol when suddenly it is pelted with mud from off-camera, exposing the fake. Canadian (?) sappers with a detonator fire another charge and then go forward to inspect the recently-blown craters by the tree line.

Notes
Production: the extra length of this film and the inclusion of scenes from **IWM 191** *The Battle of the Somme*, released August 1916, suggest that this is not the original release version.
Cameraman: for the original version this was either Malins or Tong.
Remarks: the fake patrol scene, although brief, makes interesting viewing as a comparison with suspect, but not proven, fakes.
[shotsheet available]
catalogued SDB: 11/1982

IWM 220 · GB, 31/7/1916
HOME ON LEAVE
OFFICIAL PICTURES OF THE BRITISH ARMY IN FRANCE – SIXTH SERIES (series)

b/w · 1 reel · 403' (7 mins) · silent
intertitles: English

sp War Office *pr* British Topical Committee for War Films *cam* Malins, Geoffrey H or Tong, Edward G (?)

■ British soldiers returning from the Western Front across the English Channel on leave, early 1916.

Men of various regiments board a troopship in a French port. The ship moves off and clears the harbour mouth accompanied by a P Class patrol boat. In the Channel lifebelts are issued "in case of a stray mine". The ship's captain keeps watch on the bridge while his crew act up for the camera and play leap-frog. A transport ship passes going the other way. A G Class destroyer passes. An SSZ airship on patrol comes quite low over the ship. Soldiers watch over the rail for England. After the ship's arrival the soldiers disembark. They arrive at Victoria Station in London, and drive away by bus, taxi and charabanc.

Notes
Production: the last of the final series of short features released by the War Office in 1916. By the time of its release, work was already advanced on the next War Office film venture, *The Battle of the Somme* (**IWM 191**).
Cameraman: this was either Malins or Tong.
[shotsheet available]
catalogued SDB: 11/1982

IWM 221 · Australia, (?) 1918
AUSTRALIANS ON THE MARCH

b/w · 1 reel · 157' (3 mins) · silent
intertitles: none

sp Australian War Records Section

■ Australian Infantry, probably 5th Division, on the march, Western Front, 1916-18.

The men march down a road towards the camera in a totally featureless landscape, all very smart, officers riding very clean horses. They rest by the roadside, and cheer the camera as it pans over them. The shoulder patch looks like Australian 5th Division. A small boy is with them.

Notes
Production: Australian official film.
[shotsheet available]
catalogued SDB: 11/1982

IWM 222 · GB, (?) 1917
NEWFOUNDLAND INFANTRY ON THE MARCH

b/w · 1 reel · 139' (3 mins) · silent
intertitles: none

■ Men of the Newfoundland Regiment, just out of the line, marching to their rest billets, Western Front, possibly May 1917.

The marchers, in greatcoats and helmets, are very muddy. A considerably smarter marching column is passing the other way. The Newfoundlanders look as if they have just been taken out of the line, possibly after the Battle of Arras, in which they played a key role, May 1917.

Notes
Title: this is taken from the shotsheet.
Production: very probably British official film, but there is no firm proof of this or of date of filming.
Remarks: the film gives an excellent idea of the appearance and condition of troops just out of the line in a muddy sector.
[shotsheet available]
catalogued SDB: 11/1982

IWM 223 · NO FILM

IWM 224 · GB, 1918
AMERICAN DELEGATES AT CASSEL

b/w · 1 reel · 771' (13 mins) · silent
intertitles: none

sp Ministry of Information *pr* Topical Film Company *cam* Bassill, F A

■ Delegation headed by James Wilson representing American Socialist and Union groups visits France and Britain, April-May 1918.

The tour begins at Cassel in early May, where the delegates meet British troops and are shown the SMLE rifle before being driven off. They pose on the steps of Field Marshal Haig's headquarters at Beaurepaire, firstly as a group and then individually with their escorts. As shown they are: Martin F Ryan, Leroy C Dunn, John P Fry, E T Meredith, A Secer, A O Lovejoy, George L Berry, James Wilson, Chester Wright, Harry Britain (in uniform), Gregory Butler, Sir Home Gordon, C B Davies. They then board a ship and cross the Channel. In Britain they and their wives meet women workers at a tank production factory. They ride at a test ground in Mk V tanks with all the hatches open, supervised by Royal Navy officers. They visit Buckingham Palace (the film begins to break up here into repeats and pull-backs) and the War Office, finally being posed beside the Palace of Westminster (the parliament buildings).

Notes
Title: this is taken from the shotsheet.
[*The Times*, 29 April 1918: 5B]
[*The Times*, 7 May 1918: 7D, 7E]
[*The Times*, 13 May 1918: 5A]
[*The Times*, 14 May 1918: 8C]
[shotsheet available]
catalogued SDB: 11/1982

IWM 225 · GB, 1918
BRITISH HORSE SHOW IN ITALY

b/w · 1 reel · 152' (3 mins) · silent
intertitles: none

sp Ministry of Information pr Topical Film
Company cam Raymond, H C

- British XIV Corps horse show in the
  Montello sector of the Italian Front, May
  1918.

The show is of RFA horses and limbers
being judged, a jumping contest, a view of
the audience, which contains a large
number of Italian as well as British officers,
and more of the jumping.

Notes
Title: this is taken from the shotsheet.
Remarks: senior officers showed a tendency
to 'hijack' the official cameramen to record
their sports meetings, with results that were
totally useless as propaganda: this is a
good example.
[shotsheet available]
catalogued SDB: 11/1982

IWM 226 · GB, (prod) 1918
[BRITISH TROOPS ON THE WESTERN FRONT, MAY 1918] (allocated)

b/w · 1 reel · 1089' (18 mins) · silent
intertitles: none

sp Ministry of Information pr Topical Film
Company cam McDowell, J B (?)

- Jumbled and possibly unrelated scenes
  of British forces on the Western Front,
  May 1918.

Men of the Chinese Labour Corps march
along a road. Two of the Suffolk Regiment
(?) who escaped from the Germans are
questioned by a British officer. A light
railway train carrying ammunition moves
through the rear areas of the battlefield. A
dump of 9.2-inch shells with a sign held up
"one day's rations for one gun". Troops
unload and stack shells from a light train.
Royal Engineers in a wood by the railway
make defences of cheveux-de-frise from
tree trunks and barbed wire. Gunners
remove the camouflage from shells in a
dump and fire them from a 12-inch railway
gun (film disjointed). The gunners rest and
eat. German prisoners with British soldiers
guarding them. British soldiers resting,
probably at a dressing station. Ammunition

limbers move down a road. A 6-inch Mk VII
gun battery in action. Soldiers resting in a
village. Intelligence officers inspecting
prisoners. British soldiers marching along a
road. German prisoners (some wave at the
camera). A line of Cavalrymen with their
horses by the road mount up and move off.

Notes
Date: this is taken from the store ledger.
[shotsheet available]
catalogued SDB: 11/1982

IWM 227 · GB, (prod) 1918
[AMIENS AFTER A BOMBING RAID, MAY 1918] (allocated)

b/w · 1 reel · 357' (6 mins) · silent
intertitles: none

sp Ministry of Information pr Topical Film
Company cam Bassill, F A

- Clearing up debris in Amiens after a
  German bombing raid, Western Front,
  May 1918.
The station and main square show bomb
damage. A house stands burning with a fire
engine outside it.

[shotsheet available]
catalogued SDB: 11/1982

IWM 228 · GB, (prod) 1918
[WAAC CAMP AT ABBEVILLE FOLLOWING AN AIR RAID, 22ND MAY 1918] (allocated)

b/w · 1 reel · 259' (4 mins) · silent
intertitles: none

sp Ministry of Information pr Topical Film
Company cam Bassill, F A

- Women's Army Auxiliary Corps camp at
  Abbeville following a German air raid,
  Western Front, 22 May 1918.

The camp Nissen huts show damage from
the bombs. The women stand around
watching. A view of Abbeville (?) with the
smoke rising in the background. (The film is
broken here by an unrelated scene of shells
'walking' towards a village.) In the camp the
WAACs clean up the debris and practise
running to their air raid shelters.

[shotsheet available]
catalogued SDB: 11/1982

IWM 229 · Australia, (prod) 1918
**an AUSTRALIAN BRIGADE HOLDS A
WATER CARNIVAL IN THE SOMME
BEFORE GOING INTO BATTLE**

b/w · 1 reel · 189' (3 mins) · silent
intertitles: none

sp Australian War Records Section
cam Wilkins, G H

- Very short piece of a water carnival held
  by 9th Brigade, 3rd Australian Division in
  May 1918, with punt battles, wrestling,
  diving from boards and swimming. Some
  men wear swimming costumes.

Notes
Shotsheet: this is unusually detailed and is
probably a dopesheet.
Summary: Australian official film.
[shotsheet available]
catalogued SDB: 11/1982

IWM 230 · GB, (?) 1918
**ROYAL HORSE ARTILLERY SPORTS
BEHIND THE LINES**

b/w · 1 reel · 351' (6 mins) · silent
intertitles: none

sp Ministry of Information (?) *pr* Topical Film
Company *cam* Bassill, F A

- Royal Horse Artillery horse show and a
  practice charge by 2nd Dragoons (Scots
  Greys), Western Front, early 1918.

I. At the show an RHA troop demonstrates a
fast gallop followed by a controlled trot. A
jumping race for riders of one horse while
leading another horse on a tight rein.
Wrestling on horseback and a flat race.
Among the spectators are members of the
Chinese Labour Corps.
II. A squadron of Scots Greys riding in light
order with shrapnel helmets but no heavy
equipment – a few of the horses are not
grey, and none is stained for camouflage.
They form up in a field and deliver a very
slow close order charge towards the
camera without drawing their swords.
Possibly near Montreuil on 8 May. Later, the
squadron passes a pond and farmhouse at
the walk, and some of the horses, off-
saddled, are watered in the pond.

Notes
Title: this is taken from the shotsheet.
[shotsheet available]
catalogued SDB: 11/1982

IWM 231 · GB, 1918
**CHINESE ENTERTAINING ALLIED
TROOPS**

b/w · 1 reel · 261' (5 mins) · silent
intertitles: none

sp Ministry of Information *pr* Topical Film
Company *cam* Buckstone, W A

- Show by the Chinese Labour Corps,
  Etaples area, Western Front, 13 June
  1918.

A stage has been set up in a field near the
town, and men of the Corps perform an
acrobatic and dancing show in costume for
an audience of soldiers of various
nationalities, predominantly British, and
some civilians. The Corps has a percussion
band of drums and cymbals. Stilt walkers
demonstrate a dance and men forming
Chinese dragons join in a procession.

Notes
Title: this is taken from the shotsheet.
[shotsheet available]
catalogued SDB: 11/1982

IWM 232 · GB, (prod) 1918
**HOSPITAL BOMBED BY GERMANS, AND
FUNERAL OF THE VICTIMS**

b/w · 1 reel · 488' (9 mins) · silent
intertitles: none

sp Ministry of Information *pr* Topical Film
Company *cam* McDowell, J B (?)

- Funeral at a stationary hospital near
  Etaples, probably 9 (Canadian) Hospital,
  filmed three days after a bombing raid hit
  it on the night of 31 May 1918.

The wooden huts of the hospital show
various bomb blasts but little fire damage.
Four coffins, covered in Union Flags, are
wheeled on trolleys by soldiers. A single
coffin, also covered with a Union Flag on a
wheeled trolley, is followed by a funeral
procession of nurses, soldiers with wreaths,
and a few civilians. The procession arrives
at a temporary but extensive cemetery
where a burial service is held. (Note the
official photographer, Thomas Aitken, at
work.)

Notes
Title: this is taken from the shotsheet.
[shotsheet available]
catalogued SDB: 11/1982

IWM 233 · GB, 1917
**la GUERRE ANGLAISE : grand film
documentaire en 4 parts – les tanks
anglais a la bataille de la Scarpe**
SONS OF OUR EMPIRE (export version)

b/w · 4 reels · 3683' (62 mins) · silent
intertitles: French & German

sp War Office Cinema Committee

■ British propaganda film, almost entirely
  stock or fake material, purporting to show
  their involvement in the Battle of Arras,
  Western Front, April 1917.

Mostly taken, scene-for-scene and caption-
for-caption, from the series **IWM 130** Sons
of Our Empire, which itself purported to
show the last stages of the Somme
offensive in 1916. British troops disembark
at a French port and the various arms,
Artillery, Cavalry and Infantry, prepare for
battle. The role of the tanks is stressed, and
several Mk I and Mk IV types are shown.
The preliminary bombardment runs from 18-
pounder field guns to 12-inch railway guns.
Two FE2b aircraft fly a patrol. The attack
takes place and the troops reassemble.

Notes
Intertitles: some are French, some German,
some in parallel texts of both languages.
Summary: see also the series **IWM 130**.
This film appears to have been intended to
be shown as a complete performance with
breaks, rather than episodes in a series.
The use of both French and German
subtitles suggests that this version was
intended for Switzerland.
Remarks: valueless as a historical record of
the fighting on the Scarpe, but a good
record of British propaganda techniques
aimed at neutral Europe at this date. The
film shows the classic 'big battle' structure
of the British films of 1916 and early 1917.
[shotsheet available]
catalogued SDB: 11/1982

IWM 234 · GB, (prod) 1918
HUGE BOMBING MACHINES

b/w · 1 reel · 398' (7 mins) · silent
intertitles: none

sp Ministry of Information pr Topical Film
Company cam Bassill, F A

■ Handley Page 0/400 bombers, probably
  41 Wing RAF at Coudekerque, Western
  Front, May 1918.

One of the bombers taxis, checked by
mechanics as it does so. Another is brought
out of its hangar with its wings folded and
prepared for flight, the wings being
straightened and ladders put up to the
engines. The flight mechanics lift its tail off
a trestle. The machine is fitted with three
different types of bomb, which are then
fused, and fuel is pumped into the tanks. A
Nieuport 27, with a French officer as its
pilot, has been parked directly in front of
the Handley Page for comparison of size.

Notes
Title: this is taken from the shotsheet.
[shotsheet available]
catalogued SDB: 11/1982

IWM 235 · GB, 1918
WAR MESSENGER DOGS

b/w · 1 reel · 779' (13 mins) · silent
intertitles: none

sp Ministry of Information pr Topical Film
Company cam Bassill, F A

■ Training of messenger dogs for the
  British Army, probably at XXII Corps
  headquarters kennels in Nieppe Wood,
  Western Front, 19 May 1918.

I. The dogs, a mixture of terrier mongrels,
are paraded with their handlers and taken
for walking exercises. They are given a
course to run over unescorted, which
includes fences and barbed wire to jump,
and running past soldiers who fire rifles
over the dogs' heads. At an Artillery repair
workshop the dogs are made accustomed
to the noise of guns by standing beside an
18-pounder field gun as it fires. To
demonstrate the use of the dogs one
handler writes a message and fits it into a
tube on his dog's collar, the dog runs over
a number of obstacles to arrive with the
message at the collection point. At the
kennels the dogs are held and fed by their
handlers. More demonstrations of the dogs'
ability to jump obstacles, including a small
stream. One dog at the kennels has its
paws bandaged after being burnt by
mustard gas. The exercises continue, with
one dog, encouraged by its handler,
swimming a stream too wide to jump.
II. To the end of this film has been attached
an unrelated scene of an SE5 coming in to
land at an aerodrome.

Notes
Title: this is taken from the shotsheet.

Remarks: a very interesting film indeed.
[shotsheet available]
catalogued SDB: 11/1982

IWM 236 · Australia, 1918
**a BOMBING TRIP OVER THE ENEMY
LINES**

b/w · 1 reel · 464' (8 mins) · silent
intertitles: English

sp Australian War Records Section

■ Three squadrons of the Australian Air
Corps on the Western Front, June 1918.

I. RE8s of 3 Squadron AAC, probably at
Bertangles, being prepared for a raid. Both
cockpits can be clearly seen. The machines
have 16-pounder bombs fitted and fused,
one crew gets on board, the prop is turned
over, the chocks removed, and the
aeroplane takes off.
II. Sopwith Camels of 4 Squadron AAC,
probably at Bruay, taxi towards the camera
and take off. Three overfly the airfield, stunt
flying; one finally comes in to land.
III. SE5as of 2 Squadron AAC, probably at
Savy. A flight of five taxis and takes off
(note the boomerang marking on the
fuselage). Two pilots of the squadron,
recently mentioned in despatches but not
identified, joke with each other for the
camera.

Notes
Remarks: the reproduction quality of this
film is unusually high, very clear, and some
of the shots remarkably detailed by the
standards of the time.
[shotsheet available]
catalogued SDB: 11/1982

IWM 237 · GB, 1918
**SCENES ON THE TRACK AROUND
LIEVEN AIX AND NOULETTE**

b/w · 1 reel · 546' (10 mins) · silent
intertitles: none

sp Ministry of Information *pr* Topical Film
Company *cam* Buckstone, W A

■ Film taken from on board a moving light
railway train in the British rear zones of
the battlefield around Arras, Western
Front, 1918.

Only the brake-wheel can be seen of the

train, and for part of the time a lance
corporal brakeman with his back to the
camera. The track moves through the
rubble, clay and destroyed villages of the
area, passing a few soldiers on the way. At
one point the ride is halted by sappers
doing demolition work, at another the train
halts next to a burnt-out goods train. The
train halts again to let another train pass
over a set of crossing points, and to let
soldiers load boxes from a lorry onto a
goods truck. Otherwise the train is in
motion for the duration of the film.

Notes
Title: this is taken from the shotsheet.
Summary: see also **IWM 271** *Canadian
Sector of the Western Front in July 1918.*
Remarks: the film gives an unusual view,
which is curiously evocative.
[shotsheet available]
catalogued SDB: 11/1982

IWM 238-239 · NO FILM

IWM 240 · GB, (?) 1918
AMERICANS 1
b/w · reels · 150' (3 mins) · silent
intertitles: none

sp Ministry of Information (?)

■ General John J Pershing, Major-General
Omar Bundy, and US forces on the
Western Front, probably early 1918.

Pershing addresses a group of US officers
in the open. A supply column of US wagons
moves along a road and rests in a field.
Major-General Bundy, commanding US 2nd
Division, comes out of his wooded local
command post and enters his car.

Notes
Title: this is taken from the shotsheet.
Production: the *Americans* series of films
appears to be British official material taken
of US forces, rather than US official material
given to the British. Compare with US
official material in the **IWM 501** series, **IWM
502** and **IWM 503**.
[shotsheet available]
catalogued SDB: 11/1982

IWM 241 · GB, 1918
ALDER HAY HOSPITAL SPORTS

b/w · 1 reel · 412' (7 mins) · silent
intertitles: none

pr Pathé cam Cooper, F (?)

■ Series of races at the sports day of Alder
Hay hospital in Britain, probably 1918.

Most people in the races are wounded
soldiers. A wheelchair race for cripples or
amputees (one man falls out of his chair). A
three-legged race for nurses and patients in
pairs, with the patients facing backwards. A
joke bookmaker's stand. A donkey race.
The watching crowd, mostly of wounded
soldiers. Two heats of a carrying race. A
treacle bun race, in which men on crutches
have to eat a treacle bun without using their
hands. A nurses' bicycle race. Another
donkey race. A blindfold boxing match. An
officers' donkey race. A race on crutches for
one-legged men. A confused drill
demonstration by blindfold men. A nurses'
donkey race. Prizes are awarded. The
ending shows the British and American
flags with the Red Cross flag suspended
between them.

Notes
Title: this is taken from the shotsheet.
Production: Cooper was employed by
British Pathé but worked for the Ministry of
Information from time to time, and it is hard
to ascertain if this is merely a record film or
a deliberately and officially made piece of
propaganda intended (to judge from the
ending) for the US market.
Remarks: the gaiety seems a little too slick,
and sick, for modern tastes.
[shotsheet available]
catalogued SDB: 11/1982

IWM 242 · GB, 1918
HOUNSLOW MOTOR DRIVING SCHOOL

b/w · 3 reels · 2640' (44 mins) · silent
intertitles: none

sp Ministry of Information (?) pr Pathé cam
Cooper, F (?)

■ Training film in the maintenance and
driving of the Dennis 3-ton lorry, set at
the Army Service Corps Motor Transport
Driving School at Hounslow, Middlesex,
1918.

(Reel 1) The film has a comic acted
character, the "awkward soldier". He and his
fellows arrive at the school and are
instructed in the lorry's engine and gearbox,

which are shown running opened up with
labels attached. They are taught the
principles of driving on the open road and
making a three-point turn. They clean and
maintain their lorries. *(Reel 2)* They are
taught reversing techniques on the road
and at the school. A lorry convoy is taken
out to demonstrate the importance of
correct spacing when driving, *(Reel 3)*
turning corners, hill starts and parking. The
men picnic in a field while parked. The
importance of not driving too fast is shown
by staged sequences of a horse and cart
and then some children crossing the road,
and a car skidding on an oil patch, in front
of the lorries. In each case the lorries stop
safely. The "awkward soldier" demonstrates
the starting handle, and he and the
instructor strip an engine on a test-bench to
show a cracked piston ring. Finally, an
open-air concert at which the "awkward
soldier" gives a display of tap dancing.

Notes
Title: this is taken from the shotsheet.
Summary: from its structure this is probably
the remains of a longer and more detailed
film. The PMA 2 version (1 reel of 397 feet)
consists largely of out-takes from the full
version.
Remarks: the absence of captions and
subtitles makes the film very difficult to
follow.
[shotsheet available]
catalogued SDB: 11/1982

IWM 243 · GB, 1918
**a MACHINE GUN BATTALION TRAINING
IN FRANCE, THE MEN LUDENDORFF
FEARS**
the MEN LUDENDORFF FEARS (alternative)

b/w · 2 reels · 712' (19 mins) · silent
intertitles: English

sp Ministry of Information pr Topical Film
Company prod Jury, William F
cam Buckstone, Walter A

■ Demonstrations of tactics with the Vickers
machinegun at the Machine Gun Corps
Training School at Rombly, France, 15-17
June 1918.

(Reel 1) Exercises and physical training on
a parade ground. The trainees strip and
reassemble a Vickers machinegun. This is
followed by a demonstration of a machine
which fills cartridge belts automatically. Four
machineguns blast a hole through an 18-
inch deep (50 cm) sandbag parapet at a

range of about 100 yards/metres. A machinegun section on the march with its eight pack mules entering the start of a trench system. A machinegun platform hidden in a tree. Back at the parade ground, teams of three demonstrate setting up and dismantling their machineguns. A sports interval of wrestling on horseback and officers' quoit tennis. An RE8 overflies the school slowly so that machinegunners can practise sighting on it. A section coming out of the line is "greeted" (acted?) by men at the school. The men out of the line strip and clean their weapons. *(Reel 2)* A series of demonstrations of machinegun tactics. A section of four machineguns shows how to conduct a retreat at the gallop, moving the guns in pairs from cover to cover in limber carts. Men crawl forward in long grass to set up a "nest" undetected. Machinegunners and Infantry make a practice attack under smoke and shell fire. Finally, "the dogs of war", a head-on shot of a mascot dog balanced on the barrel of a machinegun fades into a shot of a man aiming the same gun at the camera.

Notes
Remarks: an extremely valuable demonstration of the British theoretical concepts of open warfare in summer 1918.
[shotsheet available]
catalogued SDB: 11/1982

IWM 244 · GB, (prod) 1918
[EPERNAY] (allocated)

b/w · 1 reel · 50' (1 min) · silent
intertitles: none

sp Ministry of Information *pr* Topical Film Company *cam* McDowell, J B

■ Panorama taken from high ground over the town of Epernay in France, 7 June 1918.

Notes
Summary: probably an extract from a longer film.
[shotsheet available]
catalogued SDB: 11/1982

IWM 245 · GB, (?) 1918
WOMEN'S WORK

b/w · 1 reel · 1045' (17 mins) · silent
intertitles: English

sp Ministry of Information (?)

I. Women making and shaping spade cutters for guns (endless repetition) using heavy plant, a factory in Britain, 1917 or 1918.
II. Women making internal combustion engines, including some tank engines, and operating a 20-ton crane to move a heavy gun-carriage across a shop floor, a factory in Britain, 1917 or 1918.
III. Women demonstrating work with a new fluid gauge which measures in one rapid operation lengths of between 1/1000th and 1/50 000th of an inch (an inch is approximately 2.5cm), a factory in Britain, 1917 or 1918.

Notes
Title: this is taken from the shotsheet.
Summary: see also **IWM 419** *Women's Work on Munitions of War*.
[shotsheet available]
catalogued SDB: 11/1982

IWM 246 · GB, 1918
J BATTERY, 2ND CAVALRY DIVISION, 20TH JUNE 1918

b/w · 1 reel · 221' (4 mins) · silent
intertitles: none

sp Ministry of Information *pr* Topical Film Company *cam* McDowell, J B

■ Stock film of a Royal Horse Artillery 13-pounder battery manœuvring at high speed, rear areas of the Western Front, 20 June 1918.

The battery canters into a field and unlimbers, deploying its guns, then relimbers and canters off. The battery canters in column head-on out of the field and turns away when close to the camera. One limber comes back in the opposite direction. (Note the 'linked horseshoe' divisional badge on the limbers.) Limbered-up guns canter over a bump facing away from the camera – one gun overturns in the process and another is already lying wrecked nearby. The battery, including outriders canters through and along a deep stream, throwing up much spray.

Notes
Title: this is taken from the shotsheet.
Remarks: the film is intended to provide a series of spectacular stockshots, and is successful in doing so. The water sequence in particular is very impressive.

[shotsheet available]
catalogued SDB: 11/1982

IWM 247 · GB, (ca) 1917
GHQ TEST FILM

b/w · 1 reel · 71' (2 mins) · silent
intertitles: none

- Short test piece made at British GHQ
  Montreuil of soldiers with animals and
  German equipment, Western Front, 1916-
  18.

A chubby soldier, in close-up, cuddles two
lambs. Another feeds chickens from a metal
plate, letting one stand and balance on the
plate. One of the men puts on a German
helmet and trench body armour, and is
attacked in play-acting by another soldier
with a spade, whereupon he surrenders.

Notes
Title: this is taken from the store ledger.
Summary: presumably, from the title, a short
piece made either to test film equipment at
GHQ, to prove to its staff the value of film,
or for some similar purpose.
catalogued SDB: 11/1982

IWM 248 · GB (?), 1918
AMERICANS 2

b/w · 1 reel · 166' (3 mins) · silent
intertitles: none

sp Ministry of Information (?)

- US forces arriving in France, probably
  1918.

US soldiers disembark from their ship at a
French port. A group of US Navy officers
and men posed with French children they
have temporarily adopted. More Infantry on
the march. A long column of US nurses, in
navy blue capes, marching towards a
railway yard. A trooptrain carrying the
Infantry leaves the yard.

Notes
Title: this is taken from the shotsheet.
Cameraman: the store ledger gives this film
as having been taken on 16 May 1918 by
Jeapes. This seems unlikely.
Summary: from the shotsheet captions, this
was probably intended for an American
rather than a British market and may even
be US film.

Shotsheet: this is unusually detailed.
Technical: the quality of the film is very
poor, making it hard to view properly.
[shotsheet available]
catalogued SDB: 11/1982

IWM 249 · GB (?), 1918
AMERICANS 3

b/w · 1 reel · 140' (3 mins) · silent
intertitles: none

sp Ministry of Information (?)

- Stockshots of US troops on the Western
  Front, probably 1918.

French soldiers show US troops, led by a
lieutenant-colonel, the correct method of
building a command post dug-out – a large,
solid and permanent structure. German
prisoners lined up for the camera are told
by their American guard to smile and eat as
it pans over them. An early dawn
bombardment (wrong light values, virtually
nothing can be seen). A group of US
soldiers walking down a road into a village,
meant to be a company returning from a
raid.

Notes
Title: this is taken from the shotsheet.
[shotsheet available]
catalogued SDB: 11/1982

IWM 250 · GB, 1918
[AMERICANS 4] (allocated)
[the HAT IN THE RING SQUADRON]
(alternative, allocated)

b/w · 1 reel · 183' (3 mins) · silent
intertitles: none

sp Ministry of Information *pr* Topical Film
Company *cam* McDowell, J B

- Pilots of the US 94th Pursuit Squadron in
  France, early July 1918.

Portrait shots of the pilots against their
Nieuport 28c aircraft. (The squadron 'Hat in
the Ring' badge is clearly visible on the
side.) Firstly, is Major Huffer, then Major
Raoul Lufberry, then both together smoking.
Lieutenant Douglas Campbell against his
Nieuport, and Lieutenant Alan Wilson in
flying gear at the controls of his aircraft. A
group shot of 16 members of the squadron.
The French Commandant le Forest

decorates Campbell and Wilson with the Croix de guerre, and they shake each other's hand in congratulation.

Notes
Remarks: unfortunately the squadron's famous commander, Eddie Rickenbacker, the top US ace, does not appear in the film.
[shotsheet available]
catalogued SDB: 11/1982

IWM 251 · GB (?), 1918
AMERICANS 5

b/w · 1 reel · 277' (5 mins) · silent
intertitles: none

sp Ministry of Information (?)

- Meeting of Marshal Ferdinand Foch with General John J Pershing at US headquarters in France, 17 June 1918.

Foch leaves the Château de la Valdes des Ecoliers at Charmont, Pershing's own château. Pershing sees the Marshal to his car, then himself leaves by car. Pershing arrives (out of sequence) at his château, and greets Foch arriving with his staff. One of Pershing's staff officers appears to be Colonel George S Patton. Pershing and Foch walk together in the château library.

Notes
Title: this is taken from the shotsheet.
[shotsheet available]
catalogued SDB: 11/1982

IWM 252 · GB (?), (?) 1918
AMERICANS 6

b/w · 1 reel · 404' (7 mins) · silent
intertitles: none

sp Ministry of Information (?)

- US logistical build-up on the Western Front, probably 1918.

A car and truck park showing a variety of US vehicles. US Engineers building a temporary harbour (filmed from a light train). US Engineers in the early stages of building a locomotive. Men at a field bakery. French women working under US supervision, using mops to paint or dye material for camouflage purposes.

Notes
Title: this is taken from the shotsheet.
Summary: compare with **IWM 458**.
[shotsheet available]
catalogued SDB: 11/1982

IWM 253 · GB, 1918
VISIT OF THE HON J R BENNETT, MINISTER OF MILITIA OF NEWFOUNDLAND, TO FRANCE, 1918

b/w · 2 (as 1) reels · 1180' (19 mins) · silent
intertitles: none

sp Ministry of Information *pr* Topical Film Company *cam* McDowell, J B

- Mr John Bennett's visit to the Royal Newfoundland Regiment in France, 22-26 June 1918.

(Reel 1) Bennett arrives at Boulogne on 22 June, met by Major H A Timewell and war correspondents H M Beeton and Frederick McKenzie. The next day, Bennett inspects the Royal Newfoundland Regiment at Ecuires, talking briefly to the temporary commanding officer, Major A E Bernard, and to the RSM. He decorates nine NCOs and men, following which the regiment marches past. On 24 June Bennett visits Arras Cathedral, which shows the results of heavy shelling, although there are grass and flowers growing in the rubble. *(Reel 2)* On the following day, Bennett inspects the regimental transport, including a field kitchen. The transport marches past as he watches. He talks to Sergeant-Major Sampson DCM, who captured a German machinegun post single-handedly. Bennett watches a drill display at the training camp, inspects new recruits, and delivers a short speech, following which the recruits march past. On 26 June the ceremony of changing the guard takes place outside the regimental headquarters, complete with bugles and fixed bayonets.

Notes
Title: this is taken from the shotsheet.
Remarks: the transport march past gives a very good idea of the amount of horsed transport needed for even one battalion, and the amount of road space that it occupied.
[shotsheet available]
catalogued SDB: 11/1982

IWM 254 · GB (?), (prod) 1918
**[US INDEPENDENCE DAY
CELEBRATIONS IN BELGIUM, 1918]**
(allocated)

b/w · 1 reel · 294' (5 mins) · silent
intertitles: none

■ US and Belgian forces celebrate at an
   aerodrome in Belgium, 4 July 1918.

Representative officers from the various
Allies watch as the senior Belgian officer
shows the senior American officer around.
They pass a parade of Belgian cyclist
troops. The US flag is raised while the
Belgian delivers a speech. The Belgian and
American pose for the camera. The Belgian
troops (cyclists, Infantry, Cavalry and guns)
march past, and the various representatives
then depart.

Notes
Technical: the quality of this film is so poor
as to be almost unviewable.
[shotsheet available]
catalogued SDB: 11/1982

IWM 255 · GB, 20/3/1916
**IN ACTION WITH OUR CANADIAN
TROOPS**
OFFICIAL PICTURES OF THE BRITISH
ARMY IN FRANCE – SECOND SERIES
(series)

b/w · 1 reel · 623' (11 mins) · silent
intertitles: English

sp War Office *pr* British Topical Committee
for War Films *cam* Malins, Geoffrey H or
Tong, Edward G (?)

■ Canadian troops on the Western Front,
   February 1916.

Princess Patricia's Canadian Light Infantry
parade with the standard presented by the
Princess, and march to the trenches. They
enter heading towards "Prowse Point", the
shallow, waterlogged trench which forms
the junction of the British and Canadian
lines. 5th (Saskatchewan) Battalion, 1st
Division, repairs its own trenches and stops
for a meal. The men of the battalion stand
to in their trench (which like the others is
narrow, shallow and waterlogged) and send
out a reconnaissance party past some
shattered buildings and water-filled shell-
holes. One sniper is poised in the ruins of a
house's front room. The view from a front
line trench of shell-bursts over buildings in

the German positions. A short pan over the
Canadian line from an elevated position. An
officer and some men crouch in a wood
close to the enemy, possibly Mont Sorel.
Finally, a fenced enclosure for the graves of
"Canadian Heroes".

Notes
Remarks: in addition to the generally poor
film quality, which makes unit identification
difficult, much of this film does not look
right, and it may have quite a number of
fakes.
[shotsheet available]
catalogued SDB: 11/1982

IWM 256 · GB/Australia, 1916-18
**[AUSTRALIAN AND BRITISH TROOPS IN
FRANCE, 1916-18]** (allocated)

b/w · 2 reels · 1510' (25 mins) · silent
intertitles: none

■ Incoherent, jumbled collection of short
   pieces of Australian and British troops in
   France 1916-18.

Most of the film consists of unidentifiable
stockshots of guns, troops, wounded and
shell-dumps found in other films. Identifiable
and original material is as follows. *(Reel 1)*
Men of the Australian 1st and 2nd Divisions
in the Somme area in 1916; Field Marshal
Sir Douglas Haig and General Sir William
Birdwood reviewing Australian troops at
Ebblinghem on 29 August 1917; mailbags
being unloaded from a ship in a French
port; an 8-inch howitzer of 1st Australian
Siege Battery in action near Ypres on 12
September 1917. *(Reel 2)* Marching troops
and guns of 33rd Division (note the
divisional sign on limbers) and possibly
49th (West Riding) Division (note the
divisional sign on limbers again).

Notes
Summary: see also **IWM 151** *General
Birdwood Presenting Medals to Third
Australian Division.*
Remarks: the early Somme sequences are
very evocative.
[shotsheet available]
catalogued SDB: 11/1982

IWM 257 · GB, (?) 1918
AMERICANS TRAINING IN FRANCE

b/w · 1 reel · 520' (9 mins) · silent
intertitles: none

sp Ministry of Information (?)

- Training exercises for US troops under British (possibly XI Corps) supervision, Western Front, early 1918.

Sergeants of a British drill squad train US soldiers who carry British equipment and include a group of WACs. The Americans are put through bayonet practice against sandbags and parrying against a live opponent, and shown how to defend against a bayonet thrust using a knife. They go over an obstacle assault course, firing from a trench, rushing the next trench and bayoneting the sacks inside it, then firing again (some people play dead to add realism). They are shown how to deploy a Lewis machinegun, including the procedure if the machinegunner is shot and the number 3 has to take over. In a formalised open-air classroom setting the Lewis is stripped and tabletop maintenance carried out. The men practise fire-and-movement tactics from scrape trenches while wearing gas masks, smoke being laid down to simulate the barrage. Finally, they practise ordinary physical exercises.

Notes
Title: this is taken from the shotsheet.
[shotsheet available]
catalogued SDB: 11/1982

IWM 258 · GB, (ca) 1917
SCENES OF THE FRONT

b/w · 5 reels · 1725' (29 mins) · silent
intertitles: none

- Incoherent jumble of stockshots of British and Imperial forces on the Western Front, 1916-18.

Identifiable material is as follows. *(Reel 1)* A flight of Bristol F2B Fighters taking off from an aerodrome; Prime Minister W F Massey of New Zealand arriving in France, probably October 1916. *(Reel 2)* German prisoners loading captured light guns and machineguns onto lorries (compare with **IWM 105**); 4.5-inch howitzers and 18-pounders firing in the open and in an undisturbed village, possibly early 1916; British troops, probably in training, charging into smoke. *(Reel 4)* American 307th Infantry Regiment, attached to British 42nd Division for training, marching past Major-General Solly-Flood on 7 June 1918; VAD members picnicking in a wood; a fire at a large hay and fodder store. *(Reel 5)* First

aid being given at Number 3 Field Ambulance (?) possibly of the New Zealand Division. *(Reel 6)* Brigadier-General John Charteris, head of GHQ Intelligence, leaving a building in Montreuil, as despatch riders pass through the town; General Cadorna, the Italian C-in-C, entering a train; King George V at the firing of a 14-inch railway gun of 471st Siege Battery, Brayon, 8 August 1918.

Notes
Title: this is taken from the store ledger.
Summary: probably British official film throughout, perhaps compiled as background for a lecture or with a similar intention that is now lost. See also **IWM 105**, **IWM 216**, **IWM 269** and **IWM 289**.
Technical: the five reels of this film are numbered as 1, 2, 4, 5 and 6. Reel 3 appears to have once existed but cannot now be traced.
[shotsheet available]
catalogued SDB: 11/1982

IWM 259 · GB, 28/2/1916
DESTRUCTION OF A GERMAN BLOCKHOUSE BY A 9.2 HOWITZER
OFFICIAL PICTURES OF THE BRITISH ARMY IN FRANCE – SECOND SERIES (series)

b/w · 1 reel · 472' (8 mins) · silent
intertitles: English

sp War Office *pr* British Topical Committee for War Films *cam* Malins, Geoffrey H

- 9.2-inch howitzer of the Royal Garrison Artillery 'walking' its shells on top of a German blockhouse, Western Front, January 1916.

The howitzer is in a leafless wood. Its crew remove its camouflage, load the howitzer and elevate it (this is the number 4 gun of the battery). They uncover a pile of shells and roll them forward ready to be lifted up by special tongs. The howitzer fires, then is sponged out and reloaded three times. Another camera in a hide a short distance away from a German blockhouse records through a loophole the shells falling nearer to the target. Two officers in their Observation Post use trench periscopes to spot the fall of shot, and send a message via a field telephone to an RGA sergeant-trumpeter, who relays it to a second-lieutenant. Four more shells burst around the blockhouse, and the eighth shell fired scores a direct hit destroying the building.

The gunners clean out their gun and do maintenance work before re-covering it with camouflage.

Notes
Remarks: extremely entertaining, and quite well filmed, if genuine.
[Geoffrey H Malins, *How I Filmed the War*, Herbert Jenkins (1920): 76-79]
[shotsheet available]
catalogued SDB: 11/1982

IWM 260 · GB, 1918
PLUMER DECORATING WOMEN OF FANY AND VAD

b/w · 1 reel · 150' (2 mins) · silent
intertitles: none

sp Ministry of Information *pr* Topical Film Company *cam* McDowell, J B

- General Sir Herbert Plumer, commanding Second Army, presents medals for bravery to FANY and VAD officers at Blendecques, Western Front 3 July 1918.

The ceremony takes place in a field, with men of Plumer's staff watching as he pins medals for bravery onto women officers of the Queen Alexandra's First Aid Nursing Yeomanry and the Voluntary Aid Detachment, each in turn. One of the girls, and one of the staff officers, start giggling as the ceremony progresses. A final posed line of the FANY and VAD officers with their medals.

Notes
Title: this is taken from the shotsheet.
Summary: see also **IWM 268** *General Plumer Decorating Nurses* for a comparable investiture.
Remarks: Plumer, despite his undoubted military ability, had an almost caricatural appearance and was generally shy – the reaction of the staff officer and VAD member who start giggling in the middle of the ceremony is quite revealing.
[shotsheet available]
catalogued SDB: 11/1982

IWM 261 · GB, 1918
[AEROPLANE SALVAGE AND US FORCES ON THE WESTERN FRONT, JULY 1918] (allocated)

b/w · 1 reel · 661' (11 mins) · silent
intertitles: none

sp Ministry of Information *pr* Topical Film Company *cam* Buckstone, Walter A

I. Aeroplane salvage at Number 2 Army Salvage Depot, Western Front, 3 July 1918. Wrecks of crashed or damaged British aircraft arrive at the salvage depot on lorries, and the larger pieces are lifted off by crane. One almost complete fuselage is a Bristol F2B Fighter. The machines are stripped and the parts sorted. New engines are fitted to aircraft fuselages, and the results tested. Inside the sheds aeroplanes are rebuilt and the fabric doped. A group of officers watches a test flight (aircraft not shown) with binoculars, a telescope fitted to a bicycle wheel, and the naked eye. At another part of the dump the various items of salvage are thrown into bins marked "rubber", "brass", etc. Engines are removed from damaged aircraft bodies. A salvaged RE8 takes off. Wings are fitted to a rebuilt DH9.
II. British film of US forces celebrating Independence Day at or near Woirel, Western Front, 4 July 1918. Men of US 12th Engineers receive medals from the British Major-General Solly-Flood (?) at an inspection parade at Woirel (?). Solly-Flood also decorates some British soldiers, probably of his own 42nd (East Lancashire) Division. The Americans march past, and the colour party returns the two American standards to their tent. Not far away from the parade site, at the Philadelphia Hospital of Transport, a large crowd of Allied soldiers and nurses watch a baseball game. Officers and nurses stroll around as the game progresses, and a nurse helps a patient to eat.

Notes
Shotsheet: this is unusually detailed – in effect a dopesheet.
[shotsheet available]
catalogued SDB: 11/1982

IWM 262 · GB, (?) 1918
MACHINE GUNS – TANK WORKS

b/w · 1 reel · 575' (10 mins) · silent
intertitles: English

sp Ministry of Information (?)

- Lewis machinegun and tank manufacture by women, probably at the Birmingham Small Arms factory, 1918.

I. Women use various types of heavy plant, chiefly lathes or punches, to make Lewis

machineguns. One group rivets on the retaining pieces to the ammunition pans. Spraying the ammunition pans. Making the machinegun bolt, starting by profiling the camway, milling the extractor slot, boring and parting off the ferrules and profiling the receiver. One woman uses a die stamp to blank the ammunition pans, another mills the sides of the magazine centres using water as a coolant on the machinery and a third drills the centres while a fourth slots them. The captions are each headed "Woman doing...".
II. Men and women make ammunition boxes for tanks at workbenches. The women broach the roller bushes of the suspension system, using a type of lathe. Others mill the links for tank tracks, one holding up a link to the camera. The jaws of the track links are milled by machinery, drilled, chains are assembled and the whole fitted into the tracks, with the chains riveted on. One woman operates a press for riveting the outer walls of a tank, while men manœuvre the press into position. Women paint the hull of a Mk V Female tank, number 9835, which is near completion.

Notes
Title: this is taken from the shotsheet.
Remarks: the subtitling style is characteristically matter-of-fact, but the habit of starting every caption with "Woman doing..." or "Woman making...", even when there are men in shot, almost suggests that the film makers cannot quite believe that women are capable of such things. Certainly a main point of the film is not merely that the munitions are being made, but that it is women who are making them.
[shotsheet available]
catalogued SDB: 12/1982

IWM 263 · GB, (?) 1918
GUNS – BREECH MECHANISM

b/w · 1 reel · 265' (5 mins) · silent
intertitles: English

sp Ministry of Information (?) *cam* Woods-Taylor, G

- Women workers at the Armstrong Whitworth munitions works at Elswick in Yorkshire, operating heavy plant to make breeches and barrels for large calibre guns, probably 1918.

Notes
Intertitles: some of these are flashframes.
Summary: see also **IWM 419** *Women's Work*

on Munitions of War.
[shotsheet available]
catalogued SDB: 11/1982

IWM 264 · GB, (?) 1918
GUNS

b/w · 1 reel · 663' (11 mins) · silent
intertitles: English

sp Ministry of Information *cam* Woods-Taylor, G

- Women workers, supervised by men, constructing heavy guns at the Armstrong Whitworth munitions factory in Newcastle, probably 1918.

Notes
Intertitles: some of these are flashframes.
Summary: see also **IWM 419** *Women's Work on Munitions of War.*
Remarks: despite its length, this film consists of mere repetitions of women handling various pieces of heavy equipment and has no separate scenes or narrative.
catalogued SDB: 11/1982

IWM 265 · GB, 1918
the KING AND KING ALBERT INSPECTING THE GUARDS AT BUCKINGHAM PALACE

b/w · 1 reel · 71' (2 mins) · silent
intertitles: none

sp Ministry of Information
cam Woods-Taylor, G

- King George V and King Albert of Belgium inspect a reserve battalion of the Scots Guards at Buckingham Palace, 2pm, 6 July 1918.

The battalion (no clear view) marches past the sovereigns. King George wears his Field Marshal's uniform and King Albert his uniform as Colonel of the British 5th Dragoon Guards. A bouquet is presented to Queen Mary who is with them. Also present are Princess Mary, Prince Henry, Prince George, and Queen Elisabeth of Belgium with her son, the Count of Flanders.

Notes
Title: this is taken from the shotsheet.
[*The Times*, 8 July 1918: 11B, 11E]
[shotsheet available]
catalogued SDB: 11/1982

IWM 266 · GB, 1918
WITH THE BEF IN ITALY

b/w · 1 reel · 1120' (20 mins) · silent
intertitles: none

sp Ministry of Information (?) pr Topical Film
Company cam Raymond, H C

- Rear areas of the British positions on the
  Italian Front, in the Asiago valley,
  probably early 1918.

A pan over the valley with Asiago village in
the distance. A British lorry convoy comes
up a hairpin track to the top of a mountain
ridge. Asiago, filmed from the British lines
across the valley. British trenches cut out of
the rock on the valley side, with a small ski
hut used as an advanced headquarters.
One of the brigade commanders
(unidentified) sets out on foot patrol with
two of his staff across the wooded slope.
Royal Engineers use a pneumatic drill and
blasting powder to dig trenches out of the
rock on the slope. A "rope way", or
improvised rope cable system where lorries
unload supplies at the railhead and these
are taken up into the mountains by the
cables. A funeral, with full military honours,
of two British officers and an NCO killed in
an air raid, the first British casualties in Italy.
The bodies are buried at a church, possibly
Verona. General Sir Herbert Plumer, GOC
Italian Front, inspects a British brigade
which marches past. He converses with a
British divisional commander (back to
camera). A football match, possibly also in
Verona, between teams from the British
Contingent and the Italians, ending with a
posed group of both teams between the
goalposts.

Notes
Title: this is taken from the shotsheet.
Date: the store ledger gives the date of this
film as August 1918. This is impossible as
Plumer was in France at that date.
[shotsheet available]
catalogued SDB: 11/1982

IWM 267 · GB, (prod) 1918
**[US SIGNAL CORPS, ROYAL ENGINEERS
AND QMAAC ON THE WESTERN FRONT,
JULY 1918]** (allocated)

b/w · 1 reel · 328' (6 mins) · silent
intertitles: none

sp Ministry of Information pr Topical Film
Company cam Buckstone, Walter A

I. Men of US Signal Corps, probably
attached to British 42nd Division, erecting
telephone wires on top of poles, 6 July
1918.
II. Royal Engineers operating a beam
engine which bores for water. They clean
sludge out of the drill and fit new sections.
Villers-Bocage, 6 July 1918.
III. QMAAC and Red Cross work on
ambulances, Western Front, 7 July 1918.
Two girl fitters of Queen Mary's Auxiliary
Ambulance Corps doing maintenance work
on the wheels and the engine of their
ambulance. (Rather staged – the girls are
trying very hard not to be camera-
conscious.) QMAAC and Red Cross women
ambulance drivers and crews unload
stretchers from their ambulances, and go
into dug-outs wearing shrapnel helmets as
a protection against air raids. They then
start their vehicles and move off. The
ambulances have markings indicating that
they have been donated by various
charities and societies.

Notes
Shotsheet: this is unusually detailed, almost
a dopesheet.
[shotsheet available]
catalogued SDB: 11/1982

IWM 268 · GB, 1918
**GENERAL PLUMER DECORATING
NURSES**

b/w · 1 reel · 70' (1 min) · silent
intertitles: none

sp Ministry of Information pr Topical Film
Company cam McDowell, J B

- General Sir Herbert Plumer, GOC Second
  Army (back to camera) presents medals
  to a line of four British nurses in a field
  near Blendecques, Western Front, 26
  June 1918.

Notes
Title: this is taken from the shotsheet.
Summary: see also **IWM 260** Plumer
Decorating Women of FANY and VAD for a
comparable investiture.
[shotsheet available]
catalogued SDB: 11/1982

IWM 269 · New Zealand, 1918
**VISIT OF THE HON W F MASSEY AND
SIR J WARD TO THE WESTERN FRONT
30 JUNE-4 JULY 1918**

b/w · 1 reel · 1288' (22 mins) · silent
intertitles: none

cam Sanders, Henry A

- W F Massey and Sir Joseph Ward, Prime Minister and Minister of Finance of New Zealand, visit the New Zealand Division near the Bois de Warnimont, St-Léger sector, Western Front, 30 June-4 July 1918.

Massey and Ward are seen with the acting divisional commander, Brigadier-General F N Johnston (Major-General Russell was on sick leave in England) and accompanied by Brigadier-General G S Richardson, Commander NZEF (UK). They attend a church parade and address to 1st Brigade, the Engineers and the NZ (Maori) Pioneer Battalion. For the camera's benefit Ward gives a cigar to a giant Maori pioneer (Hemi) and they talk and smoke together. An inspection of the 2nd Brigade (the commander, Brigadier-General R Young, is visible), the divisional Artillery, the Squadron of Otago Mounted Rifles and the NZ Cyclist Battalion. At the 3rd NZ Rifle Brigade, accompanied by the brigade commander Colonel Stewart, they watch a demonstration of an aeroplane dropping a message and Ward takes part in a wireless demonstration. They inspect No 4 NZ Field Ambulance and talk to patients. They give speeches to the Rifle Brigade, the Entrenching Group, and to a reinforcement draft at the New Zealand Infantry and General Training Depot at Etaples. Finally, the divisional Machine Gun Battalion gives them a demonstration of setting up a Vickers machinegun at high speed. A posed shot of the battalion arranged in tiers behind the two men, while Massey, grinning broadly, menaces the camera with the Vickers and Ward acts as his loader.

Notes

Title: this is taken from the shotsheet (which, however, gives the end date as 2 July).
Technical: sequence of scenes scratched on negative. The film as held is mis-edited so that several scenes, particularly in the later part, are duplicated or out of sequence. See shotsheet for details.
Summary: this is the third of three known films taken of the New Zealand "Siamese Twins", Massey and Ward, on their visits to the NZEF in the UK and on the Western Front. The best description of the visit is by the NZ official correspondent, Captain Malcolm Ross (who can be identified in many of the scenes), in his detailed report

in the *Chronicles of the NZEF* (Vol IV, No 48 – 19 July 1918) from which it is possible to date each individual scene. Note the number of times the still photographer appears in shot: Sanders often took the still photographs himself, but on VIP visits worked with photographers from the NZ Records Section in the UK who came across with the VIP party.
Authority: additional detail from Christopher Pugsley, 12/1993.
[O E Burton, *The Auckland Regiment*, Whitcombe and Tombs (1922): 216]
[A E Byrne, *Official History of the Otago Regiment in the Great War*, J Wilkie (n.d.): 302]
[J Cowan, *The Maoris in the Great War*, Whitcombe and Tombs (1926): 140]
[shotsheet available]
catalogued SDB: 11/1982

IWM 270 · Australia (?), 1918
AUSTRALIANS AT VILLERS BRETONNEUX

b/w · 1 reel · 1089' (19 mins) · silent
intertitles: English

sp Australian War Records Section (?)

- Mixed genuine material of the village of Villers-Bretonneux after its capture by Australian forces 24-25 April and Australian training exercises, Western Front, 1918.

The village was captured at night, the remains are shown on the following morning, 25 April, with troops of 4th Australian Division moving through. A mortar team removes camouflage from a 9.45-inch 'flying pig' mortar, sponges it out and fires it. Two 6-inch mortars are also fired. Behind the lines men of the Transport sponge down their horses beside a stream. Soldiers of 2nd Australian Division assemble from a hayloft and fasten on their equipment, then form up and march away. An Infantry section trains with a Bangalore torpedo, using it to blow a hole through wire entanglements, which the men then rush through, fanning out at once. A reserve trench being dug in the rear areas. Sappers build a wooden bridge from freshly-chopped logs which they shape on a buzz-saw in a sawmill. A distant view of smoke over a heavily wooded valley, possibly Villers-Bretonneux. Australian wounded being brought out of the fighting by German prisoners (acting as Red Cross auxiliaries) and being loaded onto horse and motor ambulances. German prisoners outside an Australian YMCA in the rear areas. More prisoners marching down a road. The GOC Australian Corps, General Sir John Monash (back to camera), addresses his troops.

Notes
Title: this is taken from the shotsheet.
Production: probably Australian official film.
[shotsheet available]
catalogued SDB: 11/1982

IWM 271 · GB, (?) 1918
[CANADIAN SECTOR OF THE WESTERN FRONT IN JULY 1918] (allocated)

b/w · 1 reel · 444' (7 mins) · silent
intertitles: none

sp Ministry of Information (?) *pr* Topical Film Company

I. Visit of the Swedish Socialist leader Karl Branting to the Arras area, Western Front, 15 July 1918. Branting is in civilian clothes without shrapnel helmet or gas mask satchel, clearly in a safe part of the area, escorted by a Scottish officer. Near Vimy he talks to a British sentry and two French horsemen. He and his escort look over the ruins of Souchez church. The two, in their car, prepare to drive off; Branting raises his hat to the camera just before they do so.
II. A trip on a light railway in the Colonne area, Western Front, 16 July 1918. The area is generally devastated, and the camera, mounted on the light rail car, follows the ruins. Buildings are half-wrecked rather than pounded flat. Occasionally the brake-wheel of the car appears in the foreground. The car comes to a light railway siding showing a number of damaged trucks. Finally, the journey ends at Aix-Noulette, and the camera goes on to show the wreckage of the church and houses.
III. Canadian Engineers at Villers-Bocage starting work on a cutting for a light railway, Western Front, 13 July 1918. The Engineers use a plough to break up the ground for the cutting and mule-drawn scoops to clear the soil, coming round in a circle and building up a spoil embankment beside the cutting.

Notes
Production: probably British official film but possibly Canadian official material.
Shotsheet: this is unusually detailed, in effect a dopesheet.
[shotsheet available]
catalogued SDB: 12/1982

IWM 272 · GB, 1918
[US INFANTRY AT LE HAVRE AND WAACS AT ABBEVILLE CEMETERY, JULY 1918] (allocated)

b/w · 1 reel · 254' (5 mins) · silent
intertitles: none

sp Ministry of Information *pr* Topical Film Company *cam* McDowell, J B

I. US Infantry at Le Havre preparing to leave camp, Western Front, 10 July 1918. The men put on their equipment, showing very clearly how full marching pack and equipment was worn. They assemble by their bell tents and, led by two regimental colours (standards) and their band, they march out of camp, wearing waterproof capes and blanket rolls against the driving rain.
II. Ladies of the Women's Army Auxiliary Corps tend graves of dead soldiers at the military cemetery at Abbeville, Western Front, 19 July (?) 1918. The cemetery is large and semi-permanent (in that the crosses are of wood not stone) but is neatly laid out and well tended. The small group of ladies, very camera-conscious, lays wreaths on the graves, weeds and sweeps the path.

Notes
Date: there is some doubt as to the date of the second subject. The shotsheet gives 19 July but the apparently corresponding photographs are dated 9 February.
[shotsheet available]
catalogued SDB: 11/1982

IWM 273 · GB, (prod) 1918
CANADIAN PRESSMEN VISIT LORD BEAVERBROOK

b/w · 1 reel · 348' (6 mins) · silent
intertitles: none

sp Ministry of Information

■ Leading Canadian journalists visit Lord Beaverbrook, Minister of Information, at his home, Cherkley Court, England, 14 July 1918.

The party, in informal dress, walks in the gardens of the house. Beaverbrook's young daughter and two smaller sons (wearing kilts) are prominent. The group poses on the terrace steps, followed by a series of individual or small group portrait shots. The fourth of these is of Beaverbrook himself.

Notes
Title: this is taken from the shotsheet.
Summary: Beaverbrook appears to have arranged for visits of editors from the Dominions and India to Britain and the Western Front at approximately two-monthly intervals in summer and autumn 1918, diverting MoI cameramen and photographers onto recording this. *The Times* gives the names of the visiting party, but they remain unidentified on the film. *Remarks:* Beaverbrook's lavish treatment of the newspapermen shows the importance that, as a newspaperman himself, he placed on their role in winning the war. Sadly, the war was in the process of being won as he did so, and because of his diversion of MoI resources the record of this victory is far less complete than it might have been. The ethics of so using government employees are also questionable. The film portrait shot of Beaverbrook himself is superior to any photograph taken at the time.
[MOI(Photo) Papers]
[*The Times*, 11 July 1918: 5E]
[shotsheet available]
catalogued SDB: 11/1982

IWM 274 · GB, (prod) 1918
CANADIAN JOURNALISTS AT BRAMSHOT AND WITLEY

b/w · 1 reel · 290' (5 mins) · silent
intertitles: none

sp Ministry of Information
cam Woods-Taylor, G

■ Patchy film of leading Canadian journalists visiting the Canadian Training Division at Bramshot and Witley, near Aldershot, July 1918.

The divisional commander, Brigadier-General F S Meighan, shows the journalists around the training area. (Very broken film, extremely hard to follow.) The men are engaged in various kinds of training: a trench system, a boxing match, a battalion march past, making wire entanglements, Lewis machinegun exercises and bayonet practice.

Notes
Title: this is taken from the shotsheet.
[shotsheet available]
catalogued SDB: 11/1982

IWM 275 · GB, (ca) 1917
COOPER'S DIAGRAMS – HOUNSLOW

b/w · 1 reel · 247' (5 mins) · silent
intertitles: none

■ Short animated film on lorry driving techniques, probably made for the British Army during the First World War.

The film uses wire-controlled cutout shapes, white on a black background, to demonstrate in plan view a column of three lorries driving too close together down a road and colliding in a shunting accident when the lead one halts. Further demonstrations of a lorry correctly passing a horse and cart, and of a lorry reversing around a corner.

Notes
Title: this is taken from the shotsheet.
Summary: possibly connected with the Army Service Corps Driving School at Hounslow, see **IWM 242.**
[shotsheet available]
catalogued SDB: 11/1982

IWM 276 · GB, (prod) 1917
[GASMASKS OF THE FIRST WORLD WAR] (allocated)

b/w · 1 reel · 626' (11 mins) · silent
intertitles: none

sp War Office (?)

■ British stop-action and demonstration film of various gas masks and hoods used by both sides in the First World War, compiled about 1917.

I. The first sequence consists of static or stop-action scenes of a number of gas masks or gashoods displayed one at a time against a white background. Firstly, the British P or PH gashood of 1915, without its respirator valve in place. The German carrying case for their 1915 gashood with its Red Cross markings. The German respirator gauze pad of 1915, showing the contents of the pad. A Russian gas mask container of 1915 or 1916. An early French gashood of 1915 for the eyes and upper head only. A carrying satchel for the French respirator pad of 1915. A German gas mask with a leather facepiece, 1916, followed by its carrying canister. British mica anti-gas goggles of mid-1915. Probably a British container of detector strips for the presence of gas. A spare filter for the German 1916

pattern gas mask showing its contents. A German spare filter satchel, capable of carrying three filters, with one in place. Probably protective padding for a British small box respirator canister of 1916. A British black veiling face-mask of 1915 showing the chemically treated pad, followed by its carrying pouch. An experimental mask combining British eyepieces with the German filter system. A carrying canister for the German 1916 gas mask. The British 1917 pattern small box respirator, followed by its carrying satchel. Another view of the small box respirator, showing the detector guard and noseclip, followed by its carrying satchel. Three views of the US 1917 pattern small box respirator, including an example of the sectioned mouthpiece, followed by its carrying satchel with the record card open and another shot of the satchel. The French 'appareil respiratoire spécial' or ARS respirator of 1916, followed by its carrying case. The British large box respirator of 1916 in three versions, the second with goggles rather than eyepieces and the third opened to show the mask interior, followed by two views of the carrying satchel, showing its clip for fitting to the belt. A Russian respirator of about 1916. The British P or PH gashood with its respirator valve in place. A rare version of the British hypo gashood with a single mica window rather than eyepieces, 1915.
II. The remainder of the film shows British gas mask tests. A platoon on the march receives a gas alert and dons its small box respirators at speed, checked by its officer before continuing the march. Thick (and presumably fake) gas swirling in front of the camera being cleared by a soldier, just visible, with an Ayrton Fan. Various Royal Engineer sergeants demonstrate how to put on, as fast as possible, the P or PH gashood, the same with goggles rather than eyepieces, a version of the large box respirator with separate goggles, the German 1916 pattern respirator, and the French M2 gashood. A final, and very realistic, training exercise of British troops firing from trenches wearing the small box respirator.

[shotsheet available]
catalogued SDB: 11/1982

IWM 277 · GB, 1918
PROPAGANDA BY BALLOONS

b/w · 1 reel · 77' (2 mins) · silent
intertitles: none

sp Ministry of Information pr Topical Film Company cam Bassill, F A

- British soldiers launching balloons carrying propaganda leaflets to drift over enemy lines, near Béthune, Western Front, 4 September 1918.

A corporal and private of the Hampshire Regiment, overseen by a junior officer, use cylinders of gas to inflate medium-sized balloons. To each of these is attached a string carrying a bundle of leaflets and a slow fuse. The corporal lights the fuse (which when burnt through will release the leaflets) and launches one of the balloons. Two of the balloons float away into the sky.

Notes
Title: this is taken from the shotsheet.
[shotsheet available]
catalogued SDB: 11/1982

IWM 278 · GB, 1918
SCENES ON THE RHEIMS-EPERNAY FRONT

b/w · 1 reel · 685' (11 mins) · silent
intertitles: none

sp Ministry of Information pr Topical Film Company cam McDowell, J B

- British involvement in the Battle of Tardenois, mainly in the Bois de Reims, Western Front, July 1918.

6th Battalion, the Black Watch of 51st (Highland) Division collecting the men's packs between the Bois de Reims and St-Imoges, having just come out of line on 24 July. 1/5th Battalion, the Devonshire Regiment of 62nd (West Riding) Division, resting in the same wood on 24 July, with the sunlight on the leaves giving a dappled effect over the sleeping bodies. A nearby village after a German air raid, with American (?) troops clearing the debris while women and children watch. The view across the valley from the Bois de Reims on the same day, with British and Italian troops in the foreground. A field battery of Italian 8th Division in action while British and French troops watch. A posed group of British, French and Italian soldiers together. A British marching column, probably 8th Battalion, the West Yorkshire Regiment of 62nd Division. German prisoners help British and French soldiers bring wounded out from the wood on 23 July (the British are 2/20th Battalion, the London Regiment, of 62nd Division). German dead lying in the wood on 25 July. British, French and Italian lightly wounded posed in a group by a dressing station on the outskirts of the wood. British officers of 2/5th Battalion, the King's Own Yorkshire Light Infantry of 62nd Division consult with French officers over a map in the wood, and eat an outdoor meal with them – champagne is served. A distant puff of smoke rising from part of the wood, given as the Château Commetreuil near Cumas on fire on 25 July.

Notes

Title: this is taken from the shotsheet.
Remarks: a heavy emphasis on cooperation between the Allies marks this film. It is evocative and attractive compared to the bulk of material taken in the war, particularly in the case of the woodland scenes, which look almost too good to be true.
[A G Wauchope, *A History of the Black Watch in the Great War*, Vol 2, Medici Society (1926): 189-194]
[C T Atkinson, *The Devonshire Regiment 1914-1918*, Simpkin, Marshal, Hamilton, Kent and Company (1926): 375-378]
[dopesheet available]
[shotsheet available]
catalogued SDB: 11/1982

IWM 279 · GB, (?) 1918
PLANT AND OPERATIONS IN THE MANUFACTURE OF GASMASKS

b/w · 1 reel · 338' (7 mins) · silent
intertitles: none

sp Ministry of Information (?)

- Manufacture of the small box respirator at a Boots factory, probably Nottingham, 1918.

The workforce is mainly women working at benches or on production lines. They test rubber mouthpieces for leaks with a probe. They test the expiratory valves in the same manner. The corrugated tubes are tested for leaks by immersion in water at sinks fitted to the workbenches. The expiratory valves are tested on a vacuum machine. One bench tests the angle tubes with probes, and another by putting them in water. At another bench girls fill the canisters with chemicals, and these are then soldered shut. The join between the canister and corrugated tube is tested under water for leaks. Each canister is tested on a manometer to make sure that normal breathing is possible through it.

Another manometer is used to check pressure resistance on the cellulose pads, for the same reason. A spring balance is used to weigh the wool pads – the point is made that the balances are scratch built as an example of wartime economy. A sergeant demonstrates putting on the completed gas mask from the ready position. Women workers continue setting the valves on the angle tubes, and binding rubber round the valves to seal them. Another production line is at work wiring the angle tubes to the corrugated tubes. The finished masks are packed into satchels and the crates of satchels taken up in a conveyor belt. Outside the building the conveyor runs down to the street. After returned packages have been thrown onto it for return to the factory the completed crates come down and are loaded onto an electric platform, which drives away.

Notes

Title: this is taken from the shotsheet.
[shotsheet available]
catalogued SDB: 11/1982

IWM 280 · GB, 1918
CAVALRY EQUITATION SCHOOL

b/w · 1 reel · 480' (8 mins) · silent
intertitles: English

sp Ministry of Information *pr* Topical Film Company *cam* McDowell, J B

- British Cavalry training exercises at the Cavalry Equitation School, Cayeux, Western Front, 30 July 1918.

A Cavalry troop makes a charge across the face of the camera, thrusting with swords or lances at sacks stuffed with straw on the ground. All the demonstrators are riding light, without bandoliers, valises or helmets, throughout. Lancers charge wooden mock-ups of field guns from the flank, thrusting at targets around the guns. Swordsmen charge knockover dummies their own height, representing mounted opponents. A high jump, "Lion's Leap", is leapt by ten riders. More swordsmen, riding in extended order, charge knockover dummies representing kneeling soldiers. About ten riders make an open order charge straight at the camera. They continue over a combination jump, with one dummy to strike before the jump and one after. Another jump, "the double Oxo", is coped with. Several riders manage to jump "Lion's Leap" with a second horse on a lead rein.

Notes

Remarks: a good illustration of the open order mounted tactics of British Cavalry during the First World War, although the ease with which some very difficult pieces of riding are managed suggests that the riders are all school staff rather than trainees.
[dopesheet available]
[shotsheet available]
catalogued SDB: 11/1982

IWM 281 · GB, 1918
WITH THE VICTORIOUS BRITISH TROOPS ON THE AMIENS FRONT

b/w · 2 reels · 1514' (26 mins) · silent
intertitles: English

sp Ministry of Information *pr* Topical Film Company

- British compilation film of their own and French forces during the German 'Kaiserschlacht' offensive on the Western Front, March-April 1918.

A selection of the most visually attractive film taken by the British official cameramen during March and April (for the *German Offensive* series) without regard to date or place, padded out with stockshots of marching Allied troops and German prisoners. Starting and ending with Amiens, the film stresses that despite German efforts it did not fall. There is virtually no action and no fighting except for some distant shelling. There is heavy emphasis on cooperation between British and French forces mixed together, and on the part played by the Cavalry of both nations. The film's attitudes and limitations are conveyed by one scene of British and French soldiers relaxing captioned as "eager to meet the enemy, allied troops resting in a wood".

Notes

Summary: for the rough material from which this compilation was made, with full notes as to units, places and dates, see **IWM 178, IWM 180, IWM 182, IWM 183, IWM 184, IWM 185, IWM 186** and **IWM 190**.
[shotsheet available]
catalogued SDB: 11/1982

IWM 282 · GB, 1918
VISIT OF THE MAHARAJAH OF PATIALA TO FRANCE

b/w · 1 reel · 116' (2 mins) · silent
intertitles: none

sp Ministry of Information *pr* Topical Film Company *cam* Buckstone, W A

- The Maharajah visits British Fifth Army and Second Army areas, Western Front, July 1918.

The Maharajah's car arrives at Fifth Army headquarters on 31 July and is greeted by an honour guard. He wears a British Army uniform and a turban. He is shown a 12-inch railway gun firing at Annezin on the same day (General Sir William Birdwood, commanding Fifth Army, is present but not clearly visible). The Maharajah comes with his party on 30 July to the observation post on the Mont des Cats and looks through the twin trench periscopes. On the same day, he poses with the Second Army commander, General Sir Herbert Plumer, at his headquarters.

Notes

Title: this is taken from the shotsheet.
[shotsheet available]
catalogued SDB: 11/1982

IWM 283 · GB, 1918
WITH THE BRITISH FORCES IN ITALY – SEVEN DAYS LEAVE

b/w · 1 reel · 502' (9 mins) · silent
intertitles: none

sp Ministry of Information *pr* Topical Film Company *cam* Raymond, H C

- British troops enjoying rest and recreation, probably at Lake Garda, Italy, July 1918.

The soldiers are from various regiments and branches. One group returns from bathing in the lake, carrying towels and wearing khaki drill uniforms and 'Wolseley' pattern sun helmets with badges on the side. Outdoor lunch is served for troops at long tables. A sergeants' mess is a large white tent with tablecloths and waiter service. Soldiers rest and drink in the village square while a regimental band plays. Four sergeants from different regiments, in close-up, drink together around one table. A small paddle steamer brings more troops across the lake on leave, and as it docks they disembark, many still carrying their weapons. Officers swim, row and play in the lake itself.

Notes
Title: this is taken from the shotsheet.
Remarks: the unusually clear film quality provides some good views of the unorthodox uniforms and badges worn by the soldiers in Italy, and some good scenes of the village square.
[shotsheet available]
catalogued SDB: 11/1982

IWM 284 · GB, (prod) 1918
WATFORD MANUFACTURING COMPANY SPORTS (ledger title)

b/w · 1 reel · 1021' (18 mins) · silent
intertitles: none

sp Ministry of Information
cam Woods-Taylor, G

- Propaganda film of a company sports meeting in Watford, summer 1918.

The factory workforce (looking remarkably clean) emerges from the gates at the end of a shift, and goes on to the sports. These are a mixture of foot races, handicap races, obstacle races and a tug of war for men and women. None of the competitors wears athlete's clothing, and the absence of young men of military age becomes increasingly noticeable.

Notes
Title: this and the approximate date are taken from the store ledger. This film has no shotsheet.
catalogued SDB: 11/1982

IWM 285 · GB, (?) 1918
LIFE AT IWERNE MINSTER IN WAR TIME – AUGUST 7TH AND 8TH 1918

b/w · 1 reel · 1100' (19 mins) · silent
intertitles: English

sp Ministry of Information

- British inspirational propaganda film of a small rural community in Dorset in the last summer of the First World War.

The film stresses local personalities (some mentioned by name) and details of local life. At the village pump a notice-board is used for newspapers to spread news of the war. Children play around a maypole at the village school, which is used as a cinema in the evenings. Various thatched cottages in the village. Small-scale farming activities at a local farm, including butter-making, a farm show, and an auction where "heifers" (actually mainly bullocks) and rams are exhibited. More small activities, rabbit keeping, bee keeping, hive manufacture and poultry farming. German prisoners of war, still wearing their uniforms, work on the land with the local farmers, cutting down trees and making hay. The film's message is that "we must all pull together and everyone must do their best, then happiness and prosperity will come to our homes".

Notes
Date: the captioning suggests that the film, at least in this version, was released after the war. It has some similarities in message with the final inspirational propaganda films made by the MoI in November and December 1918.
Remarks: fascinating social history, using clichés to good effect. The portrayal of England as principally an agricultural country is in accord with the southern rural myth, rather than fact, and this film is a valuable contribution to this myth.
[shotsheet available]
catalogued SDB: 11/1982

IWM 286 · Australia, 1918
the AUSTRALIANS IN THE SOMME ADVANCE

b/w · 1 reel · 384' (6 mins) · silent
intertitles: none

sp Australian War Records Section
cam Wilkins, G H

- Australians in the Battle of Amiens, Western Front, 8 August 1918.

Probably filmed mostly before 8am (as fog is everywhere on the horizon) and on 2nd Australian Division Front. Pioneers advance in single file with spades and rifles using white tapes on the ground to guide themselves. 13th Light Horse (the Australian Corps mounted regiment) moves up with field limbers. Behind the lines, German prisoners move out of the way of a Mk V Male tank, 'Britannia' (B46) of 2nd Battalion, the Tank Corps, which comes directly into the camera, nearly knocking it over. 13th Light Horse wait in the fog. A damaged White armoured car is towed by another armoured car down a road out of the battle as ambulances pass the other way.

Notes
Title: this is taken from the shotsheet.
Summary: in the shotsheet the cameraman notes "the foggy weather made it impossible to get a connected story of good quality film".
[shotsheet available]
catalogued SDB: 11/1982

IWM 287 · GB, (ca) 1917
PIGEONS AND SEAPLANES

b/w · 1 reel · 231' (5 mins) · silent
intertitles: none

■ Carrier pigeons used to send messages from British seaplanes in the North Sea, during the second half of the First World War.

A Royal Engineers sergeant shows how to load two carrier pigeons into a small wicker basket for transport. At the Rosyth seaplane base Felixstowe F2A flying boats and Short 184 seaplanes ride at anchor or taxi through the water. One of the Shorts at rest on a choppy sea (filmed from a small boat which rises and falls with the waves). A carrier pigeon is released from the aircraft and flies away.

Notes
Title: this is taken from the shotsheet.
[shotsheet available]
catalogued SDB: 11/1982

IWM 288 · NO FILM

IWM 289 · GB, 1918
the KING'S VISIT TO FRANCE AUGUST 1918

b/w · 1 reel · 964' (16 mins) · silent
intertitles: English

sp Ministry of Information *pr* Topical Film Company *prod* Jury, William F
cam McDowell, J B (and Wilkins, G H ?)

■ Patchy review of King George V's visit to the Western Front, August 1918.

The King, in Field Marshal's uniform and unaccompanied by other members of the Royal family, arrives at Calais on HMS *Whirlwind* on 5 August. Three days later he inspects British and US pilots of RAF 1st

Brigade at Izel-les-Hameaux with General Plumer. On 6 August he reviews US 30th Division at Biezen with their commander, Major-General Lewis. At Blendecques he presents the Victoria Cross to Captain J T Crowe of 2nd Battalion, Worcestershire Regiment, Second-Lieutenant C L Knox of 150th Field Company, Royal Engineers and Sergeant C L Train of 2/14th Battalion, London Regiment (2nd London Scottish), and the GCB to General Plumer. On 7 August at Bouin he watches trees being felled by Number 365 Forestry Company, Royal Engineers. He meets Field Marshal Haig at his headquarters, Château de Beaurepaire, Montreuil, on 7 August with President Poincaré, and inspects the honour guard of Royal Guernsey Light Infantry. Back at Izel-les-Hameaux on 8 August, with General Horne, he meets pilots of 203 Squadron RAF beside their Sopwith Camels. At Sautrecourt on 10 August he watches a tank and Infantry demonstration with Brigadier-General Elles, and at Mametz on the same day meets Colonel A Barbosa, commanding 1st Portuguese Division. At Cassel on 11 August he watches a march past by Second Army troops, including US forces, and gives Americans of 30th Division some British decorations (the caption identification of General Rawlinson is incorrect). At Australian Corps headquarters, Bertangles Château, on 12 August, he knights General Sir John Monash, the Corps commander, and Major-General M W O'Keeffe, Fourth Army Director of Medical Services. Finally, he leaves Calais on board HMS *Whirlwind* on 13 August.

Notes
Cameraman: some Australian film has been used, and this was probably taken by Wilkins as the official Australian cameraman.
Summary: see also reel 99, which consists of out-takes and additional material of the visit. See also **IWM 293** *King Visits Australian Headquarters – Australian Divisional Commander Re-opens Destroyed Bridge.*
[shotsheet available]
catalogued SDB: 11/1982

IWM 290 · GB, (prod) 1918
[AUGUST OFFENSIVE 1 (?)] (allocated)

b/w · 1 reel · 646' (11 mins) · silent
intertitles: none

sp Ministry of Information *pr* Topical Film Company *cam* Bassill, F A

- British rough material of the Battle of Amiens, Western Front, August 1918.

Highland troops (possibly London Scottish of 56th Division) display captured German 76mm wheeled mortars with detachable trail pieces. A British column of veterans in shirtsleeves, possibly also of 56th Division, marches through a damaged village street. Further up the street a Mk IV Male supply tank marked "BAGGAGE" is trapped in a traffic jam. In open marshy ground a Mk V Female tank is stuck and has a hawser passed over it before being pulled out by another Mk V Female. A concert party, including a 'gypsy' violinist and a pierrot group, plays to troops from an improvised outdoor stage. A continuation of the tank being hauled out of the marsh, using its unditching beam to help. US Infantry, probably of 33rd Division, resting and waving at the camera. A marching column of Highlanders moving over open country. Two British soldiers, in a wrecked building, display for the camera two different types of captured German machinegun, the 08 pattern Maxim and the 08/15 pattern Bergmann. More US troops of 33rd Division, moving in extended single file over rolling grassland, possibly on a route march.

Notes
Summary: probably the 'missing' first episode of the *August Offensive* rough material. See also **IWM 295, IWM 296, IWM 300** and **IWM 301**.
Remarks: very difficult to interpret. The normal practice of teaming cameramen and still photographers seems to have broken down under the various pressures of August 1918, including the King's visit to France, leaving virtually no supporting evidence for the series.
[shotsheet available]
catalogued SDB: 11/1982

IWM 291 · GB, 1918
a PORTUGUESE TRAINING CAMP IN ENGLAND – ROFFEY CAMP, HORSHAM

b/w · 1 reel · 514' (9 mins) · silent
intertitles: none

sp Ministry of Information *cam* Raymond, H C

- British film of the Portuguese forces in training in England, 15 August 1918.

The Portuguese officers pose with their British liaison and training staff. A parade

ground march past, possibly gunners doing formation drill. Semaphore practice on the parade ground. Gun teams practise the full drill of loading, laying and firing the 6-inch howitzer, miming the presence of a shell. Troops do physical exercises under a British instructor. A posed group of officers and civilians watch the display, including the Portuguese 'Minister' to Great Britain (Ambassador?) Dr Augusto de Vasconcellos. A race by troops in running kit. A demonstration of Portuguese singlestick fighting (Jogo do Pau). A 'reveille race' in which the runners dress in full kit before setting off over various obstacles. Portrait shots of the Portuguese Corps commander General Rosado, firstly with his staff and then by himself.

Notes
Title: this is taken from the shotsheet where the camp name is given as 'Roffley'. This is assumed to be a misspelling of Roffey, which is near Horsham.
[shotsheet available]
catalogued SDB: 11/1982

IWM 292 · GB, (prod) 1918
FOOD CONTROL DELEGATES AT CONFERENCE (ledger title)

b/w · 1 reel · 192' (4 mins) · silent
intertitles: none

sp Ministry of Information *cam* Woods-Taylor, G

- Delegates to the International Food Control Conference at the Ministry of Food, London, late July 1918.

A portrait shot of, possibly, the chief US delegate Herbert Hoover. A group shot of the delegates, from the major Allies, descending a stairway into the Ministry grounds. Some delegates (none identified) are shown in detail. Finally, on the steps of the Ministry, beside its nameplate, appears the Minister of Food, J R Clynes.

[*The Times*, 20 July 1918: 3E]
[*The Times*, 24 July 1918: 6B]
catalogued SDB: 11/1982

IWM 293 · GB, (prod) 1918
KING VISITS AUSTRALIAN HEADQUARTERS – AUSTRALIAN DIVISIONAL COMMANDER RE-OPENS DESTROYED BRIDGE

b/w · 1 reel · 260' (5 mins) · silent
intertitles: none

sp Australian War Records Section
cam Wilkins, G H

I. The knighting of Sir John Monash by King
George V at Australian Corps headquarters,
Western Front, 12 August 1918. The King
arrives by car at Bertangles Château, the
Corps headquarters, and walks past
captured German guns and howitzers on
the lawns. In front of the château he knights
General Sir John Monash, the Australian
Corps commander, and Major-General M W
O'Keeffe, Fourth Army's Director of Medical
Services.
II. The repair of a damaged bridge at
Chérisy by 3rd Australian Pioneer Battalion
and its opening by Major-General Sir John
Gellibrand of 3rd Australian Division,
Western Front, 18 August 1918.

Notes
Title: this is taken from the shotsheet.
Summary: see also **IWM 289** The King's Visit
to France August 1918.
Shotsheet: this is unusually detailed, almost
constituting a dopesheet.
[shotsheet available]
catalogued SDB: 11/1982

IWM 294 · GB, 1918
AUGUST OFFENSIVE 3
ON THE BAPAUME FRONT – THE KEY TO
THE HINDENBURG LINE (alternative)

b/w · 1 reel · 440' (7 mins) · silent
intertitles: none

sp Ministry of Information pr Topical Film
Company cam McDowell, J B

■ British rough material of the Battle of
Amiens, Western Front, 23 August 1918.

I. A battery of Field Artillery in medium shot
moving rapidly across country, followed by
a close-up of the last two guns passing a
small hut at the trot. A stationary Medium A
Whippet tank (B37, possibly of 6th
Battalion, the Tank Corps) with all its
hatches open and two of the crew firing
Hotchkiss machineguns into the air (at
German aircraft ?). Soldiers in combat gear,
possibly 13th Battalion, Royal Fusiliers of
37th Division near Grévillers, posed in a
group shot, then resting and eating. A Field
Artillery park near Bapaume with bell tents
and horse lines. A railway cutting near
Achiet-le-Grand, captured by 13th Royal

Fusiliers on 21 August. Men digging beside
the wreck of a munitions wagon with its
dead horses still in harness. Two dead
Germans, one as if killed in the act of
throwing the stick grenade still in his hand,
the other next to an anti-tank rifle (both
probably posed while dead).
II. Attached to this is a brief scene of a
Canadian corporal buying a War Bond from
an officer seated at a table in the open air.

Notes
Title: both titles appear on the shotsheet.
Summary: see also **IWM 290**.
[shotsheet available]
catalogued SDB: 11/1982

IWM 295 · GB, (prod) 1918
ATTACK SOUTH OF ARRAS
[AUGUST OFFENSIVE 2] (alternative,
allocated)

b/w · 1 reel · 454' (8 mins) · silent
intertitles: none

sp Ministry of Information pr Topical Film
Company cam McDowell, J B

■ British rough material of the Battle of
Amiens, Western Front, mid-August 1918.

Houses in a village, already badly
damaged, being struck again by shell fire or
deliberately demolished. Shell-bursts in the
middle distance falling by a partly ruined
village. Another shell falling on a damaged
house, filmed through a window frame. 3rd
Battalion, the Grenadier Guards, occupy a
slit trench near Courcelles. Other men of
the Guards Division round up a few German
prisoners and lead them away. More
guardsmen work to expand and improve a
scrape trench. Open country with shell fire
in the distance and a few figures walking
towards it. A middle-distance view of a
single file of Cavalry on patrol in open
ground, possibly 18th Hussars on 21
August near Courcelles, possibly staged. A
single shell hits very close to the column
and when the dust clears two horses have
fallen. The riders get up safely, and the
column prepares to move on leaving the
horses, one still stirring on the ground.

Notes
Title: this is taken from the shotsheet.
Summary: see also **IWM 290**. This film is in
effect part of the August Offensive group,
but did not have that designation as part of
its title.
Remarks: impressive material giving a good

sense of action. It strains credulity that both cameraman and still photographer should happen to record the instant a shell hit a Cavalry column, but the photographs may be film stills.
[C Burnett, *The Memoirs of the 18th (Queen Mary's Own) Royal Hussars 1906-1922,* Warren and Sons (1926): 140]
[shotsheet available]
catalogued SDB: 11/1982

IWM 296 · GB, (prod) 1918
[CELEBRATIONS IN PARIS, 14TH JULY 1918] (allocated)

b/w · 1 reel · 130' (3 mins) · silent
intertitles: English

sp Ministry of Information *pr* Topical Film Company

■ Very brief film of Allied troops marching through central Paris, 14 July 1918.

Crowds watch as the procession passes. French lancers moving at the trot are followed by a French Infantry band, then more lancers. Tirailleurs in parade uniform are followed by a small US mounted contingent. A British battalion passes, led by its band. An Australian battalion passes. President Poincaré (not clearly seen) decorates a line of soldiers of various nationalities (note the American official cameraman at work in the background).

[shotsheet available]
catalogued SDB: 12/1982

IWM 297 · GB, 1918
CANADIAN JOURNALISTS LEAVE LONDON

b/w · 1 reel · 163' (3 mins) · silent
intertitles: none

sp Ministry of Information *cam* McDowell, J B (?)

■ Delegation of Canadian newsmen on a Ministry of Information tour leave London for France, July 1918.

The party assembles in twos and threes outside its hotel, and its members are seated one at a time to have formal portrait photographs taken. The man taking the photographs may be G P Lewis, the MoI official photographer. They enter taxis and

drive through central London. Arriving at their station, probably Waterloo, they are shown on board their train by two Army staff officers.

Notes
Title: this is taken from the shotsheet.
Cameraman: the store ledger gives the cameraman as McDowell but this seems unlikely unless he returned to England for the purpose.
Summary: see also **IWM 273** and **IWM 274**.
[shotsheet available]
catalogued SDB: 11/1982

IWM 298 · GB, (?) 1918
ANTI-AIRCRAFT GUNS – FRANCE
the DESTRUCTION OF A FOKKER (offcuts and mixed material)

b/w · 1 reel · 205' (4 mins) · silent
intertitles: none

sp Ministry of Information (?)
cam Buckstone, W A (?)

I. British instructional film in techniques of anti-aircraft fire using the lorry-mounted 13-pounder gun, Western Front, 1916-18. Two gunners use a rangefinder and a telescope to mark on a ranging board the correct fuse settings for anti-aircraft fire. A battery of two 13-pounders (probably Mk IXs) on Vauxhall Mk IV lorry mounts are driven along a narrow road in flat terrain. They halt, and the crews set up fire control and deploy the guns. The fire control group uses a large rangefinder, a small telescope and an angle meter. The crew ceases fire, packs up the guns and drives off. Back at the camp, a sergeant marks up numbers on the ranging board assisted by an officer, who watches for errors.
II. A brief sequence of a field gun, possibly an 18-pounder rigged for high angle fire, mounted on a firing platform in some wooded hills, filmed from the front. The crew may not be British. Perhaps Salonika Front before 1918.

Notes
Title: this is taken from the shotsheet.
Cameraman: the store ledger gives the cameraman as Buckstone, but parts of this film are taken from films made over a year before he went to the Western Front.
Summary: see also **IWM 470**.
[shotsheet available]
catalogued SDB: 11/1982

IWM 299 · GB, (?) 1918
GRAHAM WHITE'S FIRST ANNUAL SPORTS

b/w · 1 reel · 99' (2 mins) · silent
intertitles: none

- Sports day at a British Army
  convalescent camp, probably in Britain,
  1918.

The sports are held by convalescent
soldiers wearing hospital blue uniforms, and
by nurses. A man and woman in civilian
clothes, well-dressed, throw sweets to the
crowd of convalescents. The sports consist
of a tug of war, a three-legged race with
soldiers tied to nurses, a bicycle race and a
wheelbarrow joust in which the men try to
knock a bucket of water off a
counterbalance.

Notes
Title: this is taken from the shotsheet.
[shotsheet available]
catalogued SDB: 11/1982

IWM 300 · GB, (prod) 1918
[AUGUST OFFENSIVE 4] (allocated)

b/w · 1 reel · 397' (7 mins) · silent
intertitles: none

sp Ministry of Information *pr* Topical Film
Company *cam* Bassill, F A

- British rough material of the Battle of
  Amiens, Western Front, 25-27 August
  1918.

Infantry with a Lewis machinegun team
moving through rubble and wreckage,
possibly at Miraumont. British soldiers
displaying a captured German anti-tank rifle
(given by the shotsheet as Royal West
Kents at Pys, but more probably New
Zealanders near Grévillers). A cutting being
filled with rubble and a bridge built over it
by German prisoners just behind the lines
at Aveluy, north of Albert. A British
marching column, about a company strong,
38th (Welsh) Division (?) near Pozières. A
dressing station also near Pozières with bell
tents, where a line of wounded lie on
stretchers on the ground. One RAMC man
there gives a cup of water to a wounded
German officer, and an American officer
talks to some of the Germans on their
stretchers. A massed crowd of several
hundred German prisoners at Abbeville on
27 or 28 August milling around.

Notes
Summary: see also **IWM 290** and the
August Offensive group.
[shotsheet available]
catalogued SDB: 11/1982

IWM 301 · GB (?), (ca) 1917
[SHELLBURSTS] (allocated)

b/w · 1 reel · 340' (6 mins) · silent
intertitles: none

- Seven brief shell-bursts over open
  ground or the remains of houses, all
  medium or long shots with no figures
  visible. Presumably Western Front during
  the First World War.

Notes
Summary: presumably a fragment of a
longer film.
[shotsheet available]
catalogued SDB: 12/1982

IWM 302 · GB, (prod) 1918
AUGUST OFFENSIVE 7

b/w · 1 reel · 692' (12 mins) · silent
intertitles: none

sp Ministry of Information *pr* Topical Film
Company *cam* Bassill, F A

- British rough material of the Battle of
  Amiens and the Advance to the
  Hindenburg Line, Western Front, August
  1918.

A column of RFA limbers reloads from a
dump of 18-pounder shells beside a track
before moving forward, possibly near
Harlincourt. A group of soldiers, possibly
Royal Scots Fusiliers, walks in loose order
towards the camera through the dust of a
track. Transport and RFA limbers move past
Achiet-le-Grand station, which has two
captured German 150mm howitzers outside
it. Near Sapignies an officer directs the fire
of two 6-inch Mk VII guns, and the map is
reset for indirect fire. The two guns are
each hooked up to their two-wheel trail
limbers and towed to a new position by Holt
tractors. British troops dig in the remains of
a wood, clearing the trees, not far from
Bailleul. The main square at Bailleul
consists only of an open space surrounded
by rubble. Meteren, just south of Ypres, is
in a similar condition. Near Merville, a girder
bridge has been blown up and has

collapsed into the cutting below it.

Notes

Title: no record has been found of *August Offensive* episodes 5 and 6. The title has been taken from the shotsheet.
Summary: see also **IWM 290**.
Remarks: Bailleul was captured on 9 July and the other locations are similarly 'safe' areas. Either the cameraman could not get forward or he used the opportunity to cover regions which it had not been possible to film while they were being fought over.
[shotsheet available]
catalogued SDB: 12/1982

IWM 303 · GB, (?) 1918
GERMAN NAVAL INACTIVITIES

b/w · 1 reel · 152' (3 mins) · silent
intertitles: none

sp Ministry of Information (?) *pr* Messter Film (original production company)

■ British propaganda film made from German actuality material of sailors and marines relaxing in Ostend, First World War.

German naval officers, sailors and some soldiers wander through the streets of Ostend. A tram passes, pulling a line of freight carriages. At a tram stop a marching band leads a group of soldiers on board a tram, which drives off with the sailors left behind waving goodbye. A tram with Red Cross markings passes. Sailors play in the sea and sand on the beach. (According to the subtitles in the shotsheet, the British propaganda point was that the Germans were busy searching for the British Fleet – in Ostend.) A mixed group of sailors and marines beside a war memorial (perhaps the Dutch-Belgian War of 1831) near the sea front. Back on the beach the sailors continue with their games.

Notes

Title: this is taken from the shotsheet.
Intertitles: one flashframe negative title remains on the film. The titles were, according to a note on the leader tape, removed as sticky in May 1925.
Production: according to the shotsheet, this is originally German film produced by Messter Film of Berlin, found in a captured U-boat by a British destroyer. It has been re-edited by the British.
[shotsheet available]
catalogued SDB: 1/1983

IWM 304 · GB, 1918
VISIT OF AMERICAN AIRMEN TO SHAKESPEARE'S COUNTRY

b/w · 1 reel · 500' (9 mins) · silent
intertitles: none

sp Ministry of Information *cam* Cooper, F (?)

■ Highly disjointed account of a semi-official visit by US airmen to Warwickshire, August-September 1918.

The visit was organised by the Birmingham and District Professions and General Trades Fund for the Wounded. Outside Queen's College, Birmingham, Major-General Higgins (?) inspects the Americans who parade through the streets led by a band and a large dog as mascot. They then arrive in Stratford in a convoy of cars and two lorries draped with the US flag. The mayor of Stratford addresses them at a reception at Shakespeare's birthplace, making his speech from the top of a set of library steps. A baseball game at Stratford. A British Avro 504 which "just dropped in" (according to the shotsheet) takes off from a farm, cheered by the Americans. The airmen take a trip on the River Avon in a pleasure steamer. In a humorous episode, a British policeman chases one of the Americans who tries to vault the gate of a field – it collapses under him and the policeman lands on top. The men attend an official reception in a park in Leamington Spa, followed by a formal banquet in the Courthouse at Warwick and a procession led by the mayor of Warwick towards the castle. Inside Warwick Castle the men are addressed by Canon Tovey (?). A posed group of the eight members of the organising committee. The whole party then poses, including Major-General Higgins, the custodian of the castle, Mrs Marsh, and her guests, the Duke of Rutland and Earl and Countess of Denbigh. Mr J H Francis, the Fund's chairman, is posed on a bench with his wife. Children wave as the lorries carrying the airmen drive off (the film starts to break up at this point). The film ends with a posed scene of an officer of the Royal Flying Corps taking a 'Dutch' light for his cigarette from one of the US aviators, both of them keeping their cigarettes in their mouths. The effect is not unlike a kiss.

Notes

Title: this is scratched in MS on the leader.
[shotsheet available]
catalogued SDB: 12/1982

IWM 305 · GB, 1918
REMOUNTS AT RUSSLEY PARK

b/w · 1 reel · 456' (8 mins) · silent
intertitles: none

sp Ministry of Information *cam* Davis, W

- Army Remount Depot at Lady Birkbeck's
  Stud Farm, Russley Park, on the
  Hampshire Downs, August 1918.

Horses from the farm are exercised by
young ladies of the Women's Land Army
Agricultural Section, acting as grooms. The
horses are cantered around a paddock and
over a low jump. Each of the eight girls
emerges from a stable door, carrying
buckets of water, bags of oats or a saddle.
Two of them use a pole and noose to hold
up a horse's head while pouring medicine
down its throat (described as "fastening the
bit" in the shotsheet). The girls lead pairs of
horses from the stables and through the
main gate – one pair shies at the camera –
and mount up. Each riding one horse and
leading another the girls move out along
the country road at a slow trot. Each girl
holds the lead reins of her two horses while
they graze in a field. A face-on shot of a
white-faced bay fades into its girl keeper
who is handed her mascot, a tiny kitten.
Some of the girls load saddles into a
buckboard and drive off with them, waving
at the camera. Two girls clean out the
stables with rakes and a wheelbarrow. The
horses are groomed outside their loose
boxes by the girls, one having its tail
washed and soaped. Finally, the girls wear
their full Land Army riding uniform to lead
the horses out for exercise as before.

Notes
Title: this is taken from the shotsheet.
Remarks: a 'cute' but charming piece of
work, with no obvious propaganda
message.
[shotsheet available]
catalogued SDB: 12/1982

IWM 306 · NO FILM

IWM 307 · GB, (prod) 1918
DEPTFORD RED CROSS WEEK

b/w · 1 reel · 447' (8 mins) · silent
intertitles: none

sp Ministry of Information (?) *cam* Davis, W

- Parade and fête in Deptford during the
  first week in September, 1918.

A group of four police constables outside
Deptford main police station is joined by a
fifth policeman. Groups of policemen
emerge from the station, two riding past on
bicycles. A portrait shot of one constable
with a walrus moustache. People at the
fête, in the grounds of Goldsmiths' College,
playing at the various sideshows or having
tea. They include convalescent soldiers in
hospital blues. The parade goes past the
town hall and through the streets, the floats,
including a crusade tableau, a mock
aeroplane and tank, and the boy scouts, all
supervised by Army officers. Back at the
fête a conjuror demonstrates a trick and
more games are played at the sideshows,
one involving a caricature of the Kaiser,
"Come and Nail Kaiser Bill". Finally, a posed
group of the organisers, among them some
in pierrot costume.

Notes
Title: this is taken from the shotsheet.
[shotsheet available]
catalogued SDB: 12/1982

IWM 308a · GB, 12/9/1918
PICTORIAL NEWS (OFFICIAL) 368-1 [2]

b/w · 1 reel · 3' (1 min) · silent
intertitles: none

sp Ministry of Information *pr* Topical Film
Company

- Shorter version of the story held as **IWM
  308d** showing US aviators in Stratford.

[shotsheet available]
catalogued SDB: 6/1983

IWM 308b · GB, 16/9/1918
PICTORIAL NEWS (OFFICIAL) 368-2

b/w · 1 reel · 153' (3 mins) · silent
intertitles: none

sp Ministry of Information *pr* Topical Film
Company

I. An artificial hand for amputees developed
in Britain, 1918. A British soldier
demonstrates that with his artificial right
hand he can rake a garden, pick up and
open a bag, light a cigarette, drink a glass
of water, use a knife and fork, and throw

and catch a ball.

II. Lloyd George arriving in Manchester by car, 12 September 1918. A procession, led by Lloyd George and the Lord Mayor, comes down the steps of the Council Chamber and Lloyd George gets into a car. It is raining hard. Lloyd George talks to a crowd of people, including women war workers, waiting for him. A pan over a group of convalescent soldiers in hospital blues. Then Lloyd George again on the steps of Manchester Town Hall delivering a speech, then inspecting a parade of soldiers in a wet, foggy street.

Notes
Summary: note that a Spanish-language version of the second item is **IWM 682**.
[shotsheet available]
catalogued SDB: 6/1983

IWM 308c · GB, (prod) 1918
[ROYAL NEWFOUNDLAND REGIMENT (?)] (allocated)

b/w · 1 reel · 30' (1 min) · silent
intertitles: none

sp Ministry of Information *pr* Topical Film Company

■ Very brief scene of a parade of soldiers being addressed by civilians, possibly the visit of J R Bennett to the Royal Newfoundland Regiment at Ecuires, France, June 1918.

Notes
Summary: compare with **IWM 253**.
[shotsheet available]
catalogued SDB: 6/1983

IWM 308d · GB, 12/9/1918
PICTORIAL NEWS (OFFICIAL) 368-1 [1]

b/w · 1 reel · 44' (1 min) · silent
intertitles: none

sp Ministry of Information *pr* Topical Film Company

■ Visit by US airmen to Birmingham, September 1918.

The airmen are shown seated with civilians, possibly in the hall of Queen's College, Birmingham, and then formed up to enter the building. A pan over a group of civilians, probably the organisers of the Americans'

trip, from the Birmingham and District Professions and General Trades Fund.

Notes
Summary: note that a shorter version of this item is **IWM 308a**; see also **IWM 304**.
[shotsheet available]
catalogued SDB: 6/1983

IWM 309 · GB, (prod) 1918
SPORTS AT STAMFORD BRIDGE

b/w · 1 reel · 142' (3 mins) · silent
intertitles: none

sp Ministry of Information *cam* Woods-Taylor, G

■ British Army sports at Stamford Bridge football ground in Fulham, London, early September 1918.

All the competitors wear athletics kit and the stadium is quite full. There is a flat race, a pole vault, and a hurdling race. The teams parade around the ground led by a military band. More sports include the start of a long distance race, the finish of a sprint, another sprint, a long jump and a relay race. Some of the competitors are given medals and other awards, having changed into their Army uniforms.

Notes
Title: this is taken from the shotsheet.
Remarks: the film is rather grainy, and compressing so much into three minutes has meant that all the scenes are very brief indeed.
[shotsheet available]
catalogued SDB: 12/1982

IWM 310 · GB, 1918
VISIT OF CANADIAN PRESSMEN – SCENES IN ENGLAND AND FRANCE

b/w · 1 reel · 465' (9 mins) · silent
intertitles: English

sp Ministry of Information

■ Visit of a delegation of prominent Canadian newsmen to England and France as guests of the Ministry of Information, July 1918.

A party in the garden of Lord Beaverbrook's home at Cherkley Court on 14 July for the journalists and some prominent Canadian politicians. Shown in portrait shot are Sir Edward Kemp, the Canadian Minister for Overseas Forces, T C Norris, the Premier of Manitoba, George Stewart, the Premier of Alberta, and W W Martin, the Premier of Saskatchewan. The journalists are shown around the Canadian Training Division at its training grounds at Bramshot and Witley, Aldershot Command. Brigadier-General H F McDonald takes the salute as one battalion marches past. In France General Sir Arthur Currie, the Canadian Corps commander, shows the men over the old Vimy Ridge battlefield. The journalists pose with Field Marshal Haig on the steps of his Château de Beaurepaire at Montreuil on 22 July. At Hangest on 27 July they watch the Canadian Cavalry Brigade pass by in company with its commander, Brigadier-General R W Paterson. They look over Hazebruck and then go on to Ypres in a light railway train. Film taken from the train shows the remains of the Cloth Hall, which they investigate. At Verdun they are escorted by French Army guides to a high point for an overall view and are then taken into one of the deep dug-outs. They leave for England from Boulogne in a camouflaged passenger ship on 29 July.

Notes
Summary: see also **IWM 273**, **IWM 274** and **IWM 297**.
Remarks: it is noteworthy that the MoI thought this visit of sufficient importance not merely to record it but to make an edited film.
[MoI(Photo) Papers, File on H G Bartholomew]
[shotsheet available]
catalogued SDB: 12/1982

IWM 311 · GB, 1918
BLACKBERRYING IN BRENTFORD

b/w · 1 reel · 296' (5 mins) · silent
intertitles: none

sp Ministry of Information *cam* Davis, W

- Children picking blackberries for food at Brentford, Middlesex, September 1918.

A group of children, under the direction of two or three adults. Each takes a wicker basket and picks the blackberries from nearby bushes. One of the adults stands by a grocer's van with a Ministry of Food poster on it and holds up another poster, advertising the fruit, for the children. Each child comes forward to have his or her basket weighed and is paid (possibly in sweets). One of the men holds up a small silver trophy. The children all raise their hands in acknowledgement – they may have been asked if they have enjoyed themselves. A final posed group of the children with one boy and one girl in front, sitting with a large basket full of blackberries between them.

Notes
Title: this is taken from the shotsheet.
Remarks: the children have probably been told to smile at the camera, and have ended up looking sullen or hostile.
[shotsheet available]
catalogued SDB: 12/1982

IWM 312 · GB, (prod) 1918
OPEN AIR MASS IN HAVANA CUBA

b/w · 1 reel · 78' (2 mins) · silent
intertitles: none

- Celebration of Mass in an open square in Havana, Cuba, probably during the First World War.

A view down onto the square, decorated with Cuban, American and occasional British flags. From ground level, Catholic Church dignitaries seated in the foreground, with an audience of Cuban civilian men, women and children standing behind barriers – the men have all removed their hats. Seated further back from the centre of events are a few civilian and American Navy dignitaries. Some members of the crowd are holding banners, one reading "San Augustin Council". A priest delivers his sermon from a rostrum covered with the US and Cuban flags. Four small Cuban boys wearing boy scout uniform have draped themselves in a large Union Jack – they remove their hats at the cameraman's request.

Notes
Title: this is taken from the shotsheet.
Summary: probably in some way connected either with Cuba's entry into the war (one day after the USA) or with the end of the war, although there is no evidence to substantiate this; neither is there any clear indication of the production background.
[shotsheet available]
catalogued SDB: 12/1982

IWM 313 · GB, (?) 1918
HM THE KING AT THE ADMIRALTY COMPASS OBSERVATORY

b/w · 1 reel · 229' (5 mins) · silent
intertitles: none

sp Ministry of Information (?) *cam* Davis, W

- Visit of King George V and the Duke of York to the Admiralty Compass Observatory, Greenwich, 27 August 1918.

The King's Rolls-Royce pulls up outside the main door to the Observatory where his escort, Commander Sir Charles Cust, is waiting. The camera is behind the doorway, throwing everything into silhouette. The King and Duke, in civilian clothes, are led out across the lawn to inspect a ship's bell covered by a small roof (like a bird table) and on to a site where the King, given a spade by the gardener, plants a tree in commemoration. The party walks past the tennis court, where the wingless fuselage of a BE2c is being used by two officers for flight training. The King and Duke get back into their car, the radiator grill of which can be clearly seen, and depart.

Notes
Title: this is taken from the shotsheet.
[*The Times*, 27 August 1918: 9B]
[shotsheet available]
catalogued SDB: 12/1982

IWM 314 · GB, (prod) 1918
COLONIAL PRESSMEN

b/w · 1 reel · 1040' (17 mins) · silent
intertitles: none

sp Ministry of Information

- Unedited British record of leading journalists of the Dominions of Australia, New Zealand and South Africa visiting the British zone of the Western Front, September 1918.

The group of ten men arrives by car at Australian Corps headquarters, Bertangles Château, where it is met by among others Captain G H Wilkins, one of the Australian official cameramen. Captain C E W Bean (in slouch hat) is first to be seen shaking hands. They drive off again to a temporary prisoner of war camp and are shown German soldiers and guns captured by the Australians in the Battle of Amiens (Keith Murdoch identifiable in uniform with soft

hat). One soldier gets into the muzzle of a gun to demonstrate its size, two others display a 210mm mortar on a wheeled carriage. On 5 September the journalists are shown the old Vimy Ridge battlefields by men of the Canadian Corps. From a shallow trench they use binoculars, telescopes and a map to explain the battle (Bean is again identifiable – seen looking through telescope and wearing glasses). The journalists watch a race between two Mk V Female tanks at the Tank School at Etaples, after which a Medium A Whippet demonstrates its manœuvrability by driving right up to them. On 6 September, also near Etaples, they watch demonstrations by dogs at the Central Depot of the Messenger Dog Service. The dogs deliver messages which are relayed by semaphore flags. As the dogs return to their kennels, smoke and explosions are let off to accustom them to battle noises. On 7 September the men meet Field Marshal Haig at the Château de Beaurepaire, Montreuil. They are then shown on 5 September posed with General Sir Henry Horne at First Army Headquarters, Ranchicourt, going on to the ruins of Arras Cathedral on the same day and talking with an old lady who has stayed in the city throughout the war. They walk through the main square, which is reduced to rubble. On Vimy Ridge on 5 September they rest, smoke and eat, talking to three officers. Their cars drive them to a partly damaged village which they explore on foot.

Notes
Title: this is taken from the shotsheet.
Summary: identification of Bean and Murdoch was made by Christopher Pugsley, 12/1993.
[shotsheet available]
catalogued SDB: 12/1982

IWM 315 · GB, 1918
WOMEN'S ARMY IN FRANCE 1

b/w · 1 reel · 905' (16 mins) · silent
intertitles: none

sp Ministry of Information *pr* Topical Film Company *cam* Bassill, F A

- Members of the Women's Army Auxiliary Corps, probably at the Army Maintenance Depot at Etaples, France, September 1918.

In the cookhouse one woman takes a tin from the oven while another pulls a second tin from the back using a long pole. Other women work stirring porridge or cutting meat. One woman cuts off pieces of dough for loaves, a second weighs the pieces and a third rolls them into spheres. As one tray is completed it is taken away. After baking, the women carry the trays out and loosen the loaves. A posed group of the women, very camera conscious and unable to stop laughing. More tray carrying. A WAAC officer blows a whistle for a practice air raid drill and the women file out of the cookhouse to the shelter. A shift leaves work, men and women coming out of a refreshment room. Car maintenance by WAAC members, most of the lorries and cars belong to 63rd (Royal Naval) Division. The women take the engine out of the cars for work on a bench. Two women hose down and clean a car, while another woman fills a petrol tank. A final scene of several of the WAACs talking in a group.

Notes
Title: this is taken from the shotsheet.
Summary: see also **IWM 329**.
[shotsheet available]
catalogued SDB: 12/1982

IWM 316 · Canada (?), (prod) 1918
CANADIANS EAST OF ARRAS

b/w · 1 reel · 435' (8 mins) · silent
intertitles: none

sp Canadian War Records Office (?)
cam Buckstone, W A (?)

■ Unedited film of 11th Battalion, Tank Corps, and of horse-breaking by men of the Canadian Corps, in rear areas of the battlefield during the Breaking of the Hindenburg Line, Western Front, September 1918.

Not far from the Droucourt-Quéant Switch Line, tanks of 11th Battalion make their way up a gradient in the fog. The leading Mk V Male tank is marked 'Kim' and has a left-handed swastika on its nose (after Kipling). It is followed by another Male tank, and a Female 'Kitty'. Horses of the Canadian Corps unsaddled in a shallow depression. Canadian ASC men are breaking in one horse to a harness for pulling a cart. A patrol of Canadian Light Horse moves forward. Back at the horse-lines, the horses are being groomed, and the horse being broken in has been hobbled with a form of running martingale. A posed shot of the horse with his head cradled by one of the drivers. Finally, a village, mostly reduced to

rubble. Shown clearly on a wall is "O U QEEANT" (sic), presumably the village of Quéant.

Notes
Title: this is taken from the shotsheet.
Production: most probably Canadian official film, but possibly British official film.
[shotsheet available]
catalogued SDB: 12/1982

IWM 317 · GB, (prod) 1918
AUGUST OFFENSIVE (related material)
(allocated)

b/w · 1 reel · 114' (2 mins) · silent
intertitles: none

sp Ministry of Information *pr* Topical Film Company

■ British tanks preparing to go into action during the Advance to Victory, Western Front, summer 1918.

The film has at its start a very brief unrelated shot of three naval officers. The remainder shows Mk V tanks moving down a dusty road through a damaged village. As they move out of the village the tanks close up their hatches and prepare to go into action.

Notes
Summary: found in 1981 in the series *Tank Trials*, this was transferred to the *August Offensive* group to which it clearly belongs.
Remarks: very atmospheric, the tanks can clearly be seen closing up as they prepare to go into action. Unfortunately it is impossible to date with any real confidence.
[shotsheet available]
catalogued SDB: 12/1982

IWM 318 · GB, (prod) 1918
FETE AT SAINTE MARIE

b/w · 1 reel · 422' (8 mins) · silent
intertitles: none

sp Ministry of Information *pr* Topical Film Company *cam* Buckstone, W A

■ Gymnastics display by British soldiers at No 13 Convalescent Depot, Ste-Marie, near Trouville, France, 15 August 1918.

The crowd watching is mainly civilian, men and women in summer clothes. Out in the oval enclosure soldiers in athletics shorts and vests perform exercise routines with Indian clubs and rifles, after which they march off. The crowd includes a group of schoolgirls in uniform. The display continues with a tug of war and mop jousting, ending in a final close-up of the – very dirty – winning pair. A demonstration of Highland dancing. Sailors prepare for a sprint. As the winner breaks the tape at the finish he raises his arms in triumph. Children watch three clowns and a comic 'nigger minstrel' perform acrobatics. The display teams in the enclosure perform simple physical exercises of the 'Swedish drill' type. They make human pyramids, then form up and lie down in the shape of the giant letters GRV (Georgius Rex Vth), followed by the letters ST MARIE. One of the ladies watching presents prizes for the sports.

Notes
Title: this is taken from the shotsheet.
Summary: senior officers tended to 'hijack' official cameramen to record sports and similar events, and this film is a good example. Taken at the orders of GHQ France, it led the MoI to complain of its cameramen's time being wasted, and was, according to the complaint in the Aitken file, "an entire waste of time, money and material, as far as this Ministry is concerned".
[MoI(Photo) Papers, File on Thomas Aitken]
[shotsheet available]
catalogued SDB: 12/1982

IWM 319 · GB, (?) 1918
PONT REMY SPORTS

b/w · 1 reel · 430' (8 mins) · silent
intertitles: none

sp Ministry of Information *pr* Topical Film Company *cam* McDowell, J B

■ Competition between Army Forestry Companies from Britain, Australia, Canada and New Zealand at the Forestry Camp at Pont Remy, France, 15 September 1918.

The soldiers watch several forms of contest. A pillow fight between two men sitting astride a log suspended over water. A tree-stump felling contest, in which the four representatives each have to cut down a stump about ten feet high. A similar competition to cut through a short log lying on the ground, won by the Australian

whose fellows rush forward to cheer him. He poses in his shirt, shorts and bush hat with his axe beside the trunk. A third contest, including New Zealand Maoris, in chopping down medium-sized trees. Finally, a 'log rolling' contest for men keeping balance standing on a log on the river, which they cross by rolling the log forward.

Notes
Title: this is taken from the shotsheet.
[shotsheet available]
catalogued SDB: 12/1982

IWM 320 · GB, (?) 1918
OUR MERCHANT SERVICE HEROES
GEORGE ROBEY VISITS THE MERCHANT SERVICE (alternative)

b/w · 1 reel · 278' (5 mins) · silent
intertitles: English

sp Ministry of Information *pr* Topical Film Company *cam* Davis, W

■ Visit by the comedian George Robey to the crew of a recently torpedoed ship, on board another ship in dock, probably London, September 1918.

Reporters wait outside a house, including a photographer who takes details from a young sailor. Robey emerges from the house in his normal clothes rather than costume, takes the sailor by the hand and leads him back indoors. After a while they re-emerge, Robey pointing out the camera to his companion. The film jump-cuts to Robey climbing the companion-way ladder of a merchant ship and talking on deck with the sailors. He pets the ship's cat, and then catches hold of the captain as he passes, again pointing out the camera. The stokers, or "black squad", in a posed group stare at the camera. Robey looks out over the ship's side holding the cat. On deck again the officers pose in a group. Robey talks with crew members going about their work. The final shot, unlike Robey's behaviour throughout the visit, is intentionally comic – framed by a ship's lifebelt he pulls faces at the camera before flouncing off.

Notes
Title: the alternative title has been taken from the shotsheet.
Intertitles: it is likely that most of these are missing.
[shotsheet available]
catalogued SDB: 12/1982

IWM 321 · GB, (prod) 1918
**RED CROSS AMBULANCE TRAIN USED
BY GERMANS FOR AMMUNITION**

b/w · 1 reel · 95' (2 mins) · silent
intertitles: none

sp Ministry of Information *pr* Topical Film
Company *cam* Bassill, F A

▪ Unedited British propaganda film of a
German goods train captured at an
ammunition dump at Willems, near
Tournai, Western Front, 26 October 1918.

The train consists of two open-sided trucks,
guarded by British soldiers of the Machine
Gun Corps. Four of these soldiers go up to
one of the trucks, clearly marked with a Red
Cross on its roof, and take German mortar
bombs from one of the cases inside. One of
the soldiers holds three of the bombs up to
the camera. The roof of the train, also
marked with Red Crosses, has about twenty
of the soldiers gathered around it. At the
cameraman's request the men in front duck
down so that the roof may be more clearly
seen.

Notes
Title: this is taken from the shotsheet.
Remarks: fairly mild propaganda, even by
British standards. The weapons and setting
appear genuine. However, it was not
unusual for either side, if short of transport,
to use the same trains to run wounded
back from the front lines and ammunition
up to them.
[shotsheet available]
catalogued SDB: 12/1982

IWM 322 · GB, (?) 1918
the GREAT BRITISH OFFENSIVE

b/w · 2 reels · 1220' (20 mins) · silent
intertitles: English

sp Ministry of Information *pr* Topical Film
Company *prod* Jury, William F

▪ Compilation film of the British Army
during the Battle of Amiens and the
Advance to the Hindenburg Line,
Western Front, August 1918.

(Reel 1) Near Bapaume a German "anti-tank
gun" lies in an unidentifiable wreck with its
crew dead beside it. Shells burst in the
distance. Two 6-inch Mk VII guns are drawn
by Holt tractors to new positions, probably
near Sapignies, passed by a GS wagon of

the New Zealand Division. British soldiers
clear debris and trees in a thin wood near
Bailleul. Near Thiepval (?) a dead German
lies over a Maxim machinegun on a sledge.
Three British soldiers carrying German
Maxims and 08/15 Bergmanns walk past
him. "There is only one good boche – and
that is a dead boche." At a dressing station
a prostrate German officer is given water by
an RAMC corpsman. "The quality of mercy
is not strained." Just outside Abbeville a
large group of Germans, captured in the
advance, waits to move. *(Reel 2)* Men of
Princess Patricia's Canadian Light Infantry,
Canadian 3rd Division, rest against a wall in
a village "after taking Jigsaw Wood" which
they did on 29 August. British lorries have
difficulty negotiating shell craters in the road
behind the lines. In a sunken lane Royal
Engineers string telephone wires, using
German rifles stuck in the ground as posts.
In the foreground a field kitchen is covered
with a tarpaulin as line-laying wagons of the
Royal Engineers pass by loaded with
equipment. Men of 4th or 5th Battalion,
Royal Scots Fusiliers, 52nd (Lowland)
Division, in combat gear "moving forward"
(their officer has his arm in a sling). Scenes
in Achiet-le-Grand. The remains of Bailleul,
Béteran and St-Léger. Three men of 8th
Battalion, Middlesex Regiment, 56th
(London) Division, pull a cart load of
captured German mortars and
machineguns through Croisilles as
ammunition limbers pass the other way. A
group of men from 1/4th Battalion, London
Regiment, 56th (London) Division, "waiting
to go over the top in a front trench at
Bullecourt". The ruins of Bapaume station,
followed by a pan over a main street in
Bapaume, showing considerable damage.
The church at Grévillers, also showing
major shell damage.

Notes
Intertitles: most of these are flashframes.
Summary: see also **IWM 289** and the
August Offensive group for some of the
rough material from this film.
Remarks: the comparatively small-scale
compilation made from film of one of the
greatest British victories of all time is in
significant contrast to the major epic made
of the first day of the First Battle of the
Somme (**IWM 191**), one of the greatest
British disasters of all time.
[shotsheet available]
catalogued SDB: 12/1982

IWM 323 · GB, (?) 1918
PORTUGUESE TROOPS IN FRANCE

b/w · 1 reel · 718' (12 mins) · silent
intertitles: none

sp Ministry of Information pr Topical Film
Company

- British film of Portuguese Field and
Heavy Artillery men learning about their
guns and limbers, probably France,
summer 1918.

The film opens with an unrelated shot of
troops digging a trench-line. It continues as
Portuguese mule-drawn field gun limbers
come down a steep grassy bank towards
the camera. They turn and wheel on the
grassy plain below. Outriders and officers
on horseback lead the mule teams back up
the bank at the gallop, and over a deep
stream which is surrounded by foliage. A
posed group of mounted Portuguese
officers with a British liaison officer. Nearer
the front, a Portuguese gun crew marches
up a light railway track. The men break
formation on reaching a 9.2-inch howitzer
concealed under scrim netting, and
proceed to load and fire it twice. A posed
group of the gunners with a British gun
crew – one of the soldiers offers a plate of
food to another. The gunners pull
camouflage matting over the shells for the
gun. Nearby three British gunner officers
stand in conversation with each other.

Notes
Title: this is taken from the shotsheet.
[shotsheet available]
catalogued SDB: 12/1982

IWM 324 · GB, (prod) 1918
SEPTEMBER OFFENSIVE 3

b/w · 2 reels · 406' (7 mins) · silent
intertitles: none

sp Ministry of Information pr Topical Film
Company cam McDowell, J B

- Unedited film of British troops in the
Advance to Victory, Western Front,
September 1918.

(Reel 1) Stretcher-bearers with wounded,
some German, arrive at an advanced
dressing station. (Some of the bearers are
German prisoners with Red Cross
armbands.) Described as Achiet-le-Grand
but possibly 65th Field Ambulance, 21st
Division, near Epéhy on 18 September. At
the entrance to a bell tent a British doctor
removes the bandage from a German with

a head wound, wiping the blood away as
he does so. A group of British troops sit
wearing light overalls with their regimental
caps. They are described as men who have
been gassed and have changed out of their
gas-laden clothes, but show no signs of
distress. (Reel 2) A marching column
behind the lines with ammunition limbers
going the other way, probably 40th Division
(note formation sign). A house on fire with
trees nearby. A destroyed village with
British GS wagons and troops moving
through. At another location, possibly Bray-
sur-Somme, houses are damaged on both
sides of a wide main street. A small leave-
boat with camouflage markings, its deck
crowded with cheering British and Dominion
troops, leaves the quay for England.

Notes
Title: this is taken from the shotsheet.
Production: there is no record of episodes 1
and 2.
Summary: see also **IWM 325** and the
remainder of the September Offensive
series.
[shotsheet available]
catalogued SDB: 12/1982

IWM 325 · GB, (prod) 1918
SEPTEMBER OFFENSIVE 4

b/w · 1 reel · 466' (8 mins) · silent
intertitles: none

sp Ministry of Information pr Topical Film
Company cam Bassill, F A

- Unedited film of British rear echelon
troops in the Advance to Victory, Western
Front, September 1918.

Gun limbers and GS wagons move up a
sunken road in the rear areas of the
battlefield. German prisoners are marched
back in column of twos along the road,
passing the horsed transport. A horsed
vehicle park beside a partly damaged barn.
Some British soldiers rest and eat beside
the sunken road. An advanced dressing
station just off the roadside, possibly 65th
Field Ambulance, 21st Division, near Epéhy
on 18 September, where RAMC and
German Red Cross men help British and
German wounded, giving each other
cigarettes and water. The horsed wagons
continue to move up the sunken road.

Notes
Title: this is taken from the shotsheet.
Summary: see also **IWM 324** and the

remainder of the *September Offensive* series.
[shotsheet available]
catalogued SDB: 12/1982

IWM 326 · GB, (prod) 1918
SEPTEMBER OFFENSIVE 6

b/w · 1 reel · 166' (3 mins) · silent
intertitles: none

sp Ministry of Information *pr* Topical Film Company

■ Unedited film of British and captured German tanks behind British lines during the Advance to Victory, Western Front, September 1918.

Firstly, a column of Infantry marching through a town showing shell damage – the light values have been set wrongly and the film is far too dark. This is followed by British, or possibly Canadian, soldiers inspecting two captured German tanks, the A7V Sturmpanzerwagen, of which about twenty were built. One of them is marked as the 'Hagen'. Beside these tanks is a British Mk V Male tank. Another tank, a Mk V Female 'Gasper' of 7th Battalion, Tank Corps, towing a broken-down Mk V along a road.

Notes
Title: this is taken from the shotsheet.
Production: there is no record of episode 5.
Summary: see also **IWM 324** and the remainder of the *September Offensive* series.
[B H Liddell Hart, *The Tanks – the History of the Royal Tank Regiment ...*, Vol I, Cassell (1959)]
[shotsheet available]
catalogued SDB: 12/1982

IWM 327 · GB, (prod) 1918
SEPTEMBER OFFENSIVE 7

b/w · 1 reel · 272' (4 mins) · silent
intertitles: none

sp Ministry of Information *pr* Topical Film Company

I. Unedited film in the wake of the British forces in the Advance to Victory, possibly Villers-Bretonneux, Western Front, September 1918. A pan over a ruined village, Villers-Bretonneux (?) filmed from a church tower, showing British troops and transport moving in the streets below. Two soldiers look out through the crenellations of the tower, filmed from behind and caught in silhouette against the sky. The same damage from ground level; two Highlanders, possibly of 51st (Highland) Division, wave at the camera. French soldiers clear debris from the railway tracks.
II. A religious service at No 2 Aeroplane Supply Depot RAF, France, 1 September 1918. Mechanics and other ranks, mostly still wearing RFC uniform and badges, march out on parade led by their band and form a hollow square around an FE2d night bomber. The base chaplain uses the observer's front cockpit of this pusher aircraft as his pulpit to deliver a sermon, after which the band plays a hymn and marches away.
III. British wagons passing over a bridge, temporarily repaired by the Royal Engineers, across the Somme River, Monchy-Lagache, Western Front, probably 1 September 1918.

Notes
Title: this is taken from the shotsheet.
Summary: see also **IWM 324** and the remainder of the *September Offensive* series.
[shotsheet available]
catalogued SDB: 12/1982

IWM 328 · GB, (prod) 1918
WOMEN'S ARMY IN FRANCE 2

b/w · 1 reel · 134' (3 mins) · silent
intertitles: none

sp Ministry of Information *pr* Topical Film Company *cam* Bassill, F A

■ Unedited film of members of the Women's Auxiliary Army Corps in France, September 1918.

WAACs at a temporary shelter serve food to a waiting queue of other WAACs, all very camera-conscious. A WAAC platoon route marches across open moorland. WAACs erect bell tents in woodland with a village in the distance – some of them lie down to relax or write letters, and a group with towels and bathrobes prepares to take a bath. Two of the WAACs in close-up, very camera-conscious and giggling.

Notes
Title: this is taken from the shotsheet.
Summary: see also **IWM 329**, a completed

compilation film which includes some material from this film, and **IWM 315**. [shotsheet available] catalogued SDB: 12/1982

IWM 329 · GB, (?) 1918
WOMEN'S ARMY IN FRANCE (completed version)

b/w · 1 reel · 911' (16 mins) · silent
intertitles: English

sp Ministry of Information (?)

■ Compilation film of the Women's Army Auxiliary Corps in France, 1917-18.

A male sergeant-major oversees WAAC clerks at desks and benches indoors. ASC and WAAC clerks sort through a complex card index file spread out over several tables, possibly the Army Central Registry at Rouen. A WAAC officer and an elderly captain distribute money at a WAAC pay parade. WAACs and RAF personnel indoors doing draughtsmen's work at desks. WAACs erect a bell tent in a camp near a village, then strike another tent and carry it off. WAACs in bathing costumes beside the sea. WAACs cleaning and doing maintenance work on Army vehicles, possibly 41st Auxiliary Ambulance Car Company at Rouen. Three WAACs, two British soldiers and an Australian, "boys and girls come out to play", play games on the beach with waves coming over the breakwater. A WAAC in munitions uses some form of rocking device on her workbench while others perform similar precision work, apparently piston assembly, watched by RAF officers.

Notes
Title: this is taken from the shotsheet.
Intertitles: there is one flashframe, quoted in the summary.
Summary: see also **IWM 315** and **IWM 328**, unedited films from which some of the scenes of this compilation are taken.
[shotsheet available]
catalogued SDB: 12/1982

IWM 330 · NO FILM

IWM 331 · Australia, (?) 1918
AUSTRALIANS ON THE WESTERN FRONT
AUSTRALIANS IN PERONNE (ledger title)

(alternative)

b/w · 2 reels · 518' (9 mins) · silent
intertitles: none

sp Australian War Records Section
cam Wilkins, G H

■ Australian Corps in the Advance to Victory, showing Péronne after its capture and the rear areas, Western Front, September 1918.

(Reel 1) Péronne was captured by Australian 5th Division on 3 September, but this film concentrates on events behind the lines two weeks later. Wagons, including some field gun limbers and GS wagons carrying hay, move up over a stream. The Corps commander, General Monash, directs William Hughes, the Prime Minister of Australia, Lord Burnham, owner of the *Daily Telegraph*, and Sir Thomas Marlowe, editor of the *Daily Mail*, over a temporary bridge. Although Marlowe is in civilian clothes Burnham wears the uniform of a colonel. In the main square at Péronne they meet General Sir Henry Rawlinson, Fourth Army commander, and men of Australian 4th Division on 16 September. After posing for photographs the newsmen are shown over the battlefield. An Australian column in full marching kit and bush hats passes over a temporary bridge, many men cheering the camera as it pans over them. *(Reel 2)* Australian 5th Division sports, starting with a band leading a march past, then a tug of war and two heats of a hurdling race. At Mont St-Quentin a memorial in the form of a Celtic cross is unveiled to the dead of Australian 53rd Battalion. The wreaths are laid and the escort party fires into the air in salute, after which the memorial is unveiled. Australian troops listen to an address (speaker not seen).

Notes
Title: this is taken from the shotsheet. The alternative title has been taken from the store ledger.
Production: Australian official film.
[shotsheet available]
catalogued SDB: 12/1982

IWM 332 · GB, 1918
HOW THE BRITISH ARMY BROKE THE FAMOUS HINDENBURG LINE
BRITISH OFFENSIVE (alternative)

b/w · 2 reels · 1870' (31 mins) · silent
intertitles: English

sp Ministry of Information pr Topical Film Company prod Jury, William F

- Compilation film of British and Canadian forces in the Advance to Victory, Western Front, August-October 1918.

(Reel 1) Long shots of shells bursting on Bourlon Wood, and of Infantry moving up near Inchy, probably 63rd (Royal Naval) Division, on 4 September. British troops resting on the Cambrai Road with the rubble of the sugar factory behind them. 16th (Canadian Scottish) Battalion, Canadian 1st Division, moving up in column through rear area transport near Cagnicourt. A returning column of German prisoners. An advanced dressing station, probably near Epéhy, showing in some detail two RAMC sergeants bandaging the leg of a German prisoner. Men of the Royal Naval Division "who the day before had captured Braincourt and Anneux", which they did on 27 September, cheer the camera and march away. German guns, ranging from heavy pieces to machineguns, captured by the Canadian Corps, set out in a park. British or Canadian soldiers posed on the captured German A7V tank 'Hagen'. A column, possibly 1st Battalion, Duke of Cornwall's Light Infantry, 5th Division, marching through the ruins of Bapaume. The unfinished Canal du Nord, very steep at this point. A more shallow crossing, with field kitchens moving up and over a temporary bridge. Another column of German prisoners. British troops march along the bed of the canal filmed from a bank. Royal Engineers bring up rails on a flatcar to repair a light railway. An RFA 18-pounder crosses the temporary bridge. A posed group of women, children and old men in Ecourt-St-Quentin – captured by Canadian 4th Division on 4 September – with the Canadians, including three Frenchmen who hid from the Germans.
(Reel 2) The ruins of Bapaume, and of the destroyed church at Grévillers. British troops, possibly 55th (West Lancashire) Division, in the ruins of La Bassée facing east towards Bauvin. A few British soldiers cross the La Bassée Canal at a narrow point by climbing over the rubble which has choked it. Mine craters have been blown in the road. A British soldier leads a mule carrying water through the rubble. A German "concrete observation tower camouflaged to look like a house", with most of the camouflage blown away. Two horses, possibly of 55th Division, are led around a crater by a soldier. German barbed wire entanglements at Lens. A bridge being repaired near Albert. The remains of Albert basilica, "the Leaning Virgin of 1916 is no more. Probably she is melted down to make Hun shells".

Notes
Title: the alternative title has been taken from the shotsheet.
Summary: see also the August Offensive and September Offensive series, particularly **IWM 322**, **IWM 323**, **IWM 325** and **IWM 326** from which some of the scenes in this compilation come.
Remarks: a good attempt at salvaging some poor original film, but it is probable that some fakes have been used in the sections showing troop movements.
[shotsheet available]
catalogued SDB: 12/1982

IWM 333 · GB, (prod) 1918
ARRAS-LENS LINE

b/w · 1 reel · 131' (3 mins) · silent
intertitles: none

sp Ministry of Information pr Topical Film Company cam Bassill, F A

- Ruins of Lens, Western Front, captured by British forces on 4 October 1918.

A pan over the ruins of the town. There are barbed wire entanglements left on the roads between the ruins, and a British soldier walks up to and through one of the gaps in the wire. Another soldier stands in a masonry dug-out, with a sudden explosion, either shelling or demolition, behind him.

Notes
Title: this is taken from the shotsheet.
[shotsheet available]
catalogued SDB: 12/1982

IWM 334 · Australia (?), (prod) 1918
AUSTRALIANS ENTRAINING

b/w · 1 reel · 422' (7 mins) · silent
intertitles: none

sp Australian War Records Section (?)

- Men of the Australian Corps with the two US divisions loaned to it prior to the Breaking of the Hindenburg Line, Western Front, September 1918.

Headquarters rear echelon troops of Australian 1st and 2nd Divisions wait at a rail depot in bush hats and full equipment. The same men embark on a train at another place, filmed from on top of the train. The last men rush on board as the train moves off (possibly different phases of the same journey). A column of US Infantry marches up a dirt road as Australian transport comes back in the other direction. The Americans are from 27th (New York) or 30th (Old Hickory) Divisions, loaned to the Australians. American gunners try out an Australian 18-pounder field gun, probably in training, after which the gun is covered in camouflage netting. Two American soldiers, sitting in a wagon, talk casually to an Australian.

Notes
Title: this is taken from the shotsheet.
Production: possibly Australian official film.
[shotsheet available]
catalogued SDB: 12/1982

IWM 335 · GB, (prod) 1918
ON THE ST QUENTIN FRONT

b/w · 1 reel · 391' (7 mins) · silent
intertitles: none

sp Ministry of Information *pr* Topical Film Company *cam* McDowell, J B

■ Unedited film of British forces and German prisoners in the north of the St-Quentin sector, Western Front, early October 1918.

Pan over the countryside with shelling in the far distance and British troops moving up in the middle ground, probably 1st Division front north of St-Quentin. A village being bombarded by shells, close enough to shake the camera. British RAMC and German prisoners posed for the camera in a slit trench, after which they climb out and attend to wheeled stretchers. A British signal unit, including a carrier for homing pigeons, resting by the roadside. German prisoners help with the wounded at an advanced dressing station. A close-up of a German prisoner with a cap, receding hairline and heavy moustache, looking old and tired, joking for the camera. German prisoners help carry British wounded, four to a stretcher. British and German walking wounded, looking miserable, rest by a roadside. British GS wagons loaded with supplies in a park. Kilted troops, possibly Cameron Highlanders, crossing a road in widely spaced columns (Artillery Formation). Shells bursting in the open field ahead.

Notes
Title: this is taken from the shotsheet.
[shotsheet available]
catalogued SDB: 12/1982

IWM 336 · GB, (prod) 1918
SCENES ON THE HINDENBURG LINE
SOME OF THE HINDENBURG LINE
(alternative)

b/w · 1 reel · 226' (4 mins) · silent
intertitles: none

sp Ministry of Information *pr* Topical Film Company *cam* Buckstone, W A

■ Unedited film of German defences on the Hindenburg Line after their capture by British forces in the Advance to Victory, October 1918.

A British soldier walks through a forest of long, hooked metal poles set in concrete, probably as a form of reinforcement. A barbed wire entanglement more than fifty yards deep. An RAMC man emerges from the entrance to a deep dug-out – there is a second entrance nearby. A few British soldiers are digging on the surface, possibly reconstructing the defences. Another pan over belts of deep barbed wire with a light railway train making its way through them, showing the gaps between the successive belts.

Notes
Title: this is taken from the store ledger. The alternative title, probably a misreading, is from the shotsheet.
[shotsheet available]
catalogued SDB: 12/1982

IWM 337 · GB, (?) 1917
TANKS – THE WONDER WEAPON

b/w · 1 reel · 870' (15 mins) · silent
intertitles: English

sp War Office Cinema Committee (?)
pr Topical Film Company (?)

■ General British film on the uses and value of the Mk IV tank, probably at the Tank Corps Training School at Etaples, 1917 (?).

The tanks, Males and Females, are all unarmed and instead of battalion numbers carry large training numbers on their noses.

Firstly, a pan over the instructing officers in front of two of the tanks. At the "tankodrome" the parked tanks start up, emitting much smoke. The Male 416 demonstrates its ability to plunge into a deep crater and emerge slowly on the far side. Female 57 climbs over a steep bank half its own height and protected by barbed wire. The school staff doing physical training. The Male 418 in an open wood pushing over two thin trees. Three tanks emerge over the crest of a hill. View from the right-hand sponson of a tank as it travels downhill, showing the tracks churning up the ground. A wave of six tanks in very close column of twos emerges over a ridge. Male 454 comes down a very steep slope to rest. Female 108, tilted at a steep angle in a trench, shows how it can escape using an unditching beam. A crew demonstrates action if its tank is disabled, rushing out of the tank to set up a belt-fed Hotchkiss machinegun. "A tank charge" of about twenty tanks in two waves, very close together, comes over the crest of the ridge. A line abreast of Female tanks at close intervals crushes a deep barbed wire entanglement, as smoke shells explode around them. Finally, Male 454 comes down one side of a steep slope and up the other, almost on top of the camera, as the film abruptly ends.

Notes
Remarks: impressive and entertaining examples of tank movement marred by the tank formations being far too close together and by the tanks being clearly unarmed.
[shotsheet available]
catalogued SDB: 12/1982

IWM 338 · GB, (prod) 1918
BETWEEN BELLICOURT AND BELLENGLISE

b/w · 1 reel · 315' (6 mins) · silent
intertitles: none

sp Ministry of Information *pr* Topical Film Company *cam* McDowell, J B

■ Unedited material of the Australian Corps and 46th (North Midland) Division fronts during the Advance to Victory, Western Front, October 1918.

Australian soldiers, probably of 5th Division, at the south end of the St-Quentin tunnel at Bellicourt. A temporary bridge has been built just below the tunnel entrance. A view, from on top of the tunnel mouth. Three

Australians with two horses walk past two corpses on the ground. A pan from a high position of the ruins of Bellicourt (?) with soldiers in the streets below. A deep wire entanglement with gaps, through one of which comes a transport wagon and some riders. A bridge over the canal captured by 46th Division, showing some damage, probably filmed on 2 October. The canal with a narrow footbridge across it. A group of unsaddled horses, among them one foal, being fed in shallow trenches as a protection from shells.

Notes
Title: this is taken from the shotsheet.
[shotsheet available]
catalogued SDB: 12/1982

IWM 339 · GB, (prod) 1918
SCENES IN CAMBRAI 1

b/w · 1 reel · 461' (8 mins) · silent
intertitles: none

sp Ministry of Information *pr* Topical Film Company *cam* Buckstone, W A

■ Cambrai after its capture by Canadian 3rd Division, Western Front, 8 October 1918.

Canadian transport wagons move through the streets, crowded with civilians. More civilians cross a fragile-looking plank bridge over the river, which has replaced a damaged iron bridge. Marching columns and 6-inch 26cwt howitzers cross another bridge. Two of the howitzers, which are lorry-drawn, are draped with the French flag and one with the US flag. Areas of Cambrai are still on fire. A hay store burns fiercely as troops attempt to salvage some items. In the main square one building is already gutted by fire, which spreads to the others. Brigadier-General D C Draper of 8th Brigade, Canadian 3rd Division, consults a map with members of his staff on the middle of the square. More buildings are in flames. A German prisoner is escorted through a street filled with smoke.

Notes
Title: this is taken from the shotsheet.
Summary: see also **IWM 345**.
[shotsheet available]
catalogued SDB: 12/1982

IWM 340 · GB, (prod) 1918
LA BASSEE

b/w · 1 reel · 96' (2 mins) · silent
intertitles: none

sp Ministry of Information *pr* Topical Film
Company *cam* Buckstone, W A (?)

- La Bassée from across the canal,
  showing narrow boats and a pontoon
  bridge being crossed by five British
  soldiers, Western Front, 3 October 1918.

Notes
Title: this is taken from the shotsheet.
[shotsheet available]
catalogued SDB: 12/1982

IWM 341 · GB, (prod) 1918
PREMONT

b/w · 1 reel · 213' (4 mins) · silent
intertitles: none

sp Ministry of Information *pr* Topical Film
Company *cam* McDowell, J B (?)

- British troops in the village of Prémont,
  near Cambrai, shortly after its capture by
  US 30th (Old Hickory) Division during the
  Advance to Victory, Western Front, 8
  October 1918.

The main street of the village is almost
undamaged except for a prominent shell-
hole in the side of one barn. A British
Cavalry signals section of four men,
possibly Scots Greys, crouches in an open
field not far from the village as shells fall
nearby. More shells burst in the open fields.
A captured German 77mm field gun is
covered by a British (or American) soldier
with a heavily embroidered French flag (part
of the flag's embroidery is the word
"Revanche" – revenge). A British company
rests in greatcoats and helmets against an
earth bank. A small group of British support
troops rushes up over a ploughed field to a
foxhole, probably a shell crater.

Notes
Title: this is taken from the shotsheet.
[shotsheet available]
catalogued SDB: 12/1982

IWM 342 · GB, 1918
**ARRIVAL OF ITALIAN BAND AT
BLACKPOOL**

b/w · 1 reel · 864' (15 mins) · silent
intertitles: none

sp Ministry of Information *cam* Cooper, F (?)

- Fragmented film of a tour of an Italian
  Carabinieri band around Britain, autumn
  1918.

A British military band escorts the Italians
through the streets of Blackpool as civilians
watch. In various scenes the Italians wear
either undress uniforms with cloaks or their
highly ornate full dress. They are taken by
charabanc to a reception point where they
talk with British bandsmen. They play to
convalescent soldiers in London. In another
town, possibly Liverpool, they march
through the pouring rain and are inspected
by the Lord Mayor. Again they are escorted
by a British band. They discard their cloaks
and give another performance. In
Manchester (?), very foggy and damp, they
are once more escorted by a British band
and carry their national flag. The Lord
Mayor and invalid soldiers watch them play.
The Lord Mayor inspects them and presents
medals, some going to civilians and small
children. In Edinburgh a Highland pipe
band leads the Italians down Princes Street,
and they go sightseeing in the grounds of
Holyrood House. They leave by train from
Princes Street Station, waving at the
camera.

Notes
Title: this is taken from the shotsheet.
Remarks: almost too disjointed to be
comprehensible.
[shotsheet available]
catalogued SDB: 12/1982

IWM 343 · GB (?), (?) 1915
GERMAN PRISONERS IN FRANCE

b/w · 1 reel · 637' (11 mins) · silent
intertitles: English

- German prisoners being escorted
  through rear areas by French soldiers,
  Western Front, partly 1915, partly
  probably 1914.

German prisoners with a French escort
move along a trench. French wagons arrive
in a farmyard where German prisoners rest
or wander about without restraint. A large
cultivated area with German prisoners
standing in 'blocks' of a few hundred men.
French guards remove the belts, braces
and trouser buttons of their captives to

hinder escape. A few German prisoners escorted by French dragoons, the latter apparently in the uniform of 1914. A column of prisoners on foot, described as "German hussars" but probably Infantry; the escort and watching French soldiers appear to be wearing horizon blue with red trousers. A second and third column pass the same location. A group of German officers stands and waits, the camera has concentrated on one tough professional who looks amused. Germans rest in a temporary 'cage' of a few strands of barbed wire. Just off a road along which French transport passes captured German guns are on display, mainly 77mm field guns and 170mm wheeled mortars, 1915 or later.

Notes
Production: possibly French official film, but more probably film taken by the Topical Film Company before the formation of the British Topical Committee for War Films, and transferred by accident with the official film collection when Topical was sold by the WOCC back to private ownership at the end of the war.
Remarks: very difficult to date, but obviously of great rarity value. The weather looks too mild for winter. Although some of this material is clearly mid-1915 or later the bulk must be either summer 1914 or spring 1915.
[shotsheet available]
catalogued SDB: 12/1982

IWM 344 · GB, (?) 1918
YPRES – THE SHELL SHATTERED CITY OF FLANDERS [1918]

b/w · 4 reels · 3324' (36 mins) · silent
intertitles: English

■ Highly unstructured British film showing scenes in the town and area of Ypres, Western Front, 1916-18.

The scenes, in no discernible order, show Ypres and the ridges to the north and east of the town. The scenes in Ypres are chiefly of the main square showing the Cloth Hall and cathedral, the Church of St-Jacques, the theatre, and the clinic. There are several scenes of troops marching through the Menin Gate. Other identifiable points are the asylum, Hill 60, Clapham Junction, Polygon Wood, Vlamertinghe Mill, Hellfire Corner, Shrapnel Corner, Ploegsteert Wood, Sanctuary Wood and Wytschaete Ridge. Also included are scenes of Field Marshal Sir John French meeting Generals Gouraud

and Weygand, 1916 or later. One scene, of horsed transport galloping past Shrapnel Corner, has been filmed through the semi-transparent sight screens.

Notes
Production: this appears to be a compilation using as its basis the 1916 version of the film, made by the BTCFWF (**IWM 206**). It is not possible to determine whether it was a wartime official or post-war unofficial production, or whether it was ever released in this form.
Shotsheet: a detailed shotsheet and analysis of the film has been prepared and is held on file in the Department of Film.
Remarks: the film shot through the sight screens is strangely beautiful.
[shotsheet available]
catalogued SDB: 12/1982

IWM 345 · GB, (prod) 1918
SCENES IN CAMBRAI 2

b/w · 2 reels · 666' (11 mins) · silent
intertitles: none

sp Ministry of Information *pr* Topical Film Company *cam* McDowell, J B

■ Cambrai after its liberation, including a visit by Field Marshal Haig and Prime Minister Clemenceau, Western Front, probably 9 October 1918.

(Reel 1) Soldiers, probably 57th (West Lancashire) Division, use hoses and ladders to suppress a fire raging in one house. In the main square the streets have been cleared of rubble but all the buildings still show damage. One main building is still marked as the German "Kommandantur". Refugees, some in wagons carrying the French flag, others with handcarts, return to their homes. The railway station, both inside and out, shows considerable damage. The outside of the Kommandantur, including the entrance next to the "Citadelle". Buildings are still on fire. A slow pan down from a church tower, showing major shell damage. *(Reel 2)* British troops leave Cambrai Cathedral after a thanksgiving service. Priests and soldiers talk together on the steps. General Sir Henry Horne (First Army) talks candidly with General Sir Julian Byng (Third Army), neither aware of the camera. Horne and Byng talk to the officiating priest, possibly a senior church official. Prime Minister Clemenceau and Field Marshal Haig arrive in an open car, and inspect a French and British guard of honour as a

band plays. Haig introduces Clemenceau to his two Army commanders (Horne has his back to the camera). Clemenceau talks to returned refugees. The party, having looked over the town, comes back down the cathedral steps and leaves by car.

Notes
Title: this is taken from the shotsheet.
Summary: see also **IWM 339**.
[shotsheet available]
catalogued SDB: 12/1982

IWM 346 · GB, (?) 1918
FULHAM'S GUN DAY

b/w · 1 reel · 381' (6 mins) · silent
intertitles: none

sp Ministry of Information *cam* Davis, W (?)

- Parade and celebration over the purchase of a 6-inch 26cwt howitzer, Fulham, London, October 1918.

The procession is led by a car covered in Union Flags. It includes a military band, a mock stagecoach, more cars, a display of troops marching, military cadets, the 6-inch howitzer drawn by a camouflaged wagon, bands of the Girl Guides and boy scouts, and more cars. One has a large sign "Victory" and a tableau of the Kaiser, Hindenburg and Tirpitz kneeling before Britannia, supported by two British soldiers. One float has the US flag, another shows advice on air raids. The procession passes Vanston Place to Fulham Broadway, where it halts. In turn a clergyman, an Army officer, a man made up as 'Ole Bill' (the Bairnsfather cartoon character) and a man draped in Union Flags address the crowd. One of the parked cars advertises "Fulham Gun Day". A punch or stamp has been fixed to the breech of the 6-inch howitzer, and a queue of people, each in turn, places an object or donation in the breech. One small child, aided by its mother, has a pass book stamped in this fashion. As a final, posed, scene the 'Ole Bill' character talks and smokes with the Army officers and soldiers in a mock-up trench.

Notes
Title: this is taken from the shotsheet.
[shotsheet available]
catalogued SDB: 12/1982

IWM 347 · GB, (prod) 1918
ROMICOURT – ARMENTIERES NEAR ESTAIRES

b/w · 1 reel · 432' (6 mins) · silent
intertitles: none

sp Ministry of Information *pr* Topical Film Company *cam* Bassill, F A

- Unedited film of British forces on the Armentières-Estaires Road during the Advance to Victory, Western Front, mid-October 1918.

Five small Commer lorries carry British troops up the road. Civilian refugees are evacuated by another lorry, which drives off. More lorryloads of troops move up the road. The view down from a wrecked German Maxim machinegun to the trench and belts of wire it was meant to defend. Bodies can be seen between the trench and the wire. A German temporary military graveyard marked with wooden crosses. A partly destroyed church, possibly at Estaires.

Notes
Title: the name 'Romicourt' does not appear on any maps of the area between Armentières and Estaires. The title has been taken from the shotsheet.
Remarks: this film shows well the extent to which transport in the British Army had become mechanised by the end of the First World War.
[shotsheet available]
catalogued SDB: 12/1982

IWM 348 · GB, (?) 1918
MATINEE AT WEST END THEATRE (ledger title)

b/w · 1 reel · 378' (16 mins) · silent
intertitles: none

sp Ministry of Information *cam* Davis, W

- Fragmented film of military cadets and convalescent soldiers outside a theatre in Regent Street, London, October 1918 (?).

British troops of various regiments, mostly wearing hospital blues, getting down from the open top deck of a bus in Regent Street and going into a building, probably a theatre. As they enter ladies give them small gifts of cigarettes. On the far side of the road is a guard of honour of Army cadets who present arms as an officer takes the salute. The cadets march, led by their band, through the crowd which has gathered. More of the soldiers getting down from the bus top deck, some having difficulty with crutches. The cadets march away down the street led by their band. They present arms as the band plays to the crowd. (At this point the film begins to break up into pull-backs.) Across the road near the bus is a banner proclaiming "The Queen's Westminsters' Prisoners of War Fund".

catalogued SDB: 12/1982

IWM 349 · GB, (ca) 1917
GERMAN PRISONERS – SCENES AT LA BOZELLE (sic)
SONS OF OUR EMPIRE (related scenes)

b/w · 1 reel · 718' (13 mins) · silent
intertitles: English

- Mixed stock material of German prisoners of the British, Western Front, 1916-18.

A column of prisoners, "Prussians and Bavarians" moving over rough ground with an escort. A body search of prisoners in a trench. German prisoners help British RAMC men with British and German wounded at a dressing station. Parties of four British stretcher-bearers, one with a head wound, carry stretcher cases to the rear, followed by British and German walking wounded. German prisoners grin at the camera. More stretcher-bearers and columns of German prisoners. Maintenance work being carried out on tanks in a captured village. Gordon Highlanders (?) digging or reinforcing a trench-line. British soldiers cleaning up trenches, "enemy trenches at La Bozelle (sic, presumably La Boisselle) after our guns had finished with them".

Notes
Title: this is taken, including the error, from the shotsheet.
Production: possibly a post-war private compilation rather than an official film.
Summary: most of this material appears in the series *Sons of Our Empire*, see **IWM 130-01+02** to **IWM 130-09+10**. See also **IWM 324**.
[shotsheet available]
catalogued SDB: 12/1982

IWM 350 · GB, (prod) 1918
AMERICAN PRESSMEN ENTERTAINED

b/w · 1 reel · 125' (2 mins) · silent
intertitles: none

sp Ministry of Information *cam* Cooper, F (?)

- US journalists arriving at the home of Lord Beaverbrook, Minister of Information, Cherkley Court, England, October 1918.

One of the guests gets out of a car outside the main door of the house. The car, together with another, leaves through the gates. A further party of four guests emerging from another car is greeted by two civilians and an Army officer (very dark, no identification). A second car arrives with four more guests and the whole party enters the house. The party of about twenty people emerges through the French windows at the back of the house into the garden. Beaverbrook is not visible, and the camera is too far away for identification to be possible.

Notes
Title: this is taken from the store ledger.
Summary: see also **IWM 273** *Canadian Pressmen Visit Lord Beaverbrook*.
[shotsheet available]
catalogued SDB: 12/1982

IWM 351 · GB, (prod) 1918
OSTENDE (sic)

b/w · 1 reel · 325' (6 mins) · silent
intertitles: none

sp Ministry of Information *pr* Topical Film Company *cam* Bassill, F A

- Liberation of Ostend, including scenes of the wreck of HMS *Vindictive*, Belgium, 20 October 1918.

I. View from the deck of HMS *Vindictive*, sunk in the raid on Ostend, showing the rest of the harbour. The Germans have scuttled another vessel in the harbour, leaving only the funnel and masts showing. More views of the *Vindictive*. Belgian tugboats pass the wreck.
II. Ostend three days after it was liberated on 17 October. British and Belgian soldiers walk with civilians in the streets. A group of children, probably staged, runs towards the camera cheering and waving Belgian flags. The cameraman's car loaded with the

children and joined by cheering civilians runs down a street and stops in front of the camera. An iron bridge over the river estuary, still intact. The cameraman's car drives gingerly over a fragile plank bridge across a stream on the way to or from Ostend. A number of civilians, attracted by the camera, follow the car.

Notes
Title: this is taken from the shotsheet.
[shotsheet available]
catalogued SDB: 12/1982

IWM 352 · GB, (prod) 1918
LILLE NO 1 AND LILLE NO 2

b/w · 1 reel · 628' (11 mins) · silent
intertitles: none

sp Ministry of Information *pr* Topical Film Company *cam* Buckstone, W A

■ Liberation of Lille, including a thanksgiving service and parade, Western Front, 18-21 October 1918.

I. Columns of British companies march into the city on 18 October. They are Liverpool Irish, otherwise 8th Battalion, King's (Liverpool Regiment) of 57th (West Lancashire) Division. The men carry flags and flowers, some in the barrels of their rifles. The civilian population, including children, waits and watches the camera. The main square is full of cheering people and flags. A horse-drawn bus moves down the street loaded with cheering British soldiers. A civilian procession is led by the city Mayor, M Delasalle. The crowd cheers a French officer walking through. A British military band tries to make its way through the crowded square.
II. Equipment and machinery in factories deliberately wrecked by the Germans before leaving, filmed on 20 October.
III. The official celebration of liberation on 21 October. A crowd emerges from the cathedral after a thanksgiving service. There is a parade through the streets. A British battalion presents arms as General Sir William Birdwood, commanding Fifth Army, waits with other officials at one of the city gates. A car arrives and President Poincaré gets out; he and Birdwood inspect the guard of honour. Poincaré and the Mayor lead a procession down a thoroughfare and through a main gate. The crowd waits at the main gate outside the cathedral.

Notes
Title: this is taken from the shotsheet. From the length of the film it may refer to two separate reel-loads, of about 300 feet each, for the camera.
[shotsheet available]
catalogued SDB: 12/1982

IWM 353 · GB, (prod) 1918
LENS – ZONNEBEKE – MOORSELE

b/w · 1 reel · 254' (4 mins) · silent
intertitles: none

sp Ministry of Information *pr* Topical Film Company *cam* McDowell, J B

■ Unedited film of recently-liberated areas on the Western Front, October 1918.

I. Transport wagons of 12th (Eastern) Division being driven up a slope and around a corner with a push from waiting soldiers, near Lens, 14 October.
II. A dressing station, probably near Zonnebeke. British soldiers of 9th (Scottish) Division rest with Belgian soldiers, mostly wearing hats rather than helmets, so probably a safe area.
III. Pan over the village of Moorsele showing shell damage, coming to rest on an inn with the village name painted on its side.

Notes
Title: this is taken from the shotsheet, with errors in spelling corrected.
[shotsheet available]
catalogued SDB: 12/1982

IWM 354 · Australia (?), (prod) 1918
[GENERAL RAWLINSON'S HEADQUARTERS AND AUSTRALIAN TROOPS, 1918] (allocated)

b/w · 1 reel · 521' (9 mins) · silent
intertitles: none

sp Australian War Records Section (?)

I. General Sir Henry Rawlinson at his headquarters at Montigny Farm, Western Front, 17 October 1918. Firstly, a posed group of Rawlinson, Fourth Army commander, with his staff. Then, indoors, for the benefit of the camera Rawlinson traces a military manœuvre on a wall map with a pair of dividers.
II. French or Belgian refugees, old men, women and children, waiting outside a

mayor's residence. Western Front, late 1918.

III. Gunners of Australian 2nd Division drawing rations outside a farmhouse. One group of men eats its food beside a small tent made by draping gas-capes over a pole, Western Front, late 1918.

IV. Gunners of Australian 5th Division loading shells into their 18-pounder limbers, Western Front, October 1918. The limbers are in a transport park, which has a few houses in the distance. A supply train of wagons begins to move out of the park while unsaddled horses graze nearby.

V. Australian soldiers marching to board a trooptrain, probably for demobilisation, Western Front, late 1918. The men are in bush hats with greatcoats and gascapes. The weather is wet and foggy. They board the train and pose for the cameras in the doorways of their trucks. One doorway has the words "Direct To Aussie" chalked on it. The train moves off.

Notes
Production: the store ledger gives the cameraman as McDowell and suggests British official material. However, the supporting photograph is Australian, as are most of the subjects, and it seems likely that at least part of this film is Australian official material.
Remarks: the sequence of Rawlinson is candid and slightly comic in places.
[shotsheet available]
catalogued SDB: 12/1982

IWM 355 · GB, (prod) 1918
WORK OF THE METEOROLOGICAL OFFICE

b/w · 1 reel · 163' (3 mins) · silent
intertitles: none

sp Ministry of Information *pr* Topical Film Company *cam* Buckstone, W A

■ Meteorological Section, Royal Engineers, near Montreuil, Western Front, 16 October 1918.

Three members of the section, all from different regiments, use gas cylinders from a portable trailer to inflate two small weather balloons, using a lead weight to determine the gas pressure of each balloon. One soldier uses a ranging instrument to track a balloon as another releases it. The third opens a standard weather-station box and takes readings from the hygrometer and the rain gauge. He fits the wind gauge and

takes a reading from that also.

Notes
Title: this is taken from the shotsheet.
[shotsheet available]
catalogued SDB: 12/1982

IWM 356 · GB, 1918
HM THE KING'S VISIT TO THE TANK SCHOOL, WOOL, DORSET

b/w · 1 reel · 146' (3 mins) · silent
intertitles: none

sp Ministry of Information *cam* Woods-Taylor, G

■ George V's inspection of the Tank School at Bovington Camp in Dorset, 25 October 1918.

A Mk V Star tank moves away down a slope, its guns firing. Together with two other tanks it advances against dummy trenches. A Medium A Whippet moves away with the coastline visible behind it. King George V stands in Field Marshal's uniform with two other officers beside the cab of the Whippet. The King climbs out of the left side hatch of a Mk V Star. The King on top of a Whippet. Another Whippet moves off showing the royal party behind it. The King inspects American soldiers on a training course at the school, accompanied by British and American officers. Among the officers is Colonel J F C Fuller. The King inspects a Lewis machinegun and other items set out on a table for him, and talks to the soldiers at the school, who wear the distinctive Tank Corps overalls and shoulder flash. The King walks down and past a line of the soldiers, who give three cheers.

Notes
Title: this is taken from the shotsheet.
[J F C Fuller, *Tanks in the Great War 1914-1918*, Murray (1920)]
[shotsheet available]
catalogued SDB: 12/1982

IWM 357 · GB, (?) 1918
OUR WONDERFUL TANKS

b/w · 2 reels · 1402' (24 mins) · silent
intertitles: none

sp Ministry of Information *pr* Topical Film Company *cam* Bassill, F A

- Whippet, Mk V, Mk V Star, Recovery and Mk II Gun Carrier tanks demonstrating their performances, probably at the Tank Corps Central Stores at Erin, Western Front, October 1918.

(Reel 1) The setting is a large tank park with a training ground next to it. This has a number of artificial obstacles, water-filled craters and steep banks. The tanks are unmarked except for serial numbers. A Medium A Whippet drives through a water-filled crater (like a shell-hole). A Mk V Female demonstrates its ability to turn on its axis by locking one track. A Mk V Male has both sponsons removed for maintenance work. A series of races or charges across the training ground by Mk Vs and Whippets, all turning tightly to avoid collision. A line of tanks, including two Recovery tanks with crane attachments, covered with tarpaulins. Two Whippets, one carrying about eight men on its hull, manœuvre past each other. Mk V Star tanks lead off a column across the training ground. Three Whippets are driven into the park by ASC men, who park them and hose them down. (Reel 2) A long line of parked Mk Vs, mostly with hatches open. A Recovery tank with its crane comes into the park. A Mk V Male on the training ground drives through a shallow crater, then with more trouble a deeper crater. A closer view of a Mk V Male getting into and out of one of the craters. A line of Mk V Stars demonstrates that tank's ability to cross a wide trench. Two Mk II Gun Carrier tanks move across the training ground. Mk V Stars descend a steep slope followed by Mk Vs, one with an undX beam. The various tanks drive across the training ground, and one of the Mk V Stars negotiates a deep, flooded crater. A line of Mk Vs moves forward 'shoulder to shoulder' at walking pace, guided by Tank Corps men on foot. The Recovery tanks manœuvre into position beside two tanks which appear to have broken down.

Notes
Title: this is taken from the shotsheet.
Summary: see also **IWM 337**.
Remarks: entertaining material on the very late tank models of the First World War.
[shotsheet available]
catalogued SDB: 12/1982

IWM 358 · GB, (prod) 1918
ZEEBRUGGE (ledger title)

b/w · 1 reel · 408' (7 mins) · silent

intertitles: none

sp Ministry of Information *pr* Topical Film Company *cam* Bassill, F A

- Scenes showing the aftermath of the Zeebrugge raid, filmed at the time of the Allied reoccupation in October, 1918.

Long shot from a gun position, part of the Lübeck Battery on the mole, and pan right – three men stand in front of the gun, surveying the harbour. Man picks at debris in gunners' cupboard behind a 150mm gun of the Mittel Battery – pan left to show the gun and the beach it commands. Medium shot pan over the block-ship *Iphigenia*, lying across the entrance of the Bruges Ship Canal – the stern of *Intrepid* appears at frame at the very end of the take. High angle medium shot views of SS *Brussels* sunk near the end of the mole, masts and funnels showing above the water. High angle view along the mole to the lighthouse at the seaward end – two of the guns emplaced on the mole also appear in frame, the nearest with the barrel blown out at the muzzle. Long shot of the breach blown in the viaduct by the explosion of submarine C.3. Medium shot pan over rack of shells and rail lines behind the Kaiserin Battery – to the right of the lines are a series of German monuments in the form of sea mines mounted upon pedestals. Low angle medium shot behind the shield of one of the guns of the battery. Medium shots off the port bow of HMS *Thetis* lying in the harbour – the white ensign flies above the wreck. High angle medium shot along the mole as a man works the traversing wheel on one of the guns emplaced there – the gun with the blown barrel. Medium shot pan over *Iphigenia* and *Intrepid*, commencing where the previous pan finished. Barbed wire entanglements on the sloping sides of the canal – a Briton stands beside a German notice which forbids photography and drawing of the harbour mouth – camera pans to the two sunken block-ships. Long shot of *Thetis* and ML.532 in the harbour, seen from the western bank of the canal, and pan right to *Iphigenia*. Medium close-ups of the two block-ships.

catalogued NAP: 1/1983

IWM 359 · GB, (prod) 1918
[STATE ENTRY OF THE KING AND QUEEN OF BELGIUM INTO BRUGES]
(allocated)

b/w · 1 reel · 300' (5 mins) · silent
intertitles: none

sp Ministry of Information pr Topical Film
Company cam Buckstone, W A

■ Scenes in the main square of Bruges
during the state entry by King Albert and
Queen Elisabeth, Belgium, 25 October
1918.

The square is surrounded on all sides by
people waving flags and cheering. The King
and Queen are on horseback in the centre
of the square, the King wearing Belgian
Army uniform with a shrapnel helmet. The
King takes the salute as soldiers and
horsemen of the Belgian Army march past.
The two British representatives on
horseback with the party are Admiral Sir
Roger Keyes and Brigadier-General the Earl
of Athlone. The King and Queen move off to
the far side of the square, dismount and
greet various town officials, including the
local priest. Having remounted, they move
off again with their escort of the Allied
representatives, the crowd gathering behind
the procession.

[shotsheet available]
catalogued SDB: 12/1982

IWM 360 · GB, (prod) 1918
DOUAI AND LILLE

b/w · 1 reel · 246' (4 mins) · silent
intertitles: none

sp Ministry of Information pr Topical Film
Company cam Raymond, H C

■ Refugees returning to Douai and British
troops in Lille, Western Front, October
1918.

I. RAMC men help refugees in a street in
Douai to load both themselves and their
belongings into a British Army lorry. As the
last one is loaded the tailboard is closed up
and the people wave as the lorry drives
away.
II. The main square at Lille has one side
almost undamaged while the far side has
been reduced to rubble. British soldiers
clear a path through the rubble. Standing
near an old German shelter a British soldier
holds up for the camera, one after another,
the flags of the chief Allies and the United
States.

Notes
Title: this is taken from the shotsheet.
Remarks: surprisingly interesting rough
material, the excitement of refugees going
home is evident.
[shotsheet available]
catalogued SDB: 1/1983

IWM 361 · GB, (?) 1918
[ARRIVAL OF PRINCE YORIHITO OF
HIGASHI-FUSHIMI IN ENGLAND, 1918]
(allocated)

b/w · 1 reel · 517' (9 mins) · silent
intertitles: none

sp Ministry of Information

■ Prince's arrival at Dover and in London,
and visit to Woolwich (?), 28 October
1918.

The Prince is piped on board a ship in
Dover harbour and his staff line up for
inspection. He is greeted by a number of
British Army and Royal Navy officers, the
most senior being Major Prince Arthur of
Connaught, Lieutenant-General Pulteney
and Commander Sir Charles Cust. The
Prince leaves the ship to inspect his Royal
Navy escort. He is introduced to the mayor
and deputy mayor of the city, and to
Colonel the Earl of Pembroke. The
Japanese Ambassador with his naval and
military attachés are also present, and the
whole area heavily festooned with flags and
bunting. The Prince's drive from Victoria
Station (?) on the same day, through streets
hung with Japanese flags. The Prince
leaves his car at Woolwich Arsenal, the day
looking very misty and overcast. He takes
the salute as British field guns move past
slowly on a parade ground, unlimber, and
fire one shot in salute. A soldier, with his
back to the camera, demonstrates
something, possibly a gas mask, to the
Prince.

[The Times, 29 October 1918: 3A, 9B]
[shotsheet available]
catalogued SDB: 1/1983

IWM 362 · GB, (prod) 1918
CANADIAN OFFICER'S WEDDING AT ST
JAMES'S

b/w · 1 reel · 45' (1 min) · silent
intertitles: none

sp Ministry of Information (?) *cam* Cooper, F (?)

- Brief unedited record of a Canadian captain's wedding in London, possibly October 1918.

The bride and groom emerge down the steps of St James's church, Piccadilly, after the ceremony. The groom is in the uniform of a Canadian captain with raincoat, top boots and staff tabs. They pose for photographs then go past the onlookers to their car. The same captain, this time in normal uniform, walks with a major up the steps of a Whitehall building past the camera.

Notes
Title: this is taken from the shotsheet.
Remarks: a rather bizarre piece to find in an official film collection. Possibly 'abuse' of the official cameraman's time for private reasons, possibly the wedding of a hero.
[shotsheet available]
catalogued SDB: 1/1983

IWM 363 · GB, (?) 1918
GENERAL BIRDWOOD PRESENTS THE FIFTH ARMY TO THE MAYOR OF LILLE

b/w · 1 reel · 691' (12 mins) · silent
intertitles: none

sp Ministry of Information *pr* Topical Film Company *cam* Raymond, H C

- Parade of 47th (London) Division through the streets of Lille, Western Front, 28 October 1918.

The main square of Lille is crowded with civilians. The men of the division move in marching column through the crowds (filmed from a high window). The leading officer, General Sir William Birdwood, commanding Fifth Army, dismounts and greets the Mayor, M Delasalle, with the town council. The group watches from the saluting base as the division starts its march past. Watching with Birdwood and Delasalle are Lieutenant-General R C B Haking, commanding XI Corps, Major-General G F Gorringe, commanding 47th Division, and Winston Churchill, Secretary of State for War. Infantry and field guns of the division march past, the London Irish Rifles being led by a pipe band in shorts. A small French girl gives Birdwood a bouquet. Some of the soldiers have flags sticking from their rifle barrels. Birdwood and the

Mayor say goodbye. Outside the Canteleux Gate Birdwood leaves with his mounted escort. After some delay in assembly the cyclists of the division depart, followed by the rest of the troops. One mounted sergeant appears to be carrying a standard, possibly uncased battalion colours. The crowd watches the men leave.

Notes
Title: this is taken from the shotsheet.
[Alan H Maude (ed), *The 47th (London) Division*, Amalgamated Press (1922): 203-204]
[Field Marshal Lord [William R] Birdwood, *Khaki and Gown: an Autobiography*, Ward Lock (1941): 329]
[shotsheet available]
catalogued SDB: 1/1983

IWM 364-366 · NO FILM

IWM 367 · GB, (prod) 1918
DURING THE ARMISTICE (ledger title)

b/w · 1 reel · 97' (2 mins) · silent
intertitles: none

sp Ministry of Information *pr* Topical Film Company

- Brief, unedited film of refugees returning to their home towns, probably the Le Cateau Road, Western Front, 11-18 November 1918.

View down the length of a straight road lined with trees. A British staff car, probably the cameraman's, is parked by the road, and an officer watches, back to camera, as lines of refugees come up the road and exchange greetings with him. (He may be the official photographer J Warwick Brooke.) The refugees appear in a series of time cuts: a group of three with a large handcart, a large group with children riding a hay wagon, three men waving Allied flags, and carts festooned with flags.

[shotsheet available]
catalogued SDB: 1/1983

IWM 368 · GB, (prod) 1918
[FRATERNISATION BETWEEN BRITISH AND GERMAN SOLDIERS AT ATH]
(allocated)

b/w · 1 reel · 126' (2 mins) · silent
intertitles: none

sp Ministry of Information pr Topical Film
Company cam Wilson, F

- Unedited film of British and German
troops in or near Ath, Belgium, during the
Armistice, mid or late November 1918.

I. A dummy dressed in German uniform
suspended at the point of an arch, the
entrance to a brewery, with some British
soldiers passing nearby, Ath, 17 November.
II. Belgian refugees with backpacks march
up a hillside towards the camera.
III. German soldiers, one with a white flag
and the remainder carrying their rifles, talk
to a group of British soldiers who are also
carrying a white flag. They exchange
conversation and cigarettes. One of the
Germans discusses the technicalities of his
Mauser rifle with a British soldier. The
German and British officers also converse,
together with a few civilians. The four
German officers, and two escorts, prepare
to ride off, but as they leave they are halted
by Lieutenant Ernest Brooks, the British
official photographer, who checks their
passes before they ride off.

Notes
Title: the shotsheet gives the title Dummy
Boches Hanged at Courtrai but the
photographic evidence suggests Ath rather
than Courtrai.
Remarks: as with many unusual scenes, the
fraternisation looks almost too good to be
true. There is no reason, however, to doubt
its authenticity.
[shotsheet available]
catalogued SDB: 1/1983

IWM 369 · Australia, (prod) 1918
AUSTRALIAN ARTILLERY REVIEW

b/w · 1 reel · 272' (4 mins) · silent
intertitles: none

sp Australian War Records Section (?)

- Australian guns in a review, and transport
in the rear areas, Western Front, 10-11
November 1918.

I. Australian field guns pass on parade. The
inspecting officer is Lieutenant-General J J
Talbot Hobbs, commanding Australian 5th
Division, temporarily commanding the
Australian Corps. He stands at the saluting
base with his back to the camera. 10

November.
II. An open road over an old battlefield,
cratered and overgrown. Australian horsed
transport, and also a few lorries, move up
along the road. 11 November.

Notes
Title: this is taken from the shotsheet.
Production: Australian official film.
[C E W Bean, Official History of Australia in
the War of 1914-1918, Angus and
Robertson (1929-42)]
[shotsheet available]
catalogued SDB: 1/1983

IWM 370 · GB, (?) 1918
SCENES IN BRUSSELS

b/w · 1 reel · 684' (11 mins) · silent
intertitles: none

sp Ministry of Information pr Topical Film
Company cam Wilson, F

- State entry of the King and Queen of
Belgium into Brussels, 22 November
1918.

Crowds cheer the procession, which is led
by Belgian Cavalry, followed by a car
loaded with flowers, and then King Albert
and Queen Elisabeth riding in the midst of
civil and military dignitaries. The King is in
Belgian Army uniform with a shrapnel
helmet. Riding with the King are the Duke of
Brabant, Princess Marie Josée, and the
other royal children. The British dignitaries
in the contingent are the Duke of York,
together with Brigadier-General the Earl of
Athlone, Admiral Sir Roger Keyes, and three
Army commanders, Generals Plumer,
Birdwood and Horne. The parade continues
to march past. Apart from the Belgians
there are US and French troops (one
French contingent includes a black soldier)
and British soldiers, including kilted
Highlanders. (The film is broken at this
point by an extraneous scene of German
150mm guns on railway trucks captured in
the Forêt du Nord on 21 November.) The
main party forms up as a group, the King
and Queen dismount and the King talks
with the city dignitaries. The procession
then continues as the royal party, all
remounted, form again in a group for
photographs to be taken. Civilian and
military photographers, and one
cameraman, surge forward to take pictures.
The King and Queen are shown in close-up.
The procession passes in review before the
royal party. The camera, panning over the

group, picks out Generals Plumer and Birdwood together.

Notes
Title: this is taken from the shotsheet.
Summary: see also **IWM 359** and **IWM 371**.
Remarks: the best of the Belgian state entry films, with considerable movement and life, conveying well the general mood of exultation.
[shotsheet available]
catalogued SDB: 1/1983

IWM 371 · GB, (?) 1918
STATE ENTRY INTO ANTWERP 19TH NOVEMBER 1918

b/w · 1 reel · 476' (8 mins) · silent
intertitles: none

sp Ministry of Information *pr* Topical Film Company *cam* Bassill, F A

■ State entry of the King and Queen of Belgium into Antwerp, 19 November 1918.

A procession through the streets of the city, civilians mainly in formal dress, some using crutches. A convoy of cars arrives, and the city mayor gets out from one of them. A column of Belgian Cavalry led by a mounted band passes an elaborate saluting base at the side of the road. Another car arrives, King Albert (wearing Belgian Army uniform) and Queen Elisabeth get out and mount the saluting base, where they greet the waiting dignitaries and the Queen is given a bouquet of flowers. They sit on ornate brocaded chairs to watch the procession of Belgian troops. Together with the Cavalry, Infantry and Field Artillery are limber-drawn Maxim machineguns each pulled by two large dogs. After the procession the King and Queen leave in their car through a cheering crowd, followed by other cars and a mounted escort.

Notes
Title: this is taken from the shotsheet.
[shotsheet available]
catalogued SDB: 1/1983

IWM 372 · GB, (prod) 1918
NEW CHANNEL FERRY

b/w · 1 reel · 263' (4 mins) · silent
intertitles: none

sp Ministry of Information *pr* Topical Film Company

■ New British military roll-on roll-off Channel ferry for munitions trains berthing at its dock at Dunkirk, November 1918.

Seen from the shore behind the dock the ferry eases its way into its berth. Its cargo is two loaded munitions trains side by side. An engine reverses up the tracks leading to the ferry, is coupled to one of the trains and draws it out. The train carries, on flatcars, tanks with their sponsons removed (as was normal for rail travel) and covered in tarpaulin. A British official photographer, probably Second-Lieutenant Tom Aitken, can be seen at work. Another engine takes the second train, which also carries tanks in the same manner, as well as two trucks holding shells.

Notes
Title: this is taken from the shotsheet.
[shotsheet available]
catalogued SDB: 1/1983

IWM 373 · NO FILM

IWM 374 · GB, (prod) 1918
SCENES AT SPA

b/w · 1 reel · 251' (4 mins) · silent
intertitles: none

sp Ministry of Information *pr* Topical Film Company

■ Unedited material of the British Army advance towards Germany following the Armistice, 29 November-1 December 1918.

I. The gateway of the Kaiser's former headquarters at Spa with a German sentry on duty. A British staff car bearing a white flag goes through the gates followed by a German officer. A British sentry marches past on his rounds, 29 November.
II. British 1st Cavalry Division on the road with all its transport about to cross the frontier at Malmédy into Germany. Standing near the road photographing the event is J Warwick Brooke, the British official photographer, 1 December.
III. Brigadier-General A Lawson with his staff leads 2nd Cavalry Brigade, 1st Cavalry Division, led by 9th Lancers, in column into

the town of Spa, with local civilians crowding the route, 29 November.

Notes
Title: this is taken from the shotsheet.
[shotsheet available]
catalogued SDB: 1/1983

IWM 375 · GB, (?) 1918
ROYAL TOUR OF THE KING OVER FRANCE

b/w · 1 reel · 449' (7 mins) · silent
intertitles: none

sp Ministry of Information *pr* Topical Film Company

▪ King George V's visit to the British Army in France and Belgium, 1-9 December 1918.

The King (in Field Marshal's uniform) with the Prince of Wales, General Sir William Birdwood and other officers inspects graves, including that of General Maxwell, on the Ypres ridges on 8 December. On 5 December the King and Prince, together with Prince Albert and General Sir Henry Horne, are cheered through the streets of Stambruges by men of 175th Brigade, 58th (London) Division. Lieutenant-Colonel G Powell, the brigade commander, is present. On the following day the King, Horne and the Prince inspect an old battlefield, probably the ruin of Monchy-le-Preux church from the Battle of Arras. On 1 December the royal party drives over an old battlefield road, possibly the Maubeuge-Avesnes Road, in damp and overcast weather. On the next day the King walks through a crowd of jostling soldiers, very informal, possibly men of 21st Division at Le Quesnoy. On 6 December the King meets men of 15th (Scottish) Division at the crossroads at Thumaide. He leaves his car by the roadside and is taken by Birdwood to meet the divisional commander, Major-General H L Reed, who introduces him in turn to his staff, and to men of the division. The men include some Indian troops working with the RGA train attached to the division. The Infantry are lined up leaving a narrow tunnel of cheering soldiers for the King to walk down. On 7 December the King inspects 8th Division in the main square at Tournai, meeting Major-General W Heneker the divisional commander, the Bishop of Tournai and the town mayor. Birdwood is also present. They pose for a group photograph. The Prince of Wales's

car, the last of the convoy, is shown leaving the town. The royal party tours the Cloth Hall at Ypres on 8 December. Finally, probably on 9 December, the King inspects a very large shore gun emplacement at Zeebrugge.

Notes
Title: this is taken from the shotsheet.
[J H Boraston and Cyril E O Bax, *The Eighth Division in War 1914-1918*, Medici Society (1926)]
[J Stewart and John Buchan, *The Fifteenth (Scottish) Division 1914-1919*, Blackwood (1926)]
[shotsheet available]
catalogued SDB: 1/1983

IWM 376 · GB, (?) 1918
the BRITISH ENTRY INTO COLOGNE

b/w · 1 reel · 1425' (25 mins) · silent
intertitles: English

sp Ministry of Information *pr* Topical Film Company *cam* Bassill, F A

▪ British occupation of Cologne, including 1st Cavalry Division and 29th Division marching past General Sir Herbert Plumer, commanding the Army of Occupation, across the Hohenzollern Bridge, 6-14 December 1918.

I. The march past by 1st Cavalry Division on 12 December. Plumer stands with his staff to one side of the road leading across the bridge. With him are Lieutenant-General C Jacob, commanding II Corps, and Lieutenant-General Sir Charles Kavanagh commanding the Cavalry Corps. Lorries and 6-inch howitzers are parked waiting at the end of the bridge. 2nd and 9th Cavalry Brigades begin the march past, which continues for two hours, at 10am. The lancer regiment in the procession is 9th Lancers; they advance with the divisional cyclists and Austin armoured cars behind. Plumer is shown waiting to leave by his car, then standing beneath the giant statue of Kaiser Wilhelm II above the bridge, taking the salute. The division, including its transport, continues the march past.
II. On the following day, 13 December, 29th Division starts its march past at 9.30am, with Plumer again taking the salute. The Scottish battalion in the procession is 1st Battalion, King's Own Scottish Borderers. (There is an interpolation of the Cavalry from the previous day moving off the bridge.)

- 132 -

II. The lorries and 6-inch howitzers at the far end of the bridge are still in position, waiting, on 14 December.
IV. At a road bridge just north of Bayenthal, Cologne, on 6 December a corporal's guard of 'A' Squadron, 18th Hussars, sets up a Vickers machinegun and equipment. Armed German civilians, ex-soldiers employed by the British as a police force, look on.

Notes
Remarks: Lord Beaverbrook had retired for health reasons as Minister of Information in October 1918, and his ministry was closed down at the end of December. There was therefore virtually no policy directing British official films at the end of 1918. Films such as this one were taken with some sense of the need to make a historical record, but little else. It is not certain whether they were ever shown to the public in any form.
[Charles Harington, *Plumer of Messines*, Murray (1935): 187]
[shotsheet available]
catalogued SDB: 1/1983

IWM 377 · Australia, (prod) 1918
ON BOARD HMAS AUSTRALIA

b/w · 1 reel · 534' (6 mins) · silent
intertitles: none

sp Australian War Records Section

■ Crew of the battle-cruiser HMAS *Australia*, 10 December 1918.

Part of the ship's company assembled in front of the bridge tower, which shows the ship's crest and battle honours of Rabaul, German New Guinea and Samoa. A flag officer (no clear view) presents one of the ratings with a medal for his part in the Zeebrugge raid. Signal flags are raised and lowered as an exercise, with a semaphore arm in the background. A posed group of part of the ship's company. Another assembly on the fo'c's'le, the chaplain emerges and gives a brief service, following which an officer addresses the men. The men take exercise running round the deck and up and down the companion-ways. More of the crew are shown in close-up hauling the signal flags up and down, and loading shells on board the ship from a sling.

Notes
Title: this is taken from the shotsheet.
[shotsheet available]
catalogued SDB: 1/1983

IWM 378 · GB, (prod) 1918
[GERMAN TANK TRAPS 1918] (allocated)

b/w · 1 reel · 558' (9 mins) · silent
intertitles: English

■ Disjointed film of Tank Corps members inspecting types of German tank traps and anti-tank mines, Western Front, 1918.

There are three types of trap, all working on the same principle. The Tank Corps men look firstly at a simple 'hedge' of wooden stakes driven at an angle into the ground. A Mk V Male tank demonstrates how these are meant to stop tanks by driving up to the 'hedge' until one stake is directly against the forward sloped section of its right-hand track, so that any further pressure from the tank would only drive the stake more firmly into the ground. The tank then demonstrates that by approaching the stakes at a slight angle it can simply drive over and crush them without difficulty. The second type of trap is another 'hedge' of thin metal rods set closely together, probably worn railway tracks. The tank again bends and crushes these without difficulty, coming almost up to the camera. British soldiers, digging between these stakes, unearth two unexploded large calibre shells, probably intended to explode as the stakes are knocked over as a primitive form of anti-tank mine. The third type of stake defence is a combination, the thin metal rods being reinforced on either side by wooden stakes. Part of this 'hedge' has been bent right over by a tank.

Notes
Production: the shotsheet is marked "censored sections passed by GHQ", possibly censored during the war and released immediately afterwards. This film may have been taken for Army training or Intelligence purposes rather than propaganda or record.
[shotsheet available]
catalogued SDB: 1/1983

IWM 379 · GB, (prod) 1918
HUNS SURRENDERING BATTLEPLANES – BRITISH AIRMAN TAKES A TRIP IN A FOKKER

b/w · 1 reel · 269' (4 mins) · silent
intertitles: English

sp Ministry of Information *pr* Topical Film Company *cam* Wilson, F

- British or Australian airmen testing captured German aeroplanes, possibly at Birkendorf aerodrome, Cologne, December 1918.

A German aerodrome, where British aircrew (including a Captain Benson) and ground crew pose for the camera. Some of them are wearing bush hats. In front of a hangar are four Fokker DVII fighters, one with its prop turning over. A pilot gets into one of the aircraft. The wrecks of two other Fokkers with their wings missing are guarded by British soldiers. The pilot settles into the Fokker DVII and it begins to roll forward. Another pilot sits, as a joke, in the cockpit of a wreck which has one wing bent and draped over obscuring its fuselage. Two of the Fokkers taxi towards and past the camera. A partially stripped wreck of a Junkers JI ground attack aircraft is looked over by the pilots. A line of the Fokker DVIIs carrying various distinctive squadron or personal markings. A pilot boards one of the planes, the German markings of which have been obscured, and it takes off, overflying the camera. Another view of the line of Fokkers, and of the aircraft taking off.

[shotsheet available]
catalogued SDB: 1/1983

IWM 380 · GB, 26/12/1918
PICTORIAL NEWS (OFFICIAL) 383-1

b/w · 1 reel · 213' (3 mins) · silent
intertitles: English

sp Ministry of Information *pr* Topical Film Company

I. British troops guarding a road bridge near Bayenthal, Cologne, 6 December 1918. Austin armoured cars stand on the bridge, covering it with machineguns, as trams pass along and German civilians go about their business. (Note the British official photographer J Warwick Brooke at work.) At one end of the bridge a British Vickers machinegun post has been set up, manned by 'B' Squadron, 18th Hussars. With the soldiers are German civilians with rifles and armbands, acting as a temporary police force.
II. Crowds in the main square of Strasbourg wave French flags and cheer the camera in celebration of the city's liberation, November 1918.
III. "The watch on the Rhine", British sentries look out over the mists at Cologne from the Hohenzollern Bridge, December 1918.

Notes
Summary: the Strasbourg item appears to come from *Annales de la Guerre 89*, held as **IWM 508-89**.
[shotsheet available]
catalogued SDB: 1/1983

IWM 381 · GB, (prod) 1918
HAIG AT COLOGNE (ledger title)

b/w · 1 reel · 285' (5 mins) · silent
intertitles: none

sp Ministry of Information *pr* Topical Film Company *cam* Bassill, F A

I. Field Marshal Haig's farewell to the official war correspondents on the Hohenzollern Bridge, Cologne, 16 December 1918. Two cars, led by Haig's escort troop of 17th Lancers, pull up on the bridge in the mist. Haig gets out of the first car together with General Sir Herbert Plumer, commanding the Army of Occupation. Haig's Chief of Staff, Lieutenant-General Sir Herbert Lawrence, gets out from the second car. Colonel Neville Lytton, commanding the GHQ Press Section, presents each of the twenty-five correspondents, British and foreign, and Haig gives each of them a small Union Jack like his car pennant. Haig then drives away with his lancer escort.
II. The arrival of President Poincaré in Lille, 21 October 1918. Crowds wait in the streets for the President. General Sir William Birdwood, commanding Fifth Army, waits with an escort for the car carrying Poincaré to arrive. The President arrives and inspects the guard. The inhabitants of Lille cheer his car as it drives through the streets and the main square.

Notes
Summary: see also **IWM 352** for the Lille item.
[Countess [Dorothy] Haig, *The Man I Knew*, Moray Press (1936)]
[Neville Lytton, *The Press and the General Staff*, Collins (1921)]
[shotsheet available]
catalogued SDB: 1/1983

IWM 382 · Australia, (prod) 1918
the PRINCE OF WALES WITH THE AUSTRALIANS

b/w · 1 reel · 184' (3 mins) · silent
intertitles: none

sp Australian War Records Section
cam Young, S H E

■ Disjointed film of the Prince of Wales
presenting medals to men of 6th Brigade,
Australian 2nd Division, Mechelen
(Malines), Belgium, 24 December 1918.

The Prince (in Army uniform) decorates the
Australians in an open-air ceremony. View
of Belgian children, lined up for the camera.
The Australians march past the Prince. The
arrival of the Prince (?) by car with an
escort of 13th Regiment, Australian Light
Horse. Australian Infantry on guard, the
Prince emerges from a building behind
them and gets into his car (filmed from a
high position). Back at the presentation
ceremony, the soldiers present arms and
salute, and the Prince walks round
inspecting them.

Notes
Title: this is taken from the shotsheet.
Production: the store ledger gives the
cameraman for this film as F A Bassill. This
would involve a British official cameraman
working with an Australian official
photographer on an Australian subject,
which is inherently unlikely. Probably
Australian official film.
[shotsheet available]
catalogued SDB: 1/1983

IWM 383 · GB, (prod) 1915
**SECTIONS RELEASED FROM GHQ
POSITIVE BOX**
WITH THE INDIAN TROOPS AT THE
FRONT (censored sections)
the MAKING OF AN OFFICER (censored
sections)

b/w · 1 reel · 293' (5 mins) · silent
intertitles: none

sp War Office pr British Topical Committee
for War Films cam Malins, Geoffrey H
and/or Tong, Edward G (?)

I. Censored sections from **IWM 202-01** and
IWM 202-02 *With the Indian Troops at the
Front* showing units of the former Indian
Corps in rear areas of the Western Front,
November and December 1915. Men of
34th Sikh Pioneers digging a model trench,
firstly marking out the ground with white
tape. Gurkhas route marching through the
rain. Men of 1st Battalion, Seaforth
Highlanders also on the march. A supply
dump by the roadside. More of the Gurkhas
on the route march.

II. Censored sections from **IWM 203** *The
Making of an Officer* showing basic training
by the Artists Rifles at St-Omer, Western
Front, December 1915. The relief of the
guard in front of battalion headquarters at
St-Omer. Cadets going home on leave
waiting for a train at St-Omer station. The
train arrives and they board it.

Notes
Title: this is taken from the shotsheet.
Production: censored or discarded sections
of three films from the first series of features
released by the War Office in early 1916.
See **IWM 202-01**, **IWM 202-02**, **IWM 203**
and **IWM 114** for production details.
Cameraman: this was either Malins, Tong,
or both.
Remarks: it is not on first viewing obvious
why some of these scenes were cut from
the finished film. Possibly considerations of
pace played a part, as well as those of
security. Generally, scenes have been cut
of which the location was either obvious (as
in the case of St-Omer station which has a
large sign advertising the fact) or possibly
deducible. Other scenes seem to have
been cut since soldiers in them, indifferent
to the camera, have an informal or
'unsoldierly' appearance, as with the relief of
the guard at St-Omer; or to preserve an
illusion of actual combat, as with the trench-
digging scene in which traffic can be seen
on the road facing the trench. The cutting
has been clumsy, producing jolts in the
finished film. One caption in **IWM 203** in
fact promises the scene of "relieving the
guard" which has been cut. Generally, if this
represents the level of censorship the Army
was prepared to apply to the first films it
permitted of the Western Front, it lends
support to the contention of the cinema
industry of the time that the military attitude
was unrealistic.
[shotsheet available]
catalogued SDB: 1/1983

IWM 384 · Australia, (prod) 1919
**NURSE CAVELL'S GRAVE AND
MEMORIAL**

b/w · 1 reel · 287' (5 mins) · silent
intertitles: none

sp Australian War Records Section
cam Young, S H E

■ Various locations associated with nurse
Edith Cavell in Brussels, 9 January 1919.

Three Australian officers stand with a

Belgian officer as escort on the balcony of the prison where nurse Cavell was held. Then they stand by the plaque in the prison yard marking the place where she was shot. A close-up of her grave, decorated with flowers and with Red Cross and British flags, tracking out to show other graves in the cemetery. People lay flowers at the foot of the statue of nurse Cavell erected in the centre of Brussels. Australian soldiers and Belgian civilians hand out toys to children.

Notes
Title: this is taken from the shotsheet.
Production: Australian official film, among the last film taken by any of the British or Dominion camera teams.
[AWRS(Film) Papers, File 4375/60/24]
[shotsheet available]
catalogued SDB: 1/1983

IWM 385 · New Zealand, (prod) 1918
ARRIVAL OF NEW ZEALAND TROOPS AT COLOGNE
NEW ZEALANDERS AT THE FRONT
(alternative)

b/w · 1 reel · 819' (14 mins) · silent
intertitles: none

cam Sanders, Henry A; and Barton, Charles

■ Arrival of the New Zealand Division in Cologne, 26 December 1918.

Infantry in column pass through one of the frontier towns. The units of the Division led by 3rd Brigade are shown marching from the Hohenzollern Bridge with Cologne Cathedral in the background (see **Notes**). Trams pass and curious, well-dressed civilians, mainly young children, approach the camera. The scene shifts to a German restaurant at Ehrenfeld, Cologne, which has been converted into a NZ YMCA: 'diggers' file past an open window collecting bread, cakes, coffee and cocoa. Back to the transport and artillery marching into Cologne. At a railway marshalling yard transport wagons are unloaded from freight cars. The infantry continue to march over the Hohenzollern Bridge. At the marshalling yard, soldiers smoke and brew tea. A goods train loaded with troops slowly moves off with two New Zealand officers hurrying to get on board. One man playing the bagpipes dismounts and marches alongside the train playing before getting on again. At the rear of the train the troops in wagons cheer the camera. The train moves into the marshalling yards, where the troops

get off and unload their equipment and wagons.

Notes
Title: the main title is scratched on the negative; the alternative title has been taken from the shotsheet.
Production: this is the last film taken by Sanders as official NZEF cinematographer, assisted by Charles Barton. Barton was an experienced cameraman who had worked firstly as a freelance and then for New Zealand Picture Supplies, the largest film distribution company in New Zealand. He was conscripted in May 1918. After a period as a gunner in England he was appointed to succeed Sanders in December 1918, worked with him in Cologne, and replaced him after this film. In 1919 Barton filmed YMCA activities, the demobilisation of the NZEF, and the troop voyage back to New Zealand. He was discharged in April 1920.
Summary: "As the column left the bridge and entered the eastern suburbs of Cologne, the official photographer of the Division took a cinematograph film ... A more interesting spot could not have been chosen, for it has as a background the towers of the Hohenzollern Bridge and the double steeple of the Cathedral" ('With the Artillery to the Rhine' in *Chronicles of the NZEF*, 5: 61 [24 January 1919]: 303).
Remarks: gives a very good idea of the size and road space taken up by a division on the march. The train scenes may be staged, but the haphazard movements could also be accounted for by the delays in bringing the large number of trooptrains into the marshalling yards.
Authority: additional detail from Christopher Pugsley, 12/1993.
[shotsheet available]
catalogued SDB: 1/1983

IWM 386 · NO FILM

IWM 387 · New Zealand, 1917
NEW ZEALAND AMBULANCE
WORK OF THE NEW ZEALAND MEDICAL CORPS [NZMC] (alternative)

b/w · 1 reel · 938' (16 mins) · silent
intertitles: none

cam Sanders, Henry A

■ Film of the casualty evacuation system of the New Zealand Medical Corps on the Western Front in late June 1917.

Stretcher-bearers evacuate wounded by wheeled stretcher or jigger to the Advanced Dressing Station (ADS). After treatment the men are taken by ambulances (bearing the NZ Division tactical sign of a silver fern within a black circle) to 3 New Zealand Field Ambulance at Pont d'Aschelles, which is acting as the Main Dressing Station (MDS). Soldiers take pails of food to the patients' dining hall, a temporary wooden building. New Zealand and Australian wounded, including one man suffering from trench foot being carried on someone's back, enter the dining hall. An ambulance arrives at the MDS reception area and unloads its patients. Stretcher cases are carried out of the evacuating ward and taken by ambulance on the next stage of their journey to the base hospitals. Close ups are shown of the different types of labels for identifying wounds. Back at the MDS, men who have recovered queue to receive their equipment which has been stored for safe-keeping. The scene shifts to the sanitary section. Men wearing blankets and hats are seen entering the Divisional baths, and handing in their uniforms to men running the Foden Lorry Disinfector, for delousing. The ambulances return to the front lines. An ADS where medical staff sit in the sun and wait for things to happen. At a Regimental Aid Post (RAP) in Ploegsteert Wood, a stretcher case is brought in and examined by the Regimental Medical Officer (RMO) – the sun fogs the film on this scene. A wounded man with a head bandage smiles and puffs away on a cigarette. A stretcher is taken along a communication trench from the front line to the RAP, and then onto a light tramway for evacuation to the ADS – note that the stretcher-bearers are wearing Dayfield body armour. Back at No 3 NZ Field Ambulance, men leave in a horse-drawn ambulance while other ambulances line up to evacuate serious cases to hospitals. Walking wounded reach the MDS, while stretcher cases are carried between wards.

Notes
Title: this is taken from the shotsheet; the alternative title is from the WOCC invoice.
Production: this is the first film that can be dated of Sanders's work as official cinematographer for the NZEF on the Western Front (see **Notes** to **IWM 157**). Sanders reported to the NZ Division on 8 April and presumably filmed the build-up to the Battle of Messines and the battle itself in May and June 1917 – his photographs survive, and eyewitnesses describe him coming under artillery fire while filming during the battle, but no film of Messines

survives that can be attributed to Sanders.
Summary: at the time of filming, the NZ Division was in the line south of the river Douve with its front line forward of Ploegsteert Wood. It was a period of heavy fighting following the Division's capture of Messines: "During the period from the 15 to 30 June our casualties were reported to be: 106 killed; and 801 wounded. There was an increasing casualty list due to gas poisoning and there were clear signs of nervous exhaustion in many of the sick" (A D Carbery, *The New Zealand Medical Services in the Great War*, Whitcombe and Tombs (1924): 318). Sick and lightly wounded men could be held at the MDS for seven days if it was assessed they could recover in this time. The Foden Lorry Disinfector had two Thresh chambers which could each disinfect 30 blankets an hour; the baths could shower 1000 men a day, and had a laundry attached which employed 150 women to launder and repair 40 000 items of clothing a week.
Authority: additional detail from Christopher Pugsley, 12/1993.
[shotsheet available]
catalogued SDB: 1/1983

IWM 388 · GB, 2/1918
the BEDFORD REGIMENT (sic)
[the BRITISH REGIMENTS] (series, allocated)

b/w · 1 reel · 316' (6 mins) · silent
intertitles: English

sp War Office Cinema Committee *pr* Topical Film Company

■ Battalion of the Bedfordshire Regiment resting in the rear areas of the Western Front, autumn 1917.

An open-air church parade with the battalion drawn up in hollow square. The battalion marches back to its billets led by its band. A posed group of men "who have been with the battalion since 1914". A further posed group of officers and men of the battalion who have received decorations. (Both groups indistinctly filmed.) Men draw sacks of rations from a dump. Mail is distributed to the men.

Notes
Remarks: a complete failure as a historical record. Neither the scenes filmed, the camerawork nor the captioning in any way distinguish this battalion from any other in the Army of the time. This is generally true

of all the films of the series. The object was probably to encourage relatives of men serving in the various regiments to watch in the hope of seeing men they knew.
[shotsheet available]
catalogued SDB: 1/1983

IWM 389 · GB, 1/1918
the CHESHIRE REGIMENT
[the BRITISH REGIMENTS] (series, allocated)

b/w · 1 reel · 295' (5 mins) · silent
intertitles: none

sp War Office Cinema Committee *pr* Topical Film Company

■ 1st Battalion, the Cheshire Regiment, in rear areas of the Western Front, autumn 1917.

The battalion marches past its senior officer (face not visible, possibly not the commanding officer) led by its band. Battalion rations are brought up in two-man containers and stew is shovelled from these into the men's mess tins. The men sit among flowers at the edge of a wood, talking and eating. A paper-seller makes his rounds among them. A portrait shot of Private T A Jones VC serving with the battalion.

Notes
Title: this is taken from the shotsheet.
Remarks: valueless as a record of a specific battalion, consisting of a series of uninteresting stockshots.
[shotsheet available]
catalogued SDB: 1/1983

IWM 390 · GB, 1/1918
the MIDDLESEX REGIMENT
[the BRITISH REGIMENTS] (series, allocated)

b/w · 1 reel · 644' (11 mins) · silent
intertitles: English

sp War Office Cinema Committee *pr* Topical Film Company

■ Scenes of 2nd Battalion, Middlesex Regiment, in the rear areas of the Western Front, autumn 1917, with scenes of other battalions on the Western Front in 1918 added.

I. A company of the battalion on one side of a country road as the band marches up and turns before the camera. The assembled battalion cheers the camera. A group of three officers with the battalion mascot, a very small black kitten. A battalion kit inspection. A company on the march down a cobbled road showing its variety of battlefield dress and equipment. The transport section has difficulty with half-broken mules, having to tie one to a frame in order to shoe it, and to ease others into the shafts of the limber wagons. As the limbers move off some of the mules rear with excitement. A field cooker has food unloaded from it (note the divisional sign), a meal is served and the men eat at wooden tables in the open. A "sergeants' mess" made from an open hoop of corrugated iron and a more substantial officers' mess with six officers peering through the window.
II. The Middlesex involvement in the Battle of the Lys. One battalion marches, backs to camera, past watching French Infantry. Men of 8th Battalion carry captured machineguns on a cart through the ruins of St-Léger. Men of the regiment bury German dead.

Notes
Summary: see also **IWM 322** *The Great British Offensive* for the scenes of 8th Battalion. These appear to have been added to the already complete film after its first release.
Remarks: valueless as a record of a specific battalion, consisting of a series of stockshots and uninformative captions.
[shotsheet available]
catalogued SDB: 1/1983

IWM 391 · GB, 2/1918
the KING'S OWN YORKSHIRE LIGHT INFANTRY
[the BRITISH REGIMENTS] (series, allocated)

b/w · 1 reel · 573' (10 mins) · silent
intertitles: English

sp War Office Cinema Committee *pr* Topical Film Company

■ Battalion of the King's Own Yorkshire Light Infantry in the rear areas of the Western Front, autumn 1917.

A battalion manœuvre over ploughed fields with dispersed soldiers and mounted officers (filmed in long shot). Men of the battalion rest and smoke wearing field equipment. A Lewis machinegun team gives a demonstration. A second group demonstrates Swedish drill (PT), a third group bayonet fighting, a fourth the speedy donning of gas masks and a fifth a solidarity-boosting 'trust exercise'. Two field cookers arrive and stew is served to the men, who eat rather camera-consciously. The whole battalion, led by its band, marches past the camera, rifles at the trail.

Notes
Remarks: valueless as a record of a specific battalion, consisting of stockshots and uninformative captions.
[shotsheet available]
catalogued SDB: 1/1983

IWM 392 · GB, 2/1918
the NORTHANTS REGIMENT (sic)
[the BRITISH REGIMENTS] (series, allocated)

b/w · 1 reel · 382' (6 mins) · silent
intertitles: English

sp War Office Cinema Committee *pr* Topical Film Company

- Battalion of the Northamptonshire Regiment in the rear areas of the Western Front, autumn 1917.

A posed group of men of the battalion sitting or lying down. A posed shot of two soldiers together. Three soldiers clean a disassembled Lewis machinegun. A company drilling, indifferently, on open ground. A platoon practises taking aim and recovering its rifles. Signallers practise semaphore drill. An NCO, leading bayonet practice, shows a group of the men how to contain a fugitive. Officers and men stand outside a battalion headquarters made up of temporary huts. Two companies march past the huts.

Notes
Title: this and the subtitles are flashframes.
Remarks: valueless as a record of a specific battalion, consisting of stockshots and uninformative captions.
[shotsheet available]
catalogued SDB: 1/1983

IWM 393 · GB, 3/1918
the SUFFOLK REGIMENT
[the BRITISH REGIMENTS] (series, allocated)

b/w · 1 reel · 528' (9 mins) · silent
intertitles: English

sp War Office Cinema Committee *pr* Topical Film Company

- 2nd Battalion, Suffolk Regiment, in the rear areas of the Western Front, autumn 1917.

A posed group of the battalion officers. Men sitting and drinking outside a kiosk marked as the "Divisional Canteen". The camp barber at work outside his tent. The men stand outside their own tents cleaning their equipment and weapons, then wash themselves at a semi-permanent arrangement of basins and standpipes. Some of the men play cards. Food containers arrive and the men are served with a form of meat loaf. They rest beside their tents. A company in helmets and field equipment, led by its band, marches over "territory captured from the Germans". A single file of men crosses an overgrown German trench, and the men sit round as an officer, at the bottom of the trench, lectures them on German emplacements. Some of the men scramble over the wreck of a German reinforced concrete lookout tower. Two of the soldiers inspect two temporary wooden crosses marking German graves. A side view of the men defending a trench among trees in a training exercise.

Notes
Remarks: valueless as a record of a specific battalion, but the choice of items to film is rather more inspired than is typical for the series.
[shotsheet available]
catalogued SDB: 1/1983

IWM 394 · GB, 3/1918
the ESSEX REGIMENT
[the BRITISH REGIMENTS] (series, allocated)

b/w · 1 reel · 335' (6 mins) · silent
intertitles: none

sp War Office Cinema Committee *pr* Topical Film Company

- Regular battalion of the Essex Regiment in the rear areas of the Western Front, autumn 1917.

I. A posed group of men of the battalion lying on the grass. Signallers practise semaphore on the parade ground. Stretcher-bearer teams, also on the parade ground, go through the drill of helping casualties. Four battalion boot-repairers at work. The midday meal is issued to the men who queue up with their mess tins. Men of the battalion are billeted in a farm and walk up an outside stairway to a hayloft. The mail arrives and the men cluster round to receive parcels. A company marches down a country road in shirtsleeve order.

II. Two unrelated scenes have become attached to the end of the film. Recruiting bands march through city streets joined by civilians. Two observers, in a faked close-up, in a balloon basket.

Notes
Title: this is taken from the shotsheet.
Remarks: valueless as a record of a specific battalion, consisting of a series of stockshots.
[shotsheet available]
catalogued SDB: 1/1983

IWM 395 · GB, 12/1917
the HUSSARS
[the BRITISH REGIMENTS] (series, allocated)

b/w · 1 reel · 273' (5 mins) · silent
intertitles: none

sp War Office Cinema Committee *pr* Topical Film Company

■ Two troops of a British hussar regiment in the rear areas of the Western Front, autumn 1917.

The men dismount in front of a farmhouse, standing by their horses with their rifles. They then come to attention and remount with their rifles. They move off, closing up formation into column of fours. They take their horses through a stream beside a bridge, emerging to break into a trot. A second troop also passes through the stream, emerging in column of twos. The two troops trot on along a cobbled road in column of fours.

Notes
Title: this is taken from the shotsheet.
Remarks: an interesting example of wartime censorship policy whereby battalion numbers were censored from regimental titles. In this case the regimental number of the hussar regiment has been removed, making it completely unidentifiable.

[shotsheet available]
catalogued SDB: 1/1983

IWM 396 · GB, 12/1917
the YORK AND LANCASTER REGIMENT
[the BRITISH REGIMENTS] (series, allocated)

b/w · 1 reel · 409' (7 mins) · silent
intertitles: English

sp War Office Cinema Committee *pr* Topical Film Company

■ 2nd Battalion, York and Lancaster Regiment, in the rear areas of the Western Front, autumn 1917.

Close-up of a sergeant holding a football marked 2Y&L. Pan over the men of the battalion, lying, sitting or standing informally, with two Lewis machineguns in the front row. Two lance corporals sitting beside their tent. A company of men posed relaxing beside a wall. Two soldiers with a large canteen draw water from a well by the roadside. A group of battalion officers, including the current commander. The battalion, led by its band, on a route march. A "blindfold boxing march" in front of the soldiers. A pay parade in the open. A sergeant inspects rifles on parade, holding one up to the light to inspect the barrel. A portrait shot of Private Caffrey, VC.

Notes
Remarks: this film is above average for a generally poor series. It does at least convey some sense of a battalion identity. The opening shot makes nonsense of the censor's attempt to obscure the battalion's identity.
[shotsheet available]
catalogued SDB: 1/1983

IWM 397 · GB, 1/1918
the ROYAL BERKSHIRE REGIMENT
[the BRITISH REGIMENTS] (series, allocated)

b/w · 1 reel · 493' (8 mins) · silent
intertitles: English

sp War Office Cinema Committee *pr* Topical Film Company

■ Possibly 2nd Battalion, Royal Berkshire Regiment, in the rear areas of the Western Front, autumn 1917.

Opening with a close-up profile of a private of the regiment, showing the shoulder-title "Royal Berks" very clearly. A platoon walking past a damaged building. A posed group of NCOs and warrant officers who have been decorated. Two small groups of the battalion officers. Men lining up outside a building to draw "wet rations" (beer) from a barrel. Sections practise Lewis machinegun drill, using six men to a gun in rotation. Other sections practise bayonet fighting and gas alarm drill. The battalion band marches down a street. The men of the transport section ride some of their horses or mules to a billet area where a vet bandages the leg of a very placid "wounded" horse. The men use a machine to cut chaff for the horses and carry nosebags out to them. The transport camp shows the first stages of a semi-permanent wooden building being built.

Notes
Remarks: valueless as a record of a specific battalion, consisting of a series of stockshots and uninformative captions. Nevertheless some interesting material, and above average for the series.
[shotsheet available]
catalogued SDB: 1/1983

IWM 398 · GB, 1/1918
the KING'S (LIVERPOOL) REGIMENT (sic)
[the BRITISH REGIMENTS] (series, allocated)

b/w · 1 reel · 437' (7 mins) · silent
intertitles: English

sp War Office Cinema Committee *pr* Topical Film Company

■ Probably 1st Battalion, King's (Liverpool Regiment), in the rear areas of the Western Front, autumn 1917.

The battalion parades outside a virtually undamaged château. The men wear shrapnel helmets but look quite smart, if very tired. They are briefly inspected by their commanding officer (face not seen). They set out on a route march in full kit with transport limbers and wagons, the officers riding horses. The officers posed outside the château; the commanding officer may be Major H C Potter. The battalion boot repairers at work. The armourer's shop, showing maintenance work being done on a Lewis machinegun. Two field cookers in a yard comprise the "cookhouse". Several of the men emerge from the hayloft and come

down an outer stairway. A "merry group of Liverpool lads" with the regimental goat. A final close-up of a soldier wearing his cap to display the regimental badge.

Notes
Remarks: above average for the series, but by no means an outstanding film.
[shotsheet available]
catalogued SDB: 1/1983

IWM 399 · GB, 12/1917
the DURHAM LIGHT INFANTRY
[the BRITISH REGIMENTS] (series, allocated)

b/w · 1 reel · 354' (6 mins) · silent
intertitles: English

sp War Office Cinema Committee *pr* Topical Film Company

■ One or more battalions of the Durham Light Infantry in the rear areas of the Western Front, autumn 1917.

The battalion on parade is inspected by its commanding officer (not seen). Men repack their kit after an open-air kit inspection. Some of the men sit resting and eating in the open; one reads the *Daily Mail*, others smoke or play 'house' (see **Notes**). The mail is handed out but the men seem indifferent (possibly staged) reading "all the news from Blighty". The brigade commander (not clearly seen) and his staff come out of a château and get into an ornate horse-driven coach. A posed group of a Lewis machinegun platoon. A further posed group of six NCOs who have "been out since 1914".

Notes
Summary: the game of 'house' or 'housey-housey', a form of bingo, was the only game officially permitted to soldiers at the time.
Remarks: valueless as a record of a specific battalion, but containing some attractive material.
[shotsheet available]
catalogued SDB: 1/1983

IWM 400 · GB, 12/1917
the EAST KENT REGIMENT (THE BUFFS) (sic)
[the BRITISH REGIMENTS] (series, allocated)

b/w · 1 reel · 459' (8 mins) · silent
intertitles: English

sp War Office Cinema Committee *pr* Topical
Film Company

- Battalion of the Buffs (East Kent
  Regiment) in the rear areas of the
  Western Front, autumn 1917.

The battalion, led by its band, on a route
march down a tree-lined lane. A group of
the battalion officers. A party of signallers
practising training exercises. The band
marches up and turns in formation just in
front of the camera, "playing the retreat". An
out-of-focus group of "four holders of the
DCM". A pan over the men of the battalion
resting: one man juggles a bottle, other
men play their fifes and an accordion.

Notes
Remarks: valueless as a record of a specific
battalion, consisting of a series of
stockshots and uninformative captions.
[shotsheet available]
catalogued SDB: 1/1983

IWM 401 · GB, 2/1918
the ROYAL WEST KENT REGIMENT
[the BRITISH REGIMENTS] (series,
allocated)

b/w · 1 reel · 455' (8 mins) · silent
intertitles: English

sp War Office Cinema Committee *pr* Topical
Film Company

- Probably a regular battalion of the
  Queen's Own (Royal West Kent
  Regiment) on the Western Front, autumn
  1917.

The battalion and band, with mounted
officers, march along a dirt road. The men
rest outside the canteen drinking tea.
Others play in a river and millpond,
including a friendly game of water-polo. A
boxing match, in a ring, ends with a staged
knockout. A posed group of men of the
battalion "who have been out since 1914"
with the battalion mascot dog. A further
posed group of officers and men "who have
gained decorations during the present war".
A pair of transport horses, which have been
with the battalion since 1914, are awarded a
silver cup for good condition.

Notes
Remarks: slightly more varied than most of

the films in the series, but still valueless as
a record of a specific battalion.
[C T Atkinson, *The Queen's Own Royal West
Kent Regiment 1914-1919*, Simpkin Marshall
(1924)]
[shotsheet available]
catalogued SDB: 9/1981

IWM 402 · GB, 2/1918
the WEST YORKS REGIMENT
[the BRITISH REGIMENTS] (series,
allocated)

b/w · 1 reel · 281' (5 mins) · silent
intertitles: English

sp War Office Cinema Committee *pr* Topical
Film Company

- Probably a regular battalion of the Prince
  of Wales's Own (West Yorkshire
  Regiment), on the Western Front, autumn
  1917.

A posed group of the battalion's officers.
Men of the battalion, obviously camera-
conscious, rest by the roadside, then collect
their kit and move off. Led by their band,
they march in full kit through a village.

Notes
Remarks: like most of the series, this is
valueless as a record of a specific battalion.
[E Wyrall, *The West Yorkshire Regiment in
the War 1914-1918*, Lane (1924-27)]
[shotsheet available]
catalogued SDB: 9/1981

IWM 403 · GB, 2/1918
the DORSET REGIMENT
[the BRITISH REGIMENTS] (series,
allocated)

b/w · 1 reel · 463' (8 mins) · silent
intertitles: English

sp War Office Cinema Committee *pr* Topical
Film Company

- Probably 1st Battalion, the Dorsetshire
  Regiment, in the Nieuport area, Western
  Front, June-October 1917.

The battalion Transport section cleans and
maintains the wagons (note the 'four eights'
divisional sign of 32nd Division). The
wagons move out through a village. In the
blacksmith's yard the horses are shod.
Signallers of the battalion practise

semaphore. A sergeant demonstrates a signal lamp linked to a Morse transmitter. The battalion drills on a beach.

Notes
Remarks: rather more entertaining than most of the series, but still conveying nothing about the battalion.
[(C H Dudley Ward, T C [sic] Atkinson et al), *History of the Dorsetshire Regiment 1914-1919*, Ling (1932)]
[shotsheet available]
catalogued SDB: 9/1981

IWM 404 · GB, 2/1918
the WEST RIDING REGIMENT
[the BRITISH REGIMENTS] (series, allocated)

b/w · 1 reel · 407' (7 mins) · silent
intertitles: English

sp War Office Cinema Committee *pr* Topical Film Company

■ Probably a regular battalion of the West Riding Regiment on the Western Front, autumn 1917.

The guard changes over outside the battalion headquarters. The battalion sports, including "a cuddy fight" (wrestling while being carried on another man's back) and "a reveille race" of dressing in full kit before running. The medical officer gives one company a foot inspection. Pack transport mules take supplies to the headquarters (a large house). The battalion marches down a road, led by its band.

Notes
Remarks: a particularly obvious example of the shortcomings of this series, which was intended to bring involvement in the war at a more personal level for members of the civilian population in Britain. It conveys nothing of the personalities of the men or the individuality of the battalion, comprising stockshots, clichés and unhelpful captions.
[shotsheet available]
catalogued SDB: 9/1981

IWM 405 · GB, (?) 1918
the WOMEN'S AUXILIARY ARMY CORPS [sic] : the work of the WAAC at a base in France

b/w · 1 reel · 412' (5 mins)
intertitles: English

sp Ministry of Information (?) *pr* Topical Film Company

■ Work done by WAACs on a rear-area base on the Western Front, 1918 (?).

Women of the WAAC in the cookhouse serve food to soldiers. Waitresses serving in the officers' quarters. Views of the officers' mess. WAACs playing netball. WAACs tending the graves in a large cemetery. A group of WAACs marching back to camp.

[shotsheet available]
catalogued SDB: 9/1981

IWM 406 · GB, (?) 1918
[9TH DIVISION AND RAILWAY ENGINEERS] (allocated)

b/w · 1 reel · 707' (12 mins) · silent
intertitles: none

sp War Office Cinema Committee (?) *pr* Topical Film Company

■ Troops of 9th (Scottish) Division and Railway Engineers on the Western Front, 1918.

Highlanders, probably 8th/10th Battalion, the Gordon Highlanders, sit with some South African Engineers of 9th Division outside the ruins of Arras Cathedral, 24 January 1918. Royal Engineers (or possibly South African Engineers throughout) repair a broken railway wagon and shunting engine, using the syphon attached to the engine to collect water from a flooded shell-hole. Full-sized and narrow gauge railway trains cross on the level. Other narrow gauge trains, one carrying shells, pass the camera. One of the locomotives re-coals. The film returns to Highlanders (8th/10th Gordons ?) parading outside Arras Cathedral with their pipe band. A South African 6-inch 26cwt howitzer under scrim in action. Mail distribution to men of the South African Brigade in camp. Troops crowded onto a narrow gauge train, filmed from the moving train itself. Four very large soldiers posed for the camera (possibly a joke about their weight ?), not clearly seen as the film breaks up.

Notes
Title: the shotsheet gives the title as *The Gordon Highlanders*. This was the title of a film, apparently from the *British Regiments* series, of which the scenes of 8th/10th Gordons may be fragments. The South

African Brigade served with 9th (Scottish) Division until September 1918, and there were no battalions of Gordons in that division.
Remarks: given the presence of the South Africans, the value of the stills for identifying the Highlanders as Gordons and dating the film must be questionable.
[shotsheet available]
catalogued SDB: 9/1981

IWM 407 · GB, (?) 1920
COMBINED PLATOON TRAINING ON ASH RANGE

b/w · 1 reel · 798' (14 mins) · silent
intertitles: English

sp War Office for Territorial Force *pr* Baron Hartley

■ Practice assault by a platoon of 7th Battalion, the London Regiment, on a hypothetical enemy defence line, represented by the butts at Ash Range, Aldershot, probably about 1920.

Each move in the assault is shown twice, as an animated diagram, then as actuality material. The defence is a thinly-held forward position, a main position, and a redoubt or final position, at about 50 yard intervals from each other (there are no troops manning these in the exercise) and the attack is essentially frontal. The platoon consists of four sections: a Lewis gun section with one Lewis machinegun, a rifle section, a rifle grenadier section and a specialist bomber section (with particular skills in hand-grenade use). In the first phase the Lewis gun section scouts reconnoitre along the woodland to the flank of the enemy position, and on spotting the enemy at 700 yards signal to the platoon commander. He comes up to reconnoitre personally, then brings his section commanders, while the remainder of the Lewis gun section joins its scouts in their flanking position. There is a series of ridges running at regular intervals from side to side of the range concealing the deployment of the platoon. It moves out in 'artillery formation' of single-rank columns of sections. As it comes within sight of the enemy at 700 yards, two of the sections deploy into extended line, with the rifle grenadier section in line a further 100 yards behind them and the platoon commander between the two lines. At 400 yards from the enemy the front line of two sections goes to ground and, together with the

Lewis gun section, opens fire. The rifle grenadiers come forward to support the firing line by spreading evenly along it. The firing line advances in short rushes, one third of the line moving at a time, until it is 200 yards from the enemy. The Lewis gun section now advances until it is as near as is possible directly opposite the enemy flank, and resumes fire. Under cover from the Lewis gun section and its rifle grenades the platoon charges the enemy first position. With this taken, the platoon resorts itself back into sections, with the rifle grenadiers in the centre, and charges the enemy main position. As this is taken the rifle grenadiers remain in it to provide covering fire for the assault on the final position. Once this is secured the Lewis gun section comes forward with three specialist bombers to provide an advance guard while the platoon collects itself. The commander marks with a pickaxe on the ground the new line he intends to consolidate.

Notes
Remarks: a very attractive and entertaining little training film. The tactics used in both attack and defence are authentic representations of those in use in the last year of the First World War.
[C Digby Planck, *History of the 7th (City of London) Battalion, The London Regiment*, Old Comrades Association (1946)]
[shotsheet available]
catalogued SDB: 9/1981

IWM 408 · GB, 2/1918
the NORFOLK REGIMENT
[the BRITISH REGIMENTS] (series, allocated)

b/w · 1 reel · 102' (2 mins) · silent
intertitles: none

sp War Office Cinema Committee *pr* Topical Film Company

■ Pierrot show by men of the Norfolk Regiment, Western Front, autumn 1917.

The audience for the open-air show is also from the Norfolk Regiment. The pierrots are called "The Holy Boys", the nickname of the Norfolk Regiment (from its cap badge), and include a drag act.

Notes
Title: the title is taken from the shotsheet.
Summary: this is most probably an extract from the complete film.

[F Loraine Petre, *The History of the Norfolk Regiment Vol II: 4th August 1914 to 31st December 1918*, [no publisher] (1927)]
[shotsheet available]
catalogued SDB: 9/1981

IWM 409 · GB, (prod) 1917
[WOUNDED AND PRISONERS BEHIND THE LINES ON THE WESTERN FRONT]
(allocated)

b/w · 1 reel · 275' (5 mins) · silent
intertitles: none

sp War Office Cinema Committee (?)
pr Topical Film Company

■ Wounded and prisoners behind the lines during a battle on the Western Front, possibly Arras 1917.

The film opens with rolling fields, corn stacks at regular intervals. Soldiers line up for an open-air pay parade. Walking wounded come up a hill towards the camera, followed by some stretcher cases, other walking wounded, and German prisoners under escort. Water is given to the wounded. Some mounted Transport men also come up the slope towards the camera, and there is a steady trickle of men going in the other direction.

Notes
Title: the shotsheet, which bears no relation to the film, gives the title as *Black Watch and Leicesters*, clearly part of the *British Regiments* series, but now apparently missing.
[shotsheet available]
catalogued SDB: 9/1981

IWM 410 · GB, 11/1917
a CHINESE LABOUR CONTINGENT
un CONTINGENTE DE TRABAJADORES CHINOS (on copy held)

b/w · 1 reel · 589' (10 mins) · silent
intertitles: Spanish

sp War Office Cinema Committee *pr* Topical Film Company

■ Chinese Labour Corps on the Western Front, 1917.

The film, under-exposed, shows Chinese Labour Corps members working at a docks, carrying away sacks which come down on a sling from a dockside crane. They have difficulty with the sacks, but one large Chinese, after several failures, demonstrates to the camera that he can carry three sacks at once. They leave the docks marching in column. Other members of the Corps work in a stoneyard, shovelling granite chippings and road-fill out of light railway trucks. Another group works in the timber yard, carrying planks to a stack. Yet another collects water in collapsible buckets, slung on a pole between two men. At their camp, members of the Corps queue up to receive tinned rations, and a British soldier demonstrates to a bemused Chinese how to use a tin-opener. The members of the Corps form up on parade. The final scenes are of several Chinese carrying baskets suspended between poles, and of others sitting and eating.

Notes
Production: Spanish-language version of the film, the English title of which was *A Chinese Labour Contingent*. The overseas release date was January 1918.
[shotsheet available]
catalogued SDB: 9/1981

IWM 411 · GB, 1917
WITH THE PORTUGUESE EXPEDITIONARY FORCE IN FRANCE

b/w · 2 reels · 1948' (33 mins) · silent
intertitles: English

sp War Office Cinema Committee *pr* Topical Film Company

■ British film of the Portuguese Corps in training and in the line on the Western Front, 1917.

(Reel 1) General Sir Henry Horne, GOC First Army, is greeted by the GOC of the Portuguese Corps, General Tamagnini, and inspects a guard of honour which afterwards marches past. A Portuguese battalion, with all its transport, is on the march down a dirt road. A battery equipped with French-made 75mm field guns practises firing and moving off. Miners are shown entering a mineshaft. At the training school at Marthes in June 1917 the troops learn to dig trenches, revet them using wicker and build a parapet of sandbags. The men then enter this 'model' trench, line the parapet, fix bayonets, and withdraw. One man of the Portuguese 15th Battalion displays his uniform and equipment. There is more training in putting up

entanglements, bayonet fighting, bayonet charges over an obstacle course, grenade throwing, and a demonstration by an NCO of how to fire a rack of rifle grenades. A group of officers poses for the camera. The men practise setting up and firing the Stokes 6-inch mortar, and 50-pound 'plum pudding' bomb from the 2-inch mortar (described as a "French mortar"). British officers and NCOs of the school pose with Portuguese officers. The instructors give lessons in map reading and in rifle shooting, including the use of the telescopic sight. *(Reel 2)* Portuguese at the front, probably 2nd Division on 21 May 1917, enter firebays, have food served to them from backpacks, etc. Some of them are from 22nd Battalion. The battalion commander drinks tea in the front line with British officers. A Portuguese 75mm gun fires from inside a gun-pit. Another 75mm is manhandled forward, possibly in an exercise. General Gomes de Costa, commanding 2nd Division, talks to a British general. A battery of 75mm guns opens fire by a stream. A view of shell-bursts taken from a front line trench. Portuguese mule wagon teams move up, take stores from a dump, and move off again.

Notes
Summary: the front line section at the start of reel 2 was filmed under the "stage management" of Lieutenant R C G Dartford (1/19th London Regiment), liaison officer to the Portuguese, who describes the event in his diary which is held by the Museum's Department of Documents.
[Robert Blake, *The Private Papers of Douglas Haig 1914-1919*, Eyre and Spottiswoode (1952)]
[R C G Dartford, *Diary 27th March – 8th July 1917* (unpublished), entry for 21 May 1917]
[shotsheet available]
catalogued SDB: 9/1981

IWM 412 · GB, 1918
the LIFE OF A WAAC

b/w · 1 reel · 688' (8 mins) · silent
intertitles: English

sp Ministry of Information

■ Recruiting film for the Women's Army Auxiliary Corps in Britain, 1918.

The film uses actuality material backed by some acting. It begins with a WAAC recruiting march and inspection, and then shows a girl noticing the advertisement

placard for Queen Mary's Army Auxiliary Corps (the official 1918 title of the WAAC) in Trafalgar Square. She picks up a leaflet at the Ministry of Labour. After joining she is given a uniform and learns drill and physical training with other WAACs. At their camp in the countryside the WAACs form up for roll-call each morning before setting off for work. The administrator hands out tasks for each of them. Some, as cooks, peel potatoes, set tables and serve food to the soldiers. Others work as clerks. The forewoman, with her dog, pose for the camera. There is a pay parade. The girls, at their hut, wash and brush their hair. Parcels arrive. With much camera-consciousness, the girls tend the vegetable garden. In the sickbay a nurse attends to those WAACs who are ill. The tennis courts are shown. The girls demonstrate folk dancing. They tend gardens outside their huts. One girl, in a comic routine, imitates Charlie Chaplin. Other girls sit in their huts, sewing or writing letters. A march by a recruiting band of soldiers leads WAACs through a town centre. The film ends with posters showing the need for more recruits, and irises out with a WAAC holding a Union Flag.

Notes
Title: this is taken from the shotsheet.
Summary: the P 2 version has the same material with flashframes rather than captions.
[shotsheet available]
catalogued SDB: 10/1981

IWM 413 · GB, 11/1917
S AFRICAN NATIVE LABOUR CONTINGENT : somewhere in France

b/w · 1 reel · 907' (17 mins) · silent
intertitles: English

sp War Office Cinema Committee *pr* Topical Film Company

■ Work of the South African Labour Contingent in France, 1917.

The film opens with Number 1 Camp of the contingent by a wood, and a posed group of the black NCOs with their white officers. The NCOs are all "native chiefs". Members of the contingent unload boxes of supplies at a dump from railway wagons, while others use picks and shovels to dig road-mending material. The main part of the film concerns the contingent at work in a forest cutting down trees and transporting the logs by means of light rail sledges drawn by horses. The logs are cut to a manageable size by a belt-driven rotary saw. At lunchtime the men relax around a fire, one performs a dance for the camera, and there is a free-for-all, before they return to work. At the main timber yard members of the contingent unload logs from a goods train. The men march back to their camp. One of the sergeants (seen only briefly) is a "Prince in his own country", probably Muti, son of Ntshingwayo, of the Zunga tribe of Zululand.

Notes
Summary: see also **IWM 128**.
Remarks: an interesting variation on the 'personalised' approach to the war which marked the new policy of British official film in autumn 1917 and produced the *British Regiments* series.
[shotsheet available]
catalogued SDB: 5/1982

IWM 414 · GB, 2/1918
the ARTISTS RIFLES
[the BRITISH REGIMENTS] (series, allocated)

b/w · 1 reel · 180' (3 mins) · silent
intertitles: English

sp War Office Cinema Committee *pr* Topical Film Company

■ Artists Rifles, or 1/28th (County of London) Battalion, the London Regiment, in France, 1916-17.

By 1916 the Artists Rifles was not a serving battalion but a holding unit for officer trainees. A group of trainees is shown drilling on a parade ground, probably at Montreuil, and being addressed by its commanding officer. The battalion acts as the guard of honour for the visit of General Cadorna, the Italian C-in-C, to Douglas Haig in March 1916. The battalion training course shows recruits how to tie knots, construct a log bridge over a stream, make a raft from a gas cape stuffed with straw, and punt this down a river. A transport bus carrying soldiers (of the battalion ?) passes through a village, rounding the corner of the road at the top of a hill.

Notes
Title: this is taken from the shotsheet.
Summary: see also **IWM 203** and **IWM 216**. The final location may be the same as that shown in **IWM 382**.
Remarks: this is disappointing as a record

of the Artists Rifles, **IWM 203** is better.
[H A R May, *Memories of the Artists Rifles*, Howlett (1929)]
[shotsheet available]
catalogued SDB: 9/1981

IWM 415 · GB, 2/1918
the LANCASHIRE FUSILIERS
[the BRITISH REGIMENTS] (series, allocated)

b/w · 1 reel · 613' (10 mins) · silent
intertitles: English

sp War Office Cinema Committee *pr* Topical Film Company

I. Probably 1st Battalion, the Lancashire Fusiliers, Western Front, autumn 1917. A company resting. A long queue of soldiers in the camp is served with rations. Physical training exercises in the open air include a 'duck walk' and tossing a man in the air up a line. Bayonet drill for two opposing lines. The battalion marches along a dirt road while its band plays beside it.
II. A mass burial by soldiers of the British Army on the Western Front, 1916-18. The grave site is close to the battlefield and transport can be seen passing up a road in the background. The corpses are wrapped in shrouds and brought on stretchers to the mass grave, with an escort of soldiers. The battalion chaplain reads the burial service as the shrouded corpses are lowered, with some difficulty, into the grave. Some of the men handling the bodies are clearly distressed. The troops throw handfuls of earth down into the grave as the chaplain says a final prayer.

Notes
Summary: it is likely that the opening sequence represents the incomplete film of the battalion, and the burial service is an accidental addition.
Remarks: the burial service sequence is a very moving piece of film, and an excellent example of its type.
[J C Latter, *The History of the Lancashire Fusiliers 1914-1918*, Gale and Polden (1949)]
[shotsheet available]
catalogued SDB: 9/1981

IWM 416 · GB, 2/1918
the RIFLE BRIGADE
[the BRITISH REGIMENTS] (series, allocated)

b/w · 1 reel · 318' (6 mins) · silent
intertitles: English

sp War Office Cinema Committee pr Topical
Film Company

- 2nd Battalion, the Rifle Brigade, on the
Western Front, autumn 1917.

Groups of men and officers pose for the
camera. The men soap their equipment,
and clean their uniforms and rifles. One
man stands in a pit with a Lewis
machinegun on an anti-aircraft mount and a
pair of binoculars. Cooks carry dixies of
food to a temporary cookhouse, and soup
is served out. The battalion rests outside
some huts. Sides of meat are unloaded
from a wagon. Two companies from the
battalion march along a dirt road near the
front.

Notes
Remarks: as with the remainder of the
series, this conveys nothing of the feel of
the battalion as a particular organisation.
[Reginald C Berkeley, *The History of the
Rifle Brigade in the War of 1914-1918*, Rifle
Brigade Club (1927)]
[shotsheet available]
catalogued SDB: 9/1981

IWM 417 · GB, 2/1918
the KING'S ROYAL RIFLES
[the BRITISH REGIMENTS] (series,
allocated)

b/w · 1 reel · 468' (8 mins) · silent
intertitles: English

sp War Office Cinema Committee pr Topical
Film Company

- Probably 4th (but possibly 2nd) Battalion
King's Royal Rifle Corps, on the Western
Front, autumn 1917.

The battalion on the march along a
metalled road. The men march in salute
past their commanding officer (indistinctly
seen). The men, taken to a training field,
shed their packs and practise bayonet
fighting. Instruction is given in the operation
of the Lewis machinegun. This is followed
by physical training. A new issue is made of
boots and clothing. The film ends with a
half-profile portrait shot of "The
Quartermaster, who has been with the
battalion 25 years", most probably
Lieutenant T Jones of 4th Battalion.

Notes
Remarks: as with the remainder of the
series, this conveys no sense of an
individual battalion, consisting simply of a
series of stockshots. But in this case some
of the stockshots are of higher quality than
average.
[Steuart Hare, *The Annals of the King's
Royal Rifle Corps Vol V: The Great War*,
Murray (1932)]
[shotsheet available]
catalogued SDB: 9/1981

IWM 418 · GB, (?) 1918
**the KING'S TOUR ROUND THE NAPIER
MOTOR WORKS**

b/w · 1 reel · 330' (6 mins) · silent
intertitles: English

- King George V is shown around the
Napier Motor Works, London, probably
mid-1918.

The managing director, M H T Vane,
escorts the King (who is in Field Marshal's
uniform, and looks very tired) around the
plant. They pass a guard of honour made
up of the firm's contingent of the St John
Ambulance Brigade. The King talks to
workers in the machine shops. Outside he
visits the works fire brigade and women
doing welding in the motor transport
erecting shop. He inspects a line of
wounded ex-soldiers, now working for the
firm. These include Corporal C A Jarvis VC
of the Royal Engineers, the first NCO of the
war to win a VC (16 November 1914). The
King watches aero-frame and engine
construction and talks with a refugee
Belgian employee of the firm. A contract-
made RAF 3a aeroplane engine, "the latest
type of aero engine", is prominent. The King
drives away from the works to the cheers of
the workers.

Notes
Production Company: the 'C & E' trademark
which ends the film has not been identified
but is probably a private company rather
than official film.
Remarks: unconsciously a very funny film, a
better title might have been 'The King
Ignores The Napier Motor Works'. Looking
old and tired, he moves rapidly round the
factory, completely oblivious of the various
people and places of 'interest' to which the
captions draw attention.
[shotsheet available]
catalogued SDB: 10/1981

IWM 419 · GB, 1918
WOMEN'S WORK ON MUNITIONS OF WAR

b/w · 2 (as 1) reels · 718' (12 mins) · silent
intertitles: English

sp Ministry of Information

■ Women in munitions work in Britain, 1918.

I. *(Reel 1)* The Handley Page works at Cricklewood, London. Women work as clerks, help build aeroplane engines, cope with acetylene welding and complex wiring jobs, spray-paint Lewis machinegun magazines, and dope the fuselage of a partially assembled Handley Page 0/400 bomber.
II. *(Reel 2)* Women workers in unknown factories, operating various mechanisms, mainly lathes, for manufacturing guns. One woman operates an overhead crane to lift a completed 60-pounder gun across the shop floor, then the carriage of a 6-inch 26cwt howitzer across in the other direction. Women work on assembling a tank engine, and the track linkages. Other women are at work "varnishing" (?) a partly assembled Mk V Female tank.

Notes
Summary: see also **IWM 200**, **IWM 263** and **IWM 264**.
[shotsheet available]
catalogued SDB: 9/1981

IWM 420-01+2 · GB, 1919
the WORLD'S GREATEST STORY – EPISODE 1

b/w · 2 reels · 1308' (22 mins) · silent
intertitles: English

pr (War Office Official) New Era Film
dist Ashley Exclusive Films

■ Thematic, almost allegorical, account of Britain at the outbreak of the First World War.

(Reel 1) The series uses dramatised symbols to cover gaps in its actuality material. It opens, as do all the episodes, with a brief scene of an actress portraying 'Justice', blindfold with scales and sword. Next is a mailed fist crumpling a treaty. A news placard announcing the war fades to a second actress portraying 'War' with two huge dogs. In an acted scene a middle-

class family receives news of the outbreak while seated at breakfast. As the daughter consoles the mother, the father encourages the two sons to join the fight. Telephonists transmit the mobilisation order. At sea is HMS *Princess Royal*. 1st Battle Cruiser Squadron is at anchor at Rosyth. British troops disembark in France in August 1914 (note what appears to be a 13-pounder 9cwt A anti-aircraft gun, introduced 1918). Infantry, Cavalry, Artillery and Transport disembark. More transport ships are escorted by destroyers across the English Channel. The battle-cruiser squadron at sea. The 'family' says its farewells as 'War' smiles slowly. *(Reel 2)* The Guards Division (?) marches "singing Tipperary", contrasted with dead soldiers. HMS *King Edward* fires a broadside. The submarine E.23 on patrol. Members of the Chinese Labour Corps unload stockpiles of supplies and shells in a railyard. A troop of Royal Horse Artillery practises high-speed manœuvres. A squadron of 18th Hussars (?) on patrol. A 4.5-inch howitzer fires from cover. "And so began the thunder of the guns which did not cease for four and a half years." The episode ends with a brief trailer for next week's episode.

Notes
Production: some of the episodes are headed as distributed by Ashley Exclusive Films Ltd, some by Cross Pictures Ltd, some are simply given as produced by New Era Film, and some have no credits. It is likely that several firms were involved in the sponsorship and distribution of the series, and that the IWM acquired copies of different episodes from different sources.
Summary (series): the whole series consists of official film taken between 1916 and 1919 joined to staged or faked material, presented as a series of images rather than as a chronological account of the war. In this episode almost all the actuality material except that of the Royal Navy was probably filmed in 1918-19. Some of the material has been taken from **IWM 130-03+04**, **IWM 184**, **IWM 246** and **IWM 295**.
Shotsheet: there is no proper shotsheet for this film, but the list of titles and analysis of contents held by the Department of Film perform much the same function.
Remarks: the series generally is a poorly edited montage of images unrelated by location or date. Themes are briefly taken up and abruptly discarded or left dangling. The main interest value is the extreme language of the captioning when compared to the same material in British official films, rather than any merit in the finished episodes. Generally, the series is a curiosity

rather than a record. In this particular episode the value of the fictionalised characters remains unexploited; there is an over-reliance on the personification of such clichéd images as 'Death' and 'Justice', and these are presented in a hilariously inept manner. The minor exceptions in the series to this poor standard are episodes 10 and 11 dealing with the British intervention in north Russia. Compare with the series **IWM 130** Sons of Our Empire and **IWM 440** Our Empire's Fight for Freedom.
[shotsheet available]
catalogued SDB: 9/1981

IWM 420-03+4 · GB, 1919
**the WORLD'S GREATEST STORY –
EPISODE 2**

b/w · 2 reels · 1429' (24 mins) · silent
intertitles: English

dist Cross Pictures

■ Thematic treatment of the British experience in the first two years of the war on the Western Front, 1914-16.

(Reel 3) The episode starts with the figure 'Justice', which fades out. The captioning is outspoken. "We show you in this episode how extreme were the sufferings of those brave men who went with throbbing hearts and tuneful lips to the slaughter and carnage which are the offspring of war." A recruiting march through central London. A crowd being harangued in Trafalgar Square. Lord Kitchener, with General Sir William Robertson, embarks for France. A detachment of the Queen's Regiment in London led by their marching band. Sir John French (with Generals Gouraud and Weygand in 1917). Kitchener reviews recruits in France. Men of 38th (Welsh) Division are driven in buses to the Loos sector. General scenes of muddy conditions and waterlogged trenches in winter 1915. 18-pounder limbers move through muddy conditions. An observer directs the fire of a 4.5-inch howitzer using a trench periscope. An acted scene of the father and daughter of the series' fictional 'family' consoling each other at home. The Guards Division entrenched near Neuve Chapelle, winter 1915. (Reel 4) Loading and firing a 9.45-inch 'flying pig' trench mortar. In July 1916 General Haig, King George V, Marshal Joffre, Marshal Foch and President Poincaré meet. A trailer advertises the Somme offensive as next week's episode.

Notes
Production etc: see **Notes** to Episode 1, **IWM 420-01+02**.
Summary: most of the actuality material comes from **IWM 191, IWM 192, IWM 199, IWM 207, IWM 208, IWM 210, IWM 211** and **IWM 212**.
Remarks: whereas the captions suggest a date of 1914-15, the material used is all from December 1915 or later.
[shotsheet available]
catalogued SDB: 9/1981

IWM 420-05+6 · GB, 1919
**the WORLD'S GREATEST STORY –
EPISODE 3**

b/w · 2 reels · 1746' (30 mins) · silent
intertitles: English

pr (War Office Official) New Era Film

■ Thematic treatment (re-edited from **IWM 191** The Battle of the Somme) of the opening of the British offensive on the Somme, July 1916.

(Reel 5) The episode, as with all in the series, opens with the figure of 'Justice' portrayed by an actress. British troops march in column through villages near to the front. A bombardment by 60-pounders and 6-inch Mk VII guns. Troops attack, "endless waves of invincible troops swept over no man's land". Wounded are brought in by stretcher-bearers. 1st Battalion, the Lancashire Fusiliers, wait for the attack. The bombardment in no man's land. Limbers move up past the bodies of Gordon Highlanders. (Reel 6) More stretcher-bearers, "the battlefield became almost a sanctuary, so well did those brave men of the Red Cross perform their glorious task". 4.7-inch field guns firing. The dressing station at Minden Post, where "the very slightly wounded prepare to return to the fight". More bombardment. A chaplain talks to a wounded man, "through all the scarlet horrors of war was interwoven the thread of sweet compassion by the Padre forever tending to the needy". German prisoners are marched away from the battlefield.

Notes
Production etc: see **Notes** to Episode 1, **IWM 420-01+02**.
Summary: most of the actuality material comes from **IWM 191** in particular, and also **IWM 113, IWM 116** and **IWM 162**.
Remarks: even the very 'tight' material of The Battle of the Somme, filmed in three

days and in an area of a few miles, does little to improve the slap-happy approach of the series' producers.
[shotsheet available]
catalogued SDB: 9/1981

IWM 420-07+8 · GB, 1919
the WORLD'S GREATEST STORY – EPISODE 4

b/w & (partly) tinted · 2 reels · 1518' (25 mins) · silent
intertitles: English

pr (War Office Official) New Era Film

■ Thematic treatment of British rear area services on the Western Front, 1916-18.

(Reel 7) The episode starts with 'Justice'. Men of V Corps unload meat from wagons. A butcher of 16th (Irish) Division cuts up the meat. Various types of supplies are moved from rail trucks and loaded onto wagons. A rail station, probably Arras. Rail transport for soldiers. Leave boats taking soldiers "to that 'jewel set in a silver sea' and known belovedly as 'Blighty'". *(Reel 8)* Messenger dogs train at XXII Corps headquarters kennels. An RE7 of the RFC takes off on a reconnaissance flight. An observation balloon (this scene is tinted red) is shot down by enemy aircraft, not clearly seen. In response to this two lorry-mounted 13-pounder anti-aircraft guns give chase to a German aircraft and shoot it down. The reconnaissance machine lands. "Then in the silence of the eventide our machine returns home to a well earned repose."

Notes
Production etc: see **Notes** to Episode 1, **IWM 420-01+02**.
Summary: most of the actuality footage comes from **IWM 113**, **IWM 118**, **IWM 126**, **IWM 130-05+06**, **IWM 164**, **IWM 212**, **IWM 235** and **IWM 298**.
Remarks: this episode, containing more good material than usual, is slightly better quality than most of the series.
[shotsheet available]
catalogued SDB: 9/1981

IWM 420-09+10 · GB, 1919
the WORLD'S GREATEST STORY – EPISODE 5

b/w & (partly) tinted · 2 reels · 1497' (25 mins) · silent

intertitles: English

pr (War Office Official) New Era Film

■ Thematic treatment of the use of tanks and tunnelling companies by the British on the Western Front, 1916-18.

(Reel 9) The episode starts with 'Justice'. The tank race and demonstration of a tank climbing over a cottage arranged for George V's visit to France in July 1917. Post-war tests of Mk V Star tanks. A recovery tank demonstrates trench-crossing on a narrow metal support. A Female Mk V crosses a river by a temporary bridge and a Male crosses by a pontoon ferry. Three Whippet medium tanks driving through French countryside and a Female Mk V carrying Infantry. The captured German A7V tank 'Hagen'. *(Reel 10)* A tunnelling company drives to a shaft, digs, sets its mine and detonates it. (This reel is tinted grey, yellow and red.) The episode ends with a trailer for next week's episode.

Notes
Production etc: see **Notes** to Episode 1, **IWM 420-01+02**.
Summary: the second reel of this episode is a re-edited version of **IWM 219**. Most of the remaining material is **IWM 116**, **IWM 179**, **IWM 192** and **IWM 322**. For the post-war tanks see the series *Tank Trials*.
[shotsheet available]
catalogued SDB: 9/1981

IWM 420-11+12 · GB, 1919
the WORLD'S GREATEST STORY – EPISODE 6

b/w · 2 reels · 1354' (23 mins) · silent
intertitles: English

pr (War Office Official) New Era Film

■ Thematic exposition of the British military philosophy of attack on the Western Front, 1916-18.

(Reel 11) The film-makers state "We think it is well that we should have been given an opportunity in this episode to show you these terrible fields that were trampled by our deathless allies in their fight for Justice... never in the course of its pulsing narrative has the honour of a nation been so thoroughly vindicated as it was in that memorable and stupendous offensive which was undertaken in the mass by hosts of men who willingly quitted the soft ease of a

civil existence in order that they might, by their own sacrifice, prove the worth of a new and virile England." The figure of 'Justice'. The film thereafter is of an unrelated series of attacks by the British on the Western Front, with 18-pounder support, mine explosions and distant views of no man's land. "When the long waves of Khaki swept towards the breast of the enemy the first stone in the Temple of the Ultimate Civilisation was laid." A staged scene of a German Bergmann machinegun crew surrendering to the advancing British. More British attacks. The film then breaks to a physical fitness display at Ste-Marie, "war was not always grim and stern", returning *(Reel 12)* to the shelling of no man's land, a raiding party, a 9.2-inch howitzer 'walking' its shells onto a blockhouse. Back to the sports with a tug of war, various contests, Highland dancing and races. "Thus in war there is mingled the stern and gay, and happy laughter sometimes rippled o'er her harsh and sinister visage." A pierrot show and gymnastics. The episode ends with a trailer for next week's episode.

Notes
Production etc: see **Notes** to Episode 1, **IWM 420-01+02**.
Summary: most of the material in this episode comes from the series **IWM 130** *Sons of Our Empire.* See also **IWM 60, IWM 113, IWM 116, IWM 219, IWM 259** and **IWM 318**.
Remarks: this episode is a particularly good example of the character of the series, referring repeatedly to a 'British attack' without attempting to place it in a historical context, and padding it out with highly inappropriate scenes of gymnastics, held together by imaginative if lurid captioning.
[shotsheet available]
catalogued SDB: 9/1981

IWM 420-13+14 · GB, 1919
the WORLD'S GREATEST STORY – EPISODE 7

b/w · 2 reels · 1737' (29 mins) · silent
intertitles: English

■ Thematic montage of front line and behind-the-lines scenes in the British sector of the Western Front, 1916-18.

(Reel 13) After the opening with 'Justice', the episode consists entirely of unrelated scenes of the Western Front. Scottish troops in long-shot carrying barbed wire. The officer of a tunnelling company

connecting a charge. British troops in action. Others resting and swimming by a millpond. Women of the WAAC setting up a bell tent, and others playing in bathing costumes on the beach. "While men fought women worked... they found a diversion in the same way as in the piping times of peace." Vickers machineguns are set up for sustained firing. George V, in France in 1918, watches trees being felled. *(Reel 14)* Sports and exercises at Ste-Marie. Buses used as troop transport. Mk I tanks going into action. "Nothing detracted so much from the German's prestige as the Tanks, with which he was never able to cope." More tanks in action. The first train arriving at Arras station to a pipe band accompaniment. Columns of German prisoners. A Highland dance team beside Arras Cathedral. The episode ends with a trailer for the next episode.

Notes
Production etc: see **Notes** to Episode 1, **IWM 420-01+02**.
Summary: most of the material in this episode comes from **IWM 59, IWM 113, IWM 116, IWM 191, IWM 207, IWM 208, IWM 219, IWM 289, IWM 318, IWM 328, IWM 329, IWM 401** and **IWM 406**.
[shotsheet available]
catalogued SDB: 9/1981

IWM 420-15+16 · GB, 1919
the WORLD'S GREATEST STORY – EPISODE 8

b/w · 2 reels · 1755' (30 mins) · silent
intertitles: English

pr (War Office Official) New Era Film

■ Disjointed thematic treatment of British behind-the-lines services on the Western Front and of munitions manufacture during the First World War, 1916-18.

(Reel 15) The episode starts with 'Justice'. Lloyd George, as Minister of Munitions, gives a public speech from an Army staff car. A montage of women and men operating various metal presses, drop hammers, forge hammers and lathes, including manufacture of nose-caps for 18-pounders, hoists for 9.2-inch howitzers, and the manufacture of a 15-inch gun. A 12-inch railway gun being prepared for firing. A 6-inch Mk VII stuck in the mud with its tractor disabled. The Chinese Labour Corps at a light railway depot. The 12-inch railway gun still being prepared. A 15-inch shell marked

"To Willie With Compliments" and a 15-inch howitzer being fired. A Chinese band and stilt walkers, "the men of the yellow race had their own diversions too". *(Reel 16)* Stretcher-bearers of the RAMC giving first aid. Nurses at a Casualty Clearing Station with heavily bandaged patients in bed. Women ambulance drivers of the VAD doing maintenance and driving work. The 'two women of Pervyse', Baroness T'Serclaes and Marie Chisholm. More ambulances taking wounded onto special trains and a hospital ship. The Princess Louise Rest Home for nurses. Troopships returning home. The episode ends with a trailer for next week's episode.

Notes
Production etc: see **Notes** to Episode 1, **IWM 420-01+02**.
Summary: for the material in this episode see **IWM 130**, **IWM 162**, **IWM 168**, **IWM 184**, **IWM 191**, **IWM 220**, **IWM 231**, **IWM 245**, **IWM 258**, **IWM 263**, **IWM 264**, **IWM 267**, **IWM 287** and **IWM 310**.
[shotsheet available]
catalogued SDB: 9/1981

IWM 420-17+18 · GB, 1919
**the WORLD'S GREATEST STORY –
EPISODE 9**

b/w · 2 reels · 1685' (29 mins) · silent
intertitles: English

■ Thematic treatment of the Zeebrugge raid and of General Allenby's entry into Jerusalem, 1918.

(Reel 17) The episode starts with 'Justice'. Thereafter the first part is a re-edited version of **IWM 303** *German Naval Inactivities* and **IWM 358** *Zeebrugge*, showing German sailors in Ostend prior to the raid on Zeebrugge, and the aftermath of the raid itself. Seaplanes "vigilantly observing from above while the Vindictive, Iphigenia and Thetis proceed on their way" (the ships shown are HMS *Birmingham* and HMS *King Edward*). The harbour in the aftermath shows SS *Brussels* and HMS *Vindictive* blocking the mouth. *(Reel 18)* The next part is mixed images from Palestine and Mesopotamia, including the Imperial Camel Corps and HMS *Moth*. It is built around a re-edit of **IWM 13** *General Allenby's Entry into Jerusalem*. Jewish men and women (described as Moslem) are shown praying beside the West Wall ('Wailing Wall') of the Temple in Jerusalem. The episode ends with a British team

involved in a football match in a stadium, possibly north Italy.

Notes
Production etc: see **Notes** to Episode 1, **IWM 420-01+02**.
Summary: for the material in this episode see **IWM 6**, **IWM 13**, **IWM 26**, **IWM 28**, **IWM 41**, **IWM 45**, **IWM 71**, **IWM 226**, **IWM 303** and **IWM 358**.
[shotsheet available]
catalogued SDB: 9/1981

IWM 420-19+20 · GB, 1919
**the WORLD'S GREATEST STORY –
EPISODE 10**

b/w · 2 reels · 1854' (30 mins) · silent
intertitles: English

■ Thematic treatment of the British contribution to the North Russian Intervention Force, 1918-19.

(Reel 19) The episode starts with 'Justice' followed by the badge of the British Intervention Force. The actuality material opens with British troops boarding SS *Carlotta* at Tilbury docks in May 1918, and a chaplain holding a service on board. The arrival at the mouth of the River Dvina at Archangel. Brigadier-General L W de V Sadlier-Jackson is greeted on 10 June with the Slav ceremony of bread and salt. Men of the Slavo-British Legion, recruited from Russian jails. A blurred scene of General Shobelstyn (?) at Kem. Russian pony carts and views of the river. Major-General Maynard with the White Russian commander General Eugene K de Milar (or Miller). British soldiers in the forests with mosquito hoods. *(Reel 20)* A forest fire. A 4.5-inch howitzer fires by the wagon lines. Graves of men of the Royal Sussex Regiment at Kandalaksha. British troops in greatcoats and fur hats manning trenches in the winter of 1918-19. A Red Cross ambulance removes wounded during a battle in a snowstorm. British troops on skis and reindeer-drawn sleighs. A Sopwith Camel taking off from the frozen Lake Onega using skids. Tram lines across the frozen river. The icebreaker SS *War Dawn* delivers ammunition up the river.

Notes
Production etc: see **Notes** to Episode 1, **IWM 420-01+02**.
Summary: for further material on the North Russian Intervention Force see **IWM 422** and **IWM 808**.

Remarks: in contrast to the remainder of the series, this and episode 11 present beneath the usual absurd rhetoric a surprisingly complete and coherent account of the British intervention in north Russia.
[Richard Luckett, *The White Generals: a History of the White Movement and the Russian Civil War*, Longman (1971)]
[C Maynard, *The Murmansk Venture*, Hodder and Stoughton (1928)]
[Frederick Maurice (ed), *The Life of General Lord Rawlinson of Trent from his Journals and Letters*, Cassell (1928)]
[G E Livock, *To the Ends of the Air*, HMSO (1973)]
[shotsheet available]
catalogued SDB: 10/1981

IWM 420-21+22 · GB, 1919
the WORLD'S GREATEST STORY – EPISODE 11

b/w · 2 reels · 2073' (35 mins) · silent
intertitles: English

■ Continued thematic treatment of the British contribution to the North Russian Intervention Force, 1918-19.

(Reel 21) The episode starts with 'Justice' and captioned newspaper clippings, "British forces in peril... more important than Kut". The decision to send the relief force on 4 April 1919 is reported in the press. Civilian volunteers in columns of fours march out of the Central London Recruiting Office in Whitehall. Soldiers are shown in lifebelts on board a ship. The icebreaker SS *Sviatogor* breaks through the Kola Gulf. Royal Fusiliers with their pet rabbit mascot. British soldiers boarding a barge to be towed up the ice-free River Dvina. The hospital ship SS *Kalza* frozen in on the river. Tugs tow barges upstream with M Class monitors as escorts. The British camp at Troitsa showing the church in the distance. More barges move upriver escorted by two Insect Class gunboats. An observation balloon is inflated on a ship's deck. The mascot, a kitten, is fondled by the crew. *(Reel 22)* A poor view of Major-General Maynard (?) on board a barge. Fairey FIIIC seaplanes at the RAF base on Lake Onega being bombed up. The river gunboat *Jolly Roger* (later sunk by a mine) with its crew. A helmeted diver preparing to work underwater. A train transporting light barges overland with some damage to the track displayed. An armoured train. Film taken from the train of houses burning along the track. A 4.5-inch howitzer fires from the train. Bolshevik

prisoners. General Sir Henry Rawlinson, who arrived on 11 August, confers with Brigadier-General Ironside. The "White Guard", the militia of Archangel, is inspected by Ironside and General de Milar. British troops, including a detachment of Royal Marines, embark on SS *Czaritza* on 27 September and the ship clears Archangel harbour. A newspaper clipping of King George V's congratulations to Rawlinson. A final view of Archangel from the air.

Notes
Production etc: see **Notes** to Episode 1, **IWM 420-01+02**.
Summary: for material on the North Russian Intervention Force see **IWM 422** and **IWM 808**.
Remarks: in contrast to the remainder of the series, this and episode 10 display beneath the usual absurd rhetoric a surprisingly complete and coherent account of the intervention in north Russia.
[Richard Luckett, *The White Generals: a History of the White Movement and the Russian Civil War*, Longman (1971)]
[C Maynard, *The Murmansk Venture*, Hodder and Stoughton (1928)]
[Frederick Maurice (ed), *The Life of General Lord Rawlinson of Trent from his Journals and Letters*, Cassell (1928)]
[G E Livock, *To the Ends of the Air*, HMSO (1973)]
[shotsheet available]
catalogued SDB: 10/1981

IWM 420-23+24 · GB, 1919
the WORLD'S GREATEST STORY – EPISODE 12

b/w · 2 reels · 1226' (31 mins) · silent
intertitles: English

dist Cross Pictures

■ Thematic treatment of behind-the-lines life for British Infantry on the Western Front, 1917.

(Reel 23) The episode starts with 'Justice'. Bayonet drill and a march past by the Northamptonshire Regiment. A march past and open-air meal from the Cheshire Regiment, and a portrait shot of "Private Jones VC" (probably not Jones). The Dorset Regiment drilling on the sands near Nieuport. A posed group, signal section practice and postal delivery from the Essex Regiment. The Rifle Brigade on the march. The Suffolk Regiment resting and smoking,

with the camp barber at work. *(Reel 24)* The West Yorkshire Regiment marching through a French village, "one saw the new British manhood being constructed as he watched these troops march past". A parade outside headquarters and play with the regimental goat from the King's (Liverpool Regiment). Men of the KOYLI resting and smoking, "a great offering to the Goddess Nicotine". Men of the West Riding Regiment in an 'alarm race' having to dress at high speed, and queuing outside a beer tent, "the great push". The Durham Light Infantry relaxing and playing games, showing six of their NCOs who had served since 1914.

Notes
Production etc: see **Notes** to Episode 1, **IWM 420-01+02**.
Summary: nearly all the material in this episode comes from the series *British Regiments*, particularly **IWM 389, IWM 391, IWM 392, IWM 393, IWM 394, IWM 398, IWM 399, IWM 402, IWM 403** and **IWM 404**.
[shotsheet available]
catalogued SDB: 10/1981

IWM 420-25+26 · GB, 1919
the WORLD'S GREATEST STORY – EPISODE 13

b/w & (partly) tinted · 2 reels · 2076' (35 mins) · silent
intertitles: English

dist Cross Pictures

■ Thematic treatment of the British involvement in the last months of the war on the Western Front, 1918.

(Reel 25) The episode starts with 'Justice'. The opening states that this was "the great final offensive, in which the whole might of Britain's arms was concentrated, with an overwhelming force, upon one visible object... from the bases they marched in endless columns, with stern-set lips and proudly beating hearts into that maw of death and desolation". British troops move across no man's land with shells bursting. Damaged villages, including Grévillers, are shown. More of the advance. A dressing station in a sunken road. A large mine crater. Mules used as water-carriers. A German observation post disguised as a house. Guns and Highland troops advance up to the front and German prisoners are escorted back. Transport and soldiers cross a temporary bridge. British troops in La

Bassée (tinted red). Sappers cross a damaged bridge on the La Bassée Canal. A temporary bridge is being built. *(Reel 26)* A wrecked village, wounded (including Germans) on stretchers being given food and water, and one having his leg bandaged. Scenes of devastation, including the ruins of Lens. A 12-inch naval howitzer firing on a railway carriage. Traction engines carrying troops. Labour battalions constructing a railway track. British troops putting out fires in Cambrai just after its capture. Meanwhile "the Navy never ceased to harass the enemy on the seas, until at last he was rendered powerless" (actually showing the Italian Navy: fast patrol boats, cruisers in line and the battleship *Giulio Cesare* firing a broadside.)

Notes
Production etc: see **Notes** to Episode 1, **IWM 420-01+02**.
Summary: most of the material in this episode comes from the series *August Offensive* and *September Offensive*. See in particular **IWM 116, IWM 322, IWM 325, IWM 332, IWM 338, IWM 339** and **IWM 393**. For the naval material see **IWM 1163**.
[shotsheet available]
catalogued SDB: 10/1981

IWM 420-27+28 · GB, 1919
the WORLD'S GREATEST STORY – EPISODE 14

b/w · 2 reels · 2204' (37 mins) · silent
intertitles: English

pr (War Office Official) New Era Film
dist Ashley Exclusive Films

■ Continued thematic treatment of the British involvement in the last months of the war on the Western Front, 1918.

(Reel 27) The episode opens with 'Justice'. Scenes of FE2d night bombers (in daylight) interspersed with scenes of a posed group of pilots from 60 Squadron with their recently departed commanding officer Captain William Bishop. Dead horses by the roadside. Five aircraft flying in formation. British troops crossing the battlefield. The capture of various damaged villages, one still under shell fire. British and Canadian soldiers putting out the fires in Cambrai. A tank demonstrates its ability to overcome tank traps, including a land mine. *(Reel 28)* The unfinished German ferroconcrete defences on the Hindenburg Line, "the nature of the German defences was

evidence of their long preparation for their audacious attack upon unsuspecting Europe". The south side of the tunnel on the St-Quentin Canal and the bridge at Bellenglise where 46th Division crossed. Civilians celebrating the liberation of Ostend. More civilians celebrating the liberation of Lille. British troops clown for the camera, some wearing top hats and pickelhaubes, while two are pushed in a car without an engine. Field Marshal Haig greets the Prince of Wales and Prince Fushimo of Japan at his headquarters train on 11 November, about four hours after the signing of the Armistice. A posed group of Haig with his Army commanders (Generals Horne, Plumer, Byng, Rawlinson and Birdwood) after their final conference at Cambrai on the same day.

Notes
Production etc: see **Notes** to Episode 1, **IWM 420-01+02**.
Summary: most of the material for this episode comes from the series *August Offensive* and *September Offensive*. See in particular **IWM 132**, **IWM 141**, **IWM 336**, **IWM 338**, **IWM 339**, **IWM 351**, **IWM 352** and **IWM 378**.
[shotsheet available]
catalogued SDB: 10/1981

IWM 420-29+30 · GB, 1919
the WORLD'S GREATEST STORY – EPISODE 15

b/w · 2 reels · 1841' (31 mins) · silent
intertitles: English

■ Thematic treatment of the last days of the First World War and subsequent British victory celebrations.

(Reel 29) The opening justifies the series, "It is our contention that all right minded men and women will essentially look in a spirit of reverence upon all these things... This film does not depend for its interest upon sickly sentiment, nor a specious portrayal of life's true values... The final episode of this story recalls to you that happy time when a sorrowing world first knew that the terrible thunder of a thousand guns and all the dire agonies of a mighty war were leading us UNTO THE DAWN." The figure of 'Justice'. British soldiers charging across no man's land. A British cyclist patrol liberates a French village, and the soldiers fraternise with the locals (actually Arras area, spring 1917). German troops surrender. Refugees return to Cambrai after its liberation.

German dead are laid out by British soldiers. Various ruins and damaged buildings, including churches and Arras Cathedral (?). British soldiers mix with Frenchmen. *(Reel 30)* The formal British entry into Cologne across the Hohenzollern Bridge on 12-13 December 1918. General Sir Herbert Plumer, commanding the Army of Occupation, takes the salute beneath the statue of Kaiser Wilhelm I. The British victory parade in London on 19 July 1919. The parade marches past the King's temporary pavilion set up in front of Buckingham Palace, and past the temporary wooden mock-up of the Cenotaph in Whitehall. The parade starts with the Royal Navy led by Admiral Sir David Beatty, Royal Marines, WAACs and WRNS, and Sea Scouts. The Army contingent is led by Field Marshal Sir Douglas Haig, "when Field Marshal Haig passed in lordly dignity, the welkin rang with the loud shouts of a myriad lusty voices". Passing beneath Admiralty Arch, the contingent includes men of the ASC, Scottish troops, Highlanders, the massed colours of the Guards, Australians, British line regiments, and Royal Artillery limbers towing 60-pounders. The King and Queen take the salute at the pavilion as the Australians march past, followed by Canadians. American troops march past the Cenotaph, led by General John J Pershing and a mounted contingent, and followed by Belgian, Japanese, Italian naval and more Japanese troops. A pair of Medium D tanks passes very close to the camera past the King's pavilion. The series ends with crowds around the Cenotaph. "Our story, in its complete form, stands as an incomparable tribute to the men and women of our Empire who, in the time of fierce national stress, made the willing offering of their lives for the preservation of the Motherland."

Notes
Production etc: see **Notes** to Episode 1, **IWM 420-01+02**.
Summary: for the material in the first reel see the series *August Offensive* and *September Offensive*. See in particular **IWM 113**, **IWM 116**, **IWM 185**, **IWM 253**, **IWM 314** and **IWM 345**. The scenes of Cologne come from **IWM 376**. The scenes of London come from **IWM 439**.
[shotsheet available]
catalogued SDB: 10/1981

IWM 421 · GB, (prod) 1919
[NORTH RUSSIA – rough material]
(allocated)

b/w · 4 reels · 5088' (85 mins) · silent
intertitles: none

cam Gordon, K

■ Mixed material, mainly of the British intervention in North Russia, 1918-19.

Four reels of very jumbled material, mainly out-of-focus or of poor quality. The first reel is mainly of fragments from the Western Front 1916-18 taken by British official cameramen, the remainder fragments of the British presence in North Russia. Most of this material is duplicated in the series *The World's Greatest Story*, but some is unique.

Notes
Summary: see also **IWM 420-19+20**, **IWM 420-21+22** and **IWM 808**.
[shotsheet available]
catalogued SDB: 10/1981

IWM 422 · GB, (prod) 1919
BRITISH FORCES IN PERIL

b/w · 4 reels · 2198' (37 mins) · silent
intertitles: none

cam Gordon, K

■ Jumbled film of British forces in North Russia, 1918-19.

The film is mixed, often out-of-focus and poor quality. It shows, principally, Archangel, Murmansk, British transport down the River Dvina and the seaplane base on Lake Onega. In addition to British troops, some of the material is of White Russians, and Czechs of the Slavo-British Legion. The seaplanes at the base are of the Fairey FIIIC type. Identifiable British officers are General Sir Henry Rawlinson, Major-General Maynard, Major-General Ironside, and Brigadier-General Price. Identifiable White Russian generals are General de Milar (or Miller) and General Shobelstyn.

Notes
Title: the title comes from the 'newspaper' style caption which opens the film. This itself comes from the series **IWM 420** *The World's Greatest Story*.
Summary: most of the material in this film is unique although some is out-of-focus or poor quality. Some is duplicated in **IWM 420-19+20**, **IWM 420-21+22** and **IWM 808**.
Shotsheet: see the shotsheet for further details of the film.

Remarks: the film is of considerable historical interest and rarity value but contains no action material.
[Richard Luckett, *The White Generals: a History of the White Movement and the Russian Civil War*, Longman (1971)]
[C Maynard, *The Murmansk Venture*, Hodder and Stoughton (1928)]
[Frederick Maurice (ed), *The Life of General Lord Rawlinson of Trent from his Journals and Letters*, Cassell (1928)]
[G E Livock, *To the Ends of the Air*, HMSO (1973)]
[shotsheet available]
catalogued SDB: 11/1981

IWM 423 · GB, 1919
[NORTH RUSSIA – film unviewable]
(allocated)

b/w · 1 reel · 928' (10 mins) · silent
intertitles: none

■ Blurred and unviewable film of the British intervention in North Russia, 1919.

The film appears to be of the intervention in North Russia, but varies in quality from slightly out-of-focus to completely blurred.

Notes
Summary: see also **IWM 420-19+20**, **IWM 420-21+22** and **IWM 808**.
[shotsheet available]
catalogued SDB: 10/1981

IWM 424 · GB, (prod) 1917
FLAME THROWN OUT OF GAS EJECTOR (ledger title)

b/w · 2 (as 1) reels · 1123' (19 mins) · silent
intertitles: none

I. Training exercises of a British assault on German trenches, covered by smoke shells. The equipment, tactics and terrain are consistent with the Flanders offensive, Western Front, 1917.
II. A lorry-mounted 13-pounder anti-aircraft gun fires out to sea. The crew wear gas masks. The firing finishes and the gun drives off. Possibly Western Front, 1916-18.
III. A British demonstration of gas warfare on the Western Front, showing methods of releasing gas, techniques of placing gas cylinders in trenches, anti-gas drill and the correct way to wear the large box respirator, 1916.
IV. A British soldier in a flame-proof suit

demonstrates a portable flame-thrower, probably 1917.

Notes
Remarks: the 'Flanders' material is quite good.
[shotsheet available]
catalogued SDB: 10/1981

IWM 425 · GB, (?) 1917
SECOND LIFE GUARDS
[the BRITISH REGIMENTS] (series, allocated)

b/w · 1 reel · 330' (6 mins) · silent
intertitles: none

sp War Office Cinema Committee *pr* Topical Film Company

■ Behind the lines activities by 2nd Life Guards on the Western Front, probably 1917.

I. The film opens with extra scenes of 9.2-inch howitzers and 15-inch howitzers firing, followed by a sergeant and two privates in a trench spotting with a trench periscope.
II. The main body of the film shows a troop of 2nd Life Guards, including a Lewis gunner, running forward. (Note that the Hotchkiss automatic rifle replaced the Lewis machinegun in most of the Cavalry after late 1916.) The men form a prone line and open fire. A group of the soldiers attempts to move a gas cylinder stuck in mud. A dismounted squadron of 2nd Life Guards parades on a French village square, and is checked over prior to mounting.
III. The film ends with an interpolated scene of the temporary graves of men of the Canadian 7th Battalion, and soldiers at a checkpoint beside a wood.

Notes
Title: this is taken from the shotsheet.
Summary: this is probably part of the *British Regiments* series which was made in autumn 1917, but the presence of the Lewis gunner makes this less certain. What appears to be a missing scene from this film is now in **IWM 429**.
Remarks: like the remainder of the series, completely valueless as a record of a specific regiment, but good stockshot material.
[G Arthur, *The Story of the Household Cavalry, Vol III*, Constable (1926)]
[shotsheet available]
catalogued SDB: 10/1981

IWM 426 · GB, (?) 1921
ANTI-AIRCRAFT (ledger title)

b/w · 1 reel · 925' (16 mins) · silent
intertitles: English

sp War Office (?) *pr* Baron Hartley (?)

■ British training film on the use of the Lewis machinegun in an anti-aircraft role, made shortly after the First World War.

Not a finished film but the jumbled remains of one. It consists partly of long sections of subtitle captions without accompanying images, and staged actuality material of two soldiers using a Lewis machinegun in an anti-aircraft role, with aeroplanes flying overhead and apparently crashing. The aeroplanes are all British, and some have only minor damage. The bulk of the film is of repeated animated scenes of the correct alignment of Lewis gun bead sights in order to 'lead' the aircraft correctly when firing.

Notes
Production: compare with **IWM 407**, made by Baron Hartley Ltd, for possible similarities of style.
Remarks: the film is useless as it stands, but could be easily re-edited back to coherence.
[shotsheet available]
catalogued SDB: 10/1981

IWM 427 · GB, 2/1918
the EAST YORKS REGIMENT
[the BRITISH REGIMENTS] (series, allocated)

b/w · 1 reel · 375' (6 mins) · silent
intertitles: English

sp War Office Cinema Committee *pr* Topical Film Company

■ Probably 12th Battalion, the East Yorkshire Regiment, Western Front, autumn 1917.

A posed group of the battalion. One man has a small child on his knee, to whom he is chanting nursery rhymes. The men form up for an issue of beer. Men of 'C' Company are issued with hot food from carriers and eat it on trestle tables in the open. A group with towels go off to bathe. A medical orderly bandages the head of one soldier, injured while playing football, while an American doctor attached to the battalion looks on. Men outdoors play cards and drink. Private John Cunningham VC of the regiment plays with some small children and a dog.

Notes
Remarks: valueless as a record of an individual battalion or regiment, this still goes much further than most of the series in conveying the existence of personalities in the battalion, and its nature as a distinct unit.
[E Wyrall, *The East Yorkshire Regiment in the Great War 1914-1918*, Harrison (1928)]
[shotsheet available]
catalogued SDB: 10/1981

IWM 428 · GB, (ca) 1917
RICHEBOURG ST VAAST

b/w · 1 reel · 176' (3 mins) · silent
intertitles: none

■ Damage done to the village of Richebourg-St-Vaast, Western Front, possibly as early as late 1915.

General scenes of destruction with British troops in the middle distance, showing mainly the damage done to the church, inside and out, and a water-filled crater.

Notes
Date: almost certainly British official material, but no precise date is possible.
[shotsheet available]
catalogued SDB: 10/1981

IWM 429 · GB, (prod) 1918
[BRITISH INFANTRY REGIMENTS (various fragments)] (allocated)
[SCENES TAKEN FROM THE WORLD'S GREATEST STORY] (alternative)

b/w · 1 reel · 763' (12 mins) · silent
intertitles: none

■ Short segments, usually of a few seconds only, of various British regiments on the Western Front, route marching, resting or in reserve trenches unless otherwise described, 1917-18.

The regiments are as follows. The Civil Service Rifles (a battalion of the Royal Fusiliers). The London Scottish (1/14th Battalion, the London Regiment). Pipers of the Argyll and Sutherland Highlanders. The Norfolk Regiment. The Royal Fusiliers. 10th Battalion, the Northumberland Fusiliers with

12th or 13th Battalion, the Durham Light Infantry. The Devonshire Regiment. The Grenadier Guards. 9th Battalion, the Leicestershire Regiment. 10th Battalion, the East Yorkshire Regiment. The Grenadier Guards. The Worcestershire Regiment. The Welsh Guards. 2nd Life Guards troopers under cover resting and cleaning their swords. The Coldstream Guards. 7th Battalion, the Bedfordshire Regiment. The Leicestershire Regiment. Unidentified Highlanders, probably territorials. The Black Watch. 4th (Scottish) Regiment, the South African Brigade. Howe and Hawke Battalions, 63rd (Royal Naval) Division. 4th Battalion, the Worcestershire Regiment. The Welsh Guards. 1st Battalion, the Norfolk Regiment. The Gordon Highlanders. The King's Own Scottish Borderers. Troops of 1st Cavalry Division and RFA. Unidentified Highlanders, probably territorials. Welsh Guards with Grenadier Guards. The Black Watch. 20th (Blackheath and Woolwich) Battalion, the London Regiment. 17th Battalion, the Lancashire Fusiliers. The Northumberland Fusiliers with the Royal Fusiliers. The Black Watch. Men of 16th (Irish) Division. 6th Battalion, the Hampshire Regiment.

Notes
Title: the alternative title comes from one version of the shotsheet, the material of this film does not, however, in fact come from the series **IWM 420** *The World's Greatest Story*.
Summary: this selection of random offcuts and fragments was probably joined together by accident during the copying process.
[shotsheet available]
catalogued SDB: 10/1981

IWM 430 · GB, 1917
UBIQUE – OUR GUNNERS IN THE GREAT WAR
[the BRITISH REGIMENTS] (series, allocated)

b/w · 1 reel · 511' (9 mins) · silent
intertitles: English

sp War Office Cinema Committee *pr* Topical Film Company

■ Work of the Royal Field Artillery and Royal Garrison Artillery, mainly on the Western Front, 1916-17.

Drivers water their horses at a trough. A brigade of RFA 18-pounders moves off from their camp ground. Other 18-pounders move past dead Highlanders (from **IWM 191** *The Battle of the Somme*). A battery of 18-pounders in line fires. Two 60-pounders being fired. An officer climbs a ladder into a tree as an observation post. A 60-pounder battery fires under scrim. Rear view of an 18-pounder firing. Some 9.2-inch howitzers fire from a chalk pit. Finally, 60-pounders in action in Mesopotamia.

Notes
Summary: some of these scenes appear in **IWM 79**, **IWM 130-01+02** and **IWM 191**.
[shotsheet available]
catalogued SDB: 10/1981

IWM 431 · GB, (?) 1918
POPERINGHE

b/w · 1 reel · 238' (4 mins) · silent
intertitles: none

sp Ministry of Information (?)

- Damage to Poperinghe either by shelling or bombing, Western Front, probably during April 1918.

The damage is fairly minor, involving houses with a wall missing and similar ruins. British soldiers walk through the ruins and a marching column comes down the street. A wagon-load of British troops comes up another street, possibly in Vlamertinghe rather than Poperinghe.

Notes
Title: this is taken from the shotsheet.
[shotsheet available]
catalogued SDB: 10/1981

IWM 432 · GB, (ca) 1916
BRITISH EFFICIENCY

b/w · 1 reel · 438' (7 mins) · silent
intertitles: none

- Training displays given by British troops to visiting Allied military officials, probably in Britain, about 1916.

Soldiers simulate a night attack, blindfolding themselves before charging out of a trench down a course. Other soldiers build barbed wire entanglements while wearing gas masks. Two soldiers in a foxhole demonstrate a rifle grenade launcher. Dismounted Cavalry demonstrate their Hotchkiss automatic rifles, including the drill

if the operator is hit. A pack mule displays the carrying saddle for the Hotchkiss. The observers are officers from various Allied nations. Scottish troops at a rifle range demonstrate the 'mad minute' of high-speed firing. Other soldiers on a bayonet assault course. Gunners demonstrate the loading of a 6-inch 26cwt howitzer while wearing gas masks. Cavalrymen saddle their horses and lead them off while wearing gas masks. Some French officers inspect the horses. Prizes are given to various soldiers. Present at the demonstrations are the Duke of Connaught and (possibly) General Sir Horace Smith-Dorrien. The Cavalry demonstrate their ability to dismount, picket, off-saddle, and bed down at high speed, then how to remount again equally quickly, all while wearing gas masks. The film ends abruptly.

Notes
Title: this is taken from the shotsheet.
Summary: the identification of Smith-Dorrien is very tentative.
[shotsheet available]
catalogued SDB: 9/1981

IWM 433 · GB, (ca) 1917
THIRD ARMY SIGNAL OFFICE

b/w · 1 reel · 683' (11 mins) · silent
intertitles: none

- Extremely dark and out-of-focus film of the Third Army Signal Office, Western Front, 1916-18.

Soldiers deliver letters at the "Post Hatch". They are taken by motor-cycle to the Signal Office, where military clerks use telegraph, telephone and ticker tape machines to relay the information.

Notes
Title: this is taken from the shotsheet.
Technical: the entire film is out-of-focus, badly under-exposed and generally almost unviewable.
Remarks: some promising material, if it were possible to see what was going on.
[shotsheet available]
catalogued SDB: 10/1981

IWM 434 · GB, (?) 1917
VICKERS VANGUARDS (ledger title)

b/w · 1 reel · 1202' (20 mins) · silent
intertitles: English

sp Department of Information (?)

- Munitions and aircraft manufacture at Vickers Ltd works in England, 1917 (?).

I. The making of fuses for 18-pounder shells at the Ward End works. The workers are mainly women. This includes a display of all the components and gauges required to make one fuse. The manufacture of cartridge cases at the same works, again with all the components and gauges shown. The first three stages of cupping an 18-pounder shell-case.
II. The manufacture of shell-cases at the Barrow works, using various lathes to hollow the cases out.
III. The manufacture of aircraft at the Weybridge works. Most of the work, including heavy welding, is done by women. In the assembly shop two Vickers FB14 aircraft and one SE5a made under licence are being constructed.

Notes
Date: the caption style is typical of middle period WOCC and DoI material, and is probably British official film.
[shotsheet available]
catalogued SDB: 11/1981

IWM 435 · France, 1917
[SOISSONS AND RHEIMS] (allocated)

b/w · 1 reel · 942' (16 mins) · silent
intertitles: English

- English-language version of a French film of the German bombardment of Soissons in January 1915 and Rheims in March 1917, Western Front.

The film is incomplete and without its proper opening. The opening sequence alternates between shots of the diary of a German Artillery officer and captions of its contents, stating that the German bombardment of January-February 1915 deliberately used Soissons Cathedral as its aiming-point. President Poincaré visits the city, which shows severe damage. A bridge over the River Aisne has been destroyed. This is followed by a panorama of Rheims in March 1917. French soldiers walk casually through the streets, buying milk from a passing vendor who also sells to housewives in the ruins. Another woman sells newspapers to the soldiers as they clear the rubble. The Mayor, Dr Langlet, is posed with two assistants. Children run to play near the cathedral. The archbishop,

Mgr Luçon, is shown. The children play by the school wearing gas hoods since "asphyxiating shells are about to fall". More children, "the victims sought by the German batteries", play in the area. Near the city French 320mm railway guns open fire. One of the divisions presented to Poincaré on his visit. The French attack out of the trenches into a wood at Godault Farm on 6 April 1917 (possibly faked, the camera is very exposed). German prisoners are escorted back. The attack continues through the wood.

Notes
Summary: this is French official film, possibly part of the early series which continues as **IWM 508** *Annales de la Guerre.*
Remarks: the battle sequences are a marked improvement on their British counterparts, but are probably not completely genuine, looking in places a little too good to be true.
[shotsheet available]
catalogued SDB: 10/1981

IWM 436 · GB, (?) 1917
GERMAN OFFICER PRISONERS : a prisoner of war camp in England
OFICIALES ALEMANES CAUTIVOS : campos de prisioneros de guerra en Inglaterra (on copy held)

b/w · 1 reel · 576' (10 mins) · silent
intertitles: Spanish

sp Department of Information (?)

- Spanish-language version of a British propaganda film on the treatment of German officers as prisoners of war in Britain, probably 1917.

The Germans are from various branches and include some Austrians. The first camp is a large school or similar institution, with additional wooden huts built on its grounds. One group of officers poses, very smartly turned out. Another similar camp has more huts. A third camp (again a school or the equivalent) has German officers wandering about freely and playing football. A group of five, including one naval officer and one Austrian, poses by a hut. The gardens of the camp and the chapel are shown. A large group of prisoners returns to camp after a walk out on parole. The prisoners have a thatched summer house in the garden and a skittles alley for recreation. One officer, filmed while haymaking, performs impromptu acrobatics for the camera. Others join him and hold an equally impromptu wrestling match before returning to haymaking.

Notes
Summary: one of the camps is probably Donington Hall. See also **IWM 4** and **IWM 441** for comparison.
Shotsheet: the shotsheet, which is in English, gives slightly different titles and length of material than the film itself, and probably reflects the English-language version of the film.
Remarks: a good example of understated British propaganda when dealing with prisoners of war. It is almost too understated: with a few obvious alterations all these scenes, and the accompanying captions, might have come from the *British Regiments* series or films of British soldiers interned in other countries.
[shotsheet available]
catalogued SDB: 10/1981

IWM 437 · GB, (prod) 1918
[SALONIKA AND WESTERN FRONT (rough material)] (allocated)

b/w · 4 reels · 3378' (56 mins) · silent
intertitles: none

sp Ministry of Information (?)

■ Mixed and confused material, some of it unique, of the Western Front, Salonika Front and Home Front in Britain, 1918 (?).

The jumbled film consists of unrelated, very brief items. Some of these appear in other films but the majority are probably unique.

Notes
Summary: see also **IWM 130, IWM 259** and **IWM 375.**
Shotsheet: see the detailed shotsheet for further details.
[shotsheet available]
catalogued SDB: 10/1981

IWM 438 · GB, (ca) 1917
LEWIS GUN SCHOOL

b/w · 1 reel · 375' (6 mins) · silent
intertitles: none

■ Training exercises for the Lewis machinegun, demonstrated by sergeant

instructors of the Machine Gun Corps, possibly at Aldershot, probably before the end of the First World War.

I. A Machine Gun Section of seven men with one Lewis gun walking in line across an open field comes to a ridge, and the men form up for action. Four men go forward to set up the machinegun (a gunner, a loader and two ammunition carriers), while of the other three, one forms a near-flank guard and the other two cover the open flank. If the Lewis jams the gunner and loader move it behind the ridge while the near-flank guard takes their place with his rifle until the jam is cleared.
II. While the remainder watch at attention, two of the sergeant instructors demonstrate the various hand signals between a Lewis gunner and his loader. Then the sergeant-major (note the four stripes, and crown on his sleeve) stands beside them to demonstrate the signals given by a platoon commander to a Lewis gunner to alter his fire.
III. To the end of this film has been added some material of German and British machineguns from **IWM 347** *Romicourt – Armentières near Estaires.*

Notes
Title: this is taken from the shotsheet.
Summary: see also **IWM 347.**
Remarks: the drill is basically sound, but shows the British error in not using an NCO observer in addition to the two-man crew of the machinegun to direct its fire.
[shotsheet available]
catalogued SDB: 10/1981

IWM 439 · GB, 1919
the END OF A WELL FOUGHT WAR : the Peace Procession 1919

b/w · 1 reel · 763' (13 mins) · silent
intertitles: English

■ British Peace Procession, marking the end of the First World War, through the streets of London, 19 July 1919.

The first third of the film is badly jumbled and shows repeated shots of the naval contingent (including the Royal Marines) led by Admiral Sir David Beatty, passing through Admiralty Arch and about to enter Whitehall. This is followed by the Australian contingent marching past a saluting pavilion specially constructed for the King outside Buckingham Palace. Soldiers of various nations march past the Cenotaph in

Whitehall (in fact a specially constructed dummy, the stone pillar was not installed until two years later), including American, Belgian, Japanese and Italian contingents. Two Medium D tanks pass very close to the camera. The various women's contingents, including the WAAC, WRNS and FANY, pass under Admiralty Arch. They are followed by Sea Scouts, Canadians, Australians, British bands, colours, and 60-pounders of the Royal Garrison Artillery. The Portuguese contingent marches past the Cenotaph, followed by the French (?) Cavalry contingent, the Greek (?) contingent, the Italian contingent and the White Russian contingent, and by more Frenchmen. (At this point the film becomes extremely disjointed again.) A band of Royal Marines coming through Admiralty Arch. The Australian band marching past Buckingham Palace. Royal Marines passing through Admiralty Arch, followed by Field Marshal Haig with a mounted escort, and by various British contingents. In the saluting pavilion outside Buckingham Palace are King George V, the Queen, Lloyd George, Foch, Weygand and Pershing. There are more views of the procession, including WAACs marching past the saluting base. The film finally breaks up into the naval contingent again coming through Admiralty Arch.

Notes
Summary: some of this material is used in **IWM 420-29+30**.
[shotsheet available]
catalogued SDB: 10/1981

IWM 440-01 · GB, (ca) 1918
OUR EMPIRE'S FIGHT FOR FREEDOM – PART 1

b/w · 1 reel · 1475' (30 mins) · silent
intertitles: English

- Semi-contemporary material of Britain's entry into the First World War, from the Spithead review in June to the arrival of the BEF in France, 1914.

I. The film is outspoken, "The evidence – both documentary and otherwise – is now ample to prove that Germany forced this great and terrible War upon humanity to secure for herself the domination of the world."
II. The Spithead review of June 1914 shows a line of pre-dreadnoughts with HMS Implacable and HMS Vengeance, HMS Agamemnon and the Royal yacht Victoria and Albert. Two torpedo boats ride in the swell. A French Danton Class semi-dreadnought. The Japanese semi-dreadnought Kurama. The battle-cruiser HMS Indomitable. After salutes are fired HMS Victorious gets under way with dreadnoughts of the Majesty Class: HMS Magnificent, HMS Mars, HMS Illustrious and the armoured cruiser HMS Warrior. The Kurama again, briefly, with HMS Queen in the background. Rounding the stern of the dreadnought HMS Neptune. Views of the battle-cruiser HMS Lion, dreadnoughts of the Téméraire and Orion Classes, with HMS Dreadnought itself, in lozenge formation. The fleet did not disperse after manœuvres. The King's declaration of war, followed by switchboard operators relaying the information. Winston Churchill, as First Lord of the Admiralty, reviews the fleet. HMS Lion is shown. The submarine E.23 submerges. A Felixstowe flying boat passes over HMS Firedrake.
III. An Army recruiting march in London with a German 77mm field gun captured by 19th Battalion, the London Regiment. A recruiting rally in Trafalgar Square. Civilian volunteers, wearing armbands, queue to be attested at the Central Recruiting Depot in Westminster. Newly raised troops cheer the camera. The new recruits include territorials of the Argyll and Sutherland Highlanders and of the Queen's Regiment. Lord Kitchener inspects a Highland territorial battalion. The first of the BEF are transported across the Channel and disembark in France with their equipment (note what appears to be a 13-pounder 9cwt A anti-aircraft gun, introduced 1918).
IV. The film ends with HMS Queen Elizabeth patrolling the North Sea.

Notes
Summary: the series Our Empire's Fight for Freedom consists of seven episodes covering 1914-17. See Reeves for problems in dating the release of the series. It seems most likely that it was made after 1918 and is now incomplete. It was not part of the original collection of official films sent to the IWM in 1921. See also the series **IWM 130** Sons of Our Empire and **IWM 420** The World's Greatest Story.
Remarks: the series contains in its opening episodes some non-official film which may be genuine 1914-15 but is not particularly striking. For the remainder it uses official film from 1916 onwards to represent the events of earlier years. Like the series The World's Greatest Story it is chiefly a poor attempt to disguise the inept choice and use of material with overstated and ridiculous titling.

[Nicholas Reeves, *Official British Film Propaganda During the First World War*, Croom Helm (1986)]
[shotsheet available]
catalogued SDB & NAP: 11/1981

IWM 440-02 · GB, (ca) 1918
OUR EMPIRE'S FIGHT FOR FREEDOM – PART 2

b/w · 1 reel · 1070' (17 mins) · silent
intertitles: English

■ Semi-contemporary material of the first British forces in France and the creation of the massed armies in Britain at the start of the First World War, 1914-16.

Arrival of the Indian Corps in Marseilles in September 1914. A montage of recruiting posters. Civilians are exhorted to join the Army. They queue at the Central London Recruiting Office in Westminster. New recruits, and civilian cars requisitioned by the government. Welshmen of 38th Division prepare to lay up their regimental colours in the Guildhall before going overseas. "From the four corners of the World, Britain's sons rallied to the flag to save the Empire and to crush German Kaiserism, the would-be God of the universe, the despoiler of nations, the enslaver of civilisations." Troops from Canada, Australia and New Zealand (? probably Australian 1st Division) in France. Egyptians are recruited for the Egyptian Labour Corps and fighting troops, who "leave amid the cheers for the battlefields of France" (no Egyptian fighting troops served in France). British destroyers escort troop crossings over the English Channel in gale conditions. Meanwhile, for the regulars in the front line "mud was everywhere – they ate in it, drank in it, slept in it, swore and cursed in it, prayed to God and fought in it, but like true Britons they HELD ON". Troops of the Guards Division in the Loos sector in December 1915 in very muddy conditions. At a station in Britain a Highland regiment boards a trooptrain, "hold on lads, we're coming !".

Notes
Summary: probably most of the material in this reel was filmed post-1914. The 'mud' sequence comes from **IWM 207** and **IWM 208**.
[shotsheet available]
catalogued SDB: 12/1981

IWM 440-03 · GB, (ca) 1918
OUR EMPIRE'S FIGHT FOR FREEDOM – PART 3

b/w · 1 reel · 940' (16 mins) · silent
intertitles: English

■ Life for British troops in the trenches on the Western Front and munition production in Britain, 1915-16.

Troops at the Front receive letters from home (acted). The Guards Division in very muddy conditions in the Loos sector, including the 'Southerland Avenue' position. A full caption of Prime Minister Asquith's speech at the Guildhall detailing the British position on the war. Examples of the developing war industry: soldiers and civilians drilling in Hyde Park, and fully kitted-out soldiers about to embark. "Our cause is just, our arm is strong, our will inflexible and with a united Empire we shall win !" The formation of the Ministry of Munitions on 25 May 1915, showing women munition workers "for men must fight and women must work". Metalworking furnaces, "the workshops of Hades", and heavy gun manufacture. On the Western Front General Sir Douglas Haig replaces Field Marshal Sir John French (described incorrectly as a general). French talks with General Gouraud and General Weygand. Haig is shown with Marshals Joffre and Foch at Haig's château. The episode ends with a table of the amount of war material sent overseas in the first twelve months of the war, emphasised by HMS *King Edward VII* firing a broadside.

Notes
Date: the present tense used by the caption in this episode may indicate a production or release date during the war. It may, however, equally be the historic present used for dramatic effect.
Summary: some of the material from this episode also appears in **IWM 207**, **IWM 208** and **IWM 214**.
[shotsheet available]
catalogued SDB: 11/1981

IWM 440-04 · GB, (ca) 1918
OUR EMPIRE'S FIGHT FOR FREEDOM – PART 4

b/w · 1 reel · 977' (16 mins) · silent
intertitles: English

■ Review of the British war effort on all fronts and at home, 1915-16.

The episode opens with a table showing the increase in personnel of the Army and Navy in the first twelve months of the war. A new merchant ship is launched. Australian soldiers in dress uniform march through the streets of Sydney headed by Australian Light Horse. Munitions manufacture for British 60-pounders and 6-inch howitzers, then shown in action "to blast their inexorable way through the Hun defences". Meanwhile, "owing to the treachery of King Constantine of Greece in refusing to help Serbia – the nation she pledged herself to defend – and his intrigues with the Kaiser, the British and French Governments decided to help Serbia with all the means at their disposal. On Monday 4 October 1915, the Franco-British Expeditionary Force landed at Salonika." British forces on the Salonika Front in 1915 include mule trains and a 60-pounder. Egyptian troops prepare in their camps in Egypt. On his visit to France in 1916 Lord Kitchener reviews a New Army battalion and exchanges greetings with General Sir William Robertson on the quayside. Soldiers of 38th (Welsh) Division are transported by bus to the Loos sector where men of the Guards Division are digging and clearing their trenches. The episode ends with general scenes of gunfire.

Notes

Summary: although most of the material in this episode is duplicated elsewhere the scenes of the Salonika Front may be unique.

Remarks: the most significant aspect of this episode, as with the remainder of the series, is the captioning, in particular the justification for the invasion at Salonika.
[shotsheet available]
catalogued SDB: 12/1981

IWM 440-05 · GB, (ca) 1918
OUR EMPIRE'S FIGHT FOR FREEDOM – PART 5

b/w · 1 reel · 1115' (18 mins) · silent
intertitles: English

▪ British sector of the Western Front, and the battle-cruiser station at Rosyth, Scotland, 1916.

Winter on the Western Front, 1915-16. Soldiers travel on a light railway; a 6-inch howitzer and 9.2-inch howitzers firing in damp and snow; troops in snow-covered trenches, including one 'over the top' sequence; and soldiers, transport and guns

in very muddy conditions behind the lines. A kite balloon is manœuvred up by RFC personnel. A view from an aircraft at 10 000 feet over the countryside, ending with a spiralling dive from 14 000 feet. A caption gives British claims for the Battle of Jutland, 31 May 1916: German losses 18 battleships, cruisers and submarines against 13 British ships. The battle-cruiser base at Rosyth, showing a Felixstowe flying boat and various battle-cruisers, notably HMS *Lion*.

Notes

Summary: most of the material in this episode comes from the series **IWM 130** *Sons of Our Empire*.
[shotsheet available]
catalogued SDB: 12/1981

IWM 440-06 · GB, (ca) 1918
OUR EMPIRE'S FIGHT FOR FREEDOM – PART 6

b/w · 1 reel · 1177' (18 mins) · silent
intertitles: English

▪ British participation in the First Battle of the Somme (chiefly a re-edit of **IWM 191** *The Battle of the Somme*), Western Front, summer 1916.

This episode follows the normal structure of First World War 'battle' pictures. The troops in columns march up to the villages behind the lines. The guns, including a 12-inch railway gun and an 18-pounder battery directed by balloon observers, begin their bombardment. The troops gather and make the attack. The wounded and dead are counted. "They had gone to the great unknown, adding more glory to the immortal array of heroes who have given their blood for the Empire." Whereas the German prisoners are "a few of the Germans who escaped our terrific barrage and the bayonets of our boys". The episode ends, in a different caption style, with "Until Germany tears the God of despotism from her soul – her barbaric policy of blood and iron: until she chooses the path of civilisation, of honour, and of righteousness, this war MUST continue ! to save the CIVILISED human race, to save the universe".

Notes

Summary: this episode was made almost entirely by re-editing **IWM 191** and **IWM 116** and includes no original material.
Remarks: the caption in the unfamiliar style,

which may be a later or mistaken addition, is, with the caption quoted in episode 3, the only evidence to suggest that this film was released while the war was still being fought.
[shotsheet available]
catalogued SDB: 12/1981

IWM 440-07 · GB, (ca) 1918
OUR EMPIRE'S FIGHT FOR FREEDOM – PART 7

b/w · 1 reel · 1258' (20 mins) · silent
intertitles: English

■ Continuation of the British participation in the First Battle of the Somme, later stages (chiefly a re-edit of **IWM 116** *The Battle of the Ancre and the Advance of the Tanks*), Western Front, autumn 1916.

The captions are violent: "From July 1st our offensive never slackened; town after town fell to the assaults of our indomitable troops." A map of the Flers-Courcelette area. Male and Female Mk I tanks move into position. An FE2b aircraft, 'Mauritius III', takes off and flies over its camp. A motor machinegun battery leaves its camp. Tanks and soldiers move up from the rear areas. The bombardment starts. Canadian troops (from **IWM 130** *Sons of Our Empire*) make the attack. The troops and tanks advance. A Male tank in action, "trenches it laughs at, dug-outs it enjoys, shell holes and mine craters it positively revels in". German prisoners are brought back. Water is delivered to the gunners by mule. A map shows "Allies' great progress on the Somme Front from July 1st to September 16th 1916, on a front of 25 miles, maximum depth captured 7 miles and over 30,000 prisoners". George V visits France in July, and is shown in group shot with President Poincaré, General Haig, Marshal Joffre and Marshal Foch. The King leaves from Calais, watched by the Prince of Wales.

Notes
Summary: this episode is mainly a re-edited version of **IWM 116**, **IWM 130**, **IWM 191** and **IWM 192** and contains no original material.
Remarks: the whole portrayal of the offensive is highly thematic and impressionistic, with no attempt at logical or chronological sequence.
[shotsheet available]
catalogued SDB: 12/1981

IWM 441 · GB, 7/1917
GERMAN PRISONERS OF WAR : camp in England for non-commissioned officers and men

b/w · 1 reel · 768' (12 mins) · silent
intertitles: English

sp Department of Information

■ British propaganda film of the treatment of German prisoners of war at Dorchester prison camp, July 1917.

The camp is mainly of wooden huts with a few permanent buildings, for German NCOs and other ranks. Roll-call is taken early in the morning by the Germans themselves. Most are wearing patched uniforms and civilian caps, and are obviously cold. New arrivals are issued with bed boards "on which to lay their mattresses". Some of the prisoners stroll about the parade ground, others are marched off to work by armed guards. They work in the carpenter's shop, loading planks, and in the bakery making their own bread. There is a library. Prisoners are allowed to keep their own rabbits. The hospital is clean with a well-equipped operating theatre. There is a chapel and a YMCA hut for the prisoners. They have their own vegetable garden and are paid for their work. Some are shown taking heavy tubs of food out from the kitchen, others lying down "enjoying a rest and a sleep after dinner". There is a playing field where the prisoners can play football. The film ends abruptly.

Notes
Summary: this is the English-language version of a film intended mainly for export. See also **IWM 4** and **IWM 436** for comparison.
Remarks: as with the two other films on the treatment of prisoners of war, a good example of the understated British approach to propaganda.
[shotsheet available]
catalogued SDB: 11/1981

IWM 442 · GB, 1923
FIVE YEARS AGO

b/w · 2 reels · 2306' (39 mins) · silent
intertitles: English

sp Imperial War Museum

■ Compilation film of British official material of the Western Front and the War at Sea, assembled by the Imperial War Museum in 1923.

I. *(Reel 1)* The Western Front 1916, re-edited sections of **IWM 116** *The Battle of the Ancre and the Advance of the Tanks*, using the same scenes and captions as the original, but not in the same order. This covers events in the middle period of the Battle of the Somme, September-November 1916. The film stresses that "these pictures are absolutely genuine and photographed on the actual battlefield".
II. *(Reel 2)* A similar re-editing treatment of **IWM 571** *The Triumph of Britain's Sea Power* showing the surrender of the German High Seas Fleet in 1919. The re-editing shows a number of errors. From a scene of the battle-cruisers SMS *Hindenburg* and SMS *Derfflinger* the first ship has been edited out and the *Derfflinger* incorrectly described as the *Hindenburg*. The ship described as HMS *Queen Elizabeth* is probably HMS *King George V*. The reel shows the procession of the High Seas Fleet to Scapa Flow, and of the U-boat fleet to Harwich. The middle of the film contains scenes of the submarine U.35 sinking the merchant vessel SS *Parkgate* in the Western Mediterranean in 1917.

Notes
Summary: see also **IWM 116** and **IWM 571**. This and **IWM 487** are the only known examples from the interwar period of any attempt by the IWM to exploit its film collection by making its own films.
Remarks: it is disturbing that just five years after the war's end the IWM clearly had only a limited idea of what its film material contained.
[shotsheet available]
catalogued SDB & NAP: 11/1981

IWM 443 · GB, 12/1917
LONDON – BRITISH FACT AND GERMAN FICTION
LONDRES – LA VERDAD BRITANICA Y LA FICCION GERMANA (on copy held)

b/w · 1 reel · 921' (15 mins) · silent
intertitles: Spanish

sp Department of Information
pr Thanhauser Company

■ Spanish-language version of a British propaganda film on the effects of German air raids on London up to 26 September 1917.

I. The film contrasts quotes from a German newspaper, given as the *Westphalia Daily News*, reporting the damage or destruction of prominent landmarks in the centre of London with film of those places taken on dates after the report. The authenticity of the dates is established by the presence of a British special constable who holds up a placard giving the date on which filming is taking place. Care is taken to pan, rather than cut, from these placards.
II. Landmarks shown include the Tower of London, the Palace of Westminster and Westminster Bridge, all undamaged. Piccadilly Circus is undamaged at 3.40pm on 25 September (note the clock). The Bank of England and the Mansion House are also undamaged. Within the Mansion House, the bearer of the Mace announces the Lord Mayor, Colonel Sir William Dunn. German claims to have bombed a munitions factory in central London are contrasted with the actual damage to a small café, probably in King's Cross Road. Further undamaged landmarks are the church of St Martin in the Fields, Charing Cross Station, Trafalgar Square and Whitehall. This is contrasted, by way of a headline in the *Evening Standard* for 26 September, with a bomb crater outside the Bedford Hotel, Southampton Row in which eleven (actually thirteen) people were killed. An officer in the New Zealand Medical Corps who helped rescue survivors is shown. A 15th century house in Holborn, and St Paul's Cathedral, also undamaged, are contrasted with "another munitions factory" - a small dairy in Bermondsey - and with working-class houses in Burgoyne Road, Brixton, all gutted by bombs. Liverpool Street Station and Buckingham Palace (with the King in residence) are undamaged. "The population of London is 7 million, the casualties caused by air raids are 191 dead and 749 wounded or 27 dead per million. The total casualties caused by air raids during the war is therefore 940, compared to a total of victims of accidents of all kinds of 14,591." (All quotes translated.)

Notes
Title: the main title is the original English release title.
Summary: the identity of the German newspaper is difficult to establish – of those cited in the *Times* index, the *Rheinisch-Westfälische Zeitung* seems closest to the translated title given. Despite the claims attributed to the German newspaper, no air raids actually took place over London on 15 July, 16 August or 6 September.
Remarks: an excellent example of the British principle of 'the propaganda of facts'. Also a

revealing insight into British innocence in such matters. The validity of the film's conclusion depends both on its honesty in reporting German claims, and in the incorruptibility of a British special constable. Both presuppose the proven integrity of British officialdom, which is precisely the point the film is seeking to establish.
[shotsheet available]
catalogued SDB: 11/1981

IWM 444 · GB, (?) 1916
the CALL TO THE YOUNG

b/w · 1 reel · 539' (9 mins) · silent
intertitles: English

- British propaganda film for the Home Front, calling for volunteers for the Army, possibly 1916.

The film contrasts young men leaving factory gates, "still at home" with older men "who have to go to war" while their wives and families wait behind. A parade of drill sergeants shows that they are all still serving despite having two, three or four wound stripes. A home defence unit, with an average age of about fifty, drills in the open. Three of its members are seen together, "the ages of these men total 207 years and they're still doing their bit". (The uniform details suggest they are part of a volunteer or temporary unit rather than the Regular Army.) Middle-aged men, serving as special constables, don shrapnel helmets, and carry warnings against air raids. Boys drill in Royal Flying Corps uniform. All this is contrasted with the men still in the factories. "If the young men will not take their turn, thrice wounded men must go back, more fathers of families will be called up, leave may have to be stopped – is that fair ?" Soldiers are seen to be happy returning to Britain on a leave boat and walking through London. The difficulties of moving shells up through the mud of the Somme in horse-panniers (from **IWM 116** *The Battle of the Ancre and the Advance of the Tanks*) are given as the reason for young men in particular being needed.

Notes
Date: on internal evidence of scenes from **IWM 116**, the shrapnel helmets and the RFC 'maternity jacket', this film cannot have been made earlier than autumn 1916. Conscription was introduced in January 1916, making the purpose of this film by no means clear. It is either an oblique call for the non-avoidance of conscription or a private call for men in reserved occupations to volunteer. This second alternative runs contrary to the government policy of the time, and it is unlikely that this film ever received official approval. It may never have been shown.
Remarks: a real puzzler. It would have made sense in 1915, and would have been typical of the style of propaganda, very popular in that year, which appealed to guilt feelings rather than to idealism. But as it stands it seems to serve no useful purpose.
[shotsheet available]
catalogued SDB: 11/1981

IWM 445 · GB, (prod) 1918
[JAPANESE ARMY MANOEUVRES 1918 : sections from Prince Arthur's visit to Japan] (allocated)

b/w · 2 reels · 1513' (25 mins) · silent
intertitles: Japanese & English

sp Ministry of Information *pr* Universal Film Company *prod* Takiguchi, O

- Highly fragmented film (mainly covering extra incidents from **IWM 451** *The Visit of HRH Prince Arthur to Japan*) of Prince Arthur's Japanese tour, June-July 1918.

I. The film consists mainly of the Prince and his party touring Japan in June and July 1918. Some scenes are probably of a major Japanese military exercise carried on in the Prince's presence, involving Infantry with Field Artillery in very flat, waterlogged terrain. The tactics are chiefly the column charge in very close order over open ground. Radio and semaphore signalling are also practised. The second reel in particular shows Prince Arthur's visit to the sights of Japan, including a display of Samurai armour and highly intricate carvings.
II. At the start of the second reel there is an interpolated sequence from the American newsreel *Universal Animated Weekly* showing the visit of Sir Eric Geddes and Vice-Admiral Sir Allen Duff, escorted by US Secretary of the Navy Daniels and Admiral William S Benson, to see US Navy cadets in training.
III. Although most of its captions are in Japanese, this film ends with the English words "Photographed for the British Government by the Universal Film Company under the direction of O Takiguchi".

Notes
Summary: this appears to be a Japanese-

language version of **IWM 451**, or a film closely related to it.
Remarks: valuable for two separate reasons. Firstly, a demonstration of the manner in which the Ministry of Information used the Japanese subsidiary of an American firm in order to obtain its film of Japan; and secondly for its insight into Japanese military tactics, which appear to have absorbed very few of the lessons of the Western Front.
[shotsheet available]
catalogued SDB: 11/1981

IWM 446 · GB, (ca) 1918
HM QUEEN MARY AT CHATHAM AND COVENTRY

b/w · 1 reel · 330' (6 mins) · silent
intertitles: none

■ Highly fragmented film of Queen Mary's visits to Chatham dockyards and to Coventry, possibly 1918.

I. The film opens as the Queen leaves a factory escorted by a mayor. It jumps to her inspecting Royal Marines and Royal Navy ratings drawn up at Chatham. The King is also present, in naval uniform. The film, although very disjointed, apparently shows them leaving.
II. The Queen walks through a civilian crowd and enters her car. She then enters what appears to be a naval hospital and talks to wounded there. Nurses wave goodbye.
III. The Queen escorted by a bishop (of Coventry ?) gets into her car. This is followed by her being introduced to a line of people, including some wounded soldiers. She walks with her party through a crowd of workers at a factory, and watches men and women at work in a factory machine shop, possibly Coventry.

Notes
Title: this is taken from the shotsheet.
Summary: the film is highly fragmented, very difficult to follow, and nothing can be discovered of either its origins or content.
[shotsheet available]
catalogued SDB: 10/1981

IWM 447A · GB, 1918
EVERY LITTLE HELPS (first version)

b/w · 1 reel · 309' (6 mins) · silent
intertitles: English

sp Ministry of Information

■ British propaganda encouraging spare time work and food production (in Essex ?), 1918.

(Opening intertitle refers to a schoolmaster driving a tram: this sequence has been cut out.) A ditching party board vehicles to take them to a "waterlogged farm" – one of the vehicles bears the legend "Ilford Limited, Ilford". (A further title refers to their supervision by the farmer and his dog: this sequence has also been cut.) The men – "all classes, from lawyers to navvies" – are seen digging part of a field and stopping for refreshments. A group of men and women who have taken "seven acres out of town" are seen arriving at a station (on the Woodford train) and working in a field. A horse-drawn plough is seen at work. A group of schoolboys also digs a field. (Further titles refer to boys collecting refuse for pig feed: this sequence has been cut.) The feed is put out for a herd of pigs. "It is the 'little bit more' that counts. What are YOU doing ?"

Notes
Summary: the missing sequences can all be seen (together with additional footage) in version 2, **IWM 447B**. The pigs seen at the end of 447B are a different herd to those seen here.
Remarks: rather less authoritarian in tone than the second version.
catalogued DW: 6/1989

IWM 447B · GB, 1918
EVERY LITTLE HELPS (second version)

b/w · 1 reel · 608' (11 mins) · silent
intertitles: English

sp Ministry of Information

■ British propaganda encouraging spare time work and food production (in Essex ?), 1918.

The film stresses the need for part-time work to win the war. A schoolmaster drives a tram. Ladies make bandages, limb supports and other hospital items. Carpenters make crutches. Elderly part-time workers chop wood in a timber yard. Women collect rhubarb for jam. Schoolchildren collect blackberries which are then taken to a factory. Boys in their mid-teens, wearing school uniform, plant cabbages. Boys of the Naval Brigade collect waste food from door to door as pig feed. Food collected by other boys is loaded into sacks for farmers and given to pigs. Lawyers, businessmen, tradesmen and labourers work to clear a waterlogged ditch on a farm on a Saturday afternoon. The film ends with a message, "You can help. Seek out your local Part-Time Committee and find a job. If you have no such committee, start one. The Ministry of National Service will help you".

Notes
Summary: see **Notes** to the first version, **IWM 447A**.
catalogued SDB: 12/1981

IWM 447X · GB, 1918
EVERY LITTLE HELPS (second version, additional material)

b/w · 1 reel · 340' (6 mins) · silent
intertitles: English

sp Ministry of Information

- Several shots of pigs feeding from troughs (some but not all of these shots are used in **IWM 447B**). Various shots of people making bandages, artificial limbs and crutches (most material used in **IWM 447B**). Harvesting rhubarb and planting cabbages (as in **IWM 447B**). One shot of boys with refuse collected for pig feed (the final shot of the sequence in **IWM 447B**). Further shots of the pigs feeding.

Notes
Summary: this material appears to be additional material filmed for *Every Little Helps*, version 2. The remainder of the second version (apart from the blackberry picking sequence) comes from sequences apparently removed from version 1.
catalogued DW: 6/1989

IWM 448 · GB, 1917
HM KING GEORGE V INSPECTS AMERICAN TROOPS
AMERICAN TROOPS ON BRITISH SOIL – AN EPOCH MAKING INSPECTION BY OUR KING (alternative)

b/w · 1 reel · 211' (4 mins) · silent
intertitles: English

pr HP Company

- King George V visits a training camp for American Railway Engineers at Aldershot, Saturday 28 July 1917.

With the King are the Queen, Princess Mary and the Duke of Connaught. The King talks to the American officers and inspects the troops, who march past. Their commander is Colonel McKingstry. The King inspects the equipment and backpacks of two of the Railway Engineers, Master-Engineer L C Lebering and Master-Engineer W W Francis. Also among the King's party may be Winston Churchill. The King leaves to the cheers of the Americans. The film ends with the Americans taking part in a tug of war with a British team.

Notes
Title: both titles appear on the film.
Intertitles: these are all flashframes.
Summary: this film is probably by a private company under official contract. The identification of Churchill is very tentative.
[*The Times*, 30 July 1917: 6B]
[shotsheet available]
catalogued SDB: 12/1981

IWM 449 · NO FILM

IWM 450 · GB, 6/1917
ANOTHER CHAPTER OF HISTORY UNVEILED

b/w · 1 reel · 787' (13 mins) · silent
intertitles: English

sp War Office Cinema Committee

- Arrival of Lieutenant-General John J Pershing with the first contingent of the US Army in Liverpool, 8 June 1917.

The White Star liner SS *Baltic* comes into Liverpool dock at 9.30am, carrying the American party. Waiting for its arrival are the Lord Mayor and Lady Mayoress of Liverpool, Rear-Admiral Stileman (the commander of naval forces at the port), General Sir Pitcairn Campbell, GOC Western Command, and about fifty newsmen. The guard of honour is 3rd Battalion, the Royal Welch Fusiliers, complete with the regimental goat. The greeting party go on board the *Baltic*, and after a pause the Americans disembark. Pershing inspects the guard of honour. Two of his staff officers appear to be Colonel George Marshall and Major George S

Patton. The meeting then breaks up and the guard of honour leaves. More American soldiers disembark. "Look at them – do they mean it ? Why – sure !!!" Pershing's staff and the remainder of the enlisted men come across footbridges into the harbour. The mail is unloaded from the ship. Pershing formally shakes hands with Campbell. Two of the Americans, on a train, look out for their "first glimpse of London". The train arrives at King's Cross Station, where Pershing shakes hands with the driver and fireman.

Notes
Technical: some of the film is overexposed or of poor quality.
[*The Times*, 9 June 1917: 7C]
[shotsheet available]
catalogued SDB: 11/1981

IWM 451 · GB/Japan, 1918
the VISIT OF HIS ROYAL HIGHNESS PRINCE ARTHUR TO JAPAN

b/w · 7 reels · 5576' (94 mins) · silent
intertitles: English

sp Ministry of Information (?) *pr* Universal Film Company (?) *dir* Takiguchi, O (?)

■ Prince Arthur's state visit to present the Emperor of Japan with the honorary rank of Field Marshal, June-July 1918.

(Reel 1) Partly through the limitations imposed on the filming of Japanese royalty and inside the various palaces, this film shows virtually nothing of the official ceremonies. The first half concentrates on Prince Arthur in person, the second half on the scenery and culture of Japan. With Prince Arthur are the Earl of Pembroke, the Master of Sinclair, and General Sir William Pulteney. Acting as escort is the British Ambassador Sir Conyngham Greene, with Admiral Ijuin and Count Inouye. For his official duties the Prince wears his Army and diplomatic uniforms. The party arrives at Yokohama harbour (past the battle-cruiser *Hiei*) and *(Reel 2)* on to Tokyo where between parties the ceremonies take place. The Prince visits the tomb of General Nogi, hero of the Russo-Japanese War, and *(Reel 3)* is addressed by Prince Tokugawa in Shinjuku Imperial Park. *(Reel 4)* The Prince starts his informal tour of Japan with visits to Nagoya, *(Reel 5)* to Kyoto, the old capital, including the tomb of the Emperor Meiji, and a trip down the valley of the Hozu Kawa to Arashiyama. *(Reel 6)* A tour of the

Biwa (the inland sea of Japan) begins at Karasaki and looks mainly at religious shrines. *(Reel 7)* The party visits Osaka, "the Manchester of Japan, also called the Venice of Japan" including, Luna Park, "the Earl's Court of Japan". The trip also includes a visit to the headquarters of 4th Division in the arsenal of the medieval castle of Osaka. Finally, the Prince visits the home of Baron Sumitoma at Suma on the inland sea.

Notes
Shotsheet: a detailed shotsheet and analysis of the film has been prepared and is held on file in the Department of Film.
Summary: this is the English-language (with occasional mistakes) version of a film probably made by the Japanese branch of the American Universal Film Company. This version is clearly aimed at the British, not American, market. It is probably incomplete. See also **IWM 445**, which seems to be a Japanese-language version of parts of the same film. The transliteration of Japanese words given in the summary is as they appear on the film itself.
[shotsheet available]
catalogued SDB: 11/1981

IWM 452 · GB, 7/1918
TRAINING THE TANKS

b/w · 1 reel · 666' (11 mins) · silent
intertitles: English

sp Ministry of Information *pr* Topical Film Company

■ Compilation piece from other films on the British use of the tank in the First World War.

The film consists of unedited, unrelated scenes of Mk I and Mk IV tanks, at the Tank Corps training school at Bovington, on the Western Front, and in Palestine. It opens with unarmed Mk IV tanks in a training exercise at Bovington, crushing barbed wire defences and dragging a tree trunk out of a wood. In Palestine, the Mk I Male HMLS "Otazel" followed by the Female HMLS "Nut" cross a training trench. At Tank Corps headquarters in France in July 1917 two Mk IV tanks have a race for the benefit of King George V. Mk I tanks move into position during the early stages of the Battle of the Ancre in 1916. The final scene is a return to the exercises at Bovington.

Notes
Summary: see also **IWM 17** *The New*

Crusaders, **IWM 116** *The Battle of the Ancre and the Advance of the Tanks*, **IWM 198** *The Royal Visit to the Battlefields of France, July 1917* and **IWM 337** *Tanks – the Wonder Weapon.*
[shotsheet available]
catalogued SDB: 12/1981

IWM 453 · GB (?), (?) 1918
BRITISH SOLDIERS INTERNED IN SWITZERLAND

b/w · 1 reel · 730' (13 mins) · silent
intertitles: none

■ Arrival of British soldiers, mostly being repatriated via Switzerland as seriously wounded prisoners, at Interlaken, 1918.

The soldiers' train arrives at the station. Some are walking wounded, some are stretcher cases. The Swiss guards who help them are wearing the pre-1916 Swiss uniform with the shako, rather than combat uniform. Some of the British cross to another train. They are wearing either very dark khaki or hospital blues, but most have their regimental caps. Led by pipers, the men march to the Kursaal (in the main square) accompanied by Swiss officials and British military and naval officers. Some civilians gather to meet them, including the British consul, Sir Horace Rumbold, with his family, and the Swiss Major de la Harp, who is responsible for the soldiers' welfare. In a hall equipped for the soldiers some of them are presented with decorations.

Notes
Title: this is taken from the shotsheet.
Production: this film is either British official material taken directly for the MoI in Switzerland, or acquired via the Foreign Office for British purposes from a Swiss firm.
[shotsheet available]
catalogued SDB: 12/1981

IWM 454 · Switzerland, 7/1918
la SUISSE JOUE PARMI LES NATIONS LE ROLE DU BON SAMARITAIN
SWITZERLAND ACTS AS GOOD SAMARITAN TO THE NATIONS (translation)

b/w · 1 reel · 685' (11 mins) · silent
intertitles: French

pr Compagnie Générale du Cinématographie de Genève

■ Refugees from Eastern Europe arriving by train, being cared for, and reunited with their families before returning home, Basle, Switzerland, 1918.

The film states that between 5 March 1915 and 15 April 1918 over 370 000 refugees (57 000 men, 190 000 women and 123 000 children) passed through Switzerland. It does not make it clear from where they came, or whether they were permitted to stay, to return to their own country of origin, or to go elsewhere. The greatest emphasis is laid on the Swiss organisation of the scheme. This starts with a posed group of the senior Red Cross nurses at Basle: president Mlle M Paravicini, Mlle H Paravicini who is in charge of the hospital, Mme A Clavel who is in charge of clothing and Mme Wolf-Paravicini who is in charge of the nursery. It is stressed that both the nurses and the refugees come from all social classes. The refugee train arrives at Basle station, and the nurses help the refugees, mainly old people or women with children, to disembark. Some are taken to another train, where the children are bathed. The Enquiry Bureau tries to unite the families as they arrive. The children are given new clothes and small gifts or toys, including little Swiss flags. The people board another train to take them to "the land of their birth, but not to their homes".

Notes
Production: although Swiss in origin this film, or a version of it in the English language, appears to have been issued in Britain by the MoI.
[shotsheet available]
catalogued SDB: 12/1981

IWM 455 · GB (?), (?) 1918
BRITISH SOLDIERS INTERNED IN HOLLAND

b/w · 1 reel · 968' (16 mins) · silent
intertitles: English

sp Ministry of Information (?)

■ Treatment of British soldiers interned in Holland by the Dutch authorities, 1918.

The troops interned in Holland include members of the original BEF of 1914, crashed airmen, shipwrecked sailors and men in the process of repatriation from German prisoner of war camps. A large group is posed outside the camp huts. The next clear scene shows the men's dormitories, with soldiers reading and mail being distributed. The men learn new trades, working at desks, reading, in the carpentry shop or repairing boots. On the sea front they fraternise with girls in Dutch national costume. The remainder of the film is taken up mainly by a sports meeting between the interned British and members of the Dutch armed forces at the Hague. Some of the British spectators are wearing hospital blues. The sports include sprints, a hurdling race and a pole-vault. Other entertainment comes from a black-face comedian who clowns for spectators and the camera, and mock-conducts the military band. Back in the internment camp, the men dig the gardens and practise woodwork. One posed group is of a few members of the original BEF. The final scene shows some of the internees in a café at Scheveningen talking and drinking with Dutch civilians.

Notes
Summary: the film is badly disjointed, tending to jump or stay too long on one subject, making it difficult to follow. It was probably made by a Dutch firm, and possibly even for the Dutch Government. *Remarks:* long, dreary and poorly composed. Furthermore, with a very little change in the captions, this could easily have been a German propaganda film. In its anxiety to stress that interned British troops are being well treated, it carries the implicit message that desertion or escape to a neutral country would bring a life of considerable ease.
[shotsheet available]
catalogued SDB: 12/1981

IWM 456 · GB, (?) 1918
SOUTH AMERICA'S MESSAGE TO THE ALLIES

b/w · 2 reels · 2531' (42 mins) · silent
intertitles: English

sp Ministry of Information (?)

■ British mission to South America led by Sir Maurice de Bunsen, October 1918.

I. *(Reel 1)* The mission visited Brazil, Uruguay, Ecuador and Argentina. Accompanying Sir Maurice (with white beard) were Lieutenant-General Sir Charles Baxter, Mr Follett Holt, Mr T H Lyons, Mr Alan Kerr, Rear-Admiral James C Lay, Mr W S Barclay and Mr J Grant. The film is disjointed and it is not always clear which of

the various countries they are in.
II. The Uruguayan reception committee waits for the members of the mission at the Brazilian frontier. The mission arrives at Santa Anna de Libramiento, and is met by military and civilian officials. The mission arrives by train at Montevideo, being met by a Dr Delgado and escorted to the Parque Hotel. Later the mission goes to Government House to meet President Feliciano Vera. On the way, "in their enthusiasm for the cause of the Allies the crowd gave the British mission such a hearty welcome that it broke through the lines of the police". Next is Argentina, where the mission is received at Government House, Buenos Aires. *(Reel 2)* The light cruiser HMS *Newcastle* is in harbour at the time. Its captain, Commodore Aubrey C H Smith, comes ashore with Rear-Admiral Lay. A party of sailors from the *Newcastle* comes ashore and is entertained to a meal by the Argentine Government. The mission is meanwhile involved in a tour of the city, including a visit to the "National Hippodrome" for a horse race meeting and numerous encounters with fashionable society. In Rosario the mission visits the Jockey Club and watches another race. A portrait shot of the mission. Finally, the mission inspects Buenos Aires harbour before leaving on the small tug SS *Marie* for HMS *Newcastle*.

Notes
Summary: probably never shown in this form, the film has the hallmarks of an indifferent English-language version of a piece intended for the South American market.
Remarks: over-long and disjointed, valuable mainly for the horse race sequences and the various fashions worn by the women in Buenos Aires.
[shotsheet available]
catalogued SDB: 12/1981

IWM 457 · GB, 1918
FROM SOLDIER TO CIVILIAN

b/w · 1 reel · 370' (6 mins) · silent
intertitles: English

sp Ministry of Information *pr* Kinsella and Morgan

■ Partly-acted film on the discharge and relocation in civilian work of British soldiers who have served long periods on the Western Front, 1918.

Soldiers make an attack from the trenches. One such soldier (in an acted sequence) is handed his discharge notice in the trench by an officer. The men who have been discharged board a ship to cross the English Channel, arriving in Britain. From there they march to the railhead (this is actually still France). A train carrying discharged men arrives at Ripon station, and the men buy food in a nearby café (again, probably a French estaminet). Some travel in wagons and others march to the discharge centre. Each man is registered and issued with blankets. They are interviewed, medically examined and given civilian clothes. This particular group has been allocated to a shipyard as Army Reserve Munition Workers. They are told their duties by an officer and taken by wagon, lorry and train to the shipyard. Two of the men work as riveters. An incomplete cargo ship is launched from the slipway.

Notes
Title: this is taken from the shotsheet.
Intertitles: these are all flashframes.
Summary: the film contains a high proportion of staged or faked material.
[shotsheet available]
catalogued SDB: 12/1981

IWM 458 · USA, 1918
AMERICA'S ANSWER TO THE HUN

b/w · 4 reels · 3357' (57 mins) · silent
intertitles: English

sp US Committee of Public Information for Ministry of Information *pr* US Signal Corps

■ American contribution to the war effort on the Western Front, summer 1918.

I. The film is often disjointed, but covers the transfer of American manpower and material across the Atlantic, culminating in their first major engagement in the Battle of Château-Thierry in June 1918. The captioning is outspoken – "The time has come when it is America's high privilege to spend her blood upon the fields of battle already hallowed by the sacrifice of her Allies' stalwart sons" – with constant emphasis on the scale of American industrial might. "One million Americans" are in Europe, American shipping has increased by "more than two million tons", a steel and concrete landing dock is "three miles long", and a refrigeration plant is "the third largest in the world".
II. *(Reel 1)* American gunners on the

Western Front open fire with French-built 155mm howitzers and 75mm field guns. To supply these men cargo vessels cross the Atlantic under escort, unloading troops and equipment in France. *(Reel 2)* Locomotives are assembled (Austrian prisoners of war help in the work), and cars and lorries are unloaded. The troops move forward on foot and by train to their base villages, and from their trenches launch an attack through a wood. The resulting wounded are loaded onto a hospital train for a base hospital. *(Reel 3)* Trainee pilots are taught to fly French-built Nieuport 17 and 27 fighters, together with veterans of the volunteer Escadrille Lafayette, now part of the elite 94th 'Hat in the Ring' Pursuit Squadron, including Raoul Lufberry, Douglas Campbell and Alan Winslow. Back in the battle zone shells for the 75mm and 155mm guns are moved up. American soldiers eat in the trenches. The French commander, General Passaga, at Boucq on 25 April 1918 presents the Croix de guerre to Colonel Shelton, Major Doane and Chaplain de Valles of the US 104th Infantry Regiment, decorating some of the men, and pinning the Croix de guerre on the regimental colours. The ceremony is watched by the divisional commander, Major-General Clarence R Edwards (26th Division). Major Theodore Roosevelt Jr decorates men of his own battalion of 26th Infantry Regiment at Bois-l'Evêque on 5 April 1918. American 400mm railway guns of 53rd Artillery Corps north of Mailly on 15 May, with 320mm Schneider railway guns. *(Reel 4)* French, British and US troops, including some wounded, talking together near Château-Thierry. As the bombardment opens on the front, lorries and columns of soldiers move up, and ambulances carry the wounded. General John Pershing addresses his staff in the open air. President Wilson makes a speech. The American celebration march through Paris, 4 July 1918. The film ends abruptly with a brief mention of Britain, "so long as Britannia rules the waves, democracy is safe".

Notes
Summary: this film was made specially for British consumption and released via the MoI. The very abrupt ending indicates that it may well be incomplete. For the 'Hat in the Ring' sequence see **IWM 250**, and also **IWM 176**.
Remarks: the film, despite this copy being flawed, gives a good impressionistic overview of the American picture of themselves in the war. It is not noticeably superior, either in the quality of its material

or construction, to the average British war film of the period. One sequence of gunners working behind scrim in bright sunlight produces a very lovely 'dappled' effect.
[shotsheet available]
catalogued SDB: 1/1982

IWM 459 · Italy, 1918
AMID SNOW AND ICE ON MOUNT TONALE

b/w · 2 reels · 1654' (29 mins) · silent
intertitles: English

pr Italian Army, Cinematographic Section

■ Italian official film of the Italian Front just before their final offensive of June-July 1918.

(Reel 1) Food, fodder and equipment are unloaded at a railhead freightyard, and put into motorised and horse-drawn vehicles for the trip up to Mount Tonale and the River Piave valley. The convoys move along the mountain road through small villages to the snowline, where Alpini are resting and a siege gun, probably a Mortier de 220mm TR Mle 1916, is firing. An aerial cableway takes the load up above the snowline. From Austrian positions captured on 25 May it is possible to see up into the peaks and down into the Camonica valley to the village of Ponte di Legno. *(Reel 2)* Alpini carry dismantled Maxim machineguns and mountain guns up to their positions where they reassemble and fire them. A senior officer (General Cadorna ?) and his staff cross a rope bridge over a crevasse to their command post. A light railway track, taking flatcars pulled by mules, has been built over the snow, in some cases tunnelling through it. Other transport includes dog sledges and skis. Giant mortars, of the conventional 'stovepipe' shape but 2-3 metres long, bombard the Austrian positions, with the Mortier de 220mm (?) joining in. Alpini in position wearing snow suits, on Mount Presena and "hill 2921" where they have captured Austrian mountain guns, rifles and stores. Austrian prisoners come down from the mountain under escort, are fed and marched down again to the collecting station.

Notes
Production: the English-language version of an Italian official film.
[shotsheet available]
catalogued SDB: 1/1982

IWM 460 · Italy, 1918
the OTHER ITALIAN ARMY

b/w · 2 reels · 1606' (27 mins) · silent
intertitles: English

sp Italian Ministry of Munitions

■ Italian official film of the expansion of munitions production in Italy between 1914 and 1917.

The film uses actuality, graphics and animation to make the contrast between production in 1914 and 1917. *(Reel 1)* Factories run by the Army Training School for injured soldiers, including one run by "Colonial volunteers", probably from Italian Tripolitania. The massive increase in the number of women workers in munitions is shown. A grassy field in 1914 has become a massive armaments factory. Shell manufacture includes work with white-hot metal and making gas shells. Motor vehicle output has increased, including cars specially designed for mountains and fording rivers. Graphics show that "the Italian motor cars at the end of 1914 would have embodied one motor car capable of carrying the Leaning Tower of Pisa, whilst the motor cars now available might easily carry the Colosseum of Rome". The Fiat Tipo 2000 Model 17 tank is tested. *(Reel 2)* Aircraft and airship production has expanded. An airship is shown emerging from its hangar, with the armament, control car and bomb-dropping mechanism shown in detail. Aeroplane construction is followed by a Caproni Ca 42 bomber taking off. A coastal motor boat section at a quay. Naval gunnery. "And thus from the depths of the soil, from the strenuous efforts of the workshops, and the cohesion of thought and soul, Italy supplies her watchful sons with the weapons they are in need of for the final victory against barbarism." A sustained battle piece (some fakes) of a bombardment by Italian guns, including the standard Cannone da 75/27 modello 12 field gun, the 149/35 siege gun, the 152/45 siege gun and the Mortier de 220mm, followed by Italian soldiers rushing forward in broken country. A kite balloon spots for the guns, and searchlights are used at night. "And where the Italian bayonets victoriously passed, the plough will furrow amid hymns of victory and peace, the ground moistened with the blood of Italian heroes", showing a final charge fading into peasants ploughing with their oxen.

Notes
Summary: an English-language version of

an Italian film.
Remarks: a comparatively sophisticated and entertaining film, showing a number of techniques in the use of graphics and wipes which were to become clichés twenty years later but are surprising in a First World War film. This compares very favourably indeed with its British equivalent, **IWM 161** *Woolwich Arsenal and its Workers.*
[shotsheet available]
catalogued SDB: 1/1982

IWM 461a · GB, 3/10/1918
PICTORIAL NEWS (OFFICIAL) 371-1 [1]

b/w · 1 reel · 65' (1 min) · silent
intertitles: none

sp Ministry of Information *pr* Topical Film Company

- Bombardment by the gunboat HMS *Moth* from the bank of the Euphrates, Mesopotamian Front, summer 1918.

Notes
Title: the store ledger title is *Serbian Children Arrive in England*, which is an item on the newsreel issue of which this film is a fragment, but which does not itself appear to exist any longer.
Summary: see also **IWM 71** for this item. Note that another item from this issue is **IWM 461c**, later in the reel.
[shotsheet available]
catalogued SDB: 1/1982

IWM 461b · GB, 30/9/1918
PICTORIAL NEWS (OFFICIAL) 370-2

b/w · 1 reel · 81' (2 mins) · silent
intertitles: none

sp Ministry of Information *pr* Topical Film Company

- Single story from the newsreel held in a more complete form (in a French version) as **IWM 652b**. The item shows British soldiers clearing up debris in Béthune after the German retreat, September 1918.

[shotsheet available]
catalogued SDB: 1/1982

IWM 461c · GB, 3/10/1918
PICTORIAL NEWS (OFFICIAL) 371-1 [2]

b/w · 1 reel · 48' (1 min) · silent
intertitles: none

sp Ministry of Information *pr* Topical Film Company

- Private R E Cruickshank receives a gold watch from Lieutenant-General R S S Baden-Powell, Tottenham, London, 28 September 1918.

The ceremony takes place in a park. A crowd of boy scouts watches as Baden-Powell, the Chief Scout, presents Cruickshank, a former scout and VC winner with the London Scottish, with a gold watch on behalf of Cruickshank's employers, Lipton's.

Notes
Summary: note that another English item from this issue is **IWM 461a**.
[shotsheet available]
catalogued SDB: 1/1982

IWM 461d · GB, 7/10/1918
PICTORIAL NEWS (OFFICIAL) 371-2

b/w · 1 reel · 171' (2 mins) · silent
intertitles: none

sp Ministry of Information *pr* Topical Film Company

I. British troops advancing up the Cambrai Road in the Advance to Victory, Western Front, September 1918. The forces are mainly from the Cavalry Corps, including not only horsemen but Austin armoured cars, improvised armoured lorries, pontoon bridging wagons and cyclists, all in a headlong rush up the road.
II. British troops escorting German prisoners through the rear areas of the Western Front, September 1918. The prisoners are led through Cambrai. Portrait shots of two of the prisoners, one in helmet, greatcoat and spectacles, the other in a service cap.

Notes
Remarks: the advance up the Cambrai Road gives an excellent impression of a headlong pursuit.
[shotsheet available]
catalogued SDB: 1/1982

IWM 462 · GB, (ca) 1918
NACB GAZETTE

b/w · 1 reel · 650' (11 mins) · silent
intertitles: English

sp National Army Canteen Board

- Construction and ceremonial opening of a new theatre at Catterick Army Training Camp, probably immediately post-1918.

The style and tone of the film are light with attempts at humour. Its stated policy is that "items of camp interest will be specially filmed and displayed in the Board's Garrison Theatres and Cinemas from time to time". The controller of the camp, Lieutenant-Colonel Frank Towle, is shown with Sir George May cutting the first sod for the theatre. Soldiers work on its construction. The finished theatre is a permanent brick structure. For the opening the soldiers file inside, organised by Captain Stanley Hicks. The audience includes nurses and officer cadets (with the white cap-bands). The artistes arrive by car: Thorpe Bates, Douglas Furber, Mme Gleeson-White, Miss Lillian Hoare and Percy Kahn. The party of distinguished guests include the Marquis and Marchioness of Zetland, the Bishop of Ripon with his archdeacon, the headquarters staff of the Reserve Centre, the GOC-in-C Northern Command, Sir John Maxwell, the Lord Lieutenant of North Riding, Sir Hugh Bell, with Lady Bell, and bringing up the rear as guest of honour, the Duke of Connaught. All are shown entering the theatre, and the Duke's party is shown leaving, but the interior of the theatre is not shown.

Notes
Date: according to the Army List, Sir John Maxwell was GOC-in-C Northern Command from January 1917 until September 1919.
[shotsheet available]
catalogued SDB: 1/1982

IWM 463 · GB, (ca) 1917
ARMY SERVICE CORPS

b/w · 2 reels · 1474' (24 mins) · silent
intertitles: none

- Jumbled, out-of-sequence film of the Army Service Corps during the First World War, containing two main themes and a collection of unrelated scenes, all in England.

I. The first main theme is civilian recruits volunteering for the ASC outside the Central Recruiting Office in Whitehall, London. They are marched to the railway station. Arriving at a suburban station they are formed up and marched to the barracks, where they are inspected and issued with uniforms and equipment.
II. The second main theme is of ASC troops preparing to leave their camp, probably for active service. The men are inspected and their methods of folding their kit are checked. The officers are issued with their orders. The departing troops, in 3-ton lorries (mainly Thornycroft, some Maudslay) are cheered by other members of the ASC, ambulance drivers who wait beside the road for their departure. The soldiers, as they wait, are handed mail and their pay-books. They cheer the camera.
III. The remaining scenes are related to neither main theme. A group of ASC soldiers waiting in the road beside their depot joke with two passing lady bicyclists before being called to order and marched away. Rifle range practice. A pay parade for motor transport drivers. Distribution of letters. A mastiff, the depot mascot. Unloading packages from 3-ton lorries. ASC carpenters and blacksmiths at work by the roadside. A joke boxing match, including one blindfold bout, and a mop fight. Soldiers watching some form of entertainment while eating indoors. A demonstration of how to get a lorry out of a ditch with a tow-rope. A group of ASC soldiers, one walking on his hands for the camera. A meal out of doors. Two soldiers writing home (staged). An ASC driver shaving by using the window of his lorry as a mirror.

Notes
Title: this is taken from the shotsheet.
Intertitles: these are MS flashframes.
Summary: this is probably British official film. Note that while the scenes are given in a coherent order in the summary they are completely jumbled in the film as it stands.
Remarks: worthless as a film in its current condition, but the recruiting section in particular, if isolated and reassembled, could be quite good.
[shotsheet available]
catalogued SDB: 1/1982

IWM 464 · NO FILM

IWM 465 · GB, (?) 1918
OUR HEROIC CANADIAN BROTHERS

b/w · 2 reels · 1428' (25 mins) · silent
intertitles: English

pr Pathé

■ British film of the Canadian Corps forces
in Britain and on the Western Front,
1917-18.

I. *(Reel 1)* A parade by Canadian 207th
Battalion, led by Lieutenant-Colonel C W
McLean, to lay up their colours in
Westminster Abbey, probably just prior to
the battalion's absorption into 6th Reserve
Battalion on 2 June 1917. Canadian soldiers
in France parading to vote in the general
election on 17 December 1917. A village,
probably Vimy area, being shelled, filmed
from some distance away. Canadians,
probably of 3rd Division, holding a pay
parade in a shell-damaged village. A
brigade paraded to celebrate the 50th
anniversary of the Canadian Confederation
on 1 June 1917 with a service, watched by
Lieutenant-General Currie, the Canadian
Corps commander, and General Horne,
commander of First Army. Rubble and
remains of the village of Vimy; a company
of 42nd Battalion (Royal Highlanders of
Canada) returns from the village. *(Reel 2)*
Engineers, British or more probably
Canadians, constructing and operating a
narrow gauge railway. Firstly, horse-drawn
scoops flatten out the path, then complete
sections of rail, with sleepers already
attached, are laid. Flatcars are loaded with
8-inch shells and sent forward on the
railway from the dump, past "Piccadilly" and
"Crucifix" junctions to an 8-inch Mk V
howitzer battery.

Notes
Technical: it is possible that the second reel
does not belong with the first reel.
Remarks: if all this film is genuinely by
Pathé, it represents about the closest to the
front lines a cameraman who was not
controlled by an official body could expect
to be able to work.
[shotsheet available]
catalogued SDB: 1/1982

IWM 466 · GB, 1917
**the CANADIAN VICTORY AT
COURCELETTE : and the advance of the
tanks**

b/w · 3 reels · 2897' (48 mins) · silent

intertitles: English

sp War Office Cinema Committee for
Canadian War Records Office *pr* Topical
Film Company (?) *cam* Bovill, F O

I. Canadian soldiers voting in the Canadian
elections while on the Western Front, 17
December 1917.
II. Slightly jumbled film of the Canadian
forces in the Battle of Flers-Courcelette. No
tanks appear. Western Front, September
1916. *(Reel 1)* Albert basilica, mid-1916.
The Canadian 6th Brigade, 2nd Division, led
by Brigadier-General H D B Ketchen (past
German prisoners) towards the battlefield,
halts to rest at La Boisselle crossroads
before entering the trench system. A kite
balloon is raised to direct fire from 9.2-inch
howitzers. A BE2d of the RFC is bombed-up
with 112-pound, 40-pound, 20-pound and
phosphorous bombs (shown in detail)
before taking off. Ground crews signal to
the aircraft with identification panels. The
aircraft directs the fire of a 4.5-inch howitzer
battery. Carrier pigeons, taken forward,
return to a mobile loft. *(Reel 2)* A 12-inch
siege howitzer, 15-inch siege howitzer and
8-inch siege howitzer battery are directed
by Forward Observation Officers (FOOs)
onto their targets. More 8-inch shells are
brought forward, while British 18-pounders
and French 75mm guns join in. The
Canadians attack and prisoners from the
German 45th Reserve Division come back.
(Reel 3) Walking wounded, stretcher cases
and prisoners filter back to the front line
dressing stations and are evacuated by
ambulance or on foot. Canadian soldiers
watch from a safe distance as the Germans
counter-attack at the sugar factory. As they
are led back the German prisoners are
allowed to wash, "Fritz indulges in an
unfamiliar exercise", in a nearby pond.
Other Germans are shown dead, "some of
the Huns who did not get out of their trench
in time". The captured trenches at
Courcelette are a shapeless mass. Inside a
field hospital surgery is performed on
serious cases. Canadian dead are buried in
shrouds in a permanent military cemetery
after the battle.
III. Graves and a memorial to the dead of
the Canadian forces in the Battle of Vimy
Ridge, Western Front, summer 1917. The
memorial reads "To the Memory of the
Officers, NCOs and Men of the 2nd
Canadian Division and the 13th Infantry
Brigade who Fell in the Capture of Vimy
Ridge on April 9th 1917", and is followed by
a scene of graves being tended in a military
cemetery.

Notes
Title: despite being of Courcelette, this film has every appearance of being mistitled. The original *Canadian Victory at Courcelette* was probably a version made for Canadian audiences of **IWM 116** *The Battle of the Ancre and the Advance of the Tanks.* What appear to be fragments of this can be seen as **IWM 1180.** This film is Canadian material, as opposed to British material adopted for Canadians.
Summary: see also **IWM 130** for some of the same material.
Remarks: the captioning shows a snide and sarcastic hostility to the Germans very different from either the passionate anger of the French or the deliberately neutral tones of the British.
[shotsheet available]
catalogued SDB: 1/1982

IWM 467 · GB, 1917
VIMY RIDGE

b/w · 1 reel · 917' (16 mins) · silent
intertitles: English

sp War Office Cinema Committee for Canadian War Records Office *cam* Bovill, F O

■ Animated and actuality material of the Canadians in the Battle of Vimy Ridge, Western Front, 9-12 April 1917.

I. Animated graphics of a map of the battle, showing the initial dispositions, divisional boundaries, and the three phases of the Canadian offensive. The animation includes a representation of the rolling barrage in front of the attack.
II. Fragments of actuality film of the Canadian second line and rear areas during the battle from the second day, 10 April, onwards. This includes a brief scene of a kite observation balloon ascending, and a faked view from the observer's basket out over the trenches. Canadians of 3rd Division, including 42nd Battalion (Royal Highlanders of Canada) move up. Mounted troops, probably 9th Cavalry Brigade, 1st Cavalry Division, trot up a road with German prisoners being led back in the other direction. Men of the Royal Highlanders of Canada digging in. German guns and mortars captured on Vimy Ridge, chiefly 77mm field guns and mortars such as the 170mm heavy Minenwerfer and 76mm light mortar.

Notes
Summary: the poor quality of the actuality

material in this film led to Oscar Bovill being dismissed as Canadian official cameraman.
Technical: the graphics and actuality material were probably once interspersed in some manner, but it is not possible to reconstruct this.
Remarks: excellent and even amusing graphics marred by routine and poor actuality material.
[shotsheet available]
catalogued SDB: 1/1982

IWM 468 · GB, (ca) 1919
HOLMES LECTURE FILM
WAR AT FIRST HAND (former ledger title)

b/w · 5 reels · 5306' (89 mins) · silent
intertitles: none

■ Compilation of British official film to support an unknown lecture on the First World War, probably compiled immediately post-1918.

Five reels of stockshots of the Western Front, with no apparent theme or linking sequence. The majority of the material for all but the final reel comes from **IWM 191** *The Battle of the Somme.* The majority of the material for the last reel comes from **IWM 344** *Ypres – the Shell-Shattered City of Flanders* [1918 version] with fragments and items from a number of other films. All the material is British official film.

Notes
Title: this is taken from the shotsheet.
Summary: Nothing is known about either Holmes or his lectures. It would be in keeping for the IWM to ask for a print of a film made from British official material. Besides the sources noted in the summary, most of this film comes from **IWM 3, IWM 17, IWM 113, IWM 116, IWM 128, IWM 130, IWM 191, IWM 198, IWM 206, IWM 207, IWM 220, IWM 226, IWM 344** and **IWM 410.**
[shotsheet available]
catalogued SDB: 2/1982

IWM 469 · GB, 5/1917
GAUMONT GRAPHIC 534 – GRAND RECEPTION OF THE RUSSIAN TROOPS AT MARSEILLES BY THE FRENCH

b/w · 1 reel · 252' (5 mins) · silent
intertitles: none

pr Gaumont

• Arrival of the Russian Army Contingent at Marseilles, 20 April 1916.

A transport ship, the *Amiral Latouche Théville*, with Russian soldiers lining its decks, is towed into Marseilles harbour. Waiting is a predominantly French reception committee, with officers from the other Allies, including Britain. A French hussar regiment waits on parade with drawn sabres. The film changes to a view from a high window overlooking the march of the Russian Contingent, led by its band, through the streets to the cheers of civilians.

[shotsheet available]
catalogued SDB: 10/1981

IWM 470 · GB, 19/6/1916
the DESTRUCTION OF A FOKKER : our mobile anti-aircraft guns in action
OFFICIAL PICTURES OF THE BRITISH ARMY IN FRANCE – FIFTH SERIES (series)

b/w · 1 reel · 382' (6 mins) · silent
intertitles: English

sp War Office *pr* British Topical Committee for War Films *cam* Malins, Geoffrey H and/or Tong, E G (?)

• British 13-pounder anti-aircraft mobile batteries shoot down a German aircraft, Western Front, January 1916.

The film includes some fakes and a large number of stockshots. It concerns a battery of two 13-pounder Mk III anti-aircraft guns mounted on Thorneycroft lorries by Mk I lorry mounts, together with their fire control. The captain in charge sights an enemy aircraft (never actually seen) through his telescope, the details are set out on the ranging board and the men of the battery called out. The guns open fire, and as the target aircraft moves past them the lorries drive in pursuit to a new site where they again deploy and open fire. Fire control keeps track with telescopes and rangefinders. A second battery, with 13-pounder 9cwt anti-aircraft guns, joins in. The men cheer as the enemy aircraft plunges out of the sky. It is seen falling, burning while balancing on its nose, then burning on the ground (this last sequence is clearly a fake, and not recognisably a Fokker aircraft).

Notes
Cameraman: this was either Malins or Tong,

or both.
Remarks: it is interesting that the German aircraft should be described specifically as a Fokker. This may be intended as a kind of ritual exorcism – showing the vulnerability of a currently legendary enemy – but then again it may just reflect that 'Fokker' (with its convenient hint of double entendre) is a useful shorthand for 'enemy combat aircraft'.
[shotsheet available]
catalogued SDB: 1/1982

IWM 471 · GB, (ca) 1920
TACTICAL SECTION DRILL 'A' MGC

b/w · 1 reel · 1011' (18 mins) · silent
intertitles: English

sp War Office, General Staff

• British Machine Gun Corps training film on the tactical use of the Vickers machinegun in open country, 1918-1922.

The film uses a mixture of line drawings, animation and actuality material. The exercise is for a Vickers machinegun section of gunner, loader and two carriers, under the instruction of a lieutenant, with a sergeant watching the whole exercise in order to criticise the actions of each man in the debriefing. All are members of the Machine Gun Corps. The setting is an area of rolling countryside with enclosed fields, a few houses, but no trenches, strong points or Artillery support on either side. The officer takes the section number 1 (the gunner) forward with him by walk and crawl to reconnoitre the intended position, and there gives him his sector and the range and nature of his target – a gate in a hedge just beyond a red-roofed house 1000 yards distant. The number 1 returns to his section and briefs its members. At the officer's signal the section moves up to its position under cover of a hedge. The number 1 reconnoitres the sector and personally selects the site for his machinegun, which is then set up. Each section member in turn then checks the view along the gun's sights to the target. Finally, in the debriefing, the sergeant checks the line of the gun to the target, the manner in which the gun has been set up, the range on the sight, and the actions of each section member. The machinegun does not actually open fire.

Notes
Date: the Machine Gun Corps was created in 1916 and disbanded in 1922. This film

was obviously made for training in open warfare, and therefore probably after 1918. *Remarks:* although extremely interesting, in that it envisages open warfare so soon after the end of the First World War, this has a number of defects as a training film. It is hard to know exactly whom it is meant to instruct, the rank and file of the MGC or their instructors. It covers the duties of neither adequately.
[shotsheet available]
catalogued SDB: 2/1982

IWM 472 · NO FILM

IWM 473 · France, 1917
EXODUS OF THE POPULATION
RUINED VILLAGES OF FRANCE (ledger title)

b/w · 4 reels · 2749' (46 mins) · silent
intertitles: English

sp Section Cinématographique de l'Armée Française

- English-language version of a French film of German damage to French property, mainly in the Retreat to the Hindenburg Line, February-March 1917.

Damage in the Roye-Soissons area, showing many of the smaller towns and villages. Destroyed fruit trees. A desecrated cemetery at Tergnier. Damaged houses at Coucy-la-Ville and Coucy-le-Château. The French have highlighted the damage with signs such as "Musée Souvenir de la Kultur Boche". Damage to the station at Roye. Damage to the abbey at Mont des Cats to the north. Back to the River Somme area with a damaged calvary at Crapeaumesnil (just south of Roye), damaged churches at Beaulieu and at Lassigny, and more damage at Chauny. Damage to factories in the Rheims area. Back to Chauny, and Vauxrot (just north of Soissons). A mounted patrol moves in the wake of the German retreat. Seraucourt sugar factory is rubble. The sugar factory at Flavy-le-Martel (north of Noyon) is ruined. A political fact-finding mission visits the area. Agricultural equipment has been wrecked at Trosly-Loire. The glassworks is destroyed at Neuvillette (? this is east of St-Quentin and still in German hands). At Corbie factories are in ruins. Refugees are taken by trains to Paris and relocated elsewhere. At Soissons the cathedral is badly damaged. The village

of Trescourt is wrecked. French soldiers take part in worship in the rubble of the church at Missy-sur-Aisne (just north of Soissons). Near Verdun there is a pilgrimage of children, led by religious leaders, to the front lines. At Rheims the cathedral façade is intact but the roof is damaged and the floor covered with rubble, Cardinal Luçon and Monsignor Neven of the cathedral point out the damage. Another damaged calvary at Mont Renaud. Further north, at the Scherpenberg (just south of Ypres) a statuette of the Virgin Mary has been built into the trench-line. The reason given for the German retreat is that "the continuous reinforcements of French heavy artillery compelled the Germans to shorten their lines". French 400mm and 320mm railway guns in action. The country around Noyon flooded by the Germans in their retreat. French troops liberating Noyon, working to repair the railway and roads. At Roye a mine has cratered the street, partly demolishing the town hall and church. French troops follow up after the Germans.

Notes
Title: this is taken from the shotsheet and the alternative title from the store ledger.
Summary: the English-language version of a film, the material for which is probably all taken from the French official newsreel series *Annales de la Guerre*. The Rheims section comes from **IWM 508-25**.
Remarks: the film gains most of its force by repetition, a catalogue of one destroyed village after another. The smashed calvaries, which show the Christ-figure apparently 'mutilated' by the loss of a limb, make a particularly strong impact. An interesting contrast both with the British experience of the war and with British film techniques.
[shotsheet available]
catalogued SDB: 2/1982

IWM 474 · GB, 6/1918
the WAR WOMEN OF ENGLAND

b/w · 1 reel · 659' (11 mins) · silent
intertitles: English

sp Ministry of Information *pr* Topical Film Company

- Contribution of British women to the war effort as shown in the *War Office Topical Budget* newsreel 1917-18.

I. A recruiting march by girls of the

Women's Land Army in central London, April 1918. Members of the Women's Land Army form an escort for the Lord Mayor of London, Charles A Hanson, as he enters St Paul's Cathedral, probably also in April. The Duke of Portland reviews a parade of Land Girls through the streets of Nottingham, 25 May 1918. A recruiting sergeant for the Women's Land Army addresses a crowd from the top of a hay wagon in central London, May 1918. A semi-staged piece of women entering a WAAC recruiting centre in London and leaving in uniform, followed by a column of WAACs marching to Waterloo Station and boarding a train together, "for men must fight and women must work". In France the WAACs do various jobs from motor maintenance to potato peeling. The Lord Mayor's Show in London on 9 November 1917 includes a Land Girls' pageant. The opening of the WAAC recruiting hut in Trafalgar Square on 7 November 1917. At the opening the Controller of the WAAC, Mrs Chalmers Watson, invites Lieutenant-General Sir Francis Lloyd to inspect the guard of honour of "the Women's Auxiliary Army Corps, popularly known in France as the 'Waxs'". Opening the hut with Lieutenant-General Lloyd is Lieutenant-General Sir Nevil Macready.
II. In addition to war service is the question "will there be women MPs ?" showing, left to right, Christabel Pankhurst, her mother Mrs · Emmeline Pankhurst, 'General' Flora Drummond and Annie Kenney outside the Queen's Hall on 7 November 1917, on the occasion of the foundation of the Women's Parliamentary Party from the Women's Social and Political Union.
III. Further to this, Mrs C S Peel, the Director of the Women's Section of the Ministry of Food, leaves her office at Grosvenor House, December 1917. Finally, the march past Winchester Cathedral in January 1918 of "the Lady Ploughmen" of the Hampshire Women's Land Army.

Notes
Summary: this film was assembled from items in the British *War Office Topical Budget* (later *Pictorial News*) series. See also **IWM 193** for the section involving Mrs Peel.
[shotsheet available]
catalogued SDB: 4/1982

IWM 475 · GB, 1918
SCENES ON THE WESTERN FRONT

b/w · 1 reel · 818' (14 mins) · silent

intertitles: English

sp Ministry of Information (?) *pr* Topical Film Company (?)

■ British propaganda film of the Western Front, calling for greater efforts and firmness from all to win victory, 1918.

Unrelated scenes with no continuity or storyline, mainly taken from the *German Offensive* series of spring 1918, showing the British sector of the Western Front between March and April 1918. An additional attack sequence comes from **IWM 116** *The Battle of the Ancre and the Advance of the Tanks* and **IWM 466** *The Canadian Victory at Courcelette.* In so far as the film has a message, it is expressed at the end in a scene of a shell-damaged village. "This is what the German would like to do to us. He cannot, while we stand firm !", the last two words being underlined three times.

Notes
Summary: see also the *German Offensive* series for most of this film. Some of the stockshots come from **IWM 116**, **IWM 119**, **IWM 465** and **IWM 466**.
Remarks: routine and uninteresting British Western Front material, remarkable only for the tone of its captions, which appears to mark the distinct shift from the carefully neutral tone of the WOCC towards the more outspoken, demagogic approach of the MoI.
[shotsheet available]
catalogued SDB: 4/1982

IWM 476 · GB, (prod) 1918
WITH OUR BOYS AT THE FRONT (first version)

b/w · 1 reel · 657' (11 mins) · silent
intertitles: English

sp Ministry of Information *pr* Topical Film Company

■ British propaganda film of the Western Front aimed at persuading the Home population to reject any German peace offer, spring 1918.

The funeral of a nurse killed when one of the British military hospitals in France was bombed (deliberately, according to the film) by the Germans in their March offensive. The caption style which is very outspoken, has a 'late war' character that contrasts with visuals consisting of very old actuality footage of the Western Front. "Our glorious airmen give the enemy no respite" is backed by a portrait shot of Captain 'Billy' Bishop, and film of FE2d night bombers in the spring and summer of 1917. This is followed by a re-edited version of the Canadian attack on Courcelette in November 1916 (partly faked) taken from the series *Sons of Our Empire* and from **IWM 116** *The Battle of the Ancre and the Advance of the Tanks.* The film's main message is the need for those at home to support the troops. "We are moving forward to Victory and our soldiers are marching along the long road without faltering. We at home must set our teeth and have patience. What are our little hardships compared to those of our men out there ? ... The wily Hun, who sees Victory slipping from his grasp, is digging a fresh pit – a sham peace offer. However tempting are his offers, they are nothing but a trap. So let us tell him that WE WANT NO PLAUSIBLE POTSDAM PEACE."

Notes
Summary: see also **IWM 477**, which has the same title and some of the same captions backed by different actuality material. There is no direct evidence that either version was ever released to the public.
Remarks: seen with **IWM 477** this provides an extremely interesting demonstration of two separate attempts to convey the same idea in film.
[shotsheet available]
catalogued SDB: 2/1982

IWM 477 · GB, (prod) 1918
WITH OUR BOYS AT THE FRONT (second version)

b/w · 1 reel · 787' (12 mins) · silent intertitles: English

sp Ministry of Information *pr* Topical Film Company (?)

■ British propaganda film supposedly of the Western Front aimed at persuading the Home population to reject any German peace offer, spring 1918.

The film's captions are outspoken and dramatic. "We are moving forward to Victory, and our soldiers are marching along the long road without faltering. We at home must set our teeth and have patience. What are our little hardships compared with those of the men out there ?" The film material itself has every appearance of being routine camp life and

training exercises on Salisbury Plain rather than genuine Western Front material. It shows troops in a rest camp washing, officers talking, a corporal handing out mail, a man being shaved by the camp barber, a distribution of food from dixies, a pay parade, and a gas mask drill, all from various regiments. The training exercise shows soldiers entering a trench system, and resting after a "raid" with three men in German uniform, who share their food. British soldiers wearing gas capes return to their camp, and others rest beside or inside their tents. "One of our latest types of machine" is an FE2d bomber, introduced in the summer of 1916. The exercise continues with troops, described as "Guards", going over the top with no Artillery barrage and a tented camp visible behind them. Mk IV tanks move up the road as the exercise starts. Officers follow the action on a sand-tray model covered with flags. The film's message is entirely in its captions. "While they fight on and die over there, we over here live in peace. Yet there is grumbling: there are strikes! Is that right ? If the Hun won and came here our towns and villages would soon be like this:-" [film shows shell-damaged buildings] "The wily Hun, who sees Victory slipping from his grasp, is digging a fresh pit – a sham peace offer. However tempting are his offers, they are nothing but a trap. So let us tell him that WE WANT NO PLAUSIBLE POTSDAM PEACE."

Notes
Summary: see also **IWM 476**, which shares the same title as this film and some of its captions but uses different actuality material to support its message. There is no direct evidence that either version was ever released. This film is unusual in that it has no material in common with any other British official film supposedly of the Western Front.
Remarks: seen with **IWM 476** this provides an extremely interesting attempt to convey the same idea in two different ways.
[shotsheet available]
catalogued SDB: 2/1982

IWM 478 · GB, 1918
JOHN BROWN JOINS THE ARMY

b/w · 1 reel · 604' (10 mins) · silent intertitles: English

sp Ministry of Information *pr* Topical Film Company

- British administrative system whereby a conscript is identified and processed into the Army, March 1918.

The film takes a typical case, "John Brown", a clerk aged 30, single with one dependent (a sister ?) living in his own house in Catford in the suburbs of London. On the outbreak of war he attested. After the War Cabinet decides that men of his age and occupation should be conscripted, the Ministry of National Service, housed at the Windsor Hotel in London, takes up his case. The Minister, Sir Auckland Geddes, issues instructions for John Brown's class to be called up to his Parliamentary Secretary, Cecil Beck MP. John Brown's last exemption, according to his file in the ministry, was for three months expiring on 6 March. The registers pick this fact up automatically, and on 20 February notification is sent to John Brown to report on 7 March. In the meantime his cards and documents are sent to the recruiting station. On 7 March John Brown reports to the same recruiting station where he is examined by a doctor for the National Service Medical Board. As there is some doubt as to his health he is seen by a total of four doctors before being passed fit by the Board's president. On leaving he is given his first day's pay as a soldier. The Army informs the Ministry of National Service, which removes John Brown's name from the military register and informs the Registrar General at the War Office. The final scene is of John Brown in Army uniform as Private Brown.

Notes
Remarks: a neat little piece, foreshadowing many of the documentary techniques used in the Second World War. The stress on the care taken to ensure that men were fit for service is in marked contrast to the stories circulating at the time of inadequate medical checks.
[shotsheet available]
catalogued SDB: 2/1982

IWM 479 · GB, 1918
WOMEN AND THE WAR

b/w · 1 reel · 474' (8 mins) · silent
intertitles: English

sp Ministry of Information *pr* Topical Film Company

- British propaganda film of the contribution of some women to the war

effort, contrasted with the extravagance of others, 1918.

The film opens with Oxford Street in London and declares that "luxury shopping" is not helping the war effort. This is contrasted with the ways in which women do help: a mother looking after her two small children while her husband serves in the trenches, munitions workers, nurses at a hospital, drivers and mechanics of the WAAC in France, drivers of military ambulances, and women special constables in Britain. The film ends with the enquiry "CAN YOU HELP?"

Notes
Technical: the film copies of this reel made in 1956 from the badly shrunken original are unusable as the picture rolls continuously; stills may be taken, however. Recently, this fault has been largely rectified in a video version made in 1993 by the Machine Room Ltd.
Remarks: a fine example of home propaganda showing many of the techniques used again in the Second World War.
[shotsheet available]
catalogued SDB: 2/1982

IWM 480 · GB, 8/1917
the WOMEN'S LAND ARMY

b/w · 1 reel · 852' (15 mins) · silent
intertitles: English

sp Department of Information (?)
pr Broadwest Films *cast* Hopson, Violet; and Close, Ivy

- British recruiting film for the Women's Land Army, 1917.

The film uses acted material to show two "ladies of leisure" riding in Rotten Row, contrasted with the "women of action" of the Land Army practising drill. The two ladies decide to join the Land Army after receiving a letter from the brother of one of them, serving in France, who urges them to contribute to the war effort. They journey to the Department of National Service, where they are enrolled in the Land Army by Lady Crewe and her assistant, Miss Violet Markham. Wearing Women's Land Army uniform they go out with other members of the Land Army from their hostel to work on a farm. "Weeds, like U-Boats, must be exterminated." The line of women workers weeds one field, and turns over mulch in another while the farmer uses a horse-drawn reaper. The women have lunch in the shade of a tree. Some cover hay ricks while others feed chickens. Others stack hay bales onto a wagon, drive cattle, lift milk churns and feed piglets. The result of their efforts is a field of grain, with 'ghosts' of the women working appearing on it. In the same way an empty baker's window fills with loaves of bread which are then bought. The handbell recalls the women to their hostel at the end of the day. The ghost-figure of Britannia, appearing on a field of corn, blesses the Women's Land Army for its efforts.

Notes
Remarks: a well made film. The camera tricks are attractive, if the use to which they are put seems slightly absurd. But it is difficult to know at whom the film was aimed. The Women's Land Army was by no means recruited exclusively or even largely from the very small leisured class which appears to be its target.
[shotsheet available]
catalogued SDB: 2/1982

IWM 481 · GB, (?) 1916
KNOW YOUR ENEMY – SECOND SERIES

b/w · 5 reels · 4897' (82 mins) · silent
intertitles: English

■ British re-edited version of Austro-Hungarian film of their own forces on the Home Front, Italian Front, and with the Germans on the Eastern Front, in autumn and winter 1915.

(Reel 1) The departure of the Archduke (later Emperor) Karl with General Conrad von Hötzendorf from Vienna to inspect Austrian troops in the Tyrolean region, close to the Italian Front. Outside a hunting lodge Karl inspects a Tyrolean Jaeger battalion, possibly from 8th Division. The party wanders through the mountain passes. Karl, with Lobkovitz the Austrian Adjutant General, talks with divisional commanders. Karl also inspects a dragoon regiment (probably 17th Dragoons), a hussar regiment and local volunteer foot soldiers. At a barracks, Karl has various battalion commanders presented to him. Finally, Karl and his wife Zita leave a hotel in Innsbruck by car, saying goodbye to a line of officers at the station before boarding their train. *(Reel 2)* Austrian troops in a mock attack, including a 77mm field gun fitted with an obsolete semi-solid trail. In the South Tyrol, the troops are shown praying in a field

chapel and dancing to a flute. The visit of the (nominal) Austro-Hungarian Commander-in-Chief, Archduke Friedrich, to Kovel (about 80km south-east of Warsaw) following the Russian retreat of August 1915. A column of Russian prisoners is brought into the town while Austrian soldiers repair the railway. *(Reel 3)* The South Tyrol again, showing a battery of mountain guns in the Stilfersjock valley, troops climbing up the Ortler mountain, and a Red Cross orderly corporal of the Kaiserschützen, described as 68 years old. Archduke Friedrich attends a church service on the Eastern Front with von Hötzendorf, Peter Hofman, and other dignitaries, to celebrate the Emperor Franz Josef's 85th birthday (18 August 1915). In Vienna, Archduke Friedrich initiates the War Shield by knocking in the first nail. Von Hötzendorf and Archduke Friedrich wait in the Tyrol for the arrival of a German goodwill mission headed by the Kaiser. The German War Minister, General Wild von Hohenborn, arrives first, followed by Kaiser Wilhelm in Austrian uniform, together with the German Chief of Staff General von Falkenhayn. Also present are the Austrian General Graf Paar and the German General von Bülow. Friedrich talks to a court chamberlain (misidentified as Falkenhayn) and a state banquet follows. Later Kaiser Wilhelm, in German uniform, arrives at Friedrich's headquarters. *(Reel 4)* On the Galician part of the Eastern Front the Austro-Hungarian forces continue to advance in the wake of the Russian retreat. The captured fortress of Przemyśl is shown. *(Reel 5)* Moving north, the captured towns of Ivangorod and Brest-Litovsk are also shown. Included are airfields where Aviatik CII aircraft in Austro-Hungarian and German service are flying. Austrian troops march through Czernowitz. Kaiser Wilhelm visits the north part of the Eastern Front with von Falkenhayn, talking to General von Gallwitz, commanding Twelfth Army.

Notes
Title: note that the title appears at the start of the second and subsequent reels but not the first reel.
Production: Austro-Hungarian and German official film re-edited by the British, most probably as a private venture.
[Norman Stone, *The Eastern Front 1914-1917*, Hodder and Stoughton (1975)]
[shotsheet available]
catalogued SDB: 2/1982

IWM 482 · GB, (after) 1918
WARTIME FLYING FILM (ledger title)

b/w · 3 reels · 4247' (70 mins) · silent
intertitles: English

- Mixed film of unrelated scenes of British
  and Australian aircraft during the second
  half of the First World War.

The film has no plot or continuity. Almost all
the first reel comes directly from **IWM 236** *A
Bombing Trip Over the Enemy Lines*,
showing Australian aircraft, and **IWM 28**
With the Australian Forces in Palestine. The
second reel comes mostly from **IWM 570**
Our Naval Air Power, and the naval
episodes from series **IWM 130** *Sons of Our
Empire*. The third reel comes almost entirely
from **IWM 141** *With the Royal Flying Corps
(Somewhere in France)*, ending with
material from **IWM 470** *Destruction of a
Fokker*.

Notes
Summary: in addition to the sources named,
see also **IWM 118** and **IWM 551**. This may
be a film made to accompany a lecture in
the immediate post-1918 period.
[shotsheet available]
catalogued SDB: 3/1982

IWM 483-01 · Germany, 10/1915
MESSTER WOCHE 43 1915
SEMANA MESSTER 43 1915 (on copy held)

b/w · 1 reel · 727' (12 mins) · silent
intertitles: Portuguese

pr Messter Film *prod* Messter, O

- Portuguese-language version of a
  German newsreel showing their forces in
  the area of Lille, occupied France,
  autumn 1915.

British prisoners, probably from the Battle of
Loos, are marched through the streets of
Lille (?) with a mounted escort. German
wounded are taken by ambulance to a
temporary hospital in the town and
unloaded. Soldiers distribute meat to the
people (mainly old men and women) of
Lille. Nearer the battle zone, a horse from a
gun-team is coaxed out from a patch of
mud. Members of the "General Staff"
(probably not the Grosse Generalstab) visit
a ruined church. Sappers repair a trench
blown in by British shells. Work in a sawmill
and timber-yard. A dog kept as a mascot in
the rear trenches. The headquarters of a

front line battalion in a deep dug-out. A
Cavalry commander, General von Laffert (?)
with his staff beside a château. A mining
operation in which sappers take sandbags
into the forward trenches and carry earth
away from the mine. A view over no man's
land from the front trenches – a sniper fires
across at the British. The remainder of the
troops take up position on the firing-step
and open fire. (All the trenches are very well
made and dry.)

Notes
Production: Messter Woche was produced
by Oskar Messter in association with the
German Government.
Summary: all troops are German unless
otherwise stated. British official filming of
the Western Front did not start until
November 1915, and French filming at
about the same date. This series is
therefore among the earliest film of the
Western Front in existence.
Remarks: the contrast between the German
trenches and the British equivalents, as
shown in films such as **IWM 207** and **IWM
208**, is very marked. The Germans,
however, clearly suffered from the same
technical problems in filming as the British.
[shotsheet available]
catalogued SDB: 3/1982

IWM 483-02 · Germany, 10/1915
MESSTER WOCHE 44 1915
SEMANA MESSTER 44 1915 (on copy held)

b/w · 1 reel · 710' (12 mins) · silent
intertitles: Portuguese

pr Messter Film *prod* Messter, O

- Portuguese-language version of a
  German newsreel.

I. Swiss Commander-in-Chief, General Wille,
talks with officers and civilians at a review of
his troops in Switzerland, autumn 1915.
II. German troops in occupied Belgium and
on the Western Front, autumn 1915.
Soldiers just out of the front lines laugh,
joke and wrestle together while resting at a
farm. A marching column in full kit leaves its
barracks for the trenches. A boiler-distiller
for providing fresh water is demonstrated. A
steamroller helps local people to repair a
road, possibly near Brussels. Officers
fraternise with the local people at the
château where they have been billeted. A
German orderly tends and decorates the
graves of a French soldier. Two soldiers
exhibit a fragment of a British 15-inch shell

which fell one metre from the local church. Soldiers in the rear areas use sewing machines for making sandbags. Soldiers go forward in the front lines to occupy a mine crater blown by the British. Crown Prince Rupprecht of Bavaria talks to soldiers close to the front lines. A guard in a front line trench sees danger through a trench periscope and calls out the troops who man the fire-step. A training exercise for an attack supported by grenades.

Notes
Production etc: see **Notes** to **IWM 483-01**.
[shotsheet available]
catalogued SDB 3/1982:

IWM 483-03 · Germany, 11/1915
MESSTER WOCHE 45 1915
SEMANA MESSTER 45 1915 (on copy held)

b/w · 1 reel · 590' (10 mins) · silent
intertitles: Portuguese

pr Messter Film *prod* Messter, O

- Portuguese-language version of a German newsreel.

I. The Romanian Minister of Finance, Take Ionescu, at a formal meeting, probably in Bucharest, 1915.
II. Turkish troops firing German 77mm field guns and Turkish wounded, possibly at Gallipoli, 1915.
III. German forces on the Western Front, autumn 1915. A railhead behind the lines where timber is unloaded from the trains, and sacks loaded onto horse-drawn wagons. A mine shaft is pumped clear of water by a hand pump. In a training exercise troops crawl forward to simulate a "night attack" in daylight. The village of "Chelevelt", presumably Gheluvelt, destroyed "by the British", while new defensive positions are built in its ruins. A ration party moves up through the rear areas. A new 'model' set of trenches is inspected by staff officers. A Maxim machinegun on a recoiling platform in a trench is demonstrated, the platform enabling the gun to be swung down into the trench.

Notes
Production etc: see **Notes** to **IWM 483-01**.
Remarks: if the Turkish material is indeed Gallipoli, it is the only known film of land forces on that side in the campaign.
[shotsheet available]
catalogued SDB: 3/1982

IWM 483-04 · Germany, 11/1915
MESSTER WOCHE 46 1915
SEMANA MESSTER 46 1915 (on copy held)

b/w · 1 reel · 682' (10 mins) · silent
intertitles: Portuguese

pr Messter Film *prod* Messter, O

- Portuguese-language version of a German newsreel.

I. German forces on the Eastern Front, autumn 1915. Prince Heinrich of Prussia visits the Russian Orthodox Church at Kovno (Russian Poland) after the Russian retreat of summer 1915. A beached and burnt-out Russian steamer is shown on the bank of the River Nemen.
II. German forces in occupied France and Belgium, and on the Western Front, autumn 1915. Soldiers play with makeshift canoes on the Yser Canal. Food is handed out to sick or injured soldiers in a Belgian hospital. The German "military police" in Lille, a cyclist formation from various units, parades and moves off. An alarm at Lille sends "Light Truck Column 8" out from its garages. At a prisoner of war camp in Brussels British wounded prisoners, including one African, play chess as the German guards watch. Field officers move up through a trench system which leads directly through an old French cemetery, disturbing the graves. Soldiers take up defensive positions in nearby buildings. On the Flanders coast a supply column for Marines marches up the road. In Ostend sailors play on the beach and a Maxim 1-pounder practises firing out to sea.

Notes
Production etc: see **Notes** to **IWM 483-01**.
[shotsheet available]
catalogued SDB: 3/1982

IWM 483-05 · Germany, 11/1915
MESSTER WOCHE 47 1915
SEMANA MESSTER 47 1915 (on copy held)

b/w · 1 reel · 470' (8 mins) · silent
intertitles: Portuguese

pr Messter Film *prod* Messter, O

- Portuguese-language version of a German newsreel.

I. German forces on the Eastern Front, autumn 1915. The soldiers prepare wood-and-earth shelters for themselves and their horses for the forthcoming winter in Russian Poland. At "Chassina" (presumably in Poland) the town is a smoking ruin an hour after the Russians have retreated from it. II. German forces on the Western Front, autumn 1915. A marching column with mounted officers moves out of a town and towards the front lines. A supply officer delivers food and drink to troops on the Ypres ridges. A reserve line shelter, probably a regimental command post, near the Ypres ridges. A French church destroyed by shell fire, possibly near Lille. A temporary wooden bridge over the River Lys near Lille. Near the front lines soldiers dig "gas trenches" for enemy gas to collect in, away from their own positions. On the Flanders coast a column of buses is used for ambulance work.

Notes
Production etc: see **Notes** to **IWM 483-01**.
[shotsheet available]
catalogued SDB: 3/1982

IWM 483-06 · Germany, 11/1915
MESSTER WOCHE 48 1915
SEMANA MESSTER 48 1915 (on copy held)

b/w · 1 reel · 690' (10 mins) · silent
intertitles: Portuguese

pr Messter Film *prod* Messter, O

- Portuguese-language version of a German newsreel.

I. The funeral in Constantinople, with full diplomatic and military honours, of Baron von Wangenheim, German Ambassador to Turkey, who died on 25 October 1915. II. German forces on the Western Front, autumn 1915. A first aid post at work in a heavily shored-up house. Cavalry, probably a remount unit, takes part in a horse inspection. A Red Cross stretcher team, probably in a training exercise, gathers wounded on its stretchers from near a wood. At Thielt in Belgium the German garrison goes through the ceremony of 'beating retreat' as dusk falls. Sappers work to improve trench defences, probably on the Ypres ridges. In the sands of the Flanders coast a 77mm field battery, its fire directed by an observer with a trench periscope, deploys and opens fire, probably in training. A giant lamp signals from the coast out to sea.

Notes
Production etc: see **Notes** to **IWM 483-01**.

[shotsheet available]
catalogued SDB: 3/1982

IWM 484 · USA, 1934
the FIRST WORLD WAR

b/w · 8 reels · 6997' (77 mins) · comopt
intertitles: English

sp Simon and Schuster *pr* Fox Film Corporation *prod* Talley, Truman *ed* Stallings, Laurence *comm* Stallings, Laurence *comp* Powell, Bonney; Shields, Russell; Rochemont, Louis de; Lehr, Lew; and De Cordoba, Pedro *music* Rochetti, John *rec* Sponable, Earl; and Hicks, Walter

- Simplistic account of the First World War, in eleven chapters, concentrating on personalities rather than issues, but using some rare film.

I. The build-up to war from the earliest days of film record, showing the various crowned heads of Europe. II. The Balkan wars of 1912, the development of Germany's Navy, and the inauguration of President Woodrow Wilson. III. The assassination of Archduke Franz Ferdinand and the outbreak of war. IV. The war at sea, showing the various naval personalities, the Battle of Jutland (faked) and the sinking of the Austro-Hungarian ship *Szent Istvan* (or *Sankt Stefan*) V. The war in the air, showing the aces of both sides and a Zeppelin raid on London (faked). VI. The war under the sea, Germany's use of unrestricted submarine warfare leads to Wilson declaring war, and the despatch of American land and naval forces to Europe. VII. The build-up of the American forces in Europe by convoy across the Atlantic, fighting off submarine attacks (faked). VIII. The last film of the Tsar and his family before the Russian Revolution, followed by the appearance of new leaders such as Kerensky, Trotsky and Lenin. IX. The appointment of Foch as Generalissimo of the Allied armies as a consequence of the German offensive of March 1918. The arrival of substantial American forces. X. The German offensive of March-June 1918 leading to the Allied counter-offensive of July-November 1918, shown as a mixture of small fights by soldiers of all nationalities. XI. The Armistice, with peace established, but the growing threat of war as militarism and aggression increases up to the present day (1934).

Notes
Copyright: the film gives its own copyright as Fox Films Corporation 1934, adding that the British official war film used is the property of the Imperial War Museum and Crown copyright. The film was probably a gift to the IWM on that basis.
Remarks: some excellent and often very rare material ruined by the absence of any attempt to understand the issues involved in the war, and by a quite ridiculous commentary. Passing over the exaggerated role given to the American forces in the war, the film also fails to make clear why the war began, why it ended, and indeed who actually won it.
[shotsheet available]
catalogued SDB & NAP: 4/1982

IWM 485 · GB, 1933
the SOUL OF A NATION

b/w · 6 reels · 5451' (60 mins) · comopt
intertitles: English

sp Conservative Party *pr* Associated British Film Distributors *scr* Williams, J B
comp Williams, J B *music* Reynders, John
music (assistant) Beck, R E *rec* Sheridan, Harry (at Imperial Sound Studios)
comm sp Aylmer, Felix

■ Conservative Party assessment of British social and political history from 1901 to 1933.

The film emphasises the pre-war uniqueness of Britain – rich, insular, with a strong trading position and a free democracy united under the constitutional monarchy. The only pre-war violence comes in the Sidney Street siege, and perhaps from the suffragettes. Empire building creates some resentment, but is nevertheless beneficial. Only Ireland is unstable. The war is unexpected, but the decision to enter it receives great popular support. Politicians of all parties, labour leaders, and even the leaders of the Irish revolt unite to encourage men to enlist. The Empire too unites behind Britain. It is "an unsatisfactory war", principally of endurance, with determination and industrial strength counting for more than generalship. The mass participation of women leads to their achieving the franchise. Despite the loss of "over a million dead" on the Western Front, and the air raids, the nation remains united under the

monarchy. After the Armistice Britain resumes its pastimes and even Ireland finds peace. But the new Labour Government, despite its successful foreign policy, cannot cope with growing unemployment. In the General Strike the TUC insists that it has no revolutionary intent and the whole affair passes off amicably enough. Britain begins to show progress again in industry, particularly in the air, a major legacy of the war. But the slump of 1930, a consequence of the war, produces massed unemployment and a major political crisis, resulting in the forming of the National Government. British politicians and people, however, solve their differences with "doggedness, good humour and common sense" in contrast to the violence of other nations, and it is these qualities, rather than any political action, which will help the next generation to grow up in peace under "a monarchy which manifests the value of tradition as an element in progress".

Notes
Copyright: the film acknowledges that the material of the First World War which it uses is the property of the Imperial War Museum and Crown copyright. The film was probably a gift to the IWM on that basis.
Remarks: a classic, almost priceless, expression of Conservative attitudes and values in the inter-war years: calm, sardonic, patronising, tired, gentle, loyal, complacent and bankrupt. This charming and amusing film manages to make the failure of the Labour Government to keep on the gold standard appear a greater tragedy than the First World War, and the General Strike a minor disagreement. An invaluable document of political and social history, not so much for its message as for what it reveals about its makers.
[shotsheet available]
catalogued SDB: 4/1982

IWM 486 · GB, (?) 1918
DEMOBILISATION FILM

b/w · 1 reel · 181' (2 mins) · silent
intertitles: none

sp Ministry of Information (?)

■ Troops going through final demobilisation procedure in Britain at the end of the First World War.

The men, from various regiments, all go into a building marked "Entrance for Troops for Dispersal". They are checked off against a list, each handed their discharge papers (?) and issued with civilian clothing. They hand in their discharge papers and check out at the Pay Office where they receive their final pay or discharge bonus. One soldier from the Worcestershire Regiment (?) is shown laughing over his money and papers. They board a train at a suburban station. Shortly afterwards, another train arrives, carrying a new batch of soldiers.

Notes
Title: this is taken from the shotsheet.
Summary: the origins and details of the contents of this film are unknown. It is possible that it was among the last made by the MoI before its closure at the end of 1918.
[shotsheet available]
catalogued SDB: 4/1982

IWM 487 · GB, (?) 1936
WITH THE INDIAN TROOPS

b/w · 5 reels · 5349' (89 mins) · silent
intertitles: English

sp Imperial War Museum

■ Compilation film in five episodes of the Indian forces on the Western Front, Mesopotamian Front and Palestine Front, 1915-18.

I. The first reel shows men of the Indian Corps (including British soldiers) in France in January 1916. It is taken unaltered, in a slightly re-edited form, from **IWM 202** *With the Indian Troops at the Front*.
II. The middle three reels show scenes of Mesopotamia 1917-18. Although Indian soldiers appear in the film it does not in any way single them out or emphasise them above British soldiers or the events of the campaign. The material is taken directly from the series *Advance of the Crusaders into Mesopotamia*.
III. The last reel shows scenes of Palestine in 1918. Although Indian troops are shown, mainly from 7th (Meerut) Division, they are in no way given special prominence. The material is taken directly from **IWM 30** *Allenby Meets Weizmann – Tel-el-Jelil, and Arsulf*.

Notes
Summary: for the other attempt by the IWM to exploit its own film collection see **IWM 442**.
Shotsheet: an unusually detailed shotsheet or programme for this film is in the

possession of the Department of Film.
Remarks: over-long, dull, uncoordinated and entirely failing to fulfil the promise of its title.
[shotsheet available]
catalogued SDB: 4/1982

IWM 488 · GB, 1916
SCENES IN NEWCASTLE ON TYNE ON TYNESIDE SCOTTISH FLAG DAY : April 15th 1916

b/w · 1 reel · 279' (3 mins) · silent
intertitles: English

■ Tyneside Scottish flag day in Newcastle (not showing the Tyneside Scottish) 15 April 1916.

A Royal Field Artillery band marches through Newcastle to the main square. The Lord Mayor, Councillor George Lunn, arrives with his wife and poses with a group of councillors. Speeches are delivered and Lunn buys a flag. The band of 3rd Battalion, the North Staffordshire Regiment (their training battalion) marches past.

Notes
Summary: the Tyneside Scottish Brigade was 102nd Brigade, 34th Division, made up of 20th, 21st, 22nd and 23rd Battalions, the Northumberland Fusiliers. At this date they were serving in France. The film was probably a local newsreel purchased by the IWM after 1918.
[shotsheet available]
catalogued SDB: 4/1982

IWM 489-498 · NO FILM

IWM 499 · GB, (prod) 1918
[FIRST WORLD WAR FRAGMENTS] (allocated)
[WAR OFFICE OFFICIAL TOPICAL BUDGET FRAGMENTS] (alternative, allocated)

b/w · 42 reels · 25,807' (431 mins) · silent
intertitles: none

sp War Office Cinema Committee *pr* Topical Film Company

■ Duplicate or discarded material from British Official film production in the First World War.

Notes

Summary: in 1916 the War Office Cinema Committee took over the Topical Film Company to provide itself with a full-time production company. This collection represents the Topical 'film dump' of extra sections generated in the normal course of film production, including out-takes, edits, censored material and spoiled film. The 'dump' consists chiefly of British material of the Western and Home Fronts but includes fragments from Palestine, Russia and Italy, as well as material of the Japanese Navy, US Army and similar formations. Almost all of this material is duplicated elsewhere in the IWM film series, particularly in the *War Office Official Topical Budget* newsreel. Some of the scenes appear to be unique 'missing' items from the newsreel itself; while other sections may also be unique. The fragments of film come in no particular order or length, and most are, by their very nature, unidentifiable. A very few reels have captions.
Technical: this film has 42 reels numbered 1-41; reel 14 has two versions which have no scenes in common.
Remarks: a film researcher desperate to find one particular item, or a film historian trying to reconstruct a missing film, might find this monster worth watching; others are advised to leave it alone.
catalogued SDB: 1/1984

IWM 500 · NO FILM

IWM 501-01 · USA, (ca) 1919
PICTORIAL HISTORY OF THE WORLD WAR NO 1

b/w · 1 reel · 978' (16 mins) · silent
intertitles: English

sp US Army General Staff, Historical Branch, War Plans Division *pr* US Signal Corps

■ US official film of their troops on the Western Front, 11-17 October 1918.

The rail station at Châtel-Chéhéry near the Aisne on 11 October 1918 showing the limit of the German advance to Paris. A view of the town itself two days later. German prisoners of war at a camp at Souilly on 14 October building new huts for themselves. The headquarters of II Corps at St-Quentin, German prisoners passing through the town, and damage to the cathedral, 14-15

October. Headquarters of 5th Division at Bois de Tuileries-en-Fayel Farm (between Cuisy and Montfaucon), where Sergeant W B Prince of the G2 (Intelligence) Branch plots the line of advance, and Private M J Goldstein passes a note to Captain H B Payne. The divisional commander poses with his staff, left to right: Lieutenant R W Kingman, Major-General John McMahon, Lieutenant L E Devereaux, and Colonel C A Trott. General John J Pershing and Major-General Hines, the commander of III Corps, leave after a conference with McMahon. The camp of 78th Division in the River Aire valley at Apremont on 15 October, where 'F' Battery, 307th Field Artillery, practises signals. The water-supply depot of 304th Engineers, 79th Division, at Vaux-les-Palameix (which is in ruins) on 16 October. 304th Engineers at St-Remy on 17 October demolishes damaged buildings for road-fill.

Notes
Production: Pictorial History of the World War is a US official production, but does not seem to have been released as a series. It appears to have been meant as a historical record only. The first five episodes have almost excessively detailed captions and are clearly post-war. The remaining episodes have only their censored wartime captions. Note that as all the film in the series is US material all troops mentioned in it are American unless otherwise stated.
See also **IWM 502** and **IWM 503**.
Remarks: there is nothing in this series to suggest that American cameramen did not suffer the same technical and administrative problems as their British counterparts. The effort clearly made to document the film accurately as a record, however, is a considerable improvement on British methods.
[Kevin Brownlow, *The War, the West and the Wilderness*, Secker and Warburg (1979)]
[shotsheet available]
catalogued SDB: 5/1982

IWM 501-02 · USA, (ca) 1919
PICTORIAL HISTORY OF THE WORLD WAR NO 2

b/w · 1 reel · 1086' (18 mins) · silent
intertitles: English

sp US Army General Staff, Historical Branch, War Plans Division *pr* US Signal Corps

I. King Albert of Belgium in Paris with President Poincaré on a formal visit,

entering a carriage with a French Cavalry escort, late 1918.
II. The US Contingent of the North Russian Intervention Force and its Bolshevik prisoners help to build a wooden camp, "Camp Michigan", Archangel, late 1918.
III. The US Contingent on the Italian Front, 332nd Infantry Regiment (part of 83rd (Ohio) Division) crosses the River Piave by pontoon bridge and marches through the gateway of the town of Villaroba, late 1918.
IV. The centre of Metz shortly after the Armistice, Western Front, November 1918. The local people have torn down the statue of Karl Friedrich. The French Army enters the city in triumphal procession, which includes a parade of girls in local dress, and passes through the Place d'Armais.
V. Mayor Max of Brussels being greeted by a cheering crowd in front of the town hall following his release from a German prison after the Armistice, November 1918.
VI. US forces on the Western Front, 17 October 1918. A tractor in 26th (Yankee) Division sector near Beaumont pulls a line of wagons intended for road construction work. Staff of 31st (Dixie) Division at Châtel-Chéhéry waiting in reserve, left to right: Major-General L S Lyon commanding, Colonel K A Joyce Chief of Staff, Captain E R Armsbly ADC and Captain C E McDowell. General John J Pershing confers with Major-General G B Duncan, commanding 82nd (All American) Division at his divisional headquarters in the same area.
VII. US own forces on the Western Front, 18 October 1918. The town of Brieulles, behind the US lines in 32nd (Iron Jaws) Division area, with troops moving through. A "gas station", in fact a first aid post where Lieutenant A M McLeod, surgeon of 11th Infantry Regiment, checks gas and shrapnel victims. The post is at Madeleine Farm, headquarters of 5th (Red Diamond) Division, between Nantillois and Cunel. Men of 6th and 11th Infantry Regiments rest nearby. In action next to men of 5th Division is a 75mm field gun battery of 3rd (Marne) Division. The crew of one gun, in action in a wood, being, left to right: Lieutenant R W Stansbury, Sergeant Dennis Dubois, Private L Wisniewski, Corporal Alvin Carlson and Corporal D D Read. Officers of 1st Battalion, 61st Infantry Regiment, 5th Division in front of their command post, left to right: Lieutenant R E Wilson, Captain E W Sheppard commanding, and Lieutenant R V Maraist. A dump of 6000 shells for 155mm howitzers, one day's supply for III Corps, east of Sepharges. Renault FT17 light tanks undergoing repair from 321st Company, 302nd Tank Center at Varennes-en-Argonne. Furniture being unloaded for the

heavily camouflaged headquarters of 26th Division, in reserve at Bras.

Notes
Production etc: see **Notes** to **IWM 501-01**.
[shotsheet available]
catalogued SDB: 5/1982

IWM 501-03 · USA, (ca) 1919
PICTORIAL HISTORY OF THE WORLD WAR NO 3

b/w · 1 reel · 1007' (17 mins) · silent intertitles: English

sp US Army General Staff, Historical Branch, War Plans Division *pr* US Signal Corps

■ American film of French airmen and US forces on the Western Front, October 1918.

I. Captain Paul Daum, commanding the French 28ième Escadrille, attached to 79th Division, posed in his Salmson 2A2 aircraft at Rumont on 18 October. A posed group of officers of the escadrille. Left to right: Daum, Captain Morette of the air photo section, Lieutenant Dautresme, pilot, Lieutenant Dupont, pilot, Lieutenant Asnard, observer, Lieutenant Blanc, observer, Lieutenant Mettas, observer, Lieutenant Boug, observer, Sergeant-Major Moulon, pilot. Lucien Dautresme prepares to take Henry Paschen of the photographic unit for a flight in the Salmson.
II. Men of 'C' Battery, 130th Field Artillery of 35th Division carry ammunition from a dump to 155mm howitzers in a wood near Sommedieue. The divisional commander, Major-General Peter E Traub, talking to the Assistant Adjutant in Chief, Major D F Davis. The field commander of 1st Battalion, 138th Infantry Regiment, 35th Division is a lieutenant, 1st Lieutenant Lloyd C Brightfield. His battalion is in deep dug-outs, with 'D' Company in a stone quarry. The officers of the battalion to survive the Argonne drive are, left to right: Brightfield, 2nd Lieutenant W B Edmondson of 129th Machine Gun Battalion, 1st Lieutenant R S Keller, the surgeon, and 2nd Lieutenant H R Adams, the adjutant, in a posed group.
III. Chaplain J R Creighton of 101st Signal Battalion conducts a service in a ruined church in Verdun for his men on 18 October.
IV. Chaplain E J Griffiths conducts the funeral service for Sergeant-Major J W Dehaven and Sergeant M J Dobry of

Headquarters Company, 51st Artillery, on 18 October near Griscourt. The men were killed by a shell the night before. This is a full military funeral.
V. 1st Lieutenant Edward V Rickenbacker, commanding 94th 'Hat in the Ring' Pursuit Squadron, posed in his Spad 27 fighter at 1st Pursuit Group airfield, near Rembercourt, 18 October. Also present is Captain J A Meissner, commanding 147th Pursuit Squadron. A posed group of survivors of 94th Squadron, left to right: Rickenbacker, Meissner, 1st Lieutenant Reed Chambers and 1st Lieutenant J H Eastman.

Notes
Production etc: see **Notes** to **IWM 501-01**.
[shotsheet available]
catalogued SDB: 5/1982

IWM 501-04 · USA, (ca) 1919
PICTORIAL HISTORY OF THE WORLD WAR NO 4

b/w · 1 reel · 812' (14 mins) · silent
intertitles: English

sp US Army General Staff, Historical Branch, War Plans Division *pr* US Signal Corps

- US film of their forces on the Western Front, October 1918.

I. A posed group of crews and mechanics of 94th 'Hat in the Ring' Pursuit Squadron at 1st Pursuit Group airfield, Rembercourt, 18 October. Left to right: 1st Lieutenant Edward V Rickenbacker, Major Kirby Maxwell, 1st Lieutenants R L Collins, B H Smith, Reed Chambers, T C Taylor, Hamilton Civiledge, S Thayer, A B Sherry, J N Jeffers, C C Snow, C A Rankin, D G Herring, W S Sparks, H W Cook, J H Eastman, W W Palmer, S Kaye Jr, K E Hopkins, E G Garnsey, C T Crocker, C A Smith, B G Jones, W W Fowler, R J Saunders, L A Cox, R D McKenzie, 2nd Lieutenants J Davett, D M Outcalt, B B Norris, R W Witt, J DeUrtt and H B Marshall with other ranks beside a captured German Hannover CLIII. Major Hartney, the pursuit group commander, in front of the same plane with Lieutenant Cunningham, operations officer of 94th Squadron. A group of pilots and mechanics of 147th Squadron, including, left to right: 1st Lieutenant O B Meyers, 2nd Lieutenant R A O'Neill, Major H B Hartney, 1st Lieutenant J J P Heron, 2nd Lieutenant C W McDermott,

2nd Lieutenant A H Jones, 1st Lieutenant A Healy, Captain J A Meissner, 2nd Lieutenants F M Simonds, G G Willard, E H Clouser, P Porter, and 1st Lieutenants Heyward Cutting, George Brew and C C Olive. The Hannover itself is in reasonable condition. Spads are tuned up. Captain M C Cooper of the Signal Corps fits his camera to the gun position of a de Havilland DH9 fitted with a Liberty engine. The plane is said to crash on take-off but no one is hurt.
II. US gunners mechanically setting the fuses for their 75mm anti-aircraft guns using a Brocq Tachometer.
III. Lorry-mounted 75mm anti-aircraft guns of 'A' Battery, 2nd Field Artillery, Captain S B Richie commanding, near Fléville on 18 October.
IV. The camp of 101st Infantry Regiment, 26th Division, near Samogneux on 19 October, showing 'D' Company mess. Private J H Todd shaves by his tent. Private Joseph Jacobucci play-acts with a German helmet. The field kitchens of 102nd Field Artillery nearby. 'B' Company, 101st Engineers, carrying rocks for road repairs, 6-inch howitzers of 103rd Field Artillery, both 26th Division. Colonel J A Mack, Captain J Simpkins and Captain L Clayton of 102nd Field Artillery at their command post. A dug-out nearby holds Colonel Cox, Lieutenant-Colonel R E Goodwin and Captain Needham of 101st Field Artillery.

Notes
Production etc: see **Notes** to **IWM 501-01**.
Remarks: this represents the extreme example of the attempts in the early reels to the series to provide as much detail as possible. Some of the items consist of extremely long captions supporting brief scenes of almost unidentifiable men. The film in some ways conveys more when it is allowed to speak for itself.
[shotsheet available]
catalogued SDB: 5/1982

IWM 501-05 · USA, (ca) 1919
PICTORIAL HISTORY OF THE WORLD WAR NO 5

b/w · 1 reel · 918' (16 mins) · silent
intertitles: English

sp US Army General Staff, Historical Branch, War Plans Division *pr* US Signal Corps

- American film of 1st Division ('Big Red One') just before the Battle of St-Mihiel, Western Front, 9-12 September 1918.

Watering horses of 1st Field Artillery Brigade in the Forêt de la Reine, just north of Boucq, with considerable military traffic congestion. Men of 18th Infantry Regiment advancing in 'artillery formation' (ie very dispersed) across open fields. Limbers ('caissons' in American usage) of 6th Field Artillery moving past the ruins of Seicheprey, and men of 'C' Battery under Captain I R McLendon digging emplacements for their 75mm guns near Mont Sec. 'D' Battery, 7th Field Artillery, in action. American soldiers flush three Germans from a dug-out (acted ?). The first German prisoners captured in the Battle of St-Mihiel being marched away, 7am 12 September (?). Other German prisoners on the Beaumont-Seicheprey Road on 9 September. Men of 1st Ambulance Company under Captain E F Fisher at the advanced dressing station at Richecourt. 'C' Company, 1st Engineers, repairing a wooden bridge with guns of 5th Field Artillery behind them. Batteries of 6th Field Artillery cross a bridge built by 1st Engineers over the trenches. Men of 1st Division moving up between Seicheprey and St-Baussant. The ruins of St-Baussant filmed through a shell-hole in a wall.

Notes
Production etc: see **Notes** to **IWM 501-01**. *Remarks:* this episode shows well the limitations of the American 'list everything' approach to the historical use of film. In attempting to describe the known details of every scene sight has been entirely lost of the overall structure of the film and the events which it depicts.
[L Stallings, *The Doughboys*, Harper and Row (1963)]
[John Toland, *No Man's Land: the Story of 1918*, Eyre Methuen (1980)]
[shotsheet available]
catalogued SDB: 5/1982

IWM 501-06 · USA, (ca) 1919
PICTORIAL HISTORY OF THE WORLD WAR NO 6

b/w · 1 reel · 722' (12 mins) · silent
intertitles: English

sp US Army General Staff, Historical Branch, War Plans Division *pr* US Signal Corps

■ US film of their forces, mainly in the St-Mihiel salient following the Battle of St-Mihiel, Western Front, September 1918.

Secretary of State for War Newton D Baker visits American troops hospitalised at Romsey in England. The remainder of the film is of France. An American Infantry band plays in a damaged barn in the Argonne. Inside a barn one gunner tends the breech of his 75mm field gun while another rests by a pile of shells with a cat for company. In St-Mihiel itself the statue of Gerard Richier has been removed during the German occupation, leaving the plinth. The undamaged Pont-à-Mousson (despite the caption this was in Allied hands throughout the war). An American observation post in 1st Division area overlooking Hattonchâtel. A Belgian small calibre coastal defence gun recaptured from the Germans. Two American soldiers (one may be A L Browning) show that an unexploded German 220mm shell tore through their tent soon after they left it and buried itself in the ground. American sappers repair the roads in Fey-en-Haye. In recaptured Hattonville they have replaced signposts such as "Hindenburgstrasse" with "Washington St". One of their Renault FT17 light tanks (the American designation is M1917) bulldozes another sign. Shells and stores in an abandoned German supply dump at Vigneulles. A portable German searchlight captured in a deep dug-out at St-Remy. German prisoners of war being marched away. Villagers reading a French newspaper in recently liberated Hattonville.

Notes
Production etc: see **Notes** to **IWM 501-01**. *Summary:* this is the first of the reels to show a complete reversion to the wartime Signal Corps caption style and censorship limitations.
[shotsheet available]
catalogued SDB: 5/1982

IWM 501-07 · USA, (ca) 1919
PICTORIAL HISTORY OF THE WORLD WAR NO 7

b/w · 1 reel · 839' (15 mins) · silent
intertitles: English

sp US Army General Staff, Historical Branch, War Plans Division *pr* US Signal Corps

■ US film of their forces, chiefly in the Battle of Château-Thierry, Western Front, July 1918.

I. The film starts with US and French troops parading through the Place de Jena and the Avenue du Président Wilson in Paris on 4 July, followed by French troops clearing up bomb damage after a German air raid at La Ferté station on 14 July.

II. Thereafter the film concentrates on the battle. 103rd Infantry Regiment, 26th (Yankee) Division going over the top near Château-Thierry at 4.35am on 18 July. A supply column drives into the town itself, which is in ruins. By 4.40pm 101st Engineers of the same division have bridged the Marne for transport. By 4.50pm they have put a pontoon bridge across at Château-Thierry itself. An observation balloon at Picardy Farm "under attack". 155mm guns of 146th Field Artillery, 41st (Sunset) Division, used in an anti-aircraft role, while its officers man an observation post at Torcy. 2nd Balloon Company at Picardy Farm on 22 July repairing one of their damaged balloons. A posed group of men of 'D' Battery, 148th Field Artillery, 41st Division beside their gun. German prisoners being escorted down the Paris-Metz Road. American intelligence officers question some of them in a ruined village. German prisoners at Lucy-le-Bocage, near Château-Thierry, on 21 July also being questioned. Men of 102nd Infantry Regiment, 26th Division escorting German prisoners, some carrying American wounded, to the rear, near Bouresches on 20 July.

Notes
Production etc: see **Notes** to **IWM 501-01**.
[shotsheet available]
catalogued SDB: 5/1982

IWM 501-08 · USA, (ca) 1919
PICTORIAL HISTORY OF THE WORLD WAR NO 8

b/w · 1 reel · 721' (12 mins) · silent
intertitles: English

sp US Army General Staff, Historical Branch, War Plans Division *pr* US Signal Corps

■ US film of their troops after the assault on the St-Quentin Canal and in the Argonne, Western Front, September 1918.

A German 420mm railway gun captured by the Australians in the Battle of Chipilly Ridge. Four Americans "of a famous division" with the fourteen German prisoners they took in the Argonne. A German 210mm howitzer captured by Australians and Americans north of St-Quentin. The ruins of Albert, showing the basilica. US

forces passing through Malancourt, near Verdun. German prisoners captured on Côte 304 being escorted to the rear. American lorries pressing through damaged roads while French troops work to repair them (note the Signal Corps camera truck). "Young Black Joe", groups of US Colored Troops, probably 92nd (Buffalo) Division, working by the roadside. A US pilot with his crashed Bréguet Type 14, its propeller shot away. The St-Quentin Canal between Bellicourt and Riqueval, showing the German dug-outs along the banks, and men of 30th (Old Hickory) Division who captured them.

Notes
Production etc: see **Notes** to **IWM 501-01**.
[shotsheet available]
catalogued SDB: 5/1982

IWM 501-09 · USA, (ca) 1919
PICTORIAL HISTORY OF THE WORLD WAR NO 9

b/w · 1 reel · 1093' (18 mins) · silent
intertitles: English

sp US Army General Staff, Historical Branch, War Plans Division *pr* US Signal Corps

■ US film showing the battlefield of the Second Battle of the Marne and troops during the Meuse-Argonne Offensive, Western Front, October 1918.

Troops repairing bridges throw rocks to splash the camera. Varennes (where, in July, 3rd Division earned the title 'Marne') showing extensive damage. An American discovering a German booby trap (acted) with a demonstration of how they work. A US Signal Corps wireless station at Villeret. A patrol in a wood checks apparently dead Germans (acted?). American dug-outs in the hills near Varennes. 75mm guns moving into position in the Cuisy area. American troops attacking under shell fire in the Meuse advance. German prisoners being put onto a train. "Gotham Boys", presumably 27th (New York) Division at Ronssoy, their divisional headquarters, in September. A field signal unit demonstrates a mechanical wire-twister. Transport of 35th Division moving through the ruins of Cheppy. A pile of loaves showing the rations for one division for one day. Limbers of the Field Artillery move up while observers use trench periscopes. 155mm guns of V Corps on the Exermont Road. US

Engineers repair a girder bridge. An overturned 155mm gun on the road. A posed group of German prisoners. A view of Exermont with Côte 240 behind it, 35th Division area. American and French officers in an observation post at the base of a hill. US Infantry crouched in foxholes in a wood, then advancing in short rushes from hole to hole.

Notes
Production etc: see **Notes** to **IWM 501-01**.
Remarks: the two combat sequences are very attractive, and have every appearance of being genuine. The first, 'attacking under shellfire in the Meuse advance' is apparently that referred to by Brownlow in his book. [Kevin Brownlow, *The War, the West and the Wilderness*, Secker and Warburg (1979): 128-129]
catalogued SDB: 5/1982

IWM 501-10 · USA, (ca) 1919
PICTORIAL HISTORY OF THE WORLD WAR NO 10

b/w · 1 reel · 860' (15 mins) · silent
intertitles: English

sp US Army General Staff, Historical Branch, War Plans Division *pr* US Signal Corps

I. The US Contingent on the Italian Front, October 1918. Men of 332nd Infantry Regiment, detached from 83rd (Ohio) Division, being led by Italian soldiers into the second line of a trench system and going on to occupy a front line. Some of the Americans display their new mosquito-proof gloves and hoods. Other Americans assist the Italians in operating a 1-pounder pom-pom gun from a trench. Behind the lines Americans fraternise with Italian soldiers. One Italian gunner has used an American shrapnel helmet as a soundbox for an improvised mandolin.
II. US forces on the Western Front, October 1918. Views of the Freya Line near Nantillois with ruins in the foreground and a bombardment going on. A supply column moves past the ruins of Esnes, on the Cambrai Road. Tractors are used at Flirey in the St-Mihiel area to pull down damaged walls and rubble for road-fill. Nearby a girder bridge has been destroyed. A French kite balloon with flak protection bursting in front of it. A passing formation of five aircraft, too high for identification. French soldiers near Montfaucon, probably in reserve, firing a captured German 77mm

field gun. Another German gun on its side in the Bois de Sepharges being inspected by French troops. Described as "a 6-inch Krupp gun" it may be a 155mm howitzer. A portrait shot of Sergeant H J Adams who near Bouillonville (?) captured 375 Germans with an empty pistol. Inhabitants of Flirey, which shows some damage, receive food from the US Red Cross, eating with the Americans, while a baby feeds from its mother. Shelling near Montfaucon. US War Correspondents in a scrape trench, crouching because under fire (?). The correspondents group together as soldiers clear rubble nearby. General John J Pershing with Major-General William H Johnson, commanding 91st (Wild West) Division, at its divisional headquarters near Côte 290, Meuse-Argonne sector.

Notes
Production etc: see **Notes** to **IWM 501-01**.
[shotsheet available]
catalogued SDB: 5/1982

IWM 501-11 · USA, (ca) 1919
PICTORIAL HISTORY OF THE WORLD WAR NO 11

b/w · 1 reel · 34' (1 min) · silent
intertitles: English

sp US Army General Staff, Historical Branch, War Plans Division *pr* US Signal Corps

- Prince of Wales, "whose betrothal to Princess Yolanda of Italy is expected shortly", with Major-General Charles H Muir at US IV Corps headquarters at Cochem, Germany, probably early 1919.

Notes
Title: this is taken from the shotsheet although this is obviously only a fragment of the original episode.
Production etc: see **Notes** to **IWM 501-01**.
[shotsheet available]
catalogued SDB: 5/1982

IWM 501-12 · USA, (ca) 1919
PICTORIAL HISTORY OF THE WORLD WAR NO 12

b/w · 1 reel · 948' (16 mins) · silent
intertitles: English

sp US Army General Staff, Historical

Branch, War Plans Division *pr* US Signal Corps

I. US forces, chiefly 26th Division, on the Western Front, 18 October 1918. The commander of 26th (Yankee) Division, Major-General Clarence R Edwards, stands with Lieutenant-Colonel C M Dowell before their dug-out entrance at Bras. Nearby horses of 101st Field Artillery of the same division are watered. Divisional sappers have built a new wooden bridge over the Meuse Canal. At Charny a limber of 323rd Field Artillery, 83rd (Ohio) Division (? see **Notes**) pulls dead horses off the road. Members of 101st Field Artillery, 26th Division, groom their horses. Men of the Supply Column, 322nd Field Artillery, 83rd Division, around their fire.
II. The US Army of Occupation in Germany during the Armistice, December 1918. A Mobile Veterinary Section has constructed a temporary plunge bath for horses. At Molsberg American sentries challenge a lady to show her pass. Ordnance officers inspect an unexploded shell which they explode with an electric charge.
III. US forces in France, probably soon after the Armistice, November 1918. German prisoners help move stores at the US depot at Verneuil. The Minstrel Troop of First Army Tank Corps, based at 302nd Tank Center, St-Mihiel, gives a performance for the camera including, a 'cake walk' dance. The ruins of the church at Lucy. German dead in the open in the area of Château-Thierry. The first train arrives back in Amiens station and refugees return to their homes. An American divisional headquarters in an old German position on the Freya Line, possibly 2nd Division ('the racehorse brigades'). A captured dug-out used as a dressing station. A premature German mine explosion in the retreat from the Freya Line has caused much damage. Mk V tanks knocked out near Ronssoy on the Cambrai Road by running into an anti-tank minefield of spherical mines.

Notes
Production etc: see **Notes** to **IWM 501-01**.
Summary: note that 83rd (Ohio) Division did not serve in France as a formed unit, being converted into 2nd Depot Division.
Remarks: the dance routine of the minstrel troupe is of considerable interest as social history, and also very humorous.
[shotsheet available]
catalogued SDB: 5/1982

IWM 501-13 · USA, (ca) 1919
PICTORIAL HISTORY OF THE WORLD WAR NO 13

b/w · 1 reel · 982' (16 mins) · silent
intertitles: English

sp US Army General Staff, Historical Branch, War Plans Division *pr* US Signal Corps

I. US forces on the Western Front, October or November 1918. A column of men from 1st Balloon Company, in the Meuse or Moselle region, march through a village. British "8-inch Naval rifles" (in fact 6-inch Mk VII guns) being fired by gunners of 27th (New York) Division. One chalks on a shell "from first squad, New York". US Colored Troops of the Signal Corps, 92nd (Buffalo) Division, repairing wires after the capture of the Breslen trenches. US troops help issue supplies to refugees, loading the goods onto rail flatcars. French refugees return to Bohain, mainly old people and children who carry an American flag down the street. In recently-liberated Montbrehain 79 year old Madame Josephine Wassaux talks to Lieutenant C A Daniels of 105th Field Signal Battalion, 27th Division. German prisoners work carrying boxes, and sit delousing themselves, at St-Pierre-des-Corps station in the Loire area. At Puteaux five US volunteers test the effects of "sneeze gas" on American and German gas masks. All emerge from a room full of the gas. The three without masks are badly affected, as is the one wearing a German mask. The man wearing the American mask does not seem to be affected.
II. US forces on the Italian Front, October or November 1918. The contingent is 332nd Infantry Regiment. The men march through the streets of Treviso and under the main arch. At the River Sile Italian soldiers give them instructions in river crossing using punts. The Americans march to and occupy the "Royal Dyke" defences on the River Piave. Bonfires are prepared as protection against gas. A gas exercise near Varago-Maserada, with the men donning their masks. More of the trenches on the River Piave. General Charles G Treat and Mr Samuel Gompers (the American labour leader) with Colonel William Wallace, commanding 332nd Regiment, at his headquarters at Treviso. Mr Gompers talks to an Italian soldier, and in a formal ceremony the "New York Sons of Young Italy" presents its colours to the regiment, and they are carried back to its headquarters.
III. Captured German war trophies displayed

in Paris, and the state visit of George V, December 1918. The centre of the city. Captured German and Austrian 77mm field guns are parked along the Champs Elysées, and there is an exhibition of war trophies in the Place de la Concorde (the camera is on a car travelling at high speed). Enemy planes and guns are on display in the Tuileries gardens. In the Champs Elysées is a plaster of Paris study of a planned statue of "Poilu", a French soldier beside a female personification of France. A visit of King George V to France, probably December 1918. He emerges from the Bois de Boulogne station and enters a horse-drawn carriage with President Poincaré. The Prince of Wales is behind them. Their carriage and a number of others pass the camera too quickly for the occupants to be identified. With an escort of French soldiers the carriages cross the Seine into the Place de la Concorde.

Notes
Production etc: see **Notes** to **IWM 501-01**.
[shotsheet available]
catalogued SDB: 6/1982

IWM 501-14 · USA, (ca) 1919
PICTORIAL HISTORY OF THE WORLD WAR NO 14

b/w · 1 reel · 795' (14 mins) · silent
intertitles: English

sp US Army General Staff, Historical Branch, War Plans Division *pr* US Signal Corps

▪ US forces in the Advance to Victory, Western Front, 23-25 October 1918.

I. Events on 23 October. Captain J B Luckie leads 'G' Company, 313rd Infantry Regiment, 79th (Liberty) Division, over the top in a training exercise in the region of Combres. The town of Cambrai after liberation, showing the German military headquarters based in the town hall. Refugees start to return to their various homes in the town. Major-General G W Read, the commander of II Corps, with his Chief of Staff Brigadier-General G S Simonds, Captain Marshal Prentis ADC, 1st Lieutenant B F Dawson ADC and Lieutenant-Colonel J G Taylor, Chief Signals Officer, inspects a captured deep dug-out and pillbox near Le Catelet. Nearby Taylor with 1st Lieutenant E O Harris inspects the wreck of a German limber with the horses dead. Beside it are four graves marked with

German helmets.
II. Events on 24 October. Colonel J E Dent, commanding 104th Engineer Regiment, 29th (Blue and Gray) Division inspecting road traffic on horseback near Samogneux. Captain J Duffield, attached to 111th Machine Gun Battalion, 29th Division, with his men in tents near Samogneux. One of the men tells a story about his adventures, with much hand-waving and dramatic gestures.
III. Events at Cunel on 25 October. 1st Lieutenant William J Fox of the Signal Corps films a church allegedly used by the Germans as a cinema. In the village men of 90th (Alamo) Division have taken over a mansion formerly used by the Germans as a headquarters. 3rd Battalion, 358th Infantry Regiment of the division establishes its first aid post nearby. The view east down the main street followed by the view north towards the Bois de Rappes, with men of the division moving up. At a command post in the wood are, left to right: 1st Lieutenant R H Hicks, 1st Lieutenant M D Fowler and 2nd Lieutenant F P Gerling of the division. The view out of the wood towards the German position on a hill. A carrying party from 358th Infantry Regiment brings food up to the forward positions in the wood. Inside the wood, a Vickers machinegun of 'D' Company, 344th Machine Gun Battalion, has been placed in support of 358th Infantry Regiment.

Notes
Production etc: see **Notes** to **IWM 501-01**.
[shotsheet available]
catalogued SDB: 6/1982

IWM 502 · USA, (?) 1919
FLASHES OF ACTION

b/w & (partly) tinted · 5 reels · 5127' (85 mins) · silent
intertitles: English

pr US Signal Corps

▪ US film of the American Expeditionary Force, from its departure for France in 1917 to its return and triumphal parades in 1919.

(Reel 1) Men board troopships, including SS *Leviathan*, in New York harbour. On the crossing there are sports, a dance, and jive by black troops. A submarine attack is repelled by destroyers. The men disembark at Brest and board railway cars for the front. Villages close to the front show shell

damage. On 28 September 1918 men of 39th and 58th Infantry Regiments, 4th (Ivy) Division, advance under enemy fire near Montfaucon. Troops advance behind a barrage (some fakes) on 1st Division ('Big Red One') sector in front of Seicheprey on 14 September. *(Reel 2)* Scenes of trenches, sniping and wounded in the summer of 1918. Identified are the following units: 30th (Old Hickory) Division at Bellicourt on 29 September; 18th Infantry, 1st Division at Exermont on 5 October; wounded at Missy-aux-Bois on 16 July; 139th Infantry, 35th Division east of Verdun on 28 October; troops at Michelbach on 22 June; 2nd Division ('racehorse brigades') near Missy-aux-Bois on 20 July; 1st Division near Exermont on 4 October; 128th Infantry, 32nd (Iron Jaws) Division in Austerlitz Woods, Alsace, 5 June; 7th Field Artillery, 1st Division, at Varmaise on 5 July using mustard gas shells; German bombardment of Thiaucourt on 21 September and of Rambucourt on 20 April; Albatros CIII shot down by the Frenchman Raymond Varnier at Cuperly on 19 July; 155mm howitzers of 32nd Division (?) shelling German positions at Sultzeren from Gérardmer on 27 August. *(Reel 3)* 103rd Infantry, 26th (Yankee) Division attack at Torcy at 4.35am on 18 July in half-light. 305th and 307th Infantry, 77th (Metropolitan) Division approach Longueville on 5 September (the 'lost battalion' episode). General John J Pershing decorating a private. A US kite balloon near Montfaucon on 3 October defended by machineguns and 75mm anti-aircraft guns. A Fokker DVII is shot down but the pilot, Unteroffizier Hans Heinrich Marwede, survives. 75mm field guns of 6th Field Artillery, 1st Division, at Exermont on 5 October. Heavily camouflaged snipers creeping out into no man's land. Guns of 1st Division at Beaumont on 9 September. *(Reel 4)* 400mm and 320mm railway guns, and other lighter pieces, bombarding a town. American 75mm field guns in action at les Côtes de Forimont on 27 September. A Renault FT17 light tank. A British Mk V Female tank. US 155mm howitzers explode an ammunition dump. US Spad 13s being fitted with small (8-pounder ?) bombs before take-off. A caption naming Quentin Roosevelt precedes film of Sopwith Camels of 148 (American) Squadron – with which QR had no connection – in the air; similarly, reference to Eddie Rickenbacker is followed by a scene with no clear link to the American fighter ace. A night bombardment. German prisoners at Saizerais (?) on 13 September. 4th Infantry, 3rd (Marne) Division marching through Bachrach after the Armistice. An American

sentry by the River Rhine at Coblenz. A group of American gunners joking with a 75mm shell-case beside the American flag (possibly 'the last shot of the war' ?). *(Reel 5)* Post-Armistice celebrations. Pershing says formal goodbyes to Marshal Foch before boarding his ship to return. It arrives in New York to a great reception. On 10 September 1919 Pershing leads 1st Division through the streets of New York. This is followed by similar parades in Philadelphia (escorted by the Philadelphia Light Dragoons), at Wilmington in Delaware, and at Washington (this is filmed partly by airship and aircraft).

Notes
Technical: part of the first reel is tinted orange, red and green.
Remarks: "flashes" is an accurate description, and "action" more accurate than might be supposed. The film presents one lively image after another, some of them suspect or fake, but very few of them dull.
[John J Pershing, *My Experiences in the World War*, Hodder and Stoughton (1931)]
[L Stallings, *The Doughboys*, Harper and Row (1963)]
[shotsheet available]
catalogued SDB: 6/1982

IWM 503 · USA, (?) 1919
27TH AND 30TH DIVISIONS

b/w · 3 reels · 2606' (45 mins) · silent
intertitles: English

pr US Signal Corps

■ US film of their own 27th and 30th Divisions, attached to the British Army, on the Western Front, August-October 1918.

(Reel 1) King George V and General Sir Herbert Plumer, commanding Second Army to which the two divisions were attached, are greeted by 30th (Old Hickory) Division commander, Major-General Edward M Lewis and his CoS Colonel John H Kerr, Rauchicourt, 6 August. A soldier places flags on the graves of Lieutenant-Colonel Morris H Liebman and 38 enlisted men of 105th, 107th, 108th Infantry, and 104th and 105th Machine Gun Battalions, all 27th (New York) Division. Wounded of the two divisions are carried by train to Base Hospital No 37, disembarking at the station. Men of Australian 1st Division, late September, entraining for a rest camp. One

of two 12-inch railway guns of 471st Siege Battery RGA (probably 'HMG Boche Buster'). A column of German prisoners guarded by men of 115th Field Artillery, 30th Division, and 9th Infantry, 2nd Division ('racehorse brigades'). 75mm guns of 27th Division near Limey en route for Thiaucourt, 13 September. A German A7V tank 'Mephisto' (captured by 26th Battalion, Australian 2nd Division, in Monument Wood, Villerson, on 14 July after being hit by aircraft) is displayed at Poulainville on 13 September. A British Mk V Female tank captured and recaptured in the Battle of Amiens displayed with its crew at Beauquesne on 16 September. Corporal L K Knowlson, HQ Signal Platoon, 105th Infantry, the first man of 27th Division to be decorated, at Doullens, 17 September. Men of 119th Infantry, 30th Division, marching through Péronne, 27 September. A dressing station for 30th Division near Villeret, 29 September. An Australian 9.2-inch howitzer firing. *(Reel 2)* 'B' Company, 105th Machine Gun Battalion and 108th Infantry, 27th Division, return through Ronssoy, 1 October. Staff of 54th Brigade, also part of 27th (New York) Division, posed in a car. They are, left to right: 1st Lieutenant Clark, the Artillery Liaison Officer, Brigadier-General Palmer E Pierce (not Paul, as given), Lieutenant-Colonel Saulsberry, Australian 4th Division, 1st Lieutenants Baxton and R J Easton ADCs. Men of 30th Division looking for dead near Bellicourt, under fire. Two British Whippet medium tanks of 'A' Company, 6th Tank Battalion, attached to British 32nd Division (not 30th Division as given) in the Joncourt area. 'A' and 'C' Companies, 102nd Engineers, 27th Division, near Ronssoy on 4 October. Australians, probably 4th Division, at Bussu on 4 October. American propaganda balloons being released at Templeux-la-Fosse on 8 October. German prisoners of 30th Division at Bellicourt on 8 October, and of 27th Division held behind wire. The entrance to the St-Quentin Canal tunnel at Bellicourt on 9 October. 60-pounders of 1st Essex Heavy Artillery Battery in support of 30th Division near Bohain on 11 October. Field Marshal Haig, Lieutenant-Colonel Robert Bacon (ex-US Ambassador to France), Colonels Hazeltine and Fletcher ADCs, inspect the St-Quentin Canal tunnel entrance at Bellicourt 15 October. A 30th Division first aid station at Lahaie Menneresse, Le Cateau Road, 17 October. 3rd Battalion, 120th Engineers and Machine Gun Company, 105th Infantry, 27th Division, preparing to advance near Révière on 17 October. *(Reel 3)* 30th Division Engineers pass through Moslins, 18 October.

Australian gunners enter Ribeauville on 19 October shortly after 30th Division took it. Major-General George W Read, commanding II Corps, with his CoS Brigadier-General George S Simonds, visits the US cemetery at Bony on 23 October. Two wrecked Austin armoured cars on the battlefield. American troops display, at Corbei on 4 November, German body armour captured at Bellicourt. 27th Division marches past General John J Pershing, who addresses the officers. Lieutenant-General Sir David Henderson inspects the two divisions, awarding the DSO to Lieutenant-Colonel Hallahan of 27th Division and the "Medal of Bravery" to Sergeant Robert McCay (note the 30th Division 'football' sign on helmets and shoulder-flashes). A posed group, left to right, of Henderson, Major-General Lewis and Major-General John F O'Ryan, commanding 27th Division.

Notes

Remarks: together with the British *September Offensive* and *October Offensive* series this gives a good overall picture of the Battle of St-Quentin (the breaking of the Hindenburg Line).
[John J Pershing, *My Experiences in the World War*, Hodder and Stoughton (1931)]
[L Stallings, *The Doughboys*, Harper and Row (1963)]
[C E W Bean, *Official History of Australia in the War 1914-1918, Vol VI*, Angus and Robertson (1942)]
[John Terraine, *To Win a War*, Sidgwick and Jackson (1978)]
[shotsheet available]
catalogued SDB: 6/1982

IWM 504 · GB, 6/1920
GAUMONT GRAPHIC 962 – THE OPENING OF THE IMPERIAL WAR MUSEUM

b/w · 1 reel · 132' (2 mins) · silent
intertitles: English

pr Gaumont

■ George V opening the Imperial War Museum at Crystal Palace, London, 9 June 1920.

The King is with Queen Mary. They meet with Sir Alfred Mond, First Commissioner of Works, Sir Martin Conway and Major ffoulkes of the Imperial War Museum in the foyer of the Museum galleries. The guests and staff assemble for a formal ceremony of dedication. Then the King and Queen are taken on a tour of the exhibits. Also present in the party are Winston Churchill as Secretary of State for War (seen very briefly), Surgeon-Commander Parkes of the Museum, and the Duke of Connaught (?). Much of the attention of the film is taken up with the full-sized replica of an 18-inch naval gun – the shells are genuine – which dominates the main exhibition hall.

Notes

Title: both titles appear on the film. It is probably an extract from a longer newsreel. [*Imperial War Museum Handbook* (1982)] [shotsheet available] catalogued SDB: 7/1982

IWM 505 · GB, 1920
ARMISTICE DAY 1920 – HOMECOMING OF AN UNKNOWN WARRIOR

b/w · 1 reel · 413' (7 mins) · silent intertitles: English

pr Pathé

I. Scenes in the Charing Cross area of central London on Armistice Day, with crowds cheering in the streets, 11 November 1918.
II. The transport from France and burial at Westminster Abbey in London of the Unknown Warrior, 10-11 November 1920. A temporary British cemetery in France, possibly Thelus. The camera closes in to a cross marked "A British Soldier". Then the coffin of the Unknown Warrior being carried to the quay at Boulogne by senior NCOs of the Royal Army Service Corps, London Regiment, Royal Engineers, Royal Field Artillery, Machine Gun Corps, Royal Army Medical Corps, and the Australian Imperial Force and Canadian Expeditionary Force. It is escorted by French soldiers in military mourning. At the quayside Marshal Foch waits with General Weygand, Colonel Wyatt and Colonel Bradstock (?). The coffin is transferred to the destroyer HMS *Verdun*, commanded by Lieutenant-Commander Colin Thompson. The ship crosses the English Channel to Dover, where the pallbearers and escort are provided by regiments of the Dover Garrison. 10 November 1920. The ceremony of 11 November 1920. The procession comes through Admiralty Arch led by silent military bands. (The gun-carriage on which the coffin is carried went to France with the BEF in 1914.) The pallbearers (not clearly visible) are British gunners. The chief mourners

from the Army are, from the front, General Sir Julian Byng, General Sir Henry Horne, Field Marshal Sir Henry Wilson (CIGS), Field Marshal Sir Douglas Haig, Field Marshal the Earl of Ypres (John French). The naval mourners can be only occasionally and indistinctly seen. They include Viscount Jellicoe and Admiral Beatty. At the Cenotaph in Whitehall the King, in Field Marshal's uniform, places a wreath on the coffin and another at the base of the monument, after unveiling it. The Prime Minister, Lloyd George, places his wreath on the Cenotaph after the King. The procession moves off at a slow march. The King leads, behind him are the Prince of Wales, the Duke of York (the future George VI) and the Duke of Gloucester. Outside Westminster Abbey the pallbearers take the coffin from the gun-carriage and prepare to enter the building.

[*The British Legion Journal*, 9: 5 (November 1929)]
catalogued SDB: 7/1982

IWM 506 · Uruguay, 1922
el HOMENAJE DEL URUGUAY A LOS RESTOS DE SIR ERNEST SHACKLETON
URUGUAY'S TRIBUTE TO SIR ERNEST SHACKLETON (translation)

b/w · 1 reel · 667' (11 mins) · silent intertitles: Spanish

pr Maurice, Henry

■ The lying in state of the body of Sir Ernest Shackleton in Montevideo, Uruguay, and its transfer to ship for burial on the island of South Georgia, 1922.

The film opens with a portrait still of Shackleton, followed by film of one of his expedition companions, Captain Hussey RN, getting out of his car in Montevideo. Various society mourners arrive by car or on foot to pay their respects to the body, which has a military guard and is lying in a church. (The film shows only the arrival and departure of the mourners, not the interior of the building.) For transport to the quayside the coffin is given a mounted escort and full military honours. While a large crowd watches, the coffin is placed on a gun-carriage, covered with a Union Flag and has wreaths placed over it. At the quayside the Uruguayan Minister for Foreign Affairs, Doctor Juan Antonio Buero, delivers a speech (quoted in the captions) and the British chargé d'affaires replies. The coffin is loaded onto the exploration ship SS *Woodville*. The escort of lancers and the crowd departs. The *Woodville* itself then steams out of harbour.

Notes
Summary: Foreign Office papers in the Public Record Office (FO 371/8529) indicate that this film was presented to the British Government by the Uruguayan Government in 1923 and deposited at the Museum by the FO in May of that year. See also **IWM 456**.
Remarks: something of an oddity, and outside the Museum's normal terms of reference, but providing some interesting views of South American society in the early part of the century. The captioning, both in style and choice of language, is extremely florid.
[shotsheet available]
catalogued SDB: 7/1982

IWM 507 · GB, 1920
GAUMONT GRAPHIC [900 approx] – GIFT TO THE BRITISH NATION

b/w · 1 reel · 80' (1 min) · silent
intertitles: English

pr Gaumont

■ Presentation of a replica of the standard of the French 61st Artillery Regiment to the Imperial War Museum, 15 October 1920.

The replica of the standard was presented in honour of the Anglo-French cooperation in the Battle of Amiens, 8 August 1918. The presentation takes place in the street in front of the Ministry of Works in Whitehall. Making the presentation are General Viscount de la Panonse and Colonel Marie of the regiment. Receiving the standard for the Imperial War Museum are Sir Alfred Mond, First Commissioner of Works, Sir Martin Conway and Major C J ffoulkes. The ceremony has attracted the attention of a small crowd of passers-by and employees of the ministry.

Notes
Title: the title and subtitle are both flashframes. The film is an item from a Gaumont Graphic weekly newsreel.
[shotsheet available]
catalogued SDB: 7/1982

IWM 508-1 – 508-9 · NO FILM

IWM 508-10 · France, 17/5/1917
ANNALES DE LA GUERRE 10

b/w · 1 reel · 502' (9 mins) · silent
intertitles: none

pr Section Cinématographique de l'Armée Française

I. A Moroccan division's sports behind the lines in Champagne, Western Front, early May 1917. Troops of a Moroccan division behind the lines in Champagne march in road column, led by their band, through a village to their sports. The sports include a football match and a mule race as well as athletics. A Voisin 8 aircraft flies overhead. A percussion band plays various Moroccan instruments in accompaniment to a sword dance. Some local ladies give out prizes.
II. Women working on the Home Front, early May 1917. Near the front a railway siding shows some shell damage. Women in uniform help clear up the rubble. Other women work in a nearby factory and steelworks. Molten metal is poured into a Bessemer converter, and steel is forged and shaped. The factory is guarded by soldiers with a Hotchkiss machinegun on an anti-aircraft mount.
III. The award of the Croix de guerre to Madame Marchal, France, early May 1917. The award is made for Madame Marchal's help to wounded French soldiers in 1914. The military honour guard marches into position and a senior officer (not clearly seen) makes the presentation. Shown in portrait shot the lady, who is in civilian clothes, has healing face scars.
IV. Villages north of Soissons reoccupied by the French after the German retreat of February, Western Front, early May 1917. At the village of Vailly the French have captured the German trench and wire system reasonably intact. A new wooden bridge has been built across the Aisne to replace that blown up by the Germans, and French transport crosses. A pan over the new German positions on a ridge with the village of Chavonne in the foreground. The ruins of the village of Soupir. A battery of 155mm howitzers shells the German positions. A soldier explores a collapsed German dug-out.
V. French forces on the Salonika Front, April or May 1917. A Spahi Cavalry regiment makes a formal march past. General Sarrail, on horseback, presents the colonel of the regiment to the Greek Prime

Minister, M E Venizelos. The review continues and the horsemen gallop off at its end.

Notes
Title: the title of this episode has been taken from the shotsheet.
[shotsheet available]
catalogued SDB: 7/1982

IWM 508-11 · France, 24/5/1917
ANNALES DE LA GUERRE 11

b/w · 1 reel · 657' (11 mins) · silent
intertitles: French

pr Section Cinématographique de l'Armée Française

I. Carrier pigeons in a loft behind the French lines are fed by their soldier-keepers, late May 1917. In the trenches a message is fitted to one pigeon, which flies back to its loft where the message is removed. The pigeons play in a birdbath.
II. The recently reoccupied areas of the Somme region, late May 1917. Some soldiers have created an outdoor school under the blossoms on the trees. The children, about 10 years old, dance around the soldiers.
III. The observer in a kite balloon attaches his headset and the balloon, which has two baskets, ascends, late May 1917. The view down from the balloon as it goes up is shown. The cable is played out from the control vehicle. The view from one observation basket to the other. The observer in the basket checks what he can see against the map. The balloon descends again.
IV. 60th Infantry Regiment is drawn up on parade in open country and its standard decorated with the Croix de guerre, late May 1917. Smaller unit flags, called fanions, are also decorated. Private Gouvres of the regiment receives the award of Knight of the Légion d'honneur (no clear view of the awarding officer) and poses for the camera. The regiment leaves in full marching order led by its scouts and cyclists and with all its equipment.

[shotsheet available]
catalogued SDB: 7/1982

IWM 508-12 · France, 31/5/1917
ANNALES DE LA GUERRE 12

b/w · 1 reel · 540' (10 mins) · silent
intertitles: French

pr Section Cinématographique de l'Armée Française

I. A Red Cross garden fête in Salonika, Greece, late May 1917. The fête is for the various Allied contingents. The Italians and French have their national flags on display. Soldiers and civilians of various nationalities wander through the sunlight, all rather camera-conscious.
II. French forces on the Western Front, late May 1917. Near Soissons is the "Fort de Condé", taken by the French on 19 April, a large stone-and-brick construction with French soldiers walking through it. Also displayed is the collection of German guns captured in the process, chiefly 77mm field guns, 155mm howitzers and various mortars. General Maistre inspects an airfield at which two fighter squadrons are based, one of Nieuport 12 aircraft and the other of Spad 13s. The Spads have their engines started and begin to take off. The French Army Signal Service. One of the soldiers up a telegraph pole testing a line. Others erect another telegraph pole. A cable being laid in one of the trenches is paid out before being covered with sandbags. In a village not far from the front a more permanent cable is run out from a drum and installed underground via a manhole in the middle of the street. Spahi Cavalry in France practise manœuvres on a beach prior to returning to their camp.

[shotsheet available]
catalogued SDB: 7/1982

IWM 508-13 · France, 8/6/1917
ANNALES DE LA GUERRE 13

b/w · 1 reel · 469' (8 mins) · silent
intertitles: French

pr Section Cinématographique de l'Armée Française

I. A camp for Chasseurs Alpins in hill country, possibly the Vosges area, June 1917. The camp has permanent dug-outs in a hillside, while 75mm guns and limbers are being camouflaged with trees and matting. The first US forces, from US 1st Division ('Big Red One') arrive at the camp for training, firstly a small contingent marches in, then the remainder arrive in trucks. All wear American uniforms but French shrapnel helmets. They are instructed in the

French gas hood respirator. The French and American flags are raised at the camp, near the sign "camp Franco-Américain". A symbolic handshake between a French poilu and an American doughboy.
II. An American cargo ship docking at a French port, possibly Marseilles, June 1917. Its cargo of grain and flour is unloaded onto the quayside and tipped into storage vats.
III. General Pétain visits an Army rest camp, June 1917. He walks around among the troops, talks to them and samples a cup of wine. The film ends with a close-up of Pétain.

Notes
Remarks: the visit of Pétain to talk with his soldiers provides (both in the activity and in the film meant to publicise the fact) considerable insight into the manner in which he restored French morale in the summer of 1917. With no attempts at mateyness or exhortation, no handing out of cigarettes or patronising, his stately presence can be seen to act as a reassurance to the troops in the camp. A most interesting and impressive performance, all the more so for the fact that it is so understated. It has also been carefully stage-managed. According to Jeanne and Ford, Pétain pulled a face at the sour taste of the wine, and insisted on this being cut from the film before release.
[R Jeanne and C Ford, *Le Cinéma et la Presse*, Armand Colin (1961): 199-204]
[shotsheet available]
catalogued SDB: 7/1982

IWM 508-14 · France, 15/6/1917
ANNALES DE LA GUERRE 14

b/w · 1 reel · 473' (8 mins) · silent
intertitles: French

pr Section Cinématographique de l'Armée Française

I. Reoccupied Alsace, June 1917. A view of the plain of Mulhouse from the town of Thann. The town is attractive and shows no signs of war. A young lady wearing traditional Alsatian costume holds an American flag in honour of the US entry into the war.
II. The honouring of the Greek provisional Government in Salonika, June 1917. The ceremony is held in the square beside the Church of St Sophia. French and Greek troops form a guard of honour around the square while civilians watch. Prime Minister Venizelos arrives with General Danglis and

Admiral Condouriotis to general acclaim. Their departure at the end of the ceremony is then shown.
III. General Pétain decorates the standards of various units and some officers, including one from the Air Corps, Western Front, June 1917.
IV. French soldiers in the line at Laffaux, north-east of Soissons, explore a captured German command post and take rations up to the front lines, Western Front, June 1917.
V. General Pershing's visit to Paris, 14 June 1917. Pershing begins his tour, escorted by various French military officials, at Les Invalides. He goes on to visit Napoleon's Tomb and see displays of captured enemy standards at the Musée de l'Armée. At Le Bourget airfield he meets the military governor of Paris, General Dubail, and they watch aircraft stunt flying above the airfield. Pershing talks to the pilots and meets a 14 year old refugee from Arras who has been adopted by them.

[John J Pershing, *My Experiences in the World War*, Hodder and Stoughton (1931): 65]
[shotsheet available]
catalogued SDB: 7/1982

IWM 508-15 · France, 22/6/1917
ANNALES DE LA GUERRE 15

b/w · 1 reel · 456' (8 mins) · silent
intertitles: none

pr Section Cinématographique de l'Armée Française

I. A parachute, probably a message, dropping from a kite balloon near Chalais Mendon, Western Front, June 1917.
II. General Berthelot, head of the French military mission to Romania, talks with officers then goes on to meet the King and Prince Carol at a station, probably Bucharest, June 1917.
III. General Lyautey with his escort visiting the Sultan of Morocco at his palace in Rabat, June 1917.
IV. Refugees return to territory reoccupied after the German retreat to the Hindenburg Line, Western Front, June 1917. An old soldier chats to an elderly woman refugee who has returned home and is using stones and rubble to repair her house. More refugees return by horse and cart. One couple begins to weed a garden, and old men start carpentry work and roof repairs.
V. A regiment of 42nd Division receives a unit citation. Other units receive fanion

decorations. The division marches past. Western Front, June 1917.

Notes
Title: this is taken from the shotsheet.
[shotsheet available]
cataloged SDB: 7/1982

IWM 508-16 · France, 30/6/1917
ANNALES DE LA GUERRE 16

b/w · 1 reel · 534' (9 mins) · silent
intertitles: French

pr Section Cinématographique de l'Armée Française

I. The arrival of a token Russian force near Athens, Greece, June 1917. A passenger ship brings the Russian Contingent to the Piraeus, the port of Athens. French (or Russian ?) soldiers wearing sun helmets start their march from the Piraeus to Athens, establishing posts on the way.
II. Somme area: sappers bury an unexploded shell and detonate it by wire. A demonstration of a flame-thrower in a trench system. Western Front, June 1917.
III. Award of the Légion d'honneur to Captain Guynemer, the French ace pilot, Western Front, June 1917. A march past by the ground crew at the aerodrome, followed by a portrait shot of Guynemer. A visiting general (no clear picture) inspects the aerodrome's Spad 13s and decorates Guynemer with the Légion d'honneur. The troops again march past, led by their band. An additional, unexplained, scene of an explosion in open country.
IV. Farm work in central France, June 1917. Farmers harvest the hay and load it into wagons. Cattle are fenced in a field by barbed wire. Three farmers plough with "American" mechanical tractors.
V. Schoolchildren in Paris celebrate US Independence Day, waving US flags and cheering for the camera, 4 July 1917.

Notes
Title: this is taken from the shotsheet.
Date: the release date comes from the official French records. The discrepancy between this and the 4 July item is unexplained.
Intertitles: these are all flashframes.
Remarks: in this and the previous issue, the French do seem to be overplaying their willingness to receive their new American ally, not to mention their relief at the USA's entry into the war.
[shotsheet available]

cataloged SDB: 7/1982

IWM 508-17 · France, 7/7/1917
ANNALES DE LA GUERRE 17

b/w · 1 reel · 481' (8 mins) · silent
intertitles: French

pr Section Cinématographique de l'Armée Française

I. Prince Alexander of Serbia on the Salonika Front, July 1917. The Prince visits the Serbian troops in their mountain positions. He dismounts from his horse, talks with his officers and looks out over the position with binoculars before riding away.
II. French forces in the Marne area of the Western Front, July 1917. Soldiers move through the ruins of Craonnelle. A badly made trench in the Vauclerc area is manned by tired soldiers. Some of the men relax in the rear trenches or sleep in dug-outs. There are a number of temporary graves visible. A posed group of a divisional general (no identification) with his staff. Soldiers scramble and walk over the ruins of Craonne. A pan over the California plateau, with shell-bursts on the ridge in the distance.
III. Romanian field guns and limbers on the march down a road, Romanian Front, July 1917.
IV. The treatment of German prisoners and refugees near Ribécourt in the Somme area, Western Front, July 1917. The prisoners leave their tented camp and are taken into the village, where they work repairing shell damage. The work involved is mainly road and building repair, but includes a sawmill cutting timber. In the same area refugees make a temporary village of wooden huts for themselves. After work, the German prisoners wash in a nearby river.
V. The Saint Chamond tank, Western Front, July 1917. Four Saint Chamond tanks move down a village street. They are fully opened up and the crews look out through the hatches or ride on top of them. The street shows some battle damage. The fourth tank has the name 'Teddy' on its nose and a small dog is riding on top.

Notes
Title: this is taken from the shotsheet.
Intertitles: these are all flashframes.
[shotsheet available]
cataloged SDB: 7/1982

IWM 508-18 · France, 14/7/1917
ANNALES DE LA GUERRE 18

b/w · 1 reel · 530' (9 mins) · silent
intertitles: French

pr Section Cinématographique de l'Armée
Française

I. A recently recaptured area, July 1917. A
school class is held in the open air. An
officer of 102nd Infantry Regiment gives
small gifts to the children. The gifts include
small French flags. The children's faces are
shown in close-up. They race out of the
schoolyard.
II. Nesle, behind the lines, Somme area,
July 1917. A British officer hands out
chocolate to children in the main square,
one of the children is held by a French
officer, and the two men talk together. In
the square a pierrot show is about to start,
the actors are preparing and the audience,
of civilians and British and French soldiers,
is waiting. The show, on a raised stage at
one end of the square, starts with a lady
singer, followed by a paper-tearing act.
III. More recently recaptured areas, July
1917. M Viviani, the "Garde de Sceaux"
(Privy Seal) and M Leon Bourgeois, the
Minister of Labour, on a tour of enquiry
deliver speeches to a gathering in the
square of one town. At Noyon they meet
the Mayor, M Noel, and again give
speeches to the people. They pay homage
to the war dead at a temporary cemetery. At
Guiscard they are met by the town leaders,
and at Ham they again address the locals
from the main square.
IV. General Pétain at a formal parade pins
the Croix de guerre to the standard of 410th
Infantry Regiment, July 1917. As the
ceremony finishes a small girl,
accompanied by her mother, offers Pétain a
bouquet of flowers. He kisses both of them.
Later in the ceremony he also decorates the
standard of I Cavalry Corps (note that this
included Infantry and cyclist units). After this
ceremony General Féraud decorates the
fanions of cyclist units of 1st Cavalry
Division. The troops of the division,
including an Infantry regiment, march past.
A close-up of the fanion-bearer. The division
then marches back to its camp and General
Pétain congratulates the various officers.

Notes
Title: this is taken from the shotsheet.
Intertitles: these are all flashframes.
[shotsheet available]
catalogued SDB: 7/1982

IWM 508-19 · France, 21/7/1917
**ANNALES DE LA GUERRE 19 – LES
EVENEMENTS DE GRECE JUIN-JUILLET
1917**

b/w · 1 reel · 554' (9 mins) · silent
intertitles: French

pr Section Cinématographique de l'Armée
Française

■ Events following the French-backed coup
d'état in Greece, Athens 25 June-14 July
1917.

French soldiers on the Acropolis on 25
June guarding Athens from the Parthenon.
They are armed and have machinegun
posts set up, but there is an element of
sightseeing in their behaviour. This is
followed by the requiem service for Greek
soldiers killed on the Salonika Front held at
the Piraeus on 24 June, used to display the
French military presence and the new
Greek ministry. A crowd lines the way to the
church waving banners as the dignitaries
approach. Firstly, two of the new ministers,
Repoulis and Michalopoulis in procession
with the town mayor. Next is the French
Admiral de Gueydon with his staff, and
General Régnault, whose two divisions
backed the coup, with his staff. Led by the
banners, the dignitaries leave after the
ceremony. On 27 June a formal ceremony
is planned for the new Prime Minister,
Venizelos. French troops march past the
Arch of Hadrian on their way into Athens.
The crowd outside the Hôtel de Grande
Bretagne waits for the Prime Minister while
dignitaries come and go to their cheers. A
day later, back at the Arch of Hadrian,
General de Monterou watches as his troops
march past into the city. On 30 June, in the
deserted Stadium in Athens, General
Régnault decorates some of his men after
the operation. On 1 July Greek troops are
drawn up in a large hollow square to take
the oath of allegiance to the new king,
Alexander (after his father's abdication in
the coup) led by the members of the new
government. Venizelos and his cabinet take
the oath, after which General Miloth
addresses the troops while the others
watch. Senior officers of the Greek forces
then march past leading their troops. In the
crowded Stadium on 14 July Venizelos and
his cabinet watch a military revue and
demonstration of loyalty.

Notes
Titles: these and the intertitles are all
flashframes.
Remarks: the coup d'état in Greece was

thought important enough for an entire issue of the newsreel to be devoted to it. But there is no attempt to justify the French action, rather an emphasis on continuity and on the popularity of the French. The whole is remarkably naïve politically. [Alan Palmer, *The Gardeners of Salonika*, André Deutsch (1965)]
[shotsheet available]
catalogued SDB: 7/1982

IWM 508-20 · France, 28/7/1917
ANNALES DE LA GUERRE 20

b/w · 1 reel · 415' (7 mins) · silent
intertitles: French

pr Section Cinématographique de l'Armée Française

I. General Lyautey, Governor of Morocco, visits the Sultan's palace at Rabat, 14 July 1917.
The Governor, who is ex-Minister of War, has an escort of lancers. The Sultan's Guard of Zouaves, guns and lancers marches past, led by its French officers.
II. The Marne and Alsace regions of the Western Front, July 1917. The recently-captured Hurtebise plateau in the Marne area. It is badly churned-up, but soldiers are moving about quite openly. At the entrance to a heavily sand-bagged dug-out an orderly gives a message to his sector commandant. Soldiers at the entrance to, and later inside, the Cave of the Dragon, used as a shelter. French troops stand guard over a crashed Albatros CII in the Vosges region. The aircraft is in perfect condition from the tail to the gunner's cockpit, but the nose has been completely crushed. In the Marne area French troops watch as the wreck of a crashed German Aviatik CII burns.
III. Visit by M Albert Thomas, Minister of Munitions, to Romania, July 1917. Albert Thomas waits at Harlan station with General Berthelot, head of the French military mission, and with the President of the Council. King Carol arrives by train with his son Prince Carol, and performs the welcoming ceremony of bread and salt for Thomas. Together they watch a demonstration of military manœuvres. The King gives Berthelot the order of Michel the Brave, following which the Romanian soldiers with their guns pass in review.

Notes
Title: both this and the subtitles are flashframes.

[shotsheet available]
catalogued SDB: 7/1982

IWM 508-21 · France, 4/8/1917
ANNALES DE LA GUERRE 21

b/w · 1 reel · 646' (11 mins) · silent
intertitles: French

pr Section Cinématographique de l'Armée Française

■ French I Corps in the first day of the Third Battle of Ypres (Passchendaele), 31 July 1917.

Three British, one French and three Belgian soldiers walk through an archway. French soldiers of I Corps, on foot and in lorries, pass in both directions down an undamaged street with Belgian troops. (Note the signpost to the Belgian headquarters at Houthem. This may be French First Army headquarters at Rexpoëde, just inside the French border.) At a supply dump heavy shells are covered with camouflage netting. A light train is loaded with ammunition and signal rockets. Horse-drawn flatwagons carry away planks of wood from the stores. Another light train is loaded with prefabricated sections of light railway track. A 145mm naval gun, completely camouflaged except for its barrel, is loaded and fired by its marine crew. A 280mm railway gun joins in the barrage. In what looks like a training exercise, sappers pile sandbags into a river to form a breakwater and others float out light pontoon bridges allowing them to cross. In a front line trench the soldiers prepare to attack. One of the four batteries of British 6-inch howitzers with I Corps opens fire. Gunners push a light rail flatcar loaded with shells through thick mud to their guns. Wounded, some walking, some carried by German stretcher-bearers, are taken past a bridge and a lock to the rear areas. This is one of the canal branch lines, possibly passing through Loo in 51st Division area. Where the stretchers are passing, a fatigue party takes cans of water forward. Further on, on the recently-captured German front line, soldiers cross over the Yser Canal. A German captain with a head wound is led back from the front – he salutes the camera. Two soldiers inspect the remains of a German pillbox which has been heavily shelled. In the rear areas German prisoners are led past the canal lock and on to the safe area. King Albert of Belgium arrives with General Anthoine at a

French headquarters, possibly Anthoine's own headquarters at Rexpoëde. After making their inspections they leave again. The film ends with a portrait shot of Anthoine as commander of the First Army (French and Belgian forces in Flanders).

Notes
Summary: comparison with the original caption lists suggests that some scenes of this issue are missing.
Remarks: the British, particularly in writing their history, ignore or forget the contribution of 6 French and 6 Belgian divisions to the Third Battle of Ypres. This film, although itself unexciting, is a useful corrective.
[shotsheet available]
catalogued SDB: 7/1982

IWM 508-22 · NO FILM

IWM 508-23 · France, 18/8/1917
ANNALES DE LA GUERRE 23

b/w · 1 reel · 448' (7 mins) · silent
intertitles: French

pr Section Cinématographique de l'Armée Française

I. Soldiers of 5th Artillery Regiment making souvenirs, Western Front, August 1917. Three soldiers, probably of 5th Artillery Regiment, relax on top of a pile of rubble and make souvenirs from expended 75mm shell-cases. Using light hammers and punches they work intricate designs of whorls and spirals into the metal, showing the camera the finished result.
II. The Italian military mission's visit to the Western Front, August 1917. The mission, led by Admiral Thaon di Revel, is escorted by General Foch as Chief of Staff. The party looks out over a battlefield, possibly Verdun, from an observation platform. Later, an Infantry formation led by its band marches past the party through a ruined street.
III. General Guillaumat, commanding the forces at Verdun, working at his office desk. He goes outside to watch troops march past below his balcony. Western Front, August 1917.
IV. The visit of the King and Queen of Belgium to a French aerodrome, Western Front, 13 August 1917. The King and Queen are introduced to the pilots, including the French ace Lieutenant

Nungesser. He takes each in turn for a joyride in a Bréguet Type 14A2. The Queen and the King are each shown climbing into the gunner's cockpit of the aircraft.
V. General Pétain decorates the standards of regiments of 1st and 51st Division which distinguished themselves in the first day of the Third Battle of Ypres. Western Front, August 1917. The men of the divisions are drawn up in the open. Pétain presents 1st and 201st Infantry Regiments with the "fourragère" (a decorative ribbon tied to their standards). The standards of 33rd and 233rd Infantry Regiments receive the Croix de guerre. A number of officers receive individual decorations. The men then march past while Pétain watches.

[shotsheet available]
catalogued SDB: 7/1982

IWM 508-24 · France, 25/8/1917
ANNALES DE LA GUERRE 24

b/w · 1 reel · 637' (11 mins) · silent
intertitles: French

pr Section Cinématographique de l'Armée Française

I. French counter-offensive at Verdun, August 1917. The "Deuxième Bataille Offensive de Verdun" opens with a bombardment. A 145mm naval gun firing under tarpaulin, showing its loading mechanism clearly. Other guns join in – a 155mm heavy howitzer, a 75mm field gun and a 155mm gun. Troops of 126th Division cross the Canal d'Est (probably) near the Côte de Talou by a footbridge and move on through the wooded distance (possibly the Bois France Boche near Vacherauville) to take up their positions in the St-Marion trench prior to the attack. The 155mm howitzers continue to bombard no man's land. Soldiers of 31st Division, who captured Mort-Homme, inspect the entrance to the tunnel used by the Crown Prince as his headquarters. Three men fire a Maxim machinegun (captured ?) out over the plain below the position, where firing still continues. At Côte 304, north of Esnes, men of 26th Division lead their prisoners back off the hill and into the trenches. Staff of 24th Infantry Regiment lead a large number of prisoners in wide marching column along the road to Rampont. The prisoners are described as having been captured in the Bois de Corbeaux – presumably by men of XVI Corps. Another group of prisoners leaves the Bois Bourru in

the same Corps area, probably on the road to Fromeréville. At the first collection point wounded prisoners are given blankets and, after being processed by an official, are let into ambulances. The captions at this point claim that the Germans have deliberately shelled and bombed clearly marked hospitals in the Verdun area, at Dugny, Les Monthairons, Vadelaincourt and Belrupt, but no damage is shown. At Les Monthairons a bedridden soldier, with a nurse in attendance, is awarded the Médaille Militaire.
II. Marshal Joffre accepts the American "Golden Book" from General Pershing, France, August 1917. The ceremony of presenting the book takes place at the American headquarters. Joffre accepts the book from Pershing. It is to be taken by a French mission about to leave for the United States. Two staff officers, one American and one French, hold up the heavy book for the camera.
III. Field Marshal Haig inspects French troops who took part on the first day of the Third Battle of Ypres. Western Front, August 1917. Haig is escorted round the troops (who are drawn up on parade) by General Anthoine, commanding the First Army. The troops are from 1st Division and 51st Division, and from the French Marines (wearing naval caps instead of helmets). Haig talks to, and shakes hands with, some of the officers before going on to present decorations. Haig watches as the troops march past.

Notes
Title: this is taken from the shotsheet.
Summary: the scene of Haig is used very briefly at the start of **IWM 132**.
Remarks: the language used in this episode is interesting. In the Verdun attack, one caption reads "L'artillerie allonge son tir pour garantir la progression de l'infanterie", a classic statement of the French tactic of 'artillery captures, infantry occupies'. Furthermore, the German prisoners are described as being sent "vers le camp de concentration", a clear example of the correct military use of the term 'concentration camp' before the 1930s. The emphasis placed on the success of these small French operations to restore morale in the armed forces after the mutinies of the summer is also noteworthy.
[shotsheet available]
catalogued SDB: 7/1982

IWM 508-25 · France, 1/9/1917
ANNALES DE LA GUERRE 25

b/w · 1 reel · 453' (8 mins) · silent
intertitles: French

pr Section Cinématographique de l'Armée Française

I. A visit by the Queen of Belgium to a French military hospital in Roosbrugge, Belgium, August 1917. The hospital is a temporary construction of Nissen huts. The Queen and General Anthoine walk with their escort down a path between two huts and enter one of the wards.
II. The battlefield after the French counterattack at Verdun, August 1917. The village of Esnes has been reduced to rubble but it is safe for men to stand upright and look down on the battlefield. The German bombardment still continues. French soldiers occupy the badly damaged German trench system at Côte 304. Panoramas of the ruins of Cumières and Regneville, where a few German 77mm field guns have been abandoned. At the cameraman's request a French soldier handles the firing mechanism of one gun. A relief unit, with full kit and its transport carts, makes its way up the hillside to take over a set of trenches.
III. Damage done by German shelling to Rheims Cathedral, August 1917. The damage done by "les vandales" is shown. The town commandant leaves his sand-bagged headquarters. Cardinal Luçon and Monsignor Leven lead the camera around the cathedral, showing an unexploded German shell, damage done to the cathedral by shelling, and two workers trying to reconstruct the broken stained glass.

Notes
Titles: both this and the intertitles are flashframes.
Summary: comparison with original caption lists suggests that scenes are missing from this issue. See also **IWM 473**.
[shotsheet available]
catalogued SDB: 7/1982

IWM 508-26 · France, 8/9/1917
ANNALES DE LA GUERRE 26

b/w · 1 reel · 470' (8 mins) · silent
intertitles: French

pr Section Cinématographique de l'Armée Française

I. A formal display of loyalty at the town of Ammemasse, France, September 1917. The

Minister of Agriculture, Ferdinand David, and the former deputy for Colmar, the Abbé Wetterlé, leave the town hall with their followers, led by three young girls dressed in the regional costumes of the Savoi, Alsace and Lorraine. The Abbé addresses the crowd on the subject of loyalty to France, with some verve. The Abbé is then shown in portrait shot.
II. The presentation to leading French soldiers of Romanian decorations at First Army headquarters, Rexpoëde, France, September 1917. The ceremony takes place privately in the gardens of the headquarters. General Anthoine, General Velentin and the flying ace Captain Guynemer are each in turn (with timecuts) decorated with the Order of Michel the Brave by General Iliesco, head of the Romanian military mission to France.
III. The arrival of Justin Godard, the Under-Secretary of State for Health, in Salonika, Greece, September 1917. M Godard arrives in Salonika harbour by small cutter in order to inspect the medical services. He is unescorted and met by only three or four military representatives. As the party walks down the street it gains a larger entourage. General Sarrail and King Alexander get down from a train and walk along a route lined with Chasseurs Alpins. They are there to look at the damage to Salonika, but not much is in view.
IV. Celebration of the third anniversary of the Battle of the Marne. Fère-Champenoise, 6 September 1917. Members of the government and armed forces have gathered on the flat grassland, and a wooden cross has been erected. The entire cabinet, led by President Poincaré, appears to be present, together with Marshal Joffre, and Generals Pétain and Foch, and a number of other military representatives. They all approach the shrine, listen to an address being given, and then leave.
V. President Poincaré's visit to US 1st Division at Hondelaincourt, France, 6 September 1917. President Poincaré, in his blue uniform, Minister of War Paul Painlevé, and General Pétain, are taken by General Pershing to meet troops of US 1st Division in training. The President talks and shakes hands with a number of American officers before watching the division march past. French official cameramen can be seen at work.

Notes

Title: this is taken from the shotsheet.
Intertitles: these are all flashframes.
[John J Pershing, *My Experiences in the World War*, Hodder and Stoughton (1931): 152]

[shotsheet available]
catalogued SDB: 7/1982

IWM 508-27 · France, 15/9/1917
ANNALES DE LA GUERRE 27

b/w · 1 reel · 475' (8 mins) · silent
intertitles: French

pr Section Cinématographique de l'Armée Française

I. The Serbian First Army on the Salonika Front, September 1917. Colonel Stoistitch checks his maps at a command post in the mountains. 155mm guns bombard the Bulgarian positions opposite, while Serbian officers observe the effects of the fire.
II. General Berthelot decorating Romanian soldiers in Romania, September 1917. As head of the French military mission in Romania, Berthelot presents the Médaille Militaire and the Croix de guerre to a number of Romanian soldiers. Only one award is shown, followed by six soldiers with decorations in a group. A Romanian regimental standard of the 'icon' type is also decorated – shown in close-up supported by rifles.
III. A historical fête in honour of Joan of Arc held behind the lines near the Chemin des Dames by French soldiers, Western Front, September 1917. The fête is held by men from a resting division. A number of them have dressed up in 15th century costume, on foot and horseback, and parade past their curious and amused fellow soldiers.
IV. Recreation for troops resting from the Western Front, September 1917. Some soldiers are taken by their transport lorries to the beach, on the Channel coast. Having got past the wire defences, they swim in the sea. The beach shelves only very slightly. Inland another division, possibly Moroccan, holds its sports. These include Graeco-Roman wrestling, a running race, a bicycle race, a horse race with fences, and a boxing match.
V. The award of a standard to 1st Chasseur Battalion, Western Front, September 1917. In very foggy conditions, in a formal ceremony, the battalion is presented with a standard (probably a previously used historic banner – it shows considerable battle damage) in recognition of the battalion's recent fighting exploits.
VI. Soldiers attend a mass in the ruins of a church near the front lines, Western Front, September 1917.

Title: this is taken from the shotsheet.
[shotsheet available]
catalogued SDB: 7/1982

IWM 508-28 · France, 22/9/1917
ANNALES DE LA GUERRE 28

b/w · 1 reel · 512' (9 mins) · silent
intertitles: French

pr Section Cinématographique de l'Armée
Française

I. Soldiers in the Vosges cutting and
stacking peat, France, September 1917.
II. The Archbishop of Rheims holding a
mass in Gex for people killed in the war,
France, September 1917. The archbishop
and dignitaries leave the cathedral after the
mass, and go into the cemetery where the
archbishop pronounces a benediction over
the graves. Everyone then leaves.
III. A delegation of men from St-Affrique
present a sword of honour to General de
Castelnau, in an open field, France,
September 1917.
IV. French positions in the Marne area,
Western Front, September 1917. A pan over
the positions on Mont Cornillet, Mont Blond
and Mont Haut (not significant heights).
Two men carry food in containers down to
those already in the trenches. Nearby are a
few tree stumps, the remains of a wood.
Some of the soldiers wander past a
captured German pillbox.
V. The last existing film of Captain
Guynemer, who vanished while flying over
the Western Front on 11 September 1917.
Guynemer is shown on the occasion of the
award of his Légion d'honneur in June. He
explains his Spad to the awarding general
and stands bareheaded for a portrait shot.
VI. The King of Belgium, President Poincaré
and General Pétain review French troops,
Western Front, September 1917. The troops
have all taken part in the recent French
offensive at Verdun, and are on full parade
with their standards. The King and Poincaré
present medals and Pétain shakes hands
with the recipients. The formations march
past, ending with a final view of their
standards.

Notes
Title: this is taken from the shotsheet.
Intertitles: these are all flashframes.
[shotsheet available]
catalogued SDB: 7/1982

IWM 508-29 · France, 29/9/1917
ANNALES DE LA GUERRE 29

b/w · 1 reel · 447' (8 mins) · silent
intertitles: French

pr Section Cinématographique de l'Armée
Française

I. A Letord L4 or L5 bomber (described as
an artillery spotter) being wheeled out by
French and US officers and ground crew,
the crew preparing and the take-off,
Western Front, September 1917.
II. German prisoners of war at St-Dizier,
France, September 1917. Some of the
prisoners work in a wood cutting timber and
piling up sticks. Others dig up stones for
roadfill. The prisoners march back to their
camp under escort. At the camp they work
building a new barracks. One prisoner
undergoes the routine camp medical
examination. Other prisoners rest outdoors.
One has his hair cut, others wash
themselves or their clothes in a river. At
mealtime they queue for soup, then rest
and play cards.
III. Prince Arthur of Connaught visits French
troops on various parts of the Western
Front, September 1917. The Prince
decorates two men of a division in Alsace,
following which the division marches past.
Near the River Aisne he salutes the tattered
standard of a battalion of Chasseurs and
goes on to decorate one soldier. He then
performs a similar ceremony at Noyon,
decorating a soldier before watching a
march past.

Notes
Title: this is taken from the shotsheet.
[shotsheet available]
catalogued SDB: 7/1982

IWM 508-30 · NO FILM

IWM 508-31 · France, 6/10/1917
ANNALES DE LA GUERRE 31

b/w · 1 reel · 499' (9 mins) · silent
intertitles: French

pr Section Cinématographique de l'Armée
Française

I. The visit of President Machado of
Portugal to France, October 1917. Machado
with President Poincaré at Verdun inspects
the troops, and presents the mayor of

Verdun with the Order of the Tower and the Sword. The two presidents enter through the defences of the city and tour round them by car. They go on to the Aisne area, surveying the view from the Quennevières Farm plateau using maps, and walking through the ruins of Chauny. They go up into the observation tower previously used by Prince Eitel Friedrich. They then go on to the ruins of Ham Château, and finally the ruins of Nesle. There are still many children in the villages. The two presidents watch a march past by the local troops.
II. French forces resting on the Western Front, October 1917. "The right bank of the Meuse", probably the area of the counterattacks at Verdun, showing a line of soldiers marching along a road and up into some ruins near the battlefield. In the sector, obviously now quiet, "the scene of previous engagements", troops are resting and eating. A group of soldiers stands in brief silent salute over a corpse prior to placing it on a stretcher and carrying it away. The chaplain conducting the ceremony pronounces a benediction as he himself leaves.
III. A Zouave battalion is honoured by the Serbians, Salonika Front, October 1917. Colonel Karafatovitch of the Serbian Army pins the Cross of Kakageorge onto the standard of 2nd Battalion, 2nd Zouave Regiment in an open-air ceremony. General Sarrail watches with the colonel as the Zouaves then march past in salute.

Notes
Title: this is taken from the shotsheet.
[shotsheet available]
catalogued SDB: 8/1982

IWM 508-32 · France, 10/1917
ANNALES DE LA GUERRE 32

b/w · 1 reel · 533' (10 mins) · silent
intertitles: French

pr Section Cinématographique de l'Armée Française

I. Inspection of the Polish Legion at their camp by General Archinard, Western Front, October 1917. The general meets the Polish officers. He joins in a mass with the Legion, inspects the soldiers, talks to a few of them and presents decorations to members of the Legion who still survive from Bayonne in 1914. The Legion is then presented with a new standard made by the local women. The Legion marches past, and the new standard is displayed in close-up.

II. Funeral of General Baratier, killed in action. France, October 1917. The general's coffin, draped in a tricolour, is taken out of a military ambulance. The funeral procession, mainly French civilian and military personnel with some British soldiers, and the general's widow, files into the church. After the service the procession files out again and the coffin is taken on a gun-carriage to the cemetery. (The film is nearly all in long shot, making identification difficult, but General Gouraud appears to be present.)
III. First Army area during the Third Battle of Ypres ('Passchendaele'), Western Front, October 1917. The battlefield is barren except for a few crosses. One man stands at the bottom of a shell-hole, showing its depth. Two others explore a captured pillbox, while more soldiers rest in the shade of the concrete. One fatigue party with spades shores up a newly-taken position, while other parties work on improving the defences. Earth from a tunnelling operation is brought up to the surface. A supply column of wagons passes over a temporary bridge towards the fighting area. The ground is noticeably dry, almost dusty.

Notes
Title: this is taken from the shotsheet.
Intertitles: these are all flashframes.
Remarks: in view of the virtual absence of British film of the Third Battle of Ypres in its middle stages, this is a very useful record. It is in particular a corrective to the common myth that the battle was fought throughout in mud.
[shotsheet available]
catalogued SDB: 8/1982

IWM 508-33 · France, 27/10/1917
ANNALES DE LA GUERRE 33

b/w & (partly) tinted · 1 reel · 754' (13 mins) · silent
intertitles: French

pr Section Cinématographique de l'Armée Française

■ Offensive by Sixth Army from the River Aisne to the Chemin des Dames, Western Front, 23-27 October 1917.

Subtitle captions give the French gains in the offensive as the strong points Fruty, Bohery and Montparnasse, the fort at Malmaison, and the villages of d'Allemant, Vaudesson, Chavignon, Pinon and Pargny.

The effect was to secure the Chemin des Dames. The film itself shows the preparation for the offensive. A pile of 75mm, 105mm and 155mm shells being assembled at a dump with a light railway engine running alongside. Then the Infantry, in campaign dress, marching up a leafy lane to their final positions. The bombardment, by 340mm railway guns (with corresponding shell-bursts over the battlefield) and other guns, while horse-drawn wagons move supplies up the roads to the front. In the blue mists of dawn on 23 October Schneider CA1 tanks move up for the assault, very dimly seen. Engineers work on the assault trenches, and the Infantry move into position. A 400mm railway gun continues the bombardment. The Infantry file out of the trenches and across no man's land into the mist. The Red Cross men begin to bring back stretcher cases through the mist. In daylight the reserves follow up in single file through the captured German trenches and onwards, followed by men carrying boxes of equipment and supplies. German prisoners (most of them reacting to the camera) come back through the trenches. In the rear areas German and French Red Cross men work to evacuate the stretcher cases. The prisoners and walking wounded then turn away from the battlefield. Casualties from both sides are brought into a First Aid Post, from which the wounded are evacuated by stretcher or on foot. The caption claims that the French took 237 officers and 11 157 other ranks prisoner, and 180 guns. The column of prisoners, under escort, moves back to a temporary holding camp where, obviously cold and shaken, they wait behind the wire.

Notes
Title: this is taken from the shotsheet.
Colour: the film is partly tinted red for the captions, and in blue for the dawn attack sequence.
Remarks: one of the small-scale offensives by which the French Army regained its confidence in summer and autumn 1917. It is significant that the newsreel makes such a fuss about it. The use of blue tinting to go with the genuinely misty conditions is a clever and successful idea.
[shotsheet available]
catalogued SDB: 8/1982

IWM 508-34 · France, 3/11/1917
ANNALES DE LA GUERRE 34

b/w · 1 reel · 659' (11 mins) · silent

intertitles: French

pr Section Cinématographique de l'Armée Française

I. All Saints' Day on the Western Front, 1 November 1917. A procession of Chasseurs, led by priests and choirboys, makes a pilgrimage to a cemetery near the battle zone, where, as the civilian congregation watches, a monument is dedicated "To Our Dead".
II. The battlefield after the Chemin des Dames offensive from the Aisne River. Western Front, November 1917. The soldiers wait and rest in their trenches and shell-holes, passing round food and cooking on improvised fires. Some help manhandle a horse-drawn field kitchen out of the mud. Others build a corduroy road across the fields with planks. Still more collect German weapons and equipment, mainly shells and guns left behind in the retreat. One trophy is a crashed LVG CV aircraft on a trailer. The gunners dig new gun-pits by the roadside for their 75mm pieces. Soldiers on salvage work collect shells which are taken to dumps in horse-drawn carts. A 75mm anti-aircraft gun on a De Dion lorry mount opens fire. Behind the new lines, the camera pans over the ruins of the village of Allemant. On the road to Maubeuge are the remains of two farms used by the Germans as strong points, Guardian Angel and Vaurin. Transport lorries and carts move past both of them. The tunnel entry to the Montparnasse position. The fort at Malmaison, seen from a distance, then from the inside showing its various trenches and ditches, tunnel openings and shelters. The French troops settle in. A posed shot of General Maistre, whose Sixth Army made the attack, with an aide.
III. A supply column moving over the Alps towards Italy, November 1917. The lorries carry equipment and medical supplies (some are marked as ambulances). The convoy passes through the snow-covered roads on the lower reaches of the mountains and pulls up in a village for a rest before setting off again and making its way up the horseshoe mountain passes.

Notes
Title: this is taken from the shotsheet.
[shotsheet available]
catalogued SDB: 8/1982

IWM 508-35 · France, 10/11/1917
ANNALES DE LA GUERRE 35

b/w · 1 reel · 537' (10 mins) · silent
intertitles: French

pr Section Cinématographique de l'Armée Française

I. Civilians, mainly women, file past the graves at the Allied cemetery of Zeitenlick on All Saints' Day. Salonika Front, 1 November 1917.
II. M Métin, Mayor of Evian, and his council members welcome refugees from occupied areas who are to be resettled nearby. France, November 1917.
III. A demonstration that the port of Dunkirk with its Square Jean Bart is undamaged, and cargo ships are unloading there, despite German air raids. France, November 1917.
IV. Fraternisation between British and French soldiers at the junction of their lines in the Ypres area, November 1917. The men are French I Corps and British II Corps to the south. A mixed posed group of British and French soldiers talk with one another. British officers watch a French 75mm field gun crew opening fire from a gun-pit. A British relief party passes another 75mm piece. British convoys travel on the roads, which are quite muddy. These include 3-ton lorries, marching soldiers, Holt tractors pulling 9.2-inch howitzers, limbers pulling 6-inch howitzers, motor ambulances, a London bus, and horse-drawn GS wagons. French horse-drawn transport passes the other way. Other roads show more marching columns of troops and London buses used to carry them.
V. The aftermath of the Chemin des Dames offensive from the River Aisne. France, November 1917. Watched by delegations from all the regiments which fought in the offensive, General Pétain decorates the standards of the regiments which distinguished themselves most. The ceremony is held in open fields in the pouring rain. General Maistre, commanding Sixth Army which made the attack, is decorated by Pétain as a Grand Officer of the Légion d'honneur. The regiments march past in salute, and display their standards.

Notes
Title: this is taken from the shotsheet.
Remarks: the attack on the Aisne was little more than a successful line-straightening operation. It is significant that the official French newsreel should devote an entire issue – 33 – to the event and items of a further two issues to its aftermath, while virtually ignoring the French contribution to the later stages of the Flanders offensive, which was generally unsatisfactory.

[shotsheet available]
catalogued SDB: 8/1982

IWM 508-36 · France, 11/1917
ANNALES DE LA GUERRE 36

b/w · 1 reel · 572' (9 mins) · silent
intertitles: French

pr Section Cinématographique de l'Armée Française

■ French contribution to the Sherifian revolt in Arabia, November 1917.

Before leaving from Port Said, Colonel Brémond, the head of the French mission to the Hejaz forces, is made a Commander of the Légion d'honneur by General Bailloud, the chief of the French Contingent of the Egyptian Expeditionary Force. After the presentation men of the contingent, mainly mule transport and guns, march past the general. At Suez Brémond's mission begins to embark on a transport steamer. The men relax as the steamer departs. It arrives at the port of "El Ouedj" (Wejh) where it is met by the locals and brings ashore its boatloads of Lebel rifles and ammunition for the Sherifian forces. Brémond comes ashore and is greeted by local leaders. He is brought to the camp of Prince Faisal at "Gidda" (Jidda) where Faisal is shown in the shadows of his tent. His troops display the flag of Hejaz and give a small drill demonstration for the camera. French training specialists find mounting their camels rather difficult but succeed at the second attempt, and the camel train sets out into the desert. Arab tribesmen come in out of the desert to join the Sherifian Army. Turkish prisoners of war are brought in out of the desert on camels, and the wounded are given medical treatment by the Sherifian forces. There is a posed group for the camera of Prince Faisal, his army commander Djafa Pasha and members of his staff. The force then sets out, mainly on horses, a few on camels, to raid the Medina railway.

Notes
Remarks: fairly blatant propaganda, mainly for the French in their attempt to recreate 'la nation Franco-Syrienne' and other Arabian myths. The British contribution to the revolt is given no mention either in the film or its captions. Perhaps the most improbable moment is actually pro-Sherifian, rather than pro-French, propaganda, in the giving of medical aid to Turkish prisoners instead of

shooting them. But at least the French Army showed enterprise in sending a cameraman with their mission, which is more than the British did. Compare **IWM 41**.
[shotsheet available]
catalogued SDB: 8/1982

IWM 508-37 · France, 24/11/1917
ANNALES DE LA GUERRE 37

b/w · 1 reel · 585' (10 mins) · silent
intertitles: French

pr Section Cinématographique de l'Armée Française

■ French and Italian forces in the rear areas of north Italy, November 1917.

A French motor supply convoy passes through the customs posts at the Franco-Italian frontier in the mountains, and drives on through the centre of Turin. A Chasseur battalion with its pack mules marches through the crowds of people in the centre of Brescia. M Paul Painlevé, the French War Minister, returning from the Interallied Conference at Rapallo, calls at Brescia to talk with French and Italian soldiers, including the Commander-in-Chief of the French Contingent, General Fayolle. He is presented with a bouquet of flowers by Italian factory girls. At Brescia station French and Italian troops wait and watch the trains. A munitions and trooptrain draws in and some French soldiers leave the station from it. Italian ladies pass down beside the waiting trains handing out small gifts to the soldiers. Italian soldiers wave a French trooptrain out of the station. In the Piazza del Duomo in Milan French and Italian soldiers fraternise among the civilians. Garibaldists and members of local societies turn up in uniform to accompany the funeral procession of a French soldier accidentally killed in Italy. (This scene is repeated in far greater detail at the end of the film.) French marching columns with horse transport arrive in Verona and disperse to their billets, watering their horses and arranging their transport in the city. A dragoon regiment marches through the crowds in the Piazza del Municipio. (At this point the funeral scene repeats.) The crowds cheer the dragoons through the piazza and past the statue of Victor Emmanuel I on horseback.

Notes
Title: this is taken from the shotsheet.
[shotsheet available]

catalogued SDB: 8/1982

IWM 508-38 · France, 1/12/1917
ANNALES DE LA GUERRE 38

b/w · 1 reel · 471' (8 mins) · silent
intertitles: French

pr Section Cinématographique de l'Armée Française

I. French, British and Italian forces in north Italy, November 1917. French soldiers in one of the villages on Lake Garda wander around admiring the view. One addresses a letter he has been writing, others groom their horses, others buy food from the street vendors. Bersaglieri cyclists ride into the village and dismount smartly in formation. A French horse-drawn convoy begins to move out down one of the country roads. The tower at Solferino filmed from the road below the city. The monument to Napoleon at Rivoli being inspected by Italian soldiers. The bridge and monument to Napoleon at Arcola (battle 15-17 November 1796) and the house used as his headquarters during the battle. British gunners pass through the town with munitions wagons and 18-pounders, setting up camp just beyond the bridge. Italian Engineers drive piles into the bed of the Adige River to replace damaged supports for a bridge. More French soldiers and transport emerge along the road to Brescia from a tunnel ("Porta Brescia") through the hills.
II. General Anthoine decorates two pilots. Ypres area, Western Front, November 1917. Representatives of First Army and the Air Corps parade while General Anthoine presents Captain Heurteaux with the medal of Officer of the Légion d'honneur and Lieutenant Fonck with that of Knight of the Légion d'honneur. A march past follows the presentation.

Notes
Title: this is taken from the shotsheet.
Technical: in item II the light values are wrong and the film is very dark.
Remarks: the newsreel structure here betrays the film. An interesting and self-contained item on the Italian Front has had tagged onto it the inevitable, dreary (and for once poorly filmed) presentation ceremony.
[shotsheet available]
catalogued SDB: 8/1982

IWM 508-39 · France, 8/12/1917
ANNALES DE LA GUERRE 39

b/w · 1 reel · 578' (10 mins) · silent
intertitles: French

pr Section Cinématographique de l'Armée
Française

I. Japanese marines at Port Said, Egypt,
November 1917. The marines, part of the
Japanese destroyer flotilla assisting in anti-
submarine patrols in the Mediterranean, are
rowed ashore from their ship. There are
cargo vessels at anchor but no warships.
II. Visit of a Spanish diplomatic mission to
the Western Front, November 1917. At
Verdun the party of diplomats is taken to
inspect the main citadel gates and outlying
forts. They are presented to a French
Colonial unit whose band plays for them. A
Tirailleur regiment marches past for them
led by its band (note the horsetail musical
standard). The delegation goes to Pont-à-
Mousson and looks over the town, meeting
the local baker and his family, still baking
bread despite the shelling.
III. The visit of Justin Godard, Minister for
Health, to north Italy, November 1917. After
Godard's arrival, Italian officers also arrive at
the French headquarters ("Hôtel Parco")
and the various parties then leave. General
Diaz, the Italian Commander-in-Chief,
escorted by Generals Fayolle and
Duchesne, reviews a battalion of Chasseurs
Alpins who march past with their band.
IV. The French Contingent of the Egyptian
Expeditionary Force, Palestine, November
1917. Colonel Piepape, temporary head of
the contingent, reads a despatch handed to
him. A French column wearing colonial
dress and pith helmets marches into "Khan-
Yunus" (outskirts of Jerusalem ?). In near
silhouette they march past Colonel Piepape
in the open, who salutes, and march off into
the desert. A final silhouette of a soldier and
a palm tree against a setting sun.

Notes
Title: this is taken from the shotsheet.
[shotsheet available]
catalogued SDB: 8/1982

IWM 508-40 · France, 15/12/1917
ANNALES DE LA GUERRE 40

b/w · 1 reel · 469' (8 mins) · silent
intertitles: French

pr Section Cinématographique de l'Armée
Française

I. French gunners instruct US gunners in
the loading and firing of their 400mm (?)
railway howitzers, shown in detail. Western
Front, December 1917.
II. French forces on the Italian Front,
December 1917. Lorries full of French
troops drive through the village of
Montebello. French soldiers on the march in
two parallel columns come out past the
main church. Italian and French troops
share a trench on the Piave River line. The
river is visible on the horizon through the
defensive wire.
III. General Pétain decorates the standard of
27th Chasseur Battalion at its headquarters
in the Vosges, France, December 1917. The
garrison headquarters of the battalion is
shown. The men parade their standard
through the local town and back to the
barracks. General Pétain (poor shot) pins
the Médaille Militaire onto the standard.
Snow is falling, sometimes heavily,
throughout.
IV. War dogs in training, Western Front,
December 1917. War dogs of various
breeds are led off by their trainers from their
kennels into the training area, and race
forward past smoke grenade explosions in
search of wounded men. Close-ups of two
of the dogs, a St-Bernard and a beagle.
V. General Pétain arrives by car and is met
by King Albert of Belgium. Together they
review French and Belgian troops of First
Army in the Ypres area of Belgium,
December 1917.

Notes
Title: this and the subtitles are flashframes.
Remarks: it is noteworthy that two separate
and unrelated items of this newsreel should
both feature General Pétain.
catalogued SDB: 8/1982

IWM 508-41 · NO FILM

IWM 508-42 · France, 29/12/1917
ANNALES DE LA GUERRE 42

b/w · 1 reel · 683' (11 mins) · silent
intertitles: French

pr Section Cinématographique de l'Armée
Française

I. Members of the BEF of 1914 on their way
to be entertained by George V at the Albert
Hall, London, Christmas 1917. The men,
some in uniform and others in civilian
clothes, drive in a fleet of cars through

central London to the cheers of the watching crowds. (King George is not shown.) According to the caption, there are 700 veterans altogether.

II. US troops helping with Christmas celebrations in France, 1917. At Thann people emerge from a cathedral after a mass, walking into the surrounding snow. The cathedral has much supporting scaffolding. Some children play in the snow and one salutes the camera. At St-Maixent American soldiers have organised a Christmas tree. A bugler summons the children and "Uncle Sam" arrives by car to give them presents, together with ladies dressed as "Marianne" of France whom he joins on a dais. A US Army string band (guitars, violins and banjos) plays for the camera. "Uncle Sam" holds up a small child in his arms. In Noyon French nursing sisters and soldiers distribute toys to local children.

III. A counterbalanced girder bridge over a small river so built that one man can raise or lower it by hand, Western Front, December 1917.

IV. An American civilian mission to visit the graves of the first US troops killed in France, December 1917. The unidentified members of the mission approach the graves, which are neatly laid out and divided off by wooden fencing. A sign indicates that the men were killed on 3 November 1917 (probably from one of the Railway Engineer companies working near the front).

V. General Puipeyroux (?) reviewing 3rd Colonial Division, Western Front, December 1917. The men of the division first pick up and strap on their equipment. The general reviews them on horseback, and decorates some of the men. He watches the divisional march past. Finally, a close-up of one of the soldiers wearing his full display of six medals.

Notes

Remarks: it is surprising that the newsreel did not make more of Christmas as an event. It seems to have become trapped in its own stereotype.
[shotsheet available]
catalogued SDB: 8/1982

IWM 508-43 · France, 5/1/1918
ANNALES DE LA GUERRE 43

b/w · 1 reel · 782' (13 mins) · silent
intertitles: French

pr Section Cinématographique de l'Armée Française

I. A coal mine in Alsace being worked by soldiers, January 1918. The soldiers bring the full coaltrucks out to the surface of the mine. The coal is dumped from the trucks and horse-wagons are loaded from the dump. A traction engine runs a coal-crusher. A few soldiers lead a heavy ox-wagon along the roads.

II. Sergeant-Major Vitalis, at his squadron's aerodrome, Western Front, January 1918. Vitalis became the first aircraft machinegunner to win the Légion d'honneur, having scored seven kills. Firstly, a portrait shot. He poses in dress uniform beside his Bréguet Type 14A2 with his Lewis machinegun mounted in the gunner's cockpit. He demonstrates his ability as a marksman by using a rifle at about 20 paces to shoot the ash off a friend's cigar.

III. Visit by Ben Tillett, the British Labour MP, to the Western Front, January 1918. Tillett calls at Chauny Town Hall, which still shows extensive damage from the German retreat of February 1917. He then goes with his party to the Soissons area where he inspects the damage to the railway sheds and station at St-Gobain.

IV. The Italian Front, January 1918. General Pepino Garibaldi is posed together with the Commandant Sante Garibaldi, who went to fight in France at the head of the Garibaldian Legion in 1914. French soldiers lead back to the rear areas some of the Austrian prisoners they took on 30 December in the attack on Mount Tomba, with Italian women watching by the roadside, not far from Milan. The camera surveys the Austrians as they rest, picking out various types. A final portrait shot of General Fayolle, commanding the French Contingent in Italy.

V. Scenes in silhouette and semi-darkness showing the King and Queen of Belgium reviewing troops of First Army in the Ypres area, Western Front, January 1918. The troops, with their tattered battle standards, march past briskly, seen only in silhouette as they pass in review.

VI. French troops on the Western Front, probably Verdun area, January 1918. Transport mules are unhitched from light carts, some of them carrying machineguns. The carts are then loaded into lorries. Soldiers play cards and relax in a well-built dug-out. A relief unit comes down the support trench.

VII. US Secretary of State for War Baker talks with US officers beside his car on a visit to the Western Front, January 1918.

VIII. French commanders on the Western Front, January 1918. Portrait shots of General Ferdinand Foch at a formal function, General Henri Pétain decorating a soldier with the Croix de guerre and "le soldat français", an irised shot of a Chasseur.

Notes
Title: this is taken from the shotsheet.
Intertitles: these are flashframes.
[shotsheet available]
catalogued SDB: 8/1982

IWM 508-44 · France, 12/1/1918
ANNALES DE LA GUERRE 44

b/w · 1 reel · 456' (8 mins) · silent
intertitles: French

pr Section Cinématographique de l'Armée Française

I. A hospital on the French sector of the Western Front run by Scottish women, January 1918. The hospital is of prefabricated buildings, signposted as the "Hôpital Bénévole I Bis". The film captions emphasise that all the employees are women, some of whom are seen walking in the snow outside. One group carries a French soldier on a stretcher into the operating theatre where a woman doctor performs the operation. The patient is then loaded into an ambulance. In the wards food is collected by the walking wounded and distributed to the bedridden patients. The postman, also a woman, arrives on a bicycle and the staff and patients crowd round. A final posed group of the hospital staff.
II. A captured German LVG CV aircraft, which has landed intact behind French lines, Western Front, January 1918. The aircraft is watched over by French soldiers before taking off to be flown by a French pilot to the aerodrome at Villacoublay further to the rear.
III. Cooperation between French and British gunners in the Ypres area, Western Front, January 1918. Gunners of 87th Artillery Regiment are introduced to their British 8-inch howitzers by men of the Royal Artillery. The Frenchmen then fuse and fire the shells, while on an observation platform two spotters direct the fire as it falls on the enemy positions. A soldier poses by peering down a howitzer barrel at the camera. A British and a French officer joke together.
IV. The Cathedral of St Anthony at Rheims, showing shell damage and holes in the roof, Western Front, January 1918.
V. 2nd Battalion, the Foreign Legion, has its standard (shown in detail) decorated with

the Cross of the Légion d'honneur, January 1918.

Notes
Title: this is taken from the shotsheet.
Intertitles: these are flashframes.
[shotsheet available]
catalogued SDB: 8/1982

IWM 508-45 · France, 19/1/1918
ANNALES DE LA GUERRE 45

b/w · 1 reel · 595' (10 mins) · silent
intertitles: French

pr Section Cinématographique de l'Armée Française

I. Moroccan troops training in their own country, January 1918. The men are due to serve with the French Army. They practise a river crossing using pontoon ferries, drill and bayonet exercises on a parade ground, digging trenches in the scrub and making a mock attack from them. They load themselves and their equipment onto a narrow gauge trooptrain which leaves for the embarkation point for France.
II. The British extension of their front southwards to include the St-Quentin sector, Western Front, January 1918. The first contingents of Fifth Army get out of their bus transport, probably near Péronne. They form up and march away. Other contingents march along the roads with their field kitchens, GS wagons and motor transport.
III. Italian sappers on the Western Front, January 1918. The sappers, newly arrived on the Western Front, work with French Engineers on a new defensive position. They use a trench digging machine, with chain buckets, to dig a section of narrow trench. They drive stakes into the ground and wire the position between them.
IV. Alsace in the snow, Western Front, January 1918. Chasseurs and horse transport pass through the area, but the main interest is the scenery. Soldiers and civilians travel by sledge, horse or, in one case, on skis. Sledges are used as snowploughs to clear the roads so that 75mm field guns can be brought up into the hills.
V. The investiture of General Guillaumat as a Commander of the Légion d'honneur, Western Front, January 1918. General Leconte presents the decoration to General Guillemot, and goes on to decorate two other soldiers. The generals and their staffs ride to the ceremony and the presentation

is made before a divisional parade. The ceremony is brisk, followed by a march past.

Notes
Title: this is taken from the shotsheet.
[shotsheet available]
catalogued SDB: 8/1982

IWM 508-46 · France, 26/1/1918
ANNALES DE LA GUERRE 46

b/w · 1 reel · 573' (10 mins) · silent
intertitles: French

pr Section Cinématographique de l'Armée Française

I. Two French soldiers in silhouette are rowed by gondola to St Mark's Square in Venice, with the Doges' Palace nearby and other gondolas riding at rest, January 1918. The film emphasises that war has removed the gaiety from the city. A boatload of soldiers on the Grand Canal, followed by various other views of the city, ending at St Mark's Square. Nearby at an airfield four pilots are posed beside their Nieuport 12s. They then take off individually to defend the city. In Venice at the Rialto and in other areas there is some gaiety. A view of Bassano with the River Brenta flowing nearby and Mount Grappa in the background.
II. A collection of Austrian mountain guns captured in the assault on Mount Tomba, including their giant 'stovepipe' mortars, held by the men of 70th Battalion, Chasseurs Alpins, who took the position, January 1918. As the officers talk, General Fayolle arrives with General Maistre and the British "General Herring" (no such person – probably Major-General C H Harrington, Chief of Staff of the British forces in Italy). A captain in 120th Battalion, Chasseurs Alpins is given the Croix de guerre by Fayolle and the regimental fanion of 70th Battalion is also decorated, followed by the march past and review. A posed group of an Italian soldier, a French soldier of 115th Battalion, Chasseurs Alpins and a British soldier together.

Notes
Title: this is taken from the shotsheet.
Intertitles: these are flashframes.
[shotsheet available]
catalogued SDB: 8/1982

IWM 508-47 · France, 2/2/1918
ANNALES DE LA GUERRE 47

b/w · 1 reel · 583' (10 mins) · silent
intertitles: French

pr Section Cinématographique de l'Armée Française

I. The British Mk IV tank HMLS 'Intimidate' towing a captured German 150mm howitzer back to the rear areas after the Battle of Cambrai, Western Front, 29 November 1917.
II. A review of the Polish Legion in France, January 1918. The Legion, led by its band, marches up to the front of the cathedral at Puy-les-Volontaires for a mass. The Legion in the main square at Breuil holds a review before its leaders while a number of civilians watch. The officers of the Legion place a wreath at the foot of the statue of Lafayette, who fought alongside the Polish war leader Kosciusko.
III. US troops, in marching column, under training in Lorraine, Western Front, January 1918.
IV. French forces near Verdun, Western Front, January 1918. The Meuse is flooded over a wide area. Soldiers and horsed transport move past camouflaged screens on the road near Fleury. In response to an alert the gun crew of a 75mm field gun rushes out of its dug-out and opens fire, bombarding the far slopes. Near Chambrettes two officers review the position with a map, while soldiers carry duckboards or punts and cut wood. The shattered remains of Caurières Wood are shown. In the second line barbed wire is made into loops and defences set up.
V. The Allied Supreme War Council meeting at Versailles, 2 February 1918. Firstly, a view of the outside of the conference chamber, then the delegates arrive. The Italians are led by Prime Minister V E Orlando, the Americans by General Pershing, the British by Lloyd George with Colonel Hankey beside him. Clemenceau meets them with Foch, who goes on to inspect a guard of honour. (Camerawork very poor, no clear shot of anyone.)

Notes
Title: this is taken from the shotsheet.
Intertitles: these are flashframes.
Summary: the Cambrai sequence is British official film also found in **IWM 144**.
Remarks: it is a significant distortion that the French should refer to "le Secteur Américain" at this date, when there were few US troops in France and most were training in Lorraine, a quiet part of the line.

[shotsheet available]
catalogued SDB: 8/1982

[shotsheet available]
catalogued SDB: 8/1982

IWM 508-48 · France, 9/2/1918
ANNALES DE LA GUERRE 48 – EN ORIENT

b/w · 1 reel · 580' (10 mins) · silent
intertitles: French

pr Section Cinématographique de l'Armée Française

■ Life for French troops and the locals in the Salonika region of Greece, early 1918.

General Guillaumat, commanding the Army of the Orient, visits an airfield to talk with some of the pilots. The local Orthodox ceremony for Epiphany at a fishing village. The people have crowded into small boats and a priest pronounces a blessing on the sea from the quayside. A French mounted patrol near the Albanian frontier, moving along a dirt track in single file with a village in the background. Not far from Salonika, a posed group of a typical family: husband, wife, and small children beside their home, followed by an old lady knitting. A pan over the town of Vodena taken from the hills. A funeral service, with priests and people crouched low to the ground and incense swung over the grave. A pan over Verria, a town with a three-span bridge and women collecting water and washing clothes in the stream beneath it. The tombstones in an old Turkish cemetery. Festivities at an Albanian wedding, with dancing and tambourines. An Orthodox funeral procession. The peninsula and town of Kastoria on market day, with an old woman doing washing in the harbour, a number of small boys curious about the camera and people buying in the market. A small Albanian fishing boat sets out carrying two men and a veiled woman, followed by similar boats of the fishing fleet. Women in white veils go down to the mosque, which has its own minaret. Prime Minister Venizelos, General Gérome and General Zymbrakakis, visiting the front, pose in a group for the camera. They review a Greek regiment and Venizelos talks to some of the officers and men (numerous time cuts and pull-backs).

Notes
Title: this and intertitle are flashframes.
Remarks: beautiful and curious examples of Balkan peasant culture.

IWM 508-49 · France, 16/2/1918
ANNALES DE LA GUERRE 49

b/w · 1 reel · 595' (10 mins) · silent
intertitles: French

pr Section Cinématographique de l'Armée Française

I. A British Holt tractor pulling a double limber of troops through the desert, a British pack mule column crossing a bridge and another crossing the desert. Palestine 1918.
II. French forces in Italy, February 1918. The Italian General Pecori and General Maistre review the Sassari Brigade of the French Army, passing between the ranks. As the review is in progress a French Spad 13 overflies the parade twice, quite low. A formal parade by Italian troops through Venice, with watchers throwing flowers at their feet. The camera, at a high window, shows an Italian soldier (a major in the Bersaglieri), a French soldier and a British soldier leaning out of the window to watch.
III. The arrival of fresh US forces in the Marne area, Western Front, February 1918. A trooptrain arrives, the men alight, form up, lead horses from the boxes and wheel limbers off the flatcars, cinching the equipment together. More American troops march in column through a residential area. Two American soldiers pose with their horses for the camera.
IV. The visit of Georges Clemenceau to Alsace, Western Front, February 1918. The Prime Minister arrives and the staff takes him to see the new defensive positions. At Dannemarie he gives a speech and kisses little girls who wear traditional dress. He inspects a guard of honour at Massevaux, shaking hands with the officers, and goes on to meet members of the local council and clergy. His car arrives at Thann where he meets and embraces veterans of the Franco-Prussian War and is given a bouquet by a little girl. He goes on to talk with other small children.

Notes
Title: this is taken from the shotsheet.
Summary: the Palestine episode is British official film **IWM 61**.
[shotsheet available]
catalogued SDB: 8/1982

IWM 508-50 · France, (?) 23/2/1918
ANNALES DE LA GUERRE 50

b/w · 1 reel · 581' (10 mins) · silent
intertitles: French

pr Section Cinématographique de l'Armée
Française

I. The aftermath of the action at Ervantes,
near Moncel, Alsace area, Western Front,
20 February 1918. Well behind the lines, a
mass of soldiers, most probably from 123rd
Division semi-posed as if waiting for
transport. A senior officer is with them,
possibly Lieutenant-General de Riols de
Fonclare, the commander of XV Corps.
Dragoons escort the German prisoners (11
officers and 525 other ranks) to the rear.
The Germans march in step and salute the
camera and watching Frenchmen, breaking
step on command at the end of the march
past. (Whole episode acted ?)
II. US troops near the River Aisne, Western
Front, February 1918. The soldiers are
probably rear-echelon troops of II Corps.
They form up in a village and march to their
base, where their cook cuts up meat and
prepares stew. One of the men talks with a
small French girl.
III. French forces in the Marne area,
Western Front, February 1918. A trench
system in the Champagne region. One
party of four soldiers is firing rifle grenades.
A similar party is patrolling the trench. A
regimental colonel emerges from his sand-
bagged command post. A medical team
makes its way along the trench. In a dug-
out to the rear some men rest and others
carry hods of earth. Observers climb a tree
to their post, a sentry in a gas mask keeps
guard, others look out from a front line
hide. A Hotchkiss machinegun is fired on a
high angle for harassing purposes (given as
anti-aircraft).
IV. A Cavalry regiment practising
manœuvres behind the lines, Western
Front, February 1918. The regiment
marches past along a road in a quiet area
behind the lines. Arriving at an open field
the regiment deploys into column of troops
and finally full line. After an inspection one
officer receives the Légion d'honneur. A
'charge' in successive columns of troops is
made for the camera.

Notes
Title: this and the intertitles are flashframes.
Remarks: if the French really got an event
into a newsreel within two days of filming it
this speaks well for their censorship and
publicity services. However, the whole
Ervantes episode appears to have been

taken in the rear areas, the German
behaviour is strange (although not
impossible); generally the film is suspect.
[shotsheet available]
catalogued SDB: 8/1982

IWM 508-51 · France, (?) 2/3/1918
ANNALES DE LA GUERRE 51

b/w · 1 reel · 590' (10 mins) · silent
intertitles: French

pr Section Cinématographique de l'Armée
Française

I. Queen Mary and Princess Mary
inspecting a parade of women VAD
ambulance drivers in foggy conditions in
Britain, early March 1918.
II. Activity on the Aisne sector, Western
Front, March 1918. Part of the area is
flooded. A marching column sets out for the
front lines. Engineers knock in stakes for
wire defences in the second line and fix
wire to them. A relief patrol moves up in
single file through a shattered wood.
American officers in training are taken down
to watch a 220mm heavy mortar firing from
a hillside gun-pit. Three types of finned
bomb are displayed beside it. The American
officers emerge from the dug-out.
III. A bombardment by a 279mm Schneider
howitzer and 75mm field guns, the shells
falling on the German lines, Alsace area,
Western Front, March 1918.
IV. Clemenceau's visit to US 1st Division
headquarters at Ligny-en-Barrois, Western
Front, 3 March 1918. Clemenceau is
escorted by General Pershing. He talks with
the divisional commander, Major-General
John L Bullard. He presents the Croix de
guerre to a number of soldiers for the
successful repulse of a raid. He is taken to
the divisional headquarters and heavily
concealed batteries of 75mm field guns
nearby.
V. The battlefield and Fort de la Pomelle,
filmed a few days before the German attack
of 2 March. Western Front, February 1918.

Notes
Title: this is taken from the shotsheet.
Date: the release date is taken from French
official sources. However, Pershing's diary
identifies Clemenceau's visit as having
taken place one day later. This is
unexplained.
Intertitles: these are flashframes.
[John J Pershing, *My Experiences in the
World War*, Hodder and Stoughton (1931):
301]

[shotsheet available]
catalogued SDB: 8/1982

IWM 508-52 · France, (?) 9/3/1918
ANNALES DE LA GUERRE 52

b/w · 1 reel · 561' (9 mins) · silent
intertitles: French

pr Section Cinématographique de l'Armée
Française

I. The Class of 1919 conscripts honouring
French and US war dead, France, March
1918. The location is a town behind the
Western Front. The conscripts, still in
civilian clothes, march forward with US
soldiers to lay wreaths on the graves of
French and US soldiers.
II. The removal of cultural objects from
Rheims, Western Front, March 1918.
Outside the cathedral the life-size 11th
century statue "Maison des Musiciens" is
secured in a wooden frame and lifted from
its wall niche by block and tackle. The
stained glass is removed from the cathedral
windows, "this is what the Germans call
installing observation posts". The glass is
reconstructed, crated up and driven away in
lorries. M Laferre, the Minister for Public
Education and Fine Arts, visits the city and
is escorted round the work by M
Saintsaulieu, the architect responsible for
the preservation and restoration scheme.
III. Locals carrying on as normal despite an
air raid which has left an unexploded aerial
torpedo half-buried in the earth. Lorraine,
March 1918.
IV. An anti-aircraft battery, probably in
training, Western Front, March 1918. One
soldier sights on an aircraft (not shown)
using a rangefinder and calculates the
angle and fuse setting. This is shouted by
megaphone to the guns, which open fire
from their pits.
V. Two air aces, Adjutant Garaud and Sub-
Lieutenant Georges Madon, Western Front,
March 1918. Garaud, who shot down his
most recent 'kill' on 11 March, is shown
posed beside the cockpit of his Spad 13.
Madon, with 26 kills, is posed beside his
Spad, then in its cockpit.
VI. Wreck of a German aircraft shot down
near Soissons, Western Front, March 1918.
The wreck, which is burnt-out and
unidentifiable, is guarded by US soldiers.
The caption describes it as "one of the
pirates" returning from an air raid on Paris.

Notes
Title: this and the intertitles are all
flashframes.
Date: the release date is taken from French
official sources. The discrepancy between
this and the film matter is unexplained.
[shotsheet available]
catalogued SDB: 8/1982

IWM 508-53 · France, 16/3/1918
ANNALES DE LA GUERRE 53

b/w · 1 reel · 506' (9 mins) · silent
intertitles: French

pr Section Cinématographique de l'Armée
Française

I. Chasseurs Alpins skiing in the snows of
Alsace, France, March 1918. One of the
men demonstrates how to fit on a pair of
skis. The group of Chasseurs Alpins skis
from one side of a valley to the other and a
few members demonstrate ski-jumping over
a low jump, the majority falling over. Dogs
pull sledges loaded with supplies through
the snow up to the batteries nearby,
including film taken from a sledge in
motion, ending with irised shots of two of
the dogs.
II. The King of Italy and General Maistre
review troops in Italy, March 1918. The
troops are both French and Italian,
including Chasseurs. Following the Italian
march past, the King inspects and
decorates some of the Frenchmen, and
Maistre presents the Croix de guerre to
Italian officers, also one British and one
French officer. The buglers of the
Chasseurs Alpins sound the salute and the
troops march past, some of them at the
double.

Notes
Title: this is taken from the shotsheet.
[shotsheet available]
catalogued SDB: 8/1982

IWM 508-54 · NO FILM

IWM 508-55 · France, 30/3/1918
ANNALES DE LA GUERRE 55

b/w · 1 reel · 620' (11 mins) · silent
intertitles: French

pr Section Cinématographique de l'Armée
Française

- Sixth Army's relief of the British Fifth Army in the Kaiserschlacht Offensive, Western Front, late March 1918.

I. Men of Sixth Army board a trooptrain at a station. Others march along roads to the battlefield, between Noyon and Amiens. Conditions are very foggy. Soldiers rest as a horsed transport column passes by. A further column, including lorries towing 155mm howitzers and 155mm Schneider guns. One of the 155mm Schneiders is deployed and opens fire. Shells are loaded into lorries from a dump. Traffic congestion in the rear area villages as troops move up. White armoured cars, probably from 1st Cavalry Division, wait by the roadside. Men of British Fifth Army, (III Corps under French command ?) wait in the rear areas. British horsed transport moves down the Amiens-Montdidier Road, close to Moreuil. British horsemen, probably 3rd Cavalry Division, prepare to return to action – two of their observers spy from a corn rick, then the men go forward dismounted across a ridgeline. Refugees leave for safety with their property in bullock carts and horse-drawn carriages. As the French troops press forward they meet German prisoners taken at Plessis-de-Roye, escorted by dragoons to the rear.
II. A caption quotes General Pershing's declaration, which appeared in French papers on 29 March, of his willingness to place his forces at French disposal. US troops, possibly 26th (Yankee) Division near Soissons, move forward in marching column to take over parts of the French line.

[John J Pershing, *My Experiences in the World War*, Hodder and Stoughton (1931): 316-324.]
[shotsheet available]
catalogued SDB: 8/1982

IWM 508-56 · France, 6/4/1918
ANNALES DE LA GUERRE 56

b/w · 1 reel · 619' (11 mins) · silent
intertitles: French

pr Section Cinématographique de l'Armée Française

- Sixth and First Armies covering the flank of British Fourth Army in the Kaiserschlacht Offensive, Western Front, March-April 1918.

Refugees watch horsed transport move down a road by a shell-dump. The gunners attend to their 155mm howitzers. Lorries move up another road. Gunners check that a 155mm Schneider gun is properly limbered before its team brings it out of the farmyard where they have been staying. Nearer the front a similar gun is winched into position, and the bombardment starts with 75mm field guns joining in. Engineers play out a telephone line in a newly-built trench. French and British soldiers rest together in a farmyard – the French are probably First Army and the British Fourth Army. The British then march off. A stretcher-case is brought in to an aid post nearby. One of the regiments which defended Grivesnes being marched out for a rest, probably 127th Division. Improvised armoured cars of II Cavalry Corps (machinegun and gunshield on a car body) pass in the other direction. A group of German prisoners captured by 163rd Division at Mailly-Raineval are marched across country to a holding camp, being stopped for interrogation by an officer on the way. At the camp (interpolated shot of high flying aircraft) the prisoners rest, bandage and delouse themselves, and are again interrogated. One, from 66th Infantry Regiment, is shown in close-up. Medical orderlies from 77th Division at Plessis-de-Roye bury German corpses. Soldiers of 162nd Division in foxholes in front of Montdidier look out over the approaches. A view of Mount Renaud, still in French hands.

[shotsheet available]
catalogued SDB: 8/1982

IWM 508-57 · France, (?) 13/4/1918
ANNALES DE LA GUERRE 57

b/w · 1 reel · 324' (6 mins) · silent
intertitles: French

pr Section Cinématographique de l'Armée Française

- Junction of the French and British forces during the Kaiserschlacht Offensive, Western Front, 1-15 April 1918.

A 145mm naval gun is stuck in soft ground, despite all efforts to pull it clear with ropes. Finally, sledges are fitted to the wheels and it is dragged clear. A squadron of Nieuport 28s parked on an airfield. Two seater Bréguet Type 14s take off in succession. A column of De Dion lorries carrying 75mm anti-aircraft guns are halted and the guns elevated. A Mitrailleuse Saint Etienne machinegun is used from a trench for anti-aircraft fire. An Albatros DV captured intact is admired by civilians in a town square. Five captured German flyers come out from a shed in a railway yard and are taken on board a train. Most of them are in good spirits and wave at the camera. An aircraft in the distant sky spins out of control, recovering just above the ground and flying off. In the woods close to the undamaged village of Moncel an advanced post sets up its equipment and waits. A marching column in full kit with mounted officers comes in, clearly near the end of a tiring march, but not distressed.

Notes
Title: this is taken from the shotsheet.
Date: the release date is taken from official French records, the discrepancy between this and the date given on the film is unexplained.
[shotsheet available]
catalogued SDB: 8/1982

IWM 508-58 · France, (?) 20/4/1918
ANNALES DE LA GUERRE 58 – ANNIVERSAIRE DU TRAITE DE FRANKFORT

b/w · 1 reel · 313' (6 mins) · silent
intertitles: French

pr Section Cinématographique de l'Armée Française

■ Part caption, part acted and part actuality celebration of the French liberation of Alsace and Lorraine marking the anniversary of the Treaty which annexed them to Germany. France, May 1918.

The film opens with a German jackboot across the map of Alsace-Lorraine. An old couple in Alsatian costume read the news of the annexation and bemoan their fate while German officers strut outside their window. The symbolic 'Marianne' of France, in her revolutionary dress, mourns for the provinces. She hears the calls for help of the spirit of Alsace (an enchained young girl in regional dress) and can do nothing. But after forty years Germany is "avid for new conquests". A symbolic German officer tears up the Treaty of Frankfurt. The figures "1914" burn in flame behind him as he leers in anticipation. The French mobilisation order is shown as civilians in the street cheer and wave national flags. Soldiers in

the uniform of 1914 march through the streets. In a symbolic scene while other soldiers rush past on the attack a French officer embraces the girl 'Alsace'. The film ends with a quotation from President Wilson's speech of 9 January 1918, insisting that the wrong done to France by Prussia in 1871 must be redressed before peace can be signed.

Notes
Date: this has been taken from French official records; however, the discrepancy of thirty days suggests that French and British records may be mismatched.
Production etc: this is not a regular episode, but a special piece with highly decorated and artistically drawn caption titles.
Remarks: the actuality material showing the mobilisation of 1914 may well be genuine, although it is hard to judge the colour of the uniforms on monochrome film. The piece itself is a remarkable mixture, difficult to evaluate without knowing how contemporaries found it. At worst, it is disturbing rather than ridiculous.
[shotsheet available]
catalogued SDB: 8/1982

IWM 508-59 · France, 27/4/1918
ANNALES DE LA GUERRE 59

b/w · 1 reel · 397' (7 mins) · silent
intertitles: French

pr Section Cinématographique de l'Armée Française

I. General Henrys, commanding French forces, arrives by Bréguet Type 14 aircraft to visit his men on the Salonika Front, April 1918.
II. Motor-cultivators removed from the battle zone for safety, on display, Western Front, April 1918.
III. A sports meeting of 178th Artillery Regiment (?), including hurdling, wrestling, high jump, long jump, sprint and football. Behind the lines, Western Front, April 1918.
IV. An Italian Contingent led by cyclists and commanded by General di Robillant on the march through a French village, April 1918.
V. Commandant Georges Mellieur of 2nd Battalion, Chasseurs, showing the camera a citation won by his battalion for distinguished conduct on 22 April. Western Front, April 1918.
VI. Maréchal des Logis Deloche (?), who escaped after being held prisoner with his tank for two days, receiving the Médaille

Militaire, Western Front, April 1918.

Notes
Title: this is taken from the shotsheet.
Summary: the original caption lists indicate that as it stands this film is missing several items and in a confused state.
[shotsheet available]
catalogued SDB: 8/1982

IWM 508-60 · France, 4/5/1918
ANNALES DE LA GUERRE 60

b/w · 1 reel · 583' (10 mins) · silent
intertitles: French

pr Section Cinématographique de l'Armée Française

■ Events on the Western Front, May 1918.

A brief scene of Marshal Joffre receiving a civilian delegation outside his headquarters. Shells of various calibres stacked in a munitions dump, and Engineers pulling a box girder bridge into position across a river, with the piers of the old bridge standing beside the new, in the Somme region. Limbered US 155mm howitzers move up a road. US soldiers on a route march, including a machinegun company with its light carts. Most of the men wave at the camera. Soldiers move through a trench and look out from the summit of Mont Plémont. The commander of a colonial division with a Moroccan regiment attached to it (name censored) is decorated by General Humbert with the Croix de guerre. Humbert inspects the division, which marches past. 320mm railway guns "which silenced the guns bombarding Paris" are loaded and fired.

Notes
Title: this is taken from the shotsheet.
Remarks: the guns which bombarded Paris were not in fact silenced but slowed their firing rate through technical troubles and were finally withdrawn as the Allies counterattacked. See also following issue.
[shotsheet available]
catalogued SDB: 8/1982

IWM 508-61 · France, 11/5/1918
ANNALES DE LA GUERRE 61

b/w · 1 reel · 446' (9 mins) · silent
intertitles: French

pr Section Cinématographique de l'Armée Française

I. A refutation of German claims that the bombardment of Paris by long-range guns has caused serious disruption, May 1918. The item shows normal life continuing in Paris. The markets trading in the open, uncongested and normal traffic flowing in the Place de l'Opéra, and people walking through the parks and boulevards and out of a theatre performance, all emphasise that life continues as normal.
II. The decoration of General di Robillant at the Interallied Supreme Headquarters at Versailles, May 1918. Di Robillant, commanding the Italian Contingent on the Western Front, is awarded the Cross of a Grand Officer of the Légion d'honneur.
III. The creation of an independent Polish Army in France, May 1918. General Archinard reviews men of 1st Battalion, Chasseurs, of the Army of Independent Poland. A priest is present at the ceremony and the men march past Archinard at the end.
IV. Air ace Sub-Lieutenant René Fonck, Western Front, May 1918. Fonck was made an Officer of the Légion d'honneur for shooting down a total of six German aircraft in 90 minutes on 9 May. He demonstrates his shooting ability on the ground by using a carbine to shoot a hole in a 10 centimes piece at 25 paces. He takes aim, but the shot is not shown. He is then shown putting on his flying suit, getting into his Spad 13, and taking off. Finally, he poses beside his Spad.

Notes
Title: this is taken from the shotsheet.
Remarks: the differences between this episode (unfortunately marred by the absence of some important captions) and **IWM 443** *London – British Fact and German Fiction* are noteworthy. In establishing that, contrary to German newspaper reports, life in London was unaffected by air attacks, the British took elaborate and naïve precautions to establish dates using a special constable as witness. The French simply produced their film in the confident expectation that it would be taken as genuine, and the German version as false, without further consideration.
[shotsheet available]
catalogued SDB: 8/1982

IWM 508-62 · France, 18/5/1918
ANNALES DE LA GUERRE 62

b/w · 1 reel · 722' (12 mins) · silent
intertitles: French

pr Section Cinématographique de l'Armée Française

I. Visit by the Prince of Wales to the Anglo-French sector of the Italian Front. The Prince talks with French staff officers in a snowbound wood. Getting out of his car at another location he walks into a wood with his party. The group poses for the camera.
II. A British Handley Page 0/400 bomber being lined up, bombed up, and taking off, Western Front, 1918.
III. French and British troops at the junction of their lines just south of Amiens, Western Front, May 1918. The French troops have stretched gas capes over their foxholes, although one group lines a slit trench. The French and British operators share a single telephone line. At a crossroads in a nearby wood French and American transport wait to move up. Close to Villers-Bretonneux on 8 May the German A7V tank 'Elfriede', victim of the first tank-to-tank engagement on 24 April, lies on its side with its track mechanism clearly visible.
IV. Captured German aircrew and infantry prisoners, Western Front, May 1918. A German AEG GIV captured undamaged on a French airfield. The crew of four are posed, all grim-faced, for the camera. Another group of German prisoners, soldiers captured at Grivesnes on 9 May, are resting. They are curious about the camera but otherwise relaxed.
V. President Poincaré's visit to troops of the Sixth Army on the Somme, Western Front, May 1918. The President is accompanied by General Fayolle and General Humbert. His first appointment is to affix the Médaille Militaire onto the standard of 8th Tirailleur Regiment, in a formal ceremony with an inspection and band. 4th Zouave Regiment has its standard decorated with the ribbon of the Légion d'honneur. Finally, 1st Moroccan Regiment is given the Légion d'honneur, and Poincaré decorates a number of its soldiers. The officers congratulate their men, then the whole force marches past.
VI. Training of messenger dogs, Western Front, May 1918. As a demonstration, an officer fits a message to a dog's collar and the dog's handler releases it. It runs past a (pyrotechnic) explosion and on to a second handler in a scrape trench. Another dog is sent in return. One of the handlers with his dog, which has a gas mask on as another demonstration. The handler removes the mask.

Notes
Title: this is taken from the shotsheet.
[shotsheet available]
catalogued SDB: 8/1982

IWM 508-63 · France, 5/1918
ANNALES DE LA GUERRE 63

b/w · 1 reel · 629' (11 mins) · silent
intertitles: French

pr Section Cinématographique de l'Armée Française

- Disjointed French propaganda film on the welcome given to French troops billeted in Alsace, France, 1918.

The film is highly disjointed and subject to several repeats and unrelated or divided scenes. It shows two soldiers (probably actors) coming to one of the small villages near Belfort. (Views of these are in the style of picture postcards with the French, rather than German, versions of their names given – hence Dannemarie rather than Dammekirch.) The three villages shown are Lauw, Dannemarie and Kirchberg. The opening of the film after some repeats resolves into a French marching column arriving in one of the villages. Falling out, two of the soldiers ask for directions to a nearby farm. They are greeted at the farm by a woman with three small children and settle in, admiring the scenery. They play with the children, who follow them briefly when they leave. In the village soldiers sit, talk and read newspapers with the local people, while the children play round them. As one soldier shows children out of school, a number salute him. The troops shop in the market place. The families (chiefly old ladies, girls and children) dress up for church. Indoors at Kirchberg young women sew and children play. Old men and women work on spinning wheels. A woman feeds chickens. Labourers set out for the fields with ox-drawn rakes and farm equipment. A soldier drinks a formal toast with a family group. In the procession to church children carry wreaths for the cemetery. In the final scene of the jumbled film, one of the soldiers, teaching a class, encourages a small boy to write "Vive la France" on the blackboard.

Notes
Title: this is taken from the shotsheet.
[shotsheet available]
catalogued SDB: 8/1982

IWM 508-64 · France, 1/6/1918
ANNALES DE LA GUERRE 64

b/w · 1 reel · 553' (9 mins) · silent
intertitles: French

pr Section Cinématographique de l'Armée
Française

I. The Italian Contingent on the Western
Front celebrates the third anniversary of
Italy's entry into the war, 23 May 1918. The
celebrations involve an Italian Contingent
parade and march past, chiefly of the field
guns, watched by the contingent's
commander, General di Robillant. A posed
group of General Peppino Garibaldi,
commanding the Brigade Alpi in France,
Signorina Italia Garibaldi of the Red Cross
and Commandant Benitti Garibaldi who
volunteered to fight in France in 1914, with
other officers.
II. The aftermath of the fighting in the
Somme area, Western Front, May 1918.
British and French troops, and some
civilians, walk through the recently
recaptured town of Béthune. British soldiers
have repaired the German tank 'Elfriede',
captured in April, so that it now moves
under its own power. British and French
soldiers ride on top.
III. Fraternisation between French and US
flyers, Western Front, May 1918. Sergeant
Baylis, the US "Ace of Aces" with twelve
kills, talks with members of 3ième Escadrille
beside one of their Spad 13s. (Note the
Stork markings.) Baylis is posed by himself
alongside a Spad.
IV. The involvement of US and French
forces in the Battle of Cantigny, Western
Front, 28 May 1918. The action by 28th
Infantry Regiment, 1st Division, was the first
major military engagement by US forces (in
company with the French) in the First World
War. From a short distance back the
Schneider CA1 tanks are shown moving off
towards the barrage at dawn, with the
Infantry rising up from their trenches and
walking slowly after them. Later, the
Schneiders return along a dirt track, along
which filter American and French wounded
and German prisoners.
V. The decoration of two airmen, Western
Front, May 1918. Accompanied by M
Dumesnil, the Under-Secretary for Air,
Commandant Féchamp decorates two
French airmen at a parade. Lieutenant
Garros becomes an Officer of the Légion
d'honneur and Lieutenant Marchal a Knight
of the Legion. After the awards Dumesnil
congratulates both men and the parade
marches past.
VI. Prime Minister Clemenceau visits the

front near Plémont, Somme area, Western
Front, May 1918. Clemenceau uses neither
helmet nor gas mask. He begins at a senior
officer's headquarters and goes down into
the trenches to talk to the troops.
VII. Marshal Ferdinand Foch as Allied
Generalissimo, firstly with his staff, including
General Weygand, then by himself. Western
Front, May 1918.

Notes
Title: this is taken from the shotsheet.
Remarks: both subject matter and
camerawork on this issue are considerably
better than average for the series. In
particular the American attack gives a good
indication of the extent to which tactics
changed between summer 1916 and
summer 1918. A good episode.
[shotsheet available]
catalogued SDB: 8/1982

IWM 508-65 · France, 6/1918
ANNALES DE LA GUERRE 65

b/w & (partly) tinted · 1 reel · 628' (11 mins)
· silent
intertitles: French

pr Section Cinématographique de l'Armée
Française

I. Presentation by the Marquis de
Damphierre to the US 6th Infantry of its
standard, France, June 1918. The Marquis,
as a descendant of de Rochambeau,
watches the ceremony. The actual
presentation is made by the Marquise,
watched by a number of civilians. Following
the presentation the regiment marches past.
II. French forces fighting in Flanders, June
1918. Shells fired by the French fall on the
Mont Rouge position. The village of
Westouter shows some shell damage and a
large number of damaged vehicles. A
wounded man is taken by stretcher from a
temporary hospital.
III. Infantry and Cavalry on the march near
the River Oise, Western Front, June 1918.
IV. Rheims on fire, 31 May 1918. A number
of buildings (tinted red) are burning or
smouldering and there is much smoke.
Troops emerge from the cathedral, which is
not further damaged (tinting ends).
V. Milan's celebration of the third
anniversary of Italy's entry into the First
World War, 23 May 1918. There is a military
parade through the streets, including
contingents from France and America. Sgr
Bissolati, a Socialist minister, addresses the
assembled crowd in an arena from a

platform. The procession passes through the Piazza del Duomo with the crowd waving flags and cheering the Allies. A Caproni Ca 42 overflies the city, high up, during the procession through the square.

Notes
Title: this is taken from the shotsheet.
[shotsheet available]
catalogued SDB: 8/1982

IWM 508-66 · France, 6/1918
ANNALES DE LA GUERRE 66

b/w & (partly) tinted · 1 reel · 723' (12 mins) · silent
intertitles: French

pr Section Cinématographique de l'Armée Française

- Battle of the Matz, Western Front, 9-15 June 1918.

The battle began with von Hutier's offensive on the River Oise and continued with Fayolle's counter-offensive. It is shown as a series of impressions of the actions of French soldiers, rather than strategy. Cyclists move past dismounted lancers, who mount up and follow along the dusty road. Heavy guns, well dug-in but probably 145mm naval guns, fire. A Cavalry regiment canters up in open formation, dismounts and advances on foot with rifles and machineguns, still in open formation. A tractor brings a 155mm Schneider gun into position. It is unlimbered and opens fire, controlled by an observer up a tree. 155mm howitzers join in. The next scene (tinted red) shows camouflage netting on a 155mm gun catching fire and the gunners throwing earth onto it. Renault lorries in convoy bring reserves up to the front. An observation kite balloon in the sky. Troops, having just debussed, leave their motor transport and march through a village, possibly Ressons. Three Saint Chamond tanks move up the road, the first two named 'Rambouillet' and 'Loup-Carou'. Near the battle area Infantry make their way through the standing corn and dig foxholes, setting up their automatic weapons. Observers send Morse signals to the crews of 75mm guns, who strip the camouflage from the guns and open fire. The Germans bombard the plain near Belloy on 11 June while observers from Tenth Army watch the fire, and a small group of walking wounded comes past. Other troops of Tenth Army move up through the unharvested crops, dead

Germans lie in the corn and stretcher-cases are brought back to the dressing station. One German walking on crutches shows his bandaged head and foot to his French escort. In the line of advanced posts among the trees and corn the soldiers rest, eat and clean their rifles.

Notes
Title: this is taken from the shotsheet.
[shotsheet available]
catalogued SDB: 8/1982

IWM 508-67 · France, (?) 6/1918
ANNALES DE LA GUERRE 67 – L'AMERIQUE EN GUERRE

b/w · 1 reel · 820' (14 mins) · silent
intertitles: French

pr Section Cinématographique de l'Armée Française

- French propaganda film on American forces on the Western Front, June-July 1918.

The film opens with a French and US soldier shaking hands, fading into a statue of Lafayette with Washington. Scenes of American troops disembarking at a harbour to substantiate the claim that there are a million US soldiers in France, 65 000 in the Zone des Armées. The troops march out of the docks and leave by train. At a halt they receive food and talk with French soldiers by the tracks. Locals applaud as a US marching column passes through a French town. At their first training camp in the woods the Americans settle in and eat from their field cookers. Other US troops enter a YMCA hut where they play a wind-up gramophone, drink coffee, read newspapers and talk. Black troops do outdoor physical exercises with rifles. More troops train for an attack in wave formation. The waves make short rushes and go to ground; near the objective the men throw smoke grenades and rush forward supported by automatic weapons. A close-up of faces of men of 3rd Division at rest by the Marne River before assembling back into column and marching off. A few men of US 2nd Division in Belleau Wood, dug in, resting, with 155mm howitzers and 75mm field guns delivering harassing fire. At a formal ceremony Marshal Foch decorates members of 2nd Division (?) with the Croix de guerre while the divisional commander, Major-General Omar Bundy (?) watches. US soldiers play with French children, others sit reading to children in Alsatian dress, the book being "Histoire d'Alsace". The children cheer the US Army.

Notes
Remarks: the overplaying of Franco-American friendship, particularly in respect of children, is rather distasteful. It is also ludicrous that a probably German-speaking Alsatian child should be read a book in French by a US soldier. Compare with **IWM 458** *America's Answer to the Hun*.
[shotsheet available]
catalogued SDB: 8/1982

IWM 508-68 · France, (?) 29/6/1918
ANNALES DE LA GUERRE 68

b/w · 1 reel · 592' (10 mins) · silent
intertitles: French

pr Section Cinématographique de l'Armée Française

I. General Franchet d'Esperey's arrival as GOC Army of the Orient, Salonika Front, 17 June 1918. Franchet d'Esperey is met from his train by various military representatives of the Allies, British, Italian and Serbian. Franchet d'Esperey goes on with his staff to review part of the French Contingent, all wearing tropical dress. (The British representative is not General Wilson, the GOC. The Italian and Serb may be Generals Ferrero and Dojovic.)
II. Schneider CA1 tanks are driven onto railway flatcars, one reversing up to the camera, France, June 1918.
III. The Alsace area following small French attacks, Western Front, June 1918. Firstly, the small village and river valley of Montgobert, subject to an attack on 12-13 June but not obviously damaged. The villages of Coeuvres and Valséry, liberated at the same time, show some damage from shelling, but not a great deal. German prisoners captured at Ambleny and Montgobert in a surprise attack on 28 June are escorted back along a road to the holding cages by men of a colonial division.
IV. Presentation by President Poincaré of its standards to the Army of Independent Poland, France, June 1918. The presentation is part of a formal ceremony. The various standards are blessed with holy water by a priest, and the troops join in prayer and an oath-taking. M Dmowski, President of the Polish National Council, and President Poincaré both give speeches. The standard of the Polish regiment "des Bayonnais" is awarded the Croix de guerre

for its members' fighting skill in 1914. In the formal presentation Poincaré himself takes each standard briefly and hands it to a Polish soldier. The full force (formerly the Polish Legion) of Infantry, Artillery and Cavalry then marches past.
V. Field Marshal Haig and Sir Arthur Balfour sit relaxed on a bench at the Trianon Palace, 2 July 1918.
VI. Marshal Foch arrives at AEF headquarters to confer with General Pershing, Western Front, June 1918. As Foch's car arrives Pershing is waiting by the steps of his château to meet it. The two men move into the open beside the car, talking together for the benefit of the cameras.

Notes
Title: this is taken from the shotsheet.
Date: the release date is taken from official French sources. The discrepancy between this and the item on Haig is a mystery.
Remarks: taken with **IWM 508-69**, which shows a similar ceremony for the Czechs, the symbolism of the French President handing its standards to the Polish Army could scarcely be bettered in showing the origins of the Little Entente. The film of Haig is also noteworthy, showing him far more informally than any British item.
[Robert Blake, *The Private Papers of Douglas Haig 1914-1919*, Eyre and Spottiswoode (1952): 316]
[shotsheet available]
catalogued SDB: 8/1982

IWM 508-69 · France, 6/7/1918
ANNALES DE LA GUERRE 69

b/w · 1 reel · 621' (11 mins) · silent
intertitles: French

pr Section Cinématographique de l'Armée Française

I. The presentation of its standards to the Independent Army of Czechoslovakia by President Poincaré, France, July 1918. The standards, donated by the people of Paris, are presented in a formal ceremony, in the open and in very windy conditions. After the presentation and march past one of the standards is displayed for the camera. Poincaré is barely seen.
II. Two celebrations of American Independence Day in France, 4 July 1918. The first of the celebrations has been organised by the American troops for the local French people of a quite small village by a river near the front. The American

band plays, there are apple-bobbing and games of water-jousting. Local women and children watch. On the river there is punting, slippery pole climbing and swimming. The second ceremony is in Alsace, at Massevaux, and has been organised by the Americans for the locals in a formal manner. A senior US officer shares a platform in the main square with the mayor. The American and French troops, filmed by cameramen of the US Signal Corps, march on parade out of the square. III. Allied bombardment at Vaux, Western Front, 2 June 1918. The barrage is being fired prior to an attack by French and US troops, but no soldiers are visible. The camera shakes with the shelling which continues for some time with much smoke.

Notes
Title: this is taken from the shotsheet.
Intertitles: these are flashframes.
[shotsheet available]
catalogued SDB: 8/1982

IWM 508-70 · France, 13/7/1918
ANNALES DE LA GUERRE 70

b/w · 1 reel · 513' (9 mins) · silent
intertitles: French

pr Section Cinématographique de l'Armée Française

I. Events on the Italian Front, mid-July 1918. Austrian prisoners captured by the French are marched back to their prisoner of war camp. After waiting outside their huts they queue for food. French forces on the Italian Front are visited by the King of Italy, who arrives by car. He reviews the troops alongside General Diaz, the Italian GOC, and General Graziani commanding the French Contingent. The march past includes a Chasseur battalion marching at fast pace.
II. German guns captured on the Oise sector of the Western Front on display behind the lines, July 1918. The guns are of various calibres. They include a 150mm howitzer with its barrel split and some 220mm mortars, together with many trench mortars.
III. Demonstration of a Renault FT18 light tank in wooded undergrowth, Western Front, July 1918. The tank climbs a steep bank, rotates its turret, reverses into the woods and descends a steep bank, all successfully.
IV. General Gouraud reviews Cavalry regiments employed in the Marne area,

Western Front, July 1918. The general pins the Croix de guerre to the standards of 6th Dragoons and 23rd Dragoons. A whole Cavalry division marches past, led by its cyclists and horsemen throwing up dust, then the 75mm field guns and wagons, and finally the White armoured cars.

Notes
Title: this is taken from the shotsheet.
Intertitles: these are flashframes.
[shotsheet available]
catalogued SDB: 8/1982

IWM 508-71 · France, 18/7/1918
ANNALES DE LA GUERRE 71

b/w · 1 reel · 754' (13 mins) · silent
intertitles: French

pr Section Cinématographique de l'Armée Française

■ French film of the early stages of the Second Battle of the Marne, mid-July 1918.

In the Villers-Cotterêts sector French wounded and German prisoners filter back through the woods east of the village and the wagon lines. Horse-drawn supply columns make their way into Longpont. The abbey and the village are badly damaged. Men march down the tracks near Villers-Hélon, past a stagnant pond, a military traffic jam and on through mud and shell-holes towards the front. Transport moves up in the rear areas. Before Violaines soldiers dig foxholes and scrape-trenches. Batteries of 75mm guns emerge from the wood and onto the roads. German 77mm field guns have been abandoned next to the Infantry positions. Another 77mm battery has been captured in front of Chaudun. Other guns captured at St-Pierre-Aigle have been grouped together. German prisoners are in a holding camp just behind the lines. Prisoners from Lorraine are separated out and a small group is posed for the camera, still in German uniform but with their officer carrying a French flag – all are smiling but clearly nervous. The prisoners are then marched in road column to the rear. Some hide their faces from the camera, others give a salute. Back in the battle zone a Schneider CA1 tank leads a party of soldiers forwards, more troops follow through the woods and over the horizon carrying full equipment. A 75mm battery fires from the wood with horse-transport passing close by.

Notes
Title: this is taken from the shotsheet.
Intertitles: these are all flashframes.
[shotsheet available]
catalogued SDB: 8/1982

IWM 508-72 · France, 27/7/1918
ANNALES DE LA GUERRE 72
the WAR ANNALS 72 (alternative)

b/w · 1 reel · 531' (9 mins) · silent
intertitles: French & English

pr Section Cinématographique de l'Armée
Française

■ French forces during the Second Battle
of the Marne, Western Front, July 1918.

A panorama of the River Marne near
Château-Thierry. The town of Château-
Thierry itself shows extensive damage, with
German barricades and trenches still in
place. Men of XXXVIII Corps and US 26th
(Yankee) Division pass through. President
Poincaré visits the city and is shown around
by General Fayolle. He visits the town hall
and talks to the locals who stayed through
the German occupation. At Dormans, also
on the Marne, troops of III Corps clear
rubble from the streets. One soldier reads a
sign (in German): "Caution – this street is
overlooked by the enemy". The town of
Châtillon, including its church, is in ruins.
Royal Engineers of British XXII Corps build
a pontoon bridge across the Marne beside
the town. A portrait shot of a young German
prisoner, with and without his helmet.
German 77mm field guns, abandoned in
the retreat, together with dumps of their
shells, are turned by the French against the
Germans and fired repeatedly. Prime
Minister Clemenceau, accompanied by
General Berthelot, decorates the standard
of 33rd Colonial Regiment with the
"fourragère" ribbon at a formal ceremony at
its headquarters. He talks with some of the
men and receives a bouquet from a small
child.

Notes
Title: this is taken from the shotsheet. This
was the first two-language edition of the
newsreel, presumably for the benefit of
British and American troops in France.
[shotsheet available]
catalogued SDB: 8/1982

IWM 508-73 · France, 3/8/1918
ANNALES DE LA GUERRE 73
the WAR ANNALS 73 (alternative)

b/w · 1 reel · 598' (10 mins) · silent
intertitles: French & English

pr Section Cinématographique de l'Armée
Française & US Signal Corps

■ Second Battle of the Marne, Western
Front, late July-early August 1918.

The Tardenois offensive, starts with the
bombardment of Chassins (?). Oulchy-la-
Ville and Oulchy-le-Château, captured
virtually undamaged by 41st Division. British
soldiers of 34th Division rest by a first aid
post inside the village. German 77mm field
guns captured, one with its shield
shattered, others buried under rubble. Near
Grand-Rozoy German prisoners bring
wounded of British 34th Division back on
stretchers. Soissons, shortly after its capture
on 2 August with the signs for the German
officers' club still in place. An old couple
who stayed through the occupation talk
with French troops. A kitchen garden
belonging to the German 43rd Artillery
Regiment is raided by French troops
ignoring the signs forbidding this. The
soldiers pose with the marrows and
cucumbers they have stolen. A German
aeroplane, too damaged to identify but with
Maltese Cross markings, crashed behind
the front lines. A US Signal Corps film
showing a German aeroplane in the
process of crashing. The aeroplane,
probably an Albatros CV, is wrecked but the
pilot survives with a head wound. French
troops surround the plane, the pilot is
carried off and the French pilot who shot
him down poses beside the wreck. At
Villers-Cotterêts General Mangin shows
President Poincaré a display of captured
German 77mm field guns, 105mm
howitzers, 155mm howitzers and some
machineguns. The film ends with a portrait
shot of Marshal Foch.

Notes
Title: this is taken from the shotsheet.
[shotsheet available]
catalogued SDB: 8/1982

IWM 508-74 · France, 10/8/1918
ANNALES DE LA GUERRE 74
the WAR ANNALS 74 (alternative)

b/w · 1 reel · 507' (9 mins) · silent
intertitles: French & English

pr Section Cinématographique de l'Armée
Française

■ Later stages of the Second Battle of the
Marne, Western Front, August 1918.

I. Bligny village and Mont Bligny near
Rheims, showing shell damage. General
Berthelot reviews troops of British XXII
Corps under Lieutenant-General Sir
Alexander Godley. These include Godley's
escort from the Anzac Mounted Regiment,
Australians of the 4th Light Horse. Two
linked Renault lorries pull a 145mm naval
gun through the streets of Romigny,
followed by similar guns and mule
transport. French and American troops
inspect the concrete bed for a German
superheavy gun, no longer in place. Pan
over Ville-en-Tardenois and the Ardre River
in V Corps area, as lorry-drawn 75mm field
guns pass over a bridge.
II. At Lassigny (?), in preparation for the
next offensive, limbered 155mm Schneider
guns and Infantry move up (filmed through
the windows of a house). Inside the village
captured German 77mm and 155mm guns
are displayed. The bombardment of the
German positions in front of Lassigny
begins.

Notes
Date: this comes from official French
sources. However, if "Lassigny" here means
the Lassigny south of Roye, this was still in
German hands on 19 August during the
Battle of Montdidier.
[shotsheet available]
catalogued SDB: 8/1982

IWM 508-75 · France, 17/8/1918
ANNALES DE LA GUERRE 75
the WAR ANNALS 75 (alternative)

b/w · 1 reel · 570' (10 mins) · silent
intertitles: French & English

pr Section Cinématographique de l'Armée
Française

I. Refugees on foot and in carts loaded with
belongings returning home after the
German retreat following the Second Battle
of the Marne, Western Front, August 1918.
II. General Gouraud decorating troops for
valour in the Second Battle of the Marne.
Western Front, 14 August 1918. The formal
ceremony takes place at the general's
headquarters. He pins decorations on the
standards of seven regiments, including
that of 21st Battalion, Chasseurs (?). In

Châlons, close to the headquarters, the
troops are cheered by local people as they
march through back to their barracks. On
arrival they parade and dismiss to a major
banquet held later in the day.
III. US troops, probably 3rd (Marne)
Division, near the Vesle River, Western
Front, August 1918. One of the US 75mm
field guns in action near Fismes during a
German attack, with the men throwing
shells from hand to hand for stacking. A
captured German 77mm FLAK 18 anti-
aircraft gun on a lorry mount. The grave of
Quentin Roosevelt at Chamery, captured by
32nd (Iron Jaws) Division. Men of 3rd
(Marne) Division resting by the roadside at
Fismes while food containers are carried
past them.
IV. The Battle of Montdidier, the start of the
French Advance to Victory, Western Front,
14-18 August 1918. The item starts with
Ribécourt, captured on 14 August by 67th
Division, with its church heavily damaged.
Limbers of 121st Division moving through
Ressons-sur-Matz. Captured German guns
from the battle on display, mainly 77mm
field guns with 210mm howitzers, a 77mm
FLAK 18 anti-aircraft gun, machineguns and
mortars. General Humbert, the Third Army
commander, walks with his staff through the
ruins of the château at Boulogne-la-Grasse.
The railway station at Montdidier some days
after its capture. A distant view of shells
bursting over the German lines near Roye
on 18 August in preparation for the next
phase of the offensive.

Notes
Title: this is taken from the shotsheet.
[shotsheet available]
catalogued SDB: 8/1982

IWM 508-76 · France, 24/8/1918
ANNALES DE LA GUERRE 76
the WAR ANNALS 76 (alternative)

b/w · 1 reel · 668' (11 mins) · silent
intertitles: French & English

pr Section Cinématographique de l'Armée
Française

I. The end of the Battle of Montdidier and
opening of the Battle of Noyon in the
Advance to Victory, Western Front, August
1918. Men of XXXIV Corps on a German
railway line through the Bois de Loges
captured intact on 12 August together with
a derailed goods train and a dump of
shells, mainly 77mm calibre. German
prisoners, some still carrying their

Bergmann 08/15 machineguns, are led to the rear. In a gun-pit near Roye-sur-Matz a battery of 145mm naval guns of the Corps Artillery opens fire.

II. The aftermath of the Second Battle of the Marne, Western Front, August 1918. On the quiet River Marne three soldiers try out abandoned German rowing boats, which overturn. The Germans have left limbers and equipment at the water's edge. A damaged girder bridge over the river is being rebuilt and lorry traffic is getting across. Cavalry patrols move ahead down the roads followed by lorry-towed 155mm Schneider guns, while German prisoners are being marched the other way.

III. The Battle of Noyon, Western Front, August 1918. Continuing the Advance to Victory. A 75mm battery of 15th Division (?) conducts a bombardment on the Quennevières plateau. Troops, probably of 55th Division, pass through Nampcel (on the boundary between Third and Tenth Armies) past German machinegun posts. Renault FT18 tanks also move up through the villages. German prisoners march back to the holding cages where each is given a piece of bread as their first meal. Three prisoners are posed together from the "class of 1920", those who would in peacetime have been called for military service in 1920, having reached the age of 18. They are therefore 17 years old or younger.

IV. The decoration of General Pétain and Marshal Foch, France, August 1918. In a formal ceremony President Poincaré awards General Pétain the Médaille Militaire at his headquarters. In another ceremony at Versailles Poincaré, with Clemenceau watching, presents Ferdinand Foch with his baton as a Marshal of France.

Notes
Title: this is taken from the shotsheet.
[shotsheet available]
catalogued SDB: 8/1982

IWM 508-76 bis · France, 25/8/1918
ANNALES DE LA GUERRE 76 bis
the WAR ANNALS 76 part 2 (alternative)

b/w · 1 reel · 352' (6 mins) · silent
intertitles: French & English

pr Section Cinématographique de l'Armée Française

- Area and aftermath of the Battle of Noyon in the Advance to Victory, Western Front, August 1918.

Some men of IX Corps emerge from a command post dug-out in the recently captured German trench system before Roye. Views of Roye itself with X Corps troops clearing away the rubble, showing the Montdidier end of the town and the first train coming into the station. Infantry reinforcements making their way over open ground to the front. The town of Chaulnes, captured by XXXVI Corps, with most of the rubble cleared away, but extensive damage. The town square at Nesle, captured by XXXI Corps on 20 August. A patrol of Spahi Cavalry dismounted and resting with their horses in a ravine. A railway cutting near Lassigny with dead Germans lying across the tracks. A pan over Noyon, captured by XV Corps, followed by detailed views. The rue de Paris shows extensive damage and signs warn that the road is mined. One soldier demonstrates how to defuse an unexploded shell while sappers repair craters in the roads. The cathedral at Noyon shows heavy damage.

Notes
Production: this episode was released a day after episode **IWM 508-76** and was treated as a second part rather than a separate episode, hence the unusual numbering.
[shotsheet available]
catalogued SDB: 8/1982

IWM 508-77 · France, (?) 31/8/1918
ANNALES DE LA GUERRE 77
the WAR ANNALS 77 (alternative)

b/w (partly) tinted · 1 reel · 597' (10 mins) · silent
intertitles: French & English

pr Section Cinématographique de l'Armée Française

I. French forces in the Chemin des Dames region, Western Front, August 1918.
A pan over the village of Laffaux, under fire from French guns. German prisoners walk through the village of Chévillecourt. French troops wander through the ruins of the château at Coucy-le-Château.

II. French forces advance to the Hindenburg Line, Western Front, August 1918. 155mm Schneider guns of X Corps fire at the entrance of the Canal du Nord tunnel near Ercheu (east of Roye, south of Noyon). Engineers strengthen the bridge taking the Ercheu-Libermont Road across the canal while XXXIV Corps transport passes over, mainly horse-drawn. Soldiers of XXXIV Corps water their horses in the canal by the north entrance to the tunnel, which is nearly blocked by rubble, as is the south entrance. Wagon transport of XXXIV Corps drives on through Esmery-Hallon on the road to Ham, moving past the damaged church and mine craters in the road. A posed group of six young civilians who stayed in Ham during the occupation. Ham itself shows, entering by the Guiscard Road, shell damage and (tinted red) parts of the town are still on fire. The church weathercock has fallen off the roof and is held up for the camera. Two old women and an old man who hid in a cellar during the occupation re-emerge for the camera. The town is still full of smouldering rubble.

Notes
Title: this is taken from the shotsheet.
Date: this is taken from French official sources but does not fit some of the film. Ham was not liberated until 6 September.
Summary: note the English translation of the scene involving the two old women and one man, described as three old men. The mistake indicates that the translation was made by someone with no access to the film. The occasionally quaint English used suggests translation by a French, rather than a British, organisation.
[shotsheet available]
catalogued SDB: 8/1982

IWM 508-78 · France, 9/1918
ANNALES DE LA GUERRE 78
the WAR ANNALS 78 (alternative)

b/w · 1 reel · 560' (10 mins) · silent
intertitles: French & English

pr Section Cinématographique de l'Armée Française

■ Battle of St-Mihiel, Western Front, September 1918.

Men of US 2nd Division move into Thiaucourt together with their transport. The interior of the town church is badly damaged and the roof destroyed. A pan from Mount Sec, with four American soldiers in the foreground consulting a map. There is intermittent shelling in the valley below. US horse and motor transport moves through Essey, where the temporary German hospital has been taken over by Americans. The entrance, by means of a bridge, to the key fort at Camp des Romains, followed by the plains of Woëvre and St-Mihiel seen from the fort. The wreckage of the barracks at Chauvoncourt

where there was an explosion in 1915. Inhabitants of St-Mihiel, mainly women and children (described as receiving food but no sign of this). An American soldier holds up two children who wave French flags. Civilians once again cross bridges over the Meuse in the town, and the people begin to return life to normal. President and Madame Poincaré visit the town, calling at the hospital and talking to people in the streets. Three French Saint Chamond tanks move past resting US soldiers in the corner of a wood. The first is clearly named 'Lotty', but the names on the other two are less clear: one may be 'Ane Rouge'. The soldiers rouse themselves and follow on. The film ends with a French inspirational poster "On Ne Passe Pas".

Notes
Title: this is taken from the shotsheet.
[shotsheet available]
catalogued SDB: 8/1982

IWM 508-78 bis · France, 10/9/1918
ANNALES DE LA GUERRE 78 bis
the WAR ANNALS 78 part 2 (alternative)

b/w · 1 reel · 520' (10 mins) · silent
intertitles: French & English

pr Section Cinématographique de l'Armée Française

I. US forces on the River Vesle, Western Front, September 1918. Some of the troops line a trench, others a sunken road. Engineers of 3rd (Marne) Division build a light bridge over the river. Transport crosses a stone bridge as the sappers continue to repair it. A distant view of a kite balloon crashing to earth in flames as US soldiers watch it descend. The town hall at Fismes shows extensive damage, as does the railway station and the road to Soissons. Braine is also severely damaged, including the church, and the bank of the Vesle is covered with captured German wire and tank traps. One of the bridges has been damaged and the river has flooded across the water meadows. US Engineers pull down damaged buildings which threaten to collapse.
II. Places recaptured in the Battle of Noyon, Western Front, September 1918. The 'liberated' areas show battle damage. Horse-drawn 155mm Schneider guns pass through Chauny in a long column. The Crozat Canal nearby is choked with debris. A pan over Tergnier. The mayor of Noyon is briefly held up at a military checkpoint

before being allowed back into the town. Prime Minister Clemenceau visits the town, in particular the cathedral and cloisters which show severe damage. Soldiers put a French flag back above the town hall. The film ends with the inspirational poster "On Ne Passe Pas".

[shotsheet available]
catalogued SDB: 8/1982

IWM 508-79 · France, 14/9/1918
ANNALES DE LA GUERRE 79
the WAR ANNALS 79 (alternative)

b/w · 1 reel · 531' (9 mins) · silent
intertitles: French & English

pr Section Cinématographique de l'Armée Française

■ Aftermath of the Battle of St-Mihiel, Western Front, September 1918.

The town centre of Vigneulles, showing damage but cleared up, probably 13 September. Pan over Viéville-sous-les-Côtes, which is close to Hattonchâtel. German 105mm and 155mm howitzers taken at Viéville-sous-les-Côtes and Billy-sous-les-Côtes on display. Some pianos crated up by the Germans to be sent back to Germany. St-Maurice (Sous-les-Côtes ?) shows slight damage. The locals have gathered in the concert hall prior to evacuation. The rubble and remains of houses at Combres and Les Eparges just to the north. A prisoner-of-war compound with Austro-Hungarian Engineers (attached to German divisions) inside and US guards outside. US soldiers, probably 90th (Alamo) Division, marching up the road from Pont-à-Mousson to Thiaucourt, not far from Regnévelle. Other troops and transport move up to the old French lines. US Renault FT18 tanks move up also. In the ruins of Regnévelle troops of US 5th (Red Diamond) Division fill in trenches and dig their own positions on the old German lines. Other US soldiers march up the roads nearby. The film ends with the French inspirational poster "On Ne Passe Pas".

[shotsheet available]
catalogued SDB: 8/1982

IWM 508-80 · France, (?) 21/9/1918
ANNALES DE LA GUERRE 80
the WAR ANNALS 80 (alternative)

b/w · 1 reel · 721' (12 mins) · silent
intertitles: French & English

pr Section Cinématographique de l'Armée Française

I. British progress in Flanders during the Advance to Victory, September 1918. The general area of Ypres. Filmed from just outside the town itself, shells falling on buildings on the outskirts. Two Mk V tanks, one Male, one Female, both carrying soldiers, move over open country. The Male carries a British soldier with a Tank Corps flag. British Whippet tanks move up a road past abandoned German shells. A British 18-pounder battery "bombarding the Hindenburg Line". A display of captured German guns, from heavy calibres to machineguns, watched over by British and Australian soldiers. British transport limbers, possibly XI Corps (note the formation sign) make their way across the battlefield.
II. French forces in the Advance to the Hindenburg Line, Western Front, September 1918. Pan over the region near Tahure, Marne area, being bombarded by French guns. In the mist soldiers, probably of II Corps, move forward in single file to capture the German forward trenches. At a command post the soldiers work wearing their gas masks. In daylight the first lines of German prisoners are led back. Schneider CA1 tanks continue the advance. In the rear areas troops relax near a field kitchen.
III. US forces in the Meuse-Argonne Offensive, Western Front, September 1918. Men of V Corps in billets in the town of Varennes, captured 26 September. 75mm guns and transport pass through the town. A pan over Montfaucon, showing the American wire and German positions on the heights. The church has been reduced to rubble, and one of the crypts has been used by the Germans as an observation post. German prisoners are assembled and marched away. The large marching column goes past the headquarters of Fourth Army at St-Même, on the outskirts of Châlons, and the prisoners are made to march at attention and salute as they pass the building.

Notes
Title: this is taken from the shotsheet.
Date: the release date is taken from French official sources but does not fit some of the film.
Intertitles: these are flashframes.
Remarks: this is really the first episode of the newsreel to show the British, as opposed to French and American, contribution to the victories of 1918. Given

that, in terms of scale, the British and British Imperial contribution to these battles was greater than that of the other Allies combined, this is a reflection of the hostility and ill-feeling generated between the French and British during the war. British material shows a similar failure to acknowledge the French and American contributions after April 1918.
[shotsheet available]
catalogued SDB: 8/1982

IWM 508-81 · France, (?) 26/9/1918
ANNALES DE LA GUERRE 81
the WAR ANNALS 81 (alternative)

b/w · 1 reel · 684' (11 mins) · silent
intertitles: French & English

pr Section Cinématographique de l'Armée Française

I. A distant pan of Cambrai in flames as Canadian forces approach it, Western Front, early October 1918.
II. St-Quentin after its liberation, Western Front, September 1918. The town is shown from a distance, then in close-up. The suburbs are burnt-out and deserted. The main square is relatively undamaged. The collegiate church and the Church of St Martin show considerable damage.
III. French and US forces in the Advance to Victory, Marne area, Western Front, September 1918. An observation kite balloon is raised into the air near the battle zone. A wrecked tank is shown, a British-built Mk IV Female with black cross markings used by the Germans. Near Tahure Fourth Army transport moves supplies to the front. French troops use a German Maxim machinegun for anti-aircraft fire against the Germans. A German horse-drawn convoy with all the horses dead, killed by French bombardment. German prisoners are used as stretcher-bearers and begin their march to the rear. The advance continues beyond Sommepy, on the boundary between XI Corps and XXI Corps, with White armoured cars leading up the reinforcements. Men of US 2nd Division pass through Souain. Cavalry of XI Corps move up the road as mule teams of US 2nd Division come back. German prisoners are moved out from the village, passing the US soldiers. Shell-bursts around an observation kite balloon. "The enemy's artillery cannot resist the wonderful impetus of the French infantry." Distant shot of Renault FT18 light tanks and soldiers advancing through a barrage.

Notes
Date: the release date is taken from French official sources but seems early for the fall of Cambrai.
Title: this and the intertitles are all flashframes.
[shotsheet available]
catalogued SDB: 8/1982

IWM 508-82 · France, (?) 30/9/1918
ANNALES DE LA GUERRE 82
the WAR ANNALS 82 (alternative)

b/w & (partly) tinted · 1 reel · 523' (9 mins) · silent
intertitles: French & English

pr Section Cinématographique de l'Armée Française

I. A still photograph, irised in and out, of two Bulgarian officers in a car on their way to negotiate the surrender of Bulgaria to the Allies, Salonika Front, 30 September 1918.
II. British and Canadian advance through towns abandoned by the Germans, Western Front, October 1918. Armentières, set on fire by the Germans in their retreat, no longer burning but showing damage to the main streets. Lens and its church are a pile of rubble and bricks. La Bassée is only half-standing, British troops, of I Corps, inspect the ruins before marching off. Some British sappers dig through the banks of the La Bassée Canal to make a crossing point. Cambrai (tinted red) is on fire as troops of Canadian 3rd Division watch. The Canadians, one carrying a French flag, move through the city, working as fire-fighters with pumps and buckets. Lorry-towed 4.5-inch howitzers move through the town (tinting ends).
III. The entrances to the three captured forts of Nogent, l'Abbesse and Brimont from which the Germans bombarded Rheims, Western Front, October 1918.
IV. General Mangin talks with US Ambassador William G Sharp near Laon, posed for cameras, Western Front, October 1918.

Notes
Title: this and the intertitles are flashframes.
Date: taken from French official records but seems too early for some of the material.
Remarks: the red tinting makes the fires at Cambrai, which are mainly smouldering, look far worse, and more dramatic, than the normal monochrome.
[shotsheet available]
catalogued SDB: 8/1982

IWM 508-83 · France, 12/10/1918
ANNALES DE LA GUERRE 83
the WAR ANNALS 83 (alternative)

b/w · 1 reel · 551' (10 mins) · silent
intertitles: French & English

pr Section Cinématographique de l'Armée
Française

I. The Advance to Victory in the Verdun
area, Western Front, October 1918. A
75mm field gun, probably fired by gunners
of 18th Division, delivering harassing fire
near the Côte de Talou. A column of
German and Austro-Hungarian prisoners is
marched through Samogneux village by
troops of French XVII Corps and US 3rd
(Marne) Division.
II. Events in the Marne area during the
Advance to Victory, including gas
casualties, Western Front, October 1918.
There is shell damage. A view of Mount
Teton. The rubble of Nauroy, a pan over
Mont Cornillet and the village of Beine, all
just east of Rheims. German wooden
dummy tanks mounted on limbers. Troops
of US 2nd Division and French XI Corps
watch as smoke rises from the village of
Vouziers. Soldiers blinded by gas are
escorted through the streets to safety.
III. The cathedral at St-Quentin, showing
holes in the pillars to take demolition
charges the Germans had no time to fit.
Western Front, October 1918.
IV. Visit by President Poincaré to Laon after
its liberation, Western Front, October 1918.
The city, after its liberation by XVIII Corps,
shows normal civilian life. A posed scene of
M Michaut, the temporary Mayor, talking
with his staff and an officer of the Chasseur
battalion which liberated the town. A military
band plays in front of the town hall to the
delight of the small children. President
Poincaré and General Mangin arrive in
separate cars while the bands are playing,
and listen to what is probably the French
national anthem. The crowd cheers them.

Notes
Title: this and the intertitles are flashframes.
[shotsheet available]
catalogued SDB: 8/1982

IWM 508-84 · France, (?) 19/10/1918
ANNALES DE LA GUERRE 84
[the WAR ANNALS 84] (alternative)
FRENCH OFFICIAL WAR FILMS (on copy
held)

b/w · 1 reel · 702' (12 mins) · silent

intertitles: French & English

pr Section Cinématographique de l'Armée
Française

I. The liberation of Lille, Western Front, 18-
19 October 1918. The main square of the
city, soon after its liberation showing
civilians milling about but no real
celebrations. Some British troops, probably
57th (West Lancashire) Division, are
present, eventually driving off in lorries.
People read the notices stating that French
police and British military police have
replaced the German authorities, and they
are shown on duty together. The locals
display in their windows valuables they kept
hidden from the Germans. Sacks of flour
arrive at the baker's, and he displays a
German 'war loaf' of black bread. Potatoes
are on sale for the first time since 1914. The
Tournai gate to the city is damaged, as is
the nearby St Maurice quarter. The
Germans have blown up bridges and
wrecked the railway station in retreat. In the
Place de la Concorde in Paris people
gather in celebration around the statue
representing Lille.
II. General Debeney in portrait shot wearing
his newly-awarded medal of Grand Officer
of the Légion d'honneur, France, October
1918.
III. The state entry of the King and Queen of
Belgium into Bruges on 25 October 1918.
The film is entirely in long shot from a high
position. The royal party is barely
discernible. Belgian Infantry and Cavalry
march past, with many cameramen and
photographers in evidence. The crowds
gather near the town hall as the royal
procession moves away.

Notes
Title: the title *French Official War Films*
appears at the beginning of this episode
and also episode **IWM 508-85**, in a different
titling style from that normally used by the
series. In this episode the same titling style,
in English, continues until approximately
half-way through the reel when the normal
style of two-language titling returns.
Date: the release date is taken from French
official sources.
Summary: compare with the British version
of the state entry into Bruges, **IWM 359**,
and of the liberation of Lille, **IWM 352**, **IWM
360** and **IWM 382**.
[shotsheet available]
catalogued SDB: 8/1982

IWM 508-85 · France, (?) 26/10/1918
ANNALES DE LA GUERRE 85
the WAR ANNALS 85 (alternative)
FRENCH OFFICIAL WAR FILMS (on copy
held)

b/w & (partly) tinted · 1 reel · 759' (13 mins)
· silent
intertitles: French & English

pr Section Cinématographique de l'Armée
Française

I. Ostend harbour after liberation, showing
block-ships sunk in the harbour mouth,
Belgium, 20 October 1918.
II. Courtrai after its liberation by British
soldiers of II Corps, Western Front, October
1918. The canals running through the town
are undamaged but the main girder bridge
has been brought down. British soldiers of
II Corps wait in the main square.
III. The town hall and main square of
Roubaix shortly after liberation by the
British, Western Front, October 1918.
Civilians watch while the British, of 40th
Division, march in. A mounted officer,
possibly Major-General Peyton the divisional
commander, waits with his staff. The British
parade is led by bagpipers. Children peer
through windows of shops selling Allied
flags. The bridges have all collapsed into
the river. The station has been wrecked.
IV. St-Amand-les-Eaux, north-east of Douai,
on liberation by British VIII Corps, First
Army. Western Front, October 1918. French
soldiers inspect the town together with the
British. (This section is tinted red.) Some of
the factory ruins still smoulder.
V. The Canadian advance through
Valenciennes, Western Front, October 1918.
The crossroads between Valenciennes and
its suburb Anzin where French Deputy
Durre was killed. Some of the houses are
wrecked but a German cinema for the
troops is still intact. In Valenciennes itself
(this section is tinted mauve) men of the
Canadian Corps pass the rubble of the
station. A dead German lies in a doorway.
Wagons of the Canadian 4th Infantry Works
Company (note formation sign) move
through. The Canadians inspect a dead
German laid out in the street. In an office
the temporary Mayor, M Billiet, poses with
his deputy M Damien.
VI. The Prince of Wales's visit to hear a Te
Deum in celebration of the liberation of
Durre by the Canadian Corps, Western
Front, 21 October 1918. Escorted by the
Corps commander, Lieutenant-General Sir
Arthur Currie, the Prince talks to local
officials while crowds watch. The party
enters the church followed by the mass of

the people. After the service they emerge
and Currie shows the Prince to his car.

Notes
Title: all titles and intertitles are flashframes,
beginning with the title *French Official War
Films* (as with **IWM 508-84**) followed by the
main title in French and English.
Date: the release date is taken from French
official sources, despite the discrepancy
with some of the material on the film.
[shotsheet available]
catalogued SDB: 8/1982

IWM 508-86 · France, 2/11/1918
ANNALES DE LA GUERRE 86
the WAR ANNALS 86 (alternative)

b/w · 1 reel · 727' (13 mins) · silent
intertitles: French & English

pr Section Cinématographique de l'Armée
Française

I. An animated map showing the Allied
victories on the Western Front, July-
November 1918. The map, in stop-frame
action, shows the German invasion of
France and Belgium in 1914, followed by a
more detailed version of the Allied advance
to victory between July and November
1918. The Allied attacks and German
counterattacks are identified by name and
marker arrows. The Canadian and
Australian Corps in the British sector are
shown under their own national flags.
II. Zeebrugge after liberation, showing
demolished coastal defence gun positions
and HMS *Thetis* sunk in the harbour.
Belgium, November 1918.
III. The liberation of towns and villages in
Belgium and France by British and Imperial
troops, November 1918. Firstly, Tournai is
shown, comparatively undamaged, through
which British soldiers march to the cheers
of the crowd. In Audenarde (or
Oudenaarde), the village shows some shell
damage and white flags are hung out.
French soldiers with a machinegun keep a
sentry post. Tourcoing some time after
liberation. The church spire is intact but
other buildings are extensively damaged.
Australian soldiers and local people stand
by the roadside as a civic procession in
honour of the war dead passes through the
streets. Maubeuge, showing the 17th
century outer defences of the town itself.
The town is barely damaged except for
some broken glass and fallen bridges.
Civilians and British soldiers scramble
through the rubble of one area. President

Poincaré visits the town and is met by a British parade and General Sir Henry Horne, commanding British First Army. The parade includes a contingent of the New Zealand Division.
IV. "The victors", who led France to victory on the Western Front, November 1918. Prime Minister Clemenceau talking with General Pétain. A portrait shot of Marshal Foch. Finally, a line of ordinary French soldiers, "the liberators" on the march led by their band.

Notes
Title: this and the intertitles are all flashframes.
[shotsheet available]
catalogued SDB: 8/1982

troops to the cheers of the crowd. All the staff horses are very nervous and shy at the crowds. The troops pass in review. Close-ups of the faces of the local children, mainly in regional dress. The general salutes the standards of his troops.

Notes
Date: the release date, although taken from French official sources, is obviously suspect.
Summary: although in English only, the rather quaint phrasing of the language in this episode indicates that it was not written by a native English speaker, and the film was probably captioned in France.
[shotsheet available]
catalogued SDB: 10/1982

IWM 508-87 · NO FILM

IWM 508-88 · France, (?) 16/11/1918
ANNALES DE LA GUERRE 88 (English version)
the WAR ANNALS 88 (alternative)

b/w · 1 reel · 674' (11 mins) · silent
intertitles: English

pr Section Cinématographique de l'Armée Française

I. German forces leaving Brussels in the Armistice, 21 November 1918. The English is flawed, telling that "the first Deutsch troops are living the town" (sic). Riders for the German horsed transport mount up and lead their carts out, past trams and watching civilians. German Infantry follows the transport. M Max, the Mayor of Brussels, returns from prison to the town hall by car, to the cheers of onlookers (very dark).
II. Entry of the King and Queen of Belgium into Brussels, 22 November 1918. The crowds wait in the streets for the arrival of the state procession and cheer as the royal party passes on horseback. The camera stays chiefly on the crowds rather than the procession. The various Allied contingents pass – American, French and British.
III. General de Castelnau's entry into Colmar in south Alsace, France, 22 November 1918. A procession of small girls in regional dress files along the streets, which are crowded with onlookers. The girls are followed by military and civilian dignitaries walking informally. General de Castelnau enters on horseback at the head of his

IWM 508-89 · France, 23/11/1918
ANNALES DE LA GUERRE 89
the WAR ANNALS 89 (alternative)

b/w · 1 reel · 621' (11 mins) · silent
intertitles: French & English

pr Section Cinématographique de l'Armée Française

■ Alsace-Lorraine in the revolutionary period and the arrival of French troops, November 1918.

A sign in the town of Breisach, "1789-1918 Ici commence le pays de la Liberté", is shown to the camera. French and German soldiers converse and fraternise together quite happily on a bridge over the Rhine in the neutral zone. French prisoners of war line up to cross the border back into France. As they pass they cheer the camera. A British Contingent following them looks happier as it passes. A pan over the city of Strasbourg under the control of the revolutionary National Council. The Revolutionary Guard, some in German uniform, some in civilian clothes, maintain a sentry post on the Kehl bridge. Civilians pass, one with a bicycle with wooden 'tyres' as a substitute for rubber. Local civilians and released French prisoners of war make their way into the city. In the city centre the signs are in German but French and US flags are displayed. The camera, on a tram driving through the streets, is cheered by the people. A soldier and two local officials cheer and point to a clock, showing that the city is now officially within the French time zone. The statue of Kaiser Wilhelm I in front of the Imperial Palace has been knocked over and locals clamber over it. The statues of the three German emperors, Wilhelm I, Friedrich Wilhelm and Wilhelm II in front of the main Post Office have been decapitated. In Kléber square the crowds wave French flags and cheer. French troops make a ceremonial entry into Thionville in northern Lorraine. The procession, to the cheers of the crowd, is of Cavalry and Infantry led by a band. In the main square the crowds gather, including women in white (possibly a religious ceremony).

[shotsheet available]
catalogued SDB: 8/1982

IWM 508-90 · France, 30/11/1918
ANNALES DE LA GUERRE 90
the WAR ANNALS 90 (alternative)

b/w · 1 reel · 729' (12 mins) · silent
intertitles: French & English

pr Section Cinématographique de l'Armée Française

■ Reaction in Belgium, Luxembourg, Alsace and Germany to the arrival of French troops, November 1918.

French officers greet Luxembourg officers in Heiderscheid. The Luxembourg troops, all quite elderly, possibly 1870 veterans, march past followed by the French. The senior French officer is read a testimonial by a small boy and given a bunch of flowers. General Guillaumat enters Neufchâteau in Belgium at the head of his men, to the cheers of the locals. Again the mayor reads him a testimonial which he receives on horseback. The march continues. In Sarrebourg in Alsace a chain of young children, young ladies in regional costume and military cadets, dances past the camera. In Saverne, just north of Strasbourg, a crowd cheers a similar procession of young people in regional dress. The children are shown in close-up. In Phalsbourg, just north of Sarrebourg, locals watch as French troops and transport pass by. There is a similar French march through Brumath, where a young girl offers the senior officer a bouquet. In Haguenau, also in Alsace, a marching column of 1870 (Franco-Prussian War) veterans passes through. The senior French officer hears a speech from the veterans' leader and meets his men. The contingent marches past, followed by young girls in their regional dress. At Wissembourg (north of Strasbourg, just inside the new French border) General Gérard receives a kiss and

a bouquet from a local girl. He also meets veterans of 1870, and his troops march past followed by ladies in regional dress. Gérard places a wreath on the tomb of General Douay, killed in 1870. French soldiers on the march cross the new German border near Bergzabern, north of Wissembourg, led by their band. The first squadron of 19th Chasseurs enters Landau, further north still. Little boys run alongside in curiosity but no crowds gather, and the people seem to be ignoring the occupying force rather than displaying hostility. The riders halt in the main street.

Notes
Title: this and the intertitles are all flashframes.
[shotsheet available]
catalogued SDB: 10/1982

IWM 508-91 · France, 12/1918
ANNALES DE LA GUERRE 91
the WAR ANNALS 91 (alternative)

b/w · 1 reel · 670' (11 mins) · silent
intertitles: French & English

pr Section Cinématographique de l'Armée Française

■ President Poincaré in Strasbourg to accept Alsace back as part of France following the plebiscite, 9 December 1918.

In a formal ceremony, surrounded by dignitaries and cameramen, Poincaré lays a wreath at the base of the statue of General Kléber. The camera is some distance away and the President is not easily visible. It is raining softly. The procession of dignitaries, in cars and carriages, moves through streets filled with cheering crowds to the town hall, and the dignitaries enter. The camera continues to focus on the people. Poincaré makes from the town hall balcony his famous announcement "Le Plébiscite est fait" (favourably to the French) and that "Alsace with tears of joy throws herself on the neck of her refound mother". The President is shown for the first time in close-up getting into his carriage to go on to the cathedral. Prime Minister Clemenceau and Marshal Foch join him in the carriage with a fourth man, possibly the mayor of Strasbourg. The procession moves again through the streets and the crowds wait while the dignitaries enter the cathedral and shortly re-emerge, driving on to the Place de la République. Girls in regional costume are waiting there and, despite the anxiety of the soldiers controlling the event, Foch goes up to talk to the prettiest. The great parade past the President's box is about to start and people cling to the branches of trees to get a better view. The parade consists at first of French Infantry with their bands and mounted officers, including a colonial unit and a party of Marines. Renault FT18 light tanks, turrets turned in salute, follow the Infantry. The parade continues on past the President's box as darkness falls, with civilians joining the soldiers. The young girls in local costume walk past, units of Chasseurs, of sailors, of veterans in their black frock coats, all march in salute past the box containing the President, the Prime Minister and the Commander-in-Chief of France.

Notes

Titles: these and the intertitles are flashframes.
Remarks: a fine film, in which the editor has obviously taken some trouble in selecting his scenes, and which shows a high degree of sophistication compared with most episodes of the series, produced under the pressures of wartime newsreel schedules. The emphasis on the crowds not only stresses in itself the importance of the masses in the victory of France but also provides genuine suspense up to the final appearance of Poincaré in close-up. The episode ends the series on a technical high point of film construction, and an emotional high point of French achievement in the war.
[shotsheet available]
catalogued SDB: 8/1982

IWM 508-92 · France, 1/12/1918
ANNALES DE LA GUERRE 92
b/w · 1 reel · 508' (9 mins) · silent
intertitles: French

pr Section Cinématographique de l'Armée Française

I. The destruction caused in the last few months on the Western Front, 1918. The banks of the Neuville Canal, near Rheims, are lined with damaged houses. The glass factory at Neuvillette is reduced to rubble and a few walls. Old German dug-outs and fortifications cover the area east of St-Quentin. One small fort near Courcy is occupied by French soldiers. The whole area shows extensive damage, churned up earth, cratering and shattered woods. A few

soldiers wander through the badly damaged village of Beaumont, north of Verdun.
II. Damage to the cathedral and city of Rheims, France, by April 1918. The streets of the city are damaged and the town hall is burnt-out. In front of the cathedral the statue of Joan of Arc is still in place – it was subsequently removed to a place of safety. The inside of the cathedral shows more shell damage; light pours through the gaps in the roof.
III. A bombardment seen indistinctly through the fog near the River Luce. The shelling strikes a distant village, Hangard-en-Santerre. Western Front, 1918.
IV. The Schneider CA1 tank and two notable tank crews, Western Front, April 1918. While French soldiers watch, the Schneider CA1 demonstrates its ability to push over small trees. A portrait shot of Sergeant-Major Deloche, recommended for the Médaille Militaire for escaping after being held with his tank for 48 hours. A portrait shot, panned between them, of Lieutenant Domercq and Sergeant-Major Mouren with their tank 'Mets-z'y-en'. Both were awarded the Légion d'honneur for their tank exploits.

Notes

Summary: this issue was the last, and items II and IV in particular are clearly makeweights inserted from earlier material to bring the issue up to length. Compare with **IWM 508-59**.
[shotsheet available]
catalogued SDB: 10/1982

IWM 509 · France, 1929
un DEUIL NATIONAL – LA MORT DU MARECHAL FOCH
a NATION MOURNS – THE DEATH OF MARSHAL FOCH (translation)

b/w · 1 reel · 880' (14 mins) · silent
intertitles: French

pr Cinémathèque de la Ville de Paris

■ Funeral procession of Marshal Ferdinand Foch through the centre of Paris, 25 March 1928.

The body of Marshal Foch lies in state at Les Invalides. King Albert of Belgium and then a crowd of people file past to pay their last respects. For the procession the streets are lined with soldiers. A motorised hearse takes the coffin from Les Invalides and with a Cavalry escort brings it to the Arc de

Triomphe where, beside the Grave of the Unknown Soldier, it is placed on a field carriage and covered with the French flag. Crowds watch the ceremony as, following the memorial service at Notre Dame, the coffin is taken out of the cathedral and placed on the field carriage once more. One of the pallbearers is General John Pershing. The procession moves away. Among the escorts are contingents from Britain (Foch was an honorary British Field Marshal) led by Coldstream Guards in full dress and English and Scottish soldiers in khaki with arms reversed. Contingents of Belgian Infantry and Italian Alpini follow. The crowd throngs the route as the procession reaches the Place de la Concorde. President Doumergue leads the mourners on foot behind the coffin. They include the Prince of Wales, in his Welsh Guards uniform, and the Duke of York. The procession slows in front of the statue of General Galliéni. The coffin is followed by a riderless horse draped in a cloth of fleur-de-lis. At Les Invalides the mourners take their seats. Aristide Briand is seated close to the Prince of Wales and the Duke of York. Former President Poincaré mounts a lectern and delivers the address. As he talks the film shows Foch's honours: working at his desk on a train in April 1918 as Commander-in-Chief of the Allied Armies; being presented by Poincaré with his baton as Marshal of France in August 1918; being received by the City of Paris Council (together with Marshal Joffre and General Pétain) on 14 July 1919 in a procession passing under the Arc de Triomphe; arriving at Windsor to stay with the British Royal Family; on the saluting podium for the Peace Procession through London on 19 July 1919 together with George V, Queen Mary, Lloyd George, Admiral Beatty and General Pershing; and delivering an address to the new class of 1919 at the Ecole Polytechnique. Poincaré finishes his speech. The various contingents, French and Allied, pay their last respects in marching past the coffin, which is taken back to Les Invalides for burial. The crowd rushes in for a final look.

Notes
Remarks: this film compresses the time taken in the ceremony by using fades, wipes and crowd cuts. The advance in silent film technology in ten years from the First World War shows very clearly in comparison with wartime material.
[shotsheet available]
catalogued SDB: 10/1982

IWM 510 · GB, (before) 7/1917
a DAY IN THE LIFE OF A MUNITION WORKER

b/w & (partly) tinted · 1 reel · 701' (12 mins) · silent
intertitles: English

sp War Office Cinema Committee (?)

- Manual work done by women at a British munitions factory, spring 1917.

The young woman leaves her terraced house (this section is tinted blue) at 5am and takes the train to the factory (tinting ends). In the locker room she and the others change into overalls and boots, and clock on. She works on finishing 8-inch shells, pouring molten explosive in to top the cases up, capping them using a wheel to clear the screw threads, adding the detonator and stencilling them. A trolley takes another batch away. Other women, wearing masks against the fumes, top up heavier shells. The women are given a brief medical examination on site, lasting no more than a few seconds. In one suspect case a blood sample is taken. The women wear shifts to wash, which is compulsory before meals and on leaving the factory. A final close-up of the young woman, pretty without her mask and almost coy, "working for victory".

[shotsheet available]
catalogued SDB: 10/1982

IWM 511 · France, (prod) 1918
[ANNALES DE LA GUERRE – ADDITIONAL MATERIAL 1] (allocated)

b/w · 4 reels · 2753' (45 mins) · silent
intertitles: none

- Jumbled mixture, mainly from the French First World War news series *Annales de la Guerre*, with some British material, 1918.

The film is in fragments of a few seconds' duration. Apart from numerous items from the French sector of the Western Front and the Italian Front, there are three main themes. One is French forces in north Africa (or possibly Palestine) on patrol. The second is a visit of General Sir William Robertson to New Zealand officer cadets training in St John's College, Cambridge, with film of the King's College choirboys. The third is a French parade through a village in Alsace, including a girl in traditional costume handing a flower to a French soldier.

Notes

Summary: see the detailed shotsheet for further information on this film. Note that as it exists the film follows no coherent theme for any length of time.
[shotsheet available]
catalogued SDB: 10/1982

IWM 512 · GB, 1914-16
BRITISH CALL TO THE NATION

b/w · 1 reel · 254' (5 mins) · silent
intertitles: English

■ Recruiting film for the Royal Navy, 1914-16 (?).

The film consists of stockshots and doggerel verse. It opens with Trafalgar Square on Trafalgar Day, 21 October. Nelson's column has floral wreaths. The plaque on HMS *Victory* marking the spot where Nelson fell. In comparison to Nelson, a picture of Admiral Sir Charles Beresford. The submarine D.2 leaves Portsmouth harbour past HMS *Victory*. A torpedo boat patrolling the harbour. A seaplane carrier, possibly HMS *Engadine*, lowers a Fairey 42 seaplane into the harbour and it takes off. Submarine C.34 on the surface. HMS *Neptune* at anchor with crew on deck before the war. The film appeals for men to crew the ships, ending with "God Save the King".

Notes

Title: this is taken from the shotsheet.
[shotsheet available]
catalogued SDB: 10/1982

IWM 513 · NO FILM

IWM 514 · GB, 6/1918
BRITAIN'S EFFORT : drawings by Lancelot Speed

b/w · 1 reel · 1002' (17 mins) · silent
intertitles: English

sp Ministry of Information *pr* Lancelot Speed Films *prod* Speed, Lancelot

■ Cartoon of the British military and industrial contribution to the Western Front up to the end of 1917.

The film starts with a cartoonist drawing figures which then animate themselves. The Kaiser sharpens a knife to carve up the world, the figures "1914" flying from the sparks. He and Franz Josef gloat over a pile of weapons. While John Bull sleeps in England the two monarchs, as vampire bats, plot to seize Serbia as a path to India, and also Belgium. At this Britannia wakes John Bull and blows her battle horn. Across the world, in Australia, New Zealand, South Africa, India and Canada armed men arise. In Britain an aristocrat, a farmer, a clerk, a fisherman, a miner and a railwayman become soldiers, a single figure representing the army of 1914. A Canadian encouraged by a moose, an Australian with a kangaroo, a South African with a springbok, a New Zealander with a kiwi and an Indian with an elephant, all join in. By 1918, shown as single soldiers, the South African and Indian forces on the Western Front are as large as the British force of 1914, these are less than the two figures of Canada and ANZAC, and are dwarfed completely by the giant figure of the British Army by whose boot they stand. In comparison of output, British Artillery in 1914 is a small field gun and in 1917 a giant howitzer. A British soldier calls to the Home Front and a lady with a dog is transformed into a munitions worker. Whereas "woman power" in 1914 is a microscopic figure, in 1917 she engulfs the screen. Munitions production in 1914 is a single shell, in 1917 a massive shell-dump, pouring from Britain onto the Western Front, to the delight of John Bull and Lloyd George. St Paul's Cathedral will fit inside the Great Pyramid, 480 feet high, but British military artefact production in 1917 forms many larger pyramids. Ship production in 1914 is a small steamer, dwarfed by that of 1917. John Bull in a gunboat chases the Kaiser around the German colonies of the world, driving him (to the relief of the natives) back to Kiel with his fleet. For finance the cartoonist draws the figure 1 000 000 followed by a series of marks in rapid succession "at this pace, working eight hours a day, it would take a week to make a million marks". One day's British war expenditure in 1914, represented by John Bull on a gold pile, was £4 million, and in 1917 £6 million. To the end of 1917 total war expenditure was £6 951 852 472, which "in sovereigns edge to edge would circle the earth more than three and a half times". The earth transforms into an unhappy, battered Kaiser declaring "I should like Peace! – a German peace!" represented as John Bull in chains. "But this is the peace we mean to have!", Britannia victorious, guns transformed into new factories, a laurel wreath over all and the British family safe at home.

Notes
Remarks: the method of presenting complex statistics as pictures in this manner is misleading: one figure may be twice as large as another, but the image by which it is represented will also appear twice as wide and twice as long, or eight times as large altogether. This dramatises statistics in a manner which is misleading. Similarly, complex political issues are reduced to the crudest possible images in this film.
[Darrell Huff, *How To Lie With Statistics*, Pelican (1980): 64-71]
[shotsheet available]
catalogued SDB: 10/1982

IWM 515 · GB, 2/1917
the ECONOMISTS

b/w · 1 reel · 1183' (19 mins) · silent
intertitles: English

cast Paul, Lennox and De Frece, Lauri

■ British comic fictional propaganda piece on how suburban dwellers should buy National War Bonds to help the war effort rather than trying to produce their own food, early 1917.

Two friends, Mr Woodgate and Mr Sparwell, short of money and with food expensive, decide to hunt rabbits and fish locally for food. Their wives meanwhile practise home economy by decorating their own hats and "undies". At home Mr Woodgate complains that two rabbits last week cost 40s. Mr Sparwell similarly notes that 2½ pounds of plaice cost £3 10s. The next day Mr Woodgate buys a shotgun, Mr Sparwell a fishing rod, and they go out to the woods. Mr Sparwell's first cast hooks a tramp's billycan into the water for which he is forced to pay. Later Mr Woodgate injures the sleeping tramp slightly by shooting him in mistake for a rabbit and also pays him compensation. Otherwise neither has any luck. At the end of the day Mr Woodgate's dog catches and kills a rabbit which he then shoots to maintain the illusion. Mr Sparwell catches a small fish in his landing net as he is packing his equipment. They compare catches describing the fictitious

"one that got away". Their wives at dinner that night are amused by the small catch. On the week's accounts the cost of one small rabbit, including the cost of the gun and licence, is £19 4s, and of a small fish, again including the equipment, is £9 1s. On the next day both men sell off their equipment and resolve in future to practise economy by buying National War Bonds.

Notes
Title: this and the intertitles are flashframes.
Remarks: the ending, making the point of buying National War Bonds, is very abrupt, almost an afterthought. There is nothing in the remainder of the film to indicate that the country is at war, and with slightly different captioning this could have been – and may have originally been – a simple comedy.
[shotsheet available]
catalogued SDB: 10/1982

IWM 516 · GB, 6/1917
EVERYBODY'S BUSINESS
CIVILIANS FALL IN (alternative)

b/w & (partly) tinted · 2 reels · 1895' (32 mins) · silent
intertitles: English

sp Western Import Company for Ministry of Food *pr* London Film Company
prod Dewsbury, Ralph *cast* McKinnel, Norman; Du Maurier, Gerald; Lang, Matheson; O'Neill, Edward; Kelly, Renee; Rorke, Kate; and Herbert, Gwynne

■ British fictional propaganda film on the importance of the rural upper classes leading the way in the campaign to save food, 1917.

(Reel 1) "Mr Briton" is a pillar of the community, with a wife and daughter, a cook, a maid and a gardener. His son Tom is with the Army in France and his daughter Mabel is an Inspector of Female Labour in a munitions factory. On Mr Briton's birthday Tom is coming home on leave bringing Lieutenant Jack Goudron RN, Mabel's sweetheart. Mrs Briton tells her cook, whose son is also serving in France, to prepare a wartime austerity menu for dinner. She scolds the cook and gardener for throwing away bread, using seed potatoes for eating, and removing too much peel. Meanwhile Mr Keen calls on Mr Briton, asking him to join the local War Committee, but, since they are local rivals, Mr Briton refuses. When his wife tells him the evening's menu he orders his cook to

change it to a better one. Mrs Briton shows him Lloyd George's newspaper appeal for food economy. "That's not meant for people like us," he tells her. That night at dinner Tom tells of successful fighting on the Western Front, Jack of the Royal Navy patrols and Mabel of the munitions workers. The ladies retire, while Jack and Tom leave to smoke in the garden. With Tom's connivance Mabel joins Jack alone in the garden where he proposes marriage to her. Mr Briton falls asleep in his dining room chair. *(Reel 2, which is tinted, mainly yellow, throughout.)* He dreams the war is in its final stage. Despite the Royal Navy's efforts, submarines sink British ships, there is famine and bread queues. Lloyd George and Bonar Law appeal to the people, who sign voluntary food pledges, reduce their bread intake and reform their eating habits. Finally, a satisfactory and permanent peace is declared, which is announced as causing riots in Berlin and the collapse of German currency. Mr Briton wakes to find himself cheering the news, with his family around him. He tells his dream. Tom says: "Well the Army's right! The Navy's right! All that's wanted is for civilians to fall in". Mr Briton calls Mr Keen and joins his Food Committee. He tells his cook that her wasting food is keeping her son in the trenches. She gives this message to the maid and gardener, insisting on food economy. Mr Keen arrives with food campaign posters to cover the house. Mr Briton signs the food pledge issued by King George to maintain the ration scale. The final scene is HMS *Victory* riding at anchor with the legend "Britain Expects".

Notes
Title: the alternative title appeared on some release versions during 1917.
[shotsheet available]
catalogued SDB: 10/1982

IWM 517 · GB, (?) 1917
the RISING GENERATION AND THE GENERATIONS TO COME

b/w · 1 reel · 634' (11 mins) · silent
intertitles: English

pr Kinsella and Morgan *prod* Kinsella, E P; and Morgan, Horace

■ British fictional propaganda piece on the role of the shipbuilder in winning the war, and a vision of future peace, 1918 (?).

Children running to their working-class homes after school represent the future, what "Tommy" and "Jack", returning to their families, are fighting for. The shipyard workers are also part of the war. In future years a retired shipbuilder dozes and dreams of the war. His dream shows ships being launched. In an air raid a German incendiary bomb (shown) kills his wife, leaving him with two small children and her memory. She appears in ghostly form to him in her empty chair, as he makes "his solemn pledge to help his country free the world of Huns". Dreaming on, his son is older and describes enthusiastically a professional football game (shown). Soccer has returned after the war. Further on in time, his daughter's wedding day. As he dreams, his daughter and her husband watch him, with their own baby. He wakes and cuddles the child. The image of "Peace", a classical goddess figure with a Union Flag behind her, calls small children to her side.

Notes
Production: this is a Kinsella and Morgan film, but it is not certain whether it had any official sponsorship or was ever released. *Remarks:* a very odd film, which loses any political or propaganda point it may have had at the beginning in a welter of sentimentality. Its only message – that without winning the war none of the benefits of peace will come – is scarcely hinted at. This is either remarkably subtle for the time, or else the film has no message at all.
[shotsheet available]
catalogued SDB: 10/1982

IWM 518 · NO FILM

IWM 519 · GB, (?) 1918
the GREAT GAME

b/w · 1 reel · 245' (5 mins) · silent
intertitles: English

pr Kinsella and Morgan *prod* Kinsella, E P; and Morgan, Horace

■ British propaganda film of the fight between British shipbuilders and German submarines explained as a football match, 1918 (?).

The film opens with a Cup Final football match being played. Now there is "a sterner game – the World's Final – the freedom of humanity is at stake". On the German side are the submarines sinking cargo ships. On the British side are the shipbuilders launching new ones. A goal for the Germans is another sinking, a goal for the British a new launching. A final view of shipbuilders smiling at the camera.

Notes
Production: this is a Kinsella and Morgan film, but it is not clear if it had official sponsorship or was ever released in this form.
[shotsheet available]
catalogued SDB: 10/1982

IWM 520 · GB, (prod) 1918
[NATIONAL KITCHEN] (allocated)

b/w · 1 reel · 255' (4 mins) · silent
intertitles: none

sp Ministry of Information (?)

■ National Kitchen in Westminster Bridge Road, London, 25 February 1918.

The menu board at the kitchen for 25 February (the cameraman can be seen reflected in the glass). Inside women cook at the stoves and prepare food. The kitchen has advertisements on its shop-front for various government schemes, and is named "WESTMINSTER BRIDGE RD KITCHEN FOR ALL". A queue, mainly schoolchildren, has formed outside.

Notes
Summary: compare with **IWM 523**.
catalogued SDB: 10/1982

IWM 521 · GB, 10/1918
MRS JOHN BULL PREPARED

b/w · 3 reels · 2814' (48 mins) · silent
intertitles: English

sp Ministry of Information

■ Partly fictionalised account of the contribution of women to the British war effort by 1918.

(Reel 1) It is 1914 and the outbreak of the war. Mr Smith, a prosperous businessman, is starting to lose staff who have volunteered for the Army and he refuses women replacements. He also prevents his son volunteering since the war will be over

by Christmas and he needs his help. He is enraged at his two daughters, telling them that even in war "a woman's place is at home". In his garden the Spirit of British Womanhood appears and puts him to sleep for four years. She calls to women through the land who rise in a trance to the war. Mr Smith's son joins the Army with his mother's sad blessing. Four years later the Spirit wakes Mr Smith who staggers off. He sees girls of the Women's Land Army doing farm work (Byfleet Manor Farm, Old Basing) and selling milk from the farm in a town (Basingstoke). College girls work as flax pullers in their holidays. *(Reel 2)* Women work in a tannery making coats for soldiers, as railway porters at a military dock railhead, or at a station (Charing Cross). Women build buses in a factory for the London Omnibus Company, serve food in Victoria Station canteen, bake and deliver bread for Lyons Bakery in Kensington. They work at a gasworks, at a tobacco factory, for the Post Office, make aircraft at Waithead's Aircraft Factory (including acetylene welding) clean windows and make munitions. *(Reel 3)* Other women also drive ambulances, run YMCA huts, escort visiting officers in London. Queen Mary and Lloyd George are quoted stressing their importance. There are even policewomen. In a formal parade on 29 June 1918 all types of women workers march along Whitehall, through Admiralty Arch and Hyde Park to honour the King (not seen). The parade includes the Voluntary Aid Detachment, Women's Legion, WAACs, WRNS, the Women's Air Auxiliary Corps ("the Penguins"), the Women's Army Service Corps, Women's Land Army, Women's National Land Service, Women Foresters, munitions girls, TNT girls, ambulance drivers, Royal Mail drivers, bus conductors and tram drivers. Mr Smith returns home to find that his house is now a hostel for wounded soldiers run by his wife and daughters as WAACs. His son has lost an arm and is staying there. As the family dine together that night he receives his final surprise: military service age has been increased to 50 and he is being called up, he will have to salute his own son. On this comic note the film ends, with a final quotation from Lloyd George on the importance of women in war work.

Notes
Title: this is taken from the shotsheet.
Summary: the "Women's Air Auxiliary Corps" and the "Women's Army Service Corps" do not seem to have had any formal existence; these may have been convenient titles to describe the work of those particular

members of the WAAC.
[*The Times*, 1 July 1918: 10C]
[shotsheet available]
catalogued SDB: 10/1982

IWM 522 · GB, (?) 1918
the WOMAN'S PORTION

b/w · 2 reels · 1645' (28 mins) · silent
intertitles: English

pr Film Producers' Guild (?) *cast* Livesey,
Sam; and Forbes, Mary

- British fictionalised propaganda drama on
the need for women to accept separation
from, and loss of, their husbands, 1918
(?).

(Reel 1) A working-class back street slum,
with the men at war and the women largely
unable to cope with growing children. Lizzie
has a small baby that her husband Jim, a
corporal serving in France, has never seen.
From time to time the newsboy or a
telegram will tell a neighbour her husband
is dead. Lizzie is in despair. A neighbour
calls and Lizzie reads her husband's last
letter telling of German brutality and how he
would willingly die to punish them. The
vicar calls with clothes for Lizzie to mend
for a living, telling her Jim is doing his duty.
She replies that "he might have dodged it.
Plenty have!..It isn't fair to us women". After
the vicar leaves a letter arrives with the
news that Jim is missing presumed dead.
Lizzie swoons and the neighbour, unable to
console her, leaves. Lizzie falls asleep.
(Reel 2) Lizzie dreams that her husband has
returned, but is furtive and aggressive. He
tells her he has deserted, outlining how he
stole a blank leave pass and returned to
England under a false name, leaving his
comrades. She is horrified, "I'd sooner you
were dead than a deserter". He tells her
he's going north to look for work under an
assumed name and she can join him later.
Meanwhile as she dreams her husband has
genuinely returned and wakes her. He
explains that he has been given leave. "Me
desert? Not likely! We're out to finish this
job." He tells her that the telegram
announcing his death is probably to
mislead the Germans as to British
casualties, "a trick to make the Germans
overconfident – thinking I'm done for". They
embrace and he cuddles the baby as the
film irises out and ends.

Notes
Date: at one point in the film the husband

refers to "Hindenburg... building a new line".
Taken at its face value, this would suggest
a date after the breaking of the Hindenburg
Line in September and October 1918. If the
film was made after that date it is possible it
was never released.
Production: the name of the production
company is not certain, it is not known if
this film had official sponsorship or was
ever released in this form.
Remarks: it is to be hoped for the
reputations of the British propaganda
agencies that they had nothing to do with
this film. In itself it is, in acting style and
tone, firmly in the tradition of late 19th and
early 20th century melodrama. The street
scenes have considerable social realism
compared to the unrealistically spacious
and luxurious interior. But how anyone
could have been so irresponsible as to
suggest that a 'missing believed killed'
telegram could be not even an honest
mistake but a deliberate government
deception staggers belief. How much false
hope and needless suffering this film
caused if it was ever released can only be
guessed at.
[shotsheet available]
catalogued SDB: 10/1982

IWM 523 · GB, 1918
the DAILY DINNER

b/w · 1 reel · 127' (2 mins) · silent
intertitles: English

sp Ministry of Information

- British Home Front propaganda
documentary encouraging people to use
the National Kitchens, 1918.

I. A view of the rooftops of London. In every
home someone cooks a meal – as one
woman cooks at a stove. This is
uneconomical. A staff of nine women at a
"Popular National Kitchen" shows how they
can easily make 1000 dinners daily. The
dining hall is spacious and prices cheap –
the menu board for 31 May is shown. The
film advises people to use the kitchens, and
get their local mayor to start one if none
exists.
II. At the end of the film, unrelated to it,
appears the caption symbol for Pathé
Animated Gazette.

[shotsheet available]
catalogued SDB: 10/1982

IWM 524 · GB, (?) 1918
**ENROL FOR NATIONAL SERVICE AND
BACK UP THE BOYS IN THE TRENCHES**

b/w · 1 reel · 625' (10 mins) · silent
intertitles: English

sp Ministry of Information (?)

- British documentary encouraging people
  to join voluntary Home Front labour
  organisations, 1918.

Men prepare the ground for sowing spring
corn, plant the seeds in rows, water them
using hoses, and plough with horse-drawn
ploughs. The film quotes Lloyd George on
the need for more volunteers. A mechanical
reaper at work. Men pitch hay onto wagons
to take to the hayloft. A steam-driven
threshing machine pours corn into sacks. A
"farm labourer and his lass" walk and talk
romantically together. The film emphasises
the financial and health advantages of farm
labour. Skilled mechanics are also needed
to run farm machinery. A steam tractor pulls
firstly a plough, then a rake. A mechanical
thresher at work. The steam tractor pulls
wagons, then carries hurdles for a pen into
which sheep are collected.

Notes
Title: it is not clear whether this is a
complete film or a fragment. In the latter
case the title, as given here, may represent
a caption and not be correct as an issue
title.
Summary: the First World War use of the
term 'National Service' to mean, exclusively,
voluntary non-military service on the Home
Front, should be noted.
Remarks: the film uses a mixture of
promises, threats of starvation or defeat,
and moral blackmail to expound its
message.
[shotsheet available]
catalogued SDB: 10/1982

IWM 525 · GB (?), 1914-18
the LAST LESSON

b/w · 1 reel · 1290' (20 mins) · silent
intertitles: English

cast Vibart, Henry; Livesey, Barrie; and
Munro, Douglas

- British First World War fictional
  propaganda film of the imposition of
  German culture on Alsace after the
  Franco-Prussian War.

In 1872, after the end of the Franco-
Prussian War, the use of the German
language alone for all teaching purposes
was made compulsory in Alsace. The
schoolmaster in a small village is old and
amiable, loved but little respected by the
children. One evening he receives a letter
from Germany that he is being replaced by
a new German teacher. He and his wife
despair at the news. Meanwhile one of his
pupils, Philippe, would rather play than
study his French grammar and sneaks out
of the house to meet his friends, returning
before his father notices. The schoolmaster
wanders through his garden, asking "will
the flowers all have German names ?" On
the next day the German schoolmaster
arrives, middle-aged, bespectacled and
stern, but not sinister. He announces that
he will take over the old man's house, and
goes to meet him and look over the
schoolroom. After he leaves the
schoolmaster is enraged, imagining him
beating the children. He puts up a notice
asking all parents to come to school at 9am
the next day. They assemble with their
children, but Philippe, who stopped to steal
apples and talk to a boy fishing, is late as
usual. The schoolmaster explains that this is
his last lesson and stresses the importance
of French culture. "The language of a
country is the key to liberty, but when a
country is conquered both language and
liberty are lost." Philippe, asked to recite his
grammar, cannot do so, and thinks with
shame of the time he wasted playing. The
last lesson the schoolmaster gives to the
villagers is "Vive la France". The words fade
to the French flag.

Notes
Intertitles: more than one style of title is
used, including one repetition.
catalogued SDB: 10/1982

IWM 526 · GB, 1918
**LORD PIRRIE'S APPEAL TO SHIPYARD
WORKERS**
a PATRIOTIC MESSAGE (alternative)
KINKARTOONS (series)

b/w · 1 reel · 480' (8 mins) · silent
intertitles: English

pr Pathé *designer* Morgan, Horace
artist Kinsella, E P

- Cartoon appealing for unskilled men for
  shipbuilding work in Britain, 1918.

I. Before the opening credits, a portrait still

of Lord Pirrie, Controller of Shipbuilding, and his printed message that shipbuilding must be increased to counter the U-boat threat. A hand draws the head and neck of the Kaiser with an arm clutching his throat. The cartoon animates itself; the arm, marked "shipyard worker" tightens around the Kaiser's throat. This is the "shipyard grip".
II. A hand draws cartoons which animate themselves. A figure of Britannia, "Britons never shall be slaves". A family seated for a meal with a picture of a ship at sea on their wall. The figure of Death in a German helmet conjures a torpedo to sink the ship and steals the loaf from the family table. "We must have ships to bring us food". Back to Britannia and unskilled men signing up for the shipyards. Men working away from home in shipyards receive a subsistence allowance as well as pay. Back to Britannia pointing in the familiar 'Kitchener' gesture "Britannia needs YOU NOW !" Details are obtainable from any Employment Exchange or Post Office.

Notes
Title: the title appears with Lord Pirrie's message before the opening credits, which include the alternative title.
Date: the artist's hand at the end of the film signs his work with the date 1917. Lord Pirrie was appointed Controller of Shipbuilding in March 1918, and it appears that his message was tacked onto the remaining film, which was probably released before 1918 in its original form.
[shotsheet available]
catalogued SDB: 10/1982

IWM 527 · GB, 1914-18
FUN AND SPORTS AT ALDERSHOT (ledger title)

b/w · 1 reel · 360' (6 mins) · silent
intertitles: English

pr Holmfirth Production Company (?)

▪ Army sports and fête, Aldershot, 1914-18.

A crowd of civilians and soldiers watches the sports. A tug of war, the baton change on a relay race, a horse race and a football match. Teams of gymnasts give a physical training demonstration. Running races, bayonet practice, and a bayonet assault course. The crowd is entertained by a juggler, a Charlie Chaplin figure, a mock bullfight with a pantomime bull (two men dressed up) and a soldier riding a

pantomime horse. The pierrot troop, including a choir of ladies in Welsh national dress. The Charlie Chaplin figure. The whole pierrot troop. A final close-up of mothers holding twin babies.

Notes
Production company: the two negative flashframes are marked HP Co Ltd, which may refer to Holmfirth.
Intertitles: these are MS flashframes with two exceptions, which are negative flashframes.
Summary: as it stands, this is probably a random composite of more than one original film.
catalogued SDB: 10/1982

IWM 528 · GB, 1918
the PRINCE OF WALES IN GLASGOW

b/w · 1 reel · 240' (4 mins) · silent
intertitles: none

▪ Prince of Wales tours shipyards on Clydeside, probably 5 March 1918.

The riveters work in poor light on a ship's hull. The Prince (in Army uniform) joins them with his party and tries his hand at working with a rivet gun. He moves on through the shipyard and out into the open, being cheered by the workers. At another location he inspects a military parade. Back in the Clydeside area he moves with his party through the streets, watched by a crowd of local people, including children, that the police have difficulty controlling. The Prince passes through the crowd on his way to his car.

Notes
Title: this is taken from the shotsheet.
[*The Times*, 6 March 1918: 3B]
[shotsheet available]
catalogued SDB: 10/1982

IWM 529 · GB, 1918
INDIAN EDITORS AT HYDE PARK HOTEL

b/w · 1 reel · 189' (4 mins) · silent
intertitles: none

sp Ministry of Information *cam* Davis, W

▪ Arrival of the editors of leading Indian newspapers, on a goodwill tour run by the Ministry of Information, at their London hotel, 11 October 1918.

The party of five, with a guide, leave the front of the Hyde Park Hotel and go out into Hyde Park itself. The editors are J A Sandbrook of the newspaper *Englishman* (Calcutta), Hemendra Prasad Ghose of the *Basumati* (Calcutta), Kasturiranga Iyengar of the *Hindu* (Madras) and Gopal Krishna Devadlar of the *Dnyanprakash* (Poona City). They talk to a policeman in the park. They pose individually for portrait shots and then for a group shot together. A final shot of them getting out of their car back at the hotel.

Notes
Title: this is taken from the shotsheet.
[*The Times*, 12 October 1918: 9D]
[shotsheet available]
catalogued SDB: 10/1982

IWM 530 · GB, (?) 1917
SAVINGS CERTIFICATES : how to buy them, how to use them

b/w · 1 reel · 1308' (23 mins) · silent
intertitles: English

sp Department of Information (?)

■ British fictional film encouraging people to buy War Savings Certificates, 1917 (?).

A stop-action sequence of a War Savings Fund card filling with sixpenny stamps until it transforms into a 15s 6d certificate. In five years time this becomes a pound note, and in a further five years 26s. Savings have many uses. The doctor recommends a holiday for a working-class wife, so her husband cashes his certificates to pay. At the seaside they decide to save more for their children's education. Later in life they have two teenage children. Their certificates pay for their daughter to attend Pitman's secretarial school and get "a good position" as a secretary. Both she and her boss save certificates. At home both children present their parents with their savings from certificates. In another household the husband is laid off work. His wife cashes her certificates to fund his own business, a small garage which rapidly expands. Certificates and stamps are sold in public houses and post offices. A "small capitalist" buys 500 certificates from his bank manager, the maximum allowed. The bank manager suggests he buy the same number for all members of his family; there is no income tax. A £500 certificate is shown. A young suburban couple have been able to save enough War Savings

Certificates to be able to fund their wedding. Later when married they have a small child. "Over 300 million certificates have been sold. 12 million people hold them." A poster advertising the certificates is burst through by a pointing finger, "What about YOU ?" The young suburban couple kiss, happy in financial security.

Notes
Summary: the behaviour of the actors in several scenes does not fit the context of the film particularly well. This could be a very early War Savings film composed of items from other discarded productions.
Remarks: the film is occasionally ludicrous with improbably 'correct' grammar and speech from working-class characters.
[shotsheet available]
catalogued SDB: 10/1982

IWM 531 · GB, (?) 1918
MR ROBERT MIDDLEMAS'S FOOD PRODUCTION AT ILFORD

b/w · 1 reel · 565' (9 mins) · silent
intertitles: English

sp Ministry of Information (?)

■ Part-time and volunteer food production schemes at Ilford, Essex, with an exhortation to surpass them, 1918 (?).

Mr Middlemas has set up shop in the centre of Ilford where rabbits can be bought and bred for food. Men work "twitching", spiking the ground to employ drainage. Men, women and boy scouts work cultivating the hospital grounds. Boys, including "Ilford's champion digger", work on allotments. On the common a horse-drawn plough is followed by men scattering potato seeds. One month later the men work hoeing out the weeds from the patch. Sea Scouts pick blackfly off growing broad bean plants, pausing for their own meal by a tent. Men cut waste grass for hay with sickles, others work on allotments. Sea Scouts and boy scouts collect refuse for pigs from door to door. The sty is built and creosoted, then the pigs arrive by cart and car. The Ilford Boys Pig Club owns 10 breeding sows and 77 store and young pigs. A few months later, the fattened pigs and piglets are shown together in the sty.

Notes
Title: it is unclear whether this is a complete film or a fragment. If the latter, the title is in fact a caption and not the release title.

- 250 -

[shotsheet available]
catalogued SDB: 10/1982

IWM 532 · GB, (?) 1918
the NATIONAL WAR SAVINGS COMMITTEE'S CAMPAIGN FOR THE VICTORY LOAN

b/w · 1 reel · 198' (4 mins) · silent
intertitles: English

- Fund-raising rally in Trafalgar Square, possibly just after the end of the war, 1918.

In Trafalgar Square Nelson's Column is decorated with Victory Loan symbols. People queue to buy certificates at the hut nearby. On a platform Major-General Sir W S Brancker, in charge of RAF Personnel, gives a speech. Mark Hambourg gives a classical piano recital. The MP for Hull (probably Colonel Sykes) gives a speech. Madame Stralia delivers an operatic song. The signal "England Expects" is hung in flags from Nelson's Column. Miss Edith Fenton enters the hut. The mayor of Westminster gives a speech. A final view of the crowd in the square, with the injunction "Buy joy-loan NOW!".

[shotsheet available]
catalogued SDB: 10/1982

IWM 533 · GB, (before) 5/1918
HER SAVINGS SAVED
[FILM TAGS] (series, allocated)

b/w · 1 reel · 123' (3 mins) · silent
intertitles: English

sp Ministry of Information *pr* Hepworth Manufacturing Company *cast* Edwards, Henry; McAndrew, John; and White, Chrissie

- British fictional short piece encouraging people to buy War Savings Certificates, 1918.

While a working-class girl is shopping in a street market a pickpocket steals a receipt for a National Savings Certificate from her bag. A young man sees this, struggles with him and retrieves the receipt while the thief runs away. The girl offers it to him as a reward. He declines, but with a suggestion of romance confesses that the experience has inspired him to start this form of saving.

Notes
Summary: an early example of the Ministry of Information 'film tag', a successful innovation of 1918. These were very short pieces of practical or inspirational propaganda intended to be run at the start of a normal film show.
[shotsheet available]
catalogued SDB: 10/1982

IWM 534 · GB, (?) 8/1917
NATIONAL SERVICE – WOMEN'S LAND ARMY

b/w · 1 reel · 124' (2 mins) · silent
intertitles: English

pr Broadwest Films

- Partly dramatised recruiting film for the Women's Land Army in Britain, 1917.

An acted scene of a woman looking at a recruiting poster, which shows Britannia appealing for Land Army recruits. Britannia comes alive from the poster and points the woman to her job. A woman of the Land Army ploughs behind two horses. Britannia appeals for more recruits.

Notes
Summary: the First World War use of the term 'National Service' to mean, exclusively, voluntary non-military service on the Home Front, should be noted.
[shotsheet available]
catalogued SDB: 10/1982

IWM 535 · GB, 1917-18
RECRUITING MARCH OF THE OXFORDSHIRE WOMEN'S LAND ARMY

b/w · 1 reel · 437' (7 mins) · silent
intertitles: English

sp Women's War Department (?)

- Recruiting march and presentation to Princess Mary of the Women's Land Army, Oxford, 1917-18.

The march begins in St Giles with women entering the enrolment hut by the Martyrs' Memorial. The procession goes down the Cornmarket, through Carfax and into Broad Street. Some of the women are in uniform, and the procession includes a steam tractor. Mr R E Prothero, Minister of Agriculture, leads local city and university officials to Trinity College gardens, where Princess Mary presents awards to the Land Girls. One of the girls shows two baby lambs. The awards continue while the members of the council and the university, one in a Bath chair, watch.

[shotsheet available]
catalogued SDB: 10/1982

IWM 536 · GB, (?) 5/1918
GAUMONT GRAPHIC 740 – WOMEN'S LAND ARMY

b/w · 1 reel · 260' (4 mins) · silent
intertitles: English

pr Gaumont

- Recruiting rally of the forest and timber sections of the Women's Land Army through London, May 1918.

The march starts in the rain with women handing out leaflets. The film stresses that women can join for just six months. The march continues, including a hay wagon. At Trafalgar Square speeches are given (in long shot – no clear view of speakers). Two of the Land Girls in close-up each holding a duck. The girls sing a song or hymn. There are more speeches, followed by the continuation of the march.

Notes
Technical: The last scenes of the film are covered with small scratches or static marks.
[shotsheet available]
catalogued SDB: 10/1982

IWM 537 · GB, 1/1918
the ADVENTURES OF DICK DOLAN

b/w · 2 reels · 1841' (32 mins) · silent
intertitles: English

sp National War Savings Committee
pr Broadwest Films *cast* Gill, Basil; Macmahon, John; Beaumont, T; and Hopson, Violet

- British fictional film placing the saving of National War Savings Certificates among the conventional attributes of a hero in a story of working-class romance, 1918.

(Reel 1) Dolan is a London tramp living by a munitions firm at which work three men.

Mr Cambray goes to his well-kept home with a wife, an adult daughter and a younger daughter. Mr Morton lives with Mr Morrison and his wife nearby in a slovenly house. Mr Cambray gives his wife the bulk of his wages to buy War Savings Certificates. Morton and Morrison take a taxi to play cards elsewhere. At work the manager gives a speech asking the workers to save their money. Later Mr Cambray is "combed out", and called up for the Army. His wife is confident that she can get work at the factory. Meanwhile their younger daughter is nearly killed when her foot is trapped by a railway crossing with a train coming. Dick Dolan risks his life to save her, to the relief of her sister, and spectators give him a reward of a few shillings. He realises later that he has fallen in love with the elder sister. Wandering through Trafalgar Square, on impulse he buys with the reward money a War Savings Certificate from the "Tank Bank", and so becomes a "shareholder in the Empire" and begins to regain his self-esteem. *(Reel 2)* He gets work at the factory shipping cartridges. Noticing a poster that each certificate buys 124 cartridges, he adds to one box a note that he, Dick Dolan, sends that number to France. Mrs Cambray, working at the factory, often invites Dick over for Sunday tea, and he is now saving regularly. Meanwhile Mr Morrison gets into a fight in a card game, is badly hurt and laid off work for several months. On the Western Front Mr Cambray's unit fights off a German attack. He finds Dick's note among his cartridges, which are fired through a Vickers machinegun. Meanwhile Mr Morrison is in financial trouble. Dick offers to lend him the money he has saved and Morrison promises to reform when he recovers. But Mr Morton is forcing his attentions on Miss Cambray, who has come with Dick. Finding them, Dick knocks Morton senseless to the girl's relief. Mr Cambray has come home on leave and shows his family his souvenirs, including the note. His wife explains who Dick is. At this point Dick enters and declares his intention of marrying Cambray's daughter. The film ends with Dick accepted as a member of the family.

Notes
Remarks: propaganda at its best. The film is genuinely interesting and entertaining, and much too improbable to be taken as anything but fiction. The propaganda theme, the purchase of War Savings Certificates, is the mainspring of the plot: the conventional wish-fulfilment 'happy ending' comes about as a consequence of

saving. All who save are good, and display the stylised attributes of good characters. All who do not save are bad or stupid. By building the propaganda message into the film and drama conventions of the period, it has been conveyed with great simplicity and skill.
[shotsheet available]
catalogued SDB: 10/1982

IWM 538 · GB, 1918
the STORY OF THE CAMEL AND THE STRAW – NEW VERSION
KINCARTOONS (series)

b/w · 1 reel · 276' (5 mins) · silent
intertitles: English

sp National War Savings Committee
pr Kinsella and Morgan

- Cartoon appeal for the purchase of National War Savings Certificates in Britain, 1918.

The cartoonist draws a scene which animates itself. A pair of scales marked VICTORY equally balanced, with John Bull on one side and the Kaiser on the other. Money piled on the scales keeps them balanced. Finally, a working-class figure adds 15/6d to the British scale, tipping the balance and knocking the Kaiser over. John Bull congratulates him. A German face drawn on a savings card is "blotted out" with sixpenny savings stamps, encouraging child savings. John Bull encourages the scheme, stressing that certificates can be bought from banks, stockbrokers, post offices and many shops.

Notes
Summary: see also the remainder of the Kincartoons series and the Pathé Kinkartoons series.
[shotsheet available]
catalogued SDB: 10/1982

IWM 539 · GB, 1917-18
JACK AND JILL
KINCARTOONS (series)

b/w · 1 reel · 299' (5 mins) · silent
intertitles: English

sp National War Savings Committee
pr Kinsella and Morgan

- Cartoon appeal for buying National War Savings Certificates in Britain, 1917-18.

The cartoon is a parody of the nursery rhyme. Jill, a munitions worker, collects her pay and goes with her husband Jack to buy War Savings Certificates at a post office. After five years they watch their house being "built", as a line drawing, with Jack's savings, while Jill's savings pay for the furniture that is delivered. "Money saved spells victory and the end of Kaiser Bill". The figure of the Kaiser has a cone marked "War Savings Certificates" lowered over his head by a giant hand. The Crown Prince cries for his "Papa". The film invites "secure your happiness now" by purchasing War Bonds and War Savings Certificates.

Notes
Summary: see also the remainder of the Kincartoons series and the Pathé Kinkartoons series.
[shotsheet available]
catalogued SDB: 10/1982

IWM 540 · GB, (?) 1918
THERE WAS A LITTLE MAN AND HE HAD A LITTLE GUN
KINCARTOONS (series)

b/w · 1 reel · 248' (4 mins) · silent
intertitles: English

sp National War Savings Committee
pr Kinsella and Morgan

- Cartoon appeal to buy National War Savings Certificates for post-war reconstruction in Britain, probably very late 1918.

The cartoon is in the form of a parody of the nursery rhyme. It opens with the cartoonist's hand, which then draws another hand holding a pencil, which then animates itself to draw a cartoon figure of John Bull. This transforms into a soldier, then into a sailor who dances. Bonds and Savings Certificates provide the money to support them. A soldier lying down, with a bulldog beaming approval, shoots holes in the face of the Kaiser as if it were a paper target. In an underground shelter the Kaiser, the Crown Prince and Hindenburg cower, praying together. Overhead a British aeroplane drops a "War Bond Bomb" which explodes the shelter, raising lumps on their heads. More overflying aeroplanes drop paper bonds which deluge the trio. The film asks, now that the war is over, for more money to reconstruct the home industries and attain supremacy in commerce. A soldier waving a flag beside a shell-dump transforms into a factory complex with a smiling John Bull beside it.

Notes
Summary: see also the remainder of the *Kincartoons* series and the Pathé *Kinkartoons* series.
Remarks: an illustration of the virulent tone adopted by British propaganda in the last few months of the war. The scene of the Kaiser's animated face being pierced by bullets is particularly unpleasant.
[shotsheet available]
catalogued SDB: 10/1982

IWM 541 · GB, 1917-18
SIMPLE SIMON

b/w · 1 reel · 262' (4 mins) · silent
intertitles: English

sp National War Savings Committee
pr Kinsella and Morgan *cast* Robey, George

- Acted and cartoon appeal to buy War Bonds and National War Savings Certificates by George Robey in Britain, 1917-18.

The film starts with the actor Robey in normal clothes seated at a cartoonist's desk, drawing a cartoon of himself in his comedian's dress. This figure animates itself, in a parody of the nursery rhyme, as Simple Simon. Although offered a pie by the pieman, he instead goes to the Post Office and buys certificates from the serving girl. He uses the money saved to set up a general stores which proves successful. The film ends with Robey seated at the desk again, appealing for people not to waste their money but save to "rid the world of Huns".

[shotsheet available]
catalogued SDB: 10/1982

IWM 542 · GB, (?) 1917
STAND BY THE MEN WHO HAVE STOOD BY YOU
KINCARTOONS (series)

b/w · 1 reel · 299' (5 mins) · silent
intertitles: English

sp National War Savings Committee

pr Kinsella and Morgan

- Cartoon, newsreel and acted appeal for the British people to buy National War Savings Certificates, 1917 (?).

An actress "Britannia" draws aside a curtain over a screen, flanked by silhouettes of two British soldiers. On the screen appears a genuine scene of refugees fleeing out of Belgium in 1914, followed by an acted scene of the Kaiser killing a Belgian woman. An acted scene of nurse Edith Cavell being shot. The film appeals for contributions to the War Loan. Cartoon of a man feeding a 15/6d certificate into a machine which produces a shell. He fires the shell from a gun. The shell lands at the feet of the Kaiser and transforms back into a certificate, then into a British soldier who locks the Kaiser up in a box. A certificate with a line of six pennies blotting out the words "THE HUN" as an encouragement for children to save. In a hand 15/6d in silver transforms into a pound note. After a final appeal to buy certificates Britannia closes the curtain.

Notes
Title: note the change in the series title spelling of the Kinsella and Morgan *Kincartoons* from the Pathé *Kinkartoons* when the two men worked for Pathé. This was probably for copyright reasons. Compare with **IWM 526**.
[shotsheet available]
catalogued SDB: 10/1982

IWM 543 · GB, 1917-18
OLD FATHER WILLIAM
KINCARTOONS (series)

b/w · 1 reel · 356' (6 mins) · silent
intertitles: English

sp National War Savings Committee
pr Kinsella and Morgan

- Cartoon appeal for British people to buy National War Savings Certificates for social improvement, 1917-18.

The cartoon, a parody of Lewis Carroll's poem, shows a young man talking to his father after the war. A pencil draws the scene which animates itself. The old man tells how during the war he and his wife got jobs in munitions, investing the money in National War Savings Certificates, and this has given him a private income for life. Before the war over half of British goods

- 254 -

were bought from abroad, from German-looking suppliers, but (in this vision of the future) after the war the money invested in the certificates is used to make the same consumer goods at home using the industrial capacity generated by munitions production. Final shot of John Bull sitting beside a factory from which pour consumer goods.

Notes
Summary: see **IWM 542** and the remainder of the *Kincartoons* series. See also the Pathé *Kinkartoons*.
Remarks: an elegant, simple way of conveying a complex political message. So much so that, if its implications are realised, it begs several important political questions. Also unusual in that it discusses post-war society in terms of economic programmes rather than visions of eternal peace and harmony. Sadly, it cannot be precisely dated.
[shotsheet available]
catalogued SDB: 10/1982

IWM 544 · GB, 1917
the U-TUBE

b/w · 1 reel · 678' (12 mins) · silent
intertitles: English

pr Speed Cartoons *prod* Speed, Lancelot

■ Cartoon ridiculing the Kaiser and German threats to invade Britain, probably late 1916.

The cartoonist draws the figures of the Kaiser "Bill" and the Crown Prince "Billie". They play with a U-boat in a water bowl until a cargo ship marked "NOOTRAL" ('neutral' in US pronunciation) blocks it. They agree the policy has failed, and consult their astrologer Hindenburg. In his crystal ball they see an image of Admirals Jellicoe and Beatty, and First Lord of the Admiralty Arthur Balfour, blocking an invasion of Britain by sea, and Zeppelins being shot down. Hindenburg decides on an underground tunnel from Berlin to Birmingham and a scientist builds boring machines to make it. Led by the Kaiser and Crown Prince the invasion force sets off, but the Iron Crosses the Kaiser has issued to them all affect the compass and the force emerges at the North Pole. Water flooding in washes all but one of the machines back to Berlin. German newspapers announce that Birmingham, London and Liverpool have been destroyed by the raid. The

Kaiser and Crown Prince are left stuck "up the pole".

Notes
Remarks: the cartoon has a large number of puns and gags based on contemporary catch-phrases and wartime slang. The role of the Kaiser and Crown Prince in British 'hate' propaganda is well illustrated by this film. The Crown Prince speaks and acts like the conventional English 'silly young man' of comedy rather than like a German. The Germans found no equivalent figure among the Allies against whom to direct their own propaganda, except possibly Lloyd George and Lord Northcliffe in 1918.
[shotsheet available]
catalogued SDB: 10/1982

IWM 545 · GB, (?) 1918
RETURN OF THE INTERNED

b/w · 1 reel · 334' (4 mins) · silent
intertitles: none

pr Green's Film Service

■ Film taken at Leith of the arrival by ship of internees returning from Europe, with the request "Watch the picture carefully, and see if you can identify anyone."

Scenes of the returnees on deck, some waving Union Flags; on shore, kilted soldiers and nurses wait. "The most of the Civilians came from the notorious Ruhleben Camp": pan across crowd of smiling faces. "Pipes of the Gordon Highlanders playing a welcome to the returning Prisoners": the pipers stand onshore, close to the ship. "Baby Russell, Born in Berlin six weeks ago. Mrs Russell is seen coming towards the front of the picture": the baby, wrapped in an enormous amount of swaddling clothes, is held by a nurse on deck as Mrs Russell, smiling nervously, makes her way forward. "Leith gives the returning War Prisoners a right royal welcome": a street parade, including shots of a fire engine carrying local dignitaries, a military band, uniformed soldiers (carrying a banner for the Scottish Federation of Discharged and Demobilized Sailors and Soldiers), the returnees travelling in lorries covered in flags and bunting, and cheering crowds. "Another Contingent arrives at Leith Harbour from Copenhagen with Civil and Military Prisoners. The Soldiers come mostly from Brandenburg Camp": shots of cheering men, some waving handkerchiefs, on board ship; some smoke cigarettes; shot of a well-to-do woman handing out bars of chocolate. "Lieut. General Sir W R M'Cracken meets – Some of the 'Old Contemptibles'": M'Cracken greets soldiers on the dockside; others, upon disembarking, are greeted by well-wishers/loved ones. A young woman on the dockside holds the hand of one of those still on board. Final shots of parade; end caption "GREEN'S FILM SERVICE / SCOTTISH MOVING PICTURE NEWS / GLASGOW AND LONDON".

catalogued JCK: 4/1991

IWM 546 · GB, 1917-18
[GAS WORKS] (allocated)

b/w · 1 reel · 372' (7 mins) · silent
intertitles: none

■ Women workers at a gas manufacturing plant, probably in Britain, during the second half of the First World War.

The women work outside shovelling coke into sacks and loading these onto a cart. At another heap they shovel the coke onto sieves balanced on wheelbarrows to sort out the slag. The slag is taken in the barrows to another tip where it is dumped. The staff inside the gas works includes a few men. Lighting conditions are poor but the furnace doors are open and women are working shovelling coke inside.

Notes
Title: the store ledger and shotsheet title for this film is *Gas Works – Paris*. Since the lettering on objects shown on the film is in English, this is possibly a misreading of *Gas Works – Parts*.
Technical: starting with the scene of sieving coke, the film is heavily marked with static and therefore not normally suitable for commercial use.
[shotsheet available]
catalogued SDB: 10/1982

IWM 547 · NO FILM

IWM 548 · GB, 3/1918
FEEDING A NATION
ALIMENTANDO A UNA NACION (on copy held)
[the NATION'S FOOD] (alternative)

b/w · 2 reels · 1842' (32 mins) · silent
intertitles: Spanish

sp Ministry of Information

■ Spanish-language version of a British official film showing the export of meat and sugar from around the world to Britain, and production of fish and bread in the British Isles, early 1918.

I. Cattle on the plains of Argentina, the principal meat exporter to Britain, being rounded up by gauchos with a ranch in the background. The cattle are put through a dip. Sheep in Australia are rounded into pens and also put through a dip. A cargo ship carrying meat arrives at a British port (Liverpool ?) and the sides of meat are transferred to launches. As the meat is landed it is put into refrigerated warehouses by crane and conveyor belt. The ship carries a light gun against German "pirates". II. Agricultural labourers in the West Indies prepare ground for a sugar plantation by hoeing, and weed around the young cane as it grows. The cane is cut and loaded into bullock carts, then put into a crusher. One woman chews a length of cane. The pulp sugar is drained off as molasses into tanks, then barrels. A small cargo vessel takes it to Britain. At a British port sacks are unloaded. The conveyor belt has crystallised sugar running off it. (In a laboratory, sugar in two stages of crystallisation is shown on glass slides.) At the refinery the molasses is centrifuged and the resulting sugar poured from hoppers into Lyle sacks by women workers. The sacks are loaded onto lorries, taken by train to a railhead, and by ship to the Army in France. *(First reel ends.)*
III. Fishermen at a Scottish port prepare to take their boats out. The camera stays on board the trawler through a storm, and the first trawl as the men pull in the nets. The fishing fleet is guarded by patrol boats, by a destroyer (see **Notes**) and the Grand Fleet. The battleship HMS *Monarch* is shown in pre-war rig. Back in port, the catch is unloaded and men and women work together to sort it. The fish are crated or packed in barrels for transport. A display of various types of fish in ranks. IV. Wheat is harvested in the fields of Britain by horse-drawn reapers, and threshed by a threshing machine. The grain in sacks is loaded onto a ship through a chute. A horse-drawn wagon brings sacks of flour to a bakery for weighing. The automatic mixing vats make the dough, shape it into loaves, and these are baked in the oven. The men stack the loaves onto vans for the shops.

IWM 549-01 · GB, 5/1918
the SECRET
[FILM TAGS] (series, allocated)

b/w · 1 reel · 149' (3 mins) · silent
intertitles: English

sp Ministry of Information *cast* Edwards,
Henry; and White, Chrissie

■ Fictional piece showing how to use
  grated potato as a substitute for suet in
  cooking in Britain, 1918.

A working-class man expresses
dissatisfaction about dinner, protesting to
his wife that their neighbour still makes suet
puddings and dumplings. Sneaking a look
through the neighbour's window on the
following morning, his wife sees that her
neighbour uses grated potato mixed with
flour as a substitute, to compensate for the
wartime shortage. That evening she
presents her husband with a pudding.

Notes
Summary: 'Film Tags' were very short films
containing some practical piece of wartime
advice made by the Ministry of Information
to show between regular film programmes
at cinemas. See also the remainder of the
IWM 549 series.
[shotsheet available]
catalogued SDB: 10/1982

IWM 549-02 · GB, 5/1918
GIVE 'EM BEANS
[FILM TAGS] (series, allocated)

b/w · 1 reel · 102' (2 mins) · silent
intertitles: English

sp Ministry of Information

■ Short piece encouraging people in Britain
  to eat beans, with Canadian lumberjacks
  as an example of people who do, May
  1918.

Canadian lumberjacks at work stop for their
main meal of beans. In stop-action, a
packet of beans and some pork fat are
shown as their main food. "Beans are an
energiser", the lumberjacks continue work
at high speed (camera deliberately
undercranked).

[shotsheet available]
catalogued SDB: 10/1982

IWM 549-03 · GB, (?) 5/1918
[MINISTRY OF FOOD] (allocated)
[FILM TAGS] (series, allocated)

b/w · 1 reel · 31' (1 min) · silent
intertitles: none

sp Ministry of Information

■ Very short film showing the front of the
  Ministry of Food building in London,
  probably spring 1918.

[shotsheet available]
catalogued SDB: 10/1982

IWM 549-04 · GB, (before) 8/1918
a NEW VERSION
[FILM TAGS] (series, allocated)

b/w · 1 reel · 188' (4 mins) · silent
intertitles: English

sp Ministry of Information *cast* Edwards,
Henry; and White, Chrissie

■ Short fictional piece encouraging people
  in Britain to plant food in their own
  gardens, summer 1918.

The "New Version" is of the poem *Come
into the garden, Maud.* Maud is a bored
young lady whose husband invites her to
join him in their middle-class garden, which
he has turned into a kitchen garden. She
complains that he has ruined the lawn, but
he explains that otherwise people in Britain
would starve. Later in the day she helps
him plant seed potatoes, feeds the
chickens, and finally falls asleep in the hay,
tired but fulfilled. "And the moral is that one
is happier doing useful work than loafing
around in drawing rooms."

[shotsheet available]
catalogued SDB: 10/1982

IWM 549-05 · GB, (?) 5/1918
IDEAS FOR INCREASED FOOD PRODUCTION
[FILM TAGS] (series, allocated)

b/w · 1 reel · 17' (1 min) · silent
intertitles: none

sp Ministry of Information

- Fragment of a film showing the fruit trees on Mr W W Berry's farm near Faversham, Kent, probably early 1918.

[shotsheet available]
catalogued SDB: 10/1982

IWM 549-06 · GB, (?) 5/1918
DON'T WASTE DISEASED POTATOES : make them into flour
[FILM TAGS] (series, allocated)

b/w · 1 reel · 101' (2 mins) · silent
intertitles: English

sp Ministry of Information

- Short piece showing the safe method of using diseased potatoes as a substitute for flour in Britain, 1918.

The action is shown on a workbench. Firstly, the diseased pieces are cut out and discarded, and the potatoes sliced. Then flowers of sulphur are heated into a gas, which is captured in a jar. The slices of potato are put in the jar to bleach them, then taken out and put in an oven to dry. Finally, they are passed three times through a mincer and emerge as flour.

[shotsheet available]
catalogued SDB: 10/1982

IWM 549-07 · GB, 6/1918
the CURE FOR POTATO BLIGHT
[FILM TAGS] (series, allocated)

b/w · 1 reel · 137' (2 mins) · silent
intertitles: English

sp Ministry of Information *cast* Robey, George

- Short piece of the actor George Robey showing how to spray potatoes with Burgundy Mixture to prevent blight, Britain, June 1918.

Burgundy Mixture is a mix of copper sulphate with soda, shown being poured into a spraying wagon and sprayed onto the fields. Robey helps a farmer mix the fluid. A back-carried hand sprayer is used for smaller plantations. A blighted potato is the result of failing to spray properly. The film ends with Robey intoning "Let Us Spray".

[shotsheet available]
catalogued SDB: 10/1982

IWM 549-08 · GB, (?) 5/1918
HOW TO SAVE TIME WITH YOUR POTATOES
[FILM TAGS] (series, allocated)

b/w · 1 reel · 98' (2 mins) · silent
intertitles: English

sp Ministry of Information

- Short piece on tricks to speed up the cultivation of potatoes in allotments in Britain, 1918.

An allotment holder is shown making the various short cuts. The potatoes are exposed to daylight for four or five weeks so that they germinate. After two weeks, when the sprouts have appeared, all but one or two of the strongest sprouts are rubbed off. The potatoes are then ready for planting at the first fine weather.

[shotsheet available]
catalogued SDB: 10/1982

IWM 549-09 · GB, 5/1918
the RIGHT WAY TO DEAL WITH PRIVATE SPUD
[FILM TAGS] (series, allocated)

b/w · 1 reel · 114' (2 mins) · silent
intertitles: English

sp Ministry of Information

- Short piece on how to grow potatoes in gardens and allotments in Britain, 1918.

A gardener performs the actions. Larger potatoes are split in two before planting. Trenches in the garden are about two feet apart. Garden refuse is burnt as potash and spread over the trenches. The potatoes are then planted about a foot apart. Allotment holders usually plant directly rather than digging a trench first.

[shotsheet available]
catalogued SDB: 10/1982

IWM 549-10 · GB, (?) 5/1918
FIGHTING U-BOATS IN A LONDON BACK GARDEN
[FILM TAGS] (series, allocated)

b/w · 1 reel · 73' (1 min) · silent
intertitles: English

sp Ministry of Information

■ Very short inspirational piece demonstrating the amount of vegetables which can be grown in a back garden in the middle of London, 1918.

A grandmother works hoeing the vegetable patch in a working-class yard, which provides the daily vegetables for a family of five. A small child helps to water the garden. The grandmother, a "private in the civilian army", displays for the camera the turnips she has grown in the yard.

[shotsheet available]
catalogued SDB: 10/1982

IWM 550-01 · GB, 1918
[MISCELLANEOUS FIRST WORLD WAR NAVAL MATERIAL 1] (allocated)

b/w · 1 reel · 1185' (19 mins) · mute
intertitles: none

■ Eight sequences of miscellaneous footage of naval activities during the latter stages of the First World War.

I. Queenstown. Low angle medium shot from small craft crossing bows of three US destroyers moored together in the harbour with a paddle minesweeper – two of the ships are USS *Duncan* (46) and USS *Sterett* (27). American bluejackets come ashore on R and R. Close-up head and shoulders of Commander Arwyne, USN. Low sun over harbour. (*cf.* **IWM 564**)
II. Sequence showing Italian Army officers with Royal Flying Corps men on an airfield – they are watching some sort of air display and then greet the returning pilots. The Italians, like cliché Latins, are rather more effusive than the British. Aerial view of a coastal town.
III. Medium close-up of HMS *Brilliant*

prepared as a block-ship for Zeebrugge. Brief shot of Royal visit to HMS *Queen Elizabeth*. Medium shot of the crew of a trawler minesweeper (?) – one man peels potatoes, another holds a dog – all are rather scruffy and dirty but seem cheerful. Sequence showing a periscope cutting the water – taken from an unsteady small craft. Low angle view from cameraship passing under Forth Bridge. Medium shot as steam pinnace comes alongside submarine K.16 for visit of Japanese Prince Fushimi (see **IWM 550-02**). Close-up pan from top to bottom of cut-down fore-funnel of *Brilliant*. Medium shot of upper works of three submarines alongside cameraship – H.21, H.43 and H.28 (?) – a fourth submarine is just visible at frame right. Continuation of sequence showing minesweeper crew. Close-up of smokescreen billowing left to right – no other detail. Long shot of periscope cutting surface heading away from camera and towards a merchantman on the horizon – all in a circular 'telescope' frame. Medium shot on HMS *Furious* to rear of aircraft as crew open out wings of Short 184 seaplane. Frontal view as Sopwith Pup is lowered onto the forward deck and pushed into take-off position. Close-up of HMS *Brilliant*. Long shot of periscope again, now in a binocular frame. Dockyard scene – a Lieutenant performs a jokey hornpipe for the camera. Medium shot over conning towers of H.21 and H.43 to ships in the harbour beyond. Close-up as a man holds a watch up to the camera – it indicates 12 noon. Long shot over sea – muzzle of a gun trained over cameraship's starboard beam is just visible at frame left. Long shot over anchorage in low light – a V/W Class destroyer is just visible in the gloom. Onboard shot of funnels and splinter-matted bridge of *Brilliant*.
IV. Surrendered U-boats at Harwich. Medium shot as cameraship passes three U-boats moored together – U.101, U.70 and U.67. A second group comprises UB.73, U.105 and U.86.
V. HMS *Argus* at Rosyth. Good medium shot off starboard bow of the dazzle-painted carrier – C Class cruiser in the background. Tracking medium shot stern to bow along starboard side.
VI. US Navy midshipmen march past on occasion of Geddes's visit to Annapolis (*cf.* **IWM 565**). Royal party visits the flagship of the 6th Battle Squadron, USS *New York* and are given three cheers by the crew. Royal party boards HMS *Queen Elizabeth* – HMS *Canada* in the background. Cut back to Royal visit to *New York* – King George V is introduced to the ship's officers. Scenes from the First Allied Naval Conference –

Sims, Jellicoe, de Lostende, etc (*cf.* **IWM 563**).

VII. Queenstown. Low angle track past USS *Melville* with three US destroyers alongside – a man semaphores from *Melville*. Sequence showing the visit of Sir Rosslyn Wemyss to the US destroyer division (*cf.* **IWM 564**).

VIII. Wounded from Zeebrugge action are visited at the Royal Naval Hospital at Gillingham by King George V and Queen Mary accompanied by Admiral Sturdee.

catalogued NAP: 10/1986

IWM 550-02 · GB, 1918
[PRINCE FUSHIMI'S VISIT TO THE ROYAL NAVY AND JAPANESE INVESTITURE ON BOARD HMS QUEEN ELIZABETH] (allocated)

b/w · 1 reel · 636' (11 mins) · mute
intertitles: none

■ Film of the visit of Prince Fushimi of Japan to Royal Navy ships during 1918.

I. Sequence depicting the visit of Japanese Prince Fushimi to the Grand Fleet. Steam pinnace from HMS *Queen Elizabeth* conveys the Prince and his party to the flagship where he is greeted by Admiral Beatty. Cut to the Prince inspecting a V Class destroyer. Cut back to the Prince on *Queen Elizabeth* – he is in the company of Prince Arthur of Connaught – US Naval officers are also present. The Prince goes on board submarine K.16 (for this visit, see also **IWM 550-01**) – he and his party are given protective leather gloves to wear before descending into the submarine's interior.

II. Investiture on board HMS *Queen Elizabeth*. Senior officers congregate on the quarterdeck – Sturdee, Beatty and de Robeck, Madden, etc. Rear-Admiral Funakoshi comes on board and is greeted by Beatty. There is an exchange of decorations – Funakoshi returns to the quarterdeck wearing the insignia of the Most Distinguished Order of St Michael and St George. He then invests Beatty with the Order of the Rising Sun, Grand Cordon. Final shot is a pan over newly invested Admirals – Beatty, Madden, Sturdee, Evan Thomas, de Robeck, etc.

catalogued NAP: 10/1986

IWM 551 · GB, (after) 10/1918
the EMPIRE'S SHIELD : the Royal Navy

b/w · 11 reels · 11367' (190 mins) · silent
intertitles: English

sp Admiralty *pr* Engholm, F W
cam Engholm, F W

■ Film tribute to the Royal Navy and merchant marine during 1914-18.

(Reel 1) The training of a naval cadet – Pangbourne, HMS *Worcester*, HMS *Medway*. *(Reel 2)* Scenes from the building of a merchant vessel. Shots of a Standard Tanker being launched on the Clyde, female dockyard labour, dazzle-painted merchant ships, etc. *(Reel 3)* Various types of cargo unloaded at the East India Docks. Grimsby trawlers unloading and preparing for the next voyage. Medium shot groups of merchant officers and crews. *(Reel 4)* Episode portraying the bombardment of Zeebrugge, 11 May 1917 – a compilation using stock shots and some actuality material. *(Reel 5)* Preparation and execution of a sweep by drifters. Close-ups of HM.TMS *Atalanta II. (Reel 6)* Dramatic reconstruction of the clearance of a recently laid minefield – swept mines are destroyed by rifle and MG fire. Close-ups of the crew of *Atalanta II. (Reel 7)* The Royal Naval Air Service. Probationary flight officers under training at Cranwell. Squadron 'scrambles' at Manston. Aerial views of south coast. Balloons on anti-submarine patrol. *(Reel 8)* Construction and wheeling out of a Short 184. Seaplane bombed up. HMS *Furious*. Felixstowe flying boats. King George V visits the fleet – he meets the crews of various ships. *(Reel 9)* HMS *Vindictive* and material relating to the Zeebrugge raid. *(Reel 10)* Scenes on board HMS *Canada. (Reel 11)* First Battle Squadron sorties for live firing practice.

Notes
Remarks: stock shots are used very freely and without much regard for historical truth. Some of the action sequences were obviously constructed in the cutting room – Minelayer 898 leaving Dover with a cargo of deadly "pills" (Reel 5), is HMS *Melton*, a minesweeper; the five mines exploded in Reel 6 all share the same explosion; the 'Zeebrugge raid' (Reel 9) indiscriminately combines day and night action.
[shotsheet available]
catalogued NAP: 9/1977

IWM 552 · GB, (after) 3/1918
the WAY OF A SHIP ON THE SEA

b/w · 4 reels · 4731' (79 mins) · silent
intertitles: English

sp Admiralty *pr* Engholm, F W
cam Engholm, F W

■ Film tribute to the "great, gallant, glorious" men of the merchant marine, Royal Navy, and Royal Naval Air Service.

(Reel 1) Opening sequence of aerial shots showing a convoy and escort vessels. Cut to "The Making of the Men" – Nautical College, Pangbourne, HMS *Worcester*, HMS *Medway*, HMS *Arethusa*. Scenes showing cadet instruction in classroom theory, practical seamanship, navigation, signalling, squad drill, life saving, etc. *(Reel 2)* "The Birth of a Standard Ship". Shipbuilding scenes. Launch of a Standard Tanker. Female dockyard labour. Armstrong Whitworth workers. Medium shot group of merchant officers serving in the Army Supply Corps. Arrival of a hospital ship and disembarkation of the wounded. Troopship leaves harbour. *(Reel 3)* "The Work at the National Docks". Various cargoes unloaded – grain, meat, sugar, wool, timber, etc. India Line vessel in dry dock. General view of the docks and ships alongside – including a rather archaic cargo/passenger vessel with a clipper bow. *(Reel 4)* "The Toll of the Sea". Trawlers at sea and in port. Panorama across fleet anchorage taken from forward gunnery control of HMS *Canada*. Scenes on board the battleship. End sequence consisting of medium close-ups of King George V and senior naval officers, and group shots of merchant officers and crews.

Notes
Title: this is taken from the shotsheet.
Summary: much footage is shared with *The Empire's Shield* (**IWM 551**).
Remarks: reel 3 illustrates very well the wide variety of dazzle patterns used on merchantmen – one vessel is painted at the waist to resemble a paddle steamer.
[shotsheet available]
catalogued NAP: 9/1977

IWM 553 · GB, 11/1917
the STORY OF THE DRIFTERS : and of the sea dogs who man them

b/w · 2 reels · 1980' (33 mins) · silent
intertitles: English

sp Admiralty *pr* Engholm, F W
cam Engholm, F W

■ Tribute to the men of the minelaying and minesweeping drifters.

(Reel 1) Their work on shore, preparing a mined anti-submarine net – wire splicing, making nets, fitting floats, detonators, etc. Work on the water – Lowestoft drifter loads netting and cable. Two types of mines – electro-contract mine for attachment to an AS net, and the floating mine (represented on screen by a buoy?). Drifters leave port for a "secret destination". Mk H.II (?) mine is embarked. Medium shot of HMS *Melton* under way. Paddle minesweepers at sea – HMS *Sandown* (903), HMS *Albyn* (587). Grimsby drifters leave harbour for minesweeping duties: "To these men the Nation owes a vast debt of gratitude." Scenes on board destroyer leaders HMS *Swift* and HMS *Broke*: ratings embark on *Broke*; medium shot of bridge structure; crew cheers for camera; ship's dog; ship's bell; battle honours. HMS *Swift*: medium shot from the eyes as 6-inch gun is traversed HMS *Broke* in the background); high angle medium shot from crow's nest; meat ration; kitten on deck; medium shot of crew; officers pose with ship's dog. *(Reel 2)* A raid on the Belgian coast by a mixed naval force of monitors, destroyers, M/S drifters and motor launches. Admirals Ronarc'h and Bacon and Captains Bowring and Evans on HMS *Broke*. Medium shot of HMS *Swift* under way. Inboard shots of Broke's torpedo tubes. Various shots of destroyers in line ahead – Hawthorn and Admiralty M Class, Marksman Class Leader; HMS *Marshal Ney*, *Erebus*, and M15 Class monitor; drifters and MLs; C Class cruiser. HMS *Broke* – Admirals Ronarc'h and Bacon on the bridge; stern wash; anchoring at Dunkirk; Admiral Bacon goes ashore in motor boat *Muriel*.

Notes
Summary: reel 2 is very similar to reel 4 of *The Empire's Shield* (**IWM 551**).
[shotsheet available]
catalogued NAP: 2/1978

IWM 554 · GB, (?) 1918
RULE BRITANNIA

b/w · 5 reels · 2897' (48 mins) · silent
intertitles: English

sp Admiralty *pr* Engholm, F W
cam Engholm, F W

- The might of the Allied navies, represented by the dreadnoughts of the Grand Fleet, 1918.

(Reel 1) Searchlight battery at night – beams weave about and spotlight moored destroyers. Admirals Beatty and Rodman on board HMS *Queen Elizabeth*. Scenes on board HMS *Canada* – divine service (Glorious Class battle-cruiser in background), PT, re-victualling, ammunitioning, etc. Close-up of fresh water distillation apparatus – a rating chips salt from the condenser coils. Engine room scenes – men stoke and rake out boilers. Rum, soap, and tobacco rations are distributed. Sickbay. Deck games. Close-up of Challenge Cup for pulling boats of capital ships. *(Reel 2)* British and American marines go ashore for drill and inspection. Coaling and refuelling HMS *Canada*. Pan over fleet anchorage and medium-long shot of Iron Duke Class battleship with superimposed binocular effect. *(Reel 3)* Medium shots of Allied battleships – Queen Elizabeth, Wyoming, New York, and Royal Sovereign Classes. Ships of 1st and 2nd Battle Squadrons pass beneath Forth bridge: HMS *Canada*, *Emperor of India*, *Benbow*, *Iron Duke*, *Conqueror*. Destroyer pens – tracking shot past HMS *Vampire*, *Rob Roy*, *Ready*, and *Rocket*. Destroyers at sea in line ahead: Admiralty W Class, R Class, Later Marksman Class Leader, etc. "The Cradle of the Deep": destroyers in line astern in heavy weather. Medium-long shot as line of destroyers turns hard a'port into camera. Destroyer flotilla opens fire. Inboard shot from S/L position as W Class destroyer makes smoke. Medium shot of smoke screen barrier. Medium-long shot profile of R Class destroyer on sunlit sea. *(Reel 5)* Royal Sovereign Class battleships in line astern with escorting destroyers. Broadsides fired. Medium shot profile of "Leviathan afloat": HMS *Emperor of India*. End medium shot of a rating cradling a 4-inch shell, ready for loading.

Notes

Summary: reel 4 was not available for viewing when this film was catalogued. [shotsheet available] catalogued NAP: 2/1978

IWM 555-01 · GB, 1918
[FIRST WORLD WAR BATTLESHIPS AND DESTROYERS 1] (allocated)

b/w · 1 reel · 1362' (22 mins) · mute intertitles: none

- Miscellaneous naval footage of the First World War period.

Medium shot of Thornycroft V Class destroyer steaming at speed. Medium-long shot off port quarter of two battleships – the nearest is HMS *Canada* preceded by an Iron Duke flying a kite balloon. Long shot of two Iron Dukes in a choppy sea – they have guns trained over the port beam. Long shot of a Royal Sovereign Class battleship in calm coastal waters – a sistership in the background. Extreme long shot of a K Class submarine on the surface with SS airship nearby – destroyer at screen right. Medium shot off port quarter of small quarterdeck steamer as it makes away from camera – destroyer pen in the background. Extreme long shot as cameraship crosses line of approaching battleships with destroyer screen – battleships fly kite balloons. Long shot of a cruiser possibly Boadicea Class. Destroyer escorts – a destroyer comes hard a'port, an Admiralty S Class steams at speed – a V/W Class in the background, HMS *Noble* (G.9A) passes left to right. Long shot sequence as Iron Dukes steam in line for a shoot – the wind carries the dense funnel smoke ahead of the ships to merge with low clouds of the overcast sky. Medium shot in anchorage as cameraship passes HMS *Revenge*. Long shot of Royal Sovereigns at sea as line comes round to starboard. Long shot to units of 2nd Battle Squadron – a King George V, *Erin*, *Agincourt* – the sun is low on the sea and the ships are seen in silhouette. Medium shots of HMS *Valentine* (F.30) and HMS *Vesper* (F.39). Extreme long shot of Queen Elizabeth Class battleships on the horizon with escorting V Class destroyer. Medium shot of Thornycroft V Class destroyer (as opening shot). Long shots of Royal Sovereign Class battleships. Long shot over calm sea to British battleship passing one of its American counterparts. Long shots of a line of Iron Dukes at sea – once again the most notable feature is the dense pall of funnel smoke. Pan across anchorage – Iron Duke Class ships are anchored in the foreground, the nearest possibly *Benbow*. Medium shot broad on port quarter of HMS *Malaya* at sea – she has turrets trained round to starboard. Medium close-up track from stern to bow along starboard side of anchored Cambrian Class cruiser. Miscellaneous long shots of a Boadicea Class (?) cruiser, Royal Sovereign and Iron Duke Class battleships. Two Queen Elizabeths – *Barham* leading *Malaya* with an Admiralty R Class destroyer, probably HMS *Rowena* as part of the escort. Long shots of Iron Duke and Orion

Class battleships, a Marksman Class Leader and a M Class destroyer HMS *Noble* (G.9A). A destroyer at sea lowers a boat while under way. Medium shot of HMS *Queen Elizabeth* from quarterdeck of HMS *Canada* – at frame left a crewman cleans the muzzle of one of *Canada's* 6-inch guns. Medium shot over fo'c's'le of cameraship to two Iron Dukes steaming in line ahead. An anchorage – HMS *Romola* (G.15) passes left to right before an Iron Duke. At sea – Royal Sovereign Class battleship in line ahead of cameraship. Long shot of a line of Iron Dukes led by *Emperor of India* with kite balloon. Final views from a destroyer passing under Forth Bridge and out to sea.

catalogued NAP: 2/1987

IWM 555-02 · GB, 1918
[FIRST WORLD WAR BATTLESHIPS AND DESTROYERS 2] (allocated)

b/w · 1 reel · 1024' (17 mins) · mute
intertitles: none

■ Miscellaneous naval footage from the First World War period.

Medium-long shot silhouette off starboard bow of HMS *Malaya* steaming with guns trained over the beam – the cameraship changes its bearing during the sequence from starboard bow to dead ahead to port bow – second Queen Elizabeth appears in background of some shots. Medium shot as HMS *Queen Elizabeth* passes cameraship *Canada* (also on **IWM 555-01**). Sequence on board destroyer as torpedo is fired, passing left to right through lower frame. Long shot as cameraship crosses bows of Lion Class battle-cruiser in calm sea. Long shots of Thornycroft V Class destroyer (like opening shot of **IWM 555-01**) and Iron Dukes with destroyer screen. Medium shot from aft along portside of W Class destroyer with triple torpedo tube trained over the beam. Long shot of four V/W Class destroyers steaming left to right. Aerial shot of a US Birmingham Class cruiser, probably USS *Chester* – camera-aircraft passes along starboard side and circles to cross over bows. Long shot of Marksman Class Leader, HMS *Nimrod* (H.90) at speed in rough sea – other destroyers in the background. Unsteady medium shot of HMS *Valhalla* (G.45) – she slips out of bottom of the frame in latter part of the shot. Medium shot of surrendered German S.131 Class destroyer lying at anchor. Long shot from seaward to chalk cliffs on the south coast – ML.219 passes right to left, followed by ML.272. Medium shot of HMS *Noble* (G.9A), then of *Nimrod* (H.90) screening a Queen Elizabeth Class battleship. High angle view aft down starboard side of HMS *Canada* to X and Y turrets trained over the bow – X fires reduced charge by single barrels. Medium shot on board a training ship (HMS *Worcester* ?) as boy sailors march past. Medium shot of deck hockey on quarterdeck of *Canada* as she lies in anchorage. Continuation of sequence showing motor launches off the south coast – ML.272 is followed by ML.278. Medium-long shot broad on the port bow of HMS *Emperor of India* at sea. Medium-long shot of the Lion Class battle-cruiser HMS *Princess Royal* in calm waters of anchorage – funnel smoke rises nearly vertically in the calm air. Long shot of two Orion Class battleships at a shoot. M Class destroyer, part of the fleet screen. Medium shot to a Queen Elizabeth Class battleship in direct line ahead of cameraship – Y turret is trained over her starboard beam and X over the port bow. High angle view as men on destroyer ignite two smoke floats – presumably to be used as targets. Medium shot along deck of *Canada* as she replenishes in anchorage – sailors push a trolley laden with carcasses of fresh meat. Medium shot over a crowded destroyer pen – HMS *Rocket* (G.88) is present. Close-up pan over after works of V/W Class destroyer – searchlight in foreground. Medium shot as HMS *Ramillies* passes left to right – second Royal Sovereign in the background. Medium shot of HMS *Valhalla* (G.45) in a rough sea. Motor launches off the south coast – the nearest craft is ML.55. Extreme long shot of a destroyer bows on in rough sea. Medium shot as the cruiser HMS *Blonde* passes right to left in anchorage. Medium shot off starboard bow of M Class destroyer following in the wake of a companion. Long shot of Orion Class battleship and pan left to three more. Medium shot broad on the starboard bow of HMS *Versatile* (G.10) and views of rough sea from cameraship. Ship's dog gets excited as crewmen hose down the ship's side (to clean anchor cable ?). Meat cart on *Canada*. Long shot of destroyers astern of cameraship. Medium shot views forward along W Class destroyer – crew assembled around searchlight position and sitting on triple torpedo tubes. Long shots of destroyer bows on in rough sea and over calm sea to British battleship passing a US Florida Class (?) counterpart (both repeats from **IWM 555-01**).
catalogued NAP: 2/1987

IWM 555-03 · GB, 1918
[AIRCRAFT AT SEA 1] (allocated)

b/w · 1 reel · 669' (11 mins) · mute
intertitles: none

■ Miscellaneous aircraft footage from the
First World War period.

High angle view onto detachment of Royal
Marines drawn up on quayside – they
march off, arms shouldered. Detachment
passes camera, now situated in a park.
Medium shot as Royal Naval Air Service
personnel march past camera – camp
buildings in background. Close-up as sub-
Lieutenant RN takes a bearing. Cut to high
angle view as Short seaplane is brought up
from forward hangar on HMS *Furious*.
Medium shot of a DH4 and pan to a row of
Sopwiths parked beyond on grass field.
Long shot of a Short seaplane in flight low
over water. Distant aerial view of *Furious* at
sea. Medium shot of Sopwith Pup N6442 on
grass field as pilot disembarks – pan right
to two other aircraft with pilots and ground
crew about them. Various long shots of
aircraft in flight, including Handley Page
0/400 bombers. Low angle view as a kite
balloon rises on its tether. Astre-Torres type
airship C24 is brought out of its hangar.
Medium shot of the airship SSZ9 as it is
restrained by ground crew hauling on lines
– two crew are in the gondola but the
engine has not been started. Low angle
long shot as two SS airships head off at the
start of a patrol. Aerial views of a coastal
harbour, a convoy of dazzle-painted
merchantmen, RNAS air station and country
town. Low angle shot as Sopwith Pup is
lifted from forward hangar on *Furious*.
Medium shot as a French destroyer
(Gabion/Coutelas Class) passes right to left.
Medium shot broad on the port bow of a
damaged V/W Class destroyer – a light line
leads from her bows to a second vessel off
frame left, and a third ship is in close
company, but largely obscured by the first.
Long shot of Felixstowe flying boat circling
low over anchorage. Medium-long shot off
port bow of Admiralty M Class destroyer at
speed. Medium shot study of white
smokescreen left by a destroyer. Medium
shot of HMS *Llewellyn* (61) – her fo'c's'le 4-
inch gun fires to port. Continuation of earlier
sequence showing a damaged V/W Class
destroyer – the damaged ship is now down
at the stern, and the leading vessel can be
seen to be HMS *Whirlwind* (H.41) – a fourth
destroyer (American or possibly Hawthorn
M Class) is visible in background. Final shot
of the masts of a sunken small craft
breaking the surface near a rocky islet (?).

catalogued NAP: 2/1987

IWM 556 · GB, 7/1917
HM VISIT TO THE GRAND FLEET

b/w · 3 reels · 2252' (38 mins) · silent
intertitles: English

sp Admiralty *pr* Engholm, F W
cam Engholm, F W

■ King George V's visit to the Fleet at
Scapa Flow in June 1917, and investiture
of Jutland honours.

(Reel 1) Opening pan across fleet
anchorage (note HMS *Neptune*). The King
is seen on board a succession of
battleships, watching march pasts of the
crews – HMS *Queen Elizabeth* (Colossus
Class in background), HMS *King George V*
and *Ajax* of Second Battle Squadron, HMS
Barham and *Hercules*. Various senior
officers are seen waiting, or in company
with the King. The emphasis is upon the
personalities involved, and there are few
general views or details of the ships, except
for some close-ups of gun turrets. *(Reel 2)*
The King inspects a minesweeping trawler
and HMS *Plassy*, before going on board
HMS *Princess Royal* for the investiture
ceremony. Pakenham, Napier, Alexander-
Sinclair and Bruce receive honours. March
round of officers and men. High angle
medium shot as the King, standing on top
of B turret, receives the cheers of the crew
massed on the fo'c's'le. Final low angle
medium close-up of fluttering white ensign.
(Reel 3) Miscellaneous scenes after the
investiture. Medium shot group of officers
and men around after turrets. Sturdee with
KCMG. Beatty, Evan-Thomas and Nicholson
with CBs. The King and Sturdee converse.
Pan over Beatty's staff (including Japanese
naval representative), assembled for royal
presentation. Admiral de Robeck talks with
his staff. Beatty on the quarterdeck. Admiral
Madden poses with staff – Madden reads a
despatch, looks through his telescope, etc.
Ratings cheer HM. Crew leaves the fo'c's'le
and disperses after applauding the King.
Sturdee, the King, Prince Albert and Lord
Cromer stroll beneath 4-inch casemates.
The party inspects a M/S drifter. Medium
shot group – Beatty, Phillimore, Japanese
officers. US Navy shore party stands at
ease.

[shotsheet available]
catalogued NAP: 2/1978

IWM 557 · GB, 11/1918
OSTEND RE-OCCUPIED

b/w · 1 reel · 872' (15 mins) · silent
intertitles: English

sp Admiralty *pr* Engholm, F W
cam Engholm, F W

- Town of Ostend and abandoned German coastal guns, immediately after the Allied reoccupation in November 1918.

Various views of town landmarks – some of them "wantonly" destroyed by German troops. The Stars and Stripes and the Blue Ensign fly before the Kursaal. The town appears almost deserted. The Palace Battery – camouflaged 9-inch guns in shallow pits. Long shot of monitors outside the harbour. Admiral MacGregor and his staff pose for the camera. Tirpitz Battery. Hulk of the *Vindictive*, and the grave of her captain. The burgomaster talks with Captain Wedgwood Benn. Final medium shot as a small crowd cheers for the camera, and waves Union Flags and tricolours.

[shotsheet available]
catalogued NAP: 2/1978

IWM 558 · GB, 1918
PATIENT HEROES OF THE SEA

b/w · 1 reel · 814' (14 mins) · silent
intertitles: English

sp Admiralty *pr* Engholm, F W
cam Engholm, F W

- Record of a Royal visit to the naval base at Harwich, 1918.

King George V, standing on a rostrum, receives officers and watches a march past by detachments from the ships in port. The King is shown a demonstration of shot hole stopper drill, staged on the quayside. Investiture ceremonies on board flagship and at a naval air station – those honoured have their backs to the camera. The King congratulates US flying officers. RNAS march past. HM inspects officers and men from the minesweepers. The King boards a train and departs – dignitaries disperse – the guard leaps onto the train as it leaves the platform.

Notes
Summary: A catalogue of investitures, inspections and march pasts, with very little

coverage of the naval forces based at Harwich; there is a brief MS silhouette of a Motor Launch, with Caledon Class light cruisers in the background, in section eight.
[shotsheet available]
catalogued NAP: 2/1978

IWM 559 · GB, 1918
the SECRETS OF SUBMARINE HUNTING

b/w · 1 reel · 1002' (17 mins) · silent
intertitles: English

sp Admiralty *pr* British Instructional Films
ed Engholm, F W *cam* Engholm, F W

- Review of anti-submarine warfare techniques, and a tribute to the British scientists who devised the instruments which defeated the U-boat.

"U-boat's commander" (actually RN) takes bearings before submerging. Medium shot of periscope cutting the water as the U-boat approaches its "helpless victim". Merchantman sights U-boat (now surfaced), and sends SOS to fleet – cut to medium-long shot across fleet anchorage, taken from HMS *Canada* (*cf. The Empire's Shield*, **IWM 551**). PC boats leave harbour. Smokescreen laid to cover their manœuvres. Inboard medium shot as hydrophone gear is hoisted out and lowered into the sea. Close-up of operator. Destroyers in line ahead hasten to the scene (*cf.* **IWM 551**). Long shot as British "submarine cruiser" (K Class) appears towing CB airship. Various aerial and surface views as smoke bombs are dropped to screen approaching destroyers. Aerial and inboard views of a destroyer dropping depth-charges. Submarine conning tower breaks the surface, and the crew abandons ship. Patrol craft lower boats to rescue survivors. Airship SS23 is returned to its shed after a successful day. PC boats return to harbour. Final titles show the numbers of U-boats destroyed each year, 1914-18, demonstrating the growing efficiency of British ASW forces. End medium shot silhouette of London Class battleship.

Notes
Remarks: one of the worst edited pieces this cataloguer has ever seen.
[shotsheet available]
catalogued NAP: 2/1978

IWM 560 · Germany & GB, (after) 11/1918
**the EXPLOITS OF A GERMAN
SUBMARINE (U-35) OPERATING IN THE
MEDITERRANEAN**
der MAGISCHE GURTEL (original title)

b/w · 2 reels · 1987' (33 mins) · silent
intertitles: English

■ British adaptation of the German film
which records the U.35 sinking merchant
shipping in the western Mediterranean
and west of Gibraltar, 31 March-6 May
1917.

(Reel 1) The captions describe heroic fights
put up by British vessels with additional film
of U-boats at Harwich after the Armistice,
proving that "Britannia rules the waves". The
film starts with U.35 casting off at Cattaro
(not Trieste as given) and passing the
Austrian fleet at anchor. The crew of the
captured SS Parkgate row to U.35 which
the English captain boards. The destruction
party goes to the Parkgate which is then
shelled and sunk, boilers exploding. SS
Maplewood is sunk by a torpedo after the
crew abandon ship. Cleaning guns. Captain
von Arnauld de la Perière on the conning
tower. India and Stromboli are boarded and
sunk. (Reel 2) De la Perière and a warrant
officer take sightings of the sun. SS Corfu is
shelled and sunk. The U-boat crew on
deck. The boat passes through heavy seas.
Nentmoor is shelled and sunk. The captain
crosses off the names of ships sunk in
Lloyd's Register. Five captured English
captains take a stroll on the deck of U.35.
The crew of U.35 bathe in "the
Mediterranean" (Atlantic in the original). The
schooner Miss Morris sinks after the crew
abandon it. Turtles from the schooner are
lifted aboard. The captain writes a wireless
message. Meeting the cruiser SMS
Heligoland. Entering the Bay of Cattaro
bedecked with pennants. Austrian 'pilot' de
la Perière off U.35. Crew open letters from
home. Finally, surrendered U-boats at
Harwich, including de la Perière's
subsequent command, the U.139.

Notes
Summary: the original German version of
this film is held as GWY 784.
catalogued: KGTG 4/1976

IWM 561 · GB, 1919 (?)
the FATE OF A SUBMARINE

b/w · 1 reel · 234' (4 mins) · silent
intertitles: English

sp Admiralty (?)

■ Studio compilation showing a fictitious
"action", which involves the various types
of craft engaged in anti-submarine
warfare duties.

A torpedo track reveals the presence of an
enemy submarine. A destroyer (Yarrow M
Class), ML.55 and two companions, and a
trawler, Electra, close in. Electra drops a
primitive depth-charge. The "U-boat", when
forced to the surface, is clearly identifiable
as the British submarine H.47, and is flying
the white ensign. A ship's cutter picks up
"survivors". A small observation periscope
emerges from a calm sea and passes off-
screen, as the enemy "submerges for the
last time". Fish, stunned by the depth-
charge, are collected by the drifter's crew:
"To-morrow will be Friday and we've got
'some' fish today."

[shotsheet available]
catalogued NAP: 3/1977

IWM 562 · GB, 5/1917
**an HISTORICAL OCCASION : the arrival
of the advance guard of America's
fighting forces in British waters**

b/w · 2 reels · 1527' (25 mins) · silent
intertitles: English

sp Admiralty pr Engholm, F W
cam Engholm, F W

■ Record of the arrival of US 8th Destroyer
Division at Queenstown, Cork, on 4 May
1917.

Opening close-up of Admiral Sims.
Captions emphasise the kinship between
the two peoples, and the "courage and
fortitude" of the Americans. High angle long
shot pan across Queenstown harbour.
ML.181 (flying pilot's flag), ML.325, and the
Admiralty M Class destroyer, HMS Mary
Rose, go out to meet the US ships.
Medium-long shot of two "fearless
Merchantmen" passing through minefields.
Long shot of 8th Destroyer Division in line
ahead. Profile medium shot of flagship, USS
Wadsworth (60), followed by USS Porter
(59). Medium and medium close-up shots
as USS Davis (65) passes – note S/L
platform rigged beneath mainmast. Medium
shot of USS Wainwright (62). ML brings RN
officers alongside USS Porter. Tracking
medium shot from stern to bows of HMS
Mary Rose. The British destroyer leads the

US flagship and flotilla into harbour. USS *Conyngham* (58) crosses screen left to right, on her way to the Naval Dock. High angle medium shot of two destroyers lying alongside *Wadsworth*, and medium close-up of forward 4-inch gun and bridge, shot from the eyes. Commanders Taussig (USN) and Evans (RN) in medium close-up. US destroyers at moorings – including USS *McDougal* (54). Medium close-up of Flag Captain Carpendale (RN) and US consul among a reception party waiting onshore to greet the American officers, who arrive in a steam pinnace – note Arabis type Flower Class sloop in background as officers leave the pier. US officers visit Vice-Admiral Bayly at Admiralty House, and go to the US Consulate (situated over O'Reilly and Sons Machine Bakery). On board ship, American crewmen overhaul guns and machinery – close-ups of 4-inch guns, 21-inch torpedo tube, etc. Final "scene of sadness" as a rescue ship disembarks survivors from a torpedoed vessel – close-ups as walking wounded and stretcher cases come ashore.

Notes

Summary: in his book Admiral Sims describes the presence of a "moving picture operator" as one of the most "conspicuous features" of the reception given to the American officers.
[William S Sims and Burton J Hendrick, *The Victory at Sea*, Murray (1921): 40-45]
[shotsheet available]
catalogued NAP: 2/1978

IWM 563 · GB, 1918
HANDS ACROSS THE SEA

b/w · 1 reel · 988' (17 mins) · silent
intertitles: English

sp Admiralty *pr* Engholm, F W
cam Engholm, F W

■ Arrival of US Battleship Division 9 at Scapa Flow, December 1917, and first meeting of the Allied Naval Council.

The British fleet awaits its visitors – among the attendant ships are Colossus and Bellerophon Class battleships, HMS *Neptune*, and Warrior and Minotaur Class armoured cruisers. HMS *Canada*: "A link in the chain of Empire". Destroyers return from a patrol – medium shot of M Class destroyers, HMS *Offa* and HMS *Pellew* (?). Close-up of battle honours of HMS *Revenge*. Life on board ship – crew sewing and cobbling, gun-loading competition.

Scenes on a P Class patrol boat as torpedo is loaded into tube. Drifters at moorings, and an individual vessel at sea. Battleship flashes signal across anchorage (a rowing boat suddenly appears, jump cut into the foreground). "Uncle Sam's Aid" – HMS *Queen Elizabeth* passes left to right across the stern of USS *New York* in a historic meeting of flagships. Medium shot of USS *Wyoming*. Bow-on views of *Queen Elizabeth* and *New York*, contrasting their tripod and cage masts. Bluejackets learn British signalling methods – a rating semaphores. Low angle medium shot of 3-inch AA on high pedestal mount (New York Class battleship). Life on board one of the American ships – clothes scrubbed, foretop mast and whaler repaired, ship's "K.9", high angle medium shot from the bridge, taking on coal, etc. Medium shot, USS *Wyoming*. "Ave Atque Vale": visiting British officers leave American ship. The First Allied Naval Conference – individual close-ups and various shots of delegates – Sims, Wemyss, De Lostende, Twining, Funakoshi, etc.

Notes

Summary: the US Battleship Division 9 – USS *New York*, *Wyoming*, *Delaware* and *Florida* – anchored at Scapa Flow on 7 December 1917, to form 6th Battle Squadron of the Grand Fleet. The Naval Council was in operation from early on in the war, but was not officially constituted by the Allied Governments until 29 November 1917.
[shotsheet available]
catalogued NAP: 2/1978

IWM 564 · GB, 1918
AMERICA IS HERE!

b/w · 1 reel · 894' (15 mins) · silent
intertitles: English

sp Admiralty *pr* Engholm, F W
cam Engholm, F W

■ First Sea Lord, Sir Rosslyn Wemyss, visits the US destroyer base at Queenstown, Cork, in 1918.

Opening low angle long shot from a small boat as it crosses the bows of USS *Melville*, moored with two destroyers alongside (one a Tucker Class vessel). Wemyss comes on board with Commodore Brownrigg and Captain Marriott, to be greeted by Captain Pringle and the Melville's officers. Wemyss inspects crew and ship. Crew on quarterdeck, cheer for the camera and dance to the ship's band. "The Colour Problem": close-up of black orderly. Tall black rating posed alongside a shorter and fatter Caucasian as a humorous contrast (the white is a leading seaman, Gun Pointer first class, with two re-enlistments – he laughs heartily, the black rather wanly). Ship's mascot. Admiral Wemyss leaves the ship. Sequence showing survivors of a torpedoed merchantman being disembarked from a British destroyer and a steamer – some enter waiting ambulances, others walk away past camera (one acknowledges its presence by raising his hands in a triumphal gesture). US destroyers in harbour – including USS *Duncan* (46). Medium shot track along waterfront to the Royal Cork Yacht Club. Bluejackets come ashore on leave. Naval patrol falls in for inspection. Close-up of Commander Arwyne, organiser of the men's entertainments. USN Men's Club – billiard room and mess. Close-up as Wemyss commends Captain Pringle. Sunlit harbour scene. Final close-up of fluttering Stars and Stripes.

[shotsheet available]
catalogued NAP: 2/1978

IWM 565 · USA, 10/1918
VISIT OF SIR ERIC GEDDES, FIRST LORD OF THE BRITISH ADMIRALTY, TO THE US NAVAL ACADEMY, ANNAPOLIS, MD, OCTOBER 10, 1918

b/w · 1 reel · 494' (8 mins) · silent
intertitles: English

pr US Navy, Bureau of Navigation, Photographic Division (BUNAV, USN)

■ Sir Eric Geddes and others visit the US Naval Academy, Annapolis.

Geddes and Vice-Admiral Duff arrive at Annapolis with US Secretary of the Navy Daniels and Admiral W S Benson, and are greeted by Rear-Admiral Eberle and officers of the Academy. The party enters the Superintendent's house. Medium close-ups of Geddes, Daniels, Duff and Benson, as they pass the camera. Medium shot as party descends steps after visiting the chapel. Pan over facade of Bancroft Hall, and up to the clock-tower. Wipe to medium-long shot of Mahon Hall. Geddes' party watch march past of the Brigade of Midshipmen. Sir Eric makes an address – captions give his tribute to the "dauntless determination" of the United States in

rapidly training large numbers of seamen for the war. Brigade presents arms and returns to quarters. Medium shot pan along Academy waterfront. Party leaves for Washington – end effect as white ensign is carried from medium shot into camera close up.

[shotsheet available]
catalogued NAP: 2/1978

IWM 566 · GB, 1919-20
the HOME OF THE COASTAL MOTOR BOAT

b/w · 2 reels · 1686' (28 mins) · silent
intertitles: English

sp Admiralty (?)

■ Study of base for CMBs on Osea Island, Essex, ca 1920.

(Reel 1) Introductory titles. High angle shot of officer's quarters, and 360° pan around Osea, taken from the watch tower. Dressing ship. Morning prayers at an open-air service. Medium shot as Commander Walsh issues the orders of the day. Interiors of the carpenter's, machine repair and blacksmith's shops. Close-up of a notice emphasising the "painstaking precision" needed in checking torpedo equipment. Torpedo workshop – medium close-up of rack of torpedoes. 18-inch torpedo is moved by overhead gantry, and charged with compressed air. Artificer tests arming propeller on pistol – the torpedo warhead lies separately on a cradle. Gyroscope is bench tested. Artificers prepare circuitry on an instructional board. Low angle shot as torpedo is hoisted on board a CMB which rests on a cradle traverser. *(Reel 2)* Various medium shots of CMB sheds – boat 73.BD is run down the slip into the water and launched from its cradle. Naval landing pier. Moored CMB receives torpedo from a lighter – close-up of torpedo in boat's stern trough. Medium shots of CMBs leaving harbour, and under way at speed in line astern. 40ft CMB comes alongside – Commander Dobsin and crew disembark. Pan across CMB sheds. Medium shot, Reverend Mitchell in church. Naval hospital. Street scene. "Wrens at work and play." Ratings relax at cards and board games. Base animals – sow and her litter, pet dogs. Medium shot group of Captain Todd and his officers. Final close-up of fluttering white ensign.

[shotsheet available]
catalogued NAP: 2/1978

IWM 567 · GB, 1920
BOOM JUMPING TRIALS WITH COASTAL MOTOR BOAT NO 11 : as carried out off Osea Island on March 23rd – 25th 1920

b/w · 1 reel · 913' (15 mins) · silent
intertitles: none

sp Admiralty (?)

- Miscellaneous scenes showing boom jumping trials with CMBs, and life at the base at Osea.

I. CMBs approach camera to pass at speed over a boom marked by buoys – spectators watch from a barge moored in the background.
II. CMB is recovered from the water by a cradle traverser (circular frame on part of this sequence). Close-up as bilge water is drained from bleeder hole at stern of boat. Medium shot pan across CMB sheds.
III. Interior shot as Wren serves drinks in wardroom; close-up of Wren wearing headscarf; medium shot group of kitchen staff; Wrens skip for camera.
IV. Close-up of Sub-Lieutenant G G Lucas and his dog Jack. Anonymous warrant officer holds a white dog (*cf.* **IWM 566-02**).
V. Title sequence. Close-ups of stern rudder and propellers of CMB (film inverted). CMBs pass at speed between buoys. CMB approaches camera to jump boom stretched between barge and attendant vessel – having crossed the barrier, the boat loses way rapidly and turns to starboard.

catalogued NAP: 3/1978

IWM 568 · NO FILM

IWM 569 · GB, (after) 1916
FROM A LOOK-OUT'S POINT OF VIEW

b/w · 1 reel · 846' (14 mins) · silent
intertitles: English

sp Admiralty *pr* Engholm, F W
cam Engholm, F W

- Anti-submarine warfare recognition film made for the Royal Navy, ca. 1916.

I. 121ft comprised of titles shown consecutively without film.
II. Film, including only a few of the titles mentioned above, but with visual material corresponding to some of the remainder. Medium and medium-long shot views of submarine K.2 submerging – speed 4-8 knots. Medium shot off port beam as C.23 surfaces and off starboard quarter as H.33 surfaces. Periscope feather, proceeding away from camera. Aerial views of wake left by periscope on calm sea (low sun effect, M Class destroyer at frame left), and of surfaced K Class submarines. Medium shot of H.33 running at periscope depth, and K.2 running hull down. Periscope, with prominent feather, in circular frame, as if seen through a telescope – merchantman in extreme background. Medium shot as H.33 submerges. Medium-long shot of UB.III Class U-boat under way. K.2 surfacing. H Class submarine in circular frame effect. Medium shot off port bow as H.33 submerges to periscope depth. Medium close-up as U.162 passes (*cf.* **IWM 1155**). Periscope feather in choppy sea. Medium shots of torpedo track. Periscope feather in circular frame effect. Aerial long shot as aircraft closes on wake left by periscope (low sun effect). End medium shot silhouette off port beam of HMS *Gibraltar*, depot ship for the ASW School, Portland.

[shotsheet available]
catalogued NAP: 6/1978

IWM 570 · GB, 1/1918
OUR NAVAL AIR POWER

b/w · 4 reels · 4443' (74 mins) · silent
intertitles: English

sp Admiralty *pr* Engholm, F W
cam Engholm, F W

- Training and operational aircraft and airships of the Royal Naval Air Service in Great Britain, 1917-18.

(Reel 1) Aerial view of Cranwell. Medium close-up of Commodore Luce; instruction of trainee ground crew and probationary flight officers; wireless school; gunnery practice with Maxim MG and Lewis on simulator; learning to taxi a Short bomber; training flight in BE2Cs; USN officers attached for instruction; a "War Flight" of Sopwith Pups scrambles (Sopwith Camels cut in at take-off); flight of Handley Page 0/400s; aerial view of trenches and a large town; long shot of aircraft in spiral nose dive; Sopwith

1½ Strutter lands and pilot climbs out. *(Reel 2)* Kite balloon launched and towed to waiting vessel. SS airships launched for coastal patrol. Medium close-up as airship is bombed up. Aerial view of HMS *Furious*. Airships landing and returning to sheds. Pilots and mascot. Fleet anchorage – Colossus Class battleship flashes a signal – medium-long shot off port quarter of an Iron Duke, with Marksman Class Leader alongside, as No 9 Rigid, R34, passes overhead. *(Reel 3)* Seaplanes: mechanics at work; Sopwith Baby on trials; Short 184 bombed up; Short 830 and 184 take off on patrol (Lord Clive Class monitor in background). Aerial views of HMS *Courageous* and HMS *Glorious*. *(Reel 4)* Short Seaplane flies over fleet. Felixstowe flying boats are launched and taxi to take off. Aerial view of Felixstowe base and a convoy at sea. Close-up as observer takes photographs. Airmen receive medals. End medium shot of Iron Duke Class battleship, and pan across anchorage.

Notes
Summary: much of this material can be seen in reels 7 and 8 of *The Empire's Shield* **(IWM 551)**.
[shotsheet available]
catalogued NAP: 7/1978

IWM 571 · GB, (?) 1918
the TRIUMPH OF BRITAIN'S SEA POWER
GERMAN NAVY FORCED TO AN
INGLORIOUS SURRENDER (on copy held)

b/w · 2 reels · 2333' (39 mins) · silent
intertitles: English

sp Admiralty *pr* Engholm, F W
cam Engholm, F W

- Surrender of German naval forces, November 1918.

(Reel 1) Text of Admiral Beatty's message to the Empire. Beatty's flag (Vice-Admiral's) is broken out, and the Grand Fleet puts to sea: US battleships of 6th Battle Squadron in line astern; medium shots of HMS *Queen Elizabeth* and King George V and Orion Class battleships of 2nd Battle Squadron; HMS *Renown* and *Repulse* of 1st Battle Cruiser Squadron. Beatty acknowledges cheers from the Fleet. Gun crews, some in anti-flash gear, clear for action "in case of treachery". Medium shot sequence showing the "inglorious procession" of the German fleet: various battleships, including SMS *Kronprinz Wilhelm, Friedrich der Grosse*,

Bayern, Seydlitz, Kaiser, Hindenburg, Frankfurt and cruisers of the ersatz-Koenigsberg and Dresden Classes. HMS *Castor*, flying Commodore Tweedie's flag, leads in a line of German destroyers. Long shot as signal ordering the German flag to be struck is flashed across the Fleet from distant flagship (W Class destroyer in foreground). Medium-long shot of HMS *Curacao* escorting U-boats into Harwich, and views of the surrendered craft – some shots are repeated to give an impression of greater numbers. "The embarking of Germany's shame" – U-boat crews take passage home. *(Reel 2)* German fleet at Scapa Flow – battleships include *Seydlitz, Hindenburg*, Kaiser and Koenig Classes. Medium shot, SMS *Frankfurt*. Tracking medium and medium close-up shots past German destroyers – G.85 and S.53 Class ships – crew members watch at the rail, fish, gesture to camera. Royal visit to the Grand Fleet – HMS *Oak* passes between the lines of ships – K Class submarines in background. King George V and Queen Mary are greeted by Beatty on the flagship – another vessel of 5th Battle Squadron lies in the background. Final series of individual portrait close-ups of the royal couple and notable naval officers.

[shotsheet available]
catalogued NAP: 2/1978

IWM 572 · GB, 1918
NAVAL CELEBRITIES

b/w · 1 reel · 873' (15 mins) · silent
intertitles: none

sp Admiralty

- Miscellaneous stock shots of leading Allied naval officers, ca. 1918, many duplicated from other films.

I. Nelson's Column decorated for a War Bonds rally.
II. Admiral Sturdee poses with vice-admiral's flag flown at the Battle of the Falkland Islands.
III. Beatty and Rodman shake hands, posed between the 15-inch guns of Y turret, HMS *Queen Elizabeth*.
IV. Samuel Gompers and entourage go on board *Queen Elizabeth* for a meeting with Beatty.
V. Medium close-ups of Captain Crease (?), Admiral Wemyss, Captain T S Lyne, and Admiral Sims, USN.
VI. Medium shot of white ensign at head of

flagpole, and similar shot of Union Flag with iris fade effects.
VII. Medium close-up profile of Admiral R'onarch on HMS *Broke* (*cf.* **IWM 551-04**). Medium close-ups of Jellicoe, Tyrwhitt and Keyes.
VIII. King George V, Admiral of the Fleet, boards a train. Close-up of King. Sequence showing HM and Beatty being piped on board *Queen Elizabeth* for decoration of "Naval heroes". Medium close-up of King in naval uniform – background suggests he is in a park. Medium shot of Queen Mary, walking away from camera along deck of *Queen Elizabeth*. Facial close-ups of the King.
IX. Low angle medium close-up of fluttering Stars and Stripes. Close-up of Admiral Sims. Medium close-ups of Commodore Luce (*cf.* **IWM 570**), Admiral Rodman, Sir Eric Geddes, Wemyss, Tyrwhitt, and Admirals de Bon and di Revel (*cf.* **IWM 563**). Medium shot of Beatty and staff, medium close-up of Sturdee, and pan along line of newly honoured officers at presentation of the Order of the Rising Sun. Medium close-ups of Rear-Admiral Hope (?), Admiral Sims, Captain Twining, Admiral Funakoshi, de Lostende, and Rodman. Wemyss and Pringle on board USS *Melville* (*cf.* **IWM 564**). Sturdee, Pakenham, Tyrwhitt and Hope. Final medium shot group of "Heads of the greatest naval armadas the world has ever known" – Sims, de Bon, di Revel, Geddes, Duff, Jellicoe, etc.

Notes
Title: this is taken from the shotsheet.
[shotsheet available]
catalogued NAP: 6/1978

IWM 573 · GB, 1918
the STRANDING OF SS WAR-KNIGHT (ledger title)

b/w · 1 reel · 162' (3 mins) · silent
intertitles: none

■ SS *War-Knight* beached in Freshwater Bay, Isle of Wight, after striking a mine, March 1918.

High angle medium shot from cliffs overlooking the bay to starboard bow of *War-Knight* as she lies awash in slight sea – waves run over the fo'c's'le well deck. Similar shot from higher viewpoint – an oval frame appears in latter part of sequence. Medium shot off starboard beam, panning from stern to bow. High angle medium shot from the cliffs to the stranded ship in a

choppy sea – she has settled further, and waves are breaking over much of the superstructure. The funnel rocks slightly in the swell. Medium shot off the starboard beam, showing the amount by which the ship has settled.

Notes
Summary: SS *War-Knight* struck a mine on 24 March 1918. The incident cost 32 lives, including that of the Master.
catalogued NAP: 4/1977

IWM 574 · GB, 1918
[SMOKE APPARATUS] (allocated)

b/w · 1 reel · 961' (16 mins) · silent
intertitles: English

sp Admiralty *pr* Engholm, F W
cam Engholm, F W

■ Three short instructional films describing RN smoke producing equipment, ca. 1918.

I. Smoke Floats 'F' Type. Close-up of smoke float. Preparation for use – instructor indicates the relevant components, using a large hand-held cardboard arrow. Operation of the buoyancy chamber explained. Means of ignition. Trawler (practice boat) under way with smoke float operating on the quarterdeck – smoke gradually obscures the vessel. Long shot of smoke screen.
II. Close-up from alongside the quarterdeck of the Mersey type trawler *Daniel Fearall* – 'A' Type smoke apparatus is in operation.
III. Submarine recognition. Medium shots of submarine C.23 running on the surface.
IV. Smoke Apparatus 'A' Type. Instructor goes through a dry run with the apparatus.
V. Smoke Apparatus 'E' Type. Close-ups of apparatus. Method of operation explained.
VI. Miscellaneous titles (without film) relating to 'F' Type Smoke Floats (sequence I), and submarine recognition (sequence III).

Notes
Summary: the reel contains a number of titles without relevant film material, and some of the titles are placed in the wrong sequence, *eg* titles 10 and 11, sequence I, relate to 'A' Type Smoke Apparatus. The untitled sequence II should logically form a conclusion to title sequence IV.
[shotsheet available]
catalogued NAP: 5/1978

IWM 575 · GB, 1918
[PRACTICE SHOOT BY HMS ORION]
(allocated)

b/w · 1 reel · 366' (6 mins) · silent
intertitles: none

sp Admiralty *pr* Engholm, F W
cam Engholm, F W

- Ships of 2nd Battle Squadron at a
  practice shoot, ca. 1918.

I. Three Orion Class battleships, and a
Queen Elizabeth, which flies a kite balloon,
are escorted by a Marksman Class Leader,
Special I, and Admiralty M Class destroyers.
II. Long shot of HMS *King George V*,
Centurion, *Erin* and *Agincourt* in line astern
– they turn to port into line abreast for a
practice shoot (*cf.* **IWM 1174**).
III. Long shot off port bow as three Orion
Class battleships steam in line astern for a
shoot – HMS *Orion* in the van. The line
turns to port, steaming directly into camera,
which focusses on the two leading ships –
they open fire over the port beam. Medium-
long shot of second ship, bows-on to
camera, as she fires to port – a line of
spume appears across her bows, and the
camera pans left to show HMS *Orion*
holding station on her sister's starboard
bow – the spray was torn up by the blast
from *Orion*'s guns. *Orion* fires a second
time.

Documentation: the shotsheet bearing this
number has no apparent connection with
this film.
catalogued NAP: 6/1978

IWM 576 · GB, 1918
**[ADMIRAL BEATTY WITH HEROES OF
ZEEBRUGGE]** (allocated)

b/w · 1 reel · 229' (4 mins) · silent
intertitles: none

sp Admiralty *pr* Engholm, F W
cam Engholm, F W

- The 'heroes' are drawn up on the
  quarterdeck of HMS *Queen Elizabeth*.
  Admiral Beatty, his back to the camera,
  congratulates them, and talks with the
  young officers.

catalogued NAP: 7/1978

IWM 577 · GB, 9/1918
**BRITISH NAVAL ACTIVITIES AFTER THE
GREAT BRITISH VICTORY OF JUTLAND**

b/w · 1 reel · 908' (15 mins) · silent
intertitles: English

sp Admiralty *pr* Engholm, F W
cam Engholm, F W

- The Royal Navy in 1918.

I. Submarine base. (HMS *Victory* in
background – location presumably
Portsmouth). C Class submarines at
moorings: C.17, C.18, C.12. Medium shot
profile as D.2 passes; C.32 at moorings –
two ratings relaxing on deck – as the
camera craft crosses her bows, the forward
hydroplanes are prominently displayed;
high angle medium shot as E.23
approaches her moorings; B.5 takes on a
torpedo from lighter.
II. Cruiser and battleships: low angle
medium shot from fine on the starboard
bow of HMS *Phaeton* (?) at port anchor (title
identifies her as Yarmouth); low angle
medium close-ups of HMS *Commonwealth*
(before conversion to gunnery training);
medium shot of HMS *Lion*; HMS *Queen
Elizabeth* takes on 15-inch shells from a
lighter alongside.
III. Seaplane carrier. Medium shot of HMS
Engadine – camera closes on stern hangar
as seaplane is lowered into the water. Short
Seaplane takes off. Curtiss H.4 (?) goes
over. Aerial long shot of aircraft flying a
loop. Aerial medium shot of Sopwith
Schneider. Short Seaplane (Admiralty Type
184) alongside *Engadine*, folds wings and is
hoisted on board. IV. The Fleet sorties:
medium shot of fleet anchorage –
submarine D.4 crosses the foreground.
Monmouth Class armoured cruiser.
Indefatigable Class battle-cruiser. HMS
Beagle crosses left to right. High angle
medium shot as HMS *Birmingham* and
sistership pass below camera, followed by
destroyers. Medium shot of flotilla of H
Class destroyers "protecting the Battle Fleet
from U-boat attack" – HMS *Cameleon*
approaches at speed and signals, HMS
Martin and *Brisk* pass the camera.
"Encountering rough seas" – high angle
medium shot from bridge of battleship as
waves break over fo'c's'le. Final shot of shell
splashes at sea – a small target vessel is
visible, already down by the bows.

Notes
Summary: the shotsheet describes a Part II
to this film (with rather more obvious
references to Jutland – eg Boy Cornwall's

gun etc) which no longer seems to exist. [shotsheet available]
catalogued NAP: 2/1978

IWM 578-01 · GB, 1918
[AIRSHIP COOPERATION WITH SUBMARINE K5] (allocated)

b/w · 1 reel · 439' (7 mins) · mute
intertitles: none

- Sequence showing attempts by an SS airship to cooperate with submarine K.5 – the airship repeatedly closes on and hovers over the after deck of the submarine while crewmen restrain it by catching hold of the trailing tethers.

catalogued NAP: 2/1987

IWM 578-02 · GB, 1918
[MISCELLANEOUS FIRST WORLD WAR NAVAL MATERIAL 2] (allocated)

b/w · 1 reel · 341' (6 mins) · mute
intertitles: none

- Miscellaneous naval footage from the First World War period.

I. Medium close-up of Pershing and Foch at Foch's HQ. Medium shot along a line of Sopwith 1F.1 Camels of No 4 Australian Flying Corps Squadron – aircraft taxi out of the line ready to take off. II. High angle medium shot as a Sopwith Baby float plane is manhandled from shallows onto a slip. When the Sopwith has been recovered a Short 184 seaplane enters the water down the same slip and taxis away across the harbour – anchored in the background are an Admiralty R Class destroyer (HMS *Tempest* ?), a Town Class cruiser, Abercrombie and M15 Class monitors and some paddle minesweepers – a small steam pinnace enters the screen at end of the sequence. Aerial view of smoke canisters burning around airfield (wind direction indicators ?). Quayside scene – men pile up bags of mail (?). Medium shots of dazzle-painted paddle steamer ferrying troops across the Channel. Low angle medium shot as cameraship crosses bows of three US destroyers moored together in Queenstown. Tracking close-up port bow to stern past surrendered U-boats at Harwich – U.153 with UB.117, UB.114 and UB.112. Aerial view of destroyer HMS *Unity* (H.5A). Medium shot to port fore-body of HMS

Valhalla (G.45) – camera moves aft but drifts off-centre, losing the ship off the bottom of the screen. Medium shot to starboard afterbody of HMS *Agincourt* (screen right cuts forefunnel) as she steams across anchorage. Inboard close-up of torpedo tube turned over port beam of destroyer. High angle medium shot of guns of battleship's B turret trained over the starboard bow. Portside shot from bridge to stern of passing Arkansas Class battleship.

catalogued NAP: 2/1987

IWM 578-03 · GB, 1918
[AIRCRAFT AT SEA 2] (allocated)

b/w · 1 reel · 540' (8 mins) · mute
intertitles: none

- Miscellaneous aircraft footage from the First World War period.

I. Shots of Short 184 and Felixstowe flying boat. Medium shot aft down portside of HMS *Furious* over 5.5-inch gun to searchlight position as a signal is flashed. Harbour scene. Close-up as Sub-Lieutenant takes a bearing – the braid on his cuff is loose. Long shot off starboard quarter of an Erebus Class monitor. Long shots of Felixstowe flying boat alighting in a harbour, and formation of Handley Page 0/400 bombers in flight. Aerial views of airfields. II. RNAS station at Felixstowe. Sequence showing visiting senior officer – he gets into waiting staff car. Sea front. RNAS pilot relives a combat with fellow flying officers. Men carry a stripped aircraft fuselage from a hangar – this is followed by the damaged fuselage of Short 184 No 8098. Men work capstan to open hangar doors. Pilots wait at edge of airstrip. Felixstowe F3 is brought up slip from the water. Felixstowe F3 N64 warms up on the slip – a Marksman Class Leader passes left to right in the background. Sopwith Baby No 8145 is launched down slip. Medium close-up pan over Short 184 No 9065 and low angle close-up of after cockpit where flying officer holds the observer's Lewis gun. Various long shots of aircraft in flight – Fokker D.VII, Felixstowe flying boat, Short 184 and Sopwith Camel.

catalogued NAP: 2/1987

IWM 579 · GB, 1918
BOXING IN THE GRAND FLEET (ledger title)

b/w · 2 reels · 1131' (19 mins) · silent
intertitles: English

■ Collection of newsreel material, 1918.

I. *(Reel 1)* Anglo-American boxing tournament organised by the Grand Fleet. Panning medium shot across crowds of ratings assembled on quayside around raised boxing ring – two men are fighting. US flags are prominently displayed. Crowded accommodation vessel (HMS *Sutlej* ?) alongside in the background. Jump cuts between bouts – two men are knocked out. Beatty stands in the ring after awarding the prizes – Admiral Madden leads the crowd in three cheers.
II. RAF carnival at Shepperton-on-Thames in aid of military hospitals. Pan over crowd at river's edge – some sit in moored punts, the ladies wearing wide sun hats and holding parasols. Two coxed fours go by in a race. Two teams in punts stage a tug of war – after the contest, one team leaps into the water to cool off.
III. Facial close-up of the retiring US Ambassador, Mr Walter Hines Page, October 1918.
IV. Mr Samuel Gompers and delegation (see **Notes**) arrive at Liverpool, August 1918. Medium shot of Gompers and party on board liner with unidentified British Army captain – in one shot the party wear life-jackets. Medium close-up of Gompers.
V. US nurses on a Thames pleasure boat. Medium shot of nurses' boat leaving a lock – second vessel in the background is crowded with soldiers, who wave to the camera. Medium close-up of Mr S Joel, who entertained the party at Maidenhead. Medium shot of Joel greeting the nurses as they come ashore.
VI. *(Reel 2)* Additional film of the naval boxing tournament from fixed high angle medium shot viewpoint with limited panning – good stock shots of boxers, seconds, referee etc.

Notes
Summary: Samuel Gompers arrived at Liverpool on 28 August 1918, with a delegation of US trade union leaders: Mr J P Frey, International Miners Union, Mr C L Baine, Secretary of the Boot and Shoe Workers Union, Mr E Wallace, United Mine Workers, Mr W J Bowen, President of the Bricklayers', Masons' and Plasterers' International Union. Gompers' secretary was Mr G Oyster.

catalogued NAP: 4/1978

IWM 580 · GB, 29/12/1915
BRITAIN PREPARED : a review of the activities of His Majesty's naval and military forces
HOW ENGLAND PREPARED (US release title)

b/w · 12 reels · 13227' (221 mins) · silent
intertitles: English

sp Wellington House for Admiralty, Ministry of Munitions and War Office *pr* Kineto; Vickers; Kinemacolor; Gaumont; and Jury's Imperial Pictures *prod* Urban, C A *cam* Tong, E G; Wilson, F; and Weddup

■ Royal Navy, Army training camps, and Vickers' munitions and shipbuilding works in Britain, autumn 1915.

(Reel 1) Training the New Army – "cheery non-slackers" undergo PT, drill and bayonet practice, mounting and sabre drill for cavalry. *(Reel 2)* Manufacture of a 15-inch naval gun and firing trials. *(Reel 3)* King George V visits Vickers ordnance plant at Aldershot, August 1915. Troops stage mock battles in a system of demonstration trenches. *(Reel 4)* Cavalry training and care of their mounts. 18-pounder field artillery on the road. Evolutions by mounted machinegun section and cavalry. Royal Flying Corps – aircraft take off, mock aerial combat and bombing. Photo-reconnaissance aircraft returns to base. *(Reel 5)* Field telegraph and heliograph demonstrated. Wire laying and preparation of signals station. Staff officers plan an "attack". Exercise by motor-cycle machine gun battalion. *(Reel 6)* Operation of field bakery and kitchen. The King reviews 36th (Ulster) Division. Cavalry unit entrained. *(Reel 7)* Shipbuilding – construction and launch of HMS *Revenge*, Vickers, May 1915. Manufacture of 15-inch shells and gunnery trials. Minesweeping – Flower Class sloops and paddle minesweepers at work. *(Reel 8)* Manufacture of munitions and royal visit to Vickers (*cf.* Reel 3). *(Reel 9)* The Grand Fleet at Scapa Flow and in the North Sea. *(Reel 10)* Scenes on board HMS *Queen Elizabeth*. *(Reel 11)* Launching of an E-Class submarine, a staged sequence of a submarine attack, and taking on torpedoes at base. Destroyers in the North Sea, including the firing of a torpedo for training purposes. *(Reel 12)* Further scenes on board HMS *Queen Elizabeth*, this time showing firing and other "action"

material, with an "All's well" dusk return. HMS *Engadine* launching and recovering a seaplane (from **IWM 130-03+04**).

Notes
Production: the first major film made by the British Government during the First World War, produced at the instigation of the secret (and unnamed) propaganda organisation at Wellington House headed by Charles Masterman. The film was made by Charles Urban, using the resources of his own companies Kineto and Kinemacolor and a number of others. It originally included some sections in colour, ran for about 2 hours and 45 minutes, and was first shown at the Empire Theatre, London, on 29 December 1915.
Title: the film was widely exported, showing in the USA in a somewhat altered form as How England Prepared. Its use in Russia is described in the article by M L Sanders cited below, which is in turn based on the diary of Captain A C Bromhead, a copy of which is held in the Museum's Department of Documents.
Technical: the version catalogued is monochrome throughout, and its length suggests (at conventional 'silent' running speed) a duration of about 30 minutes more than that described for the original. There are also some obvious later additions, notably the HMS *Engadine* sequence in reel 12, and other anomalies such as the repeated inclusion of the Vickers visit material, reels 3 and 8. Taken together, these suggest this is not an original version of the film, but may be a version lengthened for serialisation at a later re-release.
Shotsheet: a detailed shotsheet and analysis of the film has been prepared and is held on file in the Department of Film.
[M L Sanders, "British Film Propaganda in Russia, 1916-1918", *Historical Journal of Film, Radio and Television*, 3: 2 (1983): 117-129]
[shotsheet available]
catalogued NAP: 7/1978

IWM 581 · GB, 1918
the SUBMARINE SERVICE

b/w · 1 reel · 954' (16 mins) · silent
intertitles: English

sp Admiralty *pr* Engholm, F W
cam Engholm, F W

- Submarine E.23 at Harwich and at sea, 1918.

I. Excerpt from *HM Visit to the Grand Fleet* (**IWM 556-01**), showing King George V, Admiral Beatty, Lieutenant HRH Prince Albert, and Lord Cromer on board HMS *Queen Elizabeth*.
II. Excerpt from *The Story of the Drifters* (**IWM 553-01**). Drifters embark mines and prepare to leave harbour. Minesweepers at sea – HMS *Melton* (898), HMS *Sandown* (903), HMS *Ravenswood* (588), HMS *Albyn* (587). View from crow's nest on HMS *Swift*, and medium close-up of crewman semaphoring.
III. Title sequence. Medium close-up as torpedo is taken on board submarine E.23 at Harwich – Special I Class destroyer HMS *Firedrake* (97), in the background. Submarine casts off. Medium shot of vessel under way and submerging to periscope depth. E.23 surfaces, and crew emerge to uncover and fire 12-pounder. High angle medium shot as she returns to base to be secured alongside.

Notes
Summary: the film's claim that E.23 sank a "German Dreadnought of the Nassau class" is an exaggeration. SMS *Westfalen*, hit by a torpedo fired from E.23 on 19 August 1916, had completed repairs by October of the same year.
catalogued NAP: 6/1978

IWM 582 · GB, 1918
a DAY ON A MINE-SWEEPER

b/w · 1 reel · 997' (17 mins) · silent
intertitles: English

sp Admiralty *pr* Engholm, F W
cam Engholm, F W

- Activities of drifters and paddle-minesweepers, 1918.

Drifters take on provisions from depot vessel. Commander Lyne at work in his office. Drifters leave port – medium close-up of M/S drifter *Drummer Boy*, (GY.964). ML.18 approaches, and Commander with a megaphone hails the camership to report a minefield. Medium close-up of *Victorian II* (GY.1189), with kite a-cockbill – crew pass a line to the camership, *Glenbervie* (GW.14). Onboard scenes as crew operate winch to recover kite. Camership passes moored Caledon Class light cruiser. Long shot of drifters in sweep formation. On board a drifter, crew fire rifles and Lewis guns to detonate mines (*cf.* **IWM 551-06**). Medium close-up as sweep is recovered and then payed out. Crew wash down decks. Medium shots of drifter, *Drummer Boy*, and paddle-minesweeper HMS *Eagle III*, (534) – Felixstowe flying boat goes over in far distant background. Medium shot of HMS *Kylemore* (titled as *Atalanta II*). A "cherished trophy": close-up of the sinker of a German mine. Medium close-up of a contact mine from the captured submarine UC.5, and close-ups of the access plate, cradle and detonating horns. Medium shot of officers and ship's company of *Atalanta II*. Close-up of young rating with puppies and ship's dog. Men wearing life-jackets play cards on deck. Medium shot of the Captain of *Atalanta II*, Lieutenant Budgen, with his officers and the Captain of sistership *Saint Seiriol*, Lieutenant McClymont.

[shotsheet available]
catalogued NAP: 6/1978

IWM 583 · GB, (?) 1918
SHIPYARD ACTIVITY

b/w · 1 reel · 230' (4 mins) · silent
intertitles: English

sp Admiralty (?) *pr* (cartoon sequence only) Kinsella and Morgan

■ Morale raising short urging increased production in the shipyards, ca. 1918.

Opening caption urges maximum effort "if the Hun is to be beaten". Panning medium shot across sheds. Scenes of shipyard activity. Medium shot from water as merchant hull is launched. Cartoon sequence dedicated to shipyard workers – a Teutonic head rears out of the water near a shipyard, but is repeatedly knocked about by a succession of ships coming down the ways. Slogan: "Every yard that increases the output by a ton / Is adding a weight to the mind of the Hun".

[shotsheet available]
catalogued NAP: 2/1978

IWM 584 · GB, (?) 1918
BUILDING A CONCRETE SHIP

b/w · 1 reel · 420' (7 mins) · silent
intertitles: English

sp Ministry of Information *pr* Topical Film Company

■ Construction of a concrete petrol barge, PD.25, at Barnstaple, Devon (?), 1918.

The raw material – close-up of a piece of concrete held in the hand. Travelling medium shot from a train pulling into a siding at the shipyard – seven months ago the area "consisted of open fields". Pan around interior of design office, with draughtsmen at work. Scenes during the construction of the ship: initial wooden frame built on the ways; network of reinforcing steel hull members added; concrete poured between inner and outer shells; laying down and painting of the deck; high angle medium shot into the hold, showing dividing concrete bulkhead; reverse shot from hold to deck house containing steam winch; medium close-up of plate brackets which form the ship's knees. Workers stand on the deck of the completed vessel. The launch – long shot as PD.25 enters the water, and medium shots of the barge immediately after launching and at her moorings.

Notes
Intertitles: titling is poor – several of the captions consist only of a single frame, and in one case the lettering has been printed in reverse.
Summary: in 1918 the Controller General of Shipping ordered a fleet of 86 barges and steam tugs to be constructed using the Mouchel-Hennebrique system of ferroconcrete, and in accordance with government specifications. Barges were 187ft 6in long and 13ft 6in in the beam, 20ft 9in deep, and contained three cargo holds. The yard shown may be that built by the British Construction Company, at Barnstaple, on the Taw.
[shotsheet available]
catalogued NAP: 2/1978

IWM 585 · GB, 1918
the PARAVANE – A DEVICE THAT MADE MINES USELESS : invented by Lieut Dennis Burney, RN

b/w · 1 reel · 676' (11 mins) · silent
intertitles: English

sp Admiralty (?)

■ Information film about the paravane, probably made just after the war.

Still portrait of Lieutenant Burney in an oval frame. Medium shot along Vickers assembly room. Women welders. Man finishes casings on a wheel. Paravane body tested in a small water tank. Bench assembly of paravane; women paint it, men make final adjustments. High angle medium shot as a train carries completed paravanes along a pier on their way to the ships. Camera circles bows of a merchantman to show attachment gear, and diagrams illustrate the positions of the shoe at the forefoot, and the streamed paravanes. Close-up as shoe slides down stem into the water. Medium shot as merchantman under way hoists out paravanes, and high angle medium shot inboard as paravane is lowered away. Animated diagram of streamed paravane slicing through mine cables, is intercut with film of mines surfacing in ship's wake. High angle medium shot as paravane is hoisted inboard, and medium shot as shoe is hauled up stem. Final close-up of an example of steel cable cut by a paravane.

Notes
Summary: filmed on board HMS *Accrington*, a merchantman hired as an accommodation ship, December 1915 – November 1918.
[shotsheet available]
catalogued NAP: 4/1977

IWM 586 · GB, (prod) 11/1918
[SURRENDER OF THE GERMAN FLEET] (allocated)

b/w · 1 reel · 1062' (18 mins) · silent
intertitles: none

sp Admiralty *pr* Engholm, F W
cam Engholm, F W

■ Elements of the German High Seas Fleet surrender to the British in 1918.

I. SMS *Prinz Regent Luitpold* and *Friedrich der Grosse* pass camera. Medium shot of *Friedrich der Grosse* with pan to German battleships in line ahead. SMS *Bayern* and *Kronprinz Wilhelm* pass camera. Medium shot off port bow of HMS *Cardiff* with German battle-cruisers in line astern – SMS *Seydlitz* passes off-screen, camera holding on *Moltke*.
II. German destroyers under way – V.43 Class, S.131 (with B.169 Class in background), H.145 (a G.101 in background), and V.125 Class vessels. Medium shot, passing to starboard of HMS *Anzac* (G.70).
III. King George V shakes hands with ship's officers before leaving British battleship (three K Class submarines in background).

IV. Ship's boat attempts to get a line to nearly submerged aircraft.
V. Medium shot of V.100 Class destroyer.
VI. Continuation of IV. Onboard scenes as destroyer recovers a ditched Avro 504K.
VII. Anchorage at sunset – moored V/W Class destroyers. Light cruisers in the background.
VIII. Close-ups, aft the bridge of moored G.101 Class destroyer. Medium close-up, starboard amidships, S.131 Class destroyer.
IX. Various shots showing Queen Mary and King George V with Beatty on board HMS *Canada* (HMS *Oak* and RS Class battleships in background).
X. Long shot of *Seydlitz* at Scapa – aircraft goes over anchorage – pan left to show ML hove to. Medium shot off port beam of *Seydlitz*, and medium close-up of fore-body as port anchor is let slip and ensign hauled down from foremast. Long shot as Felixstowe flying boat goes over.

catalogued NAP: 6/1978

IWM 587 · NO FILM

IWM 588 · GB, 1918
[DEPARTURE OF 6TH BATTLE SQUADRON] (allocated)

b/w · 1 reel · 420' (7 mins) · silent
intertitles: none

sp Admiralty *pr* Engholm, F W
cam Engholm, F W

■ 6th Battle Squadron under way in line ahead as it begins the voyage back to America, November 1918.

Medium shot off starboard quarter of Florida Class battleship and pan right to show 6th Battle Squadron in line ahead. Medium shot of ship's wake. Medium shot off starboard beam of Florida Class – pan right to next ship in the line (Wyoming Class), other battleships of the squadron, escorting destroyers, and a second line of capital ships. Medium shot of Marksman Class Leader, and pan left to Wyoming Class battleship and approaching Florida. Medium-long shot starboard profile as Florida comes abreast of cameraship. Long shot of approaching US line – USS *New York* and *Texas* in the van (two Queen Elizabeth Class battleships visible in extreme background at beginning of sequence). High angle medium shot of stern of cameraship (destroyer) where crewmen line the rail near depth-charge rack – camera pans onto starboard bow of the approaching line. Medium close-up as USS *New York* passes left to right through frame, followed by USS *Texas*, Nevada Class, and three other US battleships. Medium shot off starboard quarter of Nevada Class battleship. Medium shot off starboard bow and medium close-up as Wyoming Class battleship passes left to right.

catalogued NAP: 3/1978

IWM 589 · GB, 9/1918
[the LAUNCH OF SS WAR FOREST]
(allocated)

b/w · 1 reel · 659' (11 mins) · silent
intertitles: none

■ Launchings at the government-owned shipyard, Chepstow, in 1918, including that of the first standard ship.

I. Low angle medium shot of dazzle-painted hull of SS *War Forest* on slipway. Pan across crowd of soldiers and civilian workers, some of whom cheer and wave to camera. Medium close-up of (?) Lord Pirrie, Controller General of Shipbuilding. Medium close-up of anonymous colonel and captain of Royal Engineers among the spectators. Close-up as merchant hull is launched, passing left to right through frame, and pan over vessel after she has taken to the water – her dazzle-painting includes a false anchor. Medium shot as tug manœuvres the newly launched hull. Crowd disperses after the launch.
II. Chepstow. Panning high angle medium-long shot across shipyard. Medium and medium close-up shots as workers pass by, some waving to the camera – young apprentices and women are among the crowd. Medium close-up as sapper stands on railway platform and signals with a board – perhaps to signify the opening of a spur line to the shipyard – soldiers cheer and wave their caps in background.
III. Medium shot from mid-channel to SS *War Forest* on the slips – railway trucks pass along the skyline. Medium shot off port quarter during the launch. Low angle medium close-up of stern and view along the hull. Panning high angle long shot across shipyard. IV. Medium shot off port beam as SS *Petworth* is towed aft from fitting out bay – the ship swings round in mid-stream presenting bows and starboard

side to camera. Medium close-up as *Petworth* slowly passes left to right through frame, with a tug in attendance, and medium shot off her starboard quarter as she makes away from the yard.

Notes
Summary: SS *War Forest*, the first standard ship built at Chepstow, was launched on 23 September 1918, in the presence of approximately 2000 people.
catalogued NAP: 4/1978

IWM 590 · NO FILM

IWM 591 · GB, 1917
[SIR ROBERT BORDEN VISITS HMS QUEEN ELIZABETH AND HMS CANADA]
(allocated)

b/w · 1 reel · 460' (8 mins) · silent
intertitles: none

sp Admiralty *pr* Engholm, F W
cam Engholm, F W

■ Sir Robert Borden, Prime Minister of Canada, visits the British battleships in the Firth of Forth, February 1917.

Medium close-up as Sir Robert Borden comes on board HMS *Queen Elizabeth* from a motor launch – Royal Sovereign Class battleship moored in background. Commodore Brand and Admiral Beatty are among a group of officers which receives him. Borden talks with Beatty and Madden on the quarterdeck. The party goes below through the quarterdeck hatch. Cut to medium close-up of Borden and party coming up the gangway of HMS *Canada* – Captain Nicholson (?) salutes them. Borden is introduced to the ship's officers and inspects a party of ratings. Cut to medium shot from fo'c's'le to A turret (canvas hatch tent in foreground): the guns are elevated and depressed. Medium shot of crewmen preparing paravane on fo'c's'le – in the background ship's whaler is hoisted inboard. Low angle medium shot from deck to control top of foremast, and pan down to bridge and forward turrets – pan right to portside of fo'c's'le, where towing cable is secured to capstan and paravane is hoisted outboard.

catalogued NAP: 5/1978

IWM 592 · GB, (after) 4/1919
SCENES AT AROSA BAY

b/w · 1 reel · 277' (5 mins) · silent
intertitles: none

sp Admiralty (?)

- Men of the Royal Navy's Atlantic Fleet
  visit Vigo, Spain, 1919.

Harbour scene with mountains in the
background. Steam launch comes
alongside towing five ship's boats crowded
with ratings and marines. Local people
watch as the sailors disembark. Crowds
pass waterfront buildings. Sailors fraternise
with a group of local women, one of whom
mimics guitar playing with her broom. Street
scene – two policemen pass by, a crowd of
marines and ratings pose for camera.
Medium shot of a woman standing before
vegetable and fruit stalls – she chases off
one of the local men who invades the
picture – naval ratings pass by in the
background.

catalogued NAP: 4/1978

IWM 593 · GB, 1918
**MOVEMENTS OF JAPANESE WARSHIPS
IN THE MEDITERRANEAN**

b/w · 1 reel · 797' (12 mins) · silent
intertitles: English

sp Admiralty (?) *cam* Jeapes, Harold (?)

- Kaba Class destroyers of the Japanese
  flotilla assisting in anti-submarine patrols
  in the Mediterranean, possibly near
  Alexandria, 1918.

Opening long shot as Kaba Class
destroyers approach in line ahead. Medium
shot as ship bearing pendant letter 'Q'
passes camera. Low angle medium close-
up of the fo'c's'le of 'Q' showing the
4.7/40cal gun. Pan across harbour to
second destroyer. Medium shot of crewmen
paraded on quarterdeck as ensign is raised.
Medium shot of bayonet drill on board a
destroyer – in two of three contests a
practice bayonet is opposed to a kendo
stave. Battle practice – gun crews clear for
action, after torpedo tube is brought to bear
to port, air ventilator caps are rigged, crew
fall in by divisions. HIJMS *Katsura* (R)
leaves port with destroyer 'Q'. Tracking low
angle medium close-up from bow and
rounding the stern of 'Q', and final medium

shot profile.

[shotsheet available]
catalogued NAP: 5/1978

IWM 594-01 · GB, (?) 1924
**the OLYMPIC GAMES : as they were
originally practised in Ancient Greece
shown in living pictures**

b/w · 1 reel · 521' (9 mins) · silent
intertitles: English

sp Royal Navy and Royal Marines Sports
Control Board

- Tableau demonstration of the various
  athletic skills in Ancient Greece, re-
  created in Britain, probably in 1924.

The studio has a stage with a mock-
classical frieze. The demonstrators all wear
tight-fitting costumes or loincloths. A group
of them line up as the various aspects (as if
in a stop-action film) of a jumping action.
Throwing the javelin is shown in slow
motion, as well as at full speed. Discus
throwing is also shown. It is all very stagey,
with a heavy emphasis on the balletic. A
lengthy wrestling match, with women
enthusing from the side over the victor.
Tableaux of runners, of warriors, of hunters
and of athletes at rest are shown, after the
manner of Greek vase painting. One of the
athletes is saluted with palm branches.

Notes
Technical: together with **IWM 594-2+3** and
IWM 594-4-13, this was donated to the
Museum as a single film of 13 reels. The
preservation of the original numbers rather
than renumbering was decided upon in
1983 in order to maintain the same system
as that used by the British Film Institute.
Remarks: a quite astonishing film, which in
its use of mock-classical motifs and sinister
camera angles seems more typical of a
Nazi 'Master Race' epic than a Royal Navy
historical recreation.
[shotsheet available]
catalogued SDB: 4/1983

IWM 594-02+3 · France, 1924
**the OLYMPIC GAMES HELD AT
CHAMONIX IN 1924**
les FILMS SPORTIFS (series)

b/w · 2 reels · 2006' (34 mins) · silent
intertitles: English

pr Rapid Film *managing director* Rovera, Jean de

■ Winter Olympics in Chamonix, France, 1924.

(Reel 2) A view of Chamonix with Mont Blanc above it. The various national contingents mingle in procession. They dip their flags as they take the Olympic Oath. People practise at the skating rink. The start of a heat of the 500m skating race is shown firstly at normal speed, and then in slow motion. The heats continue. Vallenius of Finland, shown in portrait shot, won his heat and was fourth in the final. Miss Muckett (GB) demonstrates her technique in the ladies' figure-skating. Mrs Szabo-Plank of Austria, who won the figure skating, in action. A small child gives a demonstration. The final of the ice hockey is between Canada and the United States. The teams are posed, with the goalkeepers singled out: Cameron for Canada and Lacroix for the USA. The match is shown in detail. Some of the lady spectators watch in slacks, "masculine garb, they found it much more convenient than skirts". The Canadians win. *(Reel 3)* The marathon 50km ski race, followed by a group of the winning Swiss team. Mrs Englemann and Mr Berger, who won the figure-skating doubles, in action. Mrs Blanchard and Mr Niles, also figure-skating. In the bobsleigh races the British 4-man team, captained by W Horton, make their run to achieve second place. Other bobs make the run. The Swiss team celebrate their win. The ski-jumps are shown, sometimes in slow motion. Haugen (USA), the winner, is shown with two other team members. The Norwegian Thams is shown making a jump which broke the record, but after the games were completed.

Notes
Technical: together with **IWM 594-01** and **IWM 594-04-13**, this was donated to the Museum as a single film of 13 reels. The preservation of the original numbers rather than renumbering was decided upon in 1983 in order to maintain the same system as that used by the British Film Institute. [shotsheet available]
catalogued SDB: 4/1983

IWM 594-04-13 · France, 1924
the OLYMPIC GAMES IN PARIS 1924
les FILMS SPORTIFS (series)

b/w · 10 reels · 9732' (162 mins) · silent

intertitles: English

pr Rapid Film *managing director* Rovera, Jean de

■ Olympic Games in or near Paris, 1924, including some slow motion filming and portrait shots of the winners.

The film consists chiefly of a short extract from an event, followed by a portrait shot of the winner. *(Reel 4)* M Doumergue, the President of France, opens the games. With the guest of honour, the Prince of Wales, in the VIP box are Count Clary, President of the Olympic Committee, the Crown Prince of Sweden and Haile Selassie of Abyssinia. The procession starts and Gêo André takes the Olympic Oath for all, to open the games in celebration. *(Reel 5)* Deglane (France) defeats Nilsson (Sweden) to win the Graeco-Roman wrestling at the winter velodrome. Nurmi wins the first heat of the 3000m, with Ritola second and Tala third. The first three places are therefore taken by Finnish runners, shown running. Tootell (USA) wins the hammer. Nurmi wins the 1500m, with Scharer (Swiss) second and Stallard (GB) third. Eric Liddell (GB) wins the 400m with a world record. Nurmi wins the 5000m, with Ritola second. Myrra (Finland) wins the javelin. Houser (USA) wins the medals shot putt and Barnes (USA) the pole vault. *(Reel 6)* Ritola wins the 10km. Taylor wins the 400m hurdles. Osborn (USA) wins the high jump. Harold Abrahams (GB) wins the 100m from Paddock (USA). "The negro Hubbard" (USA) wins the long jump. Houser wins the discus. Jackson Scholz (USA) wins the 200m. Ritola wins the 3000m steeplechase. Kinsey (USA) wins the 110m hurdles from Atkinson. Lowe (GB) wins the 800m. The US team wins the 400m relay. *(Reel 7)* The United States win the 800m relay swim, with Australia second. Johnny Weissmuller (USA) wins the 100m freestyle. The diving competition. The French win the water polo. *(Reel 8)* Only 9 countries participate in the gymnastics, held in the open air, and the Italians win. The Danes give a gymnastic display. The 10km cross-country is won by Nurmi with Ritola second. Wide (GB) led at half-way. *(Reel 9)* The Swedes win the riding competition. The marathon is run from Colombes to Pontoise and back, won by Stenroos (Finland) from Bertini (Italy). De Mar (USA) leads for most of the way, overtaking Kranis (Greece) before the half-way mark. The rowing contest. The yacht race at Le Havre. The Argentinians win from the British at polo at St-Cloud, although the British "kept their end up splendidly". The

French fencer Lucien Gandin contrasts with the Italian style. Philippe Cattiau (France) wins and Mrs Osiier wins the ladies tournament. *(Reel 11)* In the football final Uruguay defeats Switzerland. *(Reel 12)* At rugby the United States wins from France. The Queen of Spain watches the tennis. Miss Wills (USA) defeats Mlle Vlasto (France). Vincent Richards (USA) defeats Cochet (France). *(Reel 13)* The 188km cycling road race is from Gisors to Colombes. Blanchonnet (France) wins. Willems (Holland) wins the 50km track race. Michard (France) in the three man pursuit. Mitchell (GB) defeats T Paterson (Denmark) at middleweight in the boxing. Smith (South Africa) defeats Tripoli (USA) at bantamweight. MacKenzy (USA) is shown against Labarba at flyweight.

Notes
Production: "The 1924 Games were the first which were marked by the production of a full-length feature-type film .... In the scale of its coverage of the Games, the 1924 epic is a hint of things to come." (Taylor Downing)
Technical: together with **IWM 594-01** and **IWM 594-02+03**, this was donated to the Museum as a single film of 13 reels. The preservation of the original numbers rather than renumbering was decided upon in 1983 in order to maintain the same system as that used by the British Film Institute.
Remarks: far too long to be seen as anything but a historical record. Nevertheless in its use of camera angles and slow motion this film provides an interesting comparison with the 1981 film *Chariots of Fire* which to some extent derives from it.
[Taylor Downing, *Olympia*, British Film Institute (1992): 13-14]
[shotsheet available]
catalogued SDB: 4/1983

IWM 595 · GB, 1918
OUR DAILY BREAD (PART 2)

b/w · 1 reel · 1001' (17 mins) · silent
intertitles: English

sp Admiralty *pr* Engholm, F W
cam Engholm, F W

■ Appeal for the War Work Volunteers, incorporating material from **IWM 552**, *The Way of a Ship on the Sea.*

Bringing food from overseas – aerial views of a convoy, escorting cruiser USS

Birmingham, and an Astre-Torres type SS airship. Unloading supplies – grain ships discharge cargo into barges. India Line ships in dry dock (*cf.* **IWM 552-03**). Fishing fleet returns to harbour – medium shots of drifters *Oceanic, Robinia, Zetland,* etc. Trawlers unload onto snow-covered wharves (*cf.* **IWM 552-04**). "The Birth of a Standard Ship": first twelve sequences from **IWM 552-02**, showing the construction and launch of a standard merchant hull, with final title exhorting "patriotic men" to become War Work Volunteers in the shipyards. "Ships that guard the Foodships": aerial view of Hunt Class minesweeper (?); medium close-up on board destroyer as torpedo is manhandled into single torpedo tube – the pointer sits astride the tube which is trained over the starboard beam; HMS *Firedrake* (97) passes left to right; medium close-up as torpedo is fired. "Dirty Weather": high angle medium shot to after deckhouse on destroyer at speed in heavy seas – man coming forward is knocked down by wind and spray, but recovers and goes below. Medium shot of destroyer closing on starboard quarter. HMS *Opportune* (G.59) passes cameraship. Medium shot from astern as HMS *King Edward VII* fires to starboard with full battery of 12, 9.2 and 6-inch guns. High angle medium close-up of 12-inch turret on *King Edward VII* as it fires by single barrels. Final title exhorts the audience to join the War Work Volunteers.

[shotsheet available]
catalogued NAP: 6/1978

IWM 596 · NO FILM

IWM 597 · GB, 11/1917
the STORY OF THE DRIFTERS (fragment of variant copy)

b/w · 1 reel · 627' (10 mins) · silent
intertitles: English

sp Admiralty *pr* Engholm, F W
cam Engholm, F W

■ Incomplete copy of the second reel of The Story of the Drifters, **IWM 553**, with minor differences in titling.

catalogued NAP: 5/1978

IWM 598 · GB, (?) 1900
[HMS ST VINCENT TAKES IN SAIL]
(allocated)

b/w · 1 reel · 67' (1 min) · silent
intertitles: none

sp Admiralty (?)

■ HMS *Saint Vincent*, training ship at
Portsmouth, practises some sail drill.

Medium shot view fine on starboard quarter
of HMS *Saint Vincent* with main yards set.
Mainsail clewed up. Main topgallant sail
furled in a body. Main topsail scandalised –
yard lowered and reef tackle hauled out.

catalogued NAP: 6/1978

IWM 599 · GB, (prod) 1918
**VISIT OF ITALIAN DELEGATION TO THE
GRAND FLEET (ledger title)**

b/w · 1 reel · 374' (6 mins) · silent
intertitles: none

sp Ministry of Information *cam* Engholm, F
W (?)

■ Disjointed film of a delegation of Italian
naval and military officers visiting HMS
Queen Elizabeth in the Firth of Forth,
March-May 1918.

The view, always in long shot, is of the
quarterdeck of the *Queen Elizabeth*. Admiral
Beatty walks and talks with his staff and
three Italian officers. The remainder of the
Grand Fleet can be seen at anchor in the
background. The Italians leave on a small
launch, which pulls away. The same launch,
ML.324, returns with more of the Italians,
who are piped on board the battleship.
There is a sudden time cut to the Italians
pacing the deck, talking with Beatty and his
staff. Lieutenant Neal, the official naval
photographer, and Lieutenant Ernest
Brooks, an official Army photographer on
secondment, can be seen taking
photographs as the delegates walk around
the deck. The delegates leave on the
launch. Brooks and Neal check their record
books.

catalogued SDB: 5/1983

IWM 600 · GB, (prod) 1918
**VISIT OF ALLIED MEMBERS TO THE
GRAND FLEET (ledger title)**

b/w · 1 reel · 319' (5 mins) · silent
intertitles: none

sp Ministry of Information *cam* Engholm, F
W (?)

■ Delegation of Allied parliamentary
representatives arrives on board HMS
Queen Elizabeth in the Firth of Forth,
March-May 1918.

The film is taken from the quarterdeck of
HMS *Queen Elizabeth*. Conditions are very
misty and the shape of another battleship
can be indistinctly seen in the distance. The
Allied representatives arrive by launch and
come up the ship's side ladder onto the
quarterdeck. They mill about, talking among
themselves and with naval officers and
press representatives. The delegates are
each introduced to Admiral Sir David
Beatty. They form up for a group
photograph. One or two are in Italian
military uniform but the majority are
civilians.

catalogued SDB: 3/1983

IWM 601 · GB, (prod) 1918
**VISIT OF USA DELEGATES TO GRAND
FLEET (ledger title)**

b/w · 1 reel · 306' (5 mins) · silent
intertitles: none

sp Ministry of Information *cam* Engholm, F
W (?)

■ Delegation of American politicians arrives
on board HMS *Queen Elizabeth* at anchor
in the Firth of Forth, March-May 1918.

Naval officers wait on the ship's quarterdeck
for the launch carrying the delegates to
arrive. They come up the ladder and are
greeted by the naval and liaison officers,
wandering about aimlessly and talking with
each other. In the background Lieutenant
Ernest Brooks, the official still photographer
(without his camera), can be seen talking to
a naval officer. After a while the delegates
file back down the ladder and motor launch
ML.324 takes them away from the ship's
side.

[shotsheet available]
catalogued SDB: 3/1983

IWM 602 · GB, (prod) 1918
VISIT OF BELGIAN KING TO GRAND FLEET (ledger title)

b/w · 1 reel · 705' (12 mins) · silent
intertitles: none

sp Ministry of Information *cam* Engholm, F W (?)

■ King Albert and Queen Elisabeth of the Belgians visit the British Grand Fleet and US 6th Battle Squadron in the Firth of Forth, probably June-July 1918.

The film starts on board the US flagship USS *New York*. The King and Queen have just come aboard and the camera, near B turret, shows the remainder of the party coming up the outer ladder and on board the ship. (Throughout the film the King and Queen contrive to remain either in long shot or just ahead of the panning camera.) With Admiral Rodman they move off to inspect the ship's company drawn up on deck. (Note the US official naval photographer at work.) The Forth Bridge is visible in the distance behind the ship. The ship's company march in review around A turret. Another New York Class battleship of the squadron is moored nearby. View of the length of the *New York*'s portside from a small launch as the King's party comes down the ladder and onto another launch. The film jumps to the battleship HMS *Queen Elizabeth*, with the camera looking down onto the quarterdeck. The King's launch arrives and his party come up on deck, where they are met by various naval officers, among them Admiral Sir David Beatty. (The British official naval photographer, Lieutenant Neal, at work.) The King inspects and meets a party of the ship's company drawn up on the quarterdeck. Navy launch ML.324 passes the stern of the *Queen Elizabeth* as they talk.

Notes
Date: this visit is not officially recorded but film **IWM 265** confirms that the King and Queen of the Belgians were in Britain in July 1918.
catalogued SDB & NAP: 3/1983

IWM 603 · GB, (prod) 1918
VISIT OF SIR H WILSON TO THE GRAND FLEET (ledger title)

b/w · 1 reel · 124' (3 mins) · silent
intertitles: none

sp Ministry of Information (?) *cam* Engholm, F W (?)

■ General Sir Henry Wilson, the Chief of the Imperial General Staff, arrives on board HMS *Queen Elizabeth* in the Firth of Forth to confer with Admiral Sir David Beatty, 21 May 1918.

The camera position looks over the *Queen Elizabeth*'s quarterdeck towards the stern. Wilson comes up the ship's ladder and shakes hands with Beatty. It is an informal, working meeting. The remainder of the party follows at a discreet distance and finally disappears altogether as the two men pace the quarterdeck in conversation. Sailors resume their normal duties. On a jump in the film the ship's Y turret has been traversed to starboard so completely blocking the camera's view.

[C E Callwell, *Field Marshal Sir Henry Wilson*, Vol II, Cassell (1927): 101]
catalogued SDB: 3/1983

IWM 604 · GB, (ca) 1916
FLAME THROWER (ledger title)

b/w · 1 reel · 1183' (20 mins) · silent
intertitles: none

■ Tests of large mounted and small hand-held flame-throwers, some of them carried out by the Royal Navy, in Britain, probably during the First World War.

A rear view, from a sand-bagged bunker, of a flame-projector nozzle angled upwards from a solid base. Pipes lead back to fuel cylinders in the bunker. These are operated by a civilian and an Army officer to produce a jet of flame from the nozzle, which is made to swing, spreading the flame and causing secondary fires. The control mechanism in the bunker is shown in close-up. A test of another mechanism – a workman pumps to produce pressure in one of two fuel barrels covered by a tarpaulin. A row of ten such barrels or cylinders in a trench. A flame-thrower nozzle (like a hose-pipe) has been mounted on a solid sledge-like platform enabling it to swivel. It throws out flame, then splutters and malfunctions, continuing to pump out liquid. With its nozzle set horizontally the same device throws out flame to about 75 yards (marked against a series of range posts) and causes a great deal of smoke in addition to the fire. Back to the bunker test – this time a malfunction again causes the nozzle to throw out liquid. Gorse burns in the heat of one of the flame-throwers, causing the image to distort with the heat. One of the devices, partly concealed by gorse, throws out flame horizontally to a considerable distance. One type of the flame-thrower or projector mounted on a lattice tower throws flame even further. In each case there are many secondary fires and a great deal of smoke. Lines of cylinders, more substantial than the earlier versions, linked together in a trench. Two men in flame-resistant suits check them over. Back to the tower version of flame-projector, showing that the liquid does not ignite until it is well clear of the nozzle. Six men in protective flame-resistant suits carry early hand-held flame-throwers down to a range. The flame-thrower consists of little more than an upright cylinder and nozzle, like a fire extinguisher. At a signal they spray the grass with flame. One man in a protective suit (with includes full head cover) creeps down a training trench. The men conclude their test and free each other from their suits. An official, possibly a naval officer, shows how the protective mica visor is fitted in position. A Royal Navy lorry arrives at a test site and the men, in their suits, get down with their flame-throwers, take up position, and advance in a skirmish line firing short bursts of flame. In the confines of a trench one man struggles into his protective suit while another prepares his partner's flame-thrower for use. The training party makes its way down a trench, and sets fire to the wooden supports. The film alternates between these two events until it returns to the men in the skirmish line still advancing, burning the grass as they do so.

Notes
Production: this may well be Admiralty sponsored film.
Remarks: visually very attractive material. Sadly it cannot be dated with any certainty.
catalogued SDB: 3/1983

IWM 605-609 · NO FILM

IWM 610 · GB, (ca) 1919
WRAF CAMP

b/w · 1 reel · 162' (3 mins) · silent
intertitles: none

- Pay parade at a Women's Royal Air Force camp in England, probably shortly after

the First World War.

The film irises up on the huts of the camp, which is large and well laid out. A column of WRAFs marches along a path in the camp. At a pay parade indoors the women come forward in turn to collect their money. A final scene of a line of officers and civilians awaiting the arrival of a dignitary – the film ends before the person arrives.

Notes
Title: this is taken from the shotsheet.
[shotsheet available]
catalogued SDB: 3/1983

IWM 611 · NO FILM

IWM 612 · GB, 1919
UXBRIDGE WRAF FORM A GUARD OF HONOUR TO QUEEN MARY AT THE SAVOY HOTEL 7/4/19

b/w · 1 reel · 125' (5 mins) · silent
intertitles: none

- Members of the WRAF and RAF, both at the Savoy as the guard of honour and relaxing in their camp at Uxbridge, April 1919.

I. WRAFs wait outside the railings of the Savoy Hotel in London. The police hold back a civilian crowd as a horse-drawn coach comes up to the hotel and the Queen gets out. The WRAF members begin to form into their squads as the guard of honour. Queen Mary emerges from the hotel, is given a bouquet of flowers and the WRAF officers are presented to her.
II. Officers and sergeants of the RAF eating at a formal banquet. WRAFs line up for a pay-parade. Men of the RAF wait outside a barracks and play with two dogs. They are curious about the camera's presence. Indoors, they play billiards and some of them read letters.

Notes
Production: probably a privately taken film.
catalogued SDB: 3/1983

IWM 613 · GB, (prod) 1917
NS 5 TRIAL FLIGHT

b/w · 1 reel · 474' (8 mins) · silent
intertitles: none

sp Admiralty

- Take-off, trial flight and landing of the Royal Navy airship NS5 ('North Sea' class) at Kingsnorth Royal Navy Airship Station, 4 December 1917.

The airship is reversed out of its shed. It carries British RNAS roundels and the gondola is clearly marked NS5. It is manœuvred into position on the landing ground and takes off. A message is dropped from the airship by parachute to the landing ground. The airship overflies the station at various altitudes providing the camera with views from all angles. The NS5 then comes in to land, its ropes are seized by the landing party and it is led back to its hangar.

[shotsheet available]
catalogued SDB: 3/1983

IWM 614 · GB, 1918
FAIREY SEAPLANES

b/w · 1 reel · 894' (15 mins) · silent
intertitles: English

sp Royal Air Force for Admiralty *pr* Royal Air Force – London Photo Centre

- Taxiing and torpedo-dropping trials by various Fairey and Short seaplanes of the Royal Air Force at the Royal Navy base on the Isle of Grain, April 1918.

The film is described in its opening captions as one of a series for naval cadets. It opens with a Fairey FIII seaplane with 190hp engine taxiing through the water. A King Edward Class battleship and some merchantmen can be seen in the distance behind it. The seaplane builds up speed and takes off, then comes back in to land. A Fairey Campania seaplane also taxis and takes off. A cruiser, possibly Monmouth Class, can be seen in the background. A Short 184 (number N 1086) on supports on land showing its experimental large Linton-Hope floats (see **Notes**). Another Short 184 with conventional floats taxis through the water. Another beached Short on supports showing the Martin Aerodynamic Stabiliser fitted to the aircraft. Film taken from the cockpit of a Sunbeam Short 184 carrying torpedoes. (The film starts to break up here and not all the scenes described by the captions appear.) Another Short 184 taxiing. A beached Short on supports showing a torpedo fitting. The various types of Fairey

and Short seaplanes practise torpedo drops with dummy torpedoes, and land, taxiing through the water.

Notes
Title: this is taken from the shotsheet. It is possible, however, that no specific title ever appeared on the film, which seems to be incomplete.
Summary: the film describes the Short fitted with large floats as N 1086. However, the book of Aircraft Serials describes N 1081 as the only Short fitted with these floats.
[shotsheet available]
catalogued SDB: 3/1983

IWM 615 · GB, (prod) 1918
EMBRYO AIRMEN

b/w · 1 reel · 890' (15 mins) · silent
intertitles: English

sp Royal Air Force (?)

- Review, ceremonial parade and athletics gathering by the Cadet Brigade of the Royal Air Force in the town of St Leonards-on-Sea (near Hastings) on Whit Monday, 20 May 1918.

The cadets are encamped near the town. They march onto a grassy 'parade ground' in PT gear and their RAF caps, and form the letters RAF in marching formation. "These letters should inspire all young men of spirit to come forward and offer themselves to the Adventure of the Air." Brigadier-General A C Critchley, commanding the Cadet Brigade, trots on horseback past the civilian spectators. Major-General F C Heath-Caldwell, commanding the South Eastern Area RAF, inspects the parade while on horseback (always in long shot). The scene changes to the sea front at St Leonards-on-Sea. Various RAF officers stand at a saluting base while the cadets of the brigade march past them. The cadets are in full uniform with their white-banded caps. Next is a cadet sports held on a grassy area of the front. The cadets compete in a 100 yards sprint, followed by a mile race around the track. A joke 'Charlie Chaplin' races past. The 120 yards hurdles is followed by the sack race. An aircraft stunt flies high overhead. The cadets give a PT display followed by a massed display of boxing.

Notes
Production: apparently the RAF Photo Centre's own film version of the event.

Compare it with **IWM 632**, which is the Ministry of Information film of the demonstration and parade. See also **IWM 625** and **IWM 635** which show the same cadet brigade.
Technical: the P 2 version of this film is identical but without title or captions. [shotsheet available]
catalogued SDB: 3/1983

IWM 616 · GB, (ca) 1916
HAULING DOWN A KITE BALLOON BY HAND (ledger title)

b/w · 1 reel · 380' (6 mins) · silent
intertitles: none

■ Long-distance view of men, probably British soldiers, pulling an observation kite balloon to the ground in snowy conditions. Probably in England during the First World War.

The men, always in long shot, are in a park or wood in snow conditions. They move as a group holding onto the ropes of the balloon, which is not seen until the end of the film. Gradually, climbing over obstacles as they move, they shorten the ropes and bring the balloon to earth.

Summary: nothing further can be discovered about this film.
catalogued SDB: 3/1983

IWM 617 · GB, (ca) 1916
HANDLING GAS CYLINDERS (ledger title)

b/w · 1 reel · 412' (7 mins) · silent
intertitles: none

■ Jumbled film of men of the Royal Navy stacking gas cylinders and testing a caterpillar tractor, interspersed with a balloon in flight. All probably in Britain during the First World War.

I. A massed pile of some hundreds of very long gas cylinders. More cylinders arrive by lorry and are rolled down onto the stack by men in uniform, either naval or munitions.
II. A spherical balloon with basket (non-military type) rising against a dramatic sky (film disfigured).
III. Men, again possibly naval, testing a commercial tractor with three driving tracks in triangular configuration by driving it up a spoil bank and over rough ground.

Notes
Summary: nothing further can be discovered about this film.
Technical: the original stock on the balloon sequence was disfigured by oil, causing a flicker effect across the film.
catalogued SDB: 3/1983

IWM 618 · GB, (ca) 1918
METEOROLOGICAL EXPERIMENTS (ledger title)

b/w · 1 reel · 170' (3 mins) · silent
intertitles: none

sp Admiralty (?)

■ Officers of the Royal Navy conduct experiments with weather balloons at a naval station near the coast of Britain, probably during the First World War.

One of the officers plays briefly outdoors with a parrot on its perch. Two officers with a theodolite on a tripod survey the area. Indoors a RNVR lieutenant makes fine adjustments to a set of scales before inflating a small meteorological balloon on one of them. Outdoors the balloon is released and tracked by the theodolite. Indoors the officer continues with his work.

catalogued SDB: 3/1983

IWM 619 · USA (?), (?) 1920
USA – SS SECTION 4 (ledger title)

b/w · 1 reel · 321' (6 mins) · silent
intertitles: none

■ Men of the US Navy Air Corps demonstrate the concealment of a Submarine Scout Airship, B or C Class, in a wood, probably in the USA shortly after the First World War.

The airship has distinctive US markings. It is pulled by the sailors out from the wood, where the tall trees have completely concealed it, and into a clearing. The crew of two in the open gondola make ready while the ground crew prepares the machine. The airship takes off. An ensign and sailor fit a message to the leg of a carrier pigeon and release it. Three of the sailors relax by a camp fire and cooking pot (for the camera's benefit) and roll their own cigarettes. The airship returns to the clearing, the men collect its ropes and guide it back under cover.

Notes
Summary: nothing further can be discovered about this film.
catalogued SDB: 3/1983

IWM 620 · GB, (prod) 1918
RAF CAMP WANTAGE (ledger title)

b/w · 1 reel · 849' (14 mins) · silent
intertitles: none

sp Royal Air Force (?)

■ RAF training camp for officer cadets at Wantage, probably summer 1918.

The camp is made up of bell tents and occasional prefabricated buildings. The cadets, some still in Army uniform but all with RAF caps, wander about talking and smoking. A physical training session of the 'Swedish drill' type. (The cadets look surprisingly old.) This includes a form of tug of war, skipping and medicine ball throwing. A game of cricket. Some of the cadets take a rowing eight out onto the Thames. A portrait shot of the commanding officer with his black labrador. The cadets build an aircraft hangar from wooden frames and canvas. The completed hangar has two aircraft outside it. One is a Martinsyde Elephant which has its propeller turned over. The other is a very smartly painted Avro 504. An officer walks around the Avro with a group of cadets, explaining how the various control surfaces work, starting with the tail rudder and moving forward to the wing surfaces and bracing wires. By this time the engine of the Elephant is running quite smoothly and it taxis away.

Notes
Summary: all the information on this film is taken from the shotsheet; nothing further can be discovered about it.
[shotsheet available]
catalogued SDB: 3/1983

IWM 621 · GB, (prod) 1917
TRIAL FLIGHT OF R9 (ledger title)

b/w · 1 reel · 592' (10 mins) · silent
intertitles: none

sp Admiralty (?)

■ One of the trial flights of the Royal Navy prototype rigid airship R9 (or Airship Number 9) at Inchinnan naval base, November 1916 to March 1917.

The airship emerges tail-first from its shed, and is steered to the take-off point by its ground crew. The camera is some distance away and shows the full length of the airship. Very slowly it begins to rise and move away into the clear sky. The camera tries to follow but gets too much flaring from the sun. The airship returns, adopting a very nose-down posture over its shed. It lands, is secured by the ground crew and is turned around back into its hangar.

Notes
Date: according to Hartcup, the R9 was completed in November 1916 and entered operational service in April 1917.
[Guy Hartcup, *The Achievement of the Airship*, David and Charles (1974): 110]
catalogued SDB: 3/1983

IWM 622 · GB, (prod) 1917
[TRIAL FLIGHTS OF RIGID AIRSHIPS NO 24 AND 25 AT INCHINNAN, OCTOBER 1917] (allocated)

b/w · 1 reel · 462' (8 mins) · silent
intertitles: none

sp Admiralty (?)

I. The take-off of R24 for its trial flight at Inchinnan airship base, Scotland, on 28 October 1917. The airship is shown facing tail-out in its hangar. It takes off from the landing ground, overflies the camera and steers towards the tree line on the horizon. It overflies the camera again, passing over the hills in the distance behind its hangar. The ground crew lines up to cheer the camera (presumably to use up the extra film).
II. Preparations for the trial flight of R25 at Inchinnan airship base, Scotland, October 1917. The airship is shown ready for take-off on the landing ground. An NS type airship in flight. A closer view of the ground crew leading R25 out to its launch spot.

[Guy Hartcup, *The Achievement of the Airship*, David and Charles (1974): 110]
[shotsheet available]
catalogued SDB: 4/1983

IWM 623 · GB, (prod) 1918
**BARROW TRIAL FLIGHT HM RIGID
AIRSHIP NO 26 : taken in heavy fog Mar
20th 1918**

b/w · 1 reel · 260' (4 mins) · silent
intertitles: English

sp Admiralty (?)

- Trial flight of Royal Navy airship R26 at
  Barrow-in-Furness, 20 March 1918.

The airship is backed out of its hangar and
prepared for flight. It lifts off and flies away.
Filmed from the ground through the fog, it
appears as a blur. It returns head-on and
nose-down to the landing site, and is
secured by the ground crew. The camera
stays in long shot throughout.

[shotsheet available]
catalogued SDB: 3/1983

IWM 624 · GB, (prod) 1918
**HM R27 TRIAL FLIGHT INCHINNAN
8/6/1918 6.15PM TO 9.30PM**

b/w · 1 reel · 469' (9 mins) · silent
intertitles: none

sp Admiralty (?)

- Royal Navy airship R27 (now under RAF
  control) making a trial flight at Inchinnan
  on 8 June 1918.

The airship is shown nose-out in its hangar
with the frame of another rigid airship being
built beside it. The ground crew leads the
R27 out to its launch ground. The camera
gets in close to show the launch and the
airship passing overhead. The airship then
flies low so that it is silhouetted against the
hills surrounding the landing field. It makes
another pass at higher altitude, comes in to
land, and is led by the ground crew to its
hangar. Probably to use up the film, the
women workers on the airship are invited to
race, cheering, past the camera. Two naval
officers watch the proceedings.

Notes
Title: this is taken from the shotsheet.
[shotsheet available]
catalogued SDB: 3/1983

IWM 625 · GB, (?) 1918
**INSPECTION OF THE ROYAL AIR FORCE
CADET BRIGADE BY HM THE KING
(GENERAL IN CHIEF) AUGUST 30 1918**

b/w · 1 reel · 1102' (18 mins) · silent
intertitles: English

sp Royal Air Force (?)

- King George V visits the RAF Cadet
  Brigade at its training camp at St
  Leonards-on-Sea (near Hastings), 30
  August 1918.

The King's train pulls in to the station
beside the camp. The King, wearing his
RAF uniform, is escorted out of the station
to face an honour guard formed by cadets
of Number 2 Wing, which he salutes and
inspects (a newsreel cameraman is moving
behind them). The full brigade is drawn up
on its parade field, where the Royal
Standard is unfurled. Cadets of Number 8
Wing out on the hill above the field form the
shape of an RAF standard and the initials
RAF. The King stands at the saluting base
(note the various cameramen at work) while
in the distance Number 8 Wing marches off.
The remaining cadets present arms and
perform a demonstration of drill. The King
takes the salute before walking from his
saluting base to the Royal Standard to take
the Royal salute. He then drives with his
party into the town, to the saluting base on
the sea front where the guard of honour
again presents arms. The cadets march
past in general salute. One of the officers
leading his squadron past is Captain HRH
Prince Albert, the Duke of York. The King
then drives to the cheers of the crowd (the
camera is in a following car) up along the
sea front and into the back streets, where
he inspects the officers' quarters and
cadets' messes. Outside one of the messes
a Women's Royal Air Force Contingent has
paraded. The King is then driven to the
main St Leonards-on-Sea station, boards
his train, and leaves to the cheers of the
cadets.

Notes
Summary: see also **IWM 615**, **IWM 632** and
IWM 635.
[shotsheet available]
catalogued SDB: 3/1983

IWM 626 · GB, 1918
**the LORD MAYOR'S SHOW : RAF well
represented**

b/w · 1 reel · 1026' (17 mins) · silent
intertitles: English

sp Royal Air Force (?) pr Royal Air Force –
London Photo Centre

- RAF film of the procession of the Lord
  Mayor of London's Show through
  Ludgate Circus, 9 November 1918.

The camera is fixed at a high position
looking down onto Ludgate Circus as the
various elements of the procession file
through. Leading are Royal Marines and
sailors, some of whom took part in the
Zeebrugge Raid. Both marines and sailors
wear full-dress blues. A large crowd of
civilians lines the route. The sailors are
followed by the boy scouts, a Belgian Army
Contingent, the Army Service Corps, the
WRNS, the WAACs, and the Forage Corps
from the Women's Land Army. Three tanks
take part in the procession, a Mk V Male, a
Mk V Star Female with fitted unditching
beam, and a Whippet. Airship R23 flies
overhead, with the dome of St Paul's
Cathedral visible in the background. The
march past continues with display floats by
the Land Army, the Ministry of Munitions,
and the Royal Field and Garrison Artillery,
which tow their various guns. The 13-
pounders of the Royal Horse Artillery lead
the Royal Field Artillery 18-pounders and
4.5-inch howitzer, followed by a 2.75-inch
mountain gun and a 4.7-inch field gun. As
R23 makes another pass the Royal Garrison
Artillery tow past a 60-pounder gun, a 6-
inch 26cwt howitzer, an 8-inch Mk VI
howitzer, and a dismantled 9.2-inch
howitzer, followed by a 13-pounder anti-
aircraft gun on a lorry mount and a float
representing an observation post. A kite
balloon overflies the crowd. One lorry
displays all the various types of British gun
ammunition, and another the various
mortars and machineguns. Also in the
procession are captured German 77mm
field guns. Airship R26 overflies the
procession. A lorry pulls a captured
German 155mm howitzer past the crowd,
followed by a 210mm howitzer, and types of
German mortars and machineguns. One
float is a pigeon loft, another is from the
Ministry of Pensions showing disabled men
at work. The massed bands of the Guards,
in khaki, are followed by the RAF band and
contingent, including the Women's Royal Air
Force. The RAF display includes lorries
carrying aircraft without their wings.
Prominent are a Felixstowe F2A flying boat
and two captured German aircraft, an
Albatros CIII and an Albatros CI (the latter
with a swastika marking on its side). Other

floats show various types of bombs, a kite
balloon in miniature, and engines being
made. At its end the film jumps to the Law
Courts, where civic, naval and military
dignitaries arrive and enter, silhouetted in
the doorway as they do so. The Lord
Mayor, also silhouetted, arrives last.

Notes
Remarks: extremely tedious, but only
because of its length. The swastika marking
is of the 'right handed', rather than the Nazi,
type.
[shotsheet available]
catalogued SDB: 3/1983

IWM 627 · GB, 1918
HMS ARGUS ALIGHTING TRIALS

b/w · 1 reel · 630' (11 mins) · silent
intertitles: English

sp Royal Air Force for Admiralty

- RAF Sopwith 1½ Strutter aircraft taking
  off and landing on the deck of the Royal
  Navy aircraft carrier HMS *Argus*, autumn
  1918.

There are two cameras filming the event, on
either side of the flight deck and forward of
midships – the cameramen can be seen at
work on a number of occasions. The ship is
steaming 15 knots and wind speed is 11
knots. The aircraft's propeller is turned over
and it takes off for the first attempt (note the
smoke pot near the bow giving wind
direction). It comes in to land and is
brought to a halt by arrester gear and a
ramp. The same take-off and landing is then
shown from the second camera's point of
view. The mechanism of the plane's rotary
engine can be seen very clearly. The
aircraft's pilot is given as Lieutenant-Colonel
Richard Bell-Davies VC, DSO, a former
naval officer. The second take-off is a
success but for the second landing the
approach is too high, the aircraft overshoots
and comes round again. The port camera
shows the landing on the second attempt.
After discussions between the pilot and the
ship's officers the ship is slowed to 4 knots,
with wind speed now 9 knots. The third
take-off is perfect but again on landing the
pilot overshoots at the first attempt and
lands the next time round with rather too
high an air speed, just stopping in time and
bouncing badly. The same landing looks
better as seen by the port camera.

Notes
Summary: from after the formation of the RAF in April 1918 to the creation of the Fleet Air Arm twenty years later, all pilots served in the RAF regardless of whether they flew from ships or land. Like many pilots, Bell-Davies was transferred from the Royal Navy with an RAF equivalent rank.
[shotsheet available]
catalogued SDB: 3/1983

IWM 628 · NO FILM

IWM 629 · GB, 1918
EXPERIMENTS IN LANDING A SOPWITH CAMEL ON WATER USING INTERNAL AIRBAGS ONLY

b/w · 1 reel · 546' (9 mins) · silent
intertitles: English

sp Royal Air Force for Admiralty *pr* Royal Air Force – London Photo Centre

■ Tests used to modify two Sopwith Camels for emergency landings in the water at the Royal Navy base on the Isle of Grain between 20 July and 28 August 1918.

The first test on 20 July is carried out with a Camel without hydrovanes or external air bags. Flying straight and level the machine glides out over the harbour and tries to belly-land on the water. As soon as the wheels touch it turns nose-up and sinks past the cockpit, although not completely. It is recovered by a launch and examined. The impact has twisted the leading edges of the wings and crushed the engine cowling. The second test on 9 August is carried out with another machine, fitted with front and rear hydrovanes – the front set is like a small third wing between the wheels, the rear fits to the tail skid. Again the machine glides in to land and noses-up the instant the wheels touch the water. The launch recovers the plane, which shows similar damage to that done on the earlier test. If anything the damage is worse, with the front hydrovane completely buckled. The third test on 28 August uses the same machine but smaller landing wheels to try and cure the problem. This time the front hydrovane is thinner and set forward of the landing wheels by means of two braces. The machine again glides in to land in the bay, and this time it lands safely, although as soon as it comes to rest the weight of

the engine tilts it nose-down and it begins to sink, so that the pilot has to crawl up onto the tail. The machine is stable in this position until the launch arrives to tow it back. (Part of the towing sequence shows B3878, the plane from the first test, also being recovered.) A final test is made using a Sopwith Snipe, also fitted with the thinner hydrovane and no external air bags, which has a device to enable it to jettison its wheels before landing. It comes in over the bay, drops its wheels, and lands in the water successfully without nosing up. It is towed back by the launch as dusk falls across the bay, throwing it into silhouette on the very calm water.

[shotsheet available]
catalogued SDB: 3/1983

IWM 630 · NO FILM

IWM 631 · GB, (prod) 1918
DECK LANDING

b/w · 1 reel · 350' (5 mins) · silent
intertitles: English

sp Admiralty (?)

■ Royal Navy trials on land of arrester gear to restrain aircraft when landing on aircraft carriers, England, probably summer 1918.

At a Royal Navy land base near the coast an artificial flight-deck has been constructed out of whitewashed wooden planks. This is roped off with white ropes like a boxing ring. The ropes which will form the arrester gear are held under tension by weighted sandbags, and their height above the deck carefully checked. An aircraft comes in to land on the 'deck'. It is N9497, a Fairey FIIID seaplane fitted with wheels and arrester hook instead of floats. On landing the left wheel buckles with the strain but the ropes prevent the machine overturning. The operation of the arrester hook is shown in detail. The nose has been fitted with a propeller guard to prevent the propeller fouling in the ropes as the aircraft lands.

Notes
Title: this is taken from the shotsheet.
Intertitles: these are all flashframes.
Summary: nothing further can be discovered about this film.
[shotsheet available]

catalogued SDB: 3/1983

IWM 632 · GB, (after) 3/1918
BRITAIN'S FUTURE AIR FIGHTERS

b/w · 1 reel · 773' (12 mins) · silent
intertitles: English

sp Ministry of Information

■ Ministry of Information version of a
ceremonial gathering by the RAF Cadet
Brigade in St Leonards-on-Sea on 20
May 1918, showing also airmen in France
in late August 1917.

The cadets are encamped near the town.
They form on their grassy 'parade ground'.
They march past Major-General F C Heath-
Caldwell, commanding South Eastern Area
of the RAF. The film jumps to their athletics
meeting in St Leonards-on-Sea later that
day. A crowd of cadets cheers the hurdles,
the sack race and a massed boxing
demonstration. The film jumps back to the
original parade, where Heath-Caldwell,
together with the brigade commander,
Brigadier-General A C Critchley, makes his
inspection. Later in the day the cadets
march past Heath-Caldwell along the front
at St Leonards-on-Sea. The film jumps
again to "the finished article", stock footage
of pilots, actually of 60 Squadron RFC in
France in August 1917. The group of pilots
shown is, left to right: Frank 'Mongoose'
Soden (with dog), Captain William 'Billy'
Bishop VC DSO MC, Keith 'Grid' Caldwell, E
W 'Moley' Molesworth, and Spencer 'Nigger'
Horn, at Ste-Marie-Cappel. Sopwith 1½
Strutters of 45 Squadron, also based at Ste-
Marie, set off on a patrol flight. One plane
stunt flies in a 'falling leaf' dive. An FE2d of
20 Night Bomber Squadron comes in to
land at Ste-Marie-Cappel past the Sopwiths
of 45 Squadron.

Notes
Summary: see also **IWM 615** which shows
the RAF version of the same visit by Heath-
Caldwell. The scenes in France come from
IWM 141.
[shotsheet available]
catalogued SDB: 3/1983

IWM 633 · GB, 1918
**BRITISH EMPIRE AND AMERICAN
SERVICES SPORTS, STAMFORD
BRIDGE, SEPT 7TH 1918**

b/w · 1 reel · 315' (5 mins) · silent
intertitles: English

sp Royal Air Force (?)

■ Athletics meeting for servicemen and
women from Britain, the Imperial forces
and the US Army at Stamford Bridge
football ground, Fulham, London, 7
September 1918.

The film starts with a posed group of the
RAF team. Three heats of the 100 yards
sprint are shown, followed by the one mile
race which is won by Corporal J Mason
from New Zealand. (Mason is not shown
clearly on the film.) Two competitors take
part in the long jump. The women's auxiliary
forces 440 yards relay is won by the RAF
team, which is shown in a posed group.
The 120 yards hurdles is won by Lieutenant
Fraser RAF, who is shown posed
afterwards. The one mile relay is won by
the RAF team, as is the tug of war. At the
end of the games Lord Beaverbrook
presents prizes to the winners.

Notes
Production: probably an RAF film, if only on
the grounds that most of the winners shown
are RAF personnel.
Remarks: an interesting film of a routine
event, with some highly inventive camera
angles. But one is left wondering why so
many obviously very fit men were still in
England while the armies in France were
involved in winning the war.
[shotsheet available]
catalogued SDB: 3/1983

IWM 634 · GB, (ca) 1955
the HORSE AND THE AEROPLANE

b/w · 2 reels · 2792' (45 mins) · silent
intertitles: English

sp Imperial War Museum (?)

■ Compilation film of the training of horses
and of aircraft pilots by the British and
Australians in Palestine, 1918.

The film is compiled, rather than edited, by
joining together 4 original films. *(Reel 1)*
Firstly, **IWM 31** *Inland Water Transport,
Egypt* and **IWM 2** *44th Remount Squadron
on the Egyptian Coast. (Reel 2)* Followed by
material taken from **IWM 38** *The Advance in
Palestine* and **IWM 28** *With the Australian
Forces in Palestine.* It shows firstly the
carriage of fodder on the Nile and the

training of remount horses, and then the training of aircrew up to a sortie and return flight out over Palestine.

Notes
Production: probably made for the Imperial War Museum for showing within the Museum itself, at some point since the Second World War.
Summary: see also for the original material from which this compilation is made **IWM 2**, **IWM 28**, **IWM 31** and **IWM 38**.
Remarks: a disappointing film, given its potentially interesting title. No attempt has been made to re-edit the film.
[shotsheet available]
catalogued SDB: 4/1983

IWM 635 · GB, (prod) 1918
[LORD WEIR'S VISIT TO THE RAF CADET BRIGADE] (allocated)

b/w · 1 reel · 463' (8 mins) · silent
intertitles: none

sp Royal Air Force

- Visit of Lord Weir, the Secretary of State for Air, to the RAF Cadet Brigade camp at St Leonards-on-Sea, summer 1918.

The day is wet and blustery. Lord Weir walks with a senior RAF officer as an escort past the waiting crowd of civilians and stands at the saluting base on St Leonards sea front. The Cadet Brigade marches past in salute and Weir doffs his hat in acknowledgement. This is followed by another march past in PT gear and an athletics match, starting with a massed boxing demonstration. On the athletics field, next to the sea front, an RAF Highland pipe band parades. Amongst the crowd is a full-sized mock-up of an aeroplane with its propeller turning. The cadets take part in various races, at middle distance, sprint distance, and over hurdles. Some of the crowd watching are members of the Women's Auxiliary Air Force. The weather deteriorates steadily and rain begins to fall heavily. The RAF still photographer can be seen at work. The brigade commander, Brigadier-General A C Critchley, directs proceedings. Near to him, wearing a raincoat against the now driving rain, is Captain Prince Albert, the Duke of York. The athletics continue despite the weather with the tug of war and a 'cuddy fight' (wrestling while being carried), followed by a race to put up a bell tent. A long-distance race finishes (note the cine cameraman at

work) and the cadets display the sign "Number 1 Cadet Wing" in front of the victor. The athletics continue with a wheelbarrow race and another tug of war, interspersed with scenes of the cheering crowd of cadets, as the film breaks up and ends.

Notes
Title: the title given for this film by the store ledger is *King George V's Visit to RAF Brigade* which is clearly incorrect.
Summary: see also **IWM 615**, **IWM 625**, **IWM 632** and **IWM 640-01** showing the cadet brigade.
catalogued SDB: 3/1983

IWM 636 · GB, 1918
TORPEDO DROPPING AT EAST FORTUNE TDS

b/w · 1 reel · 642' (11 mins) · silent
intertitles: English

sp Royal Air Force for Admiralty

- Trial torpedo attack against a British destroyer by Sopwith Cuckoo aircraft of the Royal Air Force at East Fortune Torpedo Dropping School, Scotland, 5 September 1918.

The Torpedo Dropping School was used to train pilots before they were attached to their squadrons. A stretch of hard sand on the beach at Belhaven Sands is used as a runway. An 18-inch torpedo is fitted to one of the Cuckoos and it takes off, followed by the rest of a flight of eight. For the attacks the camera is on the target ship, which is making 20 knots, and tries to pick out the Cuckoos as they make their torpedo runs. Frequently it catches only the moment of the drop at its extreme range – much the same view as an anti-aircraft gunner. The pilots are named in the captions, together with the height of the aircraft when the torpedo was dropped (between 10 and 20 feet) and the air speed (between 80 and 90 knots). Of the first wave the first attack is not shown. The second attack is from very close, only 800 yards, and hits the ship. Of the remaining ten attacks for which data are shown four were launched from too long a range and the torpedo came up short (although it would have hit if set for 2000 yards); three passed astern of the ship; one was a near miss passing 20 yards ahead of the ship and two hit the bottom. One of the torpedoes which hit the bottom is shown being recovered, its nose has been badly crushed. A number of other attacks are shown without data on the result. The aircraft come back to land at Belhaven Sands. At the end of the film is an added scene of a Cuckoo with a box-type engine, possibly a prototype.

catalogued SDB: 3/1983

IWM 637 · GB, 1918
SURRENDER OF THE GERMAN HIGH SEAS FLEET

b/w · 1 reel · 589' (10 mins) · silent
intertitles: English

sp Royal Air Force *pr* Royal Air Force – London Photo Centre

■ Film taken from a naval airship showing the surrender of the German fleet, 21 November 1918.

The German fleet "comes out": battleships in line ahead; medium shot as Kaiser Class battleship passes below; medium shots and medium close-ups of battle-cruisers – SMS *Von der Tann*, *Derfflinger*, *Moltke* and *Seydlitz*; additional shots of *Von der Tann*. Ships of US 6th Battle Squadron are part of the Allied escort: medium shots of *New York* and *Texas*. Surrendered light cruisers: two Koenigsberg (II) Class (SMS *Nuernberg* and *Emden* ?), SMS *Frankfurt*, and a Bremse Class vessel. The German flagship: medium close-up of SMS *Friedrich der Grosse* flying Rear-Admiral Reuter's flag – airship pylon obscures the view in latter part of the sequence. Medium shot off the port beam of *Seydlitz* – she passes off-screen left. "An idea of German armament": medium close-up of after turrets and port echelon turret of *Friedrich der Grosse*. "Hun Torpedo Boat Destroyers": S.131 Class vessels, S.53 Class, destroyer B.98 and companion. Medium shot of SMS *Seydlitz* with airship engine pylon in foreground. "An aerial escort": medium-long shot of German battleships in line ahead with Astre-Torres type airship above them – a second airship is visible in far distance. Medium shot of New York Class battleship – partially obscured by pylon. Medium shot of SMS *Derfflinger*. "Nearing May Island": long shot of *Seydlitz* holding station astern of HMS *Cardiff*. Long shot of *Cardiff* with Royal Sovereign Class battleship in the background.

[shotsheet available]
catalogued NAP: 4/1978

IWM 638 · GB, (?) 1918
GRAND FLEET AIRCRAFT ROYAL AIR FORCE

b/w · 1 reel · 1190' (20 mins) · silent
intertitles: English

sp Royal Air Force (?)

■ Instructional film showing how an RAF Sopwith Camel can be launched from the light cruiser HMS *Sydney*, fly to land at Rosyth seaplane base, and rejoin the ship on her return, September 1918.

The Camel is mounted on a launch platform above the light cruiser's A turret. The crew makes ready for launch, removing the safety netting and holding wires. The plane's engine is turned over (very good view of the rotary engine), it builds up speed and launches directly over the turret, which is swung out to starboard. The Camel lands conventionally at an aerodrome not far from Rosyth after flying its mission. A Royal Navy ground crew performs a quick check on the machine, then wheels it by a ramp onto a lorry. The Camel is then unbolted immediately behind the cockpit, and the two halves rearranged one under the other on the lorry for easier transportation. The lorry arrives at the seaplane base where the aircraft is reassembled and checked over. It fails to satisfy the mechanics on a second check and another Camel is provided as a substitute. This is put on a lorry (which has a long tailboard specially designed to take the aircraft in one piece) and driven to South Arm, Rosyth. Here a crane transfers the plane to the lighter *Guide Me* which takes it out to the *Sydney* or a similar Chatham Class light cruiser. The ship's derrick takes the Camel on board and it is fitted back onto its launch platform.

Notes
Remarks: an extremely well made and interesting film.
[shotsheet available]
catalogued SDB: 3/1983

IWM 639 · GB, (prod) 1918
[RAF SECTIONS] (allocated)

b/w · 1 reel · 479' (8 mins) · silent
intertitles: English

sp Royal Air Force (?)

I. A hand draws a cartoon of an RAF

biplane in flight, showing slipstream
spiralling around the aircraft.
II. RAF Avro 504 aircraft side-slip in to land
on the asphalt runway at Redcar, coming in
almost sideways on, probably 1918.
III. A demonstration of the principle of slow
motion cine-photography by having the film
slow down men in civilian clothes as they
jump over a low obstacle.
IV. A view of cloud formations from behind
a pilot's head in a biplane, showing the
pilot's view.
V. A Felixstowe seaplane rides at anchor
with a coastline behind it. The engines are
started and the mechanics leave by boat.
The plane taxis. Cut to an R Class destroyer
moving very fast through the water, 1918.

catalogued SDB: 3/1983

IWM 640-01 · GB, (prod) 1918
**[RAF CADET BRIGADE SPORTS AT
SAINT LEONARDS]** (allocated)

b/w · 1 reel · 834' (14 mins) · silent
intertitles: none

sp Royal Air Force (?)

- Disjointed film of an RAF Cadet Brigade
  athletics sports on the sea front of St
  Leonards-on-Sea, 18 June 1918.

The film jumps between the crowd, which
includes civilians and schoolboys as well as
the cadets, and the various races. Two
buglers sound a salute. The sports teams
walk around the track in parade (a newsreel
cameraman is visible). The wheelbarrow
race (in which the 'barrows' are blindfolded),
the high jump, a long distance race, a sack
race, a hurdling race, a pillow fight on a
pole, are all followed by the prize-giving,
probably by the wife of a senior officer. The
races continue with an obstacle race, a
bandsman's race (some of the men have
bagpipes) and a parade of the pipe and
drum band. One of the cadets is carried
past in a mock 'funeral'. The sports continue
again with a long distance race, a race to
put up a bell tent, and a drill exercise by
cadets wearing the 1916 pattern P gashood on backwards, so acting as a
blindfold.

Notes
Date: this is taken from the store ledger.
catalogued SDB: 3/1983

IWM 640-02 · GB, (prod) 1918
**[RAF CADETS ARRIVE IN SAINT
LEONARDS]** (allocated)

b/w · 1 reel · 1056' (17 mins) · silent
intertitles: none

sp Royal Air Force (?)

- Disjointed film of new arrivals in Hastings
  coming to join the RAF Cadet Brigade in
  nearby St Leonards-on-Sea, 1 August
  1918.

The film opens with a group of young
officer cadets filing into their temporary
billets in the Sussex Hotel in Hastings. A
large contingent of cadets has arrived at
Hastings main railway station and is forming
up outside the station under the supervision
of RAF officers. These cadets are all
transfers from other services and branches,
including a cavalryman with his blanket roll
and a number of naval officers who form up
by themselves. They are marched off. In a
back garden an RAF sergeant gives a drill
demonstration with a rifle. Back at the
station the ground crew are loading surplus
kitbags into a 3-ton truck. The new arrivals
parade at the tented camp at St Leonards-
on-Sea. The film then returns to the station,
possibly for the next arrivals, who are drilled
as they march. This contingent is taken to a
building marked as the Cadet Distribution
Depot. Back to the sergeant's drill
demonstration, this time showing how to
deliver a message to an officer with the RAF
salute (this is shown in slow motion, then at
normal speed). More recruits, in civilian
clothes, are led through the streets of
Hastings to the Distribution Depot. Back at
the tented camp the cadets are starting to
settle down.

Notes
Date: this is taken from the store ledger.
catalogued SDB: 3/1983

IWM 640-03 · GB, (prod) 1919
[RAF SPORTS IN FRANCE 1919]
(allocated)

b/w · 1 reel · 627' (11 mins) · silent
intertitles: English

sp Royal Air Force (?)

- Highly disjointed film of a sports meeting
  held by the RAF contingent in France, 28
  April 1919.

The film jumps and pulls-back frequently, making it very hard to follow. It starts with posed groups of football teams. A group of RAF officers, including a chaplain, talk together. Portrait shots, in uniform, of the winners of the various boxing heats: Sergeant Stone who won the lightweight, Corporal Garrett who won the middleweight and heavyweight and Corporal Winfield who won the welterweight divisions. The sports continue with the RAF crowd watching a football match. The winning team poses for photographs and its members are chaired away by the cheering crowd. A rugby match with, again, a posed shot of the winners. The tug of war contest also with the winners, followed by the athletes lining up for the start of the cross-country. A 'tote' takes bets. The winner of the cross-country comes in and is cheered by his supporters, who hold up a sign "Where Are They ?". Back at the football match the crowd cheers. In an acted sequence a 'toff' in the crowd has his pocket picked by two 'roughs'.

Notes
Date: this is taken from the store ledger.
Summary: both the captions and some of the signs held up in the film refer to those involved as being part of "E.R.S.". This remains unexplained.
catalogued SDB: 3/1983

IWM 641 · GB, (prod) 1918
WRNS (ledger title)

b/w · 1 reel · 564' (9 mins) · silent
intertitles: none

sp Ministry of Information for Admiralty

■ Work by members of the Women's Royal Naval Service at a Royal Navy coastal torpedo boat base on the south coast of England, probably 1917 or 1918.

Two WRNS in overalls work out of doors under the supervision of a petty officer, one reassembling a stripped Lewis machinegun and the other cleaning a pistol. Indoors, probably the WRNS officers' mess, decorated with embroidered cushions, where a few of them sit reading or writing, all very camera-conscious. Outside a supervisor marches a group of WRNS in nursing uniform past a hut. Other WRNS in overalls work whitewashing the stones on a flower bed. A close-up of three of the women, again very camera-conscious. The two women complete assembling the Lewis

gun and take it indoors. One woman works as a switchboard operator. A group of five WRNS clean the upturned hull of a coastal torpedo boat. Two others work painting the superstructure of another motor boat.

catalogued SDB: 3/1983

IWM 642 · GB, (prod) 1918
FELIXSTOWE SPORTS 13/8/1918

b/w · 1 reel · 515' (9 mins) · silent
intertitles: none

sp Royal Air Force (?)

■ Athletics meeting for RAF and Royal Navy personnel at the seaplane base at Felixstowe, 13 August 1918.

A Royal Navy bagpipe band parades around the sports field. The end of one of the races is shown. A 'reveille race' of men getting dressed. More races take place, some for WRNS and WRAFs. A 'clown' group moves around the field. The sack race is followed by competitors changing over in the relay, another women's race, the tug of war and the obstacle race. A view over the crowd, including some officers and WRNS officers. A 'rowing eight' race. A posed group of Royal Navy and RAF men followed by the prize-giving.

Notes
Title: this is taken from the shotsheet.
Intertitles: there are some MS flashframes on the print.
[shotsheet available]
catalogued SDB: 3/1983

IWM 643 · GB, (prod) 1918
COLONEL SAMSON AND DH4

b/w · 1 reel · 217' (4 mins) · silent
intertitles: none

sp Royal Air Force (?)

■ Trials by Colonel Charles R Samson RAF of a de Havilland DH4 and an SE5 fitted with landing floats, Isle of Grain, 1918.

Colonel Samson is not clearly visible in the film. The DH4, fitted with floats and no wheels, taxis through the water behind a Felixstowe flying boat, which takes off ahead of it. The DH4 then throttles back. The SE5, also fitted with floats instead of wheels, comes in to land, taxis up to the shelving beach and is secured by the ground crew. The DH4 shows how it taxis through the water, and finally it comes in to land.

Notes
Title: this is taken from the shotsheet.
[A J Jackson, *De Havilland Aircraft Since 1909*, Putnam (1962): 56]
[shotsheet available]
catalogued SDB: 3/1983

IWM 644 · GB, (?) 1918
SEAPLANES

b/w · 1 reel · 1040' (17 mins) · silent
intertitles: English

sp Royal Air Force for Admiralty

I. Seaworthiness trials of Short and Fairey seaplanes, probably Isle of Grain, 1918. A Short 184 some distance away from the camera comes in to land, then takes off. A PV5 seaplane taxis through the harbour, increasing speed to keep ahead of the camera boat. A Short 184 taxis around the harbour throwing up much spray, weaving between the small boats. A King Edward Class battleship and a Gem Class light cruiser are in the background. The seaplane finally takes off. The Short 184 number N1081 on trestles on land showing that it is fitted with standard floats, followed by the same machine taxiing through the water. The view from the rear cockpit of the seaplane over the tail as it taxis. The Fairey N9 seaplane (a prototype version of the Fairey FIII) is also shown taxiing, then stationary and moving off, then coming in to land.
II. The launch of Felixstowe flying boats at Felixstowe naval base, 12 November 1918. The Felixstowe F2A flying boat N4484 is wheeled out of its hangar by the ground crew, which has to turn the aircraft completely sideways. A second flying boat, the Felixstowe F3 number N4308 is taken down the ramp towards the sea. Another of the flying boats, probably a Felixstowe F2 but with no markings, is also taken down the ramp. The third flying boat comes back to land after a patrol. The camera boat circles around it, the camera going out-of-focus as it does so. The Felixstowe taxis and takes off, then comes back in to land again.

Notes
Summary: see also **IWM 614**.

[H A Taylor, *Fairey Aircraft Since 1915*, Putnam (1974): 67-70]
[shotsheet available]
catalogued SDB: 3/1983

IWM 645 · GB, (prod) 1921
LAUNCH OF HM AIRSHIPS R36 AND R38

b/w · 1 reel · 710' (12 mins) · silent
intertitles: none

sp Royal Air Force (?)

I. The first trial flight of the airship R36 at Inchinnan, 1 April 1921. The R36 is nose-forward in its shed. Workers turn a large capstan to wind back the doors of the shed and the airship is towed out. It is clearly marked as R36 and as G-FAAF. It takes off from its launching field, and overflies both the camera and its own shed, quite quickly. It comes in to land, stops all engines and sinks down. After being secured it is taken back to its shed by its ground crew, which includes a number of women workers.
II. The first trial flight of the airship R38 (also known by its American designation ZR2) at Cardington, from 9pm 23 June to 6am 24 June 1921. A portrait shot of Mr C Campbell, the R38's designer, in front of the airship in its shed. Air Commodore Edward C Maitland, the RAF airship base commander, talks with Air Commodore Henry Brooke-Popham, the Director of Research at the Air Ministry. They are joined by other officers, including Flight Lieutenant A H Wann, the airship's pilot. The R38, which is in US Navy markings, is to be sold to the Americans and its designated pilot, Commodore Lewis H Maxfield USN, is also present (in civilian clothes). The airship is led out and the crew get on board. The camera is right underneath it for the take-off into the dusk sky, against which the bulk of the rising airship is silhouetted. The airship comes back in to land at 6am. It manoeuvres, cuts its engines and sinks towards the waiting ground crew. It is towed back into its hangar.

Notes
Title: this is taken from the shotsheet.
Summary: the R38 crashed on a test flight shortly after this film was made, and it seems unlikely that the film was ever released in this form.
[Guy Hartcup, *The Achievement of the Airship*, David and Charles (1974): 135-152]
[shotsheet available]
catalogued SDB: 3/1983

IWM 646 · GB, 11/1918
the ARRIVAL OF THE GERMAN SUBMARINES OFF HARWICH

b/w · 1 reel · 1024' (17 mins) · silent
intertitles: English

sp Royal Air Force pr Royal Air Force – London Photo Centre

■ Surrender of U-boats and other ships of the German fleet at the end of the war.

I. Aerial medium shot of HMS *Satyr* (F.59) under way. Two surrendered U-boats pass beneath camera-airship, followed by Scott Class Leader, UC.III and U.160 Class (?) submarines. Medium shot, HMS *Melampus* (H.75) with Motor Launch alongside – R Class destroyer passes in background. Camera drifts right to pick up a line of U-boats passing right to left, diagonally down the screen – U.81 Class, U.93 Class, U.160 Class, and others.
II. "German Ships on their way to surrender to Great Britain, Nov. 21st., 1918. Photographed from *H.M.S. Castor*". Long shot of line of German light cruisers – SS airship overhead. Medium-long shot off port bow of HMS *Talisman*. Long shot of Bremse Class cruiser (?), and pan right to show German ships in line ahead. Medium-long shot as Later Marksman Class destroyer leads in German destroyers. Pan over lines of surrendered vessels. Medium shot, HMS *Seymour* (D.09). Medium shot of Dromedary Class paddle tug. Various views of anchored German destroyers, including G.101, S.131, V.67, V.125, G.85, S.31 and B.109 Class vessels. British Thornycroft torpedo boat also appears in this sequence. Tracking close-up past S.53 Class destroyer – crew on deck, German naval ensign at peak of mainmast. Medium shot of V.67 Class destroyer. Panning long shot over anchorage at sunset.
III. "Photographed from Airship N.S.7". Aerial views of surrendering German capital ships: Koenig Class battleships, British flagship HMS *Queen Elizabeth*, SMS *Baden*, *Kaiser*, *Kaiserin* (?) and *Friedrich der Grosse*, German battle-cruisers SMS *Von der Tann*, *Derfflinger*, *Hindenburg* and *Seydlitz*, light cruisers SMS *Bremse*, *Brummer*, *Frankfurt*, *Emden* (II), *Koeln* (II) and *Dresden* (II).

catalogued NAP: 6/1978

IWM 647 · GB, (?) 1918
AIRSHIPS GOING ON PATROL

b/w · 2 reels · 1417' (24 mins) · silent
intertitles: English

sp Royal Air Force (?)

■ Operation of a Royal Navy airship base with its RAF airships, possibly Toller station near Bridport, 1918.

(Reel 1) The crew of airship SSZ28 prepares for a flight. As they wait, seated in the open gondola, they are handed a basket of carrier pigeons, the pilot is given his charts and orders, and an armourer fits two 16-pound bombs, one on either side of the gondola. The wireless operator performs a final test of his equipment, and a reconnaissance camera is taken on board. The machine is checked for buoyancy, the engine is started, and the airship takes off. The camera shows the view down from the gondola (with much camera shake) over the countryside and base. Meanwhile back at the base itself the cookhouse call is sounded. The RAF men, including the sergeant-major, run to the cookhouse. Women of the WRNS drill on the parade ground. Men practise PT on the same parade ground. A detailed view of the carrier pigeons in their loft. They are released each day for exercise and return later. The petty officer "P.O. Pigeons" feeds the pigeons, which are finger-tame. The airship returns from patrol, drops a line and is hauled in, being taken to a camouflaged shed. The ceremony of lowering the flag is performed at dusk. *(Reel 2)* At the base workshop men strip down an airship's engine, and women work doping fabric. Outdoors, armourers check over the bombs. Cylinders of hydrogen gas are taken from a lorry and stacked. A lorry-load of the cylinders is taken over to a hydrogen storage tank which they are used to fill. The gas is compressed by a generator and the sludge pumped out and carted off. A sentry demonstrates the result of signalling a fire at the gas store – everyone, regardless of rank, runs to help. The same event viewed from the air. Inside the sickbay a man is given first aid. A lorry takes the deflated envelope of an SS type airship to a hangar, where the ground crew unload it. The partially-inflated envelope is protected by a rigging net. Finally, the fully-inflated airship is led out of its shed.

Notes
Title: this is taken from the shotsheet.
[shotsheet available]
catalogued SDB: 3/1983

IWM 648 · GB, (?) 1918
TAILS UP FRANCE
the LIFE OF AN RAF OFFICER IN FRANCE
(alternative)

b/w · 4 reels · 3107' (51 mins) · silent
intertitles: English

sp Royal Air Force (?)

- RAF film of how novice pilots complete
  their combat training in France and go on
  to fly operational patrols, summer 1918.

(Reel 1) The film stresses that it shows
normal RAF life and has not deliberately
selected its scenes. It begins with a training
camp for pilots in France. New pilots arrive
and are brought from the station by 3-ton
lorry with their kit. After a medical check-up
and induction they queue to be issued with
Lewis and Vickers machineguns for their
combat training, and practise pistol
shooting. They train in a flight-simulator on
rails, enabling them to shoot at deflection
targets. They learn on a dummy aircraft
how to regulate interrupter gear. Finally, on
19 August they are given their postings.
(None of the postings matches the
squadrons shown.) As they wait to leave
they are sold newspapers. At Bertangles
aerodrome between May and July the men
relax before a patrol. The Wing adjutant
phones orders to the commander of 84
Squadron, Major W S Douglas, and the
flight commanders assemble the squadron.
The squadron SE5a fighters stand wing-to-
wing ready for take-off. (Reel 2) The base
fitters strip machineguns and load the
ammunition into a Sopwith 2F1 Camel of
209 Squadron. The Camels are bombed up.
A flight of Sopwith 5F1 Dolphins of 23
Squadron starts out on patrol. 84 Squadron
also takes off with the camera following the
SE5as into the air (probably in a Bristol F2B
Fighter of 48 Squadron) as they stunt fly
around it. (Reel 3) The SE5as return to
base. Two captured German aircraft, both
intact, are displayed for the camera at the
base: a DFW Aviatik CV and a Fokker DVII.
RAF ground crew also inspect the burnt-out
remains of another DVII and a Gotha GV
with two "unexploded bombs" (fake) nearby.
The crew of a Bristol Fighter of 48
Squadron report for debriefing by the base
Intelligence officer. Fitters repair damage to
the Dolphins, some hit by anti-aircraft fire
which has torn their fabric. A wounded pilot
is taken away by ambulance. Two training
exercises in air cooperation. One has
troops advancing through a smokescreen
(no aircraft visible). The other has Cavalry
charging against sacking targets with

Camels flying overhead to "clear up
machinegun nests" for the advance. This is
presented as a genuine attack with German
prisoners being brought in. "Are they
downhearted? Ask them !" They are
counted into a holding cage and sent on by
rail. The aircraft return to Bertangles against
the dusk sky. (Reel 4) The airmen relax by
playing baseball and "bumble-puppy" (a ball
game). A bull-terrier squadron mascot.
Airmen and fitters of 209 Squadron pose
beside their Camels. An SE5a engine is
tested on a rig. A Camel has its engine
tested. "The brigadier" (?) drives off. A
chaplain conducts an open-air service. Men
socialise and play snooker in the Church
Army tent. The barber's tent has a sign
"Closed Sunday I Don't Think. Barber Abe
Pilfold Hebrew". Two officers go off on
leave, "where this sort of thing" (an RAF
wedding) "has been known to happen". A
final shot of the RAF flag.

Notes
Title: this is taken from the shotsheet. The
alternative title is part of the first intertitle.
Production: the tone of the film makes it
more likely to have been an RAF production
for internal use than an official film.
Remarks: light and jokey, occasionally
heavy-handed. The complete film holds up
well and interest seldom flags despite the
lack of 'action' shots. The simulated
'combat' would not fool the most uncritical
audience, but the training exercise itself is
very interesting.
[shotsheet available]
catalogued SDB: 3/1983

IWM 649 · GB, (prod) 1919
[RAF CRANE LAUNCH OF SEAPLANE]
(allocated)

b/w · 1 reel · 667' (11 mins) · silent
intertitles: none

sp Royal Air Force (?)

- Short 184 seaplane being placed into the
  water by a steam crane and flying on
  patrol, probably at RAF Calshot, 29
  November 1919.

The first of the Shorts is taken out of its
hangar and wheeled towards the water. Its
wings are swung forward to the flight
position. The crane derrick lifts the seaplane
up. It has bombs fitted between its floats. A
second Short is prepared for flight in a
similar way. A two-man crew prepare to
take out another Short. Once they are on

board the observer is handed a camera, a map case and two carrier pigeon boxes (?). The crane lifts the seaplane (which has its engine running) out from a quay over the water, and lowers it to the surface. The plane taxis away, takes off and overflies the base. As it returns to the quay it is hooked up to the crane and taken out of the water. The plane is shown on a second take-off, overflight and landing.

Notes
Date: the film has the words "Lieut Ashby 29/11/19" written at its start. Lieutenant Ashby may have been the cameraman.
[shotsheet available]
catalogued SDB: 3/1983

IWM 650 · France, 1915-17
WAR IN THE AIR : unique pictures by our own photographer with the Russian Navy

b/w · 1 reel · 353' (6 mins) · silent
intertitles: English

pr Pathé Frères

- Flight by a Russian seaplane out from Batum to a rendezvous with a Russian destroyer on the Black Sea, 1915-17.

The aircraft is taken out from its shed at Batum seaplane base. It appears to be a modified Farman M Type seaplane. The crew get in and the seaplane takes off from the water's edge. The view down from the aircraft shows the town and base of Batum, and the wharves with cargo ships riding at anchor. The plane flies out to rendezvous with a Bistri Class destroyer at sea, lands, and is towed back to Batum by the ship. A second seaplane, used as the camera plane, can also be seen in tow.

Notes
Summary: the English is slightly quaint, and misleading. The film refers to the ship as "a torpedo boat" rather than a torpedo boat destroyer, and to a "recognizance of the Turkish coast".
[shotsheet available]
catalogued SDB: 4/1983

IWM 651a · GB, 30/1/1918
WAR OFFICE OFFICIAL TOPICAL BUDGET 336-1

b/w · 1 reel · 108' (2 mins) · silent
intertitles: English

sp War Office Cinema Committee *pr* Topical Film Company

I. Interrogation of a Turkish spy by British troops in Mesopotamia, September 1917. 'A SPY OF THE DESERT.' The British patrol lies in a slit trench beside its Rolls-Royce Silver Ghost armoured car. The captured spy sits on top of the car's bonnet and is questioned by an Arab interpreter (?).
II. A British tented camp, with a horse column arriving, set against the background of the Italian Alps, December 1917.

Notes
Summary: see **IWM 9** for the spy item. Note that a French-language version of this item is **IWM 684e**. It is not clear exactly who is "the spy" – the captions so describe the Arab, but do not explain why the British should use a Turkish soldier to interrogate him; the synopsis offers an alternative reading.
[shotsheet available]
catalogued SDB: 5/1983

IWM 651b · GB, 2/2/1918
WAR OFFICE OFFICIAL TOPICAL BUDGET 336-2

b/w · 1 reel · 217' (4 mins) · silent
intertitles: English

sp War Office Cinema Committee *pr* Topical Film Company

I. 'THE LADY PLOUGHMAN.' A Women's Land Army march through the centre of Winchester and past the watching mayor, January 1918.
II. 'THROUGH THE WILDERNESS.' Arab workers in Palestine load horse fodder into cars and motor cars for a British supply column, late 1917.
III. 'WATER ON WHEELS.' Ford motor cars in convoy carry water through the desert in Palestine, late 1917.
IV. 'TOMMY'S TURKEY TROT.' British soldiers chase and catch turkeys for Christmas at a French farm while the farmer's wife watches, December 1917.

Notes
Summary: see **IWM 474** for the Winchester item. Note that a French-language version of items II and IV only from this issue is **IWM 684d**.
[shotsheet available]
catalogued SDB: 5/1983

IWM 651c · GB, 6/2/1918
WAR OFFICE OFFICIAL TOPICAL
BUDGET 337-1 (Spanish version)

b/w · 1 reel · 131' (3 mins) · silent
intertitles: Spanish

sp War Office Cinema Committee pr Topical
Film Company

■ Further copy of the newsreel held as
IWM 662a.

[shotsheet available]
catalogued SDB: 5/1983

IWM 652a · GB, 26/9/1918
PICTORIAL NEWS (OFFICIAL) 370-1
(French version)

b/w · 1 reel · 299' (5 mins) · silent
intertitles: French

sp Ministry of Information pr Topical Film
Company

I. "Win The War Day" parade in central
Birmingham, 21 September 1918. The
parade waits to move off from Chamberlain
Square. It includes a US Army colour party
with one man dressed as 'Uncle Sam'. A
banner proclaiming "Win The War Day" is
draped over the Town Hall. The parade as it
starts includes sailors, a single boy scout, a
Mk V Male tank, an Army contingent, a
French Army contingent, and four "Old
Contemptibles" from the BEF of 1914.
These are followed by more sailors and by
munitions workers of the area, including
women. Tractors carry the guns made in
the area (an Australian soldier watching
blocks the camera for a moment), a 9.2-
inch howitzer is pulled by a traction engine
and a 6-inch 26cwt howitzer of Coventry
Ordnance Ltd is carried by a Maudslay
lorry.
II. British forces in Palestine, March-May
1918. The captions suggest that the film
shows the destruction of the Turkish forces
in September. The first scene is of British
soldiers detraining from cattle trucks at Lod
station on 5 May. 2nd Battalion, the London
Scottish enters Es Salt in April. Another
British battalion on its way to Es Salt. British
troops escort Turkish prisoners of war out
of Es Salt. A portrait shot of General Sir
Edmund Allenby, Commander-in-Chief of
the Egyptian Expeditionary Force.
III. A band of the Italian Carabinieri visiting
London, September 1918. A British Army
band leads the Italians, who are not playing

their instruments, through the streets
crowded with cheering civilians.

Notes
Production: the material held conforms to
the 'foreign edition' – see **Notes** to issue
369-1.
Summary: see also **IWM 26, IWM 30** for the
Palestine material and **IWM 342** for the
Carabinieri band.
catalogued SDB: 6/1983

IWM 652b · GB, 30/9/1918
PICTORIAL NEWS (OFFICIAL) 370-2
(French version)

b/w · 1 reel · 293' (5 mins) · silent
intertitles: French

sp Ministry of Information pr Topical Film
Company

I. British soldiers receive the surrender of
Turkish troops, Mesopotamia, probably May
1918. The handful of Turks come in from
the desert and walk past a British 4.5-inch
howitzer. Camels and wagons carry other
prisoners across a river. A large group of
the prisoners is collected together.
II. An Italian Carabinieri band playing in
central London, September 1918. Nurses
and convalescent soldiers leave Charing
Cross Hospital and drive down the Strand
to hear the Italians play. The bandsmen
themselves arrive by horse-drawn
charabanc wearing their full dress uniforms,
and mix with British bandsmen, also in full
dress. The Italians play their instruments
outside the gates of Buckingham Palace.
III. Canadian military sports in England,
September 1918. The sports start with a
water-joust in wheelbarrows. There are
three successful attempts at the joust and
one almost perfect success. A race in which
ladies are carried in wheelbarrows. A
second wheelbarrow race in which the
soldiers pushing are blindfolded, followed
by wrestling on horseback.
IV. German damage to Béthune, September
1918. Long distance views of smoke rising
over houses, described as Béthune, set on
fire by the Germans, "these burning houses
are proof of their love of destruction". Shells
start to fall between the houses and isolated
cottages.

Notes
Intertitles: there is only one caption, for the
last item of the issue.
Production: the material held conforms to
the 'foreign edition' – see **Notes** to issue

369-1.
Summary: compare the item on Béthune
with **IWM 295**. See also **IWM 68** for
Mesopotamia and **IWM 342** for the
Carabinieri band. Note that an English-
language variant or continuation of item IV
is **IWM 461b**.
catalogued SDB: 6/1983

IWM 653a · GB, 8/7/1918
**PICTORIAL NEWS (OFFICIAL) 358-2
(French version)**

b/w · 1 reel · 363' (6 mins) · silent
intertitles: French

sp Ministry of Information pr Topical Film
Company

I. King George V and Queen Mary celebrate
their silver wedding in London, July 1918.
The open carriage with the King and Queen
leaves the Mansion House with a military
escort. The King is in Army uniform. The
coach drives to the steps of St Paul's
Cathedral where an honour guard presents
arms. They leave the carriage and go up
the steps, which are all that can be seen of
the cathedral. After the ceremony they leave
by the same coach.
II. Recruits for the Royal Navy in Ireland,
June 1918. The recruits, in civilian clothes,
are seated posed for the camera beside
sailors who carry inspirational placards.
These have slogans such as "The Germans
are sinking Irish ships and murdering
Irishmen – join us and avenge these crimes"
and "We are going to tackle Fritz and we
will let him see what Irishmen can do".
III. The loading and firing of a British 12-
inch naval railway gun on the Western
Front, May 1918. The men remove the
camouflage from the gun and shells. The
gun, named as "Bunty" on its side, is
loaded and fired. The men pose alongside
the gun.
IV. King George V presents citations at
Buckingham Palace, June 1918. The
ceremony takes place in the rear courtyard
of the palace. Nurses lead the line of
people to be commended, followed by
civilians and men of various services.
V. March of the various women's services
past George V in London, 29 June 1918.
The WAAC march past King George and
Queen Mary, followed by the Forestry
branch of the Women's Land Army. The
procession passes through Parliament
Square. In the rear courtyard of
Buckingham Palace the King and Queen
present decorations to members of the

women's services.

Notes
Date: the King's silver wedding fell on 8
July. This celebration presumably took
place a few days before this, or the release
date is incorrect.
Intertitles: note that the first item has no
titles.
Summary: see **IWM 226** for the railway gun
material.
Remarks: this issue of the newsreel is
incomplete and may be jumbled, but to
have three items out of five featuring the
King seems excessive.
[shotsheet available]
catalogued SDB: 5/1983

IWM 653b · GB, 4/7/1918
**PICTORIAL NEWS (OFFICIAL) 358-1
(French version)**

b/w · 1 reel · 198' (4 mins) · silent
intertitles: French

sp Ministry of Information pr Topical Film
Company

I. British children decorate graves at a
Canadian cemetery in England, June 1918.
II. A pacifist demonstration on Tower Hill,
London, June 1918. There is a large crowd
with a number of policemen, milling about
and uncertain. The captions say they are
ignoring pacifist speeches, but this is not
obvious.
III. A portrait shot of the late Lord Rhondda,
recent Food Controller, outside the Palace
of Westminster, June 1918.
IV. US Independence Day in London, 4 July
1918. US Navy sailors enter one horse-
drawn charabanc in London, and soldiers
enter another. King George V is shown
coming into Chelsea Football Stadium at
Stamford Bridge, accompanied by Admiral
Sims, and shakes hands with the US troops
inside. The event is recorded by numerous
still photographers and two cine
cameramen, one of whom appears to be a
Signal Corps member. The stands are
crowded as the Americans start a baseball
game.

[shotsheet available]
catalogued SDB: 5/1983

IWM 654a · GB, 8/5/1918
PICTORIAL NEWS (OFFICIAL) 350-1

b/w · 1 reel · 199' (4 mins) · silent
intertitles: English

sp Ministry of Information pr Topical Film
Company

I. A children's May Day parade through
Kent, 1 May 1918. 'THE WARRIOR'S MAY
QUEEN. Pretty incident in Kent Festival.'
The children's banners show that they come
from London or its suburbs. The procession
passes two cars full of soldiers and one
sergeant gets out and jokingly kisses the
May Queen. The May Queen is later
ceremonially crowned.
II. The break-up of a pacifist meeting in
Finsbury Park, London, May 1918.
'PACIFIST FIASCO IN LONDON.' It is raining
in the park. People in a large crowd wave at
the camera. Mounted police move through
the crowd and one man can be seen to be
led away in handcuffs.
III. 'COME, GIRLS, SIGN ON.' A Land Girl
calls for volunteers in the middle of London,
helping one lady to sign on, May 1918.
IV. 'TOMMY'S CHARACTERISTIC
HUMANITY.' British soldiers help refugees,
including old ladies, onto a train for
evacuation near Béthune, Western Front,
10-14 April 1918.

Notes
Intertitles: these are all flashframes.
Summary: See also **IWM 186** for the
refugee item. Note that a French-language
version of item IV is **IWM 673b** and a
Spanish-language version of the whole
issue is **IWM 700b**.
[shotsheet available]
catalogued SDB: 5/1983

IWM 654b · GB, 13/5/1918
PICTORIAL NEWS (OFFICIAL) 350-2

b/w · 1 reel · 267' (5 mins) · silent
intertitles: English

sp Ministry of Information pr Topical Film
Company

I. The city and cathedral at Amiens, after
the German failure to capture the city, 5-7
April 1918. 'AMIENS. A LANDMARK OF
GERMAN FAILURES.' A pan over the city
from across the river, followed by close-ups
of the cathedral showing shell damage.
According to the caption, the cathedral was
"spitefully shelled" by the Germans after
their "defeat".
II. 'NOBODY'S DOGS.' Dogs at Battersea
Dogs' Home, London, being exercised and

looked after, May 1918.
III. Lord Provost Stewart and Lord Newlands
presenting medals to civilians in Glasgow,
May 1918. 'HONOURS FOR SCOTTISH
CIVILIANS.' The presentation takes place in
the rain in front of a military parade. Both
men, in Army uniform, decorate men and
women in civilian clothes.
IV. King George V and Sir Edward Kemp,
Canadian High Commissioner, tour the
Canadian training grounds at Bramshot and
Witley, near Aldershot, May 1918.
'STRENUOUS CANADIAN FIGHTERS.' The
High Commissioner is in civilian clothes, the
King in Army uniform. They inspect the
guard of the training division, and watch a
boxing display, a display of trench digging
and wiring, and a bayonet assault course.
As the men advance over the assault
course some of them fall 'dead' to add
realism to the exercise. The men march
past and the King takes the salute. The
King and High Commissioner leave to the
cheers of the men.

Notes
Intertitles: these are all flashframes.
Summary: see **IWM 183** for the Amiens
item. Note that a French-language version
of item I is **IWM 673a** and a Spanish-
language version of the complete issue is
IWM 700c.
[shotsheet available]
catalogued SDB: 5/1983

IWM 655a · GB, 1918
LEST WE FORGET

b/w · 1 reel · 112' (2 mins) · silent
intertitles: English

sp Ministry of Information

■ Inflammatory propaganda film
   commemorating the sinking of RMS
   Lusitania by the Germans on 7 May 1915.

The film shows sailors carrying stretchers
with survivors from the sinking through the
streets of an Irish village. The formal funeral
of those who drowned in the sinking, also
in Ireland. A close-up of the 'Lusitania
medal' produced in Germany. The film
emphasises that the ship was unarmed and
sunk without warning.

Notes
Remarks: an interesting demonstration (if
the estimated date is correct) of the long life
of the *Lusitania* sinking and the medallion
sequel to it as propaganda stories.

[Philip Dutton, "'Geschäft über Alles': notes on some medallions inspired by the sinking of the *Lusitania*", *Imperial War Museum Review*, 1 (1986)]
catalogued SDB: 5/1983

camera. A man holds his (apparently unharmed) baby daughter up for the camera also.

catalogued SDB: 5/1983

IWM 655b · GB, 13/10/1917
WAR OFFICE OFFICIAL TOPICAL BUDGET 320-2

b/w · 1 reel · 56' (1 min) · silent
intertitles: English

sp War Office Cinema Committee *pr* Topical Film Company

■ 'SAVING THE NATION'S PETROL' – a single story from the newsreel held as **NTB 320-02**.

cataloqued SDB: 5/1983

IWM 655c · GB, 9/9/1916
TOPICAL BUDGET 263-2 [1]

b/w · 1 reel · 114' (2 mins) · silent
intertitles: English

pr Topical Film Company

■ 'ZEPPELIN CREW'S BURIAL' – a single story from the newsreel held in more complete form as **NTB 263-02**.

Notes
Summary: note that another fragment of this newsreel is held as **IWM 1180b**.
cataloqued SDB: 5/1983

IWM 655d · GB, 12/5/1915
TOPICAL BUDGET 194-1

b/w · 1 reel · 102' (2 mins) · silent
intertitles: English

pr Topical Film Company

■ Damage done to Southend and Westcliff by the Zeppelin raids of March and April 1915.

'SOUTHEND AIR RAID.' A hotel, the "Cromwell Board Residence", has been hit by a bomb. Firemen work to put out the various fires. The burnt-out firebombs are displayed in a heap by a policeman. A charred dead dog is held up for the

---

IWM 656a · GB, 31/10/1918
PICTORIAL NEWS (OFFICIAL) 375-1

b/w · 1 reel · 277' (5 mins) · silent
intertitles: English

sp Ministry of Information *pr* Topical Film Company

I. British residents of Lille leaving a church after the liberation of the city. They pass a German wooden dummy of a Whippet tank, Western Front, October 1918.
II. The visit of Prince Yorihito of Higashi-Fushimi to Britain, 28 October 1918. The Prince is met at Dover harbour by Prince Arthur of Connaught. The two men walk down the gangplank of Prince Yorihito's ship together and salute the flags of their nations. Next is a brief, indistinct scene of Prince Yorihito's drive through London in an open carriage with King George V.
III. The Lord Mayor of London dedicates a war shrine "In Memory of the Fallen", London, October 1918.
IV. The last known (poor quality) film of Grand Duke Nicholas, the former Russian Commander-in-Chief, seen reviewing troops in Russia, autumn 1918.
V. British soldiers clowning in the ruins of Cambrai after its liberation, October 1918. Two of the soldiers, one in a top hat and the other a pickelhaube, stare at a German sign. The two are pushed by a third through a square cleared of rubble in a wrecked German car without an engine.

Notes
Intertitles: these are all flashframes.
Production: the material held conforms to the 'foreign edition' – see **Notes** to issue 369-1.
[shotsheet available]
cataloqued SDB: 5/1983

IWM 656b · GB, 1918
the IMMORTAL STORY OF ZEEBRUGGE

b/w · 1 reel · 176' (3 mins) · silent
intertitles: English

sp Ministry of Information

I. A retrospective on the Zeebrugge raid of 22-23 April 1918, made at the end of the First World War. The film starts with a scene meant to be of the mole at Zeebrugge in 1914 (in fact showing a British Caledon Class cruiser in 1917 or 1918 at another location). The mole after the British occupation of Zeebrugge, showing the abandoned German naval guns and the mail boat SS *Brussels* sunk in the channel. More views of the area. The block-ships HMS *Iphigenia* and HMS *Intrepid* are still visible in mid-channel, as is HMS *Thetis*. Portrait shots of officers and men who won the Victoria Cross in the raid, after receiving their decorations at Buckingham Palace: Captain Alfred Carpenter, Lieutenant Richard Sandford, Lieutenant-Commander Percy Dean, Major E Bamford of the Royal Marines, and Sergeant Norman Finch, also of the Royal Marines.
II. A brief scene of wounded British and Belgian soldiers together at a dressing station, Western Front, late 1918.

Notes
Title: this and the intertitles are all flashframes.
Summary: see also **IWM 358**.
[shotsheet available]
catalogued SDB: 5/1983

IWM 657a · GB, 5/8/1918
PICTORIAL NEWS (OFFICIAL) 362-2 (French version)

b/w · 1 reel · 205' (4 mins) · silent
intertitles: French

sp Ministry of Information *pr* Topical Film Company

I. Irish fishermen rescued after a U-boat attack, July 1918. The captions state that the men were attacked and set adrift by a U-boat. A pan over a posed group of the men, now back on shore in a small harbour. Some of them board the small fishing boat N232, riding beside the quay. One of them looks very young and scared.
II. Soda-water production for British troops in Mesopotamia, near Ramadi, September 1917. An 18-pounder fires in the desert, throwing up much dust. The captions explain that the soda-water is for the gunners. The machine is portable and hand-cranked.
III. Princess Marie Louise opening an Italian Gift House in Albemarle Street, London, 31 July 1918. The house is intended as a place to sell items for Italian charities until Italian

Red Cross Day on 25 September, and is heavily decorated with banners and bunting. The Princess arrives by car and is presented with a bouquet. She is seen leaving after the opening.
IV. King George V presents Victoria Crosses to men who took part in the Zeebrugge raid, at Buckingham Palace, 31 July 1918. The ceremony takes place in the rear courtyard of the palace. The King talks to Able Seaman Albert Mackenzie (back to camera), who is walking on crutches, and presents him with his VC. Next to receive his VC is Sergeant Norman Finch of the Royal Marines. Captain A F B Carpenter is shown in portrait shot with his VC.

Notes
Summary: note that a German-language version of this issue is **IWM 683b**. See also **IWM 61** reel 1 for the soda-water item. McKernan places item I in 362-1.
[*The Times*, 1 August 1918: 9B]
[*The Times*, 3 August 1918: 9D]
[shotsheet available]
catalogued SDB: 6/1983

IWM 657b · GB, 1/8/1918
PICTORIAL NEWS (OFFICIAL) 362-1 (French version)

b/w · 1 reel · 283' (5 mins) · silent
intertitles: French

sp Ministry of Information *pr* Topical Film Company

■ French-language version of a newsreel devoted to a review of the British Empire's war effort, 1914-18.

The film starts with a declaration that the war was forced upon Britain by "Germany's sinister designs". It shows John French reviewing troops (possibly as Viceroy in Ireland in 1918, but intended as 1914) and British soldiers disembarking in France for the first time. Lord Kitchener visits New Army soldiers in France in February 1916. Australians of 2nd Division in bush hats march past. Gurkhas of 7th (Meerut) Division, also on the march in the pouring rain, and Lloyd George addressing a Canadian division from a car, all illustrate the increasing role of the Empire in the war. (Note the reporters recording the speech.) Highlanders led by a pipe band march through an English village, contrasted with an apparently unending marching column of 1918 veterans in their shrapnel helmets, typical of the current British Army.

"Meanwhile and all the while" there are ships at sea, W Class destroyers and the monitor HMS *Erebus* in the English Channel.

Notes
Summary: note that a German-language version of this issue is **IWM 683a** and a shorter and somewhat different English version is **IWM 1128a**. See also **IWM 202-2**, **IWM 213** and **IWM 553**.
[shotsheet available]
catalogued SDB: 6/1983

IWM 658a · GB, 4/1918
the NEW CRUSADERS (French version)

b/w · 1 reel · 492' (9 mins) · silent
intertitles: French

sp Ministry of Information *pr* Topical Film Company *prod* Jury, William F *cam* Jeapes, Harold (and Hurley, Frank ?)

■ Version with French-language intertitles of part of **IWM 17** *The New Crusaders*.

Men of 1/8th Battalion, the Hampshire Regiment, 54th (East Anglia) Division, on Samson Ridge, resting and eating. Some of their officers have a gramophone in a sandbag shelter. Men of 1/4th Battalion, the Norfolk Regiment, in the front trenches preparing for the Second Battle of Gaza (?) on 19 April 1917, followed by a panorama of Gaza. A Royal Engineer officer directs the building of a railway line by British troops and members of the Egyptian Labour Corps. The engine is visible as they lay the track. Soldiers clear away rubble from a damaged well, with the winding gear broken (note the shadow of the cameraman). Motor transport moves down the main street of "Bir Es Sheba" (Beersheba) after its capture in November 1917. A Holt tractor pulls a large line-laying cart, followed by a camel train coming into the town. British troops bring Turkish prisoners in from the desert. Some soldiers enter damaged houses in Beersheba. A pile of Turkish rifles after the surrender of the town. A 6-inch 30cwt howitzer is fired under scrim netting. Troops of the Australian Mounted Division march past in column of troops. In the desert are soldiers with a pile of canteens. A 13-pounder anti-aircraft gun on a lorry mount is loaded and fired.

catalogued SDB: 5/1983

IWM 658b · GB, 16/1/1918
WAR OFFICE OFFICIAL TOPICAL BUDGET 334-1 [1]

b/w · 1 reel · 53' (1 min) · silent
intertitles: English

sp War Office Cinema Committee *pr* Topical Film Company

■ 'A REAL BAD HORSE'. A single story from the newsreel held as **IWM 662b**.

catalogued SDB: 5/1983

IWM 659 · GB, 17/6/1918
PICTORIAL NEWS (OFFICIAL) 355-2 (French version)

b/w · 1 reel · 408' (7 mins) · silent
intertitles: French

sp Ministry of Information *pr* Topical Film Company

I. H S Cautley MP, opens the municipal piggeries in London. As a crowd watches, Cautley lights a fire under a bin in order to cook pigswill. He ladles out the swill and feeds it to the pigs, which eat contentedly.
II. London policemen, in civilian clothes, march as a body through the streets on their way to volunteer for the Army.
III. A commemoration service for dominion troops of Scottish origin in London. Sir Robert Borden is guest of honour at the service, which is held at St Columba's church. Various dominion troops enter the church, including a Canadian battalion in kilts and New Zealand wounded in hospital blues. Borden arrives in his carriage. The church is never seen clearly.
IV. Members of the Imperial War Cabinet arrive at 10 Downing Street. The members arrive by cars. Most of them rush through the door and inside the house before the camera can recognise them. The only ones to halt and pose for the camera are W F Massey and Sir Joseph Ward of New Zealand, and Arthur Balfour. A final view of the door of the house.
V. In a ceremony in Hyde Park, Colonel Sir E Ward decorates London special constables who have served since 1914.
VI. The burial of the dead at a Canadian hospital in France after a German air raid, May 1918. Canadian soldiers pick their way through the rubble of the hospital. The coffins of those who died are taken out for burial. The captions draw attention to the large Red Cross laid out in pebbles beside

the hospital. The coffins are draped with Union Flags. A clergyman in vestments gives the address and buglers sound the last post.

Notes
Production: according to McKernan, items I-III are from issue 355-1 while items IV-VI are from 355-2. It is not clear whether their attribution to 355-2 in this French-language version is an accurate representation of a difference between domestic and export versions or simply the result of later confusion. There is some other evidence of muddle – note the War Office Official Topical Budget logo at the end of the film.
[shotsheet available]
catalogued SDB: 5/1983

IWM 660a · GB, 20/6/1918
PICTORIAL NEWS (OFFICIAL) 356-1 (French version)

b/w · 1 reel · 199' (4 mins) · silent
intertitles: French

sp Ministry of Information *pr* Topical Film Company

I. Bristol Fighter aircraft in France being bombed up before take-off, May 1918.
II. Queen Alexandra decorates soldiers on the steps of Dollis Hill Hospital, London, June 1918.
III. Imperial and Japanese delegates to the Imperial Conference posed in a massed group outside the Palace of Westminster, London, June 1918.
IV. The arrival of W T Hughes, the Australian Prime Minister, in London, June 1918. Mr Hughes's train arrives at Paddington Station and he gets out, shaking hands with an honour guard of Australian troops. He meets and poses with Mrs Emmeline Pankhurst and her daughter Christabel.

Notes
Summary: note that a further story, identified by McKernan as belonging to this issue, is held by the Museum in a French-language version linked to two stories from issue 356-2 (**IWM 660b**).
[shotsheet available]
catalogued SDB: 5/1983

IWM 660b · GB, 24/6/1918
PICTORIAL NEWS (OFFICIAL) 356-2 (French version)

b/w · 1 reel · 103' (2 mins) · silent
intertitles: French

sp Ministry of Information *pr* Topical Film Company

■ French-language version of two stories from the issue held as **NTB 356-02**, together with an item not otherwise held.

I. The Duke of Connaught reviews US troops (on Salisbury Plain ?), June 1918. The soldiers are drawn up on parade. Connaught walks past them, talking to some of them. Of the British officers (presumably training staff) escorting him round, one has lost an arm and another walks on crutches. The US Contingent marches past.
The duplicated items are 'LONDON FLOWER FAIR' and 'SURREY RED CROSS SPORTS'.

Notes
Summary: according to McKernan, item I is from issue 356-1.
[shotsheet available]
catalogued SDB: 5/1983

IWM 661a · GB, 1/5/1918
PICTORIAL NEWS (OFFICIAL) 349-1

b/w · 1 reel · 259' (5 mins) · silent
intertitles: English

sp Ministry of Information *pr* Topical Film Company

I. General Sir William Robertson inspects Australian and New Zealand officer trainees in Cambridge, April 1918. 'HONOURS FOR ANZACS AT CAMBRIDGE.' A congregation, including Robertson and the trainees, comes out of King's College Chapel after a service. Robertson watches a drill demonstration on the backs at King's by the trainees, and presents decorations to some of the New Zealand trainees.
II. 'THE HODDEN GREY.' Earl of Scarborough inspects the reserve battalion of the London Scottish on parade in London, April 1918.
III. A munitions workers' fête at St Helens, April 1918. 'WAR TIME LANCASHIRE LASSIES.' The floats of the procession pass through the watching crowds of the town centre. One float is a tableau of "Peace" and one is a "Tank Bank" for the purchase of War Savings Certificates.
IV. 'TRIBUTES TO CIVILIAN HEROES.' Lord Crewe, in Army uniform, presents OBEs to

civilians in Green Park, London, April 1918.
V. 'YPRES TODAY.' The remains of the
Cloth Hall and the water tower, with British
troops holding a scrape trench nearby,
Western Front, March-April 1918.

Notes
Summary: note that copies of items from
this issue with French titles are **IWM 673d**
and **IWM 684a**, and a Spanish-language
version is **IWM 700d**.
[shotsheet available]
catalogued SDB: 5/1983

IWM 661b · GB, 6/5/1918
PICTORIAL NEWS (OFFICIAL) 349-2

b/w · 1 reel · 137' (3 mins) · silent
intertitles: English

sp Ministry of Information *pr* Topical Film
Company

I. King George V and Queen Mary visit
wounded survivors of the Zeebrugge raid,
probably at Chatham, April 1918. 'THE
MOLE MEN.' The King, in naval uniform,
and the Queen visit the barracks to pay
tribute to the sailors and marines involved.
The Queen goes inside a hospital ward to
talk with one of the patients. The royal
party, which includes Sir Doveton Sturdee,
prepares to leave by train.
II. 'AT THE HAMPSTEAD ORTHOPAEDIC
HOSPITAL.' A charity visit organised by
George Robey, April 1918. Lord Lurgan,
John Hodge MP and Hall Caine arrive at
the hospital for Robey's "Coliseum Charity
Concert". Robey shows them around the
hospital, where they watch a patient
receiving heat lamp treatment. They talk
with a group of patients on the hospital
lawns.
III. The funeral of Baron Manfred von
Richthofen at Bertangles, Western Front, 22
April 1918. 'THE END OF RICHTHOFEN.
How the British buried their famous enemy
air warrior in France.' Two ground crew of
the RAF display the wreckage of von
Richthofen's Fokker triplane and its two
Spandau machineguns. The burial party
from six RAF squadrons places the coffin
on a lorry. At the burial place itself the coffin
is lowered into the ground and the burial
party, of 3 Squadron, Australian Flying
Corps, fires volleys over the grave.

Notes
Summary: see **IWM 187** for the Richthofen
item, and compare with **IWM 446** for the
Chatham item. Note that a French-language

version of items I and III from this issue is
IWM 673c and a Spanish-language version
is divided between **IWM 700a** and **IWM
700e**.
[shotsheet available]
catalogued SDB: 5/1983

IWM 662a · GB, 6/2/1918
**WAR OFFICE OFFICIAL TOPICAL
BUDGET 337-1**

b/w · 1 reel · 205' (4 mins) · silent
intertitles: English

sp War Office Cinema Committee *pr* Topical
Film Company

I. Half of 38th (Jewish) Battalion, Royal
Fusiliers, marches past the Lord Mayor of
London, 4 February 1918. 'TO GARRISON
JERUSALEM ?' The men of the battalion
carry a Star of David flag, and despite the
rain have drawn quite a crowd to cheer
them. They come level with the Mansion
House where the Lord Mayor waits to
receive them as they pass.
II. 'SHIP OF THE DESERT:- NEW STYLE.' A
Holt tractor under trial pulling a limber and
men through the desert of Palestine, 1917.
III. A horsed transport column passing over
a small pontoon bridge, Palestine, 1917.
IV. Gunners water and feed their horses in a
small village near Cambrai, Western Front,
November 1917.

Notes
Intertitles: these are all flashframes.
Summary: it is not certain whether item III
belongs in this issue. See **IWM 146** for the
Cambrai item. Note that a Spanish-
language version of this issue is **IWM 651c**.
[J H Patterson, *With the Judeans in the
Palestine Campaign*, Hutchinson (1922): 43-
45]
catalogued SDB: 5/1983

IWM 662b · GB, 16/1/1918
**WAR OFFICE OFFICIAL TOPICAL
BUDGET 334-1**

b/w · 1 reel · 107' (2 mins) · silent
intertitles: English

sp War Office Cinema Committee *pr* Topical
Film Company

I. A procession of the Knights of the Order
of St John of Jerusalem through the streets
of London (?), January 1918. 'KNIGHTS OF

THE HOLY CITY.' The procession includes acolytes, banners, and the knights themselves wearing cloaks marked with the cross of their order.
II. Horse-breaking in Palestine, December 1917. 'A REAL BAD HORSE. One way of bringing an incorrigible to his senses.' A difficult horse has been fitted with a complicated harness attached to a post, which makes it difficult for him to buck or roll, or do much else but go in circles. The horse-breakers appear to be British or possibly Australian troops.

Notes
Summary: note that another copy of the second story only is held as **IWM 658b**, and that a version of both stories with Spanish titles is **IWM 697c**.
[shotsheet available]
catalogued SDB: 5/1983

IWM 663a · GB, 13/2/1918
WAR OFFICE OFFICIAL TOPICAL BUDGET 338-1

b/w · 1 reel · 269' (5 mins) · silent
intertitles: English

sp War Office Cinema Committee *pr* Topical Film Company

I. State opening of Parliament by King George V, London, 7 February 1918. 'PARLIAMENT RESUMES.' The King and Queen, in an open landau, drive out of the gates of Buckingham Palace. Their escort is composed of mounted troops of all the Imperial forces: British, Indian and Australian horsemen leading, with New Zealand, South African, Newfoundland, British West Indian and Canadian horsemen as rear escort. The procession enters the gates of the Palace of Westminster.
II. The opening of a club for non-commissioned officers of the Army and Royal Navy in London, February 1918. 'THE CHEVRONS CLUB.' Sir Francis Lloyd, Sir Arthur Conan Doyle and Lord Derby are seen arriving in turn by car for the opening of the club for petty officers and non-commissioned officers. The front of the club is shown.
III. 'INDIAN TROOPS IN PALESTINE.' A long mule train with Indian Army drivers in the deserts of Palestine, late 1917.
IV. 'THE LIMBER LINE.' A long line of limbers and GS wagons making their way forward down a road in the rear areas of the Western Front, late 1917.

Notes
Summary: note that a French-language version of item I from this issue is held as **IWM 684c**, and a further copy of stories III and IV is **IWM 1061-09d**.
[*The Times*, 1 February 1918: 7C]
[*The Times*, 8 February 1918: 9F]
[shotsheet available]
catalogued SDB: 5/1983

IWM 663b · GB, 16/2/1918
WAR OFFICE OFFICIAL TOPICAL BUDGET 338-2

b/w · 1 reel · 51' (1 min) · silent
intertitles: none

sp War Office Cinema Committee *pr* Topical Film Company

- Arab camel train in the deserts of Palestine, late 1917.

Notes
Summary: note that a French-language version of this item is **IWM 684b**.
[shotsheet available]
catalogued SDB: 5/1983

IWM 663c · GB, 20/2/1918
WAR OFFICE OFFICIAL TOPICAL BUDGET 339-1 (Spanish version)

b/w · 1 reel · 310' (6 mins) · silent
intertitles: Spanish

sp War Office Cinema Committee *pr* Topical Film Company

I. A J Balfour unveils a memorial to British war dead in Hillingdon, Middlesex, February 1918. Balfour talks with the local vicar, then the two go with a procession to the church graveyard. The monument has doors in the form of a triptych which Balfour opens.
II. Queen Mary inspects a VAD detachment in the courtyard of Wellington Barracks, February 1918. The Queen arrives with Princess Mary by car at the barracks. The VAD ladies are drawn up with their ambulances on the courtyard with the building visible in the fog behind them. The Queen with the Princess inspects the parade.
III. A football match between women workers at Southend, February 1918. The match, which takes place in a local park, is between the women munitions workers of Kynocks and of Vickers-Maxim. The teams

toss up to start and the mayor of Southend kicks off. As the game progresses other newsreel cameramen can be seen at work on the far side of the pitch.

IV. British and Indian troops supervising camels in Palestine, late 1917. The troops water the camels at a drinking trough. One of the British soldiers pets his own camel, playing with it and putting his arm in its mouth as a gesture of trust and affection.

V. Troops in a large overturned water tower at Riencourt near Bapaume, Western Front, 5 January 1918. The men, gunners of 51st (Highland) Division, enter by ladder the temporary shelter they have constructed from the water tower.

Notes
Summary: see also **IWM 163** for the water tower episode.
[shotsheet available]
catalogued SDB: 5/1983

IWM 664a · GB, 14/11/1918
PICTORIAL NEWS (OFFICIAL) 377-1

b/w · 1 reel · 368' (6 mins) · silent
intertitles: English

sp Ministry of Information *pr* Topical Film Company

- Armistice Day celebrations in London, 11 November 1918.

People surge together through the streets of central London, waving Union Flags and cheering. Charabancs and lorries pass up the Strand, their occupants also cheering. The crowd marches up the Mall to Buckingham Palace, joined by a few US troops waving and carrying the Stars and Stripes. The King and Queen, seen in long shot, appear on the palace balcony with the Duke of Connaught and Princess Mary standing beside them. Among those watching in the crowd, close to the camera by other soldiers, is Field Marshal Sir Henry Wilson, the Chief of the Imperial General Staff. Queen Mary, on the balcony, can be seen to wave a small Union Flag. Convalescent soldiers watch from inside the palace railings. The bandsmen on duty give three cheers for the King. At the Houses of Parliament the Prime Minister, David Lloyd George, appears through the cheering crowd and is driven off in a car. The royal coach drives to the thanksgiving service at St Paul's Cathedral, where the Lord Mayor of London is waiting with the aldermen. The various dignitaries follow the King into the cathedral. A view from an airship (another airship is sometimes indistinctly in sight) shows central London during the celebrations. London Bridge, Westminster Bridge and the Houses of Parliament are all prominent.

Notes
Intertitles: these are all flashframes.
Remarks: the crowd scenes are very impressive.
[*The Times*, 12 November 1918: 9-10]
[A J P Taylor, *The First World War*, Hutchinson (1963): 195]
[shotsheet available]
catalogued SDB: 6/1983

IWM 664b · GB, 18/11/1918
PICTORIAL NEWS (OFFICIAL) 377-2

b/w · 1 reel · 296' (5 mins) · silent
intertitles: English

sp Ministry of Information *pr* Topical Film Company

I. Armistice celebrations in Glasgow and Dublin, 11 November 1918. In the streets of Glasgow the crowds cheer and wave Union Flags, good-naturedly jostling the camera, which is down at street level with them. In Dublin the celebrations are more restrained, consisting of parades through the street while people stand and watch.

II. The Prince of Wales visiting Denain, France, probably 11 November 1918. The Prince emerges from the town church after a thanksgiving service. With him are Canadian troops who liberated the town and their commander, General Sir Arthur Currie. The Prince and Currie pose for photographers and receive bouquets from young ladies in local costume. The Prince talks with veterans of the Franco-Prussian War. The Canadian forces march off. The Canadian official still photographer, Lieutenant William Rider-Rider, can be seen at work.

Notes
Intertitles: these are all negative flashframes.
[shotsheet available]
catalogued SDB: 6/1983

IWM 665a · GB, 28/11/1918
PICTORIAL NEWS (OFFICIAL) 379-1

b/w · 1 reel · 181' (3 mins) · silent
intertitles: none

sp Ministry of Information *pr* Topical Film Company

- State entry of the King and Queen of Belgium into Brussels, 22 November 1918.

The film is usually in long shot, showing the crowds lining the streets and the procession led by Belgian troops. The King and Queen ride forward into the square and dismount, going forward to talk to the town mayor. Belgian photographers record the occasion. The march past continues.

Notes
Summary: see also **IWM 370**.
[shotsheet available]
catalogued SDB: 5/1983

IWM 665b · GB, 11/11/1918
PICTORIAL NEWS (OFFICIAL) 376-2

b/w · 1 reel · 164' (3 mins) · silent
intertitles: English & Spanish

sp Ministry of Information *pr* Topical Film Company

I. The visit of Prince Yorihito of Higashi-Fushimi to the Grand Fleet in the Firth of Forth, October 1918. The Prince's cutter comes alongside the flagship HMS *Queen Elizabeth* and he comes up the gangplank and onto the quarterdeck. The Prince is wearing admiral's uniform. He exchanges salutes with Admiral Sir David Beatty, who is waiting for him.
II. The procession of the Lord Mayor's Show through London, 9 November 1918. The Lord Mayor's coach leads the procession. Airship R23 flies overhead. Women munitions workers can be seen as part of the parade, followed by a Whippet tank, the US Army Contingent, and members of the Women's Land Army. One of the floats shows disabled servicemen at work. The Lord Mayor's coach arrives at the Law Courts, and he gets out.

Notes
Production: the material held conforms to the 'foreign edition' – see **Notes** to issue 369-1.
Intertitles: these are all flashframes, some in English, some in Spanish
Summary: see also **IWM 626**.
[shotsheet available]
catalogued SDB: 5/1983

IWM 665c · GB, 4/11/1918
PICTORIAL NEWS (OFFICIAL) 375-2

b/w · 1 reel · 34' (1 min) · silent
intertitles: English

sp Ministry of Information *pr* Topical Film Company

- Visit to Hampstead Orthopaedic Hospital, London, for trade union leaders, late 1918.

The trade unionist shop stewards "representing 40,000 shipyard workers" are shown around the hospital. They include some women. They are shown a patient receiving heat lamp treatment. A group of them poses for the camera.

Notes
Summary: see also **IWM 661b**.
[shotsheet available]
catalogued SDB: 5/1983

IWM 666a · GB, 11/7/1918
**PICTORIAL NEWS (OFFICIAL) 359-1
(French version)**

b/w · 1 reel · 201' (4 mins) · silent
intertitles: French

sp Ministry of Information *pr* Topical Film Company

I. Sinn Féin members march through a town in Ireland, June 1918. The men are in civilian clothes but march in formation and carry staves or other weapons. The captions say that these "misguided" men should be fighting for the British in the war for civilisation, and that Sinn Féin should be suppressed.
II. Meeting of the Anglo-Saxon Fellowship in London, July 1918. Members of the Fellowship march to their meeting hall. Some US Army officers arrive at the meeting. Also seen arriving is Winston Churchill. According to the captions, Churchill's motion that "Germany must be defeated" was passed unanimously.
III. King George V and King Albert of Belgium review the guard at Buckingham Palace, 2pm, 6 July 1918. The two kings watch as a reserve battalion of the Scots Guards parades. The King of Belgium wears his uniform as Colonel of the British 5th Dragoon Guards. Also present are Queen Mary, Princess Mary, Prince Henry, Prince George, and Queen Elisabeth of Belgium with her son the Count of Flanders.

IV. A light railway transporting shells, Western Front, May 1918.
A light train carrying shells, with troops riding on top, moves forward. A shell-dump of 9.2-inch shells is shown; a soldier holds up a notice for the camera, "one day's rations for one gun".

Notes
Summary: see also **IWM 226** and **IWM 265**.
[shotsheet available]
catalogued SDB: 5/1983

IWM 666b · GB, 15/7/1918
**PICTORIAL NEWS (OFFICIAL) 359-2
(French version) [1]**

b/w · 1 reel · 232' (4 mins) · silent
intertitles: French

sp Ministry of Information *pr* Topical Film Company

I. The funeral of Lord Rhondda at Llanwern in Wales, July 1918. The horse-drawn hearse leads a crowd of mourners, mostly civilian. The coffin is taken into the church grounds for burial.
II. George Robey raising money for the Red Cross in Liverpool, July 1918. Robey, wearing the uniform of an Army lieutenant, acts as auctioneer for a shipment of US cotton, the proceeds going to Red Cross work in France.
III. King George V invests lance corporal Harold Mugford with the VC at Buckingham Palace, July 1918. The ceremony takes place in the rear courtyard of the palace. Mugford, of the Machine Gun Corps, is in civilian clothes and in a wheelchair, having had both legs broken while winning his VC. He is shown in close-up.
IV. A visit by a French Zouave band to London, July 1918. The Zouaves, led by a British Army band, march through the streets. The Zouave band plays outside Buckingham Palace and mounts guard. They continue their march through the streets as the crowd watches.

Notes
Production: this issue ends with the logo of a Swiss distribution company, the Compagnie Générale de Cinématographie de Genève. It is obviously impossible to be sure which of the French-language versions of the newsreel were intended for Switzerland and which for France (if there was any difference between the two).
Summary: note that another two items from the French-language version of this issue

form **IWM 674a**.
[shotsheet available]
catalogued SDB: 5/1983

IWM 667 · GB, 5/9/1918
**PICTORIAL NEWS (OFFICIAL) 367-1
(French version)**
GAZETTE D'ACTUALITE (on copy held)

b/w · 1 reel · 392' (7 mins) · silent
intertitles: French

sp Ministry of Information *pr* Topical Film Company

I. Samuel Gompers and William Hughes attend the Trades Union Congress in Derby, August 1918. Gompers, President of the American Workers' Federation, and Hughes, Prime Minister of Australia, enter the hall where the congress is taking place, together with the delegates. Hughes poses beside women in the crowd outside who wave Union Flags.
II. A large crowd of German prisoners, taken in the Advance to Victory, waiting to move off in the rear areas, Western Front, August 1918.
III. Survivors of the Zeebrugge raid holding sports in Essex, August 1918. The men, described as the "heroes of Zeebrugge", participate in naval sports, including dressing up as clowns, an obstacle race and a water joust.
IV. Young French children arrive in London to spend their holidays with English children, August 1918. The children are helped out of a charabanc and arranged for the camera by the nuns looking after them. One English girl kisses a French girl hello, "they sealed the entente with a kiss".
V. The ruins of Bapaume after its recapture in the Advance to Victory, Western Front, August 1918.
VI. King George V decorates servicemen at Buckingham Palace, August 1918. The ceremony takes place in the rear courtyard of the palace. The King, in Army uniform, decorates various soldiers, including some Indian troops.

Notes
Summary: McKernan places items IV-VI in issue 367-2. See also **IWM 322**.
Remarks: the *Topical Budget* newsreel understandably 'milked' the Zeebrugge raid for its maximum propaganda value, as it was a success at a time of great uncertainty in the war, April 1918. But the item on a perfectly ordinary Royal Navy sports justified by the name of Zeebrugge a full

four months after the event seems to be going rather too far.
[shotsheet available]
catalogued SDB: 5/1983

IWM 668a · GB, 27/6/1918
PICTORIAL NEWS (OFFICIAL) 357-1 (French version)

b/w · 1 reel · 190' (3 mins) · silent
intertitles: French

sp Ministry of Information *pr* Topical Film Company

- French-language version of three items from the issue held in English as **IWM 1061-07b**. The items are those concerning Welsh Day in London, the knighting of Vice-Admiral Sir Roger Keyes and the Duke of Connaught opening a club for US officers.

Notes
Summary: note that a further English-language fragment of this issue is held as **IWM 1061-02b**.
[shotsheet available]
catalogued SDB: 5/1983

IWM 668b · GB, 1/7/1918
PICTORIAL NEWS (OFFICIAL) 357-2 (French version)

b/w · 1 reel · 205' (4 mins) · silent
intertitles: French

sp Ministry of Information *pr* Topical Film Company

I. Herbert Hoover, US Food Controller, meets British children in London. The children have had their school desks set out in the playground. A teacher chalks on a blackboard a "letter" for them to copy out to Mr Hoover, while he watches. The children cheer the US flag and the Union Flag.
II. A F Kerensky in London, June 1918. Kerensky, in civilian clothes, poses for the cameras outside a house. According to the captions, he declares that "the Russian people will never recognise the treaty of Brest-Litovsk".
III. Baby Welfare Week in London. An out of doors crèche at a maternity hospital in London, showing mothers and babies. Indoors a baby is weighed by a nurse. Mothers hold twin babies. A regimental

sergeant-major in the Scots Guards visits his wife lying in bed with their new-born baby.
IV. A review of officer cadets at Bedford School by King George V, June 1918. Queen Mary is with the King, escorted by the headmaster. The cadets march past the royal party, after which the staff is introduced to the King.

[shotsheet available]
catalogued SDB: 5/1983

IWM 668c · GB, 27/5/1918
PICTORIAL NEWS (OFFICIAL) 352-2 (French version)

b/w · 1 reel · 184' (3 mins) · silent
intertitles: French

sp Ministry of Information *pr* Topical Film Company

I. Lord French, the new Viceroy of Ireland, attends a Red Cross fête at Dublin Castle, May 1918. 'LORD FRENCH IN IRELAND.' French walks around the gardens of the castle shaking hands with people at the fête. Beside him is his aide, Lieutenant-Colonel Fitzgerald ('Fitz') Watt. The fête has a display of horse jumping, including one lady riding side-saddle. French gives a speech.
II. Lord Beaverbrook opens an exhibition of William Orpen's war paintings in London, May 1918. Beaverbrook stands next to Orpen beside the exhibition, at the Agnew Galleries, and they pose for photographs.
III. Tom Sullivan, recently returned from Germany, May 1918. 'BACK FROM RUHLEBEN.' Sullivan, a famous ex-rower, has returned from checking on the state of German prisoner of war camps. At home he digs the garden, and poses with his wife and son, and by himself.
IV. General Smuts receives the freedom of the city of Glasgow, May 1918. Smuts, on horseback, takes the salute as members of the Glasgow Boys' Brigade march past him. He emerges from a ceremony at Glasgow University and is congratulated by the dons, who include some women.

[shotsheet available]
catalogued SDB: 5/1983

IWM 668d · GB, 23/5/1918
PICTORIAL NEWS (OFFICIAL) 352-1 (French version) [1]

b/w · 1 reel · 186' (3 mins) · silent
intertitles: French

sp Ministry of Information *pr* Topical Film
Company

I. Admiral Sims opens a baseball match
between US Army and US Marine teams at
Highbury football ground, London, May
1918. The teams come out into the
crowded stadium. Admiral Sims presents
the ball and throws in the first ball, after
which the game starts to the cheers of the
crowd.
II. HMS *Iris* and HMS *Daffodil* after the
Zeebrugge raid, May 1918. The *Iris* steams
towards the camera into harbour. Its crew
disembarks and bullet holes in the
superstructure and funnel are checked. The
captain, Lieutenant John D Campbell (?), is
shown in portrait shot. A pan over the
Daffodil coming into harbour.
III. A wrecked Gotha bomber shot down
over Britain, May 1918. The burnt-out
wreckage of the plane lies beside a railway
embankment and is guarded by RAF and
WRAF personnel, and by the police.

Notes
Summary: note that two more items from
the French-language version of this issue
form **IWM 675a**.
[shotsheet available]
cataloqued SDB: 5/1983

IWM 669 · NO FILM

IWM 670a · GB, 1917
**SONS OF OUR EMPIRE EPISODE 5 :
Attacking hard (German version)**

b/w · 1 reel · 194' (3 mins) · silent
intertitles: German

sp War Office Cinema Committee *pr* Topical
Film Company *prod* Jury, William F
cam Raymond, H C; and McDowell, J B

■ German-language version of the second
part of **IWM 130-09+10**, Episode 5 of the
British documentary series *Sons of Our
Empire*.

cataloqued SDB: 5/1983

IWM 670b · France, (prod) 1917-18
**[ANNALES DE LA GUERRE –
ADDITIONAL MATERIAL 2]**

b/w · 1 reel · 385' (7 mins) · silent
intertitles: English

sp Section Cinématographique de l'Armée
Française

■ English-language version of jumbled
French official films showing events in
Brussels in 1918, and in France in 1917.

German horsed transport riders leaving
Brussels on 21 November 1918. Mayor
Max, released from prison, is cheered by
the crowd. The King and Queen of Belgium
make a state entry on 22 November. The
cathedral at Soissons in April 1917,
showing shell damage. An extract is quoted
from a captured German artillery officer's
diary to the effect that the cathedral was
deliberately used as an aiming point. A pan
over Maubeuge, which shows some
damage.

Notes
Summary: see also **IWM 435** for the
Soissons story and **IWM 508-88** for the
Brussels story.
cataloqued SDB: 5/1983

IWM 670c · USA, 1916
the POLICE DOG

b/w · 1 reel · 260' (4 mins) · silent
intertitles: English

dist Pathé *prod* Bray, J R

■ Comic cartoon involving "Pinkerton Pup"
and his handler "Officer Piffle".

The curtain goes up on the cartoon to
introduce the two characters. They set out
on patrol from a police station. The dog
sees a cat and chases it over rough ground
and through a sewer pipe. The handler,
dragged along, loses his trousers in the
process. The cat finally reaches safety up a
tree.

Notes
Summary: according to Crafton's book, this
is a unique print of a previously 'lost' film, of
which copies were no longer thought to
exist. It was probably placed by accident
into a can of *War Office Topical Budget*
newsreels at the Topical Film Company
studios and handed over with these to the

Imperial War Museum in 1921.
Remarks: Crafton suggests that the *Police Dog* series "was probably just hack work, but we cannot know until some samples are discovered". On seeing the cartoon, this appears to have been a good guess.
[Donald Crafton, *Before Mickey*, MIT Press (1982): 138-167, 219, 289]
catalogued SDB: 6/1983

IWM 671 · NO FILM

IWM 672a · GB, 23/1/1918
WAR OFFICE OFFICIAL TOPICAL BUDGET 335-1

b/w · 1 reel · 155' (3 mins) · silent
intertitles: English

sp War Office Cinema Committee *pr* Topical Film Company

I. Church parade by the National Federation of Ex-Soldiers and Sailors in Britain, January 1918. The men march in the rain through the streets, led by military bands and with a police escort. The men enter a building with a Union Flag draped over the entrance.
II. F Company, 11th US Railway Engineers, who fought at Cambrai, Western Front, December 1917. 'AMERICAN HEROES OF CAMBRAI.' The men are shown working on a railway track, after which they form up and march off. They pose in a group for the camera.
III. Jules Copin, a Frenchman freed with his family by the British during the First Battle of Cambrai, November 1917. 'RELEASED BY THE BRITISH.' A nursing home behind the lines where Copin, his wife and child, and two blind aunts are led out by nurses. Copin was a French soldier captured by Germans in September 1914 who escaped and was hidden by his wife in his own home at Masnières near Cambrai until the village was captured by the British in November 1917. He poses for the camera with his wife and child.

Notes
Intertitles: these are all flashframes.
Summary: see also **IWM 148** for the Copin story and **IWM 150** for the US Engineers story.
[shotsheet available]
catalogued SDB: 5/1983

IWM 672b · GB, 26/1/1918
WAR OFFICE OFFICIAL TOPICAL BUDGET 335-2 (extract 1)

b/w · 1 reel · 151' (3 mins) · silent
intertitles: English

sp War Office Cinema Committee *pr* Topical Film Company

■ Three stories from the newsreel held in more complete form (in a Spanish version) as **IWM 697a**. The stories concern those on Sir Edward Kemp ('CANADA IS CONFIDENT'), Walter Page ('YMCA/YOU MUST COME AGAIN') and snow in Flanders ('GENERAL SNOW TAKES COMMAND').

Notes
Intertitles: these are all flashframes.
Summary: note that an additional story is held as **IWM 1061-09a**.
[shotsheet available]
catalogued SDB: 5/1983

IWM 673a · GB, 13/5/1918
PICTORIAL NEWS (OFFICIAL) 350-2 (French version)

b/w · 1 reel · 60' (1 min) · silent
intertitles: French

sp Ministry of Information *pr* Topical Film Company

■ French-language version of a single item from the issue held in more complete form as **IWM 654b**. The item is 'AMIENS. A LANDMARK OF GERMAN FAILURE'.

Notes
Summary: note that a Spanish-language version is also held as **IWM 700c**.
[shotsheet available]
catalogued SDB: 5/1983

IWM 673b · GB, 8/5/1918
PICTORIAL NEWS (OFFICIAL) 350-1 (French version)

b/w · 1 reel · 63' (1 min) · silent
intertitles: French

sp Ministry of Information *pr* Topical Film Company

■ French-language version of an item from the issue held in more complete form as

IWM 654a. The item is 'TOMMY'S CHARACTERISTIC HUMANITY'.

Notes
Summary: note that a Spanish-language version is also held as **IWM 700b**.
[shotsheet available]
catalogued SDB: 5/1983

IWM 673c · GB, 6/5/1918
PICTORIAL NEWS (OFFICIAL) 349-2 (French version)

b/w · 1 reel · 175' (3 mins) · silent
intertitles: French

sp Ministry of Information *pr* Topical Film Company

■ French-language version of two items from the issue held in more complete form as **IWM 661b**. The items are 'THE END OF RICHTHOFEN' and 'THE MOLE MEN'.

Notes
Summary: note that a Spanish version is also held as **IWM 700a** and **IWM 700e**.
[shotsheet available]
catalogued SDB: 5/1983

IWM 673d · GB, 1/5/1918
PICTORIAL NEWS (OFFICIAL) 349-1 (French version) [1]

b/w · 1 reel · 30' (1 min) · silent
intertitles: French

sp Ministry of Information *pr* Topical Film Company

■ French-language version of an item from the issue held as **IWM 661a**. The item is 'WAR TIME LANCASHIRE LASSIES'.

Notes
Summary: note that a Spanish-language version is held as **IWM 700d**, and another French-language fragment is **IWM 684a**.
[shotsheet available]
catalogued SDB: 5/1983

IWM 674a · GB, 15/7/1918
PICTORIAL NEWS (OFFICIAL) 359-2 (French version) [2]

b/w · 1 reel · 98' (2 mins) · silent

intertitles: French

sp Ministry of Information *pr* Topical Film Company

I. J R Clynes, replacement for Lord Rhondda as Food Controller, in portrait shot, London, July 1918.
II. King George V watches a cricket match between a team from England and one from the Dominions, at Lords Cricket Ground. The England team come out to field, followed by the two Dominion opening batsmen. The King, in his Army uniform, is introduced to the two teams. Part of the match is shown. The two teams pose for group photographs.

Notes
Summary: note that another four items from the French-language version of this issue form **IWM 666b**.
[shotsheet available]
catalogued SDB: 5/1983

IWM 674b · GB, 18/7/1918
PICTORIAL NEWS (OFFICIAL) 360-1 (French version)

b/w · 1 reel · 280' (5 mins) · silent
intertitles: French

sp Ministry of Information *pr* Topical Film Company

I. A mass rally in Trafalgar Square, calling for the internment of all aliens of enemy nationalities, 13 July 1918. The camera, blocked by the crowd, shows only long shots and the view of the crowd from the speakers' platform, rather than the speakers themselves.
II. The British Army fire service extinguishing a fire at a forage dump in France, July 1918. The bales of hay are stacked over a considerable area, and the hoses are being played on those stacks which are smouldering or burning. Several stacks are completely ruined before the fire is under control.
III. Sir Edward Carson addresses a mass rally of Ulster Volunteers in Belfast, July 1918. The loyalists parade through the streets of the city holding banners. At the rally Carson addresses them from a platform covered with Union Flags. He holds up his cane – the silver-topped blackthorn of the Ulster Division (?) – in a symbolic gesture.
IV. The RAF in France, 1918. The captions state that in 1917 the RAF shot down 4102

enemy for the loss of 1203 of their own men. The film shows a DH4 of 27 Squadron being made ready for a patrol at Serny, possibly 17 February 1918. The ground crew wheel the plane out of its hangar, and fit 20-pound bombs. The gunner attaches his Lewis gun to the Scarfe ring. The plane takes off.
V. Canadian journalists visit Lord Beaverbrook at Cherkley Court, England, 14 July 1918. The journalists walk through the grounds of Beaverbrook's home. The group, including Beaverbrook and his children, poses on the terrace.

Notes
Summary: see also **IWM 273** for the Beaverbrook story.
[shotsheet available]
catalogued SDB: 5/1983

IWM 674c · GB, 22/7/1918
PICTORIAL NEWS (OFFICIAL) 360-2 (French version)

b/w · 1 reel · 276' (5 mins) · silent
intertitles: French

sp Ministry of Information *pr* Topical Film Company

I. King George V reviews an aerodrome in Britain, July 1918. The King is escorted around the base by RAF officers. A ground crew party hauls down a barrage balloon as he watches. Two other barrage balloons are seen floating side by side in the sky. The King leaves by car.
II. King George V reviews Army cadets at Woolwich, July 1918. The cadets march past while the King takes the salute. He then leaves the parade ground. (Note the local journalist taking notes.)
III. The King and Queen of Belgium visiting the US 6th Battle Squadron and British Grand Fleet, Firth of Forth, June 1918. The King and Queen come up the gangplank onto USS *New York*. Its ship's company is drawn up on the deck. A pan over the length of the *New York* from a small boat alongside. The King and Queen board HMS *Queen Elizabeth*. The King salutes the quarterdeck, and talks with Admiral Sir David Beatty. The royal party is in long shot throughout.
IV. Vegetables being grown in Buckingham Palace gardens, London, July 1918. The royal gardeners harvest turnips, which have been grown on the lawns and path verges, as part of the food economy drive. (Note the press photographer at work.)

V. Members of the FANY being decorated by King George V in the rear courtyard of Buckingham Palace, watched by convalescent soldiers and some Indians, July 1918.

Notes
Summary: see also **IWM 602** for the Belgian royal visit story. McKernan suggests that item I should be in issue 360-1.
Remarks: the persona of the King may have been a useful fall-back for the newsreels, but this issue rather overdoes it.
[shotsheet available]
catalogued SDB: 5/1983

IWM 675a · GB, 23/5/1918
PICTORIAL NEWS (OFFICIAL) 352-1 (French version) [2]

b/w · 1 reel · 108' (2 mins) · silent
intertitles: French

sp Ministry of Information *pr* Topical Film Company

I. Film of Eamon De Valera and Countess Markievicz, taken during the East Clare by-election of May 1917, issued at the time of their arrest on 17 May 1918. A band leads a crowd of people through the streets of the town. De Valera and Countess Markievicz address the crowd, two of whom are waving Sinn Féin tricolours.
II. Meat supplies to the British forces on the Western Front, May 1918. Soldiers unload whole carcasses of meat from lorries of V Corps (note the formation sign). The men cut up the meat with axes.

Notes
Summary: note that four more items from the French-language version of this issue form **IWM 668d**.
[The Earl of Longford and Thomas P O'Neill, *Eamon de Valera*, Hutchinson (1970): 63-65, 75-78]
[shotsheet available]
catalogued SDB: 5/1983

IWM 675b · GB, 30/5/1918
PICTORIAL NEWS (OFFICIAL) 353-1 (French version)

b/w · 1 reel · 351' (6 mins) · silent
intertitles: French

sp Ministry of Information *pr* Topical Film Company

I. A children's fête in London, attended by the Duchess of Marlborough, May 1918. Both the fête and the film stress the fact that the Duchess was American. The children present her with a bouquet in their school playground. She addresses them while a child waves a US flag behind her head. On the dais with her is a man in the uniform of a Chelsea Pensioner.
II. King George V presents decorations in the rear courtyard of Buckingham Palace, May 1918. The recipients of the awards are from all services. One receives a knighthood. The airship SSZ49 (described as "un avion") overflies the palace during the ceremony.
III. Lloyd George receives the freedom of the city of Edinburgh, May 1918. Lloyd George arrives for the ceremony in part of a convoy of cars. He reviews a military guard, and leaves through a cheering crowd. (Some members of the crowd are of African or West Indian origin.)
IV. A parade for Intercession for the Allies led by Cardinal Bourne through the streets of London. The Catholic procession includes ladies with banners and young girls with long white veils. May 1918.
V. A riveting contest between British shipbuilders, May 1918. The three winners are shown in turn. Firstly, R Farrant of Fraser & Fraser, London, is chaired by his mates and posed with his rivet gun. He set the record at 4376 rivets in nine hours. D Deviney of Glasgow, who raised this to 4422 rivets in the same time, is posed in his back garden in his best clothes (including fob watch and waistcoat). Finally, W Moses of Vickers Ltd, Barrow-in-Furness, who managed 5984 rivets, is shown at work with his rivet gun, then posed with it.

Notes
Summary: an English-language version of story III is held as **IWM 1061-09f**, but note that McKernan locates this story in issue 353-2.
[shotsheet available]
catalogued SDB: 5/1983

IWM 675c · GB, 3/6/1918
PICTORIAL NEWS (OFFICIAL) 353-2 (French version)

b/w · 1 reel · 351' (6 mins) · silent
intertitles: French

sp Ministry of Information *pr* Topical Film Company

- French-language version of a single item from the issue held in more complete form as **IWM 1061-02c**, showing British soldiers eating bread and jam "with proverbial coolness".

[shotsheet available]
catalogued SDB: 5/1983

IWM 676a · GB, 6/6/1918
PICTORIAL NEWS (OFFICIAL) 354-1 (French version)

b/w · 1 reel · 181' (3 mins) · silent
intertitles: French

sp Ministry of Information *pr* Topical Film Company

- French-language version of three items from the issue held as **NTB 354-01**. The items are 'BOYS OF THE OLD BRIGADE', 'KING AND BLIND KNIGHT' and 'HUN THREAT TO PARIS'.

Notes
Summary: an additional item from this issue, and the English version of story III, form **IWM 1061-02d**.
Remarks: the captions for the refugee sequence show a more overtly pro-French leaning than the captions of the original English version. The use of old film of the Battle of the Lys to suggest the British contribution to the opening Second Battle of the Marne is also noteworthy.
catalogued SDB: 6/1983

IWM 676b · GB, 10/6/1918
PICTORIAL NEWS (OFFICIAL) 354-2 (French version)

b/w · 1 reel · 165' (3 mins) · silent
intertitles: French

sp Ministry of Information *pr* Topical Film Company

- French-language version of one item (not otherwise held) from the issue held as **IWM 1061-02c**, together with item IV from that fragment.

I. Convalescent British soldiers taking a pleasure cruise on the Thames in London, June 1918. The men, in their hospital blue uniforms, board the pleasure cruiser. They are given cups of tea up on deck by the women looking after them, and later they sit

down to a meal.
II. 'THE FIGHT FOR THE WOODS'.

Notes
Summary: **IWM 1061-02a** consists of story II
and two other items, but does not include
story I. See **IWM 180** for the Cavalry
sequence.
Remarks: as for **IWM 676a**, the British have
used old material to represent British forces
involved in the Second Battle of the Marne.
catalogued SDB: 6/1983

IWM 677a · GB, 22/8/1918
**PICTORIAL NEWS (OFFICIAL) 365-1
(French version)**

b/w · 1 reel · 163' (3 mins) · silent
intertitles: French

sp Ministry of Information *pr* Topical Film
Company

I. Lord Sydenham opens an Exhibition of
British Scientific Products at King's College,
University of London, August 1918. Outside
the college, in the Strand, Lord Sydenham
is guided towards the camera, which he
acknowledges. He goes inside to the
exhibition. The exhibits are of various
industrial and chemical goods, including
coal tar dyes.
II. British soldiers display a captured
German 210mm howitzer, Western Front,
probably August 1918.
III. Portuguese troops training at Roffey
Camp near Horsham, England, 15 August
1918. The troops do physical exercises
under a British instructor. The exercise
includes a demonstration of Portuguese
singlestick fighting (Jogo du Pau). Among
those watching is the Portuguese
Ambassador to Great Britain, Dr Augusto de
Vasconcellos.

Notes
Summary: see **IWM 291** for the Portuguese
item.
[shotsheet available]
catalogued SDB: 6/1983

IWM 677b · GB, 26/8/1918
**PICTORIAL NEWS (OFFICIAL) 365-2
(French version)**

b/w · 1 reel · 191' (3 mins) · silent
intertitles: French

sp Ministry of Information *pr* Topical Film
Company

I. King George V in France, 9 August 1918.
At Rouen the King poses for a group
photograph with Field Marshal Haig,
Marshal Foch and General Pétain. At Third
Army headquarters, Frohen-le-Grand, later
in the day he decorates three men with the
Victoria Cross. They are the Reverend T B
Hardy, attached to 8th Battalion, the
Lincolnshire Regiment, and Sergeant
William Gregg and Corporal William
Beesley, both of 13th Battalion, the Rifle
Brigade. Gregg and Beesley pose together
for a photograph.
II. Members of the Ministry of Food at a
conference in London, August 1918.
Leaving Grosvenor House, the site of the
Ministry of Food, are Major E A Belcher, the
Director of the Fruit and Vegetables
Department and S Walton, Assistant Food
Controller. The delegates to the conference
come down the outside stairs of the
building into its gardens. Portrait shots of
Belcher and Walton.
III. British treatment of German prisoners,
Western Front, August 1918. British soldiers
rest beside a house equipped as a YMCA
establishment. With them are German
prisoners, some of whom are wounded. A
soldier gives a German who is lying on a
stretcher a cup of tea. The men are all
camera-conscious, but the gesture seems
nevertheless natural.
IV. General Rosado, the new Portuguese
commander, shown with his staff, then
posed by himself, probably in England,
August 1918.

Notes
Distributor: again credited as the
Compagnie Générale de Cinématographie
de Genève (see **IWM 666b**).
Intertitles: some of these are flashframes.
Summary: McKernan lists item I as
belonging to issue 365-1. See also **IWM
291** for the Portuguese item.
[shotsheet available]
catalogued SDB: 6/1983

IWM 678a · GB, 25/7/1918
**PICTORIAL NEWS (OFFICIAL) 361-1
(French version)**

b/w · 1 reel · 268' (5 mins) · silent
intertitles: French

sp Ministry of Information *pr* Topical Film
Company

. King George V visits school allotments at Merton Park, Surrey, July 1918. The King, in Army uniform, watches the children at work on an allotment. He is joined by Queen Mary, with R E Prothero, the President of the Board of Agriculture, walking behind. A girl gives the Queen a bouquet. This is followed by a portrait shot of Prothero looking out of the window in his office (in profile and half-light).
I. A rally by dissatisfied teachers in Trafalgar Square. The teachers are demanding a pay increase. They include a significant proportion of women. A vote is taken by a show of hands.
II. A march of Girl Guides past Queen Alexandra in Hyde Park. The day is quite foggy and overcast, and the Queen remains in her open carriage. Boy scouts act as markers to drill the Guides into position. One Girl Guide is shown with a complete set of proficiency badges covering most of her right sleeve.
V. Herbert Hoover, US Food Controller, poses beside his car in London, July 1918.
V. WAACs camping out in France (?), July 1918. The women parade beside their bell tents, listening for orders. Some of them picnic beside a tent. The WAACs fold up their blankets and 'sleep' (in daylight) on the forest floor near their tents. One holds a small dog up for the camera.

Notes
Remarks: it is remarkable that an officially sponsored newsreel should include a scene of industrial unrest such as the item on the teachers' protest, without apparently criticising their action. Possibly this was an attempt by the newsreel to lose its reputation as government war propaganda.
[shotsheet available]
catalogued SDB: 6/1983

IWM 678b · GB, 29/7/1918
PICTORIAL NEWS (OFFICIAL) 361-2 (French version)

b/w · 1 reel · 266' (5 mins) · silent
intertitles: French

sp Ministry of Information *pr* Topical Film Company

. Visit by leading Canadian journalists to the Canadian Training Division at Bramshot and Witley, near Aldershot, July 1918. The journalists watch a demonstration of trench fighting in the training trenches. They inspect the trenches. The men of the division march past, and their commander,

Brigadier-General F S Meighan, takes the salute.
II. Viscount French watches a boy scout meeting in the grounds of Dublin Castle, July 1918. The Scouts parade in the castle grounds and French walks down to inspect them. Next to him is, possibly, Lieutenant-General R S S Baden-Powell, the Chief Scout. The Scouts perform a 'charge', carrying a Union Flag, across the castle lawns, then give three cheers.
III. Boy scouts collect kitchen refuse, to be used in gas mask manufacture, from Buckingham Palace, July 1918. The Scouts are collecting fruit peel and nut shells, which are used to make the carbon for filters in gas masks. They collect the baskets of refuse from the palace kitchens, emptying the baskets into their barrow, which they wheel out through the gates.
IV. Sir Robert Borden receives the freedom of Cardiff while opening an exhibition of Canadian War Photographs, July 1918. Borden, the Canadian Prime Minister, is shown with the mayor and officials of Cardiff seated in the picture gallery with the Canadian photographs on the walls behind them. Directly behind them is a famous 'over the top' photograph by Ivor Castle, the Canadian Official Photographer (which was in fact of a training exercise). A portrait shot of Borden.
V. 'J' Battery, Royal Horse Artillery, manœuvring at high speed, rear areas of the Western Front, 20 June 1918. The captions describe the battery incorrectly as field artillery and suggest that it forms part of an Allied counterstroke in the Second Battle of the Marne. The men and guns of the battery splash at a canter through a shallow stream and up over a ridge (one of the limbers can be seen overturned). The battery halts and starts to deploy.

Notes
Summary: see also **IWM 246** for the artillery sequence and **IWM 274** for the Canadian journalists.
[*The Times*, 22 June 1918: 8C]
[Peter Robertson, "Canadian Photojournalism during the First World War", *History of Photography*, January 1978: 37-52]
[shotsheet available]
catalogued SDB: 6/1983

IWM 679a · GB, 8/8/1918
PICTORIAL NEWS (OFFICIAL) 363-1 (French version)

b/w · 1 reel · 266' (5 mins) · silent

intertitles: French

sp Ministry of Information *pr* Topical Film Company

I. King George V opens Australia House, London, 3 August 1918. Australia House is at the east end of the Strand. Australian soldiers march to the building. King George arrives in his carriage with Queen Mary. A view of the facade of the building with the King and Queen looking out from a balcony. The King inspects the guard of Australians.
II. King George V visits USS *New York* in the Firth of Forth, July 1918. The King and Admiral Sir David Beatty come up the gangplank onto the *New York* and salute. Rear-Admiral Rodman greets them. The ship's marines come to the salute. A portrait shot of Rodman.
III. Religious services in London on the "Day of Remembrance", the fourth anniversary of Britain's entry into the First World War, 4 August 1918. The service at St Margaret's, Westminster. King George V and Queen Mary arrive in an open landau. The church has an awning and red carpet outside. They are greeted by the Archbishop of Canterbury and enter the church. With them are the Duke of Connaught, Princess Maud and Princess Victoria. A crowd watches from behind barriers, with newsreel cameramen among them. The members of the Lords and Commons also parade into the church, led by the parliamentary officials in full robes. Lloyd George leads in the cabinet with Balfour next to him. On the same day members of the Women's Army Auxiliary Corps are seen filing up the steps of St Martin in the Fields for a similar service. Also on the same day, the Bishop of London leads an assembly of clergy in the dedication of a memorial to the war dead in Hyde Park.

[*The Times*, 5 August 1918: 4A-E]
[shotsheet available]
catalogued SDB: 6/1983

IWM 679b · GB, 12/8/1918
**PICTORIAL NEWS (OFFICIAL) 363-2
(French version)**

b/w · 1 reel · 180' (3 mins) · silent
intertitles: French

sp Ministry of Information *pr* Topical Film Company

I. A street party for the children of dead

soldiers and sailors in Southwark, London, August 1918. The party tables stretch up and down the street. Helpers give gifts and cards to the children.
II. General Sir Herbert Plumer, GOC Second Army, decorating British nurses in a field near Blendecques, Western Front, 26 June 1918. Plumer (back to camera) pins the medals on the line of four nurses. The captions say that the nurses are receiving the "Médaille Militaire" for their courage when the Germans bombed their hospitals.
III. Lloyd George at the National Eisteddfod at Neath, Wales, August 1918. The ceremonies open with a procession of women and girls in Welsh national costume. The Chief Druid mounts a slab of stone to deliver the address. Lloyd George talks with the mayor of Neath and inspects a parade of soldiers. The watching crowd cheers Lloyd George. He shakes hands with three soldiers in hospital blues (note the press photographers at work).

Notes
Summary: see **IWM 268** for the Plumer item.
Remarks: the difference between the original record film of the Plumer item and the use made of it for the newsreel shows a definite trend towards propaganda and away from information in the newsreel at this point.
[shotsheet available]
catalogued SDB: 6/1983

IWM 680a · GB, 15/8/1918
**PICTORIAL NEWS (OFFICIAL) 364-1
(French version)**

b/w · 1 reel · 123' (2 mins) · silent
intertitles: French

sp Ministry of Information *pr* Topical Film Company

I. The presentation of a gift aeroplane to the nation, Hyde Park, London, August 1918. Princess Patricia is presented with a bouquet by a small girl. With the princess is the Duke of Connaught, a clergyman and various officials. She 'christens' the aircraft, a Sopwith Camel which has the name "The Osterley M.T.T.D. No. 1" (this abbreviation remains unexplained) written below the cockpit. The pilot gets in and the plane takes off.
II. General Sir Arthur Currie showing Canadian journalists over the old Vimy Ridge battlefield, July 1918. Currie, the Canadian Corps commander, leads the journalists, all wearing shrapnel helmets

and carrying gas masks, up to the ridge, where they sit while he tells them about the battle.
III. British soldiers in a recently captured French village, probably Somme area, Western Front, August 1918. The village shows some shell damage. The troops wander through in twos and threes looking for items of interest. Two men look at a dead cat. A dead horse is in the road.

Notes
Summary: see **IWM 310** for the Currie item.
[shotsheet available]
catalogued SDB: 6/1983

IWM 680b · GB, 19/8/1918
**PICTORIAL NEWS (OFFICIAL) 364-2
(French version)**

b/w · 1 reel · 284' (5 mins) · silent
intertitles: French

sp Ministry of Information *pr* Topical Film Company

I. The wedding of a WAAC member in London, August 1918. The item opens with a misplaced caption (from a missing item in the issue about Lord Northcliffe), then shows very briefly WAACs outside the church cheering, and press photographers at work.
II. The Battle of Tardenois, July 1918. The captions describe the item as "scenes of the great Allied advance in France", as if the material were of the Advance to Victory. A distant view of smoke rising from part of the Bois de Reims, probably the Château Commetreuil near Cumas on fire on 25 July, "unable to resist Allied pressure the enemy burn their billets". 6-inch 26cwt howitzers being loaded and fired. Men "of the London Regiment" in loose marching formation moving over flat terrain. Cavalry in column of twos trotting up a road. A field battery of Italian 8th Division firing its 75mm field guns in the Bois de Reims. German dead lying in the wood on 25 July, "Allied losses were comparatively small". British, French and Italian wounded talk together beside a dressing station on the outskirts of the wood. A large group of German prisoners is marched off to the rear areas, where they have their papers and belongings checked. Men of 1/5th Battalion, the Devonshire Regiment, resting in the wood. Men of 6th Battalion, the Black Watch, collecting their packs on 24 July.

Notes
Summary: see also **IWM 278**. According to the caption transcribed in McKernan, the wedding in item I was between "Miss Beryl Wrightman of Connaught House and Lieut. J. Buchanan Wollaston" and took place at St John's, Paddington.
Remarks: although most of this material is of the Battle of Tardenois, the release date of the episode suggests that it might be intended to be taken for the Battle of Amiens. The problem of the delay of two or three weeks between film of the Western Front being shot and its being made available even to the official newsreel company underlines the difficulties faced by film makers of this period, not to mention casting some doubt over the newsreel's claim to be 'topical'.
[shotsheet available]
catalogued SDB: 6/1983

IWM 681a · GB, 27/2/1918
**PICTORIAL NEWS (OFFICIAL) 340-1
(Spanish version)**

b/w · 1 reel · 280' (5 mins) · silent
intertitles: Spanish

sp Ministry of Information *pr* Topical Film Company

■ Spanish-language version of three items from the issue held in full as **NTB 340-01**. The items are 'WORLD'S LARGEST PHOTOGRAPH', 'PRINCE IN THE PRINCIPALITY' and 'WAR AND THE WORKERS'.

catalogued SDB: 6/1983

IWM 681b · GB, 2/3/1918
**PICTORIAL NEWS (OFFICIAL) 340-2
(Spanish version)**

b/w · 1 reel · 194' (4 mins) · silent
intertitles: Spanish

sp Ministry of Information *pr* Topical Film Company

I. The building of a giant billboard poster showing the Spanish Armada in Trafalgar Square. (This story is held in an English version as **IWM 1061-09b**.)
II. The arrival of General Allenby in Cairo station on 27 June 1917. Allenby inspects the guard of British soldiers drawn up for him inside the station, and talks with local

dignitaries.

III. A memorial service for Welsh Guardsmen, Holy Trinity Church, Sloane Street, 28 February 1918. Lieutenant-General Sir Francis Lloyd is prominent supervising the arrangements outside the church. A column of the Welsh Guards arrives for the service, followed by various officers. The Prince arrives and enters for the ceremony. After the ceremony the officers emerge, and the Prince talks with Lloyd.

Notes
Summary: note that additional stories from this issue are held as **IWM 1061-05a** and **IWM 1061-09e** (both English language). See **IWM 14** for the Allenby item.
Remarks: the Allenby item seems a rather extreme example of the kind of delay experienced in getting film back from the Middle East to London; the inclusion of the poster story in a version of the newsreel produced for Spain appears somewhat tactless.
[*The Times*, 28 February 1918: 9B]
catalogued SDB: 6/1983

IWM 681c · GB, 6/3/1918
PICTORIAL NEWS (OFFICIAL) 341-1 (Spanish version)

b/w · 1 reel · 350' (6 mins) · silent
intertitles: Spanish

sp Ministry of Information *pr* Topical Film Company

I. The opening of the "Tank Bank" for war savings in Trafalgar Square, London, March 1918. The Lord Mayor opens the "Bank", which consists of the shell of a Mk IV Tank turned into a bank to sell War Bonds (no good shot of the tank). Sir Eric Geddes, the First Lord of the Admiralty, queues with some naval officers to buy his own bonds, as part of the crowd.
II. King George V visiting an exhibition of British official war photographs at the Grafton Galleries, London, 3 March 1918. The various carriages and cars are shown arriving outside the galleries, but the exhibition itself is never shown. The King leaves his carriage followed by Queen Mary, the Prince of Wales and Princess Mary. Queen Alexandra arrives by a second carriage with Princess Victoria.
III. Vice-Admiral Sir Rosslyn Wemyss decorating sailors of the Dover Patrol, at Dover, March 1918. The sailors march along the waterfront into position on a wet

and rainy day. Wemyss arrives with his staff officers, but neither he nor the investiture is clearly seen as he passes rapidly down the ranks.
IV. Mrs Margaret Lloyd George helping with St David's Day collections for Welsh charities, London, 1 March 1918. Mrs Lloyd George stands between two women in Welsh national costume, one holding a Welsh Dragon flag, the other a poster for the "Saint Nicholas Home For Raid-Shock Children". The remainder of the group includes some children in Welsh costume. Mrs Lloyd George drives off in a car covered with daffodils. She arrives to join another group collecting for the "London Welsh Flag Day". The collectors, in Welsh national costume, are shown grouped together.
V. The extension of the British line southward on the Western Front, February 1918. Men of French First Army march with their wagons down a road in the wet. British soldiers of Fifth Army come down the other way with their field cookers. The soldiers of the two armies halt and fraternise, exchanging cigarettes and talking.

Notes
Remarks: the camerawork on the Wemyss item is very poor indeed.
catalogued SDB: 6/1983

IWM 681d · GB, 9/3/1918
PICTORIAL NEWS (OFFICIAL) 341-2 (Spanish version)

b/w · 1 reel · 58' (1 min) · silent
intertitles: Spanish

sp Ministry of Information *pr* Topical Film Company

■ Spanish-language version of an item from the issue held in full as **NTB 341-02**. The item is 'DESERT WARFARE'.

catalogued SDB: 6/1983

IWM 682 · GB, 16/9/1918
PICTORIAL NEWS (OFFICIAL) 368-2 (Spanish version)

b/w · 1 reel · 68' (1 min) · silent
intertitles: Spanish

sp Ministry of Information *pr* Topical Film Company

Spanish-language version of a single item from the newsreel held in a more complete form as **IWM 682**. The item concerns Lloyd George visiting Manchester, 12 September 1918.

catalogued SDB: 6/1983

IWM 683a · GB, 1/8/1918
PICTORIAL NEWS (OFFICIAL) 362-1 (German version)

b/w · 1 reel · 283' (5 mins) · silent
intertitles: German

sp Ministry of Information *pr* Topical Film Company

■ German-language version of a newsreel devoted to a review of the British Empire's war effort, 1914-18.

Notes
Summary: note that the English version of this item is **IWM 1128a** and a French-language version is **IWM 657b**.
[shotsheet available]
catalogued SDB: 6/1983

IWM 683b · GB, 5/8/1918
PICTORIAL NEWS (OFFICIAL) 362-2 (German version)

b/w · 1 reel · 201' (4 mins) · silent
intertitles: German

sp Ministry of Information *pr* Topical Film Company

■ German-language version of the four items held in a French version as **IWM 657a**.

[shotsheet available]
catalogued SDB: 6/1983

IWM 684a · GB, 1/5/1918
PICTORIAL NEWS (OFFICIAL) 349-1 (French version) [2]

b/w · 1 reel · 84' (2 mins) · silent
intertitles: French

sp Ministry of Information *pr* Topical Film Company

■ French-language version of two items from the issue held as **IWM 661a**. The items are 'YPRES TODAY' and 'THE HODDEN GREY'.

Notes
Summary: note that a Spanish-language version is held as **IWM 700d**, and another French-language fragment is **IWM 673d**.
catalogued SDB: 6/1983

IWM 684b · GB, 16/2/1918
WAR OFFICE OFFICIAL TOPICAL BUDGET 338-2 (French version)

b/w · 1 reel · 66' (1 min) · silent
intertitles: French

sp War Office Cinema Committee *pr* Topical Film Company

■ Single newsreel story (on an Arab camel train in Palestine) which is also held as **IWM 663b**.

catalogued SDB: 6/1983

IWM 684c · GB, 13/2/1918
WAR OFFICE OFFICIAL TOPICAL BUDGET 338-1 (French version)

b/w · 1 reel · 121' (2 mins) · silent
intertitles: French

sp War Office Cinema Committee *pr* Topical Film Company

■ Single story from the newsreel held as **IWM 663a**. The story concerns the State opening of Parliament on 7 February 1918.

catalogued SDB: 6/1983

IWM 684d · GB, 2/2/1918
WAR OFFICE OFFICIAL TOPICAL BUDGET 336-2 (French version)

b/w · 1 reel · 150' (2 mins) · silent
intertitles: French

sp War Office Cinema Committee *pr* Topical Film Company

■ Two stories from the newsreel held in more complete form as **IWM 651b**. The stories concern British soldiers catching turkeys for Christmas at a French farm and Arab workers in Palestine loading horse fodder.

catalogued SDB: 6/1983

IWM 684e · GB, 30/1/1918
WAR OFFICE OFFICIAL TOPICAL BUDGET 336-1 (French version)

b/w · 1 reel · 70' (1 min) · silent
intertitles: French

sp War Office Cinema Committee *pr* Topical Film Company

■ Single story from the newsreel held in (slightly) more complete form as **IWM 651a**. The story concerns the interrogation of a Turkish spy in Mesopotamia.

catalogued SDB: 6/1983

IWM 685a · GB, 19/9/1918
PICTORIAL NEWS (OFFICIAL) 369-1

b/w · 1 reel · 249' (4 mins) · silent
intertitles: English

sp Ministry of Information *pr* Topical Film Company

I. Visit by Samuel Gompers, the US labour leader, to the Grand Fleet in the Firth of Forth, September 1918. Mr Gompers with two other labour leaders comes up the ladder and onto the quarterdeck of HMS *Queen Elizabeth*. Admiral Sir David Beatty is there with his staff to shake hands and meet him.
II. King George V and Queen Mary at a sports meeting of Canadian forestry troops in Britain, September 1918. The King and Queen leave their cars and enter the fields where the sports are being held. A Canadian pipe band marches past. The sports begin with a sprint race, followed by a shot-put. The King talks with the Canadian officers. A pole vault is shown. The Queen talks with her own companions.
III. General John J Pershing reviews French troops behind the lines on the Western Front, August or September 1918. The honour guard of French soldiers is drawn up outside a railway station. Pershing (no good shot of him) walks past reviewing them.
IV. The memorial service for Mrs V A Long,

head of the WAAC, at St Martin in the Fields Church, London, 15 September 1918. Mrs Long was drowned when the hospital ship SS *Warilda* was torpedoed by a U-boat on 3 August. Contingents representing various women's organisations, including the WAAC, the Land Army and the Girl Guides, file up the steps and into the church for the service. After the service Lieutenant-General Sir Francis Lloyd and Lieutenant-General Sir Nevil Macready leave the church.
V. English schoolboys pulling flax in their holidays as part of the harvest, September 1918. A lorry takes the boys from outside their public school, and out to the fields. There they gather flax under the supervision of an adult. The man takes a bundle of flax and separates it into fibres for the camera's benefit.

Notes
Intertitles: these are all flashframes.
Production: according to McKernan, this issue was the first occasion when a separate foreign edition was formally produced. The issue catalogued here is the 'foreign edition', despite being in English.
Summary: see **IWM 579** for the Gompers story.
[shotsheet available]
catalogued SDB: 6/1983

IWM 685b · GB, 23/9/1918
PICTORIAL NEWS (OFFICIAL) 369-2

b/w · 1 reel · 247' (4 mins) · silent
intertitles: none

sp Ministry of Information *pr* Topical Film Company

I. Bread making by members of the WAAC, probably at the Army Maintenance Depot at Etaples, France, September 1918. The women work out of doors. One woman cuts off pieces of dough for loaves, a second weighs the pieces and a third rolls them into spheres. After baking, the women carry the trays out and loosen the loaves. A posed group of the women, very camera conscious and unable to stop laughing.
II. An investiture by King George V at Buckingham Palace, September 1918. The investiture takes place in the rear courtyard. Troops of the Army and Navy receive decorations, together with some Red Cross nurses who curtsy as they collect their medals.
III. The treatment of British soldiers interned in The Netherlands by the Dutch authorities, 1918. A large group of the men, a mixture

of the original BEF, crashed airmen, shipwrecked sailors and men in the process of repatriation, is posed outside the internment camp huts. They have some Dutch children with them. Some of the men work repairing boots. One sergeant holds a small Dutch girl beside him. Inside the men's dormitories they relax. On the sea front a group of the men talks with girls in Dutch national costumes. There is a row of bathing machines along the beach behind them. Some of the internees in a café at Scheveningen talk and drink with Dutch civilians.

Notes
Production: the material held again conforms to the 'foreign edition' – see **Notes** to issue 369-1.
Summary: see **IWM 315** for the item on bread making and **IWM 455** for the item on Holland.
[shotsheet available]
catalogued SDB: 6/1983

IWM 686 · GB, (ca) 1918
[PATHE FIRE STOCKSHOTS]

b/w · 1 reel · 303' (5 mins) · silent
intertitles: English

pr Pathé

■ Stockshots of four major city fires, two in Britain, two in America, probably before 1920.

The first fire is in London, "Britain's largest timberyard" burning. The second fire is an asphalt works in New Jersey, with oil tanks and barrels ablaze. The third conflagration is at "Saint Margret's" (sic ?) railway station, probably in Scotland, showing firemen playing their hoses over the blaze, and unsafe walls being pulled down by hawsers. The last fire is a warehouse in New York. The outer shell of the building collapses as people watch.

Notes
Production: probably included by accident in the War Office Topical Budget collection when this was transferred from the Topical Film Company to the WOCC, and thence to the IWM.
catalogued SDB: 8/1983

IWM 687 · USA, (prod) 1917
UNIVERSAL CURRENT EVENTS

b/w · 1 reel · 420' (7 mins) · silent
intertitles: English

pr Universal Film Company

■ Jumble of US newsreels mainly showing various recruiting scenes for the Army and Marines in the eastern United States, 1917.

Theodore Roosevelt gives an open-air speech in support of the war to a crowd of 5000. He is shown in close-up as he speaks, face contorted with emotion. He is followed by a recruiting officer, who shakes hands with the volunteers. A Stars and Stripes is shown fluttering in a studio 'wind'. Canadian soldiers of 236th Battalion parade down the main street of Bangor, Maine, carrying French and US flags together with the Union Flag and their own colours. An officer gives a speech from a balcony, "France is calling". US soldiers parade down the streets of a city in another recruiting march. In Pittsburgh men who have already enlisted, including the dismounted Pennsylvania Dragoons in their dress uniform, march through the city in another recruiting drive. Construction starts on merchant ships, with a crane swinging the ribs of a ship into position. In New York (?) Mary Pickford, in Marine uniform, conducts a Marine recruiting band down a street, gathering recruits. At a recruiting station she holds a child on whose head is a Marine cap. (The child, most unhappy about the whole situation, is finally given back to its mother.) A portrait shot of Katherine Stinson, who recently made a non-stop record flight. "Fifteen guys who ought to be in the Army" watch "the 'Cheer Up' girls from the Hippodrome", wearing mock Army uniform, shovel snow outside the theatre and off its roof, probably New York. Red Cross nurses sit and prepare bandages, with a live tiger pacing in a cage behind them, at a zoo. Mr John Hunter of the US Shipping Board drives the first rivet on the keel of the "First Standardised Steel Ship" in a Newark, New Jersey, shipyard. The captions say that this is taking place just six days after construction of the shipyard was started. Steam whistles from other ships let off a salute. (Note the newsreel cameraman at work.) German sailors, possibly including U-boat crewmen, who are prisoners of war in the USA are led out for recreation. They play soccer, and also learn baseball. The captions emphasise how happy they are to be out of the war. In Boston, Massachusetts, some "millionaires" go out into the snow to cut down trees as part of the campaign to save coal by burning wood. They are taken on horse-drawn sledges to the forest. They stop for coffee and doughnuts in the middle of their work.

catalogued SDB: 6/1983

IWM 688-690 · NO FILM

IWM 691 · GB, (ca) 1916
BRITISCHE SPORT EN SPELEN IN TIJD VAN VREDE EN OORLOG (on copy held)
[BRITISH SPORTS AND GAMES IN TIME OF PEACE AND WAR] (translation)

b/w · 1 reel · 489' (8 mins) · silent
intertitles: Dutch

pr Topical Film Company (?)

■ Dutch-language version of a film showing sporting activities in Britain before and during the First World War.

The film shows examples of various sports. Firstly, flat racing, typified by the Epsom Derby, showing the horses coming round the final turn to the finish, and the winner's enclosure after the race. Next is steeplechasing, showing a training race for a handful of horses. Some of the riders come off or have their horses fall under them over the jumps. Soccer is described as the British national winter sport. A professional match is shown, with the teams coming out of the tunnel and the game in progress. The home team may be Aston Villa. Cricket, the national summer game, is shown as a village match, with the camera quite close in to the play. Rowing is illustrated by the finish of races at Henley Regatta, with crowds in punts surrounding the finishing line. Finally, golf, invented in Scotland. A match is in progress with a few spectators. One player just misses a long putt, after which his opponent misses a shorter putt and the hole is conceded.

Notes
Production: probably a British official film from the later part of the war, but there is no evidence for this. Professional football stopped after the 1914 season, and racing was temporarily halted during the 1917 grain shortage, so an earlier date is equally possible.
Remarks: the unstated message of the film seems to be that despite the war British culture still flourishes and the country carries on as normal. There is a heavy

emphasis on the Royal Family's interest in racing and on sports uniting people of all classes and social backgrounds. As an example of the crass awfulness of such an approach the film bears interesting comparison with MGH 332, *Listen to Britain* produced officially at the start of the Second World War, although to be fair to the propagandists of 1914-18, another Second World War film, *Britain's Youth* (UKY 242), is not noticeably superior in tackling a directly comparable message.
catalogued SDB: 6/1983

IWM 692a · GB, 9/1/1918
WAR OFFICE OFFICIAL TOPICAL BUDGET 333-1 (Spanish version)

b/w · 1 reel · 264' (4 mins) · silent
intertitles: Spanish

sp War Office Cinema Committee *pr* Topical Film Company

I. Lord Rhondda opens a communal kitchen at Silvertown, West Ham, London, 3 January 1918. Lord Rhondda, the Minister of Food, arrives by car. With him is the Mayor of West Ham, Mr Will Thorne MP. A crowd of men, women and children queue with jugs at the kitchen windows to have soup dispensed to them (there are separate windows for men and women). The children stand with their jugs of soup. Mr Thorne and Lord Rhondda watch.
II. Day of Intercession in London, showing crowds leaving St Paul's Cathedral after a service, Sunday 6 January 1918.
III. Repatriated British prisoners of war arrive in Boston, Lincolnshire, January 1918. The hospital ship is docked in Boston harbour, and the men, some with crutches, all with some physical disability, pose for the camera on board. They make their way onto the dock, saying goodbye to the nurses as they do so. A group of them are described as "Old Contemptibles" of the 1914 BEF, who have been in captivity for three years. The ship steams out of the harbour with the nurses waving. The local mayor is among those waiting to greet the soldiers.

[*The Times*, 4 January 1918: 7D]
[*The Times*, 7 January 1918: 4C]
catalogued SDB: 6/1983

IWM 692b · GB, 12/1/1918
**WAR OFFICE OFFICIAL TOPICAL
BUDGET 333-2 (Spanish version) [1]**

b/w · 1 reel · 137' (3 mins) · silent
intertitles: Spanish

sp War Office Cinema Committee *pr* Topical
Film Company

■ Women workers assembling aircraft in
   Britain, January 1918.

The women work in a hangar assembling
the aircraft. Some of the women are in the
Women's Army Auxiliary Corps. They make
the wooden frames for the aircraft wings,
then attach the fabric. A group of them
wheels out the fuselage of a BE2. Outside
the hangar, other women make final checks
on a Sopwith 1½ Strutter, tightening the
wires. The engine cowling is also checked
over. The pilot starts up the engine and the
women hold onto the aircraft's tail to enable
it to build up power.

Notes
Summary: an additional fragment of this
issue is held (also with Spanish titles) as
IWM 697b.
catalogued SDB: 6/1983

IWM 693a · GB, 13/4/1918
**PICTORIAL NEWS (OFFICIAL) 346-2
(Spanish version)**

b/w · 1 reel · 102' (2 mins) · silent
intertitles: Spanish

sp Ministry of Information *pr* Topical Film
Company

I. Princess Alice, the Countess of Athlone,
reviewing Army cadets in Reading, April
1918. The Countess is shown through a
school or college building into a courtyard
where the cadets are drawn up on parade.
She makes her inspection conducted by a
minister or teacher.
II. A public schools athletics meeting at
Stamford Bridge football ground, Fulham,
London, April 1918. According to the
caption, the meeting was won by Rugby
School. The athletics are shown in
progress, including the end of a sprint race,
the start of a long distance race, the end of
another long distance race, and a hurdles
race.

Notes
Summary: the second item is listed in

McKernan as belonging to issue 348-1
rather than 346-2; he also notes that 348-1
has an item with identical titling to the
Princess Alice story. It is therefore at least
possible that this entry should form part of
the following entry rather than standing on
its own.
[shotsheet available]
catalogued SDB: 6/1983

IWM 693b · GB, 24/4/1918
**PICTORIAL NEWS (OFFICIAL) 348-1
(Spanish version)**

b/w · 1 reel · 218' (4 mins) · silent
intertitles: Spanish

sp Ministry of Information *pr* Topical Film
Company

I. Queen Mary officially celebrating St
George's Day at Windsor, 20 April 1918.
The Queen in her open carriage drives
down the hill from Windsor Castle (visible in
the background) past an honour guard of
the Coldstream Guards to where flowers are
arranged on stalls on either side of the
street. The Queen, still in her carriage, is
presented with a bouquet.
II. A parade by women war workers through
the streets of London to St Paul's Cathedral,
April 1918. The parade is led by a military
band, followed by members of the Women's
Land Army with a hay wagon. These are
followed by the Women's Forestry Corps. A
demonstration is given of a traction engine
driving a mechanical thresher and baler,
with women overseeing the machine.
Members of the Women's Army Auxiliary
Corps file into St Paul's for the service. The
Lord Mayor, Sir Horace Marshall, arrives.
III. A delegation headed by James Wilson
representing US Socialist and Union groups
being shown over a tank works in Britain,
April 1918. Some of the men and women
ride in a Mk V Tank with its hatches open
over the test ground, then are helped out.

Notes
Summary: one additional story from this
issue, and what may well be a second
story, are listed in the entry currently
identified as issue 346-2 – see **Notes** to that
entry. See also **IWM 474** for the item on the
women war workers and **IWM 224** for the
item on the US delegates.
[*The Times*, 19 April 1918: 3C]
[*The Times*, 22 April 1918: 5C, 11C]
[shotsheet available]
catalogued SDB: 6/1983

IWM 693c · GB, 27/4/1918
PICTORIAL NEWS (OFFICIAL) 348-2
(Spanish version)

b/w · 1 reel · 239' (4 mins) · silent
intertitles: Spanish

sp Ministry of Information pr Topical Film
Company

I. Royal Navy ships in the English Channel,
1918. The film shows the monitor, HMS
Erebus, on patrol, with two torpedo boats
and two minesweepers at work in the
Channel.
II. Bonar Law's "Victory Budget", April 1918.
The item shows British troops digging a
trench as part of the war effort, followed by
a portrait shot of Bonar Law in a garden, by
himself, then with a colleague on a bench.
The caption suggests that both are
contributing to the war effort.
III. A football match between rival teams of
women workers in a park in Southend, April
1918. The two teams emerge to play. The
kick-off and some of the action of the match
are shown.
IV. The Zeebrugge raid, April 1918. The film
shows what it claims as the Zeebrugge
mole before the war, with a ship docked
alongside. (The ship is in fact a British
Caledon Class cruiser in 1917 or 1918 at
another location.) This is followed by
dockyard workers walking along what,
again, is claimed as the mole.

Notes
Summary: see **IWM 553** for the item on the
English Channel and **IWM 656b** for the item
on Zeebrugge.
[shotsheet available]
catalogued SDB: 6/1983

IWM 693d · GB, 15/4/1918
PICTORIAL NEWS (OFFICIAL) 347-1
(Spanish version)

b/w · 1 reel · 190' (3 mins) · silent
intertitles: Spanish

sp Ministry of Information pr Topical Film
Company

I. US Ambassador W H Page's delegation
visiting Liverpool and London, April 1918.
Dr Page and his group come off a ship in
Liverpool. They talk with women workers in
the street outside a factory. In London, they
pose outside the vehicle entrance to the
Palace of Westminster.
II. King George V visiting an RAF base in

England, April 1918. The King inspects the
base ground crew drawn up on parade. He
goes on to enter a hangar, making a point
of handing over his matches as he does so.
He looks inside the main cockpit of a
Handley Page 0/400. Queen Mary can be
seen with him, looking over the aircraft.
III. The "Two Women of Pervyse" on the
Western Front, 1918. The captions say that
the two ladies, Baroness T'Serclaes and
Marie Chisholm, were injured recently in a
gas attack. They are shown leaving on their
motor-cycle combination to give assistance
to a wounded man on a stretcher, then
sitting together at a table, talking.

Notes
Summary: see **IWM 162** for the item on the
two women.
[shotsheet available]
catalogued SDB: 6/1983

IWM 693e · GB, 18/4/1918
PICTORIAL NEWS (OFFICIAL) 347-2
(Spanish version)

b/w · 1 reel · 238' (4 mins) · silent
intertitles: Spanish

sp Ministry of Information pr Topical Film
Company

I. British troops near Amiens, Western Front,
late March or early April 1918. An
overturned 18-pounder field gun with the
dead bodies of its horses and crew beside
it. Soldiers including a Lewis gunner in the
foreground holding a slit trench. Cavalry
officers (dismounted) hold an open-air
briefing while German prisoners rest
nearby.
II. J R Clynes MP, opening a public food
kitchen at Stoke Newington, April 1918. The
film shows a crowd of cheering children.
Clynes arrives and performs the opening
ceremony. The children, rather camera-shy,
hold jugs of soup. A final shot of one child
in close-up eating an apple.
III. Mineworkers being recruited for the
Army in Burslem, Stoke-on-Trent, April
1918. The men pose with the recruiting
sergeants. They are the last conscripts from
the reserved occupations such as mining.
They march through the town streets. Small
children march in step as they go, and a
woman rushes out to kiss her husband
goodbye.
IV. British and French troops in the Amiens
area, Western Front, late March or early
April 1918. British troops, some resting,
hold a slit trench. Other soldiers rest, eating

from cans. British and French soldiers, looking tired and strained, wait in a village. Two of the Frenchmen pick up their rifles and leave.

Notes
Summary (item I): see **IWM 180** for the first Western Front item.
Summary (item II): an English-language version of this story is held as **NTB 347-02**.
Remarks: a well above average episode with a high standard of camerawork relative to the remainder of the series. It is tempting to associate the miners in Burslem with 46th (North Midlands) Division and its achievement in breaking the Hindenburg Line at Bellenglise, September 1918.
[shotsheet available]
catalogued SDB: 6/1983

IWM 694a · GB, 1914-18
[LONDON RALLY] (allocated)

b/w · 1 reel · 74' (1 min) · silent
intertitles: none

■ Untraced (newsreel?) fragment showing civilians walking through St James's Park with Buckingham Palace in the background. Then a street scene in London, with men and women arriving by car and on foot for a meeting at a great hall. Some hold up posters expressing "solidarity" as they enter.

Notes
Summary: this was originally tentatively identified as the 'Brotherhood Church' story from *War Office Official Topical Budget* issue 310-1. The subsequent availability of that issue for comparison (**NTB 310-01**) shows this hypothesis to be wrong, and at present the story remains a mystery.
[shotsheet available]
catalogued RBNS: 7/1993

IWM 694b · GB, 22/9/1917
WAR OFFICE OFFICIAL TOPICAL BUDGET 317-2

b/w · 1 reel · 60' (1 min) · silent
intertitles: none

sp War Office Cinema Committee *pr* Topical Film Company

■ 'THE KING ON CLYDESIDE' – a single story from the newsreel held as **NTB 317-02**.

[shotsheet available]
catalogued SDB: 6/1983

IWM 695 · GB, 1918
OUR DAY (ledger title)
[GERMAN U-BOATS LYING AT HARWICH] (alternative, allocated)

b/w · 1 reel · 276' (5 mins) · mute
intertitles: none

■ Film of surrendered U-boats at Harwich, November 1918.

Aerial sequence shot from an airship of the U-boats arriving off Harwich – Admiralty R and Modified R Class destroyers lead in Kreuzer (large) and Mittel (medium displacement) U-boats. Medium close-up of British rating standing in the eyes of cameraship looking out to sea – presumably at the beaten foe. Medium shot as a U.160 Class (?) submarine passes left to right, followed by U.99 and U.105 Class boats. Medium close-up as a U.66 Class boat passes right to left. Shots of the surrendered submarines anchored at Harwich – cameraship passes a group of three comprising U.99 and U.90 Class boats and one other – in the background is HMS *Redgauntlet* (F.97). A second group – the nearest is UB.III Class. A third group of boats – nearest is UB.133 Class. Medium close-up of ML.15 secured alongside a U-boat ready to take off some of the crew. The crew of a U.81 Class (?) boat assemble on deck with their kit ready for trans-shipment. Medium shot as cameraship passes another group of three boats – U.43 and U.99 Class and one other.

catalogued NAP: 2/1987

IWM 696 · NO FILM

IWM 697a · GB, 26/1/1918
WAR OFFICE OFFICIAL TOPICAL BUDGET 335-2 (Spanish version)

b/w · 1 reel · 258' (4 mins) · silent
intertitles: Spanish

sp War Office Cinema Committee *pr* Topical Film Company

I. French troops lead Austro-Hungarian prisoners of war through rear area villages

on the Italian Front, January 1918. The French soldiers lead a long line of prisoners along the road; Italian women and old men come out of their houses to watch as the column passes. One village has a signpost on the wall showing that Asola is nearby. A pan over a group of the prisoners.
II. Sir Edward Kemp, Canada's Minister of Militia, works at his desk and in profile against a window, January 1918. The caption states that Kemp has announced that a new army of 100 000 Canadian soldiers will shortly be joining in the fight on the Western Front.
III. US Ambassador Walter Page opening a YMCA for US officers in London, January 1918. Page arrives by car, talks to the people outside the building, then walks inside.
IV. Snow in Flanders: the cameraman's car stuck in a snowdrift, and soldiers having a snowball fight, Western Front, January 1918.

Notes
Summary: note that an English-language version of stories II, III and IV only of this issue is held as **IWM 672b** and a further copy of IV is **IWM 1061-09c**. An additional story, not duplicated elsewhere, is **IWM 1061-09a**.
[shotsheet available]
catalogued SDB: 6/1983

IWM 697b · GB, 12/1/1918
WAR OFFICE OFFICIAL TOPICAL BUDGET 333-2 (Spanish version) [2]

b/w · 1 reel · 59' (1 min) · silent
intertitles: Spanish

sp War Office Cinema Committee *pr* Topical Film Company

■ British horsed transport detours around the dry Wadi Hersi, north of Gaza, where the retreating Turks have blown the bridge, Palestine, November 1917.

Notes
Summary: an additional fragment of this issue is held (also with Spanish titles) as **IWM 692b**.
[shotsheet available]
catalogued SDB: 6/1983

IWM 697c · GB, 16/1/1918
WAR OFFICE OFFICIAL TOPICAL BUDGET 334-1 (Spanish version)

b/w · 1 reel · 120' (2 mins) · silent
intertitles: Spanish

sp War Office Cinema Committee *pr* Topical Film Company

■ Two stories from the newsreel, also held in an English version as **IWM 662b**. The stories concern a procession by the Order of St John of Jerusalem and horse-breaking in Palestine.

[shotsheet available]
catalogued SDB: 6/1983

IWM 697d · GB, 19/1/1918
WAR OFFICE OFFICIAL TOPICAL BUDGET 334-2 (Spanish version)

b/w · 1 reel · 65' (1 min) · silent
intertitles: Spanish

sp War Office Cinema Committee *pr* Topical Film Company

■ British tank brings in a captured German gun between the British offensive and German counter-offensive at Cambrai, Western Front, 29 November 1917.

A German 150mm gun is towed into a wood east of Ribecourt on the Marcoing Road by a Mk IV Female tank HMLS 'Intimidate' (of 'I' Company, Tank Corps ?) and met by men of the Royal Artillery and (probably) 6th Division.

Notes
Summary: see **IWM 144** for this item.
[shotsheet available]
catalogued SDB: 6/1983

IWM 698 · NO FILM

IWM 699a · GB, 20/3/1918
PICTORIAL NEWS (OFFICIAL) 343-1 (Spanish version)

b/w · 1 reel · 251' (4 mins) · silent
intertitles: Spanish

sp Ministry of Information *pr* Topical Film Company

■ Spanish-language version of four items from the issue held in full as **NTB 343-01**. The items (in the order in which they appear) are 'KING AND THE DOVER PATROL', 'SHAMROCK DAY', 'REMOUNTS IN EGYPT' and 'CANADIAN COMMANDER HONOURED'.

catalogued SDB: 6/1983

IWM 699b · GB, 23/3/1918
PICTORIAL NEWS (OFFICIAL) 343-2 (Spanish version)

b/w · 1 reel · 252' (4 mins) · silent
intertitles: Spanish

sp Ministry of Information *pr* Topical Film Company

I. Queen Mary inspecting Land Girls outside Buckingham Palace, March 1918. The Queen emerges into the palace courtyard. The Land Girls march past, bearing banners about the importance of the Home Front, and with a hay wagon behind them.
II. Queen Mary, the Prince of Wales and Prince Henry visiting an aircraft engine factory in England, March 1918. The Royal party shakes hands with the waiting management of the factory. The Queen goes to talk to three bedridden women whose bed-stretchers have been wheeled out of doors for the purpose. The Royal party walks through the various departments of the factory, talking with the women workers as the tour proceeds.
III. A memorial service by the South African Brigade, Western Front, 1917. Major-General H T Lukin, the divisional commander, listens to the bugles blowing the Last Post, then decorates two soldiers who won medals for the attack on Delville Wood, September 1916.
IV. British destroyers hunting submarines in the North Sea, early 1918. The conditions are overcast, with a heavy sea running, and the ships are too distant to be clearly identified as they emerge from harbour out into the open sea. An SS airship is visible in the distance.

Notes
Summary: see **IWM 169** for the item on the South African Brigade; an English-language version of this newsreel story is held as **NTB 343-02**.
[shotsheet available]
catalogued SDB: 6/1983

IWM 699c · GB, 13/3/1918
PICTORIAL NEWS (OFFICIAL) 342-1 (Spanish version)

b/w · 1 reel · 248' (4 mins) · silent
intertitles: Spanish

sp Ministry of Information *pr* Topical Film Company

I. The memorial service for John Redmond MP at Westminster Cathedral, London, 8 March 1918. The various dignitaries arrive by car for the ceremony. Prominent are Lloyd George and General Jan Smuts. At the end of the service the people leave.
II. King George V visiting the Royal Marines barracks at Deal, early 1918. The King inspects the parade of Marines. There is a march past of cadets in their blue uniforms. The King talks with the staff, then goes on to inspect the junior cadets. He stops and talks with the smallest of them, who can scarcely be 10 years old.
III. British Red Cross work on the Salonika Front, 1918. Lash-up stretchers pulled by donkeys over the rough ground make their way downhill. A mule-drawn ambulance travels over a dirt road.

Notes
Summary: see **IWM 201** for the item on Deal; a further copy of the Salonika item is held as **IWM 1129b**.
[*The Times*, 8 March 1918: 9C]
[*The Times*, 9 March 1918: 9C]
[shotsheet available]
catalogued SDB: 6/1983

IWM 699d · GB, 16/3/1918
PICTORIAL NEWS (OFFICIAL) 342-2 (Spanish version)

b/w · 1 reel · 190' (4 mins) · silent
intertitles: Spanish

sp Ministry of Information *pr* Topical Film Company

■ Spanish-language version of two items from the issue held in full as **NTB 342-02**. The items are 'KING AND QUEEN AT READING' and 'THE CHINAMAN'S NEW YEAR'.

catalogued SDB: 6/1983

IWM 700a · GB, 6/5/1918
PICTORIAL NEWS (OFFICIAL) 349-2 (Spanish version) [1]

b/w · 1 reel · 137' (3 mins) · silent
intertitles: Spanish

sp Ministry of Information *pr* Topical Film Company

- Spanish-language version of an item from the issue held in more complete form as **IWM 661b**. The item is 'THE END OF RICHTHOFEN'.

Notes
Summary: note that a French-language fragment is **IWM 673c** and another Spanish-language fragment is **IWM 700e**.
catalogued SDB: 6/1983

IWM 700b · GB, 8/5/1918
PICTORIAL NEWS (OFFICIAL) 350-1 (Spanish version)

b/w · 1 reel · 235' (4 mins) · silent
intertitles: Spanish

sp Ministry of Information *pr* Topical Film Company

- Spanish-language version of the (incomplete) newsreel issue held as **IWM 654a**.

Notes
Summary: note that a French-language fragment is also held as **IWM 673a**.
[shotsheet available]
catalogued SDB: 6/1983

IWM 700c · GB, 13/5/1918
PICTORIAL NEWS (OFFICIAL) 350-2 (Spanish version)

b/w · 1 reel · 303' (5 mins) · silent
intertitles: Spanish

sp Ministry of Information *pr* Topical Film Company

- Spanish-language version of the issue held as **IWM 654b**.

Notes
Summary: note that a French-language fragment is **IWM 673a**.
[shotsheet available]
catalogued SDB: 6/1983

IWM 700d · GB, 1/5/1918
PICTORIAL NEWS (OFFICIAL) 349-1 (Spanish version)

b/w · 1 reel · 215' (4 mins) · silent
intertitles: Spanish

sp Ministry of Information *pr* Topical Film Company

- Spanish-language version of the issue held as **IWM 661a**.

Notes
Production: in this version of the issue, in the item on Robertson, the caption states that ANZAC stands for "Australian, New Zealand and Canadian forces". This mistake suggests strongly that captions were being composed, or elaborated upon, at the country of delivery and not in Britain.
Summary: note that French-language versions of items from this issue are also held as **IWM 673d** and **IWM 684a**.
[shotsheet available]
catalogued SDB: 6/1983

IWM 700e · GB, 6/5/1918
PICTORIAL NEWS (OFFICIAL) 349-2 (Spanish version) [2]

b/w · 1 reel · 126' (3 mins) · silent
intertitles: Spanish

sp Ministry of Information *pr* Topical Film Company

- Spanish-language version of two items from the issue held in more complete form as **IWM 661b**. The items are 'THE MOLE MEN' and 'AT THE HAMPSTEAD ORTHOPAEDIC HOSPITAL'.

Notes
Summary: note that a French-language fragment is **IWM 673c** and another Spanish-language fragment is **IWM 700a**.
catalogued SDB: 6/1983

IWM 701-705 · NO FILM

IWM 706 · GB, (ca) 1927
TERRITORIAL ARMY FILM

b/w · 2 reels · 2260' (37 mins) · silent
intertitles: English

sp War Office (?)

- Recruiting film for the Territorial Army showing manœuvres by 162nd East

Midland Brigade, Northamptonshire, mid-1920s.

(Reel 1) The film opens by stating that as the basis for the expansion of the Army in wartime the TA "may be a factor in the maintenance of peace". Men of 4th Battalion, Northamptonshire Regiment, march to the station where the mayor and mayoress of Northampton are among those seeing them off to camp. They march into their tented camp at Bulford. Next morning the men get up, practise PT and hold a parade. Cooks and QMAAC members work (very camera-conscious) preparing food. Regimental barbers give men haircuts. The band practises its music. Lunch is served under canvas. After lunch the officers get a riding class under Lieutenant-Colonel Wernher, commanding 5th Battalion, Bedfordshire and Hertfordshire Regiment, who is also Master of the Fernie Hunt. The men unload footballs and beer for the YMCA tent. At the tent a conjuror performs his act, followed by a song and dance act, Arthur Line and Ireson Swann of Northampton. At the end of the week there is a pay parade and kit inspection, after which the men leave for manœuvres. Most of the transport is 3-ton lorries, but horse-drawn field kitchens are still in use. As the brigade marches past, its commander, Colonel John Brown, takes the salute with two Finnish officers watching. Brown talks with Lord Onslow, the Under-Secretary of State for War, and with Lieutenant-General Sir Hugh Jeudwine, Director-General of the Territorial Army. Two Japanese Army observers are also present, as is the mayor of Northampton. The brigade marches into the battle area, to take part in manœuvres with regular troops. Royal Tank Corps forces, including Rolls-Royce armoured cars and Vickers Medium Mk I tanks, pass up the road, followed by 18-pounder Mk IV field guns, and the remainder of the forces. *(Reel 2)* On manœuvres a section of 4th Northants piles into a ditch and 'opens fire' with rifles and a Lewis gun, using a rattle to simulate Lewis fire. Other soldiers 'play dead' as the exercise continues. The film emphasises the 'empty battlefield' of modern warfare. Obsolete Medium A 'Whippet' tanks are used to generate smokescreens which add to the confusion. As enemy aircraft (not seen) pass overhead, guns and Vickers Medium Mk II tanks hide in the woodlands. Some men of 1st Battalion, Hertfordshire Regiment, part of the brigade, relax and eat. Heliograph signallers indicate the danger is past and movement starts again. Dragon caterpillars move 18-pounder field guns to a threatened

area. 6-inch 26cwt guns open fire. Vickers machinegunners with horse-drawn limbers also set up their weapons. Other guns, including the 6-inch Mk VII and the 3.7-inch mountain howitzer, join in. Tanks and Cavalry start to pursue and 'enemy' prisoners are brought in. The cease fire is given and troops start to move out of the area. Back in camp the horses are cared for. Colonel Brown talks with Lord Exeter, the Lord Lieutenant of Northamptonshire, while Lord Onslow talks with the mayoress of Northampton and Lieutenant-Colonel Cockburn (?). Back at camp the 4th Northants commander, Lieutenant-Colonel Lowther, Master of the Pytchley Hunt, addresses his men, who then march past in dismissal. The film ends by explaining how TA training "makes a man physically fit, broadens his mind, develops his spirit of comradeship, and teaches discipline", and how the TA is "a great factor for peace".

Notes
Remarks: this film bears some of the hallmarks of having been made by a military committee. Its unimaginative title, ponderous jocularity and blatant snobbery all make it far more of a social document than a military one. However, the concern shown in manœuvres for the value of air power is noteworthy, as is the material on early tanks.
catalogued SDB: 7/1983

IWM 707-711 · NO FILM

IWM 712 · USSR, 1925
MODERN WARFARE IN CHINA 1924-1925

b/w · 5 reels · 5203' (87 mins) · silent
intertitles: English, Russian & Chinese

prod Grinevsky (Colonel) *cam* Grinevsky (Colonel); and Garutso (Lieutenant-Colonel)

■ Russian-made film of the advance of the forces of Marshal Chang Tso-Lin, warlord of Mukden, south towards Nanking, 1924-25.

Chang's Army of Fengtien, with Russian assistance, advances down the coast of the Gulf of Chihli, the territory of the warlord Wu Pei-Fu of Peking. Most of the battle sequences are clearly reconstructions after the event. The film opens *(Reel 1)* with a portrait still of Chang Tso-Lin, and then portrait shots of his senior commanders:

Chang Hsuh-Liang of the Air Force, Chang Tsung-Ch'ang of the Army, and Wu Tsi-Sheng, commander of the Northern Cavalry Group. There is a review of the forces. The Air Force has Bréguet Type 14 fighters and an amphibian. The Air Force Chief of Staff is Colonel Yao, but the "pioneer" is a Russian, Lieutenant-Colonel Koodlaienko. The Army trains for battle. Most of its equipment is Russian or Russian-derived, notably its guns, which are French 75mm field guns of Russian surplus and Russian 76.2mm mountain howitzers. Heavy mortars are carried on mules. There are both regular Cavalry and Mongol horsemen. They march past Chang Tsung-Ch'ang. General Lou has a detachment of swordsmen. *(Reel 2)* The men play with toboggans. The leaders of First Army are General King (Mongolian, Chief of Staff), General Chu as Army commander, General Netchaieff as Russian adviser, General Chen, General Pi, Colonel Hsu (commanding 55th Infantry, the main fighting force) Colonel Tchehoff (sic) 1st Brigade Chief of Staff, Colonel Makaerenko, 1st Brigade second in command, and Colonel Kostroff the battery commander. A reconstruction of the Army's attack on the Great Wall of China, defended by enemy troops. The advance continues to the sea at Chinwangtoo. The men, some brandishing German Bergmann sub-machineguns (?), watch the shoreline. On 24 November 1924 the Army enters Tientsin, which is shown in detail. *(Reel 3)* An alert by an outpost scout (acted) brings on an encounter battle with infantry rushes, supported by the guns and Maxim machineguns (the Maxim jams repeatedly). The Mongol horsemen and mortar crews move up. Colonel Chu leads 55th Regiment forward, and the enemy surrenders. The horsemen pursue and patrol. The Army occupies the next village where Chang Tsung-Ch'ang shakes hands with the local leaders. *(Reel 4)* There are further battles (also reconstructions) at Shanhaikwan and Lankow, with the Russian Artillery support proving decisive. *(Reel 5 – marked as 6)* Chang Tsung-Ch'ang arrives by train at Tsing-Hsien to review the Army. His soldiers entrain for the advance to Nanking. A river crossing by pontoon is shown. At Lankow 1st Brigade builds an armoured train, which is then shown in the fighting at Potuchen station, together with the other troops. Finally, an enemy shell-bursts on the track ahead of the train splitting the rail. The men repair the track and give some first aid to casualties. The horsemen and guns continue the advance. The film ends at this point with portrait shots of the two cameramen, Colonel

Grinevsky and Lieutenant-Colonel Garutso.

Notes
Production: this appears to have been an official film from the USSR.
Intertitles: the three languages of the titles appear together as a split screen image. The transliteration into English used in the summary for proper names is exactly as they appear in the intertitles. The English used is occasionally quaint.
Technical: the 5 existing reels of this film are numbered as 1, 2, 3, 4 and 6, but there is no obvious break in continuity between reels 4 and 6.
Remarks: the film's makers showed considerable skill in their reconstruction work, including some startling material of 'bodies' being literally blown apart by shell fire during an attack. The level of fakery is certainly good enough to convince an uncritical audience. While this enhances the value of the film as an example of early Soviet propaganda, it obviously detracts from its value as historical record. Nevertheless, its rarity value makes this a noteworthy film.
[shotsheet available]
catalogued SDB: 6/1983

IWM 713 · GB, (prod) 1918
1914-1918 ODD SECTIONS (ledger title)

b/w · 1 reel · 220' (4 mins) · silent
intertitles: none

■ Very jumbled scenes of British forces on the Western Front in the First World War.

Two German prisoners posed carrying Maxim machineguns. Scottish troops in a 3-ton lorry, which tows away a captured German 77mm field gun. A kilted Highland battalion on the march. A French colonial battery firing its 75mm field guns. British soldiers on the march in the rear areas. Back to the Highlanders on the march. A château, probably a British headquarters (very dark), the captured German guns and prisoners arrive. The prisoners help assembling the various trophies.

Notes
Summary: despite the writing on its leader, the scene of the Highland troops does not show Cameronians.
Remarks: very difficult to follow, and not worth the effort of trying.
catalogued SDB: 7/1983

IWM 714 · GB, 20/4/1916
FOR THE EMPIRE
MARTYRED BELGIUM (on copy held)

b/w · 1 reel · 467' (8 mins) · silent
intertitles: English

sp Wellington House *pr* Gaumont
prod Welsh, Thomas A *dir* Pearson, George
scenario Le Bas, Hedley

- Incomplete copy of a film combining propaganda with an appeal for the British people to buy War Bonds, April 1916.

(Missing is an opening sequence showing the tearing up of the treaty guaranteeing Belgian neutrality.) 'Martyred Belgium' is the title introducing 'scene 2'. Britannia posed beside the figure of 'Belgium' and her dead children. "What are others doing for us?" A soldier sets out for war leaving his parents in a country cottage. Muddy conditions on the Western Front are shown. A letter from the front pleads "for God's sake don't let us down". French troops train in the snow of the Vosges area. A ward for convalescent soldiers in a big hospital, "what others are suffering for us". The parents in the country cottage read in the newspaper of their son's death. Two upper-class parents hear the same news, as does a young mother with a baby and two young children, and the widow of an aristocratic naval officer, beside his portrait. The cities of France and Belgium – Rheims, Arras, Ypres – are shown ruined, but central London is untouched. A destroyer and a battle-cruiser on patrol symbolise protection. But ships must be paid for. Soldiers are shown receiving their pay. A munitions shop at work is shown. "One hand grenade can put out of action four or five persons... and six grenades cost 15/-." A War Bond costs 15/6d, which will buy six grenades or 124 rounds of ammunition. The Chancellor, R McKenna, is quoted urging people to buy the bonds, and a man is shown at the Post Office doing so. (A closing sequence also appears to be missing.)

Notes
Production: originally catalogued as *Martyred Belgium*; correctly identified following the appearance of the article by Nicholas Hiley cited below.
[Nicholas Hiley, "*The British Army Film, You!* and *For the Empire*: reconstructed propaganda films", *Historical Journal of Film, Radio and Television*, 5: 2 (1985): 165-182]
[shotsheet available]
catalogued SDB: 6/1983

IWM 715 · GB, (prod) 1916
[ASQUITH IN FRANCE, 1916] (allocated)

b/w · 1 reel · 23' (1 min) · silent
intertitles: none

sp War Office Cinema Committee (?)
pr Topical Film Company (?)

- Brief fragment showing Prime Minister Asquith on his visit to France, 7 September 1916.

Asquith has his back to the camera throughout. He is shown firstly talking with British officers near Contay, then at the Royal Flying Corps base at Fienvillers watching a Sopwith 1½ Strutter of 70 Squadron take off.

Notes
Summary: some of the information on this film derives from MS flashframes; the date on these of "7-8-16" is a misreading of 7-9-16.
[Robert Blake, *The Private Papers of Douglas Haig 1914-1919*, Eyre and Spottiswoode (1952): 164]
catalogued SDB: 6/1983

IWM 716-771 · NO FILM

IWM 772 · Germany, (?) 1917
[KAISER WILHELM VISITS TURKEY]
(allocated)

b/w & tinted · 2 reels · 1284' (22 mins) · silent
intertitles: German, Turkish & French

sp German Generalstab

- Visit of Kaiser Wilhelm II to Constantinople and the Gallipoli battlefields, Turkey, 15-16 October 1917.

(Reel 1) The Kaiser gets into the state barge and is rowed across the Bosphorus (tinted orange). On the far side he gets out to greet various German officials (tinting ends). He tours Topkapi, the old Serail, with his entourage, and relaxes briefly at the Medji Kiosk (summer house or pavilion). He visits the German battle-cruiser SMS *Goeben*, given to the Turks as the *Yavuz Sultan Selim* together with its German crew, who wear Turkish insignia on their uniforms. Drawn up on the quarterdeck, they give three cheers for the Kaiser. (Tinted orange) On the

following morning the Kaiser looks over the ship. With him is the Turkish Minister of War, Enver Pasha, Captain Ackermann of the *Goeben* and Admiral Georg von Müller. (Tinted green) The Kaiser wearing Turkish uniform boards a launch from the *Goeben* and is taken across to the fort at Hamadi. (Tinted orange) There at a conference over a map the battles of the Dardanelles are described to him by a Turkish general (tinting ends). Lunch is held in the open on the beach at Ari-Burnu. The camera pans over the Turkish positions on the coast at Ari-Burnu, with the island of Imbros indistinctly visible far out to sea. The Turkish Commander-in-Chief, Djevad Pasha, sits next to the Kaiser in a staff car and explains the battle to him as they approach Kilid-Bahr. The village itself is still in ruins as a result of British shell fire. *(Reel 2*, tinted orange) On board the *Goeben* Essad Pasha talks with the Kaiser. (Tinted green) The Turkish flag is raised on the ship and Enver joins in the salute. The Kaiser decorates members of the ship's crew and the Turkish navy. Enver consults with Colonel von Frankenburg, commander of the Asien Korps, while waiting for the Kaiser. (Tinted red) He arrives and the men talk together. The Kaiser decorates more Turkish sailors, including some senior officers. The entourage then boards a launch (note the cine camera in the background) and is taken to the shore (tinting ends). The Kaiser is taken by car to the Heragan Palace and to various mosques in Constantinople (the camera is not allowed inside). In the course of the tour a number of German nurses are presented to him. Outside the Mirasim Kiosk Turkish Janissaries in their full ceremonial dress parade past the Kaiser, complete with their musical instruments, after which he prepares to leave.

Notes
Title: this is taken from the shotsheet, but is clearly an allocated title, not an original one. [shotsheet available]
catalogued SDB: 7/1983

IWM 773-777 · NO FILM

IWM 778 · Germany, (before) 1918
VORSICHT BEI ALLEN GESPRAECHEN
[CARELESS TALK] (translation)

b/w & tinted · 1 reel · 1206' (22 mins) · silent
intertitles: German

- German First World War fictional film warning soldiers against careless talk.

The fatal consequences of accidentally letting the enemy discover secret information are illustrated by an episode set in the trenches. Orders for an attack are passed down from Hindenburg to GHQ to officers in the field. Trench mortars and gas cylinders are prepared and reinforcements arrive. The British are unaware of the forthcoming offensive until a soldier picks up a casual remark by a German over the field telephone. This gives them time to prepare their own defences and when the Germans open fire and advance across no man's land (red-tinted film) they are repulsed. While the German command wonders how the enemy gained advance warning of the attack, the soldier responsible for the failure lies wounded and has time to realise the consequences of his indiscretion before being killed by a well-aimed enemy shell.

Notes
Title: this appears at the bottom of each intertitle.
Technical: this film was previously GWY 778, acquired with German material of the Second World War under the Enemy Property Act. It was transferred to its present number in 1983.
catalogued KGTG: 2/1976

IWM 779-807 · NO FILM

IWM 808 · GB, 1919
WITH GENERAL IRONSIDE'S FORCES IN NORTH RUSSIA

b/w · 4 reels · 3517' (60 mins) · silent
intertitles: English

cam Joly, E F (Colonel) (?)

- British and other national forces in the North Russian Intervention Force in and near Archangel, and normal peasant life in the area, December 1918 to September 1919.

(Reel 1) The icebreaker SS *Canada* brings the cameraman and his colleagues into Archangel harbour in the middle of winter. The locals, in full furs, use sledges for transportation, some of them drawn by reindeer. The statue of Peter the Great still stands, as does his house in Archangel.

The city is then shown in summertime, including the cathedral and the docks. A French Montcalm Class cruiser is at anchor. A street market sells local goods. *(Reel 2)* British soldiers at a gunnery school are taught about the Vickers machinegun. In winter White Russian soldiers march across the frozen Dvina River into Archangel. In Murmansk a group of soldiers poses for the camera – British, American, French, Italian, Serbian and Russian. The main Allied warehouses are shown in Bakaritza, the harbour on the opposite bank of the river to Archangel. Soldiers in training use skis and snowshoes for patrol work. One of the trains in Archangel station has a YMCA canteen car. A supply train comes in and sleighs take the supplies out to the front. The village of Bolshayaozerka, on the way to the front, is shown. British soldiers in the front lines man trenches and rifle pits in the snow. *(Reel 3)* Sledge-ambulances bring the wounded back to the hospital in Archangel, where surgery is performed. The village of Toulgas is shown. Men of the Royal Scots Fusiliers carry out PT exercises in the snow. US troops come back to the village from the front, together with Canadian sleigh-mounted 18-pounder guns. In May 1919 the relief force arrives and marches through Archangel. Local boy scouts march at the rear of the column. Earlier, in the snow, White Russian Cossacks ride in on patrol, bringing in Bolshevik prisoners of war. In Archangel troops use the YMCA carriage, and there is a tug of war between US and Canadian soldiers. In September the last US troops evacuate the city by sea, their ship passing the repair base at Solombola. The great fire at the lumber mills at Maimaxa is shown from the river. *(Reel 4)* A "typical Russian village" is shown in the snow. More views of the peasant villages and their inhabitants. The camera is taken for a ride on a sledge. The various churches and cathedrals of the area are shown: the cathedral at Solombola in winter, that at Emetzkoe in winter, and the church at Kholmogorie, including detailed views of the church bells. The view over the Dvina valley in summer, including Kholmogorie market place on Sunday afternoon with troops wandering about. At a nearby convent the nuns clean samovars, or work in the fields gathering early wheat. The village of Kergoman on the Dvina is shown in winter. More scenes of troops in Archangel itself, including a Russian boy 'mascot' for British troops. Russian girls work under US supervision making coffee in a YMCA hut. Children play with a see-saw.

Notes
Cameraman: the film's opening credits give Colonel E F Joly DSO as the cameraman. However, the standard reference books give no such holder of the DSO before 1920, while the Army, Indian Army and Royal Air Force records show no officer with that name (the spelling Jolly occurs, but not with the initials E F). It is possible that the colonel was a Dominion officer, but his identity remains a mystery.
Summary: for further material on the North Russian Intervention Force see **IWM 420/19+20** and **IWM 422**.
Remarks: the colonel has committed most of the sins of the amateur cameraman, chiefly in failing to judge the aperture settings and cranking speeds properly and in some fairly eccentric editing, as a result of which most of the film is too dark, too jerky, and lacks any kind of flow. Nevertheless, his interest in Russian culture has produced some useful material that is worth watching.
[shotsheet available]
catalogued SDB: 7/1983

IWM 809 · GB, 14/5/1928
VISIT OF THE KING OF AFGHANISTAN TO ENGLAND (ledger title)

b/w · 7 reels · 6422' (107 mins) · silent intertitles: none

sp Foreign Office and India Office
pr Gaumont *cam* Bishop, W Herbert
ed Bishop, W Herbert *adv* Foxen Cooper, E

- Unfinished film of the visit of King Amanullah and Queen Surayya of Afghanistan to Britain, 13 March-3 April 1928.

The film is partially completed, and shows some signs of proper editing, but scenes may break off abruptly in one reel and resume in another reel. Throughout the film numerous reporters, press photographers and newsreel cameramen can be seen recording the visit. *(Reel 1)* The King tours the BSA works, Small Heath, Birmingham, on 16 March, escorted by the deputy chairman, Sir Edward Manville. The works makes both motor-cycles and weapons. The King tries out a BSA-Thompson semi-automatic rifle. The film jumps to the King and Queen's visit to the Guildhall on 14 March, escorted by Lieutenant-General Sir Francis Humphries. They are met by the Lord Mayor, Sir J E Kynaston Studd, and the aldermen. The film jumps again to the royal reception in London on 13 March. The King and Queen leave in a carriage from outside Victoria Station, with lines of Grenadier Guards stretching down Wilton Street. It is almost snowing. The streets are decorated with British and Afghan flags. The King inspects the guardsmen, who march off after his carriage leaves. The film jumps again to the arrival of the King and Queen at Dover harbour on board SS *Maid of Orleans*, being met by the Prince of Wales. Another jump to the King's escort of Royal Horse Guards and the royal coaches arriving at Buckingham Palace, to the salute of the Irish Guards. Jump again to King George V, Queen Mary, the Duke of York, Stanley Baldwin and Lord Birkenhead (among others) waiting to greet the King and Queen as their train arrives at Victoria Station, also on the same day. *(Reel 2)* A continuation of the Birmingham visit. Another jump to Hatfield House and its grounds, where the King and Queen stay with the Marquess of Salisbury. Another jump to the King and Queen visiting Portsmouth on 19 March. They are shown over HMS *Victory* and HMS *Tiger*, and the King is taken out on board submarine L.22, which dives. Jump to 17 March, the royal couple visit the RAF Technical Training Centre at Halton, being shown around the workshops. *(Reel 3)* The King visits a steel works, probably Sheffield on 27 March, and a railway engine works, where the engine "King Charles II" is on display. Jump to the L.22 surfacing again at Portsmouth, and returning alongside the *Tiger*. Jump to the Royal Tank Corps centre at Lulworth (Dorset) on 20 March, where an old Mk V Star tank demonstrates its hill climbing ability. As the King watches with the CIGS, Field Marshal Sir George Milne, a line of Vickers Medium Mk I tanks pulls up, the King climbs inside one. Jump again to the King and Queen at Hendon on 16 March watching a flying display by De Havilland DH9as, Gloucester Grebes, and Handley Page 0/1500s of the RAF. *(Reel 4)* On 22 March the King, on board the river steamer *Marchioness*, goes down the Thames to Greenwich Observatory, where the Astronomer-Royal, Sir Frank Dyson, shows him around. Jump to the boat setting out from Victoria Embankment and a repeat of the journey. On the same day the King visits Woolwich Arsenal, where he is shown Vickers Mediums and 12-inch naval guns being made. Back to the trip down the river, the steamer comes in to the main dock at Woolwich, more of the works is shown. More of the river, showing the docks area and the various cargo ships. *(Reel 5)* The King and Queen visit the Rolls-Royce works

at Derby on 27 March, followed by its Mappin and Webb factory, the Sheffield Steel works, and Port Sunlight in Birkenhead, then a textile firm. The royal party is taken across the Mersey and on to a formal reception at Liverpool Town Hall. The film jumps to the Grand National at Aintree on 30 March. In the enclosure before the race the horses "Grakle", "Koko" and "Billy Barton" are shown. The King and Queen watch the race. "Tipperary Tim" is shown winning. Jump to the King inspecting the cadets at RMA Sandhurst, probably on 26 March. Jump back to the Hendon display, with the King and Queen leaving. Jump again to the exterior of the Royal Geographical Society in Kensington Gore, visited by the royal couple on the evening of 22 March. *(Reel 6)* The King's visit to a naval demonstration on 3 April. Four R Class destroyers, led by HMS *Thruster* (nearest the camera), then HMS *Salmon*, HMS *Torrid* and HMS *Rowena* in line abreast drop depth-charges in an anti-submarine exercise. The King, with the camera, is on board HMS *Nelson*, whose sistership HMS *Rodney* is also visible. The destroyer HMS *Witch* passes through the mist, followed by a Shakespeare Class destroyer and a C Class cruiser. The film jumps to the King, in protective clothing, on 29 March descending into a coal mine in Derbyshire. Back at the Rolls-Royce works on 27 March, the King tries out a new car. The King and Queen at the end of a formal ceremony, possibly in Derby. More of the coal mine, interspersed with film of a Tootal linen factory. The royal car arrives outside another town hall. *(Reel 7)* A still picture of the King and Queen in Oxford on 23 March, where he received a DCL degree. Back to the fleet exercise, showing the King talking with Vice-Admiral Sir Hubert Brand and Rear-Admiral E J A Fullerton on board the *Nelson*. The aircraft carrier HMS *Furious* passes nearby. Jump to Longleat stately home. Jump again to the Army manœuvres on Salisbury Plain on 20 March. The King's party arrives by car to be met by Field Marshal Milne. As the band plays, Rolls-Royce armoured cars of the Royal Tank Corps start a drive past, followed by Dragon transports with 6-inch Mk VII guns and 18-pounder field guns, Carden-Loyd Mk V tankettes and Vickers Medium Mk I and Mk II tanks, all seen in long shot, with an RAF fly-past above. The film ends abruptly.

Notes

Production: the Foreign and India Offices appear to have decided to produce a British official film of the visit for propaganda usage in Kabul etc. E Foxen Cooper

("Technical Adviser to HM Government on Cinematography", and incidentally the person at the time responsible for the IWM film collection) was placed in charge of the project and obtained from Gaumont the services of Bishop as cameraman, editor etc, although it was made clear that this was not a Gaumont production. A lecturer from the School of Oriental Studies, G H Darab Khan, was employed to produce Persian translations of the intertitles. The IWM Department of Film has a file relating to the production, containing correspondence, passes, programmes of events in the tour, press cuttings etc. This file indicates that a single copy of the completed film was delivered to the FO on 14 May 1928 for despatch to Kabul. The material held by the Museum material consists presumably either of a cutting copy or of offcuts from that film. Foxen Cooper campaigned at great length for the systematic filming of events of national importance for historical purposes – the filming of this particular royal visit is perhaps the closest he ever came to success. Since the file suggests that neither he nor the FO were particularly happy with the experience, it is perhaps not surprising that the experiment was not repeated.
Remarks: unfinished and only partially edited, this film is inevitably tedious to sit through, and the finished version would probably not have been much more entertaining. Still, some of the camerawork is good, particularly in the river trip through the docklands, and there are some nice dissolves. In addition, it is useful to see what the British Government in 1928 thought that a visiting dignitary should see as significant in Britain. The visit is extensively documented in the file mentioned above. One wonders what a man from a land-locked mountain kingdom thought of battleships and of tanks on Salisbury Plain.
[18/2/1928 – 15/3/1929 : File 'References to Filming of H.M. Amir of Afghanistan visit. March 1928.' in IWM Department of Film]
[*The Times*, 1928: references as follows – 14 March: 16A and 18B; 15 March: 14A and 16B-C; 16 March: 14C; 17 March: 9A; 20 March: 11A-C; 21 March: 13D; 22 March: 11A-B; 24 March: 14D-E; 28 March: 10A; 29 March: 21C; 30 March: 13C; 31 March: 5A; 3 April: 20A-F; 4 April: 9C]
catalogued SDB & NAP: 7/1983

IWM 810 · GB, 12/1925
GAUMONT GRAPHIC 1534

b/w · 1 reel · 385' (6 mins) · silent
intertitles: English

pr Gaumont

- Newsreel on the final signing of the Locarno treaties in the Gold Room at the Foreign Office, London, 1 December 1925.

The various delegations arrive outside the Foreign Office for the ceremony. The Home Secretary, the Honourable William Joynson-Hicks, poses briefly for the camera, as does the Belgian delegate, M Vandervelde (with imperial and pince-nez). Aristide Briand arrives with the French delegation. Inside the Gold Room the delegations take their places. The British sit at the head of the table (directly across from the camera) with the Italian delegation headed by Signor Scialoja on their left (from the camera's viewpoint). Then, carrying on round the table, come the Germans led by Doktor Luther and Herr Stresemann, the Belgians led by M Vandervelde, the Poles led by Count Skrzynski, the Czechs led by Dr Beneš and finally the French delegation which is led by M Briand. Sir Austen Chamberlain chairs the meeting for the British with Stanley Baldwin on his left and Sir Cecil Hurst on his right. British cabinet ministers sit as observers immediately behind the British delegation (Winston Churchill is prominent). Chamberlain reads a speech from the King in greeting. Sitting as public observers are Lord Balfour, Mrs Baldwin and Lady Chamberlain. Hurst places the treaty in front of Stresemann to sign for the Germans. The treaty is then signed by Briand, by Baldwin, by Chamberlain as a witness, and then by Vandervelde. Baldwin gives a short speech. A brief shot of the signed treaty and the pen that Chamberlain used to witness it. The delegates are shown together with friends and wives in the grounds of 10 Downing Street after the ceremony. A final portrait shot of Chamberlain with his wife.

Notes
Summary: see also **IWM 811** which contains most of the original unedited material for this episode.
Technical: the quality of the original film for the sequences on the signing ceremony is very poor and the figures little more than blurs. The material in **IWM 811** is markedly superior in this respect.
[*The Times*, 1 December 1925: 14D, 18D]
[*The Times*, 2 December 1925: 15F, 16B-E]
[shotsheet available]
catalogued SDB: 7/1983

IWM 811 · GB, (prod) 1925
[LOCARNO PACT – rough material]
(allocated)

b/w · 2 reels · 1074' (17 mins) · silent
intertitles: none

pr Gaumont

- Unedited material on the final signing of
  the Locarno treaties in the Gold Room at
  the Foreign Office, London, 1 December
  1925.

(Reel 1) The film comes from two cameras.
For the exterior scenes of delegates arriving
at the Foreign Office the first camera is
positioned low on the steps beside which
the official cars stop. Few of the delegates
turn to or acknowledge the camera, which
mainly records the reactions of a reporter
noting the arrivals. Count Skrzynski, head of
the Polish delegation, enters on foot. Lord
Balfour arrives, also on foot. The chief
Belgian delegate, M Vandervelde (with
imperial and pince-nez) stops to
acknowledge the camera. The German
delegation led by Doktor Luther and Herr
Stresemann arrives next. After the
ceremony Sir Austen Chamberlain emerges
together with his cousin Neville. Aristide
Briand also emerges with the French
delegation. Inside the chamber the
delegates take their seats. The British are at
the head of the table, with the Italians led
by Signor Scialoja on their left (from the
camera's viewpoint). Next, going round the
table, are the Germans, then the Belgians,
then the Poles, then the Czechs led by Dr
Beneš, then finally the French. Chamberlain
chairs the meeting with Stanley Baldwin on
his left, Sir Cecil Hurst on his right and
some cabinet ministers sitting as observers
behind him. The signing ceremony takes
place, and after some speeches all
disperse. *(Reel 2)* A second view of the
Gold Room. Then the second camera's view
of the arrivals, showing rather more detail
as they come up the steps. Count Skrzynski
is first with his delegation. Lord Balfour
arrives with Mrs Baldwin and Lady
Chamberlain. Luther and the German
delegation arrive. Briand and the French
arrive. Winston Churchill arrives as an
observer. The Prince of Wales. Then again
all leave the building. Another view of the
speeches going on in the Gold Room itself.

Notes
Summary: this appears to be the unedited
material for **IWM 810**, the Gaumont
newsreel on the same subject. The detail of
the coverage, and the transfer of the film to

the Imperial War Museum, may both be
further evidence of Foxen Cooper's desire
to formalise the filming for record purposes
of important national events (see **Notes** to
IWM 809).
catalogued SDB: 7/1983

IWM 812 · Canada, (ca) 1920
**the HARVEST OF THE SUGAR MAPLE
TREE**

b/w · 1 reel · 904' (15 mins) · silent
intertitles: English

sp Canadian Department of Trade and
Commerce, Exhibits and Publicity Bureau

- Method of collecting and refining maple
  syrup in Ottawa, during or shortly after
  the First World War.

The syrup is collected in March, when the
farmer drills a small hole in the tree then
attaches a wooden "spile" for the sap to
flow out of, and a bucket in which the sap
is collected. The sap from several trees is
boiled in outdoor cauldrons to concentrate
it. A small boy drinks the sap directly from
the spile. The "modern" method is much the
same but more hygienic, using galvanised
metal spiles and buckets. The work
continues even in the snow. If there is a
sufficient slope the sap is led down pipes to
the main evaporating shed in the valley
below, where the evaporator can process
350 gallons of sap an hour. After being
tested the syrup is driven to a main factory,
where it is strained, reboiled and then
bottled or tinned. Rough cakes of sugar are
poured into moulds to set. A couple in a
restaurant are shown enjoying buckwheat
cakes with maple syrup. Meanwhile, back in
the region where the trees themselves
grow, the end of the season is marked by a
"sugaring off" outdoor party, in which the
surplus is eaten in one big gathering. This
includes pouring the syrup over snow to
make "Maple Wax, the most delectable
sweet in the world". The film ends with a
Union Flag.

Notes
Remarks: a well-made curiosity piece, which
would probably hold its interest for a
modern audience.
catalogued SDB: 7/1983

IWM 813-814 · NO FILM

IWM 815 · GB, (ca) 1925
**KOLONJE ANGIELSKIE W NOWEJ
ZELANDJI (on copy held)**
[the ENGLISH COLONY IN NEW ZEALAND]
(translation)

b/w · 1 reel · 435' (8 mins) · silent
intertitles: Polish & English

pr Kineto *dist* Alfa Warsawa Warecka

■ Polish-language version of a British film
showing the scenery in New Zealand in
the mid-1920s.

The film starts with maps showing Great
Britain, the British Empire and finally New
Zealand. It shows the Southern Alps of
South Island, New Zealand, as seen from
the ocean, leading down into the valleys of
the island, and finally to the port of
Dunedin, where goods are loaded onto
ships for export. In the farmlands nearby
shepherds and their dogs round up their
sheep. A man chops up a cake of soap
which he drops into one of the country's
geysers, producing a soapy froth when the
geyser erupts. On the farms wheat is
threshed and baled, and the bags of grain
sewn up for shipment. A view of a village
near some geysers. Various Maoris in their
village: boys, a girl, a mother and baby, and
some Maoris in a group. A Maori canoe on
the water. A view of some rapids. The film
ends with "Koniec" (Polish for "the end").

Notes
Production: the name of the distribution
company and title are in Polish, but the
maps are in English, as are the flashframe
captions, which have the Kineto logo on
them. Given, in addition to these facts, the
subject matter of the film it seems likely that
this is a Polish-language version of a Kineto
production. Correspondence with the New
Zealand Film Archive (6-7/1986), however,
failed to discover any accurate identification
for this film.
[shotsheet available]
catalogued SDB: 7/1983

IWM 816 · GB, (ca) 1925
[the ENGLISH COLONY IN INDIA]
(allocated)

b/w · 1 reel · 551' (9 mins) · silent
intertitles: none

pr Kineto (?)

■ Scenes of traditional Indian life in the
mid-1920s.

The film appears to start in Calcutta with
street scenes, and views of some of the
buildings, both Western and Eastern in
influence. A funeral procession takes place,
ending at the river. Further inland the
setting is more rural, with peasant villages.
There is a parade by the ceremonial guard
of an Indian prince, complete with jewelled
war elephants and camels. Views of one of
the main Hindu temples. Near the temple
there is a market, including a metalworker
with a hand-bellows.

Notes
Production: see production notes to **IWM
815**. This film and **IWM 815** appear to form
part of a series.
Remarks: so little information is available
concerning this film that the scenes it
shows remain virtually unidentifiable.
[shotsheet available]
catalogued SDB: 7/1983

IWM 817-841 · NO FILM

IWM 842 · GB, 1924
BRITAIN'S BIRTHRIGHT

b/w · 6 reels · 6317' (106 mins) · silent
intertitles: English

sp Admiralty and Royal Colonial Institute
pr New Era Film; and British Instructional
Films *ed* Newton, A P

■ Goodwill tour of the Royal Navy's special
service squadron around the world,
November 1923 to September 1924.

The squadron's tour takes in the principal
ports of the Empire. At each port the ships
of the squadron are thrown open to the
locals. Vice-Admiral Sir Frederick L Field
has his flag on board HMS *Hood*. The
second battle-cruiser in the squadron is
HMS *Repulse*. The remaining ships in the
squadron are the light cruisers HMS *Delhi*,
HMS *Dauntless*, HMS *Dragon* and HMS
Danae under Rear-Admiral the Honourable
Sir Hubert G Brand. Brand and his light
cruisers are rarely seen in the film. An
animated map shows the movement of the
squadron between ports, and day-to-day
scenes on board the ships are shown

during the film. *(Reel 1)* Shots of the *Hood* with Field on board, the *Repulse* and the *Delhi* are all shown. On 27 November at dawn the *Hood* leaves Portsmouth harbour and joins the remainder of the squadron in the Atlantic. On 8 December the squadron docks at Freetown, Sierra Leone. The locals look over the *Hood* and the sailors inspect the market places. On 14 December the squadron sails again. The "crossing the line" ceremony is shown with "King Neptune". *(Reel 2)* The squadron carries on to Table Bay. The Lord Mayor of Cape Town welcomes Field to the city. The flower market and memorial to Cecil Rhodes are shown. The squadron continues up the coast to Durban, where the officers meet Zulu chiefs and watch a war dance, and on to Zanzibar, reached on 12 January 1924. The Sultan, Seyyid Khalifa Bin Harub, comes on board. In Zanzibar itself the squadron's marines and sailors march past the watching crowds. Officers relax by riding camels. The squadron sails on, reaching Trincomali, Ceylon on 27 January. There is no ceremony; instead the locals wash the sailors' laundry. *(Reel 3)* On to Penang, where Chinese schoolgirls come on board the *Hood*, and to Singapore, showing the city. On the way to Australia the ships practise torpedo fire and gunnery. On 27 February they enter Fremantle harbour. The marines and sailors march through Perth. Some of the local aborigines are shown. The squadron continues around Cape Leeuwin and across the Great Australian Bight, through rough weather, and reaches Adelaide, with its parks, before going on to Melbourne on 17 March. There the Governor General, the Right Honourable Lord Forster, inspects the marines on board the *Hood* and crowds of people visit the ships. *(Reel 4)* The visit to Hobart, capital of Tasmania, is briefly shown. The squadron goes on to Sydney, where Australian soldiers lead the marines and sailors, as well as members of the Veterans Association of New South Wales, past the saluting base, on which are Field, Brand, Admiral Sir Dudley de Chair (the Governor of New South Wales) and the Prime Minister, Stanley Bruce. News cameramen record the event. The light cruiser HMAS *Australia*, scrapped under the 1922 Washington Naval Treaties, is scuttled at sea while the ships of the British squadron watch in salute, together with HMAS *Melbourne*, HMAS *Sydney* and HMAS *Adelaide*. (Although rarely seen on the film, the *Adelaide* accompanies the squadron on its tour back to Britain.) The ships continue on to New Zealand, reaching Wellington on 24 April, where the Governor General,

Viscount Jellicoe, is received on board. The following day, ANZAC day, the crews lay wreaths at the cenotaph. Mount Cook and the hot springs of Lake Rotorua are shown, as is a Maori village and its inhabitants. Having left New Zealand, the squadron on 17 May continues on to Suva, capital of Fiji, where the men watch tribal rituals, drink kava and eat sugar cane (continuing onto reel 5). The ships cross the International Date Line on 27 May, and shortly afterwards call briefly at Honolulu in the Hawaiian Islands. At sea the ships practise gunnery again. On 21 June they put into Victoria harbour on Vancouver Island, the capital of British Columbia. A dance is held for the locals on board the *Hood*. Logging in the forests is shown. The squadron sails on to Vancouver city where the ships are reprovisioned and the sailors take shore leave in the mountains. A sailor plays with a baby black bear. 5 July: the squadron sails again for San Francisco, arriving in the harbour on 7 July, and being met by the British Consul General. *(Reel 6)* On leaving San Francisco the four British light cruisers break off to tour the South American ports and do not appear again on the film until its end. The battle-cruisers and the *Adelaide* go through the Panama Canal and on to Jamaica, where Field is received in Kingston by a guard of the West Indies Regiment. There are views of the city. On 30 July the voyage continues on to Halifax, Nova Scotia where a children's party and funfair is held on the *Repulse*. The ships go up the St Lawrence seaway to Quebec, showing the old town, then on to St John's in Newfoundland. The marines again perform a march past, and there are scenes of fish curing in the harbour. Rowing races are held between the squadron's boat crews. On 17 September the ships set off across the Atlantic, meeting up with the light cruisers just west of the British Isles. A church service is held on board the *Hood*. On 28 September the *Hood*, having given three cheers to the *Repulse*, follows the *Delhi* into Devonport harbour for the end of the tour.

Notes
Remarks: considerably better than **IWM 843**, but probably not good enough to show to people today as entertainment. Contemporaries presumably found the sight of such exotic places more novel. It is also worth remembering, as the film itself points out, that the Zulu who dance for the ships' crews are the sons of the men who fought for Ctetawayo in 1879.
[shotsheet available]
catalogued SDB: 7/1983

IWM 843 · GB, 1920
50,000 MILES WITH THE PRINCE OF WALES

b/w · 6 reels · 5592' (103 mins) · silent
intertitles: English

pr Topical Film Company *dist* Film Booking Offices *cam* Barker, W (Captain)

■ World tour by Edward, Prince of Wales, on board HMS *Renown*, 1920.

(Reel 1) The Prince, wearing his naval uniform, comes on board HMS *Renown* at Portsmouth harbour on 14 March, shaking hands with Rear-Admiral Sir Lionel Halsey and Captain Dudley B N North. With the Prince as travelling companions are Lord Louis Mountbatten and Colonel Grigg (who do not really appear in the film until the final reel). An animated map shows the ship's progress. It visits firstly Barbados where the Prince inspects a detachment of the West Indies Regiment, and the governor holds a garden party. While the *Renown* passes through the Panama Canal the Prince inspects the local US Army garrison, and President Belisario Porras comes on board. At San Diego the Prince addresses the people of the USA. As everywhere on the visit, there are numerous journalists and cameramen. At Honolulu in the Hawaiian Islands the Prince meets US troops and British expatriates. *(Reel 2)* At Suva, capital of Fiji, the Prince is given a welcome ceremony and kava is brewed. The *Renown* goes on to Auckland harbour, New Zealand, where the Prince inspects the local regiment. Schoolchildren in formation spell out WELCOME in a stadium. At Rotorua the Prince talks with Maoris who served in France in the First World War, while Prime Minister W F Massey and Minister of Militia Sir Joseph Cook watch. The Prince visits the Maori villages of Chinemutu, near sulphur springs, and Whakarewarewa, *(Reel 3)* where he gives a speech and watches haka and poi dances. Back on the ship the junior officers perform a 'haka' of their own. Geysers and mud pots are shown. The ship goes on to Wellington, and the Prince visits the "Southern Alps". On to Australia. In a stadium in Melbourne children give a physical fitness demonstration and maypole dance. *(Reel 4)* The *Renown* arrives at Sydney and a military escort takes the Prince to Centennial Park. It is the Prince's birthday, 23 June. The ship continues on to Western Australia. The Prince visits Perth and goes further inland, seeing Australian fauna such as kangaroos, water buffalo and flamingos

("native wild fowl"). Loggers are seen at work in a jarrah forest. A view of Mundaring Reservoir. The train journey from Perth to Adelaide includes views of local aborigines, *(Reel 5)* and a "typical" outback railway halt. In Adelaide the Prince unveils a statue of Edward VII. For the remainder of the voyage HMAS *Australia* escorts the *Renown*, which visits Hobart, Tasmania. On board the *Renown* on the way back to Britain are various "ship's mascots" for zoos: a cockatoo, two rare lizards, emu chicks, a Dominican tortoise, opossums, parrots, and a wallaby. On arrival in Samoa the locals pay homage to the Prince. *(Reel 6)* The film jumps back to 17 April, the first occasion on which the *Renown* crossed the equator. The full "crossing the line" ceremony involves the Prince, Mountbatten and Grigg all being ducked, and Halsey receiving "the Order of the Old Sea Dog". The cruise continues, with practice for the 15-inch guns. The ship calls at Port of Spain, Trinidad, and then at Bermuda, before returning to Portsmouth. The Prince says goodbye to the ship's company and boards the train for London.

Notes
Cameraman: "Captain Barker" was the noted film producer William Barker who had run the Warwick Trading Company and Barker Motion Photography before going into retirement at the end of the war. He was called out of retirement by William Jeapes of Topical to cover this tour.
Remarks: wholly as dreadful as its title suggests it might be.
[Luke McKernan, *Topical Budget: The Great British News Film*, British Film Institute (1992): 119-120]
[shotsheet available]
catalogued SDB: 7/1983

IWM 844-858 · NO FILM

IWM 859 · Canada, (ca) 1922
IN THE WAKE OF CAPTAIN COOK

b/w · 1 reel · 708' (12 mins) · silent
intertitles: English

pr Canadian Government Motion Picture Bureau

■ Visit by flying boat to Nootka Sound on Vancouver Island, Canada, early 1920s.

The route traces one explored by Captain Cook in his search for the North-West

Passage. Two flying boats start from Vancouver city on the mainland of British Columbia. One is of the Curtiss/Felixstowe types, probably a Felixstowe F5, and the other, with a single engine, is probably a Curtiss H5. A cine cameraman fits his camera into the open-nosed cockpit of the F5. The planes take off and follow the shape of the island round to Friendly Cove, part of Nootka Sound, where they land. The "natives", North American Indians in European dress, watch as the planes taxi to the shore. A disconcerted old lady is offered a coin to pose for the camera. The children and younger people seem happier at being filmed than their elders. The village is made up of substantial, European-style timbered buildings with decorative totem poles outside them. One such pole has a timber effigy of Captain Cook at its top. The cemetery contains the carved headstones of departed chiefs, and various grave goods. The settlement has its own mission station. The planes take off from the village, "leaving behind a trail of amazed wonderment in the minds of its quaint inhabitants".

Notes

Remarks: how many of the Indians in this film had seen a camera or an aircraft before is a moot point, but they were clearly considerably more sophisticated than the commentary is trying to suggest. This is not a visit by a 'great white bird' to superstitious savages, despite the attempt to make it appear so.

catalogued SDB: 7/1983

IWM 860 · Canada, (ca) 1920
WINTER FLYING AT CAMP BORDEN

b/w · 1 reel · 690' (12 mins) · silent
intertitles: English

sp Canadian Air Force *pr* Canadian Government Motion Picture Bureau

- Flight training by Royal Canadian Air Force pilots in winter conditions at Camp Borden, Canada, early 1920s.

The film starts with some of the available aircraft, including an SE5a and a de Havilland DH9 with US 'Liberty' engine. Most of the DH9s have, to help them land on the snowbound airfield, skids fitted rather than wheels. A view of the snowbound airfield. A view over the tail of a camera plane as it takes off. The plane overflies the base several times, giving a

good aerial view of the airfield's layout. The plane then comes lower, so that the view changes from vertical to oblique, and finally comes past the aircraft sheds at hedge-hopping height, the marks of its skids occasionally showing in the snow beneath it as they touch the ground. Trainee pilots in Avro 504s start up and take off in a line, five of them flying 'circuits and bumps', coming round and just touching the ground on landing before taking off again. They fly, very low, wing-tip to wing-tip over the camera in two passes. The view from the camera plane over the airfield again shows one of the pilots flying close enough to wave. Three of the Avros, in formation, close in on the camera plane. A ground view of the Avros overflying a flagpole with the RCAF ensign on it, dipping in salute as they do so.

catalogued SDB: 7/1983

IWM 861 · Canada, (ca) 1922
FIRE FIGHTING WITH AEROPLANES

b/w · 1 reel · 685' (11 mins) · silent
intertitles: English

pr Ontario Government Pictures

- Use of flying boats and seaplanes to help prevent forest fires in Algonquin Provincial Park, Ontario, Canada, in the early 1920s.

The film stresses that timber is an important national resource, and forest fires a great danger. There are flying boat bases at Parry Sound in Georgian Bay (part of Lake Huron) and at Whitney on Cache Lake in Algonquin Park. The base at Whitney is shown. It has two flying boats, a two-engined Curtiss/ Felixstowe type, probably a Felixstowe F5, and a single-engined Curtiss H5; it has also a number of Avro 504s fitted with floats. The pilots pose for the camera, "the same dashing, daredevil, lynx-eyed fellows that used to spot the 'Boche' battery positions". The two large seaplanes set off on patrol, following the waterways of the park, one acting as a camera plane. Smoke rises from the forest: they come in for a closer look. The F5, which carries a crew of five and fire-fighting equipment, lands on a nearby lake. The crew attack the fire, using a motor to pump water from the lake for a hose. This time they are successful. The patrols, typified by one of the Avros in flight, continue.

catalogued SDB: 7/1983

IWM 862 · NO FILM

IWM 863 · GB, (prod) 1930
[RAF DEMONSTRATION 1930] (allocated)

b/w · 1 reel · 356' (6 mins) · silent & comopt
intertitles: none

sp Royal Air Force (?)

- Fragmented film of events at an RAF air
  display at Southampton, June 1930.

A civilian, presumably the inventor,
describes the workings and advantages of
the Westland Pterodactyl IV, a 'flying wing'
aircraft beside him. A test pilot takes off in
the Pterodactyl. As part of the air display a
biplane, re-creating the First World War,
makes a 'balloon busting' attack on a
tethered kite balloon, which bursts into
flames. A woman's voice can be heard
crying "Oh, look – Oh !" as this happens.
The Pterodactyl comes back in to land. RAF
rescue launches race each other in line
through Southampton water. Two
Supermarine Southampton flying boats
overfly the coastline. One comes down to
land in slow motion. Another taxis on the
water. A Vickers Wildebeest torpedo
bomber prototype (designated O-3 on its
side) takes off for a trial flight and drops its
torpedo in a mock attack.

Notes
Technical: the film has a soundtrack for its
first items, up to the end of the flight of the
Pterodactyl. Thereafter it is silent, not mute.
catalogued SDB: 8/1983

IWM 864 · NO FILM

IWM 865 · GB, (?) 1925
**ROYAL AIR FORCE : aircraft of the Fleet
Air Arm and aircraft operating from shore
bases**

b/w · 1 reel · 1043' (17 mins) · silent
intertitles: English

pr Gaumont

- Survey of the methods of using aircraft
  with ships from the First World War to the
  middle 1920s.

Firstly, the seaplane carrier. A Short 184

seaplane is lifted from a seaplane carrier
into the water and takes off. On return it is
hoisted on board again. Then the launch
from a capital ship. A Beardmore WBIII is
taken out of the hold of a ship and
launched from a short platform running
down to the bows. A Sopwith 1½ Strutter is
launched from the B turret platform of a
battle-cruiser (three views, including one
from the eyes of the ship). Then the true
aircraft carrier. A Sopwith Snipe attempts a
landing on HMS *Furious*, side-slips a great
deal and comes to rest only half on the
flight deck, finally tumbling off it into the
sea. Another attempt at a landing is
successful. A further development is the
land-based flying boat. Felixstowe (?) flying
boat base is shown, with the flying boats at
anchor. The next step is the Supermarine
Seagull amphibian, which travels down to
the water on its own wheels, takes off from
the water, and retracts its wheels against its
hull in flight. It lands in the water again and
taxis out onto land. Another Seagull is
shown taking off and landing at an
aerodrome in conventional fashion. The
Felixstowe F5 flying boat is the latest and
largest in the series. It is shown being
wheeled out of its hangar. An earlier F2A
model is launched down the slipway and
another F2A is seen taking off and landing.
The final stage so far in the evolution of
naval aircraft is the Blackburn Dart torpedo
bomber, an extremely large single-seater. It
is fitted with an 18-inch torpedo, takes off
from its airfield and overflies the sea. It
comes in to make its torpedo drop. The film
ends abruptly at this point.

catalogued SDB: 7/1983

IWM 866 · GB, 1917-19
[AIRCRAFT AT SEA 3] (allocated)

b/w · 1 reel · 721' (12 mins) · silent
intertitles: English

sp Admiralty *pr* Engholm, F W
cam Engholm, F W

- Naval aviation and other miscellaneous
  naval footage, ca 1918.

I. Sopwith 1½ Strutter is flown off starboard
echelon turret of an Indefatigable Class
battle-cruiser – an Invincible Class ship is
visible in the background as the aircraft
circles. After the launch, the flying-off
platform is stripped from the guns.
II. Sequence showing a Beardmore WB III,
N.6123, being lifted from the hangar of HMS

Nairana, positioned on the flight deck, and flown off – HMS *Furious* visible in the background.
III. Medium shot/medium close-up as airship SSZ3 comes in to alight on a grass field, and is pushed into its hangar. Five RNAS Sea Scout pilots pose with their mascot dog. IV. Panning long shot, left to right, over fleet anchorage – Saint Vincent Class (HMS *Collingwood* ?), two Colossus Class battleships, and HMS *Agincourt* (only part of which appears in frame). Long shot off the starboard bow of a Colossus Class battleship as it flashes a signal across Forth anchorage, and close-up of a rating operating a signal searchlight. Final sequence of airship R9 passing over three Iron Duke Class battleships anchored in quarter line – the nearest has a Marksman Class Leader alongside (*cf.* **IWM 551-07**).

[shotsheet available]
catalogued NAP: 4/1978

IWM 867 · GB, (?) 1918
WITH THE EYES OF THE NAVY

b/w · 1 reel · 854' (15 mins) · silent
intertitles: English

sp Ministry of Information (?) and Admiralty (?)

■ RAF cooperation with the Royal Navy at the end of the First World War.

Uses of flying boats in the war, starting with a Felixstowe flying boat coming in to land at its base, probably Hamble, followed by a rare CE1 flying boat also landing. The main subject of the film is an anti-submarine patrol by the two airships NS7 and NS8. They are led out onto their take-off site and NS7 is seen taking off. The camera, on board NS8, shows the engineers checking the external engines while at 3000 feet. A lookout spots a hostile aircraft which he shoots down with his Lewis gun. The 'enemy' goes into a steep dive and can be seen burning on the ground. The airship sends a message by signal lamp. Over the North Sea the airship spots a 'hostile' submarine (in fact a British L Class) and sends off a Morse signal, which attracts a nearby British destroyer. The submarine opens fire at the airship with its deck gun. The destroyer (not clearly seen) opens fire, forcing the submarine to dive, and then depth-charges it. The airships return to base, the reconnaissance still photographer of NS8 taking photographs over the side.

The airships overfly Arundel (?), the town and castle being visible below. They also overfly an RAF airfield. Over their own landing site NS7 drops its cable and is brought in. The larger type of patrol airship, the R23, is seen overflying London on the occasion of the Lord Mayor's show, 9 November 1918. A view, slightly blurred, of the captain in the control gondola. A final view of airships helping to escort the surrendered German High Seas Fleet across the North Sea.

Notes
Production: possibly an official production made at the end of the First World War. Compare with **IWM 118** *The Eyes of the Army.*
Summary: for the two final scenes see also **IWM 571** and **IWM 626**.
[shotsheet available]
catalogued SDB: 7/1983

IWM 868 · GB, (?) 1918
LIFE OF AN AIRSHIP SQUADRON

b/w · 1 reel · 327' (6 mins) · silent
intertitles: English

■ Routine life at an RAF airship station in Britain, probably 1918.

Officers walk out from the wooden huts of their bases. The huts have flower gardens and even a sundial. The station ground crew drill on the main square, with a band, at some length, and finally march past the guard post.

Notes
Title: this is taken from the shotsheet.
Summary: probably a fragment of a longer film.
[shotsheet available]
catalogued SDB: 7/1983

IWM 869 · GB, (?) 1918
the ROYAL AIR FORCE – PER ARDUA AD ASTRA
INSPECTION OF CADETS, SCHOOL OF MILITARY AERONAUTICS OXFORD (ledger title)

b/w · 1 reel · 264' (4 mins) · silent
intertitles: English

sp Royal Air Force

- RAF cadets training, probably at the School of Military Aeronautics, Oxford, 1918.

The cadets are paraded before a senior officer, possibly the school commandant. They march out of the school main gates. "Course Number 1" shows various planes on the nearby airfield, including a Bristol F2B Fighter with a Puma engine. A pilot and instructor remove their flying leathers after a flight. One BE2c, used for instruction, has had part of its fabric removed so that the wires can be seen joining the controls to the tail surfaces. Using stop-action, the plane is dismantled piece by piece, leaving at last the fuselage, then nothing at all.

Notes
Intertitles: these are all flashframes.
catalogued SDB: 7/1983

IWM 870 · GB (?), 1917
TRAINING PILOTS FOR THE IMPERIAL BRITISH ROYAL FLYING CORPS

b/w · 1 reel · 818' (14 mins) · silent
intertitles: English

pr Specialty Film Import (distributor ?)

- Basic RFC training for pilots in Britain, 1917.

The pilots start at a Cadet School where they are taught drill and basic skills. "The first necessity of an airman is that he must have discipline." The cadets are in various British uniforms, and include in their number some US Army and Navy cadets. From there the cadets go to one of the Schools of Military Aeronautics. There they are taught about in-line and rotary engines, and how to assemble and rig an airframe. They fit the engine to one of the aircraft they are building. From the school they are sent on to a Lower Training Squadron where they learn to fly. Their training aircraft are the same as those they helped build, the American-designed Curtiss JN4 Jenny (in this case with Canadian serial numbers). Four of these set off on a training flight together practising taking off, flying circuits, and landing. After two or three hours with an instructor they fly solo for five or six hours more, and then are sent on to a Higher Training Squadron. Two machines, one of them the camera plane, show the difficulty of following the enemy in a dogfight. They overfly the hangars and

come in to land.

Notes
Production: this appears to be an American, or possibly Canadian, release version of a British film.
[shotsheet available]
catalogued SDB: 7/1983

IWM 871 · GB, (?) 1919
ADVANCED FLYING INSTRUCTION

b/w · 2 reels · 2138' (36 mins) · silent
intertitles: English

sp Royal Air Force *pr* Royal Air Force – London Photo Centre

- Flying instruction in Avro 504 trainers at the RAF North Eastern Area Flying Instructors School, Redcar, 1918 or 1919.

(Reel 1) An instructor shows a naval trainee pilot how to fit his flying helmet and speaking tube. A pupil from the Army is shown how to fasten himself into his seat. The instructions after this are illustrated in three ways: by showing the movement of the controls in a dummy cockpit, by showing the pilot's point of view while in the air, and by showing the machine in the air performing the actual manœuvre. (The cameraman's shadow on the dummy cockpit is very noticeable and distracting.) The procedure for starting the engine, and the relationship between the controls and control surfaces is explained. A line of pupils in Avros takes off for a training flight. The effect of moving the stick and rudder bar in flight is illustrated. (The film of the pilot's viewpoint is often indistinct and it is hard to discern anything.) The pupil shows how to fly straight and level. *(Reel 2)* The pupil is taught that in a steep turn the rudder acts as an elevator, and vice versa. Correct methods of taking off are shown, covering the main faults and methods of taking off into a cross wind. Landings are covered in the same way. The pilots practise forced landings in a small, enclosed field. The film ends abruptly.

[shotsheet available]
catalogued SDB: 7/1983

IWM 872 · GB, (?) 1918
HOW TO PREPARE AN 'L' TYPE CAMERA

b/w · 1 reel · 352' (6 mins) · silent

intertitles: English

sp Royal Air Force (?)

- RAF training film for ground crew on how to make ready an aerial camera for flight, probably 1918.

A man in the uniform of an RFC flight sergeant prepares the camera on a workbench. Firstly, the lens cap is removed and the lens cleaned. Then he sets the blind aperture and the exposure indicator to zero. He shows how the shutter operation works. The locking pin secures the exposure indicator. The plate magazine is fitted and opened. A Bowden release, enabling the observer to control the camera from a distance, is fitted. Finally, the demonstrator shows how to unload the plates from the camera safely.

Notes
Title: this is taken from the shotsheet.
[shotsheet available]
catalogued SDB: 7/1983

IWM 873 · GB, (?) 1919
PHOTOGRAPHY – THE EYE OF THE AEROPLANE

b/w · 2 reels · 1374' (22 mins) · silent
intertitles: English

pr Gaumont

- Training and methods of the Photographic Section of the RAF, probably just after the First World War.

(Reel 1) Trainees are shown various types of camera, the L-Type, the C-Type, and a recently-introduced camera which uses film instead of plates. They are taught elementary chemistry for developing and fixing plates. Interpreters identify the negative plate of each reconnaissance photograph, using a map, and write in the details of the location on the negative. The latest cameras photograph a number of dials simultaneously with the ground image, giving time, height, etc. To speed up the process prints are dried by passing them through a spirit flame. A run of prints is constructed into a mosaic. The construction of the particular mosaic shown takes 1 hour 55 minutes, producing a picture which covers 50 square miles. Green light is used while the plates or film magazines are loaded. *(Reel 2)* The skeleton of an aircraft, shows how an L-Type camera is fitted to its

side: vibration from the engine is absorbed by mounting the camera on a shock absorber. The method is the same for both plate and film cameras. The observer has a sighting tube which runs down through the floor of the aircraft, which he uses to line up the shot. For a training reconnaissance flight the observer is given his map reference. He and the pilot take off in a Bristol F2B Fighter. In flight, the pilot indicates that they are near the target (in actual operations it is the observer's job to inform the pilot). Back at the aerodrome the plane is met on landing by a runner and the plates taken at once for developing. The same type of operation is shown with a film camera. Again, a member of the ground crew races to take the film on landing. A photographic developing lorry, for use when other facilities are not available, sets up its equipment. A plane comes in to land. The film ends abruptly.

catalogued SDB: 7/1983

IWM 874 · GB, 1920
the AERO COMPASS

b/w · 6 reels · 4695' (78 mins) · silent
intertitles: English

sp Royal Air Force pr Royal Air Force – London Photo Centre

- Training film on the origins, construction and uses of two types of RAF magnetic compass, 1920.

The film starts coherently, but degenerates progressively into pull-backs and misplaced scenes until the later reels are not always comprehensible. There is virtually no actuality material, all the points being explained by diagrams, models and workbench demonstrations. *(Reel 1)* "Your friend the compass", explains the cardinal and quadrantal points and the lubber line. The fact that a compass is a magnet is dealt with in some detail, and the principles of magnetism outlined *(Reel 2)* by means of bench demonstrations with iron filings and soft iron by an RAF tutor. *(Reel 4 – there is no Reel 3)* A magnet dips with the earth's magnetic field, and that magnetic variation is noted and dated on every chart. A Dip Circle is used to measure the angle of dip, which at London is 67°. This dip affects the compass needle. The difference between the magnetic and true meridian is explained, together with the angle of variation between the two and the fact that the line of no variation is the Agonic Line. A map projection of the earth gives a double Agonic Line. The variation at London in 1920 is 14° west, that of Paris 13° west. The magnetic pole moves slightly so that in "about 1976" the variation at London will be zero. The date and change in variation is used to correct the figure for magnetic north given on a chart. *(Reel 5)* The construction of the RAF Flat Type 253 Aero Compass is shown, compared to a standard ship's compass, and the evolution of the compass from the ancient type through to the present day. *(Reel 6)* More of the construction of the Type 253, followed by the construction of the RAF Upright Type 5/17 Aero Compass. The general principles of compass construction are described. A compass card (or needle) oscillates slightly in the manner of a pendulum swing. The Type 253 has an oscillation period of 25 seconds, the Type 5/17 an oscillation period of 12 seconds. The card should be allowed to oscillate gently in flight as attempts to correct each oscillation only produce a zigzag flight course which increases, rather than decreases, the swing of the compass. *(Reel 7)* In a tight turn the aircraft floor tilts to be almost perpendicular to the ground, whereupon the compass acts as a Dip Needle and swings into the line of dip. Not until the aircraft has flattened out does the compass respond properly to the direction of the turn. On turning east or west from a southerly course the compass exaggerates the extent of the turn. On turning east or west from a northerly course the compass fails to show the turn until it is complete. The film ends abruptly at this point.

Notes
Summary: it is unlikely that this was meant to be viewed as a single continuous film. It probably represents a series of some kind.
Technical: note that the 6 reels are numbered 1, 2, 4, 5, 6 and 7. There is no reel 3.
Remarks: quite entertaining educational material, if a little childish in its approach in places.
catalogued SDB: 7/1983

IWM 875 · GB, 10/1926
PILOTING A SHIP-PLANE ONTO AN AIRCRAFT CARRIER

b/w · 1 reel · 1368' (22 mins) · silent
intertitles: English

sp Royal Air Force *pr* Royal Aircraft Establishment

■ Training film on the correct method of landing a Blackburn Dart torpedo bomber on the deck of the aircraft carrier HMS *Furious*, October 1926.

The aircraft takes off from the flight deck, after which deck officers check the wind's speed relative to the ship. Most of the film shows the pilot's point of view. He overflies the carrier once, looking for the signal flag, flown aft and to port, indicating that he is clear to land. He approaches again, judging speed relative to the escort destroyer which is behind and to starboard of the carrier. The approach is shown, straight and level, from the pilot's viewpoint down almost to the moment of landing, which is seen from the deck. The flight deck is too narrow to cope with drift, and side-slip must therefore be avoided. Again the pilot's viewpoint on the approach, drifting away to starboard and correcting too much to port, resulting in the plane side-slipping over the carrier without landing. A diagram shows the ideal path of the aircraft. Back to the pilot's viewpoint, gently correcting drift to either side in order to bring the plane in on a straight, gentle descent. To undershoot, or come in too low, puts the plane into the turbulent air in the ship's wake, as shown by the diagram. The sighting line for an undershoot is the ship's hull rather than the rear of the flight deck. This is seen from the pilot's viewpoint, he comes too low, encounters turbulence and breaks away to starboard. Overshoot is caused, as the diagram shows, by diving too steeply at the end of the approach and travelling too fast to land. The sighting line for overshoot is the front of the flight deck. The pilot's viewpoint for this shows the plane clearly too high going straight over the flight deck. Both faults can be corrected early on in the approach. From the pilot's viewpoint it is shown that even with the ship throwing out a large amount of smoke it is possible to make a perfect landing. This is shown from the pilot's viewpoint all the way down to landing. The pilot keeps the engine running to avoid being blown off the deck and to provide power for taxiing towards the deck lift.

Notes
Summary: the film notes at its start that "owing to engine vibration the aerial films were taken at 20 pictures per sec, *ie* 25% faster than normal speed, thereby giving a slightly slowed down appearance".
Remarks: an excellent training film, making

its points in a clear and interesting fashion.
catalogued SDB: 7/1983

IWM 876 · GB, 1919
WITH THE ROYAL AIR FORCE IN INDIA

b/w · 3 reels · 2900' (49 mins) · silent
intertitles: English

- Everyday life for members of 99 (Madras Presidency) Squadron RAF at Ambala, India, June-September 1919.

(Reel 1) The troopship SS *Barpeta* brings a fresh contingent for the squadron into Karachi harbour. The men travel by train on to Ambala, where they get their first real view of India, including a hookah smoker, and the "local cab", a one-horse cart. Officers sit outside their bungalows and NCOs outside an open-air canteen in the cool of the evening. Out on the parade ground the airmen go through drill routines, bayonet fighting and a boxing match. Indoors other airmen, with some help from Indians, work at their trades: some repair the engines of the squadron trucks and planes: others plane wood and drill metal, while others still repair tyres. In a workshop the wings and tails of aircraft being repaired are worked on. The squadron flies Bristol F2B Fighters. Some of the pilots pose for the camera. *(Reel 2)* "Life is not always dull. A message may arrive asking for a turbulent tribal village to be bombed." An officer receives the message and briefs the crews of two aircraft while their planes are bombed up. Throwing up a large amount of dust, the Bristol Fighters take off. Later a wireless operator at base receives a request for help from one of the planes. The second plane, on return, confirms that the first has made a forced landing in a field through engine trouble. A breakdown tender drives out to assist and, finding the aircraft, starts repairs. Meanwhile recreation continues, with football and tennis matches at the squadron. At the RAF Depot in Karachi airmen go boating and bathing in the harbour. At one of the hill stations officers depart to stalk "buck", catching nothing but having time for a picnic. *(Reel 3)* Airmen shop in the bazaar at Ambala, and a civilian (the cameraman ?) joins in. 'Typical' Indians are shown. One of the camels used by the RAF for transport, "a quaint creature", is ridden by its owner. In the surrounding countryside the cameraman films mosques and Hindu temples. At this point the film breaks up into extra scenes from previous reels: the football match, the repair to the damaged aircraft, more of the football match. Then a game of billiards being played in the officers' mess. Finally, the boxing match and the bayonet fighters again.

Notes
Remarks: probably a 'home movie', this certainly has all the faults associated with that genre. Failing to allow for the intense light of India, the cameraman often produces faded images and only rarely uses close-ups. In contrast he has used dissolves, iris shots and masked shots far too often, and with no understanding of their conventional meanings. His staged scenes are frequently so obvious as to be comical. The film tells far more about the attitudes of the British in India than about the realities of life there.
[shotsheet available]
catalogued SDB: 7/1983

IWM 877 · GB, (prod) 1919
COLOGNE AIRMAIL

b/w · 1 reel · 1112' (17 mins) · silent
intertitles: none

sp Royal Air Force (?)

- Aircraft of 18 Squadron RAF flying a mail delivery service from Britain for the occupying forces in Cologne, May-August 1919.

Some of the squadron's Airco DH9 aircraft are wheeled out of their hangars at Hawkinge aerodrome near Lympne in Kent. A mail truck arrives with sacks of mail for Cologne, and these are piled into the rear gunner's seat of each aircraft. The planes take off, one of them acting as a camera plane, and fly out over Kent, passing a speeding train, before crossing the English Channel. They fly over the Belgian coast, and on inland to the squadron base at Merheim aerodrome near Cologne. They overfly Cologne and come in to land. Trucks take the mail from the planes to a sorting depot in the middle of the city. British soldiers and sailors are seen reading their letters on the banks of the Rhine. A view of Cologne Cathedral. The return journey (in fact a fake using most of the same scenes as the outward journey, and with an interpolated shot of an Avro 504 landing) shows the planes being loaded with mail again and flying back over the Channel. They come in to land at Hawkinge and trucks collect the mail from them.

Title: this is taken from the shotsheet.
Remarks: flying over water was an unusual, and still quite hazardous, activity at this time. The fact that the British would go to such lengths to provide a method for their troops to write home shows how important for morale this was seen to be.
[shotsheet available]
catalogued SDB: 7/1983

IWM 878 · GB, (ca) 1924
the CAIRO BAGHDAD SERVICE AIRMAIL

b/w · 2 reels · 1339' (23 mins) · silent
intertitles: English

- Incomplete film on the RAF airmail service between Cairo and Baghdad, 1921-26.

(Reel 1) The film compares the old ways of the desert with modern technology by starting with an Arab camel train coming to rest at an oasis. At dawn the riders wake with prayers and resume their journey. (All acted.) A bugler rouses the RAF camp at Heliopolis at dawn, the flag is raised and the airmen practise drill on the parade ground. The captions explain that the mail arrives by sea, but the final stage now takes an 11-hour flight instead of a 15-day sea trip. Two Vickers Vernon aircraft of 45 Squadron RAF are wheeled out and their controls are checked. (Both have individual identifying symbols painted on the underside of the lower wing inboard of the roundel. In one case the 'Solomon's Seal' or Star of David, in the other the left-handed swastika. These are more clearly visible later in flight.) An RAF truck arrives with the mail for the flight. This is taken on board and the planes fuelled up from petrol cans. The crews board their planes, which take off. A crude map shows the route. The aerial view as the planes overfly Cairo is shown. A third Vernon, the camera plane, takes off. The planes fly across the desert, coming in for their one refuelling stop at Amman. *(Reel 2)* The radio operator in the camera plane signals that the machines are en route to Baghdad. The message is received by the operator on the ground. At this point the film loses coherence and starts to break up into unrelated scenes, pull-backs, out-takes and brief repeats of some scenes. The Arabs in the desert again. The planes being taken out of the hangars again. British soldiers on the march beside the Suez Canal. More of the map. The wireless operator. The take-off from

Heliopolis again. The planes on the ground at Amman. The map again. The planes in flight. The map again. A view (irised) of Baghdad from the air. The camera plane's view of its own landing. A final 'romantic' shot of the camel train walking into the setting sun.

Notes
Remarks: a potentially interesting film which sadly becomes unviewable just as it gets into its stride.
[shotsheet available]
catalogued SDB: 7/1983

IWM 879 · NO FILM

IWM 880-01a · GB, 1931
BRITISH SCREEN NEWS [1931] · THE SCHNEIDER TROPHY

b/w · 1 reel · 268' (5 mins) · silent
intertitles: English

pr British Screen News

- British team in the Schneider Trophy race, Calshot, 13 September 1931.

The team lines up for a group photograph. In turn, they are Squadron Leader A H Orlebar (captain), Flight Lieutenant F W Long, Flight Lieutenant J N Boothman, Flight Lieutenant G N Stainforth, Lieutenant G L Brinton RN and Flying Officer L S Snaith. The aircraft, which Boothman is to fly, is a Supermarine S6B, number S1595. The engine is started and the plane wheeled down into the water. It takes off and is seen in flight. Then the second attempt, with Snaith at the controls (neither pilot is clearly visible). The plane is wheeled down to the water and again takes off.

Notes
Summary: Supermarine S6B number S1595 is now on display at the Science Museum.
[C F Andrews and E B Morgan, *Supermarine Aircraft Since 1914*, Putnam (1981): 199-201]
catalogued SDB: 8/1983

IWM 880-01b · GB, 1930
PATHE SUPER GAZETTE [1930] – SHOWING THE (ROYAL AIR FORCE) FLAG

b/w · 1 reel · 82' (1 min) · silent
intertitles: English

pr Pathé

- Supermarine Southampton flying boats of 201 Squadron taking off for a goodwill tour of the Baltic from Calshot, September 1930.

Notes
Summary: note that this item covers exactly the same story as the British Screen News version **IWM 880-01c** which follows it on the reel.
[C F Andrews and E B Morgan, *Supermarine Aircraft Since 1914*, Putnam (1981): 104]
catalogued SDB: 8/1983

IWM 880-01c · GB, 1930
BRITISH SCREEN NEWS [1930] – BALTIC CRUISE

b/w · 1 reel · 73' (1 min) · silent
intertitles: English

pr British Screen News

- Supermarine Southampton flying boats of 201 Squadron taking off for a goodwill tour of the Baltic from Calshot, September 1930.

Notes
Summary: note that this item covers exactly the same story as the Pathé Super Gazette version **IWM 880-01b** which precedes it on the reel.
[C F Andrews and E B Morgan, *Supermarine Aircraft Since 1914*, Putnam (1981): 104]
catalogued SDB: 8/1983

IWM 880-01d · GB, (?) 1930
BRITISH SCREEN NEWS [1930] – THE FLYING BLUES

b/w · 1 reel · 92' (2 mins) · silent
intertitles: English

pr British Screen News

- Training for Oxford University Air Squadron at Manston airfield, probably 1930.

The cadets, on the ground, study maps. Two of them climb out of a Bristol F2B

Fighter after a training flight. One has his parachute harness checked. Another tries to control his parachute on the ground, until the force of the wind takes him off his feet.

catalogued SDB: 8/1983

IWM 880-01e · GB, 1930
UNIVERSAL TALKING NEWS [1930] – A NINE TON BULLET

b/w · 1 reel · 164' (3 mins) · silent
intertitles: none

pr Universal

- Experiments in launching aircraft by means of a steam catapult at Farnborough, 1930.

A Vickers Virginia bomber is set up to be fired from one of the catapults. Firstly, a pilot gets into a smaller aircraft, a Fairey IIIF (not a seaplane) which is launched by one version of the catapult, and goes on to overfly the airfield.

Notes
Summary: despite the production company name, this item is silent, not mute. But see also **IWM 880-01h**.
[C F Andrews, *Vickers Aircraft Since 1908*, Putnam (1969): 140]
[H A Taylor, *Fairey Aircraft Since 1915*, Putnam (1974): 148]
catalogued SDB: 8/1983

IWM 880-01f · GB, 1931
PATHE SUPER GAZETTE [1931] – [SCHNEIDER TROPHY] (allocated)

b/w · 1 reel · 97' (2 mins) · silent & mute
intertitles: English

pr Pathé

- British team in the Schneider Trophy race, Calshot, 13 September 1931.

The Supermarine S6B racing seaplane S1595 comes in to land beside the monitor HMS *Medea*. The pilot, Flight Lieutenant Boothman, comes on board to the applause of the crew, and talks with the team captain, Squadron Leader Orlebar. Then the second flight, in which Flight Lieutenant Stainforth sets a new world air speed record at 378mph. He brings the seaplane in to land, gets out at the water's edge and comes up onto the land to talk with his wife and the press. Stainforth, Boothman and Orlebar pose together for the cameras.

Notes
Summary: Supermarine S6B number S1595 is now on display at the Science Museum.
[C F Andrews and E B Morgan, *Supermarine Aircraft Since 1914*, Putnam (1981): 199-201]
catalogued SDB: 8/1983

IWM 880-01g · GB, 1930
BRITISH SCREEN NEWS [1930] – [R101] (allocated)

b/w · 1 reel · 67' (1 min) · silent
intertitles: English

pr British Screen News

■ Airship R101 after a major refit, 1 October 1930.

The R101 has had an extra section added to make it the world's largest airship. It takes off lightly from its launch ground, and docks onto a mooring mast.

[Guy Hartcup, *The Achievement of the Airship*, David and Charles (1974): 215]
catalogued SDB: 8/1983

IWM 880-01h · GB, 1930
UNIVERSAL TALKING NEWS [1930] – [A NINE TON BULLET 2] (allocated)

b/w · 1 reel · 88' (1 min) · comopt
intertitles: none

pr Universal

■ Experiments in launching aircraft by means of a steam catapult at Farnborough, 1930.

A Vickers Virginia bomber is launched from the catapult. On the second launch the camera shows the view from the front of the bomber as it flies forward out of the catapult.

Notes
Summary: see also **IWM 880-01e**.
[C F Andrews, *Vickers Aircraft Since 1908*, Putnam (1969): 140]
catalogued SDB: 8/1983

IWM 880-02a · GB, 1931
GAUMONT BRITISH NEWS [1931] – LATEST 'HUSH HUSH' FLYING BOATS

b/w · 1 reel · 124' (2 mins) · mute
intertitles: none

pr Gaumont

■ Departure of RAF flying boats from Felixstowe for Basra, 1931.

The crews, of 203 Squadron, say goodbye to their families at the water's edge and take launches out to their flying boats. A number of newsreel cameramen, including one on a Pathé sound van, record the event. One crew arrives at its flying boat, a Short S818 Rangoon. Two of the Rangoons taxi and take off.

[G R Duvall, *British Flying Boats and Amphibians 1909-1952*, Putnam (1966): 158-160]
catalogued SDB: 8/1983

IWM 880-02b · GB, 1929
PATHE SUPER GAZETTE [1929] – NON-STOP INDIA HEROES HOME AGAIN

b/w · 1 reel · 57' (1 min) · silent
intertitles: English

pr Pathé

■ Return of a Fairey Long Range Monoplane to Cranwell, completing its flight to India and back, 15 June 1929.

The aircraft comes in to land at Cranwell and taxis to a halt. The crew members, Squadron Leader A G Jones-Williams and Flight Lieutenant N H Jenkins, are congratulated on their flight, which took 50 hours and 38 minutes.

catalogued SDB: 8/1983

IWM 880-02c · GB, 1932
BRITISH MOVIETONE NEWS [1932] – RAF LINKS EMPIRE'S FAR FLUNG COLONIES

b/w · 1 reel · 289' (5 mins) · mute
intertitles: none

pr British Movietone News *cam* Lieb, J H

- Aircraft of 14 Squadron flying over Mount Kenya, 21 March 1932.

The squadron pilots start up their Fairey IIIF aircraft and take off. Three of them, and the camera plane (see **Notes**), overfly the mountain, which is covered with snow.

Notes
Summary: in the early 1930s 14 Squadron was based at Amman in Transjordan. The "East African Cruise" was a flag-showing operation. Although he is never seen, it is worthy of note that the pilot of the camera plane was Wing-Commander A T Harris – to be better known as 'Bomber' Harris in the Second World War.
Remarks: the view of the mountain and snow from the open aircraft is very attractive.
[Dudley Saward, *"Bomber"* Harris, Sphere (1985): 49-50]
catalogued SDB: 8/1983

IWM 880-02d · France, 1917
la FIN D'UN RAID 19-20 OCTOBRE 1917
the END OF AN AIR RAID OCTOBRE (sic) 19.10.1917 (alternative)

b/w · 1 reel · 398' (7 mins) · silent
intertitles: French & English

- French film on the wrecks of Zeppelins forced down over French territory while returning from a raid on England, 19-20 October 1917.

The Germans lost eleven Zeppelins in the course of the raid, five of them over France. Firstly, the wreck of one of the airships is inspected by French soldiers, while two of the aircraft which shot it down fly (indistinctly) overhead. The burnt-out wreck consists mainly of the airship frame and engines. Zeppelin L49, which was forced down intact near Bourbonne-les-Bains, rests on the ground, having broken its back in landing. It is inspected by French and US soldiers.

Notes
Title: this and the intertitles are shown firstly in French, and then in English. The English is occasionally quaint.
catalogued SDB: 8/1983

IWM 881-900 · NO FILM

IWM 901 · GB, (ca) 1922
[POLICE TRAINING FILM] (allocated)

b/w · 1 reel · 496' (9 mins) · silent
intertitles: none

- Extremely dark and blurred film, possibly of police training in Britain in the 1920s.

Racks of weapons, possibly a display of police equipment. A map of the Metropolitan police divisions. An evidence case ? Men working at desks. Out-of-focus shot of fingerprints being taken. Boys working at woodwork benches. Boys and girls in an institution sitting down to a meal – a borstal ? A laundry. A dormitory for children. Police trainees receive a lecture, the instructor holds up types of number plates for cars. Another lecturer, a police sergeant, shows how to hit someone with a truncheon.

Notes
Technical: this film is, for all practical purposes, unviewable.
catalogued SDB: 10/1983

IWM 902-988 · NO FILM

IWM 989 · GB, (ca) 1936
[RAF FIGHTERS TAKING OFF] (allocated)

b/w · 1 reel · 52' (1 min) · silent
intertitles: none

- Very brief film of Hawker Harts or Demons of 23 Squadron RAF taking off from a grass airstrip, England, 1935-37.

Notes
Remarks: the Hawker Hart developed into the early Marks of Demon, and the two are difficult to tell apart.
catalogued SDB: 7/1983

IWM 990 · GB, (prod) 1951
SAPPER REUNION FILM

b/w · 1 reel · 790' (14 mins) · mute
intertitles: none

- Stockshot material of Royal Engineers in the First World War.

Not all of the material is of Royal Engineers. The opening shows Kitchener inspecting new recruits in London, and later on the Western Front. Royal Engineers dig, plant and explode a large mine under the German positions on the Western Front. Various examples of sappers repairing trenches and laying light railways. Sappers in Palestine laying telegraph wires and railway lines, including a view from a moving train of the finished railway. Pontoon bridges in Mesopotamia. Early Mk I tanks in training. The Victory Parade through the streets of London in 1919, including the Royal Engineers contingent. Finally, inland water transport barges on the Western Front and in Egypt.

Notes
Production: this compilation was made for a Royal Engineers reunion in 1951.
Summary: see the detailed shotsheet for the precise origin of each shot.
Remarks: of some interest in showing what the image of the First World War was, or was meant to be by 1951, for those who fought in it. Otherwise, this should only be used by those interested in stockshots without regard for historical accuracy.
[shotsheet available]
catalogued SDB: 8/1983

IWM 991-1003 · NO FILM

IWM 1004 · Germany, 1940
KRIEGSFLIEGER AN DER WESTFRONT :
Aufnahmen aus dem Weltkrieg
PILOTS ON THE WESTERN FRONT :
scenes from the World War (translation)

b/w · 1 reel · 420' (17 mins) · silent
intertitles: German

pr Reichsanstalt für Film und Bild in Wissenschaft und Unterricht

- Compilation film of German fliers and planes on the Western Front, 1916-18.

Poor quality film of a line of Aviatik CIIs taking off. The pilot and observer of an Aviatik CV (DFW?), with a prominent skull-and-crossbones design on its side, prepare for a sortie and take off. The plane is shown 'in flight'. The observer takes photographs, uses his machinegun to fight off an enemy, and drops a bomb by hand on the enemy below. (The plane 'in flight' resembles a LVG CII.) On the ground a Gotha GII is bombed up and takes off. It flies a bombing mission, hitting oil tanks on the ground

which burst into flames. (The plane 'in flight' is an Italian Caproni CIII.) A line of Fokker DVIIs takes off, and engages British DH4s in a dogfight. One of the DH4s is 'shot down' (a model) and burns on the ground. A lorry-mounted German 77mm anti-aircraft gun fires at the British. A French Nieuport burns on the ground as a Fokker DVII taxis past it. Back in the dogfight, the observer bales out of an observation balloon by parachute as the balloon is shot down in flames. A portrait shot of Max Immelmann. Oswald Boelcke with pilots of Jagdstaffel 2. More of the dogfight (mainly fakes). Baron Manfred von Richthofen with the pilots of Jagdgeschwader 1, with his Great Dane 'Moritz', and joking with his father, Major (Freiherr) Albrecht von Richthofen. Von Richthofen prepares for a sortie in his Fokker DrI, putting on his flying clothes while his mechanics check the engine. He briefs his pilots with a map, and then takes off with them. Von Richthofen inspects the wreck of one of the aircraft he has shot down. He talks with an uninjured British pilot he has shot down. At a troop review near Courtrai in August 1917, von Richthofen (his head bandaged after a head wound) shakes hands with Kaiser Wilhelm and General von Hoeppner, commander of the German Army Air Service. Hermann Goering, who replaced von Richthofen as commander of the Jagdgeschwader, is shown by himself, with his pilots, and with his close friend Bruno Loerzer, commander of Jagdstaffel 11. Goering, in his plane's cockpit, removes his flying helmet after a sortie.

Notes
Summary: the sequence of the Caproni making its bombing attack is also found in **IWM 484** *The First World War*, produced by Truman Talley and the Fox Film Corporation, and made in 1934.
[shotsheet available]
catalogued SDB & KGTG: 8/1983

IWM 1005 · GB, (ca) 1922
the EYES OF THE ARMY

b/w · 1 reel · 1005' (17 mins) · silent
intertitles: English

pr Gaumont

- Cooperation between the RAF and the Army during manœuvres in the Aldershot area, shortly after the First World War.

A Bristol Fighter of 4 Squadron RAF spots two 'enemy' Whippet tanks taking up position to halt the advance of 1st (Guards) Brigade, 1st Division. Oblivious of this, the Guards move towards their objective, near Bramshot Farm, in artillery formation. The pilot of the aircraft writes a message, which is dropped near the command table of the divisional commander, probably Major-General Sir E G T Bainbridge. He writes orders, which he gives to a galloper, for XII Brigade Royal Field Artillery and to 4 Squadron. The gunners, with their 18-pounder field guns and radio masts already in position, prepare to fire. The airmen brief and despatch another Bristol Fighter to act as observer for the shoot. The divisional commander writes orders to 1st (Guards) Brigade, giving them a new time for their attack. The message is fitted onto a pick-up wire between two poles, and a ground panel laid out as a signal to the first aircraft. This flies low enough to catch the message on a trailing hook, and drops it near the guardsmen. The message is brought to the brigade commander, probably Colonel J McC Steele. The second aircraft, circling over the tanks, calls down the artillery fire onto them by Morse (film blurred). The gunners can receive the Morse, and reply by using ground panels. The Whippets are shown with smoke shells bursting around them, and finally 'brewed up', covered in smoke. The Guards advance in linear formation to occupy the objective.

Notes
Title: note that this film is not to be confused with *The Eyes of the Army*, an official production made in 1916 and now held as film **IWM 118**.
Remarks: an attractive film, particularly the aerial shots of the gun batteries firing, which are most impressive.
[shotsheet available]
catalogued SDB: 7/1983

IWM 1006-1009 · NO FILM

IWM 1010 · USA, (?) 1939
COLLECTION OF ORIGINAL PLANES IN THE JARRETT MUSEUM OF WORLD WAR HISTORY : formerly maintained Moorestown NJ

col · 1 reel · 180' (7 mins) · silent
intertitles: English

- Home movie and stills of a collection of First World War aircraft.

The planes, on display in the open, include a Spad 7, a Sopwith Camel, a Fokker DVII, a Nieuport 28, a Thomas-Morse Scout, and a Pfalz DXII. As people walk around the collection a Renault FT17 tank drives past. The remainder of the film shows a Pfalz DXII rebuilt so as to be airworthy, and in flight over New Jersey, filmed from a camera plane which comes quite close to the Pfalz.

Notes
Technical: film quality is generally very poor.
catalogued SDB: 8/1983

IWM 1011-1024 · NO FILM

IWM 1025a · GB, 1900
a SKIRMISH WITH THE BOERS NEAR KIMBERLEY BY A TROOP OF CAVALRY SCOUTS ATTACHED TO GENERAL FRENCH'S COLUMN (fragment 1)

b/w · 1 reel · 60' (1 min) · silent
intertitles: none

pr Warwick Trading Company
cam Rosenthal, J

- First part of a short film on British mounted troops staging a combat manœuvre, not far from Kimberley, South Africa, May-July 1900. A copy of the complete film is held as **IWM 1081d**.

catalogued SDB: 9/1983

IWM 1025b · GB, 1900
the RETURN OF SIR GEORGE WHITE

b/w · 1 reel · 63' (1 min) · silent
intertitles: none

- Ceremonial parade through the streets of London of Sir George White and his staff, returned home after the relief of Ladysmith, April 1900.

Crowds line the streets, held back by soldiers, as the military parade (always in long shot) passes by. In the centre of the parade is General White with his staff.

Notes
Title: this is marked on the leader of the film.
Remarks: as the scene is always in long shot it is not possible to be certain about the identification of this film.
catalogued SDB: 9/1983

IWM 1025c · GB, 1900
LORD ROBERTS LEAVING FOR SOUTH AFRICA

b/w · 1 reel · 18' (1 min) · silent
intertitles: none

pr Warwick Trading Company

■ Very brief scene of Lord Roberts and his staff boarding SS *Dunottar Castle* at Southampton docks for the trip to South Africa, 23 December 1899.

Notes
Title: this is taken from the Warwick catalogue for 1900.
Production: this film is Warwick catalogue number 5521a.
Title: identified by James Barker in work for the television series *Flashback*.
catalogued SDB: 9/1983

IWM 1025d · GB, 1900
a SKIRMISH WITH THE BOERS NEAR KIMBERLEY BY A TROOP OF CAVALRY SCOUTS ATTACHED TO GENERAL FRENCH'S COLUMN (fragment 2)

b/w · 1 reel · 47' (1 min) · silent
intertitles: none

pr Warwick Trading Company
cam Rosenthal, J

■ Second part of a short film on British mounted troops staging a combat manœuvre, not far from Kimberley, South Africa, May-July 1900. A copy of the complete film is held as **IWM 1081d**.

catalogued SDB: 9/1983

IWM 1025e · GB, 1900
[INSPECTION OF THE CIV] (allocated)

b/w · 1 reel · 46' (1 min) · silent
intertitles: none

pr Warwick Trading Company (?)

■ Men of the City Imperial Volunteers being inspected at the Albany Barracks, London, by Edward, Prince of Wales, prior to their departure for South Africa, 26 January 1900.

The men are drawn up on parade for inspection. The Prince of Wales and inspecting officers move around them quickly, mainly with their backs to the camera.

Notes
Production: this film is possibly Warwick catalogue number 5535b.
Summary: identified by James Barker in work for the television series *Flashback*.
catalogued SDB: 9/1983

IWM 1025f · GB, 1902
[UNVEILING STATUE OF GORDON]
(allocated)

b/w · 1 reel · 66' (1 min) · silent
intertitles: none

■ Unveiling of the statue of General Gordon in St Martin's Place, London, 18 July 1902.

The crowds wait for the ceremony. The dignitaries arrive, and the Duke of Cambridge, the former Commander-in-Chief, unveils the statue of Gordon on his camel.

Notes
Summary: in October 1902 the statue of Gordon was moved to the Sudan, where it was erected in Gordon Avenue, Khartoum, in 1903.
[shotsheet available]
catalogued SDB: 9/1983

IWM 1026-1029 · NO FILM

IWM 1030 · GB, (?) 1962
the GOLDEN JUBILEE OF THE RFC
JUBILEE 1912-1962 (rough material ?)

b/w · 1 reel · 733' (33 mins) · silent
intertitles: English

■ Stockshot material of the work of the Royal Flying Corps, Royal Naval Air

Service, and Royal Air Force in the First World War.

A BE2 spots for a 12-inch howitzer, transmitting instructions by Morse. An RE7 comes in to land. A Lewis gun is checked before being taken on patrol by a Sopwith 1½ Strutter of 45 Squadron. A Fairey FIII seaplane is lifted out onto the deck of a ship and launched by means of a trolley and platform. A Sopwith Camel on ditching trials lands in the water at the Isle of Dogs. A Bristol Fighter of 48 Squadron comes in to land after a patrol and the crew is debriefed. An FE2 of 20 Squadron is prepared for a sortie. The squadron takes off. A (unique) view of some 'model' training trenches in England. A Farman Shorthorn in flight. The FE2s coming back to land. A German squadron prepares and takes off in Fokker DVIIs. British anti-aircraft crews with lorry-mounted 13-pounder anti-aircraft guns. Handley Page 0/400 bombers, probably of 41 Wing RAF, are bombed up for a raid and shown (unique) taking off. Bristol Fighters of 1 Squadron, Royal Australian Air Force, take off for a patrol in Palestine and come back to land. A training flight by an Avro 504 coming back in to land. Royal Naval Air Service officers receiving open-air instruction. A gunner and pilot being trained in a flight simulator. A pilot taking off in an Avro 504 at Heliopolis, Egypt. A line of Sopwith Camels on the Western Front taking off. Exercises in air cooperation with advancing Cavalry. A Short 184 seaplane being launched and overflying destroyers. The airship SSZ3, together with another SSZ Type, takes off. A sortie by airship C24.

Notes
Production: this material may be the original film given by the IWM to the Central Office of Information for the making of COI 296 Jubilee 1912-1962.
Summary: all this material comes from existing IWM films, with the exceptions noted. See in particular **IWM 28**, **IWM 38**, **IWM 130-03+04**, **IWM 141**, **IWM 175**, **IWM 218**, **IWM 234**, **IWM 470**, **IWM 629**, **IWM 648** and **IWM 871**.
Remarks: whoever put this compilation together was addicted to the half-second shot montage, and not to logical or historical continuity.
catalogued SDB: 8/1983

IWM 1031 · GB, (prod) 1918
[FIRST WORLD WAR MAPS 1] (allocated)

b/w · 1 reel · 541' (9 mins) · silent

intertitles: none

pr Topical Film Company (?)

- Animated maps of the main campaigns on the Western Front and the global effect of the declarations of war, 1914-18.

Each 'take' is introduced by a shot-board. The full map shows Europe from Dover east to Frankfurt, and Antwerp south to Orléans. In various stages the map shows the five main phase lines of the war: the furthest German advance of 1914, the line at the end of 1914, the line after the retreat to the Hindenburg Line in 1917, the line after the German offensive of 1918, and the Armistice line. Each new line is introduced by a dissolve, and traced by a pointer. This is followed by a close-up pan down the line from the Channel coast to the Somme area, and close-ups of areas of specific battles such as the Third Battle of Ypres in 1917 or the prepared defence of Paris in 1914. An animated globe of the world, centred approximately on Karachi so that Great Britain is visible but Canada and New Zealand are not. By dissolves the countries that declare war in 1914 are darkened in, with tags giving their names and dates of declaration, going from Austria-Hungary and Serbia through to the British Empire. The film ends with a map of the German advance in 1914 showing the locations of German, French and British forces by name.

Notes
Summary: this film is similar, but not identical, to **IWM 1032**.
catalogued SDB: 8/1983

IWM 1032 · GB, (prod) 1918
[FIRST WORLD WAR MAPS 2] (allocated)

b/w · 1 reel · 257' (5 mins) · silent
intertitles: none

pr Topical Film Company (?)

- Animated maps of the major campaigns on the Western Front, 1914-18.

The main map shows Europe from Dover east to Frankfurt and from Antwerp south to Orléans. Firstly, a close-up of the British positions at the end of the First Battle of Ypres. Then the main map showing the line after the Somme battles of 1916, followed by a close-up of the area. A separate map showing the British gains during the

Somme offensive and the retreat to the Hindenburg Line. The line of the furthest German advance in 1914, showing the position near Paris. A final map with all the main phase lines of the Western Front added to it by dissolves: the furthest German advance of 1914, the line at the end of 1914, the line after the retreat to the Hindenburg Line of 1917, the line after the German offensive of March-May 1918, which is traced in close-up from the Channel coast to the area of Noyon.

Notes

Summary: this is similar, but not identical, to **IWM 1031**. Note that the map of the Somme area is that used to end the IWM print of **IWM 191** *The Battle of the Somme.*
catalogued SDB: 8/1983

IWM 1033a · Austria-Hungary, (?) 1912
[FRANZ JOSEF AT BAD ISCHL] (allocated)
[HUNGARIAN ARCHIVE MATERIAL] (series, allocated)

b/w · 1 reel · 198' (4 mins) · silent
intertitles: Hungarian

- Hungarian film on Emperor Franz Josef, informal with his court at the spa of Bad Ischl, Austria, probably about 1912.

The Emperor stands with members of his court, including Prince Rainer, waiting outside one of his palaces. Coaches arrive and the party drives off. The coaches arrive at Bad Ischl. The Emperor and the King of Bavaria get out of the first coach, and the King of Saxony gets out of the second. The men are wearing hunting dress. The Emperor and the King of Bavaria re-emerge and board a train. When the train stops in a small village the Emperor gets out to the cheers of the local people; he waves to them as he gets into another horse-drawn carriage.

catalogued SDB: 11/1983

IWM 1033b · Austria-Hungary, 1912
[WILHELM II VISITS VIENNA] (allocated)
[HUNGARIAN ARCHIVE MATERIAL] (series, allocated)

b/w · 1 reel · 117' (2 mins) · silent
intertitles: Hungarian

- Hungarian film on the arrival of Kaiser

Wilhelm II by train for a state visit to Vienna, 1912.

A coach takes Emperor Franz Josef, with Prince Eugen in a second coach, to the station along a route lined with cheering people. At the station they wait (Franz Josef is wearing his German field marshal's uniform) for the train to arrive. Wilhelm emerges from the train and the two monarchs embrace. With Wilhelm are Colonel-General Helmuth von Moltke and Count Bülow. A single coach takes Wilhelm and Franz Josef past the crowds.

catalogued SDB: 11/1983

IWM 1033c · Austria-Hungary, (ca) 1912
[FRANZ JOSEF VISITS POLA] (allocated)
[HUNGARIAN ARCHIVE MATERIAL] (series, allocated)

b/w · 1 reel · 186' (3 mins) · silent
intertitles: Hungarian

- Hungarian film of a visit by Emperor Franz Josef to Pola, on the Adriatic coast, before the First World War.

Franz Josef walks with the mayor among the cheering crowds. His entourage, including Adjutant Lobkovitz, follows at a respectful distance. The Emperor walks past an exhibition of various cultures, halting beside a Japanese booth and one of Herzegovinian material. The two men walk on to a pleasure steamer moored on the river. Franz Josef gets into a carriage which drives off.

catalogued SDB: 11/1983

IWM 1033d · Austria-Hungary, (ca) 1912
[FRANZ JOSEF VISITS SANKT PÖLTEN] (allocated)
[HUNGARIAN ARCHIVE MATERIAL] (series, allocated)

b/w · 1 reel · 221' (4 mins) · silent
intertitles: Hungarian

- Hungarian film of Emperor Franz Josef's visit to Sankt Pölten in Lower Austria, probably before the First World War.

Franz Josef emerges from a building to acknowledge the cheers of the crowd. He walks with members of the local rifle club. He listens to an address at the local military academy and receives a bouquet; with him are Prince Rainer and Adjutants Lobkovitz and Graf Paar. The Emperor is shown around the local school – schoolgirls perform a kind of floral dance for him. He then goes on to inspect the cadets at the academy. His carriage then takes him back to the house where he is staying.

catalogued SDB: 11/1983

IWM 1034-01a · Austria-Hungary, 1911
[the WEDDING OF ARCHDUKE KARL AND ZITA] (allocated)
[HUNGARIAN ARCHIVE MATERIAL] (series, allocated)

b/w · 1 reel · 195' (3 mins) · silent
intertitles: none

pr Uher Filmgyar

■ Reception following the wedding of Archduke Karl and his wife Zita, near Vienna, 21 October 1911.

The Austro-Hungarian Imperial family is crowded onto the balcony of a villa. Prominent together with Karl and Zita are Archduke Franz Ferdinand (the heir apparent), the Emperor Franz Josef, King Friedrich Augustus III of Saxony and his wife Sophie. They talk and occasionally pose for the camera.

Notes
Remarks: one of the very rare good sequences of Franz Ferdinand before his assassination.
catalogued SDB: 11/1983

IWM 1034-01b · Austria-Hungary, 1917
[the CORONATION OF KARL OF HUNGARY PART 1] (allocated)
[HUNGARIAN ARCHIVE MATERIAL] (series, allocated)

b/w · 1 reel · 726' (13 mins) · silent
intertitles: Hungarian

■ Coronation of Emperor Karl of Austria-Hungary as King Karl IV of Hungary in Budapest, 30 December 1916.

Empress Zita's carriage drives past the War Ministry towards St Mathias's Church, the magnates of Hungary dipping their banners in salute as it passes. Outside the church, as the ceremony proceeds, the magnates,

including Herzog Czernin, wait. Zita and her son Otto come down the church steps and into their coach. The Hungarian Life Guard leads the procession, with Herzog Burian nearby. Karl leads the procession on horseback, wearing the Crown of St Stephen, followed by Herzog Friedrich, then Burian. Karl walks, with Adjutant Lobkovitz behind him, through the assembled magnates. Outside the church, on the coronation column, Karl takes the oath. Then the procession mounts and rides to the coronation hill. The various clergymen (of all denominations, including Jews and Moslems) who took part in the ceremony emerge from the church. Zita's coach drives off. The procession of the magnates continues. At the top of the coronation hill Karl prepares to take a further oath.

Notes
Summary: see also **IWM 1039-02.**
Remarks: rather disjointed, and in places difficult to watch.
catalogued SDB: 11/1983

IWM 1034-01c · Austria-Hungary, (?) 1917
[FRANZ JOSEF : still portraits etc] (allocated)
[HUNGARIAN ARCHIVE MATERIAL] (series, allocated)

b/w · 1 reel · 123' (2 mins) · silent
intertitles: Hungarian

■ Hungarian film showing a series of still portraits of the life of Emperor Franz Josef of Austria-Hungary.

The paintings or photographs follow in quick succession. Firstly, Franz Josef as a young man, dissolving to him as an old man. His villa at Bad Ischl. Wilhelm II of Germany with Franz Josef. Franz Josef with his grandson Otto. A symbolic 'Death' crosses out the name of Franz Ferdinand on the family tree on 29 (sic) June 1914. Franz Ferdinand's bloodstained uniform after the assassination.

catalogued SDB: 11/1983

IWM 1034-02 · NO FILM

IWM 1034-03 · Austria-Hungary, (?) 1917
[KARL VISITS BULGARIA AND TURKEY] (allocated)

[HUNGARIAN ARCHIVE MATERIAL] (series, allocated)

b/w · 1 reel · 966' (16 mins) · comopt intertitles: Hungarian

- Hungarian film on the state visits of Emperor Karl to Bulgaria and Turkey, early 1917.

Crown Prince Boris and Archduke Cyril wait to meet Karl's train at Sofia station. Karl and Empress Zita arrive. In the centre of Sofia Karl meets King Ferdinand, and they drive by coach through the crowds and parades to the palace, where Karl is introduced to a number of military commanders. Karl watches from his balcony as the parade goes by. Zita tours a hospital in Sofia, talking to convalescent patients. Karl meanwhile talks with leading military and civilian figures in Sofia. He is taken by King Ferdinand and Crown Prince Boris to a parade ground where he meets more soldiers, and watches another march past before leaving. In Constantinople Sultan Mohammed V waits for Karl and Zita's train to arrive. When it does there is, again, a formal meeting, and Karl and the Sultan get into one carriage together with Enver Pasha, the War Minister. The procession of coaches drives through the streets with a full parade escort, and arrives at the Merassim Kiosk (the summer palace). Later, Karl reviews a contingent of Austro-Hungarian troops just outside Constantinople, and then Karl and Zita walk through the parade square. They survey the Bosphoros, and get into the state barge. The film ends abruptly.

Notes
Soundtrack: the soundtrack to this film consists of military music, added by the BBC for its own purposes during the making of *The Great War* series.
catalogued SDB: 11/1983

IWM 1034-04 · Austria-Hungary, (?) 1917
[AUSTRO-HUNGARIANS ON THE ITALIAN FRONT 1] (allocated)
[HUNGARIAN ARCHIVE MATERIAL] (series, allocated)

b/w · 1 reel · 650' (11 mins) · comopt intertitles: Hungarian

pr Sascha Film

- Disjointed Hungarian film of Austro-Hungarian troops in action or training,

mostly on the Italian Front, probably 1917.

A training exercise on gently rolling slopes begins with 77mm field guns and trench mortars opening the bombardment, joined by light howitzers. An intercut scene of Austro-Hungarian troops walking down a damaged street. Back with the exercise, the bombardment of the slopes continues, and the Infantry start to move forward in waves, getting up to the first enemy wire. An intercut shot of an assault battalion on the march through some woods, then back to the staff officers directing the exercise, cutting between the two. Assault troops collect their equipment and move up through a communications trench. Austro-Hungarian Infantry advance through a wood and form a firing line, moving up by sections. Italian prisoners are led back through a town in the wet; the town shows battle damage and has temporary defences.

Notes
Soundtrack: the soundtrack to this film consists of military music, added by the BBC for its own purposes during the making of *The Great War* series.
Remarks: the training exercises, if this is what they are, look very impressive indeed, although the tactics are rather primitive for the probable date of the film.
catalogued SDB: 11/1983

IWM 1035a · Hungary, 1922
die VOLKSABSTIMMUNG IN SOPRON
[the PLEBISCITE IN ODENBURG] (translation)
[HUNGARIAN ARCHIVE MATERIAL] (series, allocated)

b/w · 1 reel · 344' (6 mins) · silent intertitles: German

pr East Newsreel Agency

- Hungarian film on the plebiscite in Sopron, 14 December 1921.

Allied troops, mainly French, patrol the streets of the town. The house of Matthias Corvinus, the 15th century King of Hungary, is shown. People queue to vote in the plebiscite. The local paper gives the result, a victory for Hungary over Austria, in a special edition. A pan over the town.

Notes
Production: the name of the production company is given in English at the start of

the film together with the title.
[Sarah Wambaugh, *Plebiscites Since The World War*, Carnegie Endowment For International Peace (1933): 271-297]
catalogued SDB: 11/1983

IWM 1035b · Austria-Hungary, (?) 1919
[AUSTRO-HUNGARIAN AND ITALIAN PRISONERS OF WAR RETURN HOME]
(allocated)
[HUNGARIAN ARCHIVE MATERIAL] (series, allocated)

b/w · 1 reel · 478' (8 mins) · silent
intertitles: Hungarian

■ Disjointed film mainly on Austro-Hungarian and Italian prisoners of war returning to their own countries during the Armistice, probably late 1918 or early 1919.

Italian soldiers and refugees walk down a road, returning home with their belongings, across the Italian-Austrian border. Austro-Hungarian troops camp in hill country, with horse transport passing. The view from one of the wagons is shown as it passes through an Italian village. At Udine (?) castle Italians guard Austro-Hungarian prisoners. At another camp Italian prisoners begin their walk back home. More returning Italians are joined by refugees. Italian Alpini at a camp in the snow. More of the castle, and of the wagons moving through the village streets. Austro-Hungarian soldiers march along a road; others move up towards a mountain. A 305mm howitzer (?) lies beside a road as more Austro-Hungarians march past. Wrecked Italian guns stand at the side of a road. More Austro-Hungarians march into the mountains. More Italian prisoners of war return. A wounded Italian has his leg bandaged beside a road.

catalogued SDB: 11/1983

IWM 1035c · Austria-Hungary, (?) 1918
[KARL VISITS THE TYROL] (allocated)
[HUNGARIAN ARCHIVE MATERIAL] (series, allocated)

b/w · 1 reel · 240' (4 mins) · silent
intertitles: German

pr Sascha Film and Messter Film

■ Austrian film of a state visit by Emperor

Karl and Empress Zita to the Tyrol region of Austria, probably 1918.

Women wait for Karl and Zita to arrive at Feldkirch station, and strew flowers in their path as they get into their carriages. With Karl are Adjutant Lobkovitz and Archduke Eugen. A line of men from the local rifle club ('Standschützen') in regional costume parades to be inspected by Karl. Zita talks with the ladies, also wearing regional dress, and looks at some cloth. The Emperor and Empress walk through the streets shaking hands with the local dignitaries, while schoolchildren throw flower petals over them. They visit another nearby town, Bregenz, arriving at the railway station. They visit the Cistercian Abbey at Mehrerau, walking through the cloisters with the abbot. They also visit the local Royal Hospital in the same town. They take a boat trip on the Bodensee. They leave by train from Bregenz.

catalogued SDB: 11/1983

IWM 1036-1037 · NO FILM

IWM 1038 · Austria-Hungary, (?) 1918
CSAPATAINK HOSI HARCA A HAVASOK SZIKLAIBAN ES JEGEBEN – PART I (incomplete version)
[OUR HEROIC TROOPS FIGHT AMONG THE SNOW-CAPPED MOUNTAINS, ROCKS AND ICE – PART I] (incomplete version) (translation)
[HUNGARIAN ARCHIVE MATERIAL] (series, allocated)

b/w · 1 reel · 946' (16 mins) · silent
intertitles: Hungarian

pr Sascha Film

■ Almost complete first reel of a Hungarian film of their own troops in the Italian Alps, probably 1918.

The troops are based at a skiing lodge in the mountains, well above the snow-line. The various groups go out on patrols, moving in single file up and down the mountain tracks at a height of 3500m. Two men ride in an aerial cable-car little bigger than they are. More men on the march like black dots in the snow. A heavy gun concealed in a gun pit, described as the highest gun in the Alps. A snow-cave dug in the mountain. A difficult climb up the mountain face. Men set out on ski patrol from the lodge. One group makes a climb with ice axes. Other patrols continue up and down the paths. Men run around the camp site for exercise. The cable-car comes up and skis are unloaded from it. General views of the mountains.

Notes
Summary: an incomplete version of the second reel of this film is held as **IWM 1043a**. Note that the complete film is held as **IWM 1084**, but that this is a master print.
catalogued SDB: 11/1983

IWM 1039-01 · Austria-Hungary, 1915
[AUSTRO-HUNGARIANS IN PRZEMYSL 1]
(allocated)
[HUNGARIAN ARCHIVE MATERIAL] (series, allocated)

b/w · 1 reel · 775' (13 mins) · mute
intertitles: Hungarian

- Hungarian film of Przemyśl and its environs after the Russian retreat, Eastern Front, June 1915.

Views of the destroyed fortress show fallen masonry blocks and dismounted guns. Austro-Hungarian and German troops move through the ruins. Austro-Hungarian transport, including bridge-building equipment and a 305mm heavy howitzer (transported in two main sections) moves down a road. The 305mm howitzer is assembled and fired. An officer at a table in a dug-out computes the firing angle, as the howitzer continues its bombardment. Back in the fortress, Austro-Hungarian and German troops pile up captured small arms. More Austro-Hungarian troops cross the San River by a pontoon bridge. Cavalry lead the advance through Przemyśl town, which is comparatively undamaged. Refugees with their carts make their way along the roads. German soldiers leave the cathedral (?) following a service of thanksgiving for the fall of Przemyśl held on 3 June.

catalogued SDB: 11/1983

IWM 1039-02 · Austria-Hungary, 1917
[the CORONATION OF KARL OF HUNGARY PART 2] (allocated)
[HUNGARIAN ARCHIVE MATERIAL] (series, allocated)

b/w · 1 reel · 70' (2 mins) · mute
intertitles: none

- Fragment from the coronation of Emperor Karl of Austria-Hungary as King Karl IV of Hungary in Budapest, 30 December 1916.

As Karl, leading the procession on horseback, reaches the coronation mound, he urges his horse up to the mound and halts to take a coronation oath.

Notes
Summary: see also **IWM 1034-01b**, which shows the bulk of the ceremony.
catalogued SDB: 11/1983

IWM 1040 · Austria-Hungary, 1916
[FRANZ JOSEF'S FUNERAL PART 3]
(allocated)
[HUNGARIAN ARCHIVE MATERIAL] (series, allocated)

b/w · 1 reel · 470' (8 mins) · silent
intertitles: Hungarian

pr Sascha Film

- Disjointed Hungarian film of mourners at the funeral of Emperor Franz Josef of Austria-Hungary, Vienna, 30 November 1916.

Firstly, the arrival by car and carriage of the various mourners at the west door of Sankt Stefan's Cathedral. Recognisable among the dignitaries arriving are Archduke Joseph, Archduke Friedrich, Archduke Eugen, King Ferdinand of Bulgaria, Prince Henry of Prussia, Prince Rupprecht of Bavaria, Crown Prince Wilhelm of Prussia and, finally, the new Emperor Karl with Empress Zita and their son Otto. At the end of the service, Kaiser Wilhelm II of Germany leaves by the west door, getting into his car. This leads a procession of cars through the streets of Vienna, past the buildings in the centre of the city. Finally, out of time sequence, is a scene of the Emperor Karl and Adjutant Lobkovitz waiting for Wilhelm's train at the main station. The train arrives and Wilhelm gets out.

catalogued SDB: 11/1983

IWM 1041a · Austria-Hungary, 1916
[FRANZ JOSEF'S FUNERAL PART 1]
(allocated)

[HUNGARIAN ARCHIVE MATERIAL] (series, allocated)

b/w · 1 reel · 406' (7 mins) · mute
intertitles: Hungarian

pr Sascha Film

■ Hungarian film of the funeral procession of Emperor Franz Josef of Austria-Hungary through Vienna, 30 November 1916.

The procession, led by priests with lighted candles, files down the steps of the Hofburg followed by the coffin and an escort of Hungarian Life Guards on foot. The coffin is loaded into a hearse. The procession moves out of the palace grounds, with an escort of guards and other soldiers. They include the Austrian Life Guard (the 'Arcièren Leibgarde'), No 1 Infantry Regiment, and No 18 Dragoons.

Notes
Summary: note that the 3 separate films on this reel follow each other without a break, which may be confusing to watch.
catalogued SDB: 11/1983

IWM 1041b · Austria-Hungary, 1914
[FRANZ FERDINAND'S MEMORIAL CEREMONY] (allocated)
[HUNGARIAN ARCHIVE MATERIAL] (series, allocated)

b/w · 1 reel · 207' (4 mins) · mute
intertitles: none

■ Procession of the coffins of Archduke Franz Ferdinand and his wife through the streets of Trieste, Austria, July 1914.

The sailors who brought the coffins up the Adriatic coast to Trieste act as escorts as the hearses and state coaches, covered with flowers, make their procession through the streets. The procession arrives at the steps of the cathedral (not clearly seen) and the coffins are taken inside. (Note the cine cameraman at work outside the cathedral.)

Notes
Summary: note that the 3 separate films on this reel follow each other without a break, which may be confusing to watch. See also **IWM 1046b**.
catalogued SDB: 11/1983

IWM 1042 · France/Czechoslovakia, 1920
[LITTLE ENTENTE CONFERENCE AT VERSAILLES] (allocated)
[HUNGARIAN ARCHIVE MATERIAL] (series, allocated)

b/w · 1 reel · 860' (14 mins) · silent
intertitles: Czech

pr Gaumont

■ Czech film of the Little Entente conference at Versailles, France, to ratify the borders of Hungary, June 1920.

Men of the Hungarian delegation arrive at Versailles, pose for the camera and go into the Château de Madrid. Handbills for the conference are printed at a machine. Three Romanian delegates, Cantacuzino, Ghika and Brediceanu, confer at a table, being joined by Pelivan and Titulescu. The full Romanian delegation confers together, consulting documents and changing places. The delegation includes, as well as those mentioned, Antonide, Caracostea, Neculcea, Serban and Raut. Seen next are the Yugoslav delegates, also debating between themselves at a table. They are named as Pasic, Trumbic, Zolger, Radovic, Rybar, Karovic, Pavlovic, Ehrlich, Jaksic, Jovanovic and Fotic. The chief Czech delegate, Osusky, is seen working at his desk. He is joined by delegate Navak, then is shown in conference with delegates Braf and Krno, then with the group of delegates, including also Kallab, Klir, Chotek and Krbec. At part of the conference the Romanian, Yugoslav and Czech delegates confer together, representative of the Little Entente ("Male Dohody"). Meanwhile the Hungarian delegate inspects a French guard of honour outside Grand Trianon, while other delegates arrive. In the Hall of Mirrors the treaty agreeing to the new borders of Hungary is signed, after which the delegates pose for the camera. The signed treaty is shown in close-up.

Notes
Remarks: rather difficult for anyone who does not understand Czech to follow. The delegates play up to the camera magnificently, 'conferring' and 'debating' in a most impressive fashion.
catalogued SDB: 11/1983

IWM 1043a · Austria-Hungary, (?) 1918
CSAPATAINK HOSI HARCA A HAVASOK SZIKLAIBAN ES JEGEBEN – PART II (incomplete version)

[OUR HEROIC TROOPS FIGHT AMONG
THE SNOW-CAPPED MOUNTAINS, ROCKS
AND ICE – PART II] (incomplete version)
(translation)
[HUNGARIAN ARCHIVE MATERIAL] (series,
allocated)

b/w · 1 reel · 792' (14 mins) · mute
intertitles: Hungarian

pr Sascha Film

- Almost complete second reel of a
  Hungarian film of their own troops in the
  Italian Alps, probably 1918.

A shell-burst lands beside an Austro-
Hungarian observation post, scattering
snow over the men. In response an assault
company is alerted from its hut, while its
37mm mountain howitzer is manhandled
into position. The men of the company run
up the snow path and climb a rope ladder
up the mountain face to reach the enemy.
The 37mm opens fire, directed from the
observation post by telephone, as the
assaulting troops scramble up the mountain
side. The shells burst against the Italian
position higher up the mountain. As the
Austro-Hungarian rush reaches the ground
directly below the Italian position they have
grenades thrown at them by the Italians.
Stretcher-bearers take away an injured
Austrian. Finally, the assault troops storm
the Italian position, using their bayonets as
knives, then taking their prisoners and
wounded with them continue on up the
mountain.

Notes
Summary: an incomplete version of the first
reel of this 2-reel film is held as **IWM 1038**.
Note that the complete film is held as **IWM
1084**, but that this is a master print.
Remarks: a very attractive reconstruction,
although it is hard to believe that these
tactics would succeed with so few
casualties.
catalogued SDB: 11/1983

IWM 1043b · Austria-Hungary, (?) 1917
[JOSEF ON THE ITALIAN FRONT 2]
(allocated)
[HUNGARIAN ARCHIVE MATERIAL] (series,
allocated)

b/w · 1 reel · 128' (2 mins) · silent
intertitles: none

- Archduke Josef, the Austro-Hungarian
  Army Group Commander, makes an

informal tour of his men's positions,
Italian Front, probably 1917.

The troops are in trenches well below the
snowline, doing general maintenance work.
The Archduke wanders along the lines of
camouflaged positions, completely
informally, occasionally stopping to talk with
the soldiers as he passes with his staff.

Notes
Summary: see also **IWM 1045b**.
catalogued SDB: 11/1983

IWM 1044 · Austria-Hungary, 1917
A POZSONYI KIRALYNAP
[the IMPERIAL VISIT TO PRESSBURG]
(translation)
[HUNGARIAN ARCHIVE MATERIAL] (series,
allocated)

b/w · 1 reel · 1009' (17 mins) · mute
intertitles: Hungarian

pr Starfilm

- Hungarian film of the visit of Emperor
  Karl to Pressburg (Pozsonyi, now
  Bratislava in the Slovak Republic) in
  Hungary, spring 1917.

Views of the city, which lies on the Danube,
show the statue of the poet Petöfi, and of
Empress Maria Teresa. The local regiment,
No 72 Infantry Regiment, parades through
the street. A river steamer approaches the
landing-stage. Emperor Karl, Empress Zita
with their son Otto, and Adjutant Lobkovitz
with their entourage, disembark. With the
entourage is an official still cameraman, and
numerous press cameramen are in
evidence throughout the trip. The Emperor
and Empress travel by carriage through the
streets, to the cheers of the crowd. At a
reception in the open Karl listens to
speeches and replies with salutes. Karl and
Zita wander over the regimental parade
ground. As their open carriage reaches the
town synagogue it halts, and the local
rabbis pronounce a blessing on Karl. They
then drive on to the cathedral where Karl
and Zita continue on foot. They are then
taken to a local girls' school where the
children make presentations to them. They
return to the river steamer, and the people
wave them goodbye.

Notes
Remarks: a well-made film by the standards
of the time; the episode with the rabbis in
particular is most impressive. The

cameraman is trying hard and is occasionally able to get in with some good close-ups, but all too often his view is blocked by still cameras and press men.
catalogued SDB: 11/1983

IWM 1045a · Germany/Austria-Hungary, 1917
MESSTER WOCHE (early 1917) (allocated)
[HUNGARIAN ARCHIVE MATERIAL] (series, allocated)

b/w · 1 reel · 347' (6 mins) · mute
intertitles: Hungarian

pr Messter Film

■ Hungarian version of a German newsreel showing Emperor Karl of Austria-Hungary visiting the German sector of the Eastern Front, 26 January 1917.

Kaiser Wilhelm waits, wearing his Austrian field marshal's uniform, with his officers in the snow. Jump cut to Wilhelm greeting Karl beside his train just after his arrival. The two emperors arrive by car at a parade ground, covered with snow, and watch while German soldiers march past them, including possibly the Alexander Guard and dismounted hussars. General Paul von Hindenburg, also wearing his Austrian uniform, talks with Karl, who then helps Wilhelm present decorations to various German officers.

Notes
Production: the Messter Woche symbol appears on the second caption of the film.
catalogued SDB: 11/1983

IWM 1045b · Austria-Hungary, (?) 1917
[JOSEF ON THE ITALIAN FRONT 1]
(allocated)
[HUNGARIAN ARCHIVE MATERIAL] (series, allocated)

b/w · 1 reel · 303' (5 mins) · mute
intertitles: none

■ Archduke Josef, the Austro-Hungarian Army Group Commander, makes an informal tour of his men's positions, Italian Front, probably 1917.

The troops are in rear-area camps and camouflaged trenches well below the snow-line. Josef, with his staff, walks around the area, completely informally, talking to the

occasional soldier. He watches the workings of a field kitchen as it prepares food. Josef and his staff make their way along a heavily camouflaged trench.

Notes
Summary: see also **IWM 1043b**.
catalogued SDB: 11/1983

IWM 1045c · Austria-Hungary, 1915
[AUSTRO-HUNGARIANS IN PRZEMYSL 2]
(allocated)
[HUNGARIAN ARCHIVE MATERIAL] (series, allocated)

b/w · 1 reel · 70' (1 min) · silent
intertitles: none

■ Brief film of the woods near Przemyśl after the Russian retreat, Eastern Front, June 1915.

An Austro-Hungarian photographer and a civilian wander through the woods, which show damage after the battle.

catalogued SDB: 11/1983

IWM 1045d · Austria-Hungary, (?) 1917
[KARL OF AUSTRIA-HUNGARY VISITS WILHELM OF GERMANY]
[HUNGARIAN ARCHIVE MATERIAL] (series, allocated)

b/w · 1 reel · 47' (1 min) · mute
intertitles: none

■ Fragment of a film of Emperor Karl of Austria-Hungary arriving by train, met by Emperor Wilhelm of Germany, probably 1917.

Wilhelm, wearing his Austro-Hungarian field marshal's uniform, stands beside the train as it halts. Karl gets off, wearing German hussar uniform, followed by members of his staff.

catalogued SDB: 11/1983

IWM 1046a · France/Hungary, 7/1914
[FRANZ FERDINAND IN SARAJEVO]
(allocated)
[HUNGARIAN ARCHIVE MATERIAL] (series, allocated)

b/w · 1 reel · 133' (2 mins) · mute
intertitles: Hungarian

pr Eclair

■ Hungarian-language version of a
newsreel showing events surrounding the
assassination of Archduke Franz
Ferdinand in Sarajevo, Bosnia, 28 June
1914.

A pan over the town of Sarajevo. People
walk past debris in the streets left after the
wrecking of Serbian-owned shops by angry
pro-Imperial mobs following the
assassination. Hungarian troops, including
dragoons, move through the streets. Franz
Ferdinand and his wife Sophie arrive by car
at the Town Hall having survived the first
attempt to kill them on the way there. They
get out, say brief greetings to the
assembled dignitaries, and walk inside. (On
their drive from the Town Hall they will be
killed.)

Notes
Remarks: the second subject is in long
shot, but has every appearance of being
genuine. As such, the significance of the
events it depicts make it one of the most
remarkable pieces of film ever taken.
catalogued SDB: 11/1983

IWM 1046b · France/Hungary, 14/7/1914
**[FRANZ FERDINAND'S MEMORIAL
CEREMONY]** (allocated)
[HUNGARIAN ARCHIVE MATERIAL] (series,
allocated)

b/w · 1 reel · 234' (4 mins) · mute
intertitles: Hungarian

pr Gaumont

■ Hungarian-language version of a
newsreel on the procession of the coffins
of Archduke Franz Ferdinand and his
wife through the streets of Trieste,
Austria, July 1914.

A crowd waits at the landing stage as a
launch carrying the coffins arrives and they
are taken off. A blessing is pronounced
over the coffins. The procession winds
through the streets of the city. Sailors and
soldiers act as escort to the hearses and
accompanying carriages. The procession
arrives at the cathedral and the coffins are
taken inside. (Note the cine cameraman at
work.) The procession returns through the
streets.

Notes
Summary: see also **IWM 1041b**.
catalogued SDB: 11/1983

IWM 1047-01 · Austria-Hungary, (prod) 1917
**[AUSTRO-HUNGARIANS AT CAPORETTO
1]** (allocated)
[HUNGARIAN ARCHIVE MATERIAL] (series,
allocated)

b/w · 1 reel · 565' (9 mins) · comopt
intertitles: Hungarian

■ Hungarian film of Austro-Hungarian
troops on the Italian Front, probably
during the Battle of Caporetto, October-
November 1917.

Austro-Hungarians on the march in the
battle zone, moving up past transport. They
include storm troops and a bridge-building
platoon. Other troops march down the
roads, or wait at the roadside. Italian
prisoners are marched back. There is snow
on the ground in some of the scenes. An
overturned truck lies beside a mountain
stream. Two horses cross a ford, with
smoke and mountains in the background.
Groups of captured Italian heavy guns of
various calibres. The troops march up the
road one way, the Italian prisoners come
back down the other. An Austrian discovers
a dead body (acted) and removes his hat in
reverence. Austro-Hungarian walking
wounded move back along the roads. More
abandoned Italian equipment by the
roadside. A shot from a lorry on the move.
The march continues, with some
refugees and prisoners crossing a
footbridge over a river.

Notes
Soundtrack: the soundtrack to this film
consists of military music, added by the
BBC for its own purposes during the
making of *The Great War* series.
Remarks: jumbled and difficult to follow. It is
not clear how much of this material relates
directly to Caporetto.
catalogued SDB: 11/1983

IWM 1047-02 · Austria-Hungary, (prod) 1917
**[AUSTRO-HUNGARIANS AT CAPORETTO
2]** (allocated)
[HUNGARIAN ARCHIVE MATERIAL] (series,
allocated)

b/w · 1 reel · 312' (5 mins) · comopt
intertitles: Hungarian

- Hungarian film of Austro-Hungarian troops and destroyed buildings on the Italian Front, probably during the Battle of Caporetto, October-November 1917.

Horses, together with their Austro-Hungarian handlers (mildly camera-conscious) rest beside a monastery which shows some shell damage. Other partly destroyed buildings, including a village square and church. Both interiors and exteriors of damaged buildings are shown.

Notes
Soundtrack: the soundtrack to this film consists of military music, added by the BBC for its own purposes during the making of *The Great War* series. catalogued SDB: 11/1983

IWM 1048 · NO FILM

IWM 1049 · GB, (prod) 1960
[the GREAT WAR : US stockshot material] (allocated)

b/w · 1 reel · 606' (10 mins) · silent intertitles: none

- Jumbled stockshot material of the USA, including Colonel House, John Pershing, Ambassador Page and Pancho Villa, 1914-18.

The material is very jumbled and hard to interpret. The film starts with a painting of a galleon, probably a reference to Columbus. Then a sign for use in US cinemas during the neutrality period, being a request from President Wilson that audiences should not show approval or disapproval when films of the war were shown. A brief scene of French bicycle troops in a village. Men in a jungle clearing the way for a road or railway, probably in Central America. A dredger scoops silt out from a lake, and another scoop clears earth from an excavation. Very poor quality film of US soldiers, including Brigadier-General J J Pershing, arriving by train in a town in the Sierra Madre, during the border trouble with Mexico in 1916. Pancho Villa, the Mexican revolutionary, poses with two other men, then by himself. A clip from a fictional (or staged) film of the Mexican revolution involving a Mexican attack on a US outpost. A lengthy scene of an unidentified pilot of the US Army being awarded the Distinguished Service Cross in a small

ceremony in the USA. A brief scene (printed out of rack) of a tailor's shop. US Ambassador Page opening a US Red Cross hospital in London in early 1918 (see Notes). Colonel Edward M House, President Wilson's adviser, seen emerging from a building, walking up a gangplank, and with Mrs House on board a ship.

Notes
Production: this material was obtained from the American firm Stock Shots Inc by the BBC for *The Great War* series, and passed on to the IWM after the series was completed. The film of Villa, almost certainly comes from the work of Charles Rosher (see Brownlow's account for this); the fictional material may be from the film *Life of Villa* also mentioned by Brownlow. The scene of Ambassador Page comes from the *War Office Official Topical Budget*, and those of Colonel House from two episodes of *Hearst-Pathé News* and *Selznick News*. *Remarks:* as the name of the firm suggests, these are stockshots and should be treated with some caution by the historian. Nevertheless they include some very rare film.
[Kevin Brownlow, *The War, the West and the Wilderness*, Secker and Warburg (1979): 87-106]
catalogued SDB: 9/1983

IWM 1050 · Belgium, (after) 1919
A LA GLOIRE DU TROUPIER BELGE 1 PARTIE
TER EERE VAN DEN BELGISCHEN SOLDAT 1 DEEL (alternative)
[TO THE GLORY OF THE BELGIAN SOLDIER PART 1] (translation)

b/w · 1 reel · 628' (11 mins) · silent intertitles: French & Flemish

- Belgian film of the outbreak of the First World War, and the activities of their own troops in Flanders, 1914-16.

The progress of the war is represented by animated maps. A hand reaches out from Germany into Belgium and grabs Liège at the start of the war. A young soldier, in an acted scene, says goodbye to his mother and sets out with his friend to the war, the start of a "calvaire sanglant et sublime". Columns of troops march to war and dig trenches. A map shows the German bombardment of the Liège fortress. German soldiers advance through woods. Belgian refugees flee before them. Belgian troops on the Yser early in the war, with shells hitting buildings for the first time. The sluices holding back the sea are opened in October and flood the lowlands between Nieuport and Dixmude. Belgian troops settle down to hold the line. They are next shown in 1916, some behind heavily piled sandbag barricades, others warming themselves by a fire in the snow. Some wash their clothes, or pick lice out of them. A platoon walks in single file over a footbridge in the flooded area. Troops enter a trench system. Two men open a tin of corned beef. A sniper uses a rifle from behind a metal shield, and two others fire from slits. In the flat, flooded countryside the trenches have been built up above the ground with sandbags, rather than dug down into it.

Notes
Summary: the whole series (see following numbers) consists of Belgian official film taken between 1914 and 1918, joined to staged or faked material, and used with little regard to geographical or chronological accuracy to present a series of images rather than a coherent account of the war. Note that as this is Belgian material the troops described in it are Belgian unless otherwise stated.
Remarks: the series generally is comparable, or superior, to **IWM 420** *The World's Greatest Story*, showing the same tendency to jumble material. Little faith should be placed in the accuracy of the material as used. On the other hand, much of the film used is attractive and, within its limits, entertaining.
catalogued SDB: 8/1983

IWM 1051 · Belgium, (after) 1919
A LA GLOIRE DU TROUPIER BELGE 2 PARTIE
TER EERE VAN DEN BELGISCHEN SOLDAT 2 DEEL (alternative)
[TO THE GLORY OF THE BELGIAN SOLDIER PART 2] (translation)

b/w · 1 reel · 691' (12 mins) · silent
intertitles: French & Flemish

■ Belgian film of general activity by their own forces in Flanders, Western Front, 1916-17.

Soldiers start digging a trench system and wiring up the positions. Finned mortar bombs for a 58mm Crapouillot (?) are carried forward into a front line trench and used to bombard the German positions. A patrol in a flooded area. A trench system near damaged buildings. A group of

soldiers leaves wattle dug-outs in response to an alert. A sniper takes aim and falls back wounded (acted ?). His friend calls for a stretcher and he is carried back through the trench system to safety. A round observation balloon is inflated. A 75mm field gun fires at a high angle. Two observers bail out from an observation balloon as it bursts into flames from an air attack. Aircraft dogfight in the sky. A soldier with a trench periscope gives the alert and a bugler blows a gas warning. The men put on 1916 pattern gas-hoods. Infantry practise an open order charge on a training ground beside their tents. A 75mm bombards the front line. A heavy gun in a fortress cupola joins in.

Notes
Title: this has been deduced from the position of the episode in the series.
Summary: see **IWM 1050**.
catalogued SDB: 8/1983

IWM 1052 · Belgium, (after) 1919
A LA GLOIRE DU TROUPIER BELGE 3 PARTIE
TER EERE VAN DEN BELGISCHEN SOLDAT 3 DEEL (alternative)
[TO THE GLORY OF THE BELGIAN SOLDIER PART 3] (translation)

b/w · 1 reel · 596' (10 mins) · silent
intertitles: French & Flemish

■ Belgian film of their own forces clearing Flanders in the Advance to Victory, Western Front, 14-16 October 1918.

Troops build a corduroy road to prepare for the advance over broken ground. A galloper rides up to a field battery with fire orders and a map. Transport on the move up a road. The attack on 14 October, marking the opening of the Battle of Thourout-Thielt, starts with a bombardment by 75mm and 105mm guns, followed by 155mm naval and 155mm Schneider guns. A 'parade' flight of aircraft passes overhead. An aerial dogfight in progress. Soldiers emerge from their trenches and walk forward in bright sunlight (training ?) through a smokescreen. German soldiers rush to reinforce their positions. The animated maps shows the Belgians taking Dzaeme, Roulers and Rumbeke in October. Soldiers with their field kitchens march forward. The Belgians take Thourout on 16 October. A German counter-bombardment falls quite close to the camera. An observation kite balloon spots, and lorries

hurry forward. 155mm Schneider howitzers
fire. Belgian planes (Nieuport 12s ?) in
'parade' flight.

Notes
Summary: see **IWM 1050**.
catalogued SDB: 8/1983

IWM 1053 · Belgium, (after) 1919
**A LA GLOIRE DU TROUPIER BELGE 4
PARTIE**
TER EERE VAN DEN BELGISCHEN
SOLDAT 4 DEEL (alternative)
[TO THE GLORY OF THE BELGIAN
SOLDIER PART 4] (translation)

b/w · 1 reel · 963' (16 mins) · silent
intertitles: French & Flemish

■ Belgian film of their own forces clearing
  Flanders of German troops in the
  Advance to Victory, Western Front, 27-29
  September 1918.

The film starts with an order of the day, in
French and Flemish, from King Albert to his
soldiers dated 27 September, telling them
that the time for the decisive attack has
come. 75mm guns start the bombardment.
German troops man their defensive
positions. Belgian troops rush forward. The
battlefield shows trees shattered by gunfire,
and captured German defences. A map
shows the positions of the two sides. The
Belgians advance. Belgian, and then
German, dead on the battlefield. German
prisoners are led to rear areas where some
are searched by Belgian soldiers. Field
guns move up. The map shows the
advance on 28 September, taking
Houthulst, Poelcappelle, Passchendaele
and Zonnebeke. A view of the Forest of
Houthulst. The village of Woumen after its
capture, followed by Dixmude, Clercken
and Moorslede, all of them virtually rubble.
Horsed transport waits to move up.
Prisoners are marched to the rear.
Abandoned German guns, 77mm, 105mm
and 155mm, lie in the mud together with
their ammunition. Belgian medics give first
aid to wounded men. Walking wounded
move to the rear; a stretcher is found for
one of them. Other stretcher-cases wait for
evacuation; German prisoners help as
stretcher-bearers. A column of motor
ambulances on the road. A forward
dressing station. The map shows that on 29
September the advance took Dixmude,
Woumen, Clercken, Moorslede,
Westboosebeke, Staden and Zarren.

Notes
Title: this has been deduced from the
position of the episode in the series.
Summary: see **IWM 1050**.
catalogued SDB: 8/1983

IWM 1054 · Belgium, (after) 1919
**A LA GLOIRE DU TROUPIER BELGE 5
PARTIE**
TER EERE VAN DEN BELGISCHEN
SOLDAT 5 DEEL (alternative)
[TO THE GLORY OF THE BELGIAN
SOLDIER PART 5] (translation)

b/w · 1 reel · 589' (10 mins) · silent
intertitles: French & Flemish

■ Belgian film of their own forces in the
  Advance to Victory and the first days of
  the Armistice, Western Front, October-
  November 1918.

German transport retreats before the
advancing Belgians. The map shows the
Belgian advance 17-31 October. Scenes of
liberation in Ostend, with cheering crowds.
Belgian transport moves through
Handzaeme. Troops liberate Roulers. More
celebrations in Ostend. The arrival of
Belgian troops in Bruges and Thielt. The
maps show the advance up to the
Armistice, and the Belgian occupation of
part of Germany under its terms. The state
entry of the King and Queen of Belgium into
Brussels on 22 November, with
accompanying troops. They halt, on
horseback, to pose for photographs. With
them are the Duke of Brabant and Princess
Marie-José. The film ends with a reminder
of the cost: three soldiers pause near the
front to salute a dead soldier on a stretcher
who is carried past. The soldier who went
off to war in the first episode (acted
sequence – see **IWM 1050**) returns home to
his mother in her cottage. Sadly, he
describes to a neighbour how his friend, the
man's son, was killed in the war. The man
goes off, leaving the soldier and his mother
together.

Notes
Title: this has been deduced from the
position of the episode in the series.
Summary: see **IWM 1050**.
catalogued SDB: 8/1983

IWM 1055a · GB, 3/6/1918
PICTORIAL NEWS (OFFICIAL) 353-2

b/w · 1 reel · 59' (1 min) · silent
intertitles: English

sp Ministry of Information pr Topical Film
Company

- Single item from the issue held in more
  complete form as **IWM 1061-02c**,
  showing British soldiers eating bread and
  jam "with proverbial coolness."

Notes
Summary: note that a French-language
version of this item is also held as **IWM
675c**.
catalogued SDB: 9/1983

IWM 1055b · GB, (?) 1915
PATHE GAZETTE [1915] (fragment 1)

b/w · 1 reel · 84' (1 min) · silent
intertitles: English

pr Pathé

- Serbian forces boarding troopships in
  Albania en route for Salonika, December
  1915.

Columns of Serbian troops, led by their
decorative regimental standards, march in
full kit out to the harbour and onto their
troopships.

catalogued SDB: 9/1983

IWM 1055c · GB, (?) 1915
[ECLAIR NEWSREEL (1915 fragment)]
(allocated)

b/w · 1 reel · 46' (1 min) · silent
intertitles: English

pr Eclair

- British machinegun team practising on a
  beach in Flanders, probably 1915.

The team has set up its Vickers
machinegun and is firing out to sea, at a
post stuck in the sand. A Belgian officer
watches with them, and nearby is a Belgian
dog-team for pulling the machinegun.

catalogued SDB: 9/1983

IWM 1055d · GB, (?) 1915
PATHE GAZETTE [1915] (fragment 2)

b/w · 1 reel · 63' (1 min) · silent
intertitles: English

pr Pathé

- Men of 1st King Edward's Horse setting
  out on a training ride in England in
  summer, probably 1915.

The men, "our gallant colonials," come from
all the colonies. They wear a mixture of
uniforms.

catalogued SDB: 9/1983

IWM 1055e · GB, 20/2/1915
TOPICAL BUDGET 182-2

b/w · 1 reel · 25' (1 min) · silent
intertitles: English

pr Topical Film Company

- Brief item of Scottish troops in training,
  firing from a shallow trench, Britain,
  February 1915.

catalogued SDB: 9/1983

IWM 1056 · GB, 1914
**SOUTH IRISH HORSE REGIMENTAL
SPORTS : Curragh May 28th 1914**

b/w · 1 reel · 290' (5 mins) · silent
intertitles: English

- Private film of the South Irish Horse at
  the Curragh Camp, near Dublin, Ireland,
  28 May 1914.

The regimental band plays a tune led by its
conductor. Various troopers and civilians
watch the sports. A jumping contest – some
of the officers wear 'No 1 Blues' uniform and
others are in mufti. An obstacle race on
horseback for the men involves riding
bareback up to a coconut shy and throwing
at it. A flat race. Some of the troopers mill
around officers in mufti – one may be
Lieutenant-Colonel Lord Decies,
commanding the regiment. A 'reveille race'
involves men leaving a tent, saddling their
horses and riding off. A sprint on foot. A
tent-pegging contest with lances. A final
view of the spectators.

Remarks: not an interesting film in itself, but it is useful to have a film of the Curragh Camp within two months of the Curragh Mutiny.

catalogued SDB: 9/1983

as a private venture.
Remarks: a very poor use of stockshots, failing to match the appearance of one shot with the next so that the fake is particularly obvious. The long march past montage is simply dull.

catalogued SDB: 9/1983

IWM 1057-01 · France (?), 1917
PLANNING AN OFFENSIVE
WITH OUR FRENCH ALLY (series)

b/w · 1 reel · 1007' (17 mins) · silent
intertitles: English

sp Section Cinématographique de l'Armée Française *pr* Pathé Frères

- Thematic description of the build-up and aftermath of a typical French offensive on the Western Front, late 1917.

Four officers around a planning table decide on the offensive. A regimental colonel receives his orders outside his dug-out. The bombardment starts, from rifle grenades, 58mm Crapouillot mortars, 105mm howitzers and 75mm field guns. Heavier guns join in, including the big railway howitzers, and shells fall on the German front line. Infantry run forward (training) under the cover of smoke. Smoke and gas fill up no man's land. Troops in shell-holes (training) advance, throwing grenades, from cover to cover. The 75s continue to fire. The second wave of troops moves up. Prisoners are led back through the trenches and march to the counting stations and cages where they are interrogated, then given food. On the battlefield French dead remain; first aid is given to the wounded, who are taken back to the dressing stations. Ambulances take the serious casualties further back. After the battle troops march in parade through a town square and out to the countryside. General Pétain reviews the troops and decorates men and standards. The review continues for some time. A soldier of 60th Infantry Regiment is shown with the Croix de guerre. A regimental standard shows battle honours from Lorraine in 1914 to the Aisne in 1917. The film ends with the SCAF logo.

Notes
Production: the material for this compilation, and for **IWM 1057-02** in the same series, comes from the French official newsreel Annales de la Guerre produced by the SCAF. This film appears to have been intended by Pathé for British or US release

IWM 1057-02 · France (?), 1917
BEHIND THE LINES
WITH OUR FRENCH ALLY (series)

b/w · 1 reel · 980' (16 mins) · silent
intertitles: English

sp Section Cinématographique de l'Armée Française *pr* Pathé Frères

- Everyday life for French soldiers in the battle zone of the Western Front, 1917.

The film opens with Marshal Joffre talking to General Pershing. It then shows French soldiers in the rear area peeling potatoes, moving around woods, saddling pack horses to take them for a ride, and generally performing routine duties. Other men build corduroy roads or join in road-mending gangs. A bridge is built over a river using a pile-driver. A pontoon bridge is built. Infantry and guns move up the roads towards the front line, including long 155mm naval guns and 75mm field guns. Piles of expended shells by the roadside. Railways, of narrow and broad gauge, are built, and rolling stock operated. Shells for the guns are brought up by light railways and offloaded at ammunition dumps. At a field hospital ambulances are started up. Patients rest inside a hospital. A hospital train has patients loaded onto it. Inside a hospital a nurse tends a patient. In a hill area mules carry a battery of 140mm mountain guns forward on pack-saddles. Horses and soldiers gallop through snow. Views of various railway guns being loaded: the 270mm, the 300mm, the 320mm and the 340mm railway howitzer. A 220mm howitzer is elevated. Engineers lay telephone cables in trenches and raise a radio mast. A 270mm and 280mm heavy howitzer fire. A 370mm railway howitzer and 400mm railway howitzer prepare to fire. Schneider CA1 tanks move with foot soldiers up a road. Soldiers in a rear area build barbed wire entanglements and move through rear trenches. Soldiers in a front line trench shovel out earth for a mine. The charge is wired up and the mine detonated (fake).

Notes
Production: see **IWM 1057-01**.
Remarks: a random assault on the senses
with no attempt to match the stockshots
into any form of visual or narrative
continuity.
catalogued SDB: 9/1983

IWM 1058 · Australia, 1920
HEROES OF GALLIPOLI

b/w · 1 reel · 1157' (20 mins) · silent
intertitles: English

sp Australian War Memorial *ed* Bean, C E W
cam Ashmead Bartlett, E; and Brooks, E

■ British and Australian forces at Anzac,
Cape Helles, and Suvla, Gallipoli, May-
August 1915.

Anzac Beach in May, a month after the
landing. Men of the ANZAC Corps help
build Watson's Pier. Further up the beach,
caves and shelters have been dug into the
hillside. Bridges's Road leads up to
MacLaurin's Hill, and men bring supplies up
it. A runner hands in a message at a
headquarters tent. While one man watches
with a trench periscope another uses a
"periscope rifle" or sniper's rifle. June at V
Beach, Cape Helles. The camera is on the
beached SS *River Clyde*, still used as a
headquarters. The fortress of Sedd-el-Bahr
is visible in the distance, and a tented
camp, probably of 29th Division, in the
foreground. On high ground horses graze
from shelter with men looking after them.
British troops, again probably 29th Division,
march up to the front. A Rolls-Royce
armoured car of the Royal Naval Division
stands hidden in a shelter trench, with its
machineguns removed. It emerges from the
trench past an RNAS lorry, and is checked
over by men of the division. The Suvla
operation in August starts with a view of a
British bombardment falling on the Suvla
positions. The harbour at Imbros island is
full of old wrecks and men swimming.
Troops of IX Corps and horses wait on the
quay for the boats to take them over for the
landing. Men of the Egyptian Labour Corps,
and Turkish prisoners of war used for
labour, walk around the quay. Among the
wrecks in the harbour is the unidentifiable
wreck of a seaplane. The men continue to
wait. At Anzac the heights leading up to
Plugge's Plateau are shown. Signallers lay
lines along the tracks. Back at Imbros the
British board their transports and lighters,
which approach Suvla Bay. The Australian

Naval Bridging Train is shown on 7 August
on the beach helping the second line
transport to land. The wounded are taken
on stretchers back to the ships. Cranes and
ropes are used to move stores and mules
from the ships to the lighters. British officers
sit in an open-air "mess" talking and eating.
Back at Anzac, Australians patrol the
trenches on Walker's Ridge. Shell fire,
filmed from the beach, falls on the Turkish
position of The Chessboard. During the
attack on Sari Bair Australian troops fire out
from their newly held trenches; Ashmead
Bartlett, at the far end of the trench, rushes
back to the camera as the fire starts. The
view from the beach of Turkish shells falling
on the 1st Australian Division position at
Lone Pine.

Notes
Production: Ellis Ashmead Bartlett was
originally sent to Gallipoli as the still
photographer for the Newspaper Proprietors
Association, taking with him also a cine
camera at the behest of Sir Cyril Burt, the
theatrical entrepreneur. At Gallipoli
Ashmead Bartlett met Ernest Brooks, the
official Royal Navy still photographer, who
helped him take his film – notably the scene
in which Ashmead Bartlett appears. The film
was subsequently given to Burt, who
showed it in London. In 1919 Burt was
approached by the Australian War Records
Section, who obtained a copy of the print
for the planned Australian War Memorial;
this was edited by Dr C E W Bean, the
Australian Official Historian, into its present
form. What became of the original film is
not known. The Imperial War Museum
obtained its copy of the Australian War
Memorial version in the 1970s. The main
source for this account is Nicholas Hiley,
researching into British propaganda in the
First World War.
Remarks: not the greatest film ever taken,
but the only one of this campaign. The
slightly primitive look gives it in places a
'surreal' appearance. The scene of
Australians firing is genuine combat but,
according to Hiley, what happened is that
Brooks asked the men to do something,
whereupon they began the fire-fight.
[shotsheet available]
catalogued SDB: 9/1983

IWM 1059 · GB, (?) 1924
EIGHT YEARS AFTER

b/w · 1 reel · 927' (16 mins) · silent
intertitles: English

- 373 -

pr Ideal Film Company *ed* Ward, W
cam Grainger, F

■ Review of the Ypres battlefields about ten
  years after the First World War.

The film describes the ground as "more
than famous – sacred" and the record as
having been made "with homage and
reverence". It starts with the view about a
mile out from Ypres on the Menin Road,
facing Menin. Then Hellfire Corner, with Hill
60 visible behind it, "The Crater" and
Hooge, with the Menin Road running
through it. The ruins of White Château
(Potize Château) with the new château built
beside it. The village of Gheluwe down the
road towards Menin still shows some
damage from shells. A tram runs through
the main street. A German pillbox still
stands in the village, and nearby is the
German military cemetery. Just off the road
in Inverness Copse is the rusting remains of
a Mk V Star tank in a flooded mine crater. A
general view of the Ypres ridges. The
Ypres-Comines Canal just south of Ypres,
showing one of the boundary stones
marking the furthest German advance in
1918, with the St-Eloi mine craters visible in
the distance. The Messines ridge, showing
the remains of pillboxes, and the ruins of
Messines itself with children playing in
them. The spot on the Wytschaete Road
north of Messines where 1st London
Scottish first came into action on 31
October 1914, marked by a monument.
Neuve-Eglise, south-west of Messines,
where people are working to repair the
damaged buildings and the crossroads at
the centre of the village, is still pitted with
bullets and shell-holes. Mount Kemel,
Ploegsteert Wood and Hill 63, covered with
old defences, are visible in the distance.
Ploegsteert village has been rebuilt and the
church spire can be seen from the camera
position on Hill 63. The wood is growing
back. Below the hill is the defensive bunker
"Gray's Inn", and going northwards "The
Strand" and "Hyde Park Corner". Nearby is
the British cemetery at Mud Corner and the
colonial cemetery at Toronto Avenue
(actually mostly containing Australians). As
people work to clear the wood they uncover
British and German equipment from the
war.

Notes
Date: despite its title, the film begins by
saying that it has been 10 years since "that
dread word war boomed forth", suggesting
a date of 1924 rather than 1922 or 1926.
[R E B Coombs, *Before Endeavours Fade*,
After the Battle (1983)]

[J H Lindsay, *The London Scottish in the
Great War*, Regimental HQ (1925): 48]
catalogued SDB: 9/1983

IWM 1060 · GB, 17/6/1916
TOPICAL BUDGET 251-2

b/w · 1 reel · 298' (5 mins) · silent
intertitles: English

pr Topical Film Company

■ Further copy of the issue held as **NTB
  251-02**.

catalogued SDB: 9/1983

IWM 1061-01 · GB, (ca) 1922
the WAR CLOUD

b/w · 1 reel · 441' (7 mins) · silent
intertitles: English

pr Pathé

■ Partly reconstructed account of Britain on
  the outbreak of the First World War,
  concentrating on the Royal Navy.

The Stock Exchange in London "closes its
doors" in 1914 – a crowd is clustered
around it. "Germany mobilises", a pre-war
German training exercise with the troops in
Prussian blue, not field grey: a 77mm gun
is fired and three resting soldiers are given
food and drink by a girl. In Britain sailors
arrive at Portsmouth railway station and join
their ships. (The fleet in Portsmouth harbour
is depicted using both pre-1914 and post-
1918 film.) The flagship, HMS *Iron Duke*, is
moored in the harbour, with the royal yacht
Victoria and Albert behind it in the distance.
King George V, in civilian clothes, inspects
a line of old sailors. A silhouette view of
HMS *Queen Elizabeth* (launched 1915)
followed by a view of the bows and fore
turrets of the same ship, and three sailors
with a bulldog and a life belt bearing the
ship's name. The Italian battleship *Sardegna*
at anchor. The light cruiser (3 funnels) HMS
Crescent semaphoring. HMS *Hercules* next
to HMS *Princess Royal* with its awnings out.
HMS *Ajax*, probably, with HMS *Neptune* in
the far distance. The camership tracks
past HMS *Indefatigable* and then HMS *Natal*
(*Neptune* in the distance again), and round
the stern of HMS *Saint Vincent* with HMS
Collingwood behind it. Submarines C.35
and D.2 are on the surface in the harbour.

HMS *Hibernia*, a float plane fitted over her A turret, flashes a signal – E Class submarines are visible in the distance. A general view of the harbour, including float planes landing. The cameraship comes round the stern of HMS *Victory*. A silhouette view of King Edward Class battleships in line.

Notes
Title: this is the first caption to appear on the film as it stands, it may not be a release title. This film appears to be the first reel of a longer narrative.
Date: the captions are marked in one corner "printed on safety film". This practice was introduced, briefly, in the early 1920s, then dropped because of costs.
catalogued SDB & NAP: 9/1983

IWM 1061-02a · GB, 10/6/1918
PICTORIAL NEWS (OFFICIAL) 354-2

b/w · 1 reel · 231' (4 mins) · silent
intertitles: English

sp Ministry of Information *pr* Topical Film Company

I. French troops guarding an overturned German A7V tank, Western Front, 8 May 1918. 'MADE IN GERMANY.' Close to Villers-Bretonneux the tank 'Elfriede', victim of the first tank-to-tank engagement on 24 April, lies on its side with its track mechanism clearly visible.
II. The visit of the Prince of Wales to the Anglo-French sector of the Italian Front, May 1918. 'PRINCE OF WALES IN ITALY.' A view of the mountain area. The Prince walks with his French escort through the snow-covered lower slopes of the area, hardly visible in his heavy winter overcoat.
III. 'MORE AND MORE AMERICANS. Heroes of Montdidier who won undying fame in defence of Paris.' US troops and guns, on the march in rear areas, Western Front, spring 1918.
IV. 'THE FIGHT FOR THE WOODS.' British cavalry and other troops on the Western Front, late March-early April 1918. "The German advance is halted – British reinforcements have counter-attacked with success." Cavalrymen, probably of 1st Cavalry Division, canter down the slope in column of twos and move through a wood. Scottish troops, some wounded, "out of the battle and all smiles", grin at the camera.

Notes
Summary: see **IWM 180** for the Cavalry

item. Note that a French-language fragment of this issue, consisting of story IV and one item not in this fragment is **IWM 676b**. The items on the German tank and the Prince of Wales appear, in slightly different form, in the French newsreel *Annales de la Guerre 62* (**IWM 508-62**).
catalogued SDB: 9/1983

IWM 1061-02b · GB, 27/6/1918
PICTORIAL NEWS (OFFICIAL) 357-1 [1]

b/w · 1 reel · 143' (2 mins) · silent
intertitles: English

sp Ministry of Information *pr* Topical Film Company

I. Lieutenant Frank Baylies, Western Front, June 1918. Baylies, shot down on 17 June (described as "reported missing") was an American flying with 3ième Escadrille. He is shown beside his Spad 13 talking with a French officer.
II. French forces near Rheims, Western Front, May or June 1918. The men move along a trench. A Saint Etienne machinegun fires on a high angle from its trench in a wood.
III. Italian Alpini on Mount Grappa, Italian Front, spring 1918. The Alpini, on skies and in white camouflage uniform, move in line over the valleys covered with snow – tiny black figures in the white expanse.

Notes
Summary: note that a further fragment of this newsreel is held as **IWM 1061-07b**, and that a French-language version of this second fragment is **IWM 668a**.
catalogued SDB: 9/1983

IWM 1061-02c · GB, 3/6/1918
PICTORIAL NEWS (OFFICIAL) 353-2

b/w · 1 reel · 431' (7 mins) · silent
intertitles: English

sp Ministry of Information *pr* Topical Film Company

I. Italian troops practising attacks, Italian Front, summer 1918. 'BATTLE SCENES ON THE ITALIAN FRONT.' The troops (quite clearly in training) practise rushing forward from slit trench to slit trench, directed by umpires. They throw their smoke grenades into the opposing trenches. They then practise "clearing out rat holes", checking the captured trenches for enemy-held dug-outs.

II. French air ace Sub-Lieutenant René Fonck, Western Front, May 1918. Fonck "recently" (on 9 May) shot down six German aircraft in 90 minutes. He is shown putting on his flying helmet, then posed in the seat of his Spad 13, which takes off.

III. 'HUNS MAKE ANOTHER BIG ATTACK. Unimpressed British taking hasty meal with proverbial coolness.' The troops, some of them Scottish, sit, rest and eat in open country: Western Front, May 1918. The point of the story is to play down the German offensive.

Notes
Summary: note that another version of story III is **IWM 1055a** and, in a French-language version, **IWM 675c**. The item on Fonck comes from the French *Annales de la Guerre* newsreel, issue 61 (**IWM 508-61**). *Remarks:* story III represents a rather extreme example of the British attempt to cover the absence of good film taken during the German offensives of spring 1918.
catalogued SDB: 9/1983

IWM 1061-02d · GB, 6/6/1918
PICTORIAL NEWS (OFFICIAL) 354-1

b/w · 1 reel · 124' (2 mins) · silent
intertitles: English

sp Ministry of Information *pr* Topical Film Company

■ 'BRITISH TROOPS IN ITALY' and 'HUN THREAT TO PARIS' – two items from the issue held as **NTB 354-01.**

Notes
Summary: note that a French-language version of story II and two additional items from this issue are held as **IWM 676b**.
catalogued SDB: 9/1983

IWM 1061-03a · GB, 4/1/1915
GAUMONT GRAPHIC 395

b/w · 1 reel · 23' (1 min) · silent
intertitles: English

pr Gaumont

■ Transport vehicles of a French squadron on the move in the rear areas of the Western Front, December 1914.

The vehicles come down a straight road. They include trailers holding the stripped fuselages of aircraft, and what appears to be a photographic developing van.

catalogued SDB: 9/1983

IWM 1061-03b · GB, 8/1912
GAUMONT GRAPHIC 151 [1]

b/w · 1 reel · 97' (1 min) · silent
intertitles: English

pr Gaumont

■ Boat and yacht races, Torquay, August 1912.

Single sculls (not racing boats) are raced. This is followed by a gondoliers' race, then coxed fours and pairs, all by the waterfront. Next shown are racing sailboats, filmed from a nearby boat which keeps up with them as they race.

Notes
Summary: another two items from this issue are held as **IWM 1061-03d**, later on this reel.
catalogued SDB: 9/1983

IWM 1061-03c · GB, 31/12/1914
GAUMONT GRAPHIC 394

b/w · 1 reel · 55' (1 min) · silent
intertitles: English

pr Gaumont

■ The wreck of the SS *Boston* at Filey, Yorkshire, December 1914.

The merchant vessel has run aground on the shoreline just below the cliffs. Nothing further is in sight.

catalogued SDB: 9/1983

IWM 1061-03d · GB, 8/1912
GAUMONT GRAPHIC 151 [2]

b/w · 1 reel · 112' (2 mins) · silent
intertitles: English

pr Gaumont

I. Seaplane races at St-Malo, France,

August 1912. Two aircraft, described as "hydroaeroplanes", are on the water. The first, a monoplane, looks like an adaptation of the Morane-Saulnier H Type, the second a variant on the Farman M Type design. The monoplane taxis, then is shown in flight. The Farman comes down to land in the bay.
II. The English steamer SS *Elenore* on the rocks at St-Malo, August 1912. The ship lies on the rocks, with her keel clean out of the water.

Notes
Summary: another item from this issue is held as **IWM 1061-03b**, earlier on this reel.
catalogued SDB: 9/1983

IWM 1061-03e · GB, 26/5/1917
WAR OFFICE OFFICIAL TOPICAL BUDGET 300-2

b/w · 1 reel · 51' (1 min) · silent
intertitles: English

sp War Office Cinema Committee *pr* Topical Film Company

■ US Army in training on the Pacific Coast of America, April or May 1917.

Field Artillery fire a 75mm M16 field gun. Riflemen practise firing lying down at a range, and then retire.

catalogued SDB: 9/1983

IWM 1061-03f · GB, 1915
the BATTLE OF CARENCY (fragment 2)

b/w · 1 reel · 57' (1 min) · silent
intertitles: English

pr Gaumont

■ Continuation of the French account of the Battle of Carency (Second Battle of Artois), Western Front, May-June 1915.

A French soldier leads a wounded German prisoner "stupefied by the force of the French bombardment" to the rear along a railway track. A French soldier holds up for the benefit of the camera a number of expended shells, "smoke cartridges for blinding assailants, shrapnel and projectiles each charged with 11lbs of Cheddite", used by the Germans in the battle.

Notes
Summary: see **IWM 1061-04a**.
catalogued SDB: 9/1983

IWM 1061-03g · GB, 6/1915
GAUMONT GRAPHIC 441

b/w · 1 reel · 23' (1 min) · silent
intertitles: English

pr Gaumont

■ Funeral service of an Indian soldier who has died of wounds, Alexandria, summer 1915.

The body, on the seashore at Alexandria, is wrapped in a burial cloth and tended by Indian soldiers. One soldier takes a bucket and pours sea water over the body. According to the caption, the body was burnt, but this is not seen.

catalogued SDB: 9/1983

IWM 1061-03h · GB, 7/2/1917
TOPICAL BUDGET 285-1

b/w · 1 reel · 148' (2 mins) · silent
intertitles: English

pr Topical Film Company

I. 'C' Battery, US 5th Field Artillery, in training at El Paso, Texas, January 1917. The men are trying out caterpillar tractors, which pull 75mm M16 field guns, complete with limbers on which men are riding, over rough ground out in the desert.
II. 'TOBOGANNING.' Children on a snow-covered slope in a park in north London, February 1917.

Notes
Remarks: the inclusion of an item on the US Army in a British newsreel shortly before the US declaration of war is noteworthy, but hard to interpret.
catalogued SDB: 9/1983

IWM 1061-03i · GB, 1911
[THANKSGIVING SERVICE FOR GEORGE V] (allocated)

b/w · 1 reel · 157' (9 mins) · silent
intertitles: English

- Fragment of a film showing George V, a week after his coronation, travelling to a thanksgiving service at St Paul's Cathedral, London, 29 June 1911.

A high angle view shows the royal parade, including the coach holding King George and Queen Mary, passing through the crowded streets. The procession arrives outside St Paul's, and the King gets out. Various military contingents file up the steps and into the cathedral.

Notes
Production: this extract may be from any of several films made of the coronation. [Harold Nicolson, *King George the Fifth: His Life and Reign*, Constable (1952): 147] catalogued SDB: 9/1983

IWM 1061-04a · GB, 1915
the BATTLE OF CARENCY (fragment 1)

b/w · 1 reel · 53' (1 min) · silent
intertitles: English

- French forces in the Battle of Carency (Second Battle of Artois), Western Front, May-June 1915.

Wrecked houses, the result of shell-damage, are shown in the suburbs which were part of the French position. A German trench captured by the French is also shown.

Notes
Date: no battle is usually referred to as the "Battle of Carency". From the style and appearance this is probably the Second Battle of Artois in spring 1915.
Production: the captions say that this film was approved by French official censors, but that does not necessarily mean it was a French official film.
Summary: see also **IWM 1061-03e** for a continuation of this film.
catalogued SDB: 9/1983

IWM 1061-04b · GB, 3/1915
GAUMONT GRAPHIC 420 [1]

b/w · 1 reel · 101' (2 mins) · silent
intertitles: English

pr Gaumont

I. A wrecked Serbian gun near Belgrade, Serbia, October 1914. The French-made gun (no identification, but possibly a 155mm naval gun) rests in its emplacement with its breech-block removed. The caption says it was destroyed in the Austrian attack which took Belgrade in October.
II. French cyclist troops in training, 1914 or early 1915. The men, still in their 1914 blue uniforms, carry their folding cycles on their backs, cycle with them, then fire from cover still carrying their cycles, following up by advancing at the jog with their cycles still on their backs.

Notes
Summary: an additional item from this issue is held as **IWM 1061-06c**.
catalogued SDB: 9/1983

IWM 1061-04c · GB, 5/1915
GAUMONT GRAPHIC 436 [1]

b/w · 1 reel · 191' (3 mins) · silent
intertitles: English

pr Gaumont

I. Damage done to the church at Barcy, on the River Ourcq near Paris, by a German bombardment, filmed early 1915. The damage was probably done during the First Battle of the Marne. The interior of the church shows slight structural damage and holes in the roof. The caption describes this as the work of "German Kultur".
II. German prisoners, captured at Liège under guard by Belgian troops at Bruges, August or September 1914. The guards are Belgian Civil Guard in their distinctive uniform of 1914. The prisoners, out for exercise in a school courtyard, have all been given clogs in place of their boots. They are normally curious about the camera, and briefly form a group for it. The caption describes them as "happier than when facing Belgian guns and swords".

Notes
Summary: the second item is very early, and it is not certain that it derives from the same newsreel as the first item. Additional material from this issue is held as **IWM 1061-06a** and **06d**, and **07d** and **07f**.
Remarks: inevitably, it is hard to view the damage done by a war of movement in 1914 other than in the perspective of later battles, and the damage done to the church scarcely seems worth noticing. But at the time such damage seemed bad enough.
catalogued SDB: 9/1983

IWM 1061-04d · GB, 3/1915
GAUMONT GRAPHIC 421 [1]

b/w · 1 reel · 64' (1 min) · silent
intertitles: English

pr Gaumont

I. The first wounded from the British landing
at Basra arrive back in India, early 1915. A
pan over the Lady Hardinge War Hospital at
Bombay. A stretcher carrying one of the
wounded is taken from an ambulance into
the hospital.
II. The aftermath of a Zeppelin raid on Paris
on the night of 9-10 March 1915. Some of
the buildings show bomb damage, and
people clear up outside them. A hand holds
up a small incendiary bomb.

Notes
Summary: an additional item from this issue
is held as **IWM 1061-04g**, later on this reel.
[H A Jones, *The War in the Air*, Vol III,
Clarendon Press (1931): 96]
catalogued SDB: 9/1983

IWM 1061-04e · GB, 3/1915
GAUMONT GRAPHIC 426 [1]

b/w · 1 reel · 59' (1 min) · silent
intertitles: English

pr Gaumont

■ German incendiary bombs dropped near
  Faversham, Kent, March 1915.

British soldiers dig the bombs out of the
ground. A major turns one over in his
hands (they are quite small).

Notes
Summary: no record of a specific attack on
Faversham in March can be found, but this
film may show part of the result of a raid
which failed to find London on 4 March.
Additional material from this issue is held as
IWM 1061-06b and **06h**.
catalogued SDB: 9/1983

IWM 1061-04f · GB, 6/1915
GAUMONT GRAPHIC 448 [1]

b/w · 1 reel · 83' (2 mins) · silent
intertitles: English

pr Gaumont

I. Convalescent Indian soldiers who have
visited the tomb of Lord Roberts, St Paul's
Cathedral, London, June 1915. The men, in
uniform and not visibly injured, come down
the steps of the cathedral after visiting the
tomb. The inside of the cathedral and the
tomb itself are not shown.
II. The arrival of Sergeant Michael O'Leary
VC in Dublin, June 1915. The crowd
gathers around O'Leary's open coach as it
arrives outside the Town Hall. He tries to
shake hands with all the people as his
coach stops. Later, he is posed with a
number of dignitaries on the back steps of
the Town Hall.

Notes
Summary: an additional item from this issue
is held as **IWM 1061-06e**.
catalogued SDB: 9/1983

IWM 1061-04g · GB, 3/1915
GAUMONT GRAPHIC 421 [2]
the EMIGRANT (alternative)
STUDDY'S WAR STUDIES (series)

b/w · 1 reel · 78' (1 min) · silent
intertitles: English

pr Gaumont *cartoonist* Studdy, G E

■ Animated cartoon ridiculing Turkey,
  March 1915.

The cartoon figure of an artist draws a
globe, from which a Turk has been kicked,
heading into space towards the sun and the
stars, asking himself "Is this what William
meant by a place in the sun?"

Notes
Title: both alternative and series titles
appear on the print, also the Gaumont
release number indicating that this is part of
issue 421, additional material from which is
held as **IWM 1061-04d** earlier on this reel.
Summary: this cartoon is presumably a
reaction to Turkey's entry into the war,
although a specific reference to the first
British naval attacks on Gallipoli in March
1915 may be intended.
catalogued SDB: 9/1983

IWM 1061-04h · GB, 23/8/1916
TOPICAL BUDGET 261-1

b/w · 1 reel · 103' (2 mins) · silent
intertitles: English

pr Topical Film Company

■ 'WELSH NATIONAL EISTEDDFOD' – a
single story from the newsreel held as
NTB 261-01.

catalogued SDB: 9/1983

IWM 1061-05a · GB, 2/3/1918
PICTORIAL NEWS (OFFICIAL) 340-2 [1]

b/w · 1 reel · 62' (1 min) · silent
intertitles: English

sp Ministry of Information *pr* Topical Film
Company

■ President Venizelos visits Greek and
French troops in Greece, early 1918.

Venizelos, with Generals Gérome and
Zymbrakakis (?) inspects French troops,
then a Greek regiment, talking with some of
the officers and men.

Notes
Summary: note that additional stories from
this issue are held as **IWM 1061-09b** and
IWM 1061-09e, and three stories are held
in a Spanish-language version as **IWM
681b**. This particular item appears to be
taken from the French newsreel *Annales de
la Guerre* 48 (**IWM 508-48**).
catalogued SDB: 9/1983

IWM 1061-05b · GB, 28/2/1917
TOPICAL BUDGET 288-1

b/w · 1 reel · 67' (1 min) · silent
intertitles: English

pr Topical Film Company

■ Belgian observation balloon section,
Western Front, early 1917.

The balloon section lorries arrive at an area
of flat ground and the men start to inflate
the balloon. The inflated balloon stands
ready to ascend. Horses, towing a car out
of a patch of soft ground, shy at the
camera. The balloon is not seen ascending
or in the air.

catalogued SDB: 9/1983

IWM 1061-05c · GB, 31/1/1917
TOPICAL BUDGET 284-1

b/w · 1 reel · 62' (1 min) · silent
intertitles: English

pr Topical Film Company

■ Men of the Royal Irish Regiment training
with rifle grenades, possibly Salonika,
early autumn 1916.

'FIRING TRENCH BOMBS.' A captain
demonstrates how the rifle grenade, which
requires no cup, fits into the rifle. His men,
using a trench periscope, fire the grenades
from a trench. All are in shirtsleeves.

catalogued SDB: 9/1983

IWM 1061-05d · GB, 17/9/1914
GAUMONT GRAPHIC 364

b/w · 1 reel · 37' (1 min) · silent
intertitles: English

pr Gaumont

■ Wrecked German ammunition limber
"destroyed by Belgian gunners", Belgium,
August 1914.

The single limber, which shows some
damage, is in a town square and draws the
attention of passing civilians.

catalogued SDB: 9/1983

IWM 1061-05e · GB, 8/10/1914
GAUMONT GRAPHIC 370

b/w · 1 reel · 78' (1 min) · silent
intertitles: English

pr Gaumont

■ Two L Class destroyers in the English
Channel, autumn 1914.

The two destroyers escort the camership
through the Channel. One comes in close
on the port bow.

catalogued SDB: 9/1983

IWM 1061-05f · GB, 24/6/1918
PICTORIAL NEWS (OFFICIAL) 356-2 [1]

b/w · 1 reel · 78' (1 min) · silent
intertitles: English

sp Ministry of Information pr Topical Film
Company

■ 'THE HUN TOUCH IN ITALY' – a single
item from the issue held as **NTB 356-02**.

Notes
Summary: note that a fragment of the
French version of this newsreel is **IWM
660b**, and that a further English fragment is
IWM 1061-05i later in the reel.
catalogued SDB: 9/1983

IWM 1061-05g · GB, 8/1912
GAUMONT GRAPHIC 157

b/w · 1 reel · 119' (2 mins) · silent
intertitles: English

pr Gaumont

I. Ostrich racing in San Francisco, summer
1912. A group of ostriches assembles with
their trainers at a race track. One of the
birds is fitted with a trotting harness, and
then races "one mile in 2 minutes 10
seconds". It is taken out of the harness after
the race.
II. Lifeboat men testing an "unsinkable"
lifeboat on the Hudson River, New York,
summer 1912. The lifeboat crew
demonstrates that the rowing boat can be
capsized and, using a special recovery drill,
righted almost at once. They row up the
river with the wharfs of New York behind
them. A final portrait shot of their coxswain.

catalogued SDB: 9/1983

IWM 1061-05h · GB, 24/5/1916
TOPICAL BUDGET 248-1

b/w · 1 reel · 114' (2 mins) · silent
intertitles: English

pr Topical Film Company

■ Two stories ('MARINES FILLING
CARTRIDGE BELTS' and 'BRITISH GUNS
IN ACTION') from the issue held in more
complete form as **NTB 248-01**.

catalogued SDB: 9/1983

IWM 1061-05i · GB, 24/6/1918
PICTORIAL NEWS (OFFICIAL) 356-2 [2]

b/w · 1 reel · 56' (1 min) · silent
intertitles: English

sp Ministry of Information pr Topical Film
Company

■ 'THE STRONG MEN OF FRANCE' – a
single item from the issue held as **NTB
356-02**.

Notes
Summary: note that a fragment of the
French version of this issue is **IWM 660b**
and that a further English fragment is **IWM
1061-05f** earlier on this reel.
catalogued SDB: 9/1983

IWM 1061-06a · GB, 5/1915
GAUMONT GRAPHIC 436 [2]

b/w · 1 reel · 52' (1 min) · silent
intertitles: English

pr Gaumont

■ National Volunteer Reserve in London,
May 1915.

Major-General Sir Francis Lloyd, on
horseback, inspects the members of the
National Volunteer Reserve in Regents Park.
They march past him, including bicycle
troops.

Notes
Summary: additional material from this issue
is held as **IWM 1061-04c, 06d, 07d** and
07f.
catalogued SDB: 9/1983

IWM 1061-06b · GB, 3/1915
GAUMONT GRAPHIC 426 [2]

b/w · 1 reel · 39' (1 min) · silent
intertitles: English

pr Gaumont

■ Inspection of 2nd London Welsh at their
barracks in London, May 1915.

Major-General Sir Francis Lloyd inspects
2nd Battalion, the London Welsh (or 18th
Battalion, Royal Welch Fusiliers) drawn up
on parade at their barracks, and then in a
nearby park. The Royal Welch 'flash' can be

clearly seen hanging from the back of several of the soldiers' collars.

Notes
Summary: additional material from this issue is held as **IWM 1061-04e** and **06h**.
catalogued SDB: 9/1983

IWM 1061-06c · GB, 3/1915
GAUMONT GRAPHIC 420 [2]

b/w · 1 reel · 40' (1 min) · silent
intertitles: English

pr Gaumont

■ Royal Artillery unit pay parade in England, March 1915.

The men line up in the open for the pay parade, and come forward in turn to collect their pay from the officers' table.

Notes
Summary: an additional two items from this issue are held as **IWM 1061-04b**.
catalogued SDB: 9/1983

IWM 1061-06d · GB, 5/1915
GAUMONT GRAPHIC 436 [3]

b/w · 1 reel · 94' (2 mins) · silent
intertitles: English

pr Gaumont

I. The Allenbury Patent gas-hood, Britain, May 1915. Troops train with the gas-hood, which fits rucked up around the cap like a cap-band. The men crouch behind a barricade of logs. Smoke, representing gas, drifts over them and they pull down the hoods. These are simple face-bags without breathing regulators and with single mica windows. The troops allow the 'gas' to float over them and then, completely unaffected, charge forward. A soldier in close-up demonstrates the hood, which covers the face only, not the ears.
II. The New South Wales Lancers, probably in Australia, 1914 (?). The lancers fold their bell tents after camping in the open. They pass on horseback on parade, carrying their lances with pennons fixed as in peacetime (poor film quality).

Notes
Summary: additional material from this issue is held as **IWM 1061-04c, 06a, 07d** and **07f**.

Remarks: the Allenbury was one of the gas-hoods rushed into production after the use of chlorine by the Germans at Second Ypres. Even presuming that it was impregnated with chemicals, it would be of extremely limited effectiveness against chlorine, and none at all against later gasses.
catalogued SDB: 9/1983

IWM 1061-06e · GB, 6/1915
GAUMONT GRAPHIC 448 [2]

b/w · 1 reel · 58' (1 min) · silent
intertitles: English

pr Gaumont

■ CLVI Brigade, Royal Field Artillery, making its farewell march through Camberwell, London, June 1915.

The brigade, raised in Camberwell, parades through the streets on its way to join 33rd Division at Bulford. The streets are lined with people as the limbers move past.

Notes
Summary: additional material from this issue is held as **IWM 1061-04f**.
catalogued SDB: 9/1983

IWM 1061-06f · GB, 6/1915
GAUMONT GRAPHIC 447

b/w · 1 reel · 102' (2 mins) · silent
intertitles: English

pr Gaumont

I. A draft of the Honourable Artillery Company leaving Victoria Station for France, London, June 1915. The men of the draft, possibly for 1st Battalion, march led by their band through the station concourse. The first train load of the men pulls out of the station, and the men remaining on the platform cheer it out.
II. French marines in Paris, spring 1915. The men, with rifles, march through the streets to the cheers of the crowd. The caption reads "Enthusiastic reception of General French in Paris", but there is no sign of him on the film (possibly a mistranslation of an original French caption ?).
III. French dragoons in Paris, spring 1915. The men walk mounted through the quiet streets. The film stresses that they are wearing their new horizon blue uniforms.

catalogued SDB: 9/1983

IWM 1061-06g · GB, 5/1915
GAUMONT GRAPHIC 438

b/w · 1 reel · 30' (1 min) · silent
intertitles: English

pr Gaumont

■ French troops at Les Invalides, Paris,
   spring 1915.

The men parade and march in the
courtyard outside the building. The caption
says that they are being inspected by
General Galopin, but he is not clearly
identifiable.

catalogued SDB: 9/1983

IWM 1061-06h · GB, 3/1915
GAUMONT GRAPHIC 426 [3]

b/w · 1 reel · 30' (1 min) · silent
intertitles: English

pr Gaumont

■ Prince Alexander of Serbia with Sir
   Thomas Lipton in Serbia, February 1915.

The two men are in a village in the rear
areas. Lipton guides the Prince up to the
camera. The Prince exchanges a few words
with a convalescent Serbian soldier. A
portrait shot of the Prince.

Notes
Summary: additional material from this issue
is held as **IWM 1061-04e and 06b**.
catalogued SDB: 9/1983

IWM 1061-06i · GB, (?) 10/1912
GAUMONT GRAPHIC 165

b/w · 1 reel · 39' (1 min) · silent
intertitles: English

pr Gaumont

■ Men of the Foreign Legion embarking
   from Marseilles for Morocco, autumn
   1912.

The men file up the gangplank of SS
Doukkala at Marseilles harbour. The ship

then sails.

catalogued SDB: 9/1983

IWM 1061-06j · GB, (?) 1914
[GAUMONT TURKISH MATERIAL]
(allocated)

b/w · 1 reel · 52' (1 min) · silent
intertitles: English

pr Gaumont

■ Turkish Army recruiting scenes, possibly
   autumn 1914.

Turkish troops parade through the streets of
Constantinople amid civilian carriages and
normal traffic. With the marchers are
recruits from the hill villages of Turkey.
Some of these pose for the camera in their
ornate local costumes.

catalogued SDB: 9/1983

IWM 1061-06k · GB, (?) 7/1915
GAUMONT GRAPHIC 451

b/w · 1 reel · 39' (1 min) · silent
intertitles: English

pr Gaumont

■ Major explosion during an engineering
   project, USA, summer 1915.

Engineers place dynamite into the holes
drilled for the blast. The charge of 26 tons
of dynamite is then used to blow a cliff face,
bringing down 300 000 tons of rock, "a
record blast".

catalogued SDB: 9/1983

IWM 1061-06l · GB, (?) 7/1918
GAUMONT GRAPHIC 775

b/w · 1 reel · 77' (1 min) · silent
intertitles: English

pr Gaumont

■ New French airship, summer 1918.

The airship is a non-rigid closely resembling
the British SS and SSZ types. It comes in to
land over a field. Its ground crew steady it

on landing, then back it into its shed.

catalogued SDB: 9/1983

IWM 1061-06m · GB, 3/1915
GAUMONT GRAPHIC 423

b/w · 1 reel · 40' (1 min) · silent
intertitles: English

pr Gaumont

- Demolition of a colliery chimney,
  Burnopfield, Durham, March 1915.

The chimney is on the colliery site. It falls
with a single explosion and men come
forward to clear the rubble.

catalogued SDB: 9/1983

IWM 1061-07a · GB, (?) 1914
**[GAUMONT GRAPHIC – SS GALICIAN
STORY]** (allocated)

b/w · 1 reel · 71' (1 min) · silent
intertitles: English

pr Gaumont

- Fragment of a reconstruction of the
  interception of SS *Galician* by SMS
  Kaiser Wilhelm der Grosse in the North
  Atlantic, 15 August 1914.

On board the *Galician* two soldiers,
Lieutenant J Deane of 1st East Lancs and
Gunner C Shurmer of the RGA are taken off
as prisoners of war. The German boarding
party rows back with its prisoners to its
ship, having ordered the *Galician* to follow.
The liner continues on its course, the
battleship is not seen. According to the
captions, British forces steaming to help
forced the German vessel to break contact.

Notes
Production: this film may be an extract from
a Gaumont newsreel.
catalogued SDB: 9/1983

IWM 1061-07b · GB, 27/6/1918
PICTORIAL NEWS (OFFICIAL) 357-1 [2]

b/w · 1 reel · 160' (3 mins) · silent
intertitles: English

sp Ministry of Information *pr* Topical Film
Company

I. Welsh Day in London, June 1918. A
service is being held at Westminster Abbey
in aid of the Prisoners of War Fund. Queen
Alexandra arrives by carriage for the
service, followed by Sir Francis Lloyd, who
arrives by car.
II. The knighting of Vice-Admiral Sir Roger
Keyes by George V at Buckingham Palace,
June 1918. The ceremony takes place in
the rear courtyard of the palace. Keyes
receives his decoration together with other
naval personnel. A crowd of spectators
watches.
III. The Duke of Connaught ceremonially
opens a club for US officers in London,
shaking hands with the organisers and
walking inside. June 1918.

Notes
Summary: note that a French-language
version of this fragment is **IWM 668a** and
that a further fragment is **IWM 1061-02b**.
catalogued SDB: 5/1983

IWM 1061-07c · GB, (?) 6/1913
GAUMONT GRAPHIC 232

b/w · 1 reel · 48' (1 min) · silent
intertitles: English

pr Gaumont

- Manchester police, June 1913.

The policemen are drawn up on parade for
their annual inspection by a civilian
commissioner. They march past, including
mounted policemen, in an open park.

catalogued SDB: 9/1983

IWM 1061-07d · GB, 5/1915
GAUMONT GRAPHIC 436 [4]

b/w · 1 reel · 18' (1 min) · silent
intertitles: English

pr Gaumont

- Motor cycle race in California, early 1915.

The 300-mile race around a dirt track at
Venice, California, is shown, very briefly, in
progress.

Notes
Summary: additional material from this issue is held as **IWM 1061-04c**, **06a** and **07f**.
catalogued SDB: 9/1983

IWM 1061-07e · GB, 6/1915
GAUMONT GRAPHIC 439 [1]

b/w · 1 reel · 26' (1 min) · silent
intertitles: English

pr Gaumont

■ Two new coastguard cutters being launched down the slipway at Newport News, Virginia, early 1915.

Notes
Summary: additional material from this issue is held as **IWM 1061-07g**, later on this reel.
catalogued SDB: 9/1983

IWM 1061-07f · GB, 5/1915
GAUMONT GRAPHIC 436 [5]

b/w · 1 reel · 141' (2 mins) · silent
intertitles: English

pr Gaumont

I. Army athletics meeting in Devonshire Park, Eastbourne, May 1915. Other troops watch as the athletics start with Graeco-Roman wrestling, then a flat race and a walking race follow.
II. Launch of the oiler USS *Maumee* at Mare Island Navy Yard, California, 17 April 1915. The oiler is described by the captions as a battleship. It slides down the slipway into the water.
III. An oil fire at Waynesburg, Pennsylvania, April 1915. The fire is described by the captions as causing $150 000 worth of damage. The firemen fight the blaze.

Notes
Summary: additional material from this issue is held as **IWM 1061-04c**, **06a**, **06d** and **07d**.
catalogued SDB: 9/1983

IWM 1061-07g · GB, 6/1915
GAUMONT GRAPHIC 439 [2]

b/w · 1 reel · 164' (2 mins) · silent
intertitles: English

pr Gaumont

I. Cavalry sports meeting at Hurlingham, London, May 1915. Members of 2/3rd County of London Yeomanry (Sharpshooters) compete fencing on horseback. Others take part in a "Victoria Cross race", rowing small coracles across a stream. This is followed by a sword demonstration by ex-Corporal-Major Eggleton of the Royal Horse Guards. On foot, using a regulation Cavalry sword, he cuts through a piece of wood held by two men. A celebrity in uniform, described as "Mr Holman James (Fred Lindsay)" holds an apple on the flat of his palm and Eggleton splits the apple with a single blow. He repeats the trick blindfold with James bent forward and the apple resting in the nape of his neck. Finally, Eggleton cuts, in one blow, through the suspended carcass of a sheep.
II. A horse show in Johannesburg, early 1915. A lady riding side-saddle over a jumping course attempts to take a high fence. She and the horse crash over it, but both recover from the fall apparently unharmed.
III. The annual Corpus Christi celebrations at Stonyhurst College, 7 June 1915. The Corpus Christi procession comes out of the college chapel into the open. The pupils, in Army uniform, present arms and lead the procession through the college grounds.
IV. The surrender of the South African rebels, probably being led to trial in Cape Town, early 1915. The leaders of the abortive rebellion of September 1915, about 50 men altogether, are marched together on foot by South African police. Although not identified, at the front of the group are probably Christiaan de Wet and Kloos de la Rey. Some of the men deliberately hide their faces from the camera.

Notes
Summary: an additional item from this issue is held as **IWM 1061-07e**, earlier on this reel.
Remarks: the South African rebellion is one of the little-known episodes of the war. The defeated Boer leaders of the Second Boer War rose, with German encouragement, under de Wet, but failed to secure any popular support and were captured within a month. Very little has even been written on this episode, and to find existing film of it is little short of astonishing.
catalogued SDB: 9/1983

IWM 1061-08a · GB, (ca) 1913
[PATHE NEWSREEL (ca 1913)] (allocated)

b/w · 1 reel · 130' (2 mins) · silent
intertitles: English

pr Pathé

I. A medical students' rag in London,
probably before the First World War.
Students from Charing Cross Hospital are
taken by an open-topped bus to Richmond
Rugby Football Club grounds, where, most
of them in fancy dress, they hold a mock
rugby match, 'fighting' for a small flag.
II. Chinese bakers' strike in New Zealand,
probably before the First World War. The
striking bakers walk in procession through
the streets of Auckland, led by a band and
carrying with them a large symbolic loaf.

Notes
Title: the reel starts with a Gaumont Graphic
newsreel title, but continues immediately
with the Pathé material. The Gaumont title
has presumably been attached by mistake.
catalogued SDB: 9/1983

IWM 1061-08b · GB, (?) 1/1916
GAUMONT GRAPHIC 503

b/w · 1 reel · 254' (4 mins) · silent
intertitles: English

pr Gaumont

I. The wedding of Field Marshal French's
son, London, January 1916. The
Honourable John R L French leaves St
Paul's church, Knightsbridge, after the
wedding ceremony with his bride, the
former Miss Olivia John. The pair are later
shown with Lady French (the Field
Marshal's estranged wife) walking in the
garden of Lady French's home. The camera
keeps a discreet distance from them.
II. British Cavalry practising a canal crossing
in Belgium, December 1915. The captions
say the film has been taken by permission
of the Belgian Government. British
horsemen, on foot, lace up inflated
groundsheets and planks to make rafts and
use these to take themselves and their
saddles across a canal.
III. The Austrian port of Cattaro in Dalmatia,
supposedly late 1915. The film shows a pan
of the port from the sea with Mount
Lovtchen behind it. The captions say that
the port was the object of recent
bombardment from the sea (by the Italians).
The film itself shows no sign of war activity,

and the view is presumably pre-war.
IV. British troops on the Salonika Front, late
1915. The captions say the film has been
taken by permission of the French
Government. British soldiers move around
their tented camp at Zeitenlick, unloading
stores and cooking meals. They are
probably rear echelon troops and tend to
hog the camera.

Notes
Summary: at this date it was forbidden for
cameramen (except for the official
cameramen on the Western Front) to film
British troops in the war zones, even in the
rear areas. Gaumont has clearly
circumvented this ban by using its privilege,
granted to newsreel firms in 1915, of filming
in the French and Belgian zones, and
taking film of British troops there in training
or rest. Stopping this would presumably
have required a protest from the British
Government to an ally, which was unlikely
to be made.
catalogued SDB: 9/1983

IWM 1061-08c · GB, (ca) 1912
[PATHE NEWSREEL (ca 1912)] (allocated)

b/w · 1 reel · 65' (1 min) · silent
intertitles: English

pr Pathé

I. The steamer SS *Espiègle* on the rocks at
Penzance, probably 1912.
II. A portrait painting of Captain R F Scott,
presumably screened to mark news of his
death, 1912.

catalogued SDB: 9/1983

IWM 1061-08d · GB, 4/12/1915
TOPICAL BUDGET 223-2

b/w · 1 reel · 57' (1 min) · silent
intertitles: English

pr Topical Film Company

■ Launch at the New York Navy Yard,
  Brooklyn, New Jersey, probably late
  1915.

'U.S.A. MAMMOTH WARSHIP ... America is
reorganising the whole of her Navy owing
to the changes involved by the European
War.' The ship's hull comes down the
slipway and into the water. It has yet to be

fitted out (see **Notes**).

Notes
Summary: the only US battleship or battle-cruiser launched from the Brooklyn yards in 1915 was USS *Arizona* on 19 June. Two further items from this issue ('KING ALBERT'S CAVALRY' and 'RUSSIAN ADVANCE') are held as **NTB 223-02**.
catalogued SDB: 9/1983

IWM 1061-08e · GB, 1/3/1916
TOPICAL BUDGET 236-1

b/w · 1 reel · 64' (1 min) · silent
intertitles: English

pr Topical Film Company

- US Marines return to League Island Navy Yard near Philadelphia from Vera Cruz in Mexico, early 1916.

'U.S.A. MARINES RETURN FROM VERA CRUZ.' Marines come down the gangplank of the transport USS *San Marcos* onto the quay. Marine officers talk among themselves. The men unload stores from two other transports, USS *City of Memphis* and USS *Denver*.

Notes
Summary: McKernan questions whether this item in fact belongs to the issue number given.
catalogued SDB: 9/1983

IWM 1061-08f · GB, 11/11/1914
TOPICAL BUDGET 168-1

b/w · 1 reel · 48' (1 min) · silent
intertitles: English

pr Topical Film Company

- 'OUR NAVAL LOSSES'. Single story from the newsreel held in a more complete form as **NTB 168-01**.

catalogued SDB: 9/1983

IWM 1061-09a · GB, 26/1/1918
WAR OFFICE OFFICIAL TOPICAL BUDGET 335-2 [1]

b/w · 1 reel · 61' (1 min) · silent
intertitles: English

sp War Office Cinema Committee *pr* Topical Film Company

- Film which actually shows a coalmine in Alsace being worked by French soldiers, January 1918, incorrectly captioned as road-building (see **Notes**).

'THE ROAD TO VICTORY. Miracles have been performed by the French in the lightning laying of the roads on which they follow up their advances.' Soldiers are shown bringing full coaltrucks out onto the surface of the mine. The coal is dumped from the trucks and horse-wagons are loaded from the dump. A traction engine runs a coal-crusher. A few soldiers lead a heavy ox-wagon along the roads.

Notes
Summary: note that three more stories from the same newsreel are held (with Spanish titles) as **IWM 697a** and shorter (English language) duplicate material as **IWM 672b** and **IWM 1061-09c**. This particular item comes from the French official newsreel *Annales de la Guerre* 43 (**IWM 508-43**). The error in interpretation of what the men are doing made by the British version suggests strongly that, as so often in British official film production in the war, the people handling the captions were not the same as those preparing the actual film.
catalogued SDB: 9/1983

IWM 1061-09b · GB, 2/3/1918
PICTORIAL NEWS (OFFICIAL) 340-2 [3]

b/w · 1 reel · 64' (1 min) · silent
intertitles: English

sp Ministry of Information *pr* Topical Film Company

- Building of a giant billboard poster in Trafalgar Square, London, February 1918.

The artist, Bert Thomas, supervises the construction of the poster. It is a mural of the Spanish Armada urging people to buy War Bonds as a defence against a comparable threat from Germany.

Notes
Summary: note that a more complete Spanish-language version of this issue is held as **IWM 681b** and additional material as **IWM 1061-05a** and **IWM 1061-09e**.
catalogued SDB: 9/1983

IWM 1061-09c · GB, 26/1/1918
**WAR OFFICE OFFICIAL TOPICAL
BUDGET 335-2 (extract 2)**

b/w · 1 reel · 59' (1 min) · silent
intertitles: English

sp War Office Cinema Committee *pr* Topical
Film Company

■ 'GENERAL SNOW TAKES COMMAND'
from the newsreel held in more complete
form as **IWM 672b** etc.

catalogued SDB: 9/1983

IWM 1061-09d · GB, 13/2/1918
**WAR OFFICE OFFICIAL TOPICAL
BUDGET 338-1 [1]**

b/w · 1 reel · 121' (2 mins) · silent
intertitles: English

sp War Office Cinema Committee *pr* Topical
Film Company

■ 'INDIAN TROOPS IN PALESTINE' and
'THE LIMBER LINE' – two stories from the
newsreel held as **IWM 663a**.

catalogued SDB: 9/1983

IWM 1061-09e · GB, 2/3/1918
PICTORIAL NEWS (OFFICIAL) 340-2 [2]

b/w · 1 reel · 63' (1 min) · silent
intertitles: English

sp Ministry of Information *pr* Topical Film
Company

■ Lloyd George arrives at Versailles for the
meeting of the Allied Supreme Council,
30 January 1918.

Lloyd George's car pulls up outside the
building entrance and he hurries inside. He
is followed by a senior US officer, possibly
General T H Bliss.

Notes
Summary: note that additional fragments of
this newsreel are **IWM 1061-05a, IWM
1061-09b** and, in a Spanish-language
version, **IWM 681b**.
catalogued SDB: 9/1983

IWM 1061-09f · GB, 30/5/1918
PICTORIAL NEWS (OFFICIAL) 353-1

b/w · 1 reel · 52' (1 min) · silent
intertitles: English

sp Ministry of Information *pr* Topical Film
Company

■ Single story from an issue held in a
French version as **IWM 675b** (but see
Notes). Lloyd George receives the
freedom of the city of Edinburgh.

Notes
Summary: note that McKernan locates this
story in issue 353-2.
catalogued SDB: 9/1983

IWM 1061-09g · GB, 17/3/1917
TOPICAL BUDGET 290-2

b/w · 1 reel · 63' (1 min) · silent
intertitles: English

pr Topical Film Company

■ Snow sculpture exhibition in Geneva,
probably February 1917.

'SCULPTURE IN THE SNOW.' In a park,
some of the sculptures are intentionally
comic but a few are obviously intended as
serious art. The various 'artists' retouch their
creations. According to the caption, one
sculpture of a German soldier 'surrendering'
(shown) was well-received.

catalogued SDB: 9/1983

IWM 1061-09h · GB, 3/12/1914
GAUMONT GRAPHIC 386 [1]

b/w · 1 reel · 114' (2 mins) · silent
intertitles: English

pr Gaumont

I. A German Army camp, possibly at
Bergen-Belsen, north of Hanover, 1914. A
pan over the wooden-hutted camp, with a
few soldiers in the distance. The caption
reads "Where they cannot pillage – German
soldiers 'lock up' at Bergen" (see **Notes**).
II. Belgian soldiers north of Ypres, Western
Front, October or November 1914. Four
soldiers gather around a brazier to keep
warm. According to the caption, they are
guarding a railway bridge on the Ypres-

Dixmude line, which, except for a small area near Elverdinghe, was nearly all in German hands.
III. A Territorial Army camp, probably in Britain, autumn 1914. The men are cooking in the open, at a large camp kitchen which gives off a considerable amount of steam; some of the men peel potatoes.

Notes
Summary: the caption to the first item is ambiguous, and the accompanying film reveals very little. "Bergen" here may possibly be the Dutch village of Bergen-op-Zoom, north of Antwerp, where some German soldiers may have been interned. Alternatively, and more probably, it may be the German village of Bergen, north of Hanover and adjacent to Belsen, where an Army camp existed. It is not impossible that a British firm might obtain such film either before or during the first year of the war. Another two items from this issue are held as **IWM 1061-09j**, later on this reel.
catalogued SDB: 9/1983

IWM 1061-09i · GB, 2/1915
GAUMONT GRAPHIC 415 [1]

b/w · 1 reel · 82' (1 min) · silent
intertitles: English

pr Gaumont

I. Moroccan troops preparing to leave for France, early 1915. Moroccan lancers and foot soldiers parade in the courtyard of a mud-walled fort, then march out into the desert for the coast.
II. Recent French conscripts in a "patriotic demonstration" in the Place Gambetta, Paris, early 1915. The young soldiers, and French boy scouts, march in salute past the statue of Léon Gambetta and the Strasbourg Memorial (poor camerawork).

Notes
Summary: additional material from this issue is held as **IWM 1061-09l** and **09n**, later on this reel.
catalogued SDB: 9/1983

IWM 1061-09j · GB, 3/12/1914
GAUMONT GRAPHIC 386 [2]

b/w · 1 reel · 94' (2 mins) · silent
intertitles: English

pr Gaumont

I. Belgian soldiers interned at Amersfoort, The Netherlands, December 1914. The internees play together, tossing corks into a circle to pass the time.
II. British wounded arrive at the Duchess of Sutherland's hospital (?), Malo-les-Bains, France, December 1914. The ambulances pull up at the military hospital and a stretcher is taken out of one with a wounded soldier on it. One of the ambulances is marked as presented by Millicent Sutherland.

Notes
Summary: another three items from this issue are held as **IWM 1061-09h**, earlier on this reel.
catalogued SDB: 9/1983

IWM 1061-09k · GB, 22/10/1914
GAUMONT GRAPHIC 374 [1]

b/w · 1 reel · 84' (2 mins) · silent
intertitles: English

pr Gaumont

I. Damage to a village school in France, autumn 1914. The school is at Cuvergnon, in the Oise Département. It shows slight damage from shells, having been "wilfully wrecked by the Germans".
II. British and Belgian soldiers in the rear areas near Ypres, October 1914. A crowd of interested soldiers has gathered before the camera. One soldier, in mechanic's overalls, dances a highly professional 'cake-walk' style of show dance, described by the caption as a "jig".
III. Belgian refugees cross into The Netherlands, September or October 1914. The scene is a frontier post between Holland and Belgium. The four Dutch soldiers on duty pose in the road for the camera, 'guarding' their post. A cart carrying Belgian refugees with their belongings comes up to the post and they let it through without bother.

Notes
Summary: another item from this issue is held as **IWM 1061-09o**, later on this reel.
catalogued SDB: 9/1983

IWM 1061-09l · GB, 2/1915
GAUMONT GRAPHIC 415 [2]

b/w · 1 reel · 43' (1 min) · silent
intertitles: English

pr Gaumont

- German prisoners at work in Brittany, early 1915.

While their French Army guards watch, the German prisoners work breaking rocks and shovelling soil, probably for road-fill.

Notes
Summary: additional material from this issue is held as **IWM 1061-09i** and **09n**, elsewhere on this reel.
catalogued SDB: 9/1983

IWM 1061-09m · GB, 1/10/1914
GAUMONT GRAPHIC 368

b/w · 1 reel · 15' (1 min) · silent
intertitles: English

pr Gaumont

- Extremely brief item on damage to a French church, August or September 1914.

The inside of the church is shown for a few seconds, it shows some shell damage. According to the caption, "the Germans show no respect for churches".

catalogued SDB: 9/1983

IWM 1061-09n · GB, 2/1915
GAUMONT GRAPHIC 415 [3]

b/w · 1 reel · 35' (1 min) · silent
intertitles: English

pr Gaumont

- Suffragettes in New York, early 1915.

The suffragettes work up ladders on a hoarding, painting various signs encouraging votes for women. They are calm and happy, there is no sense of violence.

Notes
Summary: additional material from this issue is held as **IWM 1061-09i** and **09l**, earlier on this reel.
catalogued SDB: 9/1983

IWM 1061-09o · GB, 22/10/1914
GAUMONT GRAPHIC 374 [2]
b/w · 1 reel · 52' (1 min) · silent
intertitles: English

pr Gaumont

- Trafalgar Day in London, 21 October 1914.

In Trafalgar Square a big placard has been placed across the plinth of Nelson's Column, reading "England Expects This Day That Every Man Will Do His Duty". People crowd the square. Around the plinth are wreaths, one from the "gallant sailors of France", others commemorating British ships sunk since the start of the war: HMS *Speedy*, HMS *Pathfinder* and HMS *Aboukir* have wreaths shown. British sailors contemplate the display.

Notes
Summary: another item from this issue is held as **IWM 1061-09k**, earlier on this reel.
Remarks: although apparently unofficial and perhaps unintended, this item is extremely good recruiting propaganda. Even the mention of the French as allies in the context of Trafalgar does not seem incongruous.
catalogued SDB: 9/1983

IWM 1062-01 · France (?), 1916
WITH THE RUSSIAN ARMY
WITH THE RUSSIAN ARMY IN THE CAUCASUS (alternative)

tinted · 1 reel · 775' (13 mins) · silent
intertitles: English

pr Pathé Frères

- Russian forces, including the Tsar and the General Staff, on the Caucasus Front, Easter 1916.

A field howitzer (tinted grey), part of a battery, fires from a gun pit in the snow of the mountains. General "Selivanoff" (sic) (tinted yellow) sitting in his car with another officer. A Red Cross horse-drawn ambulance (tinted blue) arrives at a permanent hospital and wounded are helped from it. Grand Duke Nicholas, the Commander-in-Chief (tinted grey) talks with other officers beside his headquarters train in a forest. A group of officers watches while their men collect Easter presents of tobacco, and start to light pipes or roll cigarettes. A senior officer (tinted yellow) inspects the horse lines – one horse tries to bite him. Cossacks (tinted grey) perform an impromptu dance to the music of an accordion. Infantry sit in the falling snow by a wood eating. A marching column of dismounted Cossacks. An Orthodox priest (tinted blue) walks on the surface along a slit trench, blessing the men in the trench as he goes. Turkish prisoners of war, some wounded, are sent to the rear. Cossacks (tinted orange) mill around on horseback, canter up a road, then make a charge in line against the camera. Tsar Nicholas (tinted grey) walks with his party down a difficult hill path. He talks with Grand Duke Nicholas beside his headquarters train. A posed group of the Tsar and Nicholas with their staff officers (Stavka) and chaplain. A camel train (tinted blue) makes its way through the snowbound hills.

Notes
Title: the alternative title appears at the end of the film.
Summary: compare with **IWM 650**.
catalogued SDB: 10/1983

IWM 1062-02a · Germany (?), (?) 1915
the TURKS

b/w · 1 reel · 147' (2 mins) · silent
intertitles: English

■ Incomplete film of a Turkish Army march past, probably not far from Constantinople, 1915.

Limbered 77mm field guns pass at the trot, then halt for the crews to dismount. The caption points out that German NCOs lead each column. A posed group of senior officers, including one German in Turkish uniform. The full force, about a division in size, including foot soldiers, horsemen and guns, starts its march past across a large training field.

Notes
Production: probably an English-language export version of German official film of Turkey.
catalogued SDB: 10/1983

IWM 1062-02b · Germany (?), (?) 1915
WITH GERMANY'S ALLY

b/w · 1 reel · 262' (5 mins) · silent
intertitles: English

■ Incomplete film of the Turkish Black Sea Fleet and scenes in Constantinople, probably 1915.

The film starts with three ships from the fleet: firstly, the four-funnelled cruiser Midilli, formerly SMS *Breslau*, riding at anchor, then a Muvanet-i-Milet Class destroyer showing the Turkish flag at her stern, then a Samsoun Class destroyer. The cameraship travels around the three warships, filming them at various angles. Then Sultan Mohammed V is shown being taken in his royal barge across the Hellespont; he meets with ministers from Bulgaria and Persia (backs to camera) at a pavilion. Enver Pasha is visible in the background. Turkish troops in the streets hold up banners, "celebrating a victory". The crowd, mainly civilian, is addressed by a speaker from a rostrum.

Notes
Production: probably an English-language export version of a German film of Turkish forces.
catalogued SDB: 10/1983

IWM 1062-03 · GB, 1916
a GREAT SERVANT OF A GREAT EMPIRE

b/w · 1 reel · 534' (10 mins) · silent
intertitles: English

sp War Office Cinema Committee (?)

■ Scenes of Lord Kitchener as Secretary of State for War, 1914-16.

Kitchener, in civilian clothes, inspects a parade of boy scouts. Next he arrives by car in his blue Field Marshal's uniform to inspect a parade, probably of the London Regiment, outside the Guildhall. He stands, this time in khaki, with the mayor of Manchester on Manchester Town Hall steps as a parade goes by. In France, February 1916, he inspects a British battalion drawn up in the snow. He shares a saluting base with King George V, and Generals Horne and Rawlinson, as British soldiers march past. He arrives by train at Compiègne station and is met by General Joffre, General Foch and Minister of War Millerand, at the start of his tour of the French Army 15 August 1915. On another part of the tour he talks with French officers while Lieutenant-General Sir Henry Wilson watches. Together with Joffre he watches French exercises from a training trench. The memorial service for Lord Kitchener at St

Paul's Cathedral, Tuesday 13 June 1916. Cars arrive at the foot of the steps of St Paul's bringing the various dignitaries, including the King and Queen. (Thanks to a misplaced scene at this point, Kitchener appears to attend his own memorial service.)

[E S Grew, *Field Marshal Lord Kitchener*, Vol III, Gresham (1916): 187-190]
[*The Times*, 14 June 1916: 7D, 8C]
catalogued SDB: 10/1983

IWM 1062-04 · France, (?) 1910
WITH THE FRENCH NAVY

b/w · 1 reel · 620' (10 mins) · silent
intertitles: English

pr Pathé Frères

■ French naval forces just before the First World War.

A line of Danton Class battleships puts to sea. Two of the Dantons with, in front of them, two destroyers, possibly Claymore Class. The destroyer *Flamberge* passes left to right, followed by the destroyer *Bombe* which fires its 3-pounder as it passes. A Voltigeur Class destroyer passes. A view of the stern of the Danton Class battleship *Jauréguiberry* with guns turned to starboard. A whaler is lowered from amidships on the cameraship and rows off. Three battleships in echelonned line astern, from nearest the camera *Bouvet*, *Jauréguiberry* and then possibly the *Suffren*. Battleships ahead of the cameraship's bow wave in rough weather. Charlemagne Class battleships plough through the rough seas. A Charlemagne Class, possibly *Saint Louis* with all turrets trained out to sea, and *Jauréguiberry* behind her. "Mosquito craft", Claymore Class destroyers in line abreast with a Charlemagne Class battleship in the distance; *Sabretache* is close to the camera as it builds up speed, with *République* and *Patrie* behind her. An Arbalète Class destroyer, or possibly the *Arc*, rolling heavily in the rough sea. The destroyer *Fanfare*, also rolling, with *Sape* beyond her. The cameraship, a battleship (possibly Danton Class) drops anchor. "In Action", a destroyer, the cameraship, fires a 4-inch gun on the port beam. A Danton Class fires a 65mm gun, then twin 9.4-inch guns in a turret. Bows-on shot of a Danton Class with six beam turrets trained on the beam and waves breaking over the bows. Waves break over the cameraship's bows, with

more Danton Class battleships astern, including the *Jauréguiberry*. A Charlemagne Class battleship running in a heavy sea, showing clearly the bulbous bow. A final shot of *Jauréguiberry* bows on.

catalogued NAP: 10/1983

IWM 1062-05 · NO FILM

IWM 1062-06 · Italy, (?) 1910
the ITALIAN NAVY (on copy held)
ITALIAN NAVAL MANOEUVRES (on copy held)

b/w · 1 reel · 540' (10 mins) · silent
intertitles: English

pr Ambrosio *dist* Jury's Imperial Pictures

■ Italian naval forces just before the First World War.

A Soldato Class destroyer passes with the coast in the background. A silhouette view of a Re Umberto Class battleship firing its forward 13.5-inch guns. Three torpedo boats manœuvre, the leader is possibly an Orione Class, the others Nembo Class. The crew of the cameraship, possibly a Re Umberto, fire a torpedo, then a 6-pounder gun, to port, then the ship's main 13.5-inch armament to starboard. A broadside from an armoured cruiser, possibly Vettor Pisani Class. A 13.5-inch barbette fires from a Re Umberto. Battleships in line ahead, stern on, the nearest being a Re Umberto. Battleships in line ahead, bows on, the nearest being Regina Margherita Class. A Re Umberto with a second Re Umberto steaming a parallel course. An observation balloon shown flying from the protected cruiser *Elba*. Armed picket boats steam past the camera towing rowing boats, with a Giuseppe Garibaldi Class battleship in the background. A demonstration of torpedo firing – a ship dead in the water launches a torpedo against a towed target, about the size of a motor boat, at about 200m range. The ship fires too soon and just catches the bow of the slowly-moving target. The cameraship takes on coal, then rations, including a cow in a sling transferred onto the ship. Onshore, a Marine detachment fires a very small mountain gun, which recoils jumping up as it is fired.

Notes
Title: both titles appear on the print. The

original release title would have been in Italian.
Production: the end credits state that Ambrosio made the film, giving Jury's exclusive rights to its use in Great Britain. catalogued NAP: 10/1983

IWM 1062-07 · Germany, (?) 1915
[GERMAN TROOPS IN RUSSIAN POLAND] (allocated)

b/w · 1 reel · 231' (4 mins) · silent
intertitles: English

- German troops in Russian Poland following the Russian retreat of August 1915.

The wreckage of a village, "destroyed by the Russians in their retreat", shows damaged houses with clothing and artifacts abandoned outside them. German soldiers in a wood emerge from a deep and well-concealed dug-out from which smoke is pouring. (According to the captions, it has been set on fire by Russian shell fire.) Nearby is a German Army blacksmith's in the open air. The stables for the horses next to the blacksmith's are camouflaged by the soldiers to prevent aerial observation. At Lyck, just over the border in East Prussia, orderlies unload wounded on stretchers from a hospital train.

Notes
Production: although the captions are in English, their tone makes it likely this is a German release for the USA and English-speaking market rather than a British re-edit of German film, such as **IWM 481**. catalogued SDB: 10/1983

IWM 1062-08 · Germany, (?) 1915
BERLIN NEWS SERVICE REPORTS

b/w · 1 reel · 745' (13 mins) · silent
intertitles: English

I. English-language version of a German newsreel item on a nurse on the bridge of a hospital ship in home waters, 1915. The hospital ship is at anchor, with other vessels in the far distance. On the bridge a nurse, assisted by a sailor, is handling the wheel.
II. English-language version of a German newsreel item on a visit by Princess Alexandra Victoria to a military hospital in Germany, early 1915. Princess Alexandra Victoria of Schleswig-Holstein, wife of Prince August Wilhelm, inspects ambulance drivers on parade in the snow, then looks over a hospital train in a siding.
III. English-language version of a German newsreel item on a visit by the King and Queen of Bavaria to a military hospital in Munich, early 1915. King Ludwig III of Bavaria and his wife inspect the exterior of the hospital buildings. Their son, Doctor Prince Ludwig of Bavaria, a qualified medical officer in charge of a hospital train, meets them beside the train as it starts to unload wounded soldiers.
IV. English-language version of a German newsreel item on cooking food by chemical means, probably early 1915. The demonstration is given in close-up, in the open, by a soldier wearing thick protective gloves. Quicklime has been inserted into the base of a tin of food. After a few minutes the soldier opens the tin with a can-opener and shows that the stew inside is boiling.
V. English-language version of a German newsreel item on troops resting, early 1915. The men appear to be holding a joke pageant, which seems to be mocking the British Army.
VI. English-language version of a German newsreel item on horsemen assembling a transport column, probably Western Front, 1915. The men dash about in all directions, harnessing and setting up the column, which then moves off. The caption, describing this as "German militia occupy a French town", is incorrect.
VII. English-language version of a German newsreel item on troops about to leave for the front lines, Western Front, early 1915. The men are the reserve battalion of an Infantry regiment. They line up in a column and an officer moves from man to man checking the condition of their rifles – a battle-check, not a parade.
VIII. English-language version of a German newsreel item on a field battery in training, probably in Germany, 1915. Six observers for the battery ride up, dismount, and take up a stance with binoculars. 77mm field guns are galloped into positions in the open and ready to fire. The captions describe this as being at the front.
IX. English-language version of a German newsreel item on German troops on the Ypres Ridges, Western Front, probably early 1915. Snow is falling quite heavily, and some of the men go down into their dug-outs. Others, including some pipe-smoking veterans, remain on the surface.
X. English-language version of a German newsreel item on a field bakery and butchers, probably Western Front, 1915. The open-air Army bakery is in the rest

areas, producing loaves while nearby butchers start to cut up carcasses draped over their tables.

XI. English-language version of a German newsreel item on the Kaiser visiting his troops, probably Eastern Front, winter 1914-15. The men are drawn up on parade beside a road in the snow. The Kaiser's car arrives and he talks with his officers before again driving off.

XII. English-language version of a German newsreel item on the Kaiserin visiting a hospital train, possibly Berlin, 1915. The train is in a mainline station. Kaiserin Auguste Victoria inspects the train (outside only) talking with the officers and nurses.

Notes
Title: this may be a first caption rather than a release title.
Production: apparently German official material intended for the USA and other English-speaking countries.
catalogued SDB: 10/1983

IWM 1062-09 · NO FILM

IWM 1062-10 · GB, 1916
GENERAL SARRAIL IN THE EAST

b/w · 1 reel · 336' (6 mins) · silent
intertitles: English

pr Topical Film Company *cam* Grant, T (?)

- Visit of General Sarrail to the British forces at Lembet Camp, Salonika Front, 12 April 1916.

Sarrail, with an escort of lancers in parade dress, rides past a guard of French soldiers and through an improvised arch ("arc de triomphe"), half-silhouetted against the sea. Sarrail arrives at Lembet Camp, and is met by the commander of the British Contingent, Lieutenant-General Sir Bryan Mahon. Sarrail decorates Mrs Catherine Harley (sister of Field Marshal Lord French) in recognition of the work done for French troops by the Scottish Women's Hospital. (Some pull-backs.) Sarrail inspects British troops on parade. Mahon decorates Sarrail with the KCMG (note the French still cameramen and newsreel cameraman at work). The troops march past in salute. Sarrail prepares to leave.

catalogued SDB: 10/1983

IWM 1062-11 · GB (?), (ca) 1925
[WESTERN FRONT – THREE SCENES FROM FEATURE FILMS] (allocated)

b/w · 1 reel · 292' (5 mins) · silent
intertitles: English

- Three extracts from fictional films showing British and Australian attacks on the Western Front, First World War.

A German officer addresses his men in a dug-out. They emerge from the dug-out and man their trench against an Australian attack. The Australians storm the trench and throw grenades down into the dug-outs. The view of a German machinegunner as a creeping barrage gets closer. British troops emerge, walk forward in line, and take cover from the machinegun in shell-holes. A German officer tells headquarters by telephone that the British are about to attack, then briefs his men in their dug-out. British troops move forward, following the white tape to the start line. The men wait in the attack trenches for the hour of the attack, while the Germans sleep in their dug-outs.

Notes
Remarks: although the origins of these films are unknown, they are significant for the image of the Western Front which they all – with remarkable consistency – present. It makes a novel contrast with the factual films in the collection.
catalogued SDB: 10/1983

IWM 1062-12 · NO FILM

IWM 1062-13 · GB, (ca) 1917
[CLERGET 9Z ENGINE CONSTRUCTION] (allocated)

b/w · 1 reel · 949' (16 mins) · silent
intertitles: English

- Incomplete instructional film on the assembly of the Clergêt 9Z Type aeroplane engine, about 1917.

The film shows in some detail, by means of stop action, the various stages in assembling the rotary engine. It starts (about half-way through) with the assembly of the rear drum and crankshaft, and continues with the pistons and cylinders, making the complete nine-cylinder engine.

Notes
Remarks: gives a good idea of the importance of ball-bearings in engine construction.
catalogued SDB: 10/1983

IWM 1062-14 · GB & Austria-Hungary (?), (?) 1916
[AUSTRO-HUNGARIAN MATERIAL 1]
(allocated)
[KNOW YOUR ENEMY – SECOND SERIES (additional scenes 1)] (related)

b/w · 1 reel · 1050' (17 mins) · silent
intertitles: English

■ Disjointed film of Austro-Hungarian forces in the Tyrol and Russian Poland, autumn and winter 1915.

Austrian horsed transport on the Italian Front below the snow-line. A hut, probably a customs post, on the road guarded by Austrian troops. A Red Cross orderly corporal in the Kaiserschützen, 68 years old. Austrian troops making their way up the mountains. Gunners fire a 77mm field gun fitted with an obsolete semi-solid trail. Ski troops on patrol over the snow. Polish civilians work repairing a road; people of the local town are given bread by the occupying "benevolent Huns" (Germans and Austro-Hungarians). Archduke (later Emperor) Karl and his wife Zita in Innsbruck talk with ladies in local costume, then leave by car. Karl with his staff inspects troops and the ground in the Tyrol, close to the Italian Front, including a hussar regiment and local volunteer foot soldiers, and a Tyrolean Jaeger battalion outside a hunting lodge. More Austrian troops on the march; part of a bombardment by 77mm guns. Discarded equipment and wrecked buildings near Przemyśl (?) following the Russian retreat of August. Karl and his staff continue their tour of the Tyrolean mountains. Austrian officers relax outside a dug-out. Soldiers clear dirt with spades.

Notes
Summary: this film and **IWM 1062-15** have some scenes in common with, and are clearly related in some way to, **IWM 481** *Know Your Enemy – Second Series.*
catalogued SDB: 10/1983

IWM 1062-15 · GB & Austria-Hungary (?), (?) 1916
[AUSTRO-HUNGARIAN MATERIAL 2]

(allocated)
[KNOW YOUR ENEMY – SECOND SERIES (additional scenes 2)] (related)

b/w · 1 reel · 1190' (19 mins) · silent
intertitles: none

■ Disjointed film of Austro-Hungarian forces in the Tyrol near the Italian Front, autumn 1915.

Austrian troops practise an attack in waves up a hillside, with some men acting as 'casualties' for the stretcher-bearers. A general view of the ground, below the snow-line, on the Italian Front. A mobile bath unit at a camp in the Tyrol, with a man having a bath. Two destroyed bridges. Senior officers, including the Archduke (future Emperor) Karl watch the exercise. 77mm field guns fire as the practice attack continues. One of the gunners sets the fuse on a shell. An observer standing astride a trench calls instructions to another with a field telephone. The Archduke Karl talks with local volunteer foot soldiers drawn up on parade, and with some hussars, as he and his staff wander over the area. At a camp an alarm is given and soldiers prepare for an alert. Men pray in a field chapel and dance to a flute. Archduke Friedrich (?) reviews some troops in the rear areas. A massed parade by a division (considerable camera-shake). Karl and his wife Zita leave Innsbruck by car. Troops are served food at their camp by a field kitchen, and carry out general repair work. Food is also taken into the officers' mess hut.

Notes
Summary: this film and **IWM 1062-14** have some scenes in common with, and are clearly related in some way to, **IWM 481** *Know Your Enemy – Second Series.*
catalogued SDB: 10/1983

IWM 1062-16 · GB (?), (?) 1915
[GERMAN PRISONERS IN FRANCE (continuation)] (allocated)

b/w · 1 reel · 438' (8 mins) · silent
intertitles: English

■ German prisoners being escorted through rear areas by French soldiers, 1914 or 1915.

The film describes the prisoners as the "result of the great French victory in Champagne". They are led into a large cultivated area, standing in 'blocks' of a few hundred men. Dragoons, apparently in the uniform of 1914, escort the prisoners back. Germans rest in a temporary 'cage' of a few strands of barbed wire – most acknowledge the camera. More prisoners are marched into the cages, being given loaves of bread by their escorts – a French officer interferes to make sure this is in camera-shot. The prisoners eat and rest.

Notes
Summary: see also **IWM 343**.
catalogued SDB: 10/1983

IWM 1062-17 · GB, 1916
SAINT PATRICK'S DAY WITH THE IRISH GUARDS

b/w · 1 reel · 820' (14 mins) · silent
intertitles: English

sp War Office *pr* Topical Film Company

▪ Visit by the King and Queen to 3rd Battalion, Irish Guards, at their Buckingham Gate barracks, London, 17 March 1916.

Field Marshal Lord Kitchener arrives by car at the barracks, followed by King George V with Queen Mary, Princess Mary and the Countess of Athlone (?), and Field Marshal Viscount French with John Redmond MP (not seen clearly until the end of the film). The King inspects the guardsmen, accompanied by Kitchener, French, the Earl of Kerry (battalion commander), Colonel D J Proby (regimental district commander), Lord de Vesci (regimental adjutant) and Lieutenant-General Sir Francis Lloyd. The Queen distributes shamrocks, firstly to Kitchener, then to the company commanders for distribution to their men. Colonel Proby, Lord de Vesci, Lord Kerry and Major P L Reid the second in command receive their shamrocks in person. The King then holds an investiture for men who have performed minor acts of bravery on the Western Front: Lieutenant F L Pusch gets the DSO for action at Loos, Company Sergeant-Major T Cory gets the DCM for the same battle, as does CSM W J Holmes. Private B Dempsey gets the DCM for an action at Cuinchy and Private J Henry for bravery at Givinchy. The King delivers a speech and receives three cheers. The regimental band, and the mascot "Leitrim Lad", an Irish wolfhound, lead the men in a march past. It starts pouring with rain as the troops dismiss. The men pose "Company Sergeant-Major

Vickers, junior", a boy of five or six in guardsman's uniform, who salutes the camera. A line of officers, including French and Lloyd, watch. The King and Queen talk with Redmond. The battalion officers pose for the camera. The King and Queen leave to the officers' cheers.

catalogued SDB: 10/1983

IWM 1062-18 · GB, (?) 1917
a DAY IN THE LIFE OF A LONDON POLICEMAN

b/w · 1 reel · 779' (13 mins) · silent
intertitles: English

▪ Rough cut of an account of typical uniformed police duties in London, probably winter 1917.

A patrol of ten constables assembles in a courtyard inside Scotland Yard. A pay parade for constables, also in Scotland Yard. Mounted policemen supervise the march of the Army relief guard and band up the Mall and through the gates of Buckingham Palace. Policemen on traffic duty at the junction of Charing Cross Road and Oxford Street help pedestrians, including convalescent soldiers, a blind man, and Australians, to cross. The traffic is heavy, including several buses. (Note the advertisement on one for "The Better 'Ole", the Bairnsfather play.) In an acted scene, an old man falls ill on a bench on the Embankment, and while one constable summons an ambulance another gives first aid. Trams pass until the ambulance comes. A policeman on duty in the East End holds up traffic for children as they rush out of school. A constable takes a lost little girl to the station to be collected by her mother. Mounted policemen leave Scotland Yard on patrol. A policeman outside the Russian Embassy directs a Russian sergeant who, according to the caption, has been twice wounded, and escaped after 20 months in Germany, "and is still keen to strike again for liberty". A constable on routine patrol checks that a shop is locked up. Two policemen off duty wander down the Embankment against the setting sun, smoking and talking.

Notes
Title: this and the intertitles are MS flashframes.
Remarks: although a few soldiers appear in this film there is virtually no sense of the country being at war.

IWM 1062-19 · Canada/GB (?), 1916
**MR LLOYD GEORGE AND SIR SAM
HUGHES REVIEW THE CANADIAN 4TH
DIVISION AT BRAMSHOT**

b/w · 1 reel · 327' (6 mins) · silent
intertitles: English

sp Canadian War Records Office

■ Visit of the Canadian Minister of Militia
and the British Secretary of State for War
to Bramshot camp, 7 August 1916.

The men of the division march past Lloyd
George and Hughes (who is in uniform).
Prominent is the division's kilted regiment,
72nd (Seaforth Highlanders of Canada)
Battalion. Lloyd George delivers a speech
standing up in his car, with Hughes beside
him and reporters taking notes as he talks.
Hughes calls for three cheers for Lloyd
George and receives a spontaneous cheer
himself. Hughes shakes hands with the
division's officers.

Notes
Summary: The Times account quotes Lloyd
George's speech in full. Unit is Division 4,
72nd Battalion (Seaforth Highlanders of
Canada); the Vancouver Highlanders.
Remarks: by varying camera distance and
angle, and by some inspired editing
between shots, the makers of this film have
done the impossible in making a march
past look interesting – a vast improvement
on the usual one-angle march past films of
the period.
[*The Times*, 8 August 1916: 3E]
catalogued SDB: 10/1983

IWM 1062-20 · France (?), 1915
**LORD KITCHENER'S VISIT TO THE
FRENCH ARMY**

b/w · 1 reel · 356' (6 mins) · silent
intertitles: English

■ Kitchener visits French Army
headquarters at Compiègne, 15 August
1915.

General Joffre, General Foch and Minister
of War Millerand wait at Compiègne station
for Kitchener's train. He arrives with his ADC
Colonel O A FitzGerald and Brigadier-
General the Honourable H Yarde-Buller (not

Major-General as in the captions), and
inspects the guard of honour. The party, led
by Kitchener and Joffre, walk through a
wood towards a slit trench. They observe
practice manœuvres (not seen) from this
trench, which is clearly in a safe area but is
described by the caption as "the front line
trenches". Lord Kitchener reviews French
colonial troops. Millerand gives Yarde-
Buller, and FitzGerald (not seen) the Légion
d'honneur, and Joffre decorates men of a
colonial division for bravery.

Notes
Title: this appears at the bottom of each of
the intertitle captions.
Production: possibly an English-language
version of French film, rather than a British
production.
Summary: according to Grew's account, the
colonial troops were part of the force
belonging to General Marchand, Kitchener's
opponent during the Fashoda Incident, and
Kitchener caused some surprise by
speaking to the troops in Arabic.
[E S Grew, *Field Marshal Lord Kitchener*,
Vol III, Gresham (1916): 187-190]
catalogued SDB: 10/1983

IWM 1062-21 · NO FILM

IWM 1062-22a · GB, 18/3/1916
TOPICAL BUDGET 238-2

b/w · 1 reel · 62' (1 min) · silent
intertitles: English

pr Topical Film Company

■ Captured German aircraft on display in a
square in Salonika, Greece, early 1916.

'AIR RAID ON SALONICA.' The aircraft, a
Rumpler Taube reconnaissance plane, has
been brought down virtually intact, and lies
guarded by French soldiers in the middle of
a square. Curious Greek civilians surround
it.

catalogued SDB: 10/1983

IWM 1062-22b · GB, (?) 1916
**WITH THE BRITISH FORCES FOR THE
DEFENCE OF SALONIKA**

b/w · 1 reel · 302' (5 mins) · silent
intertitles: English

pr Topical Film Company

- Disjointed film of British forces on the Salonika Front, probably mid-1916.

The film's scenes are out of sequence and its title appears nearly half-way through. As it stands, it opens with soldiers filling sandbags and digging a trench-line. Scottish troops on the march with shovels. Troops drinking tea in a slit trench. British soldiers escorting a Greek civilian donkey convoy. Three staff officers in a slit trench. British soldiers trying to put out a smouldering fire in a house in the town of Salonika. (The title appears here.) A digging party marches out of camp. Others carry and shovel sand for construction. The completed trench is revetted, ("rivetting a trench", according to the caption) with branches.

Notes
Summary: although some scenes of this film are missing, the numbered captions make some form of reconstruction possible. Taking the captions as a guide, the film in its current state runs as follows: scene 4, scene 9, scene 16, scene 15, title sequence, scene 1, scene 3, scene 12, scene 5.
catalogued SDB: 10/1983

IWM 1063 · Norway, 1919
FIRST VISIT OF AN ENGLISH FLYING-BOAT TO KRISTIANIA JULI 1919 (sic)

b/w · 1 reel · 613' (10 mins) · silent
intertitles: English

pr Scandinavisk Film-Central

- Arrival and overflight by an RAF Felixstowe flying boat at Kristiania (later Oslo), Norway, July 1919.

The film starts with the four-man aircraft crew posed at the water's side in Kristianiafjord, with the two pilots, Captain S D Scott and Major C J Galpin, in the centre. Their flying-boat, a Felixstowe F5 (number N4044) rides at its moorings, and a civilian party (helped by the Norwegian Army officer Captain Craster) rows out for a joyride. The plane takes off and overflies the camera. Craster and Galpin swim out to the plane after its return, and on land once more the crew and civilians talk together. The view down from the plane in its flight shows the fjord, then the city with its castle and royal palace, and Bygdo island.

catalogued SDB: 10/1983

IWM 1064-01a · USA, (ca) 1920
[US TANK EXERCISE] (allocated)

b/w · 1 reel · 315' (5 mins) · silent
intertitles: none

- US Army tank training exercise, probably in Florida, just after the First World War.

The exercises take place in swamp country as dusk begins to fall. The tanks are M1917 or M1918 (Renault) light tanks and the Tank Mk VIII "Liberty", with two scout airships above them. The tanks practise hill climbing and trench crossing on a training ground, and demonstrate their ability to push over small trees and drive through swamp. Two of the Renaults drive directly 'over' the camera. As the sun sets the exercise continues, with the airships dropping illumination flares, while the tank exhausts throw out luminescent white smoke. Some foot soldiers advance with the tanks, which fire as they move.

Notes
Remarks: really apocalyptic material, beautiful to look at but completely removed from the realities of tank trials or practical training exercises.
[shotsheet available]
catalogued SDB: 10/1983

IWM 1064-01b · GB, 1926
PATHE SUPER GAZETTE [1926] – MR WINSTON CHURCHILL INTERESTED SPECTATOR AT ALDERSHOT COMMAND MANOEUVRES

b/w · 1 reel · 120' (2 mins) · silent
intertitles: none

pr Pathé

- Winston Churchill, as Chancellor of the Exchequer, visits Army manœuvres at Tidworth, summer 1926.

Churchill is escorted past a parade of 5th Battalion, Royal Tank Corps, drawn up with their Vickers Medium Mk I tanks. Also in the parade are Carden-Loyd Mk IV tankettes and Rolls-Royce Silver Ghost armoured cars. For the exercise the Vickers Mediums cross a bridge at high speed while Churchill watches. Following the tanks are two Infantry half-tracks of the Burford-Kegresse

type and two Birch guns – self-propelled
tracked 18-pounder field guns of IX
Brigade.

Notes
Summary: despite the caption's statement
that this is Aldershot Command
manœuvres, Tidworth was in fact in
Southern Command.
[B H Liddell Hart, *The Tanks – the History of
the Royal Tank Regiment ...*, *Vol I*, Cassell
(1959): 226, 234, 242]
catalogued SDB: 10/1983

IWM 1064-02a · USA, 1931
**PATHE GAZETTE [1931] – WORLD'S
FASTEST TANK**

b/w · 1 reel · 114' (2 mins) · mute
intertitles: none

pr Pathé [USA]

■ Manufacturer's tests for the new Christie
medium tank at "Rahway", USA, winter
1931.

Spectators watch as engineers complete
the fitting of the tank's tracks for its rough
ground tests. It drives up and down slopes,
over frozen puddles, and across railway
lines. Then, with the tracks and turret
removed, it is driven on its road-wheels at
full speed down a highway, "at a mile-a-
minute", driving 'over' the camera as it does
so.

Notes
Summary: the highest speed ever claimed
by its manufacturers for the Christie was
46mph without tracks.
catalogued SDB: 10/1983

IWM 1064-02b · GB, (?) 1925
**PATHE GAZETTE [1925?] – THE SAME
OLD ... MUD**

b/w · 1 reel · 208' (4 mins) · silent
intertitles: English

pr Pathé

■ Army manœuvres on Salisbury Plain,
probably 1925.

The captions stress that, although "not quite
the Flanders variety" there is still a great
deal of mud in the battle for "our now
almost wholly mechanised Army". In the

rain small patrols of Cavalry and Infantry
make their way across the plain. Carden-
Loyd Mk II carriers and Burford-Kegresse
half-tracks follow the patrols. Rolls-Royce
armoured cars lead columns of trucks down
dirt roads (there is not, in fact, much mud,
but all look miserable).

Notes
Remarks: the first manœuvres since 1918
were held in 1925, and appear to fit this
film; but even if the date is as late as 1930,
the description of the Army as "almost
wholly mechanised" is misleading, to say
the least.
catalogued SDB: 10/1983

IWM 1064-02c · GB, 1931-33
**PATHE GAZETTE [1932 approx] –
MODERN METHODS**

b/w · 1 reel · 68' (1 min) · mute
intertitles: none

pr Pathé

■ British tank patrol in the Khyber Pass on
the North-West Frontier of India, 1931-33.

Over the rough ground of the foothills the
British drive their tanks, the Light Tank Mk
IIB. In close-up, the turret of one tank opens
and the commander (wearing a special
tanker's helmet) emerges to mop his brow.

[B H Liddell Hart, *The Tanks – the History of
the Royal Tank Regiment ...*, *Vol I*, Cassell
(1959): 405-416]
catalogued SDB: 10/1983

IWM 1064-02d · GB, 1934
**PATHE GAZETTE [1934] – MECHANISED
MANOEUVRES : 200 tanks go into action
on Salisbury Plain**

b/w · 1 reel · 178' (3 mins) · silent
intertitles: none

pr Pathé

■ Manœuvres by 1st Tank Brigade on
Salisbury Plain, 12 August 1934.

The tanks, in a 'swarm', roll over the
grassland – Vickers Medium Mk IIs and Mk
IIIs of 5th Battalion, accompanied by
Infantry carriers. A Medium Mk II Command
Tank of 5th Battalion stops near the
camera. 1st (Light) Battalion, in their Light

Tanks Mk IIB, lead the way out over the plain. Another Mk II of 5th Battalion drives off. The general manœuvres continue. (In close-up, it can be seen that the tanks have their battalion numbers painted on, eg "I(Lt)Bn R Tanks".)

Notes
Summary: see Liddell Hart's account for the details and significance of these manœuvres.
Remarks: despite Liddell Hart's claims it is hard to see, in this particular film, much evidence of tank tactics beyond a massed charge. In addition, the cleanliness and over-decoration of the tanks contrast oddly with the later myth of the 'tankies' as rough, practical men confronting an effete Army establishment.
[B H Liddell Hart, *The Tanks – the History of the Royal Tank Regiment ...,* Vol I, Cassell (1959): 317-320]
catalogued SDB: 10/1983

IWM 1064-03a · GB, (?) 1925
PATHE GAZETTE [1925?] – THE KING WITH HIS TROOPS

b/w · 1 reel · 56' (1 min) · silent
intertitles: none

pr Pathé

- King George V watches Army manœuvres at Aldershot, probably 1925.

The King, with binoculars, stands with a group of staff officers watching the exercises. King George and Queen Mary stand with a group of officers beside a NAAFI wagon. As part of the exercise the troops assemble a pontoon footbridge across a river – Infantry and mules cross after its completion, while the Royal couple watch. Then the King and Queen inspect a Dragon Medium Mk II carrier.

catalogued SDB: 10/1983

IWM 1064-03b · GB, (ca) 1923
PATHE GAZETTE [1923 approx] – REALISM AT THE ALDERSHOT MILITARY TATTOO

b/w · 1 reel · 71' (2 mins) · silent
intertitles: none

pr Pathé

- An Aldershot Military Tattoo, early 1920s.

A Medium D tank comes up to the camera, and past it on to a stream. Sappers demonstrate how to blow up a 'bridge' made of hardboard on dry land. A Vickers Medium Mk I tank manœuvres with Infantry. Sappers rebuild the 'bridge' and mule teams are led over it.

catalogued SDB: 10/1983

IWM 1064-03c · GB, 1925
PATHE GAZETTE [1925] – IF YOU WOULD HAVE PEACE ETC !

b/w · 1 reel · 91' (2 mins) · silent
intertitles: none

pr Pathé

- Army manœuvres on Salisbury Plain, summer 1925.

Infantry line up beside their bell tent camp for training. Taken out onto a road, they break ranks to have the scheme explained. A Lewis gun team (note no magazine fitted) is instructed on siting its weapon in a hayrick. A soldier shows a sniping position – he is joined by the Lewis team.

catalogued SDB: 10/1983

IWM 1064-03d · GB, 1925
PATHE GAZETTE [1925] – GETTING READY FOR THE GREAT MANOEUVRES

b/w · 1 reel · 86' (2 mins) · silent
intertitles: none

pr Pathé

- Army manœuvres on Salisbury Plain, summer 1925.

A line of Vickers Medium Mk I tanks, almost wheel-to-wheel, "greatly improved and much speedier than those in the Great War". A Dragon tows an 18-pounder Mk IV field gun along a road. At a field bakery back at the camp food is prepared for the soldiers, who are mainly Welsh Guards.

catalogued SDB: 10/1983

IWM 1064-03e · GB, 1925
PATHE GAZETTE [1925] – BRITISH ARMY MANOEUVRES : 50,000 troops take part in 'Great War of 1925'

b/w · 1 reel · 205' (4 mins) · silent
intertitles: English

pr Pathé

- Army manœuvres on Salisbury Plain, summer 1925.

Infantry march through the centre of a village, and out along the wet roads into the countryside. Back in the village signallers rig telephone wires on a barber's pole. Out on the plain lancers trot past followed by heavily camouflaged armoured cars (possibly Austin). A gun battery is using a farm as a base. A mounted signaller trails a telephone wire out along a road, behind a line-laying wagon. At the farm Royal Fusiliers have their rum ration served. The manœuvres are between a force from Mercia representing strength and one from Wessex representing mobility.

catalogued SDB: 10/1983

IWM 1064-03f · GB, 1925
PATHE GAZETTE [1925] – THE BATTLE OF QUARLEY : terminates the 'Great War of 1925'

b/w · 1 reel · 218' (4 mins) · silent
intertitles: English

pr Pathé

- Army manœuvres on Salisbury Plain, summer 1925.

A howitzer, apparently a 6-inch 26cwt without its gunshield, opens fire. An assembled group of military attachés watches – Japanese, Polish, Italian and French officers are recognisable. Gunners remove the camouflage from their 6-inch Mk VII gun, open fire and cover it again. Vickers Medium Mk I tanks burst out from the cover of a wood. "Aeroplanes, smoke screens, tanks, all played their part – but it's 'the infantry' that counts in the end." Smoke drums generate a smokescreen. Infantry in extended line advance through the smoke with tank support. The soldiers form a firing line in the open as the tanks come through on their flank. At the end of the exercise the troops march back along the road.

catalogued SDB: 10/1983

IWM 1065 · NOT INCLUDED

IWM 1066 · GB, (ca) 1915
[ARMY CAMP INSPECTION] (allocated)

b/w · 1 reel · 26' (1 min) · silent
intertitles: none

- Fragment of a film of an Army camp inspection, probably during the First World War.

A divisional general, two colonels, an ADC (in the Royal Welch Fusiliers) and a civilian walk up a slope away from a tented camp to where soldiers are cooking a meal in the open.

Notes
Summary: nothing further can be discovered about this film.
catalogued SDB: 11/1983

IWM 1067 · NO FILM

IWM 1068 · GB, 1918
[SHIPYARD FILM FRAGMENTS]
(allocated)
LORD PIRRIE'S APPEAL TO SHIPYARD WORKERS (fragments)

b/w · 1 reel · 126' (2 mins) · silent
intertitles: none

- Film fragments, part cartoon, encouraging shipyard work in Britain, 1918.

A military parade is inspected by a civilian, possibly Lord Pirrie, the Controller of Shipbuilding. Then a cartoon showing a family seated for a meal with a picture of a ship at sea on their wall. The figure of Death in a German helmet conjures a torpedo to sink the ship and steals the loaf from the family table. The figure of Britannia, "Britons never shall be slaves". In actuality, a line of men queuing to work in the shipyards.

Notes
Summary: see also **IWM 526**.
catalogued SDB: 1/1984

IWM 1069 · GB, (ca) 1919
[ROYAL NAVY SHORE BASE] (allocated)

b/w · 1 reel · 762' (12 mins) · silent
intertitles: none

pr Gaumont (?)

■ Routine on a Royal Navy shore station,
  probably just after the First World War.

The film is slightly disjointed and
concentrates almost exclusively on the
parade ground. The station clearly operates
aircraft (which are never seen) for some of
the men, mixed indiscriminately with the
others, wear RAF uniform. The action starts
with a parade ground drill, the men
marching past the Vice-Admiral in charge of
the station. Then a jump to the end of a
church parade with the chaplain ordering
'on caps'. Then more march pasts, and a
group of the men cheering the camera. (At
this point the Gaumont logo appears.) The
men march past the station commander.
Posed group shots of various officers,
including the station commander, most of
whom salute the camera. A junior officer
inspects the station transport lorries. On the
parade ground there is some confusion as
RAF and Navy men are taught their
respective drills and methods of saluting.
Physical training for the men. A pay parade.
An officer instructs men in the sundial. The
men cultivate the camp allotments and feed
the pigs. A group goes on leave. Back to
the church parade – the non-Anglicans are
dismissed and the chaplain begins. Then a
long countermarch, led by the band, past
the station commander. A posed group of
the officers. Close-ups of the station
bulldogs. The chaplain and his wife feed the
chickens. More of the march past. One
sailor receives a leave slip from another
(acted). Two Royal Naval Volunteer Reserve
officers together. Another shot of the
bulldogs. 'Eight bells' is sounded on the
station bell and the guard changed over. A
final portrait shot of an officer. (The sea is
never seen in the film.)

Notes
Remarks: for sheer pointlessness and
dullness the activities of this station deserve
some kind of prize. Surely this is not the
way the Royal Navy wished to be presented
to the world?
cataloged SDB: 11/1983

IWM 1070a · GB, 17/10/1914
TOPICAL BUDGET 164-2

b/w · 1 reel · 97' (2 mins) · silent
intertitles: none

pr Topical Film Company

I. The town of Senlis after the First Battle of
the Marne, Western Front, September 1914.
The railway station and surrounding area
show some damage after being shelled by
German guns during the battle.
II. A military parade through the centre of
New York, autumn 1914 (?). Soldiers and
Marines, led by their bands, march through
the centre of the city to the cheers of the
watching crowd.
III. The wedding of a British naval officer,
probably 1914. The newly-married couple
emerge from the church and pose for the
camera. The husband wears the uniform of
a Royal Navy commander.
IV. A Swiss Army parade through the streets
of a Swiss city, probably autumn 1914. The
marchers are wearing the old-style Swiss
parade uniform and carry Swiss national
flags. Crowds line the streets.

Notes
Summary: the title appears on the first item.
It is not certain that the remaining items
belong to the same newsreel.
cataloged SDB: 12/1983

IWM 1070b · GB, 27/2/1915
TOPICAL BUDGET 183-2

b/w · 1 reel · 60' (1 min) · silent
intertitles: English

pr Topical Film Company

■ Brigadier-General G H C Colomb and
  Lieutenant J H S Dimmer VC visit Harrow
  School OTC, February 1915.

'V.C. HERO AT HARROW.' The headmaster
accompanies the two officers (Dimmer is
described, incorrectly, as a captain) as they
inspect the cadets in the school grounds.
The cadets then march past.

Notes
Summary: Lieutenant Dimmer won his VC
during the First Battle of Ypres on 12
November 1914 with his battalion, 2nd
King's Royal Rifle Corps.
Technical: note that this item appears to
have been printed slightly out of rack and
rolls in the frame.
cataloged SDB: 12/1983

IWM 1070c · GB, 26/12/1914
TOPICAL BUDGET 174-2

b/w · 1 reel · 46' (1 min) · silent
intertitles: English

pr Topical Film Company

- British convalescent camp in France or
  Belgium, autumn 1914.

The camp is tented and quite primitive, near
some woods. The soldiers wander about,
none badly injured. Some nurses are
visible.

catalogued SDB: 12/1983

IWM 1070d · GB, (?) 1916
PATHE GAZETTE [winter 1915-16]

b/w · 1 reel · 704' (12 mins) · silent
intertitles: English

pr Pathé

I. A French "Blue Cross" veterinary hospital,
Western Front, spring 1916. A French vet
and two British vets check a bandaged
horse in the open on the 'hospital'
(obviously a farm). All the vets, including
two women, wear operating gowns from
time to time. A British vet uses a syringe to
take fluid from a horse's head wound before
rebandaging it.
II. Canadian troops training on Salisbury
Plain, early 1916. The Canadians practise
entrenching on the plain, using the turf to
hide the conspicuous white chalk thrown up
by their digging. They then rush forward
'over the top' to man the trench.
III. French gunners, Western Front, early
1916. One of the guns, described as a "6-
inch gun" is shown in detail as it is loaded
and fired. There is snow on the ground. The
gun misses fire on the first occasion.
Several firings are shown.
IV. The aftermath of a Zeppelin raid on
Yarmouth, early 1916. The wreckage of a
house is shown, Mr Ellis's house in Peter's
Plain, Yarmouth. The caption states that the
falling masonry killed two passers-by. The
house has had one wall completely stripped
away by the blast. The ruined furniture is
lined up for removal.
V. Grand Duke Nicholas of Russia,
Caucasus Front, Easter 1916. Grand Duke
Nicholas, the Russian Commander-in-Chief,
talks with his staff in a forest, then beside
his nearby headquarters train. He is joined
by Tsar Nicholas. A final posed group of the

Tsar and Grand Duke with the General Staff
members.
VI. Men of Kitchener's Army training in the
snow on Epsom racecourse, early 1916.
The men are in full uniform but some are
without rifles. They are on a route march in
the driving snow, with a number of civilians
walking alongside out of curiosity. They
come out of some trees and onto Epsom
racecourse, where, with more civilians
watching, they form up for parade.

Notes
Summary: the item on the Tsar and Grand
Duke duplicates material in **IWM 1062-01**
With the Russian Army. It is not clear
whether the various Pathé items found
together in this can are meant to form part
of one newsreel issue or not.
catalogued SDB: 12/1983

IWM 1070e · GB, 1915
**PATHE GAZETTE NORTHERN EDITION
[1915] (fragment)**

b/w · 1 reel · 80' (2 mins) · silent
intertitles: English

pr Pathé

- Donation of ambulances by the people of
  Southport, 23 April 1915.

The mayor and town council assemble
outside the Town Hall and deliver speeches
on the presentation of the ambulances. A
local clergyman gives a prayer. The
ambulances then drive past the watching
soldiers and civilians. A plaque in English,
French and Flemish explains the origins of
the gift.

catalogued SDB: 12/1983

IWM 1070f · GB, 1914
**PATHE GAZETTE [1914] – GERM-HUN
KULTUR**

b/w · 1 reel · 43' (1 min) · silent
intertitles: English

pr Pathé

- Funeral of victims of the German
  bombardment of Hartlepool, December
  1914.

The hearses, with an escort of sailors, enter
the cemetery. One coffin, draped with a

Union Jack, is taken from its hearse to its burial plot. An Army burial party fires shots over the grave. One woman is visibly in tears.

cataloguedSDB: 12/1983

IWM 1070g · GB, 1915
PATHE GAZETTE [1915] – ST GEORGE'S DAY

b/w · 1 reel · 58' (1 min) · silent
intertitles: English

pr Pathé

■ St George's Day procession through Stratford-upon-Avon, 23 April 1915.

The procession, led by the mayor and by Mr George Benson, winds through the streets. Its object, according to the caption, is to lay a wreath on Shakespeare's tomb.

cataloguedSDB: 12/1983

IWM 1070h · GB, 17/11/1915
TOPICAL BUDGET 221-1

b/w · 1 reel · 57' (1 min) · silent
intertitles: English

pr Topical Film Company

■ Explosion in rue Tolbiac, Paris, November 1915.

The area, a timber-yard, has been completely flattened by the explosion. The captions stress that this was not the result of a bombardment or air raid.

Notes
Summary: a further item from this issue ('BELGIAN ENGINEERS IN THE FIELD') is held as **NTB 221-01**.
cataloguedSDB: 12/1983

IWM 1071 · GB, 1914
BOBS

b/w · 1 reel · 342' (6 mins) · silent
intertitles: English

pr Gaumont

■ Retrospective made after the death of Lord Roberts in November 1914, showing some of his public appearances 1910-14.

The Irish Guards' St Patrick's Day parade through Hyde Park. Roberts rides with them in his uniform as Colonel-in-Chief of the regiment. Later, at their barracks, he distributes Queen Alexandra's shamrock to the men. Roberts, in civilian clothes, unveils a statue of General Sir James Wolfe and delivers a speech (probably in Westerham, Kent, where Wolfe was born). Roberts, in civilian clothes, takes part in an Empire Day parade in Hyde Park on 24 May. He shakes hands and talks with various people in an informal manner. Roberts, in Field Marshal's uniform, presents its new colours to a Territorial battalion of Infantry on Hackney Marsh. (Possibly 10th (Hackney) Battalion, the London Regiment, created in 1912.) The men are all in blue dress uniforms or in civilian clothes. They march past as Roberts takes the salute. Roberts inspects men of the National Reserve, in civilian clothes, drawn up on parade in Hyde Park in August 1914. Roberts, in civilian clothes, addresses New Army volunteers in Hyde Park in August 1914. According to the caption, he told them "this is no time for playing games". A final portrait still of Roberts in his full-dress Field Marshal's uniform with baton.

cataloguedSDB: 11/1983

IWM 1072 · Germany, 1915-16
[GERMAN NEWSREEL ITEMS] (allocated)

b/w · 1 reel · 402' (7 mins) · silent
intertitles: none

pr Messter Woche and Eiko Woche

■ Composite reel of German newsreel items on Eastern Front in 1915, plus separate items on crashed Zeppelin L31 and Turkish item on Mohammed V.

I. British soldiers guard remains of crashed Zeppelin L31 after it had been shot down at Potters Bar on 2 October 1916. Wrecked bows of Mathy's airship lie twisted round oak in mist-shrouded field.
II. Sultan Mohammed V of Turkey emerges from building and departs by coach, then is followed by succession of other Turkish dignitaries.
III. German *Messter Woche* item on Russian prisoners after the Battle near Lyck in East Prussia, February 1915. Two hundred

Russian officers captured at the battle near Lyck, and dressed in winter uniform, move under German guard past wooden building. Other prisoners at the same place include a Russian Orthodox priest in black cassock and, according to the caption, the captured Russian divisional commander. Some of the reported 65 000 prisoners of the Russian 10th Army fill a large town square dotted with short leafless trees.

IV. Misplaced *Eiko Woche* caption attached to shot of bearded German soldier demonstrating loading of captured British Short Magazine Lee Enfield Mk III with original sling. Caption in German reads: "An extremely strongly fortified position, which after heavy fighting was stormed by our troops".

V. Four *Eiko Woche* captioned items show Eastern Front scenes, possibly all related to Austro-German autumn offensive of 1915. Two columns of Austrian and German infantry march side by side across flat wintry plain, demonstrating, according to the caption, their brotherhood in arms as they pursue the fleeing Russians. German soldiers wearing Pickelhaube helmets rest by snow-covered roadside and line up with their mess tins for food from a field cooker. Small column from Landsturm Cyclist Company in black uniforms push their bicycles across a snow-covered plain. Described in the caption as "Polish traders in the rear areas", a family of Semitic appearance offer unidentified items for sale to smiling German soldiers congregated outside a thatched house. Smartly dressed Jew proffers tray (of sandwiches ?) to men while young women with baskets converse merrily with other soldiers.

Notes

Production: item I is presumably of British origin; item II is also uncredited but may be Sascha; item III is *Messter Woche*; and items IV and V are *Eiko Woche*.
catalogued KGTG: 2/1987

IWM 1073 · GB, 1917
[KENNEDY GIANT UNDER CONSTRUCTION] (allocated)

b/w · 1 reel · 364' (6 mins) · silent
intertitles: none

- Views of the prototype Kennedy Giant aircraft under construction, presumably at Northolt in 1917.

Opening panning shot across aircraft hangars, with the front of the Giant

protruding from one of them. Various shots in increasing close-up of the front of the aircraft: a man inside the cockpit can be seen operating control wheels, and the serial number (2337) and identification ("[Giant Biplane] System Kennedy No 3" – the first two words are unclear) can be read on the nose. A large number of men can be seen working out on the wings in most shots. Two men, one the designer C J H Mackenzie-Kennedy himself (dressed in pilot's clothing), the other an unidentified but prosperous-looking civilian, point out details of the starboard wing. The two seen in close-up. Interior views in hangar, showing the Giant's commodious fuselage and inadequate-looking tail, with workmen among the scaffolding that supports it. The two men again, pointing out details of the starboard engines. A shot along the interior of the fuselage, with Mackenzie-Kennedy moving away from the camera towards the cockpit. Medium close-up (from behind) of Mackenzie-Kennedy standing in the cockpit (no seats fitted) demonstrating operation of twin control wheels. Note that the aircraft is seen in its original configuration, before the wings were moved back and the tail surfaces enlarged.

Notes

Summary: the aircraft was the personal project of C J H Mackenzie-Kennedy, who claimed to have pioneered aircraft production in Russia as a collaborator of Igor Sikorsky: the Giant represented an effort to emulate in Britain the success of the large Sikorsky machines. Components were built by the Gramophone Company and by Fairey Aviation, both of Hayes, Middlesex, for assembly at Northolt. The engines provided were inadequate for the large airframe (wingspan 142ft, length 80ft), and the aircraft literally did not get off the ground. The prototype, seen in this film, was left derelict at Northolt. Identification of Mackenzie-Kennedy has been confirmed by correspondence with the RAF Museum; the identity of the other man is still unknown.
[J M Bruce, *British Aeroplanes 1914-18*, Putnam (1957): 287-289]
[Harry Woodman, "MacKenzie-Kennedy", *WW1 Aero* 106 (9/1985): 5-11 (and correspondence in 108 (2/1986): 18-19)]
catalogued DW & RBNS: 3/1987

IWM 1074 · GB, (prod) 1919
[RE-INTERMENT OF EDITH CAVELL] (allocated)

b/w · 1 reel · 558' (9 mins) · silent

intertitles: none

- Reinterment of nurse Edith Cavell in Norwich Cathedral, 15 May 1919.

Floral tributes are piled outside the door to the Cathedral's Beauchun Chapel, looked after by two nurses. The funeral procession passes through the streets of the city, including soldiers with arms reversed and members of the WAAC, VAD and FANY. The coffin is taken from its gun-carriage and taken by Army pallbearers into the cathedral. There is a large crowd and many reporters. (Note the cine cameraman carrying two cameras.) The Bishop of Norwich leads the procession inside, followed by other dignitaries and by convalescent soldiers. After the ceremony the coffin is taken out and buried. The crowd makes it impossible for the camera to get close. (Note the still photographer in a tree trying to get a better view.) After the ceremony the clergy and dignitaries lead the procession away.

Notes
Shotsheet: the shotsheet gives further information on the events surrounding this film.
Remarks: according to the shotsheet, fewer people turned up than were expected. The film gives exactly the opposite impression.
[shotsheet available]
catalogued SDB: 11/1983

IWM 1075 · Italy (?), (ca) 1919
[ITALIAN FICTIONAL FILM] (allocated)

b/w · 1 reel · 199' (4 mins) · silent
intertitles: English

- Incomplete, partially fictional film of Italian troops in the plains below the Alps, late 1918.

The Italians, in campaign hats, climb up a rugged hill below the snow-line. A bridge blown up by the Austrians is shown. The Italians crouch behind a sandbag defensive wall. A view through a telescope (masked) shows the Austrian position in the valley below. An open-air church parade before the Italian attack.

Notes
Intertitles: these show occasionally quaint English and were probably composed in Italy.
Summary: it is not clear how much of the sequence is fictional or reconstruction, but

the scenes of the Italian troops in particular do not appear genuine.
catalogued SDB: 11/1983

IWM 1076-1078 · NOT INCLUDED

IWM 1079 · USA, (ca) 1933
WITH OUR BOYS IN FRANCE

b/w · 2 reels · 2527' (105 mins) · comopt & silent
intertitles: English

pr Gaumont

- Compilation, with partial soundtrack, of Gaumont US newsreels from 1916 to 1920.

(Reel 1) The film opens with unrelated scenes of the Western Front, mainly the Marne and Château-Thierry areas. Then Theodore Roosevelt beside the grave of his son Quentin. Behind-the-lines scenes of the Western Front, including US soldiers with captured German flame-throwers, and the Signal Corps. General Gérard, commanding French Eighth Army, decorates the US aviators, Captain Peterson, Lieutenant Eddie Rickenbacker and Lieutenant J A Meissner, while Major-General C R Edwards and his staff of 26th (not 20th) Division, and men of 94th Pursuit Squadron watch. Men of 305th Military Police groom their horses among "bomb-proof" sandbags. A salvage dump. A "German tank" (in fact a French Saint Chamond). A doctor takes a letter for a wounded soldier. Josephus Daniels, Secretary of the Navy, watches the passing out of the Class of 1918 from Annapolis Naval Academy. Back in France a M1918 tank demonstrates pushing over walls. A gas sentry and gas casualties at a first aid post. Resting soldiers wash their clothes and hunt for lice. US Colored Troops ("these bronze warriors") sing to a banjo. An observation post of 'E' Company, 167th Infantry, in a wood – nearby another man of 42nd Division releases a carrier pigeon. Major-General A Cronkite and Brigadier-General E Babbit of 80th (Blue Ridge) Division meet in a trench. A machinegun post. Pits for 75mm guns ("heavy artillery"). Salvation Army girls hand out coffee and doughnuts in a trench. A sniper's post. An aerial view of training trenches (claimed as an attack). Josephus Daniels and Secretary of War Newton D Baker watch 6th Battle Squadron, led by USS *New York*, return to

New York harbour in 1919. The Navy parades down 5th Avenue. A ship's bell at Pier 'A' in memory of the dead. Troopships, including the converted cruiser USS *North Carolina*, bring the troops home. At Great Lakes, Illinois, the end of flour rationing is celebrated by pie-eating. In Washington, Baker decorates Lieutenant-General March, his CoS, with the DSC. In San Francisco, Admiral Fullam and men of the Pacific Fleet open an "Exposition" of war trophies. A view of Amerongen, Holland, home of the ex-Kaiser. In New York 5000 convalescent soldiers get a free matinee. Secretary of Commerce Wilson appeals for employment for veterans. Surplus Army mules and horses are sold at Camp Devens, and surplus DH9 aircraft in Washington. The Japanese delegate to Versailles, Baron Makino, calls in Washington. In 1916 President Wilson casts his vote in Princeton, looking over the college. In Philadelphia Mrs Wilson launches SS *Quistconck*, the first prefabricated ship (notice Franklin D Roosevelt, Assistant Secretary of the Navy). Wilson sails on the SS *George Washington* for Versailles, passing the troopship SS *Lapland*. The battleship USS *Pennsylvania* and Newport News Class destroyers act as escort. *(Reel 2)* The winter and spring of 1916 in New England, showing the grain harvest. A gymkhana for the Canadian and British Red Cross in Westbury, New York. The British steamer SS *Harpathian* in a US port. A US fast patrol boat, SC154, on anti-submarine patrol finds a submarine (acted). The Navy guards the San Francisco Golden Gate. Members of the Foreign Press Section of the Creel Publicity Bureau leave New York for Europe. Portrait shot of Charles S Hart, Director of the Division of Films. In Washington, Charles S Creel, Chairman of the Committee on Public Information, presents Italian journalists to President Wilson. In Chicago Mme Galli-Curci and other Italian opera singers auction apples for charity. Ex-Ambassador Gerard opens a YMCA hut in Bryant Park, New York, with help from Ethel Barrymore. Other women take to war charities: in Venice, California, bathing girls with elephants sell War Savings Stamps; society women in Washington make bandages. War orphans are given old clothes. Women pose in "living posters". Madame Schumann-Hemck sings outside the Treasury Building. In Chicago an old woman has made an Allies-flag blanket for General Pershing's birthday. In Dunlap, California, Mono Indians learn Red Cross work. In Denver there is a Red Cross sale of calves. (At this point the film becomes silent) Women learn to plough, and in Chicago collect food for French refugees. A mobile kitchen in Boston. Irrigation in the San Joaquin Valley, California. More grain harvest, and women picking grapes in Florin, California. In New York Governor Whitman on Wall Street, with Mme Gill, encourages war loans. Convalescent Italian troops tour New York. In Chicago the Armenian national flag is raised for the first time. An artist paints war scenes for passers-by. Fund raising in Chicago. Women gas mask makers go to the theatre in New York. In Oakland, California, the Carpenters' Union builds an Army clubhouse for nothing. Shipbuilders give demonstration boxing matches at lunchtime. In Chicago, Industrial Workers of the World leader "Big Bill" Haywood and one hundred others get 20 years hard labour and $10 000 each in fines. A new Navy shipyard is opened in Oakland. In New York shipyard a ship is named after "the Lambs", the actors' club, for charity work. Marine Cadets in Alameda, California, at a flag-raising. Girls from Charleston Navy Yard learn rifle and pistol shooting. Marine Officer Cadets from Quantico pass out, march past the Potomac, and make a charge with mounted officers. Secretary Baker and General March open a Salvation Army hostel at Camp Dix, New Jersey, aided by Commander Evangeline Booth. Governor Richard I Manning of South Carolina is shown with his family at home in Columbia. The motion picture industry war effort. In Los Angeles, mock-ups of British tanks are used to encourage war donations: D W Griffith and Mary Pickford speak from the tops of the tanks. In Van Courtlandt Park, New York, cameras film a battle scene. In Los Angeles, Griffith, on-set with Lillian Gish and his crew, receives the Chevron of Honor for his war savings efforts. Madame Petrova, the actress, sells war savings stamps in St Paul, Minnesota. In Oakland, Mary Pickford welcomes returning troops. The celebrations for 4 July 1918 in Paris, France. French soldiers lead the way followed by US troops (note the French official cine cameraman). The procession enters the Place de la Concorde. President Poincaré rides with Marshal Foch in a carriage down the Avenue Président Wilson.

Notes

Remarks: as it stands, this is almost unbelievably tedious, having neither a plot nor linking theme. However, some of the individual items are of considerable interest, particularly in revealing how the First World War was presented to US newsreel audiences, and indeed the cinema's view of

itself at the time.
catalogued SDB: 12/1983

IWM 1080a · GB, 1902
[the CORONATION OF KING EDWARD VII] (allocated)

b/w · 1 reel · 393' (7 mins) · silent
intertitles: none

- Coronation procession of King Edward VII through Central London, 19 August 1902.

An escort of Indian Cavalry, followed by the Royal Horse Guards, leads the Coronation Coach up the Mall. Just visible in the coach are Edward VII and Queen Alexandra. Various dignitaries, led by the Prince of Wales (the future George V) lead the Lifeguards behind the coach. The procession passes through Admiralty Arch to the cheers of the crowd lining the route. Among those singled out by the camera, riding among the dignitaries, are Field Marshal Lord Kitchener and Field Marshal Lord Roberts. The procession carries on up Whitehall, led by the Yeomen of the Guard on foot, then the Indian escort and the Royal Horse Guards.

catalogued SDB: 11/1983

IWM 1080b · GB, 1900
the SURRENDER OF KROONSTAD TO LORD ROBERTS

b/w · 1 reel · 150' (3 mins) · silent
intertitles: none

pr Warwick Trading Company
cam Rosenthal, J

- Troops of the Cavalry Division crossing a drift near Kroonstad, Orange Free State, South Africa, 12 May 1900.

The column of horsemen crosses the drift towards the camera. One officer has his Indian servant riding beside him. The horses are noticeably in poor physical condition. The men are carrying rifles, rather than carbines, slung on the offside of the man.

Notes
Title: this is taken from the Warwick catalogue for 1900.
Production: this film is Warwick catalogue

number 5678a.
Summary: identified by James Barker in work for the television series *Flashback*.
Remarks: according to Douglas Haig, acting as Chief Staff Officer to the Cavalry Division, Roberts exploited the surrender of Kroonstad as a major publicity stunt, to the extent of requiring the Cavalry Division to retreat slightly so that Roberts might receive the town's surrender personally in full view of the press. As his Army was then forced to halt for ten days with supply problems this may have been a wise decision.
catalogued SDB: 11/1983

IWM 1081a · GB, 1900
COLONIAL INFANTRY AND CAVALRY MARCHING ACROSS THE VELDT

b/w · 1 reel · 98' (2 mins) · silent
intertitles: none

- Cavalry and Infantry marching past on a grassy parade ground, South Africa, 1900.

The parade starts and ends with contingents of light horse. In between them are foot soldiers, two companies each with a Maxim gun on a handcart. All the men are in slouch hats and shirtsleeve order.

Notes
Summary: identified by James Barker in work for the television series *Flashback*.
Remarks: despite the title, there were no Colonial forces sent to South Africa intended as Infantry, although some were sent to be given horses as Mounted Infantry. These are therefore probably local South African recruits, referred to confusingly by the British as 'Colonials'.
catalogued SDB: 11/1983

IWM 1081b · GB, 1900
the ESSEX REGIMENT CROSSING THE VAAL RIVER ON THE WAGON PUNT

b/w · 1 reel · 98' (2 mins) · silent
intertitles: none

pr Warwick Trading Company
cam Rosenthal, J

- A company of Infantry crosses the river, the boundary between the Orange Free State and the Transvaal Republic, South Africa, 26 May 1900.

A punt is crammed full with the men, who have no room to move. It is pulled across the river and they disembark on the far side.

Notes
Title: this is taken from the Warwick catalogue for 1900.
Production: this film is Warwick catalogue number 5732a.
Summary: identified by James Barker in work for the television series *Flashback*.
catalogued SDB: 11/1983

IWM 1081c · GB, 1900
MORE AMMUNITION NEEDED

b/w · 1 reel · 71' (2 mins) · silent
intertitles: none

pr Warwick Trading Company
cam Rosenthal, J

- Light ammunition carts crossing a drift near Paardeberg, South Africa, February 1900.

The light carts cross the drift one after the other in a long continuous line.

Notes
Title: this is taken from the Warwick catalogue for 1900.
Production: this film is Warwick catalogue number 5662a.
Summary: identified by James Barker in work for the television series *Flashback*.
catalogued SDB: 11/1983

IWM 1081d · GB, 1900
a SKIRMISH WITH THE BOERS NEAR KIMBERLEY BY A TROOP OF CAVALRY SCOUTS ATTACHED TO GENERAL FRENCH'S COLUMN

b/w · 1 reel · 144' (3 mins) · silent
intertitles: none

pr Warwick Trading Company
cam Rosenthal, J

- British mounted troops staging a combat manœuvre, not far from Kimberley, South Africa, May-July 1900.

The troopers gallop towards the camera, regular cavalry first, followed by yeomanry. There is a koppie behind them on the horizon. The column gallops up to a thorn

hedge, halts beside it and deploys a Maxim machinegun from a pack-saddle. The remainder of the men dismount and come forward to form a firing line on the thorn hedge while the horseholders take the horses a little way back. The signal to retire is then given, the horses come forward, the men remount and gallop off.

Notes
Title: this is taken from the Warwick catalogue for 1900.
Production: this film is Warwick catalogue number 5545d.
Summary: identified by James Barker in work for the television series *Flashback*. Note that two fragments from this completed film are held as **IWM 1025a** and **IWM 1025d**.
catalogued SDB: 11/1983

IWM 1081e · GB, 1900
the ARRIVAL AND RECEPTION OF LORD ROBERTS AT CAPETOWN

b/w · 1 reel · 126' (2 mins) · silent
intertitles: none

pr Warwick Trading Company *cam* Hyman, E M

- Lord Roberts, the new Commander-in-Chief, arrives at Cape Town harbour, South Africa, 10 January 1900.

An honour guard of Infantry marches into position beside the dock, past Roberts's ship, the SS *Dunottar Castle*. Roberts, in Field Marshal's dress blue uniform, comes down the gangplank, followed by his staff, in khaki. Roberts gets into a horse-drawn coach, which drives off.

Notes
Title: this is taken from the Warwick catalogue for 1900.
Production: this film is Warwick catalogue number 5540a.
Summary: identified by James Barker in work for the television series *Flashback*.
catalogued SDB: 11/1983

IWM 1081f · GB, 1900
KRUGER'S DREAM OF EMPIRE

b/w · 1 reel · 64' (1 min) · silent
intertitles: none

prod Paul, R W

- British fictional propaganda film on a Boer defeat in the Second Boer War, 27 February 1900.

The film depends for its effect on stop-action camera tricks. It opens with 'President Kruger' of the Transvaal Republic gloating over a bust of himself. Beside him, a large placard reads "On Majuba Day England Was Defeated" (a reference to the British defeat at the Battle of Majuba on 27 February 1881 in the First Boer War). The placard changes to a cartoon picture of Kruger being offered an Emperor's crown. Suddenly the bust changes to one of Queen Victoria, and the placard to the news "On Majuba Day Cronje Surrendered" (a reference to the surrender of the Boer general with his forces at Paardeberg Drift on 27 February 1900). As Kruger recoils from the sight, four British soldiers rush in and cover him with a Union Flag. As he struggles beneath the flag, the soldiers line up as if they were a firing squad and shoot him. As the shot is fired, Kruger turns into a figure of Britannia; the soldiers assemble around her in a tableau.

Notes
Summary: identified by James Barker in work for the television series *Flashback*.
catalogued SDB: 11/1983

IWM 1081g · GB, 1900
the DESPATCH BEARER

b/w · 1 reel · 68' (1 min) · silent
intertitles: none

pr Mitchell and Kenyon

- Fictional piece depicting an incident in the Second Boer War, 1900.

British soldiers are engaged in a fire-fight at close range with Boers on high ground above them. One of the Boers gets close enough to a British soldier to touch him before falling hit. The Boer asks for water which the soldier gives him; but as the soldier turns away the Boer shoots him. The Boer then takes a despatch from the soldier's pocket and tries to get back up the slope to his own men, who by this time have mostly run away. Another British soldier chases after him, wrestles the despatch from him, and finally shoots him. The whole action is very quick and frenetic.

Notes
Summary: identified by James Barker in

work for the television series *Flashback*. According to this research, this film was taken on a hillside not far from Bradford in the north of England.
catalogued SDB: 11/1983

IWM 1082-01 · GB, (?) 1914
PATHE'S ANIMATED GAZETTE NO 282B

b/w · 1 reel · 294' (5 mins) · silent
intertitles: none

pr Pathé

I. French reaction to the outbreak of war, July 1914. Crowds of people are shown queuing outside the banks in the streets of Paris, as the immediate financial crisis before the outbreak of war threatens the French currency.
II. Very brief item showing a Farman Longhorn biplane in flight, probably Britain, July or August 1914.
III. A recruiting march through the streets of London, probably August 1914. The Grenadier Guards, in parade dress, lead the recruiting march through the streets, followed by sailors and marines (some of whom are pulling Maxim guns on wheels). Civilians fall in behind the march.
IV. Royal Navy ratings practising for a field gun race, probably summer 1914. The sailors are practising for a tournament in an enclosure. Teams practise disassembling and reassembling their muzzle-loading light guns in order to race with them over obstacles. Each team fires its gun.

catalogued SDB: 12/1983

IWM 1082-02a · GB, 10/10/1921
GAUMONT GRAPHIC 1104

b/w · 1 reel · 333' (6 mins) · silent
intertitles: English

pr Gaumont

I. General Pershing and the US Army of Occupation, in Britain on its way home, October 1921. A troopship carrying Lieutenant-General John Pershing and US soldiers comes into Dover harbour, where it is met by the local garrison commander. Then a formal ceremony in London, in which Pershing joins in a British military procession to Westminster Abbey, where he presents the Unknown Warrior with the US Congressional Medal of Honor. He then

goes on to lay a wreath at the Cenotaph in Whitehall (note the cine cameraman at work).
II. A student rag at a Paris Engineering College, October 1921. The camera, from a safe high angle, records the students milling around in the quadrangle, being showered with water and conducting a mock bullfight.
III. A sea angling festival at Hastings, October 1921. The Fifth Annual Festival of the National Federation of Sea Anglers starts with the small rowing boats putting out to sea and the anglers starting their rod-and-line fishing. Interested spectators watch from the beach.
IV. A Salvation Army ship about to sail from Hull to India, October 1921. According to the captions, the Salvation Army team, gathered from all over the world, is about to sail for missionary activity in India. They parade through the streets and board the SS *Calypso* for their journey. Many of them are Indian, and wear Salvation Army uniform with a turban. Some of the women, Indian or not, wear saris. They display the Salvation Army banner.

Notes
Title: this appears on the first caption, which heads the second subject of the newsreel.
catalogued SDB: 12/1983

IWM 1082-02b · GB, 1911
CORONATION OF HIS MAJESTY KING GEORGE V

b/w · 1 reel · 257' (4 mins) · silent
intertitles: English

pr Jury's Imperial Pictures *prod* Jury, William F

■ Incomplete film of the coronation procession of George V through central London, Thursday 22 June 1911.

The coronation procession passes through Admiralty Arch. It is led by the Life Guards, two of the state coaches, then the Yeomen of the Guard, senior Army officers, representative Imperial troops, and the Royal Horse Guards. The Coronation Coach itself has an escort of Life Guards. The procession arrives outside Westminster Abbey. The procession is in long shot, with the King only just visible inside his coach.

Notes
Remarks: there were a number of films made of the coronation of 1911, notably this by Jury and another by Charles Urban.

It was the popularity of these films which established British documentary cinema as a respectable and serious method of conveying news of great events.
[Harold Nicolson, *King George the Fifth: His Life and Reign*, Constable (1952): 144-148]
catalogued SDB: 12/1983

IWM 1082-02c · GB, 6/1912
PATHE'S ANIMATED GAZETTE 172

b/w · 1 reel · 380' (6 mins) · silent
intertitles: English

pr Pathé

I. A crash at an air race at Douai, France, June 1912. The wrecks of two collided aircraft are shown, neither identifiable.
II. A student rag at Kew Gardens, London, June 1912. The art students, including girls, are in fancy dress. They play leap-frog, improvise a foxtrot, and play up for the camera.
III. A flower show in Paris, June 1912. The "Battle of the Flowers" is a procession of horse-drawn or motorised floats, all decorated with flowers and driving down the boulevards. Mlle Dorgère wins ("obtains the prize", according to the caption) for her car float of a monoplane, which she is seen driving.
IV. The marriage of Graham White to Dorothy Chadwell Taylor at Chelmsford, June 1912. The bride and groom, both famous aviators, fly to their wedding. White comes in to land by the church in his own design 'Aero-Bus'. Miss Chadwell Taylor flies in a Blériot IX past the church tower. They emerge from the wedding ceremony under an archway formed by boy scouts presenting arms.
V. A coach race along the East Sheen Avenue, London, June 1912. The four-in-hand mail coaches of the coaching marathon come up the wide avenue (described as "East Sheen Road") with escorts of motor cars and some cyclists. It is a very pleasant, tree-lined, upper-class neighbourhood.
VI. King George V reviews the St John Ambulance Brigade at Windsor, 22 June 1912. The men and women of the Brigade walk into their parade position. The King, in long shot on horseback, rides among them, reviewing them. In an open carriage nearby the Queen sits with the Prince of Wales "on the eve of his birthday" in naval uniform. The King continues with his review.

catalogued SDB: 12/1983

IWM 1082-02d · GB, 6/1912
PATHE'S ANIMATED GAZETTE 173

b/w · 1 reel · 237' (4 mins) · silent
intertitles: English

pr Pathé

I. The funeral of Sir George White in
Chelsea, late June 1912. A battalion of the
Gordon Highlanders, of which White was
Colonel-in-Chief, leads the procession
through the streets, with the coffin on a
gun-carriage. Lord Roberts, on horseback,
leads the mourners.
II. Amundsen's Antarctic Expedition about to
arrive at the port of London, June 1912. The
men of the expedition are on board the SS
Highland Scot. The cameraman rows out to
meet the ship as it approaches the port. On
the deck members of the expedition pose
for the camera, firstly Lieutenant Prestrud,
then Lieutenant Gjertssen, then Mr S
Hassel, all in civilian clothes. A general shot
of members of the expedition (Amundsen is
not specifically identified).
III. A road sweepers' parade in New York,
June 1912. The municipal road sweepers
pass through the streets of New York, in a
parade which includes their water wagons.
IV. The German Zeppelin LZ10 "Schwaben"
in flight over Düsseldorf, June 1912. The
airship is shown in flight over the city. The
caption says that it exploded and was
destroyed shortly after its arrival.

catalogued SDB: 12/1983

IWM 1082-03 · GB, (ca) 1912
[WEYMOUTH CLASS CRUISER]
(allocated)

b/w · 1 reel · 213' (4 mins) · silent
intertitles: none

■ Royal Navy ship in harbour, possibly
Plymouth, before the First World War.

A long pan over a Weymouth Class light
cruiser at anchor, showing it in some detail.
On shore a Royal Navy commander hears a
speech from the local mayor, and receives
a presentation. The sailors then hold sports,
water-jousting on the open green (note the
cine cameraman at work).

Notes
Summary: nothing further can be discovered
about this film.
catalogued SDB: 12/1983

IWM 1082-04 · France, (prod) 1899
[the FUNERAL OF PRESIDENT FAURE]
(allocated)

b/w · 1 reel · 153' (2 mins) · silent
intertitles: none

■ Funeral procession of President Félix
Faure of France through Paris, 23
February 1899.

The film is of poor quality, and shows the
procession passing a fixed point. First come
the various honour guards of representative
soldiers (including horsemen) and sailors,
then the magnificent funeral hearse, and
finally the mourners (no identifications are
certain).

[*Illustrated London News*, 4 March 1899]
catalogued SDB: 12/1983

IWM 1083 · France, (?) 1896
SUBSTITUTIONS
[TRANSFORMATIONS] (translation)
VUES POUR CINEMATOGRAPHE LUMIERE
(series)

b/w · 1 reel · 131' (2 mins) · silent
intertitles: French

pr Lumière *prod* Lumière, Louis; and
Lumière, Auguste

■ Fictional comic piece illustrating the stop-
action techniques popular in the earliest
French cinema.

The stage-like set is the interior of an 18th
century drawing room (note the placard
"Lumière" on the right). A wizard mixes and
pours powders into a bowl on a pedestal.
This changes into a hunched old man
whom the wizard ushers out. A lady of the
court brings the old man back in,
whereupon the wizard makes him vanish in
a puff of smoke. He and the lady then retire
offstage, mystically summoning the next
character as they do so. The character who
enters is a pantomime young man in a
tricorn hat with a carpet bag and stick. He
puts these on a table and goes to sit in the
wizard's chair. This jumps sideways so that
he falls over, and when he goes to sit in it
again jumps back to its original place with
the same result. On the third attempt he
manages to sit. A solid but ghost-like figure
completely draped in white approaches
him. He takes up his sword and dagger to
defend himself and these change into a
broom and chamber-pot. He takes up his

stick instead and strikes at the figure, which vanishes and reappears behind him. He goes to strike again and the figure changes into the lady, to whom he bows. She sits in the wizard's chair and at once changes into a skeleton, then as the young man recoils the skeleton changes into the wizard, who seizes the young man and causes him to vanish in a puff of smoke.

Notes
Production: according to the opening credits, this is film catalogue number 2003 in the Musée du Cinéma de Lyon.
Remarks: not exactly war-related, but amusing film on a good quality print. The stop-action changes have been disguised by blurring, either in the camera or later, the two frames on either side of the change, making the whole effect surprisingly smooth.
catalogued SDB: 11/1983

IWM 1084 · Austria-Hungary, (?) 1918
CSAPATAINK HOSI HARCA A HAVASOK SZIKLAIBAN ES JEGEBEN
[OUR HEROIC TROOPS FIGHT AMONG THE SNOW-CAPPED MOUNTAINS, ROCKS AND ICE] (translation)
[SZENEN AUS DEM ERSTEN WELTKRIEG] (alternative)
[SCENES FROM THE FIRST WORLD WAR] (alternative (translation))

b/w · 2 reels · 1977' (33 mins) · silent
intertitles: Hungarian

pr Sascha Film

- Hungarian film of their own troops in the Italian Alps, probably 1918.

(Reel 1) The troops are at a skiing lodge in the mountains, well above the snow-line. The various groups go out on patrols, moving in single file up and down the mountain tracks at a height of 3500m. Two men ride in an aerial cable-car little bigger than they are. More men on the march like black dots in the snow. A heavy gun concealed in a gun pit, described as the highest gun in the Alps. A snow-cave dug in the mountain. A difficult climb up the mountain face. Men set out on ski patrol from the lodge. One group makes a climb with ice-axes. Other patrols continue up and down the paths. Men run around the campsite for exercise. The cable-car comes up and skis are unloaded from it. General views of the mountains. *(Reel 2)* A shell-burst lands beside an Austro-Hungarian

observation post, scattering snow over the men. In response an assault company is alerted from its hut, while its 37mm mountain howitzer is manhandled into position. The men of the company run up the snow path and climb a rope ladder up the mountain face to reach the enemy. The 37mm opens fire, directed from the observation post by telephone, as the assaulting troops scramble up the mountain side. The shells burst against the Italian position higher up the mountain. As the Austro-Hungarian rush reaches the ground directly below the Italian position, they have grenades thrown at them by the Italians. Stretcher-bearers take away an injured Austrian. Finally, the assault troops storm the Italian position, using their bayonets as knives, then taking their prisoners and wounded with them continue on up the mountain.

Notes
Title: the alternative title appears on the film leader.
Summary: an incomplete version of the first reel of this film is held as **IWM 1038**, and of the second reel as **IWM 1043a**; neither is markedly incomplete.
catalogued SDB: 12/1983

IWM 1085 · GB, 5/1937
GAUMONT BRITISH NEWS [5/1937] – THE CORONATION

b/w · 3 reels · 1111' (45 mins) · silent
intertitles: English

pr Gaumont

- Coronation Ceremony of King George VI at Westminster Abbey, 12 May 1937.

(Reel 1) Crowds wait, lining the processional route, for the Coronation Coach to emerge. The Duke of Norfolk, as Earl Marshal, has all prepared. The coach, with an escort of Life Guards, comes out of Buckingham Palace gates and down the Mall, then through Admiralty Arch, down Whitehall and across Parliament Square to the Abbey. The King and Queen enter the Abbey and the camera follows them inside as the procession goes up to the altar. The dignitaries take their places, and the Archbishops of Canterbury and York prepare to start the ceremony. The Queen is seated to one side while the Queen Dowager watches with the Royal Princesses from a balcony. The ceremony begins with the 'recognition' of the King by the

assembled Lords. *(Reel 2)* The King then takes his place on the throne and is anointed by the Archbishops, then given the robes and instruments of office. The Lords Spiritual and Temporal, led by the Archbishop of Canterbury, then give homage. *(Reel 3)* The Queen's coronation follows, after which the procession leaves the Abbey and the Coronation Coach takes them back to Buckingham Palace. The Royal Family appears on the balcony to the cheers of the crowd, the young Princess Elizabeth giving a very characteristic wave.

Notes
Technical: note that this film, unusually by this date, is silent rather than mute.
catalogued SDB: 12/1983

IWM 1086 · NOT INCLUDED

IWM 1087-1088 · NO FILM

IWM 1089 · NOT INCLUDED

IWM 1090 · NO FILM

IWM 1091a · GB, (?) 1913
[HENDON AIR RACE] (allocated)

b/w · 1 reel · 256' (4 mins) · silent
intertitles: English

- Air race at Hendon, Middlesex, probably 1913.

The film is very dark throughout, making identification difficult. The competing aircraft are chiefly Farman Longhorns, Farman Shorthorns and Morane-Saulnier monoplanes. They take off, crossing a start line on the ground, and fly round the turning point. A Blériot type monoplane, Number 1 in the race, has landed on Epsom Downs and is towed away, surrounded by onlookers. Mr L Noel in Number 13, a Morane-Saulnier, lands as the winner, but is later seen being told he has been disqualified.

catalogued SDB: 12/1983

IWM 1091b · Germany (?), (?) 1912
PONTOON BRIDGE BUILDING

b/w · 1 reel · 392' (7 mins) · silent
intertitles: English

pr (?) UKF

- German Army exercise in bridging a river, possibly the Rhine, before the First World War.

Scenes of a riverside town, including its castle. The river itself has steep banks, and is wide and fast-flowing. The German Engineers, in fatigue dress, row the pontoon boats with their wooden cross-beams out into the river, and link them together with ropes to form one continuous bridge. The bridging timbers are laid across the pontoons and the bridge (with a supporting side-rail) completed. Horse transport moves across the bridge. The Engineers then start to dismantle the bridge and row the pontoons back to the shore.

Notes
Title: this appears at the bottom of each intertitle.
Production: despite this being apparently a German film the titling is in English. The production company logo, appearing on each caption, is the interlinked letters UKF.
Remarks: considerably more exciting than it sounds. The river is really fast-flowing towards its centre and the flat-bottomed pontoons handle like surfboats.
catalogued SDB: 12/1983

IWM 1092-1094 · NOT INCLUDED

IWM 1095 · GB, (?) 1919
ALLENBY'S CAMPAIGN (title on can)

b/w · 1 reel · 1058' (17 mins) · silent
intertitles: English

- Animation, actuality and reconstruction film of the British campaign in Palestine, October 1917 to October 1918.

The film blames the war, and Turkey's involvement in it, completely on Germany. It uses animated maps to show how from 1415 the Duchy of Brandenburg expanded to become the German Empire and absorb Turkey in its schemes for European domination. By autumn 1917 a British and Imperial force under Allenby had been assembled in southern Palestine to oppose this threat. Actuality film emphasises the cosmopolitan nature of this force. An animated model shows the first British breakthrough at Beersheba and Gaza in October 1917, intercutting with actuality and feature film to show the capture of Jerusalem and the raids across the Jordan. The animated map shows that by 1918 Russia has been taken by Germany, and there is a new threat. In September 1918 Allenby launches his second drive, in which the cavalry reach firstly Damascus, with cooperation from Faisal and Lawrence's Arabs, and then on to Aleppo, so driving Turkey out of the war. The defeat of Turkey precipitates the defeat of Germany.

Notes
Title: this appears on the film can.
Remarks: not particularly good, even as entertainment. The film relies too heavily on its stop-action animated model to cover the gaps in its actuality material; even though it pays little attention to the correct use of such actuality film.
catalogued SDB: 12/1983

IWM 1096 · NOT INCLUDED

IWM 1097 · GB, 1918
HOW WE TREAT OUR WOUNDED (ledger title)

b/w · 1 reel · 580' (10 mins) · silent
intertitles: none

sp War Office Cinema Committee (?)
pr Topical Film Company *cam* Buckstone, W A

■ Activities at Number 13 Convalescent Depot, Trouville, France, summer 1918.

Injured soldiers on wheeled stretchers are taken from a hospital train at the depot. Other soldiers, generally more fit, arrive at the depot in light railway trucks. The troops sit on the ground outside the main depot huts (note the dining hall sign). They are served food from the field kitchens. The base commandant inspects fit men who are ready to leave; they board a train from the depot and are played out by the band. The men at the depot take part in a tug of war, a hockey match and a boxing match. Men tend the vegetable and flower gardens outside their Nissen huts. The soldiers play on the beach with local children, practise

exercises, and go swimming. A pierrot show entertains the men. More physical training, including a cross-country race and another boxing match.

[shotsheet available]
catalogued SDB: 12/1983

IWM 1098 · GB, 11/1917
REPAIRING WAR'S RAVAGES
REPARACION DE LOS DANOS CAUSADOS POR LA GUERRA (on copy held)

b/w · 1 reel · 875' (15 mins) · silent
intertitles: Spanish

sp Department of Information *pr* Imperial Film Company

■ Spanish-language version of a film on the work of the Army rehabilitation centre at Roehampton, Surrey, autumn 1917.

The inhabitants of the centre are soldiers in hospital blues, all either with an arm or a leg missing, or in wheelchairs, or blind. A group of them assembles to hear a representative of the Ministry of Pensions explain the trades the Army will teach them to help them return to civilian life. Two of the men, each with a leg missing, are taken to join others learning how to be clerks and typists. The men learn to understand account books, to type one-handed, to understand commercial correspondence and accounting. Other men are taught in a workshop how to make purses and other items from leather. In another workshop some are taught electrical work and soldering. Outdoors a teacher blinded in the war shows men the principles of poultry farming. Indoors, a one-armed man learns how to work and maintain a cinema projector. In the engineering section some men work with lathes. Others are taught car maintenance and driving, including how to repair a car tyre inner-tube. Blind or handicapped men weave baskets in the open. In the woodwork shop a one-armed man fits a chisel to his artificial arm for use with a lathe in shaping wood. Finally, wearing their civilian clothes, the men are given a discharge allowance by the Army to help them look for work.

Notes
Remarks: an interesting film, with a very positive approach. The discharge allowance does not seem very much.
[shotsheet available]
catalogued SDB: 12/1983

IWM 1099 · GB, 3/1918
the HERTFORDSHIRE REGIMENT
[the BRITISH REGIMENTS] (series,
allocated)

b/w · 1 reel · 422' (7 mins) · silent
intertitles: English

sp War Office Cinema Committee *pr* Topical
Film Company

- 1/1st Battalion, Hertfordshire Regiment
  resting in the rear areas of the Western
  Front, autumn 1917.

A pan over the men resting by their tented
camp near Brasserie. A bath parade for the
men. Tins of stew and chunks of meat are
distributed at the camp; and later this is
given out cooked at the field kitchens to the
men, who sit eating from their dixies. The
men practise physical exercises. The tailors
and bootmakers of the battalion work in the
open repairing uniforms and boots. A
posed group of several NCOs "who have
won decorations". A final shot of the
battalion Quartermaster with the Medical
Officer, a US doctor.

Notes
Summary: the Hertfordshire Regiment was
unusual in that it was exclusively a
Territorial Army regiment, technically part of
the corps of the Bedfordshire Regiment.
The Battalion's official War Diary records the
move to camp "near Brasserie" on 17
October 1917 and the entry for 22 October
reads "Cinema operator from G.H.Q. filmed
the Bn. in Camp.".
catalogued SDB: 12/1983

IWM 1100 · GB, 3/1918
the LINCOLN REGIMENT (sic)
[the BRITISH REGIMENTS] (series,
allocated)

b/w · 1 reel · 465' (8 mins) · silent
intertitles: English

sp War Office Cinema Committee *pr* Topical
Film Company

- Regular battalion of the Lincolnshire
  Regiment resting in the rear areas of the
  Western Front, autumn 1917.

A pan over the men of the battalion, posed
as a group with two dogs as mascots. The
battalion officers stand as a semi-posed
group. The battalion signallers practise
semaphore. The battalion marches past the
camera with its officers mounted. The
battalion band also marches up to the
camera. The Transport section shows off its
horses at the horse lines. Hot stew is
served to the men from food boxes. A
group of the men gather around the 'wet'
canteen, drinking beer from a barrel.

Notes
Remarks: a typical, uninteresting episode of
the series.
[C R Simpson, *The History of the
Lincolnshire Regiment 1914-1918*, Medici
Society (1931)]
catalogued SDB: 12/1983

IWM 1101 · USA, (?) 1939
the MARCH OF AVIATION

b/w · 1 reel · 253' (11 mins) · silent
intertitles: English

pr Hollywood Film Enterprises Incorporated

- Development of powered flight from 1903
  to 1939.

The earliest flights were in spherical
balloons. In 1903 the Wright brothers made
the first flight (their Mk II Flier of 1904 is
shown in flight). A 1910 Glen Curtiss
Golden Flier. A 1927 Douglas M4 mail
plane, the first commercial use of aircraft. A
flight of four USAAC Keystone B4A
bombers of 1932. A Cierva C30A autogiro
taking off. A Macon giant rigid airship in
flight over the Californian coast. A French
Caudron C460 breaking the world speed
record at 314mph over Los Angeles in
1936. The first long-range passenger
aircraft, a Douglas DC3 Dakota of American
Airlines in flight. A Short S23 flying-boat
"Caledonia", which established the first
passenger and mail flight from England to
the USA in 1937. The latest US fighter, the
Lockheed P38 Lightning, in flight. A
Douglas B18 Bolo bomber taking off,
followed by a flight of three in the air. A
flight of three RAF Fairey Battles. A flight of
four Douglas TBD1 Devastators in the air.
Curtiss P40 Hawks in flight and taxiing. A
Douglas DC4 prototype taxiing, the first
transport aircraft with retractable tricycle
undercart. A Martin M130 Clipper flying-boat
in flight. Boeing B17C Flying Fortresses
taking off and in flight over the coast.

catalogued SDB: 12/1983

IWM 1102 · GB, (?) 1917
[GAS SHELLS] (allocated)

b/w · 2 reels · 1056' (17 mins) · silent
intertitles: none

sp War Office (?)

- Demonstrations of the Livens Gas
  Projector and of gas shells, probably at
  Chapperton Down Artillery School near
  Aldershot, spring 1917.

(Reel 1) The film starts with close-ups of the
baseplate and tube of the Livens Projector.
An instructor shows how the bomb is fused
and armed. Then a view of two Livens
Projectors buried in a trench and a long
shot of the firing range, with the bombs
falling on it. The instructor shows the
propellant charge for the Livens, taking the
charge apart to show its constituents. A
number of projectors are then armed with
the propellant charge and wired up. 9.2-
inch and 8-inch howitzers nearby have
been fitted to stable platforms and are
being used to fire gas shell at the firing
range. A 4.5-inch howitzer is loaded with
gas shell and fired. A line of gas shells from
4.5-inch up to 9.2-inch calibre is shown.
The loading of the Livens Projectors with
propellant charges and gas bombs
continues. A view of the firing range
showing a camouflaged trench and buried
projectors. A repeat of the instructor taking
the propellant charge apart. (Reel 2) Views
of the target area with gas shells falling on
it, showing (in close-up) little surface
damage to the ground. Then a Livens salvo
falls on the area, producing a large gas
cloud.

catalogued SDB: 12/1983

IWM 1103 · GB, (?) 1918
[GAS FILM CAPTIONS] (allocated)

b/w · 1 reel · 361' (6 mins) · silent
intertitles: English

- Captions and extracts from an
  unidentified film on gas warfare, probably
  1918.

The film opens with an unrelated cartoon
view of no man's land. Then a stop-action
sequence of a PH gas-hood. Then troops
practising putting on the 1917 pattern Small
Box Respirator. The remainder of the film
(nearly half) consists of captions for a film
on gas training which appears not to exist.

Notes
Production: the captions are marked
"A.C.T.B." (this abbreviation remains
unexplained).
Summary: see also **IWM 276**, which may
contain some of the material relating to
these captions.
catalogued SDB: 12/1983

IWM 1104 · NO FILM

IWM 1105 · GB, 7/1918
**the STORY OF HMS VINDICTIVE AT
OSTEND**

b/w · 1 reel · 1463' (24 mins) · silent
intertitles: English

sp Admiralty pr Engholm, F W
cam Engholm, F W

- Film showing HMS Vindictive and other
  naval vessels of the type used in the raid
  on Ostend, 10 May 1918.

HMS Vindictive in port prior to the
operation. Pan over moored motor launches
as they prepare for sea. High angle medium
shot of coastal motor boat showing smoke
dischargers. Dunkirk: long shot of the
French coast. British destroyers search out
the enemy: Broke Class Leader followed by
M Class, and destroyers in line astern
laying smoke, signalling by searchlight.
CMBs pass camera at speed. ML.558
approaches to semaphore. MLs make
smoke. Long shot profile of a hospital ship
– CMB in the foreground. Monitors: stern to
bow track past Lord Clive Class monitor;
second Lord Clive bows-on; medium shot
to stern of Erebus Class monitor. The scene
shifts to the cooperating land and air forces
– various shots of Allied 12-, 9.2- and 7.5-
inch coastal batteries and their crews, pilots
being briefed and aircraft bombed up.
Medium shot profile of flagship, HMS
Warwick. French Hurricane Deck Type
destroyer cooperates with British Admiralty
M Class ships. Concluding sequence
showing close-ups of HMS Vindictive, with
the "honourable wounds" received in the
Zeebrugge raid of 23 April, and the officers
who participated in the operation. "What the
efforts of the British Navy stand for":
German flag is struck, and the white ensign
raised in its stead.

[shotsheet available]
catalogued NAP: 2/1978

IWM 1106 · GB, 1918
**WOMEN'S ROYAL AIR FORCE – LIFE ON
A BRITISH AERODROME**

b/w · 1 reel · 577' (10 mins) · silent
intertitles: English

sp Royal Air Force (?)

■ Everyday life for WRAF members at a
coastal RAF station, probably Hastings
area, summer 1918.

The women help bring a patrol airship,
SSZ13, out of its hangar, then back in again
after its flight. In their own mess the women
sit drinking tea. Some of them check the
rigging of SSZ airships, others clean and
polish the cowlings of Sopwith 1½ Strutter
aircraft. Back in their mess after dinner they
plait and arrange each other's hair or read
picture newspapers. Working again, some
cover an airframe with fabric in the
assembly sheds. Outside, a group holds a
Bristol Scout D in position while the engine
is started, then take the chocks away to let
the aircraft take off. They manœuvre the
same plane on the ground by its balance
points. One woman holds up a poster
displaying the standing orders of the WRAF.
Back indoors, they work cutting and sewing
aircraft fabric; a male NCO watches them,
and is handed a message by a boy scout.
Other women perform clerical duties. The
Bristol Scout D in flight. Another view of the
women working on cleaning disassembled
aircraft engines.

Notes
Summary: see also **IWM 1107-01** and **IWM
1107-02**. This film appears to be the
finished version of a film of which **IWM
1107-01** and **IWM 1107-02** are possible
alternatives or out-takes.
catalogued SDB: 12/1983

IWM 1107-01 · GB, (prod) 1918
BRITISH WOMEN'S AIR FORCE

b/w · 1 reel · 654' (11 mins) · silent
intertitles: English

sp Royal Air Force (?)

■ Everyday life for WRAF members at a
coastal RAF station, probably Hastings
area, summer 1918.

Two women volunteers go along to the
recruiting centre, emerging in WRAF
uniform. There is a parade at the station,
after which the women depart to their
various duties. Some work as clerks, some
as waitresses in the officers' mess, some
sewing fabric (described as "sail-making").
Others strip and repair the wings of
damaged aircraft. One group holds on to a
Bristol Scout D while the engine is run up,
then remove the chocks to let it taxi. It
comes back to land and the rotary engine
runs to a stop. They take it up by its
balance points and wheel it away. A group
of the women bring airship SSZ13 out of its
shed. Some work in a repair "shop" on
wheels. After work those who drive lorries
and motor-cycles have their vehicles
inspected. Early in the morning the women
go sea-bathing. Others play tennis, hockey,
go boating with friends, or practise waltzing
with each other. They take part in sports on
the sea front at Hastings. A final shot of "the
boys they're helping to win this war", two
RAF fliers starting up an Armstrong
Whitworth FK3.

Notes
Summary: see also **IWM 1106** and **IWM
1107-02**. This film appears to be an
alternative, or possibly discarded, version of
IWM 1106.
catalogued SDB: 12/1983

IWM 1107-02 · GB, (prod) 1918
WOMEN'S ROYAL AIR FORCE

b/w · 1 reel · 627' (11 mins) · silent
intertitles: none

sp Royal Air Force (?)

■ Everyday life for WRAF members on an
RAF coastal station, probably near
Hastings, summer 1918.

Some of the women work driving or doing
maintenance work on RAF cars and lorries.
One woman changes the tyre on a staff car,
but is unable to get the inner tube detached
from the tyre, even with the help of another
woman. A male ground crew member finally
has to help. Some of the women play
cricket outside their hut. Other women sit
outside the cookhouse peeling potatoes;
more join in. Inside the cookhouse the
women cook and wash up. One woman
does preparation work on an aerial camera,
which a ground crew member arrives to
collect, also giving her a photograph to
identify, which she does using reference
books. Women act as waitresses in the
officers' mess.

Notes

Summary: see also **IWM 1106** and **IWM 1107-01**. This film appears to be an alternative, or possibly discarded, version of **IWM 1106**.
catalogued SDB: 12/1983

IWM 1108 · NO FILM

IWM 1109-1112 · NOT INCLUDED

IWM 1113 · NO FILM

IWM 1114 · NOT INCLUDED

IWM 1115-1120 · NO FILM

IWM 1121 · GB, (before) 8/1918
ANNA
[FILM TAGS] (series, allocated)

b/w · 1 reel · 129' (2 mins) · silent
intertitles: English

sp Ministry of Information *pr* Hepworth Manufacturing Company *cast* White, Chrissie; and Edwards, Henry

- British fictional short piece encouraging people to buy War Savings Certificates, 1918.

Anna, a girl from the country, sets out through the flowers with her purse and basket for the post office (actually at Shepperton). She tells the man she meets outside the post office that she can spend 4s 6d out of a pound and still have a pound left. While he looks in amazement she goes into the post office and emerges with a War Savings Certificate, costing 15s 6d. "Foive year from now I get a pound for un" she tells him, and trips happily back into the countryside. At the end of the film there is a brief, unrelated, scene of some footballers

Notes
Remarks: a charming and entertaining little film, made all the more ludicrous by the yokel accents of the captions.
catalogued SDB: 12/1983

IWM 1122 · GB, 5/1918
FATHER AND LATHER
[FILM TAGS] (series, allocated)

b/w · 1 reel · 136' (2 mins) · silent
intertitles: English

sp Ministry of Information

- British fictional piece on the need to save soap and other fats, 1918.

A young girl works cleaning the kitchen floor of a house. When she has finished she tosses the soap and cloth into the sink, which is full of water. The cook tells her, gently, that the soap will waste if left in water and is made of fats which are scarce. Later, the girl returns home to find her father shaving. She calls her mother and explains what she has been told, and produces a soap dish for her father to use.

catalogued SDB: 12/1983

IWM 1123 · GB/Italy (?), 1911
TURKISH ITALIAN WAR – THE INVASION OF TRIPOLI

b/w · 1 reel · 445' (7 mins) · silent
intertitles: English

- Italian amphibious landing near the town of Tripoli in the Ottoman province of Tripolitania, Turkish-Italian War, 1911.

Italian battleships escort their transports towards Tripoli. The battleships *Francesco Fernuccio* and *Re Umberto* form part of the escort. View from the shore of the Italian fleet, out at sea, bombarding shore positions. Lighters tow Italian soldiers in boats ashore for an unopposed landing. Other soldiers (in tropical kit) are landed on a wooden mole. A barge brings horses ashore. As Arabs watch, the Italians start to march off the beach. They have a tented camp inland from the town where the men rest and prepare a meal.

catalogued SDB: 12/1983

IWM 1124 · Germany, 1939
LANDUNG AUF OSEL 1917 : Aufnahmen aus dem Weltkrieg
[the LANDING ON OESEL 1917 : pictures from the World War] (translation)

b/w · 1 reel · 424' (11 mins) · silent
intertitles: none

pr Reichsanstalt für Film und Bild in
Wissenschaft und Unterricht

■ German film of the amphibious landing at
Pamerort on the island of Œsel in the
Baltic, 9-12 October 1917.

At Windau on 9 and 10 October the
transport ships for 42nd Division and other
elements of XXIII Reserve Corps are loaded
with men, equipment and guns. On the
morning of 10 October the cameraship,
probably the transport Coburg carrying 2nd
Cyclist Battalion and 8th Field Artillery
Battery, is loaded, and steams out of
harbour past the light cruisers SMS Kolberg
and SMS Koenigsberg. Another camera,
probably on board SMS Koenig, watches
the other ships of 3rd Battle Squadron as
they steam to within range of Oesel and
open fire: the Grosser Kurfürst is shown
first, then probably the Markgraf. A seaplane
overflies the cameraship, followed by a
military Zeppelin, either LZ113 or LZ120.
The battleships Bayern and (probably)
Grosser Kurfürst start the bombardment.
Sailors on the cameraship load one of the
guns (view inside turret). Then back to the
Coburg for the landing at Pamerort: the
ship's boats are lowered over the side, and,
filled with bicycles and men, set off for the
shore. The horses are off-loaded from the
transports and taken by barge to the shore.
A signaller stands on top of a thatched
cottage to semaphore. As the beach-head
is established horses and supplies begin to
collect and the men line up to be inspected
by a senior officer.

Notes
Remarks: the Baltic Islands Campaign was
ostensibly to secure the flank of a possible
German drive across Livonia. In reality,
however, it was politically motivated – it was
intended to provide elements of the High
Seas Fleet with something to do after the
attempted mutiny of September 1917.
Obscure, poorly documented and (since the
collapse of Russia rendered it politically and
strategically irrelevant) largely ignored, it
was still both the first fully successful
amphibious landing of the 20th century in
European warfare and an early example of
'blitzkrieg' technique using cavalry and
bicycles to outmanœuvre a bemused
enemy. That film of it exists when there is
no film of so many more important events is
surprising; that this film also shows
battleships in action is an added bonus.
[Tschischwitz, The Army and Navy during

the Conquest of the Baltic Islands in
October 1917, R Eisenschmidt (1933)]
catalogued SDB: 12/1983

IWM 1125 · NO FILM

IWM 1126 · GB, (?) 1919
EARL KITCHENER OF KHARTOUM

b/w · 1 reel · 327' (6 mins) · silent
intertitles: English

■ Graves of British sailors washed up on
the Norwegian coast during the First
World War, with reference to the death of
Lord Kitchener.

The film opens with a still of Kitchener
superimposed on the sea. Then a Union
Flag being hoisted at a ship's stern (meant
to represent the Hampshire). A diagram of
the currents between the Orkneys and
Norway showing how bodies are carried
onto the Norwegian coast. Gravestones of
unknown British sailors buried in Norway,
all victims of the Battle of Jutland. Two
Norwegians who found the bodies, H
Iversen and L Johansen, are shown posed
together. Finally, in Britain a motor-hearse
pulls up at a side street and a packing-case
draped with a Union Flag is taken indoors.
A piece of cloth from Kitchener's jacket is
held up for the camera.

Notes
Remarks: the film certainly gives the
impression that Kitchener's was among the
bodies found by the two men, whereas his
body was never found or identified. This
may be either sensationalism or deliberate
deception.
catalogued SDB: 1/1984

IWM 1127 · GB, (prod) 1914
**the 5TH BATTALION ROYAL SUSSEX
REGIMENT AT THE TOWER OF LONDON**

b/w · 1 reel · 315' (5 mins) · silent
intertitles: none

■ Cinque Ports Battalion guarding the
Tower of London, October-December
1914.

The battalion signallers form up in the
courtyard and practise their semaphore. A
company on parade fixes bayonets and is

inspected by its company officer, following which the men march off. Men practise bayonet fighting, including the butt smash. Vickers machinegun crews practise deploying their guns on a very high tripod mount. The full ceremony of changing the Tower guard, for which the officers carry their swords. A sergeant takes a drill class.

[E A C Fazan, *Cinque Ports Battalion*, Royal Sussex Regimental Association (1971): 98-102]
catalogued SDB: 12/1983

IWM 1128a · GB, 1/8/1918
PICTORIAL NEWS (OFFICIAL) 362-1

b/w · 1 reel · 148' (3 mins) · silent
intertitles: English

sp Ministry of Information *pr* Topical Film Company

■ Incomplete newsreel devoted to a review of the British Empire's war effort 1914-18.

Lord Kitchener visits New Army soldiers in France in February 1916. Australians of 2nd Division in bush hats march past. Gurkhas of 7th (Meerut) Division, also on the march in the pouring rain, and Lloyd George addressing a Canadian division at Aldershot from a car, with Sir Sam Hughes watching (note the reporters recording the speech) all illustrate the increasing role of the Empire in the war. Highlanders led by a pipe band march through an English village in 1916, contrasted with an apparently unending marching column of 1918 veterans in their shrapnel helmets, typical of the current British Army. Douglas Haig sits with A J Balfour on a bench in Versailles. The film ends with the *War Office Official Topical Budget* logo.

Notes
Summary: note that a longer and somewhat different French-language version of this item is **IWM 657b**, and a German-language version **IWM 683a**; note also that McKernan places this item in issue 362-2.
catalogued SDB: 12/1983

IWM 1128b · GB, (before) 8/1918
[MILK SAVING FILM] (allocated)
[FILM TAGS] (series, allocated)

b/w · 1 reel · 121' (2 mins) · silent
intertitles: English

sp Ministry of Information

■ Incomplete fictional film encouraging people in Britain to save milk, spring 1918.

A young lady sits at her breakfast table drinking tea and reading the morning paper. She reads of a heavy fine imposed on someone caught watering nursery milk, and conjures up a vision of a sick child. She pours more milk into her tea, and some into a saucer for her cat. She reads of a milk shortage in the north, and thinks again of the child with its mother. "It's only a little" the caption says, "but if everyone did with less in their tea thousands of these would be saved daily for the children", showing milk churns being lined up at a dairy.

Notes
Summary: this film, although untitled on the print, appears to be a typical Film Tag of spring 1918.
catalogued SDB: 12/1983

IWM 1129a · GB, 12/9/1917
WAR OFFICE OFFICIAL TOPICAL BUDGET 316-1

b/w · 1 reel · 50' (1 min) · silent
intertitles: English

sp War Office Cinema Committee *pr* Topical Film Company

■ 'GORIZIA' – a single story from the newsreel held as **NTB 316-01**.

catalogued SDB: 12/1983

IWM 1129b · GB, 13/3/1918
PICTORIAL NEWS (OFFICIAL) 342-1

b/w · 1 reel · 50' (1 min) · silent
intertitles: none

■ Single story from the newsreel held in more complete form as **IWM 699c**. The story concerns British Red Cross work in Salonika.

catalogued SDB: 12/1983

IWM 1129c · GB, 28/11/1917
WAR OFFICE OFFICIAL TOPICAL BUDGET 327-1

b/w · 1 reel · 50' (1 min) · silent
intertitles: English

sp War Office Cinema Committee pr Topical
Film Company

- 'FLANDERS FRONT EXTENDED' – a
single story from the newsreel held as
NTB 327-01.

catalogued SDB: 12/1983

IWM 1130 · GB, 1922
MONS

tinted · 1 reel · 108' (2 mins) · silent
intertitles: English

pr British Instructional Films

- Fragment of a fictionalised reconstruction
of the Battle of Mons, Western Front, 23
August 1914.

The film reconstructs the repulse of a
German column charge by British rifle and
field artillery fire in the centre of the
battlefield, and then the defence of Nimy
bridge on the left by 4th Royal Fusiliers.

catalogued SDB: 12/1983

IWM 1131a · USA, 1927
**WITH LAWRENCE IN ARABIA : a Lowell
Thomas Adventure Film**

b/w · 1 reel · 92' (5 mins) · silent
intertitles: English

pr Eastman Kodak Company cam Thomas,
L; and Chase, H A

- Compilation film of events in Arabia,
autumn 1917 to spring 1918.

A portrait still of Colonel T E Lawrence. The
embarkation of supplies and sheep on SS
Ozarda at Port Said, the journey to Jidda,
and the disembarkation. Some irregular
Bedouin horsemen of Prince Faisal's forces
'charge' the camera. Lawrence and Faisal
drive along a road in a Ford Model T with
an escort of Bedouins. A squadron of
Lawrence's armoured cars moves along a
desert road. Faisal stands with his men.
Finally, Faisal's troops "moving up to battle"
(no enemy in sight).

Notes
Summary: see also **IWM 41**.
Copyright: the copyright to this film is
claimed in its opening captions by Eastman
Kodak. This has now lapsed.
catalogued SDB: 12/1983

IWM 1131b · USA, 1927
**WITH ALLENBY IN PALESTINE : a Lowell
Thomas Adventure Film**

b/w · 1 reel · 190' (8 mins) · silent
intertitles: English

pr Eastman Kodak Company cam Thomas,
L; and Chase, H A

- Compilation film of events in Palestine,
autumn 1917 to spring 1918.

2nd Battalion, the Black Watch, led by its
pipe band along a desert road. "The
Australian Camel Corps" (actually pack
camels). The bombardment of Gaza in
September 1917. A street scene in Jaffa;
camels and civilians moving on the
Jerusalem-Jaffa Road. British soldiers and
Indian lancers on the move. A sentry on the
Mount of Olives. The Duke of Connaught
decorating General Allenby at Mount Zion
barracks on 20 March 1918. A panorama of
Jerusalem showing the Mosque of Omar
and the Wailing Wall, the Well of David, and
the Sepulchres of David, Absolom and
Rachel.

Notes
Copyright: the copyright to this film is
claimed in its opening captions by Eastman
Kodak. This has now lapsed.
Remarks: a typical Lowell Thomas
mishmash. The use of what is apparently
British official film in this item must again
call into question how much of the film
normally attributed to Thomas was in fact
taken by him.
catalogued SDB: 12/1983

IWM 1131c · USA, 1927
**BETHLEHEM AND GETHSEMANE – NO
1536**

b/w · 1 reel · 99' (4 mins) · silent
intertitles: English

pr Eastman Kodak Company

- Compilation film of views of Bethlehem
and Jerusalem, late 1917 or early 1918.

Street scenes in Bethlehem, the Church of St Mary, the Gardens of Gethsemane, the Via Dolorosa, the Holy Sepulchre, the Valley of Kidron and (in silhouette) a tree where, according to legend, Judas Iscariot hanged himself. A final street scene.

catalogued SDB: 12/1983

IWM 1132 · France, (?) 1917
AVIATION AS A RECONNOITRING POWER

b/w · 1 reel · 340' (6 mins) · silent
intertitles: English & French

■ Disjointed French film of a reconnaissance squadron base near Soissons, probably 1917.

The film is jumbled, with the title appearing some time after the start. It opens with two FBA Hydroplanes riding at moorings, silhouetted against the sunset on the water. The captions explain how useful aircraft are for reconnaissance. (The title appears at this point.) The aerodrome is shown, with no aircraft visible. A Spad 17 fighter comes in to land. The pilot and observer of a two-seater (too close for identification) after landing. Inside the squadron darkroom the prints are developed. Outside, ground crew check the aerial cameras and plates. Two photographs of German trenches taken from 13 000 feet are shown. The photographs are identified against a large map. Officers discuss a new operation, using the photographs as an aid to planning.

Notes
Production: apparently a French official film.
catalogued SDB: 1/1984

IWM 1133 · NO FILM

IWM 1134 · GB, (?) 1917
[BRITISH ARMY AMBULANCE DRIVERS]
(allocated)

b/w · 1 reel · 50' (1 min) · silent
intertitles: English

■ Brief scene of British Army ambulance drivers racing to their ambulances and driving off.

catalogued SDB: 12/1983

IWM 1135 · NO FILM

IWM 1136 · GB, (prod) 1914
AU REVOIR ! AND GOOD LUCK : the Hallamshire Rifles leaving Sheffield, November 3rd 1914

b/w · 1 reel · 184' (3 mins) · silent
intertitles: none

■ Parade through the streets of Sheffield by 4th Battalion, York and Lancaster Regiment, 3 November 1914.

The main street is crowded with people. The battalion band leads the men down through the crowd. The camera, in the front row of the crowd, shows one rank after another in a sustained shot as they parade before it.

Notes
Remarks: the film is virtually all one long, uncut shot.
catalogued SDB: 12/1983

IWM 1137 · GB, 1922
WITH THE 5TH BATTALION, YORK AND LANCASTER REGIMENT IN CAMP AT SCARBOROUGH AUGUST 1922

b/w · 1 reel · 1004' (17 mins) · silent
intertitles: English

■ Private film of 5th Yorks and Lancs on their campsite, near Scarborough, August 1922.

The officer commanding 49th (West Riding) Division, Major-General M R Davies, and Colonel W M Withycombe, commanding 5th West Riding Infantry Brigade, to which the battalion belongs, confer with Lieutenant-Colonel S Rhodes, commanding the battalion, and his officers (all very camera-conscious throughout). The battalion forms up to be addressed by Rhodes, then marches off, with the Transport section bringing up the rear. At the tented camp the band parades for the guard to be changed. Food is prepared at the open-air cookhouse and served in the mess tent. Battalion sports include a Band Race, a bun-and-treacle race for the boys, and a tug of war. The battalion concert party, "The Jazz

Band", poses for the camera. Withycombe gives the prizes after the sports. Rhodes poses firstly with his adjutant and RSM, and then with his officers. The warrant officers and sergeants pose drinking beer. On the return home the battalion arrives at Barnsley Station by train and marches up the hill to its drill hall for dismissal at the end of two weeks' training. Crowds of people, including children, flock round the final march.

Notes

Remarks: a film made strictly for the battalion's own entertainment. Although it is quite long, it concentrates exclusively on battalion 'personalities' rather than what actually happened on a training camp. There are no scenes of actual training at all.
catalogued SDB: 12/1983

IWM 1138-1139 · NOT INCLUDED

IWM 1140 · GB, 1922
OUR PRINCE IN JAPAN

b/w · 6 reels · 4927' (55 mins) · silent
intertitles: English

pr Interest Films

- This is described as "The Official film record of the pilgrimage of HRH the Prince of Wales to the far east from Portsmouth; via Gibraltar, Malta, Ceylon, Malay States, and Hong Kong to the Land of the Sun". Also visited are Manila, Brunei and Cairo.

Notes

Summary: as no viewing print is currently held, it is not at present possible to view this film for full cataloguing.
Technical: originally held as tinted nitrate prints, which have since had to be destroyed; no viewing print is currently available.
catalogued JCK: 6/1987

IWM 1141 · GB, 7/1922
PATHE GAZETTE [1922] – THE WEDDING OF THE SEASON

b/w · 1 reel · 256' (4 mins) · silent
intertitles: English

pr Pathé

- Marriage of Lord Louis Mountbatten to Edwina Ashley at St Margaret's Church, Westminster, 18 July 1922.

The bride and groom emerge from the church through the arch of crossed swords formed by naval officers. A party of sailors pulls the bridal car along by a rope as cameramen jump out of the way. The remainder of the congregation emerges from the church, led by the King and Queen, the Dowager Queen Alexandra, and the Prince of Wales escorting Mary Ashley as maid of honour. The sailors tow the car to Brook House in Upper Brook Street. Inside, the wedding party arranges itself for photographs – the bride and groom with the Prince as best man and the maid of honour. The bride poses for a photograph alone, then with the groom.

[A Hatch, *The Mountbattens*, W H Allen (1966): 200-208]
catalogued SDB: 1/1984

IWM 1142 · GB, 7/1922
GAUMONT GRAPHIC 1182

b/w · 1 reel · 433' (7 mins) · silent
intertitles: English

pr Gaumont

- Marriage of Lord Louis Mountbatten to Edwina Ashley at St Margaret's Church, Westminster, 18 July 1922.

Mountbatten arrives at St Margaret's, Westminster, with the Prince of Wales as his best man. The King and Queen then arrive with the Queen Dowager. The bride arrives and enters the church. Outside, sailors fix a tow rope to the wedding car and tow it a short distance as cameramen move out of the way. The bridal procession emerges from the church under an arch of swords formed by naval officers, and moves down to the cars where an escort of mounted policemen waits. The sailors tow the car away down Whitehall. The King, Queen and Queen Dowager then emerge from the church with the remaining guests. The Prince of Wales walks with the maid of honour, Mary Ashley. Police hold back onlookers as the various guests leave in their cars, and the sailors in a charabanc covered with Union Flags. The police continue to hold back the crowd. Outside Brook House the bride and groom's car arrives. The King and Queen then arrive and follow them inside. The cars of the remaining guests draw up one after another.

[A Hatch, *The Mountbattens*, W H Allen (1966): 200-208]
catalogued SDB: 1/1984

IWM 1143 · GB, (ca) 1917
[JUTLAND AND AFTER 1] (allocated)

b/w · 1 reel · 738' (12 mins) · silent
intertitles: none

sp Admiralty *pr* Engholm, F W
cam Engholm, F W

- Miscellaneous British naval scenes, ca. 1918.

I. Medium shot as V/W Class destroyer crosses the screen, and pan right to long shot of line of four Iron Duke Class (?) battleships. Medium shot off port beam of HMS *Renown* under way. Royal Sovereign Class battleships in Forth anchorage – M Class destroyer alongside foremost vessel. Panning medium-long shot over Forth anchorage showing King George V Class battleship and ships of the Royal Sovereign Class, one of which has a submarine alongside.
II. Medium close-up as Lord Cromer and a party of civilians come on board a battleship to be greeted by the ship's officers.
III. Destroyers in line astern. HMS *Ready* (G.71) under way at speed – other M Class ships in the background. HMS *Norman* (G.54) passes right to left across frame. Long shot to destroyer slowly closing from astern in heavy weather, and medium shot forward along waist of the cameraship – searchlight platform in the foreground.
IV. Medium shot off port bow of Renown Class battle-cruiser. Starboard profile of Queen Elizabeth Class battleship under way, and pan to Orion Class battleship astern. Medium shot profiles of Royal Sovereign Class and Iron Duke Class battleships (the latter is incomplete as frame right cuts the ship abaft Q turret).
V. Section from ADM 574. Medium shots of smoke float and smoke screen. Submarine C.23 runs on the surface. Trawler *Daniel Fearall*, with 'A' type smoke apparatus on the quarterdeck.
VI. Medium-long shot of two Flower Class sloops at their moorings, and pan to C Class cruiser and battleships.
VII. King George V and Beatty on the quarterdeck of HMS *Princess Royal*.

VIII. Medium-long shot as V/W Class destroyer passes in front of Royal Sovereign Class battleship. Battleship flashes signal across anchorage.

catalogued NAP: 3/1978

IWM 1144 · GB, (ca) 1917
[JUTLAND AND AFTER 2] (allocated)

b/w · 1 reel · 863' (14 mins) · silent
intertitles: none

sp Admiralty *pr* Engholm, F W
cam Engholm, F W

- Miscellaneous British naval material, 1916-18.

I. Medium shot forward along portside of W Class destroyer to HMS *Renown* – a small boat spins past between the two ships. Medium-long shot across fleet anchorage – Iron Duke Class battleships at frame left. Camera tracks from starboard to port bow of HMS *Furious* – dazzle-painted HMS *Argus* in the background. Medium shot of SMS *Koenigsberg* (II), with ML.72 alongside.
II. Unsteady medium shot as a merchantman crosses frame left to right.
III. Medium shot off port quarter of an Iron Duke Class battleship, and pan to other battleships in the Forth anchorage.
IV. Medium shot as camera tracks past torpedoed merchantman lying on its beam ends – waves break over the hull.
V. Medium close-up from HMS *Queen Elizabeth* as ML.72 approaches, and Admiral Meurer and staff come on board. Medium shots of *Koenigsberg* under way with British escort.
VI. HMS *Paladin* (G.40) manœuvres to a position outboard of HMS *Nizam* (G.28) which is lying alongside the cameraship – crewmen line guard rail in foreground.
VII. Medium shot off starboard beam of Queen Elizabeth Class battleship under way at sea (frame left cuts off stern).
VIII. Medium-long shot as elements of Second Battle Squadron (*King George V, Centurion, Erin* and *Agincourt*) run abreast for a shoot.
IX. SMS *Koenigsberg* moored at Rosyth. ML.72 semaphores. Medium shot off port beam as HMS *Blonde* passes.
X. Medium-long shot of coastal airship. Medium shot of Royal Sovereign Class battleship towing a kite balloon – C Class light cruiser in the background.
XI. V/W Class destroyer approaches,

making heavy weather, then turns away to starboard to give a long-shot view of three battleships in line astern.
XII. Forth anchorage: medium shot as HMS *Colossus* passes HMS *Queen Elizabeth* and HMS *Canada* at their moorings. Medium-long shot off port quarter of HMS *Hercules* as she passes in front of *Canada*. Camera pans left to show Royal Sovereign Class battleships of First Battle Squadron at anchor.
XIII. Medium shot of Queen Elizabeth Class battleship under way at sea. S Class destroyer passes at speed. The cameraship is one of a squadron of battleships proceeding in line ahead – destroyer HMS *Ulysses* (G.77) steams right to left across bows of cameraship – in the foreground of the shot a crewman sits on a sighting hood of B turret. Camera pans left to show crewman and a companion, and three Royal Sovereign Class battleships in line on the horizon. High angle medium shot to the guns of B turret trained over the starboard bow – one gun has just fired. Long shot of Iron Duke Class battleship as it fires B turret.
XIV. Medium shot off port quarter of Royal Sovereign Class battleship under way in a slight sea – V/W Class destroyer in the background. Various shots of Royal Sovereign Class battleships returning from sea, and First Battle Squadron in line ahead with (?) HMS *Marlborough* in the van.
XV. Medium-long shot off port bow of HMS *Lion* in anchorage – Forth railway bridge in the background.

catalogued NAP: 3/1978

IWM 1145 · GB, (ca) 1917
[JUTLAND AND AFTER 3] (allocated)

b/w · 1 reel · 1142' (19 mins) · silent
intertitles: none

sp Admiralty *pr* Engholm, F W
cam Engholm, F W

■ Miscellaneous British naval material, 1916-18.

I. Battleships exercise at sea: elements of Second Battle Squadron run abreast for a shoot (*cf.* **IWM 1143**); long shots of Orion and Iron Duke Class battleships; medium shot directly astern of Queen Elizabeth Class battleship as it fires to starboard.
II. Medium shots of SMS *Koenigsberg* anchored at Rosyth (*cf.* **IWM 1143**).
III. King George V Class battleships under

way in line astern – the leading ship opens fire with Q and X turrets.
IV. Medium shot off port beam as HMS *Temeraire* passes, followed by HMS *Bellerophon*. Land in the background.
V. Random collection of individual shots: Royal Sovereign Class battleships at sea; profiles of Thornycroft V Class destroyer and HMS *Renown*; Iron Duke Class battleships under way – balloon overhead; medium shot off starboard bow of Orion Class battleship; medium shot of Lion Class battle-cruiser (HMS *Princess Royal* ?) under way; Royal Sovereign Class battleships at sea; medium shot profile of HMS *Canada* passing behind (?) HMS *Queen Elizabeth* in anchorage – steam pinnace in foreground; battleships in line astern – Iron Duke immediately astern of cameraship, flashes a signal; long shot off port bow of three battleships steaming in line, dense funnel smoke blowing away to starboard – first and second ships open fire.
VI. First Battle Cruiser Squadron: medium-long shot starboard profile of Lion Class battle-cruiser under way, and pan right to HMS *Tiger* and HMS *Renown*. Repeat pan along the line – V/W Class destroyer in the background. Medium shot off starboard bow of *Tiger*.
VII. Medium close-up of wake of cameraship – pan up to Orion Class battleship astern, and right to second line of battleships. Miscellaneous shots of battleships steaming in line – Royal Sovereign Class, Iron Dukes, Second Battle Squadron, etc.
VIII. Medium shot profile of submarine K.2.
IX. Medium shot of V/W Class destroyer at speed – second vessel in the background.
X. Medium shot of Fifth Battle Squadron in line ahead. Long shot of Iron Duke Class battleships at sea. Medium shot starboard profile of Lion Class battle-cruiser under way, guns trained over the port beam.

catalogued NAP: 3/1978

IWM 1146 · GB, (ca) 1917
[JUTLAND AND AFTER 4] (allocated)

b/w · 1 reel · 1025' (17 mins) · silent
intertitles: none

sp Admiralty *pr* Engholm, F W
cam Engholm, F W

■ Miscellaneous British naval material, 1916-18.

I. Destroyers in anchorage. Medium shot of

HMS *Parker* (G.75). Pan to neighbouring line of moored destroyers and depot ship (*Aquarius* ?).
II. Sixth Battle Squadron passes beneath Forth Bridge.
III. Medium shot of Queen Elizabeth Class battleship in line ahead as it fires to starboard. Medium shots of Iron Duke Class battleships. Medium close-up, port fore-body of an anchored Talisman Class destroyer as cameraship passes, and track onto medium shot off port beam of HMS *Whirlwind* (H.41), with an Admiralty M Class steaming left to right in the background, and a moored Hawthorn M Class destroyer. Medium shot off the port quarter of a line of destroyers at their moorings, secured bows-on to the shore – one of the ships is a Marksman Class Leader.
IV. Static medium shot port profile of HMS *Canada*.
V. Three Admiralty M Class destroyers approach in line astern.
VI. Medium-long shot off starboard quarter of a Lion Class battle-cruiser under way at sea.
VII. Long shot of line of surrendering German battleships – Koenig Class vessel in the van. Medium-long shot off the port bow of Kaiser Class battleship (*Koenig Albert* ?).
VIII. High angle medium shot as Iron Duke Class battleship passes beneath Forth Bridge (*cf*. **IWM 554-03**).
IX. Miscellaneous shots: Royal Sovereign Class battleships at sea with escorting V/W Class destroyer; medium shot off the starboard bow of an Orion Class battleship; extreme long shot of two Iron Dukes – V/W Class destroyer in the foreground; medium shot off starboard bow of HMS *Pylades* (G.62) as she passes at speed followed by a second destroyer; medium shot of an Admiralty M Class destroyer as it passes in front of a Lion Class battle-cruiser; Admiralty M Class and Marksman Class Leader with Orion Class battleship in the background – camera tracks left to Queen Elizabeth Class battleship, with Special I Class and Admiralty M Class destroyers in background; medium shot of Royal Sovereign Class battleship as cameraship approaches on the port quarter; medium shot of M Class destroyers zigzagging in line astern; Royal Sovereign Class battleships steam in line astern for a shoot – they fire to port; HMS *Canada* under way; long shot of Orion Class battleships, with escorting V/W Class destroyer in mid-ground; three Iron Dukes steam to leeward for a shoot – third ship fires to port, the second to starboard; Queen Elizabeth Class battleship at sea with escorting V/W Class destroyer. Long

shot of V/W and Admiralty S Class destroyers, and medium shot port profile of Marksman Class Leader, with Admiralty M Class in the background; SMS *Koenigsberg* under way and at Rosyth; Royal Sovereign Class battleships of First Battle Squadron at firing practice; medium shot profile as two King George V Class battleships cross the screen right to left; Orion Class ships of Second Battle Squadron steam in line led by Queen Elizabeth – escorting destroyers are Admiralty M, Marksman Class Leader, Admiralty S, and Special I Class; extreme long shot of Royal Sovereign Class battleships in line astern.

catalogued NAP: 3/1978

IWM 1147 · GB, (ca) 1917
[JUTLAND AND AFTER 5] (allocated)

b/w · 1 reel · 1319' (22 mins) · silent
intertitles: none

sp Admiralty *pr* Engholm, F W
cam Engholm, F W

- Miscellaneous British naval material, 1916-18.

I. Medium close-up of cameraship's wake, and pan up to four battleships in line astern, an Orion Class vessel leading. Kite balloon overhead.
II. Two sequences showing elements of Second Battle Squadron running abreast for a shoot (*cf*. **IWM 1143**).
III. Miscellaneous long shots of battleships at firing practice – Iron Duke, Orion, and Queen Elizabeth Classes.
IV. SMS *Koenigsberg* at Rosyth (*cf*. **IWM 1143**).
V. Medium-long shot of Orion Class battleships steaming in line astern for a shoot.
VI. Medium shot as HMS *Temeraire* and HMS *Bellerophon* pass the camera (*cf*. **IWM 1145**).
VII. Medium shot off the port beam and medium-long shot off the port quarter of a Royal Sovereign Class battleship under way at sea.
VIII. Medium shot of HMS *Renown*.
IX. Miscellaneous shots of Iron Duke, Orion and Royal Sovereign Class battleships at sea.
X. Medium shot into the wake of the cameraship, a Queen Elizabeth Class battleship, and pan up to extreme long shot of US battleships of Sixth Battle Squadron in line astern with escorting destroyers.

XI. Medium shot starboard profile of submarine, K.2.

XII. Medium shot of two V/W Class destroyers steaming at speed.

XIII. Medium shot of a Queen Elizabeth Class battleship in line ahead, after turrets trained over the port beam.

XIV. Medium shot of a Lion Class battle-cruiser under way.

XV. Medium shot off the starboard bow of an Orion Class battleship.

XVI. Lion Class battle-cruiser signals.

XVII. HMS *Canada* passes behind HMS *Queen Elizabeth* in anchorage (*cf.* **IWM 1145**).

XVIII. First Battle Cruiser Squadron – pan from Lion Class battle-cruiser to HMS *Tiger* and *Renown* (*cf.* **IWM 1145**).

XIX. Royal Sovereign Class battleships in line on the horizon – stern of an Iron Duke in the foreground. Two of the Royal Sovereign Class ships open fire.

XX. Queen Elizabeth Class battleship and Orions steam in line with a destroyer escort (Special I Class, presumably HMS *Oak*, Marksman Class Leader and Admiralty M Class).

XXI. Medium-long shot off the port bow as a line of three Iron Dukes turns to starboard.

catalogued NAP: 3/1978

IWM 1148 · GB, 17/7/1924
TOPICAL BUDGET 673-1

b/w · 1 reel · 132' (2 min) · silent
intertitles: English

pr Topical Film Company

■ Fleet assembling for the 1924 Spithead Review.

"A NAVAL OCCASION. Atlantic Fleet sweeps down Channel for the Spithead Review." Opening medium shot off the starboard bow of HMS *Caledon* (?), with superimposed binocular frame – *Caledon* turns to port. "Giant Battleships looming like castles" – Royal Sovereign and Queen Elizabeth Class battleships of First and Second Battle Squadrons steam in line ahead – the leading Queen Elizabeth fires a salute. Extreme long shot of escorting destroyers. Medium shot off the port beam as submarine M.3 surfaces "like some great sea monster", and simulates the firing of its 11-inch gun. Medium shot of HMS *Queen Elizabeth* in the van – the camera vessel crossing from a position on her starboard bow to one off the port beam.

catalogued NAP: 9/1978

IWM 1149 · GB, 31/7/1924
TOPICAL BUDGET 675-1

b/w · 1 reel · 209' (3 min) · silent
intertitles: English

pr Topical Film Company

■ 1924 Spithead Review.

"THE KING AND HIS FLEET." Opening medium shot of Queen Elizabeth Class battleships lying anchored in quarter line, dressed overall, with crews manning the sides. King George V reviews "Britain's Sure Shield" – medium and medium-long shots from *Enchantress* steaming in the wake of the Royal Yacht *Victoria and Albert* as she passes anchored *Queen Elizabeth*. Medium close-ups of some of the dignitaries on board the cameraship – Ramsay MacDonald and members of his cabinet (J H Thomas, Henderson, Olivier, Lord Thomson, etc), Lord Chelmsfield, Admiral Beatty, M Herriot of France and M Theunis of Belgium. High angle medium shot off the port bow of HMS *Royal Sovereign* in review order – she fires a salute. The King takes the salute – he has his back to the camera. High angle medium shot from the foretop to the quarterdeck of *Victoria and Albert* – the crew line the rail. Medium close-up as the Royal Yacht passes HMS *Weymouth*. "Ships die, but the Navy lives – war scarred veterans of the Battle of Jutland" – high angle view of *Royal Sovereign* and companions. *Victoria and Albert* passes a Cambrian Class light cruiser – two V/W Class destroyers in the background. Final sequence on HMS *Revenge* (?) – high angle medium shot from the control top onto the fo'c's'le, followed by reciprocal view from the centre line of the fo'c's'le, panning down from the control top to A turret.

catalogued NAP: 9/1978

IWM 1150 · GB, (?) 1917
[SOPWITH DOLPHIN] (allocated)

b/w · 1 reel · 107' (2 mins) · silent
intertitles: English

■ Final part of film showing preparation and flight of British single-seat fighter which entered service in late 1917.

Pilot tests engine and controls of Sopwith 5F.1 Dolphin (serial number C4130) and mechanic attempts to swing propeller. Line of three Dolphins start up and are lifted round so as to taxi into the position which the Squadron will take up in the air. Three Dolphins take off abreast. General airfield activity with planes taking off and caption "Overseas hangars" (numbered frame indicates that this should precede Dolphins taking off abreast). Several Dolphins fly low over airfield in different flight formations. Final shot is aerial view from one fighter to another following.

catalogued: KGTG 2/1987

IWM 1151 · GB, 1918
[MISCELLANEOUS FIRST WORLD WAR NAVAL MATERIAL 3] (allocated)

b/w · 1 reel · 586' (10 mins) · silent
intertitles: none

sp Admiralty pr Engholm, F W
cam Engholm, F W

■ Collection of miscellaneous naval scenes from the First World War.

I. Submarine K.2 runs hull down and submerged.
II. Mine-sweeping trawler *Warstar* (GY.73) recovers kite.
III. Medium close-up off the port bow and medium shot, starboard bow to stern, as an Erebus Class monitor passes.
IV. Aerial medium shot of three Motor Launches under way at speed.
V. Medium shot off the starboard quarter of two paddle mine-sweepers.
VI. Medium close-up and medium shot as HMS *Queen Elizabeth* passes the camera – HMS *Valiant* in the background.
VII. Medium shot of HMS *Collingwood* at Scapa, and pan right over Orion Class battleship, HMS *Neptune*, HMS *Saint Vincent* and other ships, to medium shot *Hercules*. Cut to MS off the port bow of moored Queen Elizabeth Class battleship with a tender alongside – mooring boom of the camership in the foreground. Medium shot along the fo'c's'le of a battleship anchored at Scapa, as Officer of the Watch and ratings wait to receive a launch on the portside – pan left over Saint Vincent/Bellerophon and Colossus Class battleships to HMS *Saint Vincent*.
VIII. High angle medium shot as ratings march round quarterdeck before King George V. Marine band in the foreground.

IX. Medium shot off the port beam of HMS *Collingwood* – trawler, crowded with sailors, crosses the foreground. Pan right to show other vessels in the anchorage, including an Orion Class battleship. Medium shot as a trawler crosses the bows of a moored Queen Elizabeth Class battleship. Medium-long shot of a Renown Class battle-cruiser. Close-up track from the stern along the starboard side of an Arethusa Class cruiser (*Aurora* or *Undaunted*). Medium shot from the fo'c's'le to the starboard echelon turret, and pan across bridge front and A position on HMS *Hercules* – a crewman is climbing out along lower boom on portside. Medium close-up as ratings and marines of *Hercules* pass camera set up on deck.
X. Medium shot of HMS *Nimrod* (H.90) under way at sea. Medium-long shot pan along line of Iron Duke Class battleships steaming in quarter line, camership holding station on port quarter of HMS *Marlborough*.

catalogued NAP: 6/1978

IWM 1152 · GB, 1919
[MISCELLANEOUS FIRST WORLD WAR NAVAL MATERIAL 4] (allocated)

b/w · 1 reel · 608' (10 mins) · silent
intertitles: none

sp Admiralty pr Engholm, F W
cam Engholm, F W

I. Sopwith 1½ Strutters taking off and landing on HMS *Argus*, 1919 (?). Medium shot pan across a group of pilots standing before the chart house of HMS *Argus*. Medium close-up as lift brings up a Sopwith 1½ Strutter, F.7562, and pilot – a second aircraft is already on deck. F.7562 runs up and takes off. Second Sopwith takes off. Medium shot of Captain Smith at well deck conning position. Medium-long shot aft to approaching Sopwith – the aircraft aborts its landing. Second aircraft lands on, and the deck handling party approach – FDCO walks into frame, holding flags. Third aircraft comes in rather high, and brakes sharply as 'dog-leash' grabs on the undercarriage engage the safety net. Fourth aircraft lands on – too far to starboard, it veers into the centre of the flight deck. Three more aircraft alight. Destroyer holding station astern, intermittently obscured by the pitching flight deck. Medium close-up of anonymous Lieutenant-Commander, and pan left as an aircraft comes ahead along flight deck.
II. Various shots of a Queen Elizabeth Class

battleship leading the Orions of Second Battle Squadron. Escorts include Marksman Class Leader, Special I, and Admiralty M Class destroyers.
III. Medium shot off the port quarter of RN *Giulio Cesare* firing its main armament over the port beam – sequence intercut with shots of shell splashes near the target, and low angle close-up of a broadside fired from a Varese Class armoured cruiser (?). Long shot from on board an Italian warship approaching a small island. Medium shot along waist to where officers watch a rating at work in a stowed lifeboat – pan to passing coastline – puffs of smoke cross the screen (from a saluting gun ?).
IV. Medium shot of feather from a raised periscope moving across a calm sea – camera slowly closing.
V. Medium shot of Admiral Madden (?) and unidentified Rear-Admiral leaving a ship – in foreground, a Lieutenant salutes.
VI. Medium close-up of the battle honours (Jutland and Dover Straits) of HMS *Broke*.
VII. Fire-fighting – Italian ratings in fatigues carry picks, axes, etc. Hose lies on the ground. Warrant officer in the foreground.

catalogued NAP: 6/1978

---

by cameraship.
V. Tracking medium close-up, stern to starboard bow, of S.49 Class German destroyer.
VI. Medium shot of an Iron Duke Class battleship with a destroyer alongside. Medium close-up track along starboard afterbody of HMS *Canada*.
VII. Continuation of sequence III. Foremost vessel is *Drake*.
VIII. Cameraship crosses the bows of a surrendered G.85 Class destroyer, and passes down the portside.
IX. Tracking medium close-up from the starboard bow of HMS *Queen Elizabeth* at moorings – note range-finding baffles.
X. Continuation of sequence IV. Medium shot of PC.43 closing on starboard quarter.
XI. Forth anchorage. Two Orion Class battleships and HMS *Agincourt* cross the screen right to left.
XII. Long shot of four Royal Sovereign Class (?) battleships steaming in line astern for a shoot – the leading ship turns to starboard.
XIII. Sequences IV and I repeated.
XIV. Long shot of R Class (?) destroyer under way at sea, and medium-long shot of following ship, HMS *Trenchant* (G.78).

catalogued NAP: 6/1978

IWM 1153 · GB, 1918
[MISCELLANEOUS FIRST WORLD WAR NAVAL MATERIAL 5] (allocated)

b/w · 1 reel · 623' (10 mins) · silent
intertitles: none

sp Admiralty *pr* Engholm, F W
cam Engholm, F W

- Collection of miscellaneous naval scenes from the First World War.

I. 'Nash Fish' (hydrophone) is winched up and swung over the side of a PC boat.
II. Medium shot from an airship holding station off the starboard quarter, and slowly coming abeam of USS *Birmingham*. Aerial long shot of a destroyer, its wake disturbed by the explosion of a depth-charge. Medium shot of HMS *Valhalla* (G.45). Medium-long aerial shot of an R Class destroyer and K Class submarine.
III. Medium shot off the port bow of two trawlers moored together in harbour – one vessel draws away from its companion. C Class cruiser in the background.
IV. Medium-long shot from a PC boat to another astern – the following ship yaws slightly as it comes hard a'starboard into line. Close-up of black smoke screen laid

IWM 1154 · GB, 1918
[MISCELLANEOUS FIRST WORLD WAR NAVAL MATERIAL 6] (allocated)

b/w · 1 reel · 364' (6 mins) · silent
intertitles: none

sp Admiralty *pr* Engholm, F W
cam Engholm, F W

- Collection of miscellaneous naval scenes from the First World War.

I. Ship's boats and steam launches come alongside carrying marines. High angle medium shot onto quayside, as Marine band and detachments of RMLI march away after disembarkation. RMLI detachment passes camera set up in a public park.
II. Two CMBs approach at speed to pass either side of a moored barge carrying observers (*cf.* **IWM 567**).
III. High angle medium shot of Ostend sea front war memorial surrounded by German marines and sailors, and pan across crowd to sea front buildings (*cf.* **IWM 303**). Panning medium shot over coastal defences at Zeebrugge.
IV. Tracking medium close-up from

starboard bow to conning tower of UC.III Class submarine lying alongside U.139 at Harwich (*cf.* **IWM 560**). Medium shot as camera vessel approaches UC.58.

V. Close-up of Admiral Keyes. Medium shot as a group of Army and Royal Naval officers come up onto a pier.

VI. Close-up of 150mm gun of the Lubeck Battery and the Mole, Zeebrugge, and pan right to show railway lines as seen in sequence III.

VII. Continuation of sequence IV – track past U.139 and UC.III Class submarine (conning tower to stern).

VIII. Admiralty M Class destroyers steaming in line astern make a turn to port. HMS *Moorsom* (H.84), and HMS *Nugent* (F.54) are among the company.

IX. Sequence from **IWM 557**, *Ostend Re-occupied*, showing Gneisenau Battery, and extreme long shot of destroyers and an Erebus Class monitor offshore.

X. Medium shot of a camouflaged UB.133 Class U-boat under way near the coast. Long shot of UB.133 and UB.III Class boats. Camera vessel closes on a UC.II Class submarine – Ex-Greek M Class, another destroyer, and an ML in the background. End shot as camera vessel approaches U.43 (?) and a UE.1 Class boat.

catalogued NAP: 6/1978

IWM 1155 · GB, 1918
[MISCELLANEOUS FIRST WORLD WAR NAVAL MATERIAL 7] (allocated)

b/w · 1 reel · 826' (14 mins) · silent
intertitles: none

sp Admiralty *pr* Engholm, F W
cam Engholm, F W

■ Collection of miscellaneous naval scenes from the First World War.

I. High angle medium close-up of submarines H.34 and H.29 alongside camership. H.29, which lies outboard, makes sternway. Close-up of the conning tower of H.34 as crew cast off – in the background, H.29 swings round from port profile to bows on. H.29 and H.34 lie off, as a third submarine, not previously visible, makes sternway from its position alongside.

II. Medium shot off the port beam, and medium-long shot off the port quarter as PC.43 passes.

III. Interior of an Italian submarine – officer descends from the conning tower to use the periscope.

IV. Onboard medium close-up as some form of submarine detection equipment (?) is lowered over a ship's side.

V. Long shot of submarine H.33 surfacing, and medium shot off the port beam as she passes the camera. Pan over slight sea to hold on periscope feather. Medium shot to medium close-up of periscope cutting the surface (camera pitching badly in the swell). Aerial long shot of periscope wake, and medium-long shot passing over two K Class submarines.

VI. Medium shot from vessel approaching an unidentified waterfront.

VII. Medium shot over the stern of a vessel operating an A Type smoke apparatus – the smoke fills the frame.

VIII. U.162 passes left to right, the camera holding on her starboard quarter as she moves away, trailing diesel exhaust fumes. Long shot of the conning tower of a submerging submarine, framed to simulate binocular vision. Close-up of controller's hands on wheel controlling bearing of asdic gear. Further shots of U.162 intercut with PC boats (*cf.* **IWM 1153**), and submarine running at periscope depth. Final medium shot of H.33 running nearly submerged.

catalogued NAP: 6/1978

IWM 1156 · GB, 1918
[MISCELLANEOUS FIRST WORLD WAR NAVAL MATERIAL 8] (allocated)

b/w · 1 reel · 404' (7 mins) · silent
intertitles: none

sp Admiralty *pr* Engholm, F W
cam Engholm, F W

■ Collection of miscellaneous naval scenes from the First World War.

I. Aerial shots of a flight of Handley Page 0/400s over town and countryside (*cf.* **IWM 551, reel 7**).

II. RNAS accommodation huts face a small green populated by ducks. Medium close-up as a kite balloon is released (*cf.* **IWM 570, reel 2**).

III. Sopwith Pup takes off from aerodrome and makes a series of low passes. BE2c and a Pup take off. Panning medium shot along a line of parked aircraft, including a Pup and a Bristol Scout D.

IV. Sopwith Baby takes off and circles – pier in the background. Medium close-up as ground crew manhandle Baby No 8145.

V. Long shot as three Handley Page 0/400s go over, and aerial shots of their formation.

VI. Medium shot of Royal Sovereign Class battleship under way in a slight sea. Medium close-up of HMS *Offa* (G.56) at speed. Medium shots of a white smoke screen at sea, then of two lines of destroyers astern of the cameraship. Moored V/W Class destroyer is passed by a torpedo boat (TB.81 at Portsmouth ?) – Botha Class Leader in extreme background. Medium close-up off the starboard bow of HMS *Moorsom* (H.84), and pan left to hold on following M Class destroyer.
VII. Aerial long shot as a patrol boat drops a depth-charge, which explodes in the ship's wake. Medium shot of ship's wake as depth-charge explodes astern.
VIII. Medium shot of M Class destroyer under way in rough sea – waves break over the fo'c's'le.
IX. Submarine E.23 submerges. Medium close-up amidships as surfaced boat fires 12-pounder (film badly scratched). Long shot of U.162 seen in a binocular frame (*cf.* **IWM 1155**).
X. Naval auxiliary (collier?) comes alongside cameraship.
XI. Forth anchorage. Medium shot of moored Royal Sovereign Class battleship with submarine alongside. Two more Royal Sovereigns in the background.
XII. Continuation of sequence X. Auxiliary makes away from the cameraship.

catalogued NAP: 6/1978

IWM 1157 · GB, 1918
[MISCELLANEOUS FIRST WORLD WAR NAVAL MATERIAL 9] (allocated)

b/w · 1 reel · 702' (12 mins) · silent
intertitles: none

sp Admiralty *pr* Engholm, F W
cam Engholm, F W

▪ Collection of miscellaneous naval scenes from the First World War.

I. Long shot across anchorage at Scapa at sunset – afterpart of a battleship, showing X and Y turrets, at frame right, and starboard profile of Arethusa Class (?) cruiser.
II. Medium shot of Admiralty Steel Drifter under way on calm sea.
III. Medium close-up of X and Y turrets on HMS *Canada*, camera holding as the camera vessel passes by on the starboard side of the battleship.
IV. Medium-long shot of merchant hull alongside in shipyard, and pan to a tug towing two barges.

V. Medium shot silhouette of HMS *Venerable* as a depot ship at Portland (*cf.* **IWM 559**).
VI. Medium close-up off port quarter of slowly passing Royal Sovereign Class battleship. Medium shot of moored Iron Duke Class battleship, an awning over Q turret, with a sistership in the background – HMS *Nonsuch* (G.38) and tender in the foreground alongside cameraship.
VII. Medium shot of HMS *Venerable* with iris fade and straight fade effects.
VIII. Medium close-up of Q turret and after superstructure of HMS *Canada*, camera moving left to show rear turrets and long shot of an Orion Class battleship. Medium shot of Queen Elizabeth Class battleship – X turret trained over port bow.
IX. US troops board lighter alongside quay.
X. Medium shot of wharf with PC boats and Later Hunt Class (?) minesweeper alongside. Medium shot as PC.56 crosses crowded harbour – minesweeper, freighter and drill ship (?) in the background.
XI. Medium-long shot of E or H Class submarine at sea.
XII. Medium shot, passing HMS *Vulcan*, depot ship at Portsmouth. PC boat in the background.
XIII. Medium shot of unidentified RN Commander on upper deck, and a bridge scene on board a PC boat.
XIV. Destroyers in line astern of cameraship. Destroyer funnel makes black smoke. Aerial long shot of M or R Class destroyer, just come hard a'port.
XV. Medium close-up of crew on the conning tower of submarine E.5 (?). HMS *Moon* (F.69) passes cameraship at sea. Medium close-up of hydrophone operator. PC boat holds station on cameraship's starboard quarter (*cf.* **IWM 1153**).
XVI. Men recover ASW detection apparatus (*cf.* **IWM 1153**).
XVII. Long shot of oil storage lighter and a flat bottomed ferry, with land background and circular frame effect.
XVIII. Long shot of Astre-Torres type C airship escorting a convoy.
XIX. Medium shot off the port beam of HMS *Gibraltar*, depot ship with *Vulcan* at Portsmouth. Frame left cuts off fo'c's'le.
XX. Medium shot off the starboard quarter of HMS *Agincourt* under way in anchorage.
XXI. As sequence XVII.
XXII. As sequence XI.

Notes
Summary: synopsis excludes some less important or repeated sequences.
catalogued NAP: 6/1978

IWM 1158 · GB, 1918
**[MISCELLANEOUS FIRST WORLD WAR
NAVAL MATERIAL 10]** (allocated)

b/w · 1 reel · 223' (4 mins) · mute
intertitles: none

- Collection of miscellaneous naval scenes
  from the First World War.

A steamer moves left to right across
anchorage. Medium shot of 150mm gun of
the Gneisenau battery in front of the Royal
Palace Hotel, Ostend in October 1918, after
the German withdrawal. Medium shot men
at work stoking ship's coal-fired boilers. HM
King George V and Beatty inspect the
hospital ship *Plassy*. Medium-long shot of
submarine hull down at sea. Medium shot
on board a United States ship – crew are
crowded onto quarterdeck around jackstaff
flying Stars and Stripes. Ground crew
straighten folding wings of a Short Bomber
and the engine is run up for take-off. A flight
of BE2cs start up. Medium shot of BE2c No
1738. Medium shot as a Felixstowe flying
boat is brought up slip to join two others.
Close-up of Admiral Sims, USN, who
salutes for the camera. Long shot as Short
seaplane goes over. Medium shot of
Felixstowe flying left to right and sequence
shot from the aircraft as it takes off in
company with a second flying boat.

catalogued NAP: 2/1987

IWM 1159 · GB, 1918
**[MISCELLANEOUS FIRST WORLD WAR
NAVAL MATERIAL 11]** (allocated)

b/w · 1 reel · 249' (4 mins) · silent
intertitles: none

sp Admiralty *pr* Engholm, F W
cam Engholm, F W

- Collection of miscellaneous naval scenes
  from the First World War.

I. Commander Taussig USN disembarks
from USS *Wadsworth*. Vice-Admiral Bayly,
back to the camera, greets the Commander
and his officers (*cf.* **IWM 562**).
II. Harwich. Medium close-up track from
port bow to stern past five U-boats moored
together after surrender – UB.143 with a
U.23 and UC.III Class boats. Long shot
along rows of moored U-boats, stern on to
the camera – the nearest group consists of
a UC.III and two U.105 Class (?)
submarines.

III. Queenstown. USS *Wadsworth* (60) and
USS *Porter* (59) pass by. Medium shot of
US destroyers in line astern at sea – USS
Davis (65) is in the van.
IV. U-boat crews being repatriated – High
angle medium shot as German sailors
come on board cameraship from Motor
Launch. Medium shot off the port beam of
SMS *Koenigsberg*. Medium close-up of
submarine UC.58 from a launch closing on
the port quarter (*cf.* **IWM 1154**), and then
making off on the same bearing. Long shot
from a vessel steaming between two lines
of surrendered U-boats.
V. Repeated medium shot of an explosion
at sea – the detonation of a mine (*cf.* **IWM
551, reel 6**).
VI. Medium shot as SMS *Derfflinger* passes
right to left (*cf.* **IWM 571**). End frame shows
amidships, portside of a Kaiser Class
battleship (*Kaiser* or *Friedrich der Grosse*).

catalogued NAP: 6/1978

IWM 1160 · GB, 1918
**[MISCELLANEOUS FIRST WORLD WAR
NAVAL MATERIAL 12]** (allocated)

b/w · 1 reel · 422' (7 mins) · silent
intertitles: none

sp Admiralty *pr* Engholm, F W
cam Engholm, F W

- Collection of miscellaneous naval scenes
  from the First World War.

I. Long shot as SS airship passes across
sky background.
II. Interior medium close-up of Italian officer
at the periscope in submarine's control
room (*cf.* **IWM 1155**).
III. Onboard low angle medium shot of
black smokescreen generated by a PC
boat. High angle medium shot from
foremast, showing W/T spreaders between
fore- and mainmast.
IV. Quarterdeck of HMS *Queen Elizabeth* –
a Japanese admiral salutes a British
counterpart (*cf.* **IWM 572**).
V. Long shot of a seaplane in flight. High
angle medium shot from the bridge of HMS
Furious to the forward aircraft hold, and pan
forward to the end of the flight deck – two
Short Admiralty Type 184 seaplanes are on
deck.
VI. A Type smoke apparatus operating on
the quarterdeck of the camera vessel (*cf.*
IWM 574).
VII. Medium shot from fo'c's'le to B turret
and bridge of HMS *Canada*, and pan up

foremast to control top. Two photographers, standing near the port semaphore, take pictures of the anchorage – partially obscured, in the background, lies HMS *Superb*.

VIII. Medium shot as officers returning from shore leave go on board steam launches lying alongside a pier.

IX. Medium shot of PC.43 as it leaves harbour, and at sea, turning hard a'starboard to follow the cameraship (*cf.* **IWM 1153**).

X. Pan across docks – merchantman alongside, barge in midstream.

XI. Low angle medium shot as airship SS24 turns to starboard. Felixstowe flying boat goes over.

XII. As sequence III. PC boats make smoke.

XIII. Radio operator receives a message (?) – RNR sub-lieutenant uses telephone in a radio shack.

XIV. Medium shot off the port beam as HMS *Revenge* passes.

XV. Medium shot to bridge of HMS *Furious* – Sopwith Pup suspended from aircraft derrick in the foreground, having been lifted from the hold. The aircraft is lowered onto the deck, and the handling party comes ahead with it, directly towards the camera.

XVI. Queenstown. British and US sailors walk the sea front – Hunt Class minesweeper in the background.

XVII. Various medium shots and tracking medium close-up from the stern to port bow of HMS *Canada* as she lies in anchorage, flying the Blue Peter. HMS *Queen Elizabeth*, and Orion and Bellerophon/Saint Vincent Class battleships in long and extreme long shot background.

catalogued NAP: 6/1978

IWM 1161 · GB, 1918
[MISCELLANEOUS FIRST WORLD WAR NAVAL MATERIAL 13] (allocated)

b/w · 1 reel · 569' (10 mins) · silent intertitles: none

sp Admiralty *pr* Engholm, F W
cam Engholm, F W

■ Collection of miscellaneous naval scenes from the First World War.

I. Medium shot off the starboard bow of Royal Sovereign Class battleship at night as the ship's searchlight battery sweeps the water. Cambrian Class light cruiser (*Calliope* or *Champion* ?) is illuminated by a battery and by a single searchlight

sweeping from the port bow to stern. Medium shot off the port bow of a Royal Sovereign Class battleship, its forepart illuminated by searchlights.

II. Quarterdeck of a battleship. Two midshipmen pass by, engrossed in conversation. Army officer walks towards the camera. Major, RA, wearing blues, sits on the guard rail, while his companion, a lieutenant, talks with one of the ship's officers, also a lieutenant.

III. Medium-long shot off port quarter of escorting Admiralty S Class (?) destroyer steaming at speed in choppy sea. Extreme long shot pan over distant line of battleships with escorting destroyers – the sky is stained with dense funnel smoke. High angle medium shot onto the fo'c's'le of HMS *Canada* as spray breaks over the bows. Medium shot of Queen Elizabeth Class battleship in line ahead with guns trained over the port beam. Long shot of escorting Modified R Class (?) destroyer, and pan along the destroyer screen. High angle medium shot to *Canada's* forward turrets, which train right. High angle medium shot aft down the starboard side, framing 6-inch casements and searchlight tower on the second funnel – Q, X and Y turrets train over the beam – camera pans down to ship's boats stowed between the funnels. Sequence showing the after turrets firing by single barrels – crewmen move about on the searchlight tower in the foreground. Medium shot from the fo'c's'le as the starboard secondaries open fire. Medium shot from the quarterdeck along the portside past X and Y turrets to range clock and 6-inch casements. Low angle medium shot of main gunnery R/F, starboard semaphore and bridge structure. Break. *Canada* in anchorage – ratings pass camera as they are dismissed by divisions from the evening inspection on the quarterdeck. A game of hockey is played on the quarterdeck.

catalogued NAP: 6/1978

IWM 1162 · GB, 1918
[MISCELLANEOUS FIRST WORLD WAR NAVAL MATERIAL 14] (allocated)

b/w · 1 reel · 152' (3 mins) · silent intertitles: English (sequence II)

sp Admiralty *pr* Engholm, F W
cam Engholm, F W

■ Collection of miscellaneous naval scenes from the First World War.

I. Admiral Wemyss on board USS *Melville* (*cf.* **IWM 564**).
II. "Arrival of the 'Devonian' at Liverpool with 59 on board". Medium shot off the port beam of SS *Devonian* under way. Medium close-up as survivors, including women and children, come down the gangway.
III. Medium shot as the crew of a lifeboat don sou'westers, life-jackets, etc. The boat is brought from its shed on a cradle traverser.
IV. Continuation of sequence I.
V. Low angle medium shot from starboard side of the fo'c's'le to forward turrets and bridge of HMS *Lion*. A rating walks out along the port gun barrel of A turret, and another, more cautious, crawls out to sit at the muzzle of port gun, B turret.

catalogued NAP: 6/1978

IWM 1163 · GB, 1918
[MISCELLANEOUS FIRST WORLD WAR NAVAL MATERIAL 15] (allocated)

b/w · 1 reel · 612' (10 mins) · silent
intertitles: none

sp Admiralty *pr* Engholm, F W
cam Engholm, F W

■ Collection of miscellaneous naval scenes from the First World War.

I. Medium shot, closing on the starboard quarter of an Italian 19 ton, Type 'B' MAS under way at speed, and a passing shot of MAS flotilla steaming in line, the camera vessel proceeding on an opposite course. RN *Aquila* crosses the screen right to left. Medium-long shot of Italian battleships in line ahead – the nearest ship is *Caio Duilio*. Sequence showing RN *Giulio Cesare* at a practice shoot (*cf.* **IWM 1152**).
II. Aerial views of a convoy escorted by an Astre-Torres type C airship.
III. Medium close-up of three drifters moored together – *Cluny Hill*, *Orion* and another.
IV. Medium shot of two Insect Class gunboats at their moorings.
V. Medium shot off the port beam of a drifter as it passes anchored transport (?).
VI. Medium shot of an Arkansas Class battleship, and pan over anchorage of the Fourth Battle Squadron from the quarterdeck of a US ship.
VII. Medium shot of HMS *Renown* under way – Thornycroft V/W Class destroyer in the background.
VIII. Long shot of Orions and Saint

Vincent/Bellerophon Class battleships in line ahead – possibly the 1914 Spithead Review.
IX. As sequence IV. Medium close-up of gunboat's crew washing in canvas baths rigged on the quarterdeck.
X. Marine (RMA) fires a Lewis gun mounted on ship's guard rail – Fusilier wearing Archangel star in the foreground. Officers observe the effects of the fire from the upper decks.
XI. Torpedo victims (?). Men disembark to be received by RSM. Motor ambulance passes by.
XII. Two Kaiser Class battleships pass right to left. Close-up as launch approaches UB.142 Class submarine – a German sailor catches boat's painter. Medium-long shot of U.43 and UE.I Class submarines (*cf.* **IWM 1154**).
XIII. As sequence VII. *Renown* under way. Thornycroft V/W Class destroyer, HMS *Woolston* (?), passes the battle-cruiser – HMS *Lion* in the background at frame left.
XIV. Medium shot as admirals walk from the quarterdeck of HMS *Queen Elizabeth* – Rodman, Phillimore, Japanese delegation.
XV. As sequence XII. Launch is secured alongside UB.142 Class U-boat.
XVI. Motor Launch poled off the side of cameraship – Caledon Class cruiser in the background. High angle medium shot to forepart of a group of MLs secured alongside.
XVII. Medium shot off the port bow of a Koenig Class battleship.
XVIII. Flotilla of German destroyers under way at speed.
XIX. Hydrophone operator at work – having obtained a fix he communicates with the bridge.
XX. Medium shot on the port quarter of HMS *Renown* under way – A and B turrets are trained over the starboard beam.

Notes
Summary: synopsis excludes some less important sequences.
catalogued NAP: 6/1978

IWM 1164 · GB, 1918
[MISCELLANEOUS FIRST WORLD WAR NAVAL MATERIAL 16] (allocated)

b/w · 1 reel · 853' (14 mins) · silent
intertitles: none

sp Admiralty *pr* Engholm, F W
cam Engholm, F W

■ Collection of miscellaneous naval scenes from the First World War.

I. 9.2-inch coastal gun is reloaded.
II. Medium shot of HMS *Walker* (G.08) steaming at speed in a slight sea. Medium close-up of a sailor of HMS *Woolston*, playing with a kitten.
III. Long shot views of surrendering German destroyers and their British escorts. Long shot of SMS *Kaiser*, and pan left to *Koenig Albert*.
IV. Medium shot off the port beam of a King George V battleship – the frame cuts bow and stern.
V. Flotilla of coastal motor boats at sea.
VI. Tracking medium close-up past starboard fore-body of a Royal Sovereign Class battleship. HMS *Iron Duke* passes beneath the Forth Bridge.
VII. Medium shot of SMS *Bremse* under way.
VIII. Medium shot off the port bow of a King George V Class battleship. The fo'c's'le is crowded with crewmen.
IX. Medium-long shot from the bridge of a battleship, her crew manning the side, as she closes on HMS *Canada*. Medium shot of *Canada* as HMS *Oak* (92) heaves to alongside. Steam launch, flying the Royal Standard, approaches from *Oak*. View from control top.
X. Admiral Wemyss and Captain Pringle USN (*cf.* **IWM 564**). Close-up of anonymous commodore RN, and junior officers.
XI. Medium shot off the starboard beam of HMS *Bellerophon* in anchorage.
XII. SMS *Koenigsberg* and *Frankfurt* pass right to left. Long shot of an airship over line of surrendering German destroyers.
XIII. HMS *Orpheus* (F.17) and HMS *Anzac* (G.70) go past – sea conditions vary between shots.
XIV. SMS *Seydlitz* under way.
XV. Frontal close-up of a destroyer's 4-inch gun.
XVI. Camera vessel closes on UC.58 (*cf.* **IWM 1154**).
XVII. HMS *Norman* (G.54) passes at speed in slight sea.
XVIII. Medium shot of SMS *Derfflinger* as camera vessel crosses her starboard bow.
XIX. Naval ratings stand with sloped arms, ready for inspection.
XX. Medium shot off the port beam of a Royal Sovereign Class battleship under way. Fo'c's'le cut by frame. Ship moves off-screen. Land background.
XXI. HMS *Vindictive* alongside jetty.
XXII. Trawlers alongside quay.
XXIII. US Men's Club, Queenstown (*cf.* **IWM 564**).
XXIV. Medium shot off the port bow of a Koenigsberg (II) Class light cruiser. Medium-long shot of UE.1 and U.43 Class submarines. Medium shot of camouflaged UB.133 Class vessel (*cf.* **IWM 1154**).
XXV. High angle medium shot from the control top down the starboard side, HMS *Canada*. Reverse low angle medium shot of the bridge and R/F.
XXVI. Medium shot as HMS *Renown* passes right to left.
XXVII. As sequence XXI.
XXVIII. High angle medium shot of motor launches moored alongside – including ML.397, ML.559 and ML.351. A crewman uncovers 3-pounder deck gun – in the background, crewmen of two other launches watch him and the camera. Sequence showing MLs laying a smokescreen at sea.
XXIX. Beatty on board HMS *Queen Elizabeth* after the presentation of the Order of the Rising Sun, Grand Cordon. Medium close-up of Beatty, Madden and Funakoshi. Facial close-up of Rear-Admiral Funakoshi – he salutes.

catalogued NAP: 6/1978

IWM 1165 · GB, 1918
[MISCELLANEOUS FIRST WORLD WAR NAVAL MATERIAL 17] (allocated)

b/w · 1 reel · 116' (2 mins) · silent
intertitles: none

sp Admiralty *pr* Engholm, F W
cam Engholm, F W

■ Scenes on board HMS *Canada*.

Medium shot from the fo'c's'le to A and B turrets and bridge – a canvas hatch tent is in the immediate foreground. Starboard barrel of A turret elevates, and port semaphore begins signalling. Camera pans right to show ship's boat being lifted inboard by a derrick – crewmen come forward to secure the wire rope around a bollard in the foreground. Pan down from the foremast control top to A turret, and right, to the portside of the ship, where a paravane is being hoisted outboard on a davit (*cf.* **IWM 591**).

catalogued NAP: 6/1978

IWM 1166 · GB, (after) 9/1917
**EXPERIMENT OF LAUNCHING
SEAPLANE BY CATAPULT METHOD :
carried out with Fairey Seaplane N9 on
HMS Slinger**

b/w · 1 reel · 518' (9 mins) · silent
intertitles: English

sp Admiralty *pr* Engholm, F W (?)
cam Engholm, F W (?)

▪ Catapult launching tests using seaplanes
   on board HMS *Slinger*.

Various close-ups of catapult on HMS
Slinger. Test baulk and a dummy aircraft
(Short 184 fuselage) are launched from the
moored vessel. Close-ups of the catapult
drive and release mechanisms. Frontal
close-up of Fairey F.127 in position on the
catapult. Medium shot of a successful
launching from *Slinger* whilst under way.
Medium shot off the port quarter of *Slinger*
while the seaplane circles the ship.

Notes
Summary: HMS *Slinger* was a steam hopper
specially commissioned for experiments
using a catapult system built by Messrs
Armstrong. First tests were made in
September 1917, in the Tyne. Also shown
are later trials conducted under Lt Col H R
Busteed, from June 1918, at the Isle of
Grain Experimental Aircraft Depot. The
Fairey F.127, Admiralty Number 9, was a
one-off development aircraft specially
strengthened for the trials. Some of this
material was used in the compilation *The
50th Anniversary of the Fleet Air Arm*, COI
302.
[shotsheet available]
catalogued NAP: 6/1978

IWM 1167 · GB, 1918
**EXPERIMENTS IN LANDING
AEROPLANES AND SEAPLANES FROM
SHIP'S DECK**

b/w · 1 reel · 708' (12 mins) · silent
intertitles: English

sp Royal Air Force for Admiralty *pr* Royal Air
Force – London Photo Centre

▪ Compilation film of various RAF methods
   of ship-launching aircraft developed in
   1917 and 1918.

I. The steam catapult trials carried out at the
Armstrong Whitworth plant, Elswick, and

later at the Experimental Aircraft Depot, Isle
of Grain. A steam catapult fitted to HMS
Slinger is used firstly to launch a dummy
seaplane, then the Fairey F127, Admiralty
Number 9, which takes off successfully
launched by the catapult.
II. Preliminary trials of a Sopwith 1½ Strutter
fitted with skids taking off from a set of
troughs at an aerodrome. Later the same
machine is launched from troughs built into
the deck of HMS *Vindex*, twice at different
air speeds.
III. Trials of launching a Sopwith Pup from
an experimental deck built on land at the
Isle of Grain. The Pup has small running
wheels fitted to the underside of its lower
wings, and these fit into raised running rails,
so that the fuselage and undercart of the
aircraft is held clear of the ground. The Pup
performs two successful launches from
these rails.

Notes
Summary: see also **IWM 1166**.
[H A Taylor, *Fairey Aircraft Since 1915*,
Putnam (1974): 67-70]
catalogued SDB: 1/1984

IWM 1168 · GB, 1918
**SEAPLANE FLYING OFF DECK OF HMS
CAMPANIA**

b/w · 1 reel · 740' (12 mins) · silent
intertitles: English

sp Royal Air Force *pr* Royal Air Force –
London Photo Centre

▪ Demonstration launching of a seaplane
   from HMS *Campania* at anchor in the
   Firth of Forth, 5 July 1918.

The aircraft is a Fairey Campania type
seaplane piloted by Lieutenant Hay. Two
camera views are shown (one after the
other rather than intercut), one from the
bows, the other from the stern. The aircraft
is hoisted up from below and prepared for
flight. It takes off, flies one circuit, lands,
taxis back to the ship and is hoisted on
board again.

Notes
Title: this is a flashframe.
[shotsheet available]
catalogued SDB: 1/1984

IWM 1169 · GB, 1918
[LAUNCH PLATFORM OF HMS REPULSE] (allocated)

b/w · 1 reel · 568' (10 mins) · silent
intertitles: English

- Demonstration launch of an aircraft from the B turret launch platform of HMS *Repulse* at anchor in the Firth of Forth, summer 1918.

Two views are shown, firstly from the bridge looking directly down onto the aircraft, then from the bow looking towards the stern. Between the two camera-views the Firth of Forth can be briefly seen with HMS *Tiger* at anchor. The aircraft is a single-seat Sopwith 1½ Strutter. Firstly, the wooden platform is fitted out over the guns of B turret, the sections fitting onto guide rails, then the turret is trained to starboard and the aircraft launched, then the platform is disassembled. At the end of the film, viewed from the bows, both forward turrets are trained to starboard and the guns elevated.

Notes
Intertitles: these are all flashframes.
Summary: this is probably an RAF official film, although there is no direct evidence for this. Compare with **IWM 1168**.
[shotsheet available]
catalogued SDB: 1/1984

IWM 1170 · GB, (after) 1918
[RAF RETROSPECTIVE FILM] (allocated)

b/w · 1 reel · 1100' (20 mins) · silent
intertitles: English

- First reel of a retrospective compilation on the role of the RAF in winning the First World War.

The film describes the achievements of "the Cavalry of the Clouds". It starts with an RAF squadron in France in 1918 (actually 84 Squadron at Bertangles) being briefed and taking off in their SE5as. They cooperate with the advance of the Cavalry and Infantry (all training scenes) before flying off into the sunset. The contribution of RAF airships to defeating German submarines is shown. An officer puts on a harness and is hoisted up into airship R26, tethered some distance above the ground. Airship NS7 on patrol over the North Sea spots a U-boat (actually a British L Class submarine) and calls in a destroyer to sink it. A Sopwith Cuckoo torpedo bomber makes an attack against

the submarine (actually training film). On return the airship flies over "the city of York" and "York Castle" (probably Windsor). An SSZ airship continues on patrol. The contribution of the "floating aerodromes", the aircraft carriers, starts with HMS *Campania*. A Fairey Campania seaplane is launched from its deck and "after a long vigil" returns and is taken on board. (Actually a training flight in the Firth of Forth, 5 July 1918.) A two-seater Sopwith 1½ Strutter is launched from the flight platform over the turret of HMS *Australia*. The flight platform is built out over B turret of HMS *Repulse* and another 1½ Strutter is launched. Finally, a Sopwith Snipe landing on the deck of the aircraft carrier HMS *Furious*. One of the landings is misjudged and the aircraft tips over into the sea. (Although claimed as more than one operational aircraft, this is in fact film of the alighting trials with a test pilot.) The film ends with "End of Part One".

Notes
Summary: although persistently described as operational material, nearly all this film is of training exercises and prototype trials. See in particular **IWM 648**, **IWM 865**, **IWM 867**, **IWM 1168** and **IWM 1169**.
catalogued SDB: 1/1984

IWM 1171 · NO FILM

IWM 1172 · GB, (ca) 1970
MRS JOHN BULL PREPARED : a shortened version of a First World War Propaganda Film

tinted · 1 reel · 366' (6 mins) · comopt
intertitles: English

music performer (pianist) de Jong, Florence

- Fictional account of the contribution of women to the British war effort by 1918.

The film has a piano accompaniment soundtrack. It begins in 1914 and the outbreak of the war. Mr Smith, a prosperous businessman, is starting to lose staff who have volunteered for the Army and he refuses women replacements. He also prevents his son volunteering since the war will be over by Christmas and he needs his help. He is enraged at his two daughters, telling them that even in war "a woman's place is at home". In his garden the Spirit of British Womanhood appears and puts him to sleep for four years. She then wakes him and he staggers off. He returns home to find that his home is now a hostel for wounded soldiers run by his wife and daughters as WAACs. His son has lost an arm and is staying there. As the family dine together that night he receives his final surprise: military service age has been increased to fifty and he is being called up. On this comic note the film ends.

Notes
Production: this version of the film was made available by the Imperial War Museum for the BBC *Yesterday's Witness* series *Women at War*.
Summary: see **IWM 521** for the full silent version of this film.
catalogued SDB: 1/1984

IWM 1173 · NOT INCLUDED

IWM 1174 · GB, (prod) 1920
[BRITISH TANKS IN COLOGNE]
(allocated)

b/w · 1 reel · 103' (2 mins) · silent
intertitles: none

■ Arrival of 5th Battalion, Royal Tank Corps, in Cologne, probably April 1920.

The British reverse their Mk V Male tanks into a courtyard in the centre of the city, to the interest of the civilian crowd. The men perform maintenance on their tanks, while soldiers and armed German civilians guard them. The crowd, including some curious children, is kept at bay by the sentries. The children are shown in close-up.

Notes
Summary: according to Liddell Hart, 5th Battalion was not part of the British occupation force until 1920.
[B H Liddell Hart, *The Tanks – the History of the Royal Tank Regiment ...*, Vol I, Cassell (1959): 203-204]
catalogued SDB: 1/1984

IWM 1175 · GB, (ca) 1925
PATHE'S ANIMATED HISTORY OF THE GREAT WAR – PART 22 CHAPTER 3

b/w · 1 reel · 749' (12 mins) · silent
intertitles: English

pr Pathé

■ Effects around the world of the outbreak of the First World War, and its progress into 1915.

In Havana, Cuba, 6000 factory hands thrown out of work by the effect of the war on trade protest outside the Congress. In Lisbon the Portuguese send troops, shown leaving by ship, to Angola (Portuguese West Africa) in case of an attack from German South-West Africa. In New York a parade led by women demonstrates in favour of immediate peace. The SS *Hamburg*, bought and equipped by the US Red Cross as a hospital ship, sails from New York for Europe. Italy, proclaiming neutrality in July 1914, sends troops to its mountain borders with Austria-Hungary for training. The troops march through the mountain passes, throwing up a lot of dust. Veterans of Garibaldi's uprising and the unification of 1860 hold a mass gathering to encourage the liberation of Italians within the Austro-Hungarian Empire. An Italian Cavour Class battleship leaves harbour and practises gunnery at sea. Lord Kitchener visits General Joffre and his staff at Compiègne. He is met by Joffre, by General Foch, and by Minister of War Millerand (August 1915). They watch a demonstration from a training trench. Kitchener is also seen in London talking on the steps of a building with the Minister of Munitions, David Lloyd George. British troops (seen from a high angle) marching through a street to the cheers of the crowd, probably in France. British and French soldiers sit together at a rough table behind a lorry, talking and drinking wine. "Meanwhile the German hoards swept through Belgium." Led by their mounted officers men of the German 36th Fusilier Regiment march though a Belgian town, and then rest by the roadside. In reaction, recruiting sergeants of the London Regiment address a London crowd calling for volunteers. The reel ends with a montage of scenes of the Western Front and the British involvement in it, mainly from the later part of the war.

Notes
Summary: the caption style changes half-way through the reel, and it is not clear that the later scenes belong to the Pathé film. The German 36th Regiment was part of von Kluck's First Army, and fought at Mons.
catalogued SDB: 1/1984

IWM 1176 · GB, 1932
BLOCKADE
Q-SHIPS (GB 1928 – re-edited version)

b/w · 7 reels · 6033' (67 mins) · comopt
intertitles: none

pr New Era Productions *dir* Croise, Hugh
scr (dialogue) Barringer, Michael; and
Croise, Hugh *story* Barringer, Michael; and
Barkas, Geoffrey *cam* Blythe, Sydney; and
Dickenson, Desmond *ed* Croise, Hugh
rec Bower, Dallas *cast* Kennedy, J P (as
Admiral Sims); Travers, Roy (as Captain von
Haag); Auten, Harold (as himself); Jellicoe
(Earl) (as himself); Butt, Johnny; Hewland,
Philip; Herald, Douglas; Emerald, Charles;
Turner, George; d'Aragon, Lionel; Hurley,
Alec; O'Brien, Terence; Douglas, Hugh; and
Gielgud, Val.

- British feature film giving a fictionalised
  account of the German naval blockade of
  Britain in 1917, and how it was countered
  with the aid of the Q-ships.

(Reel 1) Off the British coast, U-boat 32
attacks merchant ships. The German
captain, Stackmeyer, is saluted by his
Admiral, who warns that the blockade of
Britain will be tightened; later, the U-boats
declare war on Allied commercial ships.
(Reel 2) American merchant ship harassed
by U-boat – America gets involved in the
war at sea. *(Reel 3)* Seamen's tavern –
merchant crew and Royal Navy men drink
on the eve of setting sail together. A plan
has been evolved to conceal a large gun on
board a merchant ship, lure a U-boat into
surfacing, then attack it. At sea, the plan
works, and the U-boat is badly damaged
and forced to retreat. *(Reel 4)* The German
Admiralty learns of this, and warns the U-
boat crews. Engagement at sea – U-boat
taken by surprise when depth-charges are
dropped upon it. The U-boat cuts off its
engines and stays at the bottom. *(Reel 5)*
Eventually it has to surface for air, and finds
that it has escaped. Another U-boat, sent to
attack the British Fleet at Scapa Flow, is
tracked on Asdic and destroyed as it
penetrates the British lines of defence. *(Reel
6)* Stackmeyer is placed in charge of the U-
boat campaign. At sea, his U-boat attacks
the British Q-ship with a torpedo – he
watches as the merchant crew enters the
lifeboats and abandons ship. *(Reel 7)* The
U-boat warily surfaces, thinking the ship is
empty, only to discover that it is a trap – the
Royal Navy gunners are still on board. The
guns appear and the U-boat is sunk. (Many
of the Q-ship's crew are awarded VCs – a
list appears on screen.) The German fleet

surrenders, all the U-boats are captured.
The film concludes with an epigraph: "Thus
wrote an English chronicler five hundred
years ago – 'Keep then the Sea that is the
wall of England: And then is England saved
by God his hand'."

Notes
Production: this film is a 1932 reissue of the
1928 film Q-Ships; it is shorter by almost
1500 ft and has a soundtrack added (the
original film was silent). The Imperial War
Museum also possesses a 9.5mm print of
the silent version of *Q-Ships*; however, this
is incomplete, consisting of the first 4 reels
only.
catalogued JCK: 5/1987

IWM 1177a · GB, (?) 1915
[BRITISH INFANTRY MARCHING]
(allocated)

b/w · 1 reel · 147' (3 mins) · silent
intertitles: none

- British Infantry marching through a
  village, probably 1915.

The film is one sustained shot. The men are
in marching order and led by their bands,
but the march is not a parade. The sloping
road they march down is unmetalled, and
there are advertisements for theatre-shows
on the walls. A crowd of civilians watches,
and some join in to march alongside, but
there is no cheering. Probably a New Army
division marching to its port of embarkation
before leaving Britain. The men are near the
end of their march and some are obviously
tired.

catalogued SDB: 1/1984

IWM 1177b · GB, (before) 8/1918
**OLD MOTHER HUBBARD – NEW
VERSION**
[FILM TAGS] (series, allocated)

b/w · 1 reel · 115' (2 mins) · silent
intertitles: English

sp Ministry of Information *pr* Hepworth
Manufacturing Company

- Short piece encouraging people in Britain
  to save bones for munitions, summer
  1918.

In an acted scene "Old Mother Hubbard"

offers her dog (played by Mac, the Hepworth collie) a bone, which he refuses. The caption points out that bone is used in munitions, and 18 pounds of bone will fire an 18-pounder shell. The film shows these shells being stockpiled by British soldiers, and German soldiers (acted) running away under shell fire.

catalogued SDB: 1/1984

IWM 1178 · GB (?), (?) 1916
DEFENDERS OF EGYPT

b/w · 1 reel · 484' (8 mins) · silent
intertitles: English

pr Transatlantic Film Company

■ British troops defending Egypt, probably 1916.

Lord Cullen walks with the US Consul General across the lawn of the official British residence in Cairo, once occupied by Lord Kitchener. British troops relax in their camp near Cairo outside a YMCA hut. With the others gathered round, two of the men give a demonstration wrestling match. In similar vein Privates Williams and Arthur "of the 5th battery" have a boxing match. A tattooist puts a tattoo on the arm of one of the soldiers. A football match "between the 4th and 5th battery" on the baked-earth drill ground. Soldiers peel potatoes and carrots beside their tents and prepare stew for a meal. British troops pass through Cairo in an official parade, watched by the local civilians. One yeomanry regiment is pointed out as having an unusual number of white Arab horses.

Notes
Title: this appears on the bottom of each caption.
catalogued SDB: 1/1984

IWM 1179 · GB, 1919
[ARRIVAL OF PRIVATE HEAVYSIDE VC IN STANLEY] (allocated)

b/w · 1 reel · 233' (4 mins) · silent
intertitles: none

■ Arrival of Private Michael Heavyside VC in his home town of Stanley, County Durham, returning from the First World War.

The film is fragmented, switching from one scene to another and returning in a way which makes it hard to follow. Private Heavyside (of 15th Battalion, Durham Light Infantry) arrives by train at Shield Row Station where he is met by the mayor and a crowd of civilians, who shake his hand. He is taken by car in a procession through streets thronged with people cheering and waving Union Flags. In the procession are an Army contingent, a Cadet Corps contingent and a Boys Brigade contingent. Small children are led in file to take their place along the way and cheer as he passes. On the balcony of the town hall the mayor delivers a speech for him.

catalogued SDB: 1/1984

IWM 1180a · GB (?), (ca) 1916
[AUSTRALIAN AMBULANCE CONVOY] (allocated)

b/w · 1 reel · 29' (1 min) · silent
intertitles: none

■ Film fragment of an Australian convoy of wounded on mule-drawn litters, led by a mule-drawn ambulance, making its way over dusty hills, possibly Palestine, 1916-18.

Notes
Production: this is probably a British or Australian official film, but cannot be positively identified.
catalogued SDB: 1/1984

IWM 1180b · GB, 9/9/1916
TOPICAL BUDGET 263-2 [2]

b/w · 1 reel · 47' (1 min) · silent
intertitles: English

pr Topical Film Company

■ 'ALLIES CONTROL GREEK POST OFFICE' – a single item from the newsreel held in more complete form as **NTB 263-02**.

Notes
Summary: note that another fragment of this newsreel is **IWM 655c**.
catalogued SDB: 1/1984

IWM 1180c · GB, 31/3/1917
TOPICAL BUDGET 292-2

b/w · 1 reel · 55' (1 min) · silent
intertitles: English

pr Topical Film Company

■ French gunners on the Salonika Front,
spring 1917.

'ARTILLERY DUEL IN SERBIA.' A Serbian
officer scans the distance with binoculars as
the French gunners set the fuses on their
field gun's shells and fire a round. (The
caption says the gun is a 75mm, but it
appears to be an obsolete 90mm.)

catalogued SDB: 1/1984

IWM 1181 · GB, 9/2/1916
TOPICAL BUDGET 233-1

b/w · 1 reel · 237' (4 mins) · silent
intertitles: English

pr Topical Film Company

I. Ambulance dedication ceremony, North
London, February 1916. 'BISHOP
DEDICATES AMBULANCE. The Bishop of
London dedicating two ambulances given
by the inhabitants of the Borough of Stoke
Newington, for service in France.' The
Bishop delivers a speech to the people of
the borough, who have subscribed to pay
for the two ambulances.
II. A charity rugby match between members
of the New Zealand Division and the Artists
Rifles OTC at Queen's Club, West London,
February 1916. 'ANZACS BEAT ARTISTS.'
The New Zealanders, described as having
fought at Gallipoli, file out onto the pitch
first. The game is then played. The New
Zealanders win by 11 points to nil.
III. A service at Southwark Cathedral,
London, February 1916. 'MUNICIPAL
SERVICE AT SOUTHWARK.' The mayors
and aldermen of the diocese, who have
assembled for the special service, are
shown filing out of the cathedral after the
service has finished.
IV. Convalescent soldiers visit a film studio
in London, February 1916. 'ENTERTAINING
THE WOUNDED. Soldiers from London
Hospitals being taken by private motors and
entertained at a Cinematograph Studio.' The
soldiers are taken by car and charabanc to
the studio (which is not identified). Inside,
they are given a formal meal.

catalogued SDB: 1/1984

IWM 1182 · GB, 13/5/1916
TOPICAL BUDGET 246-2

b/w · 1 reel · 271' (4 mins) · silent
intertitles: English

pr Topical Film Company

I. "Lamp Day Fund" in London, May 1916.
'LADY OF THE LAMP. Lady Cowdray
receiving gifts for the "Lamp Day Fund" at
the specially decorated statue of Florence
Nightingale in Waterloo Place.' Lady
Cowdray stands with helpers selling flags
for the fund.
II. USS *Kentucky* in the Atlantic, May 1916.
'NAVAL GUN PRACTICE.' The ship is not
clearly seen as a whole. A sailor finishes
placing the tompion back in the mouth of
one of the ship's guns. One sailor shows
how to climb up one of the davits. The
ship's semaphore arm in action.
III. Queen Alexandra visits a children's
pageant in Streatham, London, May 1916.
'QUEEN ALEXANDRA'S HELP. Queen
Alexandra, accompanied by Princess
Victoria and Princess Arthur of Connaught
being received by the Mayor of Streatham.'
The pageant is on behalf of the Streatham
War Hospital Supply Depot and is held at
the town hall. The children in fancy dress
for the pageant arrive by charabanc. Then a
long shot as the royal party (not clearly
visible) arrives and enters the town hall.
IV. Lord Wimborne, Viceroy of Ireland, on
the occasion of his resignation, 11 May
1916. 'IRISH VICEROY RESIGNS.' Lord
Wimborne resigned (over the Easter Rising)
on the day the newsreel was issued. The
film shows an earlier occasion of him
inspecting the guard of honour at the
Viceregal Lodge in Dublin.

catalogued SDB: 1/1984

IWM 1183 · USA, (prod) 1918
[AMERICANS WITH RAILWAY GUN]
(allocated)

b/w · 1 reel · 50' (1 min) · silent
intertitles: none

■ American gunners with a French 400mm
railway gun, probably near Mailly,
Western Front, 15 May 1918.

The men prepare to fire the gun, elevating

the barrel. Then they are shown posed for the camera standing on and around the gun.

Notes
Production: this is probably US official film, but this is not certain
Summary: compare with **IWM 502** reel 4.
catalogued SDB: 1/1984

IWM 1184 · NO FILM

IWM 1185 · GB, 1914
the 4TH CAMERON HIGHLANDERS AT BEDFORD

b/w · 1 reel · 398' (7 mins) · silent
intertitles: none

pr Gaumont

■ Men of 4th Battalion, Cameron Highlanders, marching through Bedford, August 1914.

The battalion marches in column of fours past the fixed camera, occasionally halting for a few minutes. A shop-boy runs alongside selling chocolate to the men as they march. The battalion is headed by its Pioneer section with its pack horses and wagons, then the cyclists, then the band with its pipers.

Notes
Remarks: this gives a very good idea of how much road space was taken up by a battalion on the march.
catalogued SDB: 1/1984

IWM 1186 · GB, 1917
AMERICAN TROOPS IN LONDON

b/w · 1 reel · 337' (6 mins) · silent
intertitles: English

sp War Office Cinema Committee

■ Parade of United States soldiers through the centre of London, 15 August 1917.

The contingent forms up at Wellington Barracks before marching out, led by a band from the Coldstream Guards, on duty at the barracks. The parade passes the US Embassy, where Ambassador Dr Walter H Page and Admiral William S Sims take the salute from the balcony. The parade then passes outside Buckingham Palace. King George V stands at the gates to take the salute. With him is Queen Alexandra the Queen Mother, Field Marshal Lord French, Colonel Lassiter (the US military attaché) and Lieutenant-General Sir Francis Lloyd, in charge of London district. Also watching are Prime Minister Lloyd George and US Major-General John Biddle. The troops dip their flags in salute as they pass the King.

Notes
Remarks: this film has some scenes in common with the American-produced **IWM 1187**, and makes an interesting contrast in the way Britain and America treated the same event.
[*The Times*, 16 August 1917: 7D, 7E]
catalogued SDB: 1/1984

IWM 1187 · USA, 1917
ON THE ROAD TO BERLIN – England's Welcome To American Boys

b/w · 1 reel · 624' (11 mins) · silent
intertitles: English

sp US Government, Official Government Pictures

■ Parade of United States soldiers through the centre of London, 15 August 1917.

The parade moves through St James's Park and into Wellington Barracks, including a group of US Civil War veterans in civilian clothes with banners. Ambassador Walter Page waits for the parade outside Buckingham Palace, talking with Major-General John Biddle. The parade continues back through St James's Park. Waiting outside Buckingham Palace King George V talks with General Biddle. Also present are Queen Mary, Dowager Queen Alexandra, Lieutenant-General Sir Francis Lloyd and Lord French. The parade goes past Buckingham Palace and returns to Wellington Barracks where Lloyd talks to some of the US officers. Outside the barracks the men rest and eat, while WAAC ladies serve them with lemonade. Soldiers play with two small girls. A US sergeant shows a Coldstream Guards sergeant his copy of a letter from King George given to all US troops. Shown in close-up, this welcomes the Americans to "the great battle for human freedom".

Notes
Remarks: this film has some scenes in

common with the British-produced **IWM 1186**, and makes an interesting contrast in the way Britain and America treated the same event.
[*The Times*, 16 August 1917: 7D, 7E]
catalogued SDB: 1/1984

IWM 1188 · GB, (prod) 1917
[CANADIAN SECTIONS 1] (allocated)

b/w · 1 reel · 740' (12 mins) · silent
intertitles: none

sp Canadian War Records Office (?)
pr Topical Film Company (?)

■ Fragmentary film of Canadian troops on the Western Front, probably during the Battle of Arras, April 1917.

The Duke of Connaught is taken on a conducted tour over an old part of a battlefield (possibly Somme area), 11 March 1917. Canadians in a rear position relax and smoke in dug-outs. A tented rest camp. A long-range view of houses being shelled. More shell fire, possibly on a training range. Soldiers prepare to take heavy loads of ammunition and equipment on their backs forward from the rear areas through the trenches. Pan over an old battlefield with half-destroyed buildings. A tented camp with Canadian gunners exercising their horses. Men of the Tank Corps do maintenance work on their Mk IV tanks; one man draws an elaborate Maple Leaf on the nose of his tank.

Notes
Remarks: some good material, particularly the carrying party. Sadly, it cannot be positively dated.
catalogued SDB: 1/1984

IWM 1189 · GB, (prod) 1917
[CANADIAN SECTIONS 2] (allocated)

b/w · 1 reel · 668' (11 mins) · silent
intertitles: none

sp Canadian War Records Office (?)
pr Topical Film Company (?)

■ Fragmentary film of Canadian troops on the Western Front, probably during the Battle of Arras, April 1917.

Sunrise over a battlefield. Canadians at a front line machinegun post open fire.

Canadian wounded are brought through to the rear areas of a battle, with German prisoners helping as stretcher-bearers. At a first aid post the stretchers are loaded into a motor ambulance. German prisoners have been led back to a rear-area village, where Canadian soldiers pick up their packs and go back up the line. German prisoners, one in body-armour, sit by a tent and shake lice out of their clothing. Portrait shots of German prisoners showing various degrees of nervousness and fatigue. In a quarry in the rear troops eat and drink; a chaplain offers drinks to tired and wounded men. German and Canadian stretcher-bearers, working together, share drinks and biscuits. In a trench one party of soldiers relieves another (one man deliberately shakes hands with another). A final view of a laughing soldier.

Notes
Remarks: some very good material which, sadly, cannot be positively dated.
catalogued SDB: 1/1984

IWM 1190 · GB, (prod) 1918
[TANKS MARK IX DUCK, MARK IV HERMAPHRODITE AND MEDIUM B] (allocated)

b/w · 1 reel · 809' (14 mins) · silent
intertitles: none

■ Tank trials, probably at Bovington Camp, autumn 1918.

A Mk IX Duck amphibious tank drives into a pond, swims half-way across and reverses back out. Next, from the middle of the pond, it turns in its own length and comes back out nose first. A Mk IV Hermaphrodite (a Female on which the right-hand sponson has been replaced by a Male sponson with a 6-pounder gun) pushes over a small tree, then drives back over the tree so that the tank tilts, showing that it is well-balanced. A Medium B tank demonstrates its ability to turn in its own length and change direction sharply. The Hermaphrodite continues to demonstrate its balance techniques.

catalogued SDB: 12/1983

IWM 1191 · GB, (prod) 1918
[TANKS MEDIUM C HORNET AND PROTOTYPE 'LITTLE WILLIE'] (allocated)

b/w · 1 reel · 857' (15 mins) · silent
intertitles: English

■ Trials of the Medium C Hornet tank at the William Foster Works, Lincoln, autumn 1918.

Two Hornets move in parallel over the testing grounds, with a third just behind. They climb slopes and drive through water-filled holes in speed and stability tests. In the background is the "Little Willie" prototype tank, clearly marked on its side as "Little Willie, built September 1916". Inside the workshops Hornets are being built. Civilian observers continue to watch the trials.

Notes
Summary: the first "Little Willie" was in fact built in December 1915.
catalogued SDB: 12/1983

IWM 1192 · GB, (prod) 1918
[TANKS MARK V DOUBLE STAR AND MEDIUM B] (allocated)

b/w · 2 reels · 2472' (40 mins) · silent
intertitles: none

■ Tank trials at the Metropolitan Carriage and Wagon Company works at Wednesbury, Staffordshire, late 1918.

(Reel 1) Among the observers are Major H Buddicom, Major W G Wilson, the designer Mr Ricardo and Lieutenant Shaw. The three cameramen at work occasionally appear on each other's film, which has been joined together rather than edited. The two tanks practise repeated movements on the testing ground. *(Reel 2)* They drive up and down steep slopes and through surface water. Occasionally they can be seen together in the same shot.

catalogued SDB: 12/1983

IWM 1193 · GB, (prod) 1918
[TANK TRENCH-CROSSING TRIALS] (allocated)

b/w · 1 reel · 696' (12 mins) · silent
intertitles: none

■ Trench-crossing abilities of the Mk V Double Star and Medium C tank compared in earlier models, Britain, late 1918.

The Mk V Double Star crosses a wide but simple trench of typical 1918 pattern. A Medium B makes the same crossing, as does a Medium C, both ways. The Medium A Whippet tank HMLS 'Tarantula' gets stuck crossing the trench, having neither the length nor traction power to do so. The Medium C pulls it free. A battle-damaged Mk V Male HMLS 'Egbert' also fails to cross the trench and has to be towed out by the Mk V Double Star – the towrope breaking on the first attempt. The tanks are driven back from the testing ground at high speed to their sheds, where a number of Mk V Double Stars wait under tarpaulin.

catalogued SDB: 12/1983

IWM 1194 · GB, (prod) 1918
[TANK MARK VIII] (allocated)

b/w · 1 reel · 1043' (17 mins) · silent
intertitles: none

■ Trials of the Mk VIII "Liberty" tank, probably in Britain, late 1918.

The tank is a prototype in natural metal finish, without its fittings and with the sponsons slightly recessed for rail travel; it is flying small US flags. The troops supervising it are American, with British Army and Navy officers watching. The tank fails, after three attempts, to surmount a wooden ramp of 45°. It drives cross-country at the same rate as the US soldier marching beside it. It fails three times to drive up a steep bank. It drives well over the spoil heaps and mud of the factory testing yard, and returns to its shed. (The film is broken at this point by a brief scene of US Mail wagons collecting mail at a freight yard.) The visiting officials pose with the Mk VIII behind them. Close-ups of the guns and forward machinegun mountings being tilted and rotated. The tank again attempts the grassy slope and this time gets over on the second attempt, going on to cross a shallow trench and pushing over a medium-sized tree. The visiting officers inspect the tank. The final shot shows the driver's seat and controls.

Notes
Summary: the "Liberty" tank was a joint US-British venture, the first model being produced in England in October 1918.
catalogued SDB: 12/1983

IWM 1195 · GB/Canada, (?) 1917
[CANADIAN TANKS] (allocated)
[the BATTLE OF THE ANCRE AND THE
ADVANCE OF THE TANKS (Canadian
version extracts ?)]
[the CANADIAN VICTORY AT
COURCELETTE AND THE ADVANCE OF
THE TANKS (extracts ?)]

b/w · 1 reel · 701' (12 mins) · silent
intertitles: English

sp Canadian War Records Office (?)
pr Topical Film Company (?)

■ Fragment of a Canadian film on tanks on
the Western Front, 1916-17.

An unarmed Mk IV Male crushes barbed
wire as soldiers mark its progress. An
unarmed Mk IV Female comes up to the
camera. Tank crews perform maintenance
on HMLS 'Daphne' (from **IWM 116** The
Battle of the Ancre and the Advance of the
Tanks). Mk IV tanks are repaired in the
open at a tank base. Mk IV tanks move up
a road near a battle zone. A wireless tank
used as an observation post during the First
Battle of Cambrai. HMLS 'Oh I Say' (from
IWM 116). A training attack by a Mk IV Male
with supporting troops advancing through
smoke (note houses in background) and
firing a blank shot from one of its 6-pounder
guns. More of Mk I tanks (from **IWM 116**). A
Canadian officer poses with his tank, which
has a Maple Leaf drawn on its nose.

Notes
Production: it seems likely that this is a
Canadian official film.
Summary: see also **IWM 116**, **IWM 144** and
IWM 466.
catalogued SDB: 12/1983

IWM 1196 · GB, (prod) 1918
**[TANKS MARK IV, SCHNEIDER, AND
MARK IV UNDITCHING]** (allocated)

b/w · 1 reel · 785' (13 mins) · silent
intertitles: English

I. Trials of a Mk IV Female tank in Britain,
probably 1917. The unarmed Female tank
manages to climb a small slope without
difficulty, followed by a drop into a pit and a
climb up out again. It ends head-on to the
camera.
II. US troops in the Second Battle of the
Marne, Western Front, July 1918. The US
soldiers emerge from their trenches and
move forward for the attack, with support

from their French-made Schneider tanks.
Later, some German prisoners and one of
the tanks come back towards the rear.
III. Trials of a tank unditching beam,
probably at Bovington Camp, Britain, 1917.
Unarmed Mk IV tanks push over trees in a
wood. Unarmed Mk IV Females make a
'tank charge' (and other exercises from **IWM
337** Tanks – the Wonder Weapon). In
particular a Mk IV is shown using its
unditching beam to get out of a hole.

Notes
Summary: see also **IWM 337**.
catalogued SDB: 12/1983

IWM 1197 · GB, (prod) 1918
**[TANKS MEDIUM B AND MARK V
DOUBLE STAR IN BRIDGING EXERCISE]**
(allocated)

b/w · 1 reel · 766' (13 mins) · silent
intertitles: none

■ Tank bridging trials at Christchurch,
Dorset, late 1918.

Various types of pontoon bridge suitable for
tanks are constructed. A Medium B tank
crosses over a river on a pontoon bridge,
followed by an unarmed Mk V Double Star
supply tank. The same Mk V Double Star
then makes the crossing on a suspension-
type bridge and a pontoon ferry. A Royal
Engineers Mk V Double Star is shown fitted
with bridge-laying equipment. Another Mk V
Double Star manoeuvres a section of
bridge, about three times as long as itself,
across the ground (the bridge section has a
small caterpillar track at its centre of
balance). Finally, a number of officers take
a ride on top of a Mk V Double Star.

catalogued SDB: 12/1983

IWM 1198 · GB, (prod) 1917
[TANK SECTIONS] (allocated)
[the BATTLE OF THE ANCRE AND THE
ADVANCE OF THE TANKS (extracts)]
[TANKS – THE WONDER WEAPON
(extracts)]

b/w · 1 reel · 957' (16 mins) · silent
intertitles: none

■ Jumbled film of British tanks in the First
World War, 1916-18.

The film shows unrelated scenes of Mk IV and Mk I tanks, all from **IWM 116** *The Battle of the Ancre and the Advance of the Tanks* or **IWM 337** *Tanks – the Wonder Weapon*.

Notes
Summary: see also **IWM 116** and **IWM 337**.
catalogued SDB: 12/1983

IWM 1199 · USA (?), (prod) 1916
[BUICK TRACTOR] (allocated)

b/w · 1 reel · 451' (7 mins) · silent
intertitles: none

■ Trials of two Buick tractors, probably in the USA, about 1916.

The two tractors fly small US flags. Each has a driver on the bucket-seat and an observer in front. They demonstrate their climbing and turning characteristics on a farmyard test site. One pushes over a load of empty wooden barrels, some shrubs and a small tree without difficulty.

Notes
Summary: the Buick was adopted by the US Army for towing guns.
catalogued SDB: 12/1983

IWM 1200 · GB, (prod) 1918
[TANKS MEDIUM A, MARK V AND MARK V STAR] (allocated)

b/w · 1 reel · 806' (14 mins) · silent
intertitles: none

■ Tank Corps exercises, probably at Bovington Camp in Dorset, 1918.

The training ground is flat with deliberately constructed obstacles. A Medium A Whippet drives repeatedly through shallow flooded holes. A Mk V Hermaphrodite spins on its own axis. A stripped-down tank is repaired. A Whippet races a Mk V Male, others of both types joining in. All the tanks circle, showing that some of the Mk Vs are Hermaphrodite. A line of Mk Vs, including two recovery tanks, waits under tarpaulin. Two Whippets are joy-ridden. Mk V Stars set out for the training area. A line of Whippets is driven in to the parking area and hosed down. More Mk Vs covered with tarpaulin. Whippets and Mk Vs continue to practise – one Mk V is a Command Tank with semaphore arms.

catalogued SDB: 12/1983

IWM 1201 · GB, (prod) 1918
[TANK AND INFANTRY CO-OPERATION] (allocated)

b/w · 1 reel · 817' (14 mins) · silent
intertitles: none

■ Tank and Infantry cooperation trials, probably in Britain, late 1918.

Two Mk IV tanks, a Male HMLS 'Daisy' and a Female HMLS 'Dauntless' practise trench-crossing (some of the material is shot from inside the trench). A Mk IV command tank, waving a flag, leads other Mk IVs forward. Back with the trench-crossing trials. A brief shot of a Mk I Male tank in camouflage. A Mk IV Male advances on some 'Germans' who 'surrender' as it approaches them, being led off by supporting Infantry. More Infantry advance supported by a Mk IV tank. Shells burst around a command tank. A platoon of Infantry in battle order poses for the camera; a line of Tank Corps men also pose, firstly by themselves, and then on top of their tank. A barbed wire entanglement with 'shell-bursts' coming closer (in fact a fuse burning from one charge to another). Infantry advance in artillery formation up to the wire, then signal to a tank which advances over the wire, crushing lanes for the Infantry to advance. More shots of Mk IV tanks manœuvring around.

catalogued SDB: 1/1984

IWM 1202 · GB, (after) 1918
[MISCELLANEOUS FIRST WORLD WAR AVIATION MATERIAL] (allocated)

b/w · 1 reel · 319' (9 mins) · silent
intertitles: none

■ Collection of fragments of British and Australian aviation film of the First World War period.

The film, which appears to consist entirely of items from films held elsewhere in the IWM Series, includes material on airships and aircraft, and on both naval and land-forces machines. Conspicuous extracts include the 1 Squadron Australian Flying Corps sequence from **IWM 28** *With the Australian Forces in Palestine*, and reel 7 of **IWM 551** *The Empire's Shield*.

Notes
Summary: this film was found in the GWY series and transferred to the IWM Series in 1982.
catalogued RBNS: 5/1987

IWM 1203 · GB, (prod) 1916
LEST WE FORGET

b/w · 1 reel · 248' (4 mins) · silent
intertitles: none

■ Wreck of Zeppelin L31 on the ground at Potters Bar, Hertfordshire, after its crash on the night of 1 October 1916.

The wreck, guarded by British soldiers, is completely burnt-out, leaving only the twisted metal structure. Among the wreckage can be seen incendiary bombs, Maxim guns and ammunition belts. The soldiers start to untangle the wreckage.

Notes
Title: this is taken from the shotsheet.
[shotsheet available]
catalogued SDB: 1/1984

IWM 1204 · France/GB, (after) 2/1916
the WRECKED BABY KILLER

b/w · 1 reel · 364' (6 mins) · silent
intertitles: English

sp British Topical Committee for War Films
pr Section Cinématographique de l'Armée Française

■ English-language version of a French film on the wreck of Zeppelin LZ77 at Revigney on 21 February 1916.

The film starts with a brief scene of the Zeppelin apparently about to crash (in fact an early scene of Zeppelin L7 landing under difficulties). A French 75mm motorised anti-aircraft gun takes aim. Then the wreckage of the Zeppelin, completely burnt-out, on the ground. The camera shows the wreckage, dwelling heavily on the charred corpses of the crew lying among the pieces of metal. Adjutant Gramling and Private Pennetier, who shot the Zeppelin down, help to dismantle it.

[shotsheet available]
catalogued SDB: 1/1984

IWM 1205 · Germany, (ca) 1913
ZEPPELIN IN FLIGHT

b/w · 1 reel · 371' (6 mins) · silent
intertitles: none

■ Flight of Zeppelin LZ11 *Luise Viktoria* to rendezvous with the German merchantman SS *Imperator*, about 1913.

The airship takes off from a hovering position just above the sea, filmed from below. It overflies other ships and approaches the *Imperator*. A message or package is winched up from the ship to the LZ11. The view from a gondola is seen as the airship returns to land, crossing the coast and coming to its base, where lines are thrown down and the ground crew brings it in to rest.

Notes
Remarks: a very attractive film with some unusual and innovative camera angles.
[shotsheet available]
catalogued SDB: 1/1984

IWM 1206 · GB, 1916
the WRECKED ZEPPELINS IN ESSEX

b/w · 1 reel · 439' (5 mins) · silent
intertitles: English

sp War Office *pr* Gaumont

■ Disjointed film of the wrecks of Zeppelins L32 and L33, the morning after their crash in Essex on 24 September 1916.

The film, which claims to be "the only complete cinematograph pictures taken under official authorization", opens with shots of the twisted wreckage of the L32 which came down in flames. A number of military and naval personnel pick their way about the debris. This is followed by a film of the other Zeppelin, which came down virtually intact over a road and then burnt-out, breaking its back. There are various general shots of the metal lattice structure, in particular the undamaged nose. Attention is drawn to the nearby cottage in the background whose occupants "had a grand-stand view". There are some closer shots of a gondola, a propeller, a wrecked engine and so on. A number of military personnel are seen examining the wreckage.

Notes
Remarks: the views taken, from various

angles, of the burnt-out nose of the L33 are very attractive, as well as giving a clear idea of how the Zeppelin was constructed.
[shotsheet available]
catalogued SDB: 1/1984

IWM 1207 · GB, 1916
WRECKED ZEPPELIN BROUGHT DOWN BY BRITISH NAVAL GUNNERY

b/w · 1 reel · 178' (3 mins) · silent
intertitles: English

pr Topical Film Company

■ Wreckage of Zeppelin LZ85, brought down in the marshes near Salonika, 5 May 1916.

French and Serbian soldiers inspect and pull apart the wreckage of the Zeppelin. An unexploded bomb (?) lies in the marsh. On board one of the British ships which shot down the Zeppelin, a naval lieutenant and a gun-layer stand beside their 3-inch gun. The crew of the Zeppelin are marched back to a French camp, where they are briefly interrogated.

[shotsheet available]
catalogued SDB: 1/1984

IWM 1208 · Germany (?), (?) 1916
CRAMP IN THE NECK IN LONDON

b/w · 1 reel · 77' (2 mins) · silent
intertitles: none

■ Fragment of a cartoon on Zeppelins over London, about 1916.

The artist's hand draws the London skyline and lookouts perched on the housetops. The night sky rapidly fills with Zeppelins.

Notes
Production: it is hard to tell from so short a fragment, but the cartoon seems to be pro-German and anti-British.
[shotsheet available]
catalogued SDB: 1/1984

IWM 1209 · GB, (before) 8/1918
the LEOPARD'S SPOTS

b/w · 1 reel · 155' (3 mins) · silent
intertitles: English

sp Ministry of Information *pr* Hepworth Manufacturing Company *cast* Taylor, Alma; Edwards, Henry; and McAndrew, John

■ British propaganda piece warning against buying German goods after the war, summer 1918.

The film starts with a Belgian town in flames, and civilians lying dead in the streets. A terrified young mother with her baby is encountered by two drunken German soldiers, one carrying a smouldering torch. Despite her pleas they snatch the baby from her and throw it to the ground. "Once a German, always a German." The figures of the soldiers dissolve into the same two men, a few years older, in business suits as travelling salesmen. "They will be the same beasts then as they are now. A leopard cannot change his spots." The two salesmen come into a peaceful English village. One enters a general store and offers the shopkeeper examples of the pots and pans that he sells. The shopkeeper is keen to accept the pan, but his wife, noticing the "Made in Germany" label, objects strongly and calls the village constable; at which the salesman leaves rapidly.

Notes
Remarks: a well-made propaganda piece with an unusually virulent message, showing clearly the direction in which British propaganda was heading under the Ministry of Information.
catalogued SDB: 1/1984

IWM 1210 · GB, (?) 1919
[LONDON PEACE PROCESSION (?)]
(allocated)

b/w · 1 reel · 41' (1 min) · silent
intertitles: none

■ Fragment of a film showing cheering crowds and Medium C Hornet tanks in the streets: probably the Peace Procession in London, 19 July 1919.

catalogued SDB: 1/1984

IWM 1211 · Austria-Hungary, (ca) 1915
[RUSSIAN PRISONERS IN AUSTRIA-HUNGARY] (allocated)

b/w · 1 reel · 19' (1 min) · silent
intertitles: none

- Fragment of a film showing hygiene for Russian prisoners in Austria-Hungary during the First World War.

The prisoners are in an open compound surrounded by brick buildings. They assemble naked and are given haircuts by Austro-Hungarian troops while their own officers watch and, behind them, their clothes are burnt in incinerators.

cataloged SDB: 1/1984

IWM 1212 · GB, 1919
GAUMONT GRAPHIC [800 approx] – THE SURRENDER OF THE GERMAN NAVY

b/w · 1 reel · 803' (14 mins) · silent
intertitles: English

pr Gaumont

- Surrender of German naval forces, 21 November 1918.

Panning medium shot over HMS *Walker* at anchor with the Forth Bridge in background. Very grey long shot of Forth Bridge with destroyers directly astern of US battleships in the distance – one is Arkansas Class. German battleships coming in to surrender, led by two Koenig Class battleships. High angle medium shot astern on cameraship of a group of officers watching the Germans. Medium-long shot of three German G.101 Class destroyers. Long shot of a line of battle-cruisers, nearest is SMS *Derfflinger*, also visible are *Seydlitz*, *Moltke* and *Hindenburg*. The battleship *Kaiser* passes, followed by the *Kaiserin* (?). G.101 Class destroyers pass. Medium shot of destroyers, foremost is B.97/B.109 Class. At this point the film is broken by a sequence showing a sunken Avro 504K being lifted on board the cameraship. Medium-long shot of Arethusa Class cruiser. Medium close-up of SMS *Koeln*. King George V on board the USS *New York* shakes hands with officers. Admiral Sims, Admiral Rodman, the King and Prince Edward pose together. Admiral Tyrwhitt's cruiser squadron escorts the German U-boats into Harwich, starting with a medium-long shot of a hospital ship in fog. A rigid airship overflies it. Medium-long shot off bow of HMS *Redoubt*. High angle medium shot down the side of a destroyer at anchor – ML.13 is secured alongside. Cameraship passes HMS *Retriever* at anchor. Medium-long shot of U.66 Class submarine. Medium shot (silhouette) of

Thornycroft leader passing camera. Medium-long shot (silhouette) of UB.133 Class (?). Medium close-up of U.160 Class passing. Medium shot of U.99 Class submarine passing camera. Medium-long shot of hospital ship with destroyers anchored nearby in the fog. Medium shot of HMS *Redgauntlet*. Medium shot of HMS *Sturgeon* under way. High angle medium shot of a destroyer with ML.13 alongside taking on German submarine crewmen. High angle medium shot as the hospital ship takes on the personal kit of U-boat crewmen. The cameraship is HMS *Melampus*. German crewmen board the hospital shop. Medium shot of the crew of the *Melampus* posing for the camera.

cataloged NAP: 1/1984

IWM 1213 · GB, 1913
NEW ZEALAND'S GIFT TO THE EMPIRE
NEW ZEALAND LEADS THE WAY, SCENES ON BOARD HMS NEW ZEALAND
(alternative)

b/w · 1 reel · 127' (2 mins) · silent
intertitles: none

pr Jury's Imperial Pictures

- Inspection by King George V of the battle-cruiser HMS *New Zealand* at Portsmouth, 5 February 1913.

The King inspects the ship's company drawn up on deck. With him are the ship's captain, Captain Lionel Halsey, First Lord of the Admiralty Winston Churchill (seen briefly), C-in-C Portsmouth Admiral Sir Hedworth Meux, First Sea Lord Admiral Prince Louis of Battenberg, and Second Sea Lord Vice-Admiral Sir John Jellicoe. New Zealand dignitaries include James Allen, Minister of Defence, Thomas MacKenzie, High Commissioner, and Sir Joseph Ward MP (who as Prime Minister initiated the gift of the battle-cruiser). The party comes down the ship's gangplank and the sailors file away. The King takes his place with the ship's officers for a group photograph. Two of the sailors pose astride the barrel of a ship's gun. Other sailors cheer the camera.

Notes
Title: alternative title from shotlist held at the New Zealand Film Archive.
Authority: additional detail from Christopher Pugsley, 12/1993.
cataloged SDB: 1/1984

IWM 1214 · GB, 1914
SCOTTISH TROOPS FOR THE FRONT

b/w · 1 reel · 673' (12 mins) · silent
intertitles: English

- Training scenes with the 5th and 4th
  Royal Scots, Hawick Boy scouts,
  Yeomanry and Territorials and the
  Cameronians, probably intended to
  encourage more voluntary enlistment in
  summer 1914.

"The 5th Royal Scots who have volunteered
for the Front in training." Soldiers, including
some very young teenagers, march past a
camp of white tents erected in summer
countryside. Scenes of camp life include a
boxing match, tossing a soldier in a
blanket, packing kit, semaphore training,
washing, violent version of blind man's buff,
march past carrying rifles and queuing with
mess tins for food outdoors (two wear kilts
and all wave or grin at the camera).
"Sergeant J L Dewar, 4th Royal Scots,
Winner of the Kings Prize entering Hawick
en route for Stobs Camp." Long column of
soldiers march through the town past large
crowd of women, old men and young boys
lining street. Procession is led by brass
band and mounted officers preceding
soldiers, Scottish bagpipe band and more
officers. Popular enthusiasm is evident.
"Hawick Boy Scouts at work". Scouts
parade in summer field, then practise
Morse, signalling, erecting a tent and
crossing a stream by means of an
improvised rope and plank bridge. Two
well-dressed couples, presumably local
gentry, look on. "Yeomanry and Territorials."
Mounted soldiers ride along country road in
summer, watched by local youths, and
preceding soldiers on foot and civilian
horsecarts. "The Cameronians at Stobs."
Officers and men parade on hillside field in
summer, then stand assembled for outdoor
religious service near farm buildings. Large
encampment comprises fixed barracks and
tents. Scenes of camp life include a boxing
match, Scottish dancing, log-chopping and
signalling beside two Vickers machine
guns.

Notes
Summary: the 5th Battalion Royal Scots was
the largest Volunteer Corps in the Kingdom,
and together with the 4th Battalion took part
in the Dardanelles campaign, where the
Bisley prize marksman Sergeant Dewar
distinguished himself by killing a Turkish
sniper on 21 June 1915. By inference
therefore this film must date from the
previous summer.

catalogued: KGTG 2/1987

IWM 1215 · GB, 1915
**a DAY WITH THE BATTALION OF THE
WELSH GUARDS**

b/w · 1 reel · 397' (7 mins) · silent
intertitles: English

- Training and off-duty scenes in the exotic
  White City Exhibition Grounds with the
  1st Battalion culminate in recruitment
  appeal, spring/summer 1915.

Thirteen numbered captions separate the
following scenes. Soldiers parade and drill
in front of the ornate oriental facade of a
pavilion (Indian ?) erected for one of the
pre-war international exhibitions (Imperial of
1909 ?) held at White City, Shepherds Bush
in West London. The Prince of Wales'
Company (leading company of the 1st
Battalion) returns from a route march.
Soldiers practise bayonet exercises before
engaging each other in bayonet fighting,
using stakes and head guards. Soldiers and
several civilians watch the "Noble Art" of
boxing. Men line up on Pay-Day to salute
and collect money. Officers and sergeants
pose separately for camera against upper
level of exotic pavilion. View of sergeants
lined up drinking against bar in their mess,
and of the Men's Quarters where soldiers sit
and stand around beds in large hall. Film
concludes with scenes from football match
between the Welsh Guards and the
Gloucester Regiment in the White City
stadium and a caption appeal "His Majesty's
Welsh Guards require another 1,000 men.
CYMRU AM BYTH" (Wales for Ever – the
Welsh Guards motto).

Notes
Summary: the King authorised the formation
of the Welsh Guards on 26 February 1915
and the 1st Battalion embarked for France
on 17 August 1915, from which one may
infer that this recruitment film was made
between these two dates.
catalogued: KGTG 2/1987

IWM 1216 · GB, (?) 7/1916
**JOHN BULL'S ANIMATED SKETCHBOOK
NO 15**

b/w · 1 reel · 465' (8 mins) · silent
intertitles: none

sp Ruffell's *pr* Cartoon Company
animation Buxton, Dudley or Dyer, Anson
(?)

■ Short, humorous stop-frame animation
  propaganda film made for British Home
  Front audiences during the First World
  War.

The film consists solely of a series of
animated jokes, drawn and lettered directly
onto the screen by "our famous artist". The
artist's hand is shown (speeded up) as a
scene is drawn with a brush, and then
inhabited by animated cut-outs, moved
frame by frame. The illustrations are in a
comic style similar to Bruce Bairnsfather.
The artist interjects comments on his own
performance, *eg* "I receive remuneration for
doing this sometimes", "A little
encouragement would oblige", etc. The
principal animated episodes are as follows.
"Exclusive view of the countless prisoners
captured by the Germans" – the prisoners
are moving dummies on an endless belt
operated by the Kaiser himself. "In the
remainder of the front there is nothing to
report" – it is a shirt front. "Zeppelin
reconnoitring over Greece" – a fly and a
bowl of dripping. "The German Fleet sails
out to meet the British" – a change of
perspective reveals the drawing to be of
houses, chimneys and telegraph poles –
"Sorry my mistake". "An explanation of the
expression 'Curtain Fire'" – a curtained
window beside a fireplace: "See the point?"
– a gimlet or corkscrew. "A moon ... A star
... Two stars ... Three stars" – the three stars
are on a bottle which the moon drinks,
becoming drunk and then ("Whoa Emma ...
I'm off home") setting. "Last night we gained
three metres: Berlin" – three German
soldiers cross the screen then return, each
carrying a gas meter. "Another Zeppelin
destroyed" – a caricature Charlie Chaplin in
a wheelchair ultimately defeats the Zeppelin
by having it tie itself in knots over the
unpronounceable name of a Russian
victory, after which he grins, stands up and
pins a medal on himself.

Notes
Production: the film carries no credits.
Production information as given is derived
or deduced from Rachael Low's *History of
the British Film*. Thus, a release date of July
1916 is inferred from the issue number, the
fact that issues were released monthly, and
the date of May 1915 for issue number 1.
Sponsor/production company: Low states
the films were "nominally" made by "The
Cartoon Company" but actually sponsored
and distributed by Ruffell's, a renting firm.

Buxton and Dyer produced alternate issues
of the *Sketchbook* ("Each artist, working
separately, was able to finish one cartoon in
eight weeks, one being released each
month") but it has not been possible to
determine which was responsible for this
issue.
Remarks: the film offers confirmation of the
lack of sophistication of the First World
War's sense of humour – many of the jokes
are very obvious, but even so the point is
underlined by the artist's hand, a further
caption etc.
[Rachael Low, *The History of the British Film
1914-1918*, Allen and Unwin (1950): 172]
catalogued JCK: 5/1987

IWM 1217 · GB, (?) 1918
the WOMEN FARMERS OF BRITAIN

b/w · 1 reel · 661' (11 mins) · silent
intertitles: English

pr Pathé

■ Work of the Warwickshire branch of the
  Women's Land Army, including a march
  through the centre of Birmingham, 1918
  (?).

I. The rally in Birmingham led by a male
band. The women are mostly in uniform.
The marching column includes a steam
tractor, a horse-drawn plough and a horse-
drawn rake. The procession goes up New
Street past the cinema, and up to the Town
Hall.
II. Work on the farm, with Land Girls
cleaning out stables, chasing bullocks and
cattle out to pasture, unloading sacks from
a cart, hoeing a field by hand, thatching a
hayrick and hoeing a field of cabbages with
a horse-drawn hoe. The heavy and
monotonous nature of the work is stressed.
One girl using a mechanical horse-drawn
reaper stops to repair a jam in the
mechanism. Her technical proficiency is
stressed. The girls continue bundling corn
stooks, and ploughing with a horse-drawn
plough.

[shotsheet available]
catalogued SDB: 10/1982

IWM 1218 · GB, (?) 1918
the WRECK OF THE L33

b/w · 1 reel · 617' (11 mins) · silent
intertitles: English

pr Gaumont (?)

- Film of the wrecked Zeppelin L33 in Essex after its crash on 24 September 1916.

Opens with general views of the substantially intact metal structure of the burnt-out Zeppelin. Further shots show a gondola (with various military and naval personnel working in and around it), propellers, the engine telegraph, a badly wrecked engine, bomb droppers (an officer is seen attaching labels to them) and views of the lattice structure from inside the Zeppelin. General Sir William Robertson, Chief of the Imperial General Staff, is seen inspecting the wreckage. Lieut F Sowrey, 39 Squadron RFC, who shot down the sister Zeppelin L32 and his friend Lieut Leefe Robinson VC, also of 39 Squadron are seen passing through the barrier (presumably erected round the site of the wreck). A nearby cottage ("only 30 yards from the wreck") is shown, as is the family living there. The Secretary of State for War, David Lloyd George, and the First Lord of the Admiralty, Arthur Balfour, arrive to inspect the wreck.
[shotsheet available]
catalogued SDB: 10/1982

Topical Budget Newsreel

NTB 89-02 · GB, 10/5/1913
TOPICAL BUDGET 89-2

b/w · 1 reel · 24' (1 min) · silent
intertitles: English

pr Topical Film Company

■ Fragment of an item showing a recruiting march through East London by the Essex Field Artillery and Royal Navy cadets, May 1913.

Notes
Title: since this is the earliest example of a Topical Budget in the IWM's holdings, the exact form and layout of the title does differ slightly from later ones.
catalogued SDB: 1/1984

NTB 164-01 · GB, 14/10/1914
TOPICAL BUDGET 164-1

b/w · 1 reel · 58' (1 min) · silent
intertitles: English

pr Topical Film Company *cam* Engholm (?)

■ Conflict in Antwerp.

'THE ATTACK ON ANTWERP. Belgian infantry and artillerymen replying to the German attack on Antwerp.' Belgian troops fire from trenches at the side of a road; also shots of a gun emplacement in a field.

Notes
Summary: see also descriptive note in McKernan.
catalogued JCK: 5/1993

NTB 165-02 · GB, 24/10/1914
TOPICAL BUDGET 165-2

b/w · 1 reel ·' (1 min) · silent
intertitles: English

pr Topical Film Company

I. Troops retreating from Antwerp arrive in Ostend. 'GALLANT DEFENDERS. The arrival of allied troops at Ostend after evacuating Antwerp.' Shots of street by quayside in Ostend where a procession of pedestrians, carts and motor vehicles (including a British motor bus). Two columns of Belgian troops pass through. Tram passes in background.
II. Canadian soldiers in England. 'SONS OF THE EMPIRE. Canadian troops arrive in England prepared to defend the Empire.'

The troops are seen arriving on rail baggage wagons. Some wash themselves (outdoors), another is seen writing a letter. A group of the soldiers pose for the camera with a large Union Flag which has a border made up of miniatures of Allied flags.
III. More refugees enter Ostend. 'OSTEND IN WAR-TIME. Refugees of all sorts and conditions pour into Ostend and crowd the steamers leaving for England.' Scenes of refugees passing through the streets of Ostend in carts and on foot. Shots of the quayside (presumably taken at the same time as those in item I) showing people assembling on the quay.
IV. Trafalgar day. 'ENGLAND EXPECTS. London pays a silent tribute to Nelson's memory in Trafalgar Square.' Large crowds gather around Nelson's Column on Trafalgar Day, many of them waving their hats for the camera. The base of the column is decked with banners inscribed with patriotic slogans: "NO PRICE CAN BE TOO HIGH WHEN HONOUR AND FREEDOM ARE AT STAKE – P.M. ASQUITH", "FIGHT FOR KING" (this between the paws of one of the lions) and "ENGLAND EXPECTS EVERY MAN TO DO HIS DUTY".

Notes
Summary: see also descriptive note in McKernan.
catalogued JCK: 5/1993

NTB 168-01 · GB, 11/11/1914
TOPICAL BUDGET 168-1

b/w · 1 reel · 265' (4 mins) · silent
intertitles: English

pr Topical Film Company

I. Reports of sunken warships (including some fakes). 'OUR NAVAL LOSSES. Ships of His Majesty's Navy that have encountered the Germans. H.M.S. Monmouth sunk by German Warships off Chili (sic).' The film starts with HMS *Monmouth*, sunk in the Battle of Coronel on 1 November 1914, represented by film of HMS *Donegal*, sister to the *Monmouth*, shown in harbour before the war. 'H.M.S. Good Hope took fire during the battle and sank.' Tracking shot around prow of ship representing HMS *Good Hope*, also at anchor before the war: this time the ship shown is her sistership HMS *King Alfred*. 'H.M.S. Hogue sunk by a German submarine in the North Sea.' Genuine footage of *Hogue* (sunk on 2 September), again at anchor before the war.
II. Mexican police. 'MEXICAN UNREST. The Police of Mexico City are now armed with

rifles and will become part of the Cities Military Guard.' Large numbers of Mexico City policemen march past the camera in a formal parade. Passing pedestrians observe them. (The "unrest" alluded to in the intertitle is conspicuously absent.)
III. Grenadier Guards Band. 'THE SOUND OF THE DRUM. The Band of the Grenadier Guards stimulates recruiting by playing Martial Music through the streets.' Shots of the Guards band (and troops) marching through the streets (of London ?).
IV. The 1914 Lord Mayor's Show, London. 'LORD MAYOR'S SHOW. Colonial troops who will shortly be in the fighting line, take part in the Historic Pageant.' The Lord Mayor climbs into the coach, which sets off: high angle view of the crowds tightly packed on either side of the road while troops and cavalry march past. Item concludes with shot of the Lord Mayor alighting from the coach.

Notes
Summary: see also descriptive note in McKernan.
catalogued SDB & JCK: 5/1993

NTB 178-01 · GB, 20/1/1915
TOPICAL BUDGET 178-1

b/w · 1 reel · 480' (8 mins) · silent
intertitles: English

pr Topical Film Company

I. Men of the East Kents in barracks at Winchester. 'THE OLDEST REGIMENT. The Buffs (East Kents) stationed at Winchester is the oldest Regiment in the British Army.' Posed MS of a group of officers. Men fix bayonets and march off past camera. Rifle inspection – sergeant checks the open bolts and rifling.
II. Indian troops behind the lines in France. 'INDIANS AT ARRAS. Indian troops return to Arras for a rest after weeks of hard fighting.' Indian troops – apparently perfectly fit – board an ambulance. British, French and Indian troops stand about chatting.
III. The mayor of London reviews volunteer soldiers. 'THE PEN AND THE RIFLE. The Lord Mayor Sir Charles Johnstone inspects the Chartered Secretaries' Corps at the Mansion House.' March past of men in bowler hats and overcoats. The mayor inspects "the ranks".
IV. Soldiers on a cross country run. 'MILITARY ATHLETES. The Southend Harriers organise a military cross country run between the troops stationed in the vicinity.' Pan across a group of men in varied styles

of running gear – they wave. The men run down street past camera. Close-up of the winner of the five miles race – No 139, Rifleman Jarvis of the 14th Rifle Brigade.
V. Royal Field Artillery Territorials practise digging trenches. 'ROYAL FIELD ARTILLERY. Members of the Royal Field Artillery (Territorial) making trenches and 'dug-outs' on Hampstead Heath.' Men work with picks and shovels to dig a trench and construct a neat dug-out roofed with timber and turves. The men pose by a donkey.

Notes
Summary (item III): about 600 of the Chartered Secretaries' Drilling Corps attended a service at St Botolph's Church, Bishopsgate, with their commandant Sir Ernest Clarke. After the service the men marched to the Mansion House, accompanied by the drums and bugles of the 66th North London Scouts, where they were inspected by the Lord Mayor.
Remarks (item III): it is difficult to take this sequence seriously.
catalogued NAP: 6/1991

NTB 191-01 · GB, 21/4/1915
TOPICAL BUDGET 191-1

b/w · 1 reel · 62' (1 min) · silent
intertitles: English

pr Topical Film Company

■ The Sultan of Turkey.

'SULTAN OF TURKEY. The Sultan accompanied by the Grand Vizier and all the Ministers leaving the Palace after a war council.' Elderly dignitaries, laden with decorations, leave the palace and enter open carriages, which drive off one by one.

Notes
Summary: see also descriptive note in McKernan.
catalogued JCK: 5/1993

NTB 194-02 · GB, 15/5/1915
TOPICAL BUDGET 194-2

b/w · 1 reel · 185' (3 mins) · silent
intertitles: English

pr Topical Film Company

I. Presidents Poincaré and Deschanel. 'THE TWO PRESIDENTS. M. Poincaré offers his congratulations to M. Paul Deschanel after

visiting the crippled at the Trocadero, Paris.'
II. London demonstration and anti-German riots. 'LONDON'S PROTEST. "All Germans must go" was the unanimous verdict of an impromptu meeting held outside the Royal Exchange.' 'ANTI-GERMAN RIOTS. Anti-German feeling runs high in all parts of London, many shops wrecked and their contents thrown into the streets.'

Notes
Cataloguing: information taken largely from printed sources. This item currently exists as a negative only and is unavailabie for viewing.
catalogued JCK: 5/1993

NTB 204-01 · GB, 21/7/1915
TOPICAL BUDGET 204-1

b/w · 1 reel · 50' (1 min) · silent
intertitles: English

pr Topical Film Company

■ Women march in support of the war effort.

'WOMEN'S MARCH THROUGH LONDON. A vast procession of women headed by Mrs Pankhurst, march through London to show the Minister of Munitions their willingness to help in any war service.' Filmed from a rooftop, the procession, which is quite large, is seen walking past. The women carry banners containing such slogans as "Mobilise Brains & Energy of Women" and "Three cheers for our gallant soldiers".

Notes
Summary: see also descriptive note in McKernan; the complete issue apparently contained an item showing the culmination of the march, with the ladies meeting Lloyd George, but this does not survive in this print.
catalogued JCK: 5/1993

NTB 213-02 · GB, 25/9/1915
TOPICAL BUDGET 213-2

b/w · 1 reel · 118' (2 mins) · silent
intertitles: English

pr Topical Film Company

I. Funeral of fireman J S Green. 'FUNERAL OF FIREMAN HERO. J.S. Green whose fearless bravery was instrumental in saving 22 lives from a fire caused by a Zeppelin raid on the London District.' Brass-helmeted

firemen carry the coffin to the hearse; shots of the cortège travelling through the streets, watched by a large crowd.
II. Flag day in aid of Serbia. 'SERBIAN FLAG DAY. Many well-known actresses sell flags on behalf of gallant little Serbia, to soldiers returning on leave from the trenches.' Actresses (many of them dressed in Welsh national costume) stand on the streets (of London) and sell flags to both soldiers and civilians.

Notes
Summary: see also descriptive note in McKernan.
catalogued JCK: 5/1993

NTB 219-02 · GB, 6/11/1915
TOPICAL BUDGET 219-2

b/w · 1 reel · 171' (3 mins) · silent
intertitles: English

pr Topical Film Company

I. Trinidadian troops in London. 'TRINIDAD TO THE TRENCHES. Men from Trinidad who have answered the Empire's Call, march to the Mansion House and receive the City's welcome from the Lord Mayor.' The troops are formally inspected by officers in greatcoats, before marching (with band) through the streets of London. All the soldiers are white. (The mayor's reception is not shown.)
II. Help for Serbia. 'HELP FOR SERBIA. British and French troops landing at the base. The difficulty in disembarking the horses is vividly shown.' Shots of French troops marching past; horses and empty carts are shown passing along a country road while British soldiers stand around idly (one of them is asleep). At the quayside, a horse is lowered from a ship in a harness; the horse is in obvious distress and struggles wildly to escape.
III. Captured German artillery on display in Paris. 'GUNS FROM CHAMPAGNE. Parisians go to see the howitzers, Taubes and many machine guns, taken from the enemy during the last battle in Champagne.' A large assembly of weapons, including artillery, machineguns and even aeroplanes, is laid out in a courtyard, where a sizeable number of people wander around inspecting them.

Notes
Summary: see also descriptive note in McKernan.
catalogued JCK: 5/1993

NTB 221-01 · GB, 17/11/1915
TOPICAL BUDGET 221-1

b/w · 1 reel · 58' (1 min) · silent
intertitles: English

pr Topical Film Company

■ Belgian sappers build pontoon bridge.

'BELGIAN ENGINEERS IN THE FIELD.
Belgian engineers erecting bridges over the
rivers in Flanders. This work is vital to an
army and has to be carried out in some
cases under heavy shell fire.' A montage of
shots show the Belgian soldiers constructing
a bridge. The setting is rural and most of the
materials seem to have been taken from the
surrounding woodland.

Notes
Summary: see also descriptive note in
McKernan. A further item from this issue,
concerning a fire in a Paris timberyard, is
held as **IWM 1070h**.
catalogued JCK: 5/1993

NTB 222-02 · GB, 27/11/1915
TOPICAL BUDGET 222-2

b/w · 1 reel · 165' (3 mins) · silent
intertitles: English

pr Topical Film Company

I. Royal Field Artillery in London. 'ROYAL
FIELD ARTILLERY. Although Germany
started superior to the Allies in Artillery, the
conditions have rapidly changed. Some of
the R.F.A. on a recruiting campaign in the
City.' Horse-drawn artillery passes through
streets in the City of London; large crowds
line the streets; many spectators lurk near
the camera. The troops pass by the Mansion
House.
II. British troops in the trenches. 'LEAVING
THE TRENCHES. The methods employed in
the present "underground warfare" to pass
through traverse communicating trenches
from the front line of trenches to comparative
safety in the rear.' Troops stand in line in a
trench (one not on the battlefield); another
line of soldiers fire their guns from the cover
of a trench section. Troops are also seen
walking along a trench towards the camera
looking bored.
III. The Italian Navy. 'ITALIAN NAVY. Our Ally
in the Mediterranean is making great efforts
to bring her Navy up to full fighting strength,
in as short a time as possible.' At a shipyard,
various naval officers walk past the camera;
a bishop and members of the clergy are

also present, passing a ship's propeller. The
ship's prow is seen on a slipway, where she
is launched (viewed from the stern).

Notes
Summary: see also descriptive note in
McKernan.
catalogued JCK: 5/1993

NTB 223-01 · GB, 1/12/1915
TOPICAL BUDGET 223-1

b/w · 1 reel · 29' (1 min) · silent
intertitles: English

pr Topical Film Company

■ 'THE TOWN OF LILLE. The ruined
appearance of the Manchester of France
gives an idea of what would happen to
English towns if the Germans were able to
land in England.'

Four shots, taken from a high angle, of parts
of the town. The "ruins" referred to in the
intertitle are scarcely in evidence; indeed,
the town hardly looks damaged at all.

Notes
Summary: see also descriptive note in
McKernan; the records do not indicate what
other items, if any, were included in this
particular newsreel issue. This print has no
main title.
catalogued JCK: 5/1993

NTB 223-02 · GB, 4/12/1915
TOPICAL BUDGET 223-2

b/w · 1 reel · 119' (2 mins) · silent
intertitles: English

pr Topical Film Company

I. Belgian Cavalry in training. 'KING
ALBERT'S CAVALRY. Cavalry keeping fit for
the time when their service will be required
to drive the Hun invader out of Belgium.' The
cavalry are seen in action, galloping uphill
and across open country.
II. War damage. 'RUSSIAN ADVANCE. One
of the towns where the Russians have driven
back the German invader. Peasants are seen
returning to their ruined homes with what
remains of their personal effects.' Carts pass
down devastated street while two (British ?)
men point. Ruined buildings are seen. Shot
of children playing outside another ruined
building.

Summary: see also descriptive note in McKernan. A further item from this issue ('U.S.A. MAMMOTH WARSHIP') is held as **IWM 1061-08d**.
catalogued JCK: 5/1993

NTB 224-01 · GB, 8/12/1915
TOPICAL BUDGET 224-1

b/w · 1 reel · 134' (2 mins) · silent
intertitles: English

pr Topical Film Company

I. Ruined bridge on the Vistula. 'CROSSING THE VISTULA. The ruins of a bridge blown up by the Russians before retreating from the Germans.' The cantilevered bridge has collapsed in the centre and lies sprawled across the river. The bridge is filmed firstly from face on, and then from alongside.
II. Proxy wedding in France. 'MARRIAGE BY PROXY. The French authorities are allowing soldiers serving at the front to nominate a friend to act for them at their wedding ceremony. A French "poilu" taking the part of a bridegroom for his chum.' A brief shot of the "happy couple" as they leave the church, followed by their guests.
III. Soldiers dismantle tents prior to going to new billets. 'FROM CAMPS TO BILLETS. Nearly all the Camps have been "struck" and the men have been billeted on the neighbouring householders. A merry party clearing out their tents and marching off to their new homes.' A group of British soldiers are seen dismantling their tent (other large tents remain in the background), and then marching off, their rifles on their shoulders.

Notes
Summary: see also descriptive note in McKernan; issue has main title and first item (on Eton War Workers) missing.
catalogued JCK: 5/1993

NTB 224-02 · GB, 11/12/1915
TOPICAL BUDGET 224-2

b/w · 1 reel · 61' (1 min) · silent
intertitles: English

pr Topical Film Company

■ Patriotic pilgrimage in France.

'PATRIOTS AT CHAMPIGNY. The annual pilgrimage at Champigny la Bataill organised by M. Maurice Barres to honour the Patriots

who have died for their Country.' The procession makes its way past the cemetery at Champigny. Umbrellas are much in evidence, since it is raining, and many people are carrying wreaths. Three men (one of them presumably M Barrès) give speeches.

Notes
Summary: see also descriptive note in McKernan.
catalogued JCK: 5/1993

NTB 225-02 · GB, 18/12/1915
TOPICAL BUDGET 225-2

b/w · 1 reel · 57' (1 min) · silent
intertitles: English

pr Topical Film Company

■ Canadian troops depart for the Front.

'CANADA'S CONTINGENT. H.R.H. The Duke of Connaught inspects, at Montreal, Canada's New Army upon their departure for the Front.' The Canadians parade before departure; flag raising ceremony takes place; the Duke watches as the troops march past in the snow.

Notes
Summary: see also descriptive note in McKernan; the records do not indicate what other items, if any, were included in this particular newsreel issue. This print has no main title.
catalogued JCK: 5/1993

NTB 235-02 · GB, 26/2/1916
TOPICAL BUDGET 235-2

b/w · 1 reel · 204' (3 mins) · silent
intertitles: English

pr Topical Film Company

I. Military football match. 'ARTIST'S RIFLES V. IRISH GUARDS. The Irish Guards defeat the Artist's Rifles (O.T.C.) by four goals to all (sic) at a football match held at Warley.' Both teams are seen leaving a brick building and heading for the pitch. The match takes place, on a pitch which is in terrible condition, while an audience of soldiers watches.
II. Snow in London 'LONDON UNDER SNOW. The (Snow) Battle of London. Members of the Inns of Court O.T.C. have a pitched battle near their training camp.' Thick

snow in a park (Lincoln's Inn Fields ?) is used as ammunition as the cadets have a frantic snowball fight. A young woman enters the fray and is pelted vigorously, although she manages to keep a smile on her face. III. The Royal Baths. 'THE OLD ROMAN BATH. 2,000 years ago the Romans discovered the healing virtues of the hot mineral spring at Bath. Over 8,000 wounded soldiers suffering from rheumatism, sciatica etc. have been restored to health.' Wounded soldiers, clad in their hospital garments, stand around the hot spring and pose for the camera. Most of them are smoking.

Notes
Summary: see also descriptive note in McKernan; missing items appear to be a sequence of tobogganing in Hampstead and an item showing Viscount French visiting Bath (presumably a preliminary piece for the item included here).
Technical: several feet of blank film separate the items present.
catalogued JCK: 5/1993

NTB 237-02 · GB, 11/3/1916
TOPICAL BUDGET 237-2

b/w · 1 reel · 43' (1 min) · silent
intertitles: English

pr Topical Film Company

■ Naval guns in action.

'NAVAL BOMBARDMENT IN THE BOSPHORUS. An unique film showing the destructive power of Naval guns. Taken on board a Russian destroyer engaged in shelling the Turkish positions. Bluejackets bringing up shells for the gun.' 'THE LARGEST GUN IN ACTION. Loading the gun, the Chief Gunner gives the signal to fire and the shell is seen to burst over the Turkish entrenchments. The effect of shell fire on the large building which is completely demolished.'

Notes
Cataloguing: information taken largely from printed sources. This item currently exists as a negative only and is unavailable for viewing.
catalogued JCK: 5/1993

NTB 238-01 · GB, 15/3/1916
TOPICAL BUDGET 238-1

b/w · 1 reel · 300' (5 mins) · silent

intertitles: English

pr Topical Film Company

I. Ambulance for horses. 'MOTOR AMBULANCES FOR HORSES. One of the R.S.P.C.A.'s two horse motor ambulance (sic) in use, showing how wounded horses at the Front are conveyed to the Base.' A reluctant horse is persuaded to enter the side door of the horsebox/ambulance, "The Gift of the RSPCA Army Veteran's Hospital, Rouen". Once the horse is inside, the door is winched up. The ambulance drives back to the stable at base.
II. Artillery men relaxing. 'ARTILLERY AT THE BASE. A battery of Artillery resting at the base after a spell of hard work in the fighting line.' The artillery men are travelling home and relaxing; two men at ease on top of a gun-carriage smoke pipes, followed by another horse-drawn gun-carriage. Cavalry canter along open country road; some look at the camera as they pass.
III. Russian troops set off for the Front. 'RUSSIAN SOLDIERS OFF TO THE FRONT. The fully trained soldiers leaving for the Eastern Front. The rifles they are armed with were captured from the Austrians and have a very short bayonet.' Fairly poor shots of the parade of soldiers as they walk through the streets of Petrograd. 'SOLDIERS DRILLING IN PETROGRAD. Russian recruits called to the colours are being drilled in the streets of Petrograd. Soldiers practising in advance by a series of rushes in open order.' Further footage from same source as above (and of similarly poor picture quality). Soldiers in combat training in a large street/square: they crouch as if in hiding, then get up and charge, led by an officer brandishing a sword. At the officer's command, the men fall again, then resume their charge.
IV. 'Single Men First' protest meeting. 'MARRIED MENS' (sic) PROTEST MEETING. London attested married men hold a Single Men First protest meeting at Tower Hill. Mr W. Dyson speaking to the meeting, calling on the Government to fulfil the pledge.' On a drizzly day, Dyson addresses a large group of men, many of whom (especially those in the foreground) seem more interested in the camera. As Dyson reaches a conclusion, men raise their hands (and bowler hats) in support.

Notes
Summary: see also descriptive note in McKernan.
catalogued JCK: 5/1993

NTB 239-01 · GB, 22/3/1916
TOPICAL BUDGET 239-1

b/w · 1 reel · 295' (5 mins) · silent
intertitles: English

pr Topical Film Company

I. The German Athenaeum. 'THE GERMAN
ATHENAEUM LTD. are invoking the aid of
the English Law to forcibly eject the Services
Club, and as a protest against such action
by a Company so constituted any attempt at
entering these premises of the German
Athenaeum Ltd. will be resisted'. A sign
bearing this message (and much more) is
hoisted into position outside the German
Athenaeum in Stratford Place. Outside,
Charles Palmer, the editor of the Globe
newspaper, addresses a crowd of men
gathered in the rain.
II. Another 'Single Men First' meeting.
'LONDON HUSBANDS' PROTEST. Passing
the resolution at the protest meeting of
attested married men in Hyde Park.' Shots of
a sea of faces listening to speakers
(although neither the speakers, nor much of
the park itself, are visible). The men raise
hands (and hats) in response to speaker's
resolution.
III. Irish soldiers attend memorial service at
Westminster Cathedral. 'IRISH SOLDIERS AT
MASS. The service was held at Westminster
Cathedral for Irish soldiers who had fallen in
the war.' A company of Irish soldiers (plus
some Australians ?) march along street.
They enter the Cathedral. (The service itself
is not shown.
IV. Bomb damage in Salonika. 'DAMAGE BY
ZEPPELIN AT SALONIKA. British soldiers
operating a primitive Greek fire pump in their
efforts to quench the flames at the Ottoman
Bank.' British sailors and soldiers furiously
pump away at the handles of an extremely
antiquated pump. Poor quality long shot of
the building smouldering away. 'BOMBS ON
THE GREEKS. The Zeppelin drops on the
Greek section of the city. Several Greek
subjects were the only victims. Big hole in
the street caused by a bomb.' Further
footage of the damage in Greece. Shots of
soldiers and sailors repair tramlines and
clear streets. Men investigate an enormous
hole in the middle of a street caused by a
bomb from a Zeppelin. (Filmed by Varges ?)

Notes
Summary: see also descriptive note in
McKernan.
catalogued JCK: 5/1993

NTB 239-02 · GB, 25/3/1916
TOPICAL BUDGET 239-2

b/w · 1 reel · 285' (5 mins) · silent
intertitles: English

pr Topical Film Company

I. Ammunition column at the Front ?.
Panning shot around quayside on river
(estuary ?) in barren, rolling landscape.
Soldiers (not British ?) sit around on the
grass. In the middle distance, a large cargo
ship is docked at a makeshift quay. Boxes
are pulled along the beach on a horse-
drawn cart (probably an ammunition column
– see **Notes**).
II. The London Transport Column. 'THE
CITY'S RED CROSS MEN. The London
Transport Column, who are engaged in
transporting wounded from the London
Railway Stations march to Buckingham
Palace.' A procession of ambulances and
cars drive into the front courtyard of
Buckingham Palace. A long line of men
marches out of the gates and down the Mall.
III. 'INSPECTING RUSSIAN INFANTRY. One
of the features in the drill of a Russian
infantryman is the way he follows his officer
with his eyes ready to read his thoughts and
to obey.' Line of Russian troops stand to
attention with sabres drawn as their
commanding officer passes. After he has
passed by, the men abruptly turn their
heads in his direction. General Paget with
the Russians: officers salute him as he gets
ready to leave. 'RUSSIAN CAVALRY. Sir A.
Paget reviewing Russian Cavalry as they
pass through the snow clad forests on their
way to the Eastern Front.' General Paget,
accompanied by British and Russian officers
review a column of cavalry as it heads off
into the forest.
IV. Reception for blind soldiers at
Buckingham Palace. 'KING ENTERTAINS
WOUNDED SOLDIERS. Blinded soldiers
from St. Dunstan's arriving at Buckingham
Palace. They were entertained by the King
and Queen who personally saw to the
comfort of their guests.' Several B-type
omnibuses (one from 'Mortlake Garage')
carry the soldiers into the palace through the
Horse Guard's Parade entrance. Inside,
young women are seen getting out of cars.
The King and Queen are not seen. (Abrupt
end.)

Notes
Summary (item I): no intertitle on this item. It
is likely that this is the missing item in the
NFTVA's copy. McKernan records an
intertitle reading 'AMMUNITION FOR THE
FRONT. An ammunition column loading up
with shells at the quay side and leaving with

supplies for the front'. This broadly agrees with the footage contained here.
Summary: see also descriptive note in McKernan.
catalogued JCK: 5/1993

NTB 240-01 · GB, 29/3/1916
TOPICAL BUDGET 240-1

b/w · 1 reel · 30' (1 min) · silent
intertitles: English

pr Topical Film Company

I. Russian artillerymen fuse shells. 'ADVANCE ON THE EASTERN FRONT. Russia having replenished her ammunition supply is carrying on a great offensive on the Eastern Front. Gunners setting fuses of shrapnel shells previous to their being fired.' Three Russian artillerymen open a limber and remove 76.2mm (?) shells. The fuses are set and the shells are carried off.

catalogued NAP: 7/1991

NTB 240-02 · GB, 1/4/1916
TOPICAL BUDGET 240-2

b/w · 1 reel · 244' (4 mins) · silent
intertitles: English

pr Topical Film Company

I. Russian boy scouts. 'RUSSIAN BOY SCOUTS. One of Russia's Boy Scouts, although only fifteen. He has been decorated by the Czar for conspicuous bravery whilst on active service.' The boy, in uniform, holds the reins of a pony which, with the help of two adults, he manages to mount. He rides past a line of boy scouts, saluting them as he goes. (Poor quality film.)
II. Danish troops on parade. 'REVIEW OF DANISH TROOPS. The King of Denmark reviewing his army in Copenhagen. All the neutral nations of Europe are compelled to keep their armies in readiness.' Crowds lining the road cheer as King Christian X drives past in an open car. The review takes place in an open field, watched by a large crowd. Infantry, motor-cyclists, cavalry and horse artillery pass by.
III. Storm damage in London. 'THE GREAT BLIZZARD. The greatest blizzard for thirty five years, causes enormous damage throughout the country. Trees uprooted in London squares, fences and buildings blown down.' Branches are cleared from one of the trees blown down during the storm by a group of men; a woman with two small children talks to one of the men. A wooden hut lies wrecked; more toppled trees are shown. 'WRECKED BY THE STORM. A factory in course of construction is completely wrecked by the gale, girders and stanchions being twisted into all sorts of weird shapes.' Shots of the ruined factory, with men attempting to repair the broken beams, although it is clear that it is a hopeless case. Twisted girders are strewn across the ground. Rubble is cleared.

Notes
Summary: see also descriptive note in McKernan; the first item (on the Prince of Serbia's visit to London) is missing, although the main title is present.
catalogued JCK: 5/1993

NTB 241-01 · GB, 5/4/1916
TOPICAL BUDGET 241-1

b/w · 1 reel · 31' (1 min) · silent
intertitles: English

pr Topical Film Company

■ Boy in munitions factory.

'WOMEN WINNING THE WAR. Women and boys working in munition factories replace men who are able to join the colours. Working on capstan lathes and large vertical drilling machines.' A brief scene of a boy working on a capstan lathe (as there is no footage of women, the item is presumably incomplete).

Notes
Summary: see also descriptive note in McKernan.
catalogued JCK: 5/1993

NTB 241-02 · GB, 8/4/1916
TOPICAL BUDGET 241-2

b/w · 1 reel · 89' (1 min) · silent
intertitles: English

pr Topical Film Company

I. Versailles in use as a hospital. 'PALACE OF VERSAILLES AS HOSPITAL. Scenes in the French Red Cross hospital where the "Poilus" are cared for by charming nurses.' Nurses and a doctor attend to a patient. One of the long rooms of the Palace of Versailles has been converted into a ward, in which doctors and nurses are carrying out a tour of inspection. Some of the patients, sitting in bed or walking around.

II. Married men go to war. 'MARRIED MENS' (sic) CALL. How the first groups of married men to be called to the colours, will be trained, before they are passed as for the front.' Scenes of shirt-sleeved recruits being put through their paces: drill, exercises, weapons training (bayonet and machinegun) and practice in trenches.

III. Rowing race. 'KEEPING FIT AT SEA. Middies occupy their spare time with racing for the championship of the Fleet.' Sailors hold a rowing race. (Abrupt end.)

Notes

Summary: see also descriptive note in McKernan.
catalogued JCK: 5/1993

NTB 242-01 · GB, 12/4/1916
TOPICAL BUDGET 242-1

b/w · 1 reel · 299' (5 mins) · silent
intertitles: English

pr Topical Film Company

I. Canteen at munitions factory. 'MUNITION WORKERS CANTEEN. Women after working on munitions enjoying an excellent dinner served in the canteen at actual cost.' After a brief scene of the women at their workbenches, the sizeable canteen is shown; cups of tea are served, women sit at the tables. In the kitchen, cooks are seen preparing food (mostly rather unpleasant-looking cuts of meat).

II. The Lincolnfield Handicap horse race. 'THE LINCOLNFIELD HANDICAP. Mr. F. Philip's Clap Trap winning the Lincolfield (sic) at Lingfield Park. This is the Lincoln Handicap having been re-named under the new war racing conditions.' Horses are led out of the paddock and down to the starting post. The race itself. The paddock after the race: the winning horse Clap Trap is seen in close-up.

III. Cadets being inspected at the Guildhall, London. 'CADETS AT THE GUILDHALL. The Imperial Cadet Yeomanry (City of London) marching off from the Guildhall to be inspected by the Lord Mayor, at the Tower of London.' The cadets line up in the courtyard outside the Guildhall and are inspected by the Lord Mayor; lots of pigeons are also wandering around. Afterwards, the cadets march through the streets towards the Tower of London.

IV. Rugby match (New Zealand v South Africa). 'NEW ZEALANDERS WIN AT RUGBY. The New Zealanders have their revenge by

beating the South Africans at Richmond, by five points to three.' Both teams pose for the camera; shots of the action during the game, including scrummage.

V. US troops leave for Mexico. 'U.S. TROOPS FOR MEXICO. United States troops leaving on a transport, bound for Mexico, to protect the rights of American citizens from the insurgents.' Troops are crammed on board the US Army Transport *Kilpatrick*; most of them appear to be black. They wave as the ship puts to sea; many of them are climbing up the rigging.

Notes

Summary: see also descriptive note in McKernan.
catalogued JCK: 5/1993

NTB 242-02 · GB, 15/4/1916
TOPICAL BUDGET 242-2

b/w · 1 reel · 292' (5 mins) · silent
intertitles: English

pr Topical Film Company

I. Public School athletics. 'PUBLIC SCHOOL CHAMPIONSHIP. Mr. D.J. Bryceson wins the 100 yds., the quarter mile and the steeplechase thereby giving his school, Latymer Upper, Hammersmith, the Schools Championship.' The games take place in a huge, almost empty stadium (a cricket ground ?). Running race and hurdles are shown; the victorious Bryceson, wearing spectacles, poses for the camera. Long jump competition is shown: close-up of the winner (unnamed) in his blazer.

II. French politicians visit London. 'FRENCH SENATORS AND DEPUTIES. French Parliamentarians are received by the Lord Mayor at the Mansion House and entertained to lunch.' Poorly filmed sequence of close shots of the various deputies, mostly dressed in smart coats and top hats, entering the Mansion House.

III. Motor-cycling. 'MOTORCYCLE HILL CLIMB. Public School Boys, many of whom are members of the O.T.C. test their skill in a Motor Cycle hill climb at Snowhill Worcestershire.' Prior to the race, competitors and officials gather on a road apparently in woodland. A motor-cycle is weighed prior to the race. The climb starts: competitors set off aided by push starts. The race itself takes place on open country roads, watched by a few people sitting by the hedgerows.

IV. Allied Nations War Council, Paris. 'BROTHERS IN ARMS. Representatives of the Allied Nations, attend the last War

- 463 -

Council in Paris. *FRANCE* M. BRIAND PREMIER.' Briand descends steps of building and gets into car. (Note still photographer in background.) 'FRANCE GENERAL ROQUES WAR MINISTER AND GENERAL JOFFRE.' Roques and Joffre walk towards camera along a Parisian street followed by a small crowd of civilians. 'GREAT BRITAIN MR H.H. ASQUITH PREMIER AND SIR EDWARD GREY.' Asquith and Grey, accompanied by an unidentified third man, descend the steps first seen above and get into a car. 'GREAT BRITAIN LORD KITCHENER WAR MINISTER.' Kitchener stands at the top of the steps, firstly frowning at the camera, then looking away, then turning his stern gaze back. 'RUSSIA M. ISOVOLSKY AMBASSADOR.' He is seen getting out of a car and ascending the steps. 'RUSSIA GENERAL GILINSKY.' He does the same. 'ITALY SIGNOR SALANDRA PREMIER AND BARON SONNINO.' Salandra, Sonnino and others, dressed formally, talk together on the steps, then descend towards a waiting car. 'ITALY GENERAL CADORNA.' Cadorna and another military man walk along the street before large gates; one of them speaks to a Gendarme, presumably asking directions, then they both continue on their way, past the camera. 'BELGIUM BARON BROQUEVILLE.' The Baron ascends the steps from his car. 'SERBIA M. PACHITCH PREMIER.' The white-bearded Pachitch stands at the doorway above the steps, then walks towards the camera. Item (and issue) ends with 'Topical' lozenge-shaped logo.

Notes

Summary (item IV): this was the first war conference of all the Allies, and began in Paris on 27 March 1916.
Summary: see also descriptive note in McKernan.
catalogued JCK: 5/1993

NTB 245-02 · GB, 6/5/1916
TOPICAL BUDGET 245-2

b/w · 1 reel · 331' (6 mins) · silent
intertitles: English

pr Topical Film Company

I. Scenes in Dublin after the suppression of the Easter Rebellion. 'THE DUBLIN REBELLION. Exclusive pictures of the scene of the fighting in Dublin.' 'River Liffey and Embankment, British Troops and Artillery Marching through the streets of Dublin. Soldiers on guard over a ruined building.' HA pan over O'Connell Bridge and the street beyond showing the ruined buildings between the bridge and Nelson's Pillar. LS along the Liffey and the embankment. Soldiers with shouldered arms march past smouldering ruins. Artillery limbers and wagons pass by. MS of shattered buildings – locals stand about surveying the debris. MS past a pile of rubble and a toppled street lamp to a passing column of troops. Soldiers with fixed bayonets guard a still-smoking ruin. LS of municipal building overlooking the Liffey. 'The Post Office and Metropole Hotel after the battle, the interior of the Post Office which is completely gutted. Sackville St ruins.' Ruins of the Metropole Hotel and pan left to Post Office building. MS interior of the gutted Post Office – a few men wander about in the wreckage. A fire engine ladder is extended up into the ruins. A group of labourers start to break up debris in still smouldering interior. 'A street barricade, batches of rebels being marched off to the Quay, one of the looted shops, soldiers on guard having their meals in the street.' MS of smashed windows, the frames partially filled with sandbags. A soldier stands by a low barricade made from planks and a ladder laid across a street. Detachment of soldiers marches by followed by a Red Cross wagon – visible within the ranks of soldiers are a few prisoners. MS of the smashed window of a looted shop – the remains of the window writing suggest that it may have sold sweets – a crowd mill about in the foreground. Three soldiers sit on the pavement eating – one drinks from his canteen.
II. French, Italian and British bandsmen in Paris. 'ALLIES' BANDS IN PARIS. Bands of the Garde Republicaine, the Italian Carabineiri (sic) and the Coldstream Guards, attend the festival for wounded at the Trocadero. Mdle. Paule Andral singing the National Anthems of the Allies.' MS of Mlle Andral as she sings standing in the open air – she is dressed as a 'personification of the nation'. MS of bandsmen posing for the camera – the British very subfusc compared to their Italian and French counterparts. The men exchange hats, one pipe-smoking Guardsman donning the plumed tricorn of the Carabinieri.

Notes

Summary: a censorship certificate following the opening titles reads 'This picture "The Dublin Rebellion" has been passed for Universal Exhibition'.
catalogued NAP: 6/1991

NTB 246-01 · GB, 10/5/1916
TOPICAL BUDGET 246-1

b/w · 1 reel · 298' (5 mins) · silent
intertitles: English

pr Topical Film Company

I. Cyclist's Corps exercise. 'THE CYCLIST'S CORPS. The 25th County of London (Cyclists) carrying out 'An Attack' near their training headquarters in Middlesex.' Soldiers cycle past along a country road. Men fire prone from behind a barricade of bicycles set up across the road, while others crouch in a drainage ditch alongside. One man perches uncomfortably on a paling fence. An enemy column approaches from the opposite direction and, after dispersing at point blank range, overruns the position. There are some casualties, one man lying St Catherine-like on his bicycle. The attackers fall prone and fire past the camera after the fleeing defenders.
II. An American oil warehouse burns. 'U.S. WAREHOUSE FIRE. An enormous oil warehouse in the United States, is completely gutted, despite the efforts of the firemen to control the outbreak.' Hoses play streams of water onto burning building – the fire is obviously quite active. General scene of fire engines and hoses stretched across the ground. MCU as a fireman lays a ladder against wall of the warehouse. Firemen stand by the main entrance looking up, smoke billowing about them.
III. May Queen ceremony. 'LONDON'S MAY QUEEN. Miss Cecily Smith being crowned May Queen of London at Hayes Common.' Procession of 'Merrie England Children' with banners – small girls play violins. A May Queen of Norwood passes with her retinue. Miss Smith sits beneath a canopy on a wagon drawn by boys dressed in (?) Lincoln green. She is crowned – after some difficulty – with a flowered circlet. CU of Cecily – a helpful girl at frame left helps hold the crown in position.
IV. Czechs demonstrate in London, ostensibly about the sinking of the *Lusitania*. 'LUSITANIA DAY. Czechs in native dress, and survivors of Germany's greatest crime of piracy, marching from the Embankment to Hyde Park.' Band precedes the parade which is led by a contingent from the British Empire Union. A large model of the *Lusitania* is drawn past in a glass-sided catafalque, followed by Czechs, some in national costume and many bearing banners and flags. Among the banners are 'WITH DEEPEST SORROW THE LONDON CZECHS REMEMBER LUSITANIA', 'HANG ALL PRO-GERMAN PEACEMONGERS', and – most to the point – 'SMASH HUNISH AUSTRIA, RESTORE FREE BOHEMIA'. A steady stream of London trams passes by in the background.

V. A boy munitions worker. 'BOY MUNITIONS WORKER. A capstan lathe at work, which is producing parts for searchlights. This machine is controlled by a thirteen year old schoolboy.' CU of a capstan lathe at work – it is clearly being operated by a woman who holds out the finished components for the camera. Cut to 3/4 rear profile of a young boy in charge of another lathe – in the background a man is busy at work with a hand file.

Notes
Remarks (item V): a boy making searchlight parts is only arguably a munitions worker, and it seems unlikely that he was simultaneously attending school. Semantics apart, the work of boys in the factories is doubtless an interesting unwritten chapter in British labour history.
catalogued NAP: 6/1991

NTB 247-01 · GB, 17/5/1916
TOPICAL BUDGET 247-1

b/w · 1 reel · 294' (5 mins) · silent
intertitles: English

pr Topical Film Company

I. Crowds gather to see Roger Casement at Bow Street police court. 'TRIAL OF CASEMENT. Crowds waiting outside Bow St. Police Station in the vain hope of obtaining a glimpse of the prisoner.' HA to entrance of the station where a small crowd has gathered by the doors. During the sequence the crowd grows in size. Some press photographers are present. A policeman holding some papers stands in the doorway – perhaps preparatory to reading a statement to the crowd.
II. Asquith with Lady Wimborne and Sir John Maxwell in Dublin. 'MR. ASQUITH IN DUBLIN. Sir John Maxwell inspecting the Trinity College Officers Training Corps in the grounds of Trinity College.' MS as Maxwell and officers walk along lines of OTC and St John Ambulance Corps. 'IRISH VOLUNTEERS. Mr Asquith and Lady Wimborne watch the march past of the Irish Association Voluntary Training Corps.' Asquith, Lady Wimborne, wife of the Lord Lieutenant of Ireland, and Lieutenant General Maxwell stand at the saluting point as men march past.
III. British troops collect arms captured in the Easter Rebellion. 'GERMAN RIFLES. Rifles and pikes used by the rebels in the riots, being brought in and stacked up by soldiers.' On a Dublin street a soldier carries past a bundle of home-made pikes. Others

follow carrying rifles which they stack against a wall. MS pan over the collected firearms and pieces of kit – it is a miscellaneous collection which includes a Martini-Henry, one or two Austrian M88 Mannlichers, a double-barrelled shotgun, an under-lever repeating rifle, a Mauser 71 and an English falling block sporting or target rifle. The kit includes a French bayonet. A rather corpulent officer inspects some of the captured rifles. CUs as a soldier works the bolt on an Italian Vetterli rifle and opens the breech on a Snider, holding it up to the camera.

IV. Inspection of children at a Foundling Hospital School. 'FOUNDLINGS ON PARADE. Bishop Taylor-Smith, Maj-General Sir Francis Lloyd and the Lord Mayor attend the Founding Hospital and inspect the children.' The VIPs pass down lines of small boys and then girls all turned out in school uniform.

Notes
Summary (item I): the preliminary hearing of the charge of high treason against Sir Roger Casement and Daniel Julian Bailey, a soldier of the Royal Ulster Rifles, was opened at Bow Street police court on 15 May, and continued until 17 May, when the two were committed for trial.
Summary (item II): the Prime Minister was in Dublin on 17 May to be sworn a member of the Privy Council in Ireland. General Maxwell became a Privy Councillor at the same time.
catalogued NAP: 7/1991

NTB 247-02 · GB, 20/5/1916
TOPICAL BUDGET 247-2

b/w · 1 reel · 292' (5 mins) · silent
intertitles: English

pr Topical Film Company

I. Blind soldiers are taken boating on Regents Park lake. 'SIGHTLESS SOLDIERS RECREATION. After working at useful trades during the day, blind soldiers from St. Dunstan's Hostel, enjoying a row on the Regent's Park Lake, with a lady as coxswain.' Man leads a chain of five blind soldiers past the camera. Each man takes up the oars in a boat, directed by a lady coxswain. The boats set off.

II. Irish Republican Brotherhood rebels taken prisoner by the British. 'SINN FEIN REBELS. Disarmed rebels marching from the Military Barracks in Dublin to Kingstown for deportation.' Two lance corporals look on as a column of IRB prisoners is escorted past. A small group of rebels stand fallen in for

the camera – CU of two of the prisoners, one distinguished by a mop of dark curly hair – the soldiers standing in the background are fusiliers. CU of a prisoner of note (?) – a bearded man wearing a suit and a pince-nez.

III. Military athletics meeting. 'MILITARY ATHLETIC MEETING. Gunner H. Phillips Canadian Regt. defeats Pte. W.R. Applegarth in the 100yds. One of the most interesting races – the obstacle race with the water jump.' CU as man in running gear leaves the blocks as the race begins. LS from behind the finishing point as six runners cross the line. CU, head and shoulders of the winner, Gunner Phillips. Runners in a longer race around the stadium pass the camera to breast the tape. The obstacle race – men jump a hedge into a water obstacle on the other side. The first two men keep their footing but a third obligingly stumbles.

IV. Roman Catholic procession. 'SOLEMN PUBLIC PROCESSION. North London Catholics take part in a procession through the streets of Holloway.' HA onto Roman Catholic street procession – boys support various images and elders follow with crosses and banners.

V. Women farm workers. 'WOMEN FARM WORKERS. Women Land Workers, who are replacing men on farms driving home and milking the cows, feeding pigs and calves. More recruits are still wanted by the Womens' Land service Corps.' Women set out from a farm house. Cattle are herded through a gate. Women in farmyard, holding baskets and milking stools. Girl feeds a calf from a pail. Women fill pig trough. A woman fills a pail of water from a stream – a rather precarious undertaking.

Notes
Summary: item IV is included in issue 247-1 in McKernan.
Technical: this episode is incomplete, the original film having been broken.
catalogued NAP: 7/1991

NTB 248-01 · GB, 24/5/1916
TOPICAL BUDGET 248-1

b/w · 1 reel · 304' (5 mins) · silent
intertitles: English

pr Topical Film Company

I. Wounded soldiers have a day out. 'SIDECAR OUTING FOR WOUNDED SOLDIERS. Wounded soldiers from St Thomas's Hospital enjoy a run to Burford Bridge, where they are entertained by Alderman Duncan Watson.' The soldiers sit

on the steps; rank of motor-cycles and sidecars, complete with passengers, prepares to set off close by. They depart. The convoy of motor-cycles passes through parkland, where at one point a press photographer balances on a bike to take a photograph. One of the bikes has a small banner saying "Harley Davidson" attached to the handlebars. The climax of the trip: the travellers arrive outside the Burford Bridge Hotel. (Alderman Watson not identified.)
II. Thames rowing race. 'YEOMANRY "EIGHTS" AT PUTNEY. The 3rd County of London Yeomanry hold an inter-regimental race on the Thames. All the men taking part have fought in Gallipoli.' One of the teams of soldiers, wearing rowing shorts but still in uniform above the waist, carry their boats down to the water. Shots of the race in progress, as all three boats row past the camera positions. (No suggestion as to who won.)
III. Cycle rally. 'VETERANS OF THE ROAD. Rally of "Old Times" Cyclists on the Ripley Road. Riders of the ordinary and boneshaker bicycle of the early "Seventies" taking part.' Cyclists and their cycles congregate on the country road. A woman sits on her 'boneshaker', held stable by a man. General view of assembled multitude and the various bikes, including penny-farthings. The cyclists take to the road; the old bicycles in action, watched idly by some soldiers reclining at the roadside.
IV. Filling up cartridge belts. 'MARINES FILLING CARTRIDGE BELTS. British Marines in Salonika busily employed in filling cartridge belts for machine guns. A machine makes the work almost automatic.' Three men sit on a bench in the open air. The machine is clamped to the edge of the bench and looks like a hand-operated mincing machine. One of the men turns the handle whilst one of the others loads .303 cartridges into the top of the machine. The filled section of the belt feeds out of the bottom of the contraption and trails down onto the floor beneath the bench. (Filmed by Varges ?)
V. British artillery in Salonika. 'BRITISH GUNS IN ACTION. Huge British gun at Salonika in action sending shells into the enemy lines. The tent is used to conceal the gun from enemy aircraft observation.' Long shot of gun (possibly a 12-inch howitzer), which is almost completely enclosed in a tent with just the barrel protruding. Men stand by. Medium shot of gun firing. A still photographer takes shots of the gun/tent. Further footage is taken from the other side of the tent; the gun is fired several times. (Filmed by Varges ?)

Notes
Summary: see also descriptive note in McKernan.
catalogued JCK: 5/1993

NTB 248-02 · GB, 27/5/1916
TOPICAL BUDGET 248-2

b/w · 1 reel · 281' (5 mins) · silent
intertitles: English

pr Topical Film Company

I. The British Army takes on Balkan refugees as labourers in Salonika. 'BALKAN REFUGEES. Turk, Bulgar and Greek refugees seeking work, are examined and photographed before receiving their pass.' Two British soldiers manhandle dishevelled refugees into line. Each man holds a chit which is checked by one of two officers sitting at a desk set up in the open air. The refugees are then photographed. To oblige the film-maker, a soldier grasps the head of one of the refugees before the photographer and twists it to face the cine camera – the man's expression remains impassive. The soldier smiles.
II. French soldiers stack shells. 'MESSAGES FOR THE GERMANS. French Artillery men stacking shells before dispatching them to the Germans.' LS pan over medium calibre artillery shells piled in an open-air dump. Soldiers walk past each carrying a shell over his shoulder to stack them on top of the others.
III. Entertainment for blinded soldiers. 'THE BLIND FIDDLER. Heroes who have lost their sight in the service of the Country, dance with their nurses with a courage that defies affliction.' In the open air nurses and men waltz to the music of a solo violinist. The men are in a mixture of military and civilian dress – one is still bandaged about the eyes. The dance floor becomes more crowded, with two men sometimes dancing together. Under the circumstances there is surprisingly little confusion.
IV. Convalescent soldiers from Australia and Canada watch schoolchildren celebrate Empire Day. 'EMPIRE DAY. London School Children celebrate the First Official Empire Day. Wounded Australian and Canadian soldiers watching the Ceremony.' A column of very small children is dragooned on the playground by their teachers – most are holding small Union Flags. The children wave their flags and cadet corps salutes as wounded veterans – one on crutches – enter the schoolyard. Generally the veterans seem amused. Civic dignitaries follow the soldiers. 'SALUTING THE FLAG AS THEY MARCH

PAST.' LS as the cadets march past – they have been carefully arranged with the tallest boys on the outside and the smallest near the centre so that each rank appears as a shallow V. After the first two ranks, the boys wear school rather than military uniform. A small girl offers veterans cigars from a box. LA of Union Flag fluttering in the breeze.

catalogued NAP: 7/1991

NTB 249-01 · GB, 31/5/1916
TOPICAL BUDGET 249-1

b/w · 1 reel · 312' (5 mins) · silent
intertitles: English

pr Topical Film Company

I. Children's service at St Paul's Cathedral. 'CHILDREN OF THE EMPIRE. Children attend a very impressive service at St Paul's Cathedral, held in connection with the League of Empire.' A parade of naval cadets passes crowd of spectators lining the city streets; a long line of children travels along the street and ascends the steps of St Paul's on the way to the service. Boy scouts ascend also.
II. Founder's day at the Royal Hospital, Chelsea. 'OAK APPLE DAY. General Sir Neville Lyttelton takes the salute from the old pensioners on Founder's Day at the Chelsea Hospital.' The general inspects seated pensioners, and watches a small march past of the more active pensioners, while the seated veterans raise their hats and cheer. Close-up of medal-bedecked pensioner.
III. Drum head service. 'DRUM HEAD SERVICE. Major General Sir Francis Lloyd addresses the South London Regt. at their drum head service.' Drum head service takes place in park. The camera pans over a large crowd to whom a clergyman is preaching. The drum itself, surrounded by various dignitaries, is shown in close shot.
IV. Cadets inspected. 'CITY OF LONDON CADETS. The Lord Mayor inspecting the City of London Cadets at Regents Park and takes the salute as they march past.' The mayor, dressed in military uniform, salutes the marching Cadets. Close up of the mayor saluting.
V. Entrenching party at work. 'BRITISH TRENCH DIGGING. An entrenching party leaving the Camp and moving out through communications trenches to the front line. Building up breastworks and parapets.' Scenes of men marching along a hilltop; stone buildings are in the background. More men walk along a low trench, carrying shovels; they are then seen walking down a

deeper trench lined with sandbags. Shot from inside of trench room; men carrying sandbags pass by. (There is little or no actual digging in evidence.)

Notes
Summary: see also descriptive note in McKernan.
catalogued JCK: 5/1993

NTB 249-02 · GB, 3/6/1916
TOPICAL BUDGET 249-2

b/w · 1 reel · 312' (5 mins) · silent
intertitles: English

pr Topical Film Company

I. Queenslander's memorial statue. 'THE QUEENSLAND CONTINGENT. The Prime Minister of Queensland and Brigadier General Sellheim inspect the statue which is to be erected in Brisbane, in memory of Queenslanders who fell in the South African War.' Various dignitaries and men in uniform pose for the camera around the base of the statue. The ceremony itself, seen from high angle. Camera pans up the statue, a representation of a Queenslander soldier on horseback.
II. Countess Nada de Torby visits military hospital. 'COUNTESS TORBY AT WAR HOSPITAL. Countess Nada de Torby (fiancee of Prince George of Battenberg) presents gifts to wounded soldiers on Pound Day, at the Hampstead General Hospital.' The Countess presents gifts to various patients. One soldier, on crutches, is presented with a gift by a little girl. Item ends with close-ups of a delighted soldier cradling his parcels, and of an unidentified woman.
III. Solemn intercession at St Martin in the Fields. 'INTERCESSION SERVICE. The Bishop of Kensington leads a solemn intercession service from St Martin's-in-the-Fields to Hyde Park.' The procession leaves the church, led by the clergy; procession also contains members of the laity and a small band. In the foreground, a woman carrying leaflets bears a banner advertising various publications (?): *The Catholic Suffragist*, *Women under the Parlour*, *The Sin of Silence*.
IV. Lord Mayor visits Alton Cripple Hospital. 'ROYAL HONOUR FOR LITTLE CRIPPLE. The Lord Mayor on his visit to the Alton Cripple Hospital presents Queen Alexandra's medal to an inmate whose father is a prisoner in Germany.' Shot of hospital buildings. The mayor and other dignitaries: the mayor is introduced to a small child lying on a special raised bed in the open air

(presumably the recipient of the medal). He sees another child in a similar bed, this time indoors.

V. French anti-aircraft guns in action. 'ANTI-AIRCRAFT GUNS. French officers ascertaining the range of the enemy aircarft (sic), using different types of instruments. The anti-aircraft gun in action.' A very active group of French officers in a variety of hats use binoculars, viewfinders and other devices to watch the progress of the gun. Meanwhile, the gun itself is positioned ready to fire.

Notes

Summary: see also descriptive note in McKernan.
catalogued JCK: 5/1993

NTB 250-02 · GB, 10/6/1915
TOPICAL BUDGET 250-2

b/w · 1 reel · 302' (5 mins) · silent
intertitles: English

pr Topical Film Company

I. British soldiers guard the Greek fortress at Tuzla. 'FORT OF TUZLA. View of one of the fort's big guns with British signallers at work.' HA to rear of shielded coastal gun – a sentry guards the emplacement. MS to a sentry positioned in front of the position – a single 21 cm (?) gun.
II. Men are taken on board a hospital ship in the Mediterranean. 'HOSPITAL SHIP IN THE MEDITERRANEAN. Wounded men on board a Red Cross Ship, on their way back to England. Nurses handing little luxuries to the patients on deck.' HA.MS as a stretcher is carried up gangway onto camership. MO and nurses stand among the wounded men lying on deck. Nurses distribute "little luxuries", apparently cigarettes. Lieutenant RNR crosses the deck.
III. Wounded soldiers play golf. 'WOUNDED TOMMIES GOLF MATCH. Wounded soldiers playing a golf match under their own rules. Cigarettes being distributed to the men, and three cheers for their entertainers.' Convalescents emerge from hospital ambulance – the vehicle belongs to the motor squadron of the London Volunteer Rifles. A crowd watches as men play lawn golf – one of the competitors has one arm in a cast. A small boy dressed in a kilt and glengarry offers soldiers packs of cigarettes. HA.LS pan over crowd of patients seated in deck-chairs and around open-air tables – they wave obligingly to the camera.
IV. King George V reviews troops. 'H.M. THE KING REVIEWS TROOPS. His Majesty

attended by Capt. Godfrey Faucett (sic) R.N. and Lieutenant-Colonel Clive Wigram inspecting troops in the Eastern Command.' HM passes on horseback with the usual retinue. An open-air review, troops marching past in line abreast, the camera shooting along the passing ranks.
V. Continuation of previous episode: the King talks with Lady Frankland and Army officers. 'PRESENTATION TO HIS MAJESTY. Lady Frankland being presented to His Majesty after the review. Wounded Tommies who were asked by the King the extent of their injuries.' Lady Frankland and her two children talk with the King, who is still on horseback. Officers come forward to be presented. Pan over some convalescent soldiers, some seated on the grass, others standing behind with nurses, as for a formal group photograph.

catalogued NAP: 7/1991

NTB 251-01 · GB, 14/6/1916
TOPICAL BUDGET 251-1

b/w · 1 reel · 276' (5 mins) · silent
intertitles: English

pr Topical Film Company

I. British troops on the move in Salonika. 'THE BRITISH ARMY IN SALONIKA. Fresh British troops marching from the base to their camp. The Bay of Salonika in the distance.' LS over earthen road as a column of British troops passes diagonally left to right. Lorries pass in the opposite direction. The men are marching inland away from the scattered buildings of the base – the sea is visible in XLS background.
II. Reverend Mellish, winner of the VC, is honoured by his home town of Deptford. 'DEPTFORD'S CURATE V.C. Rev. E. Noel Mellish V.C. receives an ovation as he drives through the streets of Deptford Inspecting the Guard of Honour formed by the Boy Scouts.' HA onto Mellish in open chaise accompanied by police guard of honour. Locals look on – some from the top of a stationary bus – and a crowd follows the procession. Boy scouts line the roadside as Mellish – now on foot – passes in company with the mayor. The padre talks with a major in the Volunteer Training Force who has been acting as his sword-bearer. Mellish enters council chamber – the steps are lined with Army cadets holding Martini-Henry carbines, and he smiles and lifts his cap to the boys.
III. A parade of French 75s destined for the defence of Verdun. 'GUNS FOR VERDUN.

The Governor of Paris inspecting the new artillery at Vincennes. These new guns are to be used in the defence of Verdun.' Horse-drawn 75mm field guns pass in parade order. MS as a battery of 75s is loaded and trained in a park before crowd of spectators.
IV. King George V and Queen Alexandra attend a memorial service to Lord Kitchener at St Paul's Cathedral. 'THE KING AND QUEEN. Their Majesties with Queen Alexandra and the Royal Family arriving at the Cathedral.' HA.LS as the Royal family dismount from coaches and walk under an elaborate striped awning up the cathedral steps. HA as King George V arrives in an open coach with a mounted escort – he waves to the crowd and dismounts to go inside.

Notes
Remarks (item I): dull even by the standards of Topical Budget.
Summary (item II): the Reverend Mellish won his VC for rescuing wounded trapped by enemy bombardment at St-Eloi near Ypres in March 1916. He was the first Army chaplain to win a VC since 1879.
Summary (item IV): Kitchener had died on 5 June. Given the circumstances there was of course no burial service.
catalogued NAP: 6/1991

NTB 251-02 · GB, 17/6/1916
TOPICAL BUDGET 251-2

b/w · 1 reel · 288' (5 mins) · silent
intertitles: English

pr Topical Film Company

I. Women make roses for Queen Alexandra's Day. 'PREPARATIONS FOR ALEXANDRA DAY. Scenes at the Crippleage where the inmates are making roses for Queen Alexandra's Rose Day.' CUs of women at work – a press crimps the blanks, posies are stuck and stitched together, boxes are packed with the completed flowers.
II. Austrian POWs and the (temporarily) triumphant General Brusilov. 'RUSSIA'S GREAT OFFENSIVE. General Brusiloff the Commander of the 8th. Russian Army who is leading the victorious offensive against the Austrians, resulting in the capture of over 150,000 prisoners to date.' MS as a long column of Austro-Hungarian prisoners marches past under guard. Though unshaven the prisoners seem generally in good shape and well turned-out. MS of Brusilov and his staff standing outside a building. An officer crosses to the left to give an old woman a coin – when she attempts

to speak to others of the staff, Brusilov orders her away with a few waves of his arm.
III. Sports day of the 1/6th Kent and 1/7th Kent Field Companies, Royal Engineers. 'ROYAL ENGINEERS' MILITARY SPORTS. The Kent Field Companies R.E. make a special feature of Wrestling and Tug-of-War contests by men on horseback at their sports at Maidenhead.' CUs of a tug of war between two teams of men mounted on mules: the animals stand over the rope and are not all that happy – one throws his rider off and others caper about. Spectators watch from a good distance.
IV. Actresses learn to make munitions. 'LONDON ACTRESSES MAKING MUNITIONS. Stage favourites being taught how to turn base caps for shells and other phases of munition work.' Men at BSM Ltd teach elementary metalwork to the actresses, who are dressed in neat white overalls – it does not appear that the ladies have much natural aptitude for the work.
V. French generals inspect the military college at Vincennes. 'REVIEW AT VINCENNES. General Dubail and General Parreau inspecting the Military Preparation Societies at the French Training College.' General Parreau passes the camera – a British officer is present on his staff. General Dubail inspects a rank of men fallen in on open ground – he salutes a flag held by one of the officers. General Dubail with his staff and civilian dignitaries watch march past of soldiers and marines.

Notes
Summary (item III): the captions are marked as issue 251-1. This is believed to be an error.
Remarks (item II): it is most unlikely that any channel was open for film to travel from central Russia to London within fifteen days of the start of the Brusilov Offensive, and the newsreel is probably stock film from an earlier date.
catalogued NAP & SDB: 6/1991

NTB 252-02 · GB, 24/6/1916
TOPICAL BUDGET 252-2

b/w · 1 reel · 315' (5 mins) · silent
intertitles: English

pr Topical Film Company

I. Soldiers enjoy cups of tea at the Cook House. '"COOK HOUSE CALL. One of the most welcome bugle calls to our Tommies "The Cook House". Issuing rations to the men occupying the trenches in Greece.' The

rations seem to consist of fresh chickens, which the soldiers are seen merrily plucking. Soldiers in kilts queue up for mugs of tea. A group of men loiter around a field gun, with more kilted soldiers (one carrying a set of bagpipes) pass by in the background.
II. Artillery horses are trained. 'BREAKING IN HORSES FOR ARTILLERY. Horses whilst pulling a heavy army wagon accustomed to the sound of rapid rifle fire as part of their training.' A team of horses pull a large empty wagon through a large courtyard, with open stalls in the background. Cut to men who lie down and fire volleys from rifles; back to the horses, still cantering around the courtyard. They are well-behaved and appear to be unaffected by the rifle fire. The horses are rewarded with buckets of food.
III. Rowing race. 'PUBLIC SCHOOLS ROWING. St Pauls beat Winchester and Westminster by two lengths in a four-oared race from Beverley Brook to Hammersmith.' The race begins, filmed from moving boat. Shots of the race in progress; the three boats pass what appears to be a well-stocked lumber yard on the bank. Boats pass under Hammersmith Bridge, which is crowded with spectators. The finish, filmed from the rear. After the race, the competitors rest.
IV. Alexandra Rose Day. 'ROSE DAY. Everyone was seen bedecked with the royal flower. A prettily decorated car in one of the main streets.' Women sit in the decorated car (probably in Holborn) and sell roses to passers-by to celebrate Alexandra Rose Day.
V. Queen Alexandra passes through London. 'QUEEN ALEXANDRA'S DRIVE THROUGH LONDON. Her Majesty accompanied by Princess Victoria visits the principle depots, and sees her army of 15,000 "Girls in White".' A policeman clears crowds away from the gates (of Buckingham Palace ?) to allow Queen Alexandra's carriage and others to emerge. The carriage passes through the London streets. Many of her 'Girls in White' throw flowers at the Queen's carriage as it passes them. Cheering crowds line the streets as the carriages pass; some people follow.

Notes
Summary: see also descriptive note in McKernan.
catalogued JCK: 5/1993

NTB 253-01 · GB, 28/6/1916
TOPICAL BUDGET 253-1

b/w · 1 reel · 300' (5 mins) · silent
intertitles: English

pr Topical Film Company

I. US Fleet departs for Mexican waters. 'U.S.A. v MEXICO. In view of the grave situation the American fleet, prepared for all eventualities sails for Mexican waters.' MS off the starboard bow of USS *Michigan* – the frame cuts the picture just aft of her second funnel. MS as *New Hampshire* (22) moves left to right through frame, followed by *Virginia* (23).
II. Convalescent soldiers are entertained. 'ECCENTRIC CLUB ENTERTAIN WOUNDED SOLDIERS. Over 600 convalescent soldiers from various hospitals enjoy themselves at the entertainment given to them at the "Karsino" Hampton Court.' HA as soldiers file in through gates to an open-air restaurant – the leading two are on crutches. CU of men enjoying some general horse play – they are throwing balls (oranges ?) and one mimes throwing at the camera. Bandsmen warm up. The men eat at tables on the riverside – one waves to camera.
III. Lord French inspects the Lads' Brigade. 'CHURCH LADS' BRIGADE. The London Diocesan Church Lads' Brigade, being inspected by Lord French at Somerset House.' French inspects serried ranks of boys, some with arms shouldered – he is cheered. MS left profile of Lord French striking a martial pose. The lads pass in review – they carry Martini-Henry carbines suited to their stature.
IV. Lord Mayor of London leaves St Paul's after service. 'HOSPITAL SUNDAY. Lord Mayor and Sheriffs attend in state the service at St. Pauls.' Lord Mayor and Mayoress descend the steps of the cathedral with sheriff carrying mace.
V. Lord Chancellor leaves St Paul's after service. 'JUDGES AT ST. PAULS. The Lord Chancellor and His Majesty's Judges leaving the Cathedral after the Service.' Lord Chancellor and judges with their wives descend steps of St Paul's.

Notes
Summary (item II): the summer season of river trips on the Thames for wounded soldiers commenced in June.
catalogued NAP: 6/1991

NTB 253-02 · GB, 1/7/1916
TOPICAL BUDGET 253-2

b/w · 1 reel · 243' (4 mins) · silent
intertitles: English

pr Topical Film Company

I. French colonial troops in Salonika.

'FRENCH COLONIAL TROOPS. The French Colonial Troops from Cochin-China, who carry fans and are now on the Salonika front.' MS pan over men gathered by their tents – many wear the shallow, conical 'coolie' hats and are bare-footed. Their arms are stacked and they are setting up camp. A few Europeans stand about amidst the orientals. 'CAMP LIFE AMONG THE ANNAMITES. Indo-Chinese troops who use chopsticks instead of the customary knife and fork.' Pan over the men sitting cross-legged on the ground – some are cleaning their carbines. A group tends a fire burning in a shallow trench in which open pots are heating – one man stirs a pot. No chopsticks are evident.
II. Royal Agricultural Society's annual show. 'THE ROYAL SHOW. The Royal Agricultural Society's Annual Show at Manchester. Shetland ponies, pigs, and champion bulls being judged in the prize ring.' Men milk cows in front of spectators. Holstein-Friesland bulls are exhibited, each with its number around its neck. CU of sheep in a pen. 'THE KING'S EXHIBITS. His Majesty and the Prince of Wales were well represented in several classes.' Shire horses are led past the camera. CU of Shetland ponies being groomed. Pigs are driven past and CU of one particularly large animal grazing.

catalogued NAP: 6/1991

NTB 254-01 · GB, 5/7/1916
TOPICAL BUDGET 254-1

b/w · 1 reel · 311' (5 mins) · silent
intertitles: English

pr Topical Film Company

I. Duke and Duchess of Somerset visit a Naval Training School. 'FOUNDERS' DAY. The Duke and Duchess of Somerset at Dr. Barnardo's Homes. "Boys of the Bulldog Breed" dancing the hornpipe on the village green.' Two elderly civic dignitaries pass the camera in company with an equally ancient Rear-Admiral. The Duke and Duchess arrive by coach to be received by an honour guard of Boys in RN uniform, armed with Martini-Henry carbines. Boys' brass band plays, followed by a detachment armed with cadet rifles. About 30 boys in close ranks dance a fairly creditable hornpipe.
II. Flags from HMS *Kent* are hung in Canterbury Cathedral to commemorate the Battle of the Falkland Islands. 'FLAGS OF H.M.S. KENT. Flags presented by the Ladies of Kent to H.M.S. Kent carried by British

Bluejackets through the City of Canterbury.' HA.LS over square where soldiers – cavalry and VTC – are paraded before entering cathedral. A military band plays in the centre of the square. Civic dignitaries, many in robes of office, walk past to the service, followed by a RN detachment from HMS *Pembroke*, depot ship at Chatham. 'BATTLE OF THE FALKLAND ISLANDS. These honoured and tattered relics of the Falklands Battle were consecrated and hung in Canterbury Cathedral.' Continuation of the previous sequence – the armed RN detachment bring up the flags (*Kent*'s ensign and small jack) which are taken inside the cathedral.
III. Canadian troops are reviewed by King George V on Dominion Day. 'DOMINION DAY. The Canadians at Bramshott celebrating Dominion Day.' Horse artillery passes left to right with 18-pounder guns. 'THE KING REVIEWS CANADIANS. His Majesty accompanied by Lord French reviews the Canadians. Infantry and Artillery marching past the King who is taking the salute.' Canadian Highlanders march past King and Lord French who are on horseback – HM salutes.

Notes
Summary (item III): Canada became a dominion on 1 July 1867. The King was attended by French, C-in-C Home Forces and General Sir Archibald Hunter, C-in-C Aldershot Command.
catalogued NAP: 7/1991

NTB 254-02 · GB, 8/7/1916
TOPICAL BUDGET 254-2

b/w · 1 reel · 300' (5 mins) · silent
intertitles: English

pr Topical Film Company

I. Fund raising fête. 'REVELS FOR A WAR FUND. Sir Francis Lloyd inspects the guard of honour, composed of wounded men. An Alfresco fête in aid of funds to teach a trade to wounded soldiers.' Lloyd inspects the troops. Scenes at the fête: a male gymnast gives a display on the parallel bars, a fancy dress cricket match (a real free-for-all). A plump man in drag pulls faces for the camera in close-up.
II. Queen Mary opens a hospital. 'QUEEN MARY OPENS HOSPITAL FOR WOMEN. Arrival of Her Majesty at the SOUTH LONDON HOSPITAL, who receives purses for the support and upkeep of the institution.' Queen Mary enters the building, where small children are led up to greet her. She stands

on a dais. Later, the Queen crosses a courtyard with a small group of nurses etc. One of the nurses swings a tasselled rope hanging from a balcony; the Queen does likewise. (Nothing happens when the rope is pulled, and its significance is unclear.) A plaque on the wall a short distance away is pointed to; it is too distant to be legible. Ill. English POWs arrive in Berne. 'SWITZERLANDS RECEPTION OF ENGLISH PRISONERS. English prisoners of war receive a warm welcome on arriving at Berne.' A tram arrives at a station in Berne, where a cheering crowd is gathered. The British POWs get out and are greeted; one of them is carried off on a stretcher. Many of the men are wearing flowers that have been given them by the locals. A line of men marches away, through the crowd and past the camera. 'BRITISH MINISTER RECEIVES THE MEN. Mr E. Grant-Duff receives the men on their arrival.' Groups of soldiers stand around. Two Indian soldiers stand close to camera; children are also present. Panning shot of men and women grouped outside a building; an officer is also present, but there seems to be no sign of Mr Grant-Duff's reception. 'CANADIAN PRISONERS.' Wounded soldiers of the Toronto regiment, these were the first Canadians who fought in Belgium.' A group of (presumably Canadian) men and women pose for the camera. Men walk down the streets with their baggage, with the assistance of boy scouts. Some wounded men are carried past on stretchers.

Notes

Summary (item III): the Swiss stories do not have the issue number on the intertitle. However, they do appear to belong to this issue.
Summary: see also descriptive note in McKernan.
catalogued JCK: 5/1993

NTB 255-01 · GB, 12/7/1916
TOPICAL BUDGET 255-1

b/w · 1 reel · 45' (1 min) · silent
intertitles: English

pr Topical Film Company

Aerial footage of the armed forces. 'OVER THE LINES. An impression of an army's position as seen by our aeroplane observers when over the German lines.' (Short caption.) Aerial shots of troops at battle practice, equipment, vehicles etc.

Notes

Summary: see also descriptive note in

McKernan.
catalogued JCK: 5/1993

NTB 255-02 · GB, 15/7/1916
TOPICAL BUDGET 255-2

b/w · 1 reel · 308' (5 mins) · silent
intertitles: English

pr Topical Film Company

I. Serbian casualties. 'STRICKEN SERBIA. Serbian wounded soldiers waiting at a base depot, before being transferred to a hospital ship.' Men gather by a building, most of them bandaged or carrying crutches. Men hand out pieces of paper (tickets ?). (Possibly filmed by Varges.)
II. Charity garden party in Regent's Park. 'THEATRICAL GARDEN PARTY. Members of the theatrical profession hold their annual garden party at Regent's Park. The proceeds are in aid of the Actor's Orphanage Fund.' A costumed large girl (or small woman) sits on a donkey. José Collins (actress) poses for the camera as several eager young men jockey to light her cigarette. A line of people sell programmes. An actress and a soldier, cheek-to-cheek, are filmed in close-up. Item closes with general shot of the party.
III. Memorial service for Lieutenant Warneford VC. 'WARNEFORD MEMORIAL. Lord Derby unveiling the memorial to the late Lieut. Warneford V.C., to commemorate the heroic exploit in destroying a Zeppelin near Ghent.' Graveside ceremony is filmed from high angle. Lord Derby gives speech; priest is in attendance.
IV. Blind soldiers take part in rowing race. 'BLIND MAN'S BOAT RACES. Blind soldiers from St Dunstan's Hostel competing with students from the Worcester College for the Blind. The soldiers defeat their opponents in all the races.' The soldiers get into their boats and prepare their oars. Both two man and five man boats are shown competing. The races on the river are filmed from moving car.
V. Red Cross Day. 'FRANCE'S DAY. The French Ambassador M. Paul Cambon, buying his flag from Mdle. Marianne of the Croix Rouge.' Woman in Red Cross uniform (presumably Mlle Marianne) sells flags to a policeman, and to various people leaving (French Embassy ?) building. M Cambon descends the steps and buys his flag with some showiness. Close up of the smiling nurse; she hold up a flag for the camera.

Notes

Summary: see also descriptive note in McKernan.

cataloged JCK: 5/1993

NTB 256-01 · GB, 19/7/1916
TOPICAL BUDGET 256-1

b/w · 1 reel · 319' (5 mins) · silent
intertitles: English

pr Topical Film Company

I. Special Constabulary on parade.
'INSPECTION OF SPECIAL
CONSTABULARY. Inspection of the L,
Division of Metropolitan Special
Constabulary by the Inspector General.' In a
London park the Special Constables – some
in civilian dress with 'SC' armbands – march
past the Inspector General. In the
background are spectators sheltering under
umbrellas and the park trees.
II. Convalescent horse at a country retreat.
'SERVING THEIR COUNTRY. The horse
which was wounded in the Battle of Loos,
still doing his bit for the Country, helping the
women working on an Essex farm.' Women
use sickles to clear tall grass, hoe between
rows of potatoes, feed piglets. The horse,
wearing a halter, is led on to take a drink
from a trough – a woman rides him side-
saddle. More feeding of piglets.
III. Memorial to Liberal whip, Percy
Illingworth. 'IN MEMORY OF HIS FATHER.
Master Henry Illingworth opens the Percy
Illingworth Institute at Aldershot in memory
of the late Liberal Whip. Mrs. Lloyd George
and General Sir A. Hunter follow immediately
behind the two boys.' MCU of Mrs Lloyd
George talking with General Sir Archibald
Hunter, C-in-C Aldershot Command. The two
sons come in from frame left – they are
wearing white and an adult minder holds the
older boy's hand. The boy's facial
expressions lack the required solemnity,
presumably due to nervousness. The
procession moves off past the camera.
IV. Scots Guards entertain a French crowd
with native dancing. 'SCOTS GUARDS AT
VERSAILLES. The men of the Scots Guards
delight huge audiences by dancing national
dances to the music of the pipes.' Pan over
Guards' band. LS as they march through
gardens playing pipes – a crowd of locals
keep pace with them – two young women
laugh to see the camera present. MS as
Guardsmen perform a sword dance.
'HELPING FRENCH CHARITIES. A
successful fête held a Versailles in aid of the
various French War charities.' More sword
dancing – some of the watching crowd have
raised umbrellas against the spray from a
nearby fountain. MS, Guards' band. HA.LS
over the crowds in the palace grounds.

Notes
Summary (item I): L Division was based in
Lambeth.
Remarks (item III): anyone interested in
ladies' fashions should enjoy the concluding
procession.
cataloged NAP: 7/1991

NTB 256-02 · GB, 22/7/1916
TOPICAL BUDGET 256-2

b/w · 1 reel · 317' (5 mins) · silent
intertitles: English

pr Topical Film Company

I. US troops in training. 'U.S. TROOPS IN
TRAINING. American troops taking part in a
musical ride at New Jersey.' HA.LS across
open square/parade ground as mounted
troops form up into a square, ride round in
concentric circles and perform other
amusing evolutions.
II. Bastille Day celebrations in France.
'PAGEANT IN PARIS. M. Poincaré President
of the French Republic reviews troops taking
part in the ceremonial parade in connection
with the celebrations of the 14th. of July.'
Poincaré comes down steps with other
dignitaries. March past by French troops
with wheeled machineguns is followed by
bicycle troops and lancers. 'TROOPS OF
THE ALLIES. Led by the Scots Guards band,
English, Scottish, Canadian, Australian,
Indian and Russian troops march through
Paris.' Scots Guards band leads long
column of British and Imperial troops. The
Russians bring up the rear preceded by their
own band and marching in much wider
ranks – approximately 17 men wide
compared to the British ranks of 4 men. The
camera is looking down the Champ de Mars
to Les Invalides.
III. British cavalry training. 'CAVALRY IN
ACTION. The strenuous training of our
mounted troops enabled them to clear the
ground, broken by artillery fire, and push
through into the third line of German
defences.' Cavalry gallop through a stream –
one animal stumbles as it emerges from the
water but regains its feet, although only after
a second horse has apparently trampled
upon it. The detachment trots two abreast
along the course of the stream, the water
reaching the horses' chests.
IV. British infantry train with the bayonet.
'MERCY! CAMERADE! Some of our
"Tommies" practising with the bayonet. The
sight of cold steel drives terror into the heart
of the German and compels him to yell for
mercy.' MS of troops bayoneting filled sacks
– some suspended from an overhead beam,

others lying on the ground; a large tented encampment is visible in the background. Another group of sacks inhabit a trench – they too are killed. LS as men rise from a shallow trench to run forward with bayonets fixed – a few are shot dead and lie gazing glassily at the camera.

catalogued NAP: 7/1991

NTB 257-01 · GB, 26/7/1916
TOPICAL BUDGET 257-1

b/w · 1 reel · 281' (5 mins) · silent
intertitles: English

pr Topical Film Company

I. Captured German submarine is displayed in London. 'GERMAN SUBMARINE COMES TO LONDON. The German submarine-minelayer U.C.5 captured by the British Navy, moored off Temple Pier.' MS off the port quarter of UC.5 secured alongside the pier – old London Bridge visible in the background. The U-boat still wears the German ensign.
II. Band of the Belgian Guides visits London. 'KING ALBERT'S BAND. The Band of the Belgian Guides accompanied by the Welsh Guards on their way to Chelsea Hospital.' HA.MS as crowd accompanies along a road the band of the Welsh Guards, followed by the Belgian Contingent – only the Welsh are playing. The crowd wave to the camera and seem in a holiday mood. Two buses follow up the rear.
III. Convalescent soldiers are entertained. 'STAFFORDSHIRE HOUSE ENTERTAINS WOUNDED SOLDIERS. A donkey race and a light-the-cigarette race provide plenty of amusement for the wounded Tommies from the Hospitals.' Women run down marked-out lanes to light men's cigarettes – once the cigarette is alight the two run off together. The process is repeated with different men and women over the same course in a relay. Some of the women's cigarette-lighting technique is a little patchy. LS down the track as women run a race – there is little concession to athleticism, as all the contestants wear long dresses and some are in bonnets. They cross the finishing tape and one contestant collides with a group of soldiers watching the race – the men do not seem displeased.
IV. A procession of women war workers marches through the West End of London. 'PAGEANT OF WOMEN WAR WORKERS. The Women's procession of War workers marching through the West End with a tableau, in honour of Lord Kitchener's

memory.' Women parade past camera carrying banners: 'HELP OUR PRISONERS IN GERMANY', 'COME BACK HUGHES AND COME AT ONCE', 'HUGHES IS NEEDED HERE AND NOW', 'THE PEOPLE'S MESSAGE – COME BACK HUGHES', 'HONOUR THE MEN IN THE TRENCHES', etc. A woman rides past dressed in imitation chain-mail with a lance in hand, followed by a second horsewoman in mock medieval costume. Wagons carry various tableaux. Boadicea passes in her chariot, Queen Elizabeth I on horseback. More banners favouring Hughes, preceded by riders dressed as Australians. 'MR. LLOYD GEORGE WATCHES THE PROCESSION. The Secretary of State for War watches the women marching past the War Office.' LA to Lloyd George looking down from balcony. MSs of the procession – wagons, mock Australians, women dressed in white each carrying a staff topped with flowers, a banner calling on God to save the King. As the sequence ends, police are moving across the street to check the advance of the crowd – some of the ladies carrying flower-staves look back at the disturbance.

Notes
Summary (item I): the UC.5 was publicly exhibited from 26 July, and received 10 000 visitors on the first day at a price of 6d per visitor until 1 o'clock, and 3d thereafter. Visitors were not allowed inside, but received a postcard showing the submarine's interior arrangements. The flying of the German ensign was probably improper, as the possession of UC.5 was the result of a salvage operation.
Summary (item II): the band of the Guides was in England to help commemorate the anniversary of the Declaration of Belgian Independence on 21 July 1830. This event – not usually given much prominence in the English calendar – was celebrated in 1916 by a Te Deum in Westminster Cathedral. The concert held in the gardens of the Hospital was on behalf of Belgian charities.
Summary (item IV): the procession organised by the Women's Social and Political Union marched from the Embankment to Trafalgar Square, and was ostensibly in support of women war workers. *The Times* (24 July) noted that "There was considerable surprise, however, that by far the largest number of the bannerets were devoted to appeals to Mr. Hughes to return, giving quite secondary place to the advertised motives of the procession." Mr Hughes, Labour Prime Minister of Australia, who had visited Britain in the spring of 1916, had been a tremendous popular success. If the lady in the chain-mail can be supposed to be Joan of Arc, then that part was played by a Miss

Farmer-Bringhurst.
catalogued NAP: 6/1990

NTB 258-01 · GB, 2/8/1916
TOPICAL BUDGET 258-1

b/w · 1 reel · 321' (5 mins) · silent
intertitles: English

pr Topical Film Company

I. Large gun transported to Salonika. 'GUNS FOR SALONIKA. Unloading an enormous gun from a transport and mounting it on its gun carriage.' The barrel of a large calibre gun is lowered on ropes and pulleys over the side of a ship. Australian troops stand by to fit the barrel onto the large, two-wheeled gun-carriage. Having accomplished this task the gun-carriage is towed backwards. (Filmed by Varges ?)
II. Slavika Tomitch. 'SERBIAN GIRL HEROINE. Slavika Tomitch a girl heroine of the Serbian Army, has been decorated with the military medal, and is seen chatting with an English captain and an officer of the Serbian Army.' A smiling Slavika poses for the camera; she is offered a cigarette by the Serbian officer, which she accepts. She smiles, smokes and talks to her comrades. (Filmed by Varges ?)
III. Red Cross fête in Belgium. 'BELGIAN RED CROSS FETE. Lord Desborough takes part in a fencing bout at the fête in aid of Belgian Charities. Scenes from the pastoral play "The Magic Rose Bush".' Woman surrounded by dignitaries gives a speech; in front of her is a line of boy scouts (backs to the camera) holding staves: one of them looks around furtively to stare at the camera. Fencing match between Lord Desborough and opponent is watched by a small crowd of spectators on a raised platform, some carrying parasols. After the bout the two pose for the camera with their masks removed. Two short scenes from the play, acted in the open air with a cast largely of children dressed as fairies and elves.
IV. Princess Royal visits Australian troops. 'THE PRINCESS ROYAL AND THE AUSTRALIANS. The Princess Royal accompanied by Princess Maud, presents a silk Union Flag and a silver shield to the Australian troops.' The ceremony takes place on the parade ground at Wellington Barracks. Afterwards, a shot of the flag, with men on parade in the background.
V. Funeral of 'Boy' Cornwell. 'HERO OF JUTLAND BATTLE. The body of John Cornwell receives full Naval honours at the funeral. Dr Macnamara secretary of the Admiralty says, "His grave will be the

birthplace of heroes".' Crowds watch as the coffin, drawn by a naval detachment, arrives for the funeral; draped in a Union Flag and covered with flowers, it is carried by naval pallbearers to the graveside. A volley of shots is fire over the grave.

Notes
Summary: see also descriptive note in McKernan.
catalogued JCK: 5/1993

NTB 258-02 · GB, 5/8/1916
TOPICAL BUDGET 258-2

b/w · 1 reel · 315' (5 mins) · silent
intertitles: English

pr Topical Film Company

I. Brondesbury Hospital cricket match. 'SOLDIERS V NURSES. The soldier inmates of the Brondesbury Hospital challenge the Nurses to a cricket match, driving down to Wembley on the coaches for the match, which the soldiers won.' The game in progress; uniformed nurses bowling (underarm).
II. Fruit picking. 'SCHOOL CHILDREN FRUIT PICKING. Mr. Piggott of the Hornsey Council Schools organises a fruit picking party, girls and boys at work on a Suffolk fruit farm.' Children in a large field pick fruit and hand over their pickings.
III. Queen Amelie opens fête. 'QUEEN AMELIE OPENS FETE. H.M. Queen Amelie opens the East Surrey Regimental Fête at Richmond. The funds are in aid of the Prisoners of War and Old Comrades Association.' Queen Amelie, seated, is addressed by an officer. She stands up and delivers a short speech, standing by the tape; however, she is not filmed cutting it. Amelie is introduced to a line of wounded soldiers sitting down. Further shot of Amelie, this time sat at a table. Item concludes with a panning shot (fairly poorly filmed) of the fête.
IV. War damage in Belgium. 'TWO YEARS OF WAR. Scenes in a Belgian Town which was destroyed by the Germans two years ago at the outbreak of War.' Railway track in unidentified Belgian town; clouds of smoke rise in the distance on both sides; on the right-hand side, a large building smoulders. Cut to closer views of the building: both white smoke and then black smoke pour out from behind. 'DRIVEN FROM THEIR HOMES. Germany's ruthlessness in waging War – driving the inhabitants out of their homes. "We shall hold it our duty to exact reparation against the guilty agents in these matters".

MR ASQUITH.' Civilians/refugees, some carrying their belongings, cross a bridge (poor quality film). Shots of devastation: wrecked building, smoke rising behind it; camera pans to reveal the building shown previously.

Notes
Summary: see also descriptive note in McKernan.
catalogued JCK: 5/1993

NTB 259-01 · GB, 9/8/1916
TOPICAL BUDGET 259-1

b/w · 1 reel · 300' (5 mins) · silent
intertitles: English

pr Topical Film Company

I. American seahorse play. 'WATER PUSHBALL. American swimmers enjoying a game of water-pushball at Coney Island.' Swimmers push about a large inflated ball. Three women row about in tubs. Men in canoes engage in a scrimmage, each crew of two attempting to upset rival boats – one canoe fills with water and sinks.
II. French explosives inventor. 'FAMOUS FRENCH SCIENTIST. M. Turpin the inventor of turpenite and melinite, two high explosives that have helped to make the French "75" World famous.' MS of M Turpin standing with his back to the camera, feeding chickens in a yard. CU as he sorts chemical bottles, holding up one to examine it against the light.
III. Demonstration over the death of Captain Fryatt. 'FRYATT DEMONSTRATION. British Workers' National League, organise a demonstration in Trafalgar Square. Over 12,000 people pass a resolution in favour of the sternest reprisals for the murder of Captain Fryatt.' CU of 'worker' in a flat cap. A man addresses the crowd from a position at the foot of the column and is duly applauded. Two more speakers follow. The crowd votes with a show of hands.
IV. Sports meeting in support of disabled veterans. 'SPORTS CARNIVAL. Viscount French attends the sports meeting in aid of disabled soldiers and sailors. The mile handicap and boxing match, the marathon race won by the Norfolk Yeomanry.' Two young boys box, watched by a large stadium crowd. MS as soldiers set off running, dressed in full uniform with bandoliers and rifles – presumably this is the mile handicap. The marathon runners cross the finishing line, looking convincingly tired. A walking race around the stadium track – the winner is No 5 with No 41 a close

second. Viscount French's presence is nowhere evident.
V. Continuation of the previous episode. 'DONKEY DERBY. Celebrated jockeys who have ridden in previous "Derbys" riding a new mount to help the funds of the Star and Garter Home.' The race begins around the stadium. CU of winning jockey and his donkey.

Notes
Summary (item III): Captain Charles Fryatt was executed by the Germans on 27 July 1916. In March of the previous year he had attempted to ram a German submarine which was attacking his ship, the SS *Brussels*. This act was regarded by the British as a legitimate act of self-defence and by the Germans as a breach of the rules of war.
catalogued NAP: 6/1991

NTB 259-02 · GB, 12/8/1916
TOPICAL BUDGET 259-2

b/w · 1 reel · 299' (5 mins) · silent
intertitles: English

pr Topical Film Company

I. Serbian refugee children at work on an English fruit farm. 'SERBIAN BOYS WORKING ON THE LAND. Serbian refugee boys who are employed on a large fruit farm. They prefer marching to work to riding in the vans.' Lorry of the Chivers Company comes slowly down road carrying some of the boys – others run alongside or follow on bicycles. Column of adult workers marches along the road. Cut to open-air playground where children play on swings and at tug of war. CU of some of tug of war team.
II. Scots Guards at PT. 'SCOTS GUARDS AT PHYSICAL DRILL. Scots Guardsmen giving a demonstration of physical drill. The Brigade of Guards have always been noted for their smartness at drill.' Men wearing trousers with bayonet frogs and vests bearing emblematic thistles perform rifle drill before a large crowd. All is done with 'verve'.
III. King Nicholas of Montenegro in Paris. 'KING NICHOLAS IN PARIS. The King of Montenegro with his Staff, who are staying in Paris, being received by the French Deputies.' King Nicholas arrives by car to be greeted by a French officer. Cut to his departure – he is followed down the steps by a large crowd of officials – over the entrance is the legend 'BLESSES et MUTILES de la GUERRE'. The King doffs his hat in recognition of the crowd gathered to see him, then enters waiting car to depart.

Cut back to the King and his party inside the hospital – they are being shown something off-screen by their French hosts.
IV. Dog-fishing. 'TOPE FISHING. The Tope or Dog Fish a species of shark is fished for off the Kentish Coast. A fine specimen being landed after a severe struggle.' MS from an open boat to two more towing astern. Fisherman has reeled in his catch and gaffs it to bring it on board. Cut to scene on shingle beach – the dead fish is brought ashore to be displayed, tied to the mast of one of the boats.
V. Carnival in the United States. 'KING CARNIVAL. Citizens of the United States take advantage of their Country's freedom from War and organise a gigantic carnival.' Horse-drawn floats pass right to left – one features a dragon, jaws agape, emerging from a cave to be confronted by a armoured knight holding a sword.

Notes
Remarks (item V): not for the first time in this series the title is rather more interesting than the film.
catalogued NAP: 7/1991

NTB 260-02 · GB, 19/8/1916
TOPICAL BUDGET 260-2

b/w · 1 reel · 320' (5 mins) · silent
intertitles: English

pr Topical Film Company

I. London Division sports day. '1ST LONDON DIVISION SPORTS. Bomb throwing competition and Military Obstacle Race.' Men stand in a short length of mock trench and throw 'bombs' – officers and others look on. Camera in front of trench records men running in, throwing their grenades and then going over the top – the trench is sufficiently deep that the men first lay their rifles on the lip of the trench, climb out, then retrieve their weapons. The men advance through (not barbed) wire entanglements. Camera to the rear as men fire from their trench before advancing – some have difficulty climbing out. 'BIVOUAC ALARM. The London Division Cyclists turn out in 1 min 58 secs.' Men emerge from bivouacs and fall in.
II. The Colours of the 99th Canadian Battalion (Windsor Ontario) are deposited in Windsor Parish Church for safe keeping during the war. 'CANADIAN COLOURS. The colours of the 99th. Canadian Battalion (Windsor Ontario) are deposited in Windsor Parish Church for safe keeping during the war.'
III. Donkey derby. 'KEMPTON PARK

JUBILEE. The Jubilee Stakes meeting held by the Mechanical (sic) Transport Section of the A.S.C. Each mount carried top-weight.' MS of two soldiers at scoreboard. Soldiers place bets. Men of police and Forces race donkeys past camera – a man dressed as a huntsman is first home.
IV. US munitions factory burns. 'AMERICAN MUNITION FACTORY DISASTER. A terrific explosion causes enormous damage at a New York munition works, setting fire to many ships in the harbour.' LS of fire in waterfront building – firemen with hoses in foreground. Pan right to left over fire-fighting vessels – in the foreground are the *Slatington*, then a vessel from New York Central Lines – hoses play water onto still smouldering barges.

Notes
Summary (item IV): this episode may show the destruction on 30 July of the National Storage Company's warehouses situated on Black Tom, a peninsula in the bay near the Statue of Liberty. The warehouses contained munitions, and there were over 30 explosions causing an estimated £2 million of damage to property in New York City and New Jersey.
catalogued NAP: 7/1991

NTB 261-01 · GB, 23/8/1916
TOPICAL BUDGET 261-1

b/w · 1 reel · 315' (5 mins) · silent
intertitles: English

pr Topical Film Company

I. Serb troops receive basic training. 'RE-ORGANISING THE SERBIAN ARMY. The Serbs who are born fighters, receiving instruction in Swedish drill, preparatory to taking their place in the trenches against the Bulgars.' Men run through PT routine in open air – instructor watches them from a raised podium. MS, troops fallen in in line – they wear uniform tunics and caps but without insignia.
II. British artillery on the move in Salonika. 'ARTILLERY CROSSING THE MOUNTAINS. British artillery climbing a mountain path with their heavy guns, on the way to the Allied front at Salonika.' Column of Australian horse-drawn 60-pounder artillery passes along a dusty road, followed by French troops with supply wagons.
III. Red Cross demonstration. 'AMBULANCE COMPETITION. The spectators at the West Kent volunteer Fencibles Sports, see the way Red Cross Bandging (sic) and Stretcher Work is carried out at the Front.' Spectators

watch as 'casualties' are lifted onto stretchers and carried to Model T Ford ambulance of VAD KENT (Sydenham).

IV. Lloyd George attends Eisteddfod. 'WELSH NATIONAL EISTEDDFOD. The Gorsedd procession passing through the ruins of Aberystwyth Castle.' Man declaims to a crowd – he is in ordinary dress but next to him stands a robed figure – other 'bards' are present. Procession through the Castle ruins: police escort a banner, firemen carry a cornucopian horn on a cushion, a man bears a sword. The 'bards' follow up the rear – one is a clergyman and wears combination clerical-bardic costume. 'MR LLOYD GEORGE AT ABERYSTWYTH. The War Minister is surrounded by enthusiastic crowds on his arrival at the great Welsh Musical Festival.' Crowds in open field cheer as Lloyd George arrives by car. Police line the route. Lloyd George gets out of the car and an impetuous lady breaks through the cordon to shake his hand. As the great man walks off the crowd surges after him.

catalogued NAP: 7/1991

NTB 261-02 · GB, 26/8/1916
TOPICAL BUDGET 261-2

b/w · 1 reel · 311' (5 mins) · silent
intertitles: English

pr Topical Film Company

I. Show jumping. 'THE GUARDS SPORTS. Lifeguards give a demonstration of horse jumping over difficult obstacles, at Windsor.' Showjumping exhibition in an open field; it is raining, and the field is overgrown. The sequence involves shots of a horse refusing to jump and demolishing a fence.
II. Holloway Public Library as Hospital. 'LIBRARY AS HOSPITAL. Lord Islington opens the Public Library at Holloway. His lordship chats with the inmates after the ceremony.' Shot of the library building: it now has a sign on it reading 'Great Northern Central Hospital MILITARY SECTION B'. Lord Islington stands in the grounds and delivers a speech. Afterwards he meets a seated line of soldiers.
III. Water polo match at regatta. 'ROYAL REGATTA AT RICHMOND. The 141st Annual Watermen's Regatta, held in aid of the Richmond Royal Hospital. One of the chief items – a water polo match.' Scenes of the water polo match taking place in the river; it is raining. (Footage apparently taken from a boat.)
IV. Memorial to Lord Roberts unveiled. 'LORD ROBERTS MEMORIAL. Unveiling

ceremony by the Right Hon. Countess Roberts at Kelvingrove Park, Glasgow.' Many dignitaries pass by the camera; shot of the memorial, still draped in a Union Flag. Countess Roberts stands on podium and unveils the statue; dignitaries salute. Final shot of Countess Roberts and others on the podium.
V. Lord French at investiture. 'LORD FRENCH AT GLASGOW. Presentation of Distinguished Conduct Medals to Heroes who fought in France under Lord French.' Lord French gives medals to individuals from various regiments, including some in civilian dress, at an open-air ceremony. A line of naval officers and ratings stand in the background. (Film quality poor, and item ends rather abruptly.)

Notes
Summary: see also descriptive note in McKernan.
catalogued JCK: 5/1993

NTB 262-01 · GB, 30/8/1916
TOPICAL BUDGET 262-1

b/w · 1 reel · 330' (6 mins) · silent
intertitles: English

pr Topical Film Company

I. A game of football. 'FOOTBALL SEASON OPENS. The Football match at the Naval and Military Carnival, promoted by the 1st. Batt. City of London Regiment.' A game of football before a stadium crowd. The goal – near which the camera is situated – is merely a frame, without the conventional netting.
II. Trade Union demonstration against high food prices. 'WAR ON FOOD PIRATES. A huge demonstration marching through Trafalgar Square. "The Government must confiscate the food supplies" – Mr Ben Tillett.' HA onto procession of marchers – a banner reads 'NATIONAL UNION OF RAILWAYMEN. – HANDS OFF THE PEOPLES' FOOD – DOWN WITH THE EXPLOITERS OR UP WITH WAGES'. Another less forthrightly Socialist slogan is 'FEED THY LAMBS', and there are a series of banners representing trade union branches – Somers Town, St Pancras, etc.
III. Romania declares war. 'RUMANIA DECLARES WAR. Rumania declares herself on the side of Civilisation and the Entente Powers. Men and Artillery of the Rumanian Army who have been in strict training since the outbreak of the European War.' LS as teams of six horses drawing Maxim machineguns gallop left to right across open

ground. MS as the machinegun chariot is separated from its ammunition limber and deployed. In a town square a detachment of troops stack arms and remove their kit after a march. Despite much enthusiasm some of the drill seems rather odd – having stacked their kit in front of them one rank of soldiers steps back, whereupon the second rank turns and jumps over the kit to join their comrades.

IV. Brigade sports. 'BRIGADE SPORTS. A novel competition – the Crawling Race, which created great amusement. Maj-General Miles, presenting the prizes.' Two men sit astride a horizontal beam battering each other with pillows – no result is immediately apparent. Men crawl on all-fours, weaving in and out of lines of flags to return to their start line – even allowing for unnatural camera speeds, some of the participants are clearly accomplished crawlers. Major-General Miles presents prizes.

Notes

Summary (item II): the march ended in Hyde Park, where the men were addressed by a number of speakers, including Ben Tillett of the Dockers' Union. The thrust of Tillett's address was that the working-class made up most of the armed forces, but whatever benefit might be derived from the war would go to the capitalists, amongst whom the most outrageous were those manipulating food prices. A motion was passed in support of the executive committee of the National Union of Railwaymen, who had decided to ask for an increase of 10/- per week to meet the increased cost of living.
catalogued NAP: 7/1991

NTB 263-01 · GB, 6/9/1916
TOPICAL BUDGET 263-1

b/w · 1 reel · 260' (4 mins) · silent
intertitles: English

pr Topical Film Company

I. Wreckage of Schütte-Lanz SL11 at Cuffley. 'ZEPPELIN DESTROYED. Wreckage of the air raider, the flames of which illuminated London when it fell blazing at Cuffley.' LS of crowd gathered on open parkland. Lorries wait loaded with pieces of the wreckage, while soldiers methodically sort through the debris for anything of interest. 'GATHERING UP THE WRECKAGE. The debris being carefully gathered up and loaded on to the lorries, every fragment is of value in re-constructing the craft.' Soldiers roll up a large bale of the wire used to support the

Zeppelin fabric, and load scrap fragments onto a lorry. 'A collection of souvenirs of the destroyed Zeppelin. The cartridge cases were exploded by the terrific heat.' (This title is in a modern typeface, and is presumably a replacement for a destroyed or missing original.) CU – rather out-of-focus – of fragments of wire, individual rounds and packets of ammunition. 'FATE OF OTHER ZEPPS. Over 36 Zeppelins have been destroyed by the Allies. The remains of one brought down at Salonika.' MS pan over tangled debris amidst the tall reeds of the Vadar Marshes. A man sitting astride part of the jumbled wreckage gives scale, and as the camera pans the circular structure of girders making up the Zeppelin's nose comes into frame. A group of French soldiers examine part of one of the gondolas and cut away at the struts holding fuel tanks and propeller. 'THE CAPTURED CREW. The crew of the Zepp destroyed at Salonika, being marched off under escort, they did not share the fate of the London raider.' German crewmen enter a building, walking past a group of smiling Frenchmen – rather incongruously they are accompanied by a French cook swinging a ladle. The Germans do not seem too depressed and one manages a broad smile. MS of the airship's officers in distinctive leather greatcoats – they are being shown a picture or photograph by one of their captors. Again the atmosphere seems generally amiable.

Notes

Summary: shot down on the night of 2/3 September, the SL11 was the first Zeppelin destroyed over Britain and it marked a turning point in the war against these raiders. In the last scene between the German and French officers the racial stereotypes are so marked as to be comical – the Germans all wear their hair virtually shaven to the skull, the French are all moustachioed, some extravagantly so.
catalogued NAP: 7/1991

NTB 263-02 · GB, 9/9/1916
TOPICAL BUDGET 263-2

b/w · 1 reel · 312' (5 mins) · silent
intertitles: English

pr Topical Film Company

I. Burial of the crew of the Zeppelin which crashed near Potters Bar on 1 October 1916. 'ZEPPELIN CREW'S BURIAL. The charred remains of the Germans who set out to hurl death amongst defenceless women and children, being conveyed on an Army

transport waggon.' RFC officers and men carry coffins into churchyard. Police line the route. 'FINAL SCENES OF L21. Officers and men of the R.F.C. carrying the unnamed coffins to the grave in Potters' Bar Cemetery.' Six coffins are set down by the edge of common grave. As the dead are interred, the priest reads the burial rite and officers and men salute. LS over the heads of the crowd as the priest departs.
II. Mop fighting. 'MOP FIGHTING. Mounted on each others backs, soldiers engage in exciting mop fight. One of the items at the Military Sports at Felixstowe.' A crowd watches from a cricket (?) pavilion as two soldiers, both seated on the shoulders of others, fight with mops. The combat is quite fierce, and one man is eventually unseated.
III. Convalescent soldiers attend concert. 'KHAKI MATINEE. Miss Ellaline Terris (sic) handling (sic) cigarettes to wounded soldiers as they arrive at the theatre. Over 2,000 men from all parts of the Empire attended.' A nurse holds open the door of a car for wounded men to dismount – the first sports a large bandage over one eye, another is on crutches. Less seriously wounded men arrive by bus. A crowd of men dressed in hospital blues regard the camera – some are South Africans, one is from the Middlesex Regiment. A Yeomanry medical officer walks into frame and the men draw his attention to the camera – he turns and stares into it rather vacantly but then smiles, and the men about him laugh. MS of Miss Terris offering cigarettes to the men – they accept these and also the envelopes (perhaps containing photos of Miss Terris ?) she is giving away. Men light up and puff theatrically.
IV. Allies conquer the Salonika post office. 'ALLIES CONTROL GREEK POST OFFICE. The Greek Post Office at Salonika is now under the complete control of the Allies.' French troops, their arms stacked, stand about in front of the Post Office regarding the camera. LA.MS of main entrance of 'Postes et Télégraphes' and pan down to Australian and French troops – in left foreground locals look to camera.

Notes
Summary (item III): the occasion for the 'khaki matinee' was the opening at the Princes Theatre of a revival of *Broadway Jones* starring Mr Seymour Hicks as Jackson Jones and Miss Terriss as Josie Richards, the girl "who turns him from the gay life of New York to the cares of running a chewing-gum factory in the wilds of Connecticut" (*The Times*, 7 September 1916: 9). Seymour Hicks was later knighted, and married Miss Terriss. Lady Hicks died in 1971 at the age of 100.
catalogued NAP: 7/1991

NTB 264-01 · GB, 13/9/1916
TOPICAL BUDGET 264-1

b/w · 1 reel · 326' (5 mins) · silent
intertitles: English

pr Topical Film Company

I. Medical column on the move in Salonika. 'RED CROSS WORK AT SALONIKA. An ambulance column moving over the mountain road to the Balkan Front.' MS over flat country to Australian troops on the march – all wear Red Cross armbands. Horse-drawn Red Cross wagon and casualties pass by, lying on travois pulled by mules.
II. Orphans demonstrate their military skills to Admiral Fremantle. 'RICHMOND BOYS' NAVAL BRIGADE. Admiral Sir E.R. Freemantle (sic) inspects the Boys' Naval Brigade, who gave a display in aid of the "John Cornwell Cot" at the Star and Garter Home.' The Admiral – in civilian suit and bowler – inspects rank of small boys dressed in naval uniform – one boy near the camera wipes his nose to prepare himself for inspection. Spectators look on as the boys go through gun drill with suitably tiny cannon – in the background a second gun is pulled into frame by boys in harness – one has fallen over and is dragged in his traces by his more fleet companions. MS as boys go through a routine which approximately mimics the loading and firing of the gun. The Admiral is cheered by his diminutive hosts.
III. Mr and Mrs Churchill attend a fête. 'MR. CHURCHILL AT CHELMSFORD. The Deputy Mayor receives Mr. Winston Churchill who attended the Fete in aid of the Scottish Prisoners of War Fund.' Churchill and his wife get out of car which has pulled up in a grassy field – he is dressed in a frock coat and top hat. He delivers a speech from a platform decorated with flags. MS left profile of Churchill once more amidst the crowds, watching events – his wife stands next to him.
IV. English soldiers enjoy internment in Switzerland. 'INTERNED IN SWITZERLAND. English soldiers released from Germany and who are now interned in Switzerland receive every consideration from the Swiss.' Opening pan (very unsteady due to bad lacing in the camera) over soldiers sitting on the ground – some nurses are evident in the crowd of civilians about them. LS pan over seated audience of soldiers and civilians – in the front row a British and French officer are in animated conversation. 'VISITED BY THEIR WIVES. Special arrangements have been made for the wives of the soldiers to visit them at the Chateau d'Oex.' An elderly officer addresses a crowd from raised

platform which bears a distinctive heraldic decoration (the arms of Château d'Oex or Swiss canton ?). MS of soldiers and their wives. A soldier rocks a swaddled baby in his arms.

Notes
Summary (item III): the text of Churchill's speech can be found in *The Times*, 11 September 1916: 10.
Summary (item IV): the town of Château d'Oex is in the mountains near Montreux. According to *The Times*, the first party of 16 women did not arrive to visit their husbands until 4 October 1916.
catalogued NAP: 7/1991

NTB 265-01 · GB, 20/9/1916
TOPICAL BUDGET 265-1

b/w · 1 reel · 317' (5 mins) · silent
intertitles: English

pr Topical Film Company

I. French celebrate the second anniversary of the Battle of the Marne. 'BATTLE OF OURCQ. The inhabitants of Meaux, celebrate the 2nd anniversary of the Battle of Ourcq, which resulted in the Germans being held at the Marne.' HA.LS over crowd filing through walled graveyard. LS over dense crowd surrounding entrance to church as a procession leaves the building bearing regimental flags. MS of war memorial commemorating the battle – locals stand about it.
II. Lord Mayor visits a military hospital. 'LORD MAYOR VISITS MILITARY HOSPITAL. The Lord Mayor accompanied by the Lady Mayoress visits the City of London Military Hospital and inspects the Wards.' Mayor and Mayoress arrive in horse-drawn coach to be greeted by leading medical staff. They visit soldiers whose beds have been drawn out onto an open veranda – the soldiers seem each to have been given flowers from the Mayoress' bouquet – one who lies smoking a cigarette as he fingers his flower, seems strangely unmoved. Nurses and the mayoral party stand about a staked sapling – perhaps newly planted in honour of the occasion.
III. Women on bicycles. 'WOMEN CYCLISTS' RALLY. Women cyclists from all parts of London meet at the Angel Ditton, and cycle to Wisley.' HA.LS pan over cyclists assembled outside the Angel. They set out – despite the title men seem quite well represented. At a lakeside wood – presumably at Wisley – the ladies take a rest for refreshments. CU of two women,

probably sisters, dressed in matching outfits of turban hats with belted cardigans over chequered cotton dresses. Both are eating some sort of pasty or turnover, and while one beguiles the time with a newspaper, the other has a book.
IV. VAD nurses are inspected. 'INSPECTION OF NURSES. Surgeon-General F.G. Jencken inspects the Nurses of the Middlesex Voluntary Aid Detachment.' Jencken and staff pass ranks of nurses fallen in on grassy field. Men march past – they wear khaki with Red Cross badges and some with armbands. Women follow behind – they are dressed in white pinafores over blues. Motor ambulances follow up the rear of the column. 'AMBULANCE WORK.' VAD workers give a display at Gunnersbury Park. These volunteer workers are engaged nightly conveying wounded soldiers to hospitals.' Men place laden stretchers into the back of motor ambulances. MS of St John's nurses dressing the wounds of stretcher cases – one fortunate victim has four attendants. Officers look on.

catalogued NAP: 8/1991

NTB 265-02 · GB, 23/9/1916
TOPICAL BUDGET 265-2

b/w · 1 reel · 312' (5 mins) · silent
intertitles: English

pr Topical Film Company

I. Coatbridge Carnival. 'COATBRIDGE CARNIVAL. Wounded Scotch (sic) soldiers being well looked after by Scotch (sic) lassies at the carnival in aid of limbless soldiers and sailors.' Scottish band playing. Food and drink are served to soldiers by cheery nurses. Close-up of grinning young soldier with bad teeth eating a sandwich into the top of which somebody sticks a feather.
II. Munition workers' welfare. 'MUNITION WORKERS' WELFARE. A special department of the Ministry of Munitions look after the health of the workers. Mrs Kent inspects the girl guides (munition workers) who drill during their lunch hour.' Mrs Kent watches the Girl Guides going through their paces: several of them run to a girl lying on the ground, whom they lift up and place on a stretcher. The inspection over, one of the Guides dons an overall on top of her uniform and returns to work.
III. Wounded soldiers visit Windsor Castle. 'WOUNDED SOLDIERS VISIT WINDSOR CASTLE. At the invitation of the King, wounded soldiers from Queen Mary's Hospital drive to Windsor Castle and are

entertained at the riding school.' Various shots of the disabled soldiers arriving at the school in cars, helped out by attendants. A limbless man in a wheelchair is pushed past, followed by one-legged men on crutches. One wheelchair-bound veteran poses for the camera.
IV. Lorry-mounted AA gun. 'AIR CRAFT AT WORK. Taking up positions on the approach of hostile aircraft.' Troops climb down from a portée, and prepare the gun mounted on the back of it; stabilisers are pulled out and blocks are pushed underneath. 'IN ACTION. Gun firing at German Taube in the Salonika area. Serbian officers observing the effect through the distant gauges.' Troops load and fire the lorry-mounted AA gun, now fully prepared. After firing, the gun is reset to a new firing position. Serbian (?) officer watches through a gauge as the gun is fired; others present look through binoculars

Notes

Summary: see also descriptive note in McKernan; issue appears to have complete number of items but is lacking main title.
catalogued JCK: 5/1993

NTB 266-02 · GB, 30/9/1916
TOPICAL BUDGET 266-2

b/w · 1 reel · 315' (5 mins) · silent
intertitles: English

pr Topical Film Company

I. Lord French inspects Volunteers at Liverpool. 'LORD FRENCH AT LIVERPOOL. The Lancashire Volunteer Regiment being reviewed by Field-Marshal Lord French outside the Adelphi Hotel.' French inspects ranks of men fallen in on cobbled street – trolley-bus passes in background. Men march past – the uniforms are rather mixed in pattern and some men are in civilian dress. Lord French and his retinue depart.
II. Lord Mayor of London at fund-raising fête. 'BRUCE CASTLE FETE. The Lord Mayor of London and Lady Mayoress attend the fête at Bruce Castle Park, Tottenham, held in aid of the funds for Blinded Soldiers and Sailors.' The Mayor arrives in his full regalia. He gives a speech. MS over the crowd – one woman waves to the camera. A performance – a young girl in sylvan dress leaps about a stage while fairies and nymphs look on. The Mayor is presented with a gift (possibly chocolates) from one of the fête stalls.
III. An Orthodox priest blesses ambulances. 'BLESSING THE AMBULANCES. President Poincaré, Gen. Dubail and Gen. Pau attend

the ceremony of blessing the cars given by the Rumanians residing in Paris.' Poincaré, the generals and their retinue gather around a covered altar as Orthodox priest reads dedication. MCU as the priest daubs each car with holy water as a blessing. MS of the assembled vehicles – they are all of the same make (Peugeot ?) and model and are clearly specialised ambulance types.
IV. The London Fire Brigade lays on a demonstration for wounded soldiers. 'LONDON FIRE BRIGADE DRILL. The L.F.B. give a demonstration with their fire appliances at Headquarters to an audience of wounded soldiers.' Three fire engines speed down a road watched by a few passers-by. Vehicle 'LF 9000' raises a ladder against a building and men climb up, carrying aloft a further short scaling ladder. Man on ladder directs a hose down into the square below, adjusting it to demonstrate wide and narrow water-jets. 'SMOKE HELMET DRILL. London Firemen wearing the special helmet which is worn when entering a building full of smoke or gas.' Watched by a crowd of soldiers a man leaps from a window into a safety blanket. MS as a man emerges from a smoke-filled building wearing a respirator and carrying a hose (curiously he wears no goggles or other eye protection). A man in a respirator carries a 'casualty' out of the building. LA as a fireman on the roof directs his hose to the ground, and view below of the converging jets from several hoses. More hose gear is deployed from the fire engines.

catalogued NAP: 8/1991

NTB 267-01 · GB, 4/10/1916
TOPICAL BUDGET 267-1

b/w · 1 reel · 317' (5 mins) · silent
intertitles: English

pr Topical Film Company

I. Serbian priest blesses passing troops. 'SERBIANS GOING INTO ACTION. Serbian priest blessing the Troops as they pass on their way to the Front.' A priest stands among a group of women and young children – he faces a low building and as he reads aloud some of the women cross themselves. In the background a column of soldiers and laden mules passes through the widely scattered buildings of the village – despite the title there is no very obvious connection between the two events.
II. Territorials march at ease in the English countryside. 'LONDON TERRITORIALS. Some of the London Regiment on the

march. "A London battalion co-operated with the French at the taking of Combles".'
HA.MS over column of Territorials on the march along a country road – they are marching at ease and do not present a very military appearance – several are smoking pipes. The rifles appear to be .256 Arisakas. MS of a group of officers, two on horseback.
III. Inspection of 'Y' Division of Special Constabulary. 'SIR E. WARD INSPECTS 'SPECIALS'. The Chief of the Metropolitan Special Constabulary inspects the members of 'Y' Division.' Ward inspects ranks of Specials fallen in on grass field – terraced houses in the background. Specials march past – in rather disordered ranks – while a few spectators look on. MCU of Ward.
IV. Band of the Garde Républicaine is entertained by the Lord Mayor of London. 'GARDE REPUBLICAINE BAND. France's famous military band marches to the Mansion House and are (sic) entertained by the Lord Mayor.' MS as senior French and British military officers enter the Mansion House. (Major-General Sir Francis Lloyd, Commanding London District and the Chef de Musique Captain Balay were present.) French bandsmen arrive (without instruments) preceded by massed bands of the Brigade of Guards and followed by pipers of the Scots Guards carrying their pipes. In the background is Manfield and Sons Boots. 'CITY WELCOME. The French band standing to attention as the massed Guard's band play the "Marseillaise" on their arrival in the City.' MS of French Contingent fallen in to listen to their national anthem.

Notes
Summary (item II): Combles was retaken by Anglo-French forces on 26 September.
Summary (item IV): the French arrived in London on 28 September, and enjoyed their luncheon at the Mansion House on 30 September.
catalogued NAP: 8/1991

NTB 267-02 · GB, 7/10/1916
TOPICAL BUDGET 267-2

b/w · 1 reel · 308' (5 mins) · silent
intertitles: English

pr Topical Film Company

I. Dog teams in use in the Belgian Army. 'THE DOGS OF WAR. The training of dogs in warfare has proved of great value to the Belgian Army. The dogs at their training ground, and pulling machine guns along the road.' Soldiers put down food for the dogs who emerge from their kennels to eat – most

are on short tethers, but some are free to run about and the men make a fuss of these animals. Soldiers adjust the harness on teams of mastiff-like dogs, – there are two animals to each small cart. One soldier gives his charges a drink – some of the other dogs are muzzled. 'EXTRAORDINARY INTELLIGENCE. The soldier in charge of the gun team, goes forward to reconnoitre, and at the signal, the dogs pull the gun to the new position.' Soldier runs forward over open field and beckons to the dogs who pull the cart forward (the gun is covered with canvas) – on reaching the soldier the dogs lie down.
II. Major-General Lloyd reviews Volunteers. 'REVIEWING THE VOLUNTEERS. Major General Sir Francis Lloyd in the absence of Lord French reviews the South London Volunteers at Brockwell Park.' The General and his retinue walk towards the camera from their parked cars to be greeted by an officer. Inspection of the Volunteers – only some appear to have rifles.
III. Funeral of Lieutenant Carlot at Montreux, Switzerland. 'SWITZERLAND HONOURS HEROES. The French, Belgian and British soldiers follow the funeral of the late Lieut. Carlot at Montreux.' Preceded by a detachment of Swiss soldiers, a horse-drawn hearse passes right to left followed immediately by family and relatives (including two nuns) and then by French and Belgian officers – the British are not very evident, and if present must be at the rear of the procession.
IV. Australian artillery in action in Salonika. 'ANZACS FIGHTING THE BULGARS. Australian artillery in action against the Bulgarians on the Salonika Front.' MCU of rear of 18-pounder gun as it fires from the shelter of a canvas awning. An Australian crew serve the gun which appears to be conducting a carefully aimed bombardment – though the optical sight is not removed between shots.

catalogued NAP: 8/1991

NTB 269-01 · GB, 18/10/1916
TOPICAL BUDGET 269-1

b/w · 1 reel · 319' (5 mins) · silent
intertitles: English

pr Topical Film Company

I. Bishop of Kingston unveils war memorial. 'SOUTH LONDON HEROES. Dr. Taylor the Bishop of Kingston unveils a War Shrine in memory of local heroes at St. Mark's Kennington.' Boy scout band marches through the gates to St. Mark's – Oval tube station is in the background. A procession leaves the church, led by choristers. MS as Dr Taylor unveils the 'shrine' and unlocks the doors to reveal a roll of honour inside. Soldiers at frame right clutch bunches of lilies to place upon the shrine. The event is covered by several still photographers.

II. Fishing from the pier at Hastings. 'HASTING'S SEA ANGLING FESTIVAL. Many competitors take part in the annual sea-angling festival and despite inclement weather some fair catches were made.' Soldier baits his hook and casts. View along the pier to shore showing the array of rods over the side. Soldier lands a small conger eel. CUs of other competitors, civilian and military – one old man helps himself to a packed lunch of sandwiches.

III. Fête for convalescent soldiers in Windsor Great Park. 'ENTERTAINING 6,000 OVERSEAS WOUNDED. At the Fête organised by Mrs. Fiske in Windsor Great Park, 6,000 wounded soldiers celebrate the second anniversary of the departure of the Anzacs for the Front.' Soldiers sitting on the grass – some with crutches beside them – wave their hats in a cheer. Pan over soldiers standing on grassy slope – a few women and children are evident, and tents are visible in the background. MS as a woman shows or offers something to a seated soldier – a situation posed for the camera. Convalescents queue at one of the tents, presumably for refreshments.

IV. Training in the techniques of military mining. 'LAND MINE EXPLOSION. Officers of the Royal Engineers receive instruction in exploding land mines.' MS of two Tyneside Scottish soldiers sitting in entrenchment – one is working a hand pump to supply air to the mine – a third man looks on. HA as officers and men run out from the 'BABY MINE' and along trench toward camera. Engineer depresses plunger on exploder and cut to LS of two relatively small mines. HA as two men don Proto breathing apparatus – thus equipped, and both carrying small cages containing canaries for the detection of gas, they walk towards the mine entrance. 'OCCUPYING THE CRATER. After the mine has been fired, infantry rush forward and entrench themselves in the crater formed by the explosion.' XLS as troops advance – a model section of trench winds its way across centre-frame. MS as soldiers dig in to the lip of the crater and fill sandbags – this group have paper squares bearing the letter 'B' attached to their backs. General scene as teams of soldiers dig in. B team's strong point again – a low parapet of sandbags has been built up on the inside of the crater's lip.

Notes

Summary (item IV): to organise a fête in October in England is rather optimistic, and in this case over optimistic: most of the soldiers are in their greatcoats and it all looks pretty dismal.
catalogued NAP: 8/1991

NTB 269-02 · GB, 21/10/1916
TOPICAL BUDGET 269-2

b/w · 1 reel · 319' (5 mins) · silent
intertitles: English

pr Topical Film Company

I. Volunteers in training. 'VOLUNTEERS IN TRAINING. Men of the St. Pancras Volunteers engaged on trench digging, "Somewhere in Essex."' A sunny day. Men in civilian dress prepare the ground. They are engaged not upon digging a trench of the conventional sort but in the construction of an earthwork made of turf. The turf layers – most of whom are uniformed, in contrast to the turf cutters – appear quite expert. 'BUILDING EARTHWORKS. Volunteers spend their Sunday in training. Some of the men building a parapet.' Turf sods are cut out and laid in low walls which are neatly shaped with machetes – at the end of the sequence appears a volunteer whose age and girth would surely preclude active service unless Essex was invaded.

II. Flag day for the British Red Cross. '"OUR DAY". Indian Princesses and wounded soldiers selling flags and 'Zepp' (sic) souvenirs on behalf of the British Red Cross Society.' A soldier with tray sells paper flag badges in the street. An 'Indian princess' does likewise. LS of building decorated with Allied flags and 'Our Day' posters.

III. Rugby match in aid of Canadian prisoners of war. 'CANADIANS V PUBLIC SCHOOLS. The Rugby football match in aid of the "Canadian Prisoners of War" results in a win for the Public Schools by eight points to nil.' MS sequence showing a rugby match in progress – no score during recorded play.

IV. Cavalry in Macedonia. An improvised AA mounting for a Vickers machinegun. 'CAVALRY IN MACEDONIA. Cavalry passing through a mountain pass on their way to the Bulgarian frontier. An improvised anti-aircraft gun fixed on the wheel of a gun limber, taken in action.' Men lead horses up a low bank from a shallow stream where the animals have presumably been watered. Tethered in lines in the camp, the animals are groomed – a group of local peasants stand in left foreground doing nothing in Balkan fashion. MS of a Vickers machinegun clamped to the wheel of an overturned gun limber, the rotation of the wheel giving the gun some traverse – one man fires and another eases the feed of the belt.

Notes
Remarks (item I): the very type of the British weekend warrior.
Summary (item II): the Zepp souvenirs were made from wire recovered from the wreck of the SL11.
catalogued NAP: 8/1991

NTB 270-02 · GB, 28/10/1916
TOPICAL BUDGET 270-2

b/w · 1 reel · 324' (5 mins) · silent
intertitles: English

pr Topical Film Company

I. King Constantine of Greece visits a hospital ship. 'THE KING OF GREECE. His Majesty the King of Greece visits a hospital ship.' Honour guard of Greek sailors march along quayside (each holds his Mannlicher rifle very high, the breech resting on the shoulder). HA.MS as Constantine and party come up hospital ship's accommodation ladder from boat alongside.
II. Serbian artillery on the move and in action in the mountains. 'SERBIANS IN MACEDONIA. The immense difficulties of transport which a Serbian Mountain battery encounters in moving their guns up to the Front.' A team of six horses hauls an ammunition limber up a steep muddy slope – a rider sits astride one of each pair of horses, urging them on, and other men push on the wheels of the limber. A gun is pulled up a slope – it appears to be a 75 – followed by its ammunition limber. LS of Serbian OP in a tree in flooded country. A mountain gun (Schneider 65mm M06 ?) is fired from a covered emplacement – it is not well chocked and must be manhandled back into position after firing.
III. Wheat barges are unloaded at Paris. 'WHEAT FOR THE FRENCH ARMY. Corn being unloaded from barges at Paris. The corn is intended for the use of the French troops.' In the barge's hold men shovel wheat into a crane's bucket. The bucket discharges into a hopper which feeds the wheat into sacks. The machine-loaded sacks are topped up by hand and sealed with ties.
IV. Rugby match in New York. 'RUGBY FOOTBALL IN AMERICA. Enormous crowds watch a keenly contested rugby match, played at New York.' HA.LS of rugby match in play watched by a large crowd. LS from across the stadium – encouraged by male

cheer-leaders, a section of the crowd hold up placards which seen together make up a square bearing a huge letter 'C' – presumably representing California, which is also spelt out in 10 pendant flags at the top of the stadium. As the crowd turn the placards over, the display changes from a dark letter 'C' on a light background to the reverse.
V. Volunteer Red Cross nurses leave the USA to work in Allied hospitals in France. 'HELPING THE ALLIES. Red Cross nurses leaving the United States to help in the hospitals in France.' MS pan left to right over nurses dressed in the long dresses and short capes of the American Red Cross – they are standing on the gangway of their ship. On board, two nurses pose with a uniformed man with Red Cross armband – presumably a doctor.

Notes
Technical (item I): very bad deterioration towards the end of this sequence.
Remarks (item IV): an interesting demonstration of cultural differences.
catalogued NAP: 8/1991

NTB 271-02 · GB, 4/11/1916
TOPICAL BUDGET 271-2

b/w · 1 reel · 305' (5 mins) · silent
intertitles: English

pr Topical Film Company

I. Russian troops arrive in Salonika. 'RUSSIANS IN MACEDONIA. Russian troops disembarking from the transport to help the Allies in Macedonia.' Small paddle-steamer crowded with Russian troops runs alongside quay and men disembark. 'HELP FOR THE ALLIES. Russian Staff Officers watch their men landing. These troops are some of the finest in the Russian Army.' Officers look on as men disembark. Allied troops also watch the arrival of the Russians – on the quayside a British Army band plays to welcome them.
II. Austrian POWs in a Russian camp. 'RUSSIAN INTERNMENT CAMP. One of the camps in Russia where the Germans captured in the great offensive are being sent.' HA.LS over POWs standing in ranks – they appear to be Austrian rather than German. More prisoners are joining the queues as the camera pans slowly right to show the extent of the crowd.
III. Blinded soldiers are taught new skills. 'ST. DUNSTAN'S. The Hostel for blind soldiers where they are taught various trades. The dexterity the men show in repairing boots and making baskets is

amazing.' MS as two men work on repairing boots – the nearest man is nailing on a new heel-piece but has positioned his nail askew – he removes it and tries again. MS of men making wicker baskets – CUs of one with a nearly completed basket and another just starting work on the base plate. 'BLIND SOLDIERS TYPEWRITING. Men receive instruction in manipulating the keyboard of a typewriter.' CU of a man typing – a woman instructor is placing his fingers on the keys. MS same – the woman does not look at what she is doing and is probably herself blind. Other men type and operate (?) Comptometer.

catalogued NAP: 8/1991

NTB 272-02 · GB, 11/11/1916
TOPICAL BUDGET 272-2

b/w · 1 reel · 306' (5 mins) · silent
intitles: English

pr Topical Film Company

I. Uniformed representatives of the Allied forces fighting in the Balkans. 'THE ARMIES OF THE ALLIES. An interesting group of the nationalities fighting the Central Powers in the Balkans. British, French, Russian, Italian, Serbian, Indian, Cretan, Senegalese, Greek, and Anammite (sic) type of soldiers.' The men stand talking. Cigarettes are offered by a British officer and generally accepted. The men file past the camera one after the other. II. Inspection of the Lancashire Volunteers. 'V.T.C. Accompanied by the Lord Mayor of Manchester, Field Marshal Lord French watches the march past of the Lancashire Volunteers.' French and other military men pass the camera. The Field Marshal decorates a convalescent soldier. March past of the Lancashire Volunteers along cobbled city street – the first detachment are all in civilian dress, the second section, preceded by a small band, wear a motley combination of civilian and military clothing. III. Band of the Belgian Grenadiers arrive in Manchester. 'KING ALBERT'S BAND. The Band of the Belgian Grenadiers are inspected by Viscount French on their arrival in Manchester.' Band marches past holding their instruments – they are in a park, watched by a small crowd. Scene shifts to Belgians fallen in outside city building (the station ?) – French inspects, then talks briefly with their CO before departing. IV. Captured German weapons are exhibited at the Lord Mayor's Show in London. 'THE LORD MAYOR'S SHOW. A captured German aeroplane and three captured guns were the

special feature of the military pageant.' German light guns – a 105mm field howitzer and a (?) 75mm gun – and the wingless body of a LVG C.II are towed along the street, followed by the ornate coach carrying the Mayor. 'THE LORD MAYOR. Col. Sir W.H. Dunn arriving at the Law Courts for the initiation ceremony.' Dunn and retinue file inside – in the background a naval detachment is marching past. Dunn poses for the camera in the regalia of the Lord Mayor.

Notes
Synopsis (item I): the presence of Cretan troops, represented separately from Greek, reflects Allied support for Venizelos's rebellion against the government of King Constantine, in which the Cretan insurrection played a major part.
catalogued NAP: 8/1991

NTB 273-01 · GB, 15/11/1916
TOPICAL BUDGET 273-1

b/w · 1 reel · 311' (5 mins) · silent
intitles: English

pr Topical Film Company

I. Australian troops in Salonika are inoculated. 'FIGHTING DISEASE. Troops in the Balkans being inoculated against enteric etc., before going up to the Front.' Australian troops stand in line in the open-air, left shirt sleeves rolled up to receive their injection. Afterwards each injection mark is painted with antiseptic. II. Mayor attends a service at Southwark Cathedral. 'MUNICIPAL SUNDAY. The Mayor and Corporation attend service at Southwark Cathedral, being the first Sunday after their election.' Mayor and retinue followed by civilian dignitaries and military men file out of the cathedral past police guard. MS head and shoulders of the new mayor, in conventional dress but wearing his chain of office. He is nodding and bows at the very end of the sequence so that the last image of him is the top of his rather sparsely haired head. III. Newfoundland troops are presented with a silk Union Flag. 'LINK OF EMPIRE. Princess Henry of Battenberg presents a silk Union Flag to the contingent of Newfoundland troops at Chelsea Hospital and inspects the guard of Honour.' The Princess – who seems to be walking with some difficulty – takes a large Union Jack from one officer and quickly passes it on to another who comes forward to receive the flag. Cut to the Princess after a short speech

(?) as she steps back confusedly clutching her script, as others applaud. Newfoundland troops present arms.
IV. Soldiers grow vegetables. 'ARMY ECONOMY. Men in training at the Army Service Corps depot at Osterley Park have converted waste land into a garden, and are growing their own vegetables.' Men rake between young seedlings – huts in background. Two soldiers standing in a field of Brussels sprouts hold up two of the vegetables. An officer admires the sprouts, though rather diffidently. Men file into one of the huts – presumably to eat Brussels sprouts.
V. Russians troops arrive in Salonika. 'SOLDIERS OF THE CZAR. French and Serbian troops line the streets of Salonika as the Russians march to their camp, led by their band.' MS along city street as Russians march into camera – among the band is a uniformed but very young boy. MS as soldiers march away – French line the side of the route.

Notes

Summary (item III): the Newfoundlanders also received a silver shield, a token of appreciation from the women of Britain for the soldiers' valour and devotion. The League of the Empire had arranged similar presentations to Canadian, Australian and South African troops.
catalogued NAP: 8/1991

NTB 273-02 · GB, 18/11/1916
TOPICAL BUDGET 273-2

b/w · 1 reel · 315' (5 mins) · silent
intertitles: English

pr Topical Film Company

I. German POWs captured in Franco-Serbian offensive against Monastir. 'CAPTURED GERMANS. German prisoners of war captured by the French and Serbian Troops in the offensive which is being made towards Monastir.' German POWs fall in on station platform – the wagons of the POW train are visible in the background. The relatively small group of only about 30 prisoners is marched off, surrounded by a numerous armed guard of French soldiers.
II. A semi-comic portrayal of part of the work of the Army Remount Service. 'TRAINING REMOUNTS FOR THE ARMY. A special depot for breaking in dangerous horses which are eventually sent off for Active Service.' Officer holds halter of horse with exaggerated care – he feeds it some sugar, then leads the animal over a low jump which

consists of a single length of string between two posts. He mounts the horse, which appears to object. MS as the rider attempts the jump – the horse refuses and he falls off – clearly a contrived sequence, as the rider does not attempt to jump the horse but merely rides it into the obstacle and as it stumbles dives over its head. A second attempt, successfully clearing the jump. 'READY FOR SERVICE. After a month's training these vicious rebels are handled by lady grooms.' The officer and three 'lady grooms' demonstrate the horses' docility by standing up on the animal's backs – one horse is not quite docile enough. The trial is repeated with two horses, the officer and groom holding hands as they stand – the man's horse suddenly lunges off to the left and he neatly steps off its rump to fall to the ground. End MS of the man and grooms sitting together on a wall – he is stroking a black and white cat on his lap.
III. Wedding of Prince George of Battenberg. 'THE ROYAL WEDDING. Countess Nada de Torby daughter of the Grand Duke Michael of Russia married to Prince George of Battenberg at the Chapel Royal.' The bride arrives with her father by car and enters Russian Embassy. Cut to Queen Mary as she leaves the church and gets into waiting car. Russian officers leave and gather on the pavement outside. Two British naval officers leave – possibly Prince George and his best man. 'ANGLO-RUSSIAN ALLIANCE. Scenes at the Russian Church where the first part of the ceremony was solemnised.' Bride leaves accompanied by her father – the Russian officers congregated about the entrance salute. The bride's car departs.

Notes

Remarks (item II): by Topical Budget standards, quite a successful episode. The man's willingness to participate in this charade, and his general demeanour, suggest that he is not from the 'officer classes', but holds a commission because of his skill as a rider.
Summary (item III): this film shows the preliminary ceremony at the Russian Embassy Chapel in Welbeck Street, where the guests were predominantly Russian.
catalogued NAP: 8/1991

NTB 274-01 · GB, 22/11/1916
TOPICAL BUDGET 274-1

b/w · 1 reel · 315' (5 mins) · silent
intertitles: English

pr Topical Film Company

I. Australian mobile wireless station in Salonika. 'WIRELESS AT THE FRONT. Fixing up a temporary station which enables the officers to keep in touch with the Headquarters Staff.' Two Australian soldiers start up horse-drawn generator. CU of the generator in operation. Interior MS of Morse sender at work – he wears earphones.
II. The River Thames in flood. 'THE THAMES IN FLOOD. The enormous rainfall has flooded the Thames Valley, making the roads in some districts, impassable for traffic.' MS of man riding a horse and a horse pulling a two-wheeled cart along a flooded road. More wagons follow. A covered wagon bearing the legend 'PARIPAN LONDON & EGHAM' passes by. Another trader's wagon goes past.
III. Blinded soldiers are trained in carpentry. 'WORKING UNDER DIFFICULTIES. Blind soldiers at St. Dunstan's are developing the sense of touch to replace their lost sight, and are enabled thereby to make themselves efficient carpenters.' MS and CU as a blind man planes a piece of wood. Others saw.
IV. Women farm labour at the Royal Farm at Sandringham. 'THE ROYAL CATTLE FARMS. Miss Maxfield and the Misses Hobson who are working on the Royal Farm at Sandringham and taking the place of men in tending the King's Cattle.' Land Army girls at work – one forks turnips into a processor, others take away the resulting shredded animal feed in baskets – the device is clearly hand-cranked but this intermediate operation has been cut. One of the girls releases the cattle from their stalls while another brings up fresh hay 'GIRL FARMERS AT SANDRINGHAM. Cutting up turnips, cleaning out stalls, feeding pigs, driving up cows and milking them, all part of the work which has to be carried out every day including Sundays.' Girl carries a large pitchfork-ful of hay into cattle stalls while another rakes out the old material. A basket of feed is carried in. Girl opens gate for pigs. Two women drive cattle along a road towards the camera.

catalogued NAP: 7/1991

NTB 275-02 · GB, 2/12/1916
TOPICAL BUDGET 275-2

b/w · 1 reel · 318' (5 mins) · silent
intertitles: English

pr Topical Film Company

I. Serbian column brings up ammunition. 'SERBIAN TRANSPORT. Serbs bringing up ammunition and stores on pack mules, for the Serbian Army in Macedonia.' MS as a long column of pack mules passes over a wooden trestle bridge. To the rear of the column are some small artillery pieces. Beside the bridge lies a Serbian soldier, apparently asleep, his head and shoulders supported by his pack, his cap pulled over his face. No-one pays this man any heed, and the passing of the column does not cause him to stir.
II. Charity football match between the Army and an Essex County team. 'ESSEX V ARMY. Sir J. Bethell M.P. kicks off at the football match, the proceeds of which will be spent on Xmas parcels for men at the front.' Sir J Bethell shakes hands with the captains of the two teams. The team with striped jerseys (Essex ?) wins the toss, and Bethell kicks off. LS coverage of the game – the team in plain jerseys scores a goal.
III. Roman Catholic members of the Boys Brigade attend mass. 'WESTMINSTER CADETS. The Catholic Boys Brigade of the Westminster Cadets attend Mass at the Italian Church.' MS as cadets march past led by a band – one diminutive triangle-player seems swamped by his uniform cap. The cadets wear a variety of uniforms and some are in civilian clothes. Cut to cadets leaving the church. Crowds look on.
IV. Prince Arthur of Connaught in Paris. 'PRINCE ARTHUR IN PARIS. Prince Arthur of Connaught inspects the guard of honour at the Invalides, previous to the ceremony.' The Prince and French officers exchange salutes, and he inspects the guard of honour. 'DECORATING FRENCH GENERALS. On behalf of the King, Prince Arthur decorates Generals Balfourier and Drude with the Order of St. Michael and St. George.' Prince Arthur decorates the two Generals. A third anonymous General of Brigade is also decorated. The two French generals pose together – Drude, who has received the lesser award, fingers the ribbon of Balfourier's GCMG. Drude chats with a nursing nun, one of a group of officers, civilians, and injured soldiers who have been decorated. The nun, who is holding her medal case, seems very animated.

catalogued NAP: 7/1991

NTB 276-02 · GB, 9/12/1916
TOPICAL BUDGET 276-2

b/w · 1 reel · 315' (5 mins) · silent
intertitles: English

pr Topical Film Company

I. Troops disassemble mountain gun.
'MOUNTAIN ARTILLERY. Owing to their sure-footedness, mules are chiefly employed to carry the guns over the mountain passes. Loading up previous to moving off to the front.' MS of British troops disassembling a 2.75-inch Mountain Gun Mk 1 and loading the components onto mules held by Indian soldiers. They then unpack the parts and build up the gun again – at the end of the sequence they are preparing to put on a gun shield.
II. Slough Christmas cattle show. 'SLOUGH XMAS CATTLE SHOW. Devon and Hereford bullocks, Hampshire sheep and Berkshire porkers being sold at the Annual Christmas Cattle Show.' MSs of cattle secured in their pen by short tethers around the neck. CU of the head of one bullock. Another is fed hay. CU of phlegmatic Aberdeen Angus, his breath clouding the air. 'THE KING'S FAT STOCK. One of the pens of sheep exhibited by the King at the Show. His Majesty was a very successful exhibitor.' MS over pen of sheep 'Fed by His Majesty the King'. A man drives more animals in and packs them tightly together in the confined space. CUs of sheep. MS over pig stalls and CU of pigs sleeping together. MS of black Royal pigs. End CU of a 'porker'.
III. Lord Mayor attends memorial service in honour of fallen old LCC schoolboys. 'MEMORIAL SERVICE. The Lord Mayor attends a memorial service at St. Paul's in honour of old L.C.C. schoolboys who have fallen in the War.' In light snow, a horse-drawn coach pulls up and the Mayor in his full regalia alights and enters the Cathedral. Soldiers of a Scottish regiment file into St Paul's – a pipe band stands below in the street. A small crowd of onlookers has gathered.
IV. Clips showing the career of Lloyd George. 'MR. LLOYD GEORGE. The Rt. Hon. D. Lloyd George had an audience of the King and accepted Office as Prime Minister and First Lord of the Treasury. Mr. Lloyd George as Minister of War and Minister of Munitions.' Lloyd George, in jocular mood, presents prizes at a small fête – one soldier receives a canteen of cutlery, another a barometer – this sequence well illustrates Lloyd George's popular touch. Cut to Lloyd George being mobbed by enthusiastic crowd at Aberystwyth – see **NTB 261-01**. Lloyd George in relatively formal attire enters building – probably a recruiting centre – and talks with those inside.

Notes
Summary (item IV): Lloyd George had been sworn in as Prime Minister on 8 December.
catalogued NAP: 8/1991

NTB 277-01 · GB, 13/12/1916
TOPICAL BUDGET 277-1

b/w · 1 reel · 320' (5 mins) · silent
intertitles: English

pr Topical Film Company

I. Belgian armoured car 'in action' and troops on the move by bicycle and on foot. Horse-drawn field kitchen units. 'OFFICIAL BELGIAN FILM. ARMOURED MOTOR IN ACTION. A Belgian armoured car firing at the German lines. Cyclists moving off to a new position.' An armoured car reverses across a road as two-man gun crew fire a Hotchkiss machinegun from its open compartment. MS as a third man, clinging to the side of the vehicle, reaches over to feed a fresh strip into the gun. Bicycle troops led by bicycle buglers move along a narrow road – cycling four abreast they fill the whole width of the track. 'OFFICIAL BELGIAN FILM. FIELD KITCHEN. The travelling 'cook house' attached to the Belgian Army this kitchen cooks the meals whilst travelling. Men marching to their billets after a spell in the trenches.' Infantry column passes along a road lined with shade trees. The men rest having stacked their arms along the roadside. Horse-drawn kitchen units pass diagonally left to right along a cobbled road.
II. Major-General Sir Desmond O'Callaghan inspects the 1st London Volunteer Engineers. 'INSPECTION OF ENGINEER VOLUNTEERS. Major-General Sir Desmond O'Callaghan inspects the 1st London Volunteer Engineers.' Elderly Major-General inspects the ranks and takes salute during march past on scrubby open ground.
III. Orthodox priest prepares sacrament before open-air mass for Russian regiment. 'SACRAMENT IN THE TRENCHES. Preparing the Wafer by pouring wine over it, according to the ceremonies of the Greek Church.' Priest stands swinging censer by small table bearing a flat sacramental loaf decorated with crucifix pattern – before him stand four officers their heads bowed. In the background stands the massed ranks of the regiment. 'OFFICERS HELP THE PRIEST. Officers assisting the Russian Priest in preparing the Sacrament for the troops.' Priest scores the base of the loaf and holds it inverted as an officer pours wine over it. The priest and three of the officers then lay hands on the loaf, turning it between them. The priest then breaks the loaf in two and he and the officers kiss the opened bread.

catalogued NAP: 8/1991

NTB 277-02 · GB, 16/12/1916
TOPICAL BUDGET 277-2

b/w · 1 reel · 302' (5 mins) · silent
intertitles: English

pr Topical Film Company

I. Lewis gun on AA mounting in use in Macedonia. 'LEWIS ANTI-AIRCRAFT GUN. Troops on the Macedonian front anxiously watch the effect of the machine gun fire on an enemy aeroplane.' Australian troops look up into the sky as a man fires Lewis – the gun has been attached to the top of a wooden post by a pivot AA mount. One of the men changes the magazine, but it jams and has to be changed before firing resumes. Another fresh magazine is then fitted successfully.
II. Blinded soldiers are taught to become masseurs. 'MASSAGE BY BLIND SOLDIERS. An occupation which is particularly suitable for soldiers who have been blinded at the front. Men being taught the correct method of massage and bandaging for various complaints.' An unusually healthy and well-muscled 'patient' lies stripped to the waist on a doctor's couch as a blind man massages his chest and neck – a supervisor looks on. The masseur runs an electric vibrator along the patient's arm to stimulate the circulation – the supervisor makes an adjustment to the machine. The trainee bandages a man's hand.
III. Christmas turkeys. 'TURKEYS FOR CHRISTMAS. As a large percentage of the normal supply of turkeys from abroad, will not be available, those reared on the Norfolk farms will be much dearer.' Turkeys are driven through opened gate into a field. Four women sit in a row in the farmyard cheerfully plucking turkeys – in front of them on a pile of discarded feathers, a newly killed bird twitches spastically.
IV. Belgian soldiers enjoy a swim at a rest camp. 'SWIMMING AT THE FRONT. Belgian soldiers marching to their rest camp, and enjoying a swim in a specially constructed bathing pool, at the back of the front lines.' A Belgian detachment passes diagonally right to left preceded by buglers and a small band. Cut to a small rectangular pool surrounded by wooden staging – some men swim while one, stripped to the waist, stands at the edge rinsing his face and arms. Another man has merely rolled up his sleeves and washes his hands.
V. Convalescent sailors play football. 'LADY BEATTY'S SAILOR GUESTS. Brooksby Hall, the residence of Lady Beatty has been fitted up as a Naval convalescent hospital, some of the inmates from the Jutland Battle enjoy a game of football with the Matron-Nurse

Mortlock.' On a garden lawn a group of sailors play with a football – several of the participants are amputees, including two men with amputated legs, who perforce play on crutches. The game is played with spirit and the nurse, when she comes into possession of the ball, is treated with no exaggerated respect. The men on crutches prove to be remarkably able players.

Notes
Remarks (item III): a rather slight piece to support the message of the caption. The film demonstrates the rather insensitive attitude to animals which is often evident in these newsreels.
catalogued NAP: 8/1991

NTB 278-02 · GB, 23/12/1916
TOPICAL BUDGET 278-2

b/w · 1 reel · 304' (5 mins) · silent
intertitles: English

pr Topical Film Company

I. A French priest blesses artillery shells just before they are fired. 'BLESSING THE SHELLS. A French Priest blesses the shells as they are loaded into the famous seventy-five' (sic) guns used by the French Artillery.' Bearded priest holding a crucifix, makes a benediction over a shell held by a soldier – the shell is then loaded, and as the priest holds his cross aloft and pointing in the general direction of the enemy, the gun is fired. After a second shot the gun crew stop, obviously responding to some order from the cameraman, and all look to camera, including the priest. After a pause the firing continues for another couple of shots and then – again prompted from off-screen – the priest crosses himself and the gun crew follow suit.
II. Robust fun and games in the Belgian Army. 'OFFICIAL BELGIAN FILM. BELGIAN SOLDIERS' PILLOW FIGHT. The Belgian soldiers have adopted some of Tommies" (sic) games, and take part in a pillow fight which causes huge amusement.' A group of soldiers stand in front of a house watching two of their compatriots. Both of the 'players' are blindfolded, one holding a tin cup, the other a weighted bag. The one with the cup taps on it to lead the other on, and when contact is made, the man with the bag uses it to belabour his companion. To add to the fun there is a series of holes and trenches dug in the ground, into which the two blindfolded men stumble continually. Cut to two men sitting facing each other astride a beam. After shaking hands they commence

hitting each other with bags until one falls off – he gets back on only to be knocked off again. The next time both men fall off simultaneously. Onlookers appear amused. The fight resumes and the unlucky man is again the loser. 'OFFICIAL BELGIAN FILM. NEW WAR GAME. A favourite pastime of the Belgian soldiers. Two men are strapped together and endeavour to use one anothers hands, resulting in a real mix up.' One man sits at a table, wearing his jacket reversed, his arms not in the sleeves but close against his body, his hands inside boots which rest on the table in imitation of feet. A second man crouches behind, his arms thrust into the jacket sleeves – the hidden man plays with the front man's hat, attempts to get him to drink from a wine bottle and use a pair of fake cardboard binoculars. The natural lack of co-ordination produces the appearance of a spastic dwarf, well calculated to amuse those who look on from the background. At the end of the show, onlookers unbutton the man's coat and the hidden performer emerges.

III. Cattle at the King's farm at Sandringham. 'CHRISTMAS CATTLE. Some of the famous Angus-Dexter bullocks that are reared on the King's cattle farms at Sandringham, these are sold to grace the table on Christmas Day.' A land girl leads out a bullock from its stall. Two more follow. MS (and slightly blurred) pan and MCUs of the girls and their charges.

IV. Convalescent sailors feed Christmas turkeys. 'TURKEYS FOR H.M.S. LION. Convalescent sailors at Brooksby Hall feeding the turkeys. Two 'Gobblers' having acquired the Naval fighting instinct have to be separated by the Matron.' Turkeys in a field are fed by sailors, including a number of amputees. Two of the birds fall to fighting to the amusement of the sailors. The two birds – one pecking the neck of the other – are still locked in combat when the sequence ends, before the intervention of the matron.

catalogued NAP: 8/1991

NTB 279-01 · GB, 27/12/1916
TOPICAL BUDGET 279-1

b/w · 1 reel · 310' (5 mins) · silent
intertitles: English

pr Topical Film Company

I. California alligator farm. 'ALLIGATOR FARM. An alligator farm at Los Angeles, the reptiles answer the call at feeding time and attack a huge pile of meat fastened to the ground with iron stakes.' MLS as young adult alligator at edge of pool worries at staked meat. Others join in. Juvenile alligators in another pool pull meat off a fork – a watery mêlée ensues. Young alligators swarm over meat staked out on the ground.
II. Anonymous Anglo-French investiture on the Western Front. 'REVIEW AT THE FRONT. Cavalry marching up to the Review ground to be inspected by the Headquarter Staff, previous to going into action.' A General's escort with lances ride their horses at the walk along a French village street. The General gets out of his Daimler staff car and joins aides who include an Indian officer. The General decorates some French officers. Everybody stands after the ceremony – some of the staff officers wear armbands – possibly signifying Fifth Army.
III. Ammunition is transferred from a Belgian warehouse to trains and thence to trucks. 'BELGIAN AMMUNITION STORE. Loading up railway waggons with shells of all sizes. Some of the shells are so heavy that they have to be rolled up an inclined platform.' Soldiers file out of warehouse, each carrying a shell over his shoulder which is loaded into a waiting railway wagon. Larger shells are rolled up a wooden ramp into the wagon. 'SHELLS FOR THE GUNS. Distributing the shells. The motor lorries taking up the ammunition to the batteries.' French trench mortar rounds in wooden transit cases are transferred from railway wagon to a lorry. Shells are also rolled across on a plank.
IV. Soldiers on leave buy turkeys. '"TOMMY'S" XMAS LEAVE. Some of the trenches they have left, and some of the men back on leave, buying their Christmas dinner.' Pan over snow-covered trenches – fusiliers are heating a can by immersing it in a pot of water warming over an open fire – many of the group are smoking pipes. Cut to two soldiers of a Highland regiment wearing fur jackets as they buy turkeys (complete with feathers) from a butcher. They display their purchases to the camera – one has slipped the muzzle of his SMLE between the dead bird's tethered feet so that it hangs down his back as he stands resting the gun on his shoulder.

Notes
Remarks (item II): clearly the caption and the film have no connection except in the imagination of a Topical Budget editor.
catalogued NAP: 8/1991

NTB 279-02 · GB, 30/12/1916
TOPICAL BUDGET 279-2

b/w · 1 reel · 301' (5 mins) · silent
intertitles: English

pr Topical Film Company

I. A goose is auctioned for charity. 'GOOSE RAISES $100. A twenty six year old goose "Winsome Winnie" after repeated sales realises over $100 for charity.' A foggy day. Auctioneer in overcoat and hat stands on a step-ladder holding a gavel – in the background, on top of a parked car, is the goose standing (it can hardly sit) in a small cage. A crowd surrounds the auctioneer as he encourages the bidding. Final LA.CU of goose in its cage.

II. Christmas marathon race is run to raise funds for charity. 'BOXING DAY SPORTS. The military Marathon in aid of the British Sportsmen's Motor Ambulance Fund being run in a thick fog.' Contestants file out of a building – many wear Army greatcoats over their running gear. MS as runners set off along a road lined with spectators. Preceded by a car and followed by several men on bicycles, the leading runner comes round a corner into the final straight. Pte. Miller, contestant No 39, is supported by two men after his win – he is clearly very tired, and weaves slightly as he walks. Head and shoulders CU of Pte. Miller, a Canadian. CU of second-place man No 33 – he too is exhausted and looks into camera with a fixed stare.

III. Canadian Band in Paris. 'CANADIANS IN PARIS. Members of the Canadian Band enjoying themselves in Paris, previous to giving a charity performance at the Trocadero.' MS as a group of Canadians form a rough line to be filmed – more run up to join in. Camera pans left to right along the line. The men are in high spirits, waving to the camera. One man in the back rank plays with the cap of the man standing in front of him, to produce a comic effect. The group breaks up.

IV. Lord Mayor of London visits a children's home at Christmas. 'LORD MAYOR WITH THE CRIPPLED CHILDREN. The Lord Mayor and Sir W. Treloar spend Christmas with the children at the Alton Home.' Mayor dressed as Father Christmas walks towards the camera through a flock of sheep grazing in a field – he holds a staff and has a large bunch of holly (?) over his shoulder, the whole effect being rather eccentric and not very Santa-like. Crippled children come in from frame right to inspect the Mayor. MS as Santa, now on a donkey cart laden with gifts and led by Sir William (conventionally dressed in lounge suit and bowler), makes his way past admiring children. Gifts are dispensed from the back of the cart. CU of two boys on crutches: one is holding several

toys – a doll, soft animal, a toy Red Cross wagon. Neither he nor his companion seems much moved. 'ALDERMANIC SANTA CLAUS. Two of the City Fathers distribute Xmas gifts to the crippled children.' A dormitory or ward. Santa gives a present to a small child lying in bed – a nurse looks on from the background. Sir William shakes hands with a little boy standing by the bed and pinches the bed-ridden one on the cheek. Santa and straight man depart. Cut to girl's ward as Santa comes up ladder leant against an opened window – he cannot get in, but reaches through to hand a doll to one girl, and tosses another onto the bed of a second girl. CU of Santa and dissolve to the Mayor sans beard and wig.

Notes
Summary (item II): the term 'marathon' is used loosely: the road race was over 6½ miles. The sale of 'Winsome Winnie' was also part of this day's events, the profits of which went not only to the BSMAF, but to Richmond Royal Hospital and Richmond VAD.
Remarks (item IV): see also **NTB 280-01**.
catalogued NAP: 9/1991

NTB 280-01 · GB, 3/1/1917
TOPICAL BUDGET 280-1

b/w · 1 reel · 299' (5 mins) · silent
intertitles: English

pr Topical Film Company

I. Bob sleighing in Canada. 'BOB SLEIGHING IN CANADA. One of the many winter sports, the new Governor-General the Duke of Devonshire, will witness in Canada. Bob sleighing being an extremely popular form of enjoyment.' A team of eleven women get on a sledge and set off down a gentle slope watched by a few onlookers. A smaller sledge carrying four men follows them. The sledge run is along a town street. MS as a sledge upsets and skids over to the side of the road in a cloud of snow and ice. Onlookers scurry out of the way. The sledge is righted and the crash victims are helped up – one man is pulled upright only to fall down again immediately.

II. Serbian troops receive their pay. 'PAY DAY FOR THE SERBS. The paymaster of a Serbian Regiment issuing vouchers to the men in the Serbian village.' Man in Western-style civilian dress hands out vouchers to a motley crew of uniformed Serbs. HA.MS over the crowd – the men are in good humour and some start to wave their caps at the cameraman.

III. Belgian gun limbers are ammunitioned. 'MUNITION WORKERS EFFORTS. Owing to the enormous production of shells at the munition factories, Belgian artillerymen are well supplied with ammunition.' MS as ammunition limbers are drawn up behind parked lorries. 'FOOD FOR THE GUNS. The limber waggons are filled up and the teams drive off to the field batteries.' Chains of soldiers pass 75mm shells from lorries to limbers. Once the limbers are full they are driven off. The episode covers the ammunitioning of two separate columns, for during mid-sequence the direction of the limbers changes from head-on to a rear view, the camera position remaining unchanged.

IV. Chanukah hampers are distributed to Jewish crippled children. 'CITY'S GIFT TO CRIPPLED CHILDREN. Sir W. Treloar and the Lord Mayor dispatch hampers to the crippled children of the metropolis.' Pan over a group of bulky top-hatted dignitaries standing by the kerbside. A horse-drawn wagon of Carter Paterson and Company draws up – the front of the wagon is decorated with flyers advertising *John Bull* magazine and its leader '1917 Victory Certain' by Horatio Bottomley. The wagoner is given a letter – presumably one of instruction – and drives off. This procedure is repeated with other Carter Paterson wagons – one of the drivers is a woman. MS of the mayor and aldermen sitting about a small table on which one of the wooden hampers lies opened to reveal its contents – apparently rather spartan fare. The box bears the legend 'Crippled Childrens Homes Sir Wm TRELOAR FUND'.

Notes
Summary (item IV): this beneficence was perhaps a little less general than the caption implies. To be a recipient you had to be not only young and crippled but also Jewish. The ceremony took place at the Mile End Palladium.
catalogued NAP: 9/1991

NTB 283-02 · GB, 27/1/1917
TOPICAL BUDGET 283-2

b/w · 1 reel · 288' (5 mins) · silent
intertitles: English

pr Topical Film Company

I. Women help harvest tobacco crop. 'WOMEN LAND WORKERS. Appeals are made by the Government for help on the land. Some of the women who have answered their country's call.' Men at work in a field of tobacco – they are cutting down the mature plants. Women at work in tobacco field picking off poor leaves and collecting the cut crop and stringing it on sticks ready for drying.

II. Gymnastics demonstration on the cadet training ship *Arethusa*. 'JACK TAR KEEPS FIT. Men of the Royal Navy keeping fit for the German Navy should the latter venture out of the Kiel Canal.' Cadet sailors vault over a horse on the deck of the training ship (ex-frigate) *Arethusa*. The boys form a complicated tableaux around the horse. HA as boys practise semaphore. MS of the cadets seated for a group picture – they hold an up-ended lifebelt framing a seated dog.

III. Repair work to a railway bridge across the Missouri River. 'BRIDGE BUILDING RECORD. Fitting a new section into the Union Pacific Railway bridge over the Missouri River in twelve minutes.' LS along girder railway bridge as men work on a section of double track – to the left a train passes slowly by on another parallel section. Men work jacks to lift the bridge section and slide steel roller track underneath to be able to move it. 'MOVING 5,000 TONS. Lifting the new bridge on hydraulic jacks and rolling the double track into place. This feat constitutes a record in American engineering.' New bridge section is moved across the underlying supports into position. VIPs stand watching the process.

IV. Transport of French and Serbian wounded on the Salonika front. 'RED CROSS WORK IN THE TRENCHES. Men wounded on the Salonika front being conveyed from the trenches in rough carts drawn by oxen. One of the snipers carefully cleans his rifle in case of emergency.' A French and Serbian soldier pass down a rough trench. MS of two men relaxing in a dug-out in the side of a trench. Outside a man sits cleaning his Berthier rifle, while in the background another is engaged in lighting a cigarette. Serbs lift a stretcher onto the back of a wagon. Two oxen pull past a cart carrying French wounded – a second cart follows and then a mule carrying side panniers in which wounded men are seated.

catalogued NAP: 9/1991

NTB 284-02 · GB, 3/2/1917
TOPICAL BUDGET 284-2

b/w · 1 reel · 362' (6 mins) · silent
intertitles: English

pr Topical Film Company

I. French 75mm gun in action. 'BARRAGE FIRE. Owing to the wonderful accuracy and rapidity of fire, the French 75 m/m gun is extreamely (sic) useful for 'barrage fire' in preventing trench raids.' Rear 3/4 and rear view of 75mm gun under a wooden shelter as it fires rapidly. LS of shells bursting in open ground. The gun is an M12 and not the more famous M97.

II. President Wilson delivers a speech from the rear of a train carriage. 'PRESIDENT WILSON. The President of the United States has immense difficulties to face over the German submarine menace. Several newspapers urge that Count Bernstorff should be given his passports.' LS.MS of group of overcoated men and one woman (Edith Wilson ?) wearing furs and holding a bouquet of flowers, all standing on the rear boarding stage of stationary railway carriage. A motor car is readied – presumably for Presidential use. LA.MS of Wilson speaking from the rear of the carriage.

III. Motor Machine Gun Corps on parade. 'RECRUITS FOR THE TANKS. Men of the Motor Machine Gun Corps on parade. Those in charge of the 'Tanks' have been recruited from this Corps.' LS pan over men standing and seated in rows for group picture. CU of two men – probably brothers – in the uniform of the MGC – they doff their caps to the camera. MS of a column of motor-cycle combinations – some of them armed with Vickers machineguns – and solo motor-cycles being driven over open grassland. Men fall in with their vehicles for inspection. Cut to LS of march past by Highland regiment in full dress led by band – the men carry long Lee-Enfields and the event is probably pre-war, and clearly nothing to do with the previous material.

IV. Londoners enjoy ice skating on a frozen pond. 'SPORT ON THE ICE. Children for the first time experience the 'pleasure' of gliding or otherwise on a pair of skates. Types of skaters on a pond 'somewhere near London'.' A group of ladies sit at the edge of the pond looking to camera – one is having her skates tied on – schoolboys wave from the background. MS of three women holding hands with two small children, who are dressed alike in the manner of twins – they walk forward over the ice in line abreast. One of the children immediately loses her footing and is supported from falling by the women on either side. Boy stands on the ice staring to camera – oblivious to a line of adults skating in line abreast with hands linked, who approach from behind and nearly knock him over. Man skating – he is clearly skilled, executing neat circles and skating backwards. A man sweeps the ice. General shot of the skaters. Two women skate hand in hand, a troika of two men and

one woman skate past – one of the men in RFC uniform.

V. Lieutenant Douglas Belcher VC gets married at his local church. 'WEDDING OF SURBITON'S V.C. Lieut. Douglas Belcher the first Territorial 'ranker' to win the V.C. was married to Miss E. F. Luxford at St. Mark's Subiton (sic).' Veiled bride and her father walk from car to church. HA as Lieutenant Belcher and his bride are showered with confetti – nature also contributes, as it is snowing. MS, bridesmaid with small pageboy and other family members arriving by coach. MS of the newly-weds and pageboy (tongue sticking out of corner of his mouth) standing with the bride's parents in the doorway of the church. Lieutenant Belcher appears confused but genial.

Notes
Remarks (item II): as so often in this series, caption and film have very little to do with each other.
catalogued NAP: 9/1991

NTB 292-01 · GB, 28/3/1917
TOPICAL BUDGET 292-1

b/w · 1 reel · 297' (5 mins) · silent
intertitles: English

pr Topical Film Company

I. Army Service Corps defeats the 2nd Glamorgan Yeomanry at rugby. ['A.S.C. WINS AGAIN. The Army Service Corps (Grove Park) defeat the 2nd Glamorgan Yeomanry by 44 points to nil, their total aggregate being 1,090 points.'] LSs of a rugby match in progress – Kew Gardens pagoda visible in the background. MSs of line-outs and the general scrimmage – one player lies dramatically prone after an injury. MS of onlookers.

II. Steeplechase at Bradfield College Sports day. 'BRADFIELD COLLEGE SPORTS. The chief event at the Annual Sports being the steeplechase in which many difficult obstacles had to be negotiated.' Boys run down slope and surmount various obstacles made of brushwood and wattling, walk along balanced planks and climb over fences. 'FORDING A SLUICE. A formidable obstacle in the course. Climbing through the sluice and crossing the river.' The runners enter the river using a rope guideline. LA as boys climb the sluice – rather surprisingly, all keep their footing.

III. Wreck of Zeppelin L39 in France. 'ZEPPELIN DESTROYED. One of Germany's gas bags failed to reach Paris and was brought down by French gunners and aviators in the Boulevard Gambetta at Compiegne.' LS of mass of twisted girders – hoses are being played on the wreckage. MS pan over the debris. 'WRECK OF L39. The burning ruins taken a few minutes after the airship was brought to Earth. Masses of aluminium lying over a wall demolished by the Zeppelin in its fall.' HA.MS along the top of the wall dividing two pieces of waste ground to the wreck of the Zeppelin, and pan right to French military standing about. CU of part of one of the motors on its outrigger. MS pan over mass of wires and anonymous debris.

Notes
Technical (item I): main titles and title to first episode are missing; item title supplied by McKernan.
catalogued NAP: 9/1991

NTB 309-01 · GB, 25/7/1917
WAR OFFICE OFFICIAL TOPICAL BUDGET 309-1

b/w · 1 reel · 297' (5 mins) · silent
intertitles: English

sp War Office Cinema Committee *pr* Topical Film Company

I. French General Maistre inspects an aerodrome. 'FRENCH AVIATION CAMP. General Maistre visits an aerodrome in Soissons and inspects the fighting planes.' General Maistre and his retinue walk along a line of Nieuport XVII fighters parked on a grassy field. The General stops to talk with one of the pilots. Men prepare to board a line of Spad VIIs, and LSs as one aircraft taxis to take off.
II. Open-air concert for wounded soldiers. 'WAR ENTERTAINMENTS. A large number of wounded soldiers were entertained by a performance of "A Midsummer Nights Dream" at Hanover Lodge Regents Park.' LS as costumed actors and actresses file past. Convalescent soldiers stand looking on as fairies dance about. MS of Titania and Bottom – they embrace affectionately. Bottom, Titania and fairies approach camera.
III. Venizelos of Greece attends church service. 'PROVISIONAL CONTROL FOR GREECE. M. Venizelos accompanied by General Danglis and Admiral Condouriotis attend service at the Church of St. Sophie at Salonika.' Greek military pass camera. Venizelos wears a top hat and morning coat – his hat lifted in salute to the crowds of onlookers, including Allied officers.
IV. Scenes on the Western Front. 'ON THE WESTERN FRONT. OUR ARTILLERY AT WORK.' LS over battery of 6-inch howitzers in flat terrain. A gun opens fire from off-screen to left, and in the background, other guns – all well dug in – also fire. 'Infantry moving up to stem the German attack.' Men rest by the roadside – it is fairly muddy. MS of soldiers marching at ease along a tree-lined road, followed by bicyclists and officers on horseback.

catalogued NAP: 9/1991

NTB 310-01 · GB, 1/8/1917
WAR OFFICE OFFICIAL TOPICAL BUDGET 310-1

b/w · 1 reel · 289' (5 mins) · silent
intertitles: English

sp War Office Cinema Committee *pr* Topical Film Company

I. German POWs in France are employed in reconstruction work. 'WAR'S DEVASTATION. German prisoners employed in reconstruction work at Ribécourt 35 Kilometres behind the firing line.' LS pan as men move about with wheelbarrows shifting earth – ruined village buildings in the background. Tented POW encampment in the grounds of a château – tanned POWs walk towards and past camera. The men wear uniform jackets or fatigues, some stamped with an identifying mark (PG for Prisonniers de Guerre) and number. The men fall in. POWs at work repairing the road surface and clearing debris in Ribécourt – in the background is the quaintly named 'Hôtel de Cornet d'Or'. French guards stand about, rifles slung. POWs clean stones of mortar for re-use, construct a wooden-frame building, saw timber by hand and using a power jig-saw. 'PRISONERS' TOILET. The labours of the day ended, the prisoners take a dip.' Men sit on a wooden jetty washing in the river – a barge is alongside.
II. French tanks pass through a ruined village. 'FRENCH TANKS. French Land Cruisers on their way to the front.' HA.MS as two Saint Chamond tanks move through a ruined village. The leading vehicle, named 'Teddy', negotiates a corner. (These are early models with flat roof and 75mm Saint Chamond TR gun.)
III. The ruins of Craonne in the Champagne region. 'THE CHAMPAGNE REGION. The Ruins of Caronne (sic). The bombardment of the Californie Plateau.' Various shots as men move among shattered trees and the remains of buildings. LS pan over land gently sloping away from the camera-position – trees broken by artillery fire in the

- 496 -

foreground. LS up denuded slope as shells explode on high ground – a graphically devastated landscape.

IV. Mob storms a church to break up a pacifist meeting. 'PACIFISTS ROUTED AT BROTHERHOOD CHURCH. A pacifist meeting held at Kingsland was broken up by the forces of loyalty and patriotism. The crowd breaking into the Church.' MS of church building surrounded by a hostile crowd – one patriot is battering at the closed doors while others throw stones and kick at the windows. Having smashed one of the windows, a man climbs inside but is forced to withdraw. Mounted police sit idly by watching events. Men try once again to enter by the broken window, but are kept out by one of the congregation wielding a length of wood – those outside try to seize the defender's weapon and throw stones at those within. A second window comes under attack. The pacifists are still resisting vigorously, although losing ground, and the forces of law and order are still apparently asleep when the sequence ends.

Notes
Summary (item II): French tanks made their first appearance in the spring of 1917, playing a determining part in April in the capture of Juvincourt, east of Craonne.
catalogued NAP: 9/1991

NTB 310-02 · GB, 4/8/1917
WAR OFFICE OFFICIAL TOPICAL BUDGET 310-2

b/w · 1 reel · 287' (5 mins) · silent
intertitles: English

sp War Office Cinema Committee *pr* Topical Film Company

I. General Pétain honours an infantry regiment. 'GENERAL PETAIN. The French Commander-in-Chief receives a bouquet from a schoolgirl. Decorating the Flag of the 410th Regiment of Infantry.' A woman approaches Pétain and gives him a written paper – he responds by kissing her on both cheeks, and she seems suitably overcome. The schoolgirl is also kissed and her bouquet accepted. Pétain and his retinue inspect regiment. MS as the great man pins a medal onto the regimental flag, then kisses the standard bearer on both cheeks and shakes his hand. The inspection continues.
II. General Féraud inspects bicycle troops. 'WITH THE FRENCH ARMY. General Féraud inspects a section of cyclists attached to the 1st division of cavalry.' CU rear view of the General as he pins a medal on regimental

standard of 26th Chasseurs. March past by infantry and mounted troops.
III. French Minister of Labour attends a fête at Nesle to celebrate its recent liberation. 'CELEBRATING THEIR LIBERATION. M. Viviani and M. Leon Bourgeois, Minister of Labour, attend the Fete at Nesles (sic) and address the inhabitants on their liberation from the German rule.' LS over the heads of a crowd of soldiers to stage where a woman in French national dress gives a speech. Rear MS of a man talking to the crowd from stage – he is holding aloft and shaking a bunch of papers from which sections float free. Crowd scene – the actress seen earlier hands a programme (?) to an elderly man. M Bourgeois (?) addresses the crowd.
IV. Prince Alexander of Serbia visits the Front. 'PRINCE ALEXANDRE (sic). The Serbian Prince visits the 1st Serbian army in the field.' A Serbian officer points out something of interest to the Prince, who looks through binoculars. Prince Alexander chats with an officer. The Prince and his staff depart on horseback – as the camera pans across at the end of the sequence, the country is seen to be wooded and very mountainous.
V. Continuation of episode on the festivities at Nesle. 'FRENCH NATIONAL FETE. English officers distributing chocolates to the children of the liberated provinces.' An English staff officer distributes sweets to local children, then attempts to calm the ensuing mêlée. Actress talks with British officers. British and French officers buy programmes. A French soldier peers through a slide viewer. Actresses stand by a building ready in their costumes – a pierrot (?) appears to be peering out of a window at the beginning of the shot – pan continues over the crowd, which seems mainly to be made up of soldiers.

Notes
Summary (item III): Nesle was one of the towns liberated when the Germans withdrew to the Hindenburg Line in March 1917. Viviani, the Minister of Justice, and Bourgeois, the Minister of Labour, visited several such towns on Bastille Day.
catalogued NAP: 9/1991

NTB 312-01 · GB, 15/8/1917
WAR OFFICE OFFICIAL TOPICAL BUDGET 312-1

b/w · 1 reel · 322' (5 mins) · silent
intertitles: English

sp War Office Cinema Committee *pr* Topical Film Company

I. King Ferdinand of Romania reviews his remaining forces. 'WATCH ROUMANIA. King Ferdinand holds a great review demonstrating that the Roumanian Armies are intact. With the King are General Berthelot and M. Thomas, French Minister of Munitions.' MS of the King and his French guests as troops march past in open country. MS of the Romanian infantry, followed by (?) 105mm howitzers.

II. Canadians in England play baseball. 'THE BASEBALL BOOM. Canadian teams are making this game which is full of quick action and thrills, very popular. In particular it appeals to wounded soldiers.' MSs of baseball game in play in a stadium before a substantial crowd.

III. Delegates at the Labour Conference. 'STOCKHOLM or STOP HOME ? Famous Labour Leaders at the Conferance (sic) which resulted in Mr. Henderson's resignation. Mr. Gosling, Mr. Ramsay MacDonald and Mr. Hodge are shown.' MSs outside the Wesleyan Central Hall as Conference delegates mill about, including the named parties. 'LABOUR'S EX-CABINET MINISTER. Mr. Henderson talking to Robertson, Vice-President, Scottish Trades Unions.' MS of the two men in conversation outside the Hall.

IV. South African Labour Battalion at work felling trees in France. 'SOUTH AFRICAN LABOUR BATTALION "SOMEWHERE IN FRANCE". Tree Felling and Cutting Trunks for constructional work.' MCU as black workers use a lumberjack's saw to cut through a tree while another drives wedges in to open the cut. The tree falls. LS over men cutting up wood while in the background another detachment marches off, some with saws held over their shoulders. A horse enters frame right dragging small cars along a light railway line – the cars carry more workers. THE DAY'S WORK DONE. Marching Home: Native Chiefs "Dance of Hate" against the Boche, known at the Base as the "Whiz-bang Whirl." Detachments of blacks march along wooded path led by two white soldiers – one of them very fat. MS as African soldiers relax, sitting or lying on the ground. One man dances on the spot – he has tin cans tied around his knees, presumably acting as rattles, but is otherwise dressed in ordinary uniform – his companions do not seem much moved by his performance.

Notes
Summary (item III): early in 1917 the committee of neutral Socialists, under their Swedish leader Branting, proposed an International Socialist Conference to be held at Stockholm, and include Socialists from the belligerent countries. The intention was to lay down a set of peace terms which workers' organisations would then force upon their respective governments. The British coalition Government, which included Henderson, was opposed to the Conference and was prepared to refuse passports to any British delegates. At the Labour Conference, however, Henderson supported the Stockholm project, and the Conference voted to send representatives: this made Henderson's position in Cabinet untenable and he resigned.
catalogued NAP: 9/1991

NTB 313-01 · GB, 22/8/1917
WAR OFFICE OFFICIAL TOPICAL BUDGET 313-1

b/w · 1 reel · 303' (5 mins) · silent
intertitles: English

sp War Office Cinema Committee *pr* Topical Film Company

I. A demonstration of bayonet practice. 'THE FIGHTING DUMMY. C.S.M.I. Kenna invents a new method of teaching how to bayonet "Brother Boche".' MS of Kenna with rifle and bayonet as he dances about a dummy figure holding a wooden lance, the 'weapon' being manipulated by a man standing behind the dummy. The combat is an unequal one and Kenna kicks and stabs with impunity. MCU of Kenna, wearing a jersey with the APTC badge, standing beside the dummy, a crude representation of a German soldier.

II. The Sultan of Morocco reviews his troops. 'THE BLACK GUARD. Sultan of Morocco reviews his famous body-guard at Rabat.' Moroccan court officials bow low as, preceded by members of his guard, the Sultan rides up to take his place on review stand. European-style cavalry gallop past along street. French officers (Morocco was at this time a French protectorate) decorate men as the Sultan looks on.

III. The Duke of Connaught inspects Canadian artillery. 'CANADIAN GUNS. Duke of Connaught inspects Canadian artillery in training Camp.' The Duke of Connaught arrives to be greeted by officers and a lone civilian. Canadian's 18-pounder guns and limbers pass the Duke – in the background massed horse artillery can be seen stretching across the plain ready to pass in review. MS of the Duke as he takes the salute.

IV. The King of Belgium visits French forces in Flanders to watch artillery in action and witness a demonstration of river-crossing by French army engineers. 'KING OF THE BELGIANS VISITS THE FRENCH FRONT IN

FLANDERS. His Majesty witnesses wonders in the way of big gun manipulation.' King Albert arrives by car. Various shots of a battery of 32cm railway guns in action and CUs of shell and cartridge being loaded. Final MS as a (?) 145mm L16 Saint Chamond gun fires from a heavily camouflaged emplacement – only the barrel is visible. 'LIGHTNING BRIDGE BUILDING. Before His Majesty left, the French Engineers demonstrated that it only takes a few seconds to bridge a river.' French teams run forward to push across a river two lengths of articulated track floating on pontoons. Once the river is bridged, soldiers run across. No doubt impressed by what he has seen, the King departs.

Notes
Summary (item I): C.S.M.I. = Company Sergeant-Major Instructor.
catalogued NAP: 9/1991

NTB 314-02 · GB, 1/9/1917
WAR OFFICE OFFICIAL TOPICAL BUDGET 314-2

b/w · 1 reel · 282' (5 mins) · silent
intertitles: English

sp War Office Cinema Committee *pr* Topical Film Company

I. A society wedding. 'COLONEL MARRIES COLONEL'S WIDOW. Lord Arthur Hill receiving Mrs. George Curzon on her arrival at St. Peter's Eaton Square. Lieut Col. F. Butler and his bride leaving after the ceremony.' Mrs Curzon arrives by car with two companions, one of them a nun, to be greeted by Lord Arthur. MS as the newly married couple leave followed by family and fashionable friends – a few lesser mortals look on, including one decrepit and horribly grimacing old woman.
II. Hop picking in Kent. 'KENTISH HOP PICKERS. Soldiers help women and children to secure the hop harvest. Many hop fields have been destroyed by the gale this week.' Labourer dislodges the strings of hops with a pole, while others – mainly women and children – strip the hops from the fallen growth. Some of the girls are rather pretty. All who look to camera continue working with their hands. Army Sergeant and (?) farmer weigh the hops. CU head and shoulders of Sergeant wreathed in a garland of hops – he is of the Cheshire Regiment.
III. Salvage of a Gotha which crashed into the sea off Margate. 'MARGATE RAIDER SALVED FROM THE SEA. Diver going down to locate the Gotha.' HA.MS from on board

salvage craft as a helmet diver goes down the side into the sea. 'THE DIVER'S TRIUMPH. Having located the machine the diver fixes cables and returns to the salvage boat.' HA.MS as diver returns to the boat. 'THE AIRMAN'S BAG. Gotha's broken bones retrieved by British Sea Dogs.' The wrecked aircraft is hauled up out of the sea – its German markings are clearly visible. One of the boat's crewmen has the name 'VIGILANT EYE' on the back of his jersey.

Notes
Summary (item III): this is the wreckage of Gotha GIV/663/16 shot down off Margate on 22 August by Gerald Hervey flying a Sopwith Pup from RNAS Dover. There was one survivor, Unteroffizier Bruno Schneider, aged 19, picked up by HMS *Kestrel*.
catalogued NAP: 9/1991

NTB 316-01 · GB, 12/9/1917
WAR OFFICE OFFICIAL TOPICAL BUDGET 316-1

b/w · 1 reel · 314' (5 mins) · silent
intertitles: English

sp War Office Cinema Committee *pr* Topical Film Company

I. 'EX-QUEEN AMELIE. The Ex-Queen of Portugal inspects and presents badges to Richmond Girl Guides, afterwards being presented with a bouquet.' MS of group posed for the camera – Amelie is a tall woman, taller than the two civic dignitaries who stand to either side. The ex-Queen inspects the guides (they are very young – Brownies ?). A small boy in a white sailor suit presents a bouquet to the Queen, then immediately skips off – Amelie smiles broadly. The Queen seated at a small table – the small boy re-enters and embraces her, which favour she returns before he runs off again. Cut to Queen presenting badge to a girl and inspecting a line of diminutive guides.
II. Pictures of Gorizia after the city had fallen to the Italians. 'GORIZIA. Where the Austrians made a stubborn resistance against the Italian advance.' Pan over a damaged street front. A deserted square – a few Italian soldiers move about, one wearing a Red Cross armband. LS to an upper storey room revealed by the collapse of the front wall of a building – the wallpaper and the pictures on the wall still apparently pristine. MS of barbed-wire entanglements defending a building, and CU of an entrance fortified by sandbags and loopholes.
III. General Pétain inspects the 201st Infantry

Regiment. 'GENERAL PETAIN. The famous French General reviews the 201st Infantry Regiment who took part in the July attack in Flanders.' Rear 3/4 view of Pétain and another general officer as the Regiment passes in review. MS of the troops – they do not march in very good order. One of the soldiers is startlingly small.

IV. Australian soldiers who have had limbs amputated participate in sports. 'HANDICAPPED WAR HEROES. Australasian legless soldiers participate in sports. Much amusement is caused by the hairdressing contest.' Five Australian soldiers demonstrate their prosthetic dexterity by lying flat on the grass – the first man down lies on his back, the rest on their stomachs, so the odd man gets back on his knees and lies down in the correct posture before all stand again. A one-legged soldier executes a jump – in fact, three energetic hops ending in a controlled crouch. His finishing position is marked against that of previous contestants. Soldiers stand in a line, their trousers rolled up to show their artificial limbs. Women and young girls sit in a row while soldiers stand behind them dressing their hair – plaiting it and pinning up the braid. MS of one of the girls, her head inclined forward, her hand held up to her shoulder, the palm bent backwards. As the soldier dresses her hair he takes pins from her hand – she giggles appealingly as the work proceeds.

V. Lloyd George is given the freedom of Birkenhead. 'HONOUR FOR MR. LLOYD GEORGE. The Premier receives the freedom of the city at Birkenhead.' Lloyd George poses seated with a group which includes his wife Margaret and daughter Megan. He poses standing with two men from the group (possibly the two aldermen who proposed him, G A Solly and R J Russell). Cut to LS along fenced walkway lined with police – Lloyd George walks along briskly (rather incongruously, he is holding a bouquet), acknowledging the cheers of the public who wave to him from either side of the path. The remainder of the party follow.

Notes

Remarks (item I): ex-Queen Amelie was well known for her charitable works. At this time she was resident in Richmond.
Summary (item II): a strangely belated item as Gorizia fell to the Italians in August of the previous year.
catalogued NAP: 9/1991

NTB 317-01 · GB, 19/9/1917
WAR OFFICE OFFICIAL TOPICAL BUDGET 317-1

b/w · 1 reel · 310' (5 mins) · silent
intertitles: English

sp War Office Cinema Committee *pr* Topical Film Company

I. Land Army girls cut wood. 'WOMEN AS WOODMEN. Girls of the Womens Land Army fell trees and cut pit props.' MS as two Land Girls saw down a small pine tree. Others trim branches with axe or machete or saw up the pared trunks.

II. Italians examine the wreck of a crashed Austrian aircraft. 'ITALIAN AIRMAN'S PRIZE. Austrian aeroplane brought down in the Italian Lines on the Carso Front.' LS pan over downed Austrian aircraft – uniformed Italians, some in flying gear, examine the wreckage. CU of engine and shattered propeller. (The identity of the aircraft is unclear but it may be a Hansa-Brandenburg D1.) CU of a grinning Italian pilot – presumably the triumphant victor.

III. German POWs from the Battle for Verdun. 'A FINE HAUL OF HUNS. Some of the men who were hurled in vain against Verdun being marched into captivity by the French.' MSs of a column of German POWs led by their officers as they march along a dusty road escorted by French cavalry, sabres drawn. Wounded Germans are checked in by British and French officers and board motor ambulances.

IV. Haig reviews French division. 'SIR DOUGLAS HAIG IN FLANDERS. British Commander-in-Chief. Reviews French Division before going into action.' Haig and French officers inspect French troops fallen in on grassy field. One of the regimental flags is dramatically tattered. Haig decorates French officer. 'AT THE SALUTING BASE. Sir Douglas Haig watches a swinging march past of French Marine Infantry.' MCU head and shoulders of Haig – he salutes and pins medal on French officer. Haig salutes as troops march past – the buildings in the background suggest an aerodrome and an aircraft passes low overhead as the march past continues.

catalogued NAP: 10/1991

NTB 317-02 · GB, 22/9/1917
WAR OFFICE OFFICIAL TOPICAL BUDGET 317-2

b/w · 1 reel · 330' (5 mins) · silent
intertitles: English

sp War Office Cinema Committee *pr* Topical Film Company

I. Queen Mary visits a munitions factory in Coventry. 'QUEEN AND MUNITIONETTES. The girl War Workers of Coventry gave Her Majesty a rousing welcome. She was deeply interested in all phases of their life.' The Queen, accompanied by company dignitaries, the Mayor of Coventry, Alderman Alick Hill, and the Lord Lieutenant of Warwickshire, Lord Leigh, walks between ranks of workers. She flips through a commemorative book which she has been given – she does not seem impressed. Factory managers are presented. Workers applaud as Queen passes. She talks with a factory nurse before getting into her car. '"KEPT HERE TO WORK." An old soldier who fought in Chitral and South Africa explains to the Queen why he can't get to France.' Man wearing workshop apron, his shirt sleeves rolled up, stands talking with Queen – a con-rod is artfully displayed in the bench vice he stands beside.
II. Lieutenant Annandale marries the beautiful Miss Caldwell. 'ALL AIR WEDDING. At the wedding at Ascot of Lieut. Annandale, R.F.C. and Miss Theodora Caldwell, the best man, the chaplain, the organist and the choir were all airmen.' Guests – all airmen – and their ladies arrive at South Ascot Parish Church. Miss Caldwell arrives by coach and is led inside by her father who wears a Colonel's uniform. Once at the entrance, the bride's dress is fussed over preparatory to her going inside. Cut to the married couple emerging to be showered with rice.
III. The King bestows honours in an open-air ceremony at Ibrox Park, Glasgow. 'THE KING ON CLYDESIDE. His Majesty met with a great reception at Glasgow when he bestowed 143 honours including three V.Cs. before eighty thousand people at Ibrox Park.' HM wearing Army uniform arrives by car at the stadium – it is raining heavily. LA.MS of the King together with Lieutenant-General Ewart, C-in-C of the Scottish Command, on raised dais – HM is busy decorating. In one case a father accepts a posthumous award. 'HONOUR FOR MAIMED V.C. There was a tornado of cheering when Private H. Christian, Royal Lancaster Regiment was carried in to receive the V.C. he secured for extraordinary gallantry in a crater fight.' Draped in blankets against the inclement air, Private Christian is carried in on an invalid chair. After the award he is immediately rewrapped and carried off. MS pan over newly honoured men sitting around the stage.

Notes
Summary (item III): see also **IWM 140** for this item.
Remarks (item III): The Times referred to Christian as a "pale-faced man with a sad

smile", and indeed throughout the ceremony he does appear profoundly depressed.
catalogued NAP: 10/1991

NTB 318-01 · GB, 26/9/1917
WAR OFFICE OFFICIAL TOPICAL BUDGET 318-1

b/w · 1 reel · 325' (5 mins) · silent
intertitles: English

sp War Office Cinema Committee *pr* Topical Film Company

I. Members of the Women's Legion depart for France. 'WOMEN FOR THE FRONT. Girls of the Womens Legion leaving London to take up their duties in France. They are as plucky as the men and march like soldiers.' MS as uniformed women leave building to fall in on street outside. They march off.
II. A review of US troops in France. 'AMERICAN FIGHTING MEN IN FRANCE. Thousands of American troops are already in France. General Pershing Commanding, and the French President and General Pétain, French Commander-in-Chief reviewed a great number of them.' Pershing and French delegation pass camera to take up their positions. US troops march past.
III. Household Cavalry execute troop manœuvres. 'HOUSEHOLD CAVALRY IN FRANCE. This famous Corps is here seen in billets. Training of men and horses is complete. They only await their chance.' Cavalry troop rides out from farmyard. Column in 2's walks around a muddy pond then turns into line abreast. After a moment every other mount is walked forward to create two lines, the men then taking rifles from their buckets and dismounting to stand to their horses.
IV. Salonika is destroyed by fire. 'THE SALONIKA HOLOCAUST. The great fire at Salonika will be remembered as one of the most disastrous in history. The town was almost entirely destroyed and thousands rendered homeless.' HA.LS over gutted and still-smouldering buildings. MS as people pass along a street, smoke billowing up in the background, damaged buildings to right of frame. A hose is played on a burning building. LS down a smoke-filled street to destroyed buildings at one end – in the foreground stand some barrels which have been dragged out onto the kerb. LSs over the rooftops to the dense curtain of smoke rising from burning buildings, and pan to show the extent of the devastation – jets of water from hoses play on some of the roofs, but generally the fire seems to have the upper hand. A fire-fighting team of Italian (?)

sailors carrying axes and picks stand in a street awash with water from the hoses – thick smoke drifts across the scene. 'THE CITY OF DESOLATION. There were distressing scenes when the inhabitants tried to save their goods and when the Allied army had to provide the starving with food.' Locals carry bedding, bundles of possessions, even wooden chests and cupboards along a street. Some of the more fortunate have carts. Crowds mill about near the harbour. LS pan over an impromptu tented encampment littered with rescued furniture and goods.

catalogued NAP: 10/1991

NTB 318-02 · GB, 29/9/1917
WAR OFFICE OFFICIAL TOPICAL BUDGET 318-2

b/w · 1 reel · 272' (5 mins) · silent
intertitles: English

sp War Office Cinema Committee *pr* Topical Film Company

I. A motorised transport column on the Western Front. 'DIFFICULTIES OF TRANSPORT. Some of the troubles to be overcome by the transport to keep in touch with the advancing troops.' Wagons, carts, 18-pounder artillery and a convoy of motor lorries passes left and right along a muddy road. A column of troops also passes along the far side. Despite the heavy traffic, men are at work widening the road, and trying to keep it clear of mud and fill in holes.
II. Commemoration of French air ace Captain Guynemer. 'CAPT. GUYNEMER VICTOR OF 53 FIGHTS. Capt. Guynemer who has brought down 53 German machines, is reported to have fallen into the sea while attacking a German squadron.' French military band leads march past of troops. Watched by the men of his squadron the already medal-bedecked Captain Guynemer is received into the Légion d'honneur.
III. King George V holds a public investiture at Buckingham Palace and decorates eight VCs. 'INVESTITURE AT BUCKINGHAM PALACE. HM. the King held a Public Investiture at the Palace and decorated eight V.C.'s. Lieut. Install (sic) V.C. the airman who escaped from Germany.' Soldiers of the Reserve Battalion Grenadier Guards present arms as the King enters the forecourt of Buckingham Palace. Lieutenant Insall comes forward and receives his VC. Sergeant Edwards of the Seaforth Highlanders receives his VC, followed by Pte Ratcliffe (?)

and Skinner (?). In the background, an Army photographer covering the ceremony sets up his camera on a tripod. 'POSTHUMOUS V.C. The widow and son of the late Capt. Ackroyd receive the Victoria Cross and Military Cross, awarded that gallant officer.' The widow, dressed in black, and her small son, wearing a white sailor's suit with black armband, are each given one of Ackroyd's medals. Cut to MS pan over the VC winners as they wait their turn before the King: right to left, they are: John Skinner, King's Own Scottish Borderers (unimpressed by the proceedings, he is chewing something), William Ratcliffe, South Lancashire Regiment, Sergeant Ivor Rees of the South Wales Borderers, Sergeant Alexander Edwards, Seaforth Highlanders, Sergeant Edward Cooper, King's Royal Rifle Corps, Sergeant Robert Bye, Welsh Guards, and Lieutenant Insall. Mrs Ackroyd stands with her son in the background. Bye steps forward to receive his award. Cut to the men departing after the ceremony – most walk straight off, one to be embraced by his mother, but Lieutenant Insall is introduced to some French officers.
IV. Italian aviator Giulio Laureati flies from Turin to London. 'ITALY TO ENGLAND IN SEVEN HOURS. This was the time taken by Capt. Laureati to fly from Turin to London, a distance of 683 miles.' Italian officers stand on airfield pointing up at the arriving aircraft – they are part of a small crowd that has gathered to greet the Marquis on his arrival. LS as the SIA 7B touches down. MS of the pilot, Captain the Marquis Giulio Laureati, and his passenger, Air Mechanic Michael Angelo Tonzo, surrounded by the Italian party.

Notes
Summary (item II): Guynemer was shot down on 11 September. No trace of his body or aircraft was ever found.
Summary (item IV): early part of this sequence was subject to nitrate deterioration and the centre of the picture has gone.
catalogued NAP: 10/1991

NTB 319-01 · GB, 3/10/1917
WAR OFFICE OFFICIAL TOPICAL BUDGET 319-1

b/w · 1 reel · 312' (5 mins) · silent
intertitles: English

sp War Office Cinema Committee *pr* Topical Film Company

I. Queen Mary visits the Tank Corps. 'QUEEN AMONG THE TANKS. Wonderful

picture of Her Majesty inspecting a Tankodrome in France.' Queen Mary stands with the usual retinue by a line of Mk IV tanks – it is a sunny day and she holds a parasol. Soldiers demonstrate the function of the Gun Carrier Tank, pulling down the ramp along which the gun will be hauled onto the vehicle. 'THE KING'S GREETING. The King and the Prince of Wales waited for the return of the Queen from the Tanks. Their Majesties greeting was charming to witness.' Preceded by her lady in waiting, the Queen gets out of car to be greeted by the King – he kisses her on the right cheek. Staff officers hover about, waiting to be introduced. The Prince of Wales, standing in the background, is kissed by the Queen before she goes inside.
II. Alderman Charles Hanson becomes Lord Mayor of London. 'LORD MAYOR ELECT. With an ancient ceremony Alderman Chas. Hanson was made London's fourth War Lord Mayor elect. The Procession leaving the Guildhall.' A coach pulls up and the mayor and officers holding the regalia get out. Procession of liverymen of the various guilds pass the camera.
III. Woolwich Arsenal lose a football match against Chelsea. 'WOOLWICH ARSENAL LOSE AT HOME. The Arsenal defeated for the first time this season, Chelsea winning at Highbury by the only goal scored.' Teams run out from the stadium onto the field. MSs from near one of the goals as the game is played before a large crowd.
IV. French troops stage a historic tableau. 'THE MAID OF FRANCE. French troops found time after a bitter battle to organise a quaint costume fete in honour of Joan-of-Arc.' While soldiers stand watching a military band leads a procession of men in mock-medieval costume, including crossbowmen and mounted soldiers with spears. Joan of Arc rides past holding a lance, her horse led by a groom – beneath helmet and breastplate she appears to be genuinely female. MSs of the watching crowd – many of them wear the berets and carry the walking sticks characteristic of French Alpine infantry.

catalogued NAP: 10/1991

NTB 319-02 · GB, 6/10/1917
WAR OFFICE OFFICIAL TOPICAL BUDGET 319-2

b/w · 1 reel · 312' (5 mins) · silent
intertitles: English

sp War Office Cinema Committee *pr* Topical Film Company

I. Rear-Admiral Halsey inspects Sea Scouts in the East End of London. 'YOUNG SEA DOGS OF PORT OF LONDON. Rear Admiral Halsey C.B. Third Sea Lord inspects Sea Scouts and Roll of Honour of the Lads' fathers and brothers at Limehouse.' Rear-Admiral Halsey inspects a troop of Sea Scouts. He is accompanied by Alderman J D Riley MP, who points out a boy standing in the ranks wearing ordinary scout's uniform – Halsey chats to the lad. MCU of Halsey talking with a full-blown Sea Scout. Band leads two detachments of Sea Scouts along street – locals watch and follow along after the boys have passed. MS of Halsey looking at a printed Roll of Honour which has been framed and put up, surrounded with floral tributes, outside one of the houses.
II. General Berthelot decorates Romanian troops. 'IN BRAVE ROUMANIA. General Berthelot of the French Military Mission presenting medals and crosses to Roumanian heroes.' MS of line of Romanian soldiers – general Berthelot steps into frame from left and decorates one man, followed by the ritual kiss. LS of Berthelot watching march past of Romanian troops. MS pan along rank of newly-decorated soldiers, and MCU of two of the men – the medals are the Romanian Medal of Military Merit, Médaille Militaire (?) and Croix de guerre. MS of Romanian Mannlichers with fixed bayonets stacked so as to support the staff of a regimental colour which hangs down between the rifles.
III. Canadians practise infantry assault. '"CANNUCKS" IN TRAINING. Canadians rehearsing "Somewhere in England", the form of attack they will soon be launching "Somewhere in France".' LS over tussocky grassland to extended line of troops walking away from camera towards 'shell-bursts' in the distance. LS of pyrotechnic 'shell-burst'. Men in the trenches fire rifles, Lewis guns, throw grenades. A line of men advance with fixed bayonets – they are beset with explosions (sufficient in reality to decimate them) and go to ground.
IV. King George V visits a gas school in France. 'WITH THE KING IN FRANCE. His Majesty was greatly interested in a remarkable demonstration at a Gas School. It entirely resembles the real thing.' HM, with the Prince of Wales in attendance, chats with officers. LS of a series of air bursts, simulating gas shells – HM looks on from a respectful distance. LS of 'gas cloud' billowing up over the ground, and pan to HM talking with officers of the school.
V. Egyptian Labour Contingent at work and play. 'EGYPTIANS DO THEIR "BIT". An Egyptian Labour Contingent stacking hay at a base in France. In spare moments they break into a quaint dance.' Egyptians stand

clapping rhythmically while others dance – warehouses and cranes in the background. Watched by British soldiers, the men move boxes of Libby's tinned food products. LS as bales of hay are carried to a wooden platform where they are stacked ready to be covered with protective canvas.

Notes
Summary (item I): considering that Halsey's 30 years in the Service had never before "taken him into that part of London", the Rear-Admiral has an easy and pleasant of manner with the boys. The house in the final scene may be the Sailors' Rest in St Anne Street, Limehouse. Jack Cornwell's mother was still living in this area when the Admiral visited.
catalogued NAP: 10/1991

NTB 320-02 · GB, 13/10/1917
WAR OFFICE OFFICIAL TOPICAL BUDGET 320-2

b/w · 1 reel · 274' (5 mins) · silent
intertitles: English

sp War Office Cinema Committee *pr* Topical Film Company

I. Soldiers receive their discharge papers. 'HEROES OF MONS. Soldiers who have done their bit for England receiving their discharge prior to their return to civil life.' War Department Daimler lorry pulls up and soldiers get out with their personal kit. Cut to the men, now in civilian dress, signing for their discharge pay at a table set up in the open air. MS as a soldier throws open the door to 'Baths' and the men (still in uniform at this stage) go in with towels.
II. The Lord Chancellor attends a service at Westminster Abbey. 'JUDGES PROCESSION. The Lord Chancellor and Judges attend service at Westminster Abbey prior to re-opening the Law Courts.' The Lord Chancellor, preceded by stewards holding his regalia, walks past the camera outside the Abbey, followed by robed judges.
III. Demonstration of vehicles using coal gas. 'SAVING THE NATION'S PETROL. Demonstration in London of all types of motor vehicles using coal gas, from motor cycles to a 40 h.p. Admiralty char-a-banc.' MS of motor-cycle combination fitted with a roof which supports the gas bag. MS of a second combination which tows a 'Cox's Gas Trailer'. MSs of a car and a RN coach with gas bags on roof.
IV. Divisions on a battleship. 'Admiralty Official Film. ABOARD A DREADNOUGHT.

Sunday morning Church Parade upon a "Bulwark of Britain" Somewhere in the North Sea.' MS of a Captain talking with one of his officers. Marines are marched aft – Iron Duke Class battleship visible in the background with a Royal Sovereign beyond. HA between the guns of Y turret to quarterdeck where band is playing as divisions are marched past the King. 'Admiralty Official Film. BRITAIN'S MIGHT. The power which enables British and Allied Commerce to hold the freedom of the seas.' LS over Firth of Forth to HMS *Lion* at anchor, Forth railway bridge in the background. Between *Lion* and the cameraship are several launches and steam pinnaces, presumably standing off while ship's captains are on board the cameraship.

catalogued NAP: 10/1991

NTB 321-01 · GB, 17/10/1917
WAR OFFICE OFFICIAL TOPICAL BUDGET 321-1

b/w · 1 reel · 312' (5 mins) · silent
intertitles: English

sp War Office Cinema Committee *pr* Topical Film Company

I. Battleships at anchor. 'WHY THE GERMAN FLEET IS IDLE. A fear of the British Leviathans which make mutiny in the German Navy preferable to action.' LS off the port beam of HMS *Collingwood* and pan right to Orion Class battleship and others – a drifter crowded with men passes right to left in the foreground. LSs fine and then broad on the port bow of HMS *Queen Elizabeth* – drifter in the foreground. 'Admiralty Official Film. THE SMILE THEY HAVE IN THE NAVY. Cheery evidence that though its a "Long Long Wait for Fritz" the men of our Navy are as happy and contented as can be.' Ordinary sailors, warrant officers and marines come on board cameraship. The men are from more than one ship (*Hercules* and *Pembroke* are certainly represented) and they are at ease, smiling and even acting up to camera, many of them smoking – a party returning from shore leave ?
II. The Duke of Connaught opens a canteen at the Royal Small Arms Factory, Enfield. 'THERE IS A TAVERN – IN MUNITION TOWN. The Duke of Connaught was immensely interested in the working arrangements at the tavern controlled by the Liquor Board which H.R.H. opened at Enfield.' The Duke leaves the factory area – workers look on from left. MS of the Duke in the Tavern talking with a cook at work on a range – managerial staff point out things of

interest in the kitchens. The Duke passes crowd of workers to regain his car before leaving.

III. Lord French presents rifle proficiency medals to cadets. '"THE BRITISH RIFLE FIRE WAS DEADLY". In spite of all the machinery employed in the War, Lord French who presented the King's prize for shooting to the Royal Marine Cadets (Deal), declared that the rifle was still of vital importance.' MS of French delivering his address in the quadrangle of the War Office. He presents the King's shield to a RM sergeant instructor who (not unnaturally) wears the badge of a First Class Marksman. The cadets, rifles shouldered, are each awarded a medal for their proficiency. MS of the Deal cadets fallen in, and MCU of the shield held by their instructor.

IV. The Lord Mayor of London reviews the National Guard. 'LORD MAYOR REVIEWS THE NATIONAL GUARD. Sir Wm. Dunn took the salute when these splendid veterans marched past the Mansion House in the pouring rain.' MS as the men march past Sir William who looks down from the portico of Mansion House – the soldiers wear trench coats, and onlookers shelter under umbrellas. MCU right profile of the Mayor as he salutes the passing Guard. Cut back to MS scene – two young women seem unusually excited, perhaps recognising someone in the march past. MS of the Mayor standing with officers of the Guard in the background – he salutes for the camera. Final shot of procession past Mansion House.

Notes

Remarks (item I): the final sequence of sailors at leisure is quite unusual and worth the attention of any student of humanity.
Remarks (item II): 'The Royal Small Arms Tavern' was something of a misnomer: in modern parlance it would be a canteen, as it was designed to serve a cooked meal daily to 2500 munition workers for 1/- per head.
Summary (item III): the runners-up were C Company, 1st Cadet Battalion, London Scottish Fusiliers.
catalogued NAP: 10/1991

NTB 321-02 · GB, 20/10/1917
WAR OFFICE OFFICIAL TOPICAL BUDGET 321-2

b/w · 1 reel · 290' (5 mins) · silent
intertitles: English

sp War Office Cinema Committee *pr* Topical Film Company

I. Battleships at anchor. 'Admiralty Official Film. "GUN POWER" The enemy has already learned how terrible is our gun power. Here the great guns of a super battleship are trained seaward where floats the greatest assembly of naval guns in the world.' MS aft from forecastle down the starboard side of a Hercules Class battleship to the wing turret – the forward 4-inch guns are trained over the beam. Pan left to distant battleship of the Grand Fleet. MS pan right to left over forecastle to show A turret.

II. Red Cross flag-day. '"OUR DAY" Every one bought flags, from Princess to coster. The daughters of Lady Grace presided over the quaint "Black Cat" stall in the Haymarket.' An Army officer buys a paper flower (?) from a woman in St John's uniform. A lady sells flowers from a stall. Young women and children – all in cat-masks – hold trays full of Union Flag flags and souvenirs – the trays bear the legend 'Remember our Wounded'. The Lieutenant featured earlier buys a flag and a fashionable lady standing nearby leans forward to pin it onto his uniform. An old lady approaches from the background and makes a purchase.

III. President Machado of Portugal goes to lunch with the King. 'THE KING'S GRACIOUS WELCOME. His Majesty called at the Portuguese Legation to take the President of Portugal to lunch at Buckingham Palace.' Coach arrives and President Machado gets out and enters legation. Another coach arrives and King George V, wearing military uniform, enters the legation. A small crowd looks on as the King leaves.

IV. Prince Arthur, Duke of Connaught, in France. 'PRINCE ARTHUR ON THE FRENCH FRONT. His Royal Highness who is most popular in France takes the salute at a review of splendid troops.' LS over grassy field as French troops march past. MS 3/4 rear view of the Prince as he takes the salute. 'PRINCE ARTHUR IN NOYON. His Royal Highness visits Noyon to decorate French heroes and salutes the bullet riddled banner of the deathless Chasseurs.' Prince Arthur walks along a rank of soldiers fallen in on cobbled square in Noyon. MS profile as he decorates a soldier. He salutes as troops pass in review. Cut to Arthur and retinue walking along a tree-lined country road – a soldier stands on the grass verge holding a tattered regimental flag which the Prince salutes. Prince Arthur stops to regard the relic.

Notes

Remarks (item I): the titles are very much grander than the poor stock-shots they preface.
Summary (item II): precise identification of 'Lady Grace' seems to have been taken for

granted by the caption writer, but is now rather uncertain. Possibly she was Mildred, wife of Sir Valentine Raymond Grace, 5th Baronet of Minchenden House, Middlesex, one of the noble obscure. This couple did indeed have four daughters.
catalogued NAP: 11/1991

NTB 322-01 · GB, 24/10/1917
WAR OFFICE OFFICIAL TOPICAL BUDGET 322-1

b/w · 1 reel · 340' (6 mins) · silent
intertitles: English

sp War Office Cinema Committee *pr* Topical Film Company

I. Battleships at anchor. 'Admiralty Official Film "CLEARED FOR ACTION" Looking aft on a super Dreadnought of our great battle fleet which is cleared for action night and day.' LS aft down starboard side of quarterdeck of a Queen Elizabeth Class battleship to X and Y turrets, and pan left over anchorage – nearest the cameraship are Bellerophon Class, Hercules Class and a Saint Vincent Class battleships.
II. US officers are flown over the front line to study artillery observation. 'AMERICANS' (sic) NEARING THE DAY OF BATTLE. United States Artillery officers on the French Western front fly over the lines to study the regulation of the fire of big guns.' American and French officers stand about as a Letord 3 is wheeled out of a hangar. French help US officers don flying gear as the French pilot suits up. Two of the Americans put on goggles. Letord runs up and then takes off in a cloud of dust.
III. Queen Mary visits the Royal Dockyard at Woolwich. 'WITH THE QUEEN AT WOOLWICH. Her Majesty who was accompanied by Princess Mary was much interested in the equipment stores and the women workers at Woolwich Dockyard.' Women workers wearing smocks wave as the Queen and Princess pass. MS left profile as Queen Mary looks down at something. The party moves off, Princess Mary trailing along behind. The Queen watches a woman operating a sewing machine – as a patriotic gesture, a small Union Flag has been set up on the workbench. The Royal couple continue their tour.
IV. Open-air investiture at Buckingham Palace. 'KING HOLDS OPEN AIR INVESTITURE. His Majesty bestowed many honours including nine V.Cs four of which were presented to the relatives of fallen heroes.' Pan over guests seated in the forecourt of the Palace – crowds look on

from beyond the gates. The King enters the forecourt and shakes hands with the presiding general officer. HM decorates Sergeant Grimbaldeston, KOSB. Mrs E A Davies, widow of Corporal James Davies of the Royal Welch Fusiliers, gets a few words as she receives her husband's award.
V. VIPs attend a meeting organised by the National War Savings Committee. '"SAVE YOUR MONEY and Save the World!" Sir Edward Carson. Sir Eric Geddes, Lord Curzon, Mr. Bonar Law, Mr. Winston Churchill and Mr Lloyd George arriving at the Albert Hall where the Premier made his great speech on the need for national economy.' Dressed in top hat and overcoat, Carson talks with companions – they seem to be discussing where their tickets place them in the Hall. Sir Eric Geddes arrives by car – a police sergeant points out where he should go. Lord Curzon arrives. Bonar Law arrives with wife and daughter. Mr Churchill arrives, tips his hat to some onlookers, and studies his invitation before going inside. Lloyd George and daughter Megan arrive – he acknowledges the cheers of the crowd and they go inside.

catalogued NAP: 9/1991

NTB 323-01 · GB, 31/10/1917
WAR OFFICE OFFICIAL TOPICAL BUDGET 323-1

b/w · 1 reel · 309' (5 mins) · silent
intertitles: English

sp War Office Cinema Committee *pr* Topical Film Company

I. The King reviews the crew of a battleship. 'Admiralty Official Film. THE KING ATTENDS "DIVISIONS". In the Navy "Divisions" is the equivalent to the regimental parade in the Army, the ship's crew assemble on the quarterdeck to the playing of lively airs by the ships band.' HA from camera on Y turret as sailors and marines march past King and Admiral Sturdee (?) standing on raised dais set up on the quarterdeck – band plays 'lively airs'.
II. The Duchess of Portland christens an aeroplane presented by Nottingham City to New Zealand. 'NOTTINGHAM'S GIFT TO NEW ZEALAND. The Duke of Portland and Lord Besborough (sic) were present when the Duchess of Portland christened the aeroplane which the Midland City presented to New Zealand.' Lord Desborough leads the Duke as the two inspect a detachment of troops – a large crowd looks on. The Duchess wears a fur-trimmed coat with

matching muff. HA pan over the crowd which the Duke addresses from a raised dais draped with a Union Flag bearing the name of the Imperial Air Fleet Committee. The Duchess strikes with a mallet at a cloth-wrapped bottle attached to the propeller of the aircraft – initially she fails to break the bottle, but grits her teeth and tries again, succeeding with the second blow. The crowd cheer. The Duchess rejoins a solicitous Duke. CU of the name 'NOTTINGHAM' on the aircraft fuselage.
III. President Machado of Portugal visits France. 'PORTUGUESE PRESIDENT IN FRANCE. President Machado accompanied by President Poincaré made a tour of the French Western front and at Verdun presented the mayor with an Order, as a souvenir of the glorious defence of that famous fortress.' Machado and Poincaré pass guard of honour. Watched by an impassive Poincaré, the Portuguese President places the Order of the Tower and Sword on a cushion held by the mayor of Verdun. The two Presidents leave by car. The two men look at some of the ruins in Verdun and watch a march past by troops along one of the cobbled streets.
IV. The King and Queen attend a service for the Forces. 'SERVICE FOR FIGHTING MEN. The King and Queen attended a special service for sailors and soldiers at St. Martin's-in-the Fields.' The King and Queen accompanied by the rector pass an honour guard of boy scouts to enter the church. Lesser people follow on.
V. General Sir Francis Lloyd inspects the Motor Transport Volunteers. 'CLAPHAM JUNCTION OF THE WAR. Practically every British soldier has to cross London and the City of London Volunteer Corps provides him with transportation. General Sir Francis Lloyd inspecting cars in the grounds of the H.A.C.' General Lloyd, GOC London District, passes guard of honour to inspect an array of MTV lorries – many have been donated by American cities or states. HA over the men of the Volunteers, and the ranks of private cars parked in the grounds of the Honourable Artillery Company.

Notes
Summary (item II): Lord Desborough was President of the Imperial Air Fleet Committee, and the Duke of Portland was President of the Nottingham Chamber of Commerce.
Remarks (item III): the elderly President Machado seems rather confused during the simple presentation ceremony, and it is perhaps not surprising to learn that he was ousted from office two months later.
catalogued NAP: 11/1991

NTB 323-02 · GB, 3/11/1917
WAR OFFICE OFFICIAL TOPICAL BUDGET 323-2

b/w · 1 reel · 316' (5 mins) · silent
intertitles: English

sp War Office Cinema Committee *pr* Topical Film Company

I. Burial of Prince Christian. 'OBSEQUIES OF THE KING'S UNCLE. Prince Christian buried with full military honours in St. George's Chapel Windsor.' HA as military band (men of the 2nd Life Guards and Coldstream Guards) approaches the chapel where guard of honour is waiting. Coffin is removed from gun carriage and taken up steps into the chapel.
II. Indian troops enter Baghdad. 'WITH THE BRITISH IN BAGHDAD. Some of our splendid Indian Troops on the march through the famous City of Arabian Nights.' Indian troops – possibly from the 7th (Meerut) Division – march along 'New Street' in Baghdad. Only a few locals are evident.
III. Pan over anchored battleships. 'Admiralty Official Film. OUR ISLAND'S RAMPARTS. A wonderful and stirring panorama of the citadels afloat which guard the Empire's heart.' LS broad on the port quarter of a Saint Vincent Class battleship, and pan right to HMS *Neptune* and a second Saint Vincent. XLS off port bow of Queen Elizabeth and Orion Class battleships. MLS off the port bow of a Queen Elizabeth, a trawler lying nearby – lower boom of the cameraship intrudes from frame right.
IV. Aircraft salvage establishment in France. 'HOSPITAL FOR AEROPLANES. How British 'planes winged by Boche bullets are got ready for action again behind the lines.' MS as wing and tail section of BE 2c 2059 are taken into a hangar. Aircraft fuselages are recovered. A wing section is placed on a trestle ready to be worked upon. MS of an already extensively cannibalized BE 2c lying nosed over. Men take more parts away from aircraft scrapyard.
V. Australian 18-pounder gun in action. 'SUICIDE CORNER. Australians having worked round this dangerous spot of evil name bring one of their 18 pounders into action.' A working party moves up carrying water cans, boxes of Mills bombs, rolls of barbed wire, etc. Some glance around at the camera as they pass. Rear view of an 18-pounder gun in a sand-bagged emplacement, empty cartridge cases stacked neatly in the foreground – the gun crew (one wearing a pickelhaube) take up their positions – the gun layer arranging a spare sandbag as a cushion for himself. The gun fires three times.

Notes

Summary (item V): there were many 'Suicide Corners' on the Western Front, but this probably refers to that near the Dixmude Road, north of Ypres.

General: this is the first of the *War Office Topical Budget* issues in the NTB series to include after the main titles the declaration that the newsreel devotes all its profits to charity.

catalogued NAP: 12/1991

NTB 324-01 · GB, 7/11/1917
WAR OFFICE OFFICIAL TOPICAL BUDGET 324-1

b/w · 1 reel · 351' (6 mins) · silent
intertitles: English

sp War Office Cinema Committee *pr* Topical Film Company

I. Carrier pigeons in military service. 'THE PIGEON AS POSTMAN. Taken up on motor cycle to the trenches the birds except for casualties, never fail to reach "home" behind the lines where the telegraphist sends on the message.' Pigeons are put in baskets for transport by motor-cycles. In a training trench a RE Captain writes down a message which is put in capsule. The pigeon is released. Pigeons return to their roost and the messages are relayed by Morse sender. CU of the message form carried by a pigeon: the sender is Cpt H Dickinson, 31/10/1917, and the message is 'PLEASE DO NOT SHOOT HOMING PIGEONS. THEY ARE PERFORMING VALUABLE NATIONAL WORK.'
II. Italian artillery in the mountains. 'GREAT ITALIAN STAND. It is believed that when the Germans advance again Italy with her British and French Allies will put up one of the greatest battles in history. One of the big Italian guns which will keep the enemy at bay.' An Italian crew serve a 30.5cm Vickers-Terni howitzer (M1916 ?) emplaced in mountainous terrain. The gun is fired. LS of an explosion on a mountain ridge beyond a dense belt of pine trees. The men run to reload the gun.
III. The Polish Legion is honoured by the French. 'POLISH LEGION IN FRANCE. General Archinard distributes honours to the gallant survivors of the Polish Legion which marched from Bayonne to fight beside the French in 1914.' The General inspects the ranks. He decorates officers and a soldier wearing a dramatic head bandage. MCU as an officer holds out the regimental banner – a Polish eagle. The banner's cravat bears an inscription testifying to Franco-Polish

friendship. The troops march past – in the background are huts, each bearing an Allied flag – US, Japanese, Italian, etc.
IV. The French occupy a shattered blockhouse during the Battle of Passchendaele, and improve their own defences. 'PUSHING ON IN FLANDERS. Enemy bombarding territory wrested from them by the French. Striking specimen of a shell crater and abandoned German blockhouse.' LS over churned-up ground with shattered trees and dotted with a few crosses – shells explode in the distance – a lorry moves left to right along an invisible road – perhaps the target for the bombardment. HA.MS of a man standing in a deep shell-hole – he begins to climb out. French troops shelter in a ruined German blockhouse – the concrete structure seems to have partially subsided into a flooded shell-hole – several Frenchmen approach this pool, one unbuttoning his trousers determinedly. A French soldier sits up against the ruin reading, while a second sleeps in the sunlight. 'WATCHERS AND WORKERS. While the guns never cease observation is kept while pioneers and engineers reorganise the hard won ground as a jumping off place for the next push.' French soldiers, spades held over their shoulders, walk along duckboard. A length of trench is dug. Men observe the enemy from a ramshackle position made up of timber and corrugated iron. LS over the devastated ground of no man's land as German shells burst over an already devastated wood. Troops rest in the shelter of a sand-bagged breastwork. LS of another airburst. Troops prepare to take up a length of corrugated iron laid by the side of the road – a wagon carrying duckboards moves along the track past a stationary lorry.

catalogued NAP: 1/1992

NTB 324-02 · GB, 10/11/1917
WAR OFFICE OFFICIAL TOPICAL BUDGET 324-2

b/w · 1 reel · 332' (5 mins) · silent
intertitles: English

sp War Office Cinema Committee *pr* Topical Film Company

I. A recruiting hut for the WAAC is opened in Trafalgar Square. 'WOMEN AS GUARD OF HONOUR. General Sir Francis Lloyd at the opening of the Recruiting Hut in Trafalgar Square for the Women's Army Auxiliary Corps popularly known in France as the "Waxs".' Preceded by a (male) military band,

uniformed WAACs march along street. WAAC guard of honour lines either side of a red carpet as General Lloyd gets out of his car. Lloyd inspects ranks of WAACs.
II. A gathering of emancipationists to found a Womens' Parliamentary Party. 'WILL THERE BE WOMEN M.P.s.? Mrs Pankhurst, "General" Drummond Miss Christabel Pankhurst and Miss Kenny (sic) met with wild enthusiasm at the meeting held at Queens Hall to found a Womens Parliamentary Party.' MSs of a crowd of women – and a few men – standing outside the Hall. The party founders (minus Miss Kenney) arrive by car and go inside. MCU pan left to right over standing group – Miss Christabel Pankhurst, Miss Annie Kenney, Mrs Flora Drummond and Mrs Emmeline Pankhurst.
III. The King and Queen visit Bristol. 'KING AND QUEEN IN THE WEST. Their Majesties continuing their tour of Industrial Centres visited Bristol. The King held an Investiture on Durdham Downs.' HM and senior military officers leave after a visit to a Soldier's Rest House in Victoria Street. The King inspects local troops. Crowds lining the route wave at the royal car as it passes – a policeman runs forward to control the crowd's enthusiasm. Cut to platform set up on Durdham Downs – the Queen is seated as the King talks to Cpt. Buchanan who has just received the Victoria and Military Crosses. After a Royal handshake the blinded Captain is led off the platform by an attendant. He is succeeded by Lance Corporal Room. Cut to LA.LS past the seated Queen Mary to HM, now chatting with a nurse – she curtseys to the King and then to the Queen as she leaves, to be followed by another nurse.
IV. Lord Mayor's Show. 'LORD MAYORS WAR PAGEANT. London enjoyed a great military spectacle in this years Lord Mayors Show. Thousands of troops Women Volunteers and "All Clear" scouts taking part.' Women farm workers march along street – a hay cart is part of the procession. WAACs follow. The mayoral coach passes. 'TANK'S TRIUMPH IN LONDON. Tremendous cheering greeted the appearance of a shell-battered Tank which had fought many a hard fight against the Germans in France.' A Male and a Female Mk IV tank – neither noticeably battered – move along a street past crowds of onlookers. MS as the Mayor leaves his coach preceded by bearers carrying sword and mace.

Notes

Summary (item I): despite the attention given here to General Lloyd, GOC London District, he was not in fact the star of this particular show. The proceedings were presided over by the Minister of Labour, G H Roberts, and

the formal opening of the 'hut' was by General Sir Nevill Macready. Perhaps the cameraman turned up late.
Summary (item IV): the tanks were a popular novelty. *The Times* reported that "The pace at which they went astonished most of the onlookers, and now and again the male tank, with masculine thoughtlessness, left his consort, and had to be pulled up and slowed down.".
catalogued NAP: 12/1991

NTB 325-01 · GB, 14/11/1917
WAR OFFICE OFFICIAL TOPICAL BUDGET 325-1

b/w · 1 reel · 320' (5 mins) · silent
intertitles: English

sp War Office Cinema Committee *pr* Topical Film Company

I. Demonstration of a radio-controlled motor-boat based on the design of the German Fernlenkboote. 'MYSTERY SHIP EXPLAINED. Great interest was shown in the German electric mystery ships, one of which was captured by the British Fleet. How (sic) a similar electrically propelled ship built in America is manoeuvred from the shore.' A small launch moves about the waters of a quiet harbour. CU of the radio-controller, observing the boat's progress through binoculars.
II. The King and Queen visit Bath. 'OUR WONDERFUL WOUNDED. The King and Queen were deeply impressed with the cheeriness and courage of the wounded they visited at Bath.' The King talks with wounded soldiers – the front row of men are all seated, many with crutches beside them. King and Queen with civic dignitaries at the Pump Room. On leaving, the Royal couple chat with more convalescent soldiers – Queen Mary talking with a soldier in an invalid carriage – before moving towards their waiting car.
III. Civic service at Southwark Cathedral. 'MUNICIPAL SUNDAY. The newly elected Mayors of South London attend a special service at Southwark Cathedral.' Civic dignitaries pass camera. Detachments of police, soldiers and nurses enter the Cathedral, followed by municipal officers and the mayors preceded by their regalia. The public follow.
IV. The funeral of Sultan Hussein Kemal of Egypt. 'OBSEQUIES OF A SULTAN. Magnificent scenes of eastern splendour marked the funeral of Britain's staunch friend Hussein 1, the late Sultan of Egypt.' Procession of mourners – some holding

banners bearing the symbol of the sultanate – pass along a route lined by horsemen. The coffin is covered by a pall and surmounted by the tarbush. 'THE MOURNING OF THE FAITHFUL. Dense crowds of stricken people followed the Cortège to the Rifai Mosque the last resting place of the Rulers of Egypt.' LS as the coffin is carried up stone steps into the mosque.

Notes
Summary (item I): the German Fernlenkboote were steered by means of a trailing cable following instructions from an accompanying seaplane. They were unmanned and carried a 700kg explosive charge. On 28 October 1917, the monitor *Erebus*, then operating near Ostende, was hit by FL.12. The resulting explosion killed two and wounded fifteen of the ship's crew, destroying about fifty feet of the monitor's protective bulge. Repairs took about three weeks. A few more attacks were made but without further success, and Fernlenkboote were abandoned by the end of 1917.
catalogued NAP: 1/1992

NTB 325-02 · GB, 17/11/1917
WAR OFFICE OFFICIAL TOPICAL BUDGET 325-2

b/w · 1 reel · 301' (5 mins) · silent
intertitles: English

sp War Office Cinema Committee *pr* Topical Film Company

I. Sir Arthur Yapp appeals for economy in the use of food. 'NOTABILITIES. THE U-MEN AND THE MEN-U. Sir Arthur Yapp with the famous clock which registered the subscriptions during his hurricane campaign for the Y.M.C.A.' MS profile of Sir Arthur at his desk in a roomy and well-appointed study. He reaches down and places on his desk a placard bearing a clock-motif, moving the single hand from 2 o'clock (£10 000) to 12 o'clock (£250 000). He then puts the clock away. 'The Director of Food, Sir Arthur Yapp dons the badge of the League to Save Food and calls for ten million members.' After hunting about on his desk Sir Arthur finds the badge which, after a moment of silent contemplation, he pins to his left lapel. CU of the badge, an anchor with "FOOD ECONOMY" on the stock and "NATIONAL SAFETY" below the arms. Sir Arthur turns to his desk and begins to write purposefully.
II. German prisoners of the French after one of the battles along the Chemin des Dames. 'A SEETHING SEA OF PRISONERS. The

magnitude of the victory on the famous Chemin des Dames is attested by the masses of Boche prisoners the French marched into the cages.' German prisoners walk out of a trench to be directed onward by a French soldier. HA.MS as German POWs pass a crowd of watching French soldiers – one prisoner has a bag over his shoulder which is snatched off him by one of the onlookers. A French casualty, his head swathed in bloodstained bandages, walks along a muddy road – in the background soldiers crowd around two motor ambulances (?). French cavalry, sabres drawn, lead a column of POWs. HA.LS over barbed-wire cages crowded with prisoners, some men shifting from foot to foot to keep warm – pan right to show the extent of the cages.
III. Lord French inspects London's defences. 'INVASION IS STILL POSSIBLE. In declaring that the Volunteers were not playing at soldiers, Lord French said the unexpected happened in war and that the next suprise (sic) might be invasion. The Field Marshal inspects the Volunteer Defences of London.' Lord French and staff study maps – they are standing by a barbed-wire fence over which several have thrown their overcoats. One officer uses his walking stick to point out features of interest. French and his party stroll about the 'defences'. A party of Volunteers dig an unimpressive ditch. The party moves on.
IV. French railway guns in action. 'INFERNO OF A BARRAGE. Monster guns of our Allies put up an awful barrage before the advancing infantry swept to their great victory in the Chemin des Dames.' MS of a 400mm French railway gun, and pan right to a second gun as it opens fire. First gun fires. XLS of distant shell-bursts. The barrage continues, cutting between guns firing and shell-bursts. LA.MS of a 320mm (?) railway gun as it recoils after firing and the crew run forward to reload – the gun fires again.
V. Venizelos arrives in London. 'UNCROWNED KING OF GREECE IN LONDON. M Venizelos, the famous Patriot Premier of Greece, with the Greek Consul after his arrival with Mr. Lloyd George from the Allies' Conference in Paris.' Venizelos and the Consul walk down steps towards the camera, to stand talking at the bottom.

Notes
Summary (item I): the formation of the League of National Safety, which was to promote economy in the use of foodstuffs, had been announced by Sir Arthur, the Director of Food Economy, while at Keighley on 3 November.
Remarks (item I): at no point during this episode does Sir Arthur ever look directly at

the camera.
Summary (item III): speaking to a gathering of the Motor Volunteer Corps on 7 November, French had criticised those that sneered at the Volunteers for 'playing at soldiers', and had spoken of the need to guard against the element of surprise in wartime, citing as an example the successful German offensive in Italy, and raising the possibility of a German invasion. For raising this alarmist and rather improbable spectre, he was criticised in Parliament.
Remarks (item III): if Lord French could negotiate these defences, they could not have been very formidable.
catalogued NAP: 9/1991

NTB 327-01 · GB, 28/11/1917
WAR OFFICE OFFICIAL TOPICAL BUDGET 327-1

b/w · 1 reel · 332' (5 mins) · silent
intertitles: English

sp War Office Cinema Committee *pr* Topical Film Company

I. Tanks cross trial barbed wire defences. 'THE TANKS' SMASHING VICTORY. "The Tank Corps expects that every tank will do its damnedest." This signal was flashed by Brigadier-General Elles as he led the tanks into action and smashed the "impregnable" Hindenburg Line.' Watched by a group of soldiers, Mk IV tanks demonstrate their ability to cross a belt of barbed wire.
II. General Sir Julian Byng and his staff pose for the camera. 'GENERAL SIR JULIAN BYNG. The victorious Commander of the Third Army. (Sir Julian is seated in the centre surrounded by a group of Staff Officers.)' MLS of Byng and his staff arranged for a photo-opportunity, the front row seated, others standing behind. MS of a more select group of three seated on a bench, Byng again in the centre.
III. British troops take over a section of line from the French. 'FLANDERS FRONT EXTENDED. British Troops take over section recently held by the French.' British troops march along a paved and tree-lined road. Detachment on a muddy road, lorries moving past in the background. A column of French small arms ammunition carts moves past British troops marching in the opposite direction. A convoy of British troop-carrying buses – one carries a bicycle lashed to the roof of the driver's cabin. British troops file along duckboards – French soldiers look on, hands in pockets. French and British fraternise for the camera.
IV. Artillery on the move. 'HEAVY ARTILLERY

MOVING UP. Caterpillar tractors simplify the removal of these monsters over the shell-torn roads of Flanders.' Holt tractor tows a 9.2-inch howitzer along a muddy road. Horses move a 6-inch howitzer. Transport – a bus, motor ambulance, lorry – skirt the edge of a ruined village. Mule train of supply wagons and limbers.
V. The Tank Bank in Trafalgar Square. 'THE ARMOURED BANK. The Byng Boy is already at work in Trafalgar Square, and crowds are flocking to buy War Bonds and see "Tank 130."' MS of tank in Trafalgar – an officer emerges from a door in the rear of the starboard sponson. Sequence showing a woman seated in the sponson selling War Bonds – among the customers is an officer in an invalid chair. A civic dignitary (?) is among those in the queue to buy, and as he turns to leave he is restrained by a man who repositions him for the benefit of the camera.

Notes
Summary (item V): the Tank War Savings Bank opened in Trafalgar Square on 26 November 1917. The nickname 'Byng Boy' for the tank is a reference to General Sir Julian Byng, then celebrated for his part in the victory at Cambrai. A current popular song was 'Bynging on the Rhine'.
catalogued NAP: 12/1991

NTB 327-02 · GB, 1/12/1917
WAR OFFICE OFFICIAL TOPICAL BUDGET 327-2

b/w · 1 reel · 296' (5 mins) · silent
intertitles: English

sp War Office Cinema Committee *pr* Topical Film Company

I. Stock footage of ammunition train. 'HOT STUFF FOR FRITZ. An ammunition train of 9.2 shells going up to the Front.' HA as train passes diagonally left to right, pulling open wagons filled with 9.2-inch shells and ammunition boxes – soldiers sit in each of the wagons.
II. Cavalry training in Egypt. 'OUR CAVALRY IN EGYPT. Strenuous training, necessary, to keep men and horses fit, must be carried on in early morning on account of the fierce heat.' HA of squadron in formation, wheeling to reverse its course. Two ranks in line abreast ride through each other. Column walks along beach through shallows. Horse are ridden up a steep bank.
III. Competition for women farm workers. 'ABLE GIRL FARMERS. Farmer critics were full of praise for the agricultural work done by the women, at their efficiency test, held at

Maidstone.' Women contestants, each wearing a numbered armband, spray fruit trees – an audience of convalescent soldiers look on. Women planting with dibbers, topping a hay rick, ploughing with motor tractors.

IV. Popular author Hall Caine commences work on a propagandist screenplay. 'HALL CAINE GETS TO WORK. At the request of the Prime Minister the famous Author is doing the scenario for a great War Film.' The famous author sits at his desk, holding an open book. When prompted he opens a small can of 35mm film and holds a length up to the light for scrutiny. Hall Caine looks out of his study window. He leaves his study to step out into the garden.

V. Pétain reviews French troops after fighting in the Ailette Valley during the battle for the Chemin des Dames. 'AFTER THE AILETTE VICTORY. General Pétain reviews the Troops and decorates their Colours after the great engagement.' Troops pass in review over a grassy field. The men fallen in – Pétain salutes as he walks across in front of them. MS of soldiers holding some of the colours.

Notes

Summary (item II): more of this film can be seen in **IWM 2**.

Summary (item III): this test for Kentish women farm workers took place at Allington Farm, lent for the purpose by fruit growers Messrs James Edmonds and Sons. There were 200 competitors in 15 events. The most important test was for ploughing where each contestant had to drive one of the tractors and also ride the plough.

Summary (item IV): The Times for 10 November 1917 reported that the National War Aims Committee proposed to make as large a use as possible of the cinema in war aims propaganda. Hall Caine "promised to do his best": his scenario was for *The National Film* which was not completed until after the War and was never released – see Reeves.

[Nicholas Reeves, *Official British Film Propaganda During the First World War*, Croom Helm (1986): 125-130]
catalogued NAP: 12/1991

NTB 328-01 · GB, 5/12/1917
WAR OFFICE OFFICIAL TOPICAL BUDGET 328-1

b/w · 1 reel · 390' (7 mins) · silent
intertitles: English

sp War Office Cinema Committee *pr* Topical Film Company

I. General scenes behind the lines, ostensibly at Cambrai. 'ON THE CAMBRAI FRONT. Rushing up ammunition, building new roads and consolidating our gains.' Artillery limber crosses muddy ground at the gallop, while another stands in mid-screen, apparently bogged down – a soldier can be seen lashing the mules with a whip to no immediate effect. A second team gallops past the stranded limber. A work party stands by a road smoking as a stretcher case is carried past by German POWs. Several of the soldiers look upwards – presumably to watch some aerial activity. As some move along, others resume their work widening the road.

II. US Congressmen visit France. 'U.S.A. CONGRESSMEN ON THE BATTLEFIELD. America sends representatives to see conditions of present-day warfare.' At the Ordnance Works at Calais the group of Congressmen – some holding steel helmets – pick their way along a muddy track by a gun park – a 6-inch 30cwt gun stands nearby. Cut to Congressmen – now wearing their helmets – as they are led over old battlefield near Fricourt. The escorting British officer points out features of interest with his cane.

III. Eton wall game. 'ETON'S FAMOUS "WALL GAME". This historic contest resulted in the Oppidans beating the Collegers one shy to nil.' Boys look down from the top of the wall as the game proceeds. MS of the scrimmage. The audience applauds – one boy makes a face at the camera. The game continues.

IV. Popular entertainers fund raising at the Tank Bank in Trafalgar Square. 'STARS ON THE TANK. Miss Madge Titheradge recites "Sons of England" and George Robey sells £4,000 worth of War Bonds.' LA of the two entertainers standing on top of the tank – Mr Robey, 'The Prime Minister of Mirth', addresses the crowd, presumably introducing Miss Titheradge, then steps down. Miss T recites with appropriate gestures – in the background the National Gallery is decorated with a huge bill-board recording the sales of War Bonds in 'Provincial England'. MS as Robey buys some bonds from Miss Titheradge, now sitting at a table alongside the tank – she laughs gaily, watched by a numerous crowd of admirers (who would have the opportunity the next month to see her as Aladdin at the Garrick). HA over the dense crowd surrounding the tank.

V. Irregular Franco-Arab force fights the Turks. 'WITH THE CAMEL CORPS. A Franco-Arabian Expedition sets out for the interior.' A group of French and Arab soldiers armed with Lebel rifles mount their camels – not without difficulty for some of the French. The

- 512 -

column passes through a dry wadi – some of the camels carry ammunition boxes and the components of a French 65mm mountain gun.

Notes
Remarks (item IV): the Topical Budget seems on this occasion to have had difficulty generating a pound sign for the title.
Summary (item V): the title does not make clear the location of this sequence, but it relates to the French mission to the Hejaz forces under Colonel Brémond. For a much fuller account of this minor military episode see **IWM 508-36**.
Main titles: the customary declaration that profits go to charity undergoes a significant change. Hereafter the *War Office Official Topical Budget* devotes all its profits to "patriotic purposes".
catalogued NAP: 12/1991

NTB 329-01 · GB, 12/12/1917
WAR OFFICE OFFICIAL TOPICAL BUDGET 329-1

b/w · 1 reel · 316' (5 mins) · silent
intertitles: English

sp War Office Cinema Committee *pr* Topical Film Company

I. General Allenby and General Bailloud in Egypt. 'THE VICTOR OF JERUSALEM. General Sir Edmund Allenby who has rescued the Holy City from Turkish domination, reviews one of our mounted brigades.' Aides hold General Bailloud's horse as he mounts. MS of Allenby on his horse. The two men ride off followed by their escort. LS of 7th Mounted Brigade, Desert Mounted Corps, drawn up for inspection – one officer's horse is rather frisky.
II. The King's car is mobbed by enthusiastic crowds when he visits a factory making military equipment. 'ENTHUSIASTIC MUNITIONETTES. His Majesty receives a rousing welcome when he visits the Munition Works of Waring & Gillow.' A dense crowd of workers, many of them waving handkerchiefs, lines the route of the royal car. The crowd closes in after the car has passed, and some difficulty arises when at one point the vehicle needs to reverse.
III. French troops arrive to support the Italians after the disaster at Caporetto. 'MONSIEUR PAINLEVE AT BRESCIA. French and Italian troops fraternising at the station en route for the Front.' MCU of the French Prime Minister in conversation with an Italian officer, whose back is to the camera – the Italian gestures excitedly. A woman gives

fruit (?) to two French soldiers sitting in the open door of a railcar – she also gives one of them a pamphlet (perhaps an improving tract). A woman and a boy distribute comforts to the troops. Train passes camera in a cloud of steam – Italians look on and wave at the soldiers in the boxcars. Flatbed wagons carry vehicles and canvas-covered guns – a surprisingly 'modern' scene. 'THE RUSH TO THE ITALIAN FRONT. A regiment of French Dragoons passing through the picturesque old City of Verona.' French cavalry pass through the city, watched by crowds of waving Italians – they pass through the Piazza Bra, the wall of the amphitheatre visible in the background. 'FRENCH HURRY TO THE PIAVE. Huge demonstrations in honour of the French battalions, who, along with British forces, are rushing to help Italy hold her frontier.' MS crowd scene – French and Italian soldiers shake hands. A lorry passes through the dense crowd. Enthusiastic Italians gather in front of Verona's town hall, and around an equestrian statue in the gardens in the centre of the piazza.

Notes
Summary (item I): a typically careless use of stock footage. From the coverage the uninformed would probably suppose that the obscure General Bailloud, commander of the Détachement Français de Palestine et de Syrie, was the conqueror of Jerusalem.
Summary (item II): just as all British troop movements were advances to the Topical Budget, all equipment factories were munition works. The 8000 women employed by Waring & Gillow made tents and other canvas and leather items.
catalogued NAP: 12/1991

NTB 330-02 · GB, 22/12/1917
WAR OFFICE OFFICIAL TOPICAL BUDGET 330-2

b/w · 1 reel · 314' (5 mins) · silent
intertitles: English

sp War Office Cinema Committee *pr* Topical Film Company

I. Work of the Army Postal Service. 'XMAS PARCELS FOR TOMMY. The boys at the front are not forgotten during Yuletide, every endeavour is made to enable Tommy to receive his parcel without delay.' MS of Royal Engineer holding a chit, which another soldier examines. Men sort mail bags and load them onto horse-drawn wagons. CU of parcels – one is addressed to the CO of 1/3 Seaforth Highlanders, Salonika, another to the Coldstream Guards in France. A convoy of lorries leaves the depot.

II. French troops reinforce the Italians. 'THE ALLIES IN ITALY. By every route the French and British troops are hastening to Italy's aid in her hour of need.' Heavily laden French troops and their supply column cross a bridge to enter a walled Italian city.

III. US troops move a wooden YMCA hut to a new site. 'LIGHTNING AMERICAN METHODS. This popular YMCA hut was too far away to suit the Sammies, so they promptly carried it half a mile nearer Camp.' US soldiers leave their camp – they are unarmed and some are still in civilian dress or wearing uniform with a civilian cap. After marching through open country they come to a large (and apparently newly constructed) timber frame hall painted with a YMCA symbol. Long poles are set around the floor of the hall, and taking hold of these the soldiers lift the entire building and walk off to the new site. The hut is set down in its new location. Men cheer and wave their caps for the camera – in the background others wave from the roof of the hall.

IV. Cross-Channel ferries carry British troops home for Christmas. 'CHRISTMAS LEAVE BOATS. These boys are on the way home for a Merry Christmas. Here's to them!' Men with rifles and full kit are directed down companion-way on ferry. HA to soldiers milling about on deck – they have all been issued with regulation life-jacket. The ferry is very crowded. 'UNDER WAY FOR BLIGHTY. Many a heart will be made happy by their presence.' LS as crowded ferry makes away from quayside – a single-funnel paddle-steamer, it bears the transport number G.08. A second ship leaves the harbour, waved off by some WAACs – one of them blows a kiss to departing soldier(s).

Notes

Summary (item III): as the hall is obviously new, unglazed and internally braced for the move, the title – not for the first time – is rather fanciful.

catalogued NAP: 1/1992

NTB 340-01 · GB, 27/2/1918
PICTORIAL NEWS (OFFICIAL) 340-1

b/w · 1 reel · 306' (5 mins) · silent
intertitles: English

sp Ministry of Information *pr* Topical Film Company

I. Venice takes measures to protect historic buildings from air raids. 'VENICE IN ARMOUR. How the historic architecture of

the beautiful city is protected against possible air raids.' HA pan over the Doges' Palace – the main staircase is heavily sand-bagged and some of the architectural details have been protected with wooden casings. Wooden bracing protects the balcony colonnade.

II. A large war photograph is prepared for display. 'WORLD'S LARGEST PHOTOGRAPH. Colouring the biggest of the giant British Battle Photographs to be shown at the Grafton Galleries, London, under the direction of the Ministry of Information.' MS of two men, one of them standing on a step ladder, working with air brushes to colour a large composite photograph of a battle scene showing tanks and troops moving up. A woman enters from the right. Man and woman at work on the picture – he uses an airbrush and she adds detail with a pen.

III. The Prince of Wales visits the principality, 21 February 1918. 'PRINCE IN THE PRINCIPALITY. H.R.H. arrives at Ebbw Vale, inspects Guard of Honour and shakes hands with V.A.D. nurses.' A car arrives and the Prince, dressed in army uniform, and escorted by Sir Sidney Greville and Lord Treowan, steps out to salute an aged officer. After introductions, the Prince inspects the motley honour guard made up of cadets and men of the Monmouthshire Volunteers. He meets a group of VAD nurses at a local hospital (note the cine cameramen at work in the background). 'PRINCE OF WALES AS MINER. In overalls and lamp in hand H.R.H. sets out to visit a coal mine, and afterwards inspects a dockyard.' MS of the Prince in overalls and a flat cap as he walks off carrying his walking stick and a lamp, trailed by a retinue of police, military officers and colliery officials (the Victoria Colliery). Cut to Prince – once again in uniform and fur-collared overcoat – as he regards a collection of naval guns on quayside. A crowd wave as the Prince's car leaves the dockyard.

IV. A group of munitions workers visit Vimy Ridge. 'WAR and THE WORKERS. Representative Party of War Workers visit the Western Front to study the conditions in which our soldiers fight.' Workers' representatives, carrying gas masks and steel helmets, walk along a corduroy road. The conducting Lieutenant leads them over cratered ground – one of the party finds a broken pot.

Notes

Summary (item I): very old news. The Doges' Palace received this protection when Italy declared war in 1915.

Summary (item II): the featured photograph was entitled 'Dreadnoughts on the Battlefield'. When Lieutenant-General Sir

John Cowans opened the British Photographers Exhibition on 4 March 1918, he made special reference to this picture "so vivid that it brought the realization of a modern battle into the heart of London." Photographs of the colourists at work can be found around Q.25580 in the IWM collection.
Summary (item III): the Prince paid a two-day visit to Wales on 20-21 February, 1918. The location of the dockyard tour is a little uncertain; it may be Cardiff, visited on the first day. Ebbw Vale was visited on the second day, when the Prince descended the Victoria Coalmine to watch the miners at work. His condescension went so far as a few words of Welsh to his hosts: 'Diolch yn fawr' or 'Thank you very much'. See also **IWM 170**.
[shotsheet available]
catalogued NAP: 1/1992

NTB 341-02 · GB, 9/3/1918
PICTORIAL NEWS (OFFICIAL) 341-2

b/w · 1 reel · 308' (5 mins) · silent
intertitles: English

sp Ministry of Information *pr* Topical Film Company

I. British troops enter Bethlehem. 'BRITISH IN BETHLEHEM. Our troops headed by a band march into the Historical City of Bethlehem.' Locals look on as troops march through square.
II. Clemenceau visits Alsace. 'M. CLEMENCEAU IN ALSACE. The French War Minister visits Alsace where he receives a hearty welcome and embraces veterans of 1870.' Clemenceau embraces and kisses some young girls who are wearing Alsatian dress, inspects a guard of honour, shakes hands with civic dignitaries (?), embraces an elderly veteran, and accepts a bouquet from a young girl.
III. US troops and artillery are moved by train across France. 'AMERICAN TROOPS IN FRANCE. American troops hurried to the base to take their part in the expected offensive.' LA.MS as train passes diagonally right to left, carrying light artillery – French 75s – on open wagons and troops in boxcars. MS as heavily burdened troops disembark from train and fall in with their kit. 'U.S.A. ARTILLERY. New American guns arriving on the French Front.' Men lead horses down ramps from railcars. A limber is manhandled up to a gun. LS over column forming up and on the march.
IV. British troops build a sandbag observation post near Ramadi in Mesopotamia, 28-29 September 1917.

'DESERT WARFARE. Erecting a sandbag observation post in Mesopotamia.' Soldiers sit about the base of an elaborate sandbag observation tower. Sandbags are hauled up an improvised wooden chute to be added to the tower's ramparts.

Notes
Summary: see **IWM 59** for this item.
catalogued NAP: 1/1992

NTB 342-02 · GB, 16/3/1918
PICTORIAL NEWS (OFFICIAL) 342-2

b/w · 1 reel · 312' (5 mins) · silent
intertitles: English

sp Ministry of Information *pr* Topical Film Company

I. 'THE CHARGE. Inspiring spectacle of French Cavalry at the gallop.' French cavalry passes through a town in the rain – the column attracts the attention of a small dog drinking from a roadside puddle. LS of cavalry drawn up in a grassy field – a detachment gallops past the camera, preceded by buglers and accompanied by two enthusiastic dogs, one of them the drinker seen earlier.
II. A spectacular fire in Redding, California. 'AN INFERNO OF FLAME. Most spectacular fire of recent years wipes out the town of Redding on the Pacific Coast.' LS of the Redding Hotel and nearby offices well ablaze in a strong wind. Hoses are being played on the building, but with little apparent effect. The building starts to collapse.
III. The King and Queen visit Reading. 'KING AND QUEEN AT READING. Their Majesties inspect Sutton's war seeds and Huntley and Palmer's war biscuits.' The royal couple are shown through a long room where women are packing army ration biscuits. They stop as their escort picks up a biscuit for the King's closer attention. Cut to the seed room of Sutton's Royal Seed Establishment where women are packing paper bags. The King examines the seeds. 'KING AND A HERO'S CHILD. His Majesty shakes hands with little Master Beasley after presenting his Mother with his fallen father's medal.' The King and Queen walk through Reading Hospital grounds past nurses and convalescent soldiers. Watched by an audience of soldiers, they talk with a (just honoured ?) soldier in a wicker invalid chair – a photographer has set up his camera among the audience. King awards DCM and Military Medal to Sergeant W Dykes of the Royal Scots Greys who has lost his right arm. The

widow of Second Lieutenant A W Beasley, Royal Berkshire Regiment, comes up with her small son to receive her late husband's Military Medal. The King shakes hands with the boy, who salutes him smartly – this amuses the King, who shakes his hand again, to be rewarded with another salute. The Beasleys turn to leave and are directed towards the Queen, who seems sufficiently thawed by the boy's charm to shake his hand.

IV. Chinese Labour Battalion celebrates their New Year. 'THE CHINAMAN'S NEW YEAR. Quaint frolics of the Chinese Labour Battalion on the Western Front.' A modest Chinese New Year procession passes through a French village, watched by Chinese and British troops – the floats are stylized boats. The crowd follows on after the procession has passed. Four Chinamen caper about on stilts before onlookers.

Notes

Remarks (item III): despite the order of events in the film, it was Sutton's seed factory that was first visited. Reading's biscuit factory seems to have taxed even the Royal couple: both look bored. However, by then it was the afternoon.

Summary (item III): Master Beasley's behaviour charmed more than the *Topical Budget* editor. *The Times* commented that "The boy, a little fellow wearing a cerise coat and gaiters, clicked his heels and saluted the King with military smartness, received the medal, passed on to salute the Queen, and then having got to the end of his instructions, lingered a moment, and suddenly snatched his mother's hand to be led away."

Summary (item IV): see **IWM 168** for the Chinese item.

catalogued NAP: 1/1992

NTB 343-01 · GB, 20/3/1918
PICTORIAL NEWS (OFFICIAL) 343-1

b/w · 1 reel · 316' (5 mins) · silent
intertitles: English

sp Ministry of Information *pr* Topical Film Company

I. King George V decorates members of the Dover Patrol. 'KING & THE DOVER PATROL. H.M. presents medals to gallant skippers of the famous Drifter Patrol.' MS as the King, wearing overcoat and Army uniform, shakes hands with naval personnel – one army officer is among those presented. Medals are presented to RNR Lieutenants and warrant officers. A number of nurses watch

the ceremony. MCU of two petty officers and a Lieutenant wearing their DSCs.

II. Horses are entrained in Egypt (44th Remount Squadron). 'REMOUNTS IN EGYPT. Entraining Mules and Horses at a depot.' Australian troopers drive the animals into wagons, tying their halters to the bars once they are inside. The cars are closed up, the men fall in by the track and the train starts to move off.

III. Shamrock ceremony for reserve battalion of the London Irish Rifles on St Patrick's Day. 'SHAMROCK DAY. Presentation of Erin's Emblem to officers and men of the London Irish by the wife of the Brig. Gen.' The battalion is fallen in at its barracks. A table has been set up beneath the Regimental Flag. The wife of the CO presents shamrocks to officers, who in turn distribute them to the men. After tucking the sprigs into their cap bands, the men give the customary cheers.

IV. Clemenceau decorates US troops serving in France. 'M. CLEMENCEAU AND THE "SAMMIES". After a series of German attacks brilliantly repulsed by the Americans the French President distributes decorations.' Clemenceau with retinue of French and US officers – there is snow on the ground. A French general officer presents the decorations and after a speech by the American commander, Clemenceau shakes hands with the newly decorated men. The French depart.

V. Lieutenant-General Sir Arthur Currie is made Grand Officier of the Belgian Ordre de la Couronne. 'CANADIAN COMMANDER HONOURED. Belgian General decorates General Sir A. Currie, Commanding Canadian Corps, with the Grand Order of the Crown of Belgium.' Rather poorly focussed sequence showing a decoration in the field before a small group of Currie's staff. The Belgian general – a small figure with his back to the camera – pins the order onto the tunic of the very much bigger, taller Currie. The men exchange salutes.

Notes

Summary (item I): see **IWM 201** for the item on the Dover Patrol.

Summary (item II): see **IWM 2** for the item on the remount squadron.

Summary (item IV): Clemenceau visited the US Front on 3 March 1918, and decorated two officers and four men with the Croix de guerre with Palm for the part they had played in repelling a German raid.

catalogued NAP: 1/1992

NTB 343-02 · GB, 23/3/1918
PICTORIAL NEWS (OFFICIAL) 343-2

b/w · 1 reel · 56' (1 min) · silent
intertitles: English

sp Ministry of Information pr Topical Film Company

- Investiture in Delville Wood.

'SOUTH AFRICA IN FRANCE: Divisional Commander presenting medals to South Africans in Delville Wood'. Officer awards medals amid the devastation of the former woodland.

Notes
Summary: see also descriptive note in McKernan; a more complete Spanish-language version of this issue (with three additional stories) is held as **IWM 699b**.
catalogued JCK: 5/1993

NTB 344-01 · GB, 27/3/1918
PICTORIAL NEWS (OFFICIAL) 344-1

b/w · 1 reel · 304' (5 mins) · silent
intertitles: English

sp Ministry of Information pr Topical Film Company

I. French artillery observation post. 'WAITING AND WATCHFUL. French observers keep a sharp look out on the Champagne Front amid growing forests of wire.' MS of wire entanglements and pan right to show their extent. LS as French soldier climbs ladder up onto a platform built in a tree – below hangs a curtain of fibre matting which can be hauled up to screen the observation post. The tree is currently leafless. French troops walk along duckboards carrying rolls of barbed wire.
II. Princess Mary awards badges to Land Army women. 'PRINCESS MARY'S INVESTITURE. Presentation of chevrons and badges to Women's Land Army at Cambridge.' Princess Mary – wearing a white fox stole – is led past an honour guard of Land Girls to enter the Senate House. She re-emerges to stand on the steps for the distribution of badges and chevrons to women land workers.
III. General Pitcairn Campbell inspects tractors. 'REVIEW OF THE TRACTORS. Ploughs of many makes pass General Pitcairn Campbell at the Inspection Base.' The general and his staff stand in a field as four tractors are driven past. General and staff then return to two waiting cars. Contrary to the title there is no suggestion that these tractors are specifically agricultural and three of the four are the same model.

IV. The US Ambassador opens an American Red Cross Hospital in London. 'DR. PAGE OPENS HOSPITAL. Society attends opening of American Red Cross Hospital by U.S.A. Ambassador.' Mr and Mrs Page get out of their car to enter the hospital – their chauffeur regards the camera balefully. Page talks with one of the hospital managers. MS pan over an animated group of society people standing in the hospital gardens.
V. An Australian military band entertains Jewish children. 'SETTLING DOWN IN PALESTINE. Children listening to an Australian Band playing outside a Synagogue.' Pan left over group of children as the band plays in the background. The synagogue is a substantial building in the European style.

Notes
Summary (item IV): maintained by a wealthy philanthropist, the hospital was at 24 Kensington Palace Gardens. It was the fifth American Red Cross hospital to be opened in England, but there were no suitably injured Americans available and it was first used by British and Empire casualties.
catalogued NAP: 1/1992

NTB 344-02 · GB, 30/3/1918
PICTORIAL NEWS (OFFICIAL) 344-2

b/w · 1 reel · 295' (5 mins) · silent
intertitles: English

sp Ministry of Information pr Topical Film Company

I. Stock battle footage. 'NO BREAK THROUGH. Britain's sons win greatest battle of history.' Column of 18-pounder limbers move down road away from camera. 9.2-inch howitzer elevated and fired, cut with brickwork collapsing in a cloud of smoke and dust. Wreckage and an overturned wagon alongside a corduroy road running through muddy, shell-pocked ground – Passchendaele. HA.MS of soldiers eating in a trench – one cuts a slice of bread from a loaf while another offers his slice up to a mate to take a bite.
II. French air aces. 'PARIS RAIDERS BROUGHT DOWN. French air warriors who won great distinction in recent battle.' MS of French ace Michel Coiffard standing by his Spad – he smiles to the camera. Similar shot of second unidentified pilot. An American soldier guards the wreckage of a AEG G.IV (?).
III. US tractors undergo tests before shipment to France. 'TRACTOR'S TERRIFIC TEST. Before being shipped to the Western

Front, American tractors are tried out in Salt Marshes which are as hard to cross as shell-broken ground.' Caterpillar tractors tow over rough ground.
IV. French troops escort German POWs. 'NOT SUPERMEN. The five hundred odd prisoners taken by the French near Moncel were of poor physique and wretched appearance.' MS of French soldiers in greatcoats lining either side of the main street of a village with their commanding officer – they watch as a column of German prisoners marches through under cavalry escort.
V. Pipers of Gordon Highlanders perform in Arras. 'IN RUINED ARRAS. Pipers of the Gordon Highlanders play to the famous Regiment massed on the steps of the Cathedral.' Pipe band performs for troops gathered on grassy bank rather than steps. Pan up to show flying buttresses of Cathedral building in background.

Notes
Technical (item IV): film suffered deterioration prior to acetate transfer.
catalogued NAP: 1/1992

NTB 345-02 · GB, 6/4/1918
PICTORIAL NEWS (OFFICIAL) 345-2

b/w · 1 reel · 353' (6 mins) · silent
intertitles: English

sp Ministry of Information *pr* Topical Film Company

I. Lord Beaverbrook inspects ten 'Cine Motor-Cars'. 'GOVERNMENT'S ITINERANT WAR CINEMA. Lord Beaverbrook inspects fleet of Cine-Motors which will depict war truths in the villages.' MS over the lowered side of a truck to the rear compartment where a corporal prepares one of two projectors – pan left to show more lorries parked in the background. MS of Beaverbrook as he inspects the rank of 'Cine-Motors'. The lorries drive off – they are numbered 1-10 and each bears the legend 'Ministry of Information Cine-Motor'. A small crowd looks on.
II. American troops and French conscripts march through a French village. 'AMERICAN TROOPS AND FRENCH CONSCRIPTS. Touching tribute to heroic slain near the front.' A column of US troops precedes a group of Frenchmen through a village. More Americans follow behind.
III. Princess Alice attends Bradfield College sports, the main feature of which is a steeplechase. '"PLAYING FIELDS OF ENGLAND."' Princess Alice sees strenuous

sports tests at Bradfield College.' Chauffeur-driven car enters the school gates. Princess Alice talks with a companion. Sequence showing the steeplechase – jumping obstacles, fording the River Pang and climbing the weir. An audience of college and local children look on.
IV. Stock shots of British artillery on the move and in action. 'NO RESPITE FOR THE HUNS. British artillery moving off to action.' A limbered battery of 18-pounder guns stands bunched up in a field waiting to move out across bridge over drainage ditch. 'Firing from a village.' A 6-inch howitzer standing in a farmyard is reloaded after firing – an 18-pounder battery passes by. The howitzer fires – a party of waiting soldiers run across the line of fire as the gun is reloaded.

Notes
Summary (item I): the inspection took place on Victoria Embankment from where the lorries drove to their first engagements. The vehicles – the brainchild of one Captain Barber at the MoI – were designed to project onto a 25ft square screen over a distance of 100-120ft.
catalogued NAP: 1/1992

NTB 347-02 · GB, 18/4/1918
PICTORIAL NEWS (OFFICIAL) 347-2

b/w · 1 reel · 39' (1 min) · silent
intertitles: English

sp Ministry of Information *pr* Topical Film Company

■ Soup kitchen in Stoke Newington.

'Mr Clynes M.P. opens kitchen at Stoke Newington.' Clynes arrives and performs the opening ceremony. Shot of cheerful children holding up jugs of soup.

Notes
Summary: see also descriptive note in McKernan; a more complete Spanish-language version of this issue (with three additional stories) is held as **IWM 693e**.
catalogued JCK: 5/1993

NTB 351-02 · GB, 20/5/1918
PICTORIAL NEWS (OFFICIAL) 351-2

b/w · 1 reel · 298' (5 mins) · silent
intertitles: English

sp Ministry of Information *pr* Topical Film Company

I. Lord French is sworn in as Lord Lieutenant of Ireland, and Edward Shortt as Chief Secretary. 'LORD FRENCH IN IRELAND. New Viceroy chats with guard of Mons men at Dublin Castle.' After the ceremony of being sworn in as the new Lord Lieutenant, Lord French inspects the honour guard mounted in the Upper Yard at Dublin Castle – he speaks with several of the men. 'Mr. Edward Shortt, K.C. M.P. New Chief Secretary.' MS of Shortt in formal wear – he smiles and looks off to the left.

II. American representatives visit the Fleet at Rosyth. 'AMERICAN LABOUR DELEGATES' VISIT TO THE FLEET. They were deeply impressed by British Navy's readiness.' MS as delegates come on board from pinnace alongside to be greeted by the battleship's officers. They are shepherded off along the deck.

III. Canadian Army plays football against Londoners at Nunhead. 'BELATED, BUT KEEN FOOTBALL. Canadian Army XI. put up a good fight against Londoners at Nunhead.' The two teams enter the playing field and the game begins, watched by a sparse crowd.

IV. German POWs in French hands. 'RECENT "FRENCH OFFICIAL" ILLUSTRATED. After a successful attack at ..... we captured a few hundred prisoners.' French cavalry escort a column of German prisoners through a town – the French carry their carbines at the ready rather than the customary sabres.

V. Italian troops move along mountain roads. 'ITALIANS CROSSING THE HEIGHTS. Reinforcements moving up to a threatened sector.' HA.LS down steep slope as Italian troops file down a narrow path – a convoy of lorries is moving in the valley below. The heavily laden troops march along the main valley road.

Notes

Summary (item I): a week after his appointment French issued a proclamation declaring the discovery of a pro-German conspiracy, which was followed by the arrest of some 150 persons, including Arthur Griffith and the MPs de Valera, Cosgrave and Plunkett.

catalogued NAP: 1/1992

NTB 354-01 · GB, 6/6/1918
PICTORIAL NEWS (OFFICIAL) 354-1

b/w · 1 reel · 287' (5 mins) · silent
intertitles: English

sp Ministry of Information *pr* Topical Film Company

I. Chelsea Pensioners are inspected by General Lyttelton on Foundation Day, 1 June 1918. '"BOYS" OF THE OLD BRIGADE. Chelsea veterans reviewed by General Lyttelton on Foundation Day.' Chelsea pensioners in their formal tricorn hats march out to be inspected by the elderly General Lyttelton who is in full dress uniform. Lyttelton talks with a few of the more frail pensioners who are sitting on benches with nurses nearby. The pensioners pass in review before General Lyttelton.

II. A Buckingham Palace investiture. 'KING AND BLIND KNIGHT. Touching incident at Buckingham Palace investiture.' MS pan over audience gathered in the Quadrangle of Buckingham Palace where the King is holding an investiture. He knights an elderly civilian who is blind and is escorted away after the ceremony. MS of convalescent soldiers among the audience. Nurses receive decorations.

III. British and Italian troops man floating batteries on the Piave River. 'BRITISH TROOPS IN ITALY. Batteries on river Piave which severely punished Austrians.' MS from boat as it passes barges camouflaged with reeds secured alongside the river's edge. A fast motor boat RE.15 overtakes the cameracraft, its wake disturbing the tall reeds. Cameracraft passes a flat wooden raft carrying two Armstrong 76mm/40 AA – the Italian crew elevate the guns. A second lighter *Foca 5*, carries an Armstrong 152mm/40 naval gun. A third barge *Cane 1*, carries a Schneider 152mm/45 gun apparently served by a British crew – the barge has been deliberately listed to increase the range of the gun.

IV. German aircraft and air crew captured by the French. 'CALLOUS GERMAN HOSPITAL BOMBERS. French capture Gotha with its inglorious crew.' MS pan right to left over captured Pfalz D.III parked in a cobbled square – French troops look on. MS as five German prisoners wait by railway track before boarding a train – they seem in good spirits.

V. British troops pass a column of French refugees. 'HUN THREAT TO PARIS. British reinforcements crossing refugees in battle area.' British soldiers watch as refugees pass along a dirt road on farm wagons, bicycles and on foot. In Béthune (?) a refugee column waits while a British convoy – including a limbered 60-pounder gun – passes along the street in the opposite direction. The refugees move off after the British have passed.

Notes

Summary (item II): for this summer season the investiture ceremonies were moved from the forecourt to the less public quadrangle.

Summary (item IV): the title seems unusually imaginative. Clearly the aircraft shown is a fighter, while the German airmen are too numerous to be a Gotha crew, and seem in suspiciously good spirits for captured 'hospital bombers'.
Summary (item V): this is old film of the Battle of the Lys being recycled as the Second Battle of the Marne. See also **IWM 184**.
catalogued NAP: 1/1992

NTB 356-02 · GB, 24/6/1918
PICTORIAL NEWS (OFFICIAL) 356-2
b/w · 1 reel · 285' (5 mins) · silent
intertitles: English

sp Ministry of Information pr Topical Film Company

I. Opening of the London Flower Fair is attended by the Princess Royal. 'LONDON FLOWER FAIR. Lord Charles Beresford receives Royal party at British Ambulance Society's function in Trafalgar Square.' Admiral Lord Beresford in formal civilian dress talks with ex-Queen Amelie of Portugal – in centre frame stands the Duchess of Portland with a parasol. Beresford talks with Princess Victoria, the Princess Royal, who is standing with her niece Lady Maude Carnegie, the daughter of Princess Louise – the Duchess of Portland curtseys to the Princess. The Princess Royal and the Duchess of Portland are shown around the fair together – Princess Victoria holds a sprig of blossom.
II. A war-damaged villa at Nervesa on the River Piave, Italy. 'THE HUN TOUCH IN ITALY. Berti Solderini villa at Nervesa, containing precious frescoes by Paul Veronese, destroyed by Austrians.' MS pan over the interior of the gutted villa, and pan up to show traces of the mural work remaining high up on the walls.
III. The 301st Reserve Labour Company hold a sports day at Carshalton. 'SURREY RED CROSS SPORTS. Interesting events at 301st. Reserve Labour Coy's meeting at Carshalton.' A race is run by nurses – at the end of a length they must thread a needle (?) before running back. Soldiers race to fill buckets with stones picked up one at a time over increasing distances. A man pushes a wheelbarrow in which is seated a team-mate holding a pole which must be passed through a hole in a board suspended above the track; if the pole does not pass through the hole cleanly and the board moves, a pail of water is upset over the competitors. A pillow fight on a beam suspended over a shallow pond. An apparently conventional

100 yards dash.
IV. Clemenceau visits the Front. Foch with his staff. 'THE STRONG MEN OF FRANCE. M. Clemenceau, who embodies his countrymen's will to fight on to victory, visits the front.' Clemenceau uses neither helmet nor gas mask as he talks with staff officers at an HQ near Plémont, then visits the trenches and talks with a group of soldiers. 'General Foch, chief of Allied armies in France, with his staff.' MS pan left to right over the Marshal and his staff outside a château. Foch is talking with a US officer, and one of the staff links arms with the American for the photo-opportunity – somewhat to the latter's surprise. MCU of Foch at his ease in the grounds.
V. American forces advance at the Battle of Cantigny. 'AMERICANS GOING OVER THE TOP. The actual advance of men and tanks at Montdidier where 170 prisoners were captured.' LS as US troops rise up from trenches to advance slowly across flat grassy land – Schneider tanks support the attack. A file of men pass right to left just in front of the camera – one holds a Chauchat light machinegun.

Notes
Summary: note that English-language versions of two stories from this issue are held as **IWM 1061-05f** and **05i**, and that a French-language version is held linking two stories from this issue with one from 356-1 (**IWM 660b**).
Summary (item I): the fair was held in aid of the British Motor Ambulance Committee's work among wounded French soldiers.
Summary (item II): the Villa Berti was destroyed by bombardment on 16/11/1917. Clearly the editors were not much more artistically inclined than the Austrians, for the frescoes were by G B Tiepolo, not Veronese, and depicted allegorical scenes relating to the history of the Soderini, rather than the Solderini family. The ruins of the villa were still standing in 1925.
Summary (item IV): this particular item is taken from the French official newsreel Annales de la Guerre 64 (**IWM 508-64**).
Summary (item V): the capture on 28 May 1918, of the village of Cantigny north of Montdidier, was the first major military action by US forces in France.
catalogued NAP: 1/1992

NTB 395-01 · GB, 20/3/1919
PICTORIAL NEWS (OFFICIAL) 395-1

b/w · 1 reel · 53' (1 min) · silent
intertitles: English

sp Ministry of Information *pr* Topical Film
Company

■ Canadian soldiers embark for home after
the First World War.

'5000 CANADIANS LEAVE FOR HOME. S.S.
Olympic's historic departure from
Southampton.' Cheerful soldiers mill about
on quayside, and crowd onto the walkways
of SS *Olympic*. Caption: 'Sir Edward Kemp
(on the Right), C.F. HAYES, Capt of the
"Olympic": and Major Gen. Hogarth.' The
three men pose on board. The *Olympic*, fully
laden, prepares to set sail.

Notes
Summary: single item from newsreel issue.
catalogued JCK: 5/1993

NTB 395-02 · GB, 24/3/1919
PICTORIAL NEWS (OFFICIAL) 395-2

b/w · 1 reel · 16' (1 min) · silent
intertitles: English

sp Ministry of Information *pr* Topical Film
Company

■ Short fragment of General Allenby from
Topical Newsreel issue.

'ALLENBY WANTED IN CAIRO. Conqueror of
Palestine who was called to Peace
Conference in Paris and had to rush back to
Cairo.' Brief close-up of Allenby, in uniform,
posing for the camera.

Notes
Summary: fragment of item from newsreel
issue.
catalogued JCK: 5/1993

How to Use the Indexes

The indexes in this edition of the catalogue provide a title index, and three further indexes which give subject access by personal name, place name and unit or organisation name, respectively. Indexes refer in all cases to the film reference number (prefix IWM or NTB), *not* to pages. Many of the films described in the catalogue are too long, or too complex, for it to be possible to include in the published summary a mention of every item of interest. The indexes therefore occasionally refer to films where the presence of the person, place or unit cited is not apparent from the synopsis. Such references may be pursued at the Museum through the detailed shotsheets.

There is no index by event name as such, but the nature of the First World War means that most "events" are customarily identified by place name. There is also no index by production credit, as the level of repetition and uncertainty in the available production data makes such an index unsatisfactory. All the indexes included here are, however, edited versions of the full indexes maintained in the Department of Film, where event and credit indexes are also maintained. In order further to reduce the size of these edited indexes, the following steps have been taken.

Title · Entries for material from the *War Office Official Topical Budget* newsreel have been condensed: where material from the same issue is held under more than one film number, the index will normally point first to the most complete version held. Additional material (extra stories, or a version with foreign-language intertitles) is indicated by an *and* reference; material duplicating that which is held elsewhere is listed with the abbreviation *dup.*

Personality · Entries for several personalities have been removed. Almost all those so treated are people for whom the only entry was in one of three areas: US Army personnel identified in the series *Pictorial History of the World War* (IWM 501); athletes identified in the films of the 1924 Olympic Games (IWM 594); and delegates at the 'Little Entente' Conference at Versailles in 1920 (IWM 1042). It is hoped that by concentrating the deletions in these three areas, the reduction in usefulness of the index will be minimised.

Place · The place index is arranged by country, using country names appropriate to the period of the film. Thus, much of south-eastern Europe is listed as the Austro-Hungarian Empire, while the Middle East is similarly described, as the Ottoman Empire (subdivided by region). In countries for which there are many entries, notably England and France, places for which only a single entry was found have been consolidated at the next higher level of geographical subdivision: English counties or French départements. Many separate entries for villages in the Département of Somme have therefore been consolidated under the single heading 'Somme', although places in the region attracting several references (such as Péronne) are entered in their own right. General references to a country are grouped *after* all specific references. The arrangement of references to London is explained in the index itself.

Unit and Organisation · The index is arranged by country, using the same country names as those used in the place index. Within each country, entries are listed in the order of army, flying corps or service, navy, and civilian organisations. Within each of these categories, entries are grouped approximately by size of unit (*eg* armies, divisions, regiments, etc), and arranged alphabetically or numerically within categories. Frequently there are general references (for example, to "cavalry" or "artillery"), as well as references to specific named units.

Titles in **bold** type are main titles; ordinary type indicates other reference titles.

the **1ST BATTALION EGYPTIAN ARMY VISITS THE MOSQUE OF OMAR (sic)** (GB, 1918)
IWM 27
the **4TH CAMERON HIGHLANDERS AT BEDFORD** (GB, 1914) IWM 1185
the **5TH BATTALION ROYAL SUSSEX REGIMENT AT THE TOWER OF LONDON** (GB, 1914)
IWM 1127
[9TH DIVISION AND RAILWAY ENGINEERS] (allocated) (GB, 1918) IWM 406
27TH AND 30TH DIVISIONS (USA, 1919) IWM 503
the **44TH REMOUNT SQUADRON ON THE EGYPTIAN COAST** (GB, 1917) IWM 2
47TH STATIONARY HOSPITAL, GAZA, AND TROOPS IN PALESTINE (GB, 1918) IWM 32
1914-1918 ODD SECTIONS (ledger title) (GB, 1918) IWM 713
50,000 MILES WITH THE PRINCE OF WALES (GB, 1920) IWM 843

A LA GLOIRE DU TROUPIER BELGE 1 PARTIE (Belgium, 1919) IWM 1050
A LA GLOIRE DU TROUPIER BELGE 2 PARTIE (Belgium, 1919) IWM 1051
A LA GLOIRE DU TROUPIER BELGE 3 PARTIE (Belgium, 1919) IWM 1052
A LA GLOIRE DU TROUPIER BELGE 4 PARTIE (Belgium, 1919) IWM 1053
A LA GLOIRE DU TROUPIER BELGE 5 PARTIE (Belgium, 1919) IWM 1054
A POZSONYI KIRALYNAP (Austria-Hungary, 1917) IWM 1044
[ADMIRAL BEATTY WITH HEROES OF ZEEBRUGGE] (allocated) (GB, 1918) IWM 576
the **ADVANCE IN PALESTINE** (GB, 2/1919) IWM 38
ADVANCE OF THE CRUSADERS INTO MESOPOTAMIA - 2 (GB, 1919) IWM 78
ADVANCE OF THE CRUSADERS INTO MESOPOTAMIA - 3 (GB, 1920) IWM 79
ADVANCE OF THE CRUSADERS INTO MESOPOTAMIA - 4 (GB, 1920) IWM 80
ADVANCE OF THE CRUSADERS INTO MESOPOTAMIA - 9 (?) (alternative) IWM 82
ADVANCE OF THE CRUSADERS INTO MESOPOTAMIA (further episode) IWM 72; IWM 81
the **ADVANCE ON ST JULIEN** (GB, 7/1917) IWM 103
the **ADVANCE THROUGH NAZARETH AND DAMASCUS, SEPTEMBER 20TH-OCTOBER 1ST
1918** (GB, 2/1919) IWM 37
ADVANCED FLYING INSTRUCTION (GB, 1919) IWM 871
the **ADVENTURES OF DICK DOLAN** (GB, 1/1918) IWM 537
the **AERO COMPASS** (GB, 1920) IWM 874
AERO ENGINES (GB, 1918) IWM 200
[AEROPLANE SALVAGE AND US FORCES ON THE WESTERN FRONT, JULY 1918] (allocated)
(GB, 1918) IWM 261
[AIRCRAFT AT SEA 1] (allocated) (GB, 1918) IWM 555-03
[AIRCRAFT AT SEA 2] (allocated) (GB, 1918) IWM 578-03
[AIRCRAFT AT SEA 3] (allocated) (GB, 1917-19) IWM 866
[AIRSHIP COOPERATION WITH SUBMARINE K5] (allocated) (GB, 1918) IWM 578-01
AIRSHIPS GOING ON PATROL (GB, 1918) IWM 647
ALDER HAY HOSPITAL SPORTS (GB, 1918) IWM 241
ALIMENTANDO A UNA NACION (on copy held) IWM 548
ALLENBY IN CAIRO (1917) (GB, 1917) IWM 14
ALLENBY IN CAIRO (1918) (GB, 1918) IWM 40
[ALLENBY MEETS WEIZMANN : Tel-el-Jelil, and Arsulf] (allocated) (GB, 1918) IWM 30
ALLENBY'S CAMPAIGN (title on can) (GB, 1919) IWM 1095
AMERICA IS HERE! (GB, 1918) IWM 564
AMERICA'S ANSWER TO THE HUN (USA, 1918) IWM 458
AMERICAN CONGRESSMEN VISIT FRANCE (GB, 1918) IWM 142
AMERICAN DELEGATES AT CASSEL (GB, 1918) IWM 224
AMERICAN PRESSMEN ENTERTAINED (GB, 1918) IWM 350
AMERICAN TROOPS IN LONDON (GB, 1917) IWM 1186
AMERICAN TROOPS ON BRITISH SOIL - AN EPOCH MAKING INSPECTION BY OUR KING
(alternative) IWM 448
AMERICANS 1 (GB, 1918) IWM 240
AMERICANS 2 (GB, 1918) IWM 248
AMERICANS 3 (GB, 1918) IWM 249
[AMERICANS 4] (allocated) (GB, 1918) IWM 250
AMERICANS 5 (GB, 1918) IWM 251
AMERICANS 6 (GB, 1918) IWM 252
AMERICANS TRAINING IN FRANCE (GB, 1918) IWM 257

[AMERICANS WITH RAILWAY GUN] (allocated) (USA, 1918)   IWM 1183
AMID SNOW AND ICE ON MOUNT TONALE (Italy, 1918)   IWM 459
[AMIENS AFTER A BOMBING RAID, MAY 1918] (allocated) (GB, 1918)   IWM 227
ANNA (GB, 8/1918)   IWM 1121
ANNALES DE LA GUERRE 10 (France, 17/5/1917)   IWM 508-10
ANNALES DE LA GUERRE 11 (France, 24/5/1917)   IWM 508-11
ANNALES DE LA GUERRE 12 (France, 31/5/1917)   IWM 508-12
ANNALES DE LA GUERRE 13 (France, 8/6/1917)   IWM 508-13
ANNALES DE LA GUERRE 14 (France, 15/6/1917)   IWM 508-14
ANNALES DE LA GUERRE 15 (France, 22/6/1917)   IWM 508-15
ANNALES DE LA GUERRE 16 (France, 30/6/1917)   IWM 508-16
ANNALES DE LA GUERRE 17 (France, 7/7/1917)   IWM 508-17
ANNALES DE LA GUERRE 18 (France, 14/7/1917)   IWM 508-18
ANNALES DE LA GUERRE 19 - LES EVENEMENTS DE GRECE JUIN-JUILLET 1917 (France, 21/7/1917)   IWM 508-19
ANNALES DE LA GUERRE 20 (France, 28/7/1917)   IWM 508-20
ANNALES DE LA GUERRE 21 (France, 4/8/1917)   IWM 508-21
ANNALES DE LA GUERRE 23 (France, 18/8/1917)   IWM 508-23
ANNALES DE LA GUERRE 24 (France, 25/8/1917)   IWM 508-24
ANNALES DE LA GUERRE 25 (France, 1/9/1917)   IWM 508-25
ANNALES DE LA GUERRE 26 (France, 8/9/1917)   IWM 508-26
ANNALES DE LA GUERRE 27 (France, 15/9/1917)   IWM 508-27
ANNALES DE LA GUERRE 28 (France, 22/9/1917)   IWM 508-28
ANNALES DE LA GUERRE 29 (France, 29/9/1917)   IWM 508-29
ANNALES DE LA GUERRE 31 (France, 6/10/1917)   IWM 508-31
ANNALES DE LA GUERRE 32 (France, 10/1917)   IWM 508-32
ANNALES DE LA GUERRE 33 (France, 27/10/1917)   IWM 508-33
ANNALES DE LA GUERRE 34 (France, 3/11/1917)   IWM 508-34
ANNALES DE LA GUERRE 35 (France, 10/11/1917)   IWM 508-35
ANNALES DE LA GUERRE 36 (France, 11/1917)   IWM 508-36
ANNALES DE LA GUERRE 37 (France, 24/11/1917)   IWM 508-37
ANNALES DE LA GUERRE 38 (France, 1/12/1917)   IWM 508-38
ANNALES DE LA GUERRE 39 (France, 8/12/1917)   IWM 508-39
ANNALES DE LA GUERRE 40 (France, 15/12/1917)   IWM 508-40
ANNALES DE LA GUERRE 42 (France, 29/12/1917)   IWM 508-42
ANNALES DE LA GUERRE 43 (France, 5/1/1918)   IWM 508-43
ANNALES DE LA GUERRE 44 (France, 12/1/1918)   IWM 508-44
ANNALES DE LA GUERRE 45 (France, 19/1/1918)   IWM 508-45
ANNALES DE LA GUERRE 46 (France, 26/1/1918)   IWM 508-46
ANNALES DE LA GUERRE 47 (France, 2/2/1918)   IWM 508-47
ANNALES DE LA GUERRE 48 - EN ORIENT (France, 9/2/1918)   IWM 508-48
ANNALES DE LA GUERRE 49 (France, 16/2/1918)   IWM 508-49
ANNALES DE LA GUERRE 50 (France, 23/2/1918)   IWM 508-50
ANNALES DE LA GUERRE 51 (France, 2/3/1918)   IWM 508-51
ANNALES DE LA GUERRE 52 (France, 9/3/1918)   IWM 508-52
ANNALES DE LA GUERRE 53 (France, 16/3/1918)   IWM 508-53
ANNALES DE LA GUERRE 55 (France, 30/3/1918)   IWM 508-55
ANNALES DE LA GUERRE 56 (France, 6/4/1918)   IWM 508-56
ANNALES DE LA GUERRE 57 (France, 13/4/1918)   IWM 508-57
ANNALES DE LA GUERRE 58 - ANNIVERSAIRE DU TRAITE DE FRANKFORT (France, 20/4/1918)   IWM 508-58
ANNALES DE LA GUERRE 59 (France, 27/4/1918)   IWM 508-59
ANNALES DE LA GUERRE 60 (France, 4/5/1918)   IWM 508-60
ANNALES DE LA GUERRE 61 (France, 11/5/1918)   IWM 508-61
ANNALES DE LA GUERRE 62 (France, 18/5/1918)   IWM 508-62
ANNALES DE LA GUERRE 63 (France, 5/1918)   IWM 508-63
ANNALES DE LA GUERRE 64 (France, 1/6/1918)   IWM 508-64
ANNALES DE LA GUERRE 65 (France, 6/1918)   IWM 508-65
ANNALES DE LA GUERRE 66 (France, 6/1918)   IWM 508-66
ANNALES DE LA GUERRE 67 - L'AMERIQUE EN GUERRE (France, 6/1918)   IWM 508-67
ANNALES DE LA GUERRE 68 (France, 29/6/1918)   IWM 508-68
ANNALES DE LA GUERRE 69 (France, 6/7/1918)   IWM 508-69
ANNALES DE LA GUERRE 70 (France, 13/7/1918)   IWM 508-70

ANNALES DE LA GUERRE 71 (France, 18/7/1918) IWM 508-71
ANNALES DE LA GUERRE 72 (France, 27/7/1918) IWM 508-72
ANNALES DE LA GUERRE 73 (France, 3/8/1918) IWM 508-73
ANNALES DE LA GUERRE 74 (France, 10/8/1918) IWM 508-74
ANNALES DE LA GUERRE 75 (France, 17/8/1918) IWM 508-75
ANNALES DE LA GUERRE 76 (France, 24/8/1918) IWM 508-76
ANNALES DE LA GUERRE 76 bis (France, 25/8/1918) IWM 508-76 bis
ANNALES DE LA GUERRE 77 (France, 31/8/1918) IWM 508-77
ANNALES DE LA GUERRE 78 (France, 9/1918) IWM 508-78
ANNALES DE LA GUERRE 78 bis (France, 10/9/1918) IWM 508-78 bis
ANNALES DE LA GUERRE 79 (France, 14/9/1918) IWM 508-79
ANNALES DE LA GUERRE 80 (France, 21/9/1918) IWM 508-80
ANNALES DE LA GUERRE 81 (France, 26/9/1918) IWM 508-81
ANNALES DE LA GUERRE 82 (France, 30/9/1918) IWM 508-82
ANNALES DE LA GUERRE 83 (France, 12/10/1918) IWM 508-83
ANNALES DE LA GUERRE 84 (France, 19/10/1918) IWM 508-84
ANNALES DE LA GUERRE 85 (France, 26/10/1918) IWM 508-85
ANNALES DE LA GUERRE 86 (France, 2/11/1918) IWM 508-86
ANNALES DE LA GUERRE 88 (France, 16/11/1918) IWM 508-88
ANNALES DE LA GUERRE 89 (France, 23/11/1918) IWM 508-89
ANNALES DE LA GUERRE 90 (France, 30/11/1918) IWM 508-90
ANNALES DE LA GUERRE 91 (France, 12/1918) IWM 508-91
ANNALES DE LA GUERRE 92 (France, 1/12/1918) IWM 508-92
[ANNALES DE LA GUERRE - ADDITIONAL MATERIAL 1] (allocated) (France, 1918) IWM 511
[ANNALES DE LA GUERRE - ADDITIONAL MATERIAL 2] (allocated) (France, 1917-18) IWM 670b
**ANNUAL PROCESSION OF THE MANUNAL (HOLY CARPET) FROM THE CITADEL OF CAIRO
 TO MECCA** (GB, 8/1918) IWM 36
ANOTHER CHAPTER OF HISTORY UNVEILED (GB, 6/1917) IWM 450
ANTI-AIRCRAFT (ledger title) (GB, 1921) IWM 426
ANTI-AIRCRAFT GUNS - FRANCE (GB, 1918) IWM 298
ARMAGEDDON (GB, 1918) IWM 44
ARMISTICE DAY 1920 - HOMECOMING OF AN UNKNOWN WARRIOR (GB, 1920) IWM 505
[ARMY CAMP INSPECTION] (allocated) (GB, 1915) IWM 1066
ARMY SERVICE CORPS (GB, 1917) IWM 463
ARRAS-LENS LINE (GB, 1918) IWM 333
the **ARRIVAL AND RECEPTION OF LORD ROBERTS AT CAPETOWN** (GB, 1900) IWM 1081e
ARRIVAL OF ITALIAN BAND AT BLACKPOOL (GB, 1918) IWM 342
ARRIVAL OF NEW ZEALAND TROOPS AT COLOGNE (New Zealand, 1918) IWM 385
[ARRIVAL OF PRINCE YORIHITO OF HIGASHI-FUSHIMI IN ENGLAND, 1918] (allocated) (GB,
 1918) IWM 361
[ARRIVAL OF PRIVATE HEAVYSIDE VC IN STANLEY] (allocated) (GB, 1919) IWM 1179
the **ARRIVAL OF THE GERMAN SUBMARINES OFF HARWICH** (GB, 11/1918) IWM 646
the **ARTISTS RIFLES** (GB, 2/1918) IWM 414
[ASQUITH IN FRANCE, 1916] (allocated) (GB, 1916) IWM 715
ATTACK SOUTH OF ARRAS (GB, 1918) IWM 295
ATTACKING HARD (alternative) IWM 130-09+10
AU REVOIR ! AND GOOD LUCK : the Hallamshire Rifles leaving Sheffield, November 3rd 1914
 (GB, 1914) IWM 1136
[AUGUST OFFENSIVE 1 (?)] (allocated) (GB, 1918) IWM 290
[AUGUST OFFENSIVE 2] (alternative, allocated) IWM 295
AUGUST OFFENSIVE 3 (GB, 1918) IWM 294
[AUGUST OFFENSIVE 4] (allocated) (GB, 1918) IWM 300
AUGUST OFFENSIVE 7 (GB, 1918) IWM 302
AUGUST OFFENSIVE (related material) (allocated) (GB, 1918) IWM 317
[AUSTRALIAN AMBULANCE CONVOY] (allocated) (GB, 1916) IWM 1180a
[AUSTRALIAN AND BRITISH TROOPS IN FRANCE, 1916-18] (allocated) (GB/Australia, 1916-18)
  IWM 256
AUSTRALIAN ARTILLERY REVIEW (Australia, 1918) IWM 369
an **AUSTRALIAN BRIGADE HOLDS A WATER CARNIVAL IN THE SOMME BEFORE GOING
 INTO BATTLE** (Australia, 1918) IWM 229
AUSTRALIAN CORPS TRAINING SCHOOL (Australia, 1918) IWM 165
AUSTRALIAN ENGINEERS PREPARE A DEFENSIVE SYSTEM (Australia, 1918) IWM 173

**the AUSTRALIAN PREMIER ACCOMPANIED BY THE MINISTER FOR THE NAVY PAYS A VISIT
TO THE TROOPS IN FRANCE** (Australia, 1918)   IWM 139
AUSTRALIANS AT VILLERS BRETONNEUX (Australia, 1918)   IWM 270
AUSTRALIANS ENTRAINING (Australia, 1918)   IWM 334
AUSTRALIANS IN PERONNE (ledger title) (alternative)   IWM 331
the AUSTRALIANS IN THE SOMME ADVANCE (Australia, 1918)   IWM 286
AUSTRALIANS, ITALIANS, AND FRENCH COLONIAL TROOPS IN PALESTINE (GB, 1917)   IWM 7
AUSTRALIANS ON THE MARCH (Australia, 1918)   IWM 221
AUSTRALIANS ON THE WESTERN FRONT (Australia, 1918)   IWM 331
[AUSTRO-HUNGARIAN AND ITALIAN PRISONERS OF WAR RETURN HOME] (allocated)
(Austria-Hungary, 1919)   IWM 1035b
[AUSTRO-HUNGARIAN MATERIAL 1] (allocated) (GB & Austria-Hungary, 1916)   IWM 1062-14
[AUSTRO-HUNGARIAN MATERIAL 2] (allocated) (GB & Austria-Hungary, 1916)   IWM 1062-15
[AUSTRO-HUNGARIANS AT CAPORETTO 1] (allocated) (Austria-Hungary, 1917)   IWM 1047-01
[AUSTRO-HUNGARIANS AT CAPORETTO 2] (allocated) (Austria-Hungary, 1917)   IWM 1047-02
[AUSTRO-HUNGARIANS IN PRZEMYSL 1] (allocated) (Austria-Hungary, 1915)   IWM 1039-01
[AUSTRO-HUNGARIANS IN PRZEMYSL 2] (allocated) (Austria-Hungary, 1915)   IWM 1045c
[AUSTRO-HUNGARIANS ON THE ITALIAN FRONT 1] (allocated) (Austria-Hungary, 1917)   IWM 1034-04
AVIATION AS A RECONNOITRING POWER (France, 1917)   IWM 1132
[BAALBEC AND BEIRUT/TRIPOLI MATERIAL] (allocated) (GB, 1918)   IWM 39
BAGHDAD, BABYLON AND BAALBEC (GB, 1920)   IWM 81
[BAKU - THE OCCUPATION BY 'DUNSTERFORCE' 17TH AUGUST TO 14TH SEPTEMBER 1918]
(allocated) (GB, 1918)   IWM 73
BARROW TRIAL FLIGHT HM RIGID AIRSHIP NO 26 : taken in heavy fog Mar 20th 1918 (GB,
1918)   IWM 623
the BATTLE OF ARRAS (alternative)   IWM 113
the BATTLE OF CARENCY (fragment 1) (GB, 1915)   IWM 1061-04a
the BATTLE OF CARENCY (fragment 2) (GB, 1915)   IWM 1061-03f
the BATTLE OF THE ANCRE AND THE ADVANCE OF THE TANKS (GB, 1/1917)   IWM 116
[the BATTLE OF THE ANCRE AND THE ADVANCE OF THE TANKS (Canadian version extracts ?)]   IWM 1195
[the BATTLE OF THE ANCRE AND THE ADVANCE OF THE TANKS (extracts)]   IWM 1198
the BATTLE OF THE SCARPE (alternative)   IWM 113
the BATTLE OF THE SOMME (GB, 11/8/1916)   IWM 191
the BATTLEFIELD OF NEUVE CHAPELLE (GB, 24/4/1916)   IWM 211
the BEDFORD REGIMENT (sic) (GB, 2/1918)   IWM 388
BEHIND THE LINES (France, 1917)   IWM 1057-02
BERLIN NEWS SERVICE REPORTS (Germany, 1915)   IWM 1062-08
BETHLEHEM AND GETHSEMANE - NO 1536 (USA, 1927)   IWM 1131c
BETHLEHEM, SOLOMON'S POOL AND JERUSALEM (GB, 1917)   IWM 15
BETWEEN BELLICOURT AND BELLENGLISE (GB, 1918)   IWM 338
BLACKBERRYING IN BRENTFORD (GB, 1918)   IWM 311
BLOCKADE (GB, 1932)   IWM 1176
BOBS (GB, 1914)   IWM 1071
a BOMB PROOF LODGING (GB, 1918)   IWM 163
BOMBING SCHOOL AND SPORTS (GB, 1918)   IWM 34
a BOMBING TRIP OVER THE ENEMY LINES (Australia, 1918)   IWM 236
**BOOM JUMPING TRIALS WITH COASTAL MOTOR BOAT NO 11 : as carried out off Osea
Island on March 23rd - 25th 1920** (GB, 1920)   IWM 567
BOXING IN THE GRAND FLEET (ledger title) (GB, 1918)   IWM 579
BRITAIN PREPARED : a review of the activities of His Majesty's naval and military forces (GB,
29/12/1915)   IWM 580
BRITAIN'S BIRTHRIGHT (GB, 1924)   IWM 842
BRITAIN'S EFFORT : drawings by Lancelot Speed (GB, 6/1918)   IWM 514
BRITAIN'S FUTURE AIR FIGHTERS (GB, 3/1918)   IWM 632
BRITISCHE SPORT EN SPELEN IN TIJD VAN VREDE EN OORLOG (on copy held) (GB, 1916)   IWM 691
**BRITISH ADVANCE ON THE EUPHRATES UNDER THE COMMAND OF MAJOR-GENERAL
BROOKING** (GB, 1920)   IWM 82
[BRITISH ARMY AMBULANCE DRIVERS] (allocated) (GB, 1917)   IWM 1134
BRITISH CALL TO THE NATION (GB, 1914-16)   IWM 512

BRITISH EFFICIENCY (GB, 1916)   IWM 432
BRITISH EMPIRE AND AMERICAN SERVICES SPORTS, STAMFORD BRIDGE, SEPT 7TH 1918
   (GB, 1918)   IWM 633
the **BRITISH ENTRY INTO COLOGNE** (GB, 1918)   IWM 376
BRITISH FORCES IN PERIL (GB, 1919)   IWM 422
[**BRITISH GENERALS IN MESOPOTAMIA AND PALESTINE 1918**] (allocated) (GB/USA, 1918)
                                                                                            IWM 43
BRITISH HORSE SHOW IN ITALY (GB, 1918)   IWM 225
[**BRITISH INFANTRY MARCHING**] (allocated) (GB, 1915)   IWM 1177a
[**BRITISH INFANTRY REGIMENTS (various fragments)**] (allocated) (GB, 1918)   IWM 429
BRITISH MOVIETONE NEWS [1932] - RAF LINKS EMPIRE'S FAR FLUNG COLONIES (GB, 1932)
                                                                                            IWM 880-02c
BRITISH NAVAL ACTIVITIES AFTER THE GREAT BRITISH VICTORY OF JUTLAND (GB, 9/1918)
                                                                                            IWM 577
BRITISH OFFENSIVE (alternative)   IWM 332
[the BRITISH REGIMENTS] (series, allocated)
        IWM 388; IWM 389; IWM 390; IWM 391; IWM 392; IWM 393; IWM 394; IWM 395; IWM 396;
        IWM 397; IWM 398; IWM 399; IWM 400; IWM 401; IWM 402; IWM 403; IWM 404; IWM 408;
     IWM 414; IWM 415; IWM 416; IWM 417; IWM 425; IWM 427; IWM 430; IWM 1099; IWM 1100
BRITISH SCREEN NEWS [1930] - BALTIC CRUISE (GB, 1930)   IWM 880-01c
BRITISH SCREEN NEWS [1930] - [R101] (allocated) (GB, 1930)   IWM 880-01g
BRITISH SCREEN NEWS [1930] - THE FLYING BLUES (GB, 1930)   IWM 880-01d
BRITISH SCREEN NEWS [1931] - THE SCHNEIDER TROPHY (GB, 1931)   IWM 880-01a
BRITISH SOLDIERS INTERNED IN HOLLAND (GB, 1918)   IWM 455
BRITISH SOLDIERS INTERNED IN SWITZERLAND (GB, 1918)   IWM 453
[BRITISH SPORTS AND GAMES IN TIME OF PEACE AND WAR] (translation)   IWM 691
[**BRITISH TANKS IN COLOGNE**] (allocated) (GB, 1920)   IWM 1174
BRITISH TROOPS IN ITALY (GB, 1918)   IWM 154
[**BRITISH TROOPS IN SALONIKA - 1**] (allocated) (GB/USA, 1917)   IWM 95
[**BRITISH TROOPS IN SALONIKA - 2**] (allocated) (GB/USA, 1917)   IWM 96
[**BRITISH TROOPS IN SALONIKA - 3**] (allocated) (GB, 1917)   IWM 98
[**BRITISH TROOPS ON THE WESTERN FRONT, MAY 1918**] (allocated) (GB, 1918)   IWM 226
BRITISH WOMEN'S AIR FORCE (GB, 1918)   IWM 1107-01
[**BUICK TRACTOR**] (allocated) (USA, 1916)   IWM 1199
BUILDING A CONCRETE SHIP (GB, 1918)   IWM 584
BUILDING A NISSEN HUT (GB, 1917)   IWM 125
the **CAIRO BAGHDAD SERVICE AIRMAIL** (GB, 1924)   IWM 878
the **CALL TO THE YOUNG** (GB, 1916)   IWM 444
CAMBRAI OFFENSIVE (GB, 1918)   IWM 144
CAMELS AND JAFFA (GB, 1917)   IWM 20
[**CANADIAN CORPS HQ AND SCENES NEAR BAPAUME, MARCH 1918**] (allocated) (GB, 1918)
                                                                                            IWM 177
CANADIAN JOURNALISTS AT BRAMSHOT AND WITLEY (GB, 1918)   IWM 274
CANADIAN JOURNALISTS LEAVE LONDON (GB, 1918)   IWM 297
CANADIAN OFFICER'S WEDDING AT ST JAMES'S (GB, 1918)   IWM 362
CANADIAN PRESSMEN VISIT LORD BEAVERBROOK (GB, 1918)   IWM 273
[**CANADIAN SECTIONS 1**] (allocated) (GB, 1917)   IWM 1188
[**CANADIAN SECTIONS 2**] (allocated) (GB, 1917)   IWM 1189
[**CANADIAN SECTOR OF THE WESTERN FRONT IN JULY 1918**] (allocated) (GB, 1918)   IWM 271
[**CANADIAN TANKS**] (allocated) (GB/Canada, 1917)   IWM 1195
the **CANADIAN VICTORY AT COURCELETTE : and the advance of the tanks** (GB, 1917)
                                                                                            IWM 466
[the CANADIAN VICTORY AT COURCELETTE AND THE ADVANCE OF THE TANKS (extracts ?)]
   (related)   IWM 1195
CANADIANS EAST OF ARRAS (Canada, 1918)   IWM 316
the **CAPTURE OF MESSINES** (GB, 7/1917)   IWM 197
the CAPTURE OF PERONNE (alternative)   IWM 131
CARDINAL BOURNE VISITS THE IRISH TROOPS IN FRANCE (GB, 1917)   IWM 111
the **CARE OF OUR WOUNDED** (GB, 1918)   IWM 162
[CARELESS TALK] (translation)   IWM 778
CAVALRY EQUITATION SCHOOL (GB, 1918)   IWM 280
[**CELEBRATIONS IN PARIS, 14TH JULY 1918**] (allocated) (GB, 1918)   IWM 296

CHAPPERTON DOWN ARTILLERY SCHOOL (GB, 1916)   IWM 108
the CHESHIRE REGIMENT (GB, 1/1918)   IWM 389
CHINESE ENTERTAINING ALLIED TROOPS (GB, 1918)   IWM 231
a CHINESE LABOUR CONTINGENT (GB, 11/1917)   IWM 410
CHINESE NEW YEAR CELEBRATIONS IN FRANCE (GB, 1918)   IWM 168
CIVILIANS FALL IN (alternative)   IWM 516
[CLERGET 9Z ENGINE CONSTRUCTION] (allocated) (GB, 1917)   IWM 1062-13
COLLECTION OF ORIGINAL PLANES IN THE JARRETT MUSEUM OF WORLD WAR HISTORY :
    formerly maintained Moorestown NJ (USA, 1939)   IWM 1010
COLOGNE AIRMAIL (GB, 1919)   IWM 877
COLONEL SAMSON AND DH4 (GB, 1918)   IWM 643
COLONIAL INFANTRY AND CAVALRY MARCHING ACROSS THE VELDT (GB, 1900)   IWM 1081a
COLONIAL PRESSMEN (GB, 1918)   IWM 314
COMBINED PLATOON TRAINING ON ASH RANGE (GB, 1920)   IWM 407
un CONTINGENTE DE TRABAJADORES CHINOS (on copy held)   IWM 410
COOPER'S DIAGRAMS - HOUNSLOW (GB, 1917)   IWM 275
CORONATION OF HIS MAJESTY KING GEORGE V (GB, 1911)   IWM 1082-02b
[the CORONATION OF KARL OF HUNGARY PART 1] (allocated) (Austria-Hungary, 1917)
    IWM 1034-01b
[the CORONATION OF KARL OF HUNGARY PART 2] (allocated) (Austria-Hungary, 1917)
    IWM 1039-02
[the CORONATION OF KING EDWARD VII] (allocated) (GB, 1902)   IWM 1080a
CRAMP IN THE NECK IN LONDON (Germany, 1916)   IWM 1208
CROSSING OF THE AUJA, MULEBBIS, GUNS NEAR JERUSALEM (GB, 1917)   IWM 16
CSAPATAINK HOSI HARCA A HAVASOK SZIKLAIBAN ES JEGEBEN (Austria-Hungary, 1918)
    IWM 1084
CSAPATAINK HOSI HARCA A HAVASOK SZIKLAIBAN ES JEGEBEN - PART I (incomplete
    version) (Austria-Hungary, 1918)   IWM 1038
CSAPATAINK HOSI HARCA A HAVASOK SZIKLAIBAN ES JEGEBEN - PART II (incomplete
    version) (Austria-Hungary, 1918)   IWM 1043a
the CURE FOR POTATO BLIGHT (GB, 6/1918)   IWM 549-07
the DAILY DINNER (GB, 1918)   IWM 523
a DAY IN THE LIFE OF A LONDON POLICEMAN (GB, 1917)   IWM 1062-18
a DAY IN THE LIFE OF A MUNITION WORKER (GB, 7/1917)   IWM 510
a DAY ON A MINE-SWEEPER (GB, 1918)   IWM 582
a DAY WITH THE BATTALION OF THE WELSH GUARDS (GB, 1915)   IWM 1215
DECK LANDING (GB, 1918)   IWM 631
DEFENDERS OF EGYPT (GB, 1916)   IWM 1178
DEIR EL BELAH (GB, 1918)   IWM 10
DEMOBILISATION FILM (GB, 1918)   IWM 486
[DEPARTURE OF 6TH BATTLE SQUADRON] (allocated) (GB, 1918)   IWM 588
DEPTFORD RED CROSS WEEK (GB, 1918)   IWM 307
the DESPATCH BEARER (GB, 1900)   IWM 1081g
the DESTRUCTION OF A FOKKER (offcuts and mixed material)   IWM 298
the DESTRUCTION OF A FOKKER : our mobile anti-aircraft guns in action (GB, 19/6/1916)
    IWM 470
DESTRUCTION OF A GERMAN BLOCKHOUSE BY A 9.2 HOWITZER (GB, 28/2/1916)   IWM 259
un DEUIL NATIONAL - LA MORT DU MARECHAL FOCH (France, 1929)   IWM 509
DON'T WASTE DISEASED POTATOES : make them into flour (GB, 5/1918)   IWM 549-06
the DORSET REGIMENT (GB, 2/1918)   IWM 403
DOUAI AND LILLE (GB, 1918)   IWM 360
[the DUKE OF CONNAUGHT AND ALLENBY INSPECTING TROOPS ON THE PALESTINE
    FRONT, MARCH 1918] (allocated) (GB, 1918)   IWM 25
the DUKE OF CONNAUGHT REVIEWS THE GUARDS (GB, 1917)   IWM 117
the DUKE OF CONNAUGHT'S VISIT TO THE ARMIES (GB, 9/1917)   IWM 119
the DURHAM LIGHT INFANTRY (GB, 12/1917)   IWM 399
DURING THE ARMISTICE (ledger title) (GB, 1918)   IWM 367
DUTCH GENERALS VIEWING THE BATTLEFIELD (GB, 1917)   IWM 136
EARL KITCHENER OF KHARTOUM (GB, 1919)   IWM 1126
the EAST KENT REGIMENT (THE BUFFS) (sic) (GB, 12/1917)   IWM 400
the EAST YORKS REGIMENT (GB, 2/1918)   IWM 427
EASTER RISING, DUBLIN 1916 (GB, 1916)   IWM 194
[ECLAIR NEWSREEL (1915 fragment)] (allocated) (GB, 1915)   IWM 1055c

the ECONOMISTS (GB, 2/1917) IWM 515
an EGYPTIAN LABOUR CONTINGENT (GB, 12/1917) IWM 3
EIGHT YEARS AFTER (GB, 1924) IWM 1059
EL MEJDEL, JAFFA AND WEST COUNTRY TROOPS (GB, 1917) IWM 12
EMBRYO AIRMEN (GB, 1918) IWM 615
the EMIGRANT (alternative) IWM 1061-04g
the EMPIRE'S SHIELD : the Royal Navy (GB, 10/1918) IWM 551
the END OF A WELL FOUGHT WAR : the Peace Procession 1919 (GB, 1919) IWM 439
the END OF AN AIR RAID OCTOBRE (sic) 19.10.1917 (alternative) IWM 880-02d
[the ENGLISH COLONY IN INDIA] (allocated) (GB, 1925) IWM 816
[the ENGLISH COLONY IN NEW ZEALAND] (translation) IWM 815
ENROL FOR NATIONAL SERVICE AND BACK UP THE BOYS IN THE TRENCHES (GB, 1918)
IWM 524
[EPERNAY] (allocated) (GB, 1918) IWM 244
the ESSEX REGIMENT (GB, 3/1918) IWM 394
the ESSEX REGIMENT CROSSING THE VAAL RIVER ON THE WAGON PUNT (GB, 1900)
IWM 1081b
EVERY LITTLE HELPS (first version) (GB, 1918) IWM 447A
EVERY LITTLE HELPS (second version) (GB, 1918) IWM 447B
EVERY LITTLE HELPS (second version, additional material) (GB, 1918) IWM 447X
EVERYBODY'S BUSINESS (GB, 6/1917) IWM 516
EXODUS OF THE POPULATION (GB, 1917) IWM 473
EXPERIMENT OF LAUNCHING SEAPLANE BY CATAPULT METHOD : carried out with Fairey
Seaplane N9 on HMS Slinger (GB, 9/1917) IWM 1166
EXPERIMENTS IN LANDING A SOPWITH CAMEL ON WATER USING INTERNAL AIRBAGS
ONLY (GB, 1918) IWM 629
EXPERIMENTS IN LANDING AEROPLANES AND SEAPLANES FROM SHIP'S DECK (GB, 1918)
IWM 1167
the EXPLOITS OF A GERMAN SUBMARINE (U-35) OPERATING IN THE MEDITERRANEAN
(Germany & GB, 11/1918) IWM 560
the EYES OF THE ARMY (GB, 1922) IWM 1005
the EYES OF THE ARMY : with the RFC at the front (GB, 17/4/1916) IWM 118
FAIREY SEAPLANES (GB, 1918) IWM 614
the FATE OF A SUBMARINE (GB, 1919) IWM 561
FATHER AND LATHER (GB, 5/1918) IWM 1122
FEEDING A NATION (GB, 3/1918) IWM 548
FELIXSTOWE SPORTS 13/8/1918 (GB, 1918) IWM 642
FETE AT SAINTE MARIE (GB, 1918) IWM 318
the FIFTH BATTALION ROYAL SUSSEX REGIMENT AT THE TOWER OF LONDON (filing)
IWM 1127
FIFTY THOUSAND MILES WITH THE PRINCE OF WALES (filing) IWM 843
the FIGHT AT ST ELOI (GB, 5/6/1916) IWM 215
FIGHTING IN FLANDERS : with the Australian Imperial Forces on the Western Front (Australia,
1917) IWM 158
FIGHTING U-BOATS IN A LONDON BACK GARDEN (GB, 5/1918) IWM 549-10
[FILM TAGS] (series, allocated)
IWM 533; IWM 549-01; IWM 549-02; IWM 549-03; IWM 549-04; IWM 549-05;
IWM 549-06; IWM 549-07; IWM 549-08; IWM 549-09; IWM 549-10; IWM 1121; IWM 1122;
IWM 1128b; IWM 1177b
les FILMS SPORTIFS (series) IWM 594-02+3; IWM 594-04-13
la FIN D'UN RAID 19-20 OCTOBRE 1917 (France, 1917) IWM 880-02d
FIRE FIGHTING WITH AEROPLANES (Canada, 1922) IWM 861
FIRST BATTALION EGYPTIAN ARMY VISITS THE MOSQUE OF OMAR (filing) IWM 27
FIRST VISIT OF AN ENGLISH FLYING-BOAT TO KRISTIANIA JULI 1919 (sic) (Norway, 1919)
IWM 1063
the FIRST WORLD WAR (USA, 1934) IWM 484
[FIRST WORLD WAR BATTLESHIPS AND DESTROYERS 1] (allocated) (GB, 1918) IWM 555-01
[FIRST WORLD WAR BATTLESHIPS AND DESTROYERS 2] (allocated) (GB, 1918) IWM 555-02
[FIRST WORLD WAR FRAGMENTS] (allocated) (GB, 1918) IWM 499
[FIRST WORLD WAR MAPS 1] (allocated) (GB, 1918) IWM 1031
[FIRST WORLD WAR MAPS 2] (allocated) (GB, 1918) IWM 1032
FIVE YEARS AGO (GB, 1923) IWM 442
FLAME THROWER (ledger title) (GB, 1916) IWM 604

FLAME THROWN OUT OF GAS EJECTOR (ledger title) (GB, 1917)   IWM 424
FLASHES OF ACTION (USA, 1919)   IWM 502
FOOD CONTROL DELEGATES AT CONFERENCE (ledger title) (GB, 1918)   IWM 292
FOR THE EMPIRE (GB, 20/4/1916)   IWM 714
the FORTY FOURTH REMOUNT SQUADRON ON THE EGYPTIAN COAST (filing)   IWM 2
FORTY SEVENTH STATIONARY HOSPITAL, GAZA, AND TROOPS IN PALESTINE (filing)   IWM 32
the FOURTH CAMERON HIGHLANDERS AT BEDFORD (filing)   IWM 1185
[FRANZ FERDINAND IN SARAJEVO] (allocated) (France/Hungary, 7/1914)   IWM 1046a
[FRANZ FERDINAND'S MEMORIAL CEREMONY] (allocated) (Austria-Hungary, 1914) IWM 1041b
[FRANZ FERDINAND'S MEMORIAL CEREMONY] (allocated) (Austria-Hungary, 14/7/1914)
                                                                          IWM 1046b
[FRANZ JOSEF : still portraits etc] (allocated) (Austria-Hungary, 1917)   IWM 1034-01c
[FRANZ JOSEF AT BAD ISCHL] (allocated) (Austria-Hungary, 1912)   IWM 1033a
[FRANZ JOSEF VISITS POLA] (allocated) (Austria-Hungary, 1912)   IWM 1033c
[FRANZ JOSEF VISITS SANKT PÖLTEN] (allocated) (Austria-Hungary, 1912)   IWM 1033d
[FRANZ JOSEF'S FUNERAL PART 1] (allocated) (Austria-Hungary, 1916)   IWM 1041a
[FRANZ JOSEF'S FUNERAL PART 3] (allocated) (Austria-Hungary, 1916)   IWM 1040
[FRATERNISATION BETWEEN BRITISH AND GERMAN SOLDIERS AT ATH] (allocated) (GB,
  1918)   IWM 368
FRENCH OFFICIAL WAR FILMS (on copy held)   IWM 508-84
FRENCH OFFICIAL WAR FILMS (on copy held)   IWM 508-85
FROM A LOOK-OUT'S POINT OF VIEW (GB, 1916)   IWM 569
FROM SOLDIER TO CIVILIAN (GB, 1918)   IWM 457
FULHAM'S GUN DAY (GB, 1918)   IWM 346
FUN AND SPORTS AT ALDERSHOT (ledger title) (GB, 1914-18)   IWM 527
[the FUNERAL OF PRESIDENT FAURE] (allocated) (France, 1899)   IWM 1082-04
[GAS FILM CAPTIONS] (allocated) (GB, 1918)   IWM 1103
[GAS SHELLS] (allocated) (GB, 1917)   IWM 1102
[GAS WORKS] (allocated) (GB, 1917-18)   IWM 546
[GASMASKS OF THE FIRST WORLD WAR] (allocated) (GB, 1917)   IWM 276
GAUMONT BRITISH NEWS [1931] - LATEST 'HUSH HUSH' FLYING BOATS (GB, 1931)
                                                                          IWM 880-02a
GAUMONT BRITISH NEWS [5/1937] - THE CORONATION (GB, 5/1937)   IWM 1085
GAUMONT GRAPHIC 151 (GB, 8/1912)   IWM 1061-03b and IWM 1061-03d
GAUMONT GRAPHIC 157 (GB, 8/1912)   IWM 1061-05g
GAUMONT GRAPHIC 165 (GB, 10/1912)   IWM 1061-06i
GAUMONT GRAPHIC 232 (GB, 6/1913)   IWM 1061-07c
GAUMONT GRAPHIC 364 (GB, 17/9/1914)   IWM 1061-05d
GAUMONT GRAPHIC 368 (GB, 1/10/1914)   IWM 1061-09m
GAUMONT GRAPHIC 370 (GB, 8/10/1914)   IWM 1061-05e
GAUMONT GRAPHIC 374 (GB, 22/10/1914)   IWM 1061-09k and IWM 1061-09o
GAUMONT GRAPHIC 386 (GB, 3/12/1914)   IWM 1061-09h and IWM 1061-09j
GAUMONT GRAPHIC 394 (GB, 31/12/1914)   IWM 1061-03c
GAUMONT GRAPHIC 395 (GB, 4/1/1915)   IWM 1061-03a
GAUMONT GRAPHIC 415 (GB, 2/1915)   IWM 1061-09i and IWM 1061-09l; IWM 1061-09n
GAUMONT GRAPHIC 420 (GB, 3/1915)   IWM 1061-04b and IWM 1061-06c
GAUMONT GRAPHIC 421 (GB, 3/1915)   IWM 1061-04d and IWM 1061-04g
GAUMONT GRAPHIC 423 (GB, 3/1915)   IWM 1061-06m
GAUMONT GRAPHIC 426 (GB, 3/1915)   IWM 1061-04e and IWM 1061-06b; IWM 1061-06h
GAUMONT GRAPHIC 436 (GB, 5/1915)
            IWM 1061-04c and IWM 1061-06a; IWM 1061-06d; IWM 1061-07d; IWM 1061-07f
GAUMONT GRAPHIC 438 (GB, 5/1915)   IWM 1061-06g
GAUMONT GRAPHIC 439 (GB, 6/1915)   IWM 1061-07e and IWM 1061-07g
GAUMONT GRAPHIC 441 (GB, 6/1915)   IWM 1061-03g
GAUMONT GRAPHIC 447 (GB, 6/1915)   IWM 1061-06f
GAUMONT GRAPHIC 448 (GB, 6/1915)   IWM 1061-04f and IWM 1061-06e
GAUMONT GRAPHIC 451 (GB, 7/1915)   IWM 1061-06k
GAUMONT GRAPHIC 503 (GB, 1/1916)   IWM 1061-08b
GAUMONT GRAPHIC 534 - GRAND RECEPTION OF THE RUSSIAN TROOPS AT MARSEILLES
  BY THE FRENCH (GB, 5/1917)   IWM 469
GAUMONT GRAPHIC 740 - WOMEN'S LAND ARMY (GB, 5/1918)   IWM 536
GAUMONT GRAPHIC 775 (GB, 7/1918)   IWM 1061-06l

GAUMONT GRAPHIC [800 approx] - THE SURRENDER OF THE GERMAN NAVY (GB, 1919)
IWM 1212
GAUMONT GRAPHIC [900 approx] - GIFT TO THE BRITISH NATION (GB, 1920)   IWM 507
GAUMONT GRAPHIC 962 - THE OPENING OF THE IMPERIAL WAR MUSEUM (GB, 6/1920)
IWM 504
GAUMONT GRAPHIC 1104 (GB, 10/10/1921)   IWM 1082-02a
GAUMONT GRAPHIC 1182 (GB, 7/1922)   IWM 1142
GAUMONT GRAPHIC 1534 (GB, 12/1925)   IWM 810
[GAUMONT GRAPHIC - SS GALICIAN STORY] (allocated) (GB, 1914)   IWM 1061-07a
[GAUMONT TURKISH MATERIAL] (allocated) (GB, 1914)   IWM 1061-06j
GAZA (GB, 1918)   IWM 11
GAZETTE D'ACTUALITE (on copy held)   IWM 667
GENERAL ALLENBY'S ENTRY INTO JERUSALEM (GB, 21/2/1918)   IWM 13
GENERAL BIRDWOOD PRESENTING MEDALS TO THIRD AUSTRALIAN DIVISION (Australia,
1917)   IWM 151
GENERAL BIRDWOOD PRESENTS THE FIFTH ARMY TO THE MAYOR OF LILLE (GB, 1918)
IWM 363
GENERAL DE LISLE PRESENTING MEDALS TO OFFICERS AND MEN (GB, 1916)   IWM 107
[GENERAL PERSHING'S ARRIVAL IN FRANCE] (allocated) (GB, 1917)   IWM 137
GENERAL PLUMER DECORATING NURSES (GB, 1918)   IWM 268
[GENERAL RAWLINSON'S HEADQUARTERS AND AUSTRALIAN TROOPS, 1918] (allocated)
(Australia, 1918)   IWM 354
GENERAL SARRAIL IN THE EAST (GB, 1916)   IWM 1062-10
GEORGE ROBEY VISITS THE MERCHANT SERVICE (alternative)   IWM 320
GERMAN NAVAL INACTIVITIES (GB, 1918)   IWM 303
GERMAN NAVY FORCED TO AN INGLORIOUS SURRENDER (on copy held)   IWM 571
[GERMAN NEWSREEL ITEMS] (allocated) (Germany, 1915-16)   IWM 1072
GERMAN OFFENSIVE 1 (GB, 1918)   IWM 178
GERMAN OFFENSIVE 2 (GB, 1918)   IWM 179
GERMAN OFFENSIVE 3 (GB, 1918)   IWM 180
GERMAN OFFENSIVE 4 (GB, 1918)   IWM 181
GERMAN OFFENSIVE 5 (GB, 1918)   IWM 182
GERMAN OFFENSIVE 6 (GB, 1918)   IWM 183
GERMAN OFFENSIVE 7 (GB, 1918)   IWM 184
GERMAN OFFENSIVE 8 (GB, 1918)   IWM 185
GERMAN OFFENSIVE 9 (GB, 1918)   IWM 186
GERMAN OFFENSIVE 10 (GB, 1918)   IWM 187
GERMAN OFFENSIVE 11 (GB, 1918)   IWM 188
GERMAN OFFENSIVE 12 (GB, 1918)   IWM 189
GERMAN OFFENSIVE 13 (GB, 1918)   IWM 190
GERMAN OFFICER PRISONERS : a prisoner of war camp in England (GB, 1917) IWM 436
GERMAN PRISONERS - SCENES AT LA BOZELLE (sic) (GB, 1917)   IWM 349
GERMAN PRISONERS IN FRANCE (GB, 1915)   IWM 343
[GERMAN PRISONERS IN FRANCE (continuation)] (allocated) (GB, 1915) IWM 1062-16
GERMAN PRISONERS OF WAR : camp in England for non-commissioned officers and men
(GB, 7/1917)   IWM 441
the GERMAN RETREAT AND THE BATTLE OF ARRAS (GB, 6/6/1917)   IWM 113
the GERMAN RETREAT TO ST QUENTIN (GB, 12/1917)   IWM 121
[GERMAN TANK TRAPS 1918] (allocated) (GB, 1918)   IWM 378
[GERMAN TROOPS IN RUSSIAN POLAND] (allocated) (Germany, 1915)   IWM 1062-07
[GERMAN U-BOATS LYING AT HARWICH] (alternative, allocated)   IWM 695
GHQ TEST FILM (GB, 1917)   IWM 247
GIVE 'EM BEANS (GB, 5/1918)   IWM 549-02
GLIMPSES OF THE BRITISH NAVY IN WAR TIME (alternative)   IWM 130-03+4
the GOLDEN JUBILEE OF THE RFC (GB, 1962)   IWM 1030
GRAHAM WHITE'S FIRST ANNUAL SPORTS (GB, 1918)   IWM 299
GRAND FLEET AIRCRAFT ROYAL AIR FORCE (GB, 1918)   IWM 638
the GRAVE OF MAJOR W REDMOND (GB, 1917)   IWM 120
the GREAT BRITISH OFFENSIVE (GB, 1918)   IWM 322
the GREAT GAME (GB, 1918)   IWM 519
the GREAT GERMAN RETREAT (GB, 1917)   IWM 131
a GREAT SERVANT OF A GREAT EMPIRE (GB, 1916)   IWM 1062-03
[the GREAT WAR : US stockshot material] (allocated) (GB, 1960)   IWM 1049

GRIFFITH AT THE FRONT (GB, 1917) IWM 122
la GUERRE ANGLAISE : grand film documentaire en 4 parts - les tanks anglais a la bataille de
la Scarpe (GB, 1917) IWM 233
GUNS (GB, 1918) IWM 264
GUNS - BREECH MECHANISM (GB, 1918) IWM 263
[HAIG AND HIS ARMY COMMANDERS ON 11TH NOVEMBER 1918] (allocated) (GB, 1918)
IWM 132
HAIG AT COLOGNE (ledger title) (GB, 1918) IWM 381
HANDLING GAS CYLINDERS (ledger title) (GB, 1916) IWM 617
HANDS ACROSS THE SEA (GB, 1918) IWM 563
the HARVEST OF THE SUGAR MAPLE TREE (Canada, 1920) IWM 812
[the HAT IN THE RING SQUADRON] (alternative, allocated) IWM 250
HAULING DOWN A KITE BALLOON BY HAND (ledger title) (GB, 1916) IWM 616
HEARTS OF THE WORLD (production scenes) IWM 122
HEBRON (GB, 1918) IWM 24
[HENDON AIR RACE] (allocated) (GB, 1913) IWM 1091a
HER SAVINGS SAVED (GB, 5/1918) IWM 533
HEROES OF GALLIPOLI (Australia, 1920) IWM 1058
the HERTFORDSHIRE REGIMENT (GB, 3/1918) IWM 1099
HIS ROYAL HIGHNESS THE DUKE OF CONNAUGHT INSPECTS CADETS AT THE IMPERIAL
SCHOOL OF INSTRUCTION, ZEITOUN (GB, 4/1918) IWM 21
an HISTORICAL OCCASION : the arrival of the advance guard of America's fighting forces in
British waters (GB, 5/1917) IWM 562
HM KING GEORGE V INSPECTS AMERICAN TROOPS (GB, 1917) IWM 448
HM QUEEN MARY AT CHATHAM AND COVENTRY (GB, 1918) IWM 446
HM R27 TRIAL FLIGHT INCHINNAN 8/6/1918 6.15PM TO 9.30PM (GB, 1918) IWM 624
HM THE KING AT THE ADMIRALTY COMPASS OBSERVATORY (GB, 1918) IWM 313
HM THE KING ON THE CLYDE (GB, 1918) IWM 140
HM THE KING'S VISIT TO THE TANK SCHOOL, WOOL, DORSET (GB, 1918) IWM 356
HM VISIT TO THE GRAND FLEET (GB, 7/1917) IWM 556
HMS ARGUS ALIGHTING TRIALS (GB, 1918) IWM 627
[HMS MOTH AND HMS CADDIS FLY (?)] (allocated) (GB/USA, 1918) IWM 71
[HMS ST VINCENT TAKES IN SAIL] (allocated) (GB, 1900) IWM 598
HOLMES LECTURE FILM (GB, 1919) IWM 468
the HOME OF THE COASTAL MOTOR BOAT (GB, 1919-20) IWM 566
HOME ON LEAVE (GB, 31/7/1916) IWM 220
el HOMENAJE DEL URUGUAY A LOS RESTOS DE SIR ERNEST SHACKLETON (Uruguay, 1922)
IWM 506
the HORSE AND THE AEROPLANE (GB, 1955) IWM 634
HORSE SHOW AND SPORTS (GB, 1918) IWM 33
HOSPITAL BOMBED BY GERMANS, AND FUNERAL OF THE VICTIMS (GB, 1918) IWM 232
HOUNSLOW MOTOR DRIVING SCHOOL (GB, 1918) IWM 242
HOW ENGLAND PREPARED (US release title) IWM 580
HOW THE BRITISH ARMY BROKE THE FAMOUS HINDENBURG LINE (GB, 1918) IWM 332
HOW TO PREPARE AN 'L' TYPE CAMERA (GB, 1918) IWM 872
HOW TO SAVE TIME WITH YOUR POTATOES (GB, 5/1918) IWM 549-08
HOW WE TREAT OUR WOUNDED (ledger title) (GB, 1918) IWM 1097
HRH THE PRINCE OF WALES WITH THE GUARDS IN THE FRONT LINE (GB, 13/3/1916)
IWM 207
HUGE BOMBING MACHINES (GB, 1918) IWM 234
[HUNGARIAN ARCHIVE MATERIAL] (series, allocated)
IWM 1033a; IWM 1033b; IWM 1033c; IWM 1033d; IWM 1034-01a; IWM 1034-01b;
IWM 1034-01c; IWM 1034-03; IWM 1034-04; IWM 1035a; IWM 1035b; IWM 1035c;
IWM 1038; IWM 1039-01; IWM 1039-02; IWM 1040; IWM 1041a; IWM 1041b;
IWM 1042; IWM 1043a; IWM 1043b; IWM 1044; IWM 1045a; IWM 1045b; IWM 1045c;
IWM 1045d; IWM 1046a; IWM 1046b; IWM 1047-01; IWM 1047-02
HUNS SURRENDERING BATTLEPLANES - BRITISH AIRMAN TAKES A TRIP IN A FOKKER (GB,
1918) IWM 379
HUNTINGDON WORKSHOP (GB, 1918) IWM 167
the HUSSARS (GB, 12/1917) IWM 395
IDEAS FOR INCREASED FOOD PRODUCTION (GB, 5/1918) IWM 549-05
the IMMORTAL STORY OF ZEEBRUGGE (GB, 1918) IWM 656b
[the IMPERIAL VISIT TO PRESSBURG] (translation) IWM 1044

IN ACTION WITH OUR CANADIAN TROOPS (GB, 20/3/1916)   IWM 255
IN THE WAKE OF CAPTAIN COOK (Canada, 1922)   IWM 859
INDIAN EDITORS AT HYDE PARK HOTEL (GB, 1918)   IWM 529
INLAND WATER TRANSPORT (GB, 1917)   IWM 101
INLAND WATER TRANSPORT, EGYPT (GB, 1918)   IWM 31
INSPECTION OF CADETS, SCHOOL OF MILITARY AERONAUTICS OXFORD (ledger title) IWM 869
INSPECTION OF NEW ZEALAND TROOPS BY FIELD MARSHAL SIR DOUGLAS HAIG (New
    Zealand, 1917)   IWM 156
[INSPECTION OF THE CIV] (allocated) (GB, 1900)   IWM 1025e
INSPECTION OF THE IMPERIAL CAMEL CORPS (GB, 1918)   IWM 6
INSPECTION OF THE ROYAL AIR FORCE CADET BRIGADE BY HM THE KING (GENERAL IN
    CHIEF) AUGUST 30 1918 (GB, 1918)   IWM 625
INSPECTION OF VOLUNTEER REGIMENTS AT BEDFORD, MARCH 1918, BY FIELD MARSHAL
    VISCOUNT FRENCH (GB, 1918)   IWM 174
[ITALIAN FICTIONAL FILM] (allocated) (Italy, 1919)   IWM 1075
ITALIAN NAVAL MANOEUVRES (on copy held)   IWM 1062-06
the ITALIAN NAVY (on copy held) (Italy, 1910)   IWM 1062-06
J BATTERY, 2ND CAVALRY DIVISION, 20TH JUNE 1918 (GB, 1918)   IWM 246
JACK AND JILL (GB, 1917-18)   IWM 539
[JAPANESE ARMY MANOEUVRES 1918 : sections from Prince Arthur's visit to Japan]
    (allocated) (GB, 1918)   IWM 445
JERICHO (GB, 1917)   IWM 22
JERUSALEM (GB, 1917)   IWM 19
JEWISH COLONIES IN PALESTINE : Rishon Le Zion (GB, 1917)   IWM 18
JOHN BROWN JOINS THE ARMY (GB, 1918)   IWM 478
JOHN BULL'S ANIMATED SKETCHBOOK NO 15 (GB, 7/1916)   IWM 1216
[JOSEF ON THE ITALIAN FRONT 1] (allocated) (Austria-Hungary, 1917)   IWM 1045b
[JOSEF ON THE ITALIAN FRONT 2] (allocated) (Austria-Hungary, 1917)   IWM 1043b
JUBILEE 1912-1962 (rough material ?)   IWM 1030
[JUTLAND AND AFTER 1] (allocated) (GB, 1917)   IWM 1143
[JUTLAND AND AFTER 2] (allocated) (GB, 1917)   IWM 1144
[JUTLAND AND AFTER 3] (allocated) (GB, 1917)   IWM 1145
[JUTLAND AND AFTER 4] (allocated) (GB, 1917)   IWM 1146
[JUTLAND AND AFTER 5] (allocated) (GB, 1917)   IWM 1147
[KAISER WILHELM VISITS TURKEY] (allocated) (Germany, 1917)   IWM 772
[KARL OF AUSTRIA-HUNGARY VISITS WILHELM OF GERMANY] (Austria-Hungary, 1917)
    IWM 1045d
[KARL VISITS BULGARIA AND TURKEY] (allocated) (Austria-Hungary, 1917)   IWM 1034-03
[KARL VISITS THE TYROL] (allocated) (Austria-Hungary, 1918)   IWM 1035c
[KENNEDY GIANT UNDER CONSTRUCTION] (allocated) (GB, 1917)   IWM 1073
KINCARTOONS (series)   IWM 538; IWM 539; IWM 540; IWM 542; IWM 543
    (*see also* KINKARTOONS)
the KING AND KING ALBERT INSPECTING THE GUARDS AT BUCKINGHAM PALACE (GB,
    1918)   IWM 265
the KING HOLDS AN INVESTITURE IN HYDE PARK, LONDON (GB, 1917)   IWM 109
KING VISITS AUSTRALIAN HEADQUARTERS - AUSTRALIAN DIVISIONAL COMMANDER
    RE-OPENS DESTROYED BRIDGE (GB, 1918)   IWM 293
the KING VISITS HIS ARMIES IN THE GREAT ADVANCE (GB, 10/1916)   IWM 192
the KING'S (LIVERPOOL) REGIMENT (sic) (GB, 1/1918)   IWM 398
the KING'S MESSAGE TO HIS TROOPS (alternative)   IWM 130-05+6
the KING'S OWN YORKSHIRE LIGHT INFANTRY (GB, 2/1918)   IWM 391
the KING'S ROYAL RIFLES (GB, 2/1918)   IWM 417
the KING'S TOUR ROUND THE NAPIER MOTOR WORKS (GB, 1918)   IWM 418
the KING'S VISIT TO FRANCE AUGUST 1918 (GB, 1918)   IWM 289
KINKARTOONS (series)   IWM 526 (*see also* KINCARTOONS)
[a KITE BALLOON AND THE BELLE OF ARQUES] (allocated) (GB, 1918)   IWM 164
KNOW YOUR ENEMY - SECOND SERIES (GB, 1916)   IWM 481
[KNOW YOUR ENEMY - SECOND SERIES (additional scenes 1)] (related)   IWM 1062-14
[KNOW YOUR ENEMY - SECOND SERIES (additional scenes 2)] (related)   IWM 1062-15
KOLONJE ANGIELSKIE W NOWEJ ZELANDJI (on copy held) (GB, 1925)   IWM 815
KRIEGSFLIEGER AN DER WESTFRONT : Aufnahmen aus dem Weltkrieg (Germany, 1940)
    IWM 1004
KRUGER'S DREAM OF EMPIRE (GB, 1900)   IWM 1081f

KURKUCH (GB/USA, 1918)   IWM 69
LA BASSEE (GB, 1918)   IWM 340
the **LANCASHIRE FUSILIERS** (GB, 2/1918)   IWM 415
[the LANDING ON OESEL 1917 : pictures from the World War] (translation)   IWM 1124
LANDUNG AUF OSEL 1917 : Aufnahmen aus dem Weltkrieg (Germany, 1939)   IWM 1124
the **LAST LESSON** (GB, 1914-18)   IWM 525
LAUNCH OF HM AIRSHIPS R36 AND R38 (GB, 1921)   IWM 645
[the **LAUNCH OF SS WAR FOREST**] (allocated) (GB, 9/1918)   IWM 589
[**LAUNCH PLATFORM OF HMS REPULSE**] (allocated) (GB, 1918)   IWM 1169
LENS - ZONNEBEKE - MORSEELE (GB, 1918)   IWM 353
the **LEOPARD'S SPOTS** (GB, 8/1918)   IWM 1209
LEST WE FORGET (GB, 1916)   IWM 1203
LEST WE FORGET (GB, 1918)   IWM 655a
LETTERS FROM HOME : the work of the Postal Department at the Front (GB, 22/5/1916)
                                                                                                    IWM 214
LEWIS GUN SCHOOL (GB, 1917)   IWM 438
LIFE AT IWERNE MINSTER IN WAR TIME - AUGUST 7TH AND 8TH 1918 (GB, 1918)   IWM 285
the **LIFE OF A WAAC** (GB, 1918)   IWM 412
LIFE OF AN AIRSHIP SQUADRON (GB, 1918)   IWM 868
the LIFE OF AN RAF OFFICER IN FRANCE (alternative)   IWM 648
LILLE NO 1 AND LILLE NO 2 (GB, 1918)   IWM 352
the **LINCOLN REGIMENT (sic)** (GB, 3/1918)   IWM 1100
[**LITTLE ENTENTE CONFERENCE AT VERSAILLES**] (allocated) (France/Czechoslovakia, 1920)
                                                                                                    IWM 1042
LIVELINESS ON THE BRITISH FRONT (GB, 27/3/1916)   IWM 208
[**LOCARNO PACT - rough material**] (allocated) (GB, 1925)   IWM 811
LONDON - BRITISH FACT AND GERMAN FICTION (GB, 12/1917)   IWM 443
[**LONDON PEACE PROCESSION (?)**] (allocated) (GB, 1919)   IWM 1210
[**LONDON RALLY**] (allocated) (GB, 1914-18)   IWM 694a
LONDRES - LA VERDAD BRITANICA Y LA FICCION GERMANA (on copy held)   IWM 443
LORD KITCHENER'S VISIT TO THE FRENCH ARMY (France, 1915)   IWM 1062-20
the **LORD MAYOR'S SHOW : RAF well represented** (GB, 1918)   IWM 626
LORD PIRRIE'S APPEAL TO SHIPYARD WORKERS (GB, 1918)   IWM 526
LORD PIRRIE'S APPEAL TO SHIPYARD WORKERS (fragments)   IWM 1068
LORD ROBERTS LEAVING FOR SOUTH AFRICA (GB, 1900)   IWM 1025c
[**LORD WEIR'S VISIT TO THE RAF CADET BRIGADE**] (allocated) (GB, 1918)   IWM 635
[**LOWELL THOMAS'S FILM OF LAWRENCE OF ARABIA (reassembled by Imperial War
     Museum)**] (allocated) (USA, 1917)   IWM 42
[**LOWELL THOMAS'S FILM OF LAWRENCE OF ARABIA (rough material)**] (allocated) (USA,
     1917)   IWM 41
a **MACHINE GUN BATTALION TRAINING IN FRANCE, THE MEN LUDENDORFF FEARS** (GB,
     1918)   IWM 243
a **MACHINE GUN SCHOOL AT THE FRONT** (GB, 7/2/1916)   IWM 204
MACHINE GUNS - TANK WORKS (GB, 1918)   IWM 262
der **MAGISCHE GURTEL** (original title)   IWM 560
**MAJOR HRH PRINCE ARTHUR OF CONNAUGHT PRESENTS BRITISH DECORATIONS TO
     FRENCH OFFICERS AND OTHER RANKS** (GB, 1917)   IWM 124
the **MAKING OF AN OFFICER : with the Artists Rifles at the Front** (GB, 31/1/1916)   IWM 203
the MAKING OF AN OFFICER (censored sections)   IWM 383
the **MARCH OF AVIATION** (USA, 1939)   IWM 1101
MARTYRED BELGIUM (on copy held)   IWM 714
MATINEE AT WEST END THEATRE (ledger title) (GB, 1918)   IWM 348
the MEN LUDENDORFF FEARS (alternative)   IWM 243
[**MESOPOTAMIA (rough material)**] (allocated) (GB/USA, 1917)   IWM 59
[**MESOPOTAMIA - BABYLON AND BAGHDAD**] (allocated) (GB/USA, 1918)   IWM 66
MESOPOTAMIA - BAGHDAD AND RIVER SCENES (GB/USA, 1918)   IWM 77
[**MESOPOTAMIA - CTESIPHON AND SAMARRA**] (allocated) (GB/USA, 1917)   IWM 63
MESOPOTAMIA - DIYALA RIVER, KIFRIE ROAD, TUZ KERMATLI (sic) (GB/USA, 1918)   IWM 68
MESOPOTAMIA - EXAMPLES OF ANCIENT ARCHITECTURE (GB/USA, 1918)   IWM 75
[**MESOPOTAMIA - INDIAN TROOPS BUILD A RAILWAY**] (allocated) (GB/USA, 1918)   IWM 70
MESSTER WOCHE 43 1915 (Germany, 10/1915)   IWM 483-01
MESSTER WOCHE 44 1915 (Germany, 10/1915)   IWM 483-02
MESSTER WOCHE 45 1915 (Germany, 11/1915)   IWM 483-03

MESSTER WOCHE 46 1915 (Germany, 11/1915)   IWM 483-04
MESSTER WOCHE 47 1915 (Germany, 11/1915)   IWM 483-05
MESSTER WOCHE 48 1915 (Germany, 11/1915)   IWM 483-06
MESSTER WOCHE (early 1917) (allocated) (Germany/Austria-Hungary, 1917)   IWM 1045a
METEOROLOGICAL EXPERIMENTS (ledger title) (GB, 1918)   IWM 618
the MIDDLESEX REGIMENT (GB, 1/1918)   IWM 390
[MILK SAVING FILM] (allocated) (GB, 8/1918)   IWM 1128b
MINING ACTIVITY ON THE BRITISH FRONT (GB, 24/7/1916)   IWM 219
[MINISTRY OF FOOD] (allocated) (GB, 5/1918)   IWM 549-03
[MISCELLANEOUS FIRST WORLD WAR AVIATION MATERIAL] (allocated) (GB, 1918) IWM 1202
[MISCELLANEOUS FIRST WORLD WAR NAVAL MATERIAL 1] (allocated) (GB, 1918)
                                                                                                         IWM 550-01
[MISCELLANEOUS FIRST WORLD WAR NAVAL MATERIAL 2] (allocated) (GB, 1918)
                                                                                                         IWM 578-02
[MISCELLANEOUS FIRST WORLD WAR NAVAL MATERIAL 3] (allocated) (GB, 1918)   IWM 1151
[MISCELLANEOUS FIRST WORLD WAR NAVAL MATERIAL 4] (allocated) (GB, 1919)   IWM 1152
[MISCELLANEOUS FIRST WORLD WAR NAVAL MATERIAL 5] (allocated) (GB, 1918)   IWM 1153
[MISCELLANEOUS FIRST WORLD WAR NAVAL MATERIAL 6] (allocated) (GB, 1918)   IWM 1154
[MISCELLANEOUS FIRST WORLD WAR NAVAL MATERIAL 7] (allocated) (GB, 1918)   IWM 1155
[MISCELLANEOUS FIRST WORLD WAR NAVAL MATERIAL 8] (allocated) (GB, 1918)   IWM 1156
[MISCELLANEOUS FIRST WORLD WAR NAVAL MATERIAL 9] (allocated) (GB, 1918)   IWM 1157
[MISCELLANEOUS FIRST WORLD WAR NAVAL MATERIAL 10] (allocated) (GB, 1918) IWM 1158
[MISCELLANEOUS FIRST WORLD WAR NAVAL MATERIAL 11] (allocated) (GB, 1918) IWM 1159
[MISCELLANEOUS FIRST WORLD WAR NAVAL MATERIAL 12] (allocated) (GB, 1918) IWM 1160
[MISCELLANEOUS FIRST WORLD WAR NAVAL MATERIAL 13] (allocated) (GB, 1918) IWM 1161
[MISCELLANEOUS FIRST WORLD WAR NAVAL MATERIAL 14] (allocated) (GB, 1918) IWM 1162
[MISCELLANEOUS FIRST WORLD WAR NAVAL MATERIAL 15] (allocated) (GB, 1918) IWM 1163
[MISCELLANEOUS FIRST WORLD WAR NAVAL MATERIAL 16] (allocated) (GB, 1918) IWM 1164
[MISCELLANEOUS FIRST WORLD WAR NAVAL MATERIAL 17] (allocated) (GB, 1918) IWM 1165
MODERN WARFARE IN CHINA 1924-1925 (USSR, 1925)   IWM 712
MONS (GB, 1922)   IWM 1130
MORE AMMUNITION NEEDED (GB, 1900)   IWM 1081c
MOVEMENTS OF JAPANESE WARSHIPS IN THE MEDITERRANEAN (GB, 1918)   IWM 593
MR BEN TILLET MP VISITS BRITISH SOLDIERS IN YPRES (sic) (GB, 1918)   IWM 159
MR LLOYD GEORGE AND SIR SAM HUGHES REVIEW THE CANADIAN 4TH DIVISION AT
  BRAMSHOT (Canada/GB, 1916)   IWM 1062-19
MR ROBERT MIDDLEMAS'S FOOD PRODUCTION AT ILFORD (GB, 1918)   IWM 531
MRS JOHN BULL PREPARED (GB, 10/1918)   IWM 521
MRS JOHN BULL PREPARED : a shortened version of a First World War Propaganda Film
  (GB, 1970)   IWM 1172
NACB GAZETTE (GB, 1918)   IWM 462
a NATION MOURNS - THE DEATH OF MARSHAL FOCH (translation)   IWM 509
[the NATION'S FOOD] (alternative)   IWM 548
[NATIONAL KITCHEN] (allocated) (GB, 1918)   IWM 520
NATIONAL SERVICE - WOMEN'S LAND ARMY (GB, 8/1917)   IWM 534
the NATIONAL WAR SAVINGS COMMITTEE'S CAMPAIGN FOR THE VICTORY LOAN (GB, 1918)
                                                                                                         IWM 532
NAVAL CELEBRITIES (GB, 1918)   IWM 572
the NEBI-NUSA FESTIVALS : scenes and incidents en route (GB, 1919)   IWM 45
the NEBI-NUSA FESTIVALS (rough material)   IWM 27
NEW CHANNEL FERRY (GB, 1918)   IWM 372
the NEW CRUSADERS : with the British forces on the Palestine Front (GB, 4/1918)   IWM 17
the NEW CRUSADERS (French version) (GB, 4/1918)   IWM 658a
the NEW CRUSADERS (rough material)   IWM 5; IWM 58; IWM 60
a NEW VERSION (GB, 8/1918)   IWM 549-04
NEW ZEALAND AMBULANCE (New Zealand, 1917)   IWM 387
NEW ZEALAND DIVISIONAL RUGBY TEAM (New Zealand, 1918)   IWM 172
NEW ZEALAND FIELD ARTILLERY IN ACTION, NEW YEAR'S DAY 1918 (New Zealand, 1918)
                                                                                                         IWM 160
the NEW ZEALAND FIELD ARTILLERY IN FRANCE (New Zealand, 1917)   IWM 166
NEW ZEALAND LEADS THE WAY, SCENES ON BOARD HMS NEW ZEALAND (alternative)
                                                                                                         IWM 1213
NEW ZEALAND RIFLE BRIGADE ON THE MARCH (extracts)   IWM 166

NEW ZEALAND'S GIFT TO THE EMPIRE (GB, 1913) — IWM 1213
NEW ZEALANDERS AT THE FRONT (alternative) — IWM 385
NEWFOUNDLAND INFANTRY ON THE MARCH (GB, 1917) — IWM 222
NEWFOUNDLAND TROOPS (GB, 1917) — IWM 147
NINETEEN FOURTEEN - NINETEEN EIGHTEEN ODD SECTIONS (filing) — IWM 713
[NINTH DIVISION AND RAILWAY ENGINEERS (allocated)] (filing) — IWM 406
the **NORFOLK REGIMENT** (GB, 2/1918) — IWM 408
[NORTH RUSSIA - film unviewable] (allocated) (GB, 1919) — IWM 423
[NORTH RUSSIA - rough material] (allocated) (GB, 1919) — IWM 421
the **NORTHANTS REGIMENT (sic)** (GB, 2/1918) — IWM 392
[NORTON'S COLUMN IN MESOPOTAMIA] (allocated) (GB/USA, 1917) — IWM 9
NS 5 TRIAL FLIGHT (GB, 1917) — IWM 613
NURSE CAVELL'S GRAVE AND MEMORIAL (Australia, 1919) — IWM 384
OBSERVING FOR OUR HEAVY GUNS (GB, 3/7/1916) — IWM 217
the **OCCUPATION OF ES SALT** (GB, 1918) — IWM 26
OFF TO ENGLAND (GB, 1917) — IWM 126
OFFICIAL PICTURES OF THE BRITISH ARMY IN FRANCE - FIRST SERIES (series)
 IWM 202-01; IWM 202-02; IWM 203; IWM 204; IWM 205
OFFICIAL PICTURES OF THE BRITISH ARMY IN FRANCE - SECOND SERIES (series)
 IWM 206; IWM 207; IWM 255; IWM 259
OFFICIAL PICTURES OF THE BRITISH ARMY IN FRANCE - THIRD SERIES (series)
 IWM 118; IWM 208; IWM 209; IWM 210; IWM 211
OFFICIAL PICTURES OF THE BRITISH ARMY IN FRANCE - FOURTH SERIES (series)
 IWM 133; IWM 212; IWM 213; IWM 214
OFFICIAL PICTURES OF THE BRITISH ARMY IN FRANCE - FIFTH SERIES (series)
 IWM 114; IWM 215; IWM 216; IWM 217; IWM 470
OFFICIAL PICTURES OF THE BRITISH ARMY IN FRANCE - SIXTH SERIES (series)
 IWM 218; IWM 219; IWM 220
OFICIALES ALEMANES CAUTIVOS : campos de prisioneros de guerra en Inglaterra (on copy held)
 IWM 436
OLD FATHER WILLIAM (GB, 1917-18) — IWM 543
OLD MOTHER HUBBARD - NEW VERSION (GB, 8/1918) — IWM 1177b
the **OLYMPIC GAMES : as they were originally practised in Ancient Greece shown in living
 pictures** (GB, 1924) — IWM 594-01
the **OLYMPIC GAMES HELD AT CHAMONIX IN 1924** (France, 1924) — IWM 594-02+3
the **OLYMPIC GAMES IN PARIS 1924** (France, 1924) — IWM 594-04-13
ON BOARD HMAS AUSTRALIA (Australia, 1918) — IWM 377
ON THE BAPAUME FRONT - THE KEY TO THE HINDENBURG LINE (alternative) — IWM 294
ON THE PALESTINE FRONT (series) — IWM 6
ON THE ROAD TO BERLIN - England's Welcome To American Boys (USA, 1917) — IWM 1187
ON THE ST QUENTIN FRONT (GB, 1918) — IWM 335
OPEN AIR MASS IN HAVANA CUBA (GB, 1918) — IWM 312
OPERATIONS OF THE BRITISH EXPEDITIONARY FORCES IN EAST AFRICA (GB, 1916)
 IWM 84
OSTEND RE-OCCUPIED (GB, 11/1918) — IWM 557
OSTENDE (sic) (GB, 1918) — IWM 351
the **OTHER ITALIAN ARMY** (Italy, 1918) — IWM 460
OUR DAILY BREAD (PART 2) (GB, 1918) — IWM 595
OUR DAY (ledger title) (GB, 1918) — IWM 695
OUR EMPIRE'S FIGHT FOR FREEDOM - PART 1 (GB, 1918) — IWM 440-01
OUR EMPIRE'S FIGHT FOR FREEDOM - PART 2 (GB, 1918) — IWM 440-02
OUR EMPIRE'S FIGHT FOR FREEDOM - PART 3 (GB, 1918) — IWM 440-03
OUR EMPIRE'S FIGHT FOR FREEDOM - PART 4 (GB, 1918) — IWM 440-04
OUR EMPIRE'S FIGHT FOR FREEDOM - PART 5 (GB, 1918) — IWM 440-05
OUR EMPIRE'S FIGHT FOR FREEDOM - PART 6 (GB, 1918) — IWM 440-06
OUR EMPIRE'S FIGHT FOR FREEDOM - PART 7 (GB, 1918) — IWM 440-07
OUR GRIP ON THE HUNS : Cherry Kearton War Series (series) — IWM 84
OUR HEROIC CANADIAN BROTHERS (GB, 1918) — IWM 465
[OUR HEROIC TROOPS FIGHT AMONG THE SNOW-CAPPED MOUNTAINS, ROCKS AND ICE -
 PART I] (incomplete version) (translation) — IWM 1038
[OUR HEROIC TROOPS FIGHT AMONG THE SNOW-CAPPED MOUNTAINS, ROCKS AND ICE -
 PART II] (incomplete version) (translation) — IWM 1043a

[OUR HEROIC TROOPS FIGHT AMONG THE SNOW-CAPPED MOUNTAINS, ROCKS AND ICE]
(translation)   IWM 1084
OUR MERCHANT SERVICE HEROES (GB, 1918)   IWM 320
OUR NAVAL AIR POWER (GB, 1/1918)   IWM 570
OUR PRINCE IN JAPAN (GB, 1922)   IWM 1140
OUR WONDERFUL TANKS (GB, 1918)   IWM 357
[PALESTINE **(rough material)]** (allocated) (GB, 1917)   IWM 58
[PALESTINE SECTIONS] (GB/USA, 1917)   IWM 60
the **PARAVANE - A DEVICE THAT MADE MINES USELESS** : invented by Lieut Dennis Burney,
RN (GB, 1918)   IWM 585
[PATHE FIRE STOCKSHOTS] (GB, 1918)   IWM 686
PATHE GAZETTE [1914] - GERM-HUN KULTUR (GB, 1914)   IWM 1070f
PATHE GAZETTE [1915] (fragment 1) (GB, 1915)   IWM 1055b
PATHE GAZETTE [1915] (fragment 2) (GB, 1915)   IWM 1055d
PATHE GAZETTE [1915] - ST GEORGE'S DAY (GB, 1915)   IWM 1070g
PATHE GAZETTE [winter 1915-16] (GB, 1916)   IWM 1070d
PATHE GAZETTE [1922] - THE WEDDING OF THE SEASON (GB, 7/1922)   IWM 1141
PATHE GAZETTE [1923 approx] - REALISM AT THE ALDERSHOT MILITARY TATTOO (GB,
1923)   IWM 1064-03b
PATHE GAZETTE [1925?] - THE KING WITH HIS TROOPS (GB, 1925)   IWM 1064-03a
PATHE GAZETTE [1925?] - THE SAME OLD ... MUD (GB, 1925)   IWM 1064-02b
PATHE GAZETTE [1925] - BRITISH ARMY MANOEUVRES : 50,000 troops take part in 'Great
War of 1925' (GB, 1925)   IWM 1064-03e
PATHE GAZETTE [1925] - GETTING READY FOR THE GREAT MANOEUVRES (GB, 1925)
IWM 1064-03d
PATHE GAZETTE [1925] - IF YOU WOULD HAVE PEACE ETC ! (GB, 1925)   IWM 1064-03c
PATHE GAZETTE [1925] - THE BATTLE OF QUARLEY : terminates the 'Great War of 1925' (GB,
1925)   IWM 1064-03f
PATHE GAZETTE [1931] - WORLD'S FASTEST TANK (USA, 1931)   IWM 1064-02a
PATHE GAZETTE [1932 approx] - MODERN METHODS (GB, 1931-33)   IWM 1064-02c
PATHE GAZETTE [1934] - MECHANISED MANOEUVRES : 200 tanks go into action on
Salisbury Plain (GB, 1934)   IWM 1064-02d
PATHE GAZETTE NORTHERN EDITION [1915] (fragment) (GB, 1915)   IWM 1070e
[PATHE NEWSREEL **(ca 1912)]** (allocated) (GB, 1912)   IWM 1061-08c
[PATHE NEWSREEL **(ca 1913)]** (allocated) (GB, 1913)   IWM 1061-08a
**PATHE SUPER GAZETTE [1926] - MR WINSTON CHURCHILL INTERESTED SPECTATOR AT
ALDERSHOT COMMAND MANOEUVRES** (GB, 1926)   IWM 1064-01b
PATHE SUPER GAZETTE [1929] - NON-STOP INDIA HEROES HOME AGAIN (GB, 1929)
IWM 880-02b
PATHE SUPER GAZETTE [1930] - SHOWING THE (ROYAL AIR FORCE) FLAG (GB, 1930)
IWM 880-01b
PATHE SUPER GAZETTE [1931] - [SCHNEIDER TROPHY] (allocated) (GB, 1931)   IWM 880-01f
PATHE'S ANIMATED GAZETTE 172 (GB, 6/1912)   IWM 1082-02c
PATHE'S ANIMATED GAZETTE 173 (GB, 6/1912)   IWM 1082-02d
PATHE'S ANIMATED GAZETTE NO 282B (GB, 1914)   IWM 1082-01
PATHE'S ANIMATED HISTORY OF THE GREAT WAR - PART 22 CHAPTER 3 (GB, 1925)
IWM 1175
PATIENT HEROES OF THE SEA (GB, 1918)   IWM 558
a **PATRIOTIC MESSAGE** (alternative)   IWM 526
PHOTOGRAPHY - THE EYE OF THE AEROPLANE (GB, 1919)   IWM 873
PICTORIAL HISTORY OF THE WORLD WAR NO 1 (USA, 1919)   IWM 501-01
PICTORIAL HISTORY OF THE WORLD WAR NO 2 (USA, 1919)   IWM 501-02
PICTORIAL HISTORY OF THE WORLD WAR NO 3 (USA, 1919)   IWM 501-03
PICTORIAL HISTORY OF THE WORLD WAR NO 4 (USA, 1919)   IWM 501-04
PICTORIAL HISTORY OF THE WORLD WAR NO 5 (USA, 1919)   IWM 501-05
PICTORIAL HISTORY OF THE WORLD WAR NO 6 (USA, 1919)   IWM 501-06
PICTORIAL HISTORY OF THE WORLD WAR NO 7 (USA, 1919)   IWM 501-07
PICTORIAL HISTORY OF THE WORLD WAR NO 8 (USA, 1919)   IWM 501-08
PICTORIAL HISTORY OF THE WORLD WAR NO 9 (USA, 1919)   IWM 501-09
PICTORIAL HISTORY OF THE WORLD WAR NO 10 (USA, 1919)   IWM 501-10
PICTORIAL HISTORY OF THE WORLD WAR NO 11 (USA, 1919)   IWM 501-11
PICTORIAL HISTORY OF THE WORLD WAR NO 12 (USA, 1919)   IWM 501-12
PICTORIAL HISTORY OF THE WORLD WAR NO 13 (USA, 1919)   IWM 501-13

PICTORIAL HISTORY OF THE WORLD WAR NO 14 (USA, 1919)   IWM 501-14
PICTORIAL NEWS (OFFICIAL) - issues prior to 340-1 are listed as **WAR OFFICE OFFICIAL TOPICAL BUDGET**
PICTORIAL NEWS (OFFICIAL) 340-1 (GB, 27/2/1918)   NTB 340-01 *and* IWM 681a
PICTORIAL NEWS (OFFICIAL) 340-2 (GB, 2/3/1918)
                              IWM 1061-05a *and* IWM 681b; IWM 1061-09b; IWM 1061-09e
PICTORIAL NEWS (OFFICIAL) 341-1 **(Spanish version)** (GB, 6/3/1918)   IWM 681c
PICTORIAL NEWS (OFFICIAL) 341-2 (GB, 9/3/1918)   NTB 341-02 *and* IWM 681d
PICTORIAL NEWS (OFFICIAL) 342-1 **(Spanish version)** (GB, 13/3/1918)
                                                            IWM 699c *dup* IWM 1129b
PICTORIAL NEWS (OFFICIAL) 342-2 (GB, 16/3/1918)   NTB 342-02 *and* IWM 699d
PICTORIAL NEWS (OFFICIAL) 343-1 (GB, 20/3/1918)   NTB 343-01 *and* IWM 699a
PICTORIAL NEWS (OFFICIAL) 343-2 **(Spanish version)** (GB, 23/3/1918)
                                                            IWM 699b *and* NTB 343-02
PICTORIAL NEWS (OFFICIAL) 344-1 (GB, 27/3/1918)   NTB 344-01
PICTORIAL NEWS (OFFICIAL) 344-2 (GB, 30/3/1918)   NTB 344-02
PICTORIAL NEWS (OFFICIAL) 345-2 (GB, 6/4/1918)   NTB 345-02
PICTORIAL NEWS (OFFICIAL) 346-2 **(Spanish version)** (GB, 13/4/1918)   IWM 693a
PICTORIAL NEWS (OFFICIAL) 347-1 **(Spanish version)** (GB, 15/4/1918)   IWM 693d
PICTORIAL NEWS (OFFICIAL) 347-2 **(Spanish version)** (GB, 18/4/1918)
                                                            IWM 693e *and* NTB 347-02
PICTORIAL NEWS (OFFICIAL) 348-1 **(Spanish version)** (GB, 24/4/1918)   IWM 693b
PICTORIAL NEWS (OFFICIAL) 348-2 **(Spanish version)** (GB, 27/4/1918)   IWM 693c
PICTORIAL NEWS (OFFICIAL) 349-1 (GB, 1/5/1918)
                              IWM 661a *and* IWM 673d; IWM 684a; IWM 700d
PICTORIAL NEWS (OFFICIAL) 349-2 (GB, 6/5/1918)
                              IWM 661b *and* IWM 673c; IWM 700a; IWM 700e
PICTORIAL NEWS (OFFICIAL) 350-1 (GB, 8/5/1918)   IWM 654a *and* IWM 673b; IWM 700b
PICTORIAL NEWS (OFFICIAL) 350-2 (GB, 13/5/1918)   IWM 654b *and* IWM 673a; IWM 700c
PICTORIAL NEWS (OFFICIAL) 351-2 (GB, 20/5/1918)   NTB 351-02
PICTORIAL NEWS (OFFICIAL) 352-1 **(French version)** (GB, 23/5/1918)   IWM 668d *and* IWM 675a
PICTORIAL NEWS (OFFICIAL) 352-2 **(French version)** (GB, 27/5/1918)   IWM 668c
PICTORIAL NEWS (OFFICIAL) 353-1 **(French version)** (GB, 30/5/1918)
                                                            IWM 675b *and* IWM 1061-09f
PICTORIAL NEWS (OFFICIAL) 353-2 (GB, 3/6/1918)
                              IWM 1061-02c *and* IWM 675c *dup* IWM 1055a
PICTORIAL NEWS (OFFICIAL) 354-1 (GB, 6/6/1918)
                              NTB 354-01 *and* IWM 676a *dup* IWM 1061-02d
PICTORIAL NEWS (OFFICIAL) 354-2 (GB, 10/6/1918)   IWM 1061-02a *and* IWM 676b
PICTORIAL NEWS (OFFICIAL) 355-2 **(French version)** (GB, 17/6/1918)   IWM 659
PICTORIAL NEWS (OFFICIAL) 356-1 **(French version)** (GB, 20/6/1918)   IWM 660a
PICTORIAL NEWS (OFFICIAL) 356-2 (GB, 24/6/1918)
                              NTB 356-02 *and* IWM 660b *dup* IWM 1061-05f; IWM 1061-05i
PICTORIAL NEWS (OFFICIAL) 357-1 (GB, 27/6/1918)
                              IWM 1061-02b *and* IWM 1061-07b; IWM 668a
PICTORIAL NEWS (OFFICIAL) 357-2 **(French version)** (GB, 1/7/1918)   IWM 668b
PICTORIAL NEWS (OFFICIAL) 358-1 **(French version)** (GB, 4/7/1918)   IWM 653b
PICTORIAL NEWS (OFFICIAL) 358-2 **(French version)** (GB, 8/7/1918)   IWM 653a
PICTORIAL NEWS (OFFICIAL) 359-1 **(French version)** (GB, 11/7/1918)   IWM 666a
PICTORIAL NEWS (OFFICIAL) 359-2 **(French version)** (GB, 15/7/1918)   IWM 666b *and* IWM 674a
PICTORIAL NEWS (OFFICIAL) 360-1 **(French version)** (GB, 18/7/1918)   IWM 674b
PICTORIAL NEWS (OFFICIAL) 360-2 **(French version)** (GB, 22/7/1918)   IWM 674c
PICTORIAL NEWS (OFFICIAL) 361-1 **(French version)** (GB, 25/7/1918)   IWM 678a
PICTORIAL NEWS (OFFICIAL) 361-2 **(French version)** (GB, 29/7/1918)   IWM 678b
PICTORIAL NEWS (OFFICIAL) 362-1 (GB, 1/8/1918)   IWM 1128a *and* IWM 657b; IWM 683a
PICTORIAL NEWS (OFFICIAL) 362-2 **(French version)** (GB, 5/8/1918)   IWM 657a *and* IWM 683b
PICTORIAL NEWS (OFFICIAL) 363-1 **(French version)** (GB, 8/8/1918)   IWM 679a
PICTORIAL NEWS (OFFICIAL) 363-2 **(French version)** (GB, 12/8/1918)   IWM 679b
PICTORIAL NEWS (OFFICIAL) 364-1 **(French version)** (GB, 15/8/1918)   IWM 680a
PICTORIAL NEWS (OFFICIAL) 364-2 **(French version)** (GB, 19/8/1918)   IWM 680b
PICTORIAL NEWS (OFFICIAL) 365-1 **(French version)** (GB, 22/8/1918)   IWM 677a
PICTORIAL NEWS (OFFICIAL) 365-2 **(French version)** (GB, 26/8/1918)   IWM 677b
PICTORIAL NEWS (OFFICIAL) 367-1 **(French version)** (GB, 5/9/1918)   IWM 667

PICTORIAL NEWS (OFFICIAL) 368-1 (GB, 12/9/1918)   IWM 308d *dup* IWM 308a
PICTORIAL NEWS (OFFICIAL) 368-2 (GB, 16/9/1918)   IWM 308b *and* IWM 682
PICTORIAL NEWS (OFFICIAL) 369-1 (GB, 19/9/1918)   IWM 685a
PICTORIAL NEWS (OFFICIAL) 369-2 (GB, 23/9/1918)   IWM 685b
PICTORIAL NEWS (OFFICIAL) 370-1 **(French version)** (GB, 26/9/1918)   IWM 652a
PICTORIAL NEWS (OFFICIAL) 370-2 **(French version)** (GB, 30/9/1918)   IWM 652b *and* IWM 461b
PICTORIAL NEWS (OFFICIAL) 371-1 (GB, 3/10/1918)   IWM 461a *and* IWM 461c
PICTORIAL NEWS (OFFICIAL) 371-2 (GB, 7/10/1918)   IWM 461d
PICTORIAL NEWS (OFFICIAL) 375-1 (GB, 31/10/1918)   IWM 656a
PICTORIAL NEWS (OFFICIAL) 375-2 (GB, 4/11/1918)   IWM 665c
PICTORIAL NEWS (OFFICIAL) 376-2 (GB, 11/11/1918)   IWM 665b
PICTORIAL NEWS (OFFICIAL) 377-1 (GB, 14/11/1918)   IWM 664a
PICTORIAL NEWS (OFFICIAL) 377-2 (GB, 18/11/1918)   IWM 664b
PICTORIAL NEWS (OFFICIAL) 379-1 (GB, 28/11/1918)   IWM 665a
PICTORIAL NEWS (OFFICIAL) 383-1 (GB, 26/12/1918)   IWM 380
PICTORIAL NEWS (OFFICIAL) 395-1 (GB, 20/3/1919)   NTB 395-01
PICTORIAL NEWS (OFFICIAL) 395-2 (GB, 24/3/1919)   NTB 395-02
PIGEONS AND SEAPLANES (GB, 1917)   IWM 287
PILOTING A SHIP-PLANE ONTO AN AIRCRAFT CARRIER (GB, 10/1926)   IWM 875
PILOTS ON THE WESTERN FRONT : scenes from the World War (translation)   IWM 1004
PLANNING AN OFFENSIVE (France, 1917)   IWM 1057-01
PLANT AND OPERATIONS IN THE MANUFACTURE OF GASMASKS (GB, 1918)   IWM 279
[the PLEBISCITE IN ODENBURG] (translation)   IWM 1035a
PLUMER DECORATING WOMEN OF FANY AND VAD (GB, 1918)   IWM 260
the POLICE DOG (USA, 1916)   IWM 670c
[POLICE TRAINING FILM] (allocated) (GB, 1922)   IWM 901
PONT REMY SPORTS (GB, 1918)   IWM 319
PONTOON BRIDGE BUILDING (Germany, 1912)   IWM 1091b
POPERINGHE (GB, 1918)   IWM 431
a PORTUGUESE TRAINING CAMP IN ENGLAND - ROFFEY CAMP, HORSHAM (GB, 1918)
     IWM 291
PORTUGUESE TROOPS IN FRANCE (GB, 1918)   IWM 323
[PRACTICE SHOOT BY HMS ORION] (allocated) (GB, 1918)   IWM 575
PREMONT (GB, 1918)   IWM 341
PREPARATIONS FOR THE GREAT OFFENSIVE (alternative)   IWM 130-07+8
PREPARING A BOMBING RAID (GB, 1918)   IWM 175
PRESENTATION OF FRENCH DECORATIONS TO BRITISH TROOPS IN EGYPT BY GENERAL
   BAILLOUD (GB, 8/1917)   IWM 1
the PRESIDENT OF PORTUGAL IN FRANCE (GB, 1917)   IWM 129
[PRINCE FUSHIMI'S VISIT TO THE ROYAL NAVY AND JAPANESE INVESTITURE ONBOARD
   HMS QUEEN ELIZABETH] (allocated) (GB, 1918)   IWM 550-02
the PRINCE OF WALES IN GLASGOW (GB, 1918)   IWM 528
the PRINCE OF WALES WITH THE AUSTRALIANS (Australia, 1918)   IWM 382
PROPAGANDA BY BALLOONS (GB, 1918)   IWM 277
Q-SHIPS (GB 1928 - re-edited version)   IWM 1176
[RAF CADET BRIGADE SPORTS AT SAINT LEONARDS] (allocated) (GB, 1918)   IWM 640-01
[RAF CADETS ARRIVE IN SAINT LEONARDS] (allocated) (GB, 1918)   IWM 640-02
RAF CAMP WANTAGE (ledger title) (GB, 1918)   IWM 620
[RAF CRANE LAUNCH OF SEAPLANE] (allocated) (GB, 1919)   IWM 649
[RAF DEMONSTRATION 1930] (allocated) (GB, 1930)   IWM 863
[RAF FIGHTERS TAKING OFF] (allocated) (GB, 1936)   IWM 989
[RAF RETROSPECTIVE FILM] (allocated) (GB, 1918)   IWM 1170
[RAF SECTIONS] (allocated) (GB, 1918)   IWM 639
[RAF SPORTS IN FRANCE 1919] (allocated) (GB, 1919)   IWM 640-03
RAILWAYMEN IN FRANCE (GB, 1918)   IWM 176
READY FOR THE ENEMY (GB/USA, 1916)   IWM 99
RECRUITING MARCH OF THE OXFORDSHIRE WOMEN'S LAND ARMY (GB, 1917-18)   IWM 535
RED CROSS AMBULANCE TRAIN USED BY GERMANS FOR AMMUNITION (GB, 1918)   IWM 321
REFUGEES FROM VILLAGES ON THE CAMBRAI FRONT (GB, 1918)   IWM 148
[RE-INTERMENT OF EDITH CAVELL] (allocated) (GB, 1919)   IWM 1074
REMOUNTS AT RUSSLEY PARK (GB, 1918)   IWM 305
REPAIRING WAR'S RAVAGES (GB, 11/1917)   IWM 1098
REPARACION DE LOS DANOS CAUSADOS POR LA GUERRA (on copy held)   IWM 1098

the RESULT OF CINEMA DAY, NOVEMBER 9TH 1915 (GB, 1916)   IWM 134
the RETURN OF SIR GEORGE WHITE (GB, 1900)   IWM 1025b
RETURN OF THE INTERNED (GB, 1918)   IWM 545
REVIEW OF NEW ZEALAND TROOPS BY SIR WALTER LONG (GB, 1917)   IWM 196
RIBEMONT GAS SCHOOL (GB, 1917)   IWM 112
RICHEBOURG ST VAAST (GB, 1917)   IWM 428
the RIFLE BRIGADE (GB, 2/1918)   IWM 416
the RIGHT WAY TO DEAL WITH PRIVATE SPUD (GB, 5/1918)   IWM 549-09
the RISING GENERATION AND THE GENERATIONS TO COME (GB, 1917)   IWM 517
ROMICOURT - ARMENTIERES NEAR ESTAIRES (GB, 1918)   IWM 347
the ROYAL AIR FORCE - PER ARDUA AD ASTRA (GB, 1918)   IWM 869
ROYAL AIR FORCE : aircraft of the Fleet Air Arm and aircraft operating from shore bases (GB, 1925)   IWM 865
the ROYAL BERKSHIRE REGIMENT (GB, 1/1918)   IWM 397
ROYAL HORSE ARTILLERY SPORTS BEHIND THE LINES (GB, 1918)   IWM 230
[ROYAL NAVY SHORE BASE] (allocated) (GB, 1919)   IWM 1069
[ROYAL NEWFOUNDLAND REGIMENT (?)] (allocated) (GB, 1918)   IWM 308c
ROYAL TOUR OF THE KING OVER FRANCE (GB, 1918)   IWM 375
ROYAL VISIT TO DEAL (GB, 1917)   IWM 201
the ROYAL VISIT TO THE BATTLEFIELDS OF FRANCE, JULY 1917 (GB, 3/9/1917)   IWM 198
the ROYAL WEST KENT REGIMENT (GB, 2/1918)   IWM 401
RUINED VILLAGES OF FRANCE (ledger title)   IWM 473
RULE BRITANNIA (GB, 1918)   IWM 554
[RUSSIAN PRISONERS IN AUSTRIA-HUNGARY] (allocated) (Austria-Hungary, 1915)   IWM 1211
S AFRICAN NATIVE LABOUR CONTINGENT : somewhere in France (GB, 11/1917)   IWM 413
[SAINT OMER, SPANISH VISITORS AND CHRISTMAS SCENES, 1917] (allocated) (GB, 1917)   IWM 153
SAINT PATRICK'S DAY WITH THE IRISH GUARDS (GB, 1916)   IWM 1062-17
[SALONIKA AND WESTERN FRONT (rough material)] (allocated) (GB, 1918)   IWM 437
SAPPER REUNION FILM (GB, 1951)   IWM 990
SAVINGS CERTIFICATES : how to buy them, how to use them (GB, 1917)   IWM 530
SCENES AT AROSA BAY (GB, 4/1919)   IWM 592
SCENES AT SPA (GB, 1918)   IWM 374
[SCENES FROM THE FIRST WORLD WAR] (alternative) (translation))   IWM 1084
SCENES IN AND AROUND BRITISH HEADQUARTERS (GB, 26/6/1916)   IWM 216
SCENES IN BRUSSELS (GB, 1918)   IWM 370
SCENES IN CAMBRAI 1 (GB, 1918)   IWM 339
SCENES IN CAMBRAI 2 (GB, 1918)   IWM 345
SCENES IN CAPTURED VILLAGES ON THE CAMBRAI FRONT (GB, 1918)   IWM 146
SCENES IN NEWCASTLE ON TYNE ON TYNESIDE SCOTTISH FLAG DAY : April 15th 1916 (GB, 1916)   IWM 488
SCENES OF THE FRONT (GB, 1917)   IWM 258
SCENES OF THE WESTERN FRONT (GB, 1916)   IWM 105
SCENES ON THE EUPHRATES - MESOPOTAMIA (GB, 1918)   IWM 72
SCENES ON THE HINDENBURG LINE (GB, 1918)   IWM 336
SCENES ON THE MENIN ROAD (GB, 1917)   IWM 127
SCENES ON THE RHEIMS-EPERNAY FRONT (GB, 1918)   IWM 278
SCENES ON THE TRACK AROUND LIEVEN AIX AND NOULETTE (GB, 1918)   IWM 237
SCENES ON THE WESTERN FRONT (GB, 1918)   IWM 475
SCENES ON THE YSER CANAL (GB, 7/1917)   IWM 102
[SCENES TAKEN FROM THE WORLD'S GREATEST STORY] (alternative)   IWM 429
SCOTTISH TROOPS FOR THE FRONT (GB, 1914)   IWM 1214
SEAPLANE FLYING OFF DECK OF HMS CAMPANIA (GB, 1918)   IWM 1168
SEAPLANES (GB, 1918)   IWM 644
SECOND ARMY BOMBING SCHOOL (GB, 1917)   IWM 199
SECOND LIFE GUARDS (GB, 1917)   IWM 425
the SECRET (GB, 5/1918)   IWM 549-01
the SECRETS OF SUBMARINE HUNTING (GB, 1918)   IWM 559
SECTIONS RELEASED FROM GHQ POSITIVE BOX (GB, 1915)   IWM 383
SEMANA MESSTER 43 1915 (on copy held)   IWM 483-01
SEMANA MESSTER 44 1915 (on copy held)   IWM 483-02
SEMANA MESSTER 45 1915 (on copy held)   IWM 483-03
SEMANA MESSTER 46 1915 (on copy held)   IWM 483-04

SEMANA MESSTER 47 1915 (on copy held)   IWM 483-05
SEMANA MESSTER 48 1915 (on copy held)   IWM 483-06
SEPTEMBER OFFENSIVE 3 (GB, 1918)   IWM 324
SEPTEMBER OFFENSIVE 4 (GB, 1918)   IWM 325
SEPTEMBER OFFENSIVE 6 (GB, 1918)   IWM 326
SEPTEMBER OFFENSIVE 7 (GB, 1918)   IWM 327
[SHELLBURSTS] (allocated) (GB, 1917)   IWM 301
SHIPYARD ACTIVITY (GB, 1918)   IWM 583
[SHIPYARD FILM FRAGMENTS] (allocated) (GB, 1918)   IWM 1068
SIMPLE SIMON (GB, 1917-18)   IWM 541
[SIR ROBERT BORDEN VISITS HMS QUEEN ELIZABETH AND HMS CANADA] (allocated) (GB, 1917)   IWM 591
SIWA EXPEDITION (GB, 1917)   IWM 5
a **SKIRMISH WITH THE BOERS NEAR KIMBERLEY BY A TROOP OF CAVALRY SCOUTS ATTACHED TO GENERAL FRENCH'S COLUMN** (GB, 1900)   IWM 1081d
a **SKIRMISH WITH THE BOERS NEAR KIMBERLEY BY A TROOP OF CAVALRY SCOUTS ATTACHED TO GENERAL FRENCH'S COLUMN (fragment 1)** (GB, 1900)   IWM 1025a
a **SKIRMISH WITH THE BOERS NEAR KIMBERLEY BY A TROOP OF CAVALRY SCOUTS ATTACHED TO GENERAL FRENCH'S COLUMN (fragment 2)** (GB, 1900)   IWM 1025d
[SMOKE APPARATUS] (allocated) (GB, 1918)   IWM 574
[SOISSONS AND RHEIMS] (allocated) (France, 1917)   IWM 435
SOLDIERS VOTING AND AMERICAN HEROES AT CAMBRAI (GB, 1918)   IWM 150
SOME OF THE HINDENBURG LINE (alternative)   IWM 336
SONS OF OUR EMPIRE (export version)   IWM 233
SONS OF OUR EMPIRE (offcuts)   IWM 123
SONS OF OUR EMPIRE (related scenes)   IWM 349
SONS OF OUR EMPIRE EPISODE 1 : Winter on the Western Front (GB, 1917)   IWM 130-01+2
SONS OF OUR EMPIRE EPISODE 2 : Glimpses of the British Navy in war time (GB, 1917)   IWM 130-03+4
SONS OF OUR EMPIRE EPISODE 3 : the King's message to his troops (GB, 1917)   IWM 130-05+6
SONS OF OUR EMPIRE EPISODE 4 : Preparations for the Great Offensive (GB, 1917)   IWM 130-07+8
SONS OF OUR EMPIRE EPISODE 5 : Attacking hard (GB, 1917)   IWM 130-09+10
SONS OF OUR EMPIRE EPISODE 5 : Attacking hard (German version) (GB, 1917)   IWM 670a
[SOPWITH DOLPHIN] (allocated) (GB, 1917)   IWM 1150
the **SOUL OF A NATION** (GB, 1933)   IWM 485
SOUTH AFRICAN ARTILLERY IN ACTION (GB, 1918)   IWM 171
[SOUTH AFRICAN LABOUR CONTINGENT AT SIDING] (allocated) (GB, 1917)   IWM 195
SOUTH AFRICAN NATIVE LABOUR CONTINGENT : somewhere in France (filing)   IWM 413
SOUTH AFRICANS HOLD A MEMORIAL SERVICE IN DELVILLE WOOD (GB, 1917)   IWM 169
SOUTH AMERICA'S MESSAGE TO THE ALLIES (GB, 1918)   IWM 456
SOUTH IRISH HORSE REGIMENTAL SPORTS : Curragh May 28th 1914 (GB, 1914)   IWM 1056
SPORTS AT STAMFORD BRIDGE (GB, 1918)   IWM 309
SPORTS OF THE 7TH BLACK WATCH (GB, 1917)   IWM 110
STAND BY THE MEN WHO HAVE STOOD BY YOU (GB, 1917)   IWM 542
STATE ENTRY INTO ANTWERP 19TH NOVEMBER 1918 (GB, 1918)   IWM 371
[STATE ENTRY OF THE KING AND QUEEN OF BELGIUM INTO BRUGES] (allocated) (GB, 1918)   IWM 359
the **STORY OF HMS VINDICTIVE AT OSTEND** (GB, 7/1918)   IWM 1105
the **STORY OF THE CAMEL AND THE STRAW - NEW VERSION** (GB, 1918)   IWM 538
the **STORY OF THE DRIFTERS : and of the sea dogs who man them** (GB, 11/1917)   IWM 553
the **STORY OF THE DRIFTERS (fragment of variant copy)** (GB, 11/1917)   IWM 597
the **STRANDING OF SS WAR-KNIGHT (ledger title)** (GB, 1918)   IWM 573
STUDDY'S WAR STUDIES (series)   IWM 1061-04g
the **SUBMARINE SERVICE** (GB, 1918)   IWM 581
SUBSTITUTIONS (France, 1896)   IWM 1083
the **SUFFOLK REGIMENT** (GB, 3/1918)   IWM 393
la **SUISSE JOUE PARMI LES NATIONS LE ROLE DU BON SAMARITAIN** (Switzerland, 7/1918)   IWM 454
the **SULTAN OF EGYPT'S FUNERAL** (GB, 1917)   IWM 23
SUR LA STRUMA AVEC L'ARMEE GRECQUE (France, 1917)   IWM 97
the **SURRENDER OF KROONSTAD TO LORD ROBERTS** (GB, 1900)   IWM 1080b

[SURRENDER OF THE GERMAN FLEET] (allocated) (GB, 11/1918)   IWM 586
SURRENDER OF THE GERMAN HIGH SEAS FLEET (GB, 1918)   IWM 637
SWITZERLAND ACTS AS GOOD SAMARITAN TO THE NATIONS (translation)   IWM 454
[SZENEN AUS DEM ERSTEN WELTKRIEG] (alternative)   IWM 1084
TACTICAL SECTION DRILL 'A' MGC (GB, 1920)   IWM 471
TAILS UP FRANCE (GB, 1918)   IWM 648
[TANK AND INFANTRY CO-OPERATION] (allocated) (GB, 1918)   IWM 1201
[TANK MARK VIII] (allocated) (GB, 1918)   IWM 1194
[TANK SECTIONS] (allocated) (GB, 1917)   IWM 1198
[TANK TRENCH-CROSSING TRIALS] (allocated) (GB, 1918)   IWM 1193
[TANKS MARK IV, SCHNEIDER, AND MARK IV UNDITCHING] (allocated) (GB, 1918)   IWM 1196
[TANKS MARK V DOUBLE STAR AND MEDIUM B] (allocated) (GB, 1918)   IWM 1192
[TANKS MARK IX DUCK, MARK IV HERMAPHRODITE AND MEDIUM B] (allocated) (GB, 1918)   IWM 1190
[TANKS MEDIUM A, MARK V AND MARK V STAR] (allocated) (GB, 1918)   IWM 1200
[TANKS MEDIUM B AND MARK V DOUBLE STAR IN BRIDGING EXERCISE] (allocated) (GB, 1918)   IWM 1197
[TANKS MEDIUM C HORNET AND PROTOTYPE 'LITTLE WILLIE'] (allocated) (GB, 1918)   IWM 1191
TANKS - THE WONDER WEAPON (GB, 1917)   IWM 337
[TANKS - THE WONDER WEAPON (extracts)]   IWM 1198
TER EERE VAN DEN BELGISCHEN SOLDAT 1 DEEL (alternative)   IWM 1050
TER EERE VAN DEN BELGISCHEN SOLDAT 2 DEEL (alternative)   IWM 1051
TER EERE VAN DEN BELGISCHEN SOLDAT 3 DEEL (alternative)   IWM 1052
TER EERE VAN DEN BELGISCHEN SOLDAT 4 DEEL (alternative)   IWM 1053
TER EERE VAN DEN BELGISCHEN SOLDAT 5 DEEL (alternative)   IWM 1054
TERRITORIAL ARMY FILM (GB, 1927)   IWM 706
[THANKSGIVING SERVICE FOR GEORGE V] (allocated) (GB, 1911)   IWM 1061-03i
THERE WAS A LITTLE MAN AND HE HAD A LITTLE GUN (GB, 1918)   IWM 540
THIRD ARMY INFANTRY TRAINING SCHOOL (GB, 1917)   IWM 104
THIRD ARMY SIGNAL OFFICE (GB, 1917)   IWM 433
[TO THE GLORY OF THE BELGIAN SOLDIER PART 1] (translation)   IWM 1050
[TO THE GLORY OF THE BELGIAN SOLDIER PART 2] (translation)   IWM 1051
[TO THE GLORY OF THE BELGIAN SOLDIER PART 3] (translation)   IWM 1052
[TO THE GLORY OF THE BELGIAN SOLDIER PART 4] (translation)   IWM 1053
[TO THE GLORY OF THE BELGIAN SOLDIER PART 5] (translation)   IWM 1054
TOMMY SECURES SUITABLE FARE FOR THIS SEASON (GB, 1917)   IWM 155
TOPICAL BUDGET 89-2 (GB, 10/5/1913)   NTB 89-02
TOPICAL BUDGET 164-1 (GB, 14/10/1914)   NTB 164-01
TOPICAL BUDGET 164-2 (GB, 17/10/1914)   IWM 1070a
TOPICAL BUDGET 165-2 (GB, 24/10/1914)   NTB 165-02
TOPICAL BUDGET 168-1 (GB, 11/11/1914)   NTB 168-01 *dup* IWM 1061-08f
TOPICAL BUDGET 174-2 (GB, 26/12/1914)   IWM 1070c
TOPICAL BUDGET 178-1 (GB, 20/1/1915)   NTB 178-01
TOPICAL BUDGET 182-2 (GB, 20/2/1915)   IWM 1055e
TOPICAL BUDGET 183-2 (GB, 27/2/1915)   IWM 1070b
TOPICAL BUDGET 191-1 (GB, 21/4/1915)   NTB 191-01
TOPICAL BUDGET 194-1 (GB, 12/5/1915)   IWM 655d
TOPICAL BUDGET 194-2 (GB, 15/5/1915)   NTB 194-02
TOPICAL BUDGET 204-1 (GB, 21/7/1915)   NTB 204-01
TOPICAL BUDGET 213-2 (GB, 25/9/1915)   NTB 213-02
TOPICAL BUDGET 219-2 (GB, 6/11/1915)   NTB 219-02
TOPICAL BUDGET 221-1 (GB, 17/11/1915)   IWM 1070h *and* NTB 221-01
TOPICAL BUDGET 222-2 (GB, 27/11/1915)   NTB 222-02
TOPICAL BUDGET 223-1 (GB, 1/12/1915)   NTB 223-01
TOPICAL BUDGET 223-2 (GB, 4/12/1915)   IWM 1061-08d *and* NTB 223-02
TOPICAL BUDGET 224-1 (GB, 8/12/1915)   NTB 224-01
TOPICAL BUDGET 224-2 (GB, 11/12/1915)   NTB 224-02
TOPICAL BUDGET 225-2 (GB, 18/12/1915)   NTB 225-02
TOPICAL BUDGET 233-1 (GB, 9/2/1916)   IWM 1181
TOPICAL BUDGET 235-2 (GB, 26/2/1916)   NTB 235-02
TOPICAL BUDGET 236-1 (GB, 1/3/1916)   IWM 1061-08e
TOPICAL BUDGET 237-2 (GB, 11/3/1916)   NTB 237-02

TOPICAL BUDGET 238-1 (GB, 15/3/1916)	NTB 238-01
TOPICAL BUDGET 238-2 (GB, 18/3/1916)	IWM 1062-22a
TOPICAL BUDGET 239-1 (GB, 22/3/1916)	NTB 239-01
TOPICAL BUDGET 239-2 (GB, 25/3/1916)	NTB 239-02
TOPICAL BUDGET 240-1 (GB, 29/3/1916)	NTB 240-01
TOPICAL BUDGET 240-2 (GB, 1/4/1916)	NTB 240-02
TOPICAL BUDGET 241-1 (GB, 5/4/1916)	NTB 241-01
TOPICAL BUDGET 241-2 (GB, 8/4/1916)	NTB 241-02
TOPICAL BUDGET 242-1 (GB, 12/4/1916)	NTB 242-01
TOPICAL BUDGET 242-2 (GB, 15/4/1916)	NTB 242-02
TOPICAL BUDGET 245-2 (GB, 6/5/1916)	NTB 245-02
TOPICAL BUDGET 246-1 (GB, 10/5/1916)	NTB 246-01
TOPICAL BUDGET 246-2 (GB, 13/5/1916)	IWM 1182
TOPICAL BUDGET 247-1 (GB, 17/5/1916)	NTB 247-01
TOPICAL BUDGET 247-2 (GB, 20/5/1916)	NTB 247-02
TOPICAL BUDGET 248-1 (GB, 24/5/1916)	NTB 248-01 *dup* IWM 1061-05h
TOPICAL BUDGET 248-2 (GB, 27/5/1916)	NTB 248-02
TOPICAL BUDGET 249-1 (GB, 31/5/1916)	NTB 249-01
TOPICAL BUDGET 249-2 (GB, 3/6/1916)	NTB 249-02
TOPICAL BUDGET 250-2 (GB, 10/6/1915)	NTB 250-02
TOPICAL BUDGET 251-1 (GB, 14/6/1916)	NTB 251-01
TOPICAL BUDGET 251-2 (GB, 17/6/1916)	NTB 251-02 *dup* IWM 1060
TOPICAL BUDGET 252-2 (GB, 24/6/1916)	NTB 252-02
TOPICAL BUDGET 253-1 (GB, 28/6/1916)	NTB 253-01
TOPICAL BUDGET 253-2 (GB, 1/7/1916)	NTB 253-02
TOPICAL BUDGET 254-1 (GB, 5/7/1916)	NTB 254-01
TOPICAL BUDGET 254-2 (GB, 8/7/1916)	NTB 254-02
TOPICAL BUDGET 255-1 (GB, 12/7/1916)	NTB 255-01
TOPICAL BUDGET 255-2 (GB, 15/7/1916)	NTB 255-02
TOPICAL BUDGET 256-1 (GB, 19/7/1916)	NTB 256-01
TOPICAL BUDGET 256-2 (GB, 22/7/1916)	NTB 256-02
TOPICAL BUDGET 257-1 (GB, 26/7/1916)	NTB 257-01
TOPICAL BUDGET 258-1 (GB, 2/8/1916)	NTB 258-01
TOPICAL BUDGET 258-2 (GB, 5/8/1916)	NTB 258-02
TOPICAL BUDGET 259-1 (GB, 9/8/1916)	NTB 259-01
TOPICAL BUDGET 259-2 (GB, 12/8/1916)	NTB 259-02
TOPICAL BUDGET 260-2 (GB, 19/8/1916)	NTB 260-02
TOPICAL BUDGET 261-1 (GB, 23/8/1916)	NTB 261-01 *dup* IWM 1061-04h
TOPICAL BUDGET 261-2 (GB, 26/8/1916)	NTB 261-02
TOPICAL BUDGET 262-1 (GB, 30/8/1916)	NTB 262-01
TOPICAL BUDGET 263-1 (GB, 6/9/1916)	NTB 263-01
TOPICAL BUDGET 263-2 (GB, 9/9/1916)	NTB 263-02 *dup* IWM 655c; IWM 1180b
TOPICAL BUDGET 264-1 (GB, 13/9/1916)	NTB 264-01
TOPICAL BUDGET 265-1 (GB, 20/9/1916)	NTB 265-01
TOPICAL BUDGET 265-2 (GB, 23/9/1916)	NTB 265-02
TOPICAL BUDGET 266-2 (GB, 30/9/1916)	NTB 266-02
TOPICAL BUDGET 267-1 (GB, 4/10/1916)	NTB 267-01
TOPICAL BUDGET 267-2 (GB, 7/10/1916)	NTB 267-02
TOPICAL BUDGET 269-1 (GB, 18/10/1916)	NTB 269-01
TOPICAL BUDGET 269-2 (GB, 21/10/1916)	NTB 269-02
TOPICAL BUDGET 270-2 (GB, 28/10/1916)	NTB 270-02
TOPICAL BUDGET 271-2 (GB, 4/11/1916)	NTB 271-02
TOPICAL BUDGET 272-2 (GB, 11/11/1916)	NTB 272-02
TOPICAL BUDGET 273-1 (GB, 15/11/1916)	NTB 273-01
TOPICAL BUDGET 273-2 (GB, 18/11/1916)	NTB 273-02
TOPICAL BUDGET 274-1 (GB, 22/11/1916)	NTB 274-01
TOPICAL BUDGET 275-2 (GB, 2/12/1916)	NTB 275-02
TOPICAL BUDGET 276-2 (GB, 9/12/1916)	NTB 276-02
TOPICAL BUDGET 277-1 (GB, 13/12/1916)	NTB 277-01
TOPICAL BUDGET 277-2 (GB, 16/12/1916)	NTB 277-02
TOPICAL BUDGET 278-2 (GB, 23/12/1916)	NTB 278-02
TOPICAL BUDGET 279-1 (GB, 27/12/1916)	NTB 279-01
TOPICAL BUDGET 279-2 (GB, 30/12/1916)	NTB 279-02

TOPICAL BUDGET 280-1 (GB, 3/1/1917) — NTB 280-01
TOPICAL BUDGET 283-2 (GB, 27/1/1917) — NTB 283-02
TOPICAL BUDGET 284-1 (GB, 31/1/1917) — IWM 1061-05c
TOPICAL BUDGET 284-2 (GB, 3/2/1917) — NTB 284-02
TOPICAL BUDGET 285-1 (GB, 7/2/1917) — IWM 1061-03h
TOPICAL BUDGET 288-1 (GB, 28/2/1917) — IWM 1061-05b
TOPICAL BUDGET 290-2 (GB, 17/3/1917) — IWM 1061-09g
TOPICAL BUDGET 292-1 (GB, 28/3/1917) — NTB 292-01
TOPICAL BUDGET 292-2 (GB, 31/3/1917) — IWM 1180c
TOPICAL BUDGET 300-2 etc - from issue 300-2, the newsreel was re-titled **WAR OFFICE OFFICIAL TOPICAL BUDGET** and issues are listed under that title.
TOPICAL BUDGET 673-1 (GB, 17/7/1924) — IWM 1148
TOPICAL BUDGET 675-1 (GB, 31/7/1924) — IWM 1149
TORPEDO DROPPING AT EAST FORTUNE TDS (GB, 1918) — IWM 636
TRAINING PILOTS FOR THE IMPERIAL BRITISH ROYAL FLYING CORPS (GB, 1917) — IWM 870
TRAINING THE TANKS (GB, 7/1918) — IWM 452
[TRANSFORMATIONS] (translation) — IWM 1083
TRIAL FLIGHT OF R9 (ledger title) (GB, 1917) — IWM 621
[TRIAL FLIGHTS OF RIGID AIRSHIPS NO 24 AND 25 AT INCHINNAN, OCTOBER 1917] (allocated) (GB, 1917) — IWM 622
the **TRIUMPH OF BRITAIN'S SEA POWER** (GB, 1918) — IWM 571
TURKISH ITALIAN WAR - THE INVASION OF TRIPOLI (GB/Italy, 1911) — IWM 1123
a **TURKISH PRISONER OF WAR CAMP** (GB, 1917) — IWM 4
the **TURKS** (Germany, 1915) — IWM 1062-02a
TWENTY SEVENTH AND THIRTIETH DIVISIONS (filing) — IWM 503
the **U-TUBE** (GB, 1917) — IWM 544
UBIQUE - OUR GUNNERS IN THE GREAT WAR (GB, 1917) — IWM 430
UNIVERSAL CURRENT EVENTS (USA, 1917) — IWM 687
UNIVERSAL TALKING NEWS [1930] - A NINE TON BULLET (GB, 1930) — IWM 880-01e
UNIVERSAL TALKING NEWS [1930] - [A NINE TON BULLET 2] (allocated) (GB, 1930) — IWM 880-01h
[UNVEILING STATUE OF GORDON] (allocated) (GB, 1902) — IWM 1025f
URUGUAY'S TRIBUTE TO SIR ERNEST SHACKLETON (translation) — IWM 506
[US INDEPENDENCE DAY CELEBRATIONS IN BELGIUM, 1918] (allocated) (GB, 1918) — IWM 254
[US INFANTRY AT LE HAVRE AND WAACS AT ABBEVILLE CEMETERY, JULY 1918] (allocated) (GB, 1918) — IWM 272
[US SIGNAL CORPS, ROYAL ENGINEERS AND QMAAC ON THE WESTERN FRONT, JULY 1918] (allocated) (GB, 1918) — IWM 267
[US TANK EXERCISE] (allocated) (USA, 1920) — IWM 1064-01a
USA - SS SECTION 4 (ledger title) (USA, 1920) — IWM 619
UXBRIDGE WRAF FORM A GUARD OF HONOUR TO QUEEN MARY AT THE SAVOY HOTEL 7/4/19 (GB, 1919) — IWM 612
VICKERS VANGUARDS (ledger title) (GB, 1917) — IWM 434
VILLAGES IN FLANDERS, THE SCENES OF HARD FIGHTING, NOW HELD BY THE BRITISH (GB, 3/4/1916) — IWM 209
VIMY RIDGE (GB, 1917) — IWM 467
VISIT OF ALLIED MEMBERS TO THE GRAND FLEET (ledger title) (GB, 1918) — IWM 600
VISIT OF AMERICAN AIRMEN TO SHAKESPEARE'S COUNTRY (GB, 1918) — IWM 304
VISIT OF BELGIAN KING TO GRAND FLEET (ledger title) (GB, 1918) — IWM 602
VISIT OF CANADIAN PRESSMEN - SCENES IN ENGLAND AND FRANCE (GB, 1918) — IWM 310
the **VISIT OF HIS ROYAL HIGHNESS PRINCE ARTHUR TO JAPAN** (GB/Japan, 1918) — IWM 451
VISIT OF HRH THE PRINCE OF WALES TO EBBW VALE, FEBRUARY 21ST 1918 (GB, 1918) — IWM 170
VISIT OF ITALIAN DELEGATION TO THE GRAND FLEET (ledger title) (GB, 1918) — IWM 599
VISIT OF SIR ERIC GEDDES, FIRST LORD OF THE BRITISH ADMIRALTY, TO THE US NAVAL ACADEMY, ANNAPOLIS, MD, OCTOBER 10, 1918 (USA, 10/1918) — IWM 565
VISIT OF SIR H WILSON TO THE GRAND FLEET (ledger title) (GB, 1918) — IWM 603
VISIT OF SIR THOMAS MACKENZIE KCMG HIGH COMMISSIONER FOR NEW ZEALAND TO THE NEW ZEALAND DIVISION, SEPTEMBER 9TH AND 10TH 1917 (New Zealand, 1917) — IWM 157
VISIT OF SPANISH GENERALS TO THE WESTERN FRONT (GB, 10/1917) — IWM 115
VISIT OF THE HON J R BENNETT, MINISTER OF MILITIA OF NEWFOUNDLAND, TO FRANCE, 1918 (GB, 1918) — IWM 253

VISIT OF THE HON W F MASSEY AND SIR J WARD TO THE WESTERN FRONT 30 JUNE-4
 JULY 1918 (New Zealand, 1918)   IWM 269
VISIT OF THE KING OF AFGHANISTAN TO ENGLAND (ledger title) (GB, 14/5/1928)   IWM 809
VISIT OF THE MAHARAJAH OF PATIALA TO FRANCE (GB, 1918)   IWM 282
VISIT OF USA DELEGATES TO GRAND FLEET (ledger title) (GB, 1918)   IWM 601
VISIT TO THE NEW ZEALAND INFANTRY BASE DEPOT AT ETAPLES (extracts)   IWM 160
die VOLKSABSTIMMUNG IN SOPRON (Hungary, 1922)   IWM 1035a
VORSICHT BEI ALLEN GESPRAECHEN (Germany, 1918)   IWM 778
VUES POUR CINEMATOGRAPHE LUMIERE (series)   IWM 1083
[WAAC CAMP AT ABBEVILLE FOLLOWING AN AIR RAID, 22ND MAY 1918] (allocated) (GB,
 1918)   IWM 228
the WAR ANNALS (translation) see ANNALES DE LA GUERRE
WAR AT FIRST HAND (former ledger title)   IWM 468
the WAR CLOUD (GB, 1922)   IWM 1061-01
WAR IN THE AIR : unique pictures by our own photographer with the Russian Navy (France,
 1915-17)   IWM 650
WAR MESSENGER DOGS (GB, 1918)   IWM 235
WAR OFFICE OFFICIAL TOPICAL BUDGET 300-2 (GB, 26/5/1917)   IWM 1061-03e
WAR OFFICE OFFICIAL TOPICAL BUDGET 309-1 (GB, 25/7/1917)   NTB 309-01
WAR OFFICE OFFICIAL TOPICAL BUDGET 310-1 (GB, 1/8/1917)   NTB 310-01
WAR OFFICE OFFICIAL TOPICAL BUDGET 310-2 (GB, 4/8/1917)   NTB 310-02
WAR OFFICE OFFICIAL TOPICAL BUDGET 312-1 (GB, 15/8/1917)   NTB 312-01
WAR OFFICE OFFICIAL TOPICAL BUDGET 313-1 (GB, 22/8/1917)   NTB 313-01
WAR OFFICE OFFICIAL TOPICAL BUDGET 314-2 (GB, 1/9/1917)   NTB 314-02
WAR OFFICE OFFICIAL TOPICAL BUDGET 316-1 (GB, 12/9/1917)   NTB 316-01 dup IWM 1129a
WAR OFFICE OFFICIAL TOPICAL BUDGET 317-1 (GB, 19/9/1917)   NTB 317-01
WAR OFFICE OFFICIAL TOPICAL BUDGET 317-2 (GB, 22/9/1917)   NTB 317-02 dup IWM 694b
WAR OFFICE OFFICIAL TOPICAL BUDGET 318-1 (GB, 26/9/1917)   NTB 318-01
WAR OFFICE OFFICIAL TOPICAL BUDGET 318-2 (GB, 29/9/1917)   NTB 318-02
WAR OFFICE OFFICIAL TOPICAL BUDGET 319-1 (GB, 3/10/1917)   NTB 319-01
WAR OFFICE OFFICIAL TOPICAL BUDGET 319-2 (GB, 6/10/1917)   NTB 319-02
WAR OFFICE OFFICIAL TOPICAL BUDGET 320-2 (GB, 13/10/1917)   NTB 320-02 dup IWM 655b
WAR OFFICE OFFICIAL TOPICAL BUDGET 321-1 (GB, 17/10/1917)   NTB 321-01
WAR OFFICE OFFICIAL TOPICAL BUDGET 321-2 (GB, 20/10/1917)   NTB 321-02
WAR OFFICE OFFICIAL TOPICAL BUDGET 322-1 (GB, 24/10/1917)   NTB 322-01
WAR OFFICE OFFICIAL TOPICAL BUDGET 323-1 (GB, 31/10/1917)   NTB 323-01
WAR OFFICE OFFICIAL TOPICAL BUDGET 323-2 (GB, 3/11/1917)   NTB 323-02
WAR OFFICE OFFICIAL TOPICAL BUDGET 324-1 (GB, 7/11/1917)   NTB 324-01
WAR OFFICE OFFICIAL TOPICAL BUDGET 324-2 (GB, 10/11/1917)   NTB 324-02
WAR OFFICE OFFICIAL TOPICAL BUDGET 325-1 (GB, 14/11/1917)   NTB 325-01
WAR OFFICE OFFICIAL TOPICAL BUDGET 325-2 (GB, 17/11/1917)   NTB 325-02
WAR OFFICE OFFICIAL TOPICAL BUDGET 327-1 (GB, 28/11/1917)   NTB 327-01 dup IWM 1129c
WAR OFFICE OFFICIAL TOPICAL BUDGET 327-2 (GB, 1/12/1917)   NTB 327-02
WAR OFFICE OFFICIAL TOPICAL BUDGET 328-1 (GB, 5/12/1917)   NTB 328-01
WAR OFFICE OFFICIAL TOPICAL BUDGET 329-1 (GB, 12/12/1917)   NTB 329-01
WAR OFFICE OFFICIAL TOPICAL BUDGET 330-2 (GB, 22/12/1917)   NTB 330-02
WAR OFFICE OFFICIAL TOPICAL BUDGET 331-1 (Spanish version) (GB, 26/12/1917) IWM 193a
WAR OFFICE OFFICIAL TOPICAL BUDGET 331-2 (Spanish version) (GB, 29/12/1917) IWM 193b
WAR OFFICE OFFICIAL TOPICAL BUDGET 332-1 (Spanish version) (GB, 2/1/1918)   IWM 193c
WAR OFFICE OFFICIAL TOPICAL BUDGET 332-2 (Spanish version) (GB, 5/1/1918)   IWM 193d
WAR OFFICE OFFICIAL TOPICAL BUDGET 333-1 (Spanish version) (GB, 9/1/1918)   IWM 692a
WAR OFFICE OFFICIAL TOPICAL BUDGET 333-2 (Spanish version) (GB, 12/1/1918)
                                                             IWM 692b and IWM 697b
WAR OFFICE OFFICIAL TOPICAL BUDGET 334-1 (GB, 16/1/1918)
                                        IWM 662b and IWM 697c dup IWM 658b
WAR OFFICE OFFICIAL TOPICAL BUDGET 334-2 (Spanish version) (GB, 19/1/1918)   IWM 697d
WAR OFFICE OFFICIAL TOPICAL BUDGET 335-1 (GB, 23/1/1918)   IWM 672a
WAR OFFICE OFFICIAL TOPICAL BUDGET 335-2 (GB, 26/1/1918)
                   IWM 697a and IWM 672b; IWM 1061-09a dup IWM 1061-09c
WAR OFFICE OFFICIAL TOPICAL BUDGET 336-1 (GB, 30/1/1918)   IWM 651a and IWM 684e
WAR OFFICE OFFICIAL TOPICAL BUDGET 336-2 (GB, 2/2/1918)   IWM 651b and IWM 684d
WAR OFFICE OFFICIAL TOPICAL BUDGET 337-1 (GB, 6/2/1918)   IWM 662a and IWM 651c

WAR OFFICE OFFICIAL TOPICAL BUDGET 338-1 (GB, 13/2/1918)

          IWM 663a *and* IWM 684c *dup* IWM 1061-09d

WAR OFFICE OFFICIAL TOPICAL BUDGET 338-2 (GB, 16/2/1918)   IWM 663b *and* IWM 684b

WAR OFFICE OFFICIAL TOPICAL BUDGET 339-1 **(Spanish version)** (GB, 20/2/1918) IWM 663c

WAR OFFICE OFFICIAL TOPICAL BUDGET 339-2 (alternative)   IWM 13

WAR OFFICE OFFICIAL TOPICAL BUDGET 340-1 etc - from issue 340-1, the newsreel was
  re-titled **PICTORIAL NEWS (OFFICIAL)** and issues are listed under that title.

[WAR OFFICE OFFICIAL TOPICAL BUDGET FRAGMENTS] (alternative, allocated)   IWM 499

the WAR WOMEN OF ENGLAND (GB, 6/1918)   IWM 474

WARTIME FLYING FILM **(ledger title)** (GB, 1918)   IWM 482

WATFORD MANUFACTURING COMPANY SPORTS **(ledger title)** (GB, 1918)   IWM 284

the WAY OF A SHIP ON THE SEA (GB, 3/1918)   IWM 552

[the WEDDING OF ARCHDUKE KARL AND ZITA] (allocated) (Austria-Hungary, 1911)

                           IWM 1034-01a

the WEST RIDING REGIMENT (GB, 2/1918)   IWM 404

the WEST YORKS REGIMENT (GB, 2/1918)   IWM 402

[WESTERN FRONT (rough material)] (allocated) (GB, 1918)   IWM 123

[WESTERN FRONT CHRISTMAS - 1915 (?)] (allocated) (GB, 1916)   IWM 106

[WESTERN FRONT - THREE SCENES FROM FEATURE FILMS] (allocated) (GB, 1925)

                           IWM 1062-11

[WEYMOUTH CLASS CRUISER] (allocated) (GB, 1912)   IWM 1082-03

[WILHELM II VISITS VIENNA] (allocated) (Austria-Hungary, 1912)   IWM 1033b

WINE INDUSTRY AND LAYING OF THE FOUNDATION STONE OF THE JEWISH UNIVERSITY
  (GB, 1918)   IWM 35

WINTER FLYING AT CAMP BORDEN (Canada, 1920)   IWM 860

WINTER ON THE WESTERN FRONT (alternative)   IWM 130-01+2

WITH A CANADIAN BRIGADE AT YPRES (GB, 1917)   IWM 143

WITH ALLENBY IN PALESTINE : a Lowell Thomas Adventure Film (USA, 1927) IWM 1131b

WITH BRITAIN'S MONSTER GUNS IN ACTION (GB, 1918)   IWM 218

WITH GENERAL IRONSIDE'S FORCES IN NORTH RUSSIA (GB, 1919)   IWM 808

WITH GERMANY'S ALLY (Germany, 1915)   IWM 1062-02b

WITH LAWRENCE IN ARABIA : a Lowell Thomas Adventure Film (USA, 1927) IWM 1131a

WITH LORD KITCHENER IN FRANCE (GB, 8/5/1916)   IWM 213

WITH OUR BOYS AT THE FRONT **(first version)** (GB, 1918)   IWM 476

WITH OUR BOYS AT THE FRONT **(second version)** (GB, 1918)   IWM 477

WITH OUR BOYS IN FRANCE (USA, 1933)   IWM 1079

WITH OUR FRENCH ALLY (series)   IWM 1057-01; IWM 1057-02

WITH OUR TERRITORIALS AT THE FRONT (GB, 14/2/1916)   IWM 205

WITH THE 5TH BATTALION, YORK AND LANCASTER REGIMENT IN CAMP AT
  SCARBOROUGH AUGUST 1922 (GB, 1922)   IWM 1137

WITH THE ALLIED TROOPS IN SALONIKA (GB, 1916)   IWM 100

WITH THE AUSTRALIAN FORCES IN FRANCE (Australia, 1/1918)   IWM 138

WITH THE AUSTRALIAN FORCES IN PALESTINE (Australia, 6/1918)   IWM 28

WITH THE BEF IN ITALY (GB, 1918)   IWM 266

WITH THE BRITISH FORCES FOR THE DEFENCE OF SALONIKA (GB, 1916) IWM 1062-22b

WITH THE BRITISH FORCES IN ITALY - SEVEN DAYS LEAVE (GB, 1918)   IWM 283

WITH THE EYES OF THE NAVY (GB, 1918)   IWM 867

WITH THE FORCES IN MESOPOTAMIA - SERIES 1 (?) (GB/USA, 1917)   IWM 61

WITH THE FORCES IN MESOPOTAMIA - SERIES 4 (GB/USA, 1918)   IWM 64

WITH THE FORCES IN MESOPOTAMIA - SERIES 6 (GB/USA, 1918)   IWM 65

WITH THE FORCES IN MESOPOTAMIA (offcuts)   IWM 59

WITH THE FORCES IN MESOPOTAMIA (rough material)   IWM 64

WITH THE FRENCH NAVY (France, 1910)   IWM 1062-04

WITH THE INDIAN TROOPS (GB, 1936)   IWM 487

WITH THE INDIAN TROOPS AT THE FRONT PART I (GB, 17/1/1916)   IWM 202-01

WITH THE INDIAN TROOPS AT THE FRONT PART II (GB, 24/1/1916)   IWM 202-02

WITH THE INDIAN TROOPS AT THE FRONT (censored sections)   IWM 383

WITH THE ITALIAN FORCES IN PALESTINE (GB, 1917)   IWM 8

WITH THE KUT RELIEF FORCE IN MESOPOTAMIA (GB, 14/8/1916)   IWM 83

WITH THE NORTH AND SOUTH IRISH AT THE FRONT (GB, 1918)   IWM 212

WITH THE PORTUGUESE EXPEDITIONARY FORCE IN FRANCE (GB, 1917) IWM 411

WITH THE ROYAL AIR FORCE IN INDIA (GB, 1919)   IWM 876

WITH THE ROYAL FIELD ARTILLERY IN ACTION (GB, 10/4/1916)   IWM 210

WITH THE ROYAL FLYING CORPS (SOMEWHERE IN FRANCE) (GB, 12/1917)   IWM 141
WITH THE RUSSIAN ARMY (France, 1916)   IWM 1062-01
WITH THE RUSSIAN ARMY IN THE CAUCASUS (alternative)   IWM 1062-01
WITH THE SOUTH AFRICAN FORCES (GB, 1918)   IWM 128
WITH THE VICTORIOUS BRITISH TROOPS ON THE AMIENS FRONT (GB, 1918)   IWM 281
the **WOMAN'S PORTION** (GB, 1918)   IWM 522
WOMEN AND THE WAR (GB, 1918)   IWM 479
the **WOMEN FARMERS OF BRITAIN** (GB, 1918)   IWM 1217
WOMEN'S ARMY IN FRANCE (completed version) (GB, 1918)   IWM 329
WOMEN'S ARMY IN FRANCE 1 (GB, 1918)   IWM 315
WOMEN'S ARMY IN FRANCE 2 (GB, 1918)   IWM 328
the **WOMEN'S AUXILIARY ARMY CORPS [sic] : the work of the WAAC at a base in France** (GB, 1918)   IWM 405
the **WOMEN'S LAND ARMY** (GB, 8/1917)   IWM 480
WOMEN'S ROYAL AIR FORCE (GB, 1918)   IWM 1107-02
WOMEN'S ROYAL AIR FORCE - LIFE ON A BRITISH AERODROME (GB, 1918)   IWM 1106
WOMEN'S WORK (GB, 1918)   IWM 245
WOMEN'S WORK ON MUNITIONS OF WAR (GB, 1918)   IWM 419
the **WONDERFUL ORGANISATION OF THE RAMC** (GB, 15/5/1916)   IWM 133
WOOLWICH ARSENAL AND ITS WORKERS (GB, 3/1918)   IWM 161
the **WORK OF THE ARMY VETERINARY CORPS : and how it is helped by the RSPCA** (GB, 12/6/1916)   IWM 114
WORK OF THE METEOROLOGICAL OFFICE (GB, 1918)   IWM 355
WORK OF THE NEW ZEALAND MEDICAL CORPS [NZMC] (alternative)   IWM 387
the **WORLD'S GREATEST STORY - EPISODE 1** (GB, 1919)   IWM 420-01+2
the **WORLD'S GREATEST STORY - EPISODE 2** (GB, 1919)   IWM 420-03+4
the **WORLD'S GREATEST STORY - EPISODE 3** (GB, 1919)   IWM 420-05+6
the **WORLD'S GREATEST STORY - EPISODE 4** (GB, 1919)   IWM 420-07+8
the **WORLD'S GREATEST STORY - EPISODE 5** (GB, 1919)   IWM 420-09+10
the **WORLD'S GREATEST STORY - EPISODE 6** (GB, 1919)   IWM 420-11+12
the **WORLD'S GREATEST STORY - EPISODE 7** (GB, 1919)   IWM 420-13+14
the **WORLD'S GREATEST STORY - EPISODE 8** (GB, 1919)   IWM 420-15+16
the **WORLD'S GREATEST STORY - EPISODE 9** (GB, 1919)   IWM 420-17+18
the **WORLD'S GREATEST STORY - EPISODE 10** (GB, 1919)   IWM 420-19+20
the **WORLD'S GREATEST STORY - EPISODE 11** (GB, 1919)   IWM 420-21+22
the **WORLD'S GREATEST STORY - EPISODE 12** (GB, 1919)   IWM 420-23+24
the **WORLD'S GREATEST STORY - EPISODE 13** (GB, 1919)   IWM 420-25+26
the **WORLD'S GREATEST STORY - EPISODE 14** (GB, 1919)   IWM 420-27+28
the **WORLD'S GREATEST STORY - EPISODE 15** (GB, 1919)   IWM 420-29+30
the WORLD'S GREATEST STORY (offcuts)   IWM 123
[WOUNDED AND PRISONERS BEHIND THE LINES ON THE WESTERN FRONT] (allocated) (GB, 1917)   IWM 409
WRAF CAMP (GB, 1919)   IWM 610
the **WRECK OF THE L33** (GB, 1918)   IWM 1218
the **WRECKED BABY KILLER** (France/GB, 2/1916)   IWM 1204
WRECKED ZEPPELIN BROUGHT DOWN BY BRITISH NAVAL GUNNERY (GB, 1916)   IWM 1207
the **WRECKED ZEPPELINS IN ESSEX** (GB, 1916)   IWM 1206
WRNS (ledger title) (GB, 1918)   IWM 641
the **YORK AND LANCASTER REGIMENT** (GB, 12/1917)   IWM 396
YPRES - THE SHELL SHATTERED CITY OF FLANDERS [1916] (GB, 6/3/1916)   IWM 206
YPRES - THE SHELL SHATTERED CITY OF FLANDERS [1918] (GB, 1918)   IWM 344
ZEEBRUGGE (ledger title) (GB, 1918)   IWM 358
ZEPPELIN IN FLIGHT (Germany, 1913)   IWM 1205

Abdul Hamid II, Sultan of Turkey NTB 191-01
Abrahams, Harold M IWM 594-04-13
Ackermann (Kapitän) IWM 772
Ackroyd, Harold VC NTB 318-02
Adams, H J IWM 501-10
Adamson, Agar IWM 109
Airlie (Countess of) IWM 198
Aitken, Thomas K IWM 232; IWM 372
Albert I, King of Belgium IWM 121
  IWM 192; IWM 198; IWM 265; IWM 359;
  IWM 370; IWM 371; IWM 484; IWM 501-02;
  IWM 508-21; IWM 508-23; IWM 508-28;
  IWM 508-40; IWM 508-43; IWM 508-84;
  IWM 508-88; IWM 509; IWM 602; IWM 665a;
  IWM 666a; IWM 670b; IWM 674c; IWM 1054;
  NTB 313-01
Alcock, John W IWM 485
Alexander I, King of Yugoslavia IWM 484;
  IWM 508-17; IWM 1061-06h; NTB 310-02
Alexander, Harold R L G IWM 208
Alexander, King of Greece IWM 97;
  IWM 484; IWM 508-19; IWM 508-26
Alexander, Prince of Teck IWM 121; IWM 192
Alexander-Sinclair, Edwyn S IWM 556
Alexandra, Queen (Consort of Edward VII)
  IWM 485; IWM 660a; IWM 678a; IWM 681c;
  IWM 1061-07b; IWM 1080a; IWM 1141;
  IWM 1142; IWM 1182; IWM 1186; IWM 1187;
  NTB 251-01; NTB 252-02
Alexandra, Tsarina of Russia IWM 484
Alexandra Victoria, Princess of Schleswig-
  Holstein IWM 1062-08
Alexei, Tsarevitch of Russia IWM 484
Alfonso XIII, King of Spain IWM 484
Alice, Princess (Countess of Athlone)
  IWM 693a; IWM 1062-17; NTB 345-02
Allen, James IWM 1213
Allenby, Edmund H H IWM 1; IWM 11;
  IWM 13; IWM 14; IWM 15; IWM 17; IWM 25;
  IWM 30; IWM 33; IWM 35; IWM 37; IWM 40;
  IWM 41; IWM 43; IWM 58; IWM 484;
  IWM 652a; IWM 681b; IWM 1131b;
  NTB 329-01; NTB 395-02
Amanullah, King of Afghanistan IWM 809
Amelie, Queen of Portugal NTB 258-02;
  NTB 316-01; NTB 356-02
Amundsen, Roald IWM 1082-02d
Andral, Paule NTB 245-02
Andrew, R H IWM 13
Annandale, Arthur J NTB 317-02
Anthoine, François IWM 508-21; IWM 508-24;
  IWM 508-25; IWM 508-26; IWM 508-38
Aosta, Amadeo (Duke) IWM 484
Applegarth, W R NTB 247-02
Aranaz (General) IWM 115
Archinard, Louis IWM 508-32; IWM 508-61;
  NTB 324-01
Ariyashi (Miss) IWM 451

Arnauld de la Perière, Lothar von IWM 560
Arques, the Belle of IWM 164
Arthur, Prince (Duke of Connaught)
  IWM 13; IWM 21; IWM 25; IWM 41; IWM 97;
  IWM 109; IWM 117; IWM 119; IWM 361;
  IWM 432; IWM 445; IWM 451; IWM 508-29;
  IWM 550-02; IWM 656a; NTB 225-02;
  NTB 313-01; NTB 321-01; NTB 321-02
Arthur, Prince (of Connaught; son of above)
  IWM 119; IWM 124; IWM 132; IWM 177;
  NTB 275-02
Arwyne (Commander) IWM 550-01; IWM 564
Ashe, James IWM 120
Ashmead Bartlett, Ellis IWM 1058
Asquith, Herbert H IWM 485; IWM 715;
  NTB 242-02; NTB 247-01
Asser, John IWM 198
Astier (Captain) IWM 451
Athens, Mayor of IWM 508-19
Athlone, Alexander (Earl) IWM 359; IWM 370
Auguste Viktoria, Kaiserin of Germany
  IWM 484; IWM 1062-08
Azaña y Diaz, Manuel IWM 153
Babbit, E IWM 1079
Bacon, Reginald H S IWM 198; IWM 551;
  IWM 553; IWM 571
Bacon, Robert IWM 503
Baden-Powell, Robert S S IWM 461c;
  IWM 678b
Bailloud (General) IWM 1; IWM 7; IWM 58;
  IWM 508-36; NTB 329-01
Bainbridge, Guy T IWM 1005
Baine, C L IWM 579
Baker, Newton D IWM 484; IWM 501-06;
  IWM 508-43; IWM 1079
Baldwin, Stanley IWM 485; IWM 809;
  IWM 810; IWM 811
Balfour, Arthur J IWM 508-68; IWM 659;
  IWM 663c; IWM 679a; IWM 811; IWM 1128a;
  IWM 1206
Balfourier (General) NTB 275-02
Bamford, E VC IWM 656b
Baratier, Augustin IWM 508-32
Barbosa, A IWM 289
Barclay, W S IWM 456
Barrès, Maurice NTB 224-02
Barrymore, Ethel IWM 1079
Bates, Thorpe IWM 462
Baxter, Charles IWM 456
Baxton (1st Lieutenant) IWM 503
Baylies, Frank IWM 1061-02b
Baylis (Sergeant) IWM 508-64
Bayly, Lewis IWM 562
Bean, C E W IWM 314
Beardmore, William IWM 140
Beasley, A W NTB 342-02
Beatrice (Princess) NTB 273-01

Beatty, David IWM 439; IWM 484;
   IWM 485; IWM 505; IWM 509; IWM 550-02;
      IWM 551; IWM 552; IWM 554; IWM 556;
      IWM 571; IWM 572; IWM 576; IWM 579;
      IWM 581; IWM 586; IWM 591; IWM 599;
      IWM 600; IWM 602; IWM 603; IWM 665b;
   IWM 674c; IWM 679a; IWM 685a; IWM 1143;
         IWM 1149; IWM 1158; IWM 1164
Beaverbrook, Maxwell (Baron) IWM 273;
   IWM 310; IWM 633; IWM 668c; IWM 674b;
                                 NTB 345-02
Beck, Cyril IWM 478
Beck, John H W IWM 198
Beesley, William VC IWM 677b
Beeton, H M IWM 253
Belcher, Douglas W VC NTB 284-02
Belcher, E A IWM 677b
Belknap, Charles IWM 565
Bell, G H IWM 202-02
Bell, Hugh IWM 462
Bell-Davies, R VC IWM 627
Beneš, Eduard IWM 810; IWM 811
Bennett, John R IWM 253; IWM 308c
Benson (Captain RFC) IWM 379
Benson, George IWM 1070g
Benson, William S IWM 445; IWM 565
Beresford, Charles (Lord) IWM 512;
                     IWM 660b; NTB 356-02
Bernard, A E IWM 253
Bernstorf, Johann-Heinrich von (Count)
                                  IWM 484
Berry, George L IWM 224
Berthelot, Henri-Mathias IWM 508-15;
      IWM 508-20; IWM 508-27; IWM 508-72;
      IWM 508-74; NTB 312-01; NTB 319-02
Bertie of Thame (Lord) IWM 198
Bethell, John NTB 275-02
Bethmann-Hollweg, Theobald von IWM 484
Biddle, John IWM 1186; IWM 1187
Bingham, Edward IWM 571
Birdwood, William R IWM 121; IWM 138;
      IWM 139; IWM 151; IWM 190; IWM 198;
      IWM 256; IWM 282; IWM 352; IWM 363;
      IWM 370; IWM 375; IWM 381; IWM 484
Birkenhead, F (Earl) IWM 809
Birmingham, Mayor of IWM 652a
Bishop, William A VC IWM 141; IWM 632
Bismarck, Otto E L von IWM 484
Bissolati (Sgr) IWM 508-65
Bliss, Tasker IWM 484
Boelcke, Oswald IWM 1004
Bols, Louis J IWM 13; IWM 25; IWM 27
Bon, F J J de IWM 563; IWM 572
Booth, Evangeline IWM 1079
Boothman, J N IWM 880-01a; IWM 880-01f
Bordeaux (General) IWM 97
Borden, Robert L IWM 591; IWM 659;
                                 IWM 678b
Boris III, King of Bulgaria IWM 1034-03
Borton, W M IWM 13
Boston, Mayor of IWM 692a

Bourgeois, Léon IWM 508-18; NTB 310-02
Bourke, R VC IWM 551; IWM 1105
Bourne (Cardinal) IWM 111; IWM 143;
                                 IWM 675b
Bowen, W J IWM 579
Bowring, Humphrey IWM 553
Bradstock (Colonel) IWM 505
Brancker, Sefton IWM 532
Brand, Hubert G IWM 591; IWM 809;
                                 IWM 842
Branting, H IWM 271
Bremond (Colonel) IWM 508-36
Brewill, A W IWM 198
Briand, Aristide IWM 485; IWM 509;
      IWM 810; IWM 811; NTB 242-02
Briggs, Charles J IWM 96
Brinton, G L IWM 880-01a
Britain, Harry IWM 224
Brooke, J Warwick IWM 111; IWM 129;
            IWM 367; IWM 374; IWM 380
Brooke-Popham, Robert M IWM 645
Brooking, Harry T IWM 43
Brooks, Ernest IWM 192; IWM 215;
      IWM 216; IWM 368; IWM 599; IWM 601
Broqueville (Baron) NTB 242-02
Brown, Arthur W IWM 485; IWM 1086
Brown, John IWM 706
Browning, A L IWM 501-06
Brownrigg, Douglas IWM 564
Bruce, Henry H IWM 556
Bruce, Stanley M IWM 842
Brudenell White, C B IWM 139
Brusilov, Alexei A NTB 251-02
Brussels, Mayor of IWM 501-02;
      IWM 508-88; IWM 665a; IWM 670b
Bryan, William J IWM 484
Bryce (Viscount) IWM 484
Bryceson, D J NTB 242-02
Buchanan, Angus VC NTB 324-02
Buck, Peter IWM 196
Buddicom, H IWM 1192
Budgen, J IWM 582
Buero, Juan A IWM 506
Bulfin, Edward S IWM 13
Bullard, R L IWM 484; IWM 508-51
Bülow, Karl von IWM 481; IWM 1033b
Bundy, Omar IWM 240; IWM 508-67
Burian (Duke) IWM 1034-01b
Burney, Dennis IWM 585
Burnham (Baron) IWM 331
Butler, Francis J P NTB 314-02
Butler, Gregory IWM 224
Butler, Mabel Isabelle NTB 314-02
Byng, Julian H G IWM 132; IWM 190;
      IWM 192; IWM 198; IWM 345; IWM 484;
            IWM 485; IWM 505; NTB 327-01
Byrne, Nicholas IWM 120
Cadorna, Luigi (Count) IWM 216; IWM 258;
            IWM 414; IWM 459; NTB 242-02
Caffrey (Private) VC IWM 396
Caine, Hall IWM 661b; NTB 327-02

Caldwell, Keith   IWM 141; IWM 632
Caley (Commodore)   IWM 130-03+4
Cambon, Paul   NTB 255-02
Cambridge (Duke)   IWM 1025f
Campbell, C   IWM 645
Campbell, Douglas   IWM 250; IWM 458
Campbell, John D   IWM 668d
Campbell, Pitcairn   IWM 450; NTB 344-01
Cannon, Joseph   IWM 484
Canterbury, Archbishop of   IWM 679a;
     IWM 1085
Cape Town, Lord Mayor of   IWM 842
Cardiff, Mayor of   IWM 678b
Carlot (Lieutenant)   NTB 267-02
Carnegie, Maude (Lady)   NTB 356-02
Carol II, King of Romania   IWM 508-15;
     IWM 508-20
Carpendale (Flag Captain)   IWM 562
Carpenter, Alfred F B VC   IWM 656b;
     IWM 657a
Carson, Edward H   IWM 485; IWM 674b;
     NTB 322-01
Carter, William G   IWM 174
Casement, Roger D   NTB 247-01
Castelnau, Noel de   IWM 508-28; IWM 508-88
Caswell, A H S   IWM 198
Cautley, H S   IWM 659
Cavan, Frederic (10th Earl)   IWM 121;
     IWM 207
Cayley, George C   IWM 570
Cecilie, Princess of Mecklenburg-Schwerin
     IWM 484
Chadwell Taylor, Dorothy   IWM 1082-02c
Chalmers Watson (Mrs)   IWM 474
Chamberlain, Austen   IWM 485; IWM 810;
     IWM 811
Chamberlain, Joseph   IWM 485
Chamberlain, Neville   IWM 485; IWM 811
Chambers, Reed   IWM 501-03; IWM 501-04
Chang Hsuh-liang   IWM 712
Chang Tso-lin   IWM 712
Chang Tsung-ch'ang   IWM 712
Charles, Prince of Belgium   IWM 192;
     IWM 265; IWM 666a
Charteris, John   IWM 129; IWM 258
Chauvel, Henry G   IWM 17
Chaytor, E C W   IWM 22
Chelmsfield (Lord)   IWM 1149
Chen (General)   IWM 712
Chetwode, Philip W   IWM 7; IWM 13;
     IWM 17; IWM 38; IWM 192
Chisholm, Marie   IWM 162; IWM 693d
Christian, Harry VC   IWM 140; NTB 317-02
Christian, Prince   NTB 323-02
Christian X, King of Denmark   NTB 240-02
Chu (General)   IWM 712
Churchill, Clementine   NTB 264-01

Churchill, Winston L S   IWM 156; IWM 363;
     IWM 440-01; IWM 448; IWM 485; IWM 504;
     IWM 666a; IWM 810; IWM 811;
     IWM 1064-01b; IWM 1213; NTB 264-01;
     NTB 322-01
Clare, José   IWM 153
Clare, Luis   IWM 153
Clark (1st Lieutenant)   IWM 503
Clark, F H   IWM 551; IWM 1105
Clark, Thomas   IWM 194
Clavel, A   IWM 454
Clemenceau, Georges E B   IWM 188;
     IWM 345; IWM 484; IWM 508-47;
     IWM 508-49; IWM 508-51; IWM 508-64;
     IWM 508-72; IWM 508-76; IWM 508-78 bis;
     IWM 508-86; IWM 508-91; IWM 1061-05i;
     NTB 318-01; NTB 341-02; NTB 343-01;
     NTB 356-02
Clooton (General)   IWM 192
Clynes, J R   IWM 292; IWM 485;
     IWM 674a; IWM 693e; NTB 347-02
Cockburn (Lieutenant Colonel) (?)   IWM 706
Coiffard, Michel   NTB 344-02
Collins, Jose   NTB 255-02
Colomb, George H C   IWM 1070b
Conan Doyle, Arthur   IWM 663a
Condouriotis (Admiral)   IWM 508-14;
     NTB 309-01
Congreve, Walter N   IWM 192
Connaught [George] (HRH Duke of) IWM 448
     IWM 462; IWM 484; IWM 485; IWM 504;
     IWM 660b; IWM 664a; IWM 679a; IWM 680a;
     IWM 1061-07b; IWM 1131b; IWM 192
Constantine I, King of Greece   NTB 270-02
Conway, Martin   IWM 504; IWM 507
Cook, A J   IWM 485
Cook, Joseph   IWM 139; IWM 843
Copin, Jules   IWM 148; IWM 672a
Cornwell, John T VC
     NTB 258-01; NTB 264-01
Cory, T   IWM 1062-17
Cosgrave, William T (?)   IWM 485
Coventry, Bishop of   IWM 446
Cowdray (Lady)   IWM 1182
Craster (Captain)   IWM 1063
Crease, T E   IWM 563; IWM 572
Creel, Charles S   IWM 1079
Crewe (Lady)   IWM 480
Crewe, Robert (Marquess)   IWM 661a
Critchley, Alfred C   IWM 615; IWM 632;
     IWM 635
Cromer (Earl)   IWM 556; IWM 581; IWM 1143
Cronkite, A   IWM 1079
Crooks, Will   IWM 485
Croute, Edward   IWM 485
Crowe, J T VC   IWM 289
Cruickshank, R E VC   IWM 461c
Cullen (Lord)   IWM 1178
Cunningham, John VC   IWM 427
Curran, F   IWM 147

Currie, Arthur W IWM 198; IWM 310;
  IWM 465; IWM 508-85; IWM 664b;
  IWM 680a; NTB 343-01
Curzon, George (Marquis) NTB 322-01
Cust, Charles IWM 313; IWM 361; IWM 556;
  IWM 558
Cyril, Archduke of Bulgaria IWM 1034-03
Czernin (Count) IWM 1034-01b
D'Agostio, F IWM 13
D'Annunzio, Gabriele IWM 484
Dalmeny (Lord) IWM 13
Damien (M) IWM 508-85
Damphierre, de (Marquis) IWM 508-65
Danglis (General) IWM 508-14; NTB 309-01
Daniels, Josephus IWM 445; IWM 484;
  IWM 565; IWM 1079
Daum, Paul IWM 501-03
Dautresme, Lucien IWM 501-03
David, Ferdinand IWM 508-26
Davidson, John H IWM 129; IWM 132
Davidson, Randall T IWM 679a
Davies, C B IWM 224
Davies, E A (Mrs) NTB 322-01
Davies, M R IWM 1137
Dawnay, Guy P IWM 13
Dawson, F S IWM 128; IWM 169
Dawson, Trevor IWM 580
De Bunsen, Maurice IWM 456
De Chair, Dudley R S IWM 842
De La Rey, Kloos (?) IWM 1061-07g
de Lisle, Beauvoir IWM 107; IWM 191
De Robeck, John M IWM 550-02; IWM 556
De Valera, Eamon IWM 485; IWM 675a
De Valles (Chaplain) IWM 458
De Vesci, Ivo (Viscount) IWM 1062-17
De Vries, M IWM 557
De Wet, Christiaan R IWM 1061-07g
Dean, Percy VC IWM 656b
Debeney, Maurice-Eugene IWM 508-84
Decies, John (Baron) IWM 1056
Delgado (Doctor) IWM 456
Deloche (Sergeant-Major) IWM 508-59;
  IWM 508-92
Dempsey, B IWM 1062-17
Denbigh (Earl of) IWM 304
Derby, Edward (Earl) IWM 663a; NTB 255-02
Desborough (Lord) NTB 258-01; NTB 323-01
Deschanel, Paul NTB 194-02
Devadlar, Gopal K IWM 529
Deviney, D IWM 675b
Dewar, J L IWM 1214
Di Robillant (General) IWM 508-59;
  IWM 508-61; IWM 508-64
Diaz (General) IWM 484; IWM 508-39;
  IWM 508-70
Dickinson, H NTB 324-01
Dimmer, J H S VC IWM 1070b
Ditte (General) IWM 192
Djafa (Pasha) IWM 508-36
Djevad (Pasha) IWM 772
Dmowski, Roman IWM 508-68

Doane (Major) IWM 458
Dobsin, C C VC IWM 566
Dojovic (General) (?) IWM 508-68
Dollfuss, Engelbert IWM 485
Domercq (Lieutenant) IWM 508-92
Dorgère (Mlle) IWM 1082-02c
Douglas, Sholto IWM 648
Doumergue, Gaston IWM 509;
  IWM 594-04-13
Draper, D C IWM 339
Drude (General) NTB 275-02
Drummond, Flora IWM 474; NTB 324-02
Dubail, Augustin Y H IWM 508-14;
  NTB 251-02; NTB 266-02
Duchesne, Denis-Auguste IWM 508-39
Duff, Allen F IWM 445; IWM 565; IWM 572
Dumesnil (M) IWM 508-64
Duncan, G B IWM 501-02
Duncan, John IWM 98
Dunn, Leroy C IWM 224
Dunn, William H IWM 443; NTB 272-02;
  NTB 273-01; NTB 279-02; NTB 280-01;
  NTB 321-01
Dykes, W NTB 342-02
Dyson, Frank W IWM 809
East, J IWM 1
Eastman, J H IWM 501-03; IWM 501-04
Easton, R J IWM 503
Eberle (Rear Admiral) IWM 565
Edward VII, King IWM 485; IWM 1025e;
  IWM 1080a
Edward, Prince of Wales IWM 106;
  IWM 132; IWM 170; IWM 192; IWM 198;
  IWM 207; IWM 289; IWM 375; IWM 382;
  IWM 484; IWM 485; IWM 501-11;
  IWM 501-13; IWM 505; IWM 508-62;
  IWM 508-85; IWM 509; IWM 528; IWM 571;
  IWM 594-04-13; IWM 664b; IWM 681b;
  IWM 681c; IWM 699b; IWM 809; IWM 811;
  IWM 843; IWM 1061-02a; IWM 1082-02c;
  IWM 1140; IWM 1141; IWM 1142; IWM 1212;
  NTB 319-01; NTB 319-02; NTB 340-01
Edwards, Alexander VC NTB 318-02
Edwards, Clarence R IWM 458; IWM 501-12;
  IWM 1079
Egerton, Ralph G IWM 69
Eggleton (Corporal-Major) IWM 1061-07g
Eitel Friedrich, Prince of Prussia IWM 484
El Kuneitra, Mayor of IWM 37
Elena, Queen of Italy IWM 484
Elisabeth, Queen of Belgium IWM 192;
  IWM 198; IWM 265; IWM 359; IWM 370;
  IWM 371; IWM 484; IWM 508-23;
  IWM 508-25; IWM 508-43; IWM 508-84;
  IWM 508-88; IWM 602; IWM 665a; IWM 666a;
  IWM 670b; IWM 674c; IWM 1054
Elizabeth II, Queen IWM 1085
Elizabeth, Queen (Consort of George VI)
  IWM 1085
Elles, Hugh J IWM 198; IWM 289

Enver Pasha IWM 772; IWM 1034-03; IWM 1062-02b
Essad Pasha IWM 772
Eugen, Archduke of Austria IWM 1033b; IWM 1035c; IWM 1040
Evan-Thomas, Hugh IWM 550-02; IWM 556
Evans, Edward R G R IWM 109; IWM 551; IWM 553; IWM 562
Evian, Mayor of IWM 508-35
Ewart, John S IWM 140; NTB 317-02
Exeter, William (Marquess) IWM 706
Faisal, Prince of Hejaz IWM 37; IWM 41; IWM 508-36; IWM 1131a
Falkenhayn, Erich von IWM 481; IWM 484
Fane, Vere B IWM 25; IWM 30
Fanshawe, Edward A IWM 198
Farrant, R IWM 675b
Faure, Félix IWM 1082-04
Fayolle, Emile IWM 508-37; IWM 508-39; IWM 508-43; IWM 508-46; IWM 508-62; IWM 508-72
Féchamp (Commandant) IWM 508-64
Fenton, Edith IWM 532
Féraud (General) IWM 508-18; NTB 310-02
Ferdinand I, King of Bulgaria IWM 484; IWM 1034-03; IWM 1040
Ferdinand I, King of Romania IWM 484; NTB 312-01
Ferrero (General) IWM 508-68
Fewtrell, Albert IWM 109
ffoulkes, Charles J IWM 504; IWM 507
Field, Frederick L IWM 842
Fielding, G P T IWM 117
Finch, Norman VC IWM 656b; IWM 657a
Fiske (Mrs) NTB 269-01
Fitzgerald, O A IWM 1062-20
Fletcher (Colonel) IWM 503
Foch, Ferdinand J M IWM 192; IWM 251; IWM 439; IWM 440-03; IWM 502; IWM 505; IWM 508-23; IWM 508-26; IWM 508-43; IWM 508-47; IWM 508-64; IWM 508-67; IWM 508-68; IWM 508-73; IWM 508-76; IWM 508-86; IWM 508-91; IWM 509; IWM 578-02; IWM 677b; IWM 1062-03; IWM 1062-20; IWM 1079; IWM 1175; NTB 356-02
Fonck, René IWM 508-38; IWM 508-61; IWM 1061-02c
Forbes-Robertson, James IWM 109; IWM 147
Forster (Lord) IWM 842
Foulkes (Brigadier General) IWM 198
Fowke, George H IWM 137
Franchet d'Esperey, Louis IWM 198; IWM 508-68
Francis, J H IWM 304
Francis, W W (Master-Engineer) IWM 448
Frankenburg, von (Colonel) IWM 772
Frankland (Lady) NTB 250-02
Franz Ferdinand, Archduke of Austria-Hungary IWM 484; IWM 1034-01a; IWM 1041b; IWM 1046a; IWM 1046b

Franz Josef I, Emperor of Austria-Hungary IWM 484; IWM 1033a; IWM 1033b; IWM 1033c; IWM 1033d; IWM 1034-01a; IWM 1034-01c; IWM 1040; IWM 1041a
Fremantle, Edmund R NTB 264-01
French, John D P IWM 109; IWM 174; IWM 344; IWM 440-03; IWM 484; IWM 485; IWM 505; IWM 657b; IWM 668c; IWM 678b; IWM 1062-17; IWM 1186; IWM 1187; NTB 253-01; NTB 254-01; NTB 259-01; NTB 261-02; NTB 266-02; NTB 272-02; NTB 321-01; NTB 325-02; NTB 351-02
French (Lady) IWM 1061-08b
Frey, J P IWM 579
Frickleton, Sam VC IWM 140
Friedrich, Archduke of Austria-Hungary IWM 481; IWM 484; IWM 1040; IWM 1062-15
Friedrich, Prince of Bavaria IWM 484
Friedrich August III, King of Saxony IWM 484; IWM 1033a; IWM 1034-01a
Fry, John P IWM 224
Fryatt, Charles NTB 259-01
Fuad I, King of Egypt IWM 23
Fullam (Admiral) IWM 1079
Fuller, John F C IWM 356
Fullerton, E J A IWM 809
Funakoshi, K IWM 550-02; IWM 563; IWM 572; IWM 1164
Furber, Douglas IWM 462
Fushimi, Prince of Japan IWM 132; IWM 550-02
Galli-Curci, Amelita IWM 1079
Gallwitz, von (General) IWM 481
Galopin (General) IWM 1061-06g
Galpin, C J IWM 1063
Garaud (Adjutant) IWM 508-52
Garibaldi, Benitti IWM 508-64
Garibaldi, Italia IWM 508-64
Garibaldi, Peppino IWM 154; IWM 508-43; IWM 508-64
Garibaldi, Sante IWM 508-43
Garrett (Corporal) IWM 640-03
Garros, Roland IWM 508-64
Garutso (Lieutenant Colonel) IWM 712
Geddes, Auckland IWM 478
Geddes, Eric C IWM 445; IWM 563; IWM 565; IWM 572; IWM 681c; NTB 322-01
Gellibrand, John IWM 293
George V, King IWM 109; IWM 128; IWM 134; IWM 140; IWM 192; IWM 198; IWM 201; IWM 213; IWM 218; IWM 258; IWM 265; IWM 289; IWM 293; IWM 313; IWM 356; IWM 375; IWM 418; IWM 439; IWM 446; IWM 448; IWM 484; IWM 485; IWM 501-13; IWM 503; IWM 504; IWM 505; IWM 509; IWM 550-01; IWM 551; IWM 552; IWM 556; IWM 558; IWM 571; IWM 572; IWM 580; IWM 581; IWM 586; IWM 625; IWM 653a; IWM 653b; IWM 654b; IWM 656a; IWM 657a; IWM 661b; IWM 663a; IWM 664a; IWM 666a; IWM 666b; IWM 667; IWM 668b;

George V, King *(continued)*
IWM 674a; IWM 674c; IWM 675b; IWM 677b;
IWM 678a; IWM 679a; IWM 681c; IWM 685a;
IWM 685b; IWM 693d; IWM 699c; IWM 809;
IWM 1061-01; IWM 1061-03i; IWM 1061-07b;
IWM 1062-03; IWM 1062-17; IWM 1064-03a;
IWM 1080a; IWM 1082-02b; IWM 1082-02c;
IWM 1141; IWM 1142; IWM 1143; IWM 1149;
IWM 1151; IWM 1158; IWM 1186; IWM 1187;
IWM 1212; IWM 1213; NTB 250-02;
NTB 251-01; NTB 254-01; NTB 317-02;
NTB 318-02; NTB 319-01; NTB 319-02;
NTB 320-02; NTB 321-02; NTB 323-01;
NTB 324-02; NTB 325-01; NTB 342-02;
NTB 343-01; NTB 354-01
George VI, King   IWM 313; IWM 370;
IWM 375; IWM 484; IWM 485; IWM 505;
IWM 509; IWM 556; IWM 581; IWM 625;
IWM 635; IWM 666a; IWM 809; IWM 1085
George, Prince (Duke of Kent)   IWM 265
Gerard [Ambassador]   IWM 1079
Gérard (General)   IWM 508-90; IWM 1079
Gérome (General)   IWM 97; IWM 508-48;
IWM 1061-05a
Ghose, Hemendra P   IWM 529
Gibbs, Philip (?)   IWM 122; IWM 381
Gifford (Lady)   IWM 162
Gilfillan (Captain)   IWM 128
Gill (Mme)   IWM 1079
Gillman, Webb   IWM 43
Gish, Lillian   IWM 1079
Gjertsen (Lieutenant)   IWM 1082-02d
Glasgow, Lord Provost of   IWM 654b
Glass, W   IWM 582
Gleeson-White (Mme)   IWM 462
Godard, Justin   IWM 508-26; IWM 508-39
Godfrey-Faussett, B   NTB 250-02
Godley, Alexander   IWM 157; IWM 196;
IWM 508-74
Goering, Hermann W   IWM 1004
Gomes de Costa (General)   IWM 411
Gompers, Samuel   IWM 501-13; IWM 572;
IWM 579; IWM 667; IWM 685a
Goodenough, William E   IWM 556
Gordon, A   IWM 113
Gordon, Home   IWM 224
Gorringe, George F   IWM 363
Gosling, Harry   NTB 312-01
Gough, Hubert de la P   IWM 121
Gouraud, Henri-Joseph-Eugene   IWM 344;
IWM 440-03; IWM 508-32; IWM 508-70;
IWM 508-75
Gouvres (Private)   IWM 508-11
Gramling (Adjutant)   IWM 1204
Gray, E H   IWM 202-02
Graziani, Rodolfo   IWM 508-70
Green, J S   NTB 213-02
Greene, Conyngham   IWM 451
Gregg, William VC   IWM 677b
Greville, Sidney   IWM 170; NTB 340-01
Grey, Edward   IWM 485; NTB 242-02

Griffith, Arthur   NTB 351-02
Griffith, D W   IWM 122; IWM 1079
Grigg (Colonel)   IWM 843
Grimbaldeston, William H VC   NTB 322-01
Grinevsky (Colonel)   IWM 712
Gueydon, de (Admiral)   IWM 508-19
Guillaumat, Louis   IWM 98; IWM 508-23;
IWM 508-45; IWM 508-48; IWM 508-90
Gustav Adolf, Crown Prince of Sweden
IWM 594-04-13
Guynemer, Georges M L J   IWM 484;
IWM 508-16; IWM 508-26; IWM 508-28;
NTB 318-02
Hadow, A L   IWM 147
Haig, Douglas   IWM 110; IWM 129;
IWM 132; IWM 156; IWM 158; IWM 190;
IWM 192; IWM 198; IWM 216; IWM 256;
IWM 289; IWM 310; IWM 314; IWM 345;
IWM 381; IWM 414; IWM 439; IWM 440-03;
IWM 484; IWM 485; IWM 503; IWM 505;
IWM 508-24; IWM 508-68; IWM 677b;
IWM 1128a; NTB 317-01
Haile Selassie, Emperor of Ethiopia
IWM 594-04-13
Haking, Richard C B   IWM 363
Halahan, H G   IWM 198
Hallahan (Lieutenant-Colonel)   IWM 503
Hallam, D   IWM 558
Halsey, Lionel   IWM 843; IWM 1213;
NTB 319-02
Hambourg, Mark   IWM 532
Hamilton Benn, Ion   IWM 551; IWM 1105
Hancock, F C   IWM 551; IWM 552
Hankey, Maurice (Baron)   IWM 192;
IWM 508-47
Hanson, Charles A   IWM 474; NTB 319-01
Harding (Second Lieutenant)   IWM 192
Hardy, T B VC   IWM 677b
Harley, Catherine   IWM 1062-10
Harp, de la (Major)   IWM 453
Harper, George M   IWM 110
Harrington, C H   IWM 508-46
Hart, Charles S   IWM 1079
Hart, H   IWM 157
Hassel, S   IWM 1082-02d
Hay (Lieutenant)   IWM 1168
Hayes, C F   NTB 395-01
Haywood, William   IWM 1079
Hazeltine (Colonel)   IWM 503
Heath-Caldwell, Frederick C   IWM 615;
IWM 632
Heavyside, Michael VC   IWM 1179
Heinrich, Prince of Prussia   IWM 483-04;
IWM 1040
Henchley, A R   IWM 198
Henderson, Arthur   IWM 485; IWM 1149;
NTB 312-01
Henderson, David   IWM 503
Heneker, William C G   IWM 375
Henry, J   IWM 1062-17

Henry, Prince (Duke of Gloucester)
IWM 265; IWM 505; IWM 666a; IWM 699b
Henrys (General)   IWM 508-59
Herriot, Edouard   IWM 1149
Heurteaux (Captain)   IWM 508-38
Hicks, Stanley   IWM 462
Higgins, Harold J   IWM 304
Hill (Deputy Surgeon General)   IWM 556
Hill, Arthur (Lord)   NTB 314-02
Hillier, J H   IWM 147
Hindenburg, Paul von   IWM 484; IWM 1045a
Hines, J L   IWM 501-01
Hoare, Lillian   IWM 462
Hoare, Samuel J G   IWM 485
Hobbs, B D   IWM 558
Hobson (Miss)   NTB 274-01
Hodge, John   IWM 661b; NTB 312-01
Hodgson, H W   IWM 37; IWM 17
Hoeppner, E von   IWM 1004
Hoffmann, Max von   IWM 484
Hofman, Peter   IWM 481
Hogarth (Major-General)   NTB 395-01
Holmes, W J   IWM 1062-17
Holt, Follett   IWM 456
Hoover, Herbert C   IWM 292; IWM 484;
                          IWM 668b; IWM 678a
Hope (Rear-Admiral)   IWM 572
Hope, G P W   IWM 580
Horn, Spencer   IWM 141; IWM 632
Horne, Henry S   IWM 132; IWM 190;
    IWM 198; IWM 218; IWM 289; IWM 314;
    IWM 345; IWM 370; IWM 375; IWM 411;
    IWM 465; IWM 484; IWM 485; IWM 505;
               IWM 508-86; IWM 1062-03
Hornel, R A   IWM 558
Hotzendorf, Conrad von   IWM 481; IWM 484
Hounsell, J   IWM 147
House, Edward M   IWM 1049
Hsu (Colonel)   IWM 712
Huffer (Major)   IWM 250
Hughes, Charles E   IWM 484
Hughes, Sam   IWM 1062-19; IWM 1128a
Hughes, William M   IWM 138; IWM 139;
    IWM 331; IWM 660a; IWM 667; NTB 257-01
Hulsart, C Raymond   IWM 150
Hulton Wilson (Colonel)   IWM 115
Humbert, Georges-Louis   IWM 508-60;
                    IWM 508-62; IWM 508-75
Humphries, Francis   IWM 809
Hunter, Archibald   IWM 580; NTB 254-01;
                                  NTB 256-01
Hunter, John   IWM 687
Hurst, Cecil   IWM 810
Hussein Kemal, Sultan of Egypt   IWM 23;
                          IWM 41; NTB 325-01
Hussey (Captain)   IWM 506
Ijuin (Admiral)   IWM 451
Iliesco (General)   IWM 508-26
Illingworth, Henry   NTB 256-01
Immelmann, Max   IWM 1004
Inouye (Count)   IWM 132; IWM 451

Insall, Gilbert S M   NTB 318-02
Ionescu, Take   IWM 483-03
Ironside, Edmund (Baron)
                  IWM 420-21+22; IWM 422
Islington (Lord)   NTB 261-02
Isovolsky (Ambassador)   NTB 242-02
Iversen, H   IWM 1126
Iyengar, Kasturiranga   IWM 529
Jacob, Claud W   IWM 376
James, Holman   IWM 1061-07g
Jarvis (Rifleman)   NTB 178-01
Jarvis, C A VC   IWM 418
Jellicoe, John R   IWM 484; IWM 485;
    IWM 505; IWM 550-01; IWM 551; IWM 571;
               IWM 572; IWM 842; IWM 1213
Jencken, F G   NTB 265-01
Jenkins, N H   IWM 880-02b
Jerusalem, Chief Rabbi of   IWM 30; IWM 484
Jeudwine, Hugh S   IWM 706
Joachim, Prince of Prussia   IWM 484
Joel, S   IWM 579
Joffre, Joseph J C   IWM 192; IWM 440-03;
          IWM 484; IWM 508-24; IWM 508-26;
          IWM 508-60; IWM 509; IWM 1057-02;
      IWM 1062-03; IWM 1062-20; IWM 1175;
                                  NTB 242-02
Johansen, L   IWM 1126
John, Olivia   IWM 1061-08b
Johnson, William H   IWM 501-10
Johnston, F N   IWM 269
Johnstone, Charles   NTB 178-01
Jones, T   IWM 417
Jones, T A VC   IWM 389
Jones-Williams, A G   IWM 880-02b
Josef Ferdinand, Archduke of Austria-Hungary
          IWM 1040; IWM 1043b; IWM 1045b
Joynson-Hicks, William   IWM 810
Kahn, Percy   IWM 462
Karafatovitch (Colonel)   IWM 508-31
Karl I, Emperor of Austria-Hungary   IWM 481;
    IWM 484; IWM 1034-01a; IWM 1034-01b;
    IWM 1034-03; IWM 1035c; IWM 1039-02;
          IWM 1040; IWM 1044; IWM 1045a;
      IWM 1045d; IWM 1062-14; IWM 1062-15
Kavanagh, Charles T M   IWM 376
Keegan, K J   IWM 147
Kemp, Edward   IWM 310; IWM 654b;
          IWM 672b; IWM 697a; NTB 395-01
Kenna (Sergeant-Major)   NTB 313-01
Kenney, Anne   IWM 474; NTB 324-02
Kensington (Bishop of)   NTB 249-02
Kent (Mrs)   NTB 265-02
Keogh, Myles   IWM 120
Keppel, Derek   IWM 198
Kerensky, Alexander F   IWM 484; IWM 668b
Kerr, Alan   IWM 456
Kerr, John H   IWM 503
Kerry (Earl)   IWM 1062-17
Ketchen, H D B   IWM 466

Keyes, Roger J B IWM 359; IWM 370;
 IWM 551; IWM 571; IWM 572;
 IWM 1061-07b; IWM 1105; IWM 1154
King (General) IWM 712
Kitchener, Horatio (Earl) IWM 213;
 IWM 484; IWM 440-01; IWM 440-04;
 IWM 485; IWM 657b; IWM 1062-03;
 IWM 1062-17; IWM 1062-20; IWM 1080a;
 IWM 1128a; IWM 1175; NTB 242-02;
 NTB 251-01
Knowlson, L K IWM 503
Knox, C L VC IWM 289
Koodlaienko (Lieutenant Colonel) IWM 712
Kostroff (Colonel) IWM 712
Krupskaya, Nadezhda K IWM 484
Kynaston Studd, J E IWM 809
La Panonse, de (Viscount) IWM 507
Laferre IWM 508-52
Laffert, von (General) IWM 483-01
Lang, Cosmo G IWM 1085
Laon, Mayor of IWM 508-83
Lassiter (Colonel) IWM 1186
Laureati, Giulio (Marquis) NTB 318-02
Law, Andrew Bonar IWM 485; IWM 693c;
 NTB 322-01
Lawrence, Herbert A IWM 190; IWM 381
Lawrence, T E IWM 13; IWM 41; IWM 1131a
Lawson, Algernon IWM 374
Lay, James C IWM 456
Layton, R C IWM 1
le Forest (Commandant) IWM 250
Lebering, L C IWM 448
Leconte (General) IWM 508-45
Lefebre, Joseph IWM 192
Lejeune, John A IWM 484
Lenin, Vladimir Ilyich IWM 484
Leopold III, King of Belgium IWM 192;
 IWM 370; IWM 1054
Lewis, Edward M IWM 289; IWM 503
Lewis, G P IWM 297
Liddell, Eric IWM 594-04-13
Liggett, Hunter IWM 484
Lille, Mayor of IWM 352; IWM 363
Line, Arthur IWM 706
Lipton, Thomas IWM 1061-06h
Liverpool, Lord Mayor of IWM 342; IWM 450
Lloyd, Francis IWM 474; IWM 663a;
 IWM 681b; IWM 685a; IWM 1061-06a;
IWM 1061-06b; IWM 1061-07b; IWM 1062-17;
 IWM 1186; IWM 1187; NTB 247-01;
 NTB 249-01; NTB 254-02; NTB 267-02;
 NTB 323-01; NTB 324-02
Lloyd, Marie IWM 485
Lloyd George, David IWM 130-09+10;
 IWM 192; IWM 308b; IWM 420-15+16;
 IWM 439; IWM 484; IWM 485; IWM 505;
IWM 508-47; IWM 509; IWM 657b; IWM 664a;
 IWM 675b; IWM 679a; IWM 679b; IWM 682;
 IWM 699c; IWM 1061-04h; IWM 1061-09e;
 IWM 1062-19; IWM 1128a; IWM 1175;
 IWM 1186; IWM 1187; IWM 1206;

Lloyd George, David *(continued)*
 NTB 257-01; NTB 261-01; NTB 276-02;
 NTB 316-01; NTB 322-01
Lloyd George, Margaret IWM 681c;
 NTB 256-01; NTB 316-01
Lloyd George, Megan NTB 316-01
Lobkowitz (Prince) IWM 481; IWM 1033c;
 IWM 1033d; IWM 1034-01b; IWM 1035c;
 IWM 1040; IWM 1044
Loerzer, Bruno IWM 1004
Logue (Cardinal) IWM 212
London, Bishop of IWM 679a; IWM 1181
London, Lord Mayor of IWM 193b;
 IWM 193d; IWM 443; IWM 474; IWM 626;
 IWM 656a; IWM 662a; IWM 664a; IWM 665b;
IWM 681c; IWM 693b; IWM 809; NTB 168-01;
 NTB 178-01; NTB 242-01; NTB 249-01;
 NTB 253-01; NTB 265-01; NTB 266-02;
 NTB 272-02; NTB 273-01; NTB 276-02;
 NTB 279-02; NTB 280-01; NTB 319-01;
 NTB 321-01; NTB 324-02
Long, F W IWM 880-01a
Long, V A IWM 685a
Long, W IWM 196
Lostende, M de (Baron) IWM 563; IWM 572
Lou (General) IWM 712
Lovejoy, A O IWM 224
Lowther, J G IWM 706
Lucas, G G IWM 566; IWM 567
Luce, John IWM 570; IWM 572
Luçon (Cardinal) IWM 435; IWM 473;
 IWM 508-25; IWM 508-28
Ludendorff, Erich IWM 484
Ludwig, Prince of Bavaria IWM 1062-08
Ludwig III, King of Bavaria IWM 484;
 IWM 1033a; IWM 1062-08
Lufberry, Raoul IWM 250; IWM 458
Lukin, Henry T IWM 169; IWM 699b
Lunn, George IWM 488
Lurgan (Baron) IWM 661b
Luther, Hans IWM 810; IWM 811
Luxford, Emily F NTB 284-02
Lyautey, Louis-Hubert IWM 508-15;
 IWM 508-20
Lyne, Thomas J S IWM 551; IWM 572;
 IWM 582
Lynes (Commander) IWM 130-03+4
Lynes, Herbert IWM 551; IWM 1105
Lyon, L S IWM 501-02
Lyons, T H IWM 456
Lyttelton, Neville G NTB 249-01; NTB 354-01
Lytton, Neville IWM 381
M'Cracken, W R IWM 545
MacDonald, Ramsay IWM 485; IWM 1149;
 NTB 312-01
MacGregor (Admiral) IWM 557
Machado, Bernardino IWM 129; IWM 508-31;
 NTB 321-02; NTB 323-01
Mackensen, August von IWM 484
Mackenzie, Albert VC IWM 657a
MacKenzie, Thomas IWM 157; IWM 1213

Mackenzie-Kennedy, C J H   IWM 1073
Macnamara (Doctor)   NTB 258-01
Macready, Nevil   IWM 474; IWM 685a
Madden, Charles E   IWM 550-02; IWM 551;
   IWM 552; IWM 556; IWM 571; IWM 579;
            IWM 591; IWM 1152; IWM 1164
Madon, Georges   IWM 508-52
Mahon, Bryan   IWM 1062-10
Maistre, Paul   IWM 508-12; IWM 508-34;
   IWM 508-35; IWM 508-46; IWM 508-49;
            IWM 508-53; NTB 309-01
Maitland, Edward C   IWM 645
Maitland-Makgill-Crichton, M E   IWM 119
Makaerenko (Colonel)   IWM 712
Makino (Baron)   IWM 1079
Manchester, Lord Mayor of   IWM 308b;
      IWM 342; IWM 1062-03; NTB 272-02
Mangin, Charles M E   IWM 508-73;
            IWM 508-82; IWM 508-83
Manning, Richard I   IWM 1079
Manville, Edward   IWM 809
March, P C   IWM 1079
Marchal (Lieutenant)   IWM 508-64
Marchal (Madame)   IWM 508-10
Margaret, Princess   IWM 1085
Marie (Colonel)   IWM 507
Marie, Princess of Anhalt   IWM 484
Marie, Queen of Romania   IWM 484
Marie-Jose, Princess of Belgium   IWM 192;
            IWM 370; IWM 1054
Marie Louise, Princess   IWM 657a
Marie Therese, Queen of Bavaria
                                  IWM 1062-08
Markham, Violet   IWM 480
Markievicz (Countess)   IWM 675a
Marlborough, Consuelo (Duchess)   IWM 675b
Marlowe, Thomas   IWM 331
Marriott, T R   IWM 564
Marsh (Mrs)   IWM 304
Marshall, George C   IWM 450
Marshall, Horace   IWM 193b; IWM 193d;
   IWM 626; IWM 656a; IWM 662a; IWM 664a;
            IWM 665b; IWM 681c; IWM 693b
Marshall, Thomas R   IWM 484
Marshall, William R IWM 43; IWM 59; IWM 77
Martin, W W   IWM 310
Martinez Anido, Severiano   IWM 115
Marwede, Hans H   IWM 502
Mary, Princess (Princess Royal)   IWM 265;
   IWM 448; IWM 484; IWM 508-51; IWM 535;
   IWM 663c; IWM 664a; IWM 666a; IWM 681c;
   IWM 1062-17; NTB 258-01; NTB 322-01;
            NTB 344-01
Mary, Queen (Consort to George V)
   IWM 109; IWM 128; IWM 134; IWM 198;
   IWM 265; IWM 439; IWM 446; IWM 448;
   IWM 484; IWM 504; IWM 508-51; IWM 509;
   IWM 550-01; IWM 571; IWM 572; IWM 586;
   IWM 612; IWM 653a; IWM 661b; IWM 663a;
   IWM 663c; IWM 664a; IWM 666a; IWM 668b;
   IWM 678a; IWM 679a; IWM 681c; IWM 685a;

Mary, Queen (Consort to George V) *(continued)*
   IWM 693b; IWM 693d; IWM 699b; IWM 809;
   IWM 1061-03i; IWM 1062-03; IWM 1062-17;
   IWM 1064-03a; IWM 1082-02c; IWM 1085;
            IWM 1141; IWM 1142; IWM 1187;
   NTB 251-01; NTB 254-02; NTB 273-02;
   NTB 317-02; NTB 319-01; NTB 322-01;
   NTB 323-01; NTB 324-02; NTB 325-01;
            NTB 342-02
Mason, J   IWM 633
Massey, William F   IWM 258; IWM 269;
            IWM 659; IWM 843
Maud, Princess (Countess of Southesk)
            IWM 679a; NTB 258-01
Max, Adolphe   IWM 501-02; IWM 508-88;
            IWM 665a; IWM 670b
Maxfield (Miss)   NTB 274-01
Maxfield, Lewis H   IWM 645
Maxwell, John   IWM 462; NTB 247-01
May, George   IWM 462
Maynard, Charles C M   IWM 420-19+20;
            IWM 420-21+22; IWM 422
Mayo, Henry T   IWM 1079
McCay, J W   IWM 198
McCay, Robert   IWM 503
McClymont, D   IWM 582
McDonald, Harold F   IWM 310
McIntosh, George VC   IWM 140
McKenzie, Frederick   IWM 253
McKingstry (Colonel)   IWM 448
McLean, C W   IWM 465
McMahon, John   IWM 501-01
Meighan, F S   IWM 274; IWM 678b
Meissner, J A   IWM 501-03; IWM 501-04;
            IWM 1079
Mellieur, Georges   IWM 508-59
Mellish, Noel E VC   NTB 251-01
Mercier, Desire   IWM 484
Meredith, E T   IWM 224
Meurer (Admiral)   IWM 1144
Meux, Hedworth   IWM 1213
Michalopoulis   IWM 508-19
Middlemas, Robert   IWM 531
Mikhailovitch, Sergey (Grand Duke)
                                  NTB 273-02
Milar, Eugene K de   IWM 420-19+20;
            IWM 420-21+22; IWM 422
Miles (Major-General)   NTB 262-01
Milford Haven, George (Second Marquess)
                                  NTB 273-02
Miller, P   NTB 279-02
Millerand, Alexandre   IWM 1062-03;
            IWM 1062-20; IWM 1175
Milne, George F   IWM 809
Miloth (General)   IWM 508-19
Mitchell, G   IWM 160
Mitchell, W H   IWM 566
Mohammed V, Sultan of Turkey   IWM 484;
            IWM 1034-03; IWM 1062-02b;
            IWM 1072
Molesworth, E W   IWM 141; IWM 632

Moltke, Helmuth von (b 1848)   IWM 484;
                                  IWM 1033b
Monash, John   IWM 139; IWM 270; IWM 289;
                        IWM 293; IWM 331
Mond, Alfred   IWM 504; IWM 507
Montagu (7th Baron)   IWM 134
Montague-Bates, F S   IWM 98
Montague Cleve, S   IWM 218
Montenaro, William H F   IWM 551; IWM 552
Monterou, de (General)   IWM 508-19
Montgomery (Lieutenant-General)   IWM 132
Morocco, Sultan of   IWM 508-15
Mortlock (Nurse)   NTB 277-02
Moses, W   IWM 675b
Moulay Youseff, Sultan of Morocco
                                 NTB 313-01
Mountbatten, Louis (Earl)   IWM 843;
        IWM 1141; IWM 1142; NTB 273-02
Mountbatten, Louis (Prince; son of above)
                                 IWM 1213
Mouren (Sergeant-Major)   IWM 508-92
Mugford, Harold VC   IWM 666b
Muir, Charles H   IWM 501-11
Müller, Georg von   IWM 772
Murray, Henry   IWM 109
Muti, Prince of Zululand   IWM 128; IWM 413
Naper, W L   IWM 13
Napier, Trevylyan D W   IWM 556
Neal (Lieutenant)   IWM 599; IWM 602
Netchaieff (General)   IWM 712
Neven (Monsignor)   IWM 473; IWM 508-25
Newcastle-upon-Tyne, Mayor of   IWM 488
Newlands (Lord)   IWM 654b
Newman, Alfred W   IWM 558
Nicholas I, King of Montenegro   NTB 259-02
Nicholas II, Tsar of Russia   IWM 484;
              IWM 1062-01; IWM 1070d
Nicholas, Grand Duke of Russia   IWM 484;
        IWM 656a; IWM 1062-01; IWM 1070d
Nicholson, W C M   IWM 591
Nider (General)   IWM 97
Nikita, King of Montenegro   IWM 484
Noel, L   IWM 1091a
Norfolk (Duke of)   IWM 1085
Norris, T C   IWM 310
North, Dudley B N   IWM 843
Northampton, Mayor of   IWM 706
Norwich, Bishop of   IWM 1074
Noyon, Mayor of   IWM 508-18;
                                 IWM 508-78 bis
Nugent, Oliver S W   IWM 197; IWM 212;
                                 IWM 580
Nungesser, Charles   IWM 484; IWM 508-23
Nurmi, Paavo   IWM 594-04-13
O'Callaghan, Desmond   NTB 277-01
O'Donoughie (Lieutenant-Colonel) IWM 212
O'Donovan Rossa (Miss)   IWM 194
O'Keeffe, Menus W   IWM 289; IWM 293
O'Leary, Michael VC   IWM 1061-04f
O'Ryan, John F   IWM 503
Olivier, Sidney   IWM 1149

Onslow, Richard (Earl)   IWM 706
Orlando, Vittorio E   IWM 508-47
Orlebar, A H   IWM 880-01a; IWM 880-01f
Orpen, William   IWM 668c
Otto, Crown Prince of Austria-Hungary
        IWM 1034-01b; IWM 1040; IWM 1044
Oyster, G   IWM 579
Paar, von (Count)   IWM 481; IWM 1033d
Pachitch (Premier of Serbia)   NTB 242-02
Paddock, Charles   IWM 594-04-13
Page, Walter H   IWM 484; IWM 579;
    IWM 672b; IWM 693d; IWM 697a; IWM 1049;
              IWM 1186; IWM 1187; NTB 344-01
Paget, A   NTB 239-02
Painlevé, Paul   IWM 508-26; IWM 508-37;
                                 NTB 329-01
Pakenham, William C   IWM 551; IWM 556;
                                 IWM 572
Pankhurst, Christabel   IWM 474; IWM 660a;
                                 NTB 324-02
Pankhurst, Emmeline   IWM 474; IWM 485;
        NTB 324-02; IWM 660a; NTB 204-01
Paraskevopoulos (General)   IWM 97
Paravicini, H   IWM 454
Paravicini, M   IWM 454
Parkes (Surgeon-Commander)   IWM 504
Parreau (General)   NTB 251-02
Parsons, C   IWM 147
Passaga (General)   IWM 458
Paterson (Major Doctor)   IWM 24
Paterson, R W   IWM 310
Patiala, Maharajah of   IWM 37; IWM 282
Patricia, Princess   IWM 680a
Patton, George S   IWM 251; IWM 450
Pau, Paul M   NTB 266-02
Peck, Ambrose M   IWM 109; IWM 553
Pecori (General)   IWM 508-49
Peel, C S   IWM 193d; IWM 474
Peltier (General)   IWM 137
Pembroke (Earl)   IWM 361; IWM 451
Pennetier (Private)   IWM 1204
Pershing, John J   IWM 137; IWM 240;
    IWM 251; IWM 439; IWM 450; IWM 458;
        IWM 484; IWM 501-01; IWM 501-02;
            IWM 501-10; IWM 502; IWM 503;
        IWM 508-14; IWM 508-24; IWM 508-26;
        IWM 508-47; IWM 508-51; IWM 508-68;
    IWM 509; IWM 578-02; IWM 685a; IWM 1049;
        IWM 1057-02; IWM 1082-02a; NTB 318-01
Pétain, Philippe   IWM 198; IWM 508-13;
        IWM 508-14; IWM 508-18; IWM 508-23;
        IWM 508-26; IWM 508-28; IWM 508-35;
        IWM 508-40; IWM 508-43; IWM 508-76;
            IWM 508-86; IWM 509; IWM 677b;
    IWM 1057-01; NTB 310-02; NTB 316-01;
                NTB 318-01; NTB 327-02
Peterson (Captain)   IWM 1079
Peyton, William E   IWM 508-85
Phillimore, Richard F   IWM 556; IWM 1163
Phillips, H   NTB 247-02
Pi (General)   IWM 712

Pickford, Mary IWM 687; IWM 1079
Picot, M IWM 13
Piepape, P de IWM 13; IWM 508-39
Pierce, Palmer E IWM 503
Pinney, Reginald J IWM 188
Pirrie, William J (Earl) IWM 526; IWM 589;
 IWM 1068
Pitcher, W IWM 147
Plumer, Herbert C O IWM 132; IWM 192;
 IWM 198; IWM 260; IWM 266; IWM 268;
 IWM 282; IWM 289; IWM 370; IWM 376;
 IWM 381; IWM 484; IWM 485; IWM 503;
 IWM 679b
Poincaré, Raymond N L IWM 192; IWM 198;
 IWM 289; IWM 296; IWM 352; IWM 381;
 IWM 435; IWM 484; IWM 501-02;
 IWM 501-13; IWM 508-26; IWM 508-28;
 IWM 508-31; IWM 508-62; IWM 508-68;
 IWM 508-69; IWM 508-72; IWM 508-73;
 IWM 508-76; IWM 508-78; IWM 508-83;
 IWM 508-86; IWM 508-91; IWM 509;
 IWM 1079; NTB 194-02; NTB 256-02;
 NTB 266-02; NTB 323-01
Pola, Mayor of IWM 1033c
Pollock, B IWM 1074
Porras, Belisario IWM 843
Porte, F IWM 130-03+4
Portland, William (Duke) IWM 474;
 IWM 660b; NTB 323-01
Potter, H C IWM 398
Powell, G IWM 25; IWM 375
Pressburg, Mayor of IWM 1044
Prestrud (Lieutenant) IWM 1082-02d
Price, George D IWM 422
Primo de Rivera y Orbaneja, Miguel IWM 115
Pringle, J R P IWM 564; IWM 572; IWM 1164
Proby, D J IWM 1062-17
Prothero, R E IWM 535; IWM 678a
Puipeyroux (General) (?) IWM 508-42
Pulteney, William P IWM 361; IWM 451
Pusch, F L IWM 1062-17
Queensland (Prime Minister of) NTB 249-02
Rainer, Prince of Austria-Hungary IWM 1033a;
 IWM 1033d
Ramsey, F W IWM 111
Rawlinson, Henry S IWM 115; IWM 121;
 IWM 132; IWM 190; IWM 198; IWM 331;
 IWM 354; IWM 420-21+22; IWM 422;
 IWM 484; IWM 1062-03
Read, George W IWM 501-14; IWM 503
Reading (Lord) IWM 485
Ready, Felix F IWM 43
Redmond, John E IWM 485; IWM 1062-17
Redmond, William K IWM 120; IWM 212
Reed, Hamilton L IWM 375
Regnault (General) IWM 508-19
Reid, P L IWM 1062-17
Repoulis IWM 508-19
Rheims, Archbishop of IWM 435;
 IWM 473; IWM 508-25; IWM 508-28
Rhodes, S IWM 1137

Rhondda (Lord) IWM 653b; IWM 666b;
 IWM 692a
Ricardo, Harry IWM 1192
Richardson, G S IWM 269
Richthofen, Albrecht von IWM 1004
Richthofen, Manfred von IWM 187;
 IWM 484; IWM 661b; IWM 1004
Rickenbacker, Edward V IWM 484;
 IWM 501-03; IWM 501-04; IWM 502;
 IWM 1079
Rider-Rider, William IWM 664b
Riley, E W IWM 566
Riley, J D NTB 319-02
Riols de Fonclare, de (Lieutenant-General)
 IWM 508-50
Ripon, Bishop of IWM 462
Roberts, Frederick (Earl) IWM 1025c;
 IWM 1071; IWM 1080a; IWM 1081e;
 IWM 1082-02d; NTB 261-02
Roberts, H C IWM 198
Robertson (Mr) NTB 312-01
Robertson (Rear Admiral) IWM 565
Robertson, William R VC IWM 109;
 IWM 213; IWM 440-04; IWM 511; IWM 661a;
 IWM 1206; IWM 1218
Robey, George IWM 320; IWM 485;
 IWM 541; IWM 549-07; IWM 661b;
 IWM 666b; NTB 328-01
Robinson, Leefe VC IWM 1206; IWM 1218
Rodman, H IWM 484; IWM 554; IWM 571;
 IWM 572; IWM 602; IWM 679a; IWM 1163;
 IWM 1212
Ronarc'h, Pierre IWM 551; IWM 553;
 IWM 572
Room, Frederick VC NTB 324-02
Roosevelt, Franklin D IWM 484; IWM 1079
Roosevelt, Quentin IWM 484; IWM 502
Roosevelt, Theodore IWM 84; IWM 484;
 IWM 687; IWM 1079
Roosevelt, Theodore, Jr IWM 458; IWM 484
Roques (General) NTB 242-02
Rorison, H G IWM 580
Rosado (General) IWM 291; IWM 677b
Rose, A S IWM 147
Ross, Malcolm IWM 147
Ross-Smith (Captain) IWM 485
Rothschild, E A de IWM 27; IWM 45
Rumbold, Horace IWM 453
Runciman, Walter (Viscount) IWM 485
Rupprecht, Crown Prince of Bavaria
 IWM 483-02; IWM 484; IWM 1040
Russell, Andrew H IWM 156; IWM 157;
 IWM 196
Rutland (Duke of) IWM 304
Ryan, Martin F IWM 224
Sadleir-Jackson, Lionel W de V
 IWM 420-19+20
Saintsaulieu IWM 508-52
Salandra, Antonio (Premier of Italy)
 NTB 242-02
Salisbury, James (4th Marquess) IWM 809

Sampson (Sergeant-Major) IWM 253
Samson, C R IWM 643
Samuel, Herbert IWM 485
Samuel, John S IWM 140
Sandbrook, J A IWM 529
Sandford, F H IWM 551; IWM 1105
Sandford, Richard D VC IWM 656b
Sankey, John (Viscount) IWM 485
Sarrail, Maurice IWM 508-10; IWM 508-26;
IWM 508-31; IWM 1062-10
Saulsberry (Lieutenant-Colonel) IWM 503
Scarborough, Aldred (Earl) IWM 661a
Scholz, Jackson IWM 594-04-13
Schramm, W NTB 263-02
Schreiner (Miss) IWM 169
Schumann-Hemck (Mme) IWM 1079
Scialoja IWM 810; IWM 811
Scott, Robert F IWM 1061-08c
Scott, S D IWM 1063
Secer, A IWM 224
Selivanov (General) IWM 1062-01
Sellheim (Brigadier-General) NTB 249-02
Seymour, R H NTB 250-02
Seyyid Khalifa Bin Harub, Sultan of Zanzibar
IWM 842
Shackleton, Ernest H IWM 506
Sharp, William G IWM 508-82
Shaw (Lieutenant) IWM 1192
Shea, John IWM 22
Shelton (Colonel) IWM 458
Shobelstyn (General) IWM 420-19+20;
IWM 422
Shortt, Edward NTB 351-02
Simonds, George S IWM 501-14IWM 503
Sims, William S IWM 484; IWM 562;
IWM 563; IWM 571; IWM 572; IWM 653b;
IWM 668d; IWM 1158; IWM 1186; IWM 1212
Sinclair (Master of) IWM 451
Skrzynski, Alexander (Count) IWM 810;
IWM 811
Smith, Aubrey C H IWM 456
Smith, Cecily NTB 246-01
Smith-Dorrien, Horace L (?) IWM 432
Smuts, Jan C IWM 668c; IWM 699c
Snaith, L S IWM 880-01a
Snowden, Philip IWM 485
Soden, Frank IWM 141; IWM 632
Solly-Flood, Arthur IWM 258; IWM 261
Somerset (Duke) NTB 254-01
Sonnino, Sidney (Baron) NTB 242-02
Sophie, Countess of Austria-Hungary
IWM 484; IWM 1046a
Sophie, Duchess of Oldenberg IWM 484
Sophie, Queen of Saxony IWM 1034-01a
Southend, Mayor of IWM 663c
Southport, Mayor of IWM 1070e
Sowrey, F IWM 1206; IWM 1218
Stacy, Samuel H IWM 130-09+10
Stainforth, G N IWM 880-01a; IWM 880-01f
Stamfordham, Arthur IWM 198
Stanley, Mayor of IWM 1179

Steele, J McC IWM 1005
Stewart (Lord Provost) IWM 654b
Stewart (Miss) IWM 25
Stewart, George IWM 310
Stileman, Harry H IWM 450
Stinson, Katherine IWM 687
Stoistitch (Colonel) IWM 508-27
Stone (Sergeant) IWM 640-03
Storrs, Ronald IWM 27; IWM 45
Stralia (Madame) IWM 532
Strasbourg, Mayor of IWM 508-91
Stratford-upon-Avon, Mayor of IWM 304;
IWM 1070g
Strathclyde (Lord) IWM 140
Stresemann, Gustav IWM 485; IWM 810;
IWM 811
Stuart-Wortley, Richard M IWM 43
Sturdee, Doveton IWM 484; IWM 550-01;
IWM 550-02; IWM 551; IWM 556; IWM 571;
IWM 572; NTB 323-01
Sullivan, Thomas IWM 668c
Sumitoma (Baron) IWM 451
Surayya, Queen of Afghanistan IWM 809
Sutherland (Duchess) IWM 198
Swann, Ireson IWM 706
Swinton, Philip (Viscount) IWM 485
Sydenham (Lord) IWM 677a
Sykes, Mark IWM 532
T'Serclaes, Elsie (Baroness) IWM 162;
IWM 693d
Taft, William H IWM 484
Talbot Hobbs, J J IWM 369
Tamagnini (General) IWM 411
Taussig, J K IWM 562; IWM 1159
Taylor (Doctor) NTB 269-01
Taylor-Smith (Bishop) NTB 247-01
Tchehoff (Colonel) IWM 712
Temple, William IWM 1085
Terriss, Ellaline NTB 263-02
Thadeus, André IWM 484
Thaon di Revel (Count) IWM 508-23;
IWM 563; IWM 572
Theunis, George IWM 1149
Thomas, Albert IWM 508-20; NTB 312-01
Thomas, Bert IWM 681b
Thomas, J H IWM 485; IWM 1149
Thomas, Lowell IWM 41
Thompson (Major) IWM 192
Thompson, A E IWM 558
Thompson, Colin IWM 505
Thomson (Lord) IWM 1149
Thorne, Will IWM 692a
Thornton, R IWM 1
Thorpe, H IWM 1
Tillett, Ben IWM 159; IWM 508-43;
NTB 262-01
Timewell, H A IWM 253
Titheradge, Madge NTB 328-01
Todd, G T IWM 566
Tokugawa (Prince) IWM 451
Tomitch, Slavika NTB 258-01

Tonzo, Michael Angelo NTB 318-02
Torby, Nada de (Countess) NTB 249-02;
NTB 273-02
Tournai, Bishop of IWM 375
Tournai, Mayor of IWM 375
Tovey (Canon) IWM 304
Towle, Frank IWM 462
Train, C L VC IWM 289
Traub, Peter E IWM 501-03
Treat, Charles G IWM 501-13
Treloar, William NTB 279-02; NTB 280-01
Trenchard, Hugh M IWM 198
Treowan (Lord) IWM 170; NTB 340-01
Triand, André IWM 153
Trotsky, Leon IWM 484
Tsolacopolos (Colonel) IWM 97
Tufnell, D H C IWM 198
Turpin, Eugène NTB 259-01
Twining, M C IWM 563; IWM 572
Tyrwhitt, Reginald Y IWM 551; IWM 571;
IWM 572
Valenciennes, Mayor of IWM 508-85
Vandervelde, Emile IWM 810; IWM 811
Vane, M H T IWM 418
Varnier, Raymond IWM 502
Vasconcellos, Augusto de IWM 291;
IWM 677a
Vaughan, Bernard IWM 193c
Vaughan, Louis R IWM 132
Velentin (General) IWM 508-26
Venizelos, Eleutherios IWM 97; IWM 484;
IWM 508-10; IWM 508-14; IWM 508-19;
IWM 508-48; IWM 1061-05a; NTB 309-01;
NTB 325-02
Vera, Feliciano IWM 456
Verdun, Mayor of IWM 508-31; NTB 323-01
Vickers (Junior) IWM 1062-17
Victor Emmanuel III, King of Italy
IWM 484; IWM 508-53; IWM 508-70
Victoria, Princess IWM 679a; IWM 681c;
NTB 252-02; NTB 356-02
Victoria Eugenie, Queen of Spain
IWM 594-04-13
Villa, Pancho IWM 1049
Vitalis (Sergeant-Major) IWM 508-43
Viviani, René IWM 508-18; NTB 310-02
Wakefield, Charles C NTB 247-01
Wallace, E IWM 579
Wallis, W H St J IWM 582
Walsh, J G IWM 566
Walton, S IWM 677b
Wangenheim, von (Baron) IWM 483-06
Wann, A H IWM 645
Ward, Edward IWM 659; NTB 267-01
Ward, Joseph IWM 269; IWM 659; IWM 1213
Warneford (Lieutenant) NTB 255-02
Warwick, Mayor of IWM 304
Waterfield, J R IWM 147
Watt, Fitzgerald IWM 668c
Wavell, Archibald P IWM 13
Wedgwood Benn (Captain) IWM 557

Weir, William D IWM 635
Weissmuller, Johnny IWM 594-04-13
Weizmann, Chaim A IWM 27; IWM 30;
IWM 35; IWM 45
Wemyss, Rosslyn IWM 484; IWM 550-01;
IWM 551; IWM 563; IWM 564; IWM 571;
IWM 572; IWM 681c; IWM 1162; IWM 1164
Wernher, H A IWM 706
West Ham, Mayor of IWM 692a
Westminster, Mayor of IWM 532
Westmoreland, George W IWM 15
Wetterle (Abbé) IWM 508-26
Weygand, Maxime IWM 344; IWM 439;
IWM 440-03; IWM 505; IWM 508-64;
NTB 356-02
White, George IWM 1025b; IWM 1082-02d
White, Graham IWM 1082-02c
Whitman, Charles S IWM 1079
Wigram, Clive IWM 558; NTB 250-02
Wild von Hohenborn (General) IWM 481
Wilhelm II, Kaiser of Germany IWM 481;
IWM 484; IWM 485; IWM 772; IWM 1004;
IWM 1033b; IWM 1040; IWM 1045a;
IWM 1045d; IWM 1062-08
Wilhelm II, King of Wurttemberg IWM 484
Wilhelm, Crown Prince of Germany IWM 484;
IWM 1040
Wilkins, G H IWM 314
Wille, Ulrich IWM 483-02
Williams (Private) IWM 1178
Wilson, Alan IWM 250
Wilson, Henry F M IWM 98; IWM 485;
IWM 505; IWM 603; IWM 664a; IWM 1062-03
Wilson, James IWM 224; IWM 693b;
IWM 1079
Wilson, W G IWM 1192
Wilson, Woodrow IWM 458; IWM 484;
IWM 485; IWM 1079; NTB 284-02
Wilson-Barker, D IWM 551; IWM 552
Wimborne (Lady) NTB 247-01
Wimborne (Lord) IWM 1182
Winchester, Mayor of IWM 651b
Winfield (Corporal) IWM 640-03
Winnington-Ingram, A IWM 679a; IWM 1181
Winslow, Alan IWM 458
Withycombe, W M IWM 1137
Wolf-Paravicini (Mme) IWM 454
Wright, Chester IWM 224
Wu Tsi-sheng IWM 712
Wyatt (Colonel) IWM 505
Yao (Colonel) IWM 712
Yapp, Arthur IWM 193c; NTB 325-02
Yarde-Buller, Henry IWM 1062-20
Ynglanda, Pierre IWM 153
Yokohama, Mayor of IWM 451
Yorihito, Prince of Japan IWM 361;
IWM 656a; IWM 665b
York, Archbishop of IWM 1085
Young, R IWM 269
Ypres, John (2nd Earl) IWM 1061-08b
Zahroam of Amara IWM 65; IWM 79

Zetland (Marquis)   IWM 462
Zita, Empress of Austria-Hungary   IWM 481;
    IWM 484; IWM 1034-01a; IWM 1034-01b;
       IWM 1034-03; IWM 1035c; IWM 1040;
      IWM 1044; IWM 1062-14; IWM 1062-15
Zymbrakakis (General)   IWM 97;
        IWM 508-48; IWM 1061-05a

ALBANIA   IWM 508-48; IWM 1055b

ARABIA see OTTOMAN EMPIRE, ARABIA

ARGENTINA   IWM 456; IWM 548

AUSTRALIA   IWM 440-04; IWM 485;
IWM 548; IWM 842; IWM 843; IWM 1061-06d

AUSTRO-HUNGARIAN EMPIRE (including
Bosnia, Dalmatia etc.)
Bad Ischl   IWM 1033a
Caporetto area   IWM 1047-01; IWM 1047-02
Cattaro, Dalmatia   IWM 1061-08b
Budapest   IWM 1034-01b; IWM 1039-2
Innsbruck   IWM 481; IWM 1062-14;
                                 IWM 1062-15
Pola   IWM 1033c
Pozsonyi/Pressburg   IWM 1044
Sankt Pölten   IWM 1033d
Sarajevo, Bosnia   IWM 1046a
Sopron   IWM 1035a
Trieste   IWM 1041b; IWM 1046b
Tyrol   IWM 481; IWM 1035c; IWM 1062-15
Vienna   IWM 481; IWM 484; IWM 1033b;
                      IWM 1040; IWM 1041a

(General references)   IWM 481; IWM 560;
IWM 1034-01a; IWM 1034-01b; IWM 1034-04;
              IWM 1035a; IWM 1038; IWM 1043a;
              IWM 1062-15; IWM 1084; IWM 1211

BARBADOS   IWM 843

BELGIUM
Antwerp   IWM 371; NTB 164-01
Ath   IWM 368
Bruges   IWM 359; IWM 508-84; IWM 1054
Brussels   IWM 370; IWM 384; IWM 483-04;
          IWM 501-02; IWM 508-88; IWM 665a;
                      IWM 670b; IWM 1054
Courtrai   IWM 508-85
Dickebusch   IWM 218
Dixmude   IWM 1053
Elverdinghe   IWM 122; IWM 1061-09h
Gheluvelt   IWM 483-03
Locre   IWM 120; IWM 197; IWM 212
Louvain   IWM 484
Malines   IWM 382
Messines   IWM 158; IWM 197; IWM 212
Meteren   IWM 302
Mont des Cats   IWM 122; IWM 187; IWM 188;
                      IWM 282; IWM 473
Mont Saint Eloi   IWM 209; IWM 215
Mont Sorel   IWM 255
Neufchâteau   IWM 508-90
Nieuport   IWM 403

Ostend   IWM 303; IWM 351; IWM 483-04;
          IWM 508-85; IWM 557; IWM 1054;
          IWM 1154; IWM 1158; NTB 165-02
Pervyse   IWM 162; IWM 693d
Ploegsteert   IWM 197
Poperinghe   IWM 431
Roosbrugge   IWM 508-25
Spa   IWM 374
St-Julien   IWM 103
Tournai   IWM 375; IWM 508-86
Wytschaete   IWM 122; IWM 197
Ypres   IWM 122; IWM 143; IWM 158;
          IWM 159; IWM 206; IWM 310; IWM 344;
     IWM 375; IWM 508-80; IWM 661a; IWM 714;
                                 IWM 1062-08
Ypres area   IWM 127; IWM 197; IWM 473;
          IWM 483-05; IWM 483-06; IWM 508-32;
          IWM 508-35; IWM 508-40; IWM 508-43;
              IWM 508-44; IWM 1051; IWM 1059;
     IWM 1061-09k; IWM 1134; NTB 318-02;
                                 NTB 324-01
Yser Canal   IWM 102; IWM 106;
          IWM 483-04; IWM 508-21; IWM 1050
Zeebrugge   IWM 358; IWM 375;
     IWM 508-86; IWM 656b; IWM 1154

(General references)   IWM 122; IWM 123;
     IWM 143; IWM 158; IWM 192; IWM 197;
     IWM 198; IWM 209; IWM 212; IWM 254;
     IWM 281; IWM 282; IWM 310; IWM 353;
          IWM 374; IWM 375; IWM 420-03+4;
              IWM 420-17+18; IWM 420-23+24;
              IWM 420-25+26; IWM 420-27+28;
          IWM 420-29+30; IWM 430; IWM 431;
          IWM 473; IWM 483-02; IWM 483-04;
     IWM 483-05; IWM 483-06; IWM 508-65;
          IWM 508-85; IWM 508-86; IWM 656b;
     IWM 672b; IWM 678b; IWM 697a; IWM 1051;
              IWM 1052; IWM 1053; IWM 1054;
     IWM 1055c; IWM 1061-05b; IWM 1061-05d;
     IWM 1061-08b; IWM 1061-09k; IWM 1154;
          IWM 1175; NTB 221-01; NTB 258-02;
                                 NTB 343-01

("British Western Front" - less certain
identification)   IWM 118; IWM 155;
     IWM 160; IWM 165; IWM 166; IWM 173;
     IWM 195; IWM 210; IWM 217; IWM 219;
     IWM 221; IWM 226; IWM 246; IWM 258;
     IWM 259; IWM 298; IWM 354; IWM 369;
     IWM 401; IWM 402; IWM 404; IWM 408;
     IWM 411; IWM 415; IWM 416; IWM 417;
     IWM 424; IWM 427; IWM 433; IWM 470;
IWM 663a; IWM 666a; IWM 675a; IWM 678a;
     IWM 713; IWM 1061-02c; IWM 1062-08;
                      IWM 1070c; NTB 223-02

BERMUDA   IWM 843

BULGARIA　　　　IWM 484; IWM 1034-3

CANADA
Halifax　　　　　　　　　　IWM 842
Montreal　　　　IWM 485; NTB 225-02
Ottawa　　　　　　　　　　IWM 812
Quebec　　　　　　　　　　IWM 842
Vancouver　　　　IWM 842; IWM 859

(General references)　　　　IWM 549-02;
　IWM 697a; IWM 842; IWM 860; IWM 861;
　　　　　　　　　　　　　NTB 280-01

CEYLON (SRI LANKA)　　　IWM 842

CHINA　　　　　　　　　　IWM 712

CUBA　　　　　IWM 312; IWM 1175

DENMARK　　　　　　　NTB 240-02

EGYPT
Alexandria　　　IWM 58; IWM 1061-03g
Cairo　IWM 14; IWM 23; IWM 36; IWM 40;
　IWM 41; IWM 681b; IWM 878; IWM 1178;
　　　　　　　　　　　　　NTB 325-01
Heliopolis　　IWM 38; IWM 634; IWM 878
Ismailia　　IWM 1; IWM 25; NTB 329-01
Kantara　　　　　　　　　　IWM 25
Nile (River)　　　　IWM 31; IWM 634
Port Said　IWM 41; IWM 508-36; IWM 508-39;
　　　　　　　　　　　　　IWM 1131a
Siwa　　　　　　　IWM 5; IWM 17
Suez　　　　　　IWM 17; IWM 878
Timsah (Lake)　　　　　　　IWM 25
Zeitoun　　IWM 21; IWM 38; IWM 634

(General references)　　　IWM 2; IWM 3;
　IWM 4; IWM 440-02; IWM 440-04;
　　　　　　　NTB 327-02; NTB 343-01

ENGLAND *see* UNITED KINGDOM,
　ENGLAND

FIJI　　　　　　　　　　IWM 843

FRANCE
Abbeville (Somme)　　IWM 115; IWM 128;
　IWM 198; IWM 228; IWM 272; IWM 300;
　　　　　　　　　　　　　IWM 322
Achiet-le-Grand (Pas-de-Calais)　　IWM 294;
　　　　IWM 302; IWM 322; IWM 324
AISNE　　　　IWM 112; IWM 121; IWM 341;
　IWM 473; IWM 501-01; IWM 501-07;
　IWM 501-12; IWM 501-13; IWM 501-14;
　IWM 503; IWM 508-10; IWM 508-17;
　IWM 508-34; IWM 508-67; IWM 508-68;
　IWM 508-69; IWM 508-71; IWM 508-73;
　IWM 508-77; IWM 508-78 bis; IWM 508-83
Aisne (River)　　IWM 508-10; IWM 508-29;
　IWM 508-33; IWM 508-50; IWM 508-51

Albert (Somme)　　　　IWM 142; IWM 198;
　　　　　　　IWM 332; IWM 501-08
ALSACE　　IWM 501-13; IWM 502; IWM 508-13;
　IWM 508-20; IWM 508-24; IWM 508-28;
　IWM 508-29; IWM 508-40; IWM 508-43;
　IWM 508-45; IWM 508-47; IWM 508-50;
　IWM 508-51; IWM 508-52; IWM 508-53;
　IWM 508-58; IWM 508-63; IWM 508-67;
　IWM 508-69; IWM 508-89; IWM 508-90;
　IWM 511; IWM 1061-09a; NTB 341-02
Amiens (Somme)　　　IWM 183; IWM 185;
　IWM 189; IWM 190; IWM 227; IWM 501-12;
　　IWM 508-55; IWM 508-62; IWM 654b
ARDENNES　　　　IWM 501-04; IWM 501-09;
　　　　IWM 508-83; NTB 344-02
Arras (Pas-de-Calais)　　IWM 113; IWM 121;
　IWM 133; IWM 182; IWM 189; IWM 222;
　IWM 233; IWM 253; IWM 354; IWM 406;
　　IWM 714; IWM 1188; IWM 1189;
　　　　　　NTB 178-01; NTB 344-02
Aubers Ridge (Nord)　　IWM 207; IWM 208;
　　　　　　　　　　　　　IWM 212
Bailleul (Somme)　　　IWM 110; IWM 198;
　　　　　　　　IWM 302; IWM 322
Bapaume (Pas-de-Calais)　　　　IWM 113;
　　IWM 130-01+2; IWM 177; IWM 294;
　　　IWM 322; IWM 332; IWM 667
BAS-RHIN　　　　　　　　IWM 508-90
Beaumont (Meuse)　IWM 501-02; IWM 508-92
Bellicourt (Aisne)　　　IWM 338; IWM 502;
　　　　　　　　　　　　　IWM 503
Bertangles (Somme)　　IWM 187; IWM 236;
　IWM 289; IWM 293; IWM 314; IWM 648;
　　　　　　　　　　　　　IWM 661b
Béthune (Pas-de-Calais)　　　　IWM 184;
　IWM 185; IWM 186; IWM 187; IWM 190;
　IWM 207; IWM 208; IWM 277; IWM 461b;
　　IWM 508-64; IWM 652b; IWM 654a;
　　　　　　　　　　　　　NTB 354-01
Blendecques (Pas-de-Calais)　　IWM 260;
　　　　IWM 268; IWM 289; IWM 679b
Bohain (Aisne)　　　IWM 501-13; IWM 503
Boucq (Meurthe-et-Moselle)　　IWM 458;
　　　　　　　　　　　　　IWM 501-05
Boulogne (Pas-de-Calais)　　　　IWM 137;
　IWM 253; IWM 310; IWM 505; NTB 330-02
Bras (Meuse)　　IWM 501-02; IWM 501-12
Brayon (Somme)　　　IWM 218; IWM 258
Brest (Finistère)　　　　　　　IWM 502
Butte de Warlencourt　　IWM 115; IWM 198
Calais (Pas-de-Calais)　　IWM 192; IWM 198;
　IWM 213; IWM 216; IWM 289; NTB 328-01
Cambrai (Nord)　　　　IWM 132; IWM 332;
　IWM 339; IWM 345; IWM 367; IWM 461d;
　　IWM 501-14; IWM 503; IWM 508-47;
　　IWM 508-81; IWM 508-82; IWM 656a;
　　IWM 662a; IWM 1195; NTB 328-01
Canal du Nord (Nord)　　IWM 144; IWM 332
Cassel (Nord)　IWM 122; IWM 188; IWM 224;
　　　　　　　　　　　　　IWM 289
Châlons (Marne)　　IWM 508-75; IWM 508-80

Chamonix (Haute-Savoie)   IWM 594-02+3
Château-Thierry (Aisne)   IWM 458;
    IWM 501-07; IWM 501-12; IWM 508-72;
    IWM 1079
Châtel-Chéhéry (Ardennes)   IWM 501-01;
    IWM 501-02
Chauny (Aisne)   IWM 473; IWM 508-31;
    IWM 508-43; IWM 508-78 bis
Combres (Eure et Loire)   IWM 501-14;
    IWM 508-79
Compiègne (Oise)   IWM 1062-03;
    IWM 1062-20; IWM 1175; NTB 292-01
Corbie (Somme)   IWM 181; IWM 473;
    IWM 503
Coucy-le-Château-Auffrique (Aisne)
    IWM 473; IWM 508-77
Courcelette (Somme)   IWM 130-07+8;
    IWM 130-09+10; IWM 466
Craonne (Aisne)   IWM 508-17; NTB 310-01
Cunel (Meuse)   IWM 501-02; IWM 501-14
Dannemarie (Haut-Rhin)   IWM 508-49;
    IWM 508-63
Delville Wood (Somme)   IWM 169;
    IWM 699b; NTB 343-02
Dieppe (Seine-Maritime)   IWM 133
Douai (Nord)   IWM 360; IWM 1082-02c
Dunkirk (Nord)   IWM 198; IWM 372;
    IWM 508-35; IWM 553
Ebblinghem (Nord)   IWM 190; IWM 256
Ecuires (Pas-de-Calais)   IWM 253; IWM 308c
Epéhy (Somme)   IWM 324; IWM 325;
    IWM 332
Erin (Pas-de-Calais)   IWM 198; IWM 357;
    NTB 319-01
Esnes (Nord)   IWM 501-10; IWM 508-25
Etaples (Pas-de-Calais)   IWM 162; IWM 198;
    IWM 231; IWM 232; IWM 314; IWM 315;
    IWM 337; IWM 685b
Evian (Haute-Savoie)   IWM 508-35
Fismes (Marne) IWM 508-75; IWM 508-78 bis
Flesquières (Nord)   IWM 144; IWM 146
Fricourt (Somme)   IWM 142; IWM 191
Gex (Ain)   IWM 508-28
Grévillers (Pas-de-Calais) IWM 198; IWM 294;
    IWM 322; IWM 332
Ham (Somme)   IWM 508-18; IWM 508-31;
    IWM 508-77
HAUT-RHIN   IWM 508-63; IWM 508-88
HAUTE-MARNE   IWM 880-02d
Helfaut (Pas-de-Calais)   IWM 119; IWM 198
Jeancourt (Aisne)   IWM 121; IWM 503
La Bassée (Nord)   IWM 340; IWM 508-82
La Bassée Canal   IWM 101; IWM 185;
    IWM 186; IWM 187; IWM 332; IWM 340;
    IWM 508-82
La Boisselle (Somme)   IWM 115; IWM 191;
    IWM 349; IWM 466
Laffaux (Aisne)   IWM 508-14; IWM 508-77
Laon (Aisne)   IWM 508-82; IWM 508-83
Lassigny (Oise)   IWM 473; IWM 508-74;
    IWM 508-76 bis

Le Havre (Seine-Maritime)   IWM 272;
    IWM 594-04-13
Lens (Pas-de-Calais)   IWM 333; IWM 353;
    IWM 508-82
Lille (Nord)   IWM 352; IWM 360; IWM 363;
    IWM 381; IWM 483-01; IWM 483-04;
    IWM 483-05; IWM 508-84; IWM 656a;
    NTB 223-01
Loos (Nord)   IWM 205; IWM 440-02;
    IWM 440-03; IWM 440-04
Lumbres (Pas-de-Calais) IWM 117; IWM 151;
    IWM 156; IWM 157
MARNE   IWM 244; IWM 251; IWM 278;
    IWM 435; IWM 501-07; IWM 501-13;
    IWM 502; IWM 508-10; IWM 508-15;
    IWM 508-17; IWM 508-20; IWM 508-25;
    IWM 508-26; IWM 508-27; IWM 508-34;
    IWM 508-49; IWM 508-50; IWM 508-72;
    IWM 508-74; IWM 508-75; IWM 508-76;
    IWM 508-77; IWM 508-80; IWM 508-81;
    IWM 680b; IWM 1062-03; IWM 1079;
    NTB 224-02; NTB 356-02
Marne (River)   IWM 501-07; IWM 508-67;
    IWM 508-72; IWM 508-76
Marseilles (Bouches-de-Rhône)
    IWM 440-02; IWM 469; IWM 508-13;
    IWM 1061-06i
Maubeuge (Nord)   IWM 508-34; IWM 508-86;
    IWM 670b
Metz (Moselle)   IWM 501-02
MEURTHE-ET-MOSELLE   IWM 501-03;
    IWM 501-05; IWM 501-10; IWM 502;
    IWM 508-78; IWM 508-79
MEUSE   IWM 473; IWM 501-01; IWM 501-02;
    IWM 501-03; IWM 501-05; IWM 501-06;
    IWM 501-08; IWM 501-09; IWM 501-12;
    IWM 508-24; IWM 508-25; IWM 508-47;
    IWM 508-51; IWM 508-78; IWM 508-79;
    IWM 1204
Meuse (River)   IWM 508-47; IWM 508-78
Monchy-le-Preux (Pas-de-Calais)   IWM 113;
    IWM 375
Mont Blanc   IWM 594-02+3
Mont Bligny   IWM 508-74
Mont Blond   IWM 508-28
Mont Cornillet   IWM 508-28
Mont Haut   IWM 508-28
Mont Plemont   IWM 508-60
Mont Renaud   IWM 473; IWM 508-56
Mont Sec   IWM 508-78
Montdidier (Somme)   IWM 508-56;
    IWM 508-75; IWM 1196
Montfaucon (Meuse)   IWM 501-01;
    IWM 508-80
Montreuil (Pas-de-Calais)   IWM 129;
    IWM 224; IWM 230; IWM 247; IWM 258;
    IWM 289; IWM 310; IWM 314; IWM 355;
    IWM 414
Moreuil (Somme)   IWM 181; IWM 183;
    IWM 508-55
MOSELLE   IWM 508-89; IWM 508-90

Mouquet Farm (Somme)   IWM 121; IWM 138
Nesle (Somme)   IWM 508-18; IWM 508-31;
        IWM 508-76 bis
NORD   IWM 132; IWM 144; IWM 146;
    IWM 198; IWM 234; IWM 235; IWM 237;
    IWM 302; IWM 321; IWM 347; IWM 375;
    IWM 508-82; IWM 508-85; IWM 508-86;
        IWM 664b; IWM 1061-09j
Noyon (Oise)   IWM 473; IWM 508-18;
    IWM 508-29; IWM 508-42; IWM 508-76 bis;
        IWM 508-78 bis; NTB 321-02
OISE   IWM 473; IWM 508-18; IWM 508-56;
    IWM 508-66; IWM 508-75; IWM 508-76;
        IWM 1061-09k; IWM 1070a
Oise (River)   IWM 508-65; IWM 508-66;
        IWM 508-70
Paris   IWM 172; IWM 296; IWM 458;
    IWM 473; IWM 484; IWM 485; IWM 501-02;
    IWM 501-07; IWM 501-13; IWM 508-14;
    IWM 508-16; IWM 508-61; IWM 508-84;
    IWM 509; IWM 594-04-13; IWM 1061-04c;
IWM 1061-04d; IWM 1061-06f; IWM 1061-06g;
    IWM 1061-09i; IWM 1070h; IWM 1079;
IWM 1082-01; IWM 1082-02a; IWM 1082-02c;
    IWM 1082-04; NTB 194-02; NTB 219-02;
    NTB 242-02; NTB 245-02; NTB 256-02;
    NTB 259-02; NTB 266-02; NTB 270-02;
    NTB 275-02; NTB 279-02; NTB 344-02
PAS-DE-CALAIS   IWM 111; IWM 113;
    IWM 115; IWM 116; IWM 119; IWM 124;
    IWM 128; IWM 129; IWM 133; IWM 138;
    IWM 146; IWM 147; IWM 150; IWM 158;
    IWM 164; IWM 182; IWM 183; IWM 192;
    IWM 197; IWM 198; IWM 208; IWM 211;
    IWM 212; IWM 236; IWM 237; IWM 243;
    IWM 271; IWM 282; IWM 289; IWM 293;
    IWM 316; IWM 322; IWM 332; IWM 501-07;
    IWM 505; IWM 508-57; IWM 508-71;
        IWM 1061-04a
Péronne (Somme)   IWM 113; IWM 171;
    IWM 130-09+10; IWM 131; IWM 142;
    IWM 331; IWM 503; IWM 508-45
Pont-à-Mousson (Meurthe-et-Moselle)
        IWM 501-06; IWM 508-39
Pozières (Somme)   IWM 121; IWM 138;
        IWM 198; IWM 300
Rembercourt (Meuse)   IWM 501-03;
        IWM 501-04
Ressons (Oise)   IWM 508-66; IWM 508-75
Rexpoëde (Nord)   IWM 508-21; IWM 508-26
Rheims (Marne)   IWM 435; IWM 473;
    IWM 508-25; IWM 508-44; IWM 508-51;
    IWM 508-52; IWM 508-65; IWM 508-82;
    IWM 508-83; IWM 508-92; IWM 714;
        IWM 1061-02b
Rhine (River)   IWM 508-89
Ribécourt (Nord)   IWM 144; IWM 508-17;
    IWM 508-75; IWM 697d; NTB 310-01
Richebourg-Saint-Vaast (Pas-de-Calais)
        IWM 207; IWM 428
Riencourt (Somme)   IWM 163; IWM 663c

Ronssoy (Somme)   IWM 501-09; IWM 501-12;
        IWM 503
Rouen (Seine-Maritime)   IWM 115; IWM 198;
    IWM 329; IWM 677b; NTB 238-01
Roye (Somme)   IWM 113; IWM 473;
        IWM 508-75; IWM 508-76 bis
St-Affrique (Aveyron)   IWM 508-28
St Léger (Pas-de-Calais)   IWM 269; IWM 322;
        IWM 390
St Malo (Ille-et-Vilaine)   IWM 1061-03d
St Mihiel (Meuse)   IWM 458; IWM 501-05;
    IWM 501-06; IWM 501-12; IWM 502;
    IWM 503; IWM 508-78; IWM 508-79;
        IWM 1183
St Nazaire (Gard)   IWM 484
St Omer (Pas-de-Calais)   IWM 153; IWM 198;
    IWM 203; IWM 214; IWM 216
St Pierre-des-Corps (Indre-et-Loire)
        IWM 501-13
St Quentin (Aisne)   IWM 121; IWM 335;
    IWM 501-01; IWM 508-45; IWM 508-81;
        IWM 508-83; IWM 508-92
St Quentin Canal   IWM 338; IWM 501-08
Ste-Marie-Cappel (Nord)   IWM 141; IWM 632
Samogneux (Meuse)   IWM 501-04;
        IWM 501-14; IWM 508-83
Sapignies (Pas-de-Calais) IWM 302; IWM 322
SEINE   IWM 501-03; IWM 501-13
SEINE-ET-MARNE   IWM 1061-04c; NTB 265-01
SEINE-MARITIME   IWM 114; IWM 176;
        IWM 318
Soissons (Aisne)   IWM 435; IWM 473;
    IWM 508-12; IWM 508-43; IWM 508-52;
    IWM 508-55; IWM 508-73; IWM 1132;
        IWM 670b; NTB 309-01
SOMME   IWM 115; IWM 116; IWM 121;
    IWM 130-05+6; IWM 130-09+10; IWM 131;
    IWM 136; IWM 138; IWM 139; IWM 178;
    IWM 179; IWM 180; IWM 183; IWM 191;
    IWM 192; IWM 196; IWM 212; IWM 256;
    IWM 261; IWM 280; IWM 286; IWM 290;
    IWM 295; IWM 300; IWM 302; IWM 310;
    IWM 319; IWM 322; IWM 324; IWM 331;
    IWM 336; IWM 420-05+6; IWM 440-06;
    IWM 440-07; IWM 442; IWM 501-09;
        IWM 503; IWM 508-11; IWM 508-15;
    IWM 508-16; IWM 508-31; IWM 508-56;
    IWM 508-57; IWM 508-62; IWM 508-64;
IWM 508-76; IWM 508-76 bis; IWM 508-77;
    IWM 508-92; IWM 677a; IWM 677b;
IWM 680a; IWM 681c; IWM 693e; IWM 715;
    IWM 1061-02a; IWM 1061-05i; IWM 1195;
        NTB 310-02; NTB 327-01
Somme (River)   IWM 131; IWM 229;
        IWM 327
Strasbourg (Bas-Rhin)   IWM 380;
        IWM 508-89; IWM 508-91
Tahure (Marne)   IWM 508-80; IWM 508-81
Tergnier (Aisne)   IWM 473; IWM 508-78 bis
Thann (Haut-Rhin)   IWM 508-14;
        IWM 508-42; IWM 508-49

Thiaucourt (Meurthe-et-Moselle)   IWM 508-78;
IWM 508-79
Thumaide (Hainaut)   IWM 375
Tramecourt (Pas-de-Calais)   IWM 119;
IWM 198
Trouville (Seine-Maritime) IWM 318; IWM 1097
Varennes-en-Argonne (Meuse)   IWM 501-02;
IWM 508-80
Verdun (Meuse)   IWM 310; IWM 473;
IWM 501-03; IWM 501-09; IWM 501-10;
IWM 501-12; IWM 501-14; IWM 502;
IWM 508-23; IWM 508-24; IWM 508-25;
IWM 508-31; IWM 508-39; IWM 508-43;
IWM 508-47; IWM 508-80; IWM 508-83;
NTB 323-01
Versailles (Yvelines)   IWM 172; IWM 508-47;
IWM 508-61; IWM 508-68; IWM 508-76;
IWM 1042; IWM 1061-09e; NTB 241-02;
NTB 256-01
Vesle (River)   IWM 508-75; IWM 508-78 bis
Vigneulles (Meuse) IWM 501-06; IWM 508-79
Villeret (Aisne)   IWM 501-09; IWM 503
Villers-Bocage (Somme)   IWM 267; IWM 271
Villers-Bretonneux (Somme)   IWM 181;
IWM 185; IWM 270; IWM 327; IWM 508-62;
IWM 1061-02a
Villers-Cotterêts (Aisne)   IWM 508-71;
IWM 508-73
Vimy (Pas-de-Calais)   IWM 142;
IWM 153; IWM 198; IWM 310; IWM 314;
IWM 465; IWM 466; IWM 467; IWM 680a;
NTB 340-01
Vincennes (Val-de-Marne)   NTB 251-02
Vosges area   IWM 714

(General references)   IWM 3; IWM 104;
IWM 105; IWM 121; IWM 123; IWM 126;
IWM 134; IWM 141; IWM 148; IWM 153;
IWM 164; IWM 168; IWM 175; IWM 176;
IWM 177; IWM 192; IWM 193a; IWM 198;
IWM 199; IWM 202-01; IWM 202-02;
IWM 204; IWM 220; IWM 240; IWM 248;
IWM 249; IWM 250; IWM 252; IWM 257;
IWM 261; IWM 267; IWM 276; IWM 281;
IWM 282; IWM 289; IWM 301; IWM 317;
IWM 322; IWM 326; IWM 327; IWM 328;
IWM 334; IWM 343; IWM 354; IWM 378;
IWM 383; IWM 387; IWM 388; IWM 391;
IWM 392; IWM 393; IWM 394; IWM 395;
IWM 396; IWM 397; IWM 398; IWM 399;
IWM 400; IWM 405; IWM 409; IWM 410;
IWM 413; IWM 420-01+2; IWM 420-03+4;
IWM 420-07+8; IWM 420-09+10;
IWM 420-11+12; IWM 420-13+14;
IWM 420-15+16; IWM 420-23+24;
IWM 420-25+26; IWM 420-27+28;
IWM 420-29+30; IWM 424; IWM 425;
IWM 430; IWM 440-03; IWM 440-05;
IWM 452; IWM 457; IWM 458; IWM 466;
IWM 473; IWM 474; IWM 475; IWM 476;
IWM 483-01; IWM 483-02; IWM 483-05;

(General references) (continued)
IWM 484; IWM 485; IWM 501-01; IWM 501-02;
IWM 501-12; IWM 503; IWM 508-10;
IWM 508-11; IWM 508-12; IWM 508-14;
IWM 508-15; IWM 508-16; IWM 508-17;
IWM 508-23; IWM 508-24; IWM 508-26;
IWM 508-27; IWM 508-28; IWM 508-29;
IWM 508-32; IWM 508-34; IWM 508-35;
IWM 508-38; IWM 508-40; IWM 508-42;
IWM 508-43; IWM 508-44; IWM 508-45;
IWM 508-47; IWM 508-50; IWM 508-52;
IWM 508-59; IWM 508-60; IWM 508-61;
IWM 508-62; IWM 508-64; IWM 508-65;
IWM 508-67; IWM 508-68; IWM 508-69;
IWM 508-70; IWM 508-72; IWM 508-74;
IWM 508-76; IWM 508-84; IWM 508-85;
IWM 508-86; IWM 508-92; IWM 511;
IWM 640-03; IWM 648; IWM 651b;
IWM 653a; IWM 657b; IWM 659; IWM 660a;
IWM 667; IWM 672a; IWM 674b; IWM 685a;
IWM 778; IWM 990; IWM 1004; IWM 1030;
IWM 1057-01; IWM 1057-02; IWM 1061-02a;
IWM 1061-02b; IWM 1061-02c;
IWM 1061-03a; IWM 1061-04b;
IWM 1061-04c; IWM 1061-06l; IWM 1061-09l;
IWM 1061-09m; IWM 1062-16; IWM 1070d;
IWM 1099; IWM 1100; IWM 1128a;
IWM 1150; IWM 1170; IWM 1188;
IWM 1189; IWM 1198; NTB 224-01;
NTB 248-02; NTB 313-01; NTB 317-01;
NTB 319-02; NTB 342-02; NTB 354-01

("British Western Front" - less certain
identification)   IWM 107; IWM 118;
IWM 125; IWM 143; IWM 155; IWM 160;
IWM 165; IWM 166; IWM 173; IWM 195;
IWM 210; IWM 217; IWM 219; IWM 221;
IWM 226; IWM 246; IWM 259; IWM 298;
IWM 323; IWM 354; IWM 369; IWM 389;
IWM 390; IWM 401; IWM 402; IWM 404;
IWM 408; IWM 411; IWM 415; IWM 416;
IWM 417; IWM 424; IWM 427; IWM 433;
IWM 470; IWM 663a; IWM 666a; IWM 675a;
IWM 678a; IWM 678b; IWM 713;
IWM 1061-02c; IWM 1062-08; IWM 1070c;
NTB 238-01; NTB 249-02

GERMAN EAST AFRICA   IWM 84

GERMANY
Berlin   IWM 484; IWM 1062-08
Cologne   IWM 376; IWM 379; IWM 380;
IWM 381; IWM 385; IWM 420-29+30;
IWM 877; IWM 1174
Düsseldorf   IWM 1082-02d
Friedrichshaven   IWM 484
Kiel Canal   IWM 484; IWM 485
Koblenz   IWM 502
Leipzig   IWM 484
Munich   IWM 1062-08

(General references)   IWM 484;
IWM 501-02; IWM 501-11; IWM 501-12;
       IWM 502; IWM 508-90; IWM 877;
IWM 1061-09h; IWM 1062-07; IWM 1062-08;
       IWM 1072; IWM 1091b; IWM 1205

(less certain identification)   IWM 1045d;
                                        IWM 1062-08

GREAT BRITAIN see UNITED KINGDOM

GREECE
Athens   IWM 97; IWM 508-16; IWM 508-19
MACEDONIA   NTB 269-02; NTB 270-02;
                                        NTB 275-02
Salonika (Macedonia)   IWM 41; IWM 60;
IWM 95; IWM 96; IWM 97; IWM 98; IWM 99;
       IWM 100; IWM 440-04; IWM 508-10;
       IWM 508-12; IWM 508-14; IWM 508-17;
       IWM 508-26; IWM 508-27; IWM 508-31;
       IWM 508-35; IWM 508-48; IWM 508-59;
       IWM 508-68; IWM 699c; IWM 1061-05a;
IWM 1061-05c; NTB 239-01; NTB 248-01;
NTB 252-02; NTB 258-01; IWM 1061-08b;
IWM 1062-10; IWM 1062-22a; IWM 1062-22b;
       IWM 1180b; IWM 1180c; IWM 1207;
       NTB 248-02; NTB 250-02; NTB 251-01;
       NTB 253-02; NTB 261-01; NTB 263-01;
       NTB 263-02; NTB 264-01; NTB 267-02;
       NTB 271-02; NTB 272-02; NTB 273-01;
       NTB 273-02; NTB 274-01; NTB 277-02;
       NTB 283-02; NTB 309-01; NTB 318-01
Skra (River)   IWM 97
Struma (River)   IWM 97

HUNGARY see AUSTRO-HUNGARIAN
   EMPIRE

INDIA   IWM 816; IWM 876; IWM 1061-04d;
                                        IWM 1064-02c

IRAQ (see also OTTOMAN EMPIRE,
   MESOPOTAMIA)   IWM 878; NTB 323-02

IRELAND (see also UNITED KINGDOM,
   IRELAND)   IWM 485

ITALY
Adige (River)   IWM 508-38
Brenta (River)   IWM 508-46
Brescia (Lombardy)   IWM 508-37;
                                       IWM 508-38;
                                        NTB 329-01
Camonica (River)   IWM 459
CAMPANIA   IWM 225; IWM 1047-01;
                                       IWM 1047-02
FRIULI   IWM 1035b
Garda (Lake)   IWM 508-38; IWM 283
Gorizia (Friuli)   NTB 316-01
LOMBARDY   IWM 508-38; IWM 697a

Milan (Lombardy)   IWM 508-37;
                    IWM 508-43; IWM 508-65
Mount Grappa   IWM 508-46; IWM 1061-02b
Mount Presena   IWM 459
Mount Tonale   IWM 459
Piave (River)   IWM 154; IWM 459;
       IWM 501-02; IWM 501-13; IWM 508-40;
              IWM 1061-05f; NTB 354-01
PIEDMONT   IWM 508-37; IWM 508-38
Sile (River)   IWM 501-13
VENETO   IWM 154; IWM 266; IWM 501-13;
       IWM 508-38; IWM 508-40; IWM 508-46;
       IWM 1061-05f; NTB 317-01; NTB 356-02
Venice (Veneto)   IWM 508-46; IWM 508-49;
                                        NTB 340-01
Verona (Veneto)   IWM 508-37; IWM 266;
                                        NTB 329-01

(General references)   IWM 193d; IWM 460;
       IWM 484; IWM 501-10; IWM 508-37;
       IWM 508-39; IWM 508-49; IWM 508-53;
       IWM 508-62; IWM 508-70; IWM 651a;
IWM 1035b; IWM 1061-02a; IWM 1061-02c;
       IWM 1075; IWM 1175; NTB 222-02;
       NTB 324-01; NTB 330-02; NTB 351-02

(less certain identification)   IWM 1034-04;
       IWM 1038; IWM 1043a; IWM 1043b;
              IWM 1045b; IWM 1084

JAMAICA   IWM 842

JAPAN   IWM 445; IWM 451

KENYA   IWM 880-02c

LEBANON see OTTOMAN EMPIRE,
   SYRIA/LEBANON

LUXEMBOURG   IWM 508-90

MALAY STATES   IWM 842

MESOPOTAMIA see OTTOMAN EMPIRE,
   MESOPOTAMIA

MEXICO   NTB 168-01; IWM 1049

MONTENEGRO   IWM 484

MOROCCO   IWM 508-15; IWM 508-20;
       IWM 508-45; IWM 511; IWM 1061-09i;
                                        NTB 313-01

THE NETHERLANDS   IWM 455; IWM 685b;
       IWM 1061-09j; IWM 1061-09k; IWM 1079

NEW ZEALAND   IWM 485; IWM 815;
       IWM 842; IWM 843; IWM 1061-08a

NORWAY   IWM 1063; IWM 1126

OTTOMAN EMPIRE
ARABIA
El Wejh   IWM 508-36
Jidda   IWM 41; IWM 508-36; IWM 1131a
Petra   IWM 41

MESOPOTAMIA
Abu Rumman   IWM 83
Aq Su   IWM 64
Babylon   IWM 60; IWM 66; IWM 75; IWM 81
Baghdad   IWM 59; IWM 60; IWM 61;
    IWM 63; IWM 66; IWM 77; IWM 79; IWM 80;
                                                IWM 81
Basra   IWM 65; IWM 79; IWM 83
Birs Nimrud   IWM 81
Ctesiphon   IWM 63; IWM 75; IWM 78
Diyala River   IWM 64; IWM 68; IWM 82
Euphrates River IWM 71; IWM 72; IWM 82;
                                                IWM 461a
Fallahiya   IWM 83
Hindiya   IWM 72
Kahm Baghdadie   IWM 80
Khasradala   IWM 64
Khora Creek   IWM 79
Kurkuch   IWM 69
Kut al Amara   IWM 65; IWM 77; IWM 79
Masina   IWM 68; IWM 82
Narim Kopris   IWM 64; IWM 68; IWM 79
Ora   IWM 83
Qurna   IWM 65; IWM 77; IWM 79; IWM 83
Ramadi   IWM 59; IWM 60; IWM 61; IWM 78;
    IWM 79; IWM 80; IWM 657a; NTB 341-02
Samarra   IWM 59; IWM 61; IWM 63; IWM 78
Tigris River   IWM 65; IWM 66; IWM 71;
                    IWM 77; IWM 79; IWM 80
Tuz Khurmatli   IWM 68

(General references)   IWM 9; IWM 43;
    IWM 70; IWM 430; IWM 651a; IWM 652b;
                                               IWM 990

PALESTINE
Arsulf   IWM 30
Auja River   IWM 16
Beersheba   IWM 17; IWM 30
Belah   IWM 10; IWM 25
Bereit Salaam   IWM 34
Bethlehem   IWM 15; IWM 1131c; NTB 341-02
Dead Sea   IWM 28
El Arish   IWM 5; IWM 17; IWM 60
El Ghoranyeh   IWM 12; IWM 26
El Kuneitra   IWM 37
Es Salt   IWM 26; IWM 652a
Gaza   IWM 10; IWM 11; IWM 28; IWM 32;
                    IWM 697b; IWM 1131b
Haifa   IWM 38
Hebron   IWM 24; IWM 72
Jaffa   IWM 12; IWM 20; IWM 28; IWM 634;
                                                IWM 1131b
Jericho   IWM 16; IWM 22; IWM 28

Jerusalem   IWM 12; IWM 13; IWM 15;
    IWM 16; IWM 19; IWM 22; IWM 27; IWM 28;
    IWM 30; IWM 32; IWM 35; IWM 37; IWM 41;
    IWM 45; IWM 193c; IWM 1131b; IWM 1131c
Jordan River   IWM 28; IWM 37
Khan-Yunus (?)   IWM 508-39
Lake Tiberias   IWM 38
Lod   IWM 30; IWM 652a
Mount Zion   IWM 13; IWM 25; IWM 32
Mulebbis   IWM 16; IWM 78
Nablus   IWM 38
Nazareth   IWM 37
Ramleh   IWM 30
Rishon le Zion   IWM 18; IWM 32; IWM 33;
                          IWM 35; IWM 72
Sea of Galilee   IWM 38
Shellal   IWM 10
Tel-el-Jelil   IWM 30; IWM 34
Wadi Auja   IWM 30
Zimmaria   IWM 38

(General references)   IWM 6; IWM 7; IWM 8;
        IWM 32; IWM 33; IWM 43; IWM 58;
    IWM 420-17+18; IWM 452; IWM 508-39;
        IWM 508-49; IWM 651b; IWM 662a;
    IWM 662b; IWM 663a; IWM 663b; IWM 663c;
    IWM 990; IWM 1030; IWM 1095; IWM 1180a;
                                          NTB 344-01

SYRIA/LEBANON
Aleppo (?)   IWM 44
Baalbec   IWM 39; IWM 60; IWM 81
Beirut   IWM 39
Damascus   IWM 37
Tripoli   IWM 39

TURKEY
Constantinople   IWM 483-06; IWM 484;
        IWM 772; IWM 1034-03; IWM 1061-06j;
    IWM 1062-02a; IWM 1062-02b; IWM 1072;
                    NTB 191-01; NTB 237-02
Dardanelles (?)   IWM 483-03
Gallipoli   IWM 772; IWM 1058
Imbros   IWM 1058

PALESTINE see OTTOMAN EMPIRE,
    PALESTINE

PANAMA   IWM 842; IWM 843

POLAND see RUSSIA, RUSSIAN POLAND

PORTUGAL   IWM 1175

ROMANIA   IWM 483-03; IWM 508-15;
    IWM 508-17; IWM 508-20; IWM 508-27;
                                      NTB 319-02

RUSSIA
Archangel Area   IWM 420-19+20;
        IWM 420-21+22; IWM 422; IWM 808

Baku (Azerbaijan) IWM 73
Batum IWM 650
Brest Litovsk IWM 481
Chassina IWM 483-05
Czernowitz IWM 481
Galicia NTB 251-02
Kovno IWM 483-04
Moscow IWM 484
Œsel Island IWM 1124
Petrograd IWM 484; NTB 238-01
Przemyśl IWM 481; IWM 1039-01;
   IWM 1045c; IWM 1062-14
Russian Poland IWM 1045a; IWM 1062-07;
   IWM 1062-08; IWM 1072; NTB 223-02;
   NTB 224-01

(General references) IWM 656a;
   IWM 1062-01; NTB 239-02; NTB 240-02

SCOTLAND *see* UNITED KINGDOM,
   SCOTLAND

SERBIA IWM 484; IWM 1061-04b;
   IWM 1061-06h; NTB 255-02

SIERRA LEONE IWM 842

SINGAPORE IWM 842

SOUTH AFRICA IWM 485; IWM 551;
   IWM 842; IWM 1061-07g; IWM 1080b;
   IWM 1081a; IWM 1081c; IWM 1081d;
   IWM 1081e

SPAIN IWM 484; IWM 592

SRI LANKA *see* CEYLON

SWITZERLAND IWM 453; IWM 454;
   IWM 483-02; IWM 485; IWM 1061-09g;
   IWM 1070a; NTB 254-02; NTB 264-01;
   NTB 267-02

SYRIA *see* OTTOMAN EMPIRE,
   SYRIA/LEBANON

TRANSJORDAN (*see also* OTTOMAN
   EMPIRE, ARABIA) IWM 878

TRINIDAD IWM 843

TRIPOLITANIA IWM 1123

TURKEY *see* OTTOMAN EMPIRE, TURKEY

UNITED KINGDOM
ENGLAND
Aldershot (Hants) IWM 108; IWM 274;
   IWM 310; IWM 407; IWM 438; IWM 448;
   IWM 527; IWM 580; IWM 654b; IWM 678b;
   IWM 1005; IWM 1062-19; IWM 1064-03a;

Aldershot (Hants) *(continued)*
   IWM 1064-03b; IWM 1102; NTB 254-01;
   NTB 256-01
Barrow-in-Furness (Lancs) IWM 434;
   IWM 623; IWM 675b
Bedford IWM 174; IWM 668b; IWM 1185
BEDFORDSHIRE IWM 645
BERKSHIRE IWM 551; IWM 620; IWM 809;
   NTB 317-02
Birkenhead (Ches) IWM 809; NTB 316-01
Birmingham IWM 262; IWM 304;
   IWM 308d; IWM 485; IWM 652a; IWM 691;
   IWM 809; IWM 1217
Bovington (Dorset) IWM 356; IWM 452;
   IWM 1190; IWM 1196; IWM 1200
Bradfield (Berks) NTB 292-01; NTB 345-02
BUCKINGHAMSHIRE NTB 276-02; NTB 328-01
Calshot (Hants) IWM 649; IWM 880-01a;
   IWM 880-01b; IWM 880-01c; IWM 880-01f
Cambridge IWM 511; IWM 661a; NTB 344-01
Chatham (Kent) IWM 446; IWM 661b
Chelmsford (Essex) IWM 1082-02c;
   NTB 264-01
CORNWALL IWM 1061-08c
Coventry IWM 446; NTB 317-02
Cranwell (Lincs) IWM 551; IWM 570;
   IWM 880-02b
Deal (Kent) IWM 201; IWM 699c
Derby IWM 667; IWM 809
DERBYSHIRE IWM 809
DEVON IWM 484; IWM 584; IWM 842;
   IWM 1061-03b
DORSET IWM 285; IWM 441; IWM 647;
   IWM 809; IWM 1197
Dover (Kent) IWM 192; IWM 198; IWM 212;
   IWM 361; IWM 485; IWM 505; IWM 551;
   IWM 656a; IWM 681c; IWM 809;
   IWM 1082-02a; NTB 343-01
DURHAM (County) IWM 1061-06m; IWM 1179
Elswick (Lancs) IWM 263; IWM 1167
English Channel IWM 192; IWM 1148;
   IWM 1149
Epsom (Surrey) IWM 485; IWM 691;
   IWM 1070d
ESSEX IWM 655d; IWM 1206; NTB 235-02;
   NTB 254-01; NTB 256-01; NTB 269-02;
   NTB 275-02
Farnborough (Hants) IWM 880-01e;
   IWM 880-01h
Faversham (Kent) IWM 549-05; IWM 1061-04e
Felixstowe (Suff) IWM 551; IWM 578-03;
   IWM 642; IWM 644; IWM 865; IWM 880-02a;
   NTB 263-02
Grimsby (Lincs) IWM 552; IWM 553
HAMPSHIRE IWM 305; IWM 440-01;
   IWM 501-06; IWM 521; IWM 867;
   IWM 1064-01b; IWM 1064-03f; NTB 249-02
Harwich (Essex) IWM 551; IWM 558;
   IWM 560; IWM 571; IWM 1154; IWM 1212

Hastings (Sussex)   IWM 635; IWM 640-02;
    IWM 1082-02a; IWM 1106; IWM 1107-01;
        IWM 1107-02; NTB 269-01
Hendon (Middx)   IWM 809; IWM 1091a
Henley-on-Thames (Oxon) IWM 485; IWM 691
HEREFORDSHIRE   NTB 310-01
HERTFORDSHIRE   IWM 284; IWM 809
Horsham (Sussex)   IWM 291; IWM 677a
Hounslow (Middx)   IWM 242; NTB 318-02
Huntingdon (Hunts)   IWM 167; IWM 200
Ilford (Essex)   IWM 447; IWM 531
Isle of Grain (Kent)   IWM 614; IWM 629;
    IWM 643; IWM 644; IWM 1166; IWM 1167
Isle of Wight   IWM 573
KENT   IWM 420-19+20; IWM 551; IWM 552;
    IWM 613; IWM 654a; IWM 877; IWM 1071;
        NTB 259-02; NTB 314-02; NTB 254-01;
            NTB 327-02
LANCASHIRE   IWM 342; IWM 485; IWM 661a;
        IWM 1061-07g; IWM 1070e
LINCOLNSHIRE   IWM 692a; IWM 1191
Liverpool   IWM 241; IWM 342; IWM 450;
    IWM 548; IWM 666b; IWM 693d; IWM 809;
        IWM 1162; NTB 266-02

LONDON
[Note that, apart from general references,
    London entries have been subdivided
    geographically, the first letter or two
    letters of the Post Office codes providing
    the basis for most of the subdivisions]
LONDON [Buckingham Palace, Westminster
    and Whitehall]   IWM 134; IWM 224;
        IWM 265; IWM 362; IWM 412;
    IWM 420-21+22; IWM 439; IWM 440-01;
    IWM 440-02; IWM 463; IWM 465; IWM 478;
    IWM 480; IWM 485; IWM 505; IWM 507;
    IWM 521; IWM 652b; IWM 653a; IWM 653b;
    IWM 656b; IWM 657a; IWM 659; IWM 660a;
    IWM 663a; IWM 663c; IWM 664a; IWM 666a;
    IWM 666b; IWM 667; IWM 674c; IWM 675b;
    IWM 678b; IWM 679a; IWM 685b; IWM 693d;
    IWM 694a; IWM 699b; IWM 714; IWM 809;
        IWM 810; IWM 811; IWM 1061-07b;
    IWM 1062-18; IWM 1080a; IWM 1082-02a;
        IWM 1082-02b; IWM 1085; IWM 1141;
            IWM 1142; IWM 1182; IWM 1186;
        IWM 1187; NTB 239-01; NTB 239-02;
    NTB 275-02; NTB 318-02; NTB 320-02;
            NTB 322-01; NTB 354-01
LONDON [City]   IWM 193d; IWM 443;
    IWM 474; IWM 485; IWM 626; IWM 653a;
    IWM 653b; IWM 662a; IWM 664a; IWM 665b;
        IWM 692a; IWM 693b; IWM 809;
    IWM 1061-01; IWM 1061-03i; IWM 1061-04f;
    IWM 1062-03; IWM 1127; NTB 168-01;
    NTB 178-01; NTB 194-02; NTB 219-02;
    NTB 222-02; NTB 238-01; NTB 242-01;
    NTB 242-02; NTB 249-01; NTB 252-02;
    NTB 253-01; NTB 267-01; NTB 276-02

LONDON [East]   IWM 320; IWM 485;
    IWM 549-10; IWM 552; IWM 692a;
        IWM 1062-18; NTB 89-02
London [North and North West]   IWM 200;
    IWM 419; IWM 450; IWM 461c; IWM 485;
    IWM 654a; IWM 660a; IWM 661b; IWM 665c;
        IWM 668d; IWM 674a; IWM 693e;
    IWM 1061-03h; IWM 1061-06a; IWM 1071;
        IWM 1181; NTB 178-01; NTB 247-02;
    NTB 249-01; NTB 255-02; NTB 258-02;
    NTB 261-02; NTB 266-02; NTB 309-01;
            NTB 347-02
LONDON [South East]   IWM 161; IWM 297;
    IWM 307; IWM 313; IWM 361; IWM 474;
        IWM 478; IWM 504; IWM 520;
    IWM 664a; IWM 674c; IWM 679b; IWM 809;
    IWM 1061-06e; IWM 1181; NTB 256-01;
    NTB 267-02; NTB 269-01; NTB 273-01;
    NTB 319-01; NTB 322-01; NTB 325-01;
            NTB 351-02
LONDON [South West (excluding Westminster
    and Whitehall)]   IWM 193b; IWM 220;
    IWM 309; IWM 346; IWM 361; IWM 443;
    IWM 633; IWM 653b; IWM 654b; IWM 659;
    IWM 661a; IWM 677b; IWM 681b; IWM 693a;
    IWM 699c; IWM 1061-06f; IWM 1061-08b;
    IWM 1071; IWM 1082-02c; IWM 1082-02d;
        IWM 1182; NTB 239-01; NTB 249-01;
    NTB 257-01; NTB 258-01; NTB 259-01;
    NTB 273-01; NTB 322-01; NTB 354-01
LONDON [West]   IWM 109; IWM 193d;
    IWM 292; IWM 348; IWM 362; IWM 418;
    IWM 443; IWM 485; IWM 521; IWM 529;
    IWM 657a; IWM 659; IWM 660a; IWM 678a;
    IWM 679a; IWM 680a; IWM 1061-07g;
    IWM 1062-17; IWM 1062-18; IWM 1071;
    IWM 1082-02c; IWM 1141; IWM 1142;
        IWM 1181; IWM 1215; NTB 239-01;
    NTB 252-02; NTB 265-01; NTB 344-01
LONDON [West Central]   IWM 193c; IWM 412;
        IWM 420-03+4; IWM 443; IWM 474;
    IWM 478; IWM 479; IWM 485; IWM 505;
    IWM 508-42; IWM 512; IWM 521; IWM 532;
    IWM 536; IWM 537; IWM 549-03; IWM 572;
    IWM 612; IWM 652b; IWM 654a; IWM 659;
    IWM 664a; IWM 668c; IWM 674b; IWM 677a;
        IWM 678a; IWM 679a; IWM 681b;
        IWM 681c; IWM 685a; IWM 1025f;
    IWM 1061-07b; IWM 1061-09o; IWM 1062-18;
    NTB 165-02; NTB 247-01; NTB 249-02;
    NTB 253-01; NTB 259-01; NTB 263-02;
    NTB 314-02; NTB 324-02; NTB 327-01;
    NTB 328-01; NTB 340-01; NTB 356-02
LONDON [General references]
    IWM 130-09+10; IWM 342; IWM 420-29+30;
    IWM 484; IWM 523; IWM 652a; IWM 656a;
    IWM 659; IWM 660b; IWM 661a; IWM 662a;
    IWM 662b; IWM 663a; IWM 666a; IWM 667;
    IWM 668b; IWM 674a; IWM 675b; IWM 678a;
    IWM 681c; IWM 686; IWM 697a; IWM 867;
        IWM 1025b; IWM 1025e; IWM 1049;

LONDON [General references] *(continued)*
 IWM 1061-06b; IWM 1082-01; IWM 1175;
  IWM 1181; IWM 1210; NTB 194-02;
 NTB 204-01; NTB 213-02; NTB 235-02;
 NTB 240-02; NTB 246-01; NTB 247-01;
 NTB 251-02; NTB 252-02; NTB 254-02;
 NTB 255-02; NTB 257-01; NTB 262-01;
 NTB 265-01; NTB 266-02; NTB 272-02;
 NTB 274-01; NTB 279-02; NTB 280-01;
 NTB 284-02; NTB 312-01; NTB 319-01;
 NTB 320-02; NTB 321-02; NTB 324-02;
  NTB 329-01; NTB 340-01; NTB 345-02
Maidenhead (Berks)   IWM 579; NTB 251-02
Manchester   IWM 308b; IWM 342;
 IWM 682; IWM 1061-07c; IWM 1062-03;
  NTB 253-02; NTB 272-02
Manston (Kent)   IWM 551; IWM 880-01d
Margate (Kent)   IWM 551; NTB 314-02
Mersey (River)   IWM 809
Mickleham (Surrey)   IWM 273; IWM 310;
  IWM 350; IWM 674b
MIDDLESEX   IWM 311; IWM 612; IWM 663c;
 IWM 809; IWM 1070b; IWM 1073;
 NTB 246-01; NTB 253-01; NTB 260-02;
 NTB 263-01; NTB 273-01; NTB 321-01
Newcastle upon Tyne (Northd)   IWM 264;
  IWM 488
NORFOLK   IWM 1070d; IWM 1074;
  NTB 277-02
NORTHAMPTONSHIRE   IWM 706
Nottingham (Notts)   IWM 279; IWM 474;
  NTB 323-01
Osea Island (Essex)   IWM 566; IWM 567
Oxford (Oxon)   IWM 535; IWM 809;
  IWM 869; NTB 248-01
Plymouth (Devon)   IWM 598; IWM 1082-3
Portsmouth (Hants)   IWM 512; IWM 577;
 IWM 809; IWM 842; IWM 843; IWM 1061-01;
  IWM 1157; IWM 1213
Potters Bar (Middx)   IWM 655c; IWM 1072;
  IWM 1203; NTB 263-02
Reading (Berks)   IWM 693a; NTB 342-02
Redcar (Yorks)   IWM 639; IWM 871
Richmond (Surrey)   IWM 128; IWM 1061-08a;
 NTB 242-01; NTB 258-02; NTB 261-02;
  NTB 264-01; NTB 316-01
St Leonards-on-Sea (Sussex)   IWM 615;
 IWM 625; IWM 632; IWM 635; IWM 640-01;
  IWM 640-02
Salisbury Plain (Wilts)   IWM 477; IWM 551;
  IWM 580; IWM 660b; IWM 809;
  IWM 1064-01b; IWM 1064-02b;
  IWM 1064-02d; IWM 1064-03c;
  IWM 1064-03d; IWM 1064-03e;
  IWM 1064-03f; IWM 1070d
Sandringham (Norfolk)   NTB 274-01;
  NTB 278-02
Sheffield (Yorks)   IWM 809; IWM 1136
Shepperton (Middx)   IWM 579; IWM 1121
SOMERSET   NTB 235-02; NTB 324-02;
  NTB 325-01

Southampton (Hants)   IWM 863;
  IWM 1025c; NTB 395-01
Southend-on-Sea (Essex)   IWM 655d;
  IWM 663c; IWM 693c; NTB 178-01
STAFFORDSHIRE   IWM 134; IWM 693e;
  IWM 1192
Stratford-upon-Avon (Warks)   IWM 304;
  IWM 308a; IWM 1070g
SUFFOLK   NTB 258-02
SURREY   IWM 434; IWM 678a; IWM 1098;
 NTB 242-01; NTB 248-01; NTB 265-01;
  NTB 284-02; NTB 356-02
SUSSEX   IWM 867; IWM 1061-07f
Thames (Valley, River and Estuary)   IWM 579;
 IWM 614; IWM 620; IWM 629; IWM 643;
 IWM 644; IWM 676b; IWM 1166; IWM 1167;
  NTB 248-01; NTB 274-01
Tyne (River)   IWM 551; IWM 1166
WARWICKSHIRE   IWM 304; IWM 434
WILTSHIRE   IWM 706; IWM 809; NTB 251-01
Winchester (Hants)   IWM 474; IWM 651b;
  NTB 178-01
Windsor (Berks)   IWM 484; IWM 485;
 IWM 509; IWM 693b; IWM 1082-02c;
 NTB 260-02; NTB 261-02; NTB 265-02;
  NTB 269-01; NTB 323-02
WORCESTERSHIRE   NTB 242-02
YORKSHIRE   IWM 457; IWM 462;
 IWM 1061-03c; IWM 1070f; IWM 1082-02a;
  IWM 1137

(General references)   IWM 213; IWM 245;
 IWM 394; IWM 412; IWM 420-01+2;
 IWM 420-15+16; IWM 426; IWM 436;
 IWM 440-03; IWM 440-04; IWM 444;
 IWM 463; IWM 471; IWM 479; IWM 480;
 IWM 484; IWM 485; IWM 486; IWM 510;
 IWM 515; IWM 516; IWM 517; IWM 519;
 IWM 522; IWM 524; IWM 530; IWM 534;
  IWM 546; IWM 548; IWM 549-07;
 IWM 549-08; IWM 604; IWM 610; IWM 618;
 IWM 631; IWM 641; IWM 652b; IWM 653b;
 IWM 657b; IWM 668b; IWM 668c; IWM 668d;
 IWM 672a; IWM 674c; IWM 680b; IWM 685a;
 IWM 691; IWM 692b; IWM 693b; IWM 693c;
 IWM 693d; IWM 699b; IWM 870; IWM 873;
  IWM 989; IWM 990; IWM 1055d;
 IWM 1061-06c; IWM 1061-06d; IWM 1070a;
  IWM 1128a; IWM 1170; IWM 1175;
  IWM 1177a; IWM 1193; IWM 1198;
  IWM 1201; NTB 165-02; NTB 168-01;
 NTB 224-01; NTB 241-01; NTB 241-02;
 NTB 242-01; NTB 242-02; NTB 254-02;
 NTB 255-02; NTB 257-01; NTB 258-01;
 NTB 265-01; NTB 265-02; NTB 321-01;
  NTB 342-02; NTB 343-01

IRELAND
ARMAGH (County)   IWM 212
Belfast   IWM 212; IWM 485; IWM 674b
CLARE (County)   IWM 675a

CORK (County)   IWM 212
Dublin   IWM 194; IWM 485; IWM 664b;
              IWM 668c; IWM 678b; IWM 1056;
          IWM 1061-04f; IWM 1182; NTB 245-02;
          NTB 247-01; NTB 247-02; NTB 351-02
LIMERICK (County)   IWM 212
Queenstown (Co Cork)   IWM 551; IWM 562;
              IWM 564; IWM 1159; IWM 1160

(General references)   IWM 653a; IWM 655a;
                         IWM 657a; IWM 666a

SCOTLAND
East Fortune (E Loth)   IWM 551; IWM 636;
EAST LOTHIAN   IWM 636
Edinburgh   IWM 342; IWM 675b;
Firth of Forth   IWM 484; IWM 599;
          IWM 600; IWM 601; IWM 602; IWM 603;
    IWM 665b; IWM 674c; IWM 679a; IWM 685a;
    IWM 1143; IWM 1144; IWM 1145; IWM 1146;
    IWM 1147; IWM 1156; IWM 1164; IWM 1168;
              IWM 1169; IWM 1212; NTB 320-02
Glasgow   IWM 140; IWM 485; IWM 528;
      IWM 551; IWM 654b; IWM 664b; IWM 668c;
              IWM 675b; NTB 261-02; NTB 317-02
Inchinnan (Renf)   IWM 621; IWM 622;
                         IWM 624; IWM 645
LANARK   NTB 265-02
Leith (Mloth)   IWM 545
Rosyth (Fife)   IWM 130-03+4; IWM 287;
      IWM 440-05; IWM 551; IWM 638; IWM 1144;
              IWM 1145; IWM 1146; IWM 1147;
                                    NTB 351-02
ROXBURGH   IWM 1214
Scapa Flow (Orkney)   IWM 556; IWM 563;
      IWM 571; IWM 580; IWM 586; IWM 1151;
                                    IWM 1157

(General references)   IWM 548; IWM 686;
                         IWM 691; IWM 1055e

WALES
Aberystwyth (Card)   IWM 1061-04h;
                                    NTB 261-01
Cardiff   IWM 170; IWM 678b; NTB 340-01
Chepstow (Mon)   IWM 589
Ebbw Vale (Mon)   IWM 170; NTB 340-01
Llanwern (Mon)   IWM 666b
Neath (Glam)   IWM 679b

(General reference)   IWM 485

UNITED STATES OF AMERICA
Annapolis (MD)   IWM 565; IWM 1079
Bangor (ME)   IWM 687
Boston (MA)   IWM 687; IWM 1079
Camp Dix (NJ)   IWM 1079
Chicago (IL)   IWM 1079
Columbia (SC)   IWM 1079
Denver (CO)   IWM 1079
El Paso (TX)   IWM 1061-03h;

Honolulu (HI)   IWM 842; IWM 843
Los Angeles (CA)   IWM 1079; NTB 279-01
Mare Island Navy Yard (CA)   IWM 1061-07f
New York (NY)   IWM 484; IWM 502;
          IWM 686; IWM 687; IWM 1061-05g;
      IWM 1061-08d; IWM 1061-09n; IWM 1070a;
      IWM 1079; IWM 1082-02d; IWM 1175;
          NTB 246-01 NTB 256-02; NTB 259-01;
                         NTB 260-02; NTB 270-02
Newark (NJ)   IWM 687; IWM 1010
Newport News (VA)   IWM 1061-07e
Oakland (CA)   IWM 1079
Pacific Coast   IWM 1061-03e
Philadelphia (PA)   IWM 502; IWM 1061-08e;
                                          IWM 1079
Pittsburgh (PA)   IWM 687
Princeton (NJ)   IWM 1079
Quantico (VA)   IWM 1079
Redding (CA)   NTB 342-02
Saint Paul (MN)   IWM 1079
San Francisco (CA)   IWM 842;
                         IWM 1061-05g; IWM 1079
Venice (CA)   IWM 1061-07d; IWM 1079
Washington (DC)   IWM 484; IWM 502;
                                          IWM 1079
Waynesburg (PA)   IWM 1061-07f

(General references)   IWM 445; IWM 484;
          IWM 619; IWM 1049; IWM 1061-06k;
      IWM 1064-01a; IWM 1064-02a; IWM 1199;
                                    NTB 259-02

URUGUAY   IWM 456; IWM 506

WALES *see* UNITED KINGDOM, WALES

"WEST INDIES"   IWM 548

ZANZIBAR   IWM 842

ARABIA
ARABIAN ARMY (Army of Hejaz)   IWM 32;
   IWM 37; IWM 41; IWM 508-36; IWM 1131a

ARMENIA
ARMENIAN ORGANISATIONS
[Baku defence force]   IWM 73

AUSTRALIA
AUSTRALIAN ARMY (Australian Imperial Force)
   IWM 7; IWM 11; IWM 12; IWM 13; IWM 17;
   IWM 18; IWM 22; IWM 25; IWM 28; IWM 32;
   IWM 34; IWM 37; IWM 38; IWM 60; IWM 72;
   IWM 109; IWM 113; IWM 121; IWM 127;
      IWM 130-09+10; IWM 138; IWM 139;
   IWM 143; IWM 165; IWM 187; IWM 192;
   IWM 194; IWM 197; IWM 199; IWM 236;
   IWM 289; IWM 293; IWM 296; IWM 314;
   IWM 319; IWM 344; IWM 354; IWM 369;
   IWM 382; IWM 384; IWM 439; IWM 440-02;
   IWM 440-04; IWM 484; IWM 485; IWM 505;
      IWM 508-80; IWM 508-86; IWM 578-02;
   IWM 634; IWM 661b; IWM 663a; IWM 679a;
      IWM 842; NTB 258-01; NTB 273-01;
   NTB 274-01; NTB 277-02; NTB 316-01

1st Division   IWM 116; IWM 138; IWM 162;
   IWM 198; IWM 256; IWM 334; IWM 503
2nd Division   IWM 116; IWM 130-05+6;
   IWM 138; IWM 139; IWM 158; IWM 162;
   IWM 256; IWM 270; IWM 286; IWM 334;
   IWM 354; IWM 382; IWM 657b; IWM 1128a
3rd Division   IWM 139; IWM 151; IWM 197;
                          IWM 229; IWM 293
4th Division   IWM 139; IWM 270; IWM 331;
                                    IWM 503
5th Division   IWM 130-01+2; IWM 158;
   IWM 198; IWM 221; IWM 331; IWM 338;
   IWM 354 - 5th Division Gas School IWM 112

ANZAC Corps   IWM 138; IWM 192
ANZAC Division   IWM 12; IWM 25; IWM 38;
                       IWM 194; IWM 1058g
Australian Light Horse   IWM 7; IWM 11;
   IWM 13; IWM 18; IWM 22; IWM 25; IWM 28;
   IWM 32; IWM 34; IWM 37; IWM 60; IWM 72;
      IWM 286; IWM 382; IWM 508-74
Australian Militia   IWM 843
   - New South Wales Lancers IWM 1061-06d
Egyptian Expeditionary Force   IWM 7;
   IWM 11; IWM 12; IWM 13; IWM 17; IWM 18;
   IWM 22; IWM 25; IWM 28; IWM 32; IWM 34;
      IWM 37; IWM 38; IWM 60; IWM 72;
      IWM 662b; IWM 1095; IWM 1180a
Imperial Camel Corps   IWM 17; IWM 28

Artillery   IWM 130-05+6; IWM 256;
   NTB 261-01; NTB 267-02; NTB 323-02

Cadets   IWM 661a
Cavalry   NTB 269-02
Engineers   IWM 173; IWM 319
Machine Gun Corps, Motorised   IWM 138
Medical Corps   NTB 264-01

AUSTRALIAN AIR CORPS (Royal Australian Flying
   Corps)   IWM 187
1 Squadron   IWM 28; IWM 634
2 Squadron   IWM 236
3 Squadron   IWM 187; IWM 236; IWM 661b
4 Squadron   IWM 236; IWM 578-02

AUSTRALIAN NAVY
Adelaide   IWM 842
Australia   IWM 377; IWM 842; IWM 843;
                                    IWM 1170
Melbourne   IWM 842
Sydney   IWM 638

AUSTRALIAN ORGANISATIONS
Veterans Association of New South Wales
                                    IWM 842

AUSTRO-HUNGARIAN EMPIRE
AUSTRO-HUNGARIAN ARMY   IWM 481;
   IWM 1034-03; IWM 1034-04; IWM 1035b;
   IWM 1038; IWM 1039-01; IWM 1041b;
   IWM 1043a; IWM 1043b; IWM 1045b;
   IWM 1046a; IWM 1046b; IWM 1047-01;
   IWM 1047-02; IWM 1062-14; IWM 1062-15;
      IWM 1072; IWM 1084; IWM 1211
Arcièren Leibgarde   IWM 1041a
18th Dragoon Regt   IWM 1041a
Hungarian Life Guard   IWM 1034-01b;
                                   IWM 1041a
1st Infantry Regt   IWM 1041a
72nd Infantry Regt   IWM 1044
Standschützen   IWM 1033d; IWM 1035c
Cadets   IWM 1033d

AUSTRO-HUNGARIAN NAVY   IWM 1041b;
                                   IWM 1046b
Szent Istvan   IWM 484

BELGIUM
BELGIAN ARMY   IWM 122; IWM 162;
   IWM 254; IWM 353; IWM 359; IWM 370;
   IWM 371; IWM 384; IWM 439; IWM 484;
   IWM 509; IWM 508-21; IWM 508-84; IWM 508-88;
   IWM 509; IWM 626; IWM 656b; IWM 665a;
   IWM 670b; IWM 1050; IWM 1051; IWM 1052;
      IWM 1053; IWM 1054; IWM 1055c;
   IWM 1061-09h; IWM 1061-09j; IWM 1061-09k;
   NTB 164-01; NTB 165-02; NTB 221-01;
   NTB 223-02; NTB 267-02; NTB 277-01;
      NTB 277-02; NTB 278-02
1st Guides   NTB 257-01

Artillery   NTB 280-01
Balloon Corps   IWM 1061-05b
Civil Guard   IWM 1061-04c
Grenadiers   NTB 272-02
Infantry   IWM 192

BELGIAN ORGANISATIONS
Catholic Church   IWM 122

BULGARIA
BULGARIAN ARMY   IWM 484; IWM 508-82;
                                          IWM 1034-03

CANADA
CANADIAN ARMY (Canadian Expeditionary
   Force)   IWM 109; IWM 130-07+8;
       IWM 138; IWM 143; IWM 177; IWM 192;
       IWM 212; IWM 216; IWM 219; IWM 222;
       IWM 232; IWM 253; IWM 274; IWM 294;
       IWM 314; IWM 319; IWM 326; IWM 362;
    IWM 439; IWM 440-02; IWM 466; IWM 485;
    IWM 505; IWM 508-85; IWM 652b; IWM 653b;
    IWM 657b; IWM 659; IWM 663a; IWM 664b;
    IWM 680a; IWM 685a; IWM 1128a; IWM 1188;
          IWM 1189; IWM 1195; NTB 165-01;
       NTB 254-01; NTB 279-02; NTB 312-01;
       NTB 319-02; NTB 343-01; NTB 351-02;
                                          NTB 395-01

1st Division   IWM 255; IWM 332
2nd Division   IWM 466
3rd Division   IWM 150; IWM 322; IWM 339;
             IWM 465; IWM 467; IWM 508-82
4th Division   IWM 332; IWM 1062-19
Training Division   IWM 274; IWM 310;
          IWM 654b; IWM 678b; IWM 1070d
Cavalry Brigade   IWM 181; IWM 310
7th Brigade   IWM 150

15th Bn   IWM 130-05+6
16th Bn   IWM 107; IWM 332
25th Bn   IWM 192
26th Bn   IWM 192
42nd Bn (Royal Highlanders of Canada)
          IWM 150; IWM 465; IWM 467
49th Bn   IWM 150
99th Bn   NTB 260-02
207th Bn   IWM 465
236th Bn   IWM 687

Canadian Light Horse   IWM 316
Irish Canadian Rangers, 55th Bn   IWM 212
Princess Patricia's Canadian Light Infantry
          IWM 150; IWM 255; IWM 322
Royal Canadian Regt   IWM 150
Toronto Regt   NTB 254-02

Army Service Corps   IWM 316
Artillery   IWM 191; NTB 313-01
Medical Corps   IWM 192; IWM 232

Engineers   IWM 176; IWM 219;
          IWM 271; IWM 319; IWM 465
Infantry Works Coy 4   IWM 508-85

CANADIAN ORGANISATIONS
Algonquin Provincial Park Fire Service
                                          IWM 861

CHINA
CHINESE ARMY   IWM 193a

CHINESE ORGANISATIONS
Army of Fengtien   IWM 712
Chinese Labour Corps   IWM 176; IWM 184

CRETE
CRETAN ARMY   NTB 272-02

CUBA
CUBAN ORGANISATIONS
Boy Scouts   IWM 312
Roman Catholic Church   IWM 312

CZECHOSLOVAKIA
CZECHOSLOVAK ARMY   IWM 508-69

DENMARK
DANISH ARMY   NTB 240-02

EGYPT
EGYPTIAN ARMY   IWM 23; IWM 27; IWM 41;
                                          IWM 45

EGYPTIAN MARINES   IWM 23

"ENTENTE POWERS"
International Food Control Commission
                                          IWM 292

FIJI
FIJIAN ARMY   IWM 706

FRANCE
FRENCH ARMY   IWM 97; IWM 99;
       IWM 113; IWM 124; IWM 137; IWM 154;
       IWM 159; IWM 172; IWM 180; IWM 189;
       IWM 198; IWM 249; IWM 251; IWM 271;
       IWM 278; IWM 281; IWM 296; IWM 310;
       IWM 327; IWM 343; IWM 344; IWM 370;
       IWM 435; IWM 439; IWM 469; IWM 473;
        IWM 484; IWM 501-02; IWM 501-07;
        IWM 501-08; IWM 501-09; IWM 501-10;
         IWM 505; IWM 508-10; IWM 508-11;
       IWM 508-13; IWM 508-14; IWM 508-15;
       IWM 508-16; IWM 508-17; IWM 508-19;
       IWM 508-20; IWM 508-23; IWM 508-24;
       IWM 508-25; IWM 508-26; IWM 508-27;
       IWM 508-28; IWM 508-29; IWM 508-31;
       IWM 508-32; IWM 508-33; IWM 508-34;
       IWM 508-37; IWM 508-38; IWM 508-39;
       IWM 508-40; IWM 508-42; IWM 508-43;

FRENCH ARMY *(continued)*
IWM 508-45; IWM 508-47; IWM 508-49;
IWM 508-50; IWM 508-51; IWM 508-52;
IWM 508-53; IWM 508-57; IWM 508-58;
IWM 508-59; IWM 508-61; IWM 508-62;
IWM 508-63; IWM 508-64; IWM 508-65;
IWM 508-67; IWM 508-68; IWM 508-69;
IWM 508-70; IWM 508-71; IWM 508-73;
IWM 508-74; IWM 508-75; IWM 508-76;
IWM 508-77; IWM 508-78; IWM 508-78 bis;
IWM 508-84; IWM 508-85; IWM 508-86;
IWM 508-88; IWM 508-89; IWM 508-90;
IWM 508-91; IWM 508-92; IWM 509; IWM 511;
IWM 652a; IWM 680b; IWM 685a; IWM 693e;
IWM 697a; IWM 714; IWM 880-02d;
IWM 1035a; IWM 1042; IWM 1057-01;
IWM 1057-02; IWM 1061-02a; IWM 1061-02b;
IWM 1061-03f; IWM 1061-05a; IWM 1061-05i;
IWM 1061-06g; IWM 1061-09a; IWM 1061-09i;
IWM 1061-09l; IWM 1062-03; IWM 1062-10;
IWM 1062-16; IWM 1062-20; IWM 1062-22a;
IWM 1079; IWM 1082-04; IWM 1175;
IWM 1180b; IWM 1180c; IWM 1204;
IWM 1207; NTB 219-02; NTB 251-02;
NTB 272-02; NTB 278-02; NTB 317-01;
NTB 324-01; NTB 329-01; NTB 330-02;
NTB 356-02

1st Army   IWM 508-26; IWM 508-38;
IWM 508-40; IWM 508-43; IWM 508-56;
IWM 508-62; IWM 681c; IWM 1061-02a
3rd Army   IWM 508-75; IWM 508-76
4th Army   IWM 508-81
6th Army   IWM 508-35; IWM 508-55;
IWM 508-56; IWM 508-62
10th Army   IWM 508-66; IWM 508-76

I Corps   IWM 508-21; IWM 508-35;
NTB 324-01
II Corps   IWM 508-80
III Corps   IWM 508-72
V Corps   IWM 508-74
IX Corps   IWM 508-76 bis
X Corps   IWM 508-76 bis; IWM 508-77
XI Corps   IWM 508-81; IWM 508-83
XV Corps   IWM 508-76 bis
XVI Corps   IWM 508-24
XVII Corps   IWM 508-83
XVIII Corps   IWM 508-83
XXI Corps   IWM 508-81
XXV Corps   IWM 508-50
XXXI Corps   IWM 508-76 bis
XXXIV Corps   IWM 508-76; IWM 508-77
XXXVI Corps   IWM 508-76 bis
XXXVIII Corps   IWM 508-72
I Cavalry Corps   IWM 508-18
II Cavalry Corps   IWM 183; IWM 186;
IWM 508-56

1st Division   IWM 508-23; IWM 508-24
6th Division   IWM 508-75

15th Division   IWM 508-76
18th Division   IWM 508-83
26th Division   IWM 508-24
29th Division (?)   IWM 181; IWM 183
31st Division   IWM 508-24
41st Division   IWM 508-73
42nd Division   IWM 508-15
51st Division   IWM 508-21; IWM 508-23;
IWM 508-24
55th Division   IWM 508-76
77th Division   IWM 508-56
121st Division   IWM 508-75
126th Division   IWM 508-24
127th Division   IWM 508-56
156th Division   IWM 100
162nd Division   IWM 508-56
163rd Division   IWM 508-56
1st Cavalry Division   IWM 508-18;
IWM 508-55; NTB 310-02
2nd Cavalry Division   IWM 188
3rd Colonial Division   IWM 508-42

5th Artillery Regt   IWM 508-23
61st Artillery Regt   IWM 507
87th Artillery Regt   IWM 508-44
178th Artillery Regt   IWM 508-59
Chasseurs   IWM 508-29; IWM 508-34;
IWM 508-37; IWM 508-43; IWM 508-45;
IWM 508-53; IWM 508-70; IWM 508-91;
NTB 321-02 - 1st Bn IWM 508-27;
IWM 508-75 - 2nd Bn IWM 508-59
- 27th Bn IWM 508-40
19th Chasseurs à Cheval   IWM 508-90
Chasseurs Alpins   IWM 100; IWM 508-13;
IWM 508-26; IWM 508-39; IWM 508-53;
NTB 319-01 - Bn 70 IWM 508-46 - Bn 115
IWM 508-46 - Bn 120 IWM 508-46
Colonial Infantry Regt 33   IWM 508-72
6th Dragoons   IWM 508-70
23rd Dragoons   IWM 508-70
Garde Republicaine NTB 245-02; NTB 267-01
24th Infantry Regt   IWM 508-24
60th Infantry Regt IWM 508-11; IWM 1057-01
102nd Infantry Regt   IWM 508-18
201st Infantry Regt   NTB 316-01
410th Infantry Regt IWM 508-18; NTB 310-02
Moroccan Infantry Regt 1   IWM 508-62
Spahis   IWM 508-10; IWM 508-12;
IWM 508-76 bis
1st Spahi Cavalry Regt   IWM 7; IWM 38
Tirailleurs   IWM 508-39
8th Tirailleur Regt   IWM 508-62
Zouaves (band)   IWM 666b
2nd Zouave Regt   IWM 508-31
4th Zouave Regt   IWM 508-62

Artillery   IWM 508-40; IWM 508-45;
IWM 508-47; IWM 508-51; IWM 508-52;
IWM 508-56; IWM 508-57; IWM 508-60;
IWM 508-66; IWM 508-74; IWM 1070d;
NTB 248-02; NTB 249-02; NTB 313-01;

Artillery *(continued)*
    NTB 325-02; NTB 344-01
Cavalry   IWM 508-48; IWM 508-50;
    IWM 508-65; IWM 508-66; IWM 508-76;
    IWM 508-81; IWM 509; IWM 1061-06f;
    NTB 342-02; NTB 351-02
Colonial Troops   IWM 508-10; IWM 508-27;
    IWM 508-39; IWM 508-45; IWM 508-60;
    IWM 508-68; IWM 508-91; IWM 1061-09i;
    IWM 1062-20; NTB 253-02; NTB 272-02
Cyclists   IWM 508-66; IWM 1049;
    IWM 1061-04b
Dragoons   IWM 508-37; IWM 508-50
Engineers   IWM 508-45; IWM 508-51;
    IWM 508-56; IWM 508-60; NTB 313-01
Infantry   IWM 121; IWM 190
Lancers   IWM 508-66; IWM 1061-09i;
    IWM 1062-10
Military mission   IWM 508-27
Military Police   IWM 508-84
Signal Service   IWM 508-12

Czech Legion   IWM 508-69
Foreign Legion   IWM 1061-06i
    - 2nd Bn IWM 508-44
Polish Legion   IWM 508-32; IWM 508-47;
    IWM 508-68
Sassari Brigade   IWM 508-49
Egyptian Expeditionary Force (French
  Contingent)   IWM 7; IWM 13; IWM 38;
    IWM 44; IWM 58; IWM 193c; IWM 508-36;
    IWM 508-39; NTB 328-01

Ecole Polytechnique   IWM 509
Saint Cyr Cadets   IWM 1082-04
Vincennes Military College   NTB 251-02

FRENCH AIR CORPS   IWM 508-12;
    IWM 508-14; IWM 508-16; IWM 508-23;
    IWM 508-26; IWM 508-28; IWM 508-29;
    IWM 508-38; IWM 508-43; IWM 508-44;
    IWM 508-46; IWM 508-48; IWM 508-49;
    IWM 508-52; IWM 508-57; IWM 508-61;
    IWM 508-64; IWM 1061-03a; IWM 1061-06l;
    IWM 1132; NTB 309-01; NTB 318-02;
    NTB 344-02
Escadrille 3   IWM 508-64; IWM 1061-02b
Escadrille 28   IWM 501-03

FRENCH NAVY   IWM 137; IWM 440-01

Arc   IWM 1062-04
Bombe   IWM 1062-04
Bouvet   IWM 1062-04
Condorcet   IWM 484
Enseigne Henry   IWM 484
Fanfare   IWM 1062-04
Flamberge   IWM 1062-04
Jauréguiberry   IWM 1062-04
Patrie   IWM 1062-04
République   IWM 1062-04

Sabretache   IWM 1062-04
Saint Louis   IWM 1062-04
Sape   IWM 1062-04
Suffren   IWM 1062-04

Marines   IWM 508-21; IWM 508-24;
    IWM 508-91; IWM 1061-06f; NTB 251-02

FRENCH ORGANISATIONS
Asiatic Petroleum Company   IWM 198
Blue Cross   IWM 1070d
Boy Scouts   IWM 1061-09i
Fire service   IWM 227
Ministry of Agriculture   IWM 508-26
Ministry of Health   IWM 508-26; IWM 508-39
Ministry of Public Education and Fine Arts
    IWM 508-52
Paris City Council   IWM 509
Red Cross   IWM 508-12; IWM 508-42;
    NTB 241-02; NTB 255-02
Revolutionary Guard   IWM 508-89
Roman Catholic Church   IWM 667

GERMANY

GERMAN ARMY   IWM 368; IWM 374;
    IWM 481; IWM 483-01; IWM 483-02;
    IWM 483-03; IWM 483-04; IWM 483-05;
    IWM 483-06; IWM 484; IWM 485; IWM 508-88;
    IWM 508-89; IWM 670b; IWM 778;
    IWM 1039-01; IWM 1045a; IWM 1050;
    IWM 1052; IWM 1053; IWM 1054;
    IWM 1061-01; IWM 1061-09h; IWM 1062-07;
    IWM 1062-08; IWM 1062-14; IWM 1072;
    NTB 257-01; NTB 263-01; NTB 263-02;
    NTB 273-02; NTB 292-01
XIX Corps [Saxon]   IWM 138
XXII Reserve Corps   IWM 1124

Alexander Guard   IWM 1045a
Asien Korps   IWM 772
Cuirassiers of the Guard   IWM 484
36th Fusilier Regt   IWM 1175
66th Infantry Regt   IWM 508-56
18th Jaeger Bn   IWM 215
Prussian Guard   IWM 484
109th Wurttemberg Reserve Regt (?)
    IWM 191
Landsturm [cyclists]   IWM 1072

Artillery   IWM 1062-08
Cavalry   IWM 483-06
Engineers   IWM 1091b
Medical Service   IWM 1062-08
Military Police   IWM 483-04

GERMAN AIR SERVICE   IWM 1030;
    IWM 1082-02d; IWM 1124
Jagdgeschwader 1   IWM 1004
Jagdstaffel 2   IWM 1004
Jagdstaffel 11   IWM 1004

GERMAN NAVY   IWM 303; IWM 483-04;
                     IWM 1124

Baden   IWM 646
Bayern   IWM 571; IWM 586; IWM 1124
Blucher   IWM 484
Bremse   IWM 646; IWM 1164
Breslau   IWM 1062-02b
Brummer   IWM 646
Coburg   IWM 1124
Derfflinger   IWM 484; IWM 637; IWM 646;
         IWM 1159; IWM 1164; IWM 1212
Dresden (II)   IWM 646
Emden (II)   IWM 646
Frankfurt   IWM 484; IWM 571; IWM 637;
                                IWM 1164
Friedrich der Grosse   IWM 571; IWM 586;
                     IWM 637; IWM 646
Gneisenau   IWM 484
Goeben   IWM 772
Grosser Kurfurst   IWM 1124
Heligoland   IWM 560
Hindenburg   IWM 571; IWM 646; IWM 1212
Kaiser   IWM 571; IWM 646; IWM 1164;
                                IWM 1212
Kaiserin   IWM 646; IWM 1212
Koeln   IWM 1212
Koeln (II)   IWM 646
Koenig   IWM 484; IWM 1124
Koenig Albert   IWM 1164
Koenigsberg   IWM 1124; IWM 1144;
          IWM 1145; IWM 1146; IWM 1147;
                     IWM 1159; IWM 1164
Kolberg   IWM 1124
Kronprinz Wilhelm   IWM 571; IWM 586
Markgraf   IWM 1124
Moltke   IWM 586; IWM 637; IWM 1212
Prinz Regent Luitpold   IWM 586
Seydlitz   IWM 484; IWM 571; IWM 586;
     IWM 637; IWM 646; IWM 1164; IWM 1212
U.35   IWM 484; IWM 560
U.67   IWM 550-01
U.70   IWM 550-01
U.86   IWM 550-01
U.101   IWM 550-01
U.105   IWM 550-01
U.124   IWM 571
U.139   IWM 484; IWM 560; IWM 571;
                                IWM 1154
U.162   IWM 569; IWM 1155; IWM 1156
U.164   IWM 571
UB.73   IWM 550-01
UB.122   IWM 571
UB.143   IWM 571; IWM 1159
UC.58   IWM 1154; IWM 1159
UC.96   IWM 571
Von der Tann   IWM 637; IWM 646

Marines   IWM 303; IWM 483-04

GERMAN ORGANISATIONS
Hamburg Line   IWM 1205
Imperator   IWM 1205
Occupation police   IWM 376; IWM 380
Red Cross   IWM 1062-08
Revolutionary Guard   IWM 508-08

GREECE
GREEK ARMY   IWM 97; IWM 439;
        IWM 508-14; IWM 508-19; IWM 508-48;
        IWM 1061-05a; IWM 1180b; NTB 272-02

GREEK NAVY   IWM 548

GREEK ORGANISATIONS
Post Office   IWM 1180b

INDIA
INDIAN ARMY   IWM 487; IWM 663a;
        IWM 667; IWM 674c; IWM 1061-03g;
        IWM 1061-04f; NTB 178-01; NTB 272-02;
                              NTB 323-02

Indian Corps   IWM 440-02
7th Division   IWM 25; IWM 30; IWM 33;
        IWM 34; IWM 39; IWM 59; IWM 61;
        IWM 202-01; IWM 202-02; IWM 657b;
                                IWM 1128a
13th Division   IWM 64; IWM 68; IWM 69
14th Division   IWM 68
15th Division   IWM 82
1st Cavalry Division   IWM 25; IWM 121;
        IWM 68; IWM 115; IWM 130-05+6
2nd Cavalry Division   IWM 37; IWM 38;
                           IWM 130-05+6
38th Brigade   IWM 69
7th Cavalry Brigade   IWM 9

Bengal Lancers   IWM 80
93rd Burma Infantry   IWM 202-02
Burma Sappers and Miners   IWM 68; IWM 82
Guides Infantry Regt   IWM 61
Gurkha Rifles   IWM 44; IWM 68; IWM 82;
              IWM 383 - 3/3 Bn IWM 10
Hong Kong-Singapore Mountain Bty   IWM 6;
                     IWM 28; IWM 58
1st Hyderabad Lancers   IWM 12; IWM 32
[Jat infantry]   IWM 68
Patiala Infantry Regt   IWM 37
121st Pioneer Regt   IWM 30
[Punjab infantry]   IWM 68
20th Punjab Infantry   IWM 61
69th Punjab Infantry   IWM 202-02
4th Cavalry Regt   IWM 202-01
57th Rifles   IWM 202-01
58th Rifles   IWM 19; IWM 45; IWM 202-01;
                            IWM 202-02
[Sikh infantry]   IWM 68
47th Sikhs   IWM 202-01
34th Sikh Pioneers   IWM 202-01; IWM 383

Egyptian Expeditionary Force   IWM 6;
IWM 10; IWM 11; IWM 12; IWM 13; IWM 15;
IWM 19; IWM 21; IWM 25; IWM 28; IWM 30;
IWM 32; IWM 33; IWM 34; IWM 37; IWM 38;
IWM 39; IWM 44; IWM 45; IWM 58;
IWM 508-49; IWM 663a; IWM 663c;
IWM 1095; IWM 1131b
Imperial Camel Corps   IWM 28; IWM 58
Kut Relief Force   IWM 83
Mesopotamian Expeditionary Force
IWM 9; IWM 59; IWM 61; IWM 63; IWM 64;
IWM 68; IWM 69; IWM 70; IWM 77; IWM 78;
IWM 80; IWM 81; IWM 82; IWM 83

Artillery   IWM 95
Cavalry   IWM 1080a
Lancers   IWM 15; IWM 130-07+8
Sappers and miners   IWM 70

INDIAN ORGANISATIONS
Lady Hardinge War Hospital   IWM 1061-04d

IRELAND
IRISH ORGANISATIONS
Irish Republican Army   IWM 194;
IWM 485; IWM 666a; IWM 675a
Irish Republican Brotherhood   NTB 245-02;
NTB 247-02
Ulster Defence Force   IWM 485

ITALY
ITALIAN ARMY   IWM 154; IWM 439; IWM 460;
IWM 484; IWM 501-10; IWM 501-13;
IWM 508-23; IWM 508-37; IWM 508-38;
IWM 508-39; IWM 508-40; IWM 508-46;
IWM 508-49; IWM 508-53; IWM 508-59;
IWM 508-61; IWM 508-64; IWM 508-65;
IWM 599; IWM 1035b; IWM 1061-02c;
IWM 1075; IWM 1123; IWM 1175;
NTB 222-02; NTB 272-02; NTB 316-01;
NTB 351-02
8th Division   IWM 278; IWM 680b

Alpini   IWM 459; IWM 509; IWM 1061-02b
Army Training School   IWM 460
Artillery   NTB 324-01
Bersaglieri   IWM 508-38
Carabinieri   IWM 342; IWM 652a;
IWM 652b; NTB 245-02
Engineers   IWM 508-38; IWM 508-45
Italian Contingent, Egyptian Expeditionary
Force   IWM 7; IWM 8; IWM 13

ITALIAN AIR CORPS   IWM 508-65; NTB 318-02

ITALIAN NAVY   IWM 599; IWM 1062-06;
IWM 1175

Alfredo Cappellini   IWM 484
Aquila   IWM 1163
Caio Duilio   IWM 1163

Cane 1   NTB 354-01
Dante Alighieri   IWM 484
Elba   IWM 1062-06
Faa di Bruno   IWM 484
Foca 5   NTB 354-01
Francesco Fernuccio   IWM 1123
Giulio Cesare   IWM 1152; IWM 1163
Monfalcone   IWM 484
Re Umberto   IWM 1123
Sardegna   IWM 1061-01
[Submarines]   IWM 1155

Marines   IWM 1062-06

ITALIAN ORGANISATIONS
Garibaldists   IWM 508-37

JAPAN
JAPANESE ARMY   IWM 30; IWM 439;
IWM 445; IWM 451; IWM 706

JAPANESE NAVY
Hiei   IWM 451
Katsura   IWM 593
Kurama   IWM 440-01

Marines   IWM 508-39

LUXEMBOURG
LUXEMBOURG ARMY   IWM 508-90

MEXICO
MEXICAN ORGANISATIONS
Mexico City Police   NTB 168-01

MOROCCO
MOROCCAN ARMY   IWM 508-45; NTB 313-01
Sultan's Guard   IWM 508-20

THE NETHERLANDS
NETHERLANDS ARMY   IWM 136; IWM 455;
IWM 1061-09k

NEW ZEALAND
NEW ZEALAND ARMY (New Zealand Division)
IWM 130-05+6; IWM 130-09+10; IWM 138;
IWM 157; IWM 160; IWM 166; IWM 172;
IWM 196; IWM 258; IWM 269; IWM 300;
IWM 319; IWM 385; IWM 485;
IWM 508-86; IWM 633; IWM 659;
IWM 1181
ANZAC Mounted Division   IWM 12;
IWM 17; IWM 22; IWM 508-74
New Zealand Mounted Brigade   IWM 13;
IWM 17; IWM 22
Auckland Mounted Rifle Regt   IWM 22
Auckland Regt   IWM 157; IWM 843
New Zealand Mounted Rifles   IWM 663a
New Zealand Rifle Brigade   IWM 140;
IWM 269
Otago Mounted Rifles   IWM 269

Otago Regt   IWM 157
Egyptian Expeditionary Force   IWM 12;
         IWM 13; IWM 17; IWM 22

Artillery   IWM 166; IWM 269
Cadets   IWM 511; IWM 661a
Cyclists   IWM 269
Engineers   IWM 269; IWM 319
Medical Corps   IWM 443
Field Ambulance   IWM 258; IWM 269;
                          IWM 387
Machine Gun Bn   IWM 269
New Zealand Militia   IWM 843
Pioneer Bn   IWM 269

NEW ZEALAND ORGANISATIONS
YMCA   IWM 385

NEWFOUNDLAND
Newfoundland Regt   IWM 147; IWM 222;
  IWM 253; IWM 308c; IWM 663a; NTB 273-01

NORWAY
NORWEGIAN ARMY   IWM 1063

OTTOMAN EMPIRE
TURKISH ARMY   IWM 483-03; IWM 772;
  IWM 1034-03; IWM 1061-06j; IWM 1062-02a

Janissaries   IWM 772
Prisoners   IWM 4

TURKISH NAVY
Black Sea Fleet   IWM 1062-02b
Midilli   IWM 1062-02b
Yavuz Sultan Selim   IWM 772

POLAND
POLISH ARMY   IWM 508-68
Chasseurs, 1st Bn   IWM 508-61; NTB 324-01
Polish Legion   IWM 508-32

POLISH ORGANISATIONS
Polish National Council   IWM 508-68

PORTUGAL
PORTUGUESE ARMY   IWM 129; IWM 291;
  IWM 439; IWM 677a; IWM 677b; IWM 1175

1st Division   IWM 289
2nd Division   IWM 184; IWM 411
Artillery   IWM 323
Cyclists   IWM 187

ROMANIA
ROMANIAN ARMY   IWM 508-17; IWM 508-20;
   IWM 508-27; NTB 262-01; NTB 312-01;
                       NTB 319-02
Military mission   IWM 508-26

RUSSIA
RUSSIAN ARMY   IWM 73; IWM 469;
     IWM 484; IWM 508-16; IWM 656a;
   IWM 1062-01; IWM 1062-18; IWM 1070d;
   NTB 239-02; NTB 251-02; NTB 256-02;
   NTB 271-02; NTB 272-02; NTB 273-01;
                      NTB 277-01

8th Army   NTB 251-02
10th Army   IWM 1072
Artillery   NTB 240-01

RUSSIAN NAVY   IWM 650

RUSSIAN ORGANISATIONS
Baku defence force   IWM 73
Boy Scouts   IWM 808; NTB 240-02
Orthodox Church   IWM 808
Slavo-British Legion   IWM 420-19+20;
                      IWM 422
White Russians   IWM 420-19+20;
   IWM 420-21+22; IWM 422;
          IWM 439; IWM 808

SERBIA
SERBIAN ARMY   IWM 96; IWM 508-17;
  IWM 508-31; IWM 1055b; IWM 1061-06h;
   IWM 1180c; IWM 1207; NTB 258-01;
   NTB 261-01; NTB 265-02; NTB 267-01;
        NTB 272-02; NTB 275-02

1st Army   IWM 508-27; NTB 310-02
Artillery   NTB 270-02
Pay Corps   NTB 280-01

SOUTH AFRICA
SOUTH AFRICAN ARMY (South African Brigade)
  IWM 128; IWM 169; IWM 406; IWM 485;
            IWM 663a; IWM 699b

1st Regt   IWM 113
Artillery   IWM 171
South African Labour Contingent   IWM 128;
         IWM 195; NTB 312-01

SOUTH AFRICAN ORGANISATIONS
Police Force   IWM 1061-07g
Boer Rebels   IWM 1061-07g

SPAIN
SPANISH ARMY   IWM 115

SWITZERLAND
SWISS ARMY   IWM 453; IWM 483-02;
                   IWM 1070a

SWISS ORGANISATIONS
Red Cross   IWM 454

TRINIDAD AND TOBAGO
TRINIDADIAN TROOPS   NTB 219-02

TURKEY *see* OTTOMAN EMPIRE

UNITED KINGDOM
BRITISH ARMY   IWM 97; IWM 99; IWM 105;
IWM 107; IWM 109; IWM 122; IWM 123;
IWM 124; IWM 126; IWM 132; IWM 137;
IWM 142; IWM 153; IWM 155; IWM 164;
IWM 175; IWM 177; IWM 190; IWM 193d;
IWM 220; IWM 224; IWM 233; IWM 271;
IWM 276; IWM 281; IWM 282; IWM 296;
IWM 299; IWM 309; IWM 310; IWM 342;
IWM 344; IWM 346; IWM 347; IWM 361;
IWM 368; IWM 370; IWM 380; IWM 409;
IWM 411; IWM 415; IWM 420-01+2;
IWM 420-03+4; IWM 420-05+6;
IWM 420-07+8; IWM 420-09+10;
IWM 420-11+12; IWM 420-13+14;
IWM 420-15+16; IWM 420-17+18;
IWM 420-23+24; IWM 420-25+26;
IWM 420-27+28; IWM 420-29+30; IWM 424;
IWM 426; IWM 428; IWM 431; IWM 432;
IWM 439; IWM 440-05; IWM 440-06;
IWM 440-07; IWM 444; IWM 453; IWM 455;
IWM 461b; IWM 461d; IWM 475; IWM 476;
IWM 477; IWM 478; IWM 484; IWM 485;
IWM 486; IWM 505; IWM 508-18; IWM 508-21;
IWM 508-24; IWM 508-42; IWM 508-64;
IWM 508-86; IWM 508-88; IWM 508-89;
IWM 509; IWM 527; IWM 604; IWM 616;
IWM 633; IWM 648; IWM 651a; IWM 651b;
IWM 652a; IWM 652b; IWM 653a; IWM 654a;
IWM 654b; IWM 656a; IWM 656b; IWM 657b;
IWM 660b; IWM 661a; IWM 662a; IWM 663a;
IWM 664a; IWM 666b; IWM 667; IWM 668c;
IWM 674c; IWM 676b; IWM 677a; IWM 677b;
IWM 679b; IWM 680a; IWM 685b; IWM 692a;
IWM 693c; IWM 693e; IWM 697a; IWM 713;
IWM 714; IWM 1025b; IWM 1025c;
IWM 1055c; IWM 1055e; IWM 1061-02a;
IWM 1061-02c; IWM 1061-04e;
IWM 1061-04h; IWM 1061-06d;
IWM 1061-07f; IWM 1061-08h; IWM 1061-09h;
IWM 1061-09k; IWM 1062-03; IWM 1062-10;
IWM 1062-18; IWM 1062-22b; IWM 1064-02b;
IWM 1064-03a; IWM 1064-03c;
IWM 1064-03d; IWM 1064-03e; IWM 1064-03f;
IWM 1066; IWM 1070b; IWM 1070c;
IWM 1070d; IWM 1070f; IWM 1072;
IWM 1074; IWM 1081c; IWM 1081e;
IWM 1128a; IWM 1134; IWM 1177a;
IWM 1178; IWM 1179; IWM 1181; IWM 1182;
IWM 1201; IWM 1206; NTB 219-02;
NTB 222-02; NTB 224-01; NTB 235-02;
NTB 245-02; NTB 248-01; NTB 249-01;
NTB 251-01; NTB 252-02; NTB 255-01;
NTB 265-02; NTB 272-02; NTB 279-01;
NTB 283-02; NTB 314-02; NTB 327-01;
NTB 354-01

1st Army   IWM 508-85; IWM 508-86
2nd Army   IWM 289; IWM 503

3rd Army   IWM 677b
4th Army   IWM 115; IWM 121; IWM 354;
                          IWM 508-56; IWM 508-62
5th Army   IWM 381; IWM 508-45; IWM 681c

I Corps   IWM 508-82
II Corps   IWM 508-35; IWM 508-85
III Corps   IWM 508-55
V Corps   IWM 675a; IWM 1058
VIII Corps   IWM 508-85
XI Corps   IWM 257; IWM 508-80
XXII Corps   IWM 235; IWM 508-74
Cavalry Corps   IWM 461d

Dunsterforce   IWM 73
Egyptian Expeditionary Force   IWM 1;
IWM 2; IWM 5; IWM 6; IWM 10; IWM 11;
IWM 12; IWM 13; IWM 14; IWM 15; IWM 16;
IWM 17; IWM 21; IWM 22; IWM 24; IWM 25;
IWM 26; IWM 27; IWM 28; IWM 30; IWM 32;
IWM 33; IWM 34; IWM 37; IWM 38; IWM 39;
IWM 40; IWM 41; IWM 43; IWM 44; IWM 58;
IWM 60; IWM 78; IWM 508-49; IWM 651b;
                IWM 652a; IWM 662a; IWM 662b;
                IWM 663c; IWM 681b; IWM 697b;
                          IWM 1095; IWM 1131b
 - 44th Remount Squadron IWM 634;
NTB 327-02; NTB 343-01 - Desert Mounted
Corps IWM 1; IWM 17; IWM 33 NTB 329-01
 - French Contingent IWM 7; IWM 13;
IWM 38; IWM 44; IWM 58; IWM 193c;
                          IWM 508-36; IWM 508-39
 - Italian Contingent IWM 7; IWM 8;
                IWM 13; IWM 266; IWM 283
Hodgson's Force   IWM 5; IWM 17
Kut Relief Force   IWM 83
Mesopotamian Expeditionary Force
IWM 9; IWM 43; IWM 59; IWM 60; IWM 61;
IWM 63; IWM 64; IWM 65; IWM 66; IWM 68;
IWM 69; IWM 70; IWM 73; IWM 77; IWM 78;
IWM 79; IWM 80; IWM 82; IWM 83;
                IWM 651a; IWM 652b; IWM 657a
North Russian Intervention Force
                IWM 420-19+20; IWM 420-21+22;
                          IWM 422; IWM 808
Norton's Column   IWM 9

1st Division   IWM 335; IWM 1005
2nd Division   IWM 382
4th Division   IWM 191
5th Division   IWM 154; IWM 332
6th Division   IWM 144; IWM 697d
7th Division   IWM 191
8th Division   IWM 375
9th Division   IWM 113; IWM 128; IWM 169;
          IWM 171; IWM 353; IWM 406; IWM 699b
10th Division   IWM 100
12th Division   IWM 353
15th Division   IWM 144; IWM 197; IWM 375
16th Division   IWM 111; IWM 116; IWM 120;
                          IWM 197; IWM 212

18th Division   IWM 181; IWM 191
21st Division   IWM 375
22nd Division   IWM 98
23rd Division   IWM 154
25th Division   IWM 197
29th Division   IWM 113; IWM 116; IWM 191;
                       IWM 376; IWM 1058
31st Division   IWM 191
32nd Division   IWM 403
33rd Division   IWM 187; IWM 188;
                     IWM 256; IWM 1061-06e
34th Division   IWM 508-73
35th Division   IWM 130-05+6;
                            IWM 130-09+10
36th Division   IWM 102; IWM 120;
           IWM 197; IWM 212; IWM 580
37th Division   IWM 191; IWM 294
38th Division   IWM 208; IWM 300;
           IWM 440-02; IWM 440-04
39th Division   IWM 103
40th Division   IWM 324; IWM 508-85
41st Division   IWM 154; IWM 193c;
                                  IWM 193d
42nd Division   IWM 261
47th Division   IWM 144; IWM 146; IWM 205;
                  IWM 363; NTB 260-02
49th Division   IWM 256; IWM 1137
51st Division   IWM 133; IWM 144;
   IWM 146; IWM 163; IWM 184; IWM 186;
   IWM 187; IWM 278; IWM 327; IWM 663c;
                                  IWM 680b
52nd Division   IWM 12; IWM 16; IWM 17;
                       IWM 25; IWM 322
53rd Division   IWM 16
54th Division   IWM 17
55th Division   IWM 184; IWM 185;
                     IWM 186; IWM 332
56th Division   IWM 130-07+8; IWM 182;
                     IWM 191; IWM 322
57th Division   IWM 345; IWM 352;
                                IWM 508-84
58th Division   IWM 183; IWM 185; IWM 375
59th Division   IWM 131
60th Division   IWM 10; IWM 12; IWM 22;
                     IWM 26; IWM 28
62nd Division   IWM 278; IWM 680b
63rd Division   IWM 116; IWM 332;
                                  IWM 1058
73rd Division   NTB 251-02
75th Division   IWM 10; IWM 11; IWM 12
1st Cavalry Division   IWM 180; IWM 186;
   IWM 374; IWM 376; IWM 467; IWM 508-55;
                               IWM 1061-02a
2nd Cavalry Division   IWM 246; IWM 374;
                                  IWM 678b
3rd Cavalry Division   IWM 181
4th Cavalry Division   IWM 25; IWM 115;
             IWM 121; IWM 130-05+6
5th Cavalry Division   IWM 37; IWM 38;
             IWM 115; IWM 130-05+6

Guards Division   IWM 117; IWM 121;
                IWM 130-05+6; IWM 130-07+8;
         IWM 130-09+10; IWM 207; IWM 208;
         IWM 295; IWM 440-02; IWM 440-03;
                     IWM 440-04; IWM 626
Royal Naval Division   IWM 116

48th Brigade   IWM 111
157th Brigade   IWM 25
179th Brigade   IWM 26
181st Brigade   IWM 26
1st Guards Brigade   IWM 1005
2nd Guards Brigade   IWM 121
7th Mounted Brigade   IWM 1

1st King Edward's Horse   IWM 1055d
2nd Dragoons (Royal Scots Greys) IWM 230;
                                  IWM 341
5th (Princess Charlotte of Wales's) Dragoon
   Guards   IWM 192
7th (Queen's Own) Hussars IWM 60; IWM 80
8th (King's Royal Irish) Hussars   IWM 144
9th (Queen's Royal) Lancers   IWM 376
17th (Duke of Cambridge's Own) Lancers
                       IWM 192; IWM 381
18th Hussars   IWM 295; IWM 376; IWM 380
19th Hussars   IWM 113
Argyll and Sutherland Highlanders
   IWM 179; IWM 213; IWM 440-1 - 2nd Bn (?)
      IWM 187; IWM 188 - 11th Bn IWM 116
Bedfordshire Regt   IWM 130-05+6;
   IWM 174; IWM 388 - 1st Bn (?) IWM 154
   - 1/1st Bn IWM 1099 - 5th Bn IWM 706
                       - 7th Bn IWM 191
Berkshire Regt (Princess Charlotte of Wales's
   Royal), 2nd Bn   IWM 397
Black Watch   IWM 98; IWM 130-05+6
   - 2nd Bn IWM 25; IWM 30; IWM 39; IWM 59;
      IWM 61; IWM 1131b - 6th Bn IWM 278;
         IWM 680b - 7th Bn IWM 110
British West Indies Regt, 1st Bn   IWM 10
Buffs (East Kent Regt)   IWM 400;
         NTB 178-01 - 7th Bn IWM 191
Cameron Highlanders (Queen's Own)
   IWM 116; IWM 335 - 4th Bn IWM 1185
Cameronians (Scottish Rifles)   IWM 1214
                     - 9th Bn (?) IWM 113
Cheshire Regt   NTB 314-02
                     - 1st Bn IWM 389
City Imperial Volunteers   IWM 1025e
Coldstream Guards   IWM 207; IWM 509;
      IWM 693b; IWM 1186; IWM 1187;
                                NTB 245-02
Connaught Rangers   IWM 212
                     - 1st Bn IWM 64
Devonshire Regt   IWM 130-05+6; IWM 191
   - 1/5th Bn IWM 10; IWM 278; IWM 680b
Dorsetshire Regt, 1st Bn   IWM 403
   - 2/4th Bn IWM 15; NTB 341-02

Duke of Cambridge's Own (Middlesex Regt),
1st Bn   IWM 188 - 2nd Bn IWM 390
          - 8th Bn IWM 322; IWM 390
          - 16th Bn IWM 191
Duke of Cornwall's Light Infantry, 1st Bn
          IWM 332
Duke of Wellington's (West Riding Regt)
          IWM 404
Durham Light Infantry   IWM 116; IWM 127;
          IWM 130-05+6; IWM 399
          - 15th Bn IWM 1179
East Lancashire Regt, 6th Bn   IWM 68
East Surrey Regt   NTB 258-02
East Yorkshire Regt, 10th Bn   IWM 191
          - 12th Bn IWM 427
Essex Regt   IWM 116; IWM 394; IWM 1081b
          - 1st Bn IWM 191
Gloucestershire Regt   IWM 1215
Gordon Highlanders   IWM 113; IWM 140;
          IWM 146; IWM 349; IWM 545;
          IWM 1082-02d; NTB 344-02
- 2nd Bn IWM 191 - 8/10th Bn IWM 406
Grenadier Guards   IWM 102; IWM 208;
          IWM 809; IWM 1082-01; NTB 168-01
          - 1st Bn IWM 119; IWM 207
          - 3rd Bn IWM 295 - 4th Bn IWM 207
Guernsey Light Infantry   IWM 289
Gurkha Rifles   IWM 383 - 3/3rd Bn IWM 10
Hampshire Regt   IWM 277
          - 2nd Bn IWM 191 - 1/8th Bn IWM 17
Herefordshire Regt   IWM 174
Highland Light Infantry   IWM 121;
          IWM 130-01+2; IWM 140
Honourable Artillery Company   IWM 1061-06f
Honourable Artillery Company, Bty A
          IWM 38
Irish Guards   IWM 102; IWM 207; IWM 485;
          IWM 809; IWM 1061-04f; IWM 1071;
          NTB 235-02 - 2nd Bn IWM 208; IWM 212
          - 3rd Bn IWM 1062-17
King's African Rifles   IWM 84
King's (Liverpool Regt), 1st Bn   IWM 113;
          IWM 398 - 8th Bn IWM 352
King's Own (Royal Lancaster Regt)
          IWM 185; NTB 317-02 - 6th Bn IWM 68
King's Own Scottish Borderers   IWM 116;
          NTB 322-01 - 1st Bn IWM 376
          - 2nd Bn IWM 154
King's Own Yorkshire Light Infantry
          IWM 391 - 2/5th Bn IWM 278
King's Royal Rifle Corps   IWM 127
          - 4th Bn IWM 417 - 16th Bn IWM 188
King's (Shropshire Light Infantry)   IWM 113
Lancashire Fusiliers   IWM 140
          - 1st Bn IWM 415 - 2nd Bn IWM 191
Lancashire Regt (Prince of Wales's
Volunteers)   NTB 266-02
Leicestershire Regt   IWM 121; IWM 130-07+8
          - 2nd Bn IWM 25; IWM 30
Life Guards   IWM 425; IWM 1080a;
          IWM 1082-02b; IWM 1085; NTB 261-02

Lincolnshire Regt   IWM 131; IWM 1100
          - 8th Bn IWM 677b
London Regt   IWM 680b; IWM 1062-03;
          IWM 1175; NTB 249-01; NTB 267-01
- 1st Bn NTB 262-01 - 1/4th Bn IWM 322
          - 7th Bn IWM 407 - 8th Bn IWM 205
          - 10th Bn IWM 1071 - 2/10th Bn IWM 183
          - 14th Bn (London Scottish) IWM 461c;
          IWM 661a - 1/14th Bn IWM 130-07+8;
          IWM 182; IWM 191; IWM 290
- 2/14th Bn IWM 26; IWM 289; IWM 652a
          - 15th Bn IWM 130-09+10; IWM 205
          - 18th Bn NTB 343-01 - 1/18th Bn
          IWM 130-09+10 - 19th Bn IWM 440-1
- 2/20th Bn IWM 278 - 25th Bn NTB 246-01
          - 28th Bn (Artists Rifles) IWM 383;
          IWM 414; IWM 1181; NTB 235-02;
          - 1/28th Bn IWM 203; IWM 216
Loyal North Lancashire Regt   IWM 130-05+6;
          IWM 131
Manchester Regt, 22nd Bn   IWM 191
          - 24th Bn IWM 191
Monmouthshire Regt   IWM 170
Norfolk Regt   IWM 408 - 2nd Bn IWM 68
          IWM 82 - 1/4th Bn IWM 17
Northamptonshire Regt   IWM 130-05+6;
          IWM 174; IWM 192; IWM 392
          - 2nd Bn IWM 116 - 4th Bn IWM 706
Northumberland Fusiliers   IWM 130-07+8
          - 1st Bn IWM 215
Prince of Wales's (North Staffordshire Regt)
          IWM 192 - 3rd Bn IWM 488 - 7th Bn IWM 73
Prince of Wales's Own (West Yorkshire Regt)
          IWM 402 - 2nd Bn IWM 116
          - 8th Bn IWM 278 - 11th Bn IWM 154
Queen's Own (Royal West Kent Regt)
          IWM 113; IWM 127; IWM 300; IWM 401
          - 1/5th Bn IWM 59
Queen's (Royal West Surrey Regt)
          IWM 129; IWM 440-01
Rifle Brigade, 2nd Bn   IWM 416
          - 13th Bn IWM 677b
Royal Dublin Fusiliers   IWM 197
Royal Fusiliers   IWM 420-21+22;
          IWM 1064-03e - 2nd Bn IWM 191
          - 10th Bn IWM 113 - 13th Bn IWM 191;
          IWM 294 - 25th Bn IWM 84
          - 38th Bn IWM 662a - 40th Bn IWM 30
Royal Horse Guards   IWM 134; IWM 809;
          IWM 1061-07g; IWM 1080a; IWM 1082-02b
Royal Inniskilling Fusiliers   IWM 197;
          IWM 212
Royal Irish Regt   IWM 1061-05c; NTB 324-02
Royal Irish Rifles   IWM 188; NTB 343-01
          - 6th Bn (?) IWM 197 - 7th Bn IWM 212
Royal Munster Fusiliers   IWM 131; IWM 212
Royal Scots   IWM 1214 - 8th Bn IWM 144
Royal Scots Fusiliers   IWM 302; IWM 808
          - 4th Bn IWM 322 - 5th Bn IWM 322
          - 13th Bn IWM 116 - 17th Bn (?)
          IWM 130-05+6

Royal Sussex Regt   IWM 130-05+6;
     IWM 420-19+20 - 5th Bn IWM 1127
Royal Warwickshire Regt   IWM 121
                          - 2nd Bn IWM 191
Royal Welch Fusiliers   IWM 116; IWM 208;
          IWM 1066 - 1st Bn IWM 191
- 3rd Bn IWM 450 - 4th Bn (?) IWM 205
                     - 18th Bn IWM 1061-06b
Scots Guards   IWM 207; IWM 265; IWM 485;
          IWM 666a; IWM 668b; NTB 256-01;
               NTB 256-02; NTB 259-02
Seaforth Highlanders   NTB 318-02
     - 1st Bn IWM 34; IWM 39; IWM 202-02;
          IWM 383 - 2nd Bn IWM 191
Sherwood Foresters (Nottinghamshire and
  Derbyshire Regt)   IWM 131
South Irish Horse   IWM 1056
South Wales Borderers   NTB 324-02
Suffolk Regt   IWM 189; IWM 226
     - 2nd Bn IWM 393 - 8th Bn IWM 191
Welsh Guards   IWM 681b; IWM 1064-03d;
     NTB 257-01 - 1st Bn IWM 207; IWM 1215
West India Regt   IWM 663a; IWM 842;
                              IWM 843
Worcestershire Regt, 2nd Bn   IWM 289
          - 4th Bn IWM 116; IWM 191
York and Lancaster Regt, 2nd Bn   IWM 396
     - 4th Bn IWM 1136 - 5th Bn IWM 1137

Machine Gun Corps   IWM 154; IWM 180;
     IWM 243; IWM 321; IWM 438; IWM 471;
     IWM 666b - Machine Gun School IWM 204
- Motor Machine Gun Corps IWM 130-07+8;
               IWM 131; NTB 284-02
Tank Corps (Machine Gun Corps, Heavy
  Branch)   IWM 116; IWM 130-05+6;
IWM 130-07+8; IWM 130-09+10; IWM 144;
     IWM 158; IWM 178; IWM 179; IWM 182;
     IWM 184; IWM 198; IWM 286; IWM 289;
     IWM 290; IWM 294; IWM 314; IWM 316;
     IWM 317; IWM 326; IWM 356; IWM 357;
     IWM 378; IWM 452; IWM 502; IWM 503;
          IWM 508-47 IWM 508-80; IWM 626;
     IWM 665b; IWM 697d; IWM 706; IWM 809;
               IWM 1064-01b; IWM 1064-02c;
IWM 1064-02d; IWM 1064-03b; IWM 1174;
IWM 1188; IWM 1190; IWM 1191; IWM 1192;
IWM 1193; IWM 1194; IWM 1195; IWM 1196;
IWM 1197; IWM 1198; IWM 1200; IWM 1201;
               IWM 1210; NTB 319-01
     - Tank Corps, Training School IWM 337

Royal Artillery   IWM 508-80; IWM 662a;
     IWM 1178; NTB 238-01; NTB 248-01;
                         NTB 354-01
Royal Field Artillery   IWM 210; IWM 225;
     IWM 298; IWM 302; IWM 430; IWM 470;
     IWM 488; IWM 508-38; IWM 580; IWM 626;
     IWM 657a; IWM 1061-06c; NTB 178-01;
     NTB 222-02; NTB 341-02; NTB 345-02
                       - XII Bde IWM 1005

Royal Field Artillery *(continued)*
          - CLVI Bde IWM 1061-06e
     - CCXXXV Bde IWM 144; IWM 146
          - CCLXVII 267 IWM 16
Royal Garrison Artillery   IWM 95; IWM 113;
IWM 130-05+6; IWM 138; IWM 178; IWM 217;
     IWM 226; IWM 259; IWM 302; IWM 323;
     IWM 430; IWM 439; IWM 508-44; IWM 626;
          IWM 653a; IWM 666a; NTB 354-01
     - Chapperton Down Artillery School
               IWM 108; IWM 1102
          - Essex Heavy Bty 1 IWM 503
     - Siege Bty 15 IWM 191 - Siege Bty 89
          IWM 218 - Siege Bty 115 IWM 192
- Siege Bty 471 IWM 218; IWM 258; IWM 503
Royal Horse Artillery   IWM 106; IWM 146;
          IWM 230; IWM 626; NTB 252-02
     - Bty J IWM 246 - Bty S IWM 9; IWM 678b
                    - Essex Bty IWM 37
     - Light Armoured Motor Bty 14 IWM 9
          - Nottinghamshire Bty IWM 38

Royal Engineers   IWM 16; IWM 17; IWM 34;
     IWM 98; IWM 102; IWM 125; IWM 127;
     IWM 154; IWM 178; IWM 180; IWM 226;
     IWM 267; IWM 287; IWM 322; IWM 327;
          IWM 332; IWM 406; IWM 508-72;
     IWM 508-82; IWM 990; IWM 1064-03b;
     IWM 1064-03e; IWM 1197; NTB 251-02;
     NTB 269-01; NTB 324-01; NTB 330-02
               - Field Coy 150 IWM 289
          - Forestry Coy IWM 319; IWM 289
               - Kent Field Coy NTB 251-02
          - Meteorological Section IWM 355
               - Special Bde IWM 1102
               - Tunnelling Coy IWM 219

Royal Army Medical Corps IWM 17;
          IWM 24; IWM 25; IWM 32; IWM 102;
     IWM 133; IWM 134; IWM 162; IWM 191;
     IWM 192; IWM 198; IWM 318; IWM 322;
     IWM 324; IWM 325; IWM 329; IWM 332;
     IWM 335; IWM 349; IWM 360; IWM 699c;
          IWM 1097; IWM 1098; NTB 318-02
     - First Aid Nursing Yeomanry IWM 162;
     IWM 260; IWM 439; IWM 674c;   IWM 1074
Motor Ambulance 1   IWM 205
     - Queen Mary's Auxiliary Ambulance Corps
                              IWM 267

Army Bombing School 2   IWM 199
Army Central Registry   IWM 329
Army Pay Corps   NTB 320-02
Army Physical Training Corps   NTB 313-01
Army Postal Service   IWM 214; NTB 330-02
Army Remount Service   NTB 273-02
Army Salvage Depot 2   IWM 261
Army Service Corps   IWM 96; IWM 159;
     IWM 329; IWM 463; IWM 626; NTB 260-02;
               NTB 273-01; NTB 292-01
     - Motor Transport Driving School IWM 242

Army Signal Office 3   IWM 433
Army Training School 3   IWM 104
Army Veterinary Corps   IWM 114; IWM 115;
                                   IWM 1070d
BEF Locomotive Shop   IWM 176
Cadet Corps   IWM 170; IWM 348; IWM 1179
Cavalry Equitation School   IWM 280
Dover Garrison   IWM 505
Eastern Command   IWM 174
GHQ Press Section, Censorship and Press
   Branch   IWM 381
Imperial Camel Corps   IWM 6; IWM 17
Imperial School of Instruction, Zeitoun
          IWM 21; IWM 38; IWM 634
Inland Water Transport   IWM 101
Messenger Dog Service   IWM 314
Military Police   IWM 65; IWM 508-84
National Army Canteen Board   IWM 33;
                                   IWM 462
National Reserve   IWM 1061-06a; IWM 1071
Officers' Training Corps   IWM 1061-07g;
                       IWM 1070b; NTB 235-02
Remount Sqdn 44   IWM 2
Royal Hospital, Chelsea   IWM 675b;
                                  NTB 354-01
Royal Military Academy, Sandhurst   IWM 809
Trench School of Instruction, Helfaut
                                   IWM 119
Women's Army Auxiliary Corps   IWM 228;
   IWM 272; IWM 315; IWM 328; IWM 329;
   IWM 405; IWM 412; IWM 439; IWM 474;
   IWM 479; IWM 485; IWM 521; IWM 626;
 IWM 653a; IWM 678a; IWM 679a; IWM 680b;
 IWM 685a; IWM 685b; IWM 693b; IWM 706;
        IWM 1074; IWM 1187; NTB 324-02

Chinese Labour Corps   IWM 168; IWM 226;
   IWM 230; IWM 231; IWM 410; NTB 342-02
Egyptian Labour Corps   IWM 3; IWM 17;
   IWM 20; IWM 30; IWM 77; IWM 440-02;
        IWM 440-04; IWM 1058; NTB 319-02
South African Labour Contingent   IWM 413
West African Labour Contingent
                               IWM 130-05+6

Territorial Army - East Midland Brigade 162
                                   IWM 706
Territorial Army - Essex Field Artillery
                                  NTB 89-02

Volunteer Training Corps   IWM 174
Volunteers, 1st London Engineer NTB 277-01
Volunteers, Lancashire   NTB 272-02
Volunteers, South London   NTB 267-02
Volunteers, St Pancras   NTB 269-02

Yeomanry   IWM 96; IWM 127; IWM 131;
      IWM 580; IWM 1081d; IWM 1178
Yeomanry, Glamorgan   NTB 292-01
Yeomanry, Imperial Cadet   NTB 242-01
Yeomanry, Norfolk   NTB 259-01

Yeomanry, London County   IWM 1061-07g;
                                  NTB 248-01
Yeomanry, Sherwood Rangers, 1/1st Bn
                                    IWM 1
Yeomanry, Surrey (?)   IWM 121
Yeomen of the Guard   IWM 1080a;
                                 IWM 1082-02b

Cadets   IWM 668b; IWM 674c; IWM 693a;
                                  NTB 249-01
Cavalry   IWM 130-07+8; IWM 136; IWM 172;
      IWM 226; IWM 395; IWM 432; IWM 580;
      IWM 648; IWM 680b; IWM 1061-08b;
      IWM 1064-02b; IWM 1080b; IWM 1081d;
               NTB 238-01; NTB 256-02
[Household Cavalry]   NTB 318-01
Colonial troops   NTB 168-01
             [Trinidadian] NTB 219-02
Cyclists   IWM 113; IWM 121; IWM 131;
                       IWM 181; IWM 189
Escort   IWM 136
Fire services   IWM 674b
Highlanders   IWM 219; IWM 342; IWM 657b;
                       IWM 713; IWM 1128a
Infantry   IWM 96; IWM 130-01+2; IWM 213
Lancers   IWM 1064-03e
Reserve   IWM 457

ROYAL FLYING CORPS/ROYAL AIR FORCE
      IWM 84; IWM 118; IWM 186; IWM 187;
      IWM 217; IWM 218; IWM 258; IWM 289;
   IWM 304; IWM 329; IWM 379; IWM 444;
   IWM 466; IWM 508-62; IWM 612; IWM 614;
      IWM 624; IWM 626; IWM 627; IWM 629;
      IWM 631; IWM 633; IWM 638; IWM 639;
   IWM 640-03; IWM 642; IWM 643; IWM 644;
      IWM 645; IWM 647; IWM 649; IWM 660a;
         IWM 661b; IWM 668d; IWM 674c;
      IWM 693d; IWM 809; IWM 863; IWM 865;
      IWM 867; IWM 868; IWM 870; IWM 872;
         IWM 874; IWM 875; IWM 880-01e;
      IWM 880-01h; IWM 1030; IWM 1063;
      IWM 1069; IWM 1101; IWM 1107-01;
   IWM 1150; IWM 1167; IWM 1168; IWM 1169;
      IWM 1170 NTB 317-02; NTB 318-02

Aeroplane Supply Depot 2   IWM 327
Air College, Cranwell   IWM 570
Balloon Section 49   IWM 28
Cadet Bde   IWM 615; IWM 620; IWM 625;
         IWM 632; IWM 635; IWM 640-01;
                                  IWM 640-02
High Speed Flight   IWM 880-01a;
                                  IWM 880-01f
Kite Balloon Section   IWM 68; IWM 79;
                                   IWM 164
Long Range Flight   IWM 880-02b
North Eastern Area Flying Instructors School
                                   IWM 871
Oxford University Air Squadron IWM 880-01d
Photographic Section   IWM 873

RAF Technical Training Centre, Halton
 IWM 809
School of Military Aeronautics IWM 869;
 IWM 870
Senior Officers' School IWM 634
Senior Officers' School, Heliopolis IWM 38
Torpedo Dropping School IWM 636
Women's Army Auxiliary Corps, RFC
 IWM 692b
Women's Royal Air Force IWM 38;
 IWM 521; IWM 610; IWM 612; IWM 625;
 IWM 626; IWM 633; IWM 634; IWM 635;
 IWM 642; IWM 668d; IWM 1106;
 IWM 1107-01; IWM 1107-02

41 Wing IWM 234
4 Squadron IWM 1005
14 Squadron IWM 880-02c
18 Squadron IWM 877
20 Squadron IWM 130-05+6; IWM 141;
 IWM 632
23 Squadron IWM 648; IWM 989
25 Squadron IWM 878
27 Squadron IWM 175; IWM 674b; IWM 876
39 Squadron IWM 1206; IWM 1218
45 Squadron IWM 141; IWM 154; IWM 632
48 Squadron IWM 648
52 Squadron IWM 198
60 Squadron IWM 141; IWM 632
70 Squadron IWM 715
72 Squadron IWM 63
84 Squadron IWM 648; IWM 1170
99 Squadron IWM 876
201 Squadron IWM 880-01b; IWM 880-01c
203 Squadron IWM 289; IWM 880-02a
209 Squadron IWM 648

Royal Navy IWM 65; IWM 77; IWM 109;
 IWM 126; IWM 130-03+4; IWM 140;
 IWM 220; IWM 224; IWM 289;
IWM 420-01+2; IWM 420-17+18; IWM 439;
 IWM 446; IWM 485; IWM 505; IWM 556;
 IWM 558; IWM 563; IWM 588; IWM 592;
 IWM 604; IWM 614; IWM 617; IWM 618;
 IWM 626; IWM 629; IWM 631; IWM 636;
 IWM 639; IWM 642; IWM 643; IWM 644;
 IWM 647; IWM 652a; IWM 653a; IWM 656b;
 IWM 657a; IWM 657b; IWM 661b; IWM 667;
 IWM 685b; IWM 699b; IWM 865; IWM 867;
 IWM 1061-05e; IWM 1061-07b;
 IWM 1061-09o; IWM 1069; IWM 1070a;
 IWM 1070f; IWM 1082-01; IWM 1082-03;
 IWM 1141; IWM 1142; IWM 1145; IWM 1146;
 IWM 1147; IWM 1148; IWM 1152; IWM 1163;
 IWM 1206; IWM 1207; NTB 237-02;
 NTB 277-02; NTB 320-02; NTB 354-01

Admiralty IWM 681c
Admiralty Compass Observatory IWM 313
Cadets NTB 89-02
Cardiff Naval Docks IWM 170; NTB 340-01

CMB Depot, Osea IWM 566; IWM 567
Dover Patrol IWM 201; IWM 681c;
 NTB 343-01
Women's Royal Naval Service IWM 439;
 IWM 521; IWM 567; IWM 626; IWM 641;
 IWM 642; IWM 647

Accrington IWM 585
Achilles IWM 563
Agamemnon IWM 440-01
Agincourt IWM 552; IWM 575;
 IWM 578-02; IWM 580; IWM 866;
 IWM 1144; IWM 1153; IWM 1157
Ajax IWM 556; IWM 1061-01
Albyn IWM 551; IWM 553; IWM 581
Anzac IWM 586; IWM 1164
Arethusa IWM 551; IWM 552; NTB 283-02
Argus IWM 550-01; IWM 627; IWM 1144
Atalanta II IWM 551; IWM 582
Australia IWM 377; IWM 843; IWM 1170
B.5 IWM 577; IWM 580
Barham IWM 555-01; IWM 556
Bellerophon IWM 1145; IWM 1147;
 IWM 1164
Benbow IWM 551; IWM 554
Birmingham IWM 577
Blonde IWM 555-02; IWM 1144
Brilliant IWM 550-01
Brisk IWM 577; IWM 580
Broke IWM 551; IWM 553; IWM 1152
C.12 IWM 577
C.17 IWM 577
C.18 IWM 577
C.23 IWM 569; IWM 574; IWM 1143
C.32 IWM 577
C.34 IWM 512
C.35 IWM 1061-01
Caddis Fly IWM 71; IWM 82
Caledon IWM 1148
Cameleon IWM 577; IWM 580
Campania IWM 1168; IWM 1170
Canada IWM 484; IWM 550-01; IWM 551;
 IWM 552; IWM 554; IWM 555-01;
 IWM 555-02; IWM 559; IWM 563; IWM 580;
 IWM 586; IWM 591; IWM 1144; IWM 1145;
 IWM 1146; IWM 1147; IWM 1153; IWM 1157;
 IWM 1160; IWM 1161; IWM 1164; IWM 1165
Cardiff IWM 586; IWM 637
Castor IWM 551; IWM 554; IWM 571
Centurion IWM 575; IWM 1144
Charing (decoy name) IWM 559; IWM 1153;
 IWM 1155; IWM 1160
Collingwood IWM 866; IWM 1061-01;
 IWM 1151; NTB 321-01
Colossus IWM 1144
Commonwealth IWM 577; IWM 580
Courageous IWM 570
Crescent IWM 1061-01
Curacao IWM 571
Cyclamen IWM 551
D.2 IWM 512; IWM 577; IWM 1061-01

D.4	IWM 577
Daffodil	IWM 668d
Danae	IWM 842
Daniel Fearall	IWM 574
Dauntless	IWM 842
Delhi	IWM 842
Dominion	IWM 580
Donegal	NTB 168-01
Dragon	IWM 842
Dreadnought	IWM 440-01; IWM 580
Drummer Boy	IWM 551; IWM 582
Drusilla	IWM 581
E.23	IWM 440-01; IWM 577; IWM 581; IWM 1156
Eagle III	IWM 551; IWM 582
Emperor of India	IWM 551; IWM 554; IWM 555-01; IWM 555-02; IWM 580
Enchantress	IWM 1149
Engadine	IWM 512; IWM 577; IWM 580
Erebus	IWM 551; IWM 553; IWM 657b; IWM 693c
Erin	IWM 575; IWM 1144
Firedrake	IWM 440-01; IWM 581; IWM 595
Furious	IWM 551; IWM 555-03; IWM 570; IWM 578-03; IWM 809; IWM 865; IWM 866; IWM 875; IWM 1144; IWM 1160; IWM 1170
Gibraltar	IWM 569; IWM 1157
Glenbervie	IWM 582
Glorious	IWM 570
Good Hope	NTB 168-01
H.21	IWM 550-01
H.29	IWM 1155
H.33	IWM 569; IWM 1155
H.34	IWM 1155
H.43	IWM 550-01
H.47	IWM 561
Hercules	IWM 551; IWM 556; IWM 1061-01; IWM 1144; IWM 1151; NTB 321-01
Hibernia	IWM 1061-01
Hogue	NTB 168-01
Hood	IWM 842
Illustrious	IWM 440-01
Implacable	IWM 440-01
Indefatigable	IWM 1061-01
Indomitable	IWM 440-01; IWM 714
Intrepid	IWM 358; IWM 656b
Iphigenia	IWM 358; IWM 656b
Iris	IWM 668d
Iron Duke	IWM 554; IWM 580; IWM 1164
K.2	IWM 569; IWM 1147; IWM 1151
K.5	IWM 578-01
K.16	IWM 550-01; IWM 550-02
Kent	NTB 254-01
King Alfred	NTB 168-01
King Edward VII	IWM 440-03; IWM 595
King George V	IWM 556; IWM 575; IWM 1144
Kylemore	IWM 551; IWM 582
L.22	IWM 809
Lance	IWM 551
Legion	IWM 551
Linnet	IWM 551
Lion	IWM 440-01; IWM 440-05; IWM 551; IWM 577; IWM 1144; IWM 1162; IWM 1163; NTB 278-02; NTB 320-02
Llewellyn	IWM 555-03
Lochinvar	IWM 551
M.3	IWM 1148
Magnificent	IWM 440-01
Malaya	IWM 555-01; IWM 555-02
Marlborough	IWM 1144; IWM 1151
Mars	IWM 440-01
Marshal Soult	IWM 551
Martin	IWM 577; IWM 580
Mary Rose	IWM 562
Medea	IWM 880-01f
Medway	IWM 551; IWM 552
Melampus	IWM 646; IWM 1212
Melton	IWM 551; IWM 553; IWM 581
Midge	IWM 580
ML.15	IWM 695
ML.18	IWM 551; IWM 582
ML.55	IWM 553; IWM 555-02; IWM 561
ML.72	IWM 1144
ML.181	IWM 562
ML.219	IWM 555-02
ML.272	IWM 555-02
ML.275	IWM 553
ML.278	IWM 551; IWM 553; IWM 555-02
ML.279	IWM 553
ML.324	IWM 602
ML.325	IWM 562
ML.351	IWM 1164
ML.397	IWM 1164
ML.532	IWM 358
ML.558	IWM 1105
ML.559	IWM 1164
Monarch	IWM 548
Monmouth	NTB 168-01
Moon	IWM 580; IWM 1157
Moorsom	IWM 551; IWM 1105; IWM 1154; IWM 1156
Moth	IWM 71; IWM 461a
Nairana	IWM 866
Natal	IWM 1061-01
Nelson	IWM 809
Neptune	IWM 440-01; IWM 512; IWM 556; IWM 563; IWM 1151; NTB 323-02
Nereide	IWM 580
New Zealand	IWM 1213
Newcastle	IWM 456
Nimrod	IWM 555-02; IWM 1151
Nizam	IWM 1144
Noble	IWM 555-01; IWM 555-02
Nonsuch	IWM 1157
Norman	IWM 1143; IWM 1164
North Star	IWM 551
Nugent	IWM 1105; IWM 1154
Oak	IWM 571; IWM 586; IWM 1147; IWM 1164
Offa	IWM 563; IWM 1156

Opportune	IWM 595
Orion	IWM 484; IWM 575
Orpheus	IWM 1164
Owl	IWM 580
Paladin	IWM 1144
Parker	IWM 1146
PC.43	IWM 559; IWM 1153; IWM 1155; IWM 1160
PC.56	IWM 1157
Pellew	IWM 563
Pembroke	IWM 551; NTB 254-01; NTB 321-01
Phaeton	IWM 577
Pitfour	IWM 581
Plassy	IWM 551; IWM 556; IWM 1158
Porpoise	IWM 580
Princess Royal	IWM 551; IWM 555-02; IWM 556; IWM 1061-01; IWM 1143
Pylades	IWM 1146
Queen	IWM 440-01
Queen Elizabeth	IWM 440-01; IWM 484; IWM 550-01; IWM 550-02; IWM 551; IWM 552; IWM 554; IWM 555-01; IWM 555-02; IWM 556; IWM 563; IWM 571; IWM 572; IWM 576; IWM 577; IWM 580; IWM 581; IWM 586; IWM 591; IWM 599; IWM 600; IWM 601; IWM 602; IWM 603; IWM 646; IWM 665b; IWM 674c; IWM 685a; IWM 1061-01; IWM 1144; IWM 1146; IWM 1147; IWM 1148; IWM 1149; IWM 1151; IWM 1153; IWM 1160; IWM 1163; IWM 1164; NTB 321-01
Ramillies	IWM 555-02
Ravenswood	IWM 551; IWM 581
Ready	IWM 551; IWM 554; IWM 1143
Redgauntlet	IWM 695; IWM 1212
Redoubt	IWM 1212
Renown	IWM 551; IWM 571; IWM 843; IWM 1143; IWM 1144; IWM 1145; IWM 1147; IWM 1163; IWM 1164
Repulse	IWM 571; IWM 842; IWM 1169; IWM 1170
Retriever	IWM 1212
Revenge	IWM 551; IWM 555-01; IWM 563; IWM 580; IWM 1149; IWM 1160
Rob Roy	IWM 551; IWM 554
Rocket	IWM 551; IWM 554; IWM 555-02
Rodney	IWM 809
Romola	IWM 555-01
Rowena	IWM 555-01; IWM 809
Royal Sovereign	IWM 1149
Salmon	IWM 809
Sandown	IWM 551; IWM 553; IWM 581
Sappho	IWM 551
Satyr	IWM 646
Seymour	IWM 646
Slinger	IWM 1166; IWM 1167
Saint Seiriol	IWM 582
Saint Vincent	IWM 598; IWM 1061-01; IWM 1151
Strathdevon	IWM 581
Sturgeon	IWM 1212
Swift	IWM 551; IWM 553; IWM 581
Sydney	IWM 638
Talisman	IWM 646
TB.81	IWM 1156
Temeraire	IWM 1145; IWM 1147
Thetis	IWM 358; IWM 508-86; IWM 656b
Thruster	IWM 809
Tiger	IWM 809; IWM 1145; IWM 1147; IWM 1169
Torrid	IWM 809
Trego (decoy name)	IWM 559; IWM 1153; IWM 1155; IWM 1160
Trenchant	IWM 1153
Ulysses	IWM 1144
Unity	IWM 552; IWM 578-02
Valentine	IWM 555-01
Valhalla	IWM 555-02; IWM 578-02; IWM 1153
Valiant	IWM 1151
Vampire	IWM 551; IWM 554
Venerable	IWM 1157
Vengeance	IWM 440-01
Versatile	IWM 555-02
Vesper	IWM 555-01
Victor	IWM 580
Victoria and Albert	IWM 440-01; IWM 1061-01; IWM 1149
Victorian II	IWM 551; IWM 582
Victorious	IWM 440-01
Victory	IWM 512; IWM 516; IWM 577; IWM 809; IWM 1061-01
Vindex	IWM 1167
Vindictive	IWM 351; IWM 551; IWM 557; IWM 1105; IWM 1164
Vulcan	IWM 1157
Walker	IWM 1164; IWM 1212
Warrior	IWM 440-01
Warstar	IWM 1151
Warwick	IWM 551; IWM 1105
Weymouth	IWM 1149
Whirlwind	IWM 555-03; IWM 1146
Witch	IWM 809
Woolston	IWM 1164
Worcester	IWM 551; IWM 552
Zealandia	IWM 580
Royal Marines	IWM 420-21+22; IWM 439; IWM 446; IWM 484; IWM 555-03; IWM 626; IWM 656b; IWM 657a; IWM 661b; IWM 842; NTB 248-01; IWM 1082-01
Royal Marine Artillery	IWM 191
Royal Marine Cadets	IWM 201; IWM 699c
Royal Marine Cadet Corps, Deal	NTB 321-01
Royal Naval Air Service	IWM 130-03+4; IWM 198; IWM 287; IWM 555-03; IWM 558; IWM 570; IWM 578-03; IWM 580; IWM 613; IWM 621; IWM 622; IWM 623; IWM 624; IWM 648; IWM 866; IWM 1030; IWM 1058; IWM 1156
Royal Naval Division	IWM 116; IWM 332; IWM 1058

BRITISH ORGANISATIONS
Agnew Galleries   IWM 668c
Alton Home for Crippled Children
                                         NTB 279-02
American Workers' Federation   IWM 667
Anglo-Saxon Fellowship   IWM 666a
Armstrong Whitworth   IWM 263; IWM 264;
                         IWM 552; IWM 1167
Army Reserve Munition Workers   IWM 457
Aston Villa Football Club   IWM 691
Baptist Union   NTB 256-01
Battersea Dogs' Home   IWM 654b
Beardmore and Company   IWM 140
Bedford School   IWM 668b
Birmingham and District Professions and
   General Trades Fund   IWM 304; IWM 308d
Birmingham Small Arms   IWM 262;
                         IWM 809; NTB 251-02
Board of Agriculture   IWM 678a
Bombay Presidency War Relief Fund,
   Women's Branch   IWM 77
Boots   IWM 279
Boy Scouts   IWM 14; IWM 307; IWM 346;
     IWM 461c; IWM 531; IWM 626; IWM 652a;
       IWM 678a; IWM 678b; IWM 1062-03;
       IWM 1082-02c; IWM 1106; IWM 1214
Boys' Brigade   IWM 668c; IWM 1179
Boys, Gilson   IWM 140
Boys' Naval Brigade   NTB 264-01
Bradfield College   NTB 292-01; NTB 345-02
British and Foreign Sailors' Society
                                   NTB 319-02
British Motor Ambulance Committee
                                   NTB 356-02
British Sportsmen's Motor Ambulance Fund
                                   NTB 279-02
British Workers' National League NTB 259-01
Brondesbury Hospital   NTB 258-02
Brooksby Hall   NTB 277-02; NTB 278-02
Burnopfield Colliery   IWM 1061-06m
Cambridge University   IWM 485; IWM 661a
Carter Paterson   NTB 280-01
Catholic Boys Brigade   NTB 275-02
Charing Cross Hospital   IWM 1061-08a
Chartered Secretaries' Drilling Corps
                                  NTB 178-01
Chelsea Football Club   NTB 319-02
Church Army   IWM 648
Church of England   IWM 679a; NTB 269-01
City of London Motor Volunteer Corps,
   Group II   NTB 323-01
Clydeside Steel Works   IWM 140
Conservative Party   IWM 485
Coventry Ordnance   IWM 652a
Dockers' Union   NTB 262-01
Dr Barnardo's Homes, Girls' Village Home
   Barkingside   NTB 254-01
Dunsmuir and Jackson   IWM 140
Ebbw Vale Company   NTB 340-01
Eton School   NTB 328-01
Fernie Hunt   IWM 706

Fire Brigade   IWM 655d; IWM 686;
                                  NTB 213-02
Fire Brigade, London   NTB 266-02
Fraser and Fraser   IWM 675b
Girl Guides   IWM 346; IWM 678a;
                       IWM 685a; NTB 265-02
Girl Guides, Richmond District   NTB 316-01
Glasgow University   IWM 668c
Grafton Galleries   NTB 340-01
Greenock and Grangemouth Dockyard
                                  IWM 140
Guest, Keene and Nettlefold   IWM 170
Hampstead Orthopaedic Hospital IWM 661b;
                                  IWM 665c
Handley Page   IWM 200; IWM 419
Harrods   IWM 193b
Harrow School   IWM 1070b
Highland Scot   IWM 1082-02d
Huntley and Palmers   NTB 342-02
Imperial Air Fleet Committee   NTB 323-01
Imperial War Museum   IWM 504; IWM 507
Irish Association Voluntary Training Corps
                                  NTB 247-01
Irish Republican Army   IWM 194;
            IWM 485; IWM 666a; IWM 675a
Irish Republican Brotherhood   NTB 245-02;
                                  NTB 247-02
James Edmonds and Sons   NTB 327-02
Joseph Rank   IWM 552
Kincaid, J and Company   IWM 140
Kynock   IWM 663c
Labour Party   IWM 485; NTB 312-01
Lanarkshire Steel Company   IWM 140
League of National Safety   NTB 325-02
League of the Empire   NTB 273-01
Lever Brothers   IWM 809
Liberal Party   IWM 485
Liptons   IWM 461c
London County Council   NTB 276-02
London Diocesan Church Lads' Brigade
                                  NTB 253-01
London Omnibus Company   IWM 521
London Transport Column   NTB 239-02
London University, King's College IWM 677a
Lyons Bakery   IWM 521
Mappin and Webb   IWM 809
Marylebone Cricket Club   IWM 674a
Merchant Marine   IWM 320
Metropolitan Carriage and Wagon Company
                                  IWM 1192
Ministry of Agriculture   IWM 535
Ministry of Food   IWM 193d; IWM 292;
     IWM 474; IWM 520; IWM 523; IWM 549-03;
            IWM 677b; IWM 692a; IWM 693e
Ministry of Information   IWM 668c;
                     NTB 340-01; NTB 345-02
Ministry of Munitions   IWM 626
Ministry of National Service   IWM 478;
                                  IWM 480
Ministry of Pensions   IWM 626; IWM 1098
Ministry of Works   IWM 507

Motor Transport Volunteers   NTB 323-01
NAAFI   IWM 1064-03a
Napier Motor Works   IWM 418
National Army Canteen Board   IWM 462
National Federation of Ex-Soldiers and Sailors
                                             IWM 672a
National Federation of Sea Anglers
                                          IWM 1082-02a
National Motor Volunteers No 1 Bn
                                              NTB 265-01
National Union of Railwaymen   NTB 262-01
National War Aims Committee   NTB 327-02
National War Savings Committee
        NTB 322-01; NTB 327-01; NTB 328-01
Nelson Line   IWM 1082-02d
Officers Training Corps, Trinity College
                                              NTB 247-01
Order of Saint John of Jerusalem   IWM 662b
Oxford University   IWM 485; IWM 535;
                          IWM 809; IWM 880-01d
Pathé   IWM 880-02a
Percy Illingworth Soldiers' Home and Club
                                              NTB 256-01
Pitman's Secretarial School   IWM 530
Police Force   IWM 307; IWM 443; IWM 444;
      IWM 479; IWM 485; IWM 521; IWM 612;
   IWM 653b; IWM 654a; IWM 655d; IWM 659;
              IWM 1061-07c; IWM 1062-18
Police Force, Metropolitan Police   IWM 1142
Post Office   IWM 521; IWM 714; IWM 1121
Pytchley Hunt   IWM 706
Queen Alexandra's Charities   NTB 251-02
Queen's College Birmingham   IWM 308d
Red Cross   IWM 109; IWM 134; IWM 232;
    IWM 241; IWM 267; IWM 268; IWM 508-44;
  IWM 652b; IWM 660b; IWM 668c; IWM 679b;
         IWM 685b; IWM 1070e; NTB 258-01;
       NTB 261-01; NTB 269-02; NTB 321-02;
                     NTB 354-01; NTB 356-02
Richmond Rugby Football Club
                                          IWM 1061-08a
Rolls-Royce   IWM 809
Roman Catholic Church   IWM 675b
Royal Agricultural Society   NTB 253-02
Royal Dockyard, Equipment and Stores
   Inspection Division   NTB 322-01
Royal Geographical Society   IWM 809
Royal Greenwich Observatory   IWM 809
Royal Hospital, Chelsea   NTB 249-01
Royal Seed Establishment   NTB 342-02
Royal Small Arms Factory   NTB 321-01
Royal Society for the Prevention of Cruelty to
   Animals   IWM 114; NTB 238-01
Rugby School   IWM 693a
Russian Wounded Fund   NTB 264-01
Salvation Army   IWM 1082-02a
Scottish Prisoners of War Fund   NTB 264-01
Scottish Women's Hospital   IWM 1062-10
Sea Scouts IWM 439; IWM 531; NTB 319-02
Sheffield Steel   IWM 809
Sinai Police   IWM 5

Sinn Féin   IWM 666a; IWM 675a
Sir William Treloar Fund   NTB 279-02;
                                              NTB 280-01
Southend Harriers   NTB 178-01
Special Constabulary   NTB 256-01;
                                              NTB 267-01
St Dunstan's School for the War Blinded
      NTB 255-02; NTB 271-02; NTB 274-01;
                                              NTB 277-02
St John Ambulance   IWM 134; IWM 418;
      IWM 1082-02c; NTB 247-01; NTB 265-01
St Nicholas Home For Raid Shock Children
                                              IWM 681c
Staffordshire House   NTB 257-01
Star and Garter Home   NTB 259-01;
                                              NTB 264-01
Star Engineering Company   IWM 134
Stock Exchange   IWM 1061-01
Stonyhurst College   IWM 1061-07g
Sutton War Seeds   NTB 342-02
Tootal   IWM 809
Trades Union Congress   IWM 485;
                            IWM 665c; IWM 667
Treowan Steelworks   IWM 170
Ulster Defence Force   IWM 485; IWM 674b
Vickers   IWM 434; IWM 580; IWM 585;
                    IWM 663c; IWM 675b
Victoria Colliery   IWM 170; NTB 340-01
Victoria Shipping Line   IWM 31; IWM 634
Voluntary Aid Detachment (VAD)   IWM 169;
      IWM 170; IWM 213; IWM 258; IWM 260;
             IWM 508-51; IWM 521; IWM 663c;
        IWM 1074; NTB 265-01; NTB 340-01
Volunteer Training Reserve, National Guard
                                              NTB 321-01
Waithead's Aircraft Factory   IWM 521
Waring and Gillow   NTB 329-01
Watt's Naval Training School   NTB 254-01
White Star Line & Baltic   IWM 450
William Foster   IWM 1191
Women's Forestry Corps IWM 521; IWM 693b
Women's Land Army   IWM 305; IWM 474;
      IWM 480; IWM 521; IWM 534; IWM 535;
      IWM 536; IWM 626; IWM 651b; IWM 653a;
      IWM 654a; IWM 665b; IWM 685a; IWM 693b;
            IWM 699b; IWM 1217; NTB 274-01;
       NTB 278-02; NTB 317-01; NTB 344-01
Women's Legion   IWM 521; NTB 318-01
Women's National Land Service Corps
                                              NTB 247-02
Women's Party   NTB 324-02
Women's Social and Political Union
           IWM 474; IWM 485; NTB 257-01;
                                              NTB 324-02
Woolwich Arsenal   IWM 161; IWM 809
Woolwich Arsenal Football Club NTB 319-01
YMCA   IWM 441; IWM 521; IWM 677b;
   IWM 706; IWM 808; IWM 1178; NTB 325-02

UNITED STATES OF AMERICA
US ARMY (American Expeditionary Force)
    IWM 119; IWM 137; IWM 240; IWM 248;
    IWM 249; IWM 250; IWM 251; IWM 252;
    IWM 254; IWM 257; IWM 258; IWM 261;
    IWM 267; IWM 272; IWM 278; IWM 289;
    IWM 290; IWM 296; IWM 300; IWM 304;
    IWM 308a; IWM 308d; IWM 334; IWM 356;
    IWM 370; IWM 439; IWM 448; IWM 450;
    IWM 458; IWM 484; IWM 501-01;
    IWM 501-02; IWM 501-03; IWM 501-04;
    IWM 501-05; IWM 501-06; IWM 501-07;
    IWM 501-08; IWM 501-09; IWM 501-10;
    IWM 501-11; IWM 501-12; IWM 501-13;
IWM 501-14; IWM 502; IWM 503; IWM 508-13;
    IWM 508-24; IWM 508-29; IWM 508-40;
    IWM 508-42; IWM 508-43; IWM 508-47;
    IWM 508-49; IWM 508-50; IWM 508-51;
    IWM 508-52; IWM 508-55; IWM 508-60;
    IWM 508-64; IWM 508-65; IWM 508-67;
    IWM 508-68; IWM 508-69; IWM 508-72;
    IWM 508-74; IWM 508-75; IWM 508-78;
IWM 508-78 bis; IWM 508-79; IWM 508-80;
    IWM 508-81; IWM 508-83; IWM 508-88;
IWM 558; IWM 652a; IWM 653b; IWM 660b;
IWM 664a; IWM 665b; IWM 666a; IWM 668d;
IWM 672a; IWM 687; IWM 843; IWM 870;
IWM 880-02d; IWM 1049; IWM 1061-02a;
    IWM 1061-03e; IWM 1061-07b;
IWM 1064-01a; IWM 1070a; IWM 1079;
IWM 1079; IWM 1183; IWM 1186; IWM 1187;
    IWM 1194; IWM 1196; NTB 256-02;
    NTB 318-01; NTB 330-02; NTB 343-01;
    NTB 345-02

4th Army   IWM 508-80
II Corps   IWM 501-01; IWM 501-14;
    IWM 503; IWM 508-50
III Corps   IWM 501-01
IV Corps   IWM 501-11
V Corps   IWM 501-09; IWM 508-80

1st Division   IWM 458; IWM 501-05;
    IWM 501-06; IWM 508-13; IWM 508-26;
    IWM 508-51; IWM 508-64; NTB 356-02
2nd Division   IWM 240; IWM 501-12;
    IWM 502; IWM 503; IWM 508-67;
    IWM 508-78; IWM 508-81; IWM 508-83
3rd Division   IWM 501-02; IWM 502;
IWM 508-67; IWM 508-75; IWM 508-78 bis;
    IWM 508-83
4th Division   IWM 502
5th Division   IWM 501-01; IWM 501-02;
    IWM 508-79
26th Division   IWM 458; IWM 501-02;
    IWM 501-04; IWM 501-07; IWM 501-12;
    IWM 502; IWM 508-55; IWM 508-72;
    IWM 1079
27th Division   IWM 334; IWM 501-09;
    IWM 501-13; IWM 503
29th Division   IWM 501-14

30th Division   IWM 289; IWM 334;
    IWM 501-08; IWM 502; IWM 503
31st Division   IWM 501-02
32nd Division   IWM 501-02; IWM 508-75;
    IWM 502
33rd Division   IWM 290
35th Division   IWM 501-03; IWM 501-09;
    IWM 502
41st Division   IWM 501-07
42nd Division   IWM 1079
77th Division   IWM 502
78th Division   IWM 501-01
79th Division   IWM 501-01; IWM 501-03;
    IWM 501-14
80th Division   IWM 1079
82nd Division   IWM 501-02
83rd Division   IWM 501-02; IWM 501-10;
    IWM 501-12; IWM 501-13
90th Division   IWM 501-14; IWM 508-79
91st Division   IWM 501-10
92nd Division   IWM 501-08; IWM 501-13

4th Infantry Regt   IWM 502
6th Infantry Regt   IWM 501-02; IWM 508-65
9th Infantry Regt   IWM 503
11th Infantry Regt   IWM 501-02
18th Infantry Regt   IWM 501-05; IWM 502
26th Infantry Regt   IWM 458
28th Infantry Regt   IWM 508-64; NTB 356-02
39th Infantry Regt   IWM 502
58th Infantry Regt   IWM 502
61st Infantry Regt, 1st Bn   IWM 501-02
101st Infantry Regt, D Coy   IWM 501-04
102nd Infantry Regt   IWM 501-07
103rd Infantry Regt   IWM 501-07; IWM 502
104th Infantry Regt   IWM 458
105th Infantry Regt   IWM 503
108th Infantry Regt   IWM 503
119th Infantry Regt   IWM 503
125th Infantry Regt, Machine Gun Coy
    IWM 503
128th Infantry Regt   IWM 502
138th Infantry Regt, 1st Bn   IWM 501-03
139th Infantry Regt   IWM 502
167th Infantry Regt, E Coy   IWM 1079
305th Infantry Regt   IWM 502
307th Infantry Regt   IWM 258; IWM 502
313th Infantry Regt, G Coy   IWM 501-14
332nd Infantry Regt [Italian contingent]
    IWM 501-02; IWM 501-10; IWM 501-13
358th Infantry Regt, 3rd Bn   IWM 501-14
101st Machine Gun Bn   IWM 501-14
105th Machine Gun Bn, B Coy   IWM 503
129th Machine Gun Bn   IWM 501-03
344th Machine Gun Bn   IWM 501-14
Pennsylvania Dragoons   IWM 687
Philadelphia Light Dragoons   IWM 502

Ambulance Coy 1   IWM 501-05
Army of Occupation   IWM 1082-02a

Artillery   IWM 458; IWM 501-01; IWM 501-02;
     IWM 501-03; IWM 501-04; IWM 501-05;
     IWM 501-07; IWM 501-12; IWM 501-13;
          IWM 502; IWM 503; IWM 508-40;
     IWM 1061-03h; IWM 1183; NTB 322-01;
                              NTB 341-02
Balloon Coy 1   IWM 501-13
Balloon Coy 2   IWM 501-07
Base Hospital 37   IWM 503
Black troops   IWM 501-08; IWM 501-13;
     IWM 508-67; IWM 1079; NTB 242-01
Engineers   IWM 252; IWM 261; IWM 501-01;
     IWM 501-04; IWM 501-05; IWM 501-07;
     IWM 501-09; IWM 501-14; IWM 503;
                         IWM 508-78 bis
Railway Engineers   IWM 150; IWM 448;
                              IWM 672a
Military Police   IWM 1079
North Russian Intervention Force
               IWM 501-02; IWM 808
Signal Corps   IWM 267; IWM 501-03;
     IWM 501-04; IWM 501-08; IWM 501-09;
     IWM 501-13; IWM 501-14; IWM 508-69;
               IWM 653b; IWM 1079
Tank Corps   IWM 501-02; IWM 501-12;
               IWM 502; IWM 1196
Veterinary Corps   IWM 501-12
West Point Officer Cadets   IWM 484
Women's Army Corps   IWM 257

US ARMY AIR CORPS   IWM 289; IWM 304;
     IWM 308a; IWM 308d; IWM 501-08;
     IWM 502; IWM 508-29; IWM 508-64;
     IWM 558; IWM 1049; IWM 1079; IWM 1101
Pursuit Group 1, 94th Squadron   IWM 250;
     IWM 458; IWM 501-03; IWM 501-04;
                              IWM 1079
Pursuit Group 1, 147th Squadron
               IWM 501-03; IWM 501-04

US MARINE CORPS   IWM 668d; IWM 687;
          IWM 1061-08e; IWM 1070a
Cadets   IWM 1079

US NAVY   IWM 248; IWM 668d; IWM 870;
                              IWM 1079

6th Battle Squadron   IWM 1079
9th Battleship Division   IWM 563; IWM 588
8th Destroyer Division   IWM 562; IWM 1159
US Navy Air Corps   IWM 570; IWM 619;
                              IWM 1101
Annapolis Naval Academy   IWM 1079
Cadets   IWM 445
Charleston Navy Yard   IWM 1079

Birmingham   IWM 551; IWM 552; IWM 595;
                              IWM 1153
Chester   IWM 555-02
Conyngham   IWM 562
Davis   IWM 562; IWM 1159

Delaware   IWM 484
Duncan   IWM 550-01; IWM 564
Florida   IWM 484
Kentucky   IWM 1182
Kilpatrick   NTB 242-01
Maumee   IWM 1061-07f
McDougal   IWM 562
Melville   IWM 550-01; IWM 564; IWM 1162
Michigan   NTB 253-01
New Hampshire   NTB 253-01
New York   IWM 484; IWM 550-01;
     IWM 563; IWM 588; IWM 637; IWM 674c;
          IWM 679a; IWM 1079; IWM 1212
North Carolina   IWM 1079
Oregon   IWM 1079
Pennsylvania   IWM 1079
Porter   IWM 562; IWM 1159
SC.154   IWM 1079
Sterett   IWM 550-01
Texas   IWM 588; IWM 637
Virginia   NTB 253-01
Wadsworth   IWM 562; IWM 1159
Wainwright   IWM 562
Wyoming   IWM 484; IWM 563
York   IWM 602

US ORGANISATIONS
American Airlines   IWM 1101
American Federation of Labour   NTB 351-02
Carpenters' Union   IWM 1079
Coastguard   IWM 1061-07e
Congress   IWM 142
Creel Committee on Public Information
                              IWM 1079
Fire Dept   IWM 686; IWM 1061-07f;
                              NTB 246-01
Industrial Workers of the World   IWM 1079
Jarrett Museum of World War History
                              IWM 1010
Lambs Actors' Club   IWM 1079
Life Boat Service   IWM 1061-05g
Loyal Order of the Moose   IWM 177
New York Sons of Young Italy   IWM 501-13
Princeton University   IWM 1079
Red Cross   IWM 248; IWM 261;
     IWM 501-10; IWM 687; IWM 1049;
     IWM 1079; IWM 1175; NTB 270-02;
                              NTB 344-01
Salvation Army   IWM 1079
Socialist and Union Groups   IWM 224;
                              IWM 693b
St John Ambulance   IWM 198
Union Pacific Railway   NTB 283-02
US Wheel and Track Layer Corporation
                              IWM 1064-02a
YMCA   IWM 508-67; IWM 672b; IWM 697a;
     IWM 808; IWM 1079; NTB 330-02

URUGUAY
URUGUAYAN ARMY   IWM 506

ZIONIST ORGANISATIONS
International Zionist Commission   IWM 27;
                           IWM 30; IWM 45
Maccabi Athletic Association   IWM 27;
                           IWM 35; IWM 45